FROM ANIMALS TO ANIMATS

Complex Adaptive Systems

John H. Holland, Christopher Langton, and Stewart W. Wilson, advisors

Adaptation in Natural and Artificial Systems: An Introductory Analysis with Applications to Biology, Control, and Artificial Intelligence, John H. Holland

Toward a Practice of Autonomous Systems: Proceedings of the First European Conference on Artificial Life, edited by Francisco J. Varela and Paul Bourgine

Genetic Programming: On the Programming of Computers by Means of Natural Selection, John R. Koza

From Animals to Animats 2: Proceedings of the Second International Conference on Simulation of Adaptive Behavior, edited by Jean-Arcady Meyer, Herbert L. Roitblat, and Stewart W. Wilson

FROM ANIMALS TO ANIMATS 2

Proceedings of the Second International Conference on Simulation of Adaptive Behavior

edited by Jean-Arcady Meyer, Herbert L. Roitblat, and Stewart W. Wilson

A Bradford Book

The MIT Press
Cambridge, Massachusetts
London, England

This book was printed and bound in the United States of America.

Library of Congress Cataloging-in-Publication Data

International Conference on Simulation of Adaptive Behavior (2nd : 1992 : Honolulu, Hawaii)
From animals to animats 2 : proceedings of the Second International Conference on Simulation of Adaptive Behavior / edited by Jean-Arcady Meyer, Herbert L. Roitblat, and Stewart W. Wilson.
p. cm. — (Complex adaptive systems)
"A Bradford book."
Includes bibliographical references and index.
ISBN 0-262-63149-0
1. Animal behavior—Simulation methods—Congresses. 2. Adaptation (Psychology)—Simulation methods—Congresses. 3. Robotics—Congresses. 4. Artificial intelligence—Congresses. I. Meyer, Jean-Arcady. II. Roitblat, H. L. III. Wilson, Stewart W. IV. Title. V. Title: From animals to animats two. VI. Series.
QL751.65.S55I58 1992
591.51—dc20 93-12410
CIP

CONTENTS

ACTION SELECTION AND BEHAVIORAL SEQUENCES

COGNITIVE MAPS AND INTERNAL WORLD MODELS

LEARNING

EVOLUTION

COLLECTIVE BEHAVIOR

ONE-PAGE SUMMARIES

PREFACE

On December 7-11, 1992, in Honolulu, Hawaii, just steps from Waikiki Beach, 125 researchers from Europe, North America, and Japan met to report from, debate, and push forward the frontier of an exciting new approach to understanding intelligence: the simulation and building of artificial animals ('animats') which must survive and adapt in progressively more challenging environments. Representing fields as diverse as ethology, psychology, connectionism, evolutionary computation, and robotics, the participants shared the belief that the creation of whole, coping, animal-like systems—however simple at the moment—may be one of the best routes to understanding intelligence in both natural and artificial systems. The conference was entitled "From Animals to Animats: The Second International Conference on Simulation of Adaptive Behavior" (SAB92). It succeeded one held with equal enthusiasm in Paris in September, 1990.

These proceedings contain 59 papers and constitute the most comprehensive and up-to-date source on the field. The book is divided into sections corresponding to the conference sessions. In each section, papers presented as talks are followed by related papers that were presented as posters. (Eleven additional contributions could not be included in full in this book, but were given as posters and are represented in a final section by summaries.)

The first section, The Animat Approach to Adaptive Behavior, contains papers on the nature of the animat enterprise, on simulating the evolution of adaptive behavior with minimal prior assumptions, and on sexual selection—a significant and underrated adaptive force.

Papers in Perception and Motor Control address from diverse angles the question of obtaining useful percepts from the available sensory profusion, and report on adaptive locomotion, especially walking.

The need for practical action hierarchies is brought out by several papers in Action Selection and Behavioral Sequences. Others address action choice in relation to motivation and how plans can emerge from the interplay of simple computational units.

In the section on Cognitive Maps and Internal World Models several papers show how local information can yield large-scale maps of the environment. Other papers concern extraction of landmarks from route data, and the kinds of internal 'representations' that localist behavior control produces.

The Learning section contains leading-edge papers on hierarchy, internal states, experiential memory, and associative extension of existing competences. The aim of understanding learning problems better is furthered in a paper offering a perspicuous categorization of learning environments.

The Evolution section contains papers on evolving—rather than designing—robots, and on evolution of behaviors, including group behaviors, that satisfy multiple fitness demands.

The section on Collective Behavior has papers on identifying primitive individual competences which permit principled design of group behavior, adaptive cooperation among relatively high-level animats, and emergence of explicit communication.

SAB92 could not have taken place without the assistance of many people and organizations. We are especially grateful to members of the Program Committee, whose conscientious reviewing selected the papers here from the 105 submitted. The Committee members were:

Alain Berthoz, Collège de France, France
Lashon Booker, MITRE Corporation, USA
Rodney Brooks, MIT Artificial Intelligence Lab, USA
Patrick Colgan, Canadian Museum of Nature, Canada
Juan Delius, Universität Konstanz, Germany
Anthony Dickinson, University of Cambridge, UK
Jacques Ferber, Université Paris VI, France
Simon Goss, Université Libre de Bruxelles, Belgium
Paul Nachtigall, University of Hawaii, USA
Luc Steels, VUB AI Lab, Belgium
Richard Sutton, GTE Laboratories, USA
Frederick Toates, The Open University, UK
Peter Todd, The Rowland Institute for Science, USA
Saburo Tsuji, Osaka University, Japan
William Uttal, Arizona State University, USA
David Waltz, Thinking Machines Corp. and Brandeis University, USA

We thank each of the following conference sponsors:

Air Force Office of Scientific Research
Defense Advanced Research Projects Agency
Ministère de l'Education Nationale et de la Culture
Office of Naval Research

and are grateful to John Tangney for his continuing intellectual support and excellent advice.

The members of the Organizing and Local Arrangements Committee worked long and hard to make the conference a success. We thank Agnès Guillot, Heidi Harley, David Helweg, Constance Susan Manos, Patrick Moore, Philippe Tarroux, Pierre Vincens, and Satoru Yamamoto.

We thank Yvonne Yamashita of the University of Hawaii Conference Center for handling the fiscal arrangements for the conference and the University of Hawaii Department of Psychology, especially Karl Minke and Sheryl Nakahara, for their support.

Finally, we are particularly indebted to Gilbert Roger for the artistic conception of the SAB92 poster and the Proceedings cover.

We invite readers to enjoy and profit from the papers in this book, and look forward to the next conference, SAB94, which is planned for August 8-12, 1994, in Brighton, England.

Aloha,

Jean-Arcady Meyer Herbert L. Roitblat Stewart W. Wilson
Conference Co-Chairs

THE ANIMAT APPROACH TO ADAPTIVE BEHAVIOR

Behavior-Based Artificial Intelligence

Pattie Maes
MIT Media-Laboratory
20 Ames Street Rm 489
Cambridge, MA 02139
pattie@media.mit.edu

Abstract

This paper attempts to define Behavior-Based Artificial Intelligence (AI) as a new approach to the study of Intelligence. It distinguishes this approach from the traditional Knowledge-Based approach in terms of the questions studied, the solutions adopted and the criteria used for success. It does not limit Behavior-Based AI to the study of robots, but rather presents it as a general approach for building autonomous systems that have to deal with multiple, changing goals in a dynamic, unpredictable environment.

1. Why this paper?

Since 1985, a new wave has emerged in the study of Artificial Intelligence (AI). At the same moment at which the popular, general belief is that AI has been a "failure", many insiders believe that something exciting is happening, that new life is being brought to the field. The new wave has been termed "behavior-based AI" as opposed to main-stream "knowledge-based AI", or also "bottom-up AI" versus "top-down AI". Finally, the term "animat approach", which was coined by Wilson (1985), is also frequently used. This paper attempts to describe what Behavior-Based AI is about and how it differs from Knowledge-Based AI. It argues that Behavior-Based AI poses problems in a different way, investigates interesting new techniques and applies a set of different criteria for success.

Several people have tried to define Behavior-Based AI, among others Brooks (1991), Wilson (1991) and Meyer (1991). There are several reasons for giving it yet another try. First of all many researchers are still sceptical about the approach. Some claim that it isn't very different from what they have been doing all along. Others are still not convinced that the approach is founded and scientific. A second reason is that this account is different from the papers listed above. Brooks, being one of the main originators of this new approach, presents a picture which is restricted towards robotic forms of intelligence (Brooks, 1991).

This paper presents a more general perspective. It argues that the behavior-based approach is appropriate for the class of problems that require a system to autonomously fulfill several goals in a dynamic, unpredictable environment. This includes applications such as interface agents (Maes, 1992b), process scheduling (Malone et.al., 1988), and so on. Wilson's account (1991) focuses on a scientific methodology for Animat research, while Meyer (1991) aims to give an overview of the research performed so far.

Defining a new approach is a difficult and tricky thing to do. In particular, it is dangerous to draw solid lines between the different approaches and to force examples of research to fit into one of them. For the sake of clarity the remainder of the paper presents Knowledge-Based AI and Behavior-Based as two extremes. The reader should keep in mind that concrete examples of research are often situated along the continuum between the two extreme positions presented here and that those intermediate positions are valid ones to adopt.

The paper is structured as follows. Section 2 distinguishes the goal and emphasis of Knowledge-Based AI with those of Behavior-Based AI. Section 3 discusses the solutions investigated by the Knowledge-Based Approach. The next chapter lists some of the key insights which underlie the Behavior-Based approach. Section 5 elaborates upon the solutions adopted by Behavior-Based AI. Section 6 discusses some examples contrasting the two approaches. Finally section 7 contains some critical comments about the progress made so far.

2. Goals of the Two Approaches to AI

The goal of both Knowledge-Based AI and Behavior-Based AI is to synthesize computational forms of intelligent systems. Both approaches attempt to model intelligent phenomena such as goal-directed behavior, prediction, learning, communication and cooperation. Knowledge-Based AI has traditionally emphasized the modeling and building of systems that "know" about some problem domain. These systems model the domain and can answer questions about this problem domain, often involving extensive problem solving and reasoning. Behavior-based AI on the other hand has emphasized the modeling and building of systems that "behave" in some problem domain.

More specifically, "main-stream" Knowledge-Based AI can be characterized as typically studying systems with the following characteristics:

1. They model isolated, often advanced, competences (e.g. medical diagnosis, chess playing, etc). They rather provide "depth" than "width" in their expertise.

2. They are "closed", in the sense that there is no direct interaction with the problem domain about which they encode knowledge and solve problems. Their only connection with the environment is the user. The user recognizes a problem in the domain, describes it to the system in the symbolic language which the system understands. The system then returns a symbolic description of an answer or solution, which then has to be implemented by the user in the actual domain.

3. They deal with one problem at a time. Often, they do not have time constraints for solving the problem (although the user might) and do not have to deal with interrupts. From the system's point of view the problem domain does not change while the system is computing. They also do not have to deal with multiple problems simultaneously. They are given one problem at a time by the user.

4. They have declarative "knowledge structures", which model aspects of the domain of expertise. All of the internal structures, apart from an interpreter are static. The system is only active when a problem is posed by the user, in which case the interpreter uses the static knowledge structures to determine the solution to the problem.

5. They are not usually concerned with the developmental aspect, or how the knowledge structures got there in the first place and how they should change over time. They do not have to be adaptive to changing situations (components breaking down, etc). At the most some form of knowledge compilation or knowledge optimization is incorporated.

6. In the few cases where an autonomous system (e.g. a robot or an interface agent) is being modelled, a central system which has all of the above characteristics is augmented with a perception module and an execution module which take over part of the role of the human interface. The perception module has to recognize the current situation and translate it into a symbolic description for the central system. The "problem" or goal is usually still specified in symbolic terms by a human. The execution module is responsible for "implementing" the description of the solution produced by the central system in the problem domain.

In contrast, Behavior-Based AI has typically studied the following type of system:

1. It has multiple integrated competences. Typically the competences are lower-level (as opposed to expert level). For a robot these are competences such as locomotion, navigation, survival, collecting objects, etc. For other systems these might be other simple competences, like reacting in a market system by simple bidding and buying behaviors (Malone et.al., 1988) or executing a simple routine in the case of an interface agent (Maes, 1992b) (Kozierok and Maes, 1992).

2. The system is "open" or "situated" in its environment. It is directly connected to its problem domain through sensors and effectors. It can affect or change this domain through its output. The problem domain is typically very dynamic, which means that the system has a limited amount of time to act. The domain is usually also very complex. Unpredictable events happen all the time. It typically also involves other acting agents (human and/or artificial).

3. The emphasis is on autonomy: the system is completely self-contained. It has to monitor the domain and figure out by itself what the problem to be solved next is. Typically it has to deal with many conflicting goals simultaneously.

4. Rather than on knowledge, the emphasis is on the resulting behavior of the system. Its internal structures are active "behavior producing" modules as opposed to static "knowledge structures". They do not have to be initiated by a goal formulation from the user. It is less important that the system can answer questions about its problem domain (such as how to solve particular problems). It is also less important that the user is able to inspect the internal structures and identify those that are responsible for particular aspects of the behavior. For example, it is acceptable for goals or planning to be emergent observable properties, which cannot be attributed to particular internal structures.

5. Finally, there is a strong emphasis on "adaptation" and on a "developmental approach". This often means that the system improves its own structures (and thus behavior) over time based on its own experience in the environment. In other cases, this means that an incremental approach is taken: the user gradually evolves a more sophisticated system by adding structure to an already existing "working" system.

One can conclude from the above discussion that it is hard to compare the Knowledge-Based and Behavior-Based approach because they typically study different classes of problems: knowledge versus behavior, a single high-level competence versus a range of low-level competences, user-driven computation versus autonomous systems, and so on. Both classes of problems are interesting in their own right. So far, neither approach has shown much success dealing with the problem classes concentrated on by the other approach. As long as it remains to be seen whether either one will be able to broaden its domain of success in significant ways, both types of research are necessary and complementary.

3. Solutions investigated by Knowledge-Based AI

The difference between Knowledge-Based AI and Behavior-Based AI lies not only in the problems that are studied, but also in the techniques and solutions that are explored. The solutions typically adopted in mainstream AI projects can be characterized as follows:

Function-Oriented Decomposition

The intelligent system is decomposed along "functional modules" such as perception, execution, natural language communication (the peripheral components), a learner, planner and inference engine (the central systems components). These modules are typically developed independently. They rely on the "central representation" as their means of interface. The central representation includes things such as beliefs (updated by perception, also read and augmented by the inference engine and the natural language component), desires (or goals) and intentions (produced by planner).

Approach

Typically all of these functional components are as general and domain-independent as possible. The hope is that the same functional components can be used for different problem domains (a general domain-independent planner, learner, etc). The only component which needs to be adapted is the central representation, which contains domain-specific information such as heuristic knowledge.

Role of Representation

The key issue on which emphasis is laid is a complete, correct internal model, a perfect copy of the world (with all its objects and relationships) inside the system, which the system can rely on to predict how the problem can be solved.

Organization

The organization of the different modules within the system is completely sequential. The modules take turns being "active" or processing and changing the internal representations. Perception and inference first update the internal model (beliefs and goals). After that, planning or problem solving produce a description of the solution to the problem (a plan or the answer to a question). Finally either the execution module or a human implements the solution in the domain (the latter one having more knowledge and understanding of the situation than the former one).

Model of Activity

Activity is modeled purely as the result of a "deliberative thinking" process. The central system evaluates the current situation (as represented in the internal model) and uses a search process to systematically explore the different ways in which this situation can be affected so as to achieve the desired goals.

Role of Learning

Learning typically consists of compilation or reformulation of what the system already knows. For example, the system might cache a plan for later reuse. Very seldom is there learning of new information or correction of existing knowledge based on environmental feedback. This implies that the programmer is completely responsible for creating an initial complete and correct model.

The Knowledge-Based approach has produced several successes, in particular in the area of knowledge systems assisting experts with the modelling of and reasoning about a specific problem domain. For a range of reasons the approach has proven non-satisfactory when dealing with the class of problems Behavior-Based AI is interested in. Several experiments which attempted to use the above approach for constructing autonomous systems operating in dynamic environments have run into the following problems[1].

- The resulting systems can be slow, because of the sequential processing of information and because of the high computational cost involved in maintaining a model and doing general perception and planning.
- The resulting systems can be inflexible. They have difficulty reacting fast to changes in the environment. They do not deal very well with unexpected opportunities or contingencies. This is partly due to the fact that changes have to propagate through many sequential layers before they affect the actions taken by the system. Another reason is that these systems are built on the assumptions that few or no unpredictable changes will happen.
- The resulting systems tend to be brittle. They fail in situations that only differ slightly from the ones they are programmed for. They do not show graceful degradation of performance as components break down. For example, if the perception module cannot make sense of the current situation, the whole system might break down.
- In practice it proves to be hard to relate the symbols in the internal model (representing objects and relations in the domain) to physical stimuli. It is hard to keep track of object identities, often the sensor data are ambiguous, erroneous, inconsistent, and so on.
- In practice it also proves to be hard to hand-build a complete and consistent model of the environment which the system can rely on to make predictions.
- Another practical problem is that of combinatorial explosions. General planning and problem solving have proven to be a computationally expensive process (Chapman, 1987).
- Several theoretical problems have come up, which remain unsolved in satisfactory ways. Examples of such problems are the frame problem and the problem of non-monotonic reasoning.

[1] See for example the literature on the Shakey project (Nilsson, 1984) or the more recent Ambler project (Bares et.al., 1989) for examples of this approach in the study of autonomous robots. Sullivan and Tyler (1991) present an example of this approach in the area of interface agents.

4. Important Insights of Behavior-Based AI

The methods developed by Behavior-Based AI in response to the problems of Knowledge-Based AI techniques listed above, are grounded in two important insights[2]:

- Looking at complete systems changes the problems often in a favorable way.
- Interaction dynamics can lead to emergent complexity.

A first realization is that viewing the problem of building an intelligent system in its context can make things a lot easier. This observation is true at several levels:

1. The intelligent functions which are being modelled are part of a complete intelligent system. Building systems in an integrated way (rather than developing modules implementing these functions independently) often makes the task a lot easier. For example, a system which can learn has to rely less on planning (because it can cache computed plans). A system which has sensors and actuators can perform tests in the environment and as such has less of a need for modelling and inference. A system which has sensors has an easier job disambiguating natural language utterances and so on.

2. The complete system is part of some environment, it is situated in some space. This implies that there is less of a need for modeling, because the "world is its own best model" (Brooks, 1991). The environment can also be used as an external memory (e.g. for reminding the system which tasks still have to be performed and which ones it already did perform (Suchman, 1987). The environment usually has particular characteristics which can be exploited by the system (offices consist of vertical walls and horizontal floors, doors typically have a particular size, etc). These "habitat constraints" can be exploited by the system, making its task much easier (Horswill, 1992).

3. The system is not only situated in space, but also in time. This implies that the system can evolve itself so as to become better at its task, if time and the particular task admits (either through individual learning or some sort of artificial evolution). Time also allows for the construction of an iterative, incremental solution to a problem. For example, a natural language system situated in time does not need to disambiguate every utterance. It can go back and forth asking questions or making particular remarks which will help to gradually disambiguate whatever the other speaker wants to convey.

4. Finally the system is typically also part of a society. Other agents in the same environment are dealing with similar problems. Therefore there is no need for the agent to figure everything out by itself. For example, a mobile robot could use the strategy of closely following a person passing by, so as to achieve the competence of navigating in an office environment without bumping into things. Kozierok and Maes (1992b) report on some experiments in which interface agents learned to perform certain tasks by observing and imitating users.

[2]Notice that I do not credit Behavior-Based AI with the discovery of these insights.

As a consequence of the above ideas, Behavior-Based AI has concentrated on modelling systems in their context. While traditional AI has concentrated on simulated toy examples, Behavior-Based AI has built "real" systems which solve an actual (small) problem in a concrete environment.

A second major insight of Behavior-Based AI is that interaction dynamics among simple components can lead to emergent complexity (see also Resnick, 1992). Also this idea applies at several different levels (Brooks, 1991b):

1. Simple interaction dynamics between the system and its environment can lead to emergent structure or emergent functionality. Simon (1968) gives an example of an ant on the beach. He notes that the complexity of its behavior is more a reflection of complexity of environment than of its own internal complexity and postulates that the same might be true of human behavior. Agre (1991) shows how behavior as complex as goal-directed action sequences can be an observable, emergent property of the interaction dynamics between the environment and a reflex-guided person. This means that often it is sufficient to study the particular properties of the environment and find an interaction loop, a set of simple feedback or reflex mechanisms, which will produce the desired behavior. One of the implications is that we need a better understanding of environments (Horswill, 1992), (Wilson, 1991). It also means that if we want to prove aspects about the resulting performance of Behavior-Based systems, we have to model these systems as well as their environments.

2. Simple interaction dynamics between the components of the system can lead to emergent structure or emergent functionality. For example, Mataric's wall-following robot does not have a single component to which the expertise of wall-following can be attributed (Mataric, 1991). One module is responsible for steering the robot towards the wall when the distance to the wall is above some threshold while another module is responsible for steering the robot away from the wall when the distance is below some threshold. Neither one of these modules is primarily "responsible" for the wall following behavior. It is their interaction dynamics which makes the robot follow walls reliably. In Maes' networks (1990), none of the component modules is responsible for action selection. The action selection behavior is an emergent property of some activation/inhibition dynamics among the primitive components of the system.

3. Finally interaction dynamics between the component systems in a social system can lead to emergent struc-

ture or functionality. Deneubourg (1991, 1992) describes how social insects following simple local rules can produce emergent complexity such as a path to a food source, food foraging trees, etc. Malone's collection of autonomous bidding systems solves the complicated task of process-processor allocation (Malone et.al., 1988). Finally, anthropologists have studied the social construction of different concepts and methods (Suchman, 1987) (Shrager and Callanan, 1991).

Important is that such emergent complexity is often more robust, flexible and fault-tolerant than programmed, top-down organized complexity. This is the case because none of the components is really in charge of producing this complexity. None of the components is more critical than another one. When one of them breaks down, the system demonstrates a graceful degradation of performance. Since all of the components interact in parallel, the system is also able to adapt quicker to environmental changes. Often the system explores multiple solutions in parallel, so that as soon as certain variables change, the system is able to switch to an alternative way of doing things. For example, in Maes' system (1990) several sequences of actions are evaluated in parallel, the best one determining the behavior of the agent. Also in Malone's system (Malone et.al., 1988) several mappings of processes to machines can be said to be explored in parallel.

5. Solutions Investigated by Behavior-Based AI

In section 3 we listed the techniques adopted by Knowledge-Based AI and discussed why they proved to be inadequate for building autonomous systems situated in dynamic environments. This section contrasts these techniques with those adopted by Behavior-Based AI.

Task-Oriented Decomposition

Instead of building general functional modules like perception and planning, Behavior-Based AI develops competence modules, modules which are an expert at (and are responsible for) a particular small task-oriented competence. These modules interface to one another via extremely simple messages (rather than a common representation of beliefs, etc). The communication is almost never of a "broadcast" nature, but happens rather on a one-to-one basis. Typically the messages consist of activation energy, or simple suppression and inhibition signals, or simple tokens in a restricted language. Each of the modules is directly connected to relevant sensors and actuators.

Approach

There are no "general" or task-independent modules. There is no general perception module, no general planner, etc. Each of the competence modules is responsible for doing all the representation, computation, "reasoning", execution, etc, related to its particular competence. For example, an obstacle avoidance module might need one bit of information to represent whether an obstacle is perceived or not, and it might do some very simple computation to decide how an obstacle should be avoided. Competence modules are self-contained, black boxes. They might employ completely different techniques (even different hardware) to achieve their competence. Part of the reason for this more pragmatic approach is a pessimistic vision about whether it is possible at all to build a general vision system, a general planner, etc (a view also expressed in (Minsky, 1986).

Role of Representation

There is much less emphasis on modeling the domain. First of all, there is no central representation shared by several modules. The system also does not attempt to integrate the information from different sensors into one coherent, objective interpretation of the current situation. Instead every task-oriented module represents whatever it needs to represent to achieve its competence. These representations are not related and might be inconsistent or redundant. Within one competence module, the usage of representations is minimized in favor of employing the environment as a source of information (and a determiner of action). The representations within one module are often of a less propositional, objective and declarative nature than those employed in Knowledge-Based AI. For example they might index objects according to the features and properties that make them significant to the task at hand (Agre, 1991) rather than their identities. They can be of a numeric, procedural or analog nature. Often a lot of task-specific "problem solving" is performed in the perception part of a particular competence (Steels, 1990b) (Chapman, 1992) (Ballard, 1989).

Organization

The systems built are highly distributed. All of the competence modules operate in parallel. None of the modules is "in control". However, some simple arbitration method is often included in order to select or fuse multiple conflicting actuator commands. This arbitration network might be a winner-take-all network, as in (Maes, 1990) or a hardcoded priority scheme as in (Brooks, 1986). Because of its distributed operation, a behavior-based system is typically able to react very fast to changes in the environment or changes in the needs of the system.

Model of Activity

Activity is not modelled as the result of a deliberative process. Instead complex and goal-directed activity is modeled as an emergent property of the interaction among competence modules internally, and among competence modules and the environment. There is no internal structure corresponding to "the plan" of the system.

Role of Learning

Learning and development are considered crucial aspects of a Behavior-Based System (Wilson, 1985) (Maes, 1992). Building an adaptive system that will develop into one that achieves the tasks, is often considered a better approach than building a static system which will not change when the environment or task changes (e.g. a robot breaking one of its legs). In some systems, the evolution (towards increasingly more sophisticated behavior) is simulated by the programmer, e.g. by incrementally adding more structure to existing successful systems (Brooks, 1991). Other systems employ artificial evolution (Koza, 1991) or learning by the individual (Maes, 1992) (Maes and Brooks, 1990) (Wilson, 1985) (Drescher, 1991) (Kaelbling, 1992) (Sutton, 1991). In almost all cases, the system concentrates on learning new information (or behavior) from its environmental, rather than compiling existing information. The learning algorithms are implemented in a distributed way: typically a similar learning algorithm runs in different competence modules. Related to the idea of learning is that of redundancy: often the system has multiple modules for a particular competence. Experience sorts out which of these modules implements the competence in a more reliable way (Maes, 1992) (Payton et.al., 1991) (Drescher, 1991).

Systems built using the above principles suffer less from the problems listed in section three. They act fast, because (1) they have less layers of information processing, (2) they are more distributed and often non-synchronized, and (3) they require less expensive computation. They are able to deal with unforeseen situations (opportunities as well as contingencies), because they rely much more on the environment as a source of information and a determiner of action. They are less brittle, because (1) none of the modules is more critical than the others, (2) they do not attempt to fully understand the current situation, (3) they incorporate redundant methods and (4) they adapt over time. They have less trouble relating representations to sensor stimuli, because they do not attempt to maintain objective representations of the environment. Finally they are not prone to problems of combinatorial explosions, because they do not employ traditional search processes.

6. Three Examples Contrasting the Two Approaches

A Mobile Robot

Consider a mobile surveillance robot which has to watch over some offices. Its task requires that it navigates from room to room. The Knowledge-Based version of this robot could work as follows. The perception module processes the different sensor data and integrates them into a representation of the environment. It attempts to update this model as often as possible. The model includes information such as the location of the robot in the environment, the location and type (often even identity) of other objects in this environment such as chairs, tables, etc. The model is used by the planning module to decide how to fulfill the goal of finding the door in the current room, while avoiding obstacles. The planner goes through a systematic search to produce a list of actions which will according to the model fulfill both goals. The execution module executes this plan while possible checking at certain points whether things are going as predicted. If not, control is returned to the planner.

A Behavior-Based robot for the same task could be constructed in the following way. In an incremental way, several modules would be implemented corresponding to the different competences necessary for the task: a module for recognizing and going through doors, a module for wall following (actually wall following is often modeled as an emergent property of two to three lower-level modules), a module for obstacle avoidance (or even a couple redundant ones, using different sensors, since this is a very critical competence), and so on. All of these modules operate in parallel. A simple arbitration scheme (some simple suppression and inhibition wires among these modules) suffices to implement the desired priority scheme: the obstacle avoidance modules always have priority over going through doors which has priority over wall following. This robot does not plan a course of action. However from an observer's point of view it will appear to operate in a systematic, rational way. Brooks (1986)(1991) has argued convincingly in writing and in actual demonstrations, which of the two above robots will be more able to fulfill the task in a robust and reliable way.

An Interface Agent

Consider the problem of building a "software agent" or "interface agent" which assists the user with certain computer-based tasks. Its goal is to offer assistance to the user and automate as many of the actions of the user as possible. Knowledge-Based AI approaches this problem in the following way (Sullivan and Tyler, 1991). The agent is given an elaborate amount of knowledge about the problem domain by some Knowledge Engineer. This knowledge contains: a model of the user and possibly the user's organization, a model of the tasks the user engages in, including a hierarchical specification of the subtasks, knowledge about the vocabulary of these tasks, and so on. At run time, the agent uses this knowledge to recognize the intentions and plans of the user. For example, if a UNIX user enters a command like "emacs paper.tex", the system deduces that the user is planning to produce a written document. It then plans it's own course of action (the goal being to assist the user), which for example might consist of the action sequence: the text formatting command "latex paper.tex", followed by the preview command "xdvi papr.dvi" and the printing command "lpr paper.dvi". The problems with this approach are exactly the same ones as those for mobile robots (cfr. list in section three): it is hard to provide such a complete and consistent model, the model is quickly outdated (as the user's ways of performing tasks change). Because of the computational complexity of the approach, the system would react very slow. All sorts of unpredicted events might take place which the agent cannot deal with (the user might change his/her mind about what to do in the middle of things, or might perform tasks in unorthodox non-rational ways), etc.

Instead a Behavior-Based interface agent can be built as follows (Maes, 1992) (Kozierok and Maes, 1992). Several competence modules are constructed which are experts (or try to become experts) about a small aspect of the task. For example, one module might be responsible for invoking a particular command (like "lpr") at a particular moment. The agent is situated in an environment containing an ideal source for learning: the user's behavior. Each of the modules gathers information by observing the user and keeping statistics about a particular aspect of the user's behavior. For example, the above mentioned module will keep track of the situations in which the user executed the "lpr" command. Whenever a new situation comes up which is very similar to one of one or more memorized situations, it actually offers to the user to execute the "lpr" command. If we have several experts for the different commands listed above, each of these will know when to become active and offer their assistance to the user. From an observer's point of view, it will seem as if the system "understands" the intentions of the user, as if it knows what the task of producing a document involves. Nevertheless, the action sequences are just an emergent property of a distributed system. The system will smoothly adapt to the changing habits of the user, will react in a fast way, will never completely break down, and so on.

A Scheduling System

Finally, consider the problem of building a scheduling system, whose goal it is to allocate processes to processors in real-time. Again the domain is a very dynamic one: new processing jobs are formulated in different machines all the time. The decision to be made is whether to run these processes locally or on a different machine, the global goal being to minimize the average amount of time it takes to run a process. The loads of the different available machines vary continuously. Certain machines might suddenly become unavailable for scheduling processes, requiring a rescheduling of the jobs that were running on those machines at the time, and so on. A Knowledge-Based system for this task would contain a lot of knowledge about scheduling and about the particular configuration of machines and typical processing jobs at hand. The system would update its representation of the current situation as often as possible. This requires gathering all the data from the different machines in the network on whether they are still available, what their workload is, which processes they are running, which new processes were formulated on them, etc. Once all this information has been centralized, the system would perform a systematic search (possibly involving some heuristics) for the most optimal allocation of processes to processors. Once that schedule has been produced, the processing jobs can actually be sent to the different machines that they have been assigned to. This centralized way of solving the problem is present in the majority of the traditional work in this area (Kleinrock and Nilsson, 1981).

Malone has proposed a different solution to this problem (Malone et.al, 1988), which one could call Behavior-Based. In his "Enterprise" system, each of the machines in the network is autonomous and in charge of its own work load. The system is based on the metaphor of a market. A machine on which a new processing task originates, sends out a "requests for bids" for the task to be done. Other machines respond (if they feel like it) with bids giving estimated completion times which reflect their speed and currently loaded files. For example, if the task to be performed is a graphics rendering job and some machine has that software loaded, it will be more interested in running the new job (because it does not have do waste time and space loading the necessary software). The machine which sent out the request for bids will collect the bids it receives over some small period of time and allocate the job to the machine which made the best bid (either remote or local). This distributed scheduling method was found to have several advantages. The system is very robust because none of the machines is more critical than another one (there is no central scheduler). A user can make a machine unavailable for external processing jobs at run-time. The whole system will adapt smoothly to this unexpected situation. The system is very simple and yet very flexible in terms of the kind of factors it can take into account.

7. Discussion

Behavior-Based AI represents an exciting new approach to the study of intelligence. So far, Behavior-Based AI has demonstrated several "proofs-of-concept" of its approach. In particular, successes have been booked in the area of autonomous, situated systems. Several prototypes have been built which have shown to solve some reasonable difficult task in a real, dynamic domain. These initial results are very promising, but are far from representing a solid, systematic methodology.

In order for the new approach to be more founded, more fundamental research has to be undertaken. First of all, we need to understand the classes of problems Behavior-Based AI is trying to deal with much better, so that it becomes possible to critically compare particular systems and proposals. For example, many different models of action selection have been proposed, but unless we understand the problem of action selection better, and have a list of desiderata for solutions, we do not have any ground to compare the different proposals[3].

Aside from better evaluation criteria, we need a better understanding of the underlying principles of Behavior-Based AI. Without an underlying theory, it will not be possible to scale the approach. In particular, it is important to understand the mechanisms and limitations of emergent behavior. How can a globally desired structure or functionality be designed on the basis of local rules? What are the conditions and limitations under which the emergent structure is stable? and so on. Some first steps towards a theory of emergent functionality have been proposed, using tools from complex dynamics (Steels, 1991) (Kiss, 1991).

[3]Some people have started making such lists, e.g. (Brooks, 1991b), (Tyrell, 1992) and (Maes, 1990, 1990).

Acknowledgements

Parts of this paper were prepared for a public discussion on the topic of Behavior-Based AI with Marvin Minsky and Mike Travers. Karl Sims provided comments on an earlier draft.

References

Agre P.E, 1991, The Dynamic structure of Everyday Life, Cambridge University Press.

Ballard D.H, 1989, Reference Frames for Animate Vision, Proceedings of IJCAI-89 conference, Detroit.

Bares J., Hebert M., Kanade T., Krotkov E., Mitchell T., Simmons R., Whittaker W., 1989, Ambler: An Autonomous Rover for Planetary Exploration, IEEE Computer, June 1989.

Brooks R.A., 1986, A Robust Layered Control System for a Mobile Robot, IEEE Journal of Robotics and Automation, RA-2, April.

Brooks R.A., Maes P., Mataric M.J., and More G., 1990, Lunar Base Construction Robots, Proceedings of the IROS-90 conference, Japan.

Brooks R.A., 1991, Intelligence without Reason, Computers and Thought lecture, Proceedings of IJCAI-91, Sidney, Australia.

Brooks R.A., 1991b, Challenges for Complete Creature Architectures, In: From Animals to Animats, Proceedings of the First International Conference on the Simulation of Adaptive Behavior, Edited by Meyer J.-A. and Wilson S.W., MIT-Press, 1991.

Chapman D., 1987, Planning for Conjunctive Goals, Journal of Artificial Intelligence, 32, 3.

Chapman D., 1992, Vision, Instruction and Action, MIT-Press, in press.

Deneubourg J.L., Goss S., Franks N., Sendova-Franks A., Detrain C., Chretien L., 1991, The Dynamics of Collective Sorting: Robot-like Ants and Ant-like Robots, In: From Animals to Animats, Proceedings of the First International Conference on the Simulation of Adaptive Behavior, Edited by Meyer J.-A. and Wilson S.W., MIT-Press, 1991.

Deneubourg J.L, Theraulaz G. and Beckers R., 1992, Swarm-Made Architectures, In: Toward a Practice of Autonomous Systems, Proceedings of the First European Conference on Artificial Life, edited by F.J. Varela and P. Bourgine, MIT-Press.

Drescher G.L, 1991, Made-Up Minds: A Constructivist Approach to Artificial Intelligence, MIT-Press.

Holland J.H., 1986, Escaping Brittleness: the Possibilities of General-Purpose Learning Algorithms applied to Parallel Rule-Based Systems, In: Machine Learning, an Artificial Intelligence Approach, Volume II, edited by R.S. Michalski, J.G. Carbonell and T.M. Mitchell, Morgan Kaufmann.

Horswill I., 1992, Characterizing Adaptation by Constraint, In: Toward a Practice of Autonomous Systems, Proceedings of the First European Conference on Artificial Life, edited by F.J. Varela and P. Bourgine, MIT-Press.

Kaelbling L.P., 1992, An Adaptable Mobile Robot, In: Toward a Practice of Autonomous Systems, Proceedings of the First European Conference on Artificial Life, edited by F.J. Varela and P. Bourgine, MIT-Press.

Kiss G., 1991, Autonomous Agents, AI and Chaos Theory, In: From Animals to Animats, Proceedings of the First International Conference on the Simulation of Adaptive Behavior, Edited by Meyer J.-A. and Wilson S.W., MIT-Press, 1991.

Kleinrock L. and Nilsson A., 1981, On Optimal Scheduling Algorithms for Time-Shared Systems, Journal of the ACM, 28, 3, July 1981.

Koza J.R., 1991, Evolution and Co-evolution of Computer Programs to Control Independently-Acting Agents, In: From Animals to Animats, Proceedings of the First International Conference on the Simulation of Adaptive Behavior, Edited by Meyer J.-A. and Wilson S.W., MIT-Press, 1991.

Kozierok R. and Maes P., 1992, A Learning Interface Agent for Scheduling Meetings, Proceedings of the ACM SIGCHI International Workshop on Intelligent User Interfaces, ACM, Orlando, Florida.

Maes P., 1990, Situated Agents Can Have Goals, In: Designing Autonomous Agents: Theory and Practice from Biology to Engineering and Back, edited by P. Maes, MIT Press.

Maes, P., 1990b, Designing Autonomous Agents: Theory and Practice from Biology to Engineering and Back, MIT-Press

Maes P. and Brooks R.A., 1990, Learning to Coordinate Behaviors, Proceedings of AAAI-90, Boston.

Maes P., 1992, Learning Behavior Networks from Experience, In: Toward a Practice of Autonomous Systems, Proceedings of the First European Conference on Artificial Life, edited by F.J. Varela and P. Bourgine, MIT-Press.

Maes P., 1992b, Learning Interface Agents, Submitted to the ACM SIGCHI International Workshop on Intelligent User Interfaces, ACM, Orlando, Florida.

Malone T.W., Fikes R.E., Grant K.R., and Howard M.T., 1988, Enterprise: A Market-like Task Scheduler for Distributed Computing Environments, In: The Ecology of Computation, edited by B. Huberman, North-Holland.

Mataric M., 1991, Behavioral Synergy without Explicit Integration, In: Special Issue of SIGART on Integrated Cognitive Architectures, Volume 2, Number 4.

Meyer J.-A. and Guillot A., 1991, Simulation of Adaptive Behavior in Animats: Review and Prospects, In:

From Animals to Animats, Proceedings of the First International Conference on the Simulation of Adaptive Behavior, Edited by Meyer J.-A. and Wilson S.-W., MIT-Press, 1991.

Minsky M., 1986, the Society of Mind, Simon and Schuster, New York.

Nilsson N., 1984, Shakey the Robot, SRI A.I. Center Technical Note 323.

Payton D.W., Keirsey D., Krozel J. and Rosenblatt K., 1991, Do Whatever Works: A Robust Approach to Fault-Tolerant Autonomous Control, to appear in Journal of Applied Intelligence, Vol. 3, 1992.

Resnick M., 1992, Beyond the Centralized Mind Set: Explorations in Massively Parallel Microworlds, Ph.D. Thesis, MIT Media-Laboratory Epistemology and Learning Group.

Roitblat H.L., 1991, Cognitive Action Theory as a Control Architecture, In: From Animals to Animats, Proceedings of the First International Conference on the Simulation of Adaptive Behavior, Edited by Meyer J.-A. and Wilson S.W., MIT-Press, 1991.

Shrager J. and Callanan M., 1991, Active Language in the Collaborative Development of Cooking Skill, Proceedings of the Cognitive Science Conference, Lawrence Erlbaum.

Simon H., 1969, The Sciences of the Artificial, MIT-Press.

Steels L., 1990, Cooperation between Distributed Agents through Self-Organization, In: Decentralized AI, edited by: Y. Demazeau and J.-P. Muller, Elsevier, North-Holland.

Steels L., 1990b, Exploiting Analogical Representations, In: Designing Autonomous Agents: Theory and Practice from Biology to Engineering and Back, edited by P. Maes, MIT Press.

Steels L., 1991, Towards a Theory of Emergent Functionality, In: From Animals to Animats, Proceedings of the First International Conference on the Simulation of Adaptive Behavior, Edited by Meyer J.-A. and Wilson S.W., MIT-Press, 1991.

Suchman L.A., 1987, Plans and Situated Actions: The Problem of Human-Machine Communication, Cambridge University Press.

Sullivan J.W., and Tyler S.W. (editors), 1991, Intelligent User Interfaces, ACM Press.

Sutton Richard S., 1991, Reinforcement Learning Architectures for Animats, In: From Animals to Animats, Proceedings of the First International Conference on the Simulation of Adaptive Behavior, Edited by Meyer J.-A. and Wilson S.W., MIT-Press, 1991.

Tyrrell T., 1992, Defining the Action Selection Problem, In: Proceedings of the 14th Conference of the Cognitive Science Society.

Wilson S.W., 1985, Knowledge Growth in an Artificial Animal, In: Proceedings of the First International Conference on Genetic Algorithms and their Applications, edited by Greffenstette, Lawrence Erlbaum Assoc.

Wilson S.W., 1991, The Animat Path to AI, In: From Animals to Animats, Proceedings of the First International Conference on the Simulation of Adaptive Behavior, Edited by Meyer J.-A. and Wilson S.W., MIT-Press, 1991.

Environment Structure and Adaptive Behavior From the Ground Up

Peter M. Todd **Stewart W. Wilson**
The Rowland Institute for Science
100 Edwin H. Land Boulevard
Cambridge, MA 02142 USA
ptodd@spo.rowland.org wilson@smith.rowland.org

Abstract

We describe a framework for exploring the evolution of adaptive behaviors in response to different physical environment structures. We focus here on the evolving behavior-generating mechanisms of individual creatures, and briefly mention some approaches to characterizing different environments in which various behaviors may prove adaptive. The environments are described initially as simple two-dimensional grids containing food arranged in some layout. The creatures in these worlds can have evolved sensors, internal states, and actions and action-triggering conditions. By allowing all three of these components to evolve, rather than prespecifying any of them, we can explore a wide range of behavior types, including "blind" and memoryless behaviors. Our system is simple and well-defined enough to allow complete specification of the range of possible action-types (including moving, eating, and reproducing) and their effects on the energy levels of the creature and the environment (the bioenergetics of the world). Useful and meaningful ways of characterizing the structures of environments in which different behaviors will emerge remain to be developed.

1 Introduction

We are interested in the effects that the environment can have on an organism's adaptive behavior. Since this question encompasses essentially the whole of psychology and biology, we must pare it down a bit before we can make much headway. We focus here on how the physical, spatial structure of the environment can foster the evolution of, and be in turn exploited by, particular adaptive behavior-generating mechanisms. We leave aside for now the fascinating questions that arise when the environment is considered not only in terms of the physical selectors at work in it, but also the biotic (e.g. parasites and hosts) and psychological (e.g. conspecifics and mimics) selectors (see Miller, 1992). Our work here may in fact be seen as complementary to explorations elsewhere attempting to characterize the effects of the social environment on adaptive behavior and evolution (Todd & Miller, 1991; Todd & Miller, submitted). As it turns out, even without this added complexity and realism, the sorts of behaviors that can evolve to take advantage of static spatial environments are still varied and interesting. This work is also intended to provide theoretical support for the behavior-based approach to AI described by Maes (these proceedings). By categorizing environments and describing the sorts of behaviors that are adaptive in them, we hope to provide not only insights into natural evolved systems, but also useful guidelines for the design of artificial agents existing in various application domains.

Creating simple simulated worlds and seeing what sorts of simulated behaving creatures will evolve in them is certainly not a new approach. Ackley and Littman (1992) and Werner and Dyer (these proceedings) have developed sophisticated simulations that embody many of the ideas described here, and serve as positive examples of what is possible with such an approach. But our goals here are different from those embodied in many similar research efforts. Rather than manipulating the environment with the specific aim of evolving creatures that can navigate, or communicate, or learn, we want to explore a more general question: what *will* creatures evolve to do, given certain environmental regularities or structures? What behaviors will prove adaptive in various types of environments? These questions require us to do two very intertwined things in our research program: both elucidate the sorts of environment-exploiting behavioral mechanisms that creatures might employ, and describe and characterize how environments can vary in ways that lead to the evolution of different forms of adaptive behavior. Obviously such goals are very ambitious, and perhaps still beyond our reach, but at least by beginning to formalize our thinking about these questions, we can hope to make some progress in our understanding of the complexities involved in the behavioral interactions between environments and organisms.

In a simulated 2-dimensional world across which food is distributed in some fashion, creatures attempting to find and eat that food may get along fine with no sensory systems, or without memories or internal states, or with very few motor commands; or the creatures may find it virtually essential to possess long-distance sensors, sophisticated internal world models, and finely-tuned motor sequences before they can achieve any adaptive advantage at all. What sensors, states, and actions prove adaptive depends on the environment in which the population of creatures evolves. But since it is exactly those three components (at least) which define an organism's adaptive behavior, in order to study the effects of the environment on adaptive behavior we must instantiate our study in a framework which allows the evolution of all three components, something not usually attempted in evolutionary simulations. Cariani (1990) and Pattee (1989) in particular have issued the call to consider the evolution of sensors and effectors in addition to the behavioral links in between, since it is only through the former two that creatures can ground themselves in connection to the outside world. We hope that the framework we present here will allow the exploration of the evolution of exactly those sensors and effectors, the process that Cariani calls *semantic-adaptation,* along with the *syntactic-adaptation* of evolving information-processing mechanisms, thereby yielding a more complete picture of the evolution of behavior in general.

To try to achieve these grand ends, we focus primarily in this paper on an open-ended scheme for the evolution of simulated creatures in terms of their sensors, internal states, and actions. Only after this framework has been laid down can we turn to the question of the structure of environments, and the effects they can have on these evolving creatures and their behaviors. In this combined context, we discuss briefly our planned explorations of the interactions of these two parts of our system, and what we can hope to learn from such an investigation.

2 The World and the Organism

The creature and its environment cannot be described separately; each is shaped by and shapes the other. Different types of environments call for different behavioral mechanisms to respond to them adaptively; and different behavioral mechanisms, including internal representations and sensory inputs, change the very structure of the world-lived-in for the creature living in it, or, via emitted actions, the structure of the world experienced by others. To understand the interactions of the physical world and behavior, then, we must consider the two in an intertwined fashion. In this section we first describe possible worlds and adaptive behaviors in them with an eye toward showing what components we'll need to create those behaviors, and then we discuss those components themselves, and how they can work together to create adaptive behavior in the world.

2.1 The Structure of the World

To begin with the simplest interesting (and easily visualizable) case, we use a 2-dimensional hexagonal-grid world consisting of N by M positions. (A hexagonal rather than a square grid is used to avoid the anisotropies in distances between orthogonally and diagonally adjacent squares in the latter.) Each position $W(x,y)$ in the world can contain food, one or more creatures, both, or nothing. Time in the world passes by in discrete clock-ticks, t. The currency in this world is simply energy; creatures live on it and use it up, and food contains it -- the greater the amount of food in a particular location, the greater the amount of energy available to a grazing organism. (This is in contrast to Holland's ECHO system, which works on a flow of metabolic products equivalent to organic chemical compounds -- see Holland, 1992.)

The exact layout of food in the world over time constitutes the spatio-temporal structure of the environment, in response to which the creature should behave adaptively. This layout is created primarily by the real-valued function, $\phi(x,y,t)$, which indicates the new food being added to each position in the world at each time-step (so that it can be thought of as specifying the "plant growth" in the world). Since creatures may, through their actions, cause the amount of food in the world to change, the contents of W at time t can be computed as the contents of W after time $t-1$ (including the effects of creature actions) plus $\phi(x,y,t)$, the new food appearance/growth that occurs.

2.2 The Structure of the Organisms

The world can contain one or more simulated organisms running around in it at a time. Each organism in the world has associated with it a 3-tuple (x,y,E) which codes its current position and internal energy level, and a behavior-generating component which defines its possible actions and triggering conditions, internal state variables, and sensors. The position-energy 3-tuple can change during a creature's lifetime; the beginning values for each creature are determined at the time of their creation, as will be described later. The behavioral portion of each creature is created by an evolutionary process, and is fixed throughout the creature's lifetime (thus we are for the moment ignoring learning processes). To introduce the subcomponents of the creature's behavioral mechanisms, we will first look at a few example environmental situations.

Consider four possible worlds, and the types of creatures that might do well in them. First, there could be food everywhere in the world, evenly and equally distributed (see Figure 1a -- while the world is shown with squares in this figure, it is represented as hexes in the simulation). In this case a creature really does not need very sophisticated behavior to maximize its food input: it can basically just move about the environment in a straight line, perhaps turning every now and again, eating as it goes. Thus, if the creature merely has a small set of motor commands, such as "eat," "go straight," and "turn right," which it selects from stochastically in a fixed proportion, say 1:1:0.1, then this creature will do about as well as possible (in terms of gaining food energy) in this world. It has no need for any sensory input, nor for any memory of what it's already done or seen, that is, no internal state is necessary (or helpful). Thus in this case, evolution need only supply the creature with the appropriate motor commands, and appropriate rates of firing them stochastically.

If the world is laid out slightly differently, for instance with food in a regular "zig-zag" pattern stretching across the whole 2-d plain (see Figure 1b), then a slightly more sophisticated set of behavioral mechanisms could prove useful. A creature which performs the action sequence "eat, move forward, move left, eat, move forward,

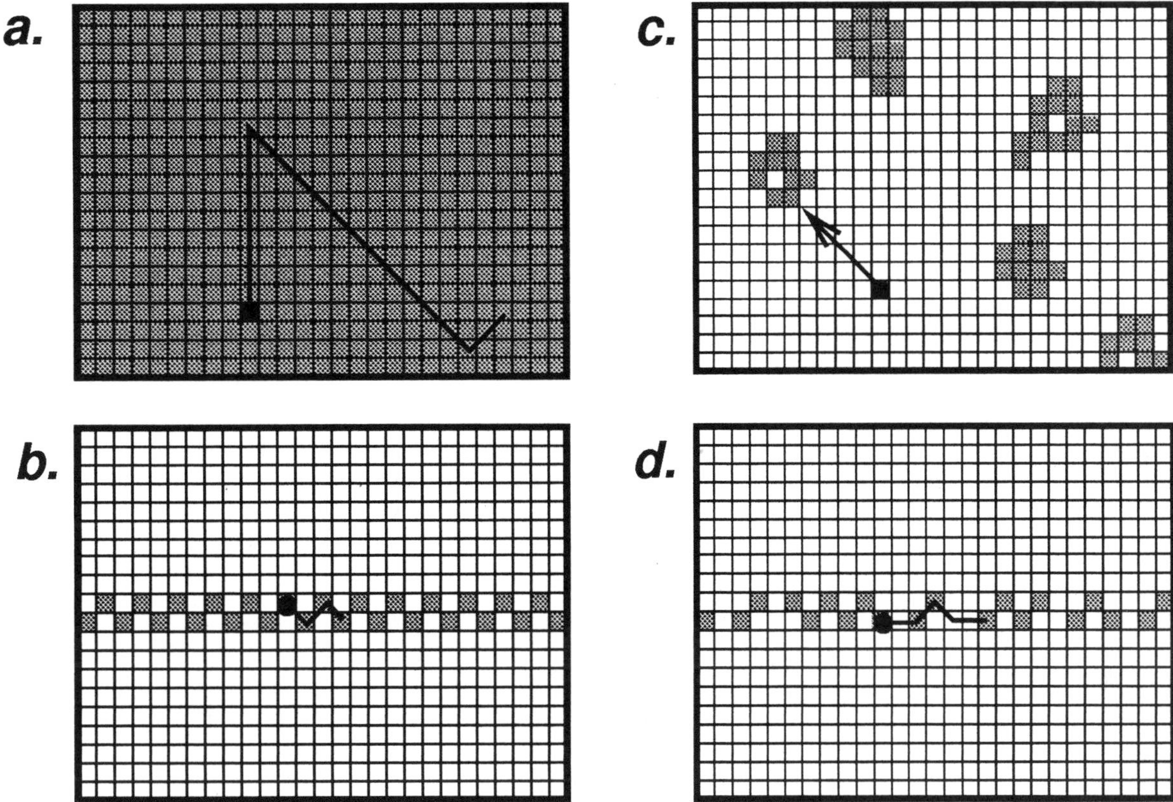

Figure 1. Environments with differing behavioral component requirements. a. An environment with food everywhere (dark grey), showing a creature (black circle) and the mostly-straight path it might take. b. A zig-zag environment, showing a creature and the regular path it might take. c. A clumpy environment, showing a creature heading toward one of the clumps. d. A zig-zag-with-gaps environment, showing a creature adjusting its regular path to take the missing food-squares into account.

move right, eat..." over and over again (provided it starts off at an appropriate position!) will find as much food as possible. Here there is still no need for any sensory input, since the world is very regular and so evolved models of the world can mirror it exactly; but internal state *is* very important in this case. Essentially the creature must utilize an evolved "central pattern generator" (CPG) that produces this string of motor commands over and over. Since this CPG must keep track of where it is in the action-cycle, it must use some state information. In this situation, then, both appropriate actions triggered by certain internal states, and the means of properly generating those internal states, must evolve.

Next, consider a world in which food is distributed sparsely and randomly, in small clumps, as shown in Figure 1c. In this case, a creature would do well to have some sensory input. If it just moves in a fixed or random manner, as in the first situation, or in a blind preprogrammed fashion, as in the second, it is quite unlikely to run across much of the widely separated food in its lifetime. But if it has a sensory apparatus which indicates the direction of the nearest source of food, the creature can base it movements on this input and head in that direction, eating when it arrives at the food. Here, evolved actions can be based solely on the outputs of evolved sensors; there is no need for internal state to guide the actions.

Finally, imagine a modification of the "zig-zag" world of Figure 1b, in which there are occasional gaps in the zags, as shown in Figure 1d. In this case, if we drop one of our previously-evolved zig-zag creatures into this world, it will do fine for a while, but when it comes to one of the gaps, it will be thrown off by one position, and will miss all the food until the *next* gap comes. Obviously, it should be able to do better than this. What it needs so it can do better is again some sensory input, which this time modifies the action of the central pattern generator by adding an extra "move forward" whenever it detects a gap in the food pattern. So in this scenario, all three behavioral components will prove adaptive and could be expected to evolve: a set of actions including "eat," "move forward," "move left," and "move right"; a set of internal state variables which successively influence each other to trigger the proper actions in sequence; and a set of sensors which can detect gaps in the zig-zag sequence in the world, and modify the action of the internal state CPG loop to keep the sequence of generated behaviors in sync with the structure of the world. (This is similar to the sensor-modulated CPGs that Gallagher and Beer, these proceedings, have evolved to control artificial insect locomotion.)

We can see from these four examples that actions, internal states, and sensors can all combine independently in a variety of ways to create adaptive behavior in different environments. Thus to explore the evolution of such adaptive behaviors, we need a system which can evolve each of these components independently. Moreover, to be able to analyze the simulated creatures which result from our evolutionary scenarios in terms of these behavioral components, it is important that they be kept modularly distinct; if we were just to evolve big unstructured neural networks or Lisp code representations of our creatures, for instance, it would be very difficult to say when a network was using internal state, or whether or not a Lisp routine instantiates a central pattern generator. (It is typically easier to determine what actions and sensory inputs such systems are employing than what they're doing internally, but even that may not be so clear in more complex situations.) To help alleviate this difficulty of both evolution and analysis, we have developed a modular system of evolving lists of actions and triggering conditions, internal state variables, and sensory input systems. These lists of variables are restricted in how they can interact with each other, so that modularity and interpretability can be maintained. Evolution creates and builds up the entries in each of these lists within each individual creature. For now, we will remain agnostic in our choice of representation and implementation of the elements in these lists; they should merely be thought of as some sort of simple information-processing mechanisms. (We will return to the issue of implementation in a later section.) We now consider each of these three behavioral components in detail.

2.2.1 Sensors

The ultimate role of sensory systems is to tell creatures about what's out there in the world that might be important. Sensors are not for informing about spectral intensity, or airborne polypeptides, or modulated pitch formants; rather, they are for indicating the presence of a colorful ripe fruit, or a sexually-ready conspecific, or a snarling predator. That is, sensors should be thought of as signalling *fitness affordances,* things in the world which can have a positive or negative effect on the individual's ongoing fitness (see Miller & Todd, in preparation, for a more detailed account of this topic, patterned after Gibson's 1966 notion of perceptual affordances). As such, we will define the sensors in the present system as providing information about just those things that are out there in the world, that is, about the contents of $W(x,y)$.

Each individual has a list of sensors, $S[i]$, where i can go from 1 to some preset maximum number of sensors n_S. If n_S is preset to 0, then none of the creatures in this world can have any sensors -- this is how we can restrict our experiments to the first two types of environmental situations presented earlier. Each $S[i]$ is defined as a function $f_{S[i]}$ of just the category-based contents of the world, $W_c(x,y)$, for a particular category c. That is, $S[i] \equiv f_{S[i]}(W_c(x,y))$, where c in the current simple worlds can be either food or (other) creatures, so that two general classes of sensors are possible. The categories c that sensors can respond to are just those classes of objects or entities that the creatures can act on -- the granularity of actions and sensors is always equal. (There is no proprioception possible through the sensory inputs in S, but this can sneak in through the internal state variables described next.)

Each $S[i]$ can be as complicated or as simple as evolution deigns to make it. For instance, one creature might have $S[18] = log(W(1,1))+8.73$, a complex function of an absolute position in the world, and another might have $S[7] = W(x_p+1,y_p) + W(x_p-1,y_p)$, where x_p and y_p indicate the individual's current position, in which case this sensor looks at what's above and below the creature in the 2-d world. Sensors can also be noisy or inaccurate, delivering an only more-or-less realistic view of the objects in the world. If a particular ith sensor is not present (which can be signified by an "inactive" flag for that sensor in the evolving list of sensors), $S[i]$ is defined to be 0.

Such "direct-perception" sensors may not seem to match the sorts of indirect windows on the world our own sensors sometimes feel like, and one might object that there's nothing here like propagating chemical gradients or reflecting light or sound waves to carry information around in the environment. But again, it is the ultimate sources of these signals that we (and all living creatures) are really interested in, rather than the particular form of their proximal cues, and the sensory scheme presented here captures just this notion. In addition, by focussing on the objects in the world and their action consequences, we hope to make the behavioral orientation of this work clearer, and at the same time avoid the complicated (and important) problems of sensory transduction.

2.2.2 Internal States

The internal state variables available to an individual creature are designated in a manner similar to the sensors. They are indexed in a list $I[i]$, for i from 1 to n_I, the preset maximum number of internal state variables. Again, if n_I is preset to 0, all creatures will evolve without any internal state. Each $I[i]$ is defined as a function of (some of) the current sensory inputs, the previous internal states, and the previous action-states (indicating whether or not a particular action fired on the previous time-step); that is, $I[i] \equiv f_{I[i]}(S^t, I^{t-1}, A^{t-1})$. The inclusion of the previous action as one of the possible inputs to the internal state variables allows for limited proprioception, as mentioned in the previous section. Each $I[i]$ is set to 0 if not defined (inactive), just as for each $S[i]$.

Internal state variables allow further processing on the sensory inputs. For example, $I[3] = logistic(S[7])$ would perform a gentle thresholding of the results of sensor 7 (looking up and down). They can also provide a memory for past events or actions, as in the pair $I[52] = A^{t-1}[3]$, which remembers whether or not action 3 was just performed, and $I[17] = I^{t-1}[52]$, which returns the performance-status of action 3 two time steps ago. More complicated systems, like the central pattern generators mentioned earlier, can also be evolved (though it may take quite a while for such things to be hit upon in such an open-ended framework). The outputs of the internal state variables, along with the current sensory values, are then made available to the final component of the behavioral triptych, the actions and their triggers.

2.2.3 Actions and their Triggers

Each action $A[i]$ an individual can perform is defined as a two-part structure consisting of an action-type and a triggering function. (Here again i can vary from 1 to n_A, the maximum number of different actions an evolved behavioral system can contain; in this case, n_A will never be set to 0, or else we'd end up with an uninteresting, unbehaving creature.) Action-types $A[i]_{act}$ can be primitive motor commands such as "move forward," "turn," "eat," etc.; we will discuss these in more detail in the next section. These actions can be thought of as very simple "fixed action patterns" which are fired off and run to completion without any environmental influence either before or during their execution. Thus they are not functions of either the sensory inputs or the internal state variables, but rather are impenetrable units.

The way sensory inputs and internal states *are* able to affect emitted behavior is by controlling which behaviors actually get emitted at all, through the triggering functions. Triggering functions $A[i]_{trig}$ are real-valued functions of the individual's current sensory inputs and current internal states (if there are any of each) which are used to determine when a particular action is invoked. That is, $A[i]_{trig} \equiv f_{A[i]}(S', I')$. To determine which action an individual will perform at a given time-step, all of the creature's (active) trigger functions are evaluated, giving a real value representing the strength with which each possible (active) action is being triggered. From here, there are several ways that the final single action to be performed can be chosen, including selecting the action $A[i]$ with the highest trigger value, choosing an action stochastically based on the normalized trigger values interpreted as a discrete probability distribution function, or picking an action at random from among all those above some trigger threshold. Different selection schemes will result in different observed patterns of behavior, and therefore also in different evolved behavioral systems to achieve the same behavioral ends.

2.3 A Catalogue of Action-types

The things that an organism can do in its world depend on what there is in that world to act on and affect. In the system we've described here there is not all that much in the world for the creatures to alter: basically, there is only food/energy, and the creatures themselves. As a result, the number of action-type primitives that we can define for this world will also be limited. We view this as a plus, though, since it will keep our analysis and understanding of the evolutionary and behavioral dynamics of this system that much simpler.

First of all, creatures can change the distribution of food in the world, that is, change the food entries in $W(x,y)$. The most obvious action in this category is "eating" -- lowering the food-value at a particular world location. (This will in turn result in an increase the creature's own energy level, E, and a decrease in the energy of the food, but we will consider these as energetic "side-effects" of the direct action, described in the next section.) Though this behavior seems simple, a variety of possible action-types are subsumed under this category. For instance, what (x,y) locations do we allow a creature to eat from? Only their own current location? Or neighboring locations? How big a "reach" should we allow creatures in that case? And how much of the food will the creatures eat? All of it at once? Or can they opt to eat a lesser amount? If there's a lot of food to be eaten at a certain location, should it take longer for the creature to do so? We plan to extend this system so that the eating command (and others) will itself be a 3-tuple, (x,y,E), specifying what location to eat from, and how much to eat (i.e., the amount of energy to absorb). This action will be generated as a function of the current internal state and sensory inputs, just as the triggering values now are. How difficult each such action is (i.e., how much effort, in terms of energy, it takes the creature to perform it), and what the energetic benefits and side-effects are, would again be specified in the bioenergetics of the world. But in the meantime, we can restrict this class of actions simply to "eat everything that's in your current hex, in one time-step."

Besides just eating the food in the world, though, there are other ways creatures can alter its distribution. For example, we might want to allow creatures to *increase* the amount of food at a given location, by "fertilizing" that position (certainly at a cost in energy terms to the creature itself, another side-effect). Or creatures could "farm" the food in the world, by "pushing" the food spread in some large area into a smaller region for easier later harvest or hoarding from other creatures. (This could also be achieved through a combination of "eating," "moving," and "fertilizing" actions.) Both of these actions could again be described via a 3-tuple (x,y,E) indicating the positions and amounts of food/energy involved. For now we will leave these possible actions out of the system, but for completeness later we anticipate including them in the evolutionary pot, to see whether or not any creatures find them adaptively useful. (It is important to try to begin with as few possible actions as we can, and let the selectable pool of them build up slowly, preferably also through a non-arbitrary evolutionary process.)

Another thing in the world that a creature can change is itself. At present, we do not allow a creature to alter its own behavior-generating mechanisms, that is, its list of usable sensors, internal state variables, and actions and triggers; in particular, as mentioned earlier, since the behavior-generators are fixed, no learning is possible yet. (Note that the *values* that the sensory, internal state, and trigger functions return can all be affected by what the creature does, since its actions can change its internal states and its view of the world, but the *functions themselves* cannot be altered, except by the action of evolution.) But a creature can change its own (x,y) location, moving about in the world. Just as for the eating action, questions arise as to how far and in what directions a creature can travel in a single time-step. Again for now, just to keep things simple, we will only allow single-hex movement to any of the positions currently adjacent to the creature, making six movement action-types.

With more than one organism in the world at a time, there comes the possibility for a wide range of other "social" (or anti-social!) behaviors, as one creature affects another: for instance, "move-other" or "eat-other." Once again, to start off simple, we are setting these types of creature interactions aside for the moment. But there is one final aspect of the world that the creatures should be able to influence: the *number* of the creatures themselves. To this end, we add a final action-type, "split." When a creature performs this action, it creates one or more copies of itself as new individuals in the world. In this case, we need to determine how many new individuals are created, how much energy each one gets, what location each one ends up at, and whether or not the new copies are exact or altered versions of the original. In our simple first instantiation of this system, we allow an individual creature to just split into two, with each getting an equal amount of the "parent's" energy, and each occupying the same hex as the original. Finally, one of the two new creatures that replace the original is kept identical to the original, and the other is mutated slightly, so that new behavioral mechanisms can enter the population. Without such mutation, the system would be more or less static, with no evolutionary change possible. In future versions of the system, we can imagine sexual reproduction through a "combine-with-other" action-type, as well as more morbid behaviors like "mutate-self," "mutate-other," and "split-other"....

We have described all the possible action-types in our simple world, in terms of all the things in the world that can be changed. As more types of objects are introduced into the world (more categories of entities, c, as described earlier in section 2.2.1), and more inter-organism interactions are allowed, correspondingly more action-types for changing each of those things will be created. By allowing *any* possible change in the world and its contents to be a potential action-type (subject to the bioenergetic constraints of the world), we hope to enable every possible type of action in these simple worlds to appear, whether or not they have analogs in the "real" world. Such generality is essential for the study of adaptive agency (Miller & Todd, 1990), construed as the investigation of adaptive behavior by *any* sort of behaving agent, whether real or hypothesized, terrestrial or extraterrestrial, biological or artificial.

2.4 Bioenergetics of the World

As we indicated in the previous section, every action a creature can perform in its simulated world may have energetic side-effects, in terms of changing the distribution of energy in the world (that is, transferring it from one entity to another). In particular in the current simple world, these effects will be manifested as raising or lowering the individual organism's own personal energy level, E, and changing the energy level in food-plants. How each action-type affects the world's energy-distribution is determined by the bioenergetics of the world. For now, we will just assign the energy side-effects of actions by fiat, but we will describe briefly at the end of this section a way in which the bioenergetics, like the behaviors themselves, can emerge during the evolutionary process.

The main rule governing the bioenergetics of our system is that *nothing any creature does can raise the energy in the world.* The only way the total world-energy can ever increase is via the food/growth function, $\phi(x,y,t)$. Energy can be transferred from one entity to another, and certainly can be lowered or lost, but never increased through creature actions. If we did not impose such a restriction, then obviously the best thing a creature could do in its lifetime (in terms of survival or ongoing existence) would be to increase its own energy level directly, resulting in essentially a perpetual-motion organism. The only other global rule is that once an individual's energy level E drops to (or below) zero, it dies and is removed from the world and the simulation.

In the previous section, we ended up allowing our initial creatures to perform only three main action-types: eat everything from the current hex, move to one of the adjacent hexes, and split into two. Thus for the energetics of this world, we need only specify the energy side-effects associated with each of these actions. (In general, the bioenergetics of a given world consists of a table or list of all the action-types possible in that world, along with their associated energetic consequences.) For eating, the energy effects will simply be to lower the individual's energy by an eating-exertion cost (for example, 0.5), and then increase the individual's E by the amount of energy absorbed from the food in its current hex. Furthermore, the food-energy in that hex is set to zero (since it is all eaten). The eating-exertion cost guarantees that creatures that always just try to eat, even when there is no food around, will eventually run out of energy and die. Thus the creatures must evolve to only try to eat when it's adaptive, that is, when there *is* food present, rather than attempting to constantly shovel everything around them down their gullets.

For movement, we will charge the creature (i.e., lower its energy E) a movement-exertion cost (e.g. 1.0) for each step in any direction. For splitting, we impose a splitting-exertion cost (e.g. 1.0) on the parent creature, and divide the remaining energy equally between the two resulting offspring. Finally, if the creature does nothing in a given time-step, we still impose a small energy sloth-cost on it (e.g. 0.3), so that completely useless sedentary organisms will eventually be weeded out, dying and being removed when their energy slowly leaks away to nothing.

All of the other action-types that we chose not to include in our initial system could in fact appear in the bioenergetic specification of the world. But they would have a prohibitively high energetic cost associated with them so that no creature could ever perform these actions. In general, this is how particular action-types are "disallowed" in our system, through unpayable energy penalties for performing them. Thus when we introduce the general location-energy 3-tuple (x,y,E) action-type form, we will be able to allow or disallow "reaching" in the world by how we assign energy costs to actions with $x \neq x_p$ and $y \neq y_p$; similarly for movement beyond adjacent hexes or multiple-offspring splitting, etc. (Note that there is no energy cost associated with either sensing or performing cognitive computations, e.g. in the internal state variables, but this could also be introduced at some point, no doubt with profound effects on the sensors and behaviors evolved.)

The energetic costs and benefits of the actions we have described here have all been set by hand, in what we hope are reasonable ways that will allow interesting organisms and behaviors to evolve. But we would be happier if this aspect of the world as well could emerge through evolution, rather than being predetermined in what might be an ultimately uninteresting way. One idea we have for how to allow such emergence of the basic bioenergetic laws of the world is to let every organism "vote" or "bid" for the energy costs and benefits that *it* would like to see associated with various action-types. If we have only roving, eating creatures evolving in the world as we have so far described here, we can imagine that they will all vote or bid to lower the movement cost to 0, so that they can roam about the world eating over as long and far a range as they want without incurring any cost. This would not be particularly interesting. However, if we also allowed the *food itself* to evolve, akin to say plants or sedentary or immobile prey organisms, and let *these* entities also vote on the bioenergetics of the world, they would no doubt call for very *high* movement costs, to cripple the roving eaters and keep them from getting close enough to devour the food organisms.

With both organism types voting, each with different self-interests, and with the bioenergetics coming out of this conflict-based democratic process, we expect that much more interesting dynamics would emerge. Perhaps some sort of energetic cost/benefit compromise would be settled upon, allowing an uneasy truce where individuals in both species could survive; or maybe there would be a continuous predator-prey cyclic pattern as first one faction and then another gathered enough votes to sway the bioenergetics temporarily in their own favor. In this way perhaps "evolution at the edge of chaos" (Langton, 1992) could be achieved and maintained, along with the ongoing interesting patterns that this entails.

3 Evolutionary Dynamics and a Day in the Life

Creatures in our simulations obviously have rather simple lives. To begin each run, we just create a random initial organism via abiogenesis (generation of life from inanimate substance), with random sensors, internal state variables, and actions and triggers, as well as a specific amount of energy to get it started. We then set it loose in the world and see what happens. We introduce new such random creatures by abiogenesis every so often (after a typically fixed interval of many time-steps), to keep up a constant trickle of potentially adaptive creatures into the world. Some of these creatures will move about in the world, but do little else. Others will sit and eat, but never move. Still others will split repeatedly, until their energy is too low to allow any further splitting. All of these will burn up or waste away their energy until they reach zero and die, with their ineffectual behavioral endowments being removed from the world. Some lucky few in any given run though may combine these actions in an appropriate fashion, moving, then eating, then splitting and spreading their successful behavior-generating mechanisms to new offspring. In turn, some of the new offspring, mutated slightly, will improve upon the behaviors of their parents, and more and more adaptive behavior will evolve over time. In any given time-frame, this emergence of surviving creatures may not occur; but as we continue to introduce new random creatures into the world, eventually an interesting (i.e. adaptive) one will show up, and the system will take off, bubbling with life.

There are two important subtleties to this evolutionary scheme. First, reproduction is not imposed on any individual. For evolution to work, some of the creatures must hit upon "reproductive behavior" (i.e., splitting) themselves. Otherwise, the best they can do is just be long-lived. An immortal creature that works its way around the world and eats enough to remain alive time-step after time-step may be impressive, but without such creatures splitting and having slightly mutated offspring, behavioral improvements will not be introduced into the population. Furthermore, our creature-controlled reproduction scheme allows a fitness measure to emerge naturally from the simulation. Fitness will be defined exactly in terms of those creatures who behave appropriately to produce the most offspring. (This is in sharp contrast to the usual fitness measures imposed from above by hand, e.g. by forcing any creature above a certain energy threshold to split, or by running the simulation in generations and giving each individual a number of offspring in the next generation proportional to its amassed energy.) Note that with our current method, we will also have (perhaps widely) fluctuating population sizes; however, this should not be seen as a disadvantage, but rather as an added measure of realism.

Second, one of the most important things that a creature can know about its world, namely, its own energy level E, is never directly available to it. An individual's energy level could be crucial for knowing when to split, when to head toward food, when to sit and wait for it to grow back, etc. However, we do not allow any creature direct access to this important piece of information. Rather, if creatures are to make use of this information, they must evolve an internal representation of it which is updated appropriately in response to the actions the individual organism emits. Thus, if an individual eats, it should increase its internal assessment of its energy level by an appropriate amount; if it moves or splits, it should likewise lower its energy-level internal variable. We expect the most adaptively-behaving individuals will make use of just such an internal constructed bit of "self-knowledge," so we are on the lookout for any such feature in our evolving scenarios.

4 Actual Implementation Methods

The behavioral evolution system we have presented here is intended to be implementable by a variety of methods; the description has been purposefully placed at a high level to be agnostic in terms of implementation details. We are focussing our own efforts though on two very different types of implementations which we will describe briefly in this section: evolving Lisp routines, and evolving neural network architectures.

The lists-of-functions representation we used for the actions and triggers, internal state variables, and sensors earlier is obviously readily translatable into Lisp code and s-expressions. In such a form, we can use a "genetic programming" method to try to evolve these functions, such as that of Koza (1992) or Sims (1991). Since our creatures currently just split and mutate, the latter method may be more suited to our purposes at present, because it emphasizes mutational changes to the Lisp code, rather than the recombination of s-expressions primarily used in the former. In either case, while the translation of our system into Lisp may be clear, the evolutionary process itself could still be quite extended and tortuous.

When compared to the obvious Lisp representation, it may seem very unclear how we could construct neural network architectures that will precisely embody the modularized lists of sensors, internal state variables, and actions and triggers that we want our creatures to be able to use. But there is also a natural interpretation in this case, in terms of a structured network with each layer of nonlinear units interpreted as one of the three categories just mentioned. First of all, we can have a set of possible output unit types, each of which is associated with one of the possible action-types. Every network will have an evolutionarily-determined selection of these. Each output unit in every creature has an evolved bias level associated with it, which forms part (or all) of its triggering function. Actions are selected from among the active output units based on one of the selection schemes listed in section 2.2.3. If the network has only such output units, as shown in Figure 2a, and uses the probability-based action selection scheme, we will end up with a stochastically-behaving creature like that described in the first scenario in section 2.2.

Now we can add the internal state variables as another layer of (hidden) units in the network, as shown in Figure 2b. These units receive recurrent connections from the output units, and from themselves, and pass their logistic-function activations forward in turn to the output units. In this case, the evolutionary mutation process would determine not only the number and type of output units, but also the number of internal state units, and the weights on all the connections between these two layers. With such a network, we would get the memory-guided creature described in the second scenario in section 2.2.

Finally, we can add sensors to this network as another layer of (input) units, as shown in Figure 2c, and end up with the full-blown sensory-guided behavior of the fourth scenario. As can be seen in the figure, each sensor unit (which is sensitive to one particular category) has direct connections to positions in the world, that is, $W(x,y)$. Sensors are in turn connected both to the internal state units, and to the output units, since both are functions of the current sensory input (as described in sections 2.2.2 and 2.2.3). Evolution will determine the number and types of sensory units in each creature's network, and the connectivity pattern and weights between the world and the sensors, and between the sensors and the internal state units and output units. (The final recurrent structure of the full network here resembles that of an Elman- or Jordan-style recurrent network -- see Elman, 1988, and Jordan, 1986. Here we have drawn the input units offset, to emphasize their secondary role in guiding and adjusting internally-generated behavior.)

For the genetic and evolutionary representation and modification of these neural networks, we use a scheme like that developed by Miller, Todd, and Hegde (1989). Units can use various activation functions, allowing a wide range of nonlinear functions to be implemented between different variables in the three layers; but obviously this framework does not allow the unlimited flexibility that evolving entire Lisp routines does. Still, we believe it will be flexible (and manipulatable) enough to yield very interesting results in this system (as it has in many earlier studies), and so we are eager to compare the results of this representation scheme to the Lisp-based one. (If further computational power is needed in the network, we can add additional hidden layers of computing units between the existing layers.)

5 Characterizing the Environment, and Other Research Directions

At this point, we do not have space (nor results) enough left to do much other than describe some of the types of environments, and environmental classifications, that we are beginning to explore with the framework we have just laid out. We choose to consider two-dimensional grid world environments in general because they are easily visualizable and concrete (rather than described by unintuitive parameter settings). They should also be more readily translatable into real-world settings so that we can tie in with empirical, ecological data. However, classifying these environments will probably require returning to abstract parameters and categories; but we will maintain the link to the grid world description and the valuable visualization it allows.

Traditional machine-learning conceptions of environments, as "noisy," "regular," "unknown," etc., are crude and unhelpful in our current endeavor. Slightly more sophisticated conceptions of environments as finite state automata (FSA's), which return sensory inputs to the creature in response to its motor outputs, can describe quite complex environment/behavior interactions (see, e.g., Mozer & Bachrach, 1991; Rivest & Schapire, 1987). We are interested in developing mappings between such models of environments, and our 2-d grid world representation. However, there are at least three drawbacks to the FSA approach to environmental characterization: first, for environments of reasonable size (like our grid worlds), the FSA will have to be enormous to capture all the possible states and transitions between them (e.g., for a small

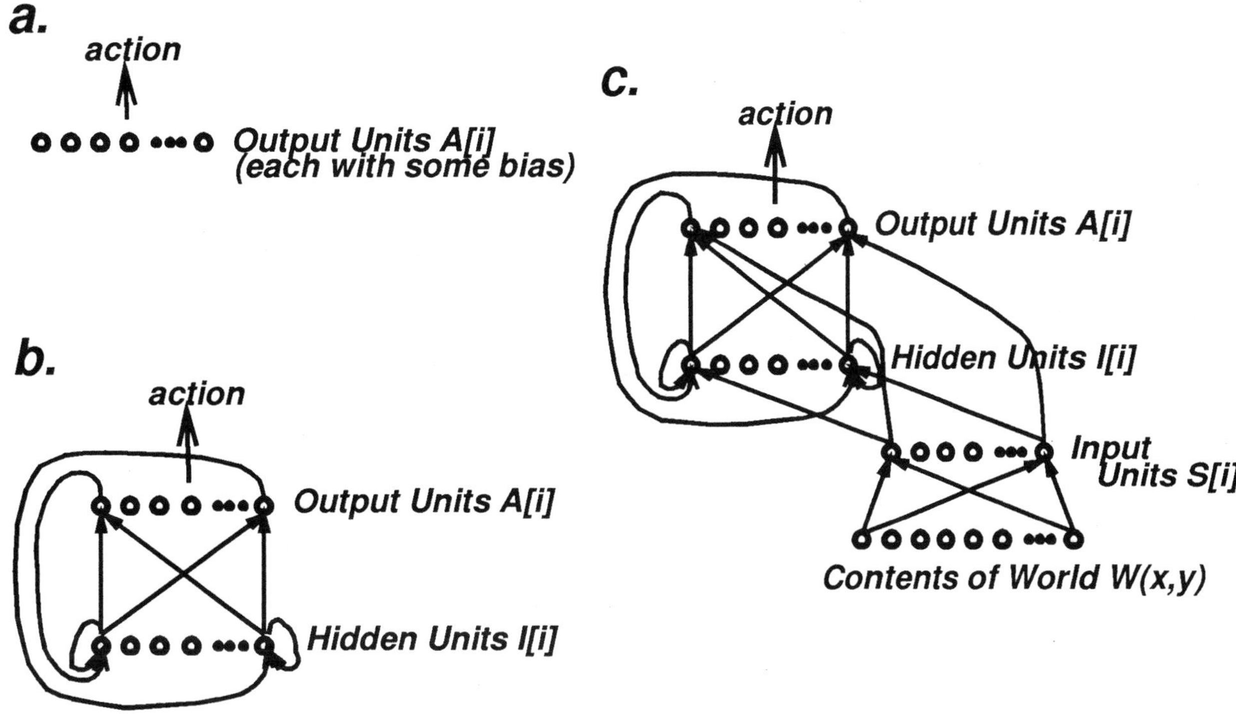

Figure 2. Network implementations of behavioral components. a. A simple network for producing actions stochastically. b. A network for generating actions based on internal states. c. A network that uses both internal states and sensory inputs from the contents of the world to produce its actions.

10x10 grid which either contains food or nothing at each location, there are 2^{100}, or approximately 10^{30}, possible states); second, the actions and sensations are all assumed to be defined, rather than allowed to emerge through the course of evolutionary adaptation; and third, in focussing on the sensory consequences of actions, the FSA model overlooks the interesting possibilities where no sensors are used.

Wilson (1991), Smith (1991), and Littman (these proceedings) have proceeded from the FSA environment models to more abstract categories based on the amount of memory or state a creature needs to exploit an environment, and how long the creature must wait for rewards following its behavior. Littman carries this further, characterizing environments in terms of the creatures that can behave optimally in them. These approaches also seem promising, and certainly emphasize the interrelationship between environmental structure and the creatures that behave in those environments. But it is not easy to see how to move back and forth between these conceptions of environments and more concrete visualizable forms like the grid world representation. Also, the notion of reward, while important for learning systems, again obscures the important classes of non-learning, and even non-sensing, creatures and behaviors, as well as their evolution. And finally, we believe that it should be possible to describe some aspects of the environment in terms that are not entirely creature-centric, that is, in ways that do not rely solely on the capabilities of creatures themselves; but we may be forced to recant this position.

An example classification scheme closer to what we are hoping for was indicated in the third scenario in section 2.2, where we spoke of food being distributed in the world in separate clumps or patches. We are working on a way of parameterizing the clumpiness of food in a 2-d world (which we have already done in one way for the 1-d case -- see Todd, 1992, chapter 5). With this characterization in hand, we will be able to construct worlds of different clumpinesses, and see what sorts of behaviors evolve to exploit them, and whether there are interesting correlations between the two. Patch finding and foraging is a well-studied area in the animal behavior literature, so we will have much to draw on and compare to there.

As we have mentioned earlier, we are also interested in how well creatures without various of the behavioral components might fare in different environments. Thus we might compare creatures without internal state to those with, or ones with limited sensory abilities to others with sophisticated senses. Another interesting variation would be to explore the tradeoffs that evolution makes when it must choose *between*, say, senses and internal states: by keeping the sum $n_S + n_I$ fixed during evolution, we could see how evolution balances the two when it has limited resources to work with.

We are clearly embarked on an exploratory, open-ended research program, but one which we believe will yield useful insights into the nature of environments and the behaviors that are adaptive in them. By starting at the ground-level, creating a system in which all aspects of a creature's behavior-generating mechanisms can evolve as needed, and working our way up to consideration of different types of environments where this evolution will take place, we hope to have a framework rich enough to lead us to understanding of phenomena beyond those we have already imagined.

References

Ackley, D., and Littman, M. (1992). Interactions between evolution and learning. In C.G. Langton, C. Taylor, J.D. Farmer, and S. Rasmussen (Eds.), *Artificial life II* (pp. 487-509). Redwood City, CA: Addison-Wesley.

Cariani, P. (1990). Adaptive connection to the world through self-organizing sensors and effectors. In A. Meystel, J. Herath, and S. Gray (Eds.), *Proceedings of the 5th IEEE International Symposium on Intelligent Control,* vol. 1 (pp. 73-78). Los Alamitos, CA: IEEE Computer Society Press.

Elman, J.L. (1988). *Finding structure in time.* Technical Report 8801. La Jolla, CA: Center for Research in Language, University of California at San Diego.

Gallagher, J.C., and Beer, R.D. (these proceedings). A qualitative dynamical analysis of evolved locomotion controllers.

Gibson, J.J. (1966). *The senses considered as perceptual systems.* Boston: Houghton-Mifflin.

Holland, J.H. (1992). *Adaptation in natural and artificial systems.* Cambridge, MA: MIT Press.

Jordan, M.I. (1986). *Serial order: A parallel, distributed processing approach.* Technical Report ICS-8604. La Jolla, CA: Institute for Cognitive Science, University of California at San Diego.

Koza, J. (1992). *Genetic programming.* Cambridge, MA: MIT Press/Bradford Books.

Langton, C.G. (1992). Life at the edge of chaos. In C.G. Langton, C. Taylor, J.D. Farmer, and S. Rasmussen (Eds.), *Artificial life II* (pp. 41-91). Redwood City, CA: Addison-Wesley.

Littman, M.L. (these proceedings). An optimization-based categorization of reinforcement learning environments.

Maes, P. (these proceedings). Behavior-based artificial intelligence.

Miller, G.F. (1992). *The evolution of protean behavior through psychological selection: Adaptive unpredictability, sexual selection, and human encephalization.* Unpublished doctoral thesis. Stanford, CA: Psychology Department, Stanford University.

Miller, G.F., and Todd, P.M. (1990). Exploring adaptive agency I: Theory and methods for simulating the evolution of learning. In D.S. Touretzky, J.L. Elman, T.J. Sejnowski, and G.E. Hinton (Eds.), *Proceedings of the 1990 Connectionist Models Summer School* (pp. 65-80). San Mateo, CA: Morgan Kaufmann.

Miller, G.F., and Todd, P.M. (in preparation). *A theory of perception based on fitness affordances.* Unpublished manuscript. Stanford, CA: Psychology Department, Stanford University.

Miller, G.F., Todd, P.M., and Hegde, S.U. (1989). Designing neural networks using genetic algorithms. In J.D. Schaffer (Ed.), *Proceedings of the Third International Conference on Genetic Algorithms* (pp. 379-384). San Mateo, CA: Morgan Kaufmann.

Mozer, M.C., and Bachrach, J. (1991). SLUG: A connectionist architecture for inferring the structure of finite-state environments. *Machine Learning, 7,* 139-160.

Pattee, H.H. (1989). Simulations, realizations, and theories of life. In C.G. Langton (Ed.), *Artificial life* (pp. 63-77). Redwood City, CA: Addison-Wesley.

Rivest, R.L., and Schapire, R.E. (1987). A new approach to unsupervised learning in deterministic environments. In P. Langley (Ed.), *Proceedings of the Fourth International Workshop on Machine Learning* (pp. 364-375). San Mateo, CA: Morgan Kaufmann.

Sims, K. (1991). Artificial evolution for computer graphics. *Computer Graphics, 25,* 319-328.

Smith, R.E. (1991). *Default hierarchy formation and memory exploitation in learning classifier systems.* Unpublished doctoral thesis. Tuscaloosa, AL: Department of Engineering Mechanics, University of Alabama.

Todd, P.M. (1992). *The evolution of learning: Simulating the interaction of adaptive processes.* Unpublished doctoral thesis. Stanford, CA: Psychology Department, Stanford University. (Available from UMI.)

Todd, P.M., and Miller, G.F. (1991). On the sympatric origin of species: Mercurial mating in the Quicksilver model. In R.K. Belew and L.B. Booker (Eds.), *Proceedings of the Fourth International Conference on Genetic Algorithms* (pp. 547-554). San Mateo, CA: Morgan Kaufmann.

Todd, P.M., and Miller, G.F. (submitted). *Evolution "without" natural selection: Sexual selection for speciation and learning.* Submitted to the Proceedings of the Third Artificial Life Conference.

Werner, G.M., and Dyer, M.G. (these proceedings). Evolution of herding behavior in artificial animals.

Wilson, S.W. (1991). The animat path to AI. In J.-A. Meyer and S.W. Wilson (Eds.), *From Animals to Animats: Proceedings of the First International Conference on Simulation of Adaptive Behavior* (pp. 15-21). Cambridge, MA: MIT Press/Bradford Books.

Evolutionary wanderlust: Sexual selection with directional mate preferences

Geoffrey F. Miller
School of Cognitive and Computing Sciences
University of Sussex
Falmer, Brighton, BN1 9QH England
geoffm@cogs.sussex.ac.uk

Peter M. Todd
The Rowland Institute for Science
100 Edwin H. Land Boulevard
Cambridge, MA 02142
ptodd@spo.rowland.org

Abstract

In the pantheon of evolutionary forces, the optimizing Apollonian powers of natural selection are generally assumed to dominate the dark Dionysian dynamics of sexual selection. But this need not be the case, particularly with a class of selective mating mechanisms called 'directional mate preferences' (Kirkpatrick, 1987). In previous simulation research, we showed that non-directional assortative mating preferences could cause populations to spontaneously split apart into separate species (Todd & Miller, 1991). In this paper, we show that directional mate preferences can cause populations to wander capriciously through phenotype space, under a strange form of runaway sexual selection, with or without the influence of natural selection pressures. When directional mate preferences are free to evolve, they do not always evolve to point in the direction of natural-selective peaks. Sexual selection can thus take on a life of its own, such that mate preferences within a species become a distinct and important part of the environment to which the species' phenotypes adapt. These results suggest a broader conception of 'adaptive behavior', in which attracting potential mates becomes as important as finding food and avoiding predators. We present a framework for simulating a wide range of directional and non-directional mate preferences, and discuss some practical and scientific applications of simulating sexual selection.

1 Overview

The dynamics of evolution and the mechanisms of cognition interact in complex and often surprising ways. For example, once psychological mechanisms of mate choice emerge through natural and sexual selection, they can have profound effects on the further course of evolution. In previous papers (Todd & Miller, 1991; Todd & Miller, submitted), we showed that certain kinds of simple assortative mate preference mechanisms alone are sufficient to result in a sympatric population of simulated organisms splitting apart into distinct species. In this paper, we go one step further to explore a new class of mate choice mechanisms called 'directional mate preferences' (Kirkpatrick, 1987). With non-directional mate preferences, one's ideal mate just has some degree of similarity (or dissimilarity) to one's own phenotype. With directional mate preferences, one's ideal mate is some distance away in phenotype space in a particular phenotypic direction (e.g. is much bigger, smarter, or richer than oneself). These two kinds of mate preferences result in very different evolutionary dynamics and make populations move around in phenotype space in very different ways.

In the simulations presented here, genetically coded mate preferences evolve to exploit currently available phenotypes, and phenotypic traits evolve to fulfill currently popular mate preferences. Thus, sexual selection sets up a complex reciprocal interaction between evolving mate preferences and evolving phenotypes. Over the short term, both preferences and phenotypes adapt to each other under strong sexual-selective pressures. But over the long term, the population follows a capricious trajectory through phenotype space that looks a bit like sped-up genetic drift. One might expect that imposing moderate natural selection pressures would eliminate this capricious wandering, but we show that it doesn't. Even when there are clearly defined natural-selective peaks in an adaptive landscape, a population subject to sexual selection with directional mate preferences will still wander through the landscape, often climbing adaptive peaks but seldom staying there for long. These results provide more evidence for our previous suggestions (Todd & Miller, 1991) that apparently trivial changes in the psychological mechanisms of mate choice can have substantial effects on the evolutionary dynamics of an entire population.

This paper progresses from historical background to simulations methods, simulation results, possible applications, and finally conclusions. An intellectual context for this work is provided in section 2, through a short historical look at sexual selection theory. Section 3 presents our methods for simulating sexual selection with a variety of mate-choice mechanisms. Our results are summarized in section 4, after which section 5 offers some suggestions for how simulations of sexual selection might be used in practical applications and in further scientific research. Conclusions about the importance of this line of research are offered in section 6.

2 A Brief Review of Sexual Selection Theory

Darwin postulated two kinds of sexual selection: male competition for female mates, and female choice of male mates. Male competition was widely accepted by Victorian biologists as an important, necessary, and general evolutionary process. But the possibility of female choice was almost universally mocked and dismissed, at least until Fisher (1930) proposed his model of 'runaway sexual selection'. In this process, an evolutionary positive-feedback loop gets established between female preferences for certain male traits, and the male traits themselves. As a result, both the elaborateness of the traits and the extermity of the preferences increase at an exponential rate. Fisher's model could account for the wildly exaggerated male traits seen in many species, such as the peacock's plumage, but he did not explain the evolutionary origins of female preferences themselves, nor did he develop formal genetic models of runaway sexual selection. After Huxley (1938) presented many ill-conceived but often-cited arguments against the possibility of female choice and against Fisher's model, both the specific runaway model and the general notion of female choice were left to languish unexamined until quite recently.

In the last 15 years, however, there has been an explosion of work in biology on sexual selection through mate choice. The new population genetics models of O'Donald (1980), Lande (1981), and Kirkpatrick (1982) showed the mathematical feasibility of Fisher's runaway sexual selection process. New behavioral experiments on animals showed that females of many species do exhibit strong preferences for certain male traits (e.g. Andersson, 1982; Catchpole, 1980; Ryan, 1985). New comparative morphology has supported Darwin's (1871) claim that capricious elaboration is the hallmark of sexual selection: Eberhard (1985) argued that the only feasible explanation for the wildly complex and diverse male genitalia of many species is evolution through female preference for certain kinds of genital stimulation. New evolutionary computer simulation models such as those of Collins and Jefferson (1992) confirmed the plausibility, robustness, and power of runaway sexual selection. Once biologists started taking the possibility of female choice seriously, evidence for its existence and significance came quickly and ubiquitously. Cronin (1991) provides a readable, comprehensive, and much more detailed account of this history.

This peculiar historical saga suggests that the scientific neglect of Darwin's process of female choice was due to sexist biases in biology, not to its infeasibility or objective unimportance. What we have, then, is a major evolutionary process that has been neglected in biology until quite recently for demonstrably ideological reasons, and yet has been shown to be widespread, important, and powerful. We suggest that it is time we dust off Darwin's long-neglected theory of sexual selection through mate choice, and use the power of computer simulation to explore its nuances.

In natural selection, the causal flow of evolutionary forces is often one way: organism adapts to environment, but not vice-versa. This makes natural selection easier to study empirically and formally, because one can often specify a stable external set of conditions (e.g. a predefined 'fitness function') to which a species adapts. In sexual selection, though, the selective 'environment' itself always evolves. The mate preferences that serve as the selective environment to which sexually selected phenotypic traits adapt, themselves evolve under various forces. Indeed, there is a fierce debate in sexual selection theory between advocates of 'viability indicators', who suggest that mate choice mechanisms always evolve to prefer traits that indicate high natural-selective viability, and advocates of 'arbitrary preferences', who suggest that sometimes preferences are due to intrinsic sensory, perceptual or cognitive biases, such as the greater salience of the large, the colorful, the symmetric, and the novel. This is exactly the sort of debate that can be illuminated best by computer simulation, because it involves such complex interactions between coevolving traits. Just as computer simulation has been important in understanding the dynamics of coevolution between species (e.g. Hillis, 1992; Kauffman & Johnson, 1992), we expect that it will be critical in understanding the reciprocal interactions within a species between mate preferences and sexually selected traits. And as we will show, directional mate preferences *can* often evolve to be quite arbitrary, driving populations away from natural-selective peaks.

3 Simulation Methods

To explore the intricacies of sexual selection with directional mate preferences, we modified our previous genetic algorithm method of simulating sexual selection with non-directional preferences (Todd & Miller, 1991). Our general framework for simulating mate preferences is cast within the context of an n-dimensional phenotype space. Every individual in our evolving populations has a particular phenotype, which can be represented as a particular location in that space. Each individual also has associated with it its own genetically determined probability-of-mating (POM) function. This function is defined across the entire phenotype space, determining not only the phenotypic location of an individual's ideal mate, but also willingness to mate with non-ideal mates. The individual's POM function assigns to every phenotypic location, and thus every potential mate, a certain probability-of-mating, which can be represented as a height in the n+1st dimension. This probability represents the individual's willingness to mate with some prospective paramour: a zero probability indicates total disdain and disinterest, while a probability of one indicates wild, unquenchable, obsessive lust (or its simulated equivalent). Sexual selection is then driven by the topography of evolved POM functions interacting with the evolved frequency distribution of available mates in phenotype space.

To make the phenotype space easy to visualize, we restrict it to two dimensions in these simulations. Each individual thus embodies, and has preferences for, just two phenotypic traits, and can be represented as a particular (x,y) location in phenotype space. Individual phenotypes and ideal mate preferences can thus be displayed together in the same plot. We furthermore use a toroidal phenotype space, plotted as a square with its opposite edges effectively connected, just to avoid edge effects. It is important to remember that positions in this abstract 2-D phenotype space are not spatial locations in some simulated world, and that phenotypic separation between individuals does not imply geographic separation. Mate preferences permitting, it is as easy for two individuals far apart in phenotype space to meet and mate as for two individuals close together in that space.

In the work described here, the POM function always has a conical shape, such that probability-of-mating peaks at some point in phenotype-space and falls off linearly until it hits zero at some radial distance away from that point. Thus if we plotted an individual's POM function in three dimensions, it would look like a conical mountain poking up from the two-dimensional plane of phenotypes. A whole population's mate preferences could be represented as an overlapping set of such conical mountains. Across a whole population, if one summed the heights of every individual's POM function for every point in phenotype space, one would obtain a whole complicated mountain range of mating probabilities. Those individuals who are lucky enough to have phenotypes perched at a high elevation in this mountain range will be sought after by many other individuals wishing to mate with them. This abstract mountain range formed from individuals' POM functions is literally the environment to which individuals adapt through sexual selection.

But because POM functions are determined by genes which can evolve, this apparently stable mountain range of sexual preferences is actually, at a longer time scale, more like a storm-tossed ocean with wave-peaks rising and falling as generations go by. Mate preferences evolve because individuals with POM functions that peak in deserted, mate-poor regions of phenotype space will tend to die virgins. In contrast, individuals with POM functions that peak in densely populated regions of phenotype space will find a plethora of acceptable mates, and will likely have more offspring. So the peaks of POM functions will generally evolve towards the peaks in the current frequency distribution of individuals across phenotype space (i.e. the preferences will evolve to exploit the available phenotypes). And sexual selection will drive the peaks in that population frequency distribution itself to evolve towards the peaks of the POM functions (i.e. the phenotypes will evolve to fulfill the preferences).

One might expect both sorts of peaks to converge on one another and thereby reach a stable equilibrium. But this need not happen for two reasons. First, with small populations especially, sampling error (genetic drift) operating on all genes can keep mate preferences and phenotypic traits from converging perfectly onto one another, and thereby maintain the sexual-selective tension between them that drives the population's movement through phtnotype space. Second, with directional preferences, a given individual's POM peak can be forced to be some distance away from the individual's own location. In this case, the POM mountain range obtained by summing together POM functions across individuals could never completely coincide with the population's frequency distribution peaks, and the two would endlessly chase each other across phenotype space in a futile attempt at mutual satisfaction. The dynamics of sexual selection thus depend critically on the way POM functions are defined and genetically determined. We now explore some of the possibilities.

To begin with, each individual has its own *sexual reference position* (SRP) somewhere in the phenotype space. This SRP can determined in one of four ways, depending on the model of sexual selection being explored: (1) with "individual-relative preferences", the SRP is identical to the individual's own phenotype-location; (2) with "parent-relative preferences" (which can result from sexual imprinting at a young age), the SRP is the phenotype of a parent; (3) with "population-relative preferences", the SRP is the average of all phenotypes in the population or some specified sub-population; (4) with "space-relative preferences", the SRP is some absolute position in phenotype-space. To illustrate this somewhat whimsically: in humans, individual-relative preferences correspond to narcissism, parent-relative preferences correspond to an Oedipus or Electra complex, population-relative preferences to sexual conformism, and space-relative preferences to romantic idealism. We concentrate here on parent-relative preferences because they are better-documented in the biological literature, but we have discussed the other three types elsewhere (Todd & Miller, 1991; Todd & Miller, submitted).

Given a particular SRP, the peak of the cone-shaped POM function can be determined in two general ways. First, the POM peak could simply be centered on the SRP itself to yield *non-directional* preferences. We showed in previous work (Todd & Miller, 1991) that such non-directional assortative mate preferences can result in spontaneous sympatric speciation. Second, individuals can have *directional* preferences, in which the POM function is offset some distance away from the SRP in a particular direction, with both distance and direction parameters genetically specified. These directional preferences can be plotted as *mate preference vectors* in phenotype space, originating at the SRP and ending at the center of the POM function. Directional preferences are of interest primarily because they can facilitate runaway sexual selection (Kirkpatrick, 1987), and because they seem quite common in nature. Many species probably use a combination of non-directional preferences for some phenotypic dimensions and directional preferences for others. We focus here on the effects of directional preferences.

The genotypes in this simulation encode the elements just described in the following way. Two genes determine the individual's phenotypic traits. Two genes determine the direction in phenotype space along which the POM function is offset from the SRP, and one gene determines the distance in phenotype space by which the POM function is offset from the SRP. Together, these three genes determine the individual's mate preference vector. Finally, one gene determines the width of the base of the POM function: the wider the base, the less steeply the POM function slopes off from its peak down to zero probability, and the less 'picky' the individual is about its potential mates in terms of the area in phenotype space that its POM function covers. The resulting binary genotype for each individual is about 120 bits long.

The population size is fixed in these simulations (as it is in most genetic algorithms); here we use 100 individuals. To create the next generation of individuals, we use the following sexual selection method (an earlier version of which was described in greater detail in Todd & Miller, 1991). First, one individual is selected to play the role of "mom" and another is selected to play the role of a potential "dad" -- these are temporary gender roles, not genetically determined sexes. Both mom and dad are selected probabilistically according to whatever *natural* selection fitness function has been imposed over phenotype space, or at random if there is no natural selection at work. Next, mom's POM function is constructed based on her *directional* preferences, and dad's is constructed based on his *non-directional* preferences (i.e. by centering his POM function on his SRP). We do not use the directional preferences of both individuals, because, for complicated theoretical reasons, this has been found to make it almost impossible for any individual to find mates in our simulations. Other possible methods for determining directional preferences may not have this trouble, but powerful directional selection still results even with this asymmetric scheme.

Next, mom's probability of mating with dad is determined, given her POM function and his phenotype, and dad's probability of mating with mom is determined, given his POM function and her phenotype. These two probabilities are multiplied (representing mutual consent) to yield an overall probability of mating, a die is thrown, and if the parents are lucky then two new offspring are created and put into the next generation. The offspring are made by applying 2-point crossover to the two parental bit-string genotypes, and then mutating the resulting children slightly (mutation rate .01 per bit). If the mom and dad prove unlucky, failing to meet each others' preferences, a new dad is chosen and tried again with the same mom. This continues until a successful match is found for this mom, or until she has proven too finicky (our criterion is going through 500 failed mating attempts). The entire mating process is repeated until the next generation is filled (that is, until 50 successful matings have occurred, each yielding two new offspring).

It is important to remember just what is evolving in this population. The phenotypic locations of individuals will change from generation to generation, evolving in response to sexual selection pressures exerted by the mate preferences of the population as a whole, and to any natural selection pressures present. The preferences themselves also evolve from generation to generation, tracking the locations of the individuals (i.e. potential mates) in the population. For the simulations in this paper, we specified a small minimum length for the directional preference vectors to ensure that they wouldn't devolve to be effectively non-directional; and we used a (small) fixed width for the POM functions to keep overly indiscriminate individuals who'll mate with anything from evolving. But the phenotypes and the direction of the preference vectors are always free to evolve, even when we preset their initial values in the first generation; and these are the genes of most interest here, as we will now see.

4 Simulation Results

4.1 Sexual Selection Alone

To understand the basic effects of directional mate preferences on the course of evolution, our initial simulations used sexual selection alone without natural selection. Thus, every individual has an equal chance of being picked as a potential parent, so only their success at choosing mates and at being chosen determines their reproductive ability. Our initial population was clustered in the center of phenotype space, with all of their directional mate preferences pointing to the upper-right corner of this abstract space. To simplify our discussion, we will use compass-point terminology, and call this corner of abstract phenotype space the "northeast" (NE), This initial population of 100 individuals at generation 0 is shown in Figure 1. Each individual's phenotypic location is shown as a dot, and each individual's directional mate preference is shown as an arrow-vector. The mate preference vector originates at the individual's SRP (which in this parentless first generation is just the phenotypic location of the individual itself) and extends in a genetically determined direction for a genetically determined distance.

The NE-pointing vectors shown here mean that every individual would prefer to mate with another who has a higher x-value (e.g. bigger antennae) and a higher y-value (e.g. greener wings) on their phenotypic traits than did their parent (their SRP). But remember that only the "mom" in each mating pair *expresses* this directional preference; the preference vectors for everyone are displayed because we can't know ahead of time who will play a mom-role and who will play a dad-role during mating. For clarity, we do not display each individual's cone-shaped POM function here, but these are simply centered at the arrowhead-end of the preference vector when the individual plays the mom-role, or at the SRP end of the vector for the dad-role. The conical 3-D POM functions would project down onto this 2-D space as circles, with radii in these simulations about half the length of the average preference vector.

After starting these initial individuals in the center of phenotype-space, we turn them loose, letting both phenotypes and preferences evolve freely, and see where sexual selection takes the population over successive generations. Since every individual's mate preference vector pointed NE, we expected the population as a whole to move initially in that direction. As we see in Figure 2, showing the population at generation 10, this is exactly what happens: most individuals have evolved higher values on both of their phenotypic traits, so are now closer to the NE corner of phenotype-space. (Note that in this plot there are some dots not connected to arrows, and some arrows not connected to dots -- this is because each dot shows an individual's own phenotypic location, while each associated arrow shows that individual's preference vector, which originates at its SRP, a parental phenotypic location.) Moreover, most of the preference vectors still point NE. But because they are free to evolve, a few have started to diverge, mutating to point NW instead; one (extending off the E edge of phenotype space) has

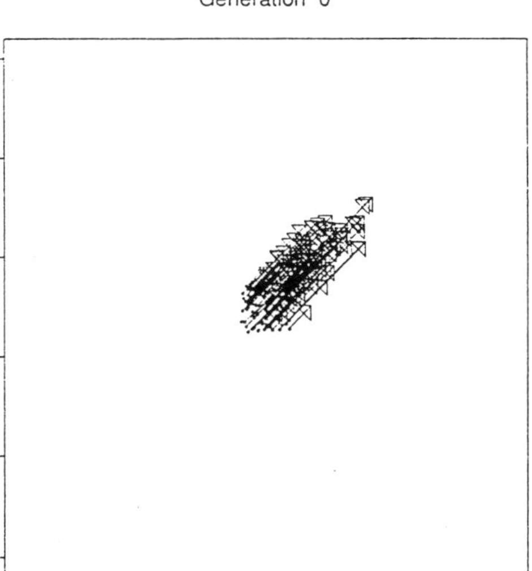

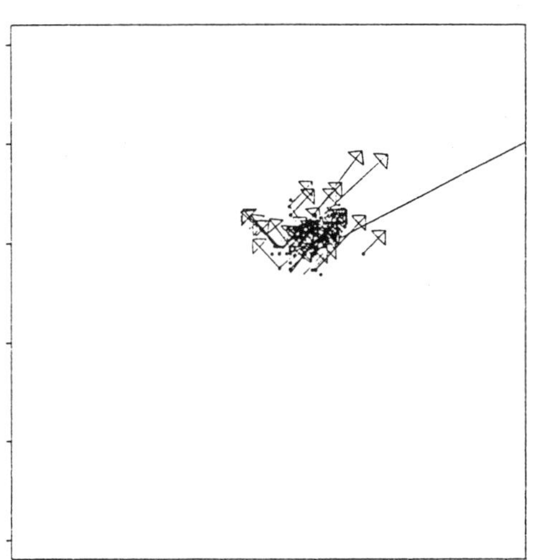

Figure 1. The initial population, clustered in the middle of phenotype space with preferences pointing NE.
Figure 2. The population after 10 generations, now shifted NE and with some diversity of preferences.

mutated to a much larger magnitude. But overall, the population is still headed in the same direction, with the phenotypes evolving to match the preferences, and the preferences evolving to match the phenotypes.

This NE migration of population phenotypes continues for 50 generations, as we can see in the "time-lapse" view of generation 0 to 300 shown in Figure 3. Here we have plotted a dot at the average phenotype of the entire population every two generations (or a circle to mark every 50th generation), and a line segment to show the population average preference vector. After starting in the center of phenotype space (the central circle) with NE preferences, the population marches steadily upwards in that direction, with its preference average continuing to point that way. In general the population average evolves in the direction that the average preference vector points, and the average preference vector evolves to point in the direction that the population is heading. This pattern seems to be violated after generation 50, when the population reaches the end of its first NE run; the population average phenotype then moves straight S (down), while the preferences continue to point NNE. But this is an artifact of how the population average is determined given the toroidal wrap-around of our phenotype space. The population has actually moved off the top edge of phenotype space, and reappeared at the bottom; but the phenotype averages don't take this into account, and so seem to move S. In fact, the phenotype/preference coupling is still working all along. We can see this in SE corner after generation 150, when once again the population heads NE, following the NE-pointing preference vectors.

But this feedback coupling between phenotypes and preferences is somewhat noisy and inaccurate, due to the noisy, stochastic nature of the evolutionary process (e.g. genetic drift due to selectional sampling error with small populations). This evolutionary noise can affect both phenotypes and preferences, weakening the reciprocal interaction between them. The population can drift in phenotype space, meaning that new preferences must evolve to ensure that individuals will find mates. Perhaps even more importantly, the direction of the preference vectors can drift, as we saw in Figure 2. This starts to happen noticeably around generation 200, in the middle of the E edge of phenotype space. Preference vectors which before had pointed NE, now begin to slowly shift, pointing more and more straight N, which in turn causes the phenotypes to evolve in that direction. The preference vectors continue to swing counter-clockwise around the compass dial, pointing more and more westerly: first NW,

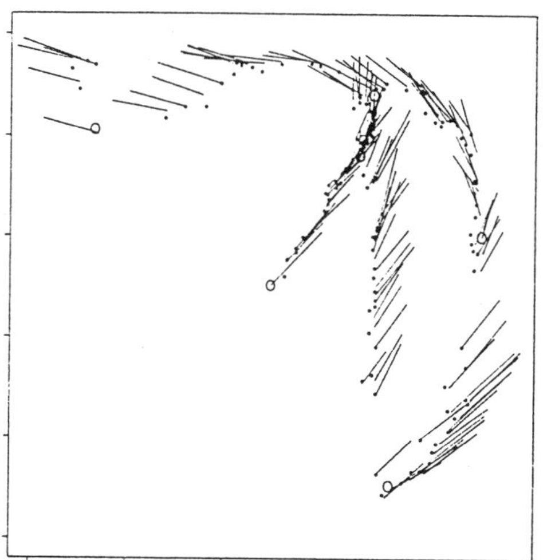

Figure 3. Sexual selection alone over 300 generations, showing population average phenotype and directional mate preference every two generations.

and then, after generation 250, straight W. The population follows (or maybe leads?) this trend, curving around the N (top) edge of phenotype space until it ends up in the NW corner at generation 300.

The coupling between preferences and phenotypes under sexual selection ensures that neither will shift too rapidly, and changes in one will force congruent changes in the other. This can result in a kind of evolutionary hysteresis, wherein the population's movement through phenotype space has a sort of momentum represented by the average mate preference vector. The interplay between this momentum effect, which drives the population in a consistent direction, and the genetic drift effects, which change the population's direction, result in the unique type of evolutionary trajectory shown in Figure 3. If we let the simulation keep running and allowed the population to evolve further (which we have done many times), it would continue wandering about in phenotype space, powered by directional mate preferences that impose strong sexual selection from generation to generation, but with nothing to guarantee a consistent direction or ultimate goal for the population's movement.

This simulation shows the capricious nature of directional sexual selection, and the way in which it can drive a population along a rapid but winding trajectory through phenotype space. In a flat fitness landscape (no natural selection), with directional mate preferences initialized to point in some direction but free to evolve in any direction thereafter, the short-term evolution is 'adaptive': phenotypic traits adapt to the current mate preferences, and mate preferences adapt to the current phenotypic traits, yielding effective sexual selection. But the long-term course of evolution is continuously capricious: neither phenotypic traits nor mate preferences ever settle down to a stable, optimal, equilibrium, because there is no stable 'adaptive landscape' external to the population. Rather, the two play catch-up with each other, engaged in a kind of arms-race that neither preferences nor traits can ever win, but which keeps them running quixotically across phenotype space. Directional mate preferences thus can indeed lead to runaway sexual selection, but the direction in which evolution runs cannot be predicted.

4.2 Sexual and Natural Selection Combined

What happens when we introduce natural selection into our model, to operate simultaneously with sexual selection? Whereas the population in the previous simulation wandered capriciously through phenotype space, one might expect that imposing some stern natural-selective fitness function would bring an end to all that sexual-selective rambling, and force the population responsibly upwards to some adaptive peak. But with directional mate preferences at play, the population's wanderlust can be surprisingly robust.

To investigate the interplay between natural and sexual selection, we constructed a single-peaked natural-selective fitness function as follows: phenotypes in the SW (lower left) corner are given the highest fitness, those in the NE are given the lowest, and the fitness of those in between falls off linearly from SW to NE. Thus, the isofitness contours in this landscape are just straight lines running diagonally from NW to SE. If a standard genetic algorithm were run in this fitness space, its population would sprint up these isofitness contours, heading S and W, and would quickly end up clustered at the peak in the SW corner. But in our simulations, these natural-selective fitnesses simply influence the probability of an individual being chosen as a potential parent; that individual's final reproductive success will also depend on sexual selection. Thus, there is an ever-shifting sexual-selective landscape overlaid on the fixed natural-selective fitness function; their combination determines actual final fitness.

To see what happens when sexual selection forces are in direct opposition to natural selection, we again initialized a starting population in the center of phenotype-space with preference vectors pointing NE, away from the SW direction of the natural-selective fitness peak. Moms and dads are now sampled from the population according to their natural-selective fitness, but they still will only get to mate and have offspring if they each meet the other's mate preference. The population's movement under the influence of both selective forces is shown over 500 generations in Figure 4a.

At first, sexual selection seems to dominate. The population starts heading NE in the direction of the mate preference vectors, just as it did in the previous run with sexual selection alone. But after about a dozen generations, this movement has stopped. The population then dithers around a bit, but finally succumbs to the pull of natural selection, and starts heading straight W, obliquely up the fitness function's slope, despite the preferences vectors continuing to point NE. After 50 generations, the population does a switch-back, changing direction to heads straight S up the fitness function slope. At this point, the preference vectors try to catch up with the phenotypic movement, shifting to point more southward, and the population hovers at a high-fitness point slightly E of the peak for several generations. Finally the population closes in on the peak in the SW corner. The preferences then swing around to point SW, reflecting the fitness landscape and reinforcing its selective pressures, so that high-fitness mates are also sexually preferred. And there the population stays, generation after generation.

But this appearance of happy optimality does not last forever. For the dark forces of sexual selection, first reigning, then overthrown, and then joining ranks with natural selection, remain powerful and capricious. And they reassert their command over the population after about 150 generations. For a while, all is well at the fitness peak -- the individuals in the population remain clustered there, and their preference vectors continue to point predominately SW, as shown for generation 226 in Figure 4b. But by generation 378, in Figure 4c, the preference vectors escape the magnetic pull of the fitness function and no longer point towards its peak. They now point in all directions, with many starting to point northward. The mate preference vectors continue to drift about in different directions until a general northward consensus is reached, around generation 400. Wanderlust returns: sexual selection entices the population towards the north, away from the natural-selective peak. By generation 450, in Figure

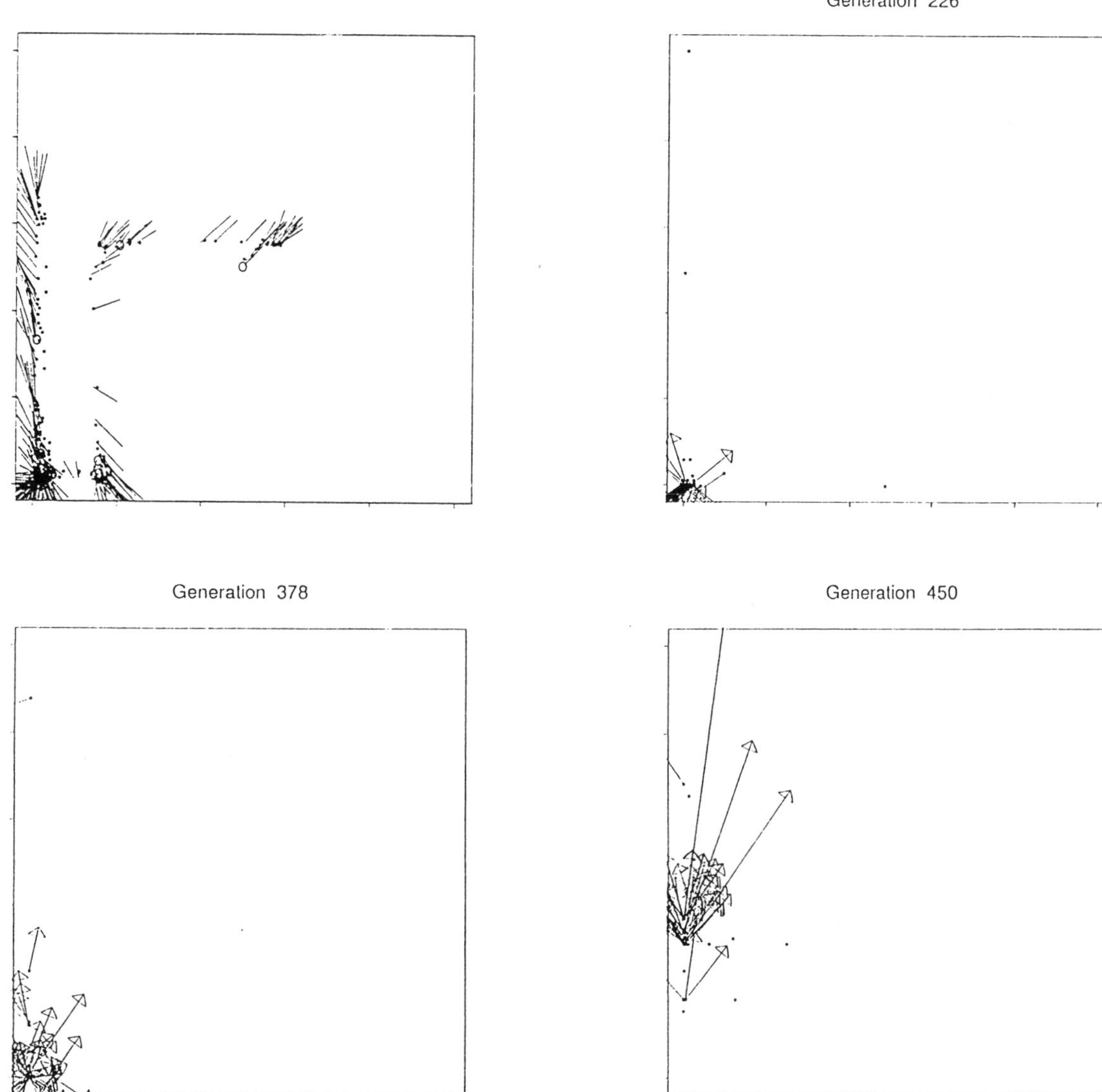

Figure 4. a. Sexual selection and natural selection initially pointing in opposite directions, plotted for 500 generations. b. The population clustered at the natural-selective fitness peak at generation 226, with SW directional preferences. c. The population still clustered near the fitness peak at generation 378, with varied directional preferences. d. The population shifted in position significantly by sexual selection at generation 450, with N directional preferences.

4d, the population has moved significantly northwards, and this progress continues over many generations, as Figure 4a showed.

If we ran this simulation further, we would see a continual battle between homesickness and wanderlust, with natural selection pulling the population towards its comfortable home on the fitness peak, and sexual selection compelling the population to wander through the wilderness of phenotype space under the momentum of the directional mate preferences. Of course, one of these forces could be made stronger, so that it alone controls the population's path. But we believe that in nature as in this simulation, the two are often balanced in a tenuous tug-of-war, with both affecting the course of evolution.

We next explored the effect of pointing the initial population's preference vectors SW, towards the natural-selective peak, so that natural and sexual selection pull in the same direction at first. The results over 500 generations are shown in Figure 5. This time, as we would expect, the population moves very rapidly toward the fitness peak, first heading SW, then straight S, and then straight W. The population converges on the peak within 50 generations here, compared to the 200 generations it took in the previous case of opposition. As before, the population remains at the peak, with preferences continuing to point SW, for many generations. But once again, the directional preferences begin to drift after a while, sexual selection soon rears its seductive head, and the population begins to

Figure 5. Sexual selection and natural selection initially pointing in the same direction, plotted for 500 generations.

move N in phenotype space, leaving the fitness peak behind. Thus, even though the directional mate preferences were initialized to complement natural selection, there is nothing to keep them in line. The preferences can ultimately evolve their own agenda, to which the population is (at least partially) subject.

Overall, these simulations show some of the capricious power of directional mate preferences to affect the course of evolution under sexual selection, with or without natural selection. Without natural selection, directional sexual selection can make a population wander through phenotype space at a fairly steady rate, along a trajectory that shows high directional consistency and momentum over the short term, but that changes directions unpredictably over the long term. When natural selection is applied as well, directional sexual selection can result in more rapid evolution toward an adaptive fitness peak, slower evolution toward such a peak, or even divergence away from a peak, depending on the directions the preference vectors evolve. Clearly, sexual selection forces in general and directional mate preferences in particular can play powerful roles in evolution, sometimes even dominating strong and consistent natural selection pressures. We will now turn to ways that simulating sexual selection may prove useful, both in assisting the evolution of human technology and in understanding evolution in nature.

5 Applications of Simulating Sexual Selection

5.1 Practical/Applied Uses

The relationship between natural selection and design optimization has been explored at great length and used to great effect in many practical contexts. But because sexual selection has often been considered a pathological, minor, non-adaptive force, it has often been overlooked as a design tool. We present three possible ways that methods for design optimization through simulated natural selection might be aided by including some simulated sexual selection.

First, to the extent that mate preferences evolve to be 'utilitarian' preferences for viability rather than 'pathological' preferences for arbitrary displays, sexual selection can reinforce ongoing natural selection, making it faster, more robust, and more consistent. In this paper, we have focused more on arbitrary preferences, but there is strong evidence from biology that many mate preferences do pick out viability indicators (e.g. Hamilton & Zuk, 1982). The ability of mate preferences to respond to viability indicators may be particularly useful and important when the mapping from phenotype to natural-selective fitness is noisy. In essence, selective mate preferences can allow a population to internalize natural-selective pressures, conferring some sexual-selective momentum on a population while it climbs an adaptive peak under the influence of natural selection.

Second, sexual selection can be thought of as imposing an automatic, emergent form of 'fitness scaling', so that ad-hoc methods such as pre-defined scaling algorithms and rank-based selection do not have to be used. Selective mate preferences based on the observed viability of potential mates will tend to increase the effective fitness variance in a population. Among many bird species for example, most male adults are healthy enough to survive, so there is little variance in their natural-selective fitness. But only a few are healthy enough to produce brilliant, sexually-preferred plumage (Hamilton & Zuk, 1982), so there is large variance in their sexual-selective fitness. Since sexual-selective fitness is highly correlated with natural-selective fitness in such cases, the former can be thought of as magnifying the latter. In general, sexual selection's ability to magnify natural-selective fitness differences may increase the power and consistency of natural selection in a way analogous to fitness scaling. So sexual selection could keep a population evolving along even when the objective variance in natural-selective fitness is rather small.

Finally, sexual selection can allow spontaneous sympatric speciation (see Todd & Miller, 1991). This sort of speciation may allow more efficient niche exploration and exploitation in complex adaptive landscapes with multiple peaks. If a population does not have the ability to spontaneously speciate, then it must remain fairly coherent and climb only one adaptive peak at a time. To explore a complex adaptive landscape then, one would have to go through many simulation runs to be sure that different adaptive peaks have been explored. But with spontaneous speciation, a population can split up to climb different adaptive peaks as they are encountered, without the experimenter knowing ahead of time how many peaks there are or where they can be found. With a large enough initial population, a single evolutionary run might be sufficient to explore most of the peaks in the fitness space, because the run will generate a branching phylogeny with separate species exploring separate peaks.

In essence, searching without spontaneous speciation through sexual selection is like sampling with replacement over many computationally expensive runs (i.e. it can be highly inefficient). Searching *with* spontaneous speciation on the other hand is like sampling with replacement during one big integrated run. For example, there may be many different ways of designing an efficient jet engine, but a normal one-species genetic algorithm will only be able to explore one adaptive peak in the space of possible designs at a time, and may keep climbing that same peak in run after run. But a large simulation with sexual selection and spontaneous speciation may be able to produce a range of species corresponding to a range of distinct, highly optimized engine designs.

In further research, we hope to substantiate these applications. We suspect that some combination of mate preference types may prove very useful in optimization. Directional preferences for viability indicators could be used to facilitate the exploitation of adaptive peaks and speed hill-climbing. Directional preferences for arbitrary traits may facilitate the exploration of complex phenotype spaces. And non-directional assortative mate preferences may facilitate spontaneous sympatric speciation and therefore efficient and automatic niche specialization.

5.2 Scientific/Theoretical Uses

Sexual selection has been such a neglected part of evolutionary biology and evolutionary psychology, and involves such mathematically intractable dynamics, that computer simulations of sexual selection will probably play a critical role in our scientific understanding of evolution in general. In the following three areas computer simulation may prove particularly fruitful; we intend to explore these in future research.

(1) Simulations can very probably help theoretical evolutionary biologists and mathematical population geneticists understand the complex dynamics of sexual selection, especially formally intractable interactions between evolving mate preferences and evolving phenotypes. Sexual selection dynamics may underlie both the microevolutionary processes that generate capriciously elaborated traits, and certain macroevolutionary processes such as speciation. If so, sexual selection may be primarily responsible for the vast biodiversity of sexually reproducing animals and flowering plants (which themselves undergo a kind of cross-species sexual selection by pollinators). We suspect that much of the evolution assumed driven by natural selection could turn out to be better explained as a product of sexual selection, and that computer simulation will be valuable in demonstrating this.

(2) Simulations may help comparative biologists and paleontologists better understand the ubiquity, structure, function, and origin of adaptations resulting from sexual selection. Likewise, they may help comparative and evolutionary psychologists understand the origins, mechanisms, and functions of mate preferences, and their effects on the emergence of certain kinds of behaviors, especially those associated with courtship. This use may prove critical in human psychology because it seems to us likely that the human brain itself has been enlarged and elaborated through runaway sexual selection, and functions conspicuously as a long-term courtship device (Miller, 1993).

(3) Simulations of sexual selection may help establish the general importance of 'psychological selection' (Miller, 1993), i.e. the causal effect of evolved mental mechanisms (such as selective mate preferences) on the further course of evolution. As such, simulations of sexual selection may illuminate other evolutionary processes (e.g. the evolution of camouflage, warning coloration, mimicry, and protean behavior) wherein the nervous systems of other animals constitute the primary selective environment. Because nervous systems are very different from other kinds of selective environments, we might expect that they can lead to distinctive kinds of evolutionary processes and outcomes.

6 Conclusions

Natural selection typically results in convergent evolution onto a few (locally) optimal solutions given pre-established problems posed by the econiche. Sexual selection in contrast often results in an unpredictable, divergent pattern of evolution, with lineages speciating spontaneously and exploring the space of phenotypic possibilities according to their capriciously evolved mate preferences. Some evolutionary biologists view sexual selection as a maladaptive process because it results in highly elaborated, physiologically expensive traits that sometimes impair an organism's ability to cope with other organisms (e.g. conspecifics, pathogens, parasites, prey, and predators) or with the physical environment. But this is an overly restricted view of what adaptive behavior means. In runaway sexual selection, members of a population adapt to the mate preferences of their conspecifics. These mate preferences are perceptual, motivational, emotional, and behavioral mechanisms that are just as real and important as the perceptual mechanisms that predators use to locate prey: if camouflage and warning coloration are legitimate adaptations, then so must be sexually-selected traits. And the adaptations produced through sexual selection, such as the peacock's tail, the mandrill's face, and the human's brain (Darwin, 1871; Miller, 1993), fulfill all the usual criteria for being legitimate complex adaptations (Williams, 1966): clarity of function, complexity of design, and efficiency and reliability of operation.

Traditionally, empirical evolutionary biology has had trouble with sexual selection because the mechanisms that drive it (that is, mate choice mechanisms) are hidden away in the heads of animals rather than displayed out in the open like more obvious aspects of the econiche. Also, the adaptations that sexual selection produces (e.g. courtship displays) can only be evaluated if one understands the mate choice mechanisms that they are designed to excite. Indeed, empirical studies of mate choice in animals did not really begin in earnest until theoretical population geneticists (e.g. O'Donald, 1980; Lande, 1981; Kirkpatrick, 1982) confirmed the possibility of runaway sexual selection. The history of sexual selection research is a clear example of good theory preceding and priming the acquisition of empirical data. However, there are frustrating limits on how much theory one can build with mathematically tractable formal models of evolution. Computer simulation can circumvent these limits. Furthermore, the mate choice mechanisms that cause evolution by sexual selection are themselves subject to evolution, leading apparently to problems of circular causality. But it is in such situations of apparent circular causation that explicit simulation modelling of complex interactions can be most useful. The complex interactions we investigated among evolving mate choice mechanisms, assortative mating, sexual selection, and speciation would have been difficult if not impossible to derive by traditional mathematical analysis. Thus, the study of sexual selection offers unique prospects for computer simulation to guide biological theory and empirical research.

Normal sexual selection is a process of a species equilibrating to its own sexual preferences; runaway sexual selection is a process of a species catalyzing its own directional evolution driven by its own sexual preferences. Computer simulations of both processes can take on a simpler, more elegant, more self-referential form than simulations of natural selection that require the researcher to construct an arbitrary, pre-defined, external fitness function or environment. For this reason, we suspect that simulation results concerning sexual selection may sometimes prove more robust, generalizable, and biologically relevant than results concerning natural selection that require very precise modelling of pre-existing environmental conditions and selection forces. We invite other researchers interested in the simulation of adaptive behavior to come in from the dry, glaring parking lot of natural selection, where species adapt to their niches like Buicks scraping their way into parking spaces, and enter the enticing fantasy-land of sexual selection, which overflows with dark tunnels of love, roller-coaster rides of exponential ascent and decline, mirrored funhouses in which species get caught in infinite cycles of self-reflection and self-distortion, and vast, seductive mazes of bizarre phenotypic extravagance, from which no species emerge untransformed.

Acknowledgments

Geoffrey Miller's portion of this work was partially supported by National Science Foundation research grants BNS 90-21684 to Roger Shepard at Stanford University, and INT-9203229 for postdoctoral research.

References

Andersson, M.B. (1982). Female choice selects for extreme tail length in a widowbird. *Nature, 299,* 818-820.

Catchpole, C.K. (1980). Sexual selection and the evolution of complex song among European warblers of the genus *Acrocephalus. Behavior, 74,* 149-166.

Collins, R.J., and Jefferson, D.R. (1992). The evolution of sexual selection and female choice. In F.J. Varela and P. Bourgine (Eds.), *Toward a practice of autonomous systems: Proceedings of the First European Conference on Artificial Life* (pp. 327-336). Cambridge, MA: MIT Press/Bradford Books.

Cronin, H. (1991). *The ant and the peacock: Altruism and sexual selection from Darwin to today.* New York, NY: Cambridge University Press.

Eberhard, W.G. (1985). *Sexual selection and animal genitalia.* Cambridge, MA: Harvard University Press.

Fisher, R.A. (1930). *The genetical theory of natural selection.* Oxford: Clarendon Press.

Hamilton, W.D., and Zuk, M. (1982). Heritable true fitness and bright birds: A role for parasites? *Science, 218,* 384-387.

Hillis, W.D. (1992). Co-evolving parasites improve simulated evolution as an optimization procedure. In C.G. Langton, C. Taylor, J.D. Farmer, and S. Rasmussen (Eds.), *Artificial Life II* (pp. 313-324). Redwood City, CA: Addison-Wesley.

Huxley, J.S. (1938). The present standing of the theory of sexual selection. In G.R. de Beer (Ed.) *Evolution: Essays on aspects of evolutionary biology* (pp. 11-42). Oxford: Clarendon Press.

Kauffman, S.A. and Johnson, S. (1992) Co-evolution to the edge of chaos: Coupled fitness landscapes, poised states, and co-evolutionary avalanches. In C.G. Langton, C. Taylor, J.D. Farmer, and S. Rasmussen (Eds.), *Artificial Life II* (pp. 325-370). Redwood City, CA: Addison-Wesley.

Kirkpatrick, M. (1982). Sexual selection and the evolution of female choice. *Evolution, 36,* 1-12.

Kirkpatrick, M. (1987). The evolutionary forces acting on female preferences in polygynous animals. In J.W. Bradbury and M.B. Andersson (Eds.), *Sexual selection: Testing the alternatives* (pp. 67-82). New York: Wiley.

Lande, R. (1981). Models of speciation by sexual selection on polygenic traits. *Proc. Natl. Acad. Sci., 78,* 3721-3725.

Miller, G.F. (1993). *The evolution of protean behavior through psychological selection: Adaptive unpredictability, sexual selection, and human encephalization.* Unpublished doctoral thesis. Stanford, CA: Psychology Department, Stanford University.

O'Donald, P. (1980). *Genetic models of sexual selection.* Cambridge, UK: Cambridge University Press.

Ryan, M.J. (1985). *The Tungara frog.* Chicago: University of Chicago Press.

Todd, P.M., and Miller, G.F. (1991). On the sympatric origin of species: Mercurial mating in the Quicksilver model. In R.K. Belew and L.B. Booker (Eds.), *Proceedings of the Fourth International Conference on Genetic Algorithms* (pp. 547-554). San Mateo, CA: Morgan Kaufmann.

Todd, P.M., and Miller, G.F. (submitted). *Evolution "without" natural selection: Sexual selection for speciation and learning.* Submitted to the Proceedings of the Third Artificial Life Conference.

Williams, G.C. (1966). *Adaptation and natural selection.* Princeton, NJ: Princeton University Press.

Designing efficiently navigating non-goal-directed robots

Rolf Pfeifer and Paul F.M.J. Verschure
AI Lab, Institute for Informatics, University of Zürich
Winterthurerstrasse 190
CH-8057 Zürich, Switzerland
e-mail: pfeifer/verschur@ifi.unizh.ch
Fax.: +41-1-363 00 35

Abstract

The basic problem in robot design is, how a given task description can be translated into mechanisms which produce the desired robot behavior. The solution proposed by classical artificial intelligence (AI) has been to "endow" the agent with a set of goals. These goals are then used to derive the robot's actions. However, this approach has proved to be inappropriate for a number of reasons. Using the example of a navigation task we will demonstrate that goal-oriented behavior can be accomplished by non-goal-directed designs. Our approach is based on two key ideas, self-organized learning and a value system to constrain the process of self-organization. This way structures can be acquired by the agent which control the agent's actions based on purely local system-environment interactions. The resulting performance of the agent on the navigation task is significantly better than random. Moreover, the behavior is adapted to the particular environment. It is concluded that non-goal-directed designs are more efficient, adaptable, and cheaper than goal-directed ones.

1. Introduction

The basic problem in robot design is, how a given task description can be translated into mechanisms which produce the desired robot behavior. The solution of classical artificial intelligence (AI) has been to "endow" the agent with a set of goals. These goals, designated by symbols, are then used to direct the robot's actions. Typically this is done by executing plans which are associated with a goal. However, this approach has proved to be inappropriate for the reasons which will be elaborated below. We start by discussing the traditional notion of goals and argue why it fails to deal appropriately with explaining behavior in scientific terms[1]. We then show some of the fundamental problems of goal-directed designs. It is demonstrated how agents can be disgned which navigate efficiently without resorting to the idea of goals. This is illustrated with a navigation task. The underlying architecture, distributed adaptive control, will briefly be exposed and it is shown how the navigation task is solved through self-organized Hebbian learning. We will then show that non-goal-directed designs are superior to goal-directed ones in many respects.

2. Problems with goal-directed systems

Goals: the traditional view. Since there is considerable confusion about this topic in the literature we will discuss the notion of goals in some detail. The dominant view on behavior in AI — the cognitivistic view — is based on the physical symbol system hypothesis (PSSH) (Newell and Simon, 1976, Newell, 1980). Roughly speaking, a PSS consists of a memory containing symbol structures, and a set of actions. It can be viewed as containing a "body of knowledge" that specifies the relations between the events in the world and the actions of the system. We can also refer to this body of knowledge as a world model. The actions of the system, either in the world or in the form of internal inferences, are organized around the goals of the system. They are executed according to the principle of rationality: briefly, a system will use its knowledge to reach its goals. Newell (1980) argues:

> "A general intelligent system must somehow embody aspects of what is to be attained prior to attainment of it, i.e. it must have goals. Symbols

[1]We use the term "scientific" to contrast it with common sense folk psychological explanations.

that designate the situation to be attained (including that it is to be attained, under what conditions, etc.) appear to be the only candidate for doing this. It might seem an alternative to build goal-orientation into the structure of the system at design time (as is often done in programs that have a single fixed task, such as playing a game). However, this does not suffice for a general intelligence facing an indefinite sequence of novel and sufficiently diverse goal situations." (p. 172).

Thus, according to Newell (1980) intelligent behaving systems require goals. These goals must have explicit representations. In other words, they must obey the "representation law": decode[encode(*T*)(encode(*X*))] = *T*(*X*), where *X* is the original external situation and *T* is the external transformation (Newell, 1990, p. 59). The "representation law" is illustrated in Figure 1.

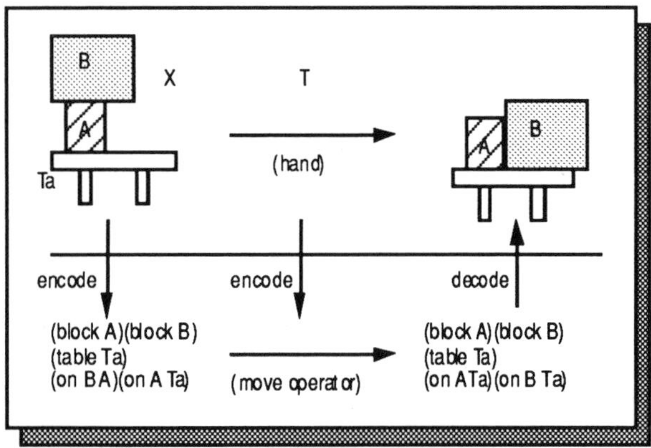

Figure 1: Schematic illustration of the "representation law" (adopted from Newell, 1990). Any representation, goals or otherwise, must fulfill this law.

Unless it can be shown that this law holds, we cannot sensibly talk about goals. The term goal is sometimes (inappropriately) used in a more broad sense, namely to designate certain internal states. For example, animals (*and animats*) need to keep a certain set of internal variables, the *essential variables* within the so-called viability zone (Ashby, 1952). Calling the level at which the physiological variable is to be maintained (or the range within which it should be kept) a *goal* of the agent would be inadequate since the value of the physiological variable per se does not obey the "representation law" in any obvious way[2]. McFarland (1989) uses the term *goal-directed* for a system which has an explicit representation of the to-be-achieved goal (i.e. — in our interpretation — it must obey the "representation law") and this goal representation is instrumental in guiding its actions: the agent works towards the goal. Below it is shown that goals which are broadly used in everyday explanations of behavior are highly problematic as scientific concepts.

Typically goal-directed behavior is accomplished by associating plans with goals. Plans can be generated in various ways. Examples are the use of a distance metric as in GPS (Newell and Simon, 1963) or the instantiation of certain types of predefined memory structures (e.g. Schank and Abelson, 1977). The important point about plans is that they all incorporate some kind of world model. The world model need not be complete but it must go beyond the immediate environment of the agent which is accessible through the sensors. The information contained in the world model can be viewed as "global" information since it can be accessed at any time.

In AI the vast majority of systems have been, and still are, *goal-directed* systems. Famous historical examples are GPS for problem solving, Schank and Abelson's programs for natural language processing, and STRIPS (Fikes and Nilsson, 1971), a planning system used in the Stanford robot Shakey. Modern AI programs are also largely goal-directed, e.g. expert systems which are sophisticated problem solving programs. An example of a recent goal-directed architecture, specifically designed for autonomous agents, is Maes (1990) which is based on STRIPS and uses the idea of add-lists and delete-lists which describe the effects of actions on the environment. In addition there is a controlled spreading-activation mechanism in a network of actions for action selection. The system is goal-directed since it employs explicit representations of goals and they are instrumental in directing the agent's actions. There is a data-driven component which has the effect that alternative goals can be activated. In this system the world model is essentially encoded in the add-lists and delete-lists. In spite of the reactive component the system is still entirely goal-directed since the purpose of the reactive component is basically to activate alternative goals which enable the system to react to the current situation.

[2]Of course, the term goal can be used in this broad sense, too, but then valuable distinctions are lost and confusion will emerge easily.

The world model must contain the information that allows the system to reduce the difference to the goal state. If there are many alternatives this process in turn has to be based on some heuristic search principles since exhaustive search would make it impossible to act in real time. An important conclusion is that if an agent built on the bases of these principles (i.e. as a goal-directed system) is to act successfully in the world, it already must possess a body of knowledge.

In order to discuss the problems with goal-directed systems we distinguish between observation and design. Let us begin by discussing observation.

Observing agents

First, we have to deal with the frame-of-reference problem (Clancey, 1991). We must make a clear distinction between the attributions made by an observer and the mechanisms which are actually responsible for an agent's actions. Goals are ascribed by an observer to an agent and thus only exist in the eye of the observer — they are intentional-level concepts (Dennett, 1987). They are used to organize an observer's thoughts about an agent in order to come up with some predictions (e.g. about what it will probably do next), to communicate with others about the agent's behavior, or to influence the behavior of the agent. Since goals are entirely observer-based descriptions no conclusions can be drawn about the processes within the agent which lead to behaviors that the observer describes in these terms. In particular it cannot be concluded that the agent's behavior is goal-directed.

Second, there is the problem of the indeterminacy of goal ascriptions. If we assume that the agent's behavior *were* goal-directed, it would not be possible to determine its goals. For example, if someone heads towards the cafeteria early in the morning we can attribute the goal of drinking coffee or tea to the person, and we interpret change in the agent's behavior when the alleged goal is achieved (e.g. drinking the coffee) as confirming evidence for our hypothesis. However, if along the way, the person meets a friend, starts talking and never ends up in the cafeteria, we have no way of knowing whether the person actually ever had the goal to go there. Of course, we can ask, but that is highly unreliable and leads to post-hoc rationalizations (Nisbett and Wilson, 1977).

Moreover, the goals attributed to an agent can also be at very different levels. In the cafeteria example our agent's behavior can be described in terms of having the following goals: reducing thirst, drinking coffee, talking to someone in the cafeteria, being in good spirits for the exam which is coming up, passing the exam, getting a PhD, being famous, etc., i.e. there is a lot of arbitrariness in attributing goals. And there is no way for an observer to come to a definite decision on which is the right one, i.e. there is no experimental procedure. It is therefore not possible to derive the agent's actions on the basis of its (his or her) goals.

Therefore, one might want to find additional evidence for the existance of goals. Iran-Nejad et al. (1984) argue that we have to look for evidence from other levels of description, i.e. we need inter-level constraints (in contrast to intra-level ones). The obvious candidate for such a level is physiology. However, and this is the *third* point, there is no physiological evidence for goal-directed behavior in natural agents and perhaps there never will be (McFarland, 1989). We can conclude that, although from a cognitivistic perspective explaining behavior in terms of goal-directedness has high value (see, for example, Schank and Abelson, 1977), and although from a common sense perspective explanations in terms of goals are plausible and useful, from a scientific point of view the notion of goal-directedness is not well-founded and it is a better strategy to explain behavior without reference to the notion of goal-directedness.

Similar arguments hold for animal behavior, with the obvious difference that we cannot ask animals about their goals. But, as we know from humans — whom we *can* ask — this would not make any difference, since introspection yields unreliable data anyway (Nisbett & Wilson, 1977).

An illustration: the navigation problem

To illustrate this point let us look at a simple example, the classical navigation problem: how does an agent get from location A to location B? (Figure 2). Studies in animal navigation (Orr, 1970, Baker, 1978, Swingland and Greenwood, 1983) show that sometimes animals can travel long distances from one location to another. For example, certain types of fish (salmon, eel) can travel back to their place of birth over thousands of miles. Their behavior could be described by attributing to them the goal of being at the place where they came from (location B) and viewing them as goal-directed. If their behavior were goal-directed this would on one hand require an explicit representation of the environmental situation of location B in order for the fish to test whether a particular location corresponds to location B (and this representation would have to obey the "representation law") and on the other a mechanism by which this goal representation becomes effective in choosing an action. This mechanism could be based on some kind of a "map" of their environment that they can use for guidance and for testing whether they have reached the goal. If the fish had an explicit goal representation and a map of the environment that they could use for guiding their actions towards the goal they could be considered *goal-directed* systems.

However, as just discussed goal-directed explanations are highly problematic and arbitrary. Therefore we should look for alternatives. And indeed in the case of the fish there is a comparatively simple explanation: the fish seem to be following a concentration gradient of some chemicals. Salmon appear to be following a chemical gradient, at least once they are back in fresh water (Haseer, 1978) and in combination with a rheotactic response (a tendency to orient against the direction of the water flow — Hara, 1970) this leads to the observed behavior.

In other words, the behavior of the fish can be explained on the basis of purely local mechanisms (following a gradient), without the need to resort to global goal-directed mechanisms. By a local mechanism

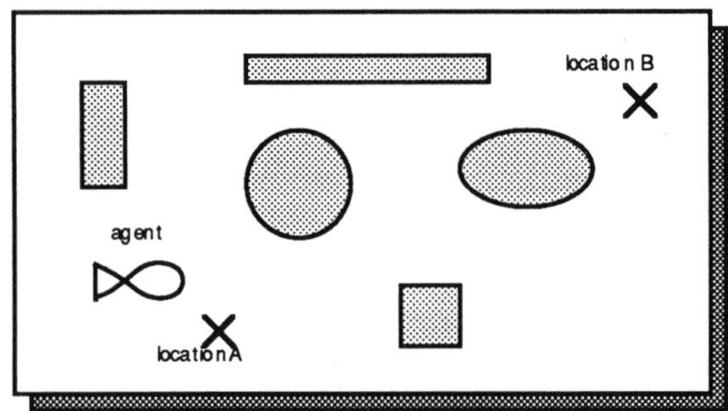

Figure 2: The classical navigation problem: the agent (in our example, the fish) is at location A. Its task is to go to location B. The shaded areas represent obstacles.

we mean one which is based directly on the immediate system-environment interaction. Mechanisms involving world models are global, as argued earlier. In the example of the fish a behavioral program is triggered by some physiological state (e.g. an essential variable approaching its boundery) which leads to the gradient-following behavior whenever a gradient is present, and is shut off again when a physiological or sensory state corresponding to being at location B is detected. In other words, the behavior of the fish is *not goal-directed*: one would be hard-pressed to argue that there is some sort of goal respresentation (obeying the "representation law"), and even more that there is some kind of global map.

This example can be used to illustrate a point which applies generally to autonomous agents. Behavior is always the result of the dynamics of internal physiological variables which through the physical setup of the agent (sensors, actuators) interact with the environment. The notion of goals is observer-based. Although goals have been — and are — often used in AI to direct the behavior of an agent they are intentional-level constructs which do not pertain in any direct sense to internal mechanisms. As illustrated the behavior under investigation, that we might want to call goal-directed, pertains to a continuous interaction between an agent and its environment. Therefore, this goal-directed description cannot be reduced to processes which are stricly internal to an agent. Consequently, equating goal ascriptions with internal mechanisms to explain goal-oriented behavior would be a category mistake (e.g. Clancey, 1989). It would be better, whenever talking about internal mechanisms, to employ a completely different terminology, namely the one of dynamical systems which is appropriate for the dynamics to be accounted for.

Designing agents

Designing an agent means translating a task description, e.g. keeping the Bahnhofstrasse in Zürich clean, into a physical set-up and into mechanisms that will accomplish the task. Note that the term "task" is neutral with respect to the agent: it is defined by an outside observer. What are the implications of the previous considerations for designing agents? What we have shown so far is that behavior which can be described by using the idea of goals does not necessarily imply that the system is goal-directed. However, we have not yet demonstrated that when designing a system, it would be inappropriate to take a goal-directed approach. The fact that the behavior of animals is presumably not directed by explicit goal representations does not necessarily imply that artifacts should not be goal-directed.

There are several reasons why building goal-directed systems might not be the best way of designing autonomous agents. *First*, goal-directed systems as explained earlier, need to — one way or other — resort to the notion of plans. Plans require a world model. Such a world model is hard to obtain (because the world is only partially knowable) and difficult to maintain (because the world is continuously changing). Moreover, plan based approaches quickly run into combinatorial problems (e.g. Fikes and Nilson, 1971; Chapman, 1987) which make it hard for an agent to act in real time. *Second*, systems which are based on static designer-defined ontologies — and such ontologies are needed when world modelling is involved — tend to be less adaptive. Since the knowledge of the system which is expressed in a world model must be defined in advance the designer has to transfer his of her own domain ontology to the system. But there is little reason to believe that this domain ontology can serve as a sound base for an adaptive system because the real world is constantly changing and only partially predictable. *Third*, the task description has to be translated into goal structures. For the cleaning task one might be able to come up with a certain list ("broom in hand", "bucket empty", "Bahnhofstrasse clean", etc.). But on one hand this list is highly arbitrary — there is no principled way of compiling it — and on the other we would still have to work out the plans (and the pertinent aspects of the world model) implying the problems just mentioned. *Fourth*, if we use goals and plans in our agent (which are symbolic represetations) we have to establish the connections of these symbols to the outside world, which has been a notoriously hard problem throughout the history of AI systems interacting with the real world. *Fifth*, and this is a pragmatic argument, there are efficient simpler alternatives which work well in nature, are highly adaptive, and obviously do not have the problems mentioned above: the fish in our example are flexible and they do not suffer from combinatorial problems in action selection.

But if our agent should not be goal-directed, what then is the right way of modeling its behavior? How then would we design the agent such that it could, for example, achieve the navigation task of going from A to B? It seems very hard *not* to think of goals which is probably the reason why goals are ubiquitous in the AI literature. Clearly there is no definite answer yet but we will discuss some pertinent ideas below.

Conclusion for autonomous agent design

Traditional models have been conceived as goal-directed systems where all behavior was generated by explicit goal representations and associated plans or world models. We showed that this approach has significant limitations and that it neither seems plausible from a biological nor from a design perspective. We want to present an alternative that demonstrates that powerful agents with high plasticity can be developed which are not goal-directed.

3. Designing non-goal-directed robots to perform tasks

Distributed adaptive control (DAC).

In this section we will show how a robot can be designed to perform a navigation task without having to resort to the notions of goal, plan, or world model. The agent we will consider is developed according to the design methodology of distributed adaptive control (Pfeifer & Verschure, 1992; Verschure et al., 1992). We will base our example on a simulated agent that has to learn to avoid obstacles and locate food sources in an environment. The description of the approach will be short since it has been described elsewhere (see also Verschure and Pfeifer, this Volume).

The basic idea of DAC is as follows. The agent is a simple mobile robot which is equipped with a number of sensors (collision detector, range finder, target detector) and can move forward, reverse, and turn. The central ingredient is a so-called *value scheme* (or value system) which encodes the agent's essential variables (e.g. to maintain a certain energy or temperature level), its reflexes (e.g. if a collision to the left is registered, reverse and turn right), parameter settings, and properties of the sensors and the motor apparatus. In other words, the value scheme encodes those aspects of the genetic setup which constrain or direct the process of self-organization (e.g. Edelman, 1986). In our architecture the agent learns whenever an action is triggered. This implies that the agent will acquire *action-based* categories (see also Verschure and Pfeifer, this volume). The agent has a neural network-based architecture, derived from a model of classical conditioning (Verschure & Coolen, 1991) which enables it to integrate more sophisticated sensors (e.g. a range finder) with the basic reflexes (see Figure 3).

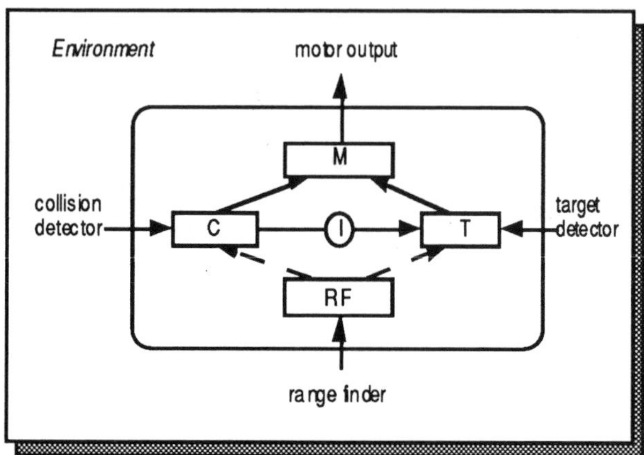

Figure 3: Schematic representation of the control architecture. RF: range finder group; C: collision detector group; T: target detector group; M: motor output group; I: inhibitory unit. The solid lines between the groups represent prewired connections, the dashed lines are modifiable through Hebbian learning.

Sensors: The agent has three sensors: range finder, collision detector, and target sensor. The range finder spans over -90° and 90° from the center of the robot. It consists of 37 elements that each cover a part of this receptive field. The receptive fields of these elements decrease when they get closer to the center of the agent. The system has 37 collision detectors that cover the same region as the range finder. The two target detectors can each calculate their own distance to the target. They are placed at -90° and 90° degrees from the center of the robot. The calculation of the difference in activation between the two target sensors yields whether the target is to the left or right from its center.

Actions: The agent can perform 5 actions which are "reverse-turn-left", "reverse-turn-right", "turn-left", "turn-right", and "advance". The latter action will be executed when none of the others is active.

Control: The control architecture consists of four neural groups and one inhibitory unit. The first group (RF) which consists of 37 units receives its input from the range finder. Activation a_i of each unit is determined roughly by the inverse value of a corresponding unit r_i in the range finder. The units in the second group (C), which also consists of 37 units, receive their input from the collision detectors. Also here there is a one to one mapping between units and elements of the sensor. If one collision detector is triggered the corresponding unit will get activation value 1. The third group (T), consisting of two units, receives its input from the target sensors. The last group (M) consists of 5 command neurons which code the basic actions the system can perform.

The connections between T, C and M are prewired (the solid lines in Figure 3). A collision to the left will automatically trigger a "reverse-turn-right" action and symmetrically for a collision to the right. If the target is detected to the left of the system a "turn-left" action will be executed and symmetrically for turning right. One unit in C or T can trigger a unit in M. In addition there is a special unit I that regulates the relation between C and T. Activation in C will increase its activation. When the activation of I is above a certain threshold the output from T to M will be inhibited. The inhibitory element represents an important aspect of the value scheme. In essence, it encodes the basic value "avoidance has preference over approach" which prevents the agent from being damaged.

Experiments

The environment for our experiments is depicted in Figure 4. As the agent moves around it will initially hit obstacles which will trigger the basic reflexes of "reverse-turn-left" and "reverse-turn-right". Whenever such a reflex is triggered learning takes place between RF and C. This is an example of the way in which the value scheme directs the learning process. As a result, after a while the agent will avoid the obstacles because it has learned to use range finder input to control its actions. In a sense, it starts anticipating obstacles which enables it to turn away before it is hitting (the result of this process can be seen in Figure 4). The agent keeps learning even after it is no longer moving into obstacles. This is important since there may be changes in the environment to which the agent has to adapt.

In the experiment which we performed to demonstrate non-goal-directed designs, a target was put behind the hole in the wall (indicated by the small circle on the right). The agent can detect the target once it is in its vicinity (the region bounded by the larger circle) in which case it will move towards it. This can be viewed as following a gradient. In this environment the agent acquired a behavior that one might want to call "wall-following" (Figure 4).

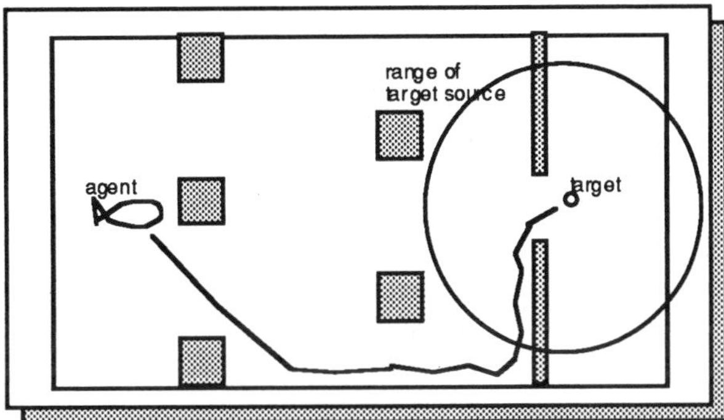

Figure 4: Environment for the simulation experiments. The agent is shown on the left, the target on the right. The range of the target source is indicated by the larger circle. The shaded areas represent obstacles. It is important that the target source is located behind a whole in the wall (the Figure has been adopted from Pfeifer and Verschure, 1992).

How does this wall-following behavior come about? If the agent is within the range of the target source it will turn towards it because of one of its approach reflexes. Because the target is behind a hole in the wall this also means turning towards the wall. At the same time there will be high activation on one side of the range finder RF because there is a wall. This pattern in the range finder will, through Hebbian learning, be associated with the target group T. This implies that over time, whenever there is a wall (i.e. high activation on one side of the range finder RF) the action of turning towards the wall will be triggered. Because avoidance has priority over approach the agent will then turn away from the wall. But then the approach behavior will be triggered again, etc. until it reaches the target. This accounts for the wiggly trail of the agent which can be interpreted as "wall-following". This acquired behavior can now be exploited to solve the navigation task depicted in Figure 1 (see below). From this description the importance of the value scheme can be seen: self-organization only works if it is directed essentially by what is "good" for the agent.

It is interesting to note that wall-following only develops if there is this particular regularity of targets in the environment. If the agent moves around, it will after some time start following walls and if somewhere in the wall there is a hole it will turn into it. To an outside observer this looks as if the agent were pursuing a goal, namely to seek targets. The agent is clearly not goal-directed: its goal-oriented behavior emerges through self-organization and is entirely based on local mechanisms. In other words, the system is not "working towards" a goal. If the agent is placed in an environment in which there are no target sources behind holes in walls it will not develop "wall-following". For certain behaviors to emerge there must be certain environmental conditions to activate the pertinent part of the value system, e.g. the reflexes (e.g. turning towards a target). Since we are the designers of the system we have, of course, insight into its internal mechanisms. We can therefore say that the system is *by design* not goal-directed.

Solving the navigation task. Let us go back to the problem of how the agent can be told to do something, i.e. to achieve a task, say to go from location A to location B, without resorting to some notion of goals, plans or models. If it is released in an environment in which there are target sources behind holes in walls it will eventually learn to follow walls. After having acquired this wall-following behavior, if the agent is released anywhere in the environment (let's call this location A) it will move straight while avoiding obstacles, until it gets near a wall. It will then follow the wall until there is indeed a target source behind a hole in the wall. If we take this to be our target location B we do indeed have a robot that will go from location A (which is the agent's starting location) to location B which is defined by the designer. The path will not be the shortest one the system could take (from the point of view of the observer) but it will be much better than random search if there is this particular regularity in the environment. It is important to note that the task description is entirely designer based: all the designer has to do is to place a target behind the hole in the wall where he or she wants the robot to go (location B) and the robot will find the location efficiently. What needs to be defined by the designer is a value scheme that enables the agent to establish the interation with the environment in such a way that the desired behavior can emerge. This implies that target locations are not defined for the agent, but only ways to generate sequences of actions to find targets. Of course, navigation problems can be solved, for instance, by programming a map (a world model) into the agent and use this map to generate a sequence of actions. This might be an appropriate design strategy in highly engineered environments but for the real world they will not do, as argued earlier.

A criticism of this bottom-up approach could be that instead of specifying trajectories in an internal world model this approach places them in the world by relying on certain kinds of gradients which will "draw" the agents to the target from any position (see our example of the fish). The goal-oriented behavior of such agents, e.g. the fish, is therefore constrained by the presence of these gradients in the environment. However, if no such gradients are currently there the system should be able to exploit regularities which have been associated earlier with these gradients (when they were still there). In our example the gradient is defined by the field which extends from the target source behind the hole in the wall, and the regularity is given by the wall. The association of the gradient with the wall leads to goal-oriented behavior which is independent of the presence of the gradient.

One of the distinctions between the traditional approach and the one presented here is the way in which a target is defined. In the traditonal approach this definition is in terms of coordinates or a position on a map. If we assume that the target represents "food" then the "wall following" behavior is useful for efficiently finding food (always provided that the environment does have the regularitiy that food is behind holes in walls), then this behavior should only be triggered if the agent has a need for this type of food. This can be accomplished by designing the agent such that its target related reflexes are only triggered when an internal variable, the energy supply, is moving towards the boundary of its viability zone (the pertinent simulations are not shown in this paper). Especially when talking about animals it is obvious that the location of the food sources cannot be genetically prespecified. Thus, there must be mechanisms by which efficient navigation strategies for food searching can be acquired.

This non-goal-directed design is robust since it can adapt to a variety of environments and to unanticipated situations. It is also cheap because it relies upon the properties that are already present in the environment and does therefore not have to be represented in the form of models within the agent: local mechanisms are sufficient to exploit them.

4. Summary and conclusion

We have argued that viewing agents as goal-directed is inappropriate if we want to understand their behavior. We also showed that goal-based designs are fraught with problems and demonstrated, using the example of a simple navigation task, how agents can be designed in a non-goal-directed way. The approach is based on two key issues, self-organization and a value scheme to direct the process of self-organization. Important aspects of the value scheme are the reflexes which determine when the agent learns. Another one which is a prerequisite for the wall-following is the inhibitory element which gives preference to avoidance over approach. Goal oriented behavior of the agent (which to an observer may look goal-directed) is not designed into the agent but emerges from the system-environment interaction.

Thinking in terms of self-organization, value schemes, and emergence is more difficult than thinking in terms of goals and plans. It requires a particular attitude towards programming which Rod Brooks called the "Zen of robot programming". The difficulty in adopting this attitude may be one of the reasons why goal-directed designs have dominated — and still dominate — autonomous agent design.

Acknowledgments

This research was partly sponsored by grant # 21-34119.92 of the Swiss National Science Foundation to Rolf Pfeifer. We thank René te Boekhorst for many valuable comments and discussions.

References

Ashby, W.R. (1952). *Design for a brain.* Chapman & Hall.

Baker, R.R. (1973). *The evolutionary ecology of animal migration.* London: Hodder & Stoughton.

Chapman, D. (1987). Planning for conjunctive goals. *Artificial Intelligence*, **32**, 333-337.

Clancey, W.J. (1992). The frame of reference problem in the design of intelligent machines. In K.v. Lehn (ed.). *Architectures for intelligence*. Proc. 22nd Carnegie Symposium on Cognition. Hillsdale, N.J.: Erlbaum, 357-423.

Clancey, W.J. (1989): The knowledge level reinterpreted. *Machine Learning*, **4**, 285-291.

Dennett, D.C. (1987). *The intentional stance*. Cambridge, Mass.: MIT Press.

Edelman, G. M. (1987). *Neural Darwinism: The theory of neuronal group selection*. New York: Basic Books.

Fikes, R.E., & Nilsson, N.J. (1971). STRIPS: A new approach to the application of theorem proving to problem solving. *Artificial Intelligence*, **2,** (no. 3&4), 1971.

Hara, T.J. (1971). Chemoreception. In: W.S. Hoar & D.J. Randall: *Fish Physiology*. Volume V Sensory systems and electric organs, 19-120. New York: Academic Press.

Iran-Nejad, A., Clore, G.L., & Vondruska, R.J. (1984). Affect: a functional perspective. *The Journal of Mind and Behavior*, **5**, 279-310.

Maes, P. (1990). Situated agents can have goals. *Robotics and Autonomous Systems*, **6**, 49-70.

McFarland, D. (1989). Goals, no-goals and own goals. In A. Montefiore and D. Noble (eds.). *Goals, no-goals and own goals. A debate on goal-directed and intentional behavior*. London: Unwin Hyman, 39-57.

Newell, A. (1980). Physical symbol systems. *Cognitive Science*, **4**, 135-183.

Newell, A. (1990). *Unified theories of cognition*. Cambridge, Mass.: Harvard University Press.

Newell, A., and Simon, H.A. (1963). GPS, a program that simulates human thought. In E. A. Feigenbaum and J. Feldman (eds.). *Computers and Thought*. New York: McGraw-Hill.

Newell, A., and Simon, H.A. (1976). Computer science as empirical enquiry: symbols and search. *Comm. ACM*, **19**, 113-126.

Nisbett, and Wilson (1977). Telling more than we can know: Verbal reports on mental data. *Psychological Review*, **84**, 231-259.

Orr, R.T. (1970). *Animals in migration*. London: McMillan.

Pfeifer, R., & Verschure, P.F.M.J. (1992). Distributed adaptive control: a paradigm for designing autonomous agents. *Toward A Practice of Autonomous Systems: Proceedings of the First European Conference on Artificial Life*. Cambridge, Mass.: MIT-Press, 21-30.

Pfeifer, R., & Verschure, P.F.M.J. (in press). Beyond rationalism: symbols, patterns, and behavior. *Special Issue of Connection Science on Philosophical Issues of Connectionism*.

Schank, R.C., & Abelson, R.P. (1977). *Scripts, plans, goals, and understanding*. Hilssdale N.J.: Erlbaum.

Singland, J.R., & Greenwood, P.J. (1983). *The ecology of animal movement*. Oxford: Clarendon Press.

Verschure, P.F.M.J., & Coolen, A.C.C. (1991). Adaptive fields: distributed representations of classically conditioned associations. *Network:*, **2**, 189-206.

Verschure, P.F.M.J, Kröse, B.J.A., & Pfeifer, R. (1992). Distributed adaptive control: The self-organization of structured behavior. *Robotics and Autonomous Systems*, **9**, 181-196.

PERCEPTION AND MOTOR CONTROL

Anuran Visuomotor Coordination for Detour Behavior: From Retina to Motor Schemas

Michael A. Arbib and Hyun Bong Lee
Center for Neural Engineering
University of Southern California
Los Angeles, CA 90089-2520, U.S.A.
arbib@pollux.usc.edu, hblee@rana.usc.edu

Abstract

Anurans (frogs and toads) show a quite flexible behavior when confronted with stationary objects on their way to a prey or when escaping from a threat. Rana computatrix (Arbib, 1989) is an evolving computer model of anuran visuomotor coordination. To model a complex behavior such as detour around a stationary barrier on the way to prey requires an understanding of anuran prey and barrier recognition, depth perception, and appropriate motor pattern generation mechanisms. The aim of this paper is to trace and model such processes. This paper begins with an overview of anuran detour behavior, which also includes new data from our lab, followed by a model of anuran stationary object recognition and localization. A brief comparison between anuran behavior and robot navigation is presented. The stationary barrier signal and prey signal have to be integrated to generate appropriate motor commands for detour behavior. The paper concludes with a schema-theoretic model of the integration that builds on the Arbib and Cobas (1991).

1. Introduction

Ingle (1983) and Collett (1982) have observed that a frog or toad's approach to prey or avoidance of a threat are also determined by the stationary objects in the animal's surround. A frog or toad, viewing a vertical paling fence barrier through which it can see a worm, may either approach directly and snap at the worm, or detour around the barrier. However, if no worm is present, the animal does not move. Thus, it is the worm that triggers the animal's response but when the barrier is present, the animal's trajectory to the worm changes in a way that reflects a relative spatial configuration of the worm and the barrier. Arbib and House (1987) offered a model of this using a "potential field" approach, which was also adopted by Arkin (1989) to build a mobile robot that can navigate around obstacles on its way to a destination.

Our aim in this paper is to trace and model those processes required in such detour behavior. More specifically, we seek to unravel the mechanisms behind the stationary object (paling fence barrier in particular) recognition, depth perception, integration of sensory signals, and the mechanism that transforms the result of sensory perception into appropriate motor commands.

1.1. Overview of Anuran Detour Behavior

Fig.1 shows the results of several of Collett's experiments where he presented toads with various prey-with-barrier configurations. When prey is at 12cm behind the barrier, the toad shows 75% detours and 25% direct approaches as illustrated in Fig.1.a. As shown in Fig.1.b, if a barrier with a passable gap (henceforth called "internal gap") is introduced, the animal usually aims to the gap (90%). When a double fence, constructed from single fences Fig.1.a and Fig.1.b, was presented as in Fig.1.c, the toad showed a response that was nearly an average of the two responses, with detours on about 50% of the trials and the other 50% directed to the gap in the front fence. As the two constituent fences are brought closer together, the toad detours around the barrier more often. When the gap in the front fence was filled as in Fig.1.d, most of the toad's approaches were detours (94%). Collett's data further show that toads possess a quite capable visual perception ability that detects sophisticated spatial arrangements of two fences, gaps, and a prey, meaning that a toad can acquire global knowledge of its surroundings.

New data: Collett's data make one think that the frog/toad is a simple automaton. Recently, our pilot observations suggest that it may be more flexible than we thought earlier.

Initially, when the frogs were first introduced to the experimental arena from a closed confinement, frogs always approached the worm directly, ignoring the barrier irrespective of prey, barrier, or animal location. Then, they tried to squeeze their way through an aperture between the neighboring palings (inter-paling aperture). They often tilted their bodies when passing through the aperture and were successful in about 50% of the trials. For another 30%, after the failed squeeze, they sidestep laterally usually poking their nose to some inter-paling apertures on the way, to a barrier edge where they reorient and approach a prey. In the remaining 20%, they either moved away from the barrier or remained inactive. When they were frightened, the animals often jumped into the barrier even though it was located in the direction of escape.

The animals began to show detour behavior after a week in the experimental arena. About a month later, they usually showed detours when the prey-barrier-frog configuration was appropriate. Even when the frogs made an initial direct approach, after poking at one or two apertures, they tend to initiate detour behavior. In some instances, they backstep about 3-5cm and then initiate detour behavior. It was as if the animal was trying to reexamine the barrier from a more distant, global perspective.

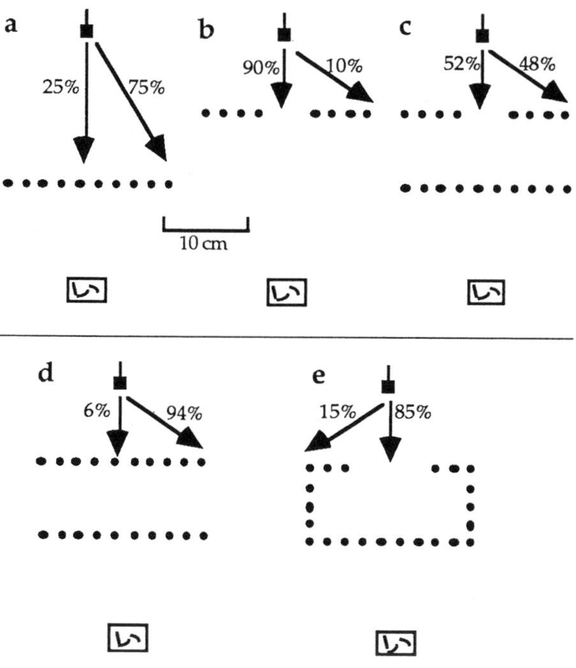

Fig.1: Approaches to prey with single and double barriers interposed. In each case, the "hammer" indicates the toad's starting position and orientation, the filled circles show the fence, and the arrows summarize the directions of the approaches. The results are given in terms of the percentage of approaches made in a particular direction. **a.** Single fence with prey 12cm behind. **b.** Single fence with 6cm gap and with prey 22cm behind. **c.** Double fence composed from single fences of **a** and **b**. **d.** Double fence with no gap. **e.** Approaches to prey behind the "cage". Cage is formed from double fence with palings connecting the ends. (From Collett, 1982).

When frightened, they seldom jumped into the barrier even though its location was in the typical escape direction. After about two months stay in the experimental arena, the frogs were relocated to the confined aquarium. When the frogs were put back to the experimental arena after two weeks stay in the aquarium, the animals acted just like when they were first introduced to the place: They did not detour. Gradually they began to exhibit detour behavior after three experimental sessions.

Although more experiments are needed, we believe some form of learning is involved in the animal's gradual shift from direct approach to detour behavior as the experiment progresses. Vertical plants and stems constitute many of natural stationary objects to the frogs but because many of them are pliant, they may not be perceived as impassable obstacles to the frogs. Perhaps because the palings resemble plants and stems, inexperienced frogs initially may opt to approach directly to the prey. But after some failures, frogs may gradually learn that the palings could not be toppled over so they shift to detour instead.

1.2. Frog vs. Robot

In the mobile robotics circle, the potential field method for path planning has gained popularity in part due to its simplicity and elegance. In this approach, obstacles exert repulsive forces onto the robot, while the target applies an attractive force to the robot. The resultant sum of all forces determines the subsequent direction and speed of travel. Arkin (1989) used the method for his mobile robot's, AuRA, path planning model. Warren (1990) used a similar technique for coordinating the paths of multiple robots in the presence of obstacles. Tilove (1990) offers an overview of the potential field method, and Koren & Borenstein (1991) present inherent problems/shortcomings associated with the method.

Arbib & House (1987) presented a model of anuran detour behavior based on the potential field method. Here, a prey sets up a radially symmetric attractant field whose strength decays gradually with distance from itself. A barrier sets up a repellent field whose effect is more localized than that of prey. The barrier field is not radially symmetric but has a lateral component that is stronger but decays more rapidly with distance than does its rostro-caudal component. Associated with a toad itself is a radially diverging field that represents the animal's "urge" to move. When prey, barrier, and toad are present simultaneously, the interaction of the associated fields determines the animal's path. The model was able to explain detour behavior when the barrier configuration was simple as in Fig.1.a and Fig.1.b.

Let us analyze the toad detour behavior when the barrier configuration is more complex as in Fig.1.c. The toad usually approaches the gap even though the rear fence still effectively blocks its approach to prey. This behavior cannot be explained using the potential field method unless the gap itself is treated as a target exerting an attractant field similar to prey. Another clue that the maladaptive behavior in Fig.1.c is caused by the toad's response to the gap is shown in Fig.1.d where the approaches are mostly detours when the gap in the front barrier is filled. Note that the barriers/gaps themselves do not elicit any movements from the animal. Thus, a toad can attach a new meaning to the gap, from a neutral object to an intermediate target, when prey is present. Using the analogy from toad, it will be interesting to think of a robot that can not only change the shape of potential field but also a meaning of an object, e.g., from an attractor to a repellor, as it encounters new elements in its workspace.

Based on the potential field method, neighboring potential fields of front and rear barriers gradually lump into one as the distance between them shrinks. This lumping effect can explain why toad approaches the gap less as the two constituent fences are brought closer together. When the distance between two barriers becomes less than 5cm, approaches to the gap fall to less than 30% (Collett, 1982), suggesting the gap's attractant force should be less powerful than the repulsive forces of the barriers. A mobile robot using the potential field method could be stuck in local minima as when it is trapped inside a U-shaped obstacle (Koren & Borenstein, 1991). Similar things happen to the toad as shown in Fig.1.e.

Collett also reports that an internal gap in the rear fence also influences the toad behavior, sometimes even when the front fence has no gap and the inter-fence distance is not small. Because, the gap in the rear barrier cannot cancel the repulsive force of the frontal barrier due to its weaker intensity, we find it difficult to explain the aforementioned behavior with the potential field theory. So, while much of frog behavior can be replicated based on potential field method, some subtle problems still remain.

How does the toad's "intelligence" compare with that of a potential field based mobile robot? Obviously, toads' behavior suggests that they are bad at formulating a global path plan which requires them to integrate the spatial information which they have, whereas there are mobile robots capable of doing that (e.g. Warren, 1989). Many robots capable of global path planning employ search methods to find the best path from the initial state to the goal state among many alternative paths. Toad behavior, however, seems to be based on average response to a linear sum of *"unit"* responses. Unit response is based on a *"unit"* rule which is applicable only to a specific prey-barrier configuration consisting of prey and an individual fence but not to the integrative features of a double fence. In a way, each unit rule is like a reflexive stimulus-reaction paradigm. For instance, the response of a frog in Fig.1.c is the average of unit responses in Fig.1.a and Fig.1.b. The unit rules may be summarized as follows: i) Aim for a gap in the barrier (gap in this case also includes the two barrier ends). ii) If there is a choice, select the most salient. iii) If there is no suitable gap, aim for the prey. The saliency of a gap depends on its location w.r.t. toad→prey axis, width, and depth. A gap in the frontal fence may have more influence to the animal than that of the rear fence.

In the following chapters, we will present models of how the anurans may recognize the barrier/gap and its depth, and how these could be integrated with prey information to generate appropriate actions based on the physiology and anatomy of the animal.

2. Model of Stationary Object Recognition and Depth Perception

While considerable efforts have been taken to analyze and to model anuran perception and behavioral mechanism w.r.t. moving stimuli (prey or predator) at a neuronal level, rather little work is done w.r.t. stationary objects (henceforth called SO). Anuran visual perception is the result of cooperation of many different classes of neurons located in different brain regions. Anuran retina cells have been classified into five or six classes depending on their characteristic responses to different stimuli and light conditions (Grüsser & Grüsser-Cornehls, 1976). Retinal signals converge onto *tectum* and *pretectum* in anuran midbrain region and through their interactive or independent processes further visual perception is accomplished. Certain cells in tectum and pretectum have been associated as grandmother cells signaling the detection of certain visual stimuli: T5-2 as a worm detector (Ewert, 1987) and Th6 (Ewert, 1971) as a looming threat detector. Neural network models for the above cells have been proposed using appropriate cells from retina, tectum and pretectum (Cervantes-Perez et al., 1985; Liaw & Arbib, 1991).

Ingle (1983) showed that a main locus for anuran SO recognition is the pretectum. His observation also suggests that not only the pattern but also the size and the depth relationship w.r.t. the background are the important cues for the recognition of the object, especially during figure-ground segmentation: A smaller barrier has a better chance to get detected than a larger one, and the same horizontally striped pattern is interpreted differently when its depth is identical to the background (a place to hide) compared to when it is located in front of the background (a place to avoid) during the escape behavior.

We do not think that there are different pretectal neurons sensitive to different SOs, and there are no data suggesting such neurons exist (see next section). Rather, we posit that the recognition should be based on application of recognition algorithms to neuronal representations of the SO. This section presents a neural process of pattern formation of SOs in pretectum, an important part to understand the recognition mechanism, and a depth perception process that depends on visual features extracted by pretectum. Based on the patterns formed in pretectum, a brief description of anuran paling fence recognition will be offered.

2.1. Cells involved in SO Recognition

Among the retinal ganglion cells, only R3 and R4 cells are positively identified to project to pretectum (Ewert, 1971; Grüsser & Grüsser-Cornehls, 1976).

- *Class R3 neurons:* With ERF of about 8°, these cells can be simply described as detectors of *moving* contrast. These cells show brief phasic response to diffuse ON and OFF light stimulation but do not discharge to stationary stimuli.
- *Class R4 neurons:* With a large ERF of 12-16°, these cells exhibit continuing discharge when lights are turned off or when a dark object is introduced to their ERF and stays there.

Ewert (1971) found in toad's pretectum, units that give continued discharge in the presence of a large dark stationary object.

- *Class Th10 neurons:* With ERF of about 30 - 90°, these neurons exhibit prolonged discharge to large dark stimuli that are stationary in their ERFs even when the SOs were revealed by turning on the room light without prior motion.
- *Class Th7 neurons:* These neurons are luminance detectors. Among 3 major subclasses, Th7(1) responds to any reduction of the general illumination with a prolonged tonic discharge lasting 5 minutes or longer.

2.2. Stationary Object Recognition Model

A layer (surface) of pretectal Th10 neurons will be the substrate of SO recognition. Since a SO forms a 2-D pattern on the pretectal surface due to the topographical retina→pretectal projection, features for SO recognition should be based on 2-D firing pattern on the Th10 layer. Since one subclass, Th10(4), has a binocular ERF, frogs and toads could have a stereoscopic cue to estimate the depth, which is one important cue for SO recognition. The Th10 cells are modeled to receive direct excitatory R3 and R4 retinal inputs and inhibitory inputs from Th7(1) neurons. The retinal model is from Teeters and Arbib (1991) and all models are written in NSL (Weitzenfeld, 1991) running on a Sun workstation.

Because a Th7(1) class neuron is a general dimness detector, it is modeled to receive R4 (retinal dimness detector) inputs through its receptive field which is modeled to be the entire view field of the animal. The cell is made to generate prolonged tonic discharge so long as the R4 summation across its receptive field remains above the specified threshold. Fig.2 shows the schematic diagram.

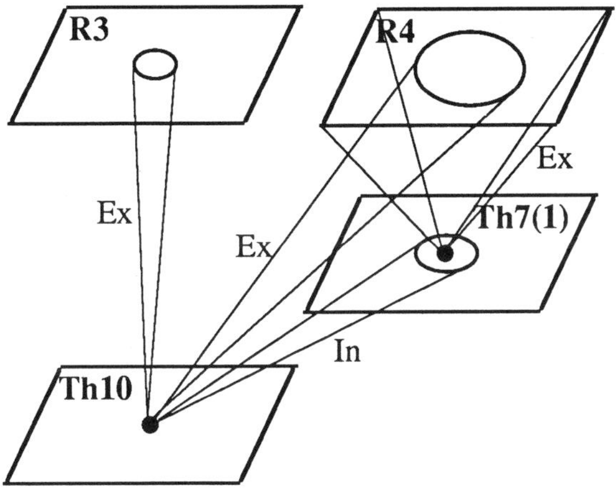

Fig.2: Schematic diagram illustrating the connection patterns of Th10 network. R3s and R4s excite Th10 directly. Th7(1) receives excitatory input from entire R4 view field and inhibits Th10. For the details, see the text. (Ex: excitatory connection, In: inhibitory connection).

The pretectal Th10 based SO recognition model should satisfy the following criteria: i) A simulated Th10 cell should replicate the response of a real cell. ii) A SO pattern on Th10 surface should offer neuronal cues for identification. An understanding of SO pattern formation on Th10 surface requires knowledge of distribution of retinal projections to pretectum and dendritic process of Th10 cells. Lacking both data, we modeled Th10's R4 receptive field to be large (45°) to account for Th10's large receptive field and its increasing response to large dark objects. Convergence of R3 explains Th10's On-Off response to light changes. We posit that R3 activation should signal edge location. In order to preserve an edge location, Th10's R3 receptive field is modeled to be much more focused than that of R4. Simulation shows that the R3 receptive field should be either very narrow (less than 3°) or could be somewhat broader (up to about 10°) if the receptive field is modeled as a center-on, surround-off Difference-Of-Gaussian (DOG) mask. Th10 response shown in the next two figures is based on the DOG mask. Fig.3. shows that the simulated Th10 neuron responds similar to a real neuron.

Ingle has shown that frogs view a dark horizontally striped barrier and the same sized dark solid patch similarly, whereas a vertically striped barrier (similar to Collett's paling fence barrier) is interpreted differently: Frogs jump into the horizontally striped barrier and also to the solid dark patch but avoid the vertically striped barrier during an escape. This suggests that the Th10 representation of horizontally striped barrier and solid dark patch should show similarity while that of the vertically striped barrier should be different. Due to R4's large ERF and aforementioned broad projection characteristic to Th10, its boundary sensitivity is very poor. R3 is sensitive to edges and has better resolution (due to smaller ERF and focused projection to Th10) but how could a stationary object elicit retinal image movement to generate R3 activation?

Anurans have ways to generate retinal image movements through diverse self induced motions. Pigarev et al. (1971) report that R3 neurons are activated by each active head and body movement. Burghagen and Ewert's (1983) observation also suggest similar conclusions. Grüsser and Grüsser-Cornehls (1976) elicited R2 and R3 responses from incompletely immobilized frogs and toads during eye-retraction/lid-closure. Respiration causes periodic and predominantly vertical eye movement of about 0.5° every 0.63 seconds (Schipperheyn, 1963). Schipperheyn proposed that the respiration-induced eye movement produces moving retinal image and thus elicits activation of movement specific ganglion cells such as R3s. Grüsser and Grüsser-Cornehls report that they observed the most sensitive R3 neurons were activated when a stationary contrast object smaller than the size of ERF is placed in their ERFs and when small shifts in the retinal image occur during respiratory eye movement. However, Pigarev, and Burghagen & Ewert failed to see the respiration induced R3 firings.

Given these conflicting data, we set out to see, through retinal modeling (Teeters et al. 1992, submitted), if respiration induced R3 excitation is possible. Simulation showed that it is possible. Thus, the Th10 model is

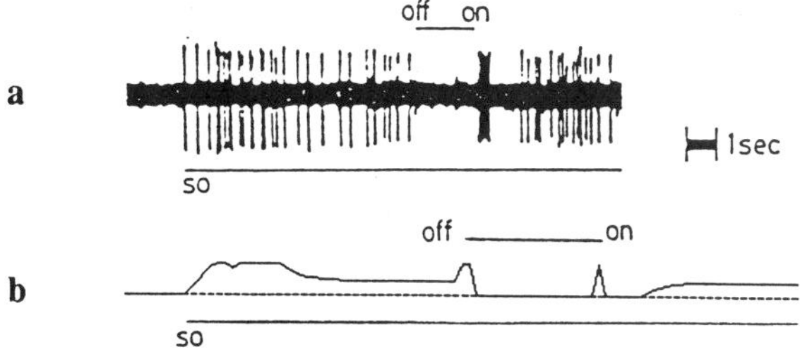

Fig.3: **a.** Pretectal Th10(3) unit, a subclass of Th10, sensitive to stationary objects. The frequency increased when a dark object moved into the receptive field and remained stationary in the field (SO). After turning the light off, the activity ceased. Turning the lights on again elicited a short burst, followed, after a delay, by renewed response to the SO. (from Ewert, 1971). **b.** Simulated Th10(3) cell against 20×20° dark SO.

constructed to receive a respiratory induced R3 signal as well as the R4 signal. Because respiration is mostly vertical oscillations, respiration induced R3 activation usually signals horizontal edges. Fig.4 shows the pretectal image of a vertically striped barrier, a solid dark patch, and a horizontally striped barrier. We can see that the solid dark object and horizontally striped barrier form similar patterns across the Th10 surface in that they both do not present conspicuous features along the horizontal axis. However, the image of the vertically striped barrier clearly delineates the horizontal eccentricities of vertical stripes along the lower and upper boundaries. Thus, anurans could detect a paling fence as follows: i) See if the pretectal image has overall activity above the spontaneous level. ii) See if there are two rows of succession of local maxima along the horizontal axis within the region of supra-spontaneous level. iii) Use the feature from (ii) to segment and to estimate the depth (see below) of the barrier.

Gap detection could be as follows: A potential gap would be detected due to its discontinuity in barrier (discontinuity could take place along horizontal or depth axis). Once the discontinuity is detected, the animal could measure the width of the region to estimate the probability of it being a gap.

2.3. Depth Perception Model

We stated that depth perception is an important cue in recognizing the different classes of SOs. How then do anurans estimate the depths? In this section, we will present an anuran depth perception model of stationary objects such as a paling fence barrier.

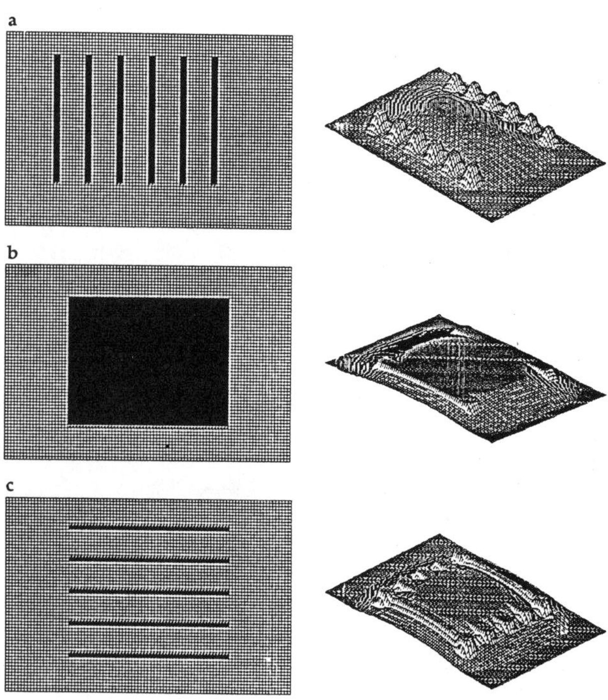

Fig.4: Stationary Objects (left) and corresponding pretectal Th10 images (right) induced by respiratory eye movement. **a.** Vertically striped barrier. **b.** Dark solid patch. **c.** Horizontally striped barrier.

Collett (1977) showed that frogs and toads use both binocular and monocular cues to determine depth. Collett found that while binocular toads utilize binocular cues predominantly (94%) when estimating the depth of prey in the binocular field, nevertheless their depth estimation does include a small (6%) effect from monocular accommodation. Deprived of binocular cues, monocular toads still retain an ability to judge distance through accommodation cues. Thus, data exist regarding frog/toad's depth perception against prey. However, very little is known about how the animal might estimate the depths of SOs.

House (1989) offered a cooperative model, the cue-interaction model, of SO depth perception in which the lens accommodation cue is used to help disambiguate the correspondence problem of stereopsis. The model is constructed based on the physiology and anatomy specific to frogs/toads. House insists that any anuran depth perception model i) should not depend on eye vergence, ii) must account for use of an active process like accommodation, iii) must not depend on the tectal map, and iv) must be able to operate on sparse images, because the visual maps cannot be assumed to represent local illumination level since the visual input from the retina is feature encoded. We believe his claims are still valid.

House assumed that binocular disparity cues are processed similar to a Dev-Marr (Dev, 1975; Marr and Poggio, 1976) type cooperation/competition algorithm. The model demonstrated its ability to estimate the depth of a single object (prey or predator) and a paling fence. It also predicts that concave lenses will have a consistent effect, with stronger lenses causing a fence to appear closer to the animal. Prisms, on the other hand, should have a more variable effect, even causing the fence to be fragmented, so that the animal may occasionally behave as if there were gaps in the fence.

One of the problems with House's model was that it was not able to resolve the double barrier as in Collett's experiment. By replacing the Dev-Marr algorithm in House's model with Prazdny's (1985) stereo correspondence algorithm, we were able to overcome the double-fence problem. Prazdny formed his algorithm based on a *"coherence"* principle. The coherence principle recognizes that for transparent surfaces, where proximal points on the (retinal) projection surface may arise from widely separated 3D objects, image proximity does not necessarily imply disparity continuity. Thus by relaxing the smoothness constraint of typical cooperation/competition stereo algorithm, the model is better equipped to handle quasi-transparent objects like bushes, and double paling fences. Obviously, an animal cannot focus on two barriers simultaneously, so the model assumes that the animal changes the focus intermittently to each barrier.

Input features to the revised cue-interaction model come from the Th10 pattern of the SO as explained in the section earlier. The cue-interaction model samples locations of local maxima points on the Th10 surface along the horizontal axis, which are the horizontal eccentricity coordinates of the constituent palings forming the barrier. This information is used as an input to the stereopsis component of the cue-interaction model. Accommodative state directly influences the firing profile of R3 neurons. A correct focus will give a stronger and sharper R3 profile than a defocused state. Thus, by varying the accommodative state and measuring the R3 firings (actually Th10 firings), the animal obtains an accommodative cue which is the other component of the cue-interaction model. Fig.5.a shows a double barrier as an input stimulus, and Fig.5.b shows the frog's estimation of the barrier location after the cue-interaction process. Fig.5.b is generated from the retina_angle - disparity map where cue-interaction takes place.

a

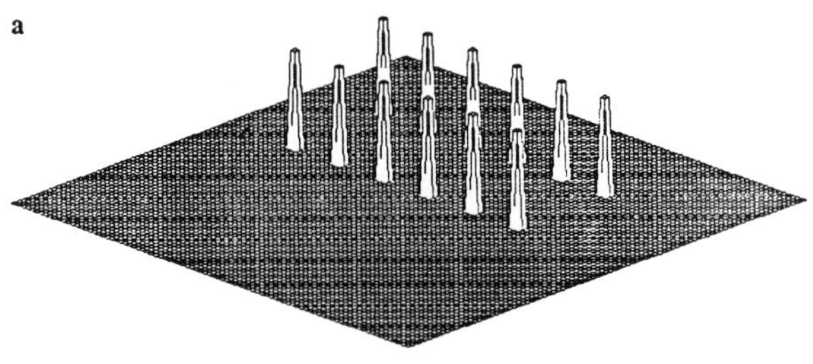

b

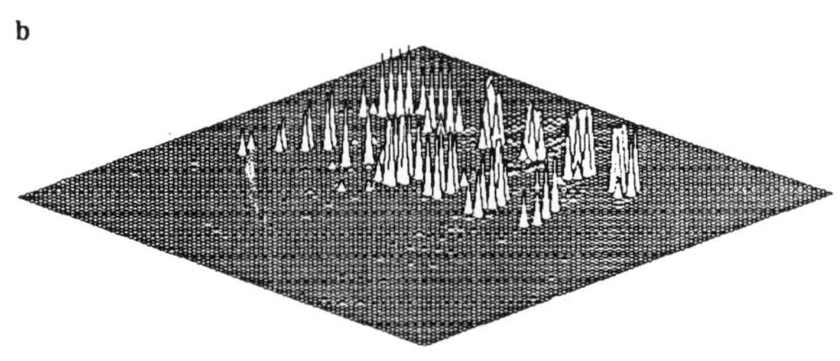

Fig.5: Revised Cue-Interaction model for a double barrier. **a.** A double barrier is given as input stimulus. **b.** Frog or toad's estimation of the depth of the double barrier. Estimation of the barrier location is represented in a probabilistic measure.

3. Anuran Detour Model

In this section, we integrate barrier perception and depth-estimation models with the schema model of prey capture (Arbib & Cobas, 1991) to explain the behavior of normal and lesioned animals engaged in detour behavior. Because the detour model builds on it, we present a brief summary of the prey capture model. But first, since the model is rooted in experimental data of Grobstein (1988), a short account of his ideas is given.

Grobstein and his colleagues observed that the tectal signal conveying the prey location at the caudal midbrain level shows lateralization and parcellation traits and is population (frequency) coded: The horizontal eccentricity signal conveying the prey location of one visual hemifield runs through the ipsilateral body side but not the contralateral side (lateralization). Different components of the prey location (eccentricity, elevation, and depth) are handled through different pathways that can be disturbed independently (parcellation). The prey location is represented relative to the animal's body (body-centered) which is different from its retinotopic representation in the tectum. Grobstein reports that somatosensory and tectal prey information are integrated at the level of midbrain *tegmentum*.

A schema model for prey capture: The model consists of the dotted portion in Fig.6, showing the schemas for one half of the visual field. First, the Prey-Selector schema, located in tectum, detects and selects a unique prey and returns the eccentricity (x) and elevation (y) of the prey. Depth-Translator then calculates the depth (d) to the prey through x and y values furnished by Prey-Selector. Prey Heading-Translator uses x, y, and d values to obtain the body-centered angle to the selected prey from the animal. The Depth-Map schema provides the transition from a spatially-coded representation to a frequency coded information and furnishes "closeness" (1/d) signal for output. Similarly, Heading-Map, using the prey heading signal as input, calculates the target location of the required motor heading and outputs it population coded. Note that the Heading-Map signal codes the *target* location of the required motor response and not the location of the prey per se, the *Motor Heading Map* hypothesis.

Orient, Snap, and Approach motor schemas activate corresponding pool of motor neurons in the spinal cord that actually carry out the action. The more strongly Orient is activated by larger heading value, the more strongly will it stimulate motoneurons controlling the turn muscles. The activity of Snap is an increasing function w.r.t. the closeness of the prey from Depth-Map and a decreasing function w.r.t. the animal's heading toward the prey as calculated by the Orient schema. In a similar way, the Approach schema determines the distance for the animal to advance as a function of the closeness to the prey and the activation level of the Orient schema. Several of these motor schemas may be active at the same time. In this way, the final motor behavior will result from the combined activity of these motor schemas. The model was successful in simulating the experimental data on anuran prey catching behavior with and without brain lesions.

3.1. Some Issues on Prey, Barrier Integration

An integration of barrier and prey signals has to take place in order to determine detour or direct approach to prey depending on prey-barrier configuration. A question is then where and how the integration take place.

Does the integration take place at tectum via topographical projection from pretectum to tectum? Ingle's (1983) lesion data showing that the atectal frog avoids barriers while escaping noxious cutaneous stimulation suggest that pretectal barrier signal is not disturbed by the tectal lesion, and so tectum is not likely the place of prey-barrier integration. Could pretectum be the integration site? A lesion at pretecto-tectum connection could shed some light: If pretectum is the integration site, the lesioned animal should exhibit more direct approach to prey than normal animal in the same situation.

Currently we favor a tegmental integration hypothesis following Grobstein's data (1988). However, to develop the integration model, we need to know more about the nature of pretectal outflow. For instance, we lack the data

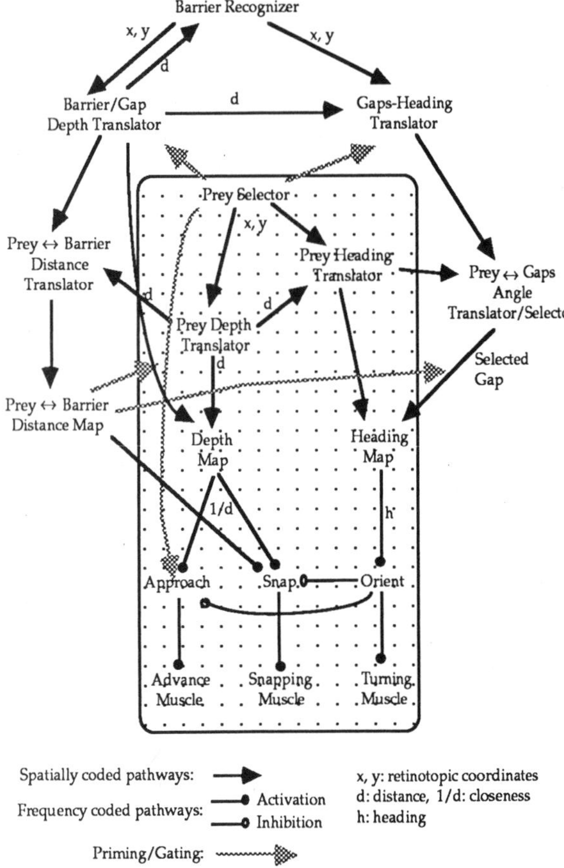

Fig.6: A schematic model of anuran detour behavior. Schemas in the dotted region correspond to the Prey-Capture model of Arbib & Cobas.

on whether pretectal outflow arriving at tegmentum is spatially coded or population coded. We will assume that the pretectal signal is spatially coded and thus, pretectal (barrier) signal and tectal (prey) signal can be integrated in the spatial domain and the resultant motor heading signal will leave the tegmentum population coded after the signal conversion. We will also assume that the pretectal signal is parcellated and lateralized.

3.2. Detour Model

Fig.6 illustrates a schematic overview of the complete detour model of unit response for one half of the visual field. The dotted portion shows Arbib & Cobas' prey capture model and the schemas in the non-dotted region are responsible for recognition/localization of a barrier and integration to the prey capture model. In this section, we present a schematic explanation of the barrier recognition/localization network, modifications to the schemas in the prey capture model, and how these are integrated as a detour model.

Barrier Recognizer: Barrier-Recognizer schema is implemented in a neural network as described in section 2.2. It detects the barrier and the gap. The schema provides the x and y coordinates of each paling to the Barrier/Gap Depth Translator and a set of x and y coordinates of the gaps to the Gaps-Heading Translator. The Barrier-Recognizer resides in pretectum and is assumed to become activated, at least the pattern formation part, regardless of detection of prey. It is because some stationary objects like a paling fence barrier seem to be recognizable by their patterns alone. Depth estimation and gap detection need further processing with inputs (features) furnished by the Barrier-Recognizer.

Barrier/Gap Depth Translator: The Barrier/Gap Depth Translator schema is implemented as mentioned in section 2.3. Using x and y coordinates of the palings received from the Barrier-Recognizer, it computes depth to the barrier and the gaps (gap-depth is considered to be an average of depth(s) of neighboring paling(s)). An activation of the Prey-Selector is necessary for the activation of Barrier/Gap Depth translator: Activation of Barrier-Recognizer alone does not activate the schema. This relationship between the Prey-Selector and the Barrier/Gap Depth Translator schema is depicted by priming signal going from the former to the latter. The schema efferents its output to Gaps-Heading Translator, Prey↔Barrier Distance Translator, Barrier-Recognizer, and Depth Map schemas.

Gaps-Heading Translator: Using x and y coordinates of the gaps from the Barrier-Recognizer and the depth (d) from the Barrier/Gap Depth Translator, the Gaps-Heading Translator computes the body-centered angles to the gaps. Similar to the Barrier/Gap Depth Translator, this schema becomes activated only after the reception of the priming signal from the Prey-Selector.

Prey↔Barrier Distance Translator: Using d values of the barrier and the prey from the Barrier/Gap Depth Translator and the Prey Depth Translator respectively, the Prey↔Barrier Distance Translator computes the distance between the prey and the barrier. It also determines if the prey is behind or in front of the barrier.

Prey↔Gaps Angle Translator/Selector: Using heading values of the prey and the gaps from the Prey-Heading Translator and the Gaps-Heading Translator respectively, the Prey↔Gaps Angle Translator/Selector computes the angles between the prey and the gaps. Note that the barrier endings are also considered to define the gaps. The schema first searches for internal gaps and selects the gap that has the least angle between the prey and the gap. When there is only one internal gap, then that is chosen. When there is no internal gap, the schema selects a barrier ending with smaller prey↔gap angle. The schema outputs the heading value of the selected gap to the Heading Map.

Prey↔Barrier Distance Map: Prey↔Barrier Distance Map schema converts spatially coded Prey↔Barrier Distance information into a frequency coded signal: When the prey lies behind the barrier, the greater the distance between the prey and the barrier, the stronger is the activity level of its output. The activity level will be set to 0 when the prey is in front of or at the same depth relative to the barrier. The schema acts like a switch in the sense that its output level serves as a criterion to determine whether the gap-depth from the Barrier/Gap Depth Translator or the prey-depth from the Prey-Depth Translator should be sent to the Depth Map. The output level is also used to determine whether the gap-heading value from the Prey↔Gaps Angle Translator/Selector or the prey-heading value from the Prey-Heading Translator should be gated to the Heading Map. As prey↔barrier distance increases, the chances of the gap-depth and the gap-heading being gated to the Depth Map and the Heading Map increases. The output of the schema also inhibits the Snap schema: The larger the prey↔Barrier distance, the less likely the snap will occur.

Modifications to Prey Capture Model: The basic organization of the Prey Capture network is unchanged. Modifications to Depth Map, Heading Map, and Snap schemas do not change the original information flow nor the performance of the Prey Capture model because the changes can be made on top or independent of the original schemas which could be encapsulated to preserve modularity and integrity.

The Heading Map is modified to have two input ports, one for gap-heading and the other for prey-heading signal. Both ports can be active simultaneously. The modified Heading Map includes a competition network where probability of one port selected over the other depends on the relative activity levels of two input ports. The activity level of gap-heading input port positively correlates to the gating signal level from the Prey↔Barrier Distance Map. So, as the prey↔barrier distance increases, the activity level on the gap-heading port increases, which makes the gap-heading signal have increased probability to be gated to the Heading Map. If the gap heading port is selected, the Heading Map translates the heading value into a population coded signal, which then excites the Orient schema to innervate the motor neuron pools to make the animal turn to the direction of the selected gap. If the prey is in front of or not far behind the barrier, zero or weak gating signal from the Prey↔Barrier Distance Map may not raise the activity level of the gap-port high enough to have it gated. In this case, the prey heading signal will be selected and the animal turns to the prey.

The principle of the modified Depth Map is identical to the modified Heading map. In this case, the Depth Map has to select between prey-depth and gap-depth coming from Prey Depth Translator and Barrier/Gap Depth Translator respectively. Just like the Heading Map, the probability that the gap-depth is chosen increases as the prey↔barrier distance increases. Since both the Heading Map and the Depth Map have to agree on their selection, the model forces both schemas to vote for the selection until they agree.

The Snap schema is modified to receive an inhibitory signal from the Prey↔Barrier Distance Map. Thus, when a frog approaches a gap, the possibility of it snapping during the way is almost nil due to inhibitions from both Orient and Prey↔Barrier Distance Map schemas.

Note that the pretectal barrier/gap signal is parcellated and lateralized. Both the prey related signal and the barrier/gap related signal from tectum and pretectum respectively remain spatially coded until they are integrated at the Heading Map and the Depth Map, presumed to be located at midbrain tegmentum, where they are then translated to a population signal.

4. Performance of the Model

The schemas related to the integration of barrier and prey signal such as Prey↔Barrier Distance Translator, and modified Depth Map have not been simulated yet. However, we believe we know the model well enough to offer a first account of what could be expected of the model when asked to simulate the data on the behavior of normal and lesioned animals.

4.1. Normal functions

First, we look at simpler cases when only prey or barrier alone is present. When the barrier is absent, the Barrier-Recognizer schema is not activated and so the prey signal is gated to the Heading and Depth Maps. Thus our model performs just like the Prey Capture model. With barrier alone, even though the Barrier-Recognizer performs pattern formation, because of no priming signal from the Prey-Selector, Barrier/Gap Depth Translator and Gaps Heading Translator are not activated. Thus, Depth and Heading Map receive neither prey signal nor gap signal. As a result, the animal does not show any movement, which conforms to the behavioral data.

Prey close behind the barrier: In this situation, frogs usually approach prey directly, presumably because the worm is within the snapping distance from the barrier. In our model, the behavior can be replicated by a weak gating signal from the Prey↔Barrier Distance Map making prey signals more gateable to the Depth and Heading Maps resulting in a direct approach to prey.

Prey far behind the barrier: In this situation, frogs usually detour around the barrier. Due to a high level of gating signal from Prey↔Barrier Distance Map, selected gap (barrier end) signal will be routed to the Depth and Heading Maps. Thus, our computational frog will detour in this case.

A passable gap within the barrier: A frog/toad in this situation seems to prefer the internal gap over the two lateral barrier endings, even if one of the latter gaps offer a closer path to prey. This situation is handled in our model because the Prey↔Gaps Angle Translator/Selector prefers internal gaps over barrier endings by searching them first.

4.2. Lesion effects

According to Ingle, a pretectum lesioned frog seems to be unaware of a large hemifield barrier. This behavior can be replicated in our model by unavailability of Barrier-Recognizer in pretectum. Ingle also observed that a frog with "split pons" seems to know whether or not to approach/snap a prey behind the barrier. But it will always collide to the barrier if the critical barrier edge is in monocular view field and located on the same side of prey. We believe this behavior can be replicated by severing the Prey↔Gaps Angle Translator/Selector link coming from the contralateral side which is responsible for the gap in the ipsilateral monocular view field: Due to presumed lateralization of the pretectal signal, information of the gap in the ipsilateral view field comes solely from the contralateral pretectal lobe. Splitting the pons severs this pretectal decussation but preserves tectal decussation responsible for the lateralization of tectal signal.

5. Discussion

While we tried to construct the model reflecting as much known data of real animal as possible, much of the formulation is based on hypotheses that need to be verified by experiments. For instance, the model is based on the assumption that prey and barrier signal are integrated spatially at the tegmentum. The assumption that only one Heading map and Depth Map exist and that the prey signal and the gap signal have to compete each other to deposit their contents to the maps suggests that there should be a competition circuit between them. It could simply be a mutual inhibitory circuit. We should also ask how Prey↔Barrier Distance Translator and the Prey↔Gaps Angle Translator/Selector might be realized in the anuran brain. However, in the model, they can be implemented as a simple spatial domain comparator.

Collett's data also show that an animal's behavior is stochastic: Even during the same experimental session with the prey-barrier configuration unchanged, a frog sometimes show detour and in another trials a direct approach. Our model can account for this stochasticity because selection of prey or gap in the Depth and Heading Map schemas is modeled as a stochastic process.

We have seen that the potential field method can account for many anuran detour behaviors. However, the method is not based on the neuroanatomy of the animal, whereas the schema model is neurally inspired in the sense that it addresses the parcellation and lateralization of the signal flow. But the latter model also has a drawback in that it contains some schemas that are hard to implement in neural networks but can be easily implemented in sequential algorithms. So, an aspect of the future research is to develop a new detour model that has the best features of the above two that can also simulate the new behavioral data we observed in our preliminary study.

References

Arbib, M.A. : *The Metaphorical Brain 2: Neural Networks and Beyond.* Wiley Interscience. (1989).

Arbib, M. A., Cobas, A. : Schemas for Prey-Catching in Frog and Toad. (in *From animals to animats,* J-A. Meyer & S.W.Wilson, Eds) *Proceedings of the First International Conference on Simulation of Adaptive Behavior.* 142-151 (1991).

Arbib, M.A., House, D.H. : Depth and Detours: An essay on visually guided behavior. (in *Vision, Brain and Cooperative computation,* M.A.Arbib & A.R. Hanson, Eds), A Bradford Book/MIT Press. 129-163 (1987).

Arkin, R. : Motor Schema based mobile robot navigation. *Int, J, Robotics, Res.* Vol. 8, No 4, 92-112 (1989).

Burghagen, H., Ewert, J. P. : Influence of the background for discriminating object motion from self-induced motion in toads *Bufo bufo* (L.). *J. Comp. Physiol,* 241-249 (1983).

Cervantes-Perez, F., Lara, R., and Arbib, M.A. : A Neural Model of Interactions Subserving Prey-Predator Discrimination and Size Preference in Anuran Amphibia. *J, Theor. Biol,* 113, 117-152 (1985).

Collett, T. : Stereopsis in toads. *Nature* 267, 349-351 (1977).

Collett, T. : Do toads plan routes? A study of detour behavior of B.viridis. *J. Comp. Physiol.A,* 146. 261-271 (1982).

Dev, P. : Perception of depth surfaces in random-dot stereograms: a neural model. *Int. J. Man-Machine Studies,* 7, 511-528 (1975).

Ewert, J.P. : Single unit response of the toad's (*Bufo americanus*) caudal thalamus to visual objects. *Z. vergl. Physiol.* 74, 81-102 (1971).

Ewert, J.P. : Neuroethology of releasing mechanisms: Prey-catching in toads. *Behavioral and Brain Sciences,* 10, 337-405 (1987).

Grobstein, P. : Between the retinotectal projection and directed movement: Topography of sensorimotor interface. *Brain Behav. Evol.* 31, 34-48 (1988).

Grüsser, O.J., Grüsser-Cornehls, U. : Neurophysiology of the Anuran Visual System. (*Frog Neurobiology,* R.Llinas and W.Precht, Eds), 297-385 (1976).

House, D.H. : Depth Perception in frogs and toads. *Lecture Notes in Biomathematics* 80, Springer-Verlag, (1989).

Ingle, D. : Brain mechanisms of visual localization by frogs and toads. (*Advances in Vertebrate Neuroethology,* J. -P. Ewert, R.R.Caprinica and D.J.Ingle, Eds), 177-226 (1983).

Koren, Y., Borenstein, J. : Potential Field Methods and their Inherent Limitations for Mobile Robot Navigation. *Proceedings of the 1991 IEEE International Conference on Robotics and Automation,* Sacramento, California, 1398-1404 (1991).

Liaw, J.S., Arbib, M.A. : A neural network model for response to looming objects by frogs and toads. (in *Visual Structures and Integrated Functions,* M.A.Arbib & J.-P. Ewert, Eds), Research notes in Neural Computing, Springer-Verlag. 167-180 (1991).

Marr, D., Poggio, T. : Cooperative computation of stereo disparity. *Science,* 194, 283-287 (1976).

Pigarev, J.N., Zenkin, G.M., Girman, S.B.: The detectors of the frog retina. Responses in unrestrained frogs. *Sechenov J. Physiol.* USSR 57, 1448-1458 (1971).

Prazdny, K. : Detection of binocular disparities. *Bio. Cybernetics.* 52, 93-99 (1985).

Schipperheyn, J.J. : Respiratory eye movement and perceptions of stationary objects in the frog. *Acta. Physiol. Pharmacol. Neerl.* 12. 157 - 159 (1963).

Teeters, J.L., Arbib, M.A. : A model of anuran retina relating interneurons to ganglion cell responses. *Biol. Cybern.* 64, 197-207 (1991).

Teeters, J.L., Arbib, M.A., Corbacho. F., Lee. H.B. : Quantitative modeling of Responses of Anuran Retina: Stimulus shape and size dependency. Submitted to *Vision Research.* (1992).

Tilove, R.B. : Local Obstacle Avoidance for Mobile Robots Based on the Method of Artificial Potentials. *Proceedings of the 1990 IEEE International Conference on Robotics and Automation,* Cincinnati, Ohio, 566-571 (1990).

Warren, C.W. : Global Path Planning Using Artificial Potential Fields. *Proceedings of the 1989 IEEE International Conference on Robotics and Automation,* Scottsdale, AZ, 316-322 (1989).

Warren, C.W. : Multiple Robot Path Coordination Using Artificial Potential Fields. *Proceedings of the 1990 IEEE International Conference on Robotics and Automation,* Cincinnati, Ohio, 500-505 (1990).

Weitzenfeld, A. : NSL, Neural Simulation Language, Version 2.1, CNE-TR 91-05, Center for Neural Engineering, University of Southern California. (1991)

Artificial neural nets for controlling a 6-legged walking system

Holk Cruse, Uwe Müller-Wilm, Jeffrey Dean
Dept. of Biol. Cybernetics, Fac. of Biology, University of Bielefeld,
Postfach 100131, D-4800 Bielefeld 1, FRG
E-mail: holk at bio128.uni-bielefeld.de

Abstract

A system that controls the leg movement of an animal or a robot walking over irregular ground has to ensure stable support for the body and at the same time propel it forward. To do so, it has to react adaptively to unpredictable features of the environment. As part of our study of the underlying mechanisms we present here a model which describes the control of the leg movement of a 6-legged walking system. The model is based on biological data obtained from the stick insect. It represents a combined treatment of realistic kinematics and biologically motivated, adaptive gait generation. The model extends a previous algorithmic model in substituting simple artificial neurons for the algorithms previously used to control leg state and interleg coordination. The model is able to walk at different speeds over irregular surfaces. The control system rapidely reestablishes a stable gait when the movement of the legs is disturbed or the model begins walking from an arbitrary starting configuration.

1 Introduction

Neural networks which initiate and control the behavior of animals embody several features. One feature concerns the role of sensory input. At one extreme are networks which mediate actions that are direct responses to sensory input, i.e., reactive or sensory-driven actions. At the other are networks which themselves generate the basic activation or movement parameters for the behavior, i.e. autonomous activity or actions controlled by central pattern generators. For a system to produce suitable actions in an unpredictable environment, however, the control system usually contains elements of both kinds. A second feature concerns the structure of the control network. In most complex biological networks, control functions, whether sensory-driven or autonomous, are dispersed among several subsystems which interact more or less strongly.

Both aspects are especially true for walking. Although it is sometimes regarded as quite a simple behavior, it involves a very strong and complex interaction with the physical environment. Typical control systems involve autonomous elements as well as simple reflexes and more complex sensory-driven modulations of central activity (Cruse Dean Heuer Schmidt 1990). The combination makes the walking system independent of particular stimulus inputs but at the same time enables the walking system to adapt to changes in the environment. The flexible control appears to arise from the cooperation of several autonomous control centers (in the terminology of Minski (1985) these may be called "agents") each of which controls the movement of one leg. Each center is responsible for two mutually exclusive microbehaviors ("states"), stance or power stroke and swing or return stroke. On a higher level the control systems for the individual leg have to cooperate to produce a suitable behavior of the overall system, propelling the body while maintaining postural stability.

From a biological point of view, walking is simple enough that one can hope to gain a complete understanding of the basic mechanisms. In fact, a lot of information has been collected in recent years on how animals control the movement of the legs during walking (review Cruse 1990). A study of this system might therefore be of interest not only in itself but also as a model for the control of other, more complicated behaviors. From an applied control point of view, the next step is to incorporate the insights gained from the biological experiments into a model able to control a walking system.

To reach this goal, several problems have to be solved. One question concerns the way the movement of the individual leg is controlled. The second question refers to the coordination between legs. From biological experiments - most of the information comes from experiments using the stick insect - the following answers can be given. First, each leg has its own control system which generates rhythmic step movements (review Bässler 1983). The behavior of this control system corresponds to that of a relaxation oscillator in which the change of state, the transition between power and return strokes, is determined by thresholds based on leg position. Second, the coordination of the legs is not determined by a hierarchically superior control system. Instead, the gait pattern emerges from the cooperation of the separate control systems of the individual legs. This cooperation is based on different types of signals which convey information on the actual state of the sender to the control systems of the neighboring legs. The receiving system collects this information and, on this basis, decides on its own action. This distributed architecture results in a very stable gait but nevertheless allows the whole system to react flexibly to disturbances. At the present time no detailed information is available concerning the control of the individual leg joints of the walking animal and the control of the dynamics.

In an earlier paper (Müller-Wilm et al., 1992) a model was presented based on these biological results and, where necessary, several ad hoc assumptions. This model was constructed using the classical algorithmic approach. Because models using distributed networks show a number of advantages, such as error tolerance, generalisation etc., we plan to replace successively the algorithms of this earlier model by modules of artificial neural nets. In the present report we describe neural network moduls for controlling the oscillatory movement of the individual leg and the coordination of legs. The movement of the individual joints of a leg is still controlled by the classical methods described in Müller-Wilm et al. (1992) and Pfeiffer, Weidemann, Danowski (1990).

The movement of the individual leg consists of two parts, the power stroke and the return stoke. During the power stroke, the leg is on the ground, supports the body and, in the forward walking animal, moves backwards with respect to the body. During the return stroke, the leg is lifted off the ground and moved in the direction of walking where it can begin a new power stroke. The anterior transition point, i.e. the transition from return stroke to power stroke in the forward walking animal, has been called the anterior extreme position (AEP) and the posterior transition point has been called the posterior extreme position (PEP). Either as a hypothesis or on the basis of experimental results several authors (Wendler 1968, Bässler 1977, Graham 1972, Cruse 1985b) proposed the idea that the transition from one mode to the other occurs when the leg reaches a given criterion position and that the step generator can thus be considered a relaxation oscillator. The role of load in modifying this criterion will be neglected here (see however Bässler 1977, Cruse 1983, Dean 1991a).

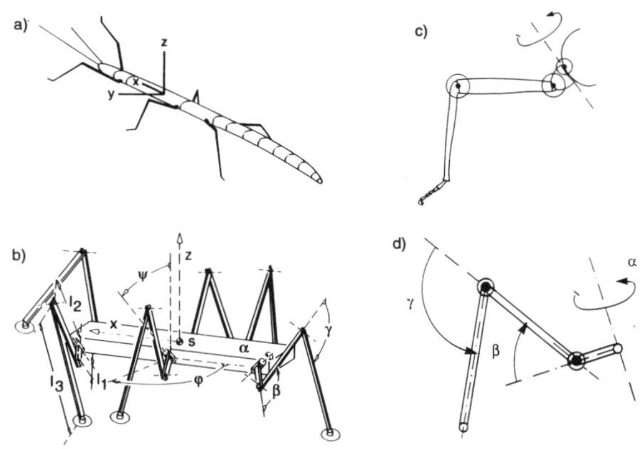

Fig 1. (a) Schematic drawing of a stick insect wqith the location of the body-centered coordinates, (b) mechanical model: arrangement of the joints and their axes of rotation, (c) single leg of a stick insect showing the axes of rotation, (d) the joints of the simplified leg of the model.

As in the model of Müller-Wilm et al. (1992), each leg is represented by three segments which are connected to each other and to the body by three simple hinge joints.

Contact with the ground is assumed to occur at a non-slipping hemisphere at the end of the distal segment. This simplified leg omits the set of short segments forming the tarsus or foot of the insect. The structure of the leg and the definition of the angles are shown in Fig 1. The axes of rotation of the basal joints are arranged in the same way as in the stick insect and, therefore, are not orthogonal with respect to the body-fixed coordinate system shown in Fig 1. In the stick insect the basal joint actually is a ball and socket joint. However, the primary movement during walking involves only one axis of rotation (Cruse 1976). Therefore, for the present model we assume that the basal joint is used only to move the leg in the forward-backward direction and that all the up-down movement is performed at the coxa-trochanter joint.

2 Model

The movement of the individual leg is controlled in the following way. In order to simplify the model, we assume for the straight walking considered here that the tarsus always moves in a vertical plane parallel to the long axis of the body. The rhythmic movement in the direction of the x-axis (Fig 1), i.e. the axis parallel to the long axis of the body, is controlled by an oscillatory system. How can this be done using a neuronal system?

The oldest and simplest proposal for a network oscillator with neuronal elements is the Brown half center model

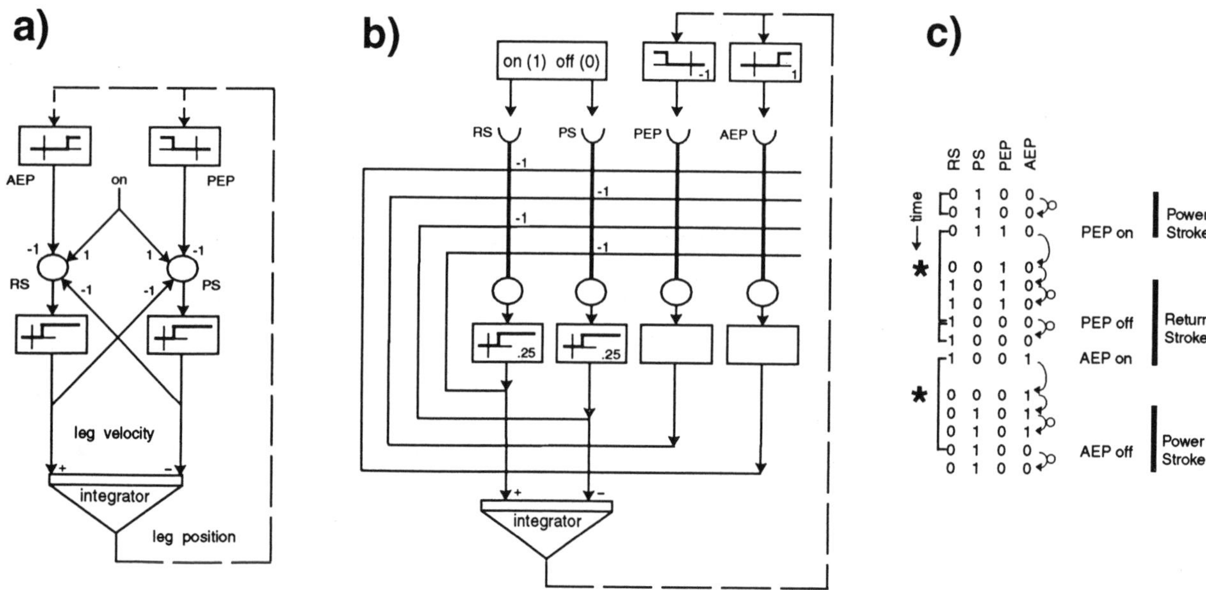

Fig 2. A model for the control of rhythmic leg movement using mutual inhibition between the motor units RS (return stroke) and PS (power stroke). Leg position is obtained by integration of the output of RS and PS. Once the leg has reached a given threshold (AEP, PEP), the system switches from one state to the other. (a) classical version. (b) the same system constructed as a fully recurrent network. (c) the output vector for consecutive iteration steps in one complete step. The square brackets on the left side indicate the input and output vectors used for training.

(Brown 1911). Two neurones are connected by mutual inhibition (Fig 2a), forming a bistable system (flip-flop), in which either one neuron or the other is active. If the inhibitory channels are provided with high pass properties and tonic excitation is applied, the system oscillates. Alternative, two-neuron networks are discussed by Camhi (1984). For example, oscillation can also occur if the mutual inhibition is replaced by mutual excitation passed through a delay element. Some central pattern generators which have been characterized physiologically contain neurons with still more complex dynamical properties and connections (e.g. Getting and Dekin 1985).

As mentioned above, the step pattern generator of arthropods is better described as a relaxation oscillator which depends on sensory feedback. This means that the periphery has to be included in the system. In this case, as shown in Fig 2a, the signals from sensory feedback can provide appropriate feedback to produce a rhythmic movement (Land 1972, Bässler 1977, for a general discussion see Bässler 1986): the motor output of motor unit RS in Fig 2a, interpreted as a velocity signal moving the leg forward, is applied to the leg until a sense organ signals that the AEP has been reached. This sensory unit turns off the motor unit PS. This unit in turn inhibits RS and causes the leg to move to the rear until a sense organ signals that the PEP has been reached. This sense organ turns off the unit RS which in turn inhibits PS. As a result the system oscillates rhythmically moving the leg between AEP and PEP. The transformation from leg velocity to leg position is symbolized by the integrator in Fig 2a.

Fig 2b shows the same system in another, more general format. The four units are now part of a fully connected recurrent network. The weights of the synapses are given. If no number is given this means that the weight after training is zero. Again the integrator represents the mechanical periphery, the movement of the leg under the influence of RS and PS. The leg position oscillates as long as both motor units receive an input of 1 which can be interpreted as an "on" signal from higher centers. Fig 2c shows the output of the system for consecutive iteration steps.

An advantage of the artificial neural network approach is that training procedures can be used to find alternative and possibly better solutions. In order to test whether other versions of such oscillatory systems exist we started with a fully connected recurrent network with randomly distributed weights because, apart from the absence of hidden units, this is the most general form. We trained networks with this structure using a linear activation

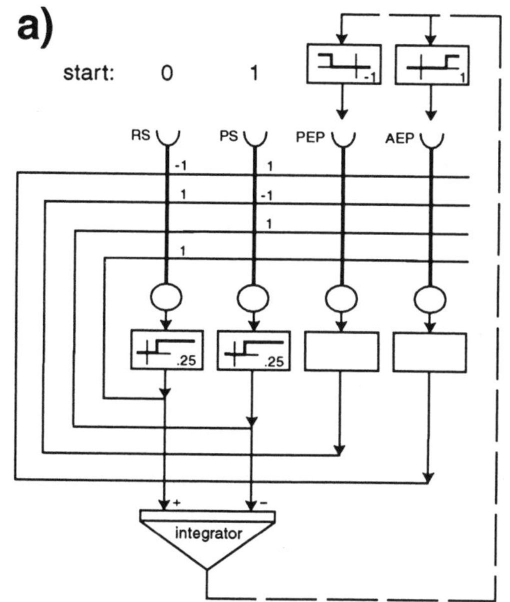

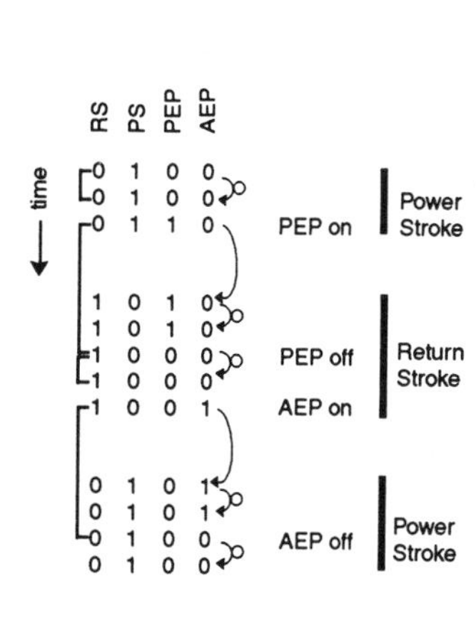

Fig 3. A model, obtained by training, for the control of the rhythmic leg movement. The oscillatory behavior of the system corresponds to that shown in Fig 2 except for the intermediate vectors marked by stars in Fig 2c.

function and the Delta rule as proposed by Levin (1990) for the training. In a recurrent system the output vector is also the feedback vector and therefore the input vector for the next iteration. Therefore the Delta rule can be applied using the output vector of one time step as input for the next. In this way the net was trained on two autoassociative tasks: when the net is in power stroke (output vector: 0100), it should stay in that state, and the same should be the case for the return stroke (output vector: 1000). In addition, the net was trained on two heteroassociative tasks: the desired reponse to the feedback vector 1001, i.e. "return stroke on" and "AEP reached", was "power stroke on" (i.e. 0100) and the desired response to the feedback vector 0110, i.e. "power stroke on" and "PEP reached" was "return stroke on" (i.e.1000). Using the Delta rule with an learning rate of 0.1 the error decreased to zero. The resulting weights are shown in Fig 3a. In this net the motor units receive a self-excitation instead of reciprocal inhibition. The sensory units have two different effects on the two motor units. One is excitatory, the other is inhibitory: Fig 3b shows the output of the system after training. This output lacks one cycle present in the results of Fig 2c.

For training vectors with values symmetrically distributed around zero, i.e. values of 0.5 or -0.5 instead of values of 0 and 1, another set of weights is obtained (Table 1). The network looks like a mixture of both the "inhibitory system" of Fig 2a and the "excitatory system" of Fig 3a. The behavior of the system corresponds to that shown in Fig 2b.

Table 1 The weight distribution of a network producing rhythmic oscillations. The format is the same as in Figs 2b and 3a.

	receiver			
sender	RS	PS	PEP	AEP
AEP	-0.5	0.5	0	0
PEP	0.5	-0.5	0	0
PS	-1.5	0.5	0	0
RS	0.5	-1.5	0	0

Although the unperturbed behavior of all three systems is nearly the same, they might still differ in stability when noise is present. To investigate this, the performance of all three oscillators was tested with noise of increasing amplitude range added to all four feedback lines. The stability was measured by observing the oscillatory behavior of the systems. When the noise amplitude exceeded a certain threshold, the oscillatory behavior suddenly vanished in all three systems. The inhibitory system (Fig 2) was most sensitive and the excitatory system (Fig 3) was least sensitive to noise. Quantitatively, a noise amplitude of +/- 0.25 is sufficient to disrupt the oscillatory behavior of the inhibitory system whereas amplitudes of about +/- 0.50 and +/- 0.76, repsectively, are required to disturb the mixed system (Table 1) and the excitatory system (Fig 3) to the same extend. These differences in the stability correspond to the size of the mean error during the training procedure. For the excitatory system the sum of the total squared error was smaller than 0.01 after 180 epochs and approximated zero. For the mixed system this error could not be made smaller than 4.2. The inhibitory system was never obtained through training, even when the starting weights were chosen to correspond exactly to this solution.

It should be mentioned that the systems shown in Fig 3 and Table 1 can be switched on by a short impulse to one of the motor units. They do not require a continuous input as the inhibitory system does. As the excitatory system has proved to be the most stable we decided to use this module to control the state (power stroke, return stroke) of each leg. For the stick insect it has been shown that in both the power stroke and the return stroke the movement of the tarsus is controlled by a velocity controlling feedback system (Cruse 1985a, Dean 1984, Weiland and Koch 1987). Therefore, we use the output values of the state controller as reference signals for a velocity feedback controller. However, the state value is first put through a low pass filter. This causes the reversals in the direction of movement to be less abrupt and therefore more realistic.

This reference signal is used to control the movement of the leg tip (tarsus) in the horizontal and vertical directions, i.e. parallel to the x-axis and parallel to the z-axis, respectively (Fig 1). However, the movement along the x-axis is governed by a velocity controller, that along the z-axis by a position controller. When walking on irregular surfaces, the end of the downward movement during the final part of the return stroke has to be determined by an additional sensor which is assumed here to be a contact sensor ("ground contact" GC in Fig 4). The determination of the tarsus trajectory is described in detail by Müller-Wilm et al. (1992) and therefore not repeated here. Once the trajectory of the tarsus relative to the body is selected, the values of the joint angles can be calculated.

This is done here using the inverse kinematic solution described by Pfeiffer et al. (1990). The calculation of the tarsus trajectory and the required joint movements is symbolized by the box marked (TT-JC) in Fig 4.

How are the movements of these oscillators coordinated? In all, six different coupling mechanisms have been found for the stick insect (review Cruse 1990). Two of these will not be considered here. (One serves to correct errors in leg placement, the other has to do with distributing propulsive force among the legs). The other four mechanisms were successfully implemented in an earlier model (Dean 1991b,c 1992a,b) which formed the basis for the coordination module in the present model. The beginning of a return stroke, and therefore the end-point of a power stroke (PEP), is modulated by three mechanisms arising from ipsilateral legs: (1) a rostrally directed inhibition during the return stroke of the next caudal leg, (2) a rostrally directed excitation when the next caudal leg begins active retraction, and (3) a caudally

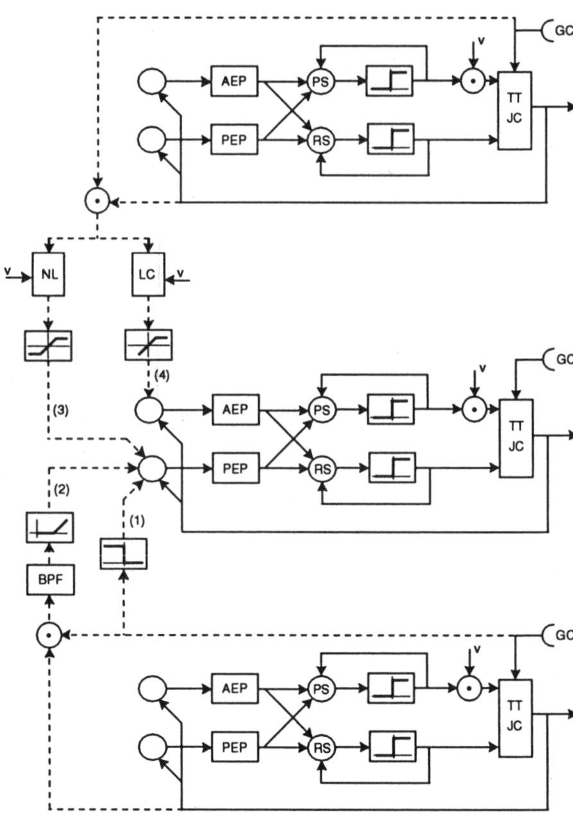

Fig 4. The four coordinating influences used in the model illustrated for a middle leg receiving the signals. Two influences occur from the front leg and two from the hind leg onto a centrally located middle leg. The oscillator, which corresponds to that of Fig 3, controls the state and forward-backward movement of the leg. The derivation of the corresponding tarsus trajectory and joint angles occurs in the box marked (TT-JC). The sensory input GC registers ground contact. See text for further explanations.

directed influence depending upon the position of the next rostral leg. The beginning of the power stroke (AEP) is modulated by a single, caudally directed influence (4) depending on the position of the next rostral leg; this mechanism is responsible for the targeting behavior. Influences (2) and (3) are also active between contralateral legs.

Fig 4 shows, as an example, the influences from the front leg and the hind leg onto the ipsilateral middle leg. Influences (1), (2), and (3) act on the PEP unit, whereas influence (4) acts on the AEP unit. Influence (1) is only active, i.e. different from zero, when the caudal leg has no ground contact. Influence (2) is zero when the caudal leg has no ground contact. In neuronal terms these conditional effects (in Fig 4 shown by a multiplication symbol for convenience) are represented by inhibition

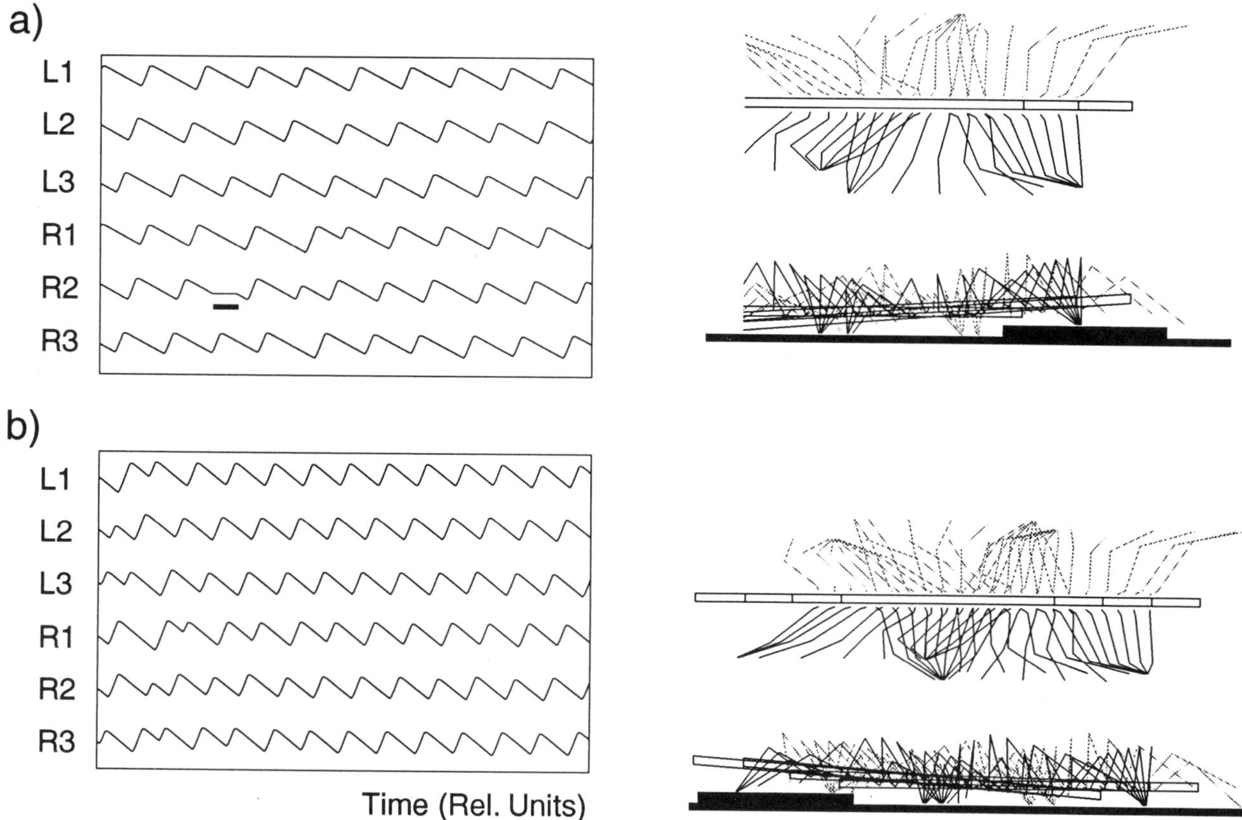

Fig 5. Stability of the coordination pattern. (a) movement of the legs when the power stroke of the right middle leg is interrupted for a short time. (b) Illustration of how the normal contralateral alternation is established when contralateral legs start from the same position.

Fig 6. Two sections of superimposed frames from a video film showing the model walking over an obstacle. Upper part: top view, lower part side view. Leg position is shown only for every 5th frame, body position is shown only for every 15th frame. (a) The model approaches the obstacle and places the front legs onto it. (b) The model leaves the obstacle. The left hind leg steps onto the obstacle whereas the right hind leg touches the ground beyond the obstacle.

subsequent rectification. If the caudal leg has ground contact, influence (2) corresponds to the band pass filtered value of the position signal of the caudal leg. The band pass filter (BPF in Fig 4) which is constructed of a small recurrent network consisting on six linear units (not shown) is followed by a rectifier. Influence (3) is zero when the rostral leg is lifted (again this is represented in Fig 4 by a multiplication symbol) and depends on the position of the rostral leg when the latter is in power stroke. This value passes through a non-linear characteristic (NL in Fig 4) the form of which depends logarithmically on a central command, v, corresponding to the general walking velocity. This command also serves as a gain factor in all power stroke units. The output of the NL - characteristic passes a non linear clipping function. Influence (4), which determines the AEP, is determined in a similar manner as influence (3). The main difference is that the position value depends on the parameter v, the retraction velocity, in a linear way (LC in Fig 4). The activation function is clipped only for values in the positive range. The contralateral influences correspond to the ipsilateral influences (2) and (3) and are not shown in Fig 4. In the contralateral form of influence (3), the dependence on the parameter v is linear.

3 Results

The model shows a proper coordination of the legs when walking at different speeds on a horizontal plane. With increasing walking speed the typical change of coordination from the tetrapod to the tripod gait (Graham 1972) is found. As the movement of the legs is very similar to those found in the algorithmic model (Müller-Wilm et al., 1992) this is not shown here in detail.

The coordination pattern is very stable. For example, when the movement of the right middle leg is interrupted briefly during the power stroke, the normal coordination is regained immediately at the end of the perturbation (Fig 5a). A critical test of the stability of the coordination pattern is to consider the behavior of the model when starting to walk from arbitrary leg positions. The start is particularly difficult when contralaterally neighboring legs begin from the same x- position. In this case, contralaterally neighbouring legs reach their PEP thresholds at the same time, whereas they normally alternate. Fig 5b shows such a test: the normal coordination is regained after a very few steps. The 3-dimensional plot, which is not shown here, demonstrates that the model also maintains postural stability except for starts from some unnatural starting configurations.

The height control is illustrated in Fig 6. Here the model has to step over an obstacle. This figure represents two sections of a video film. Different frames are superimposed here to give an impression of the movement of the whole model. The figure also indicates that the leg glides over the ground for a short time after touch down. This gliding would correspond to a force decelerating the body if the tarsi were fixed to the substrate.

4 Discussion

The model proposed here represents a combined treatment of realistic kinematics and of biologically motivated, adaptive gait generation. In contrast to earlier biologically motivated models it contains the joint geometry and, with some simplifying assumptions, describes the movement of the joints and the tarsi. The movement of the tarsus is also more realistic in the sense that the velocity profile is rounded at the transition points. The results show that the information obtained from biological experiments can be incorporated into a 6-legged model which is able to walk at different speeds at different speeds over irregular surfaces. The model shows a stable gait even when the movement of the legs is disturbed. The system can control walks beginning from arbitrary leg positions. Thus, the control system described here can be used to control a real walking machine. To increase the stability for difficult starting positions, the introduction of load feedback might be helpful.

The system is based on extremely simple connections. Unlike the model proposed by Müller-Wilm et al. (1992), the model consists of simple artificial neurons, except for that part which controls the movement of the individual joints of the leg. The connections of the state controller were learned.

The connections which provide the coordination between legs were hard-wired based on biological experiments. Current work with various, biologically based optimization methods (reinforcement learning, genetic algorithms, etc.) is testing whether these mechanisms can be further improved. (In our modelling of a six-legged walker, we relied heavily on results with stick insects, but it should be noted that other animals walking under different conditions use different coordinating mechanisms (crayfish: Cruse Müller 1986, Müller Cruse 1991, cat: Cruse Warnecke 1992).

Other approaches to modelling walking have incorporated biological features to different degrees. Knowledge of the neural control of walking in any animal is still quite rudimentary. Brown's (1911) half-center hypothesis, that alternating activity for stepping arises from two subsystems coupled by reciprocal inhibition, is still the most applicable model. Vertebrate walkers have proved quite intractable neurophysiologically. However, work on a simple model system, lamprey swimming (Grillner et al. 1991), has shown that even simple systems embodying this reciprocal inhibition depend upon complex neuron properties and interconnections. Pearson (1972), working with an insect, proposed a model of alternation in which activity of one center is periodically interrupted by activity in a second center initiated either by peripheral sensory signals or by intrinsic neural properties.

This organization has parallels in the subsumption architecture created by Brooks to step control in a successful hexapod robot (1986, 1989). For interleg coordination this robot used a typical insect gait, the alternating tripod gait, but this gait was generated by a single timing center. Hence, interleg coordination in this robot did not emerge out of interactions among semi-autonomous centers in the way that is more typical of animals. This property was exhibited by a later version in which the subsumption architecture was extended to control interactions among independent leg controllers (Maes Brooks 1990). These interactions were not based on biological models. Nevertheless, they were able to learn the tripod coordination.

Such decentralized mechanisms have been considered by several researchers. Based on physiological results from an insect preparation, Pearson and Iles (1973), studying a non walking insect preparation, described intersegmental activation which could mediate reciprocal inhibition serving for interleg coordination, an idea proposed by Wilson (1966) on the basis of behavioral studies. This inhibition resembles mechanism 1 in the present model. As discussed elsewhere (Cruse 1980, Dean 1991c, 1992b), this mechanism alone provides incomplete control of step phase. Moreover, it can easily produce tripod gait but requires a gradient of natural step frequencies in different legs if metachronal rhythms are to occur. Nevertheless, this type of inhibition has been incorporated into several robot control systems (Donner 1984, Beer, Chiel and coworkers 1989, 1992). Beer and Gallagher (1992) have also used genetic algorithms to successfully train intra- and interleg coordination under conditions where tripod gait is the gait of choice. Our results show that a combination of mechanisms provides a better control of phase, which is necessary for example in controlling starts from unfavorable leg configurations.

Our future studies are directed toward removing three restrictions in the present model. First, the movement of the tarsus is restricted to a vertical plane parallel to the long axis of the body. Besides being somewhat artificial, this does not permit turns to be simulated. Second, our model does not take into account the dynamics of the system, i.e. the forces needed to perform the described movements. Third, we did not consider the mechanical coupling of the legs in power stroke through the substrate and the resulting effects when the legs attempt to move with different velocities. The reader is referred to Müller-Wilm et al. (1992) for a more detailed discussion of these restrictions. Fourth, all robots mentioned above use relatively simple legs, possessing two degrees of freedom and fixed to the body in an orthogonal and bilaterally symmetrical manner. We hope that a leg geometry more similar to that evolved in animals will provide greater flexibility.

Acknowledgements

This work was supported by BMFT grant no. 01 IN 104 B/1.

References

Bässler,U. (1977): Sensory control of leg movement in the stick insect Carausius morosus. Biol.Cybern.25, 61-72

Bässler,U. (1983): Neural basis of elementary behavior in stick insects. Springer, Berlin, Heidelberg, New York

Bässler,U. (1986): On the definition of central pattern generator and its sensory control. Biol. Cybern. 54, 65-69

Beer,R.D., Chiel,H.J., Sterling,L.S. (1989): Heterogenous neural networks for adaptive behavior in dynamic environments. In: Advances in Neural Information Processing Systems 1, D.S. Touretzky (ed.) 577-585. Morgan Kaufmann, San Mateo, CA

Beer,R.D., Chiel,H.J., Quinn,R.D., Espenschied,K.S. Larsson,P. (1992): A distributed neural network architecture for hexapod robot locomotion. Neural Computation 4, 356-365

Beer,R.D., Gallagher,J.C. (1992): Evolving dynamical neural networks for adaptive behavior. Adaptive Behavior 1, 91-122

Brooks,R.A. (1986): A robust layered control system for a mobile robot. IEEE Journal of Robotics and Automation, RA-2, 14-23

Brooks,R.A. (1989): A robot that walks: emergent behavior from a carefully evolved network. Neural Computation 1, 253-262

Brown,T.G. (1911): The intrinsic factors in the act of progression in the mammal. Proc. of the Royal Soc. 84B, 308-319

Camhi,J.M. (1984): Neuroethology. Sinauer Ass.. Inc, Sunderland, Massachusetts

Cruse,H. (1976): On the function of the legs in the free walking stick insect Carausius morosus. J.comp.Physiol.112,235-262

Cruse,H. (1980): A quantitative model of walking incorporating central and peripheral influences. II. The connections between the different legs. Biol. Cybern.37,137-144

Cruse,H. (1983): The influence of load and leg amputation upon coordination in walking crustaceans: A model calculation. Biol.Cybern.49, 119-125

Cruse,H. (1985a): Which parameters control the leg movement of the walking insect. I. Velocity control during the stance phase. J.exp.Biol. 116, 343-355

Cruse,H. (1985b): Which parameters control the leg movement of a walking insect? II. The start of the swing phase. J.exp.Bio. 116, 357-362

Cruse,H. (1990): What mechanisms coordinate leg movement in walking arthropods? Trends in Neurosciences, 13, 15-21

Cruse,H., Dean,J., Heuer,H., Schmidt,R.A. (1990): Utilization of sensory information for motor control. In: O. Neumann, W. Prinz (eds.) Relationship between action and perception. pp. 43-79. Springer, Berlin

Cruse,H., Müller,U. (1986): Two coupling mechanisms which determine the coordination of ipsilateral legs in the walking crayfish. J.exp.Biol. 121, 349-369

Cruse,H., Warnecke,H. (1992): Coordination of the legs of a slow-walking cat. Exp. Brain Res. 89, 147-156

Dean,J. (1984): Control of leg protraction in the stick insect: a targeted movement showing compensation for externally applied forces. J.comp.Physiol. A. 155, 771-781

Dean, J. (1991a): Effect of load on leg movement and step coordination of the stick insect Carausius morosus. J. exp. Biol. 159, 449-471

Dean, J. (1991b): A model of leg coordination in the stick insect, Carausius morosus. I. A geometrical consideration of contralateral and ipsilateral coordination mechanisms between two adjacent legs. Biol. Cybern. 64, 393-402

Dean,J. (1991c): A model of leg coordination in the stick insect, Carausius morosus. II. Description of the kinematic model and simulation of normal step pattern. Biol.Cybern. 64, 403-411

Dean,J. (1992a): A model of leg coordination in the stick insect, Carausius morosus. III. Responses to perturbations of normal coordination. Biol. Cybern. 66, 335-343

Dean,J. (1992b): A model of leg coordination in the stick insect, Carausius morosus. IV. Comparison of different forms of coordinating mechanisms. Biol.Cybern. 66, 345-355

Donner,M.D. (1984): Control of walking. Local control systems and real time systems. PhD thesis, Carnegie-Mellon University, Pittsburgh, PI

Getting,P.A., Dekin,M.S. (1985): Tritonia swimming: a model system for integration within rhythmic motor systems. In: A.I.. Selverston (ed.) Model Neural Networks and Behavior. pp. 3-20. Plenum Press, New York, London

Graham,D. (1972): A behavioural analysis of the temporal organisation of walking movements in the 1st instar and adult stick insect. J.comp.Physiol.81, 23-52

Grillner,S., Wallen,P., Brodin,L., Lansner,A. (1991): Neuronal network generating locomotor behavior in lamprey: circuitry transmitters membrane properties and simulation. Ann.Rev.Neurosc. 14, 169-199.

Land,M.F. (1972): Stepping movements made by jumping spiders during turns mediated by lateral eyes. J.exp.Biol. 57, 15-40

Levin,E. (1990): A recurrent network: limitations and training. Neural Networks 3, 641-650

Maes,P. Brooks,R.A. (1990): Learning to coordinate behaviors. Proc. Eighth Natl. Conf. AI (AAAI-90), 796-802

Minski,M. (1985): The Society of Mind. Simon and Schuster, New York

Müller,U., Cruse,H. (1991): The contralateral coordination of walking legs in the crayfish Astacus leptodactylus. I. Experimental results. Biol. Cybern. 64, 429-436

Müller-Wilm,U., Dean,J,. Cruse,H., Weidemann,H.J., Eltze,J., Pfeiffer,F. (1992): Kinematic model of a stick insect as an example of a 6-legged walking system. Adaptive Behavior 1, 33-46

Pearson,K.G. (1972): Central programming and reflex control of walking in the cockroach. J.exp.Biol.56,173-193

Pearson, K.G., Iles, F.J. (1973): Nervous mechanisms underlying intersegmental co-ordination of leg movements during walking in the cockroach. J.exp.Biol. 58,725-744

Pfeiffer,F., Weidemann,H.J., Danowski,P. (1990): Dynamics of the walking stick insect. Proceed. of the 1990 IEEE Int. Conf. on Robotics and Automation, 1458-1463

Weiland,G., Koch,U.T. (1987): Sensory feedback during active movements of stick insects. J.exp.Biol. 133, 137-156

Wendler,G. (1968): Ein Analogmodell der Beinbewegungen eines laufenden Insekts.
In: Kybernetik 1968, Beihefte zu "elektronischen Anlagen"18, 68-74, Oldenbourg,
München

Wilson,D.M. (1966): Insect walking. Ann. Rev. Ent. 11, 103-122

A Neural Network Based Behavior Hierarchy for Locomotion Control

Sunil Cherian and Wade O. Troxell
Department of Mechanical Engineering
Colorado State University
Fort Collins, Colorado 80523 USA

Telephone : (303) 491-6618
Fax : (303) 491-1055
E-mail : wade@longs.lance.colostate.edu

Abstract

This paper describes how simple, biologically inspired, networks of model neurons generate simple behaviors in a small, legged robot - the Micro-Rover. Behaviors are investigated at three levels of system organization: i) networks of artificial neurons, ii) properties of individual behaviors, and iii) organization of multiple behaviors. We draw upon ethological concepts, neuroscientific models, and recent AI techniques to guide system design.

Neural elements within the central nervous system generate oscillatory activity patterns that forms a basis for rhythmic movement in vertebrates and invertebrates alike. Similar oscillatory networks are built with model neurons in order to control the locomotion rhythm of the Micro-Rover. Multiple behaviors are integrated within a behavior hierarchy. Behavior adaptation is viewed as environment sensitive optimization.

1 Introduction

We are interested in understanding how networks of neuron like elements generate specific behaviors, how multiple behaviors are integrated within a common framework, and how behaviors adapt to satisfy environmental constraints. Although mathematical models and computer simulations have increased our understanding of how model neural networks might generate behavior, we seek a fuller understanding of real world control systems by building machines that operate in the real-world.

Understanding can come through devising theoretical models, conducting physiological and anatomical studies, computer simulations, and building real world machines. Each approach has its own advantages and disadvantages. Theoretical models are amenable to formal verification practices and may prove consistent in themselves, but they may only describe the activity of a mechanism rather than account for the actual mechanism. Empirical studies are needed to more closely match the formal world to the natural world. Empirical studies often result in the destruction of the mechanism under study or are impractical to carry out.

Simulations introduce computational constraints that neither the actual nor a constructed system would face. Simulated worlds lack the richness and uncertainty of the natural world. The simplifications made may be unreasonable for real world applications. Interactions are often contrived and limited. Here, we advocate the construction of robots that operate in the real world. This approach eliminates some of the disadvantages inherent in the other approaches while it draws together many of their advantages to provide a useful testing ground. In particular, we focus on designing biologically-inspired networks that generate task-achieving activity patterns and mapping the model to a simple, robotic system.

A central pattern generator (CPG), based on recurrent cyclic inhibition, forms the basis for controlling walking in the Micro-Rover robot. Other networks that are modulated by sensory inputs control the local actuation of legs, translation of the frames, and the relative rotation of frames for turning. Different behaviors were developed independently and integrated within a behavior hierarchy derived from the instinct models proposed by Tinbergen and Baerends.

Braitenberg's work on abstract vehicles [4], Brooks's

work on architectures for mobile robots [6], and Smither's work on behavior-based robotics [17] serve as inspiration and motivation for this project. Recent work investigating the neural basis of locomotion in a hexapod has been reported in [2] and [7]. Section 2 contains a brief overview of the biological basis of rhythmic movement; we outline some of the basic features of network oscillators and focus on the multiphasic properties of recurrent cyclic inhibition networks. In Section 3 we discuss the notion of neuro-control, review some neural models, and introduce a simple model for the neuro-control of locomotion. We present an implementation scheme for the controller in Section 4. Section 5 discusses the integration of multiple behaviors within a unified framework. Section 6 discusses temporal dynamics of neurons as a source for network plasticity and we conclude the paper in Section 7.

2 Biological Locomotion

Animals move continuously; much of their movement is rhythmic. They exhibit both autonomous rhythmic movement such as breathing and heartbeat and voluntary rhythmic movement such as swimming or walking. The latter are examples of episodic movement and are subject to modulation on a cycle-by-cycle basis. The neural basis of behaviors has been studied extensively in invertebrates since their neural activity can be recorded with relative ease during the performance of complex behaviors [8, 19, 10, 1]. Invertebrate locomotion appears to result from the endogenous activity of their neural networks, as opposed to a stage-by-stage procedure where peripheral feedback from a previous stage evokes the following stage. Grillner and others [11, 12] have presented strong evidence for the existence of central pattern generators in vertebrates as well. Studies conducted on fish such as lamprey have shown that the isolated spinal cord, deprived of all movement related sensory information, can produce a motor pattern with a similar phase lag, burst, and cycle duration as the intact lamprey swimming in a swimmill. These studies present strong evidence that the spinal cord contains central pattern generators for rhythmic activity such as locomotion.

Neural networks distribute control, making a system more fault tolerant, and are readily extensible. By changing the nature of the connections between elements or by adding elements, a network acquires additional properties such as polyphasic activity. For example, a network oscillator with recurrent cyclic inhibition characteristics (described below) appears to govern swimming in the leech [20]. More complex animals, such as vertebrates, have many times more neurons than the leech and perform more varied movements. As the numbers of neurons increase, network analysis increases in difficulty.

During locomotion proprioceptors provide sensory feedback for such parameters as touch and strain and can thus modulate motor activity. The ratio of sensory neurons to motor neurons is typically high, indicating considerable interneuronal convergence and integration. Afferent neurons diverge to several interneurons, systematically distributing sensory signals over many parallel pathways. The receptive fields of many interneurons converge and contribute to the activation of pools of motor neurons. The interconnections between the afferents, local interneurons, and motor neurons make up local networks which underlie reflexive behaviors. Interneurons play an important role in the generation of distinct behavior patterns for their varying levels of activity enables the same sensory and motor neurons to participate in the generation of more than one behavior [10].

2.1 Network Oscillators

Pattern generators within the central nervous system, known as central pattern generators or central nervous oscillators, are responsible for generating rhythmic movement in animals. Models of central nervous oscillators are divided into two classes. In the first class, individual neurons have special oscillatory properties that produce endogenous polarization rhythms. These neurons appear to generate chronic rhythms. In the second class, neurons have endogenously stable polarization levels while their interconnections give rise to oscillatory properties that produce network oscillations. Network oscillators appear to govern episodic movement. Several types of network oscillators have been proposed, including self-excitatory networks, reciprocal inhibition networks, and recurrent cyclic inhibition networks [20].

2.1.1 Self-Excitatory Networks

Self-excitatory networks contain a minimum of two neurons linked by mutually excitatory connections. The network generates a two-phase oscillatory cycle. The active phase occurs when the net gain of the neuronal connections is positive, i.e., creates a positive feedback loop. Each cell then drives the other, each gradually increasing membrane depolarization and producing impulses at progressively higher frequencies. The inactive phase occurs once a critical impulse frequency is reached. A restorative mechanism terminates impulse production and repolarizes the network cells. An inhibitory cell that becomes activated may serve as a possible impulse termination mechanism. A simple network realization is given in Figure 1a.

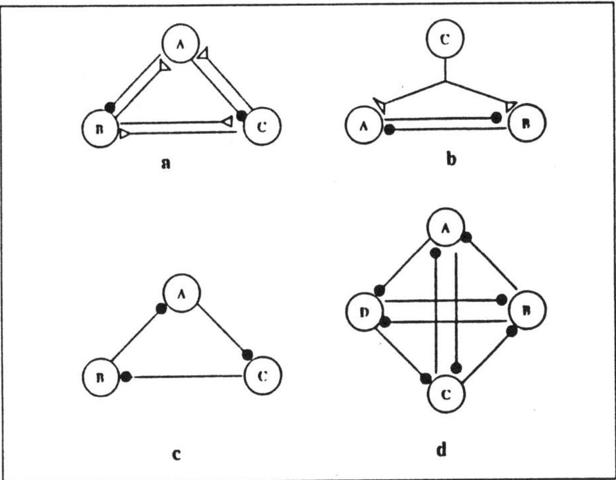

Figure 1: Oscillatory networks

2.1.2 Reciprocally Inhibitory Networks

Networks that are reciprocally inhibitory, rather than self-excitatory, can also form oscillatory rhythms. A basic, reciprocal inhibition network is depicted in Figure 1b. In this example, a tonically active cell excites a pair of reciprocally inhibited cells. The pair will alternate impulse bursts if the inhibitory effect of one cell on the other decreases as a consequence of past activity. Mechanisms producing such a restorative, hysteretic process may involve postinhibitory rebound, where past inhibition results in a transient reduction of the impulse threshold level, or adaptation, where a neuron's impulse frequency declines in response to a constant excitation.

2.1.3 Recurrent Cyclic Inhibition

A hysteretic process is not necessary in networks having recurrent cyclic inhibition. Recurrent cyclic inhibition networks require a minimum of three neurons to generate oscillatory activity. A simple network realization is given in Figure 1c. Three tonically excited neurons form an inhibitory ring by each cell making an inhibitory contact with one cell and receiving an inhibitory contact from another. An oscillatory cycle begins with a cell, say C in Figure 1c, generating impulses, i.e., it is depolarized. Because the connection is inhibitory, its postsynaptic cell, B, is inactivated, i.e., B is hyperpolarized, and thus A can recover from past inhibition. Once A recovers, it begins firing and inhibits C. When C ceases firing, B is no longer inhibited and begins recovery. On recovery, B fires, inhibiting A and enabling C to enter its recovery phase. C's recovery marks the start of a new cycle. Hence the network is capable of producing triphasic rhythms. A closer look at the properties of recurrent cyclic inhibition networks reveals the advantages of using them as a model for a multiphasic rhythm generator.

2.1.4 Multiphasic Rhythm Generators

Multiphasic rhythms enables polyphasic motor routines such as those required in locomotion. Recurrent cyclic inhibition networks consisting of a simple, inhibitory ring with an odd number of neurons, N, can generate N phases. If the recovery time, R, is large compared to the time for establishing inhibition, the cycle period is $P = NR$. The $N-1$ cells of the N-membered ring form a sequence of alternating active and inactive phases while the remaining cell is in recovery. A simple, even-numbered ring cannot oscillate for no cells can be in the recovery phase while the ring assumes one of two stable states: when either all the even-numbered or odd-numbered cells are active.

Rings containing more than three cells can form topologically more complex networks. Under these circumstances, even-numbered rings can also generate oscillatory activity patterns. For example, in Figure 1d, each of the four tonically excited neurons contact two other cells through inhibitory connections and receive inhibitory contact from two cells. Suppose cell A is in the active phase, its postsynaptic cells, C and D, are inhibited and thus inactive, allowing their postsynaptic cell, B, to enter its recovery phase. When B recovers, it inhibits A and D, enabling C to enter recovery. Continuing in this manner, the network generates a four-phase activity pattern with a cycle period of $4R$.

Another property of recurrent cyclic inhibition networks also makes them useful candidates for generating rhythmic movements. Changes in the neuron recovery time, R, correspond to changes in the oscillatory cycle period. Recovery time is related to characteristics of the cell membrane. A value for R can be formulated when the cell membrane acts as a passive element in response to voltage transients and is given by

$$R = \rho_i C_i \ln[(V_I - V_E)(V_T - V_E)] \tag{1}$$

Recall that the cells in cyclic inhibition networks are tonically active. The cell membrane has an impulse initiation zone having an input resistance ρ_i, capacitance C_i, and threshold potential V_T. Following the most recent inhibitory synaptic event, the membrane potential is V_I. Synaptic inhibition prevents depolarization. In the absence of inhibition, tonic excitation would depolarize the cell to a steady state potential of V_E. Increases (or decreases) in V_E, the level of tonic excitation, thus shortens (or lengthens) the value of R and consequently the period P of the rhythm.

Many rhythmic movements show variable phase relations among their component features. The cycle of the underlying rhythm generator appears to be divided between a variable time block and a constant time block. The above recurrent cyclic inhibition networks maintain phase-constancy, e.g., the corresponding onset of an impulse train among the cells is invariant. Varying the recovery time in the above networks varies the length of the period, but the phase relations remain fixed. Adding a constant time delay element to the network disrupts phase relations.

Network connectivity gives rise to multiphasic activity; however, the properties of individual neurons also constrain network activity. In the following, we turn to neural models. Neural models span the entire spectrum from simple threshold computational units to much more complex models that are based on the anatomical structure and the physiological characteristics of actual biological networks.

3 Neuro-control

The response of a neural network depends upon the properties of the individual neuron, properties of synaptic connections, and the connectivity of the network. The choice of an appropriate network model depends upon the underlying motivation. Many mathematicians and computer scientists are at one end of a network model spectrum while most neurobiologists are found at the other. Mathematicians and computer scientists are primarily concerned with computation and information processing in artificial networks composed of threshold units.

Neurobiologists are more interested in modeling the actual biophysical dynamics of real neurons, in part to deduce the function of biological networks and to bridge the gap between neural functioning and higher level behaviors [9].

Somewhere in between these camps falls neuro-control, the control of real machines by networks of artificial neurons. The robustness and generality of such networks along with their ability to 'learn' makes them ideal candidates for autonomous control purposes [3]. Successful neural models for control purposes require an appropriate level of abstraction. Neuro-control is not concerned with computation *per se*, although some form of computation is obviously involved, nor is it constrained by biological plausibility, even though many of its metaphors are drawn from the biological world. In this paper, we present networks that are tailored for achieving specific tasks rather than generic networks with high connectivity that somehow 'learn' those tasks. Some of the more common neural models are briefly presented below and a simple model that seems suitable for the neuro-control of locomotion is introduced.

3.1 Neural Models

A simple model proposed by McCulloch and Pitts abstracts the neuron to a binary threshold unit [13].

$$n_i(t+1) = sgn\left(\sum_j w_{ij} n_j(t) - \theta_i\right) \qquad (2)$$

where

$$sgn(x) = \begin{cases} 1 & \text{if } x \geq 0 \\ 0 & \text{otherwise} \end{cases}$$

Here, n_i is either 1 or 0, and represents the state of the neuron i as *firing* or *not firing* respectively. Time t is discrete, with one time unit elapsing per processing step. The strength, or weight, of the synapse connecting neuron j to neuron i is represented by w_{ij}. θ_i is a cell-specific parameter for neuron i called its *threshold value*. The weighted sum of inputs must reach or exceed the threshold for the neuron to fire. A synchronous assembly of McCulloch-Pitts neurons has been shown to be capable of **universal computation** for suitably chosen weights w_{ij}. A lot of effort in neural computation centers around exploiting the notion of universal computation. One of the drawbacks of this approach is that the previous behavior of a unit can only affect its current behavior by influencing its synaptic weights during training. However, most real neurons are influenced by their recent history and integrate their inputs over some period.

At the other end of the spectrum neurobiologists attempt to model the electrophysiological properties of real neurons in order to better understand neuron dynamics, the Hodgkin-Huxley equations being a good example [14]. These equations are generally quite complex and difficult to analyze.

Klienfield and Sompolinsky have developed an associative network model for the generation of multiple, coherent patterns by a highly interconnected network [16]. Network output consists of temporally coherent patterns of linear or cyclic sequences of states. Rhythmic output emerges as a collective property of the network. Desired output patterns are encoded in the connections between the model neurons. Each connection T_{ij} is functionally separated into two components, denoted T_{ij}^S and T_{ij}^L. The two components have different characteristic response times. The synaptic connections T_{ij}^S act on the shorter of the two time scales and determines the time required for the network to settle into a particular pattern. The T_{ij}^L component acts on a much longer time scale than T_{ij}^S and sets the time for the transition from one state to the next. T_{ij} is defined in terms of a formal version of Hebb's learning rule. In this model high interconnectivity of the network is favored over connection specificity.

3.2 Dynamic Neuron Model

We develop a simple neuron model incorporating three major properties: *delayed excitation, squashing*, and *thresholding*. Delayed excitation is manifested as a delay between the onset of a depolarizing stimulus and the first spike. Delayed excitation captures some of the temporal dynamics of real neurons and is one way of generating rhythmic activity within networks. The depolarizing stimulus increases activity within the model neuron, exponentially approaching the maximum activity level. The maximum activity level is computed as a non-linear function of the summed inputs to the neuron. The non-linear squashing function is a hyperbolic tangent that keeps neural activity constrained between +1 and -1. The output of the neuron is "all or none", depending upon whether its dynamic activity is above or below the threshold value. The following equation models the neuron.

$$n_i(t+1) = sgn\left[sqsh(n_j,t) \times \left(1 - \exp^{rst(t_i)/\tau_i}\right) - \theta_i\right] \quad (3)$$

where

$$sgn(x) = \begin{cases} 1 & \text{if } x \geq 0 \\ 0 & \text{otherwise} \end{cases},$$

$$sqsh(n_j,t) = \tanh\left(\sum_j w_{ij} n_j(t)\right),$$

and

$$rst(t) = \begin{cases} 0 & \text{if } sqsh(n_j,t) \times sqsh(n_j,(t-1)) < 0 \\ t & \text{otherwise} \end{cases}$$

Two key synaptic properties are modeled that effect network activity. The sign of a synaptic connection determines whether its action is excitatory or inhibitory. The strength of a connection determines what portion of pre-synaptic activity is propagated to the post-synaptic neuron. Connections are not required to be symmetric. However, they are constrained by functional requirements placed on the network.

As described below, locomotion in the Micro-Rover robot requires a four-phasic oscillator. A network with recurrent cyclic inhibition generates the desired rhythm pattern; the network connectivity allows for decentralized control. The model follows from biology in that the central pattern generator (CPG) determines the overall rhythm while local movements are modulated by sensory feedback. The local networks are therefore structurally specific and carry out a predefined function.

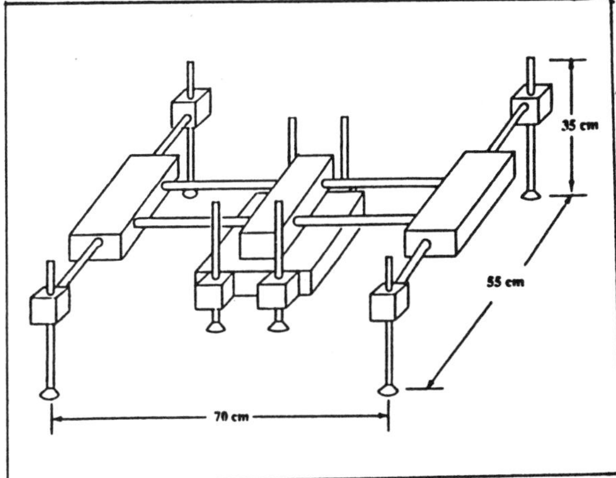

Figure 2: Micro-Rover

4 Micro-Rover Robot Testbed

A very small, legged robotic system, the Micro-Rover, is to be used as (i) a testbed to evaluate the performance potential of very small robotic systems and (ii) a demonstration and exhibition tool for walking machine activities related to the Space Exploration Initiative. The Micro-Rover prototype is a miniature version of the Rover prototype developed by Martin Marietta Astronautics Group in 1989. The beam-walker locomotion concept is retained in the Micro-Rover; however, the areas of control, actuation, and sensing are re-examined under new design concepts. The approach does not rely on any detailed, predefined world map nor on accurate guidance systems. Instead, effective operation depends on environmental contingencies such as avoiding obstacles. A design schematic of the Micro-Rover is given in Figure 2.

4.1 Micro-Rover Platform

The beam walker design consists of two, rectangular base frames that are attached to each other by a revolute joint. Each base has four legs, one at each corner. The prototype has a total of ten joints: eight *leg drive* joints, one *beam drive* prismatic joint between the frames, and one *turn drive* rotary joint between the frames. The leg drives lower the feet of the beam walker, allowing a frame to stand and support the robot, or retract the feet, allowing the frame to move to a new location. The turn drive rotates the beam that connects the two frames while the beam drive translates the leg-retracted frame with respect to the leg-extended frame along the beam. Robot mobility arises from sequencing the standing-moving action of the two frames.

The outer base of the Micro-Rover is approximately

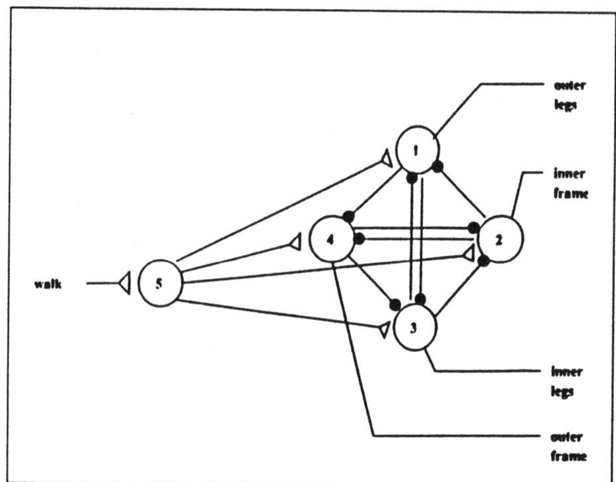

Figure 3: CPG for Micro-Rover locomotion.

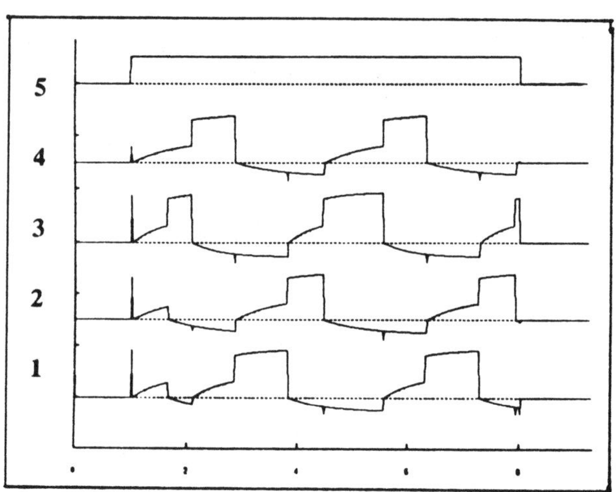

Figure 4: Dynamic response of the CPG.

55 cm wide by 70 cm long and the inner base 20 cm wide by 30 cm long. With its legs retracted, the Micro-Rover does not exceed 35 cm in height. The walking stride is approximately 25 cm. The feet are durable and capable of support in soft soils. The power plant is self-contained, can operate for at least an hour, and has easily interchangeable power packs. The components used are "off the shelf" and commercially available. The entire robot weighs less than 10 kilograms. The robot can operate either autonomously or connected to a control tether.

4.2 Locomotion Implementation

The controller for Micro-Rover locomotion consists of several networks that carry out predefined tasks locally. The control methodology is homogeneous in the sense that the entire controller is built up of neural elements alone. The neural elements are divided into three categories: sensory neurons, motor neurons, and inter-neurons. Sensory neurons are activated by exteroceptive or proprioceptive stimuli. They, in turn, connect to either inter-neurons or motor neurons. Inter-neurons receive inputs from and pass their outputs to other neurons. Motor neurons excite actuators that are the mechanical equivalent of muscles. They may also connect to other sensory or inter neurons. Synaptic connections are either excitatory or inhibitory. At present, the Micro-Rover controller consists of seven semi-independent networks: the central pattern generator for gait control, a leg control network, a frame control network, a turn control network, a network that keeps the two frames aligned, an obstacle avoidance network, and a pseudo-random wander network.

The pattern generator shown in Figure 3 generates a four-phasic rhythm with a constant phase relationship. The period for which each neuron is active during a cycle is determined by the time constant associated with its pre-synaptic neuron. The dynamic response of the five neurons in the recurrent inhibitory ring is shown in Figure 4. Neuron 5 becomes tonically active at $t = 1$. After start up transients die out, a stable four-phasic pattern is maintained by the network. At $t = 8$, when neuron 5 stops firing, oscillator activity stops. During this simulation neuron 5 had to be maintained tonically active for oscillatory behavior of the network. However, within a complete behavior hierarchy, higher command centers can turn neuron 5 on or off as desired. Arbitrary time constants were assigned to the neurons in order to obtain this simulation trace: these time constants do not correspond to actual values required for Micro-Rover locomotion.

The forward locomotion rhythm of the Micro-Rover consists of the actuation sequence:

outer-legs → inner-frame → inner-legs → outer-frame

Rhythmic output from the CPG activates 'control neurons' of appropriate local networks. Each corner of the Micro-Rover has two legs, an inner leg and an outer leg. Only one leg at each corner is needed for supporting the rover at any given time. For translational Forward movement of the inner frame, the outer legs support the rover and the inner legs are retracted. The order is reversed for movement of the outer frame. Figure 5 shows the network that locally controls the inner and outer legs at each corner. A leg is extended by exciting its corresponding 'extend' motor neuron. In addition to extending the appropriate leg, an active motor neuron also inhibits the inter-neurons that excite the opposing 'retract' motor neuron. As soon as the extended leg is firmly placed on the ground, its 'step' sensor is activated. This sensory neuron inhibits the active motor neuron, terminating further extension of

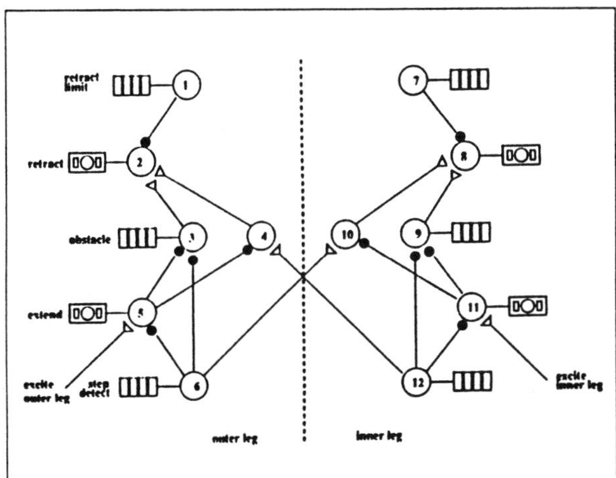

Figure 5: Leg control network that modulates leg actuation based upon local sensory input.

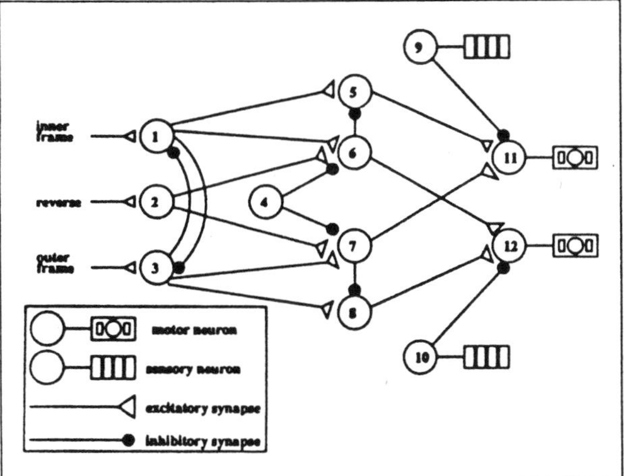

Figure 6: Local network for forward and reverse frame translation.

the leg. The step sensory neuron also excites the interneuron responsible for retracting the opposite leg, thereby preparing for frame translation. Sensory input therefore modulates leg movement.

The translation of one frame with respect to the other results in the overall forward or backward movement of the Micro-Rover. Figure 6 depicts the network that controls frame movement. The network receives input from the CPG two times every cycle for moving the inner or the outer frame. The 'reverse' command comes from possibly higher network centers and results in the reversal of the frame translation direction, thus reversing the direction of locomotion in the Micro-Rover. Sensory inputs that provide information about translation limits modulate frame actuation.

The rotary joint between the two frames facilitate

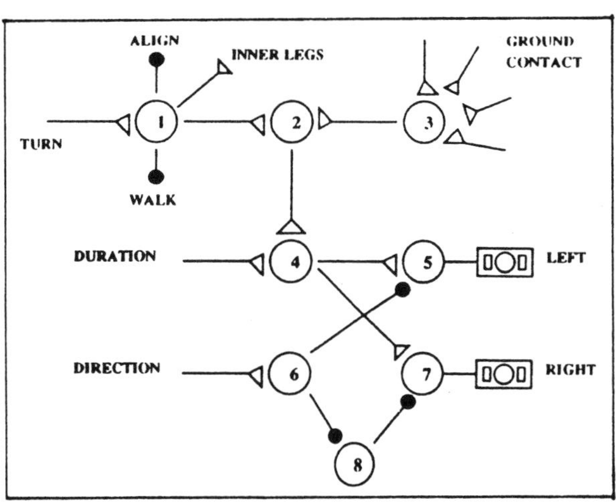

Figure 7: Network for turning the inner frame of the Micro-Rover with respect to the outer one.

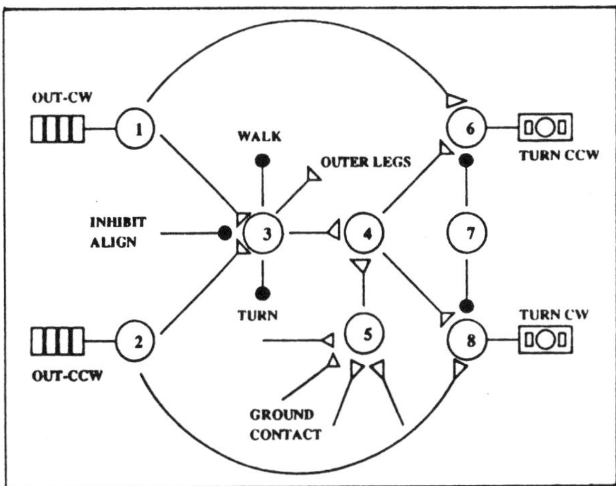

Figure 8: Network that aligns the inner and outer frames in the direction of travel.

turning. A schematic representation of the 'turn' network is shown in Figure 7. Inputs to three neurons control turning. A command neuron initiates turning by inhibiting the 'align' and 'walk' networks and extending the inner legs. Once the inner legs contact the ground, the outer legs are automatically retracted by the leg control network. The 'left-' or 'right-' turn motor neurons are activated depending upon the state of the direction control neuron. Turning is continued as long as the 'duration' neuron is active. As soon as the 'turn' command neuron is disabled, 'align' and 'walk' are no longer inhibited. Since the two frames are not aligned after turning the 'align' network is excited and it turns the inner frame to bring it into alignment with the outer frame. The network is shown in Figure 8.

The Micro-Rover can now exhibit simple behaviors

such as walking and turning. In addition, a very simple network extension can enable the rover to avoid obstacles. Direct connections from obstacle detectors to appropriate 'turn' command neurons form a reflexive pathway that allows the rover to continue locomotion avoiding obstacles along the way. This type of reflexive pathway is similar to those suggested in Braitenberg's vehicles. We are also testing a 'wander' behavior that consists of a network with neurons with large time constants excited while 'walk' is active. It also receives inputs from pseudo-random devices corresponding to environmental influences, saturating the wander command neuron and exciting the network at apparently random intervals. The 'wander' network then inhibits 'walk' and changes its heading.

5 Behavior Organization

In addition to building independent behaviors that achieve different tasks, we also investigate mechanisms for integrating these diverse behaviors within a common framework. Ethology provides several explanatory models for the organization of animal behavior which appears to be useful preliminary abstractions for the organization of robot behaviors. Since we are interested in building machines with 'insect level' competence, with little or no apparent cognitive capabilities, it appears that ethological models of simple animal behavior might serve as a useful yardstick for analyzing robot behaviors. Schnepf [18] presents a tentative framework for research into autonomous intelligent systems based on the study of behavioral sequences in robot beings.

The study of animal behavior is primarily concerned with the sequence and temporal structure of behavior patterns, their causation, and their hierarchical organization, the aim of which is to predict future behavior and to justify current behavior. This study is carried out at different levels of system organization ranging from the cellular level to societies of animals. Description of the sequence and temporal organization of behavior patterns can be made observationally, whereas statements about the causation of behavior can be made only after careful manipulation of the behavior. Experimental ethology involves the manipulation of animal behavior in order to study their causation. Experimental ethology and descriptive ethology strive to develop models of behavior organization while neuroethology tries to discern the neural basis of animal behavior.

In the case of artificial autonomous systems however, prior to the description and analysis of behavior they have to be designed and built. This necessitates a synthesis component in the robot equivalent of ethological investigation.

The organizing principle for animal behavior involves the concept of 'instinct'. Although controversial, the notion of instinct is widely used in ethology. Tinbergen (quoted in [15]) defines the term *instinct* as

> *"... hierarchically organized nervous mechanism which is susceptible to certain priming, releasing and directing impulses of internal as well as external origin, and which responds to these impulses by coordinated movements that contribute to the maintenance of the individual and the species."*

Tinbergen's instinct model, distinguishes between several levels of instincts each of which comprises a subset of several behavior patterns that are components of the next higher level of organization. An 'excitatory potential' flows from a higher center to the next lower one and is normally inhibited by a 'block'. This block can be removed by appropriate stimuli or releasers. A 'block' also called a 'releasing mechanism', can be seen as a lock that can be opened only with the right 'key', consisting of the proper stimulus configuration, called the 'key stimuli'. The prevailing key stimuli determines which lower behavior will be released. If all blocks remain in place due to inadequate stimuli, then an appetitive behavior is activated that seeks to find stimuli that releases one of the behaviors. When appropriate stimuli is encountered, the next lower centers are released and the process is repeated.

Although Tinbergen's instinct model is out of favor in modern ethological theories, it appears to be quite useful as a conceptual model for describing the numerous regularities observed in animal behavior and of course desired in robot behavior.

Figure 9 shows a schematic representation of the behavior hierarchy for the Micro-Rover. Each behavior receives external and/or internal stimuli. A behavior 'block' prevents the expression of the behavior until a proper stimulus configuration making up the 'key stimuli' is detected. Some of the desirable features of the model are:

1. It clearly accounts for situations where the same behavior pattern is present as a component of several other behaviors: instead of being duplicated in several behaviors, a single behavior is activated by higher level behaviors as needed.

2. Finite machine resources are shared by several behaviors, and the organization of those motor resources are accounted for within the model.

3. The stimulus combination that activates a particular behavior is explicitly shown in the form of a releasing mechanism.

4. Layering of behaviors is well structured: behaviors belong to the lowest level where its datapath

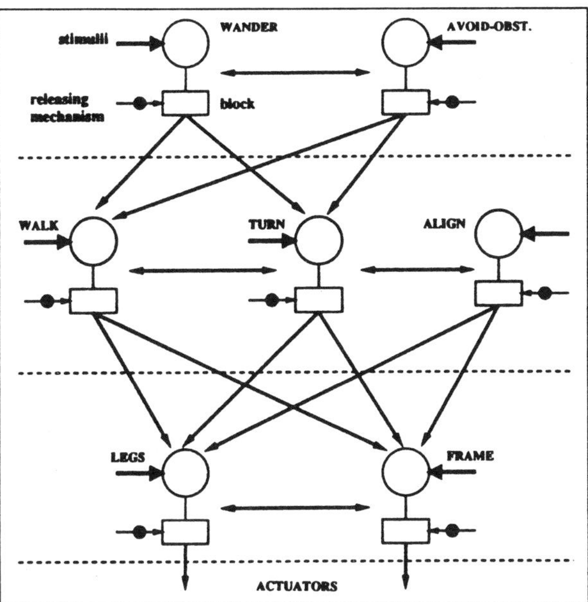

Figure 9: Behavior hierarchy that integrates the different local behaviors.

is not required to project to higher levels.

5. New behaviors are added either horizontally on a particular level, or vertically on higher levels. Adding new behaviors does not require taking apart behaviors already in place much like Brooks' subsumption architecture [5].

6. Mutual inhibition between behaviors at the same level within the same functional group makes sure that only one behavior is active, thus avoiding conflict situations.

The generality of this model remains to be determined through further experimentation. Since this is only a preliminary model, we expect it evolve through future empirical evaluation.

6 Behavior Adaptation

Terrain conditions constrain Micro-Rover locomotion rhythm by placing lower bounds on the time required for leg and frame actuation. Constraints on upper bounds arise out of optimality considerations. Predefined periods for each phase of the network activity cycle results in sub-optimal performance when new terrain is encountered. For optimal locomotion, the time for which each phase is active has to be modulated by sensory information about the terrain being traversed. The biological solution is often in the form of probabilistic modulation of the central rhythm. Recent sensory history is utilized for probabilistic predictions that lead to near-optimal performance. The recovery time R described in Section 2.1.4, is a biological mechanism for varying the period P of the network rhythm.

In the case of the Micro-Rover, the active period of each phase of the four-phasic network oscillator depends on the time dynamics of the corresponding presynaptic neuron. We are currently designing a simple reward/punish scheme for generating optimal time constants for the neurons that constitute the network oscillator. It takes into account the constraints that must be met for optimal network performance. Some of the constraints currently considered are: (i) minimize dead-time between the termination of leg or frame actuation during one phase and the initiation of the next phase, (ii) minimize variation in mean ground clearance (This accounts for the shortening of effective leg height if the leg extension phase is too short), and (iii) maximize stride length. The probabilistic rhythm modulator is embedded within the controller as an integral part of the 'walk' behavior.

7 Conclusions

This paper presents a neural controller for an autonomous walking machine called the Micro-Rover. Static and dynamic properties of real neurons were incorporated within our neuron model. The pattern generation capability of networks of biological neurons were studied in order to choose an appropriate gait controller. A four-phasic network with recurrent inhibition was found to be suitable for generating the locomotion rhythm. Sensory modulation of the locomotion rhythm takes place within local networks that coordinate leg and frame actuation. Networks were developed independently and tested numerically. Work is currently underway to implement the controller on the Micro-Rover.

Factors motivating the current implementation are: (i) incorporation of static and temporal dynamics within the neuron model, (ii) utilizing structural specificity of networks, (iii) exploiting oscillatory properties of networks, (iv) investigating the structure of individual behaviors as well as collections of behaviors, and (v) investigating behavior adaptation as an integral part of task-achieving behaviors.

Simple algorithms are being developed that can alter the dynamic properties of the neural units, rather than just their synaptic strengths. This type of learning is advantageous when temporal rhythms with constant phase relationships are more important than the recall of multiple patterns. This may have direct significance for the neural coordination of robot motor activity. Future research is aimed at investigating the evolution of the structured networks once the assumption of connection specificity is relaxed.

Acknowledgements

Support for the Micro-Rover robotic project has been in the form of a gift from Martin Marietta Astronautics Group. We gratefully acknowledge the efforts and support of Steve Price of Martin Marietta. The Colorado Advanced Software Institute has also provided grant support. Tim Smithers at the Free University of Brussels has provided welcome insights and vision into this research over the years.

At Colorado State University, Stanley Kater, Gearold Johnson, Bryan Willson, and Michael Histand are gratefully acknowledged for discussions leading up to this manuscript. Anne M. Sjöström helped with earlier drafts of this paper and Muhammad M. Ali has been instrumental in the construction of the Micro-Rover robot prototype; their assistance and insight are much appreciated.

References

[1] Michael A. Arbib. *The Metaphorical Brain 2: Neural Networks and Beyond.* John Wiley and Sons, 1989.

[2] Randall D. Beer and Hillel J. Chiel. The neural basis of behavioral choice in an artificial insect. In Jean-Arcady Meyer and Stewart W. Wilson, editors, *From Animals to Animats: Proceedings of the First International Conference on Simulation of Adaptive Behaviorr*, pages 247–254. MIT Press, 1991.

[3] Randall D. Beer, Hillel J. Chiel, and Leon S. Sterling. A biological perspective on autonomous agent design. In Pattie Maes, editor, *Designing Autonomous Systems: Theory and Practice from Biology to Engineering and Back*, pages 169–186. MIT Press, 1990.

[4] Valentino Braitenberg. *Vehicles: Experiments in Synthetic Psychology.* MIT Press, Cambridge, MA, 1984.

[5] Rodney A. Brooks. A robust layered control system for a mobile robot. In *IEEE Journal of Robotics and Automation, RA-2(1)*, March 1986.

[6] Rodney A. Brooks. Challenges for complete creature architectures. In Jean-Arcady Meyer and Stewart W. Wilson, editors, *From Animals to Animats: Proceedings of the First International Conference on Simulation of Adaptive Behavior*, pages 434–443. MIT Press, 1990.

[7] Hillel J. Chiel, Randall D. Beer, Roger D. Quinn, and Kenneth S. Espenschied. Robustness of a distributed neural network controller for locomotion in a hexapod robot. *IEEE Transactions on Robotics and Automation*, 8(3):293–303, 1992.

[8] William J. Davis. Organizational concepts in the central motor networks of invertebrates. In Richard M. Herman, Sten Grillner, and Paul S.G. Stein, editors, *Advances in Behavioral Biology*, pages 265–292. Plenum Press, 1976. Volume 18.

[9] Richard Durbin, Christopher Miall, and Graeme Mitchison, editors. *The Computing Neuron.* Addison-Wesley Publishing Company, 1989.

[10] Peter A. Getting. Reconstruction of small neural networks. In Christof Koch and Idan Segev, editors, *Methods in Neuronal Modeling: From Synapses to Networks*, pages 171–194. MIT Press, Cambridge, MA, 1989.

[11] Sten Grillner. Neurobiological bases of rhythmic motor acts in vertebrates. *Science*, 228:143–149, 1985.

[12] Sten Grillner, James T. Buchanan, Peter Wallén, and Lennart Brodin. Neural control of locomotion in lower vertebrates: From behavior to ionic mechanisms. In Avis H. Cohen, Serge Rossignol, and Sten Grillner, editors, *Neural Control of Rhythmic Movements in Vertebrates*, pages 1–40. John Wiley and Sons, 1988.

[13] John Hertz, Anders Krogh, and Richard G. Palmer, editors. *Introduction to the Theory of Neural Computation.* Addison-Wesley Publishing Company, 1991.

[14] A. L. Hodgkin and A. F. Huxely. A quantitative description of membrane current and its application to conduction and excitation in nerve. *J. Physiology (London)*, 117:500–544, 1952.

[15] Klaus Immelmann. *Introduction to Ethology.* Plenum Press, New York, 1980.

[16] David Kleinfeld and Haim Sompolinsky. Associative network models for central pattern generators. In Christof Koch and Idan Segev, editors, *Methods in Neuronal Modeling: From Synapses to Networks*, pages 195–246. MIT Press, 1989.

[17] Ulrich Nehmzow and Tim Smithers. Mapbuilding using self-organising networks in "really useful robots". In Jean-Arcady Meyer and Stewart W. Wilson, editors, *From Animals to Animats: Proceedings of the First International Conference on Simulation of Adaptive Behavior*, pages 152–159, Cambridge, MA, 1990. MIT Press.

[18] Uwe Schnepf. Robot ethology : A proposal for the research into intelligent autonomous systems. In Jean-Arcady Meyer and Stewart W. Wilson, editors, *From Animals to Animats: Proceedings of the First International Conference on Simulation of Adaptive Behavior*, pages 465–474. MIT Press, 1991.

[19] Allen I. Selverston. Neuronal mechanisms for rhythmic motor pattern generation in a simple system. In RichardM. Herman, Sten Grillner, and Paul S.G. Stein, editors, *Advances in Behavioral Biology*, volume 18, pages 377–399. Plenum Press, 1976.

[20] Gunther Stent. Neural circuits for generating rhythmic movements. In F. Eugene Yates, editor, *Self-organiaing Systems–the Emergence of Order*, pages 245-263. Plenum Press, 1987.

A Qualitative Dynamical Analysis of Evolved Locomotion Controllers

John C. Gallagher[1] **and Randall D. Beer**[1,2]
Departments of [1]Computer Engineering and Science, and [2]Biology
Case Western Reserve University
Cleveland, OH 44106 USA
{johng, beer}@alpha.ces.cwru.edu

Abstract

In previous work, we demonstrated the use of continuous-time recurrent neural networks as a means to control autonomous agents. Such networks are capable of exhibiting a rich repertoire of complex behavior. Due to this complexity, both synthesis and analysis of these systems is often difficult. We have elsewhere addressed the synthesis problem. In this work, we intend to address the analysis problem by taking a dynamical systems perspective and re-examining several previously developed controllers. In so doing, we not only demonstrate the utility of the dynamical systems approach, but also explain the mechanics underlying network function. In particular, we focus on our systems' ability to make appropriate use of sensory information, and demonstrate that adaptive behavior need not be the product of changes in network structure, but rather, a natural consequence of the network's dynamics.

1 Introduction

The adaptive behavior approach (Meyer and Wilson, 1991) proposes that a large amount of intelligent behavior arises from the dynamic coupling between an agent's environment and its internal control mechanisms (Maes, 1991). A successful controller is one that, when coupled with the agent and supplied with information about the environment, produces outputs that drive the agent's effectors in appropriate fashion. Several questions, however, need to be asked. What kinds of control mechanisms are appropriate for the generation of adaptive behavior? How can these mechanisms be designed or developed? How can we go about understanding how the developed controllers generate adaptive behavior?

In previous work (Beer and Gallagher, 1992), we focused on the first two questions by exploring the use of genetic algorithms to generate continuous-time dynamical neural networks to control several autonomous agents. Since these controllers were evolved, rather than designed, they often lacked any obvious internal organization. In this paper, we adopt a dynamical systems perspective and focus on the problem of understanding how these evolved controllers generate appropriate control signals. We will make a qualitative analysis of system phase portraits to illustrate the dynamical basis of several adaptive features of some evolved locomotion controllers. Using the results of these analyses as examples, we will discuss the appropriateness of continuous-time neural networks as a means of control for autonomous agents.

2 Locomotion Controllers

We have successfully used genetic algorithms to develop dynamical neural networks to control a number of autonomous agents (Beer and Gallagher, 1992). In those studies, we assumed that both the dynamics of the agents' bodies and the dynamics of the environment in which the agent was to function were fixed *a priori*. We also assumed that there existed some measure of each agents' overall level of performance within that environment. Using as a performance function the agents' fitness in the environment, we employed a genetic algorithm to find controllers that optimized the agents' overall performance. Among the networks developed were several variations of a legged locomotion controller. In this section, we present a brief review of the portions of that work that are of concern in this paper.

2.1 Agent Body Model

We employed an insect-like body which is an extension of a model used in previous work (Figure 1; Beer, 1990). Two versions of the insect body were utilized. We employed a one-legged version to study the generation of control signals needed to drive the stepping of individual legs, and a six-legged version to study the interactions necessary to properly coordinate the steppings of multiple legs. Since this work concerns itself

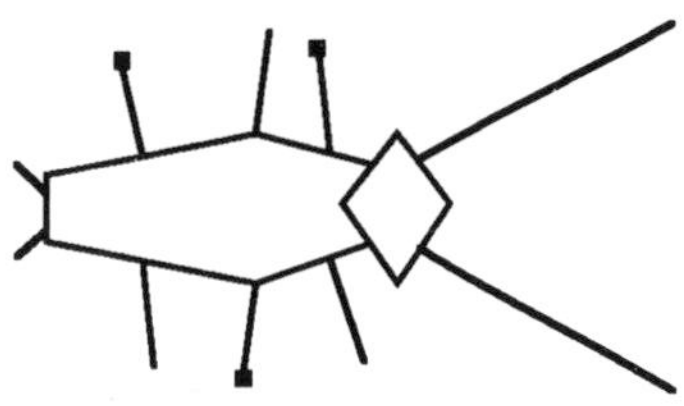

Figure 1: Insect Body Model

with the analysis of stepping behavior, we will focus on the single legged model.

Each leg has a foot that may be either up or down. When its foot is down, a leg provides support and can generate forces which move the body. When its foot is raised, a leg is incapable of providing support, and any forces it generates serve only to swing the leg about its joint with the body. A leg contains three effectors: one governs the state of the foot, and the other two generate opposing torques about the leg's single joint. The single legged insect is considered to be stably supported when its single foot is on the ground; the six legged insect is considered to be stably supported if its center of mass is inside the polygon formed by the positions of the feet that are down. When the body is stably supported, the forces are summed and translate the body under Newtonian dynamics.

In addition to the effectors, legs are equipped with a single sensor which returns the leg's angular position relative to the body.

2.2 Dynamical Neural Networks

The behavior of all of the agents discussed here is controlled by continuous time, recurrent neural networks (*dynamical neural networks*) with a state equation of the form:

$$\tau_i \frac{dy_i}{dt} = -y_i + \sum_{j=1}^{N} w_{ji}\sigma_j(y_j) + I_i(t) \qquad (1)$$

where y can be interpreted as the mean membrane potential of the neuron, $\sigma_j(\xi) = (1 + e^{(\theta_j - \xi)})^{-1}$ is a sigmoidal (S-shaped) function which can be interpreted as its short-term average firing frequency, θ is a bias term which controls the firing threshold, τ is a time constant associated with the passive properties of the cell membrane, w_{ji} represents the strength of the connection from the jth to the ith neuron, and $I_i(t)$ represents an external input to the network such as from a sensor. Networks with this state equation have been studied by Hopfield (1984). Because Hopfield assumed zero diagonal symmetry of the weights, his networks were capable only of fixed point behavior. Since we do not make this assumption, our networks can exhibit more complicated dynamics.

Single legged insects are controlled by five-neuron fully-interconnected dynamical neural networks. Three of these are motor neurons and govern the state of the foot, the forward swing torque, and the backward swing torque. The remaining two units are interneurons with no specified role. In addition to inputs from other neurons in the network, each neuron also receives a weighted input from the leg's angle sensor (i.e. $I(t)$ in equation (1) is $w_i\theta(t)$, where $\theta(t)$ is the leg angle in radians and w_i is the weight of the sensory input to neuron i). Six legged insects are controlled by six coupled, single leg controllers. Each neuron in a leg controller is connected to corresponding neurons in the controllers of adjacent legs.

We used the public domain genetic algorithms package GAucsd 1.1 (Schraudolph and Grefenstette, 1991) (Goldberg, 1989) (Holland, 1975) to search the space of network parameters for settings that produced controllers that would produce walking behavior when coupled to the described artificial insect body.

2.3 Results

A successful leg controller must produce rhythmic control signals that have the following properties: (1) The activations of the foot neuron and the backward swing neuron must be in phase, and the activations of the forward swing neuron must be out of phase with the activations of both the foot and backward swing neurons. (2) The durations of the phases must be matched to both the kinematic range of motion and the dynamic force/acceleration properties of the leg. In addition to these, six legged controllers must also be able to coordinate the actions of all legs such that stability is maintained at all times. We succussfully evolved controllers for both the single legged and the six legged locomotion problem.

In one series of experiments, we evolved single leg controllers that were always provided with accurate leg angle information via the sensory input term of equation [1]. In all cases, successful controllers were developed. However, all of these controllers lacked the ability to function properly in the absence of sensory feedback. In some cases, deprivation of sensors (setting $I(t)$ in equation (1) to zero) caused insects with this type of controller to take one step and stop. In other insects of this type, such deprivation simply caused the insect to stand motionless. Because of their functional similarity to early chained reflex theories of legged locomotion (Sherrington, 1898), controllers of this class were named *reflexive pattern generators*.

In another series of experiments, we evolved single

leg controllers that operated in the absence of sensory input by depriving the network of sensory feedback during evolution. These controllers were capable of producing appropriate rhythmic behavior without sensory input. However, since they were evolved without sensory feedback, they lacked the ability to make use of sensory information. Controllers of this class are called *central pattern generators* (Delcomyn, 1980).

To produce a single leg controller that could operate in the absence of sensory information, yet be able to take advantage of it if available, we used a compound evaluation function in which each candidate network was evaluated twice, once with and once without sensory feedback. A network's fitness score was taken to be the average of its performance with and without sensory information. In all cases, we evolved controllers that could operate under either condition, and would often take advantage of sensory information, when available, to improve performance. Since controllers in this class could operate either as reflexive or central pattern generators, we named these *mixed pattern generators*.

Figure 2 details the operation of a mixed pattern generator. The plots shown represent the behavior of the coupled body/controller system with the leg initialized to 95% of its full backward position. The top set of plots shows body velocity and neuron activation levels when the controller is deprived of sensory feedback. The velocity plot shows the forward velocity of the body, while the remaining plots show the activation levels of the labeled neurons. The bottom set of plots shows the same information for the same controller operating with sensory feedback. In addition, the bottom set of plots shows the value of the sensory input ($I(t)$).

Note that in the top set of plots, there is a longer transient before normal rhythmic walking (denoted by the periodic "saw tooth" velocity pattern) begins. The stereotyped control signal generated when no sensory information is available directs the insect to stance (place leg on ground and rotate leg to full backward position). Since the insect's leg is already nearly all the way back, generating a full stance phase causes the insect to move its leg all the way back, then waste time attempting to move the leg further back than it can actually go. An insect with its leg already near the mechanical limit should generate a swing (lift leg and rotate to full forward position) before stepping. The mixed controller can, when provided with a leg angle signal, shorten the length of initial stance phase – thereby generating a swing phase more quickly if needed.

Each series of experiments was repeated with full, six legged artificial insects. All were successful in producing effective, coordinated walking. Like single legged controllers evolved with sensors, six legged controllers evolved with reliable sensory information available could not function in the absence of this information, nor could six legged controller evolved without sensors take advantage of that information when it was present. Six legged controllers evolved with a compound evaluation function operated better with sensory information, but could function without it if necessary.

3 Dynamical Systems

The dynamical neural networks introduced in the last section are instances of dynamical systems (Thompson and Stewart, 1986). Such systems are characterized by a finite set of *state variables* and a *dynamical law* that governs how the values change in time. For a given dynamical neural network, the mean membrane potentials (y_i) are the state variables, and the set of neuron state equations is the dynamical law. The set of all possible values that the state variables may assume constitute the system's state space. In the case of dynamical neural networks, this space is both real-valued and euclidian.

Starting from a given point in the state space (*initial state*), the sequence of states generated by the action of the dynamical law is called a *trajectory* of the system. The trajectories of some systems will simply diverge to infinity as time goes on. Others will converge to *limit sets*, which are sets of points that are invariant with respect to the dynamical law. In other words, if the state of a dynamical system ever falls in a limit set, the action of the system will keep it within that set indefinitely. For the purposes of this paper, we are most interested in the stable limit sets, or *attractors*. An attractor is a limit set that has the property that all trajectories passing through nearby states eventually converge to the attractor. The set of points that converge to an attractor are known as the attractor's *basin of attraction*. The portions of trajectories that lie outside of attractors are known as transients. Of the several classes of attractors, only two are important in understanding the controllers we examined. *Fixed point* attractors are stable limit sets consisting of only one point. *Limit cycles* are stable limit sets that form a closed trajectory in state space. A trajectory under the influence of a fixed point will flow to that point and never again leave it. A trajectory under the influence of a limit cycle will flow to the cycle, and will become constrained to move forever on that closed curve.

Further, dynamical systems can be viewed as being either *autonomous* or *nonautonomous*. In an autonomous dynamical system, the parameters of the dynamical law are held constant as the state follows a trajectory. In a nonautonomous system, one or more of those parameters are allowed to vary in time as a trajectory is being traced. Dynamical neural networks can be either autonomous or nonautonomous, depending on the presence of external input ($I(t)$ in equation [1]).

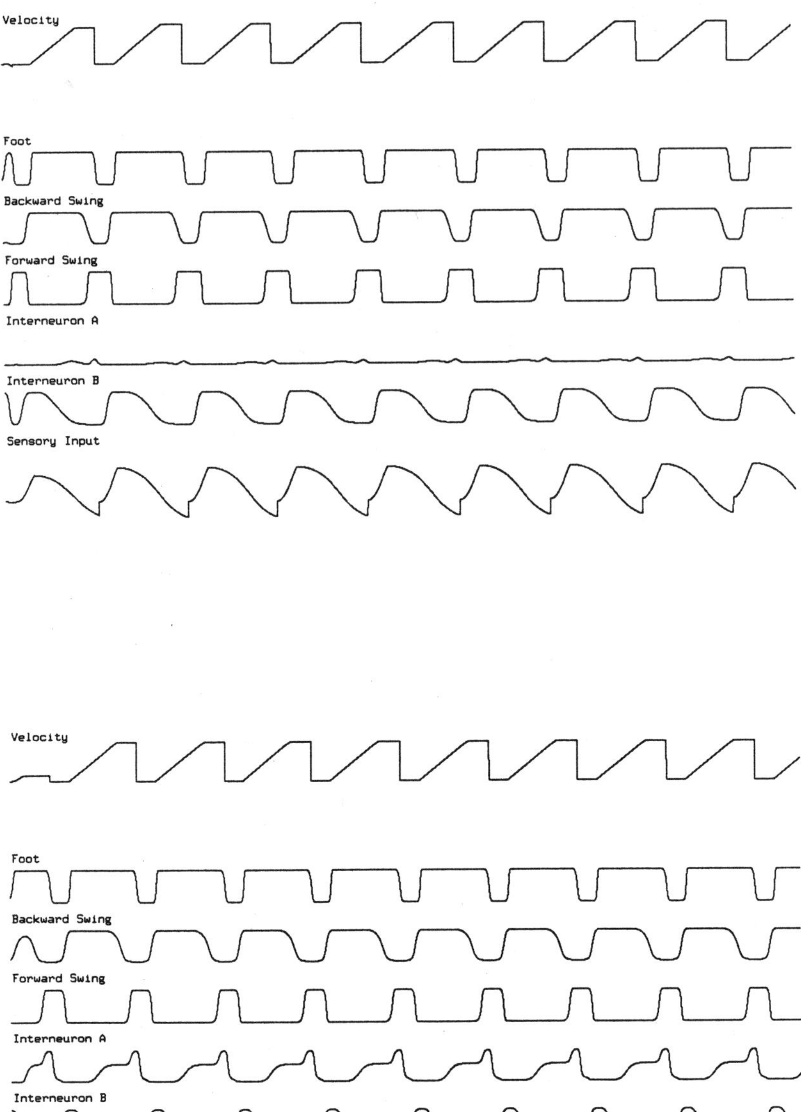

Figure 2: Activity of a typical mixed leg controller with (top) and without (bottom) sensors. The leg was initialized to 95% of its full backward position. Velocity is the forward velocity of the body, sensory input is the value returned by the leg sensor in radians. The remaining signal traces are neuron activation levels.

4 Analysis of a Reflexive Pattern Generator

Each neuron in a reflexive pattern generator receives as a sensory signal the leg's angular position in radians. None of the reflexive pattern generators we evolved were capable of operation when deprived of sensory feedback. This observation suggests that such feedback is vital, but does not tell us much about exactly what the sensory signal is doing.

By making a qualitative study of system *phase plots* (trajectory plots), it is possible to uncover important details that might otherwise go unseen. To illustrate this, we selected a reflexive pattern generator for analysis. A single leg controller has five state variables and thus, a five dimensional trajectory. Since it is difficult to envision spaces of higher that three dimensions, we utilized three dimensional projections of the five space trajectories.

A phase plot of the activities of the foot, forward swing, and backward swing neurons (from here on referred to as a *motor space projection* - see center of Figure 3) demonstrates that this controller is both properly phased and periodic. The foot and backward swing neuron activations are high at the same time, generating a stance, and the forward swing neuron activation is high when both the foot and backward swing are low. The trajectory forms a closed loop, indicating that the generated motor signals are periodic.

In this particular controller, the A and B interneurons both produce constant, zero valued activations. This suggests that the A and B interneurons are not contributing to the generation of this behavior. In fact, we can remove these neurons entirely, replacing them with appropriate constant valued biases, and see no difference in network operation. One should note, however, that other reflexive controllers do use their interneurons to assist in the generation of behavior. In those controllers, removing the interneurons will, in general, damage the generation of appropriate motor signals.

The fact that interneurons can be doing such vastly different things, yet the whole system be able to generate appropriate behavior, is not surprising. The only feature of the controller that is important in determining its fitness is that the system's motor space projection is appropriately phased and periodic. Indeed, we have examples of controllers whose motor space projections are nearly identical, yet show vastly different behaviors in other projections.

The trajectory observed in the center of Figure 3 is an attractor of the coupled body/controller system. At every instant, the trajectory of the coupled system is determined by the dynamics of the controller with sensory input clamped to the value of the leg's angular position at that time. When sensory input changes, the dynamical law governing the system also changes, moving and changing the shapes of both attractors and flows. We can study the attractors governing the behavior of the coupled system trajectory at a given angular position by fixing the sensory input to the value of interest and examining the behavior of the resulting autonomous dynamical system.

The surrounding plots in Figure 3 are motor space projections of the controller with the sensory inputs clamped to values corresponding to the shown leg positions. In each plot, the grey circles denote the state the normally operating, non clamped system, is in when the leg is at the shown position. The black circles denote the fixed points governing the system behavior at those times, and the curves from the gray to black circles show the trajectories the system follows at that leg position. The early portions of each trajectory match closely the path taken by the normally running system (Figure 3, center). This is to be expected, as the path of the body/controller system follows these trajectories instantaneously.

At any given time, the controller is tracking a fixed point. Periodic behavior is being generated because the governing fixed point, and flows to that point, are being continuously shifted as the dynamical law is changed by varying sensory inputs. The switch between swing and stance phases is precipitated by a series of bifurcations which moves the governing fixed point between two corners of the phase space. A detailed discussion of this can be found in Beer, 1992.

We would expect, then, that in this controller, clamping the sensor to any constant value should cause the system to flow to a fixed point and prevent normal, rhythmic walking. THis is exactly what occurs, and is why the reflexive controller can not function without its normal sensory input.

5 Analysis of a Mixed Pattern Generator

Mixed pattern generators operate both with and without sensors. The center of Figure 4 is a motor space plot of the operation of a mixed pattern generator when coupled with the body and provided with normal sensory input. The shape of the trajectory is different than that of the previously discussed reflexive controller. It is, though, periodic and appropriately phased. Since this is all that was selected for, it is the only property we would expect must be shared by successful controllers.

The surrounding plots in Figure 4 are motor space projections taken for the same leg angle values used in Figure 3. As before, each plot shows the flow from the state the system is normally in when the leg is at that position to the attractor governing its flow at that position. As with the previously discussed reflexive con-

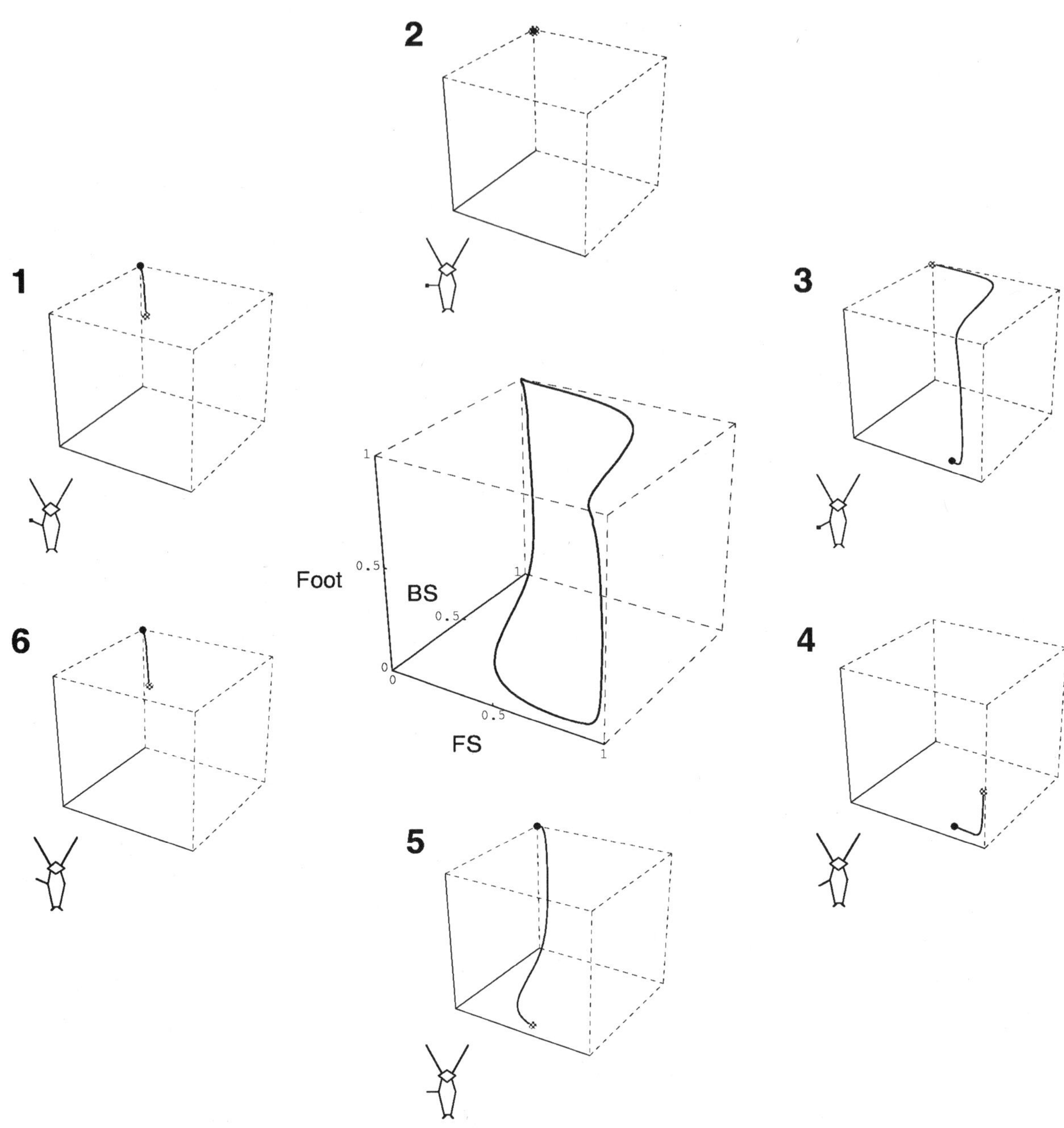

Figure 3: Motor Space Plots of Reflexive Controller. Center plot shows the motor space projection of the activity of the coupled controller/body system. The coupled body/controller system has a limit cycle attractor that is appropriately phased to drive stepping behavior. Surrounding plots show the instantaneous flows the same controller follows at shown leg positions. The coupled system limit cycle is generated as a result of the system following a series of constantly changing, leg position determined, trajectories.

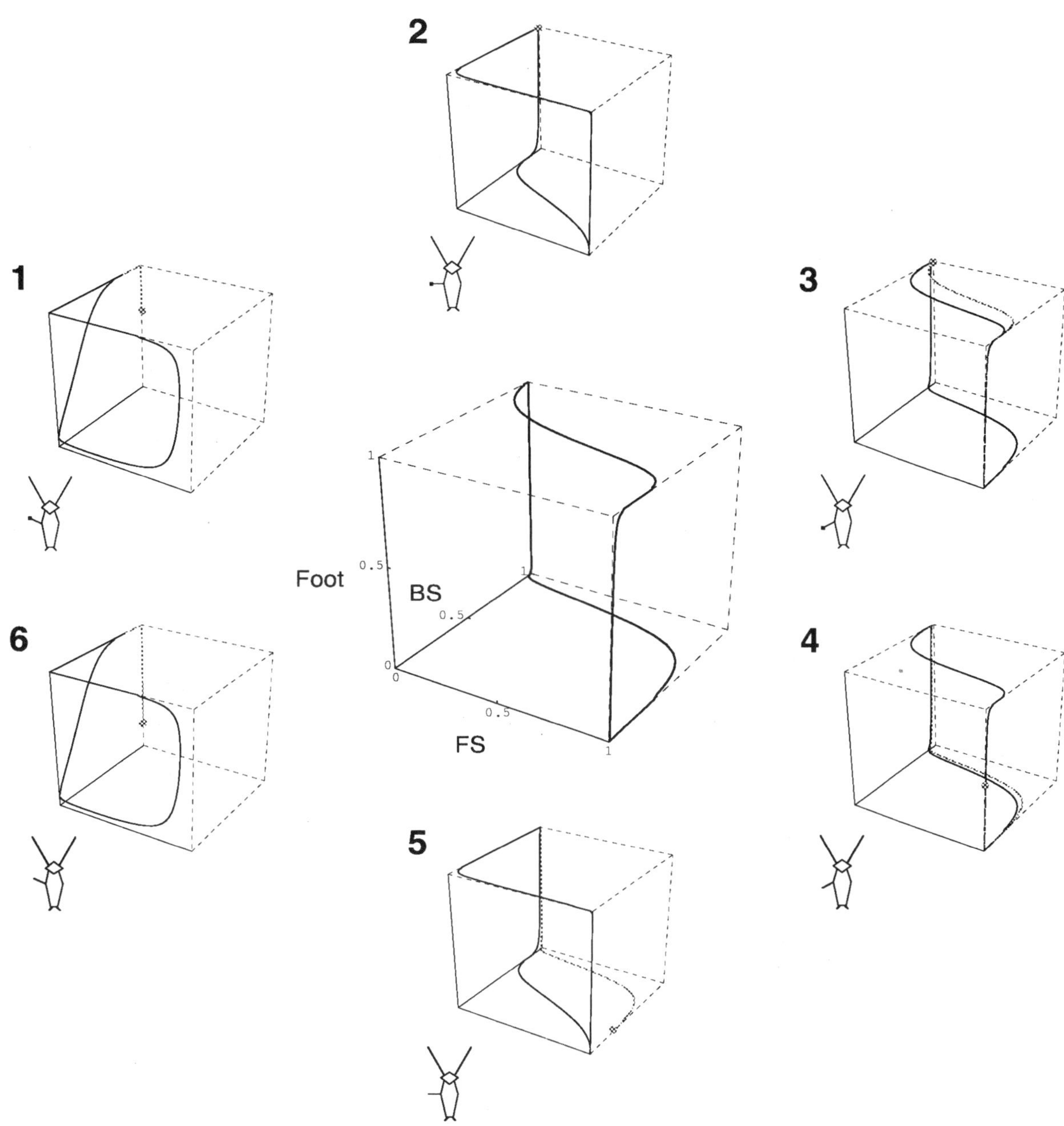

Figure 4: Motor Space Plots of Mixed Controller. Center plot shows motor space projection of coupled controller/body system. Surrounding plots show motor space projections of the same controller with legs fixed at the shown positions. Plotting conventions and system initial conditions for all plots are identical to those used in Figure 3. Attractors are shown with solid lines, transients with dotted lines, and initial state with grey circles. Some plots show no transient because the initial state is already on the attractor.

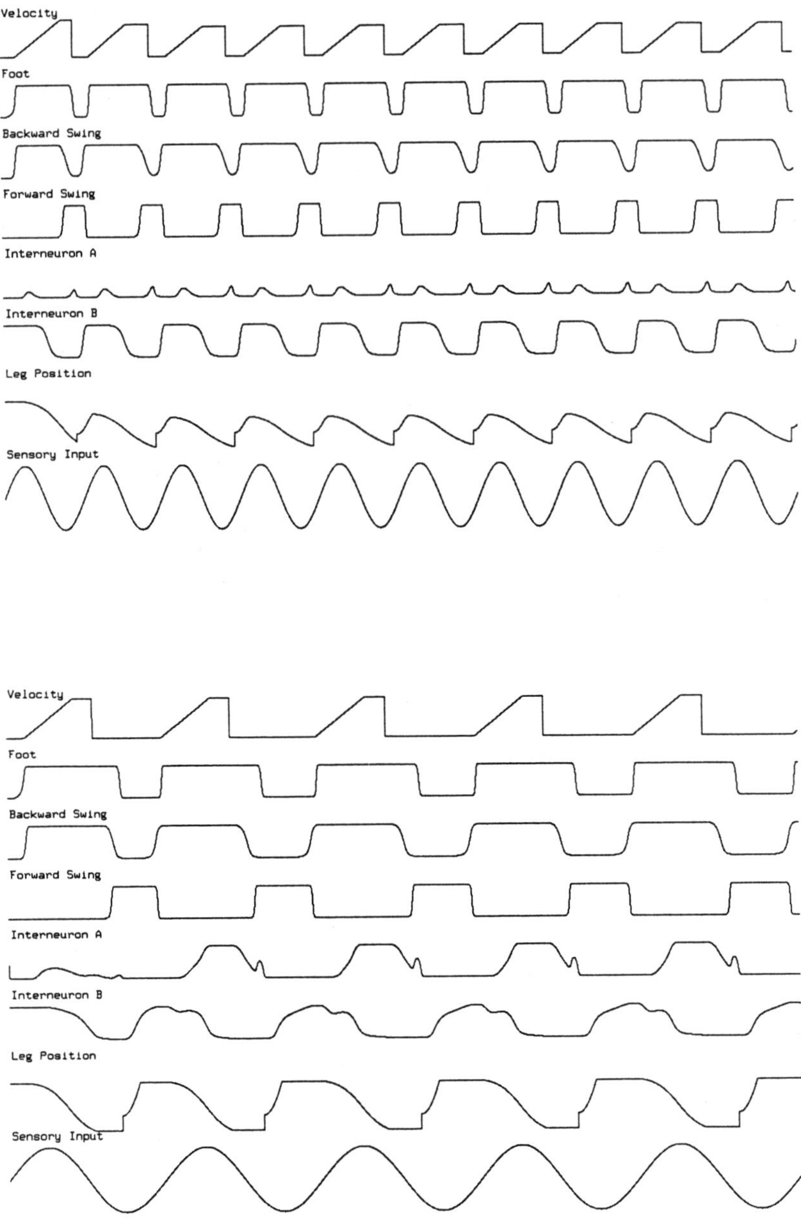

Figure 5: Using entrainment to modify controller frequency. The mixed controller of Figure 2 is driven with faster (top) and slower (bottom) than normal sensory signals. Note the one to one entrainment between the input sensory signal and the motor activation levels.

troller, the trajectory observed when the system is provided with sensory information is a result of the many instantaneous flows generated by the dynamical systems corresponding to each leg position. Unlike with the previous controller, however, the governing attractors are usually limit cycles. The limit cycle corresponding to a sensor value of zero (deprivation of sensors) is appropriately phased to drive stepping behavior. Therefore, unlike with the reflexive controller, removing sensory input does not destroy the generation of appropriate stepping. The system merely flows to its attractor, which itself is appropriately phased to drive stepping.

Since the mixed controller, like the reflexive controller, makes use of its sensory signal to shift the flows and attractors governing the system trajectory, one might think that by changing the rate at which the sensors change, we can also change the rates at which the attractors and flows change, thus either making longer or shorter the periods of the generated control signals. To test whether such entrainment behavior was possible, we detached the mixed controller from the body and drove the sensory input with sine waves of various frequencies. To check that a sine wave was not too gross a distortion of the normal sensory signal, we first supplied the network with a sine signal whose frequency was identical to the normal sensory signal. No difference in activation was observed in any of the five neurons making up the controller.

In the range from about one half to twice the normal sensory frequency, the network's output is 1:1 entrained with the sensory input. This entrainment results in faster or slower, but otherwise normal looking stepping behavior (Figure 5). Below this range, more complicated phase lockings are seen, because the system state has time to orbit the governing limit cycles several times during each period of the sensory input. Above the range of 1:1 entrainment, other entrainment ratios are observed, as several sensory input periods pass in the time it takes the system state to orbit the governing limit cycles. Some of these more accelerated sensory signals, most notably those that entrain 2:1 with the output, also produce normal looking stepping behavior.

6 Adaptation of Mixed Pattern Generator to a Changing Body

Natural control systems, in many cases, do not need many trials to adjust to damage or other changes in the body. A cockroach after a leg amputation, for example, does not stumble about for extended periods of time learning how to deal with its damaged body. It almost immediately reorganizes its gait to compensate for the missing leg (Graham, 1985).

As pointed out in the last section, the frequency of

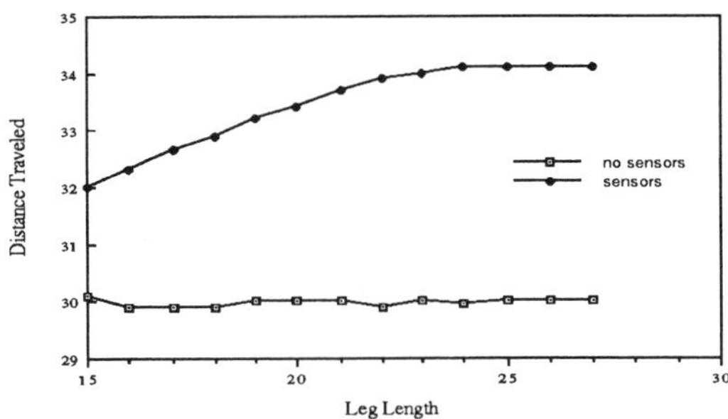

Figure 6: Performance of mixed controller with and without its sensors as the leg grows in length. Note that performance does not improve unless sensory information is available.

the mixed pattern generator's oscillations is entrained by the frequency of the sensory input. An interesting behavioral implication of this fact is that this network is able to adapt its control effort to appropriately drive legs of different lengths. If a leg were to grow in length while the agent was walking, for example, the change in angular position for a given applied torque would be smaller. The mixed controller would entrain to the resulting slower leg frequency and generate longer stance phases. These longer stance phases would utilize the full range of motion of the longer leg. The controller not capable of using sensory information in this way, however, would continue to generate stereotyped control signals that would not take advantage of properties of the changed leg (Figure 6).

The mixed controller shows ability reminiscent the ability of naturally occurring neural controllers to adapt quickly to differing conditions. It also demonstrates that adaptation need not be the result of an explicit learning procedure or overt changes to network structure, but rather, as a natural consequence of the non-linear dynamics governing the controller.

7 Discussion

By using a qualitative analysis of motor space projections, we have been able to understand the dynamics underlying some adaptive features of two evolved locomotion controllers. In so doing, we have demonstrated both the utility of a dynamical system viewpoint, and some of the strengths of dynamical neural networks as a vehicle for implementing controllers for autonomous agents.

Our evolved networks were free to exhibit any dynamics, as long as their motor space projections provided control efforts that moved the body forward. It was not surprising, then, that evolved controllers rarely possed clean architectures whose structures easily relate to their functions. However, by applying dynamical systems techniques, we were nevertheless able to understand their operation. Indeed, we believe that the language of dynamical systems may provide a powerful theoretical framework for autonomous agent research (Beer, 1992).

Our analysis has demonstrated several adaptive features of the evolved controllers. First, we have clearly characterized the role sensory information plays in both the controllers presented. We have explained, in terms of the attractors governing the coupled body/controller systems, why the reflexive pattern generator fails to work without its sensors, and why the mixed pattern generator continues to operate under the same restriction. We have shown that the mixed controller can adapt its motor output to a appropriately drive a changing body because the controller is entrained by the sensory feedback. That such range of function is expressible in only five neurons is testament to the potential power of neural network controllers.

Acknowledgements

We would like to thank Michael Gallagher and Leslie Picardo for their comments on earlier drafts of this paper. This work was supported by Office of Naval Research grant N00014-90-J-1545. Additional support was provided by the Howard Hughes Medical Institute and the Cleveland Advanced Manufacturing Program through the Center for Automation and Intelligent Systems Research at CWRU.

References

Beer, R.D. (1990). *Intelligence as Adaptive Behavior: An Experiment in Computational Neuroethology*. Academic Press.

Beer, R.D. (1992). *A Dynamical Systems Perspective on Autonomous Agents*. Technical Report CES 92-11. Department of Computer Engineering and Science, Case Western Reserve University.

Beer, R.D. and Gallagher, J.C. (1992). Evolving Dynamical Neural Networks for Adaptive Behavior. *Adaptive Behavior* **1**:92-122.

Delcomyn, F. (1980). Neural basis of rhythmic behavior in animals. *Science* **210**:492-498.

Goldberg, D.E. (1989). *Genetic Algorithms in Search, Optimization, and Machine Learning*. Addison-Wesley.

Graham, D. (1985). Pattern and control of walking in insects. *Advances in Insect Physiology*, **18**:31-140.

Holland, J. (1975). *Adaptation in Natural and Artificial Systems*. University of Michigan Press.

Maes, P., Ed. (1991). *Designing Autonomous Agents*. MIT Press.

Meyer, J.A. and Wilson, S.W., Eds. (1991). *From Animals to Animats: Proceedings of the First International Conference on Simulation of Adaptive Behavior*. MIT Press.

Schraudolph, N.N. and Grefenstette, J.J. (1991). A User's Guide to GENESIS 1.1ucsd.

Sherrington, C.S. (1898). Decerebrate Rigidity and Reflex Coordination of Movements. *J. Physiol* (London) **22**:319-332.

Thompson, J.M.T. and Stewart, H.B. (1986) *Nonlinear Dynamics and Chaos*. J. Wiley and Sons.

NEURONAL PARAMETER MAPS AND SIGNAL PROCESSING

Richard A. Altes
Chirp Corporation
8248 Sugarman Drive
La Jolla, CA 92037

ABSTRACT

Animal sensory systems utilize multiple neuronal maps of parameters such as estimated stimulus/source location, instantaneous frequency, delay, amplitude, and motion variables. Maximum (best) responses of tuned neurons comprising such maps are ordered with respect to values of the mapped parameters, but the neurons have overlapping tuning curves. Spatially registered maps from different sensors are overlaid in the optic tectum or superior colliculus, and are connected to corresponding motor maps via large neurons that penetrate through the sensory layers. These properties can be exploited for Bayes optimum estimation of time varying parameters, sequential hypothesis testing, distortion compensation, sensor fusion, and robust multitarget tracking, as well as for interpretation of ongoing experiments in vision, animal echolocation and machine recognition of speech. Comparison with man made signal processors indicates advantages of map-based processors that can be exploited for sensor fusion, radar/sonar imaging, and tracking.

1. INTRODUCTION

In many animals, multiple neuronal maps representing ordered variation of various signal parameters are found in different parts of the brain. Neurons within such maps respond best to particular stimulus parameters; locations of tuned neurons are correlated with ordered values of a mapped parameter. Neighboring neurons within a map often have overlapping tuning curves.

In somatosensation, positions within a cortical map are correlated with different points on the body surface [1], and signal parameters thus represent location. For hearing, vision, electroreception, infrared processing, and animal sonar, location maps are extended beyond the body surface and into the external environment; neurons in internal maps respond best to stimuli at specific points in the space surrounding the animal [2-6]. Overlaid maps extracted from different sensory modalities (vision, hearing, somatosensation) are spatially registered in the superior colliculus of mammals [3] and in the optic tectum of lower order vertebrates [4,5]. In electric fish, motor maps corresponding to sensor or whole animal position are in spatial register with the sensory maps. The motor maps are excited by relatively large neurons with extended dendritic trees that penetrate through the layered sensory maps, combining information from all sensors to control direction of movement [7].

Position or place of origin of a stimulus or echo describes only part of biologically significant information about an object; a map of location represents a subset of important signal parameters. Other parameters include instantaneous frequency and amplitude for hearing, form, motion and color for vision, etc. Neuronal maps for some of these parameters can also be found [6]. How are such maps exploited by animals, and how might artificial versions be used for optimum signal processing and control?

2. AN INTERPRETATION OF NEURONAL EXCITATION IN PARAMETER MAPS

Each neuron in a parameter map is assumed to represent a hypothesis about the mapped parameter vector x corresponding to the neuron's position in the map. Neural excitation may then be related to conditional probabilities or detection statistics such as the log-likelhood function or log-likelihood ratio, prior probability, or posterior probability corresponding to a particular value of x. This viewpoint provides insights into biological data, e.g., (i) the possible utilization of overlapped tuning curves as interpolation functions to compensate for coarseness of neuronal sampling in cortical maps [8], (ii) training mechanisms that exploit imperfect design data via utilization of lateral inhibition or sharpening [9], and (iii) the role of facilitation of some groups of neurons and/or antifacilitation of other groups as a means of reducing the significant degradation (OR-ing effect) that can occur when a large number of equally likely hypotheses are simultaneously tested in the presence of additive noise [8].

3. SEQUENTIAL PROCESSING OF SIGNALS WITH TIME VARYING PARAMETERS

The interpretation of neuronal maps as ordered hypothesis tests provides further insight into neurophysiological data and artificial map-based processors by using concepts from sequential statistical hypothesis testing. Suppose, for example, that node activations in an artificial neuronal map represent updated conditional probabilities of feature values or hypotheses. A mathematical description of such a map follows.

New data at time k consist of a data vector r_k composed of signal samples corrupted by samples of noise and interference. The corresponding signal vector is composed of samples of the signal $s(t,x_k,H_m)$ in an interval starting at time k; the signal is affected by a vector of parameters or features x_k as well as by the signal class H_m. Some of the features represent kinematic variables such as position and motion, while others describe signal attributes (e.g., the frequency band of an auditory stimulus) that are independent of position. The signal classes $\{H_m;\ m=1,\ldots,M\}$ could consist of different phonemes in speech, differently shaped objects in vision, or different targets in animal sonar.

The cumulative set of all data vectors $r_1,r_2,\ldots,r_k$ obtained at and before time k is denoted R_k. The conditional probability of a given feature vector x_k is written $p(x_k|R_k,H_m)$ to represent the fact that feature estimates depend not only on observed input data vectors $R_k=r_1,\ldots,r_k$, but also on signal classification hypotheses $H_1,\ldots,H_M$.

Equations for sequential updating of neuronal excitations are [10,11]

$$p(H_m|R_k,x_k) = \frac{p(r_k|x_k,H_m)p(H_m|R_{k-1},x_k)}{\sum_j p(r_k|x_k,H_j)p(H_j|R_{k-1},x_k)} \quad (1)$$

and

$$p(x_k|R_k,H_m) = \frac{p(r_k|x_k,H_m)p(x_k|R_{k-1},H_m)}{\sum_{x_k} p(r_k|x_k,H_m)p(x_k|R_{k-1},H_m)}. \quad (2)$$

For maximum posterior probability hypothesis testing, the hypothesis that maximizes $p(H_m|R_k)$ is needed, where

$$p(H_m|R_k) = \sum_{x_k} p(H_m|R_k,x_k)p(x_k|R_k) \quad (3)$$

and

$$p(x_k|R_k) = \sum_{m=1}^{M} p(x_k|R_k,H_m)p(H_m|R_{k-1}). \quad (4)$$

Starting with prior probabilities (initial contextual information) $p(x_0|R_0,H_m)$ and $p(H_m|R_0, x_0)$, posterior probabilities can be formed by converting observations into likelihood functions $p(r_k|x_k,H_m)$. Posterior probabilities for observation vector r_1 are used as priors for r_2, and the process is iterated [10]. The likelihood functions $p(r_k|x_k, H_m)$ can be estimated from training data or obtained from predetermined probability distributions (often based on an additive white Gaussian noise assumption). For example, a signal emanating from a specified direction with given delay can be represented as $s(t,x_k,H_m)$, where delay and direction effects are embedded in the parameter vector x_k. In additive, zero-mean Gaussian noise, $p(r_k|x_k,H_m)$ is a multivariate normal distribution with mean vector composed of samples of $s(t,x_k,H_m)$ and covariance matrix determined from the noise.

In the absence of contextual knowledge, the initial prior probabilities for k=1 are uniform over all x_0 and H_m values. The most probable hypothesis after k observations is the one that maximizes $p(H_m|R_k)$ on the left hand side of (3). The right hand side of (3) indicates that such a choice depends on $p(x_k|R_k)$, and (4) shows that this quantity depends on the updated posterior probability of each hypothesis, $p(H_m|R_{k-1})$, m=1,2,..., M. One feature can be favored over another depending upon which hypothesis is favored, and this feature affects the choice of hypothesis on the next iteration of (3). If features are letters in printed text, this phenomenon can be used to explain human insensitivity to typographical errors during rapid reading. Hypothesis dependent feature perception also explains perceptual alternation in some well known visual patterns [11].

The left hand side of (2) at time k-1 is $p(x_{k-1}|R_{k-1},H_m)$, while the right hand side of (2) at time k depends on $p(x_k|R_{k-1}, H_m)$. Sequential utilization of (2) requires prediction of $p(x_k|R_{k-1},H_m)$ from $p(x_{k-1}|R_{k-1},H_m)$, e.g.,

$$p(x_k|R_{k-1},H_m) = \sum_{x_{k-1}} p(x_k|x_{k-1},H_m)p(x_{k-1}|R_{k-1},H_m). \quad (5)$$

For a Markov process, $p(x_k|x_{k-1}, H_m)$ corresponds to a transition probability matrix [12]. Inclusion of (5) in a sequential hypothesis test allows the test to exploit temporal feature variations (e.g., motion-induced changes) that are different for different hypotheses, e.g., different transition probability matrices for H_i and H_j [13]. Sequential estimation of a parameter x is illustrated in Fig. 1, where the dynamic model is given by (5).

4. SEQUENTIAL HYPOTHESIS TESTING AND INTERACTIVE ACTIVATION

A sequential hypothesis test for maximum a posteriori detection/classification is similar to recursive updating found in a variety of cognitive models [14], especially in interactive activation networks [15]. As in interactive activation, neural excitations at time k+1 are recursively updated using excitations of all neurons in a map (or in several interconnected maps) at time k together with input data observed at time k+1.

Sequential hypothesis testing differs from many interactive activation networks, however, in that repeated iterations based on the same input observation are unnecessary; a single iteration of the sequential test combines new input data with past excitations to determine current excitations. This iteration theoretically extracts all relevant information from the input data. Multiple iterations based on the same input signal, as in interactive activation networks, are useful for sequential hypothesis testing only if the signal is corrupted by different, decorrelated external or internal noise samples for different observations, or if different observations have different resolution as in peripheral vs. foveal vision.

5. DISTORTION COMPENSATION

Many biological sensory systems are capable of recognizing time-warped signals (as in continuous speech) and distorted images. Dynamic distortion compensation [24] can be implemented via sequential processing with neuronal maps by finding the admissible distortion of each hypothesized template such that the distorted template best fits the data.

For distortion compensation, the parameter vector x describes the new locations of signal/image samples or instantaneous frequency components that are originally uniformly spaced. Admissible distortions determine the transition probability matrix in (5). For additive, white Gaussian noise, the admissibly distorted template at time k that has the highest correlation with data up to time k yields the posterior probability distribution with the largest peak value.

6. SENSOR FUSION

An important capability of biological systems is the synthesis or fusion of data from dif-

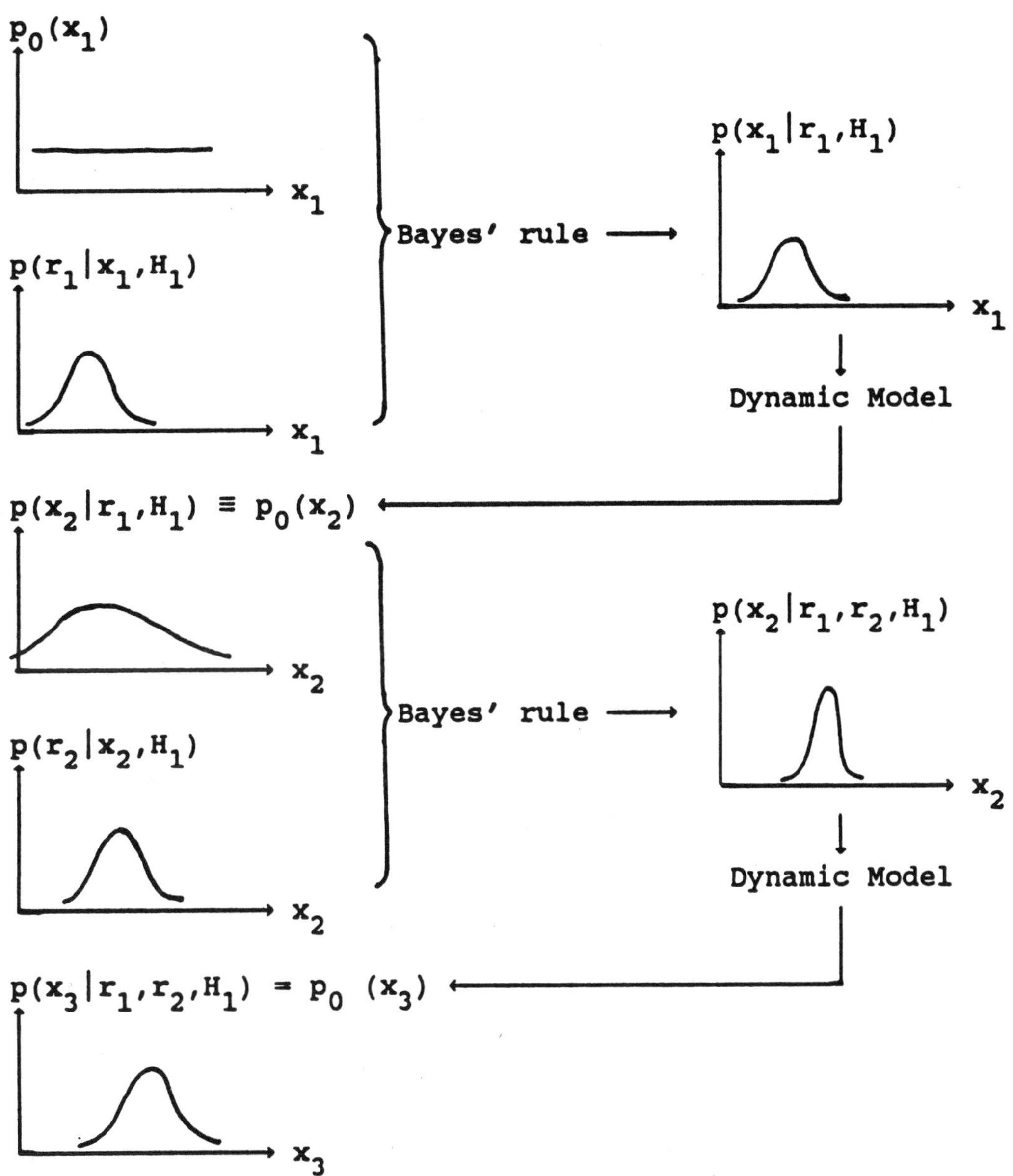

Figure 1. Sequential likelihood estimation of a time varying parameter x (tracking); r_k = observation vector at time k; x_k = unknown random variable at time k. The smaller the variance of $p(x_k|r_1,\ldots,r_k,H_1)$, the more accurate the parameter estimate. In an artificial neuronal map, sample values of probability distributions along the x-axis correspond to excitations of neurons at ordered locations within the map; neural excitations at time k correspond to sample values along the x_k axis. The illustrated operations could involve three different maps or could be performed on a single map with appropriate interconnections between processing elements.

ferent sensory modalities so as to respond appropriately to a real-world event. A multivariate classifier for sensor fusion can use overlaid, spatially registered sensor maps as in [3]-[5]. Data corresponding to each point in the environment at time k, as simultaneously perceived by each of the different sensors, is represented on each map. A composite data vector r_k is constructed by combining data samples from a given environmental location x_k as measured by the various sensors at time k. An expected composite signal vector corresponding to hypothesis H_m is compared with the concatenated data vector r_k to generate the likelihood function $p(r_k|x_k,H_m)$. Sequential processing as in (1)-(5) is then used to update the posterior probabilities of H_1, $\ldots,H_M$ given observed data R_k = $r_1,r_2,\ldots,r_k$ at various positions. This process is simplified by using spatially registered maps as in animal sensory systems, such that environmental location x_k corresponds to the same point in maps obtained from different sensors.

Acoustic and visual data, for example, could contribute to each observation vector r_1,r_2,r_3 in Fig. 1. Inconsistent versions of such data for hypothesis H_1 (e.g., a flying insect) will cause spreading and a smaller peak value of the posterior distribution $p(x_3|r_1,r_2,r_3,H_1)$ in the Figure.

The model can be used to interpret neurophyological data as well as to design man made fusion systems. If the sensor outputs are statistically independent, the log-likelihood function obtained with a concatenated data vector is the same as the sum of log-likelihood functions from the individual sensors. The large, multipolar neurons used to combine neuronal excitations in overlaid, spatially registered maps from different sensors should then function as linear summation devices, as observed in [16].

An equivalent approach to sensor fusion [17] is to apply the procedure in (1)-(5) to each sensor in turn, repeating the process for each new observation. This method is useful if signal parameters are time invariant or vary slowly relative to processing time. For time varying parameters, however, it is advantageous to use a concatenated data vector or sum of log-likelihood functions that represents the outputs of all the different sensors at the same time and at the same point in space. Overlaid, spatially registered sensor output representations, as in biological sensory systems, are well designed to perform the desired operations. At point x_k, sensor fusion is performed by neurons with synaptic connections in all the sensory maps [7]; such neurons physically penetrate through all the overlaid, spatially registered maps from different sensors at each position.

A biomimetic approach thus uses parallel processing of large signal and data vectors derived from simultaneous observation of spatial position x_k by all available sensors, as opposed to sequential processing of smaller data vectors from each sensor in turn. The biomimetic method is advantageous for rapidly time varying parameters and is easily implemented with overlaid, spatially registered maps.

7. MULTITARGET TRACKING AND DATA INTERPRETATION

The formulation in (1)-(5) automatically allows multiple objects to be tracked simultaneously with a sensor fusion system, provided that each object or target corresponds to a different hypothesis. Tracking of the mth object involves updating position and velocity variables in a kinematic feature vector x_k for hypothesis H_m, as in (2). Pruning hypotheses by dropping inconsistent tracks is easily accomplished, since such tracks will have low posterior probability $p(H_m | R_k)$ relative to more promising trajectories. The sequential hypothesis test differs from an error-driven tracker such as a Kalman filter in that a single predicted parameter vector and the corresponding observation is avoided; probabilities of all possible future parameter values are predicted at each iteration. Sequential likelihood ratio tracking is thus robust against loss of track induced by a large difference between predicted and actual observations.

If different hypotheses represent different data interpretations, e.g., different interpretations of connected speech, then correct interpretations can theoretically be accentuated and erroneous interpretations can be pruned via sequential signal processing with neuronal maps. A data understanding system can be conceived as a multi-target (multiple hypothesis) tracker in a suitable parameter space. Unconscious visual tracking capability in brain damaged humans [18] can be explained by an autonomic version of the tracker in Fig. 1. Conscious awareness of a stimulus in a normal brain could occur when a posterior distribution on the right side of Fig. 1 becomes sufficiently concentrated that its maximum value exceeds a threshold of consciousness.

8. MEMORY-EFFICIENT IMAGING FOR RADAR, SONAR, AND ECHOLOCATION

An environmental map based on sequentially processed echolocation data is a biologically inspired concept that has immediate application to man made radar/sonar imaging systems. Using a line segment (rotated wavelet) transform [11,19], a radar/sonar with poor azimuth/bearing resolution but with fine range resolution can use multiple observations from different locations to construct a target image with fine resolution in two dimensions rather than just one. The space-time transmission patterns used by echolocating dolphins are similar to the line segment (rotated wavelet) basis functions that are needed to implement this process [11], suggesting that a similar technique may be exploited by the animals.

An environmental map composed of recursive sum-and-store elements can be used for memory efficient, real-time line segment transform imaging [11]. If the map can be referenced to a point in the environment rather than to the transmitter/receiver location, then the same storage element in the internal map can refer to the same location in the environment, regardless of transmitter/receiver position. In line segment transform processing, cumulative summation of match-filtered echo data from a given object, as perceived from different transmitter/receiver locations, yields an image of the object. A radar/sonar image can then be recursively constructed by updating echo data at each point in an environmental map as the transmitter/receiver changes position. This process uses memory very efficiently during image construction; if data from each transmitter/receiver position were stored separately, memory requirements would be extremely demanding.

Utilization of this concept by echolocating animals would require the capability to associate the same external point perceived on different self-referenced maps for different positions of the animal.

9. SEQUENTIAL ESTIMATION IN ANIMAL ECHOLOCATION

Sequential estimation, as implemented by an artificial neural network, has been used to model pulse to pulse accumulation of information by a dolphin during target discrimination [20,21]. Estimation of echo energy spectral density via a cumulative average is represented in Fig. 1 as a more general process for estimating the probability distribution of the energy of each frequency component. Sequential estimation of a probability distribution as in Fig. 1 is equivalent to a receiver based on simple averaging of squared frequency components if the distribution can be constructed from the averaged quantities, as in the case of the gamma distribution [22]. The resulting hypothesis test for target classification is synthesized as in (3), and is not necessarily the same as substituting estimated parameters (feature values) into a classifier (e.g., nearest neighbors in feature space).

10. INSIGHT INTO SOMATOSENSATION

It has been assumed that neurons within a parameter map represent ordered hypothesis tests for stimuli with the relevant parameters. Although this viewpoint is useful for biomimetic signal processing, is it relevant to actual biological sensory systems? The concept of neurons as hypothesis tests can in fact be used to understand somatosensory receptive field changes after digit amputation in monkeys [23].

Observed receptive field changes are explained by a model in which the stimulus location hypothesis made by each cortical neuron is unaffected by ampution or equivalent damage, imperfect exemplars are used for training, and lateral inhibition exists between peripheral receptors [9].

11. SUMMARY AND CONCLUSION

Sensory parameter maps similar to those found in the brain can be exploited for Bayes optimum sequential signal processing. The resulting architecture yields efficient implementation of a variety of signal processors and cognitive models.

REFERENCES

[1] E.R. Kandel and J.H.Schwartz, Principles of Neural Science, 2nd Ed. New York: Elsevier, 1985.
[2] M. Konishi, "Centrally synesized maps of sensory space," Trends in Neuro Sciences 9 (1986) 163-168.
[3] V.C. Drager and D.H. Hubel, "Responses to visual stimulation and relationship between visual, auditory, and somatosensory inputs in the mouse superior colliculus," J. Neurophysiol. 38 (1975) 690-713.
[4] C.E. Carr and L. Maler, "Electroreception in gymnotiform fish," in Electroreception, T.H. Bullock and W. Heiligenberg, eds. (Wiley, New York, 1986) 319-373.
[5] E.A. Newman and P.H.Hartline, "The infrared 'vision' of

snakes," Sci. Amer. 246 (1982) 116-124.

[6] N. Suga, "The extent to which biosonar information is represented in the bat auditory cortex," in Dynamic Aspects of Neocortical Function, G.M. Edelman, W.E.Gall, and W.M. Cowan, eds. (Wiley, New York, 1984) pp. 315-373.

[7] W. Heiligenberg and G.J. Rose, "The optic tectum of the gymnotiform electric fish, Eigenmannia: Labelling of physiologically identified cells," Neuroscience 22 (1987), 331-340.

[8] R.A. Altes, "An interpretation of cortical maps in echolocating bats," J. Acous. Soc. Am. 85 (1989) 934-942.

[9] R.A. Altes, "A histogram-based recursively trained classifier as a model for somatosensation," IEEE Trans. on Systems, Man, and Cybernetics 21 (1991) 1586-1593.

[10] L.W. Nolte, "Theory of signal detectability: Adaptive optimum receiver design," J. Acoust. Soc. Am. 42 (1967) 773-777.

[11] R.A. Altes, "The line segment transform and sequential hypothesis testing in dolphin echolocation," in Sensory Abilities of Aquatic Mammals, J. Thomas, R. Kastelein, and A. Supin, eds. (Plenum, New York, 1992).

[12] E. Parzen, Modern Probability Theory and Its Applications (Wiley, New York, 1960) 136-141.

[13] L.W. Nolte, "Adaptive processing: Time-varying parameters," in Signal Processing, J.W. R. Griffiths, P.L. Stocklin, and C. van Schooneveld, eds. (Academic Press, London, 1973) 647-656.

[14] S. Grossberg, "Nonlinear neural networks: Principles, mechanisms, and architectures,"Neural Networks 1 (1988) 17-61.

[15] D.L. Waltz and J.B. Pollack, "Massively parallel parsing: A strongly interactive model of natural language interpretation," Cognitive Science 9 (1985) 51-74.

[16] J. Bastian, "Electrolocation: Behavior, anatomy, and physiology," in Electroreception, op. cit., 577-612.

[17] R.R. Tenney and N.R.Sandell, Jr., "Detection with distributed sensors," IEEE Trans. on Aerosp. and Electron. Sys. AES-17 (1981) 501-510.

[18] F. Crick and C. Koch, "The problem of consciousness," Sci. Am. 267, No. 3 (Sept. 1992) 153-159.

[19] Altes, R. A., "Generalized wavelet analysis, the line segment transform, tomography, and vision," Proc. 1991 IEEE International Symposium on Information Theory, Budapest, Hungary, IEEE Cat. No. 91CH3003-1 (1991) 130.

[20] H.L. Roitblatt, P.W.B.Moore, P.E. Nachtigall, and R.H. Penner, "Natural dolphin echo recognition using an integrator gateway network," in Advances in Neural Information Processing Systems 3, R. P. Lippmann, J. E. Moody, and D. S. Touretzky, eds. (Morgan Kaufmann, San Mateo, 1991) 273-281.

[21] H.L. Roitblatt, R.H. Penner, and P.E. Nachtigall, "Matching-to-sample by an echolocating dolphin," J. Exp. Psych: Animal Behav. Proc. 16 (1990) 85-95.

[22] A.D. Whalen, Detection of Signals in Noise (Academic, New York, 1971) 112.

[23] M.M. Merzenich, R.J. Nelson, M.P. Stryker, M.S. Cynander, A. Schoppmann, and J.M. Zook, "Somatosensory cortical map changes following digit amputation in adult monkeys," J. Comp. Neurol. 224 (1984) 591-605.

[24] H. Sakoe and S. Chiba, "Dynamic programming algorithm optimization for spoken word recognition," IEEE Trans. on Acoust., Speech, Sig. Proc. ASSP-26 (1978) 43-49.

Representation and Processing of Acoustic Information in a Biomimetic Neural Network

Herbert L. Roitblat,[1] Patrick W. B. Moore,[2] David A. Helweg,[1] & Paul E. Nachtigall[2]

[1]University of Hawaii-Manoa, [2]NRaD/NCCOSC

Abstract

The effectiveness of artificial neural network models, depends strongly on the way in which the information to be learned is presented to the network. Use of biologically relevant mechanisms is likely to yield effective synthetic systems as well as understanding the performance of biological systems. We developed a model of the dolphin cochlea and used this model to produce the representations used by a neural network to model the delayed matching-to-sample performance of a bottlenosed dolphin. The model yielded psychophysical functions and matching choice accuracy similar to those obtained from the dolphin.

1. Introduction

The deployment of robots and other artificial creatures or "animats" depends strongly on the development of adequate perceptual and conceptual mechanisms for perceiving and recognizing objects and for navigation. Artificial neural networks are uniquely suited for solving problems in pattern recognition, signal detection in noise, speech recognition and adaptive control, and are likely to play an important role in animat development. These networks also offer a useful computational technique for modeling and studying biological processes both because of their effectiveness in biologically important tasks and because their structure resembles natural biological information processing architectures. Complementarily, we can use the information gained from investigations of biological performance to guide the structural development of artificial systems that accomplish analogous tasks. We can, in a sense, "reverse engineer" computational models from successful biological systems to aid in understanding the biological system.

The effectiveness of artificial neural network models, depends, in large part, on the way in which the information to be learned is presented to the network. There are no well established rules to guide the selection of these representations. However, an obvious and plausible source for direction in this process, is to incorporate what is already known about the way in which the biological systems being modeled represent important information, that is, to identify the features of the environment that control the animal's behavior and to identify the means by which such information is represented. Construction of artificial systems that implement functions performed by biological systems can benefit from the same, or close to the same mechanisms, as those used by the biological system. Use of biologically relevant mechanisms, represented with increasing fidelity, is likely to help us produce increasingly effective synthetic systems and to help us to understand the performance of their biological counterparts. Models aid understanding and they facilitate applications.

2. Dolphin Hearing & Sonar

Dolphins provide an excellent paradigm for developing artificial neural network models of biological signal categorization. Their categorization performance has been well studied, so there is ample background and a well-developed methodology for investigating these capabilities. They provide a well-bounded problem and demonstrate the solution of that problem, thereby indicating that biological-sonar-based recognition of various kinds of targets is feasible. Dolphins are of immediate practical importance in that they can be trained to recognize practical signals from real objects and to perform important tasks with those objects. Finally, this laboratory has already begun the development of various kinds of models for the decision processes (Roitblat et al., 1990) and for the sensory processes (Au, 1980) that the dolphin uses in object recognition, and have developed some preliminary neural network models (Moore et al., 1991; Roitblat et al., 1991).

In addition to excellent visual capabilities comparable to those seen in other terrestrial mammals, dolphins interrogate their environment by sending out clicks from their rounded forehead or melon. The clicks reflect from objects that are directly in front of the dolphin and return characteristic echoes, from which the dolphin can extract information about the location and many features of the object (Nachtigall, 1980). Because the dolphin must emit clicks in order to engage its biological sonar and because the clicks are separated in time from other clicks, each echo corresponds to a discrete packet of information. The quantal nature of dolphin echoes greatly simplifies the problems associated with modeling continuous information acquisition mechanisms.

The biological sonar capabilities of the bottlenose dolphin (*Tursiops truncatus*) far exceed those of any artificial systems at object detection, recognition and many other close-range (i.e., with in about 100 m) tasks. Dolphin echolocation signals emerge as a series of ultrasonic clicks from the melon as a highly directional sound beam with 3 dB (half power) beam widths of approximately 10° in both the vertical and horizontal planes (Au, Moore, & Pawloski, 1986). Dolphin echolocation clicks are broadband, have peak energy at frequencies ranging from 40 to 130 kHz, and source levels of up to 220 dB re: 1 uPa or higher (Au, 1980; Moore & Pawloski, 1990). Bottlenose dolphins have excellent directional hearing (Au & Moore, 1984) and a wide range of frequency sensitivity, spanning over seven octaves. The dolphin is sensitive to frequencies seven to 10 times (four octaves) higher than can be detected by humans, and can detect frequencies as high as 150 kHz (Johnson, 1966). The animal is maximally sensitive to frequencies in the 40 - 80 kHz range (e.g., Johnson, 1967).

Both the dolphin's signal production and hearing are specifically adapted to the underwater acoustic environment. Although both bats and dolphins use echolocation, the characteristics of the medium in which their signals are emitted, the mechanisms by which the signals are produced, the type of signals and the neurological apparatus they use to processes those signals differ substantially (Zook, Myron, Ilya, & Morgane, 1988; Zvorykin, 1959, 1963). Bat biosonar is adapted for use in air, whereas dolphin biosonar is adapted for use underwater. Bat biosonar signals are relatively long in duration (up to several ms), and contain both narrow band constant-frequency and FM-modulated components depending on the species (Bellwood, 1988; Fenton, 1988; Suthers, 1988). By contrast the dolphin echolocation signal is very broadband and extremely short (about 50 μsec).

The anatomy of the dolphin ear also displays aquatic specialization. Cetacean cochleas correspond generally to the standard mammalian design, with certain specializations. The standard mammalian ear consists of a tympanic membrane, which is in contact with the atmosphere and is the typical means by which sounds are transduced from the environment into the hearing system. The tympanic membrane connects via a series of ossicles to the cochlea, which in most mammals is a spiral rather snail-shaped structure. If the cochlea were to be unrolled, it would have a cone-like shape with the oval window occupying its base. Within, and running the length of the cochlea is the basilar membrane. Sounds enter the cochlea through the oval window and excite vibrations on the basilar membrane. Because of the shape and stiffness characteristics of the basilar membrane, different frequencies differentially excite standing waves at specific locations along the membrane (Bekesy, 1944; Fletcher, 1940; Helmholtz, 1863). The inner hair cells contact the basilar membrane and transduce the movement of the membrane into neural signals for processing by the brain (Hudspeth, 1985).

Species-specific anatomical characteristics of the ears of whales and dolphins relate to the echolocation signals they produce and to the particular habitat and feeding behavior these animals exploit (Ketten, 1992). Among the specializations seen in the cetacean ear are isolation of the bulla from the surrounding skull, fusion and enlargement of the ossicular chain, and specializations in the shape of the basilar membrane and osseous spiral laminae, which support it. The thickness and width of the dolphin basilar membrane, like that of other mammalian species varies monotonically from the base to the apex. Highest frequencies are encoded in the thicker, narrower portions of the membrane near the base and progressively lower frequencies are represented toward the apex as the membrane thins and broadens (Ketten, 1984, 1992; Wever, 1971a, 1971b). The dimensions of the basilar membrane suggest that dolphin ears are capable of an exceptionally wide frequency response. This prediction is consistent with the audiometric data.

Hair cells are approximately evenly distributed along the membrane at the density of about 100 inner hair cells per mm (Ketten, 1992). The hair cells synapse on ganglion cells, whose axons form the auditory eighth nerve. Tursiops ears contain approximately 105,000 ganglion cells distributed about evenly along the 41.6 mm length of the basilar membrane (i.e., averaging about 2,526 ganglion cells per mm of membrane length). In comparison the human ear contains about 30,500 ganglion cells distributed along 31 mm of basilar membrane, for an average of about 984 ganglion cells per mm. Ganglion cell densities are higher in odontocetes than in any other mammal and the ratio of

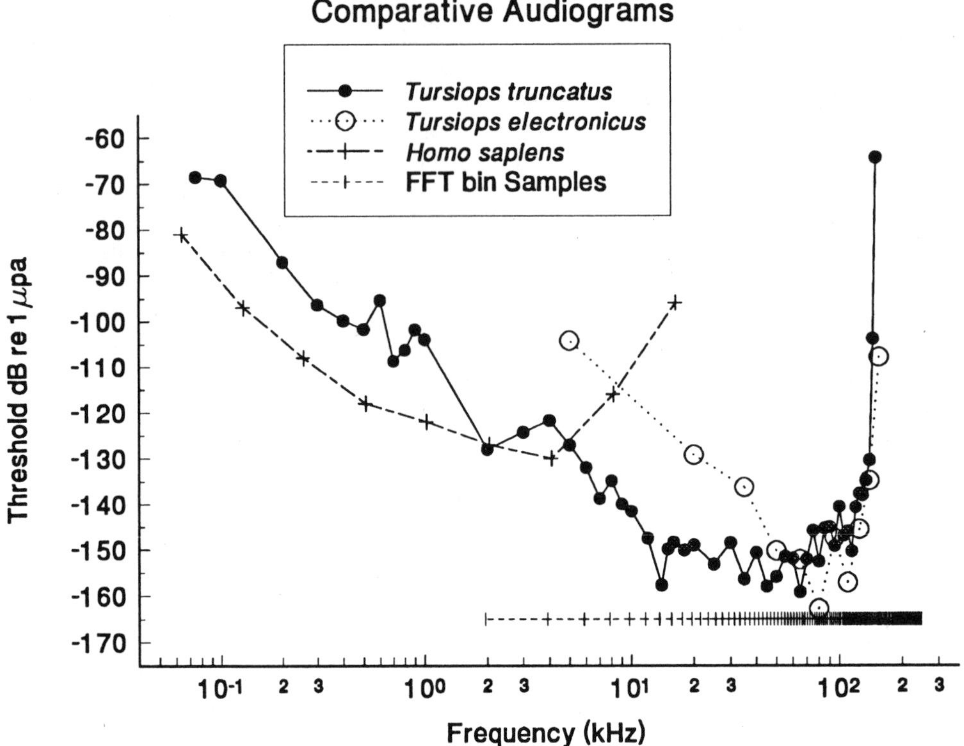

Figure 1. Dolphin, human, and simulated audiograms. FFT bin samples show the frequency resolution of the underlying spectrum on which the simulations were based.

ganglion cells to inner hair cells is about twice that in bats and about three times that in humans (Ketten & Wartzok, 1990).

Some properties of dolphin psychophysics are known. For example, dolphin frequency discrimination limens (ΔF) correspond approximately to Weber's Law: A stimulus must be increased by a constant proportion (ΔF) of its value to be "just noticeably different" (Weber, 1846). If the dF is the smallest discriminable difference, then $\Delta F/F = K$, a constant. Another way of stating this relationship is that the graph of log ΔF versus log F is a straight line. At frequencies near 1 kHz, dolphins can discriminate frequencies differing by about 6 Hz; at 100 kHz, the smallest discriminable difference is approximately 800 Hz (Herman & Arbeit, 1972; Thompson & Herman, 1975). An exponential function fit to these data had an exponent of approximately 1.09, supporting the near linearity of this function.

Figure 1 shows the dolphin's audiogram (Johnson, 1967; Morozov, Akopian, Burdin, Donskov, Zaytseva, & Sokovykh, 1971). The dolphin's hearing is relatively insensitive at low frequencies and at very high frequencies above 150 kHz. Hearing tends to be most sensitive in the range between 40 and 80 kHz.

The frequency response of the basilar membrane and the distribution of inner hair cells and ganglion cells suggest that each ganglion cell functions as a band-pass frequency filter. Because of the cochlear characteristics described earlier, specific frequencies differentially excite the hair cells located in specific portions of the basilar membrane. Hence, each hair cell responds maximally to a limited range of frequencies according to how much those frequencies affect its location on the membrane. The ganglion cells combine activation from multiple hair cells distributed along a limited range on the membrane, and as a result, are differentially sensitive to a particular frequency band.

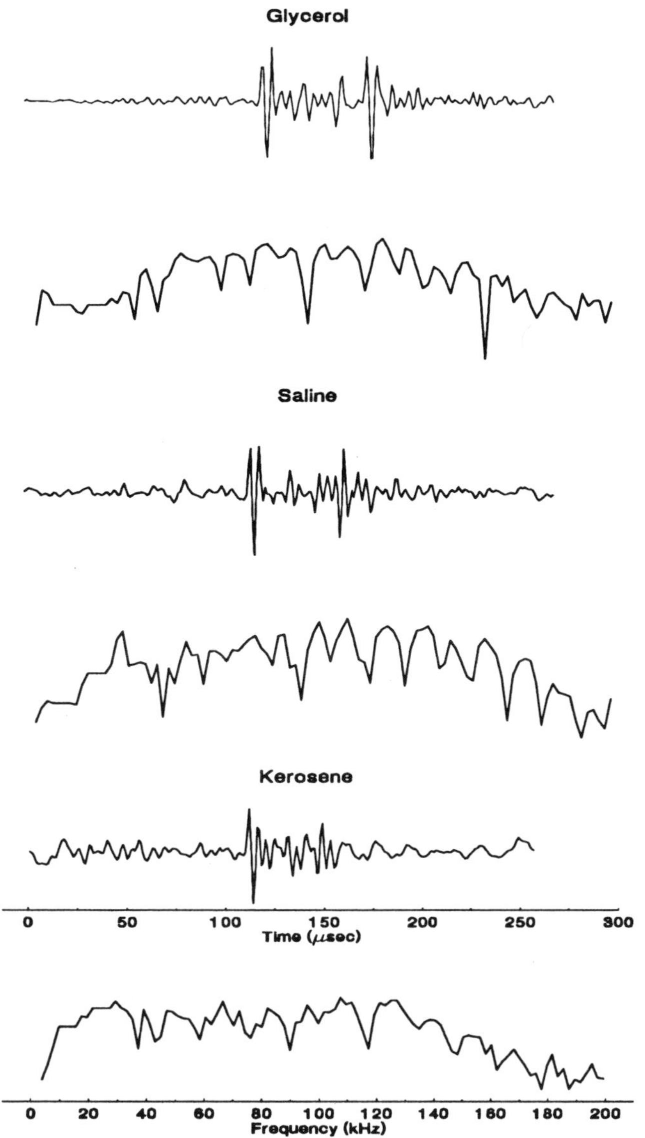

Figure 2. Example waveforms and spectra for the three target types used.

3. The Dolphin's Task

The dolphin performed a matching-to-sample task (see Roitblat et al., 1990 for details). Wearing soft removeable eyecups, the dolphin stationed under water and directed its echolocation clicks at a submerged target located in front of it. Following the dolphin's examination of this target, it was removed from the water and three other targets were placed in the water. The dolphin then echolocated on these targets and selected the target that most resembled the sample. The identity of the sample varied randomly from trial to trial and the location of the matching alternative also varied randomly from trial to trial, so the dolphin had to identify and remember the sample in order to correctly chose the matching comparison target.

We captured and digitized the dolphin's outgoing clicks and returning echoes that were directed at and reflected from the sample and the center comparison target. Clicks were obtained using a B&K 8103 hydrophone placed in the path between the dolphin and the center targets and echoes were obtained using a custom-built hydrophone placed next to dolphin. Signals were digitized at 500 kHz using an RC-Electronics A/D converter and custom-written software.

The stimuli used for the matching task were fuel bottles containing different materials--glycerol, physiological saline, and kerosene. All stimuli were identical in their outer form, differing only in their internal constituents. Example echo waveforms and spectra are

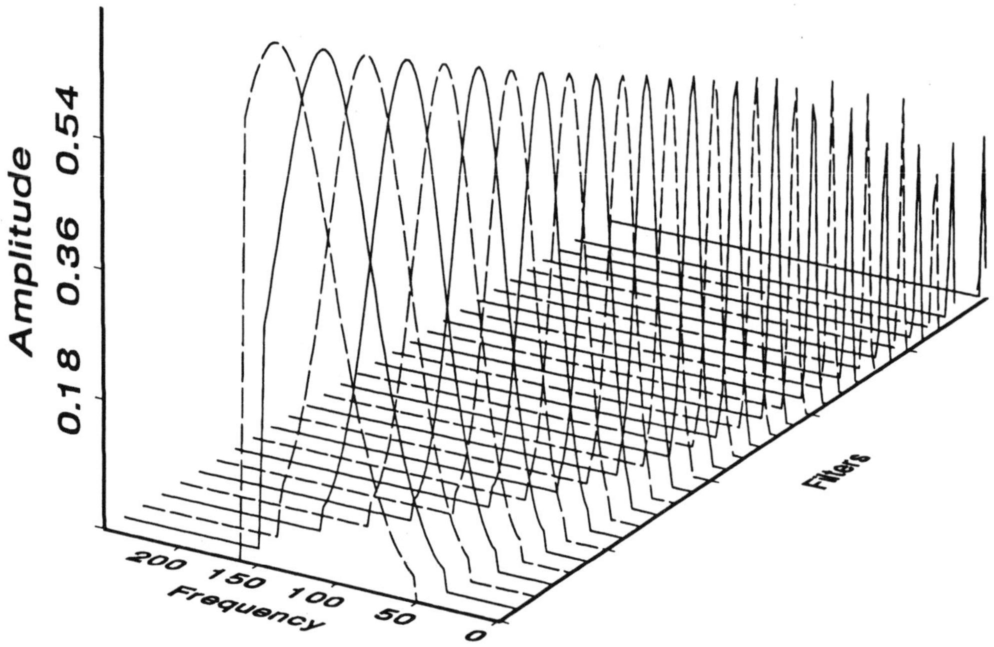

Figure 3. The filters used in the cochlear model.

shown in Figure 2. These stimuli were apparently very difficult to discriminate because the dolphin's choice accuracy was only 50%. Chance accuracy with three alternatives is 33%.

4. Model

We used the known facts about the dolphin ear and hearing to construct a computational model of the dolphin's ear that could be used to create principled inputs for our neural net model of the dolphin's decision processes. In developing any model, one must necessarily make simplifying assumptions. Some of these assumptions are dictated by computational constraints (e.g., the capacity of the computer's memory and time to perform the computations), some are dictated by other physical or electronic constraints. Our model also includes a further constraint in that we wanted to be able to compare the performance of the model with that of previous models we developed for similar tasks, and we wanted to compare the model to the dolphin's performance.

Our basic data for input to the network consist of digitized 256-point waveforms, sampled at 500 kHz and transformed via an FFT to a 128 bin spectrum. Each bin represents the energy in an approximately 1.95 kHz wide band. Because the hearing of the dolphin falls off so sharply between 140 and 150 kHz we selected the first 85 bins for further processing. For computational reasons and in order to compare the present model to previous models, we needed a 30 bin vector to summarize the relevant frequency information. In previous investigations we had averaged pairs of adjacent frequency bins between 31 and 150 kHz. All frequencies in this earlier model were represented equally--each bin represented a constant bandwidth. The evidence described above, however, suggests that in the ear, bandwidth varies with the frequency being measured. Lower frequencies are represented with narrower band "channels" than higher frequencies. The number of inner hair cells and ganglion cells in the dolphin ear is approximately constant over the length of the basilar membrane suggesting that each unit of length contributes about equally to representation of the signal. The range of frequencies represented by each segment of basilar membrane, however, is not constant. Near the base, each unit of basilar membrane length represents a broader range of high frequencies relative to the narrow range of lower frequencies represented near the apex.

In the present model we sought to generate the representational vector to correspond to known features of dolphin ears. Many of the parameters were selected on the basis of rough estimates, and the resolution of the model was fairly crude, nevertheless, such exercises are likely to be valuable in the long run in the development of effective biomimetic mechanisms.

The sensitivity of the ear was represented as a bank of 30 bandpass filters. Each filter had a Gaussian shape, meaning that it was most sensitive to its center frequency and had diminished sensitivity with increasing distance from the center. The center frequency of each of the 30 filters was selected according to Eq. 1:

$$\text{CenterFreq} = 160 \times \text{EXP}(-.1392 \times (i)) \qquad (1)$$

in which i ranged from 1 to 30. This equation (Ketten, 1992, personal communication) is an estimate derived from the stiffness and size of the basilar membrane. According to this equation, the filters are approximately equally spaced along the length of the basilar membrane.

Each of the filters is characterized by its width as well as its center frequency. Bandwidth also varied as a function of the filters location on the basilar membrane as in Eq. 2:

$$\sigma = 40 \times 0.00201 \times (\mathit{CenterFreq}^{1.093}) \times \mathit{stepsize} \qquad (2)$$

Stepsize is a constant corresponding to the bandwidth of the FFT bin (1.953125 kHz) in the underlying original FFT spectral distribution. This bandwidth is determined by the number of points sampled in the original signal and the sampling rate. The total sensitivity of each filter was set according to Eq. 3:

$$\mathit{sensitivity} = (\sigma \times 2)^{0.139} \qquad (3)$$

The rationale for Eq. 3 is that the spacing of inner hair cells and ganglion cells is about constant over the length of the basilar membrane, so the number of cells that are likely to contribute to the filter should be inversely proportional to the spacing between filters (Eq. 1). Filters that are spaced farther apart are expected, in other words, to receive inputs from a wider range of inner hair cells than filters that are spaced closer together.

The sensitivity of each filter was set to be proportional the height of the Gaussian distribution at the corresponding frequency. Figure 3 shows the resulting filters.

In producing the 30-element vector representing the eighth-nerve response of the simulated ear, the power in each bin of the underlying FFT distribution was multiplied by the height of the Gaussian distribution for that filter at that frequency and added to the output of that filter. Notice that the bins are arithmetically symmetrical. On a log scale, they would appear to cut-off more sharply at higher than at lower frequencies relative to each filter's center frequency.

5. Results

A simulated audiogram was obtained by comparing the response of the simulated ear when confronted with noise only versus when the system was confronted with a signal of a particular frequency in addition to the noise. Each simulated trial consisted of two parts. During the first part of the trial each frequency bin was set to a small random value. These values were then fed to the bank of filters (the matrix product of the noise vector and matrix of filter vectors was computed resulting in a 30-element vector). A new noise vector was then specified and the bin corresponding to the tested frequency for that trial was incremented by a fixed value. This vector was also fed to the bank of filters, also resulting in a 30-element vector. The discriminability of the two conditions was taken to be the Euclidean distance between the noise-only and signal+noise vectors. Each comparison was repeated 10,000 times. The resulting audiogram is also shown in Figure 1.

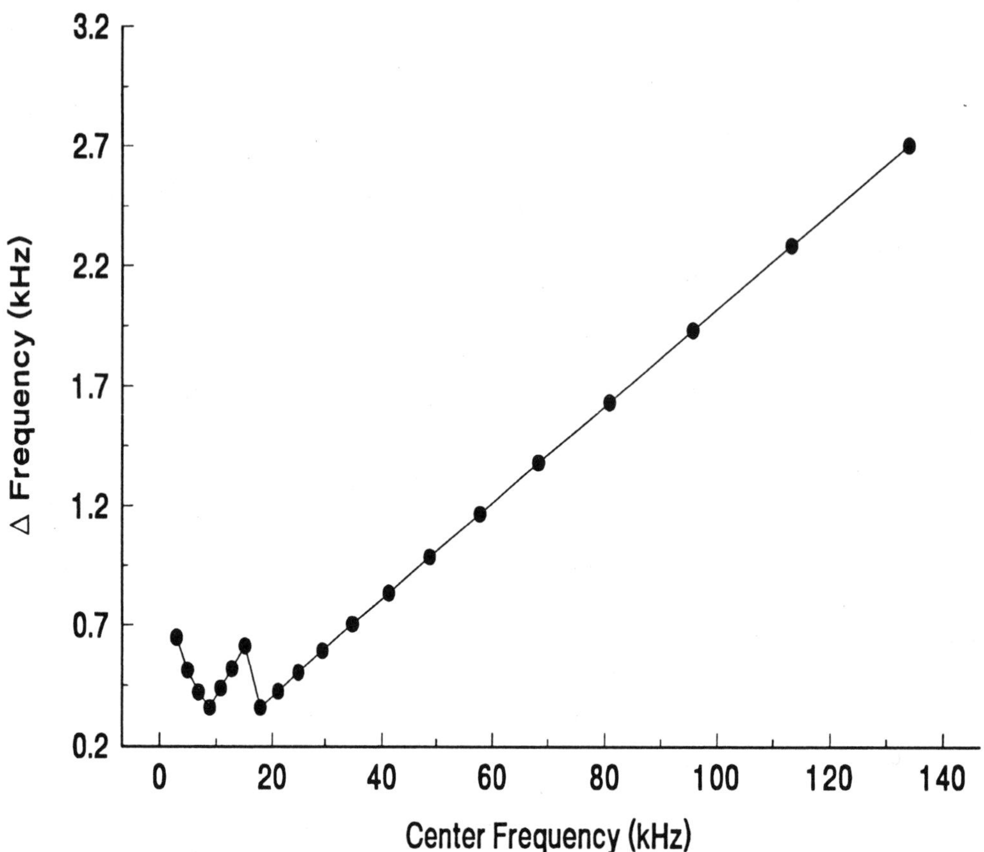

Figure 4. Smallest discriminal difference as a function of frequency.

In another simulated experiment we compared the difference limens predicted by the model with those observed in actual dolphins. These limens are shown in Figure 4. These limens correspond closely to the observed frequency limens, at least in the middle range of the dolphin's sensitivity. The crudeness of the underlying frequency analysis (i.e., the fact that our original representation uses 1.95 kHz wide bins) limits our ability to make fine discriminations at low frequencies.

Finally, we compared the performance of a neural network using the model as the input transducer to the neural network and comparing the network's performance to that of the dolphin on the difficult task of recognizing the substance inside the test bottles. That is, we used the cochlear model as the "front end" of the network transforming the underlying FFT into a vector of 30 filtered amplitudes. We implemented the cochlear model as a preprocessor, but it could just as easily be implemented directly in the network by setting the strengths of the connections from the input layer proportional to the sensitivity of the filters.

For the neural network we used the integrator gateway model described earlier by Moore et al. (1991) and Roitblat et al. (1991). This network was designed to implement the underlying item-recognition processes thought to be used by dolphins in the delayed matching-to-sample task (Roitblat et al., 1990). It takes advantage of the observation that dolphins tend to emit a series of clicks to the same object and hence of the redundancy between successive echoes.

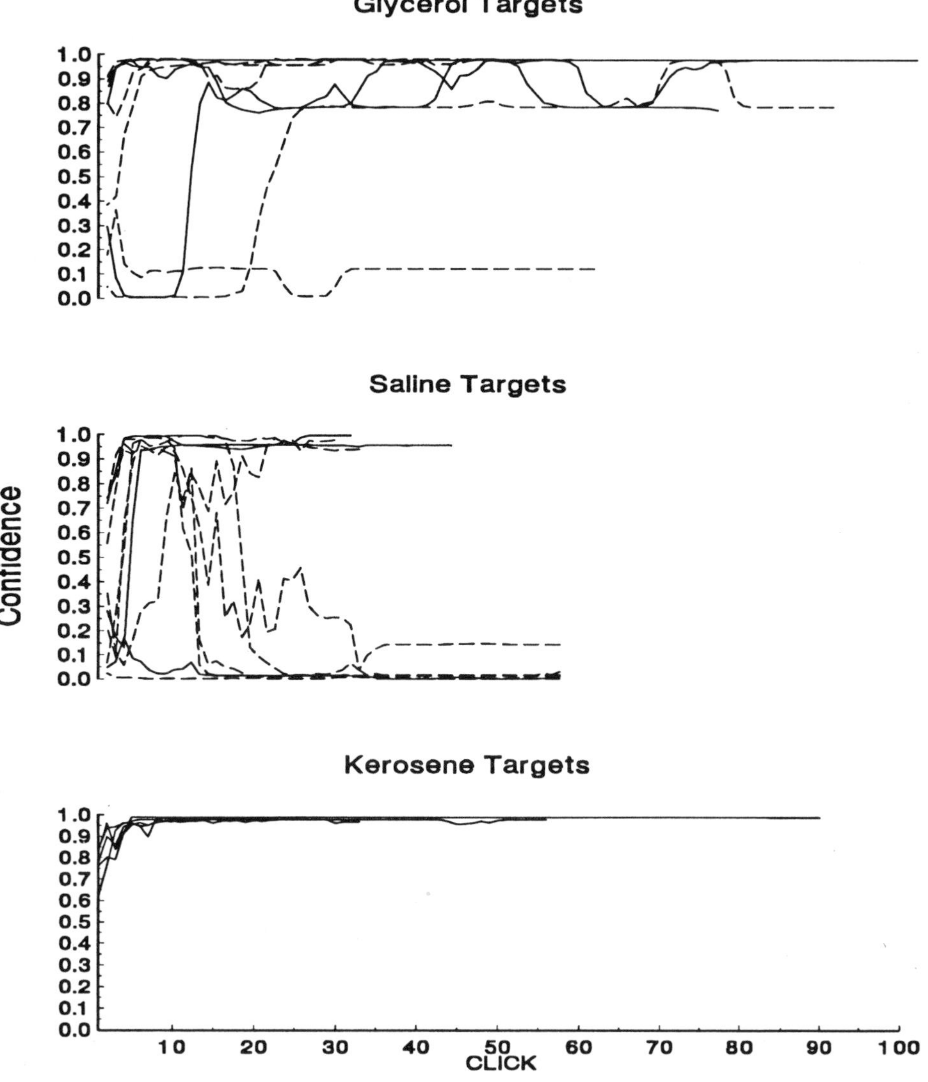

Figure 5. The confidence of a correct classification based on network output.

The network combines successive echoes in a train and computes a function similar to a running average.

The performance of this network is shown in the form of confidence ratios (see Moore et al., 1991; Roitblat et al. 1991). A confidence ratio of 1.0 indicates that the item was correctly and reliably identified by the network. A confidence ratio of 0.0 indicates that the network has misidentified the target as one of the alternative items. By convention we have chosen 0.96 as the dolphin's criterion of confidence. Ideally the dolphin should continue to emit clicks to a target until its confidence ratio reaches 0.96 and then stop clicking. In every experiment with this dolphin, however, he has continued to click beyond the point at which our network reaches this confidence criterion, suggesting either that the dolphin does not control his echolocation click production on a click by click basis or we over estimate his ability to extract information form the signal.

Table 1 shows the number of clicks the network incorporating the cochlear model needed to reach a 0.96 confidence criterion and the number of clicks emitted by the dolphin on each trial. Figure 5 shows the course of the change in confidence over successive clicks.

6. Conclusions

The biomimetic approach holds significant promise for the development of artificial systems that mimic the functions performed by biological organisms. The present

Table 1. Integrator Gateway Network and Dolphin Decisions

Train #	Target	Decision	Number of Clicks	Dolphin Correct
1	Glycerol	Glycerol	3	-
2	Glycerol	Glycerol	3	+
3	Glycerol	Glycerol	6	-
4	Glycerol	Glycerol	2	-
5	Glycerol	Glycerol	12	-
6	Glycerol	Kerosene	23	-
7	Glycerol	Glycerol	3	+
8	Glycerol	Kerosene	3	+
9	Glycerol	Glycerol	3	-
10	Glycerol	Kerosene	13	-
1	Saline	Saline	3	+
2	Saline	Saline	3	-
3	Saline	Saline	3	-
4	Saline	Saline	19	+
5	Saline	Saline	21	-
6	Saline	Kerosene	7	+
7	Saline	Saline	4	-
8	Saline	Kerosene	6	-
9	Saline	Kerosene	17	-
10	Saline	Saline	5	-
1	Kerosene	Kerosene	4	+
2	Kerosene	Kerosene	8	+
3	Kerosene	Kerosene	4	+
4	Kerosene	Kerosene	6	+
5	Kerosene	Kerosene	2	-
6	Kerosene	Kerosene	2	+
7	Kerosene	Kerosene	17	+
8	Kerosene	Saline	9	-
9	Kerosene	Kerosene	2	-
10	Kerosene	Kerosene	5	+

Note: A train is a sequence of echolocation clicks to the same Target. The third column shows the decision that the network reached. Number of clicks is the number of clicks/echoes the network needed in order to reach the confidence criterion. The last column indicates whether the dolphin chose the correct (+) or incorrect target (-) on the indicated trial.

model incorporates what we know about dolphin cochlear and neural anatomy, psychophysics, and behavior, to develop an effective model of echolocation object recognition. Dolphins are capable of exquisite object detection and recognition performance. Incorporation of even a small portion of their capabilities in artificial systems would greatly enhance their effectiveness and capabilities.

References

Au, W. W. L. (1980). Echolocation signals of the Atlantic bottlenose dolphin (*tursiops truncatus*) in open waters. In R. G. Busnel & J. F. Fish (Eds.), *Animal sonar systems* (pp. 251-282). New York: Plenum Press.

Au, W. W. L. (1988). Detection and recognition models of dolphin sonar systems. In P. E. Nachtigall & P. W. B. Moore (Eds.), *Animal Sonar: Processes and performance* (pp. 753-768). New York: Plenum Press.

Au, W. W. L. & Moore, P. W. B. (1984). Receiving beam patterns and directivity indices of the Atlantic bottlenose dolphin *Tursiops truncatus*. *Journal of the Acoustical Society of America*, 75, 255-262.

Au, W. W. L., Moore, P. W. B. & Pawloski, D. (1986). Echolocating transmitting beam of the Atlantic bottlenose dolphin. *Journal of the Acoustical Society of America*, 80, 688-691.

Bekesy, G. von (1944) Uber die Frequenzauflosung in der menslichen Schnecke. *Acta oto-laryngologica*, 32, 60-84.

Bellwood, J. (1988). Foraging behavior, prey selection, and echolocation in *phyllostomine* bats (*phyllostomidae*) In P. E. Nachtigall & P. W. B. Moore (Eds.) *Animal sonar: Processes and performance* (pp. 601-605). New York: Plenum.

Fenton, M. B. (1988) Variations in foraging strategies in five species of insectivorous bats--implications for echolocation call design. In P. E. Nachtigall & P. W. B. Moore (Eds.) *Animal sonar: Processes and performance* (pp. 607-611). New York: Plenum.

Fletcher, H. (1940) Auditory patterns. *Reviews of Modern Physics*, 12, 47-65.

Helmholtz, H. L. F. (1863) *Die Lehre von den Tonempfindungen als physiologische Grundlage fur die Theorie der Musik.*

Herman, L. M. & Arbeit, W. R. (1972) Frequency difference limens in the bottlenose dolphin: 1-70 kHz. *Journal of Auditory Research*, 12, 109-120.

Hudspeth, A. J. (1985) The cellular basis of hearing: The biophysics of hair cells. *Science*, 230, 745-752.

Johnson, C. S. (1966). *Auditory thresholds of the bottlenosed porpoise, Tursiops truncatus (Montague)* (Naval Ordnance Test Station Technical Publication No 4178). Naval Ordnance Test Station.

Johnson, C. S. (1967) Sound detection thresholds in marine mammals. In W. N. Tavolga (Ed.), *Marine bioacoustics*, (vol. 2, pp. 247-260). New York: Pergamon Press.

Ketten, D. R. (1992) The marine mammal ear: Specializations for aquatic audition and echolocation. In D. R. Webster, R. R. Fay, & A. N. Popper (Eds.) *The evolutionary biology of hearing.* (pp. 717-750) New York: Springer Verlag.

Ketten, D. R. & Wartzog, D. (1990) Three dimensional reconstruction of the dolphin cochlea. In J. Thomas & R. Kastelein (Eds.) *Sensory abilities of cetaceans* (pp. 81-106). New York: Plenum Press.

Moore P. W. B. & Pawloski, D. (1990). Investigations on the control of echolocation pulses in the dolphin (*Tursiops truncatus*). In J. Thomas & R. Kastelein (Eds.) *Sensory abilities of cetaceans* (pp. 305-316). New York: Plenum Press.

Moore, P. W. B., Roitblat, H. L., Penner, R. H., & Nachtigall, P. E. (1991). Recognizing successive dolphin echoes with an integrator gateway network. *Neural Networks*, 4, 701-709.

Morozov, V. P., Akopian, A. I., Burdin, V. L., Donskov, Zaytseva, K. A., & Sokovykh, Y. A. (1971) Repetition rate of ranging signals of dolphins as a function of distance to target. *Biofisika*, 17, 49-55.

Morozov, V. P., Akopian, A. I., Zaytseva, K. A., & Sokovykh, Y. A. (1972). Tracking frequency of the locations signals of dolphins as a function of the distance to the target, *Biofizika*, 17, 139-143.

Nachtigall, P. E. (1980). Odontocete echolocation performance on object size, shape, and material, In R. G. Busnel & J. F. Fish (Eds.), *Animal Sonar Systems* (pp. 71-95). New York: Plenum Press.

Roitblat, H. L., Moore, P. W. B., Nachtigall, P. E. & Penner, R. H., (1991). Natural Dolphin Echo Recognition Using an Integrator Gateway Network. In D. S. Touretsky, & R. Lippman (Eds.), *Advances in neural information processing systems* 3. (pp. 273-281). San Mateo, CA: Morgan Kaufmann.

Roitblat, H. L., Penner, R. H., & Nachtigall, P. E. (1990) Matching-to-sample by an echolocating dolphin. *Journal of Experimental Psychology: Animal Behavior Processes*, 16, 85-95.

Thompson, R. K. R. & Herman, L. M. (1975) Underwater frequency discrimination in the bottlenosed dolphin (1-140kHz) and human (1-8kHz). *Journal of the Acoustical Society of America*, 57, 943-947.

Suthers, R. (1988) The production of echolocation signals by bats and birds. In P. E. Nachtigall & P. W. B. Moore (Eds.) *Animal sonar: Processes and performance* (pp. 23-45). New York: Plenum.

Weber, E. H. (1846) Tastsinn Gemeingefuhl. *Handworterbuch der Physichen Wagner*, 3, 481-588.

Wever, E. G., McCormick, J. G., Palin, J., & Ridgway, S.H. (1971a) The cochlea of the dolphin, *Tursiops truncatus*: General morphology. *Proceedings of the National Academy of Science*, 68, 2381-2385.

Wever, E. G., McCormick, J. G., Palin, J., & Ridgway, S.H. (1971b) The cochlea of the dolphin, *Tursiops truncatus*: The basilar membrane. *Proceedings of the National Academy of Science*, 68, 2908-2912.

Zook, J. M., Myron, S. J., Glezer, I., & Morgane, P. (1988) Some comparative aspects of auditory brainstem cytoarchitecture in echolocating mammal—— Speculations on the morphological bases of time-domain signal processing. In P. E. Nachtigall & P. W. B. Moore (Eds.) *Animal sonar: Processes and performance* (pp. 311-316). New York: Plenum.

Zvorykin, V. P. (1959) Morphological basis of locative and supersonic abilities in bat. *Arkh. Ant. Gistol. Embriol.*, 36, 19.

Zvorykin, V. P. (1963) Morphological substrate of ultrasonic and locational capacities in the dolphin. *Arkh. Ant. Gistol. Embriol.*, 45, 3.

AN INTEGRATED COMPUTATIONAL MODEL OF A PERCEPTUAL-MOTOR SYSTEM

William R. Uttal
Thomas Shepherd
Sriram Dayanand
Robb Lovell

The Perception Laboratory
Department of Industrial and Management Systems Engineering
Arizona State University
Tempe, Arizona 85287
e-mail - AOWRU@ASUACAD.BITNET

ABSTRACT

This paper presents a report on the progress made on the development of a computational model of the perceptual-motor behavior of a predatory "SWIMMER". Brief discussions of the visual image processing, decision making, and navigational aspects of the simulation are presented. The work can be considered to be either a psychological theory or the necessary programming for autonomous visual control of an underwater vehicle.

I. Introduction:

We report the development of a computational model of an entire perceiving and responding organism. Our project is both a unified theory of a perceptual motor process and a step towards an autonomous, visually guided, underwater vehicle. We shall concentrate on the general organization of the system in this presentation. We place primary emphasis on the integration of a suite of algorithms and processes that constitute a theory of a perceptual-motor system, but we also report considerable progress in improving the logic of a number of individual programming modules. Each of the functional steps in our simulation is considered to be tentative and replaceable as the technology for executing that particular subprocess evolves.

The actions that have to be simulated range from the initial transduction of photic energy to the appropriate interpretation of a stimulus scene to the construction of a map of the world of the simulated entity to a specific effector response. Thus, our simulation -- to the degree that it is successful -- represents a descriptive transformational theory of this kind of behavior from an entire organism as opposed to a model restricted to a single internal stage of information processing. It is not intended to be a valid reductive explanation of the actual inner workings of the brain or mind of any real organism but a description of the transformations and processes that have to be accounted for if we are to understand the complexities involved in perceptual-motor behavior.

We have chosen, as a prototypical microworld system to be studied, an underwater SWIMMER capable of acquiring images of food objects, recognizing and discriminating among salient (edible) and irrelevant (inedible) objects, establishing a three-dimensional world model of its environment and the objects in it (including itself), and then demonstrating its understanding by swimming through a turbulent ocean to those objects. Involved in such a simulation must be consideration of visual, localization, interpretative, decision making, and motor functions as well as some challenging new problems of how one integrates all of these functions.

The general framework of our simulation is made up of a number of stages of transformation that we believe must be included if the system is to perform in a comparable way to an organism. Specifically, we see the correspondences shown in Table 1. as some examples of the relations between our program components and the processes of the visual system:

COMPUTER	HUMAN
Image Acquisition	Receptor Transduction
Pixel Sampling	Retinal Mosaic Sampling
Image Smoothing and Noise Reduction	Local Retinal Averaging
Edge Detection	Lateral Inhibition
Object Segmentation	
From Attributes of Form	Figure Ground Segregation
From Attributes of Motion	Common Motion Grouping
From Attributes of Depth	Stereopsis
From Attributes of Color	Color Discrimination
From Attributes of Texture	Texture Discrimination
From Attributes of Lightness	Lightness Discrimination
Object Reconstruction	Closure and Completion
Object Classification	Naming, Recognizing
Object Discrimination	Organic Discrimination
The World Map	Egocentric Localization
Navigation	Locomotion

TABLE 1. A comparison of the computational and organic visual domains indicating the processes that have to be simulated in a model such as the one described in this paper.

In this presentation, a variety of displays will be presented that illustrate the outcome of the simulation. The main philosophical point we wish to emphasize is that good image processing is more likely to come from integration or combination of the efforts to produce a single robust algorithm. This is the way the organic nervous system accomplishes its powerful image processing capabilities and it is the way that our programs are organized. In other words, it is not necessarily the case that GIGO (Garbage In produces Garbage Out). Sometimes, at least, it can be GIBO (Garbage In produces Beauty Out).

Let us now consider the main modules in our simulation model of the SWIMMER which is flowcharted in its entirety in Figure 1.

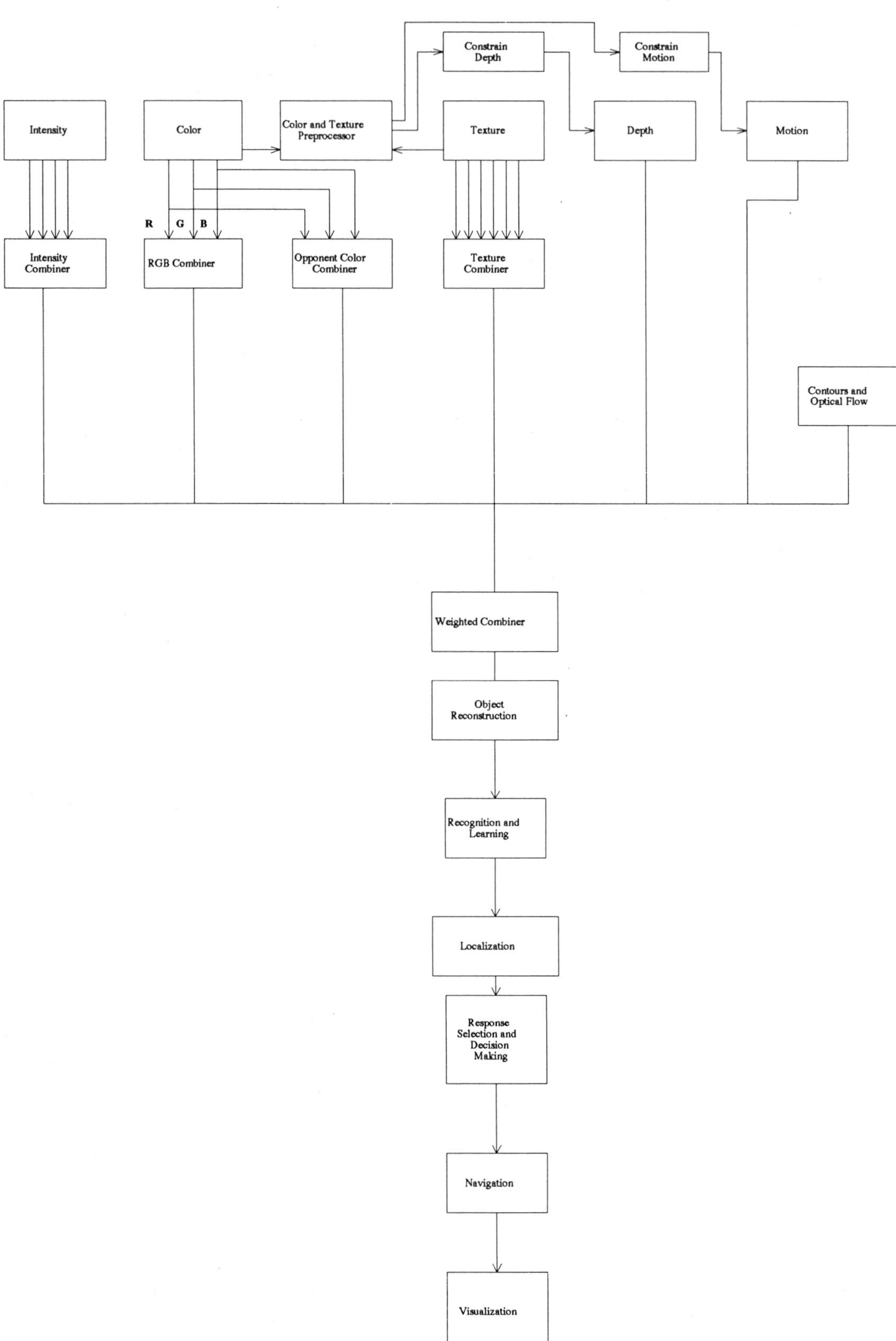

FIGURE 1. A block diagram of the computational model presented in this paper.

II. DISCUSSION:

The following is a brief description of many of the steps in our simulation of the SWIMMER. A full discussion of our progress and philosophy can be found in Uttal, Bradshaw, Dayanand, Lovell, Shepherd, Kakarala, Skifsted, and Tupper (1992). The general philosophy we champion is that of combination and integration of relatively weak and fallible operators individually acting on the several attributes of human vision as shown in Figure 1. Following the lead of new developments in organic physiology and psychology (e.g., Livingstone and Hubel, 1988; Cavanagh, Arguin, and Treisman, 1990) our model organizes the computer simulation so that the relatively independent operators initially work on their respective stimulus attributes in order to produce a more or less accurate estimate of the boundaries between distinguishable regions. We assume that this contour information can be obtained by analyzing an image on the basis of its luminance, color, texture, depth and motion attributes. (At the present stage of development of our model we have not yet incorporated programs to deal with contour and optical flow lines.) A corollary of our model is that we should not make any attempt to polish each of these modules to a fine level of performance, but rather to accept the sometimes poor estimates of the boundaries they individually produce. We then look for "spatial statistical" central tendencies that collectively produce a much improved estimate of the boundaries.

At the topmost level of Figure 1, it can be seen there is a horizontal combination phase. Both our shape-from-motion and our version of the Marr-Poggio-Grimson shape-from-disparity algorithms are fraught with artifacts and noise. To improve their outputs, we constrain their operation by information that has been obtained by combining the color and texture algorithms indicated in Figure 1.

Similarly, there are many points of vertical combination among the operators acting on single attributes. For example, the intensity attribute operator produces the pooled output of four separate operators, whose outputs are combined prior to the major intensity combiner. These include selective mean, minimum, maximum, and range operators.

In addition to a more or less conventional trichromatic combination (R + G + B) of the output of the three color images captured by our camera, we also have a version of trichromatic vision in which the three color outputs are more completely manipulated. (R - G, G - B, B - R, R +G, G + B, B + R, R - [G + B], G - [B + R], and B - [R + G]).

Six texture operators (which produce between 15 and 20 different output boundary estimates) are also used. These include three well known in the literature (Fractal Dimension, Law's Microtextures, and the co-occurrence Matrix) and three others that we invented to emphasize other properties (Sample and Match, Area Differential, and Redundancy).

The combination and integration of the output information from the partially combined family of operators discussed so far occurs in a number of ways. The vertical combination of all of the operator outputs is shown in Figure 1. The main point of combination is indicated by the box labeled "Weighted Combiner." At this point we invoke one of two possible combination algorithms. The first (Lovell, Uttal, Shepherd, and Dayanand, 1992) is a relatively straight forward spatial statistical averager that plots all of the outputs onto a single image and then calculates the center of gravity of all of the points from the operator suggested boundaries within a local region.

The second combiner (Dayanand, Uttal, Shepherd, and Lunskis, 1992) is a slower, but more sophisticated, procedure in which the gravitational field of the points on the operator suggested boundaries controls the trajectory of a moving point. The trajectory, as it is traced out, produces an excellent estimate of the true boundaries in the original image. To illustrate the combination process, Figure 2 shows the individual outputs from the texture operators. Figure 3 shows the superimposed outputs as well as the final combined output from the gravitational field operator.

We have also developed procedures that reconstruct or fill in incompletenesses in the combined images. Some of these are capable of closing up two dimensional images that may have short breaks in them. However, in anticipation of our upcoming move to three dimensional images, we have also made an effort to develop procedures that interpolate from the punctate samples coming from the stereoscopic analysis system to produce complete surfaces.

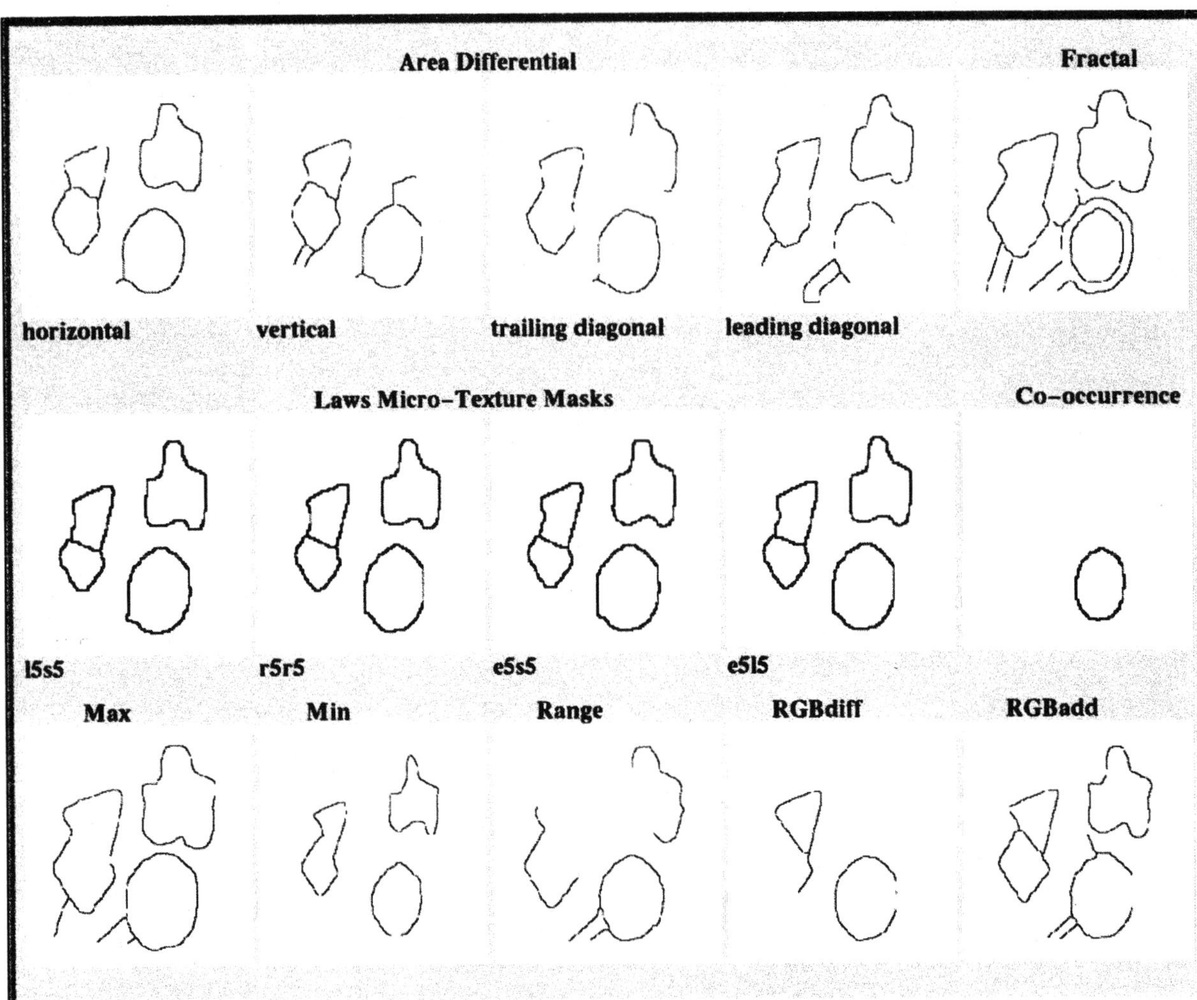

FIGURE 2. The outputs from a sample set of boundary detecting operators. These are the separate estimates of boundaries from a scene in which four objects were placed. The area differential, fractal, micro-texture masks, and co-occurrence procedures operate on image texture. The max, min, and range operate on image intensity, and the RGB diff and add are "opponent color" type operators. Note the wide variation in the resulting images. In other situations, some that work well here (e. g., the Law's micro-texture method) will not succeed in defining the boundaries. Others, on the other hand, might work. It is for this reason that the combination process is required.

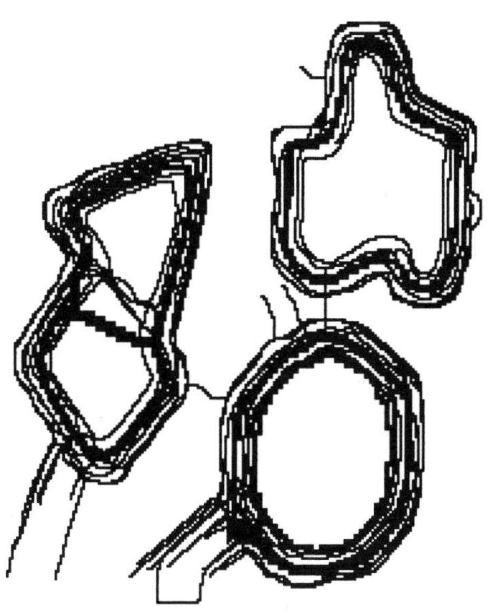

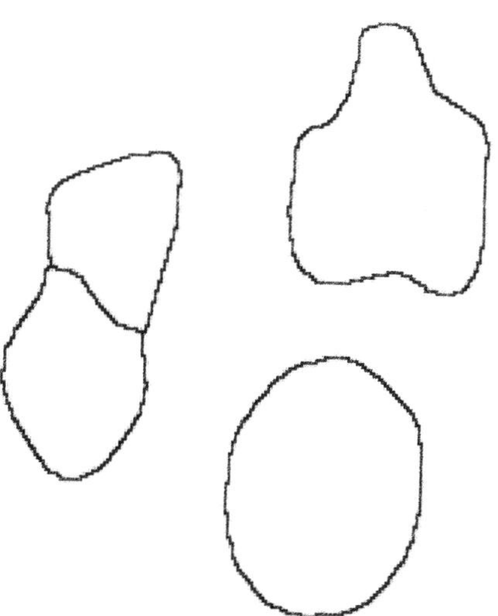

FIGURE 3. The top picture shows the superimposition of all of the operator outputs from Figure 2. When combined by either one of the combining algorithms described in the text, a single pixel wide "best" estimate of the boundaries of the four objects will be obtained as shown in the lower picture.

Once the combination and reconstruction processes described in the previous paragraphs has produced satisfactory boundary information and estimates made of the depth of the objects in the camera's field of view, we simulate knowledge (on the part of the SWIMMER) of the arrangement of the objects in an underwater scene. Objects of the correct shape are placed at locations in the visualized simulation corresponding to their location in the real scene captured by the camera.

Our recognition program (Shepherd, Uttal, Dayanand, and Lovell, 1992) is particularly powerful. This program was written not only to be invariant to rotation, translation and magnification, but also to adapt to new objects that it had not seen previously. The program is written so that a perfect correlation is not required for identification. Indeed, the simulation of stimulus generalization is so great that the recognition program is capable of identifying partially occluded objects as shown in Figure 4.

The visualization portion of the simulation program is then initiated. Our SWIMMER moves about following a set of decision rules (go to the nearest object first, recognize its shape, swim through regular objects and around irregular objects) which, though simple, produce complex behavior. Rules of navigation allowing adaptive responses to currents and impulses are built into the program to assist in its "search, recognize, and appropriately respond" mission. The entire behavior of the simulated system is graphically presented for experimental manipulation in this manner.

ACKNOWLEDGMENTS

At the present time we are working in collaboration with Ms. Barbara Fletcher of the Naval Ocean Systems Center -- San Diego Laboratory to link our computation model and simulation to the control logic of a remotely controlled submersible. We believe this will lead to an operational visually guided, autonomous, adaptively behaving system in the near future.

This project has been supported by Grant N00014-91-J-1456 from the Office of Naval Research. We are especially indebted to Dr. Harold Hawkins for his sustained support during the course of our work.

REFERENCES

CAVANAGH, P., ARGUIN, M. , & TRIESMAN, A. (1990). Effect of surface medium on visual search for orientation and size features. Journal of Experimental Psychology: Human Perception and Performance. 16, 479-491.

DAYANAND, S. UTTAL, W. R., SHEPHERD, T. S., & LUNSKIS, C. (1992). A particle system model for combining edge information from multiple segmentation modules. (Submitted -- Available from the authors.)

LIVINGSTONE, M. S., & HUBEL, D., (1988). Segregation of form, color, movement, and depth: anatomy, physiology, and perception. Science, 240, 740-750.

LOVELL, R., UTTAL, W. R., SHEPHERD, T. S., & DAYANAND, S. (1992). A model of visual texture discrimination using multiple weak operators and spatial averaging. Pattern Recognition, 25.

SHEPHERD, T. S., UTTAL, W. R., DAYANAND, S., & LOVELL, R. (1992). A Method for shift, rotation, and scale invariant pattern recognition using the form and arrangement of pattern specific features. Pattern Recognition. 25, 343-356.

UTTAL, W. R., BRADSHAW, G., DAYANAND, S., LOVELL, R., SHEPHERD, T., KAKARALA, R., SKIFSTED, K, AND TUPPER, K. (1992) The Swimmer: An Integrated Computational Model of a Perceptual-Motor System, Hillsdale, NJ: Erlbaum.

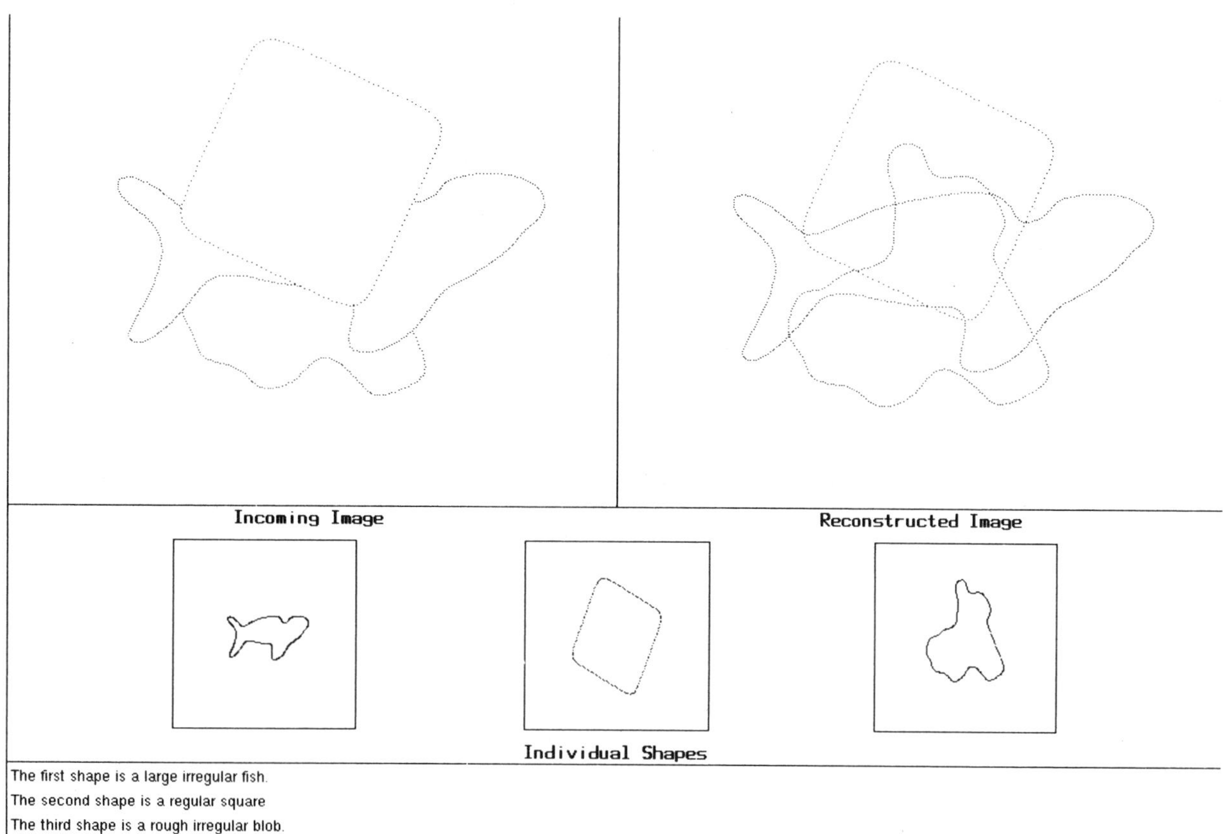

FIGURE 4. A sample of the pattern recognition procedure's ability to identify occluded images on the basis of a partial match. The left hand upper picture depicts the original image, the left hand upper picture, the reconstructed image, and the three lower pictures the best matches from the library of stored images. The text output from the recognition program is also indicated.

Reactive Behaviors of Fast Mobile Robots in Unstructured Environments : Sensor–based Control and Neural Networks

R. Zapata, P. Lépinay, C. Novales, P. Deplanques

*Laboratoire d'Informatique, de Robotique et de Microélectronique de Montpellier
UMR CNRS C9928Université de Montpellier II
Place E. Bataillon 34095 Montpellier cedex 5 FRANCE
Tel : (+33) 67–14–34–45 FAX : (+33) 67–52–14–96
E–mail : zapata@frmop53.bitnet

Abstract

This paper addresses the problem of reactive behaviors for collision avoidance of fast mobile robots evolving in unstructured and dynamic environments.

The first approach is based on the description of a deformable virtual zone (DVZ) surrounding the robot. The deformations of this *risk zone*, due to the intrusion of proximity informations, control the robot reactions.

The second approach is based on the Neural Network technology. The network inputs are the measured distances of obstacles on the robot way and its velocity;its outputs are the controls of the robot acceleration, direction and braking actuators.

These two approaches have been first simulated and compared, then implemented on two different autonomous wheeled robots : an outdoor and an indoor fast mobile vehicles. They will also be tested on a walking artificial grasshopper which, today, is under development.

1. Introduction

Reactive behaviors for mobile robots can be defined as the capability to react when unscheduled events occur. For instance, and this will be the case here, when unknown and dynamic obstacles can collide the vehicle.

Generally, this problem is solved by a *behavioral approach*, consisting in directly relating inputs (stimuli) to outputs (actions) through state machines [1], [2], [3], [4].

In another hand, we can consider the *sensor–based control approach* which directly feedbacks sensory information to the robot control loop [5], [6], [7].

In this paper, we focus our attention on two different methods we have developed for solving this problem. The first one is a member of the Sensor–based methods family and was previously explained in [7] and [8]. The second one is based on the Neural Network technology [9][10].

These two methods were simulated and compared in the case of moving robots evolving in unstructured (unknown) and dynamic worlds. They were then implemented on an outdoor fast vehicle and on an indoor fast wheeled robot. The results obtained with these two systems are being implemented on a walking machine which will demonstrate learning capabilities in locomotion and collision avoidance skills.

In the second part of this paper, we will describe the two wheeled robots used in collision avoidance experiments and, more briefly, the walking machine. The third and the fourth parts will focus on the description of the two approaches that we have developed. Finally, the last part of the paper will present a few results, obtained both in simulation and during real experiments.

2. Motion machines

2. 1. *SNAKE : A Fast Outdoor Mobile Robot*

SNAKE (Sensor–based Navigation Autonomous Kinetic Expert) is a 1/4–scale car–like vehicle equipped with an optical velocity sensor, an electronic orientation sensor (magnetic compass) and a 7–sensor ultrasonic proximity system.

The main motion is provided by an internal combustion engine driven by a DC servo–motor controlling an acceleration cable. Another servo–motor drives the brakes and two other electric motors control the robot direction.

The software has been developed in C language on a Motorola™ 68020/VME architecture for the first version SNAKE I, and on a 7–Transputer network for the second version SNAKE II.

Input/Output boards and timers for controlling sensors and motors complete the structure [11].

Roughly based on the Brooks approach of robot control [1], four modules relating sensors to actuators allow an hierarchical description of behaviors. These modules are parallel asynchronous processes.

The two high-level modules (Emergency Stops and Dynamic Collision Avoidance) have been both implemented with Sensor-based Control concepts (Figure 1).

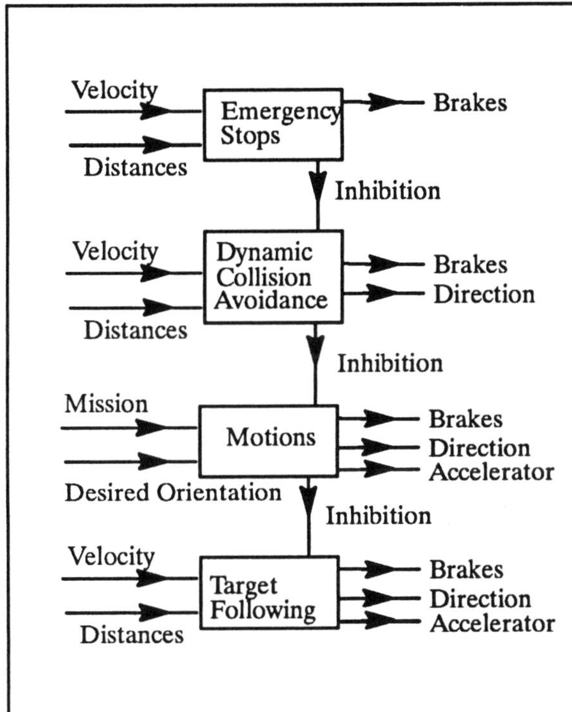

Figure 1 : *Hierarchical architecture*

2. 2. RAT : A Fast Indoor Mobile Robot

RAT (Autonomous Robot with Transputer) has almost the same design than SNAKE, except that this electric 1/10-scale car-like robot can also move backward and therefore has increased dynamic capabilities.

Three ultrasonic sensors protect the robot front space while a single ultrasonic sensor protects its back. Artificial whiskers are used to detect close obstacles and also allow this vehicle to follow walls.

The perception-action loop is carried out by a single transputer board, controlling the sensors and the actuators.

The process board is a INMOS™ T800 Transputer with 1 megabyte of RAM. The programs are developed in Parallel C.

The Emergency Stops and Dynamic Collision Avoidance modules have been implemented on this board using either the DVZ method or the Neural Network technology approach.

2. 3. WAAL : A 6-leg artificial Locust

WAAL (Walking Autonomous Artificial Locust) is a 6-leg, 6 degrees of freedom robot with only forward motion capabilities. Its purpose is also to demonstrate indoor safe motion in presence of unknown obstacles.

A 3-sensor ultrasonic system and artificial whiskers allow it to avoid collisions with its environment.

WAAL has been designed to be able of avoiding unknown obstacles when moving at important speeds (from 0.5 to 1 m/s).

3. Sensor-based Control

3. 1. General overview

The robot/environment interaction can be described as a deformable virtual zone surrounding the robot. This zone is a 2-dimensional imbedding of the sphere in $\mathbb{R}^2$. The deformations of this *risk zone* are due to the intrusion of proximity information and control the robot reactions.

The *robot internal state* is defined to be a couple (π, Ξ) where the first component π characterizes the robot dynamics (its translational and rotational velocities) and the second component Ξ, called the *interaction component*, characterizes the geometry of this deformable zone. Figure 2 is a simple illustration of this principle.

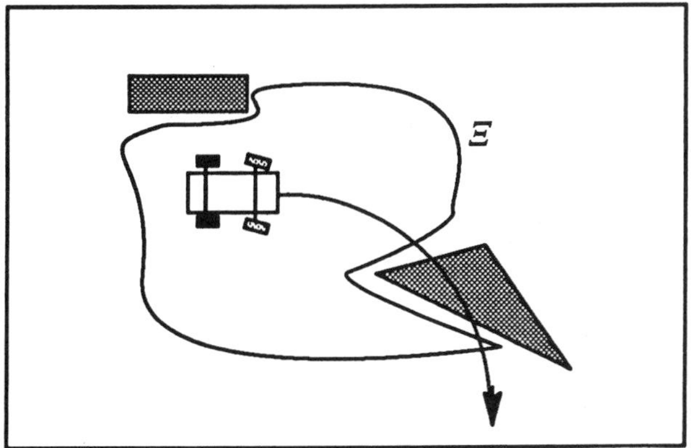

Figure 2 : *Three different activation functions*

The *internal control* -or reactive behavior- is a relation ϕ, linking these two components, namely $\Xi = \phi(\pi)$.Figure 3 shows a possible influence of translational and rotational velocities on the general shape and dimensions of the DVZ. The faster the robot is, the larger the DVZ will be. This also hold for the rotational velocity. This way, the DVZ can play its protecting role in the directions of motions.

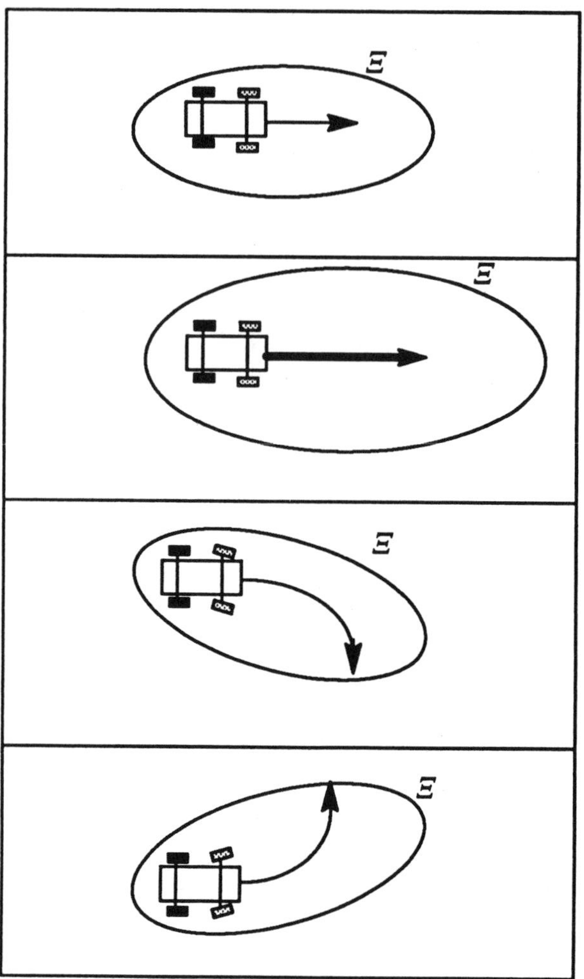

Figure 3 : *Dependance between dynamics and the DVZ*

The relevant information for collision avoidance purposes is the distance polar function relating the closest impact point distance in each direction to this direction of observation.

The range of all sensors is defined to be a surrounding zone, called **R** , and which deformations will lead to a new surrounding information zone, named **B**.

The *intrusion vector field* I is defined on **R** by the vector difference between the information boundary **B** in each direction, and the range **R** of the virtual sensor in the same direction.

A *deformation vector field* Δ is defined from this intrusion vector field. During information intrusion, the risk zone Ξ is deformed into $\tilde{\Xi}$ (Figure 4).

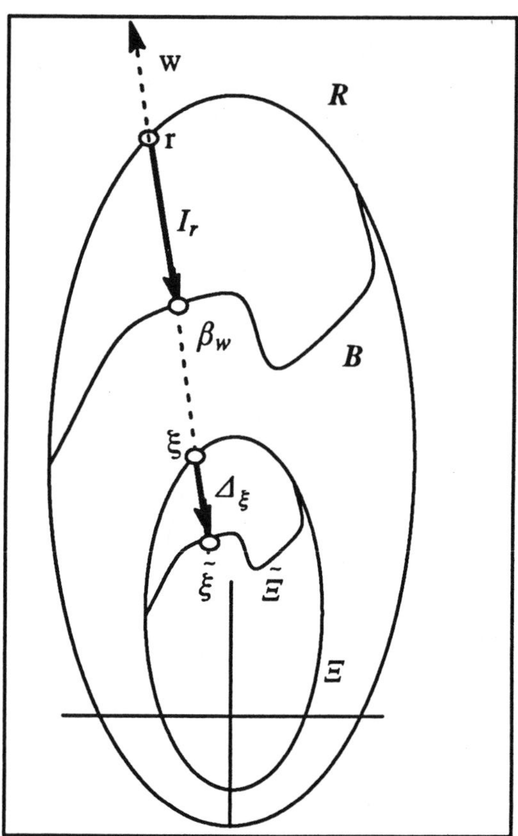

Figure 4 : *Intrusion and deformation vector fields*

The control of the internal state is done after comparing a reference interaction component Ξ_0 with the deformed component $\tilde{\Xi}$. This reference depends on the accepted risk taken by the vehicle and is a matter of choice.

3. 2. Implementation

The Sensor–based Control method described above, has been implemented on SNAKE and RAT.

The interaction component Ξ was chosen as a deadband value for the information boundary **B**.

In this case, Ξ is deformed if and only if the information boundary manifold **B** is 'smaller' than Ξ.

Therefore, the control problem consists in rebuilding the initial state interaction component Ξ through an action on the robot rotation (dynamic avoidance), or by modifying the robot dynamics in order to attain another acceptable stable state Ξ'.

These concepts have been implemented on SNAKE. The virtual zone **R** has been sampled in the 7 directions of the ultrasonic observations :

* The robot dynamics π is given by its translational velocity v and its rotational velocity $\dot{\Theta}$. These ones are directly related to the inter–axle distance L and to the turn angle δ of the robot by : $\dot{\Theta} = \frac{v}{L} \times \tan(\delta)$.

* The range manifold **R** is an arc of circle and can be deformed along the 7 directions into the information boundary manifold **B**.

* Two circular interaction zones (Ξ_{Stop} for the Emergency Stops procedure and Ξ_{Avoid} for the Dynamic Collision Avoidance procedure) are sampled by using the proximity data provided by the 7 ultrasonic sensors. The sizes of Ξ_{Stop} and Ξ_{Avoid} are proportional to the translational velocity v. For Ξ_{Avoid} we have: $R_{\Xi_{Avoid}} = k \times v + R_0$

where $R_{\Xi_{Avoid}}$ is the radius of Ξ_{Avoid}. The parameters k and R_0 (0–velocity risk radius) have been experimentally identified. These coefficients highly depend on the characteristics of the ground and on the reaction times of the servo–motors and of the ultrasonic system.

* The sampled interaction components $\hat{\Xi}_{Stop}$ and $\hat{\Xi}_{Avoid}$ are computed as the intersections of homothetic transformations of **R** and 2 limiting δ–oriented angular zones working as blinkers. These virtual blinkers make the robot look the direction it will move on. These two zones are deformed when **B** is smaller than Ξ. Otherwise, there is no reaction (Figure 5).

3. 3. The Collision Avoidance Algorithm

The internal security zone Ξ_{Stop} (Emergency Stops) is just a triggering space which produces a complete braking of the robot. The use of the external security zone Ξ_{Avoid} is more sophisticated and leads to the following algorithm:

STEP 1 : Check the deformation of **R**. If there is no deformation: Exit.

STEP 2 : Compute Ξ_{Avoid} with respect to the velocity of the robot and its rotational speed.

STEP 3 : Check the deformation of Ξ_{Avoid}. If there is not such a deformation: Exit.

STEP 4 : Look for a motion (rotation in the robot reference frame) which allows a rebuilding of Ξ_{Avoid} while minimizing the robot rotation. If such an avoidance motion exists: Goto STEP 1.

STEP 5 : Change the robot velocity in order to obtain a homothetic deformation of Ξ_{Avoid} (by slowing down).

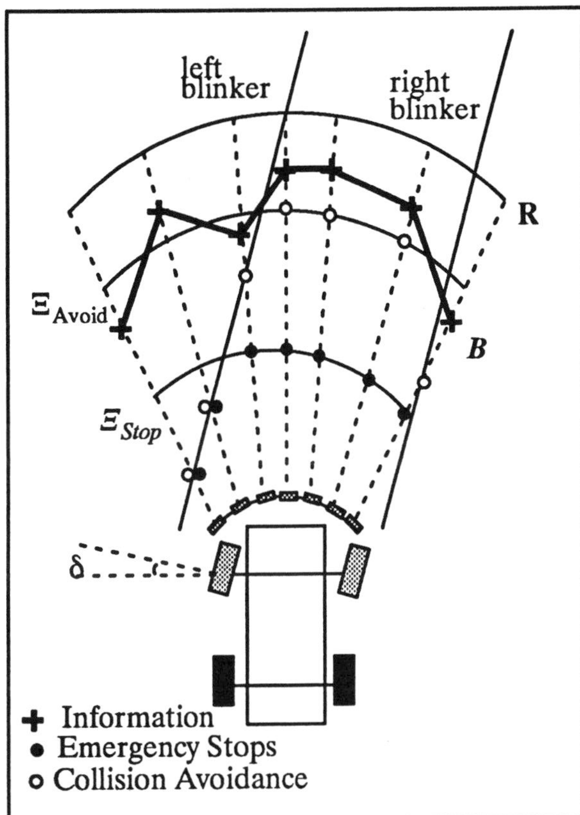

Figure 5 : *Sampled protecting virtual zones*

This algorithm works till the robot has dynamically found a way of rebuilding an interaction zone Ξ_{Avoid} and hence to avoid obstacles. If such is not the case, the internal state will continue to deform and the Emergency Stops process will react (after a deformation of Ξ_{Stop}).

4. The Neural Network Approach

4. 1. General overview

The Elementary Neural Cell : A Neural Network is composed of several neural cells interconnected; the way to connect these neural cells, called neurons, determines the architecture of the Neural Network.

A neuron is a computed entity which has several inputs, one output, and two functions (Figure 6) :

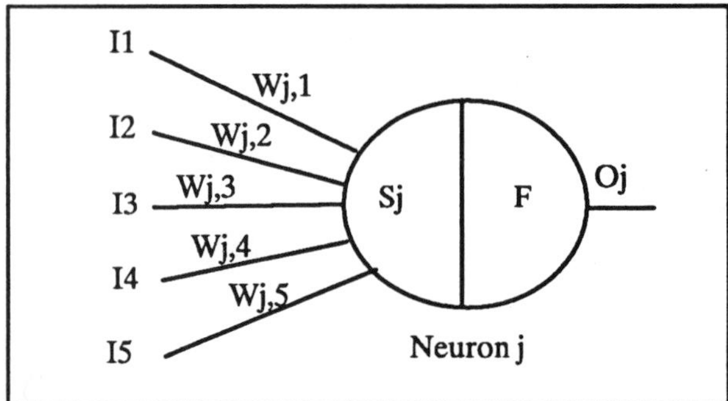

Figure 6 : *Single Neuron*

For the jth neuron :

* each input I_i is weighted by a scalar $W_{j,i}$,

* the first function of the neuron is to add all the weighted inputs : $S_i = \sum (W_{j,i} \times I_i)$

* the second function is an activation function which gives the state of the neuron *j*, i.e. its output.

This activation function outputs a result between -1 and 1. Generally, it shape depends of the use of the neural network ; in our case we used the following activation function (Figure 7) :

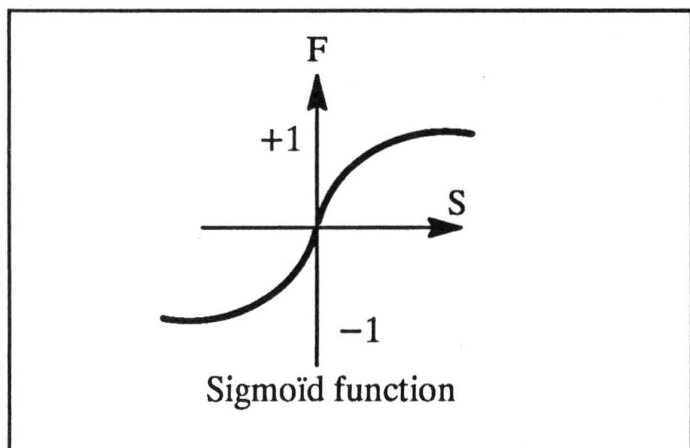

Figure 7 : *Three different activation functions*

The output O_j of the jth neuron is "connected" to one input of one or several neurons. The result of the neuron j is: $Oj = \mathcal{F}(\sum_i W_{j,i} * I_i)$

The Neural Network : The layered association of several neurons forms a Neural Network ;

The first layer is the input layer : all the data needed by the Neural Network are entered at this stage.

The last layer is the output layer : all the informations delivered by the Neural Network are available at this stage.

Between this two layers, there is one or more hidden layers.

The network can be fully−connected or partially connected (Figure 8)

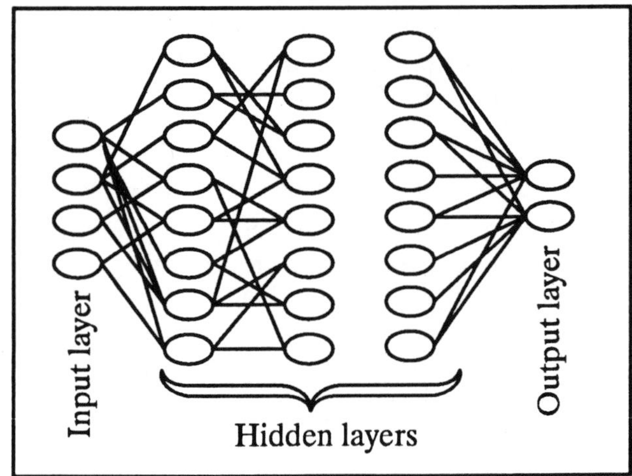

Figure 8 : *Example of partially connected multi−layer network*

The Learning Process : In our implementation, we use fully−connected networks with two hidden layers, and the activation function is a "sigmoïd". Our target was to have an on−line learning of the network while the robot moves. Indeed, in unstructured environments, there is too many types of scenes to learn them before the robot moves.

During the learning phase, we use the retrogression algorithm that minimize the quadratic error : $E = \sum_i (O_{id} - O_i)^2$

with O_i : the real output of the neuron *i*,
O_{id} : the desired output of the neuron *i*.

This criterion is used with known examples ; we present the inputs to the Neural Network which computes the outputs by propagation, and we give the wanted outputs to the retrogression program. Then, the retrogression process modifies the weight of the connections to obtain better outputs. At each steps, the modification of the weights is carried out by using:

$$W_{i,j} = W_{i,j} - n . e_i . O_j \qquad 2$$

with :
$W_{i,j}$: the weight of the connection between the neuron *j* and the neuron *i* in the next layer,
n : a coefficient called "gradient step",
O_j : the state of the neuron *j*,
$e_i = 2.(O_{id} - O_i).\mathcal{F}'(Si)$ for the output layer,
$e_i = \sum_h e_h . W_{h,i} . \mathcal{F}'(Si)$ for the hidden layers,

$\mathcal{F}'(Si)$: the derivate of activation function at the point S_i.

Error estimation : The Neural Networks outputs are "connected" on the accelerator, brakes and direction control of a mobile robot. The inputs are the distances of obstacles ahead the robot, the robot velocity and the orientation of the front wheels .

The main problem is that we cannot have the exact wanted output needed by the retrogression process. As a mater of fact, when the robot runs to an obstacle, we do not know how much to turn or to brake.

We are only able to evaluate a good answer following a definite qualitative criterion.

This qualitative criterion must be translated in a analytic function : the error estimation function will be the computation basis for the retrogression process. In order to be efficient, this error estimation must follow a few rules :

* It must be equal or close to zero for the desired output (following a qualitative criterion).

* It must be convex. With this, the retrogression process, based on the gradient descent, will never be locked in a local minimum.

* All the variables used in the error estimation function must be inputs of the neural network.

By experience, even if these three restrictive conditions hold, we cannot say that the process converge to a stable state, we can only say that the process is locally stable.

On–line learning algorithm : The 6–step algorithm used in our on–line learning Neural Networks is the following :

STEP 1 : Data acquisition for the network inputs,

STEP 2 : Data propagation in the network,

STEP 3 : Robot control with the network outputs (accelerator / brakes / direction),

STEP 4 : Error evaluation,

STEP 5 : Retrogression and correction of the weights,

STEP 6 : GoTo Step 1.

4. 2. Sub–networks

This approach of reactive behaviors is based on the development of a neural network system composed of several sub–networks :

* An *Emergency Stops Module* (ESM) which can generate a maximal braking force (action on the braking actuator). Its inputs are the robot velocity, an estimation of the braking distance and the measured distance of front obstacles.

* A *Braking Modeling Module* (BMM) modeling the robot braking dynamics in order to generate an estimation of the braking distances when the vehicle velocity and the braking force are given.

* *A Dynamic Collision Avoidance Module* (CAM) generating accelerations, braking, changes of directions when the robot velocity, its orientation and the field of surrounding obstacles (proximity informations) are given.

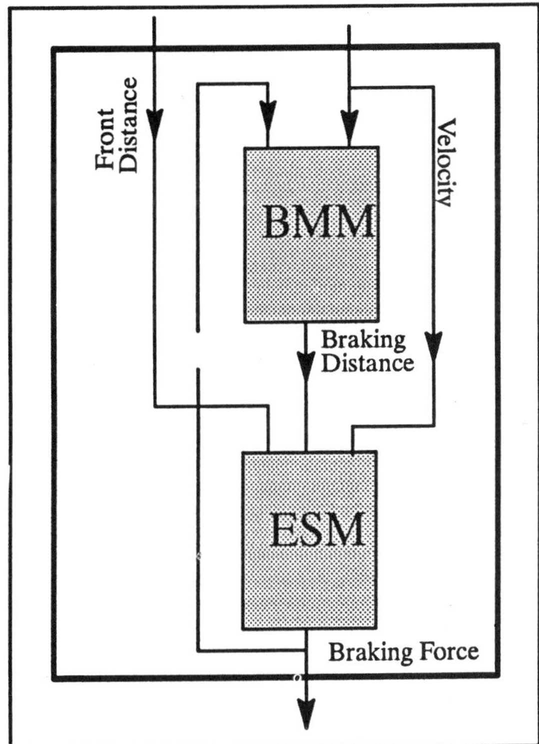

Figure 9 : *Emergency Stops Level*

These networks are combined in order to create the two levels of reactive behaviors (The *Emergency Stops Level* and the *Dynamic Collision Avoidance Level)*

5. Main Results

5. 1. Simulation [12]

These 3 networks were simulated in Turbo C on a PC compatible. A dynamic model of the robot was taught to

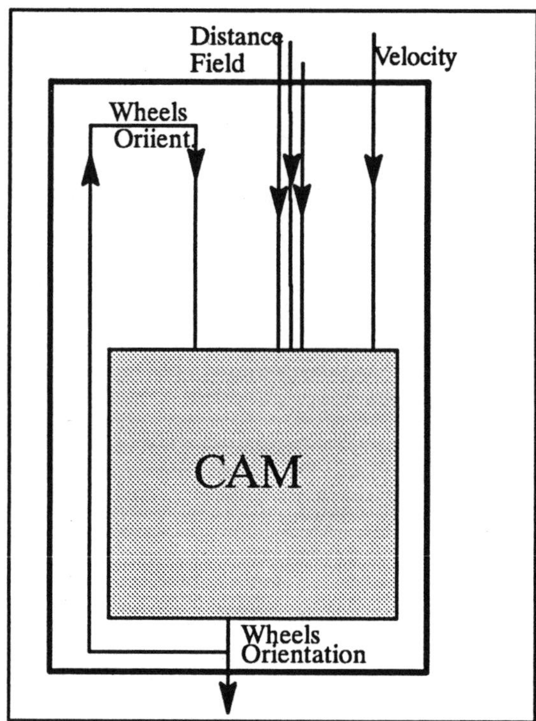

Figure 10 : Collision Avoidance Level

the network and several experiments about collision avoidance were carried out.

The reaction time of the networks (each sub−network has about 40 neurons) is better than real time (with respect to the robots dynamics and control). Thus, the learning process can be executed by two ways :

* An *off line learning*, carried out during the simulation process,

− for BMM alone, and then
−for CAM using these two previous modules in order to run its own retrogression process.

* An *on line learning*, carried out during the motions of the real vehicle, with the same procedure (BMM and then CAM).

To simulate the motion of a car−like robot, we have developed a dynamic behavior program. This simulator uses simplified dynamic equations of a mobile robot and manages a graphic User Interface.

To teach the dynamic behavior to the BMM network, we measure on the simulator the braking distances after throwing the vehicle with different initial velocities and braking forces. After the off−line learning phase of the BMM network, both Neural Networks, BMM and ESM, are implemented in the simulator.

From the first try, the vehicle thrown on a front obstacle stops before the collision. As long as we make different tries with different initial velocities, ESM network learns how to optimally brake, and to stop exactly at the specified distance X_{stop}.

To implement the Dynamic Collision Avoidance Level, we have defined a perception system which gives the same proximity information as the real sensors. We have chosen three ultrasonic sensors with 10 meters range ; one on the front of the robot, and two at thirty degrees from the main direction on the both sides of the robot.

With only this perception, the CAM network was tested alone. Obstacles are randomly placed in the scene. In the first try, the Neural Network avoids obstacle, but with jerk motions. After several tries, the direction control is smoothed and the curves described by the robot become more homogeneous.

In the last simulation phase, we implemented together both the Emergency Stops level and the Dynamical Collision Avoidance level. We obtained a robot which can avoid obstacle and stop itself when it is jammed (no free way to avoid obstacles), whatever the environment.

5. 2. Experiments

Several experiments on the 2 wheeled vehicles have been carried out in unknown and dynamic environments (outdoor and indoor).

The results provided by the two approaches are qualitatively similar and allow fast collision avoidances in unknown and dynamic worlds (5m/s for SNAKE and 2m/s for RAT).

A videotape demonstrates the skills of these robots in the problem of avoiding moving and unknown obstacles.

6. Conclusion

This paper addressed the problem of autonomous reactive behaviors in the important case of collision avoidance. Our contribution is more in the development of efficient collision avoidance procedures than in the inter−connections between different levels of behaviors, .

Simulation experiments and real world experiments on two wheeled robots have both demonstrate the validity of sensor−based control approaches and behavioral approaches (neural networks).

These experiments will be soon extended to the case of walking machines.

REFERENCES

[1]R.A. Brooks "Robot Beings", International Workshop on Intelligent Robots and Systems '89, Sep 1989, Tsukuba, Japon .

[2]T.L. Anderson "Autonomous Robots and Emergent behaviors : A Set of Primitives Behaviors for Mobile Robot Control",IROS'90, Tsukuba 1990, Japan

[3]M. Soldo "Reactive and Preplanned Control in a Mobile Robot", Proc. IEEE Int. Conf. on Rob. and Aut.,Cincinnati, Ohio, USA, May 90

[4]D. Lawton "Qualitative Spatial understanding and Reactive Control for Autonomous Robot", IROS'90, Tsukuba 90, Japan

[5]B. Espiau & *al* , "Nouvelle approche de la relation vision−commande en robotique", rapport INRIA RR−1172, 1990

[6] Holenstein, E. Badreddin "Collision Avoidance in a Behavior−based Mobile Robot Design", Proc. IEEE Int. Conf. on Rob. and Aut., Sacramento, California, April 1991.

[7]R. Zapata "Quelques aspects topologiques de la planification de mouvements et des actions réflexes en robotique mobile", Thèse d'Etat, Université de Montpellier II,1991.

[8]R.Zapata & *al* "Reactive Behaviors of Fast Mobile Robots", Journal of Robotic Systems, proposed in July 1991

[9]B.Jouvencel, P.Lépinay, R. Zapata "Reactive Behaviors and Local Navigation for Fast Mobile Robots" Journal of Automation and CIM, Volume 1, N°1, February 1992

[10]T.W. Miller, F.H.Glanz, L.G. Kraft "Application of a General Learning Algorithm to the Control of Robotic Manipulators", The International Journal of Robotics Research, Vol.6. N°2, 1987

[11]Guillaume Euvrard "Modèles connexionnistes", Rapport final MRT, 89PO713, janvier 1991

[12]P. Deplanques "Application des réseaux de neurones aux actions réflexes des robots mobiles" Rapport de DEA, Université de Montpellier 2, juillet 1992

The Adaptive Nature of 3D Perception

Allen Brookes
Department of Computing Science
Linfield College
McMinnville, Oregon 97128
(503) 472-4121 x576
allenb@audrey.linfield.edu

Abstract

The perception of the three-dimensional qualities of an image has long been treated as a deterministic process based on geometric constraints detected from cues such as motion, shading and stereo disparities. Recent psychophysical evidence suggests that the process is adaptive and that the interpretation of cues, alone or in combination, depends on learning, expectation and attention. Treating the 3D visual system as adaptive provides an efficient and robust method for dealing with a very large and complex set of cue interactions that would be much more difficult using a purely feed forward process.

1. Introduction

One of the standard methods for studying vision is the computational approach. The idea is to look at vision as an information processing problem. In such a problem one needs to determine the inputs, the outputs and the computations that are required to transform one into the other. This approach has been used widely in the study of three dimensional image understanding. In this case the input is one or two, two dimensional arrays of points with particular color and intensity values. Our experience tells us that the output should be a hierarchical structure consisting of groupings of objects, objects, parts of objects and points that all have a labeling of, among other things, distance and orientation. Since the input only has two dimensions while the output has three, the computation involved in making a transformation to three dimensions must come from information within the image.

In natural images there are many possible sources of 3D information. Among these are, shading, perspective, occlusion, motion parallax, surface contours, surface texture, and stereo disparity. Each source is interpreted in a different way. For example, the basic idea for interpreting shading is that brightness values in an image vary with surface orientation. Differences in brightness may indicate different angles away from the illuminant and the rate of change of brightness indicates the degree of curvature. Sharp changes in brightness may indicate discontinuities in surfaces. For pairs of overlapping images the difference in position of objects and parts of objects, within a left and right view of the same scene, is an indication of the relative positions in space of those objects.

In both these cases the input provides pointalistic information that varies with distance and surface orientation. Since these are some of the quantities earlier indicated as part of the desired output it seems logical that the computation be a direct calculation from point sources of disparity or brightness to that of depth, distance or surface orientation.

The problem with using these cues as sources of 3D information directly is that there is no unique way to interpret the information. For example, to determine surface orientation from shading one needs to determine where the light is coming from and the reflectance properties of the surface. Without knowing these things a particular brightness can have an infinite number of interpretations. There is no way of knowing a priori where the illuminant is or what the reflectance of the surface is so there is no unique solution to the problem.

In contrast, stereopsis is more constrained in theory than the other cues. In principle, depth can be computed from disparity, given the interpupilary distance (the distance between the eyes), and the vergence angle (the angle formed by the eyes converging on a single point).

It is difficult to know in general the location of the light source or surface reflectance properties but it seems plausible that one could know from experience the distance between ones eyes and at any moment the vergence angle of ones eyes. For this reason most of the work in stereopsis has been done on the matching process, assuming that once points are matched it is a simple calculation to find depth.

Studies of the human visual system have shown behavior that is not consistent with computational models for interpreting 2D images as 3D scenes. In particular, these behaviors are not consistent with many of the models of stereopsis that compute depth in a manner consistent with that outlined above. From the input of a pair of images, depth is calculated at each point based on how the individual points of each image are matched to their counterpart in the other image. While this appears to be a reasonable method given that the data for these computations is available and seemingly more reliable than what is provided by other cues, this does not appear to be the way in which the human visual system interprets stereo disparities. Various studies have shown that perceived depth sometimes differs from that predicted by disparities. Several studies have reversed the disparities of familiar figures such as faces and found that the familiar percept generally overpowers that of the reversed disparities. McKee (1983) and Mitchison and Westheimer (1984) showed that the depth of pairs of lines can be effected by the addition of other nearby lines. Youngs (1976) showed that in planar stimuli disparities had little effect on perceived slant. These studies cast some doubt on the theories for computing depth from disparities. The following confirm that there is no direct relationship between depth and disparities and suggest a different way of looking at the computation that is more consistent with observed behavior.

2. Evidence for Indirect Depth from Stereopsis

Stevens & Brookes (1988) studied the roles of stereopsis and shape from contours. They pitted two 3D cues against each other to see how the contradictory information would be interpreted. It was found that stereopsis is remarkably impotent in influencing perceived orientation and 3D shape. For example, given a pair of stereo points, the one with the greater (more positive) disparity is seen as relatively farther away. But if these points are embedded in a continuous 3D surface in which the monocular interpretation suggests an alternative relative depth between the two points, that monocular interpretation dominates. Figure 1 shows a planar grid stereogram with a pair of probe points. The subjects judged the left point to be closer even though the disparities are consistent with it being farther away.

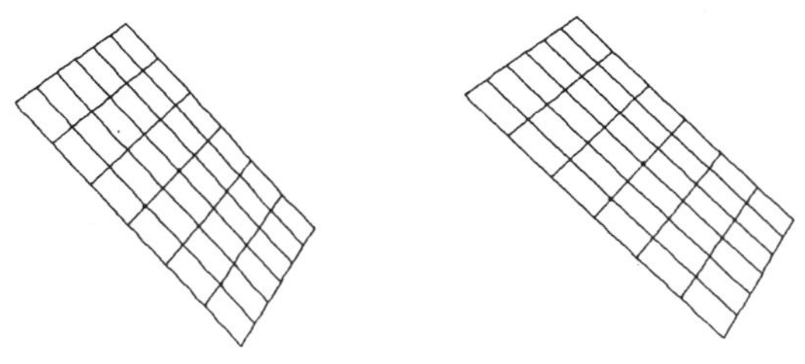

Figure 1. Example stimulus in which subjects judged relative distance of a probe point. Stereo gradient was varied while monocular gradient was kept fixed.

Examination of control stimuli indicate that sufficient stereo information is available for such a task yet with the competing interpretation the disparities are not effective. Thus stereo disparities across a planar surface are not effectively analyzed in 3D. Figure 2 shows an example of a grid with non-planar disparities. In such figures subjects tend to interpret the figure according to the disparity information.

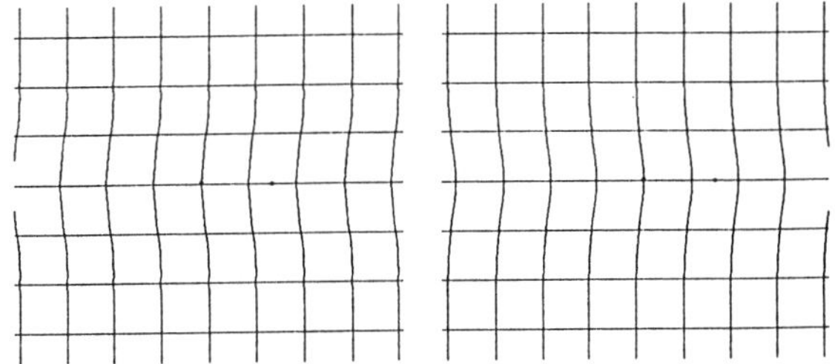

Figure 2. A horizontal Gaussian ridge defined by the disparities with a flat plane defined by the contour lines.

These results suggest that depth is derived from disparity only where the surface exhibits continuous curvature or sharp discontinuities. Also, that depth is reconstructed from multiple sources of evidence about surface topography. This means that the depth one experiences is a consequence of how this information is interpreted and reconciled. Depending on how the monocular information is interpreted, radically different depth distributions might be experienced. This is very different from the notion that depth is derived directly from stereo disparity.

If depth were computed directly from disparities then surfaces would be computed subsequently from the resulting depth maps. The results described in Brookes and Stevens (1989) show that binocular depth is computed *subsequent* to surface detection and that depth is computed from the surface descriptions. This provides a proof that, at least in certain instances, depth is a reconstructed quantity. An experiment was performed to test this conjecture. Given a random dot stereogram of four slanted panels arranged at roughly the same distance, the overall impression is of a set of slanted stairsteps. Subjects judged the relative depth of a pair of probe points according to this misperception rather than according to the values of the disparities. As a control they used a stimulus with the same set of points in which the disparities were chosen at random. The same disparities were used for the probe points within the volume created by the random disparities. In this case subjects judged the relative depth of the probe points very accurately. Figure 3 shows both types of stimuli. In both cases the disparities of the dots should indicate that the dot on the left is farther than the dot on the right.

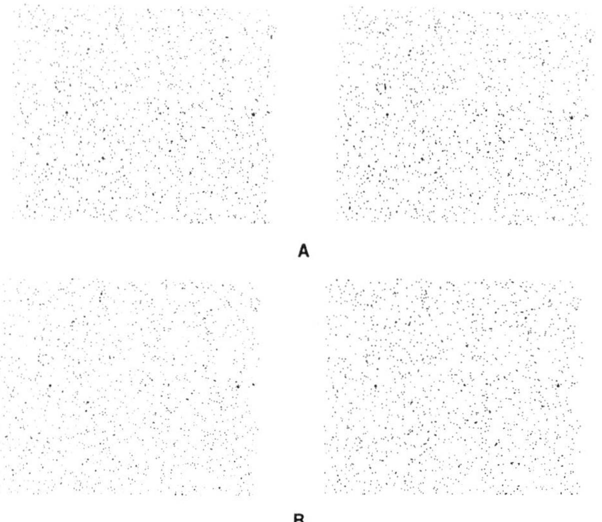

Figure 3. In *a* the disparities are distributed randomly, giving the appearance of a volume of points. In *b*, the disparities correspond to a triangle-wave surface, but seen as having an overall staircase variation in depth changing the relative distances of the probe points.

If the depth of the pair of probe points were determined by a direct comparison of the disparities then the disparities of adjacent points should not affect the judgment. It appears that adjacent points which do not provide evidence of a surface do not affect the judgment. When the adjacent points are consistent with a surface, however, the judgment seems to be consistent with the properties of the perceived surface. This not only shows that the depth is reconstructed from surface discontinuities but also adds support to the conjecture that surface properties such as slant are inaccurately derived from disparities.

3. Integration of 3D cues

The evidence above shows that the human visual system does not compute depth directly from disparities. As stated earlier, disparities have the possibility for giving the most reliable 3D information since the information needed seems to be available. If disparities do not give reliable depth information then the next best possibility for interpreting 3D information is to use combinations of cues so that the various cues may mutually constrain each other to provide an unambiguous interpretation of the image.

One of the main impediments to integrating 3D information is that different cues provide seemingly incompatible and ambiguous information. For example, shading provides information about surface curvature, rather than about the distance of the surface from the observer. To interpret a shading gradient as implying surface curvature requires some (occasionally unreliable) assumptions about the uniformity of the incident illumination and of the reflectance properties of the surfaces. Information about surface curvature is fundamentally different from, say, information about the overall distance to a surface, and if the corresponding cues are to be combined, their information must be made commensurate.

It is not clear that this is done. When looking at a picture there is often a vivid impression of 3 dimensions despite the fact that the picture is flat. This impression may be an illusion. There are several possibilities for how the qualitatively different information may be interpreted: (1) The cues are not commensurate and the impression of depth from monocular, or flat binocular images is illusory; (2) Cues are commensurate only where there is a reasonable computation for comparing them (no restrictive assumptions); (3) Cues are converted to common representation using assumptions if necessary to do conversion.

Stevens and Brookes (1987) showed that depth is derived from both orthographic and perspective projections as a scaled quantity that is commensurate with the depth perceived from stereopsis in the near field. The fact that the cues are comparable suggests that they may be combinable as well. If 3D information is in fact combinable the problem becomes finding how they are combined. Many of the computational models for interpreting 3D information try to combine 3D information to constrain the problem. For example, Richards (1984) uses stereo and motion to constrain each other and shows that only with such constraints can rigid structure be recovered from motion. However, there are few models that attempt to model the general problem for how to integrate 3D information. Bulthoff and Mallott (1988) describe a set of possible methods for combining 3D information. These include accumulation, combining information from cues, perhaps in a statistical way, disambiguation, using one cue where another is ambiguous, cooperation, and veto, where cues disagree one wins and provides the percept. The model that they develop from their experiments consists of an accumulation model where cues agree and a winner-take-all integration strategy where they do not. Bruno and Cutting (1988) propose an algebraic summation model for the integration of 3D information from multiple monocular cues. In their experiments, simple addition explains all of their results. Algebraic summation of the strength of evidence given by independent cues has also been suggested by Dosher, Sperling and Wurst (1986).

In each of these models, including the less general models, the integration is proposed to be a procedure that relies on direct comparisons of the cues without regard to context. Experiments using more complex stimuli show that this is not the case.

Stevens, Lees and Brookes (1991), generated a series of stimuli similar to those in Stevens and Brookes (1988), in which different planar and curved patterns were independently defined by surface contours and by binocular disparity. The results showed that, although with planar stimuli there a a winner-take-all domination of one cue over another, when each cue presents non-planar information the results depend on many factors.

Where both stereo and monocular interpretations indicate inconsistent surface curvature features, the results seem to involve such things as: subjects experience, focus of attention, subjects mindset, and the impression may be either the stereo or the mono interpretation, or a compromise between both, but varying among observers and among presentations for the same observer.

In cases where both stereo and monocular interpretations indicate surface curvature features which are qualitatively consistent, but different in amplitude, different observers show markedly different response patterns in a quantitative comparison task.

An example of one of the stimuli used is shown in Figure 4. The figure consists of a stereogram rendered using contour lines in which the disparities are not consistent with the normal geometric interpretation of surfaces formed by the contours. The contour information suggests a smooth edge with Gaussian profile. The disparities suggest a Gaussian edge rotated 90 degrees. Subjects impressions ranged from entirely consistent with the contours to entirely consistent with the disparities or somewhere in between. The inset shows the two extremes as well as the compromise.

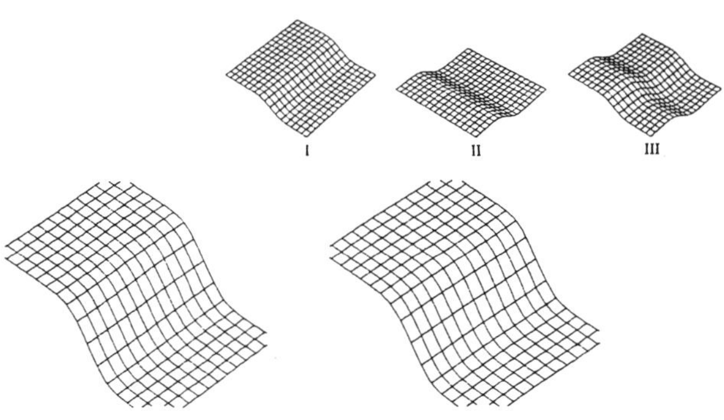

Figure 4. Stereo and mono edges intersecting at right angles. For most observers the appearance is of four steps of differing depths. The inset shows the two extremes as well as the compromise.

The ways in which these stimuli are interpreted appear to rule out any simple additive model for the integration of 3D information from surface contour and disparity processing, unless one is willing to propose a separate mechanism for cases in which the stereo and mono curvature information conflict and for cases in which it is consistent.

4. Discussion

The lesson from the above is that no simple model for deriving depth from 3D cues will account for human behavior in this area. What such models lack is the top-down component that allows the behavior of the system to to depend on subject experience and mindset. The three dimensional percept seems to be based as much on our expectations of what we will see, as on what we are actually looking at. In order to model this sort of behavior we need to model a dynamic memory that molds the percept according to stored patterns and that allows the addition of unfamiliar forms for subsequent processing.

We propose that such a memory for surface shape consists of extended surface feature assertions representing the individual cues. These surface feature assertions constitute a common language for combining cues, rather than local, pointwise primitives such as depth, or surface orientation. Constructing the surface descriptions consists of separately constructing surface feature assertions by stereo and mono processes in a bottom up manner, then combining the separate surface feature assertions top down by comparing with the stored forms, and finally filling in consistent smooth surfaces between those features. The idea that surface features are compared with stored models for their interpretation and then pasted together into larger units, provides a simple account for the difficulties observed in images with contradictory curvature information from each source. The expected interpretations of these comparisons might be: the overwriting of a feature assertion from one source with that from the other, resulting in either a stable percept determined by one process, (i.e. winner-take-all,) or an unstable percept in which each feature repeatedly overwrites the other or a compromise from the filling and smoothing processes. This prediction is consistent with our observations, although we expect that a more complete explanation could be obtained if we had a better understanding of how the integration is affected by changes in the focus of attention.

Why should the visual system be set up this way when there appears to be a simpler solution to the problem? Why, in particular, is stereopsis not used more extensively when it appears to be the most reliable cue? There are several possible reasons why this may be. One reason is generality. Stereopsis is only possible in places where the stereo disparities can be accurately perceived. In general, that is within about 200 feet of the viewer. There are also regions of the visual field where there can be no stereopsis due to a lack of binocular cells or due to an obstruction such as the nose. Also, in regions that are relatively homogeneous there will be a great deal of ambiguity in the matching process and stereopsis will be unreliable. Thus for the system to operate in a similar way under all conditions it is useful to have stereopsis as one of several contributing sources rather than as the primary source. Finally, if the visual system were to compute depth at each point from disparities the result is a point-wise depth map. The problem of imposing structure has not been solved but instead is more difficult since there is now a third dimension to consider.

The problem of combining cues is very difficult. The numbers of ways in which cues can combine makes it difficult to implement general rules for the combinations. Thus, the use of previous knowledge to provide expectations to constrain the problem seems like a reasonable solution.

Basing each percept on stored information seems like a rather complex solution to the problem. It is true that the behavior of such a system is complex. However, the principles behind this behavior may be relatively simple. If we look at the visual system as a dynamical, adaptive system, the behavior is still complex but the explanations for the behavior become much less so. In this case, for each set of features the best match is sought from conditions within the systems experience. Descriptions for such systems can be fairly simple. In fact, there are already models that display many of the characteristics of the behavior we have found in human 3D processing.

One example of such a model is Adaptive Resonance Theory or ART (Carpenter and Grossberg, 1987). ART is a theory of category recognition in which recognition consists of a network settling to a stable state where there is a match between the input and a stored template. This stable state, or resonance as they call it, may be a compromise between the input and the template. The resonance can be affected by attentional priming as well as vigilance, the degree of similarity required for the match. When an input is fed into the network each of the categories that have features in common with the input are stimulated. These categories in turn inhibit other categories. If one category has many more features of the input than others then all other categories will be inhibited and if the similarity is within the vigilance parameter then that category will be selected. The ART models do not specifically deal with different sets of cues, however, so the model must be adapted for this. Despite this, the model already has some of the important behaviors we find in integrating depth cues. First, objects that are more familiar are more easily recognized and properties such as depth, extracted. Objects with incomplete information, such as objects rendered with a single 3D cue can be recognized with partial information and compared with other objects rendered with different cues. Objects that contain inconsistent 3D cues can settle to the closest match with the available information which may be with winner-take-all or some sort of compromise. Weak matches may be unstable relative to changes that make another match stronger. These changes may include eye movements, attentional shifts or mindset.

5. Conclusions

Many of the approaches for interpreting 3D information in images do not adequately model the behavior found in humans. One of the main reasons seems to be the inappropriateness of the basic model of vision assumed by many of these approaches. This basic model contains the idea that individual features can be treated as symbols that have a predetermined 3D interpretation. This allows for systems in which the processing contains no feedback. Thus there is no effect of previous experience or current state. With such a model human behavior seems incredibly complex, different types of processing occur in different parts of the visual field, processing differs depending on the relationships of different cues, and different people behave in different way to the same stimuli. If instead the visual system is treated as a dynamical, adaptive system, the behaviors become more easily understood. The interpretation of any one feature at any particular time depends on how that feature, with its context, fits a stored model of surface curvature and discontinuity features. This process of comparisons with stored models allows for quickly discounting a combinatorially large set of possibilities and thus enabling a quick interpretation of a scene. It also allows one to adapt to new circumstances that might arise and that would cause a deterministic system to fail.

6. References

Brookes, A. & Stevens, K.A. 1989 Binocular depth from surfaces vs. volumes. *Journal of Experimental Psychology* 15(3) 479-484.

Bruno N, Cutting J E, 1988 Minimodularity and the perception of layout *Journal of Experimental Psychology: General* 117(2) 161-170

Bulthoff H H, & Mallot H A 1988 Integration of depth modules: stereo and shading *Journal of the Optical Society of America* 5 1749 - 1758

Carpenter, G.A. & Grossberg, S. 1987 A massively parallel architecture for a self-organizing neural pattern recognition machine. *Computer Vision, Graphics and Image Processing* 37, 54-115

Dosher B A, Sperling G, Wurst S A, 1986 "Tradeoffs between stereopsis and proximity luminance covariance as determinants of perceived 3D structure" *Vision Research* 26 (6) 973-990

Gillam B J, 1968, "Perception of slant when perspective and stereopsis conflict: Experiments with aniseikonic lenses" *Journal of Experimental Psychology* 78 299-305

Gillam B J, Flagg T, Finlay D, 1984 "Evidence for disparity change as the primary stimulus for stereoscopic processing" *Perception and Psychophysics* 36 559-564

Gillam B J, Chambers D, Russo, T, 1988 "Postfusional latency in stereoscopic slant perception and the primitives of stereopsis" *Journal of Experimental Psychology: Human Perception and Performance* 14 163-175

McKee S.P., 1983 The spatial requirements for fine stereoacuity. *Vision Research,* 23, 191-198.

Mitchison, G.J. and Westheimer G.. 1984 The perception of depth in simple figures. *Vision Research* 24, 1063-1073.

Richards W, 1984 Structure from stereo and motion, AI Memo 731, Artificial Intelligence Laboratory, MIT.

Rogers B J, Graham M E, 1983 "Anisotropies in the perception of three-dimensional surfaces" *Science* 221 1409-1411

Stevens, K.A. & Brookes, A. 1987 Probing depth in monocular images. *Biological Cybernetics* 56, 355-366.

Stevens K A, Brookes A, 1988 "Integrating stereopsis with monocular interpretations of planar surfaces" *Vision Research* 28 (3) 387-396

Stevens, K.A., Lees, M. & Brookes, A. Combining binocular and monocular curvature features. *Perception.* 20(4) 425-440.

Wheatstone C, 1852 On some remarkable, and hitherto unobserved phenomena of binocular vision *Phil. Mag. Ser.* 4 504-523.

Yellott J I, Kaiwi J L, 1979 "Depth inversion despite stereopsis: the appearance of random-dot stereograms on surfaces seen in reverse perspective" *Perception* 8 135-142

Youngs W M, 1975 “The influence of perspective and disparity cues on the perception of slant” *Vision Research* 16 79-82

Propulsion and Guidance in a Simulation of the Worm *C. Elegans*

Ralph Hartley

Navy Center for Applied Research
in Artificial Intelligence,
Naval Research Laboratory,
Washington, DC 20375-5000

Abstract

A simulation of the mechanics of the Nematode worm *C. Elegans* was constructed and used to study its locomotory behaviors. This simulation shed light on the mechanisms that must be used by any animal or robot using the same type of propulsion and also on aspects of the behavior of the real worm. The simulation of locomotion is an important step in the understanding of the overall behavior of an animal.

1. Introduction

An extension of the strategy of learning about robotics by building robots [Brooks86] is to build animals. In [Hartley92] it was suggested that the complete simulation of an actual animal could be feasible and would almost certainly be instructive. *C. Elegans* the is only animal for which this is likely to be possible.

C. Elegans is a small nematode worm which lives in soil and rotting vegetation. It has been used by biologists as a model system, and consequently there is a great deal of information available about it [Wood88]. The anatomy (including all synapses) of all 302 neurons in its nervous system (and of the rest of its 959 cells) has been completely mapped [White86]. The developmental history of each cell, including each cell division, is known. There is also currently a *C. Elegans* genome project, which expects to complete its job before the turn of the century.

As a first step in the simulation of the worm's behavior, a simulation study of the mechanics of the worm's body and of the control of locomotion has been carried out. This is a necessary first step because of the way in which all behavior is coupled to locomotion.

[Erdos90] also built a simulation of the body and some of the neural circuitry of *C. Elegans*, but was unable to perform experiments as extensive as those described here. [Rowley91] has done some simulation of the motor circuits of a related worm but did not simulate the associated mechanics.

2. Real Worms

C. Elegans, like all other nematodes, uses a form of locomotion known as "undulatory propulsion" [Gray53]. Undulatory propulsion is also used by most snakes, some fish, and some protozoa. The worm propagates bending waves from head to tail to move itself forward (waves propagate from tail to head to move backward). This works because the part of the body which forms the "side" of the wave is moving backward while the parts near the crest and trough are moving forward. The coefficients of drag are different for these two regions because the crest and trough are moving tangentially while the side is moving at an angle. This produces a net thrust.

C. Elegans is approximately 1mm long and about 1/20th as thick. For an animal in this size range, the dominant forces are not gravity and inertia (which are in fact negligible), but surface tension and viscosity. *C. Elegans*' behavior has mostly been studied in a thin film of water covering a rigid (or nearly rigid) surface. In this situation surface tension mainly serves to pull the worm down tightly onto the substrate. The force with which the worm is pressed into the substrate along with the composition of the substrate largely determines the resistance to motion (the effective viscosity). The resistance to motion along its axis and to slipping sideways can vary greatly.

This form of locomotion has several important properties. The most important of which is that locomotion uses the entire body of the animal. Unlike locomotion by legs or wheels, it is impossible to decouple locomotion from other behaviors. Undulatory propulsion is suitable for complex environments where there are many small obstacles. It is also well suited to three dimensional environments such as between soil particles and inside the body of another animal.

3. The simulator

To study the problems of this type of locomotion, a simulator was constructed. Only the relatively simple situation of a worm on a flat unobstructed surface was simulated. The simulator is sufficiently flexible that other, more complex, environments for the worm can also be simulated. The simulation is inherently three dimensional, but in all the experiments that were performed the worm was restricted to one plane.

3.1. Model of worm

In order to produce a simulation which is both fast and accurate, it is important to be very careful in selecting the variables to be simulated. If important variables are left out, the simulation will not represent the phenomena being studied. On the other hand, extra variables can decrease the stability of the simulation, so that it becomes computationally intractable. Furthermore, the model can be made more elaborate than is justified by what is known of the system being simulated. This can produce extraneous phenomena in the simulation.

Three models of the worm were tried, using different levels of detail. All three models break the worm into small segments which interact with each other and with the substrate. Interaction with the substrate is by viscous forces which are proportional to velocity, but which may have different coefficients in different directions.

Figure 1 shows the first model. The worm is modeled as a chain of segments connected by springs. This model is a simplification of the one used by [Erdos90] which was to complex and too slow to be used in extensive experiments. The primary difference is that variations in thickness (which are too small to be dynamically important) are not modeled. The model consists of a

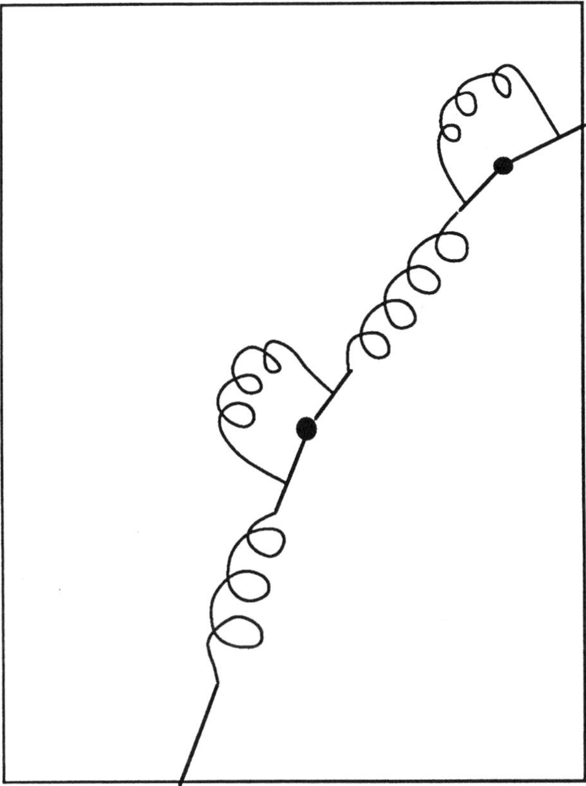

Figure 1 - The first, Most complex, model of the worm.

chain of lengthwise springs, connected by universal joints held straight by springs. The lengthwise springs can change in length, but may not bend, bending forces are controlled by the springs on the joints. The velocity of each segment can be computed from the spring forces and the hydrodynamic coefficients.

The lengthwise springs represent the symmetric component of the elastic and hydrostatic forces. The springs mounted on the joints represent bending forces due to asymmetry in the cuticle tension and muscle forces. This model assumes that all musculoskeletal forces are essentially longitudinal. The forces of the two sets of springs represent the sum and difference of forces on opposite sides of the body.

This model has the following problems. Though bending motions are most important in undulatory locomotion, it is longitudinal stretching and contraction which consumes most of the simulation effort. Suppose the worm's body is straight and a lengthwise force is applied to one end. The force will propagate to the other end by the successive stretching of each segment in turn.

This requires a number of simulation time steps roughly proportional to the number of segments. On the other hand, a lateral force need only bend a few segments near the point of application. Combine this with the fact the the worm is relatively resistant to stretching but bends easily, and that the lateral coefficients of friction are generally greater, and the result is that much finer time steps must be used to obtain stability in length than in bending.

The second model does not simulate forces between segments at all. Instead, the relative positions of the segments are set independently of the dynamics and only the motion of the worm as a whole is modeled. This is appropriate if the elastic and muscular forces are large compared to viscous forces. In this case (which may occur when the worm is swimming) the body approaches static equilibrium on a short time scale relative to the rate of motion. However, this will generally be the case only when the ratio of lateral to longitudinal friction is near one. Otherwise movement is fast enough that viscous forces make a significant contribution to determining the worm's shape.

The third model (figure 2), which was found to be most suitable, is a simplification of the first. The lengthwise springs are replaced by rigid rods, so that the length of each segment is kept fixed. Unlike the first model, the velocities of the segments can no longer be computed independently. They are coupled together by the constraint on the segment lengths. This means that a set of simultaneous linear equations must be solved to get the velocities. Because the constraints are only between adjacent segments, however, the only non-zero matrix elements are near the diagonal, and the equations can be solved quickly.

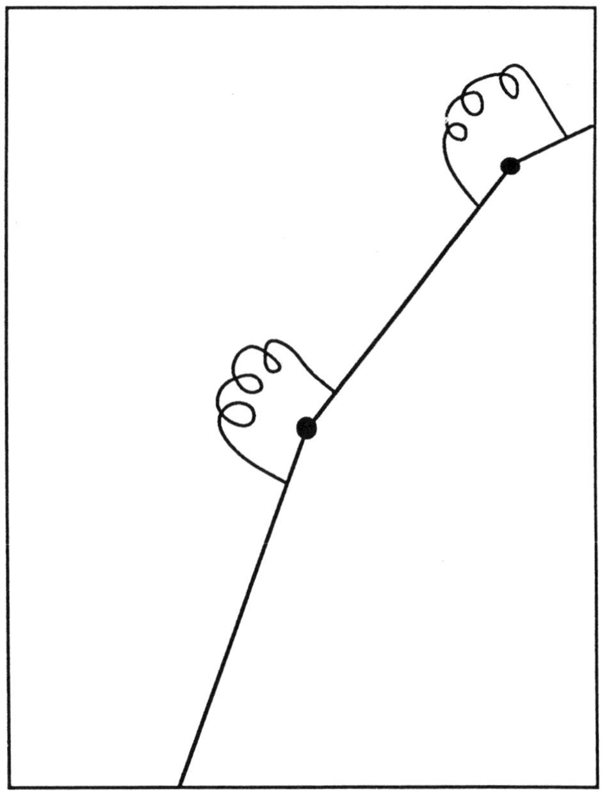

Figure 2 - Simplified model of worm.
This model was used for all experiments.

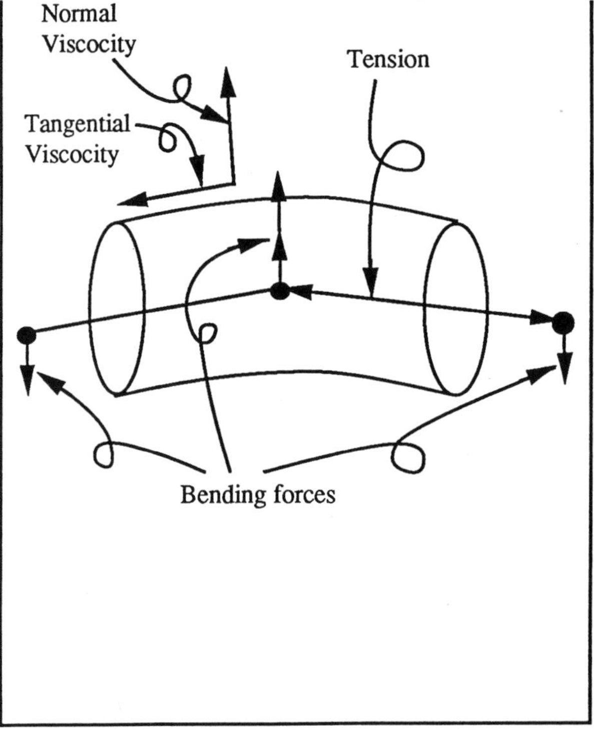

Figure 3 - Forces on a small section of the worm.

The forces acting on a segment are shown in figure 3. The viscous force is proportional to velocity. The viscous force has two parts: the component in the tangent direction and the part perpendicular to this direction. Each of these components is proportional to the corresponding component of the velocity and is oppositely directed. The drag coefficients must differ (the perpendicular component is usually larger) for undulatory propulsion to be possible.

Bending forces F_i are produced by the elasticity of the cuticle combined by the force produced by internal presure as well as the forces generated by muscles. These forces produce a bending moment consisting of a force applied to the segment and an equal and opposite force divided equally between its two neighbors.

The remaining force is the net tension or compression required to keep the segment lengths constant.

The velocity at each segment can be computed by solving a system of 4N-1 equations in 4N-1 variables. The variables are the 3 components of velocity at each segment and the tension between each pair of segments. The 3N equations

$$-F_i = -C_i V_i - T_{i-1} U_{i-1} + T_i U_i$$

ensure that the total force on each segment is zero. The remaining N-1 equations

$$0 = -V_{i+1} \cdot U_i + V_i \cdot U_i$$

keep the lengths of the segments constant.

Once the muscle forces are given, solving these equations gives the velocity of each segment. The equations were integrated over time by the second order Runge-Kutta method [Press88].

3.2. Parameters of simulation

The spring constant of the elastic forces, and the viscosity, are used in the simulation only in the form of their ratio. However, even this is not dynamically important. Because velocity is proportional to force and inversely propulsional to viscosity, changing this ratio only changes the time scale of the simulation. For some methods of controlling locomotion (for instance any that use an internal oscillator) this parameter needs to be known. It must be noted that the real worm is able to function even when the effective viscosity varies widely.

The ratio of muscle forces to the passive elastic and internal presure forces is more important. This ratio controls the amplitude of the waves used in locomotion. There is little or no information available for setting this parameter other than the observed waveform of the worm.

The most important parameter is the "slip ratio", the ratio of the drag coefficients for motion perpendicular to the body axis and tangent to the axis. This ratio, which also varies greatly with environmental conditions, determines the efficiency of undulatory propulsion. If the slip ratio were 1, then propulsion would be impossible[Gray63]. Some protozoa [Lighthill76] have specialized structures that make the ratio less than one, and propel themselves with forward propagating waves. All nematodes, however, have slip ratios greater than one, and propel themselves forward by means of backward propagating waves.

4. Experiments

Many qualitative and some quantitative experiments on the mechanics and control of undulatory propulsion were performed using the simulation. The results show that previous studies of undulatory propulsion [Gray63] miss some key issues. The results also explain some observed aspects of the behavior of real worms [Croll75].

4.1. Propulsion

In the simple case examined in the literature[Gray63], where the sinusoidal body wave is already established and only instantaneous motion is considered, undulatory propulsion is not difficult. A sinusoidal wave of muscle contraction, ninety degrees ahead of the body wave, produces forward motion. What is left out is how to establish the body wave, and once established how to maintain it while moving.

The simplest and most general control algorithm that was used in the experiments was a sinusoidal wave of muscle action. The phase of the muscle wave was set to a fixed offset from the phase of the body wave, which was measured globally at each time step. A phase of 0 degrees acts to increase the amplitude of the current body waveform, while an offset of 90 degrees produces the simple forward propulsion discussed above.

[Chalfie85] describes a theory of how the control of propulsion in *C. Elegans* could actually be implemented. In this theory, the muscle action at a given position along the worm's body is determined by the curvature at a point some distance from that position. The head is controlled independently. This is similar to the method described in the previous paragraph except that the phase of the body wave is measured locally instead of over the whole body. This algorithm was implemented, and was found to give similar results. This model is more complex, however, with many parameters that must be adjusted, and was not therefore mot considered suitable for quantitative experiments.

The simple global wave algorithm was used to study the dynamics of propulsion. The most striking observation is that under some conditions the system is bistable.

Efficient propulsion is possible, and self-maintaining, but the necessary body wave does not form spontaneously.

The critical parameters for propulsion are the slip ratio (an environmental variable beyond the worm's control), and the phase offset between the body wave and the muscle wave. In the ideal case, where the problems of maintaining the body wave are not considered (as would occur in a sinusoidally bent capillary tube), a phase offset of 90 degrees is clearly best. All muscle forces are then contributing to forward motion. For offsets less than this, there is a component of the muscle forces that act to maintain the waveform.

Figure 4 shows the distance traveled in 60 simulated seconds, as a function of the phase offset, for different values of the slip ratio, and for different initial conditions. The "cold start" curve shows the performance when the worm's body was initially straight, while the "warm start" curve shows the performance after the waveform was first established by 60 seconds with an offset of 60 degrees. Propulsion is bistable in the region between the drop off in the cold start curve and that of the warm start curve. The length of the tests was long enough that starting transients have only minor effects, they can be seen, however, as the dip in the cold start curve just before it drops off.

4.2. Turning

Turning in *C. Elegans* is a relatively simple matter; turn the head and the rest of the body follows. Complications arise because of the fact that propulsive waves must be occurring at the same time. Because the functions of propulsion and turning cannot be uncoupled, synchronization between these functions could be important.

There are two possible ways in which turning and propulsion can be synchronized. The worm can either skip one half wave, or exaggerate one. Figure 5 shows both types of turn. Both behaviors can produce turns of any magnitude, but they have dramatically different effects on propulsive efficiency. When the head is turned in the same direction as the current propulsive wave, so as to exaggerate one half wave, locomotion proceeds smoothly. If the head is turned in the opposite direction, reducing the magnitude of a half wave, a straight section is formed in the body. This section can produce no thrust, and greatly reduces propulsive efficiency. If the worm is operating in the bistable regime, it can loose its propulsive body wave altogether.

It has been noted from observations of actual worm's [Croll75] that, whenever they make a large change in direction, the worms use a behavior known as an "omega wave" (due to the shape of the worm's track). This waveform corresponds exactly to our exaggerated half wave.

5. Conclusions

The simulation of the mechanics of *C. Elegans* clarifies much of the behavior of the real worm. It also reveals additional issues. It is unclear how the actual worm maintains its body waveform. There are several possibilities. The worm may use a phase offset small enough that it never operates in the bistable region. This would require a sacrifice of speed, however, because the fastest speed is always in the bistable region.

The worm may also use a small phase offset to establish the body wave and then switch to a larger value. This would work, but there is no evidence of a neural mechanism for changing the offset. It should be noted that, with all the neural connections mapped, such a mechanism should be apparent. Circuits capable of generating a fixed offset are fairly obvious.

Another possibility is that the phase offset for backward motion may be smaller than for forward motion. This would be a solution because of the way in which the worm used forward and backward motion. Most of the time, the worm moves forward. Whenever the worm hits an obstruction, or occasionally at random, the worm reverses for about three waves, and then continues forward, sometimes with a change of direction. Because relatively little time is spent in backward motion, the low speed implied by a low phase offset is acceptable. The body waveforms required for forward and backward motion are identical.

Further studies with the simulation will include sensing and seeking behaviors. These behaviors can not be studied in isolation because the nature of undulatory locomotion and the motion based gradient detection apparently used by *C. Elegans* [Ward73] couples them tightly to propulsion. *C. Elegans* is also a good model system for studying reactive behavior. The amount of long range planning possible in its environment is very limited. The worm gets very limited information about what lies ahead, and is never able to retrace its path.

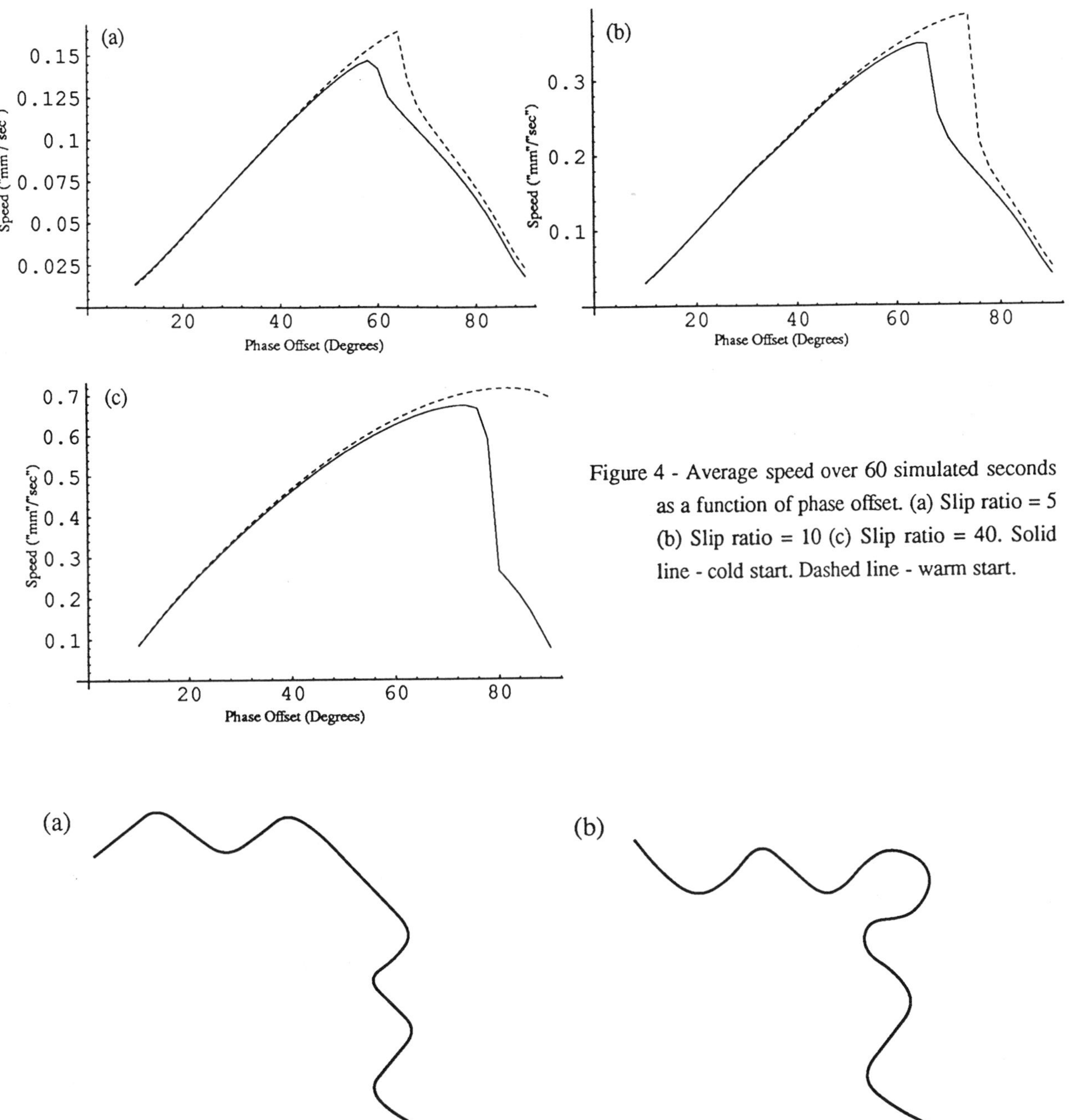

Figure 4 - Average speed over 60 simulated seconds as a function of phase offset. (a) Slip ratio = 5 (b) Slip ratio = 10 (c) Slip ratio = 40. Solid line - cold start. Dashed line - warm start.

Figure 5 - (a) Turning by Skipping a half wave.
(b) Turning by exaggerating a half wave.

References

[Brooks86] R. Brooks, "Achieving Artificial Intelligence Through Building Robots", MIT AI Memo 899, 1986

[Chalfie85] M. Chalfie, J. Sulston, J. White, E. Southgate, J. Thomson, S. Brenner, "The Neural Circuit for Touch Sensitivity in Caenorhabditis Elegans", *The Journal of Neuroscience*, Volume 5, Number 4, pp 956-964, 1985

[Croll75] N. Croll, "Components and Patterns in the Behavior of the Nematode Caenorhabditis Elegansρq, *Journal of Zoology* Volume 176, pp 159-176, 1975

[Erdos90] P. Erdos, E. Niebur, he Neural Basis of the Locomotion of Nematodes", *Statistical Mechanics of Neural Networks*, L. Garrido (ed), Springer-Verlag, 1990

[Gray53] J. Gray, "Undulatory Propulsion", *Quarterly Journal of Microscopical Science*, Volume 94, Part 4, pp 551-578, 1953

[Gray63] J. Gray, H. Lissmann, "The Locomotion of Nematodes", *Journal of Experimental Biology*, Volume 41, pp 135-154.

[Hartley92] R. Hartley, "Caenorhabditis Elegans: a Proposal to simulate a Simple Animal", Talk given at *Artificial Life III*, 1992

[Lighthill76] M. Lighthill, "Flagellar Hydrodynamics", *SIAM Review* Volume 18, Number 2, 1976

[Press88] W. Press, B. Flannery, S. Teukolsky, W. Vetterling, *Numerical Recipes in C*, Cambridge University Press, 1988

[Rowley91] S. Rowley, C. Rockland, " The design of Simulation Languages for Systems with Multiple Modularities", *Simulation*, Volume 56, Number 3, pp 153-163, 1991

[Ward73] S. Ward, "Cemotaxis by the Nematode Caenorhabditis Elegans: Identification of Attractants and Analysis of the Response by Use of Mutants", *Proccedings of the National Academe of Science* Volume 70, Number 3, pp 817-821

[White86] j. White, E. Southgate, J. Thomson, S. Bremner, "The Structure of the Nervous System of the Nematode, Caenorhabditis Elegans", *Philosophical Transactions of the Royal Society of London*, Section B, Volume 314, Issue 1165, pp 1-340, 1986

[Wood88] B. Wood, and the community of *C. Elegans* researchers, *The Nematode Caenorhabditis Elegans*, Cold Spring Harbor Laboratory, 1988

A simple, cheap, and robust visual navigation system

Ian Horswill
MIT Artificial Intelligence Laboratory
545 Technology Square
Cambridge, MA 02139, USA
ian@ai.mit.edu

Abstract

In this paper I will discuss a system which uses vision to guide a mobile robot through corridors and freespace channels. The system runs in an unmodified office environment in the presence of both static and dynamic obstacles (*e.g.* people). The system is among the simplest, most effective, and best tested systems for vision-based navigation to date. The performance of the system is dependent on an analysis of the special properties of robot's environment. I will describe these properties and discuss how they simplify the computational problems facing the robot.[1]

1 Introduction

Navigation is one of the most basic problems in robotics. Since the ability to safely move about the world is a prerequisite of most other activities, navigation has received a great deal of attention in the AI, robotics, and computer vision communities. One of the limiting factors in the design of current navigation systems, as with many other robotic systems, has been the availability of reliable sensor data. Most systems have relied on the use of sonar data [7][8], or on vision [9][3][5][6][13][1]. In all cases, the unreliability of the available sensor data was a major concern in the research. Some researchers have even avoided the use of sensor data entirely in favor of precompiled maps [10].

In this paper, I will discuss a very simple vision-based corridor following system which is in day-to-day use here at MIT. The system is notable in that it is very fast (15 frames per second in the current system), very well tested, and uses only cheap "off-the-shelf" hardware. A major source of this simplicity is an analysis of the agent's niche. Such an analysis helps make clear the dependence of an agent on its environment and provides guidance for the design of future systems.

1.1 The Polly project

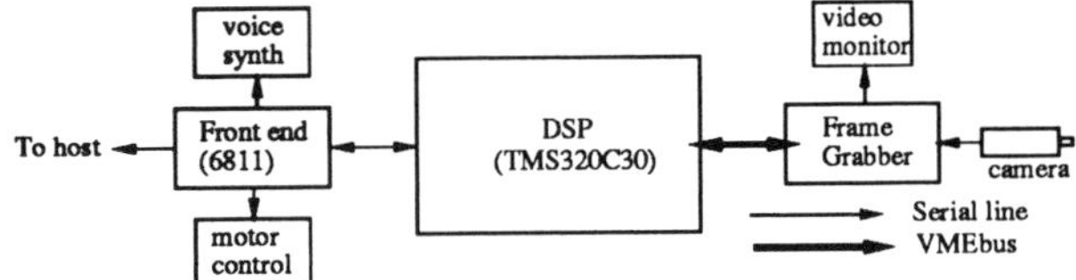

Figure 1: Hardware architecture of Polly.

Polly is a low cost, vision-based, autonomous robot built to help study how properties of the environment can simplify the computational problems facing an agent.[2] The theoretical goal of the project is to articulate a number of useful ***computational properties*** of office environments, and to develop a theory of how those properties can simplify the design of an agent. For example, one such property is that office environments do not generally have any moving objects other than people; thus, motion is a cue to agency. Rather than having to do a complicated analysis of the various objects in view to determine if they look or act like agents, the robot can simply check if they're moving, a much simpler test. This property does not hold of all habitats–trees blow in the wind and waves crash upon the shore, but they are not agents–and so the property partly determines of the set of habitats in which an agent that assumes it may survive. For this reason, I will refer to such properties as ***habitat constraints*** (see Horswill [4] for a more detailed discussion).

In this paper, I will discuss how habitat constraints can allow "optimizations" to be performed on the control systems of simple agents. The optimizations we will examine take the form of replacing a subsystem of the agent with another system which is in some way less expensive, but which nonetheless does the same job, provided that the habitat constraint holds. The motion constraint outlined above allows a motion detector to be substituted for a more complicated recognition system. This substitution is an optimization in the sense that the motion detector is less expensive than the recognition system. Depending on the context, we may mea-

[1]Support for this research was provided in part by the University Research Initiative under Office of Naval Research contract N00014–86–K–0685, and in part by the Advanced Research Projects Agency under Office of Naval Research contract N00014–85–K–0124.

[2]Polly was built for $20K (parts cost in the U.S.), but today, a roughly comparable, or perhaps even faster, system could be bought for roughly $10K US.

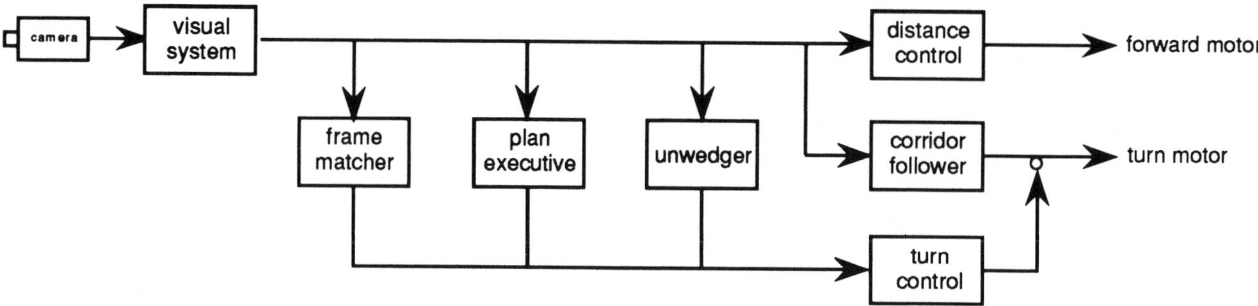

Figure 2: Conceptual architecture of the current version of the navigation system, as implemented in software.

sure expense as the actual monetary cost of building a robot, or the biological cost of growing and feeding extra neurons, or some other measure entirely. By analyzing an agent's specialization in terms of habitat constraints and optimizations, we can place specific properties of the environment into correspondence with specific computational problems facing the agent and the solutions which those properties allow. Such an analysis makes very explicit the way in which an agent is adapted to its environment, the possible consequences of changing that environment, and what facets of the agent would have to change to adapt to the new environment.

The implementation goal of the project is to use this approach to design to develop an efficient visual system which will allow the robot to run unattended for extended periods (hours) and to give primitive "tours" of the MIT AI lab. Our general approach to design has been to determine what particular pieces of information are needed by the agent to perform it's activities, and then to design complete visual systems for extracting each piece of information. Thus, the agent might have distinct systems for answering questions such as "am I about to hit something?" and "what is the axis of this corridor?" If these systems are simple enough, they can be run in parallel very efficiently. In the system presented here, they are indeed simple enough so that each one can be run for each image frame, using an inexpensive computer.

The computational hardware on Polly consists of a 16MIP digital signal processor (Texas Instruments TMS320C30) with 64K 32-bit words of high speed ram[3], a video frame buffer/grabber, a simple 8-bit microcontroller (M68HC11) for I/O tasks, and commercial microcontrollers for voice synthesis and motor control (see figure 1). Nearly all computation is done on the DSP. The fact that Polly uses only vision for sensing was due to lack of engineering time and experience, *not* because we feel that vision should be used for everything.

1.2 Work to date

At present, Polly consists of:

- A system for navigating corridors and relatively uncluttered spaces (reported on here)
- A rudimentary place recognition system
- A plan executive for forcing the robot to perform fixed sequences of actions (useful for debugging)
- A simple person detector based on bilateral symmetry
- An "unwedger," which pilots the robot out of cul-de-sacs and dead ends.
- A unit which overrides the corridor follower to perform open-loop turns
- A carpet-boundary detector (see section 7)

The connectivity of the navigation components is shown in figure 2. All these components are run in pseudo-parallel fashion on the DSP: at each moment in time, the robot grabs a new frame from the camera, runs each of the components, yielding a motor command, issues the motor command, and repeats the cycle.

The corridor follower nearly always controls the robot when it is moving. Even when the robot is not in a corridor, the corridor follower is still used to attempt to go forward without hitting obstacles. All other modules are built upon the corridor follower: the turn box can override the corridor follower to turn a corner; the place recognition system, the unwedger, and the plan executive can issue turn requests to the turn box. As of this writing, the corridor follower, unwedger, carpet boundary detector, and plan executive are essentially finished. The place recognition system and person detector are still under active development.

2 Corridor following

Corridor following is a common navigation task in office environments. Office buildings tend to consist of long corridors lined with rooms on either side, thus much of the work of getting from one room to another consists of driving along a series of corridors. The corridor follower described here is intended to be used as one component among many which cooperate to allow the robot to participate in its projects.

Corridor following can be broken into the complementary problems of keeping aligned with the axis of the corridor and keeping away from the walls. This amounts to keeping the variable θ in figure 3 small, while simultaneously keeping l and r comfortably large. Since Polly can only move in the direction in which it's pointed,

[3]The DSP includes an additional 1Mb of low speed ram, which is not presently in use. At present, only approximately 10KW of RAM are in use.

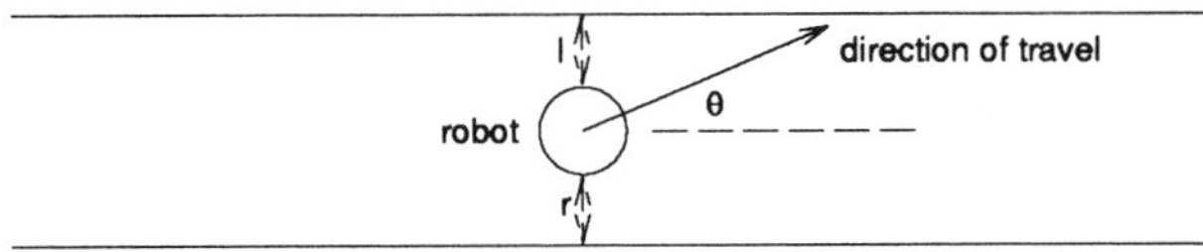

Figure 3: Corridor following.

these variables are coupled. In particular, if the speed of the robot is s, then we have that:

$$\frac{dl}{dt} = -\frac{dr}{dt} = s \sin\theta$$

so moving away from a wall requires that Polly temporarily turn away from the axis of the corridor. Thus the problem for the control system amounts to controlling s and $\frac{d\theta}{dt}$ so as to keep l and r large and θ small and the problem for the visual system amounts to determining when one of these conditions is violated.

There is a huge space of possible solutions to this problem. Consider the subtask of aligning with the corridor. An obvious way of performing this task would be to use a system that first constructs a 3D model of the environment, then finds the walls of the corridor in the model, then computes the axis, θ, of the corridor from the walls, and finally, multiplies the axis by some gain to drive the turning motor. We can represent this schematically as:

$$\Rightarrow \boxed{\text{3D model}} \rightarrow \boxed{\text{corridor}} \rightarrow \boxed{\theta} \rightarrow \boxed{\text{gain}} \rightarrow \text{motor}$$

Here the double arrow at be beginning represents input from the sensors and the boxes are successive transformations of the sensory data. This is not a particularly efficient design however, since 3D models are both difficult and computationally expensive to build. Intuitively, building an entire model of the environment, only to compress down to a single number, θ, seems a waste of energy.

Of course, any system which computes θ, in whatever manner, and then turns to minimize θ, that is, any system of the form,

$$\Rightarrow \boxed{\theta} \rightarrow \boxed{\text{gain}} \rightarrow \text{motor}$$

will do the trick. Furthermore, it can be shown that given the right conditions, we don't even need to compute θ *per se*; we can substitute any monotonic function of θ which is zero when θ is zero.[4] Thus we can use any system of the form:

$$\Rightarrow \boxed{f(\theta)} \rightarrow \boxed{\text{gain}} \rightarrow \text{motor}$$

where f is the monotonic function.

[4]The conditions are that the motor must be controlled in velocity space, meaning that we have direct control over its speed, rather than just its acceleration, and that the control system must be fast enough so that we can treat it as having zero delay. If these conditions are not met, then the system may oscillate.

The point of this analysis is simply that the constraints imposed by the task on the architecture of agent are actually quite modest, and that they admit a huge space of possible architectures. The choice of what architecture is best will depend on the resources available to the agent, the other tasks which the agent may have to perform, and the relative expense of the design.

3 The control system

At any given time, the corridor follower has to make a decision about what direction to turn, if at all, how fast to turn, and how fast to move forward. Since our robot has independent motors for turning and driving forward, we can treat these problems separately. In this section, I will discuss how the corridor follower computes the turn and drive rates from five numbers describing the situation: l', r', and θ', which are estimates of l, r, and θ, respectively, c', a measure of the distance to the nearest obstacle in front of the robot, and σ, a measure of the visual system's confidence in its estimate of θ. The control problem is actually much easier than the perceptual problem of estimating these numbers. In section 4, I will discuss two special properties of the environment which can make it easier for the visual system to estimate these numbers, and then in section 5, I will discuss the actual design of the visual system.

3.1 *Steering for corridor following*

the steering rate $\frac{d\theta}{dt}$ is controlled by θ', σ, l', and r', which are measured by the visual system. The system drives the steering motor at a rotational velocity of

$$\frac{d\theta}{dt} = \alpha(l' - r') + \beta\theta'$$

if it is confident of it's measure of θ', otherwise with a velocity of $\alpha(l' - r')$. Here α and β are gains (constants) adjusted empirically for good results.

In practice, we have not measured the variable θ' directly, but instead have used the image plane x coordinate of the projection of the axis of the corridor, which is more easily measured. The projection x is equal to $k \tan^{-1}\theta$, where k is determined by the focal length and resolution of the camera Thus the actual control law used in our system is:

$$\frac{d\theta}{dt} = \alpha(l' - r') + \beta \tan^{-1}\theta'$$

One could solve for θ given x and an accurately calibrated camera, but in our experience, this control system has worked perfectly well.

3.2 *Controlling forward motion*

The two constraints on forward velocity are that the robot should move forward when there's nothing in its way, and that it should stop when there is something close to it. We want the robot to move at full speed when the nearest obstacle is more than some safe distance, d_{safe}, and to stop when it's less than some distance d_{stop}. We use the rule

$$s = \min\left(v_{max}, \frac{v_{max}}{d_{safe} - d_{stop}}(c' - d_{stop})\right)$$

Constraint	Computational problem
Ground plane	Depth perception
Background-texture	Figure/ground separation
Long corridor edges	Vanishing point
Strong corridor edges	Edge detection (for vanishing point)
Known camera tilt	Vanishing point
Uniform non-corridor intersections	Vanishing point

Figure 4: Habitat constraints assumed by the visual system and the problems they helped to simplify. Note that "known camera tilt" is more a constraint on the agent, than on the habitat.

which causes the robot to smoothly decelerate as it approaches an obstacle, and to back up if it gets too close to an obstacle. Backing up is useful because it allows one to herd the robot from place to place.

4 Computational properties of office environments

Estimating distance and parsing the visual world into objects are both very difficult problems in the general case. For example, figure/ground separation can be arbitrarily difficult if we consider pathological situations such as camouflage or crypsis, which can require preditors to learn to recognize prey on a case by case basis (see Roitblat [12], p. 260). Fortunately, office environments, Polly's habitat, are actively structured by both designers and inhabitants so as to facilitate their legibility (see Passini [11] for an interdisciplinary discussion of the navigational properties of buildings). The special properties of office environments allow much simpler architectures to be used than would be necessary for an agent which was to follow arbitrary paths in arbitrary environments.

One such property is that office environments have a flat ground plane, the floor, upon which most objects rest. For a given height and orientation of the camera, the distance of a point P from the camera will be a strictly increasing function of the height of P's projection in the image plane, and so image plane height can be used as a measure of distance to objects resting on the floor[5]. While this is not a linear measure, and the exact correspondence between heights and distances cannot be known without first knowing the specifics of camera, it is still a perfectly useful measure for determining which of two objects is closer, whether an object is closer than a certain threshold, or even as an (uncalibrated) measure of absolute distance. This property was referred to as the *ground plane constraint* in [4].

Another important property of office environments is that they are generally carpeted, and their carpets generally have only fine-scale texture. That is to say, that from a distance, the carpet will appear to have a uniform reflectance. If this is true, and if the carpet is uniformly illuminated, then the areas of the image which correspond to the floor should have uniform image brightness, and so any violation of this uniformity must be an object other than the floor. This property, called the *background texture constraint* in [4], can greatly simplify the computational problem of figure-ground separation.

[5]This observation goes back at least to Euclid. See [2].

5 Design of the visual system

The visual system estimates the axis of the corridor and three distance measures from 64×48 pixel grey-scale images covering a field of view of 110 degrees (1.9 radians). All vision computations are performed for each frame. The overall structure of the visual system is shown in figure 5. The constraints used in the optimization of the system are given in figure 4.

5.1 *Computing the vanishing point*

As was mentioned above, the axis of the corridor is represented by the x coordinate of it's image-plane projection. This can be estimated by finding the vanishing point of the parallel lines forming the edges of the corridor. Bellutta *et al* [1] report on a such a system which extracts vanishing points by running an edge finder, extracting straight line segments, and performing 2D clustering on the pairwise intersections of the edge segments.[6] We can represent this schematically as:

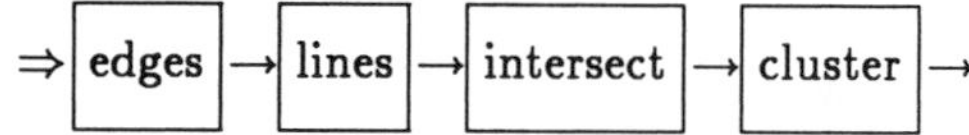

This algorithm, while less computationally expensive than 3D modeling, is still rather expensive. We can simplify the system if we make stronger assumptions about the environment. We can remove the step of grouping edge pixels into segments by treating each edge pixel as its own tiny segment:

⇒ edges → intersect → cluster →

Note that this system will effectively weight segments by their length. This will be fine provided that the long lines in the scene are the lines directed toward the vanishing point.

Edge detectors can also be extremely expensive. Since the edges we're looking for should be very strong and straight, we should be able to use a very simple edge detector, such as a gradient threshold. Computing the

[6]The algorithm of Bellutta *et al.* is actually more complicated than this in that it extracts multiple vanishing points, but for our purposes we can treat it as extracting only the forward vanishing point.

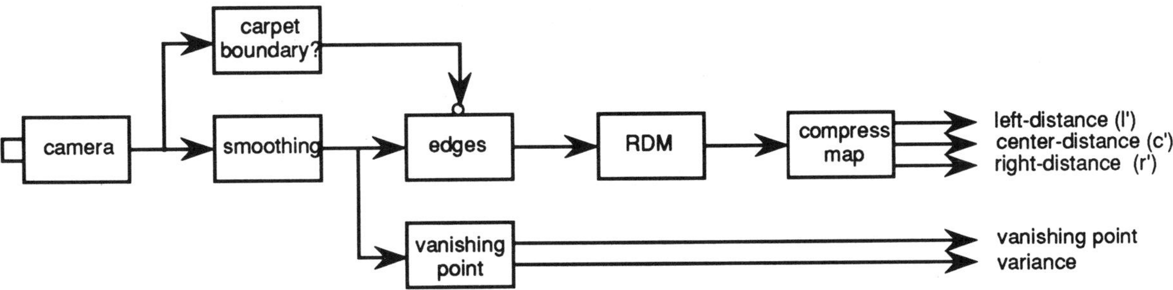

Figure 5: The portion of the visual system devoted to corridor following. Note that smoothing is performed prior to edge detection to remove noise. The vanishing point unit is shown as a single box because all the steps of the vanishing computation are performed simultaneously. The carpet boundary detector is discussed in section 7.

intensity gradient (the rate of change in image brightness, denoted by ∇) at a pixel and testing its magnitude can be done using only a few machine instructions. The resulting system is then:

$$\Rightarrow \boxed{|\nabla|} \rightarrow \boxed{\text{intersect}} \rightarrow \boxed{\text{cluster}} \rightarrow$$

If the tilt-angle of the camera is held constant by the camera mount, then the vanishing point will always have the same y coordinate, that is, it will lie in the line $y = y_0$ for some y_0. We can then replace the pair-wise intersections with the intersections of the edges with $y = y_0$. This reduces the number of points to consider from $O(n^2)$ to $O(n)$, where n is the number of edge pixels, and also reduces the clustering to a 1D problem, which is also more efficient:

$$\Rightarrow \boxed{|\nabla|} \rightarrow \boxed{y \text{ intersect}} \rightarrow \boxed{\text{1D cluster}} \rightarrow$$

Finally, if we assume that the intersections of the edges not pointing toward the vanishing point are uniformly distributed, then we can replace the clustering operation, which looks for modes, with the mean of the x coordinate:

$$\Rightarrow \boxed{|\nabla|} \rightarrow \boxed{y \text{ intersect}} \rightarrow \boxed{\bar{x}} \rightarrow$$

This does have the disadvantage that if there are many non-corridor edges in view, then the mean will tend to move toward the center of the screen. The sign will still be correct however, and so the robot will still steer in the correct direction.

5.2 Computing distances

There are two problems involved in estimating the left, right, and center distances: figure/ground separation to find the walls in the image, and depth estimation to determine the distances to them. Suppose we had computed a radial depth map, *RDM*, of the scene. A radial depth map gives the distance of the nearest object in each direction. Then we could find the distance to the left wall by finding the minimum distance given in the left side entries of the radial depth map:

$$\Rightarrow \boxed{RDM} \rightarrow \boxed{\min_{\text{left-side}}} \rightarrow$$

If we had already somehow solved the figure-ground problem, that is, if we had already labeled every pixel as being either "floor" or "not floor", then we could use the ground-plane constraint to generate the RDM: the distance to the closest object in a given direction is a monotonic function of the height in the image plane of the lowest non-floor pixel in the image plane. Since columns of the image correspond to directions, the distance is then simply the height of the lowest non-floor pixel in a given column. Thus:

$$RDM(x) = \min\{y | \text{the point } (x, y) \text{ isn't floor}\}$$

so now our system looks like this:

$$\Rightarrow \boxed{\text{F/G}} \rightarrow \boxed{RDM} \rightarrow \boxed{\min_{\text{left-side}}} \rightarrow$$

where "F/G" is the figure/ground system. If the floor is textureless but the walls generate edges where they meet with the floor, then, by the background-texture constraint, it too can be replaced, in this case, by an edge detector (*e.g.* thresholded gradients):

$$\Rightarrow \boxed{|\nabla|} \rightarrow \boxed{RDM} \rightarrow \boxed{\min_{\text{left-side}}} \rightarrow$$

A number of things are worth noting here. First of all, l' and r' are not necessarily the distances to the walls. They are simply the distances to the nearest non-floor objects on the left and right sides of the image. This is not actually a problem however, since if there are other objects in the way it will simply cause the robot to steer around them, thus conferring on the robot a limited object avoidance capability. If there are no such objects, then there is no difference anyhow. Thus having the system make no distinctions between walls and other obstacles is actually advantageous in this situation. The second thing worth noting is that the distance measures are nonlinear functions of the actual distances[7]. For some applications this might be unacceptable, but for this application we are mostly just concerned with whether a given object is too close or whether the left side or the right side is closer, for which these nonlinear measures

[7]The actual function is a quotient of linear equations whose coefficients are determined by the camera parameters.

Test	Time (sec)	Frames/sec
Full system	67	15
Corridor follower	67	15
I/O only	67	15
No I/O	15	67
No VP	10	100

Figure 6: Execution times for 1000 frames. "Full system" is all code presently implemented, including the person detector. "No I/O" is the corridor follower without any frame grabbing or output to the base (a single frame is grabbed at the beginning and processed repeatedly). "No VP" is the collision avoidance system run without I/O or the vanishing-point box. All execution times are for a Texas Instruments TMS-320C30-based DSP board (a Pentek 4283) running with no wait states. The processor has a 60ns instruction time. The first three lines are the same because the system cannot digitize frames faster than 15 FPS.

are quite adequate. Finally, since no camera has a 180 degree field of view, l' and r' are not even measures of the perpendicular distances to the walls, l and r, but rather are measure of the distance to the closest point *in view*. Again, this is not a problem in practice, partly because our camera has a relatively wide field of view, and partly because for a given orientation of the robot, the perpendicular distance is another monotonic and strictly increasing function of the measured distance, and *vice versa*.

6 Evaluation

The corridor follower has been running for nine months and is quite stable. It has seen at least 200 hours of service with many continuous runs of one hour or more. This makes it one of the most extensively tested and reliable visual navigation systems to date. We have been able to run the system as fast as our robot base could run without shaking itself apart (approximately 1 m/s). While there are cases which will fool the braking system (see below), we have found the system to be quite reliable in general.

6.1 Efficiency

The system is very efficient computationally. The present implementation runs at 15 frames per second, which is a fast as the system can read data from the camera (see figure 6). All computation boxes in figure 5 are run on every frame in (simulated) parallel. This implementation is heavily I/O bound however, and so it spends much of its time waiting for the serial port and doing transfers over the VMEbus to the frame grabber and display. We expect that performance would be noticeably better on a system with a more tightly coupled DSP and frame grabber. This efficiency of the system allows it to be implemented with a relatively simple and inexpensive computer such as the DSP. The modest power requirements of the computer allow the entire computer system to run off of a single motorcycle battery for as long as nine hours.

The simplicity and efficiency of the system make it quite inexpensive compared to other real-time vision systems. C30 DSP boards are now available for personal computers for approximately $1-2K US and frame grabbers can be obtained for as little as $400 US. Thus the corridor follower would be quite cheap to install on an existing system. We are also working on a very inexpensive hardware platform for the system which we hope will cost less than $200 US.

6.2 Failure modes

The system runs on all floors of the AI lab building on which it has been tested (floors 3-9) except for the 9th floor, which has very shiny floors. There the system brakes for the reflections of the overhead lights in the floor. The present system also has no memory and so cannot brake for an object unless it is actually in its field of view. This sometimes causes problems. The system also cannot brake for an object unless it can detect an edge on or around it, but this can more or less be expected of all vision systems. The system's major failure mode is braking for shadows. If shadows are sufficiently strong they will cause the robot to brake when there is in fact no obstacle. This is less of a problem than one would expect because shadows are generally quite diffuse and so will not necessarily trigger the edge detector. Finally, the 7th floor of the lab, where the robot spends most of its time, does not have a single carpet, but several carpets, each with a different color. The boundaries between these carpets can thus be mistaken for obstacles. This problem was dealt with by explicitly recognizing the boundary (see section 7).

6.3 Performance outside corridors

While the system was designed to navigate corridors, it is also capable of moving through more complicated spaces. Its major deficiency in this situation is that there is no way of specifying a desired destination to the system. Effectively, the system acts in a "point and shoot" mode: it moves forward as far as possible, veering away from obstacles, and continuing until it reaches a dead end or is stopped externally. The system is also non-deterministic in these situations. When the robot is blocked by an object, it will turn either left or right depending on the exact position and orientation of the robot and object. Since these are never exactly repeatable, the robot is effectively non-deterministic. Thus in a "forest environment" such as figure 7, the robot could emerge at any point or even get turned around completely. The system's performance is good enough however that a higher-level system can lead it though a series of corridors and junctions by forcing the robot to make a small open-loop turn when the higher-level system wants to take a new corridor at a junction. The corridor follower then realigns with the new corridor an continues on its way.

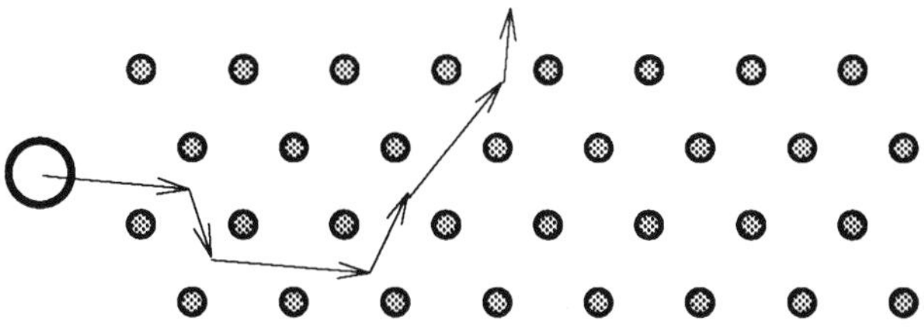

Figure 7: A forest environment.

7 Extensions

A number of minor modifications to the algorithm described above are worthwhile.

Vertical biasing

As discussed above, shadows and bright lights radiating from office doors can sometimes be sufficiently intense to trigger the edge detector. Since these shadows always radiate perpendicular to the wall, they appear horizontal in the image when the robot is successfully aligned with the corridor. By biasing the edge detector toward vertical lines, we can make it less sensitive to these shadows. A previous version of the system dealt with the problem by weighting vertical lines twice as much as horizontal lines. The system now explicitly searches for carpet boundaries and briefly disables the detection of horizontal lines when a carpet boundary is found. The criterion for a carpet boundary is that it must be a weak horizontal line with no surrounding texture.

Fear of the dark

The system, as described above, will happily drive through a dark room and hit the nearest obstacle. Similarly, if the robot somehow misses the boundary between the floor and a blank wall, and drives close enough to the wall for it to fill the robot's visual field, then it will treat the blank wall as being an empty floor and attempt to drive up the wall. Polly avoids these problems by treating dark pixels as obstacles to be avoided, and by refusing to drive forward if there is insufficient texture in the image. A better solution would be to add other sensory modalities to the system, such as touch or sonar, but those sensors were not available on the robot.

Wall following

When the system described above reaches a large open space, the single wall which is in view will act as a repulsive force, causing the robot to turn away from it until there is nothing in view whatsoever. Thus it naturally tends toward situations in which it is effectively blind. While this is sufficient for following corridors, and is in fact a very good way of avoiding obstacles, it is a very bad way of actually getting to a destination unless the world consists only of nice straight corridors. This problem can be fixed by modifying the steering control so that when only a single wall is in view, the robot will try to keep that wall at a constant distance. Thus, in the case where only the left wall is in view, the control law becomes:

$$\frac{d\theta}{dt} = \alpha(l' - d)$$

Where d is the desired distance to the wall.

8 Conclusions

Curiously, the most significant things about the system are the things which it does not do. It does not build or use detailed models of its environment; it does not use carefully calibrated depth data; it does not use high resolution imagery; and it is not designed to run in arbitrary environments. Indeed, much of its power comes from its specialization.

One may be tempted to object that this system is too domain specific and that more complicated techniques are necessary to build practical systems for use in the real world. I think that this is misguided however. To begin with, even if one had a single truly general navigation algorithm, its very generality would likely make it much slower than the system discussed here. The general system may also require allocating scarce cognitive or attentive resources which would be better used for other concurrent tasks. One approach would be to build a hybrid which used the simple system when possible, and the more cumbersome system only when necessary.

Another possibility would be to build a system which could rapidly switch between a number of domain-specific strategies. Ullman's Visual Routine Processor [14] is a particularly attractive architecture for this approach. A VRP could be quickly configured by the central system to use different strategies for different situations. Ideally, such a system would be able to recognize and learn to use domain-specific strategies for visual tasks, thus making it truly adaptive (see Whitehead and Ballard for an interesting example of learning visual routines [15]).

It remains to be seen how far we can go with simple, domain-specific strategies which rely on special properties of the environment. I suspect that quite a lot can be done with them. In either case, the system described here is a demonstration that it is practical to build simple, inexpensive vision systems which perform useful tasks, and that the solutions to vision problems do not necessarily involve buying better cameras and bigger computers.

Acknowledgements

Both this paper and the system described within benefitted from discussions with Lynn Stein, Rod Brooks, Eric Grimson, Maja Mataric, Mike Bolotski, Jose Robles, and David Michael.

References

[1] P. Bellutta, G. Collini, A. Verri, and V. Torre. Navigation by tracking vanishing points. In *AAAI*

Spring Symposium on Robot Navigation, pages 6–10, Stanford University, March 1989. AAAI.

[2] James E. Cutting. *Perception with an Eye for Motion.* MIT Press, 1986.

[3] Y. Goto and A. Stenz. The cmu system for mobile robot navigation. In *1987 IEEE Internation Conference on Robotics and Automation*, pages 99–105. IEEE, March 87.

[4] Ian Horswill. Characterizing adaptation by constraint. In *Proceedings of the First Annual European Conference on Artificial Life*, 1991.

[5] Ian D. Horswill. Reactive navigation for mobile robots. Master's thesis, Massachusetts Institute of Technology, June 1988.

[6] A. Kosaka and A. C. Kak. Fast vision-guided mobile robot navigation using model-based reasoning and prediction of uncertainties. *To appear in Computer Vision, Graphics, and Image Processing*, 56(2), September 1992.

[7] Maja Mataric. A distributed model for mobile robot environment-learning and navigation. Technical Report 1228, Massachusetts Institute of Technology, Artificial Intelligence Lab, May 1990.

[8] Hans P. Moravec. Certainty grids for mobile robots. Unpublished memo.

[9] Hans P. Moravec. The stanford cart and cmu rover. Technical report, Robotics Institute, Carnegie-Mellon University, February 1983.

[10] ed. Nils J. Nilsson. Shakey the robot. Technical Report 323, SRI International, April 1984.

[11] Romedi Passini. *Wayfinding in Architecture*, volume 4 of *Environmental Design Series.* Van Norstrand Reinhold, New York, 1984.

[12] Herbert L. Roitblat. *Introduction to Comparitive Cognition.* W. H. Freeman and Company, 1987.

[13] K. Storjohann, T. Zeilke, H. A. Mallot, and W. von Seelen. Visual obstacle detection for automatically guided vehicles. In *Proceedings of the IEEE International Conference on Robotics and Automation*, pages 761–766, May 1990.

[14] Shimon Ullman. Visual routines. *Cognition*, 18:97–159, 1984.

[15] S. Whitehead and D. Ballard. Active perception and reinforcement learning. *Neural Computation*, 2(4), 1990.

ACTION SELECTION AND BEHAVIORAL SEQUENCES

The Use of Hierarchies for Action Selection

Toby Tyrrell
email: lrtt@uk.ac.ed.cns
Centre for Cognitive Science
University of Edinburgh
Edinburgh EH8 9LW
Great Britain

Abstract

Several researchers studying animal behaviour, such as Tinbergen and Baerends, have proposed hierarchical mechanisms for action selection. Maes, amongst others, has argued against mechanisms of this type because of the top-down control and lack of robustness inherent in these *hierarchical decision structures*, in which decisions are made at every level. Two alternatives exist to these hierarchical decision structures: **(1)** Maes has designed a non-hierarchical action selection mechanism, and **(2)** Rosenblatt & Payton have outlined a hierarchical mechanism which does *not* make decisions at each level. In this paper the use of the two types of hierarchies for action selection is discussed and the Rosenblatt & Payton approach with free flow of information, combination of evidence and the ability to select compromise candidates is supported. Evidence from animal behaviour is used to back up this claim.

1. Introduction

Before commencing with the body of the paper it is necessary to define some terms. Several of these terms are illustrated in figure 1.

The term *action* here refers to an entity at the 'lowest' level, that of the behavioural final common path [e.g. McFarland, 1975]. That is to say, the demands of each action on the effectors of the animal are mutually exclusive so that only one action may be carried out at any one time. Some actions in figure 1 are retrieving eggs, trampling, lining of the nest and combing of the feathers. *Action selection* is the process of choosing, by whatever means, one out of a set of candidate actions.

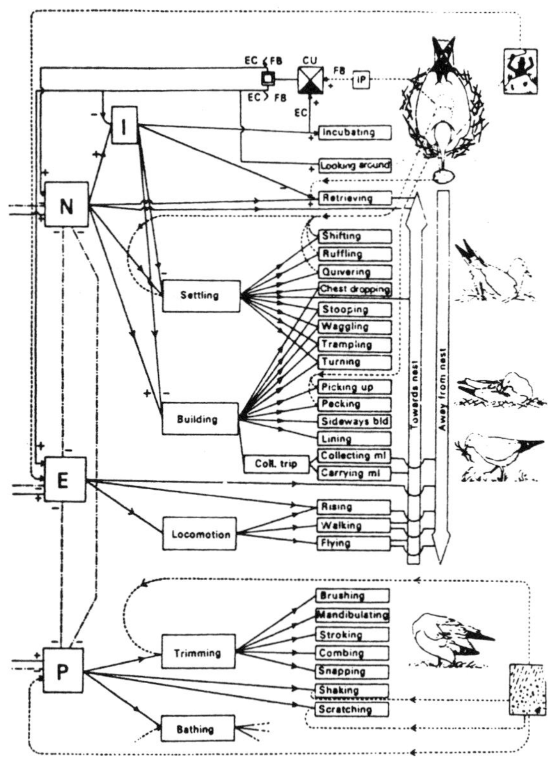

Figure 1: Baerend's model to account for incubation behaviour of the herring gull. Actions or fixed action patterns are in the far right column. "Superimposed control systems" of higher order are to the middle and left. **N** = incubation system, **E** = escape system and **P** = preening system. The three systems mutually suppress each other. © acknowledged to Bailliere Tindall.

Animals are vehicles for the transmission and propagation of their genes [Dawkins, 1989]. The global *action selection problem* for an animal is therefore how to choose successive actions so as to maximise the number of copies of its genes in future generations. Action selection mechanisms have evolved to provide a solution to this problem, i.e. to make the animal reproduce, and to make it help conspecifics with similar sets of genes (e.g. siblings, parents, offspring) to do the same. In order to achieve the above the animal needs to stay alive and to help conspecifics to do so as well. The main action selection problem thus engenders more specific *sub-problems* such as the need to obtain food, the need to avoid predators, the need to care for young and the need to find mates. Each of these sub-problems will have its own requirements on the animal's time which will need to be interleaved by the action selection mechanism.

Most mechanisms have separate parts devoted to each of the separate sub-problems, which will be referred to here as *systems*. Some systems of the mechanism shown in figure 1 are nesting, escaping and preening. Parts of the mechanism at any level between that of the system level and the action level will be known as *sub-systems*.

The terms just defined, while being very similar to those used by Baerends, differ from those defined by McFarland [1975].

The definition of a *hierarchy* used here is taken from [Dawkins, 1976]. For two nodes A and B then A *'is boss of'* B if A has a direct causal influence on B. *Direct* is meant to imply that A is immediately above B in the hierarchy (i.e. its influence on B is not mediated through another node), and *causal influence* is meant to imply that the state of node B is to some extent dependent on the state of node A. For a set of nodes A, B, C, etc, A is said to be *superior* to B if **(1)** A is boss of B, or if **(2)** A is boss of a node which is superior to B. Using this recursive definition of the term superior it is now possible to define a hierarchy as a set of nodes A, B, C, etc. which satisfy:

(i) there is no node in the set which is superior to itself, and

(ii) there is one element in the set which is superior to all others in the set.

Figure 2 shows some example hierarchies. The hierarchical mechanisms discussed here are all composed of sets of overlapping hierarchies (one for each system) as in figure 2(e).

The rest of this introductory section is given over to a discussion of other work relevant to the theme of this paper. Firstly two hierarchical mechanisms for action selection, due to the ethologists Tinbergen and Baerends, are reviewed. They are both the product of extensive observation of animal behaviour. Following this is a description of a different type of hierarchical mechanism, proposed by Rosenblatt & Payton, two roboticists.

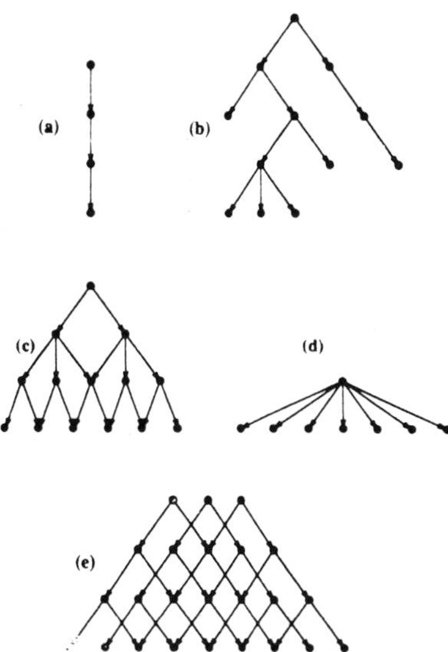

Figure 2: Some example hierarchies. **(c)** is an overlapping hierarchy, **(e)** is a set of overlapping hierarchies (after [Dawkins, 1976]).

1.1. Tinbergen

This mechanism [Tinbergen, 1950 & 1951] was put forward as a "working hypothesis" and as such was only described fairly vaguely, rather than being specified exactly. There is a hierarchy of nodes (see figure 3), each of which (except for the very top-most one) is gated by an *innate releasing mechanism*. The highest level nodes correspond to systems such as 'reproduction' and 'cleaning/preening'. The lowest level nodes correspond to actions such as 'lay eggs' and 'comb feathers'.

The top-most nodes are activated by motivations such as 'internal food deficit'. Their activation energy will then pass down to lower nodes in turn as long as the innate releasing mechanism (IRM) for each node is activated (an inactivated IRM 'blocks' its node). Each IRM consists of a device for summing several incoming stimuli and a threshold. If the sum of the stimuli exceeds the threshold then the IRM 'frees' the node, allowing it to pass activation down to lower layers. The IRM's act to block any nodes not relevant to the current situation.

In addition to the IRM threshold, each node has its own separate threshold which needs to be surpassed by the activation it receives from several different sources

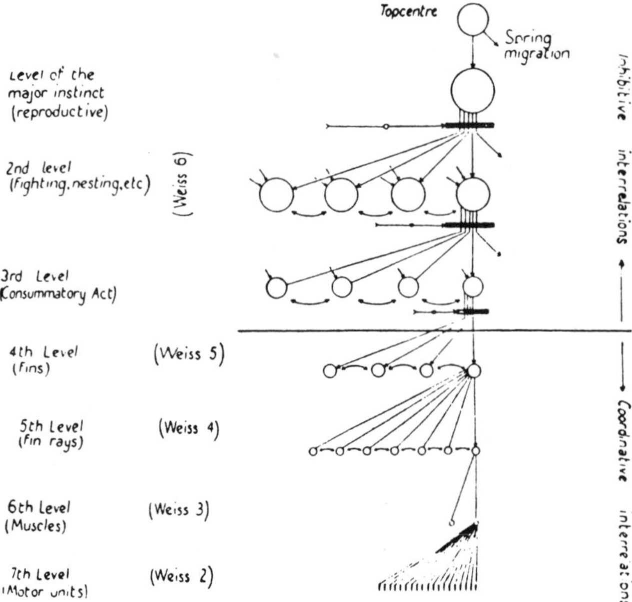

Figure 3: Tinbergen's 'Hierarchy of Instincts' (the bottom half shows motor control and can be ignored). Circles = centres, downwards arrows = causal factors, horizontal arrows = innate releasing mechanisms, and two-way arrows between centres on the same level = mutual suppression. © acknowledged to Clarendon Press.

(see figure 4). The most important of these inputs to a node, for the purposes of this paper, are the inhibitory inputs from other nodes at the same level. It is unclear exactly how Tinbergen expected the intra-layer inhibition to work, except that "as a rule, the strong activation of instinctive behaviour of one kind prevents the functioning of another pattern" [Tinbergen, 1951] and "centres of the same level mutually suppress each other's activities" [Tinbergen, 1950]. The desired effect of the IRM's and the inhibition amongst nodes at the same level is that in most cases only one node at any level is allowed to be active. That is to say, there is a *winner-take-all* operation at each level. It is this aspect of the mechanism that is of interest here.

1.2. Baerends

Figure 1 shows a model that Baerends postulated to account for the incubation behaviour of the herring gull [Baerends, 1976], and figure 5 shows a similar diagram for the reproductive behaviour of the digger wasp [Baerends, 1976]. The two are different instantiations of the same type of architecture. As with Tinbergen's 'hierarchy of instincts', there is a feeding of activation down through the hierarchy (or rather from left to right in Baerends' diagrams). There are no IRM's, but system-level nodes inhibit one another so that only one is active, and below that level each higher-level node controls (in some unspecified way) which one of its subordinates receives activation. Baerends specifies that internal and external stimuli affect which node (at any level) becomes active, and also that once a node becomes active, it tends to remain active for some time.

Again, the details of the mechanism are not important here, only the fact that (as with Tinbergen's mechanism) only one node at any one level is allowed to be active. That is to say, a *decision* is made at each level as to which system or sub-system is the most appropriate and all others are subsequently disregarded. This type of mechanism is called here a *hierarchical decision structure.*

1.3. Maes's Criticisms

Maes [1991)] has argued against the use of such hierarchical decision structures, in particular because of the top-down, preprogrammed sort of control they exert. Maes designed a mechanism of her own [Maes, 1991] which is distributed and non-hierarchical with no central control. The behaviour of the network is an emergent property of interactions amongst the nodes, and of

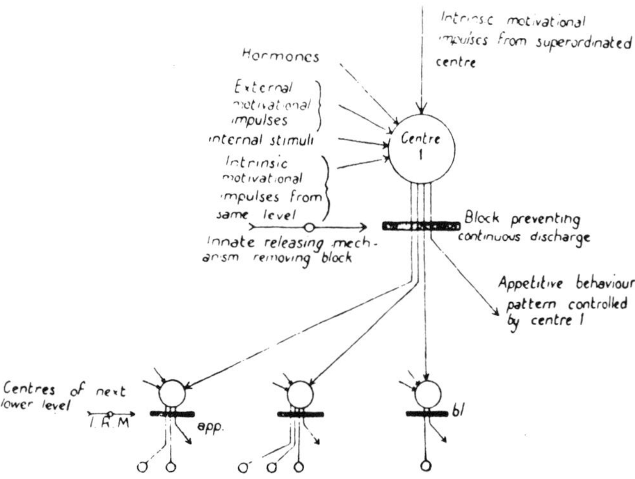

Figure 4: Tinbergen's 'tentative representation' of a node or centre from an intermediate level in the hierarchy. © acknowledged to Clarendon Press.

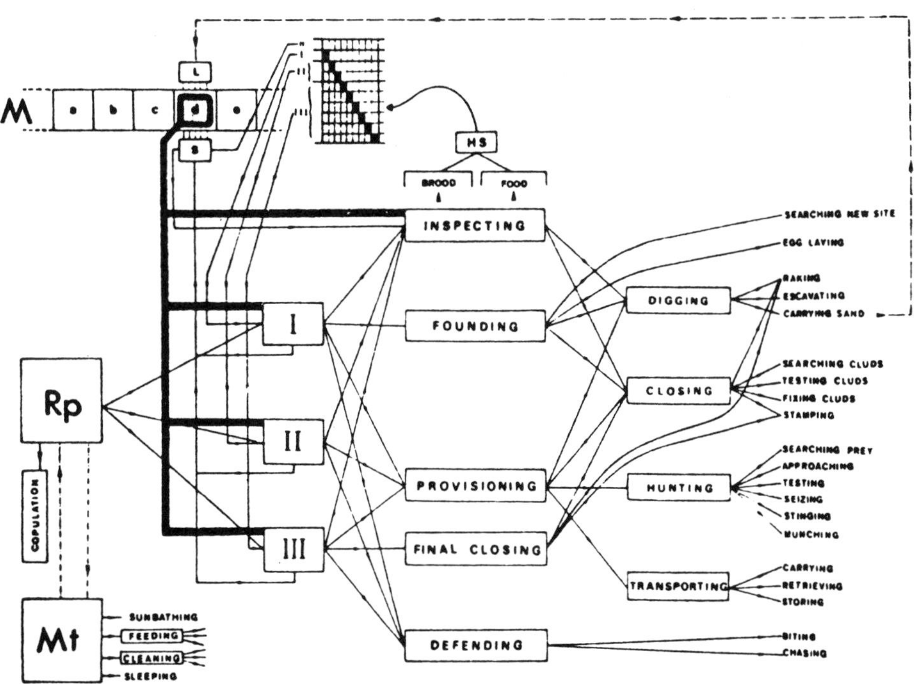

Figure 5: Baerend's model to account for nest provisioning behaviour of the digger wasp. As in the last diagram, actions or fixed action patterns are in the far right column and systems and sub-systems are to the left and middle. **Rp** = reproductive system, and **Mt** = 'maintenance' system. **I, II** and **III** are sub-systems controlling the completion of three separate phases of nest provisioning, each of which require the execution of several different lower-level sub-systems. © acknowledged to Bailliere Tindall.

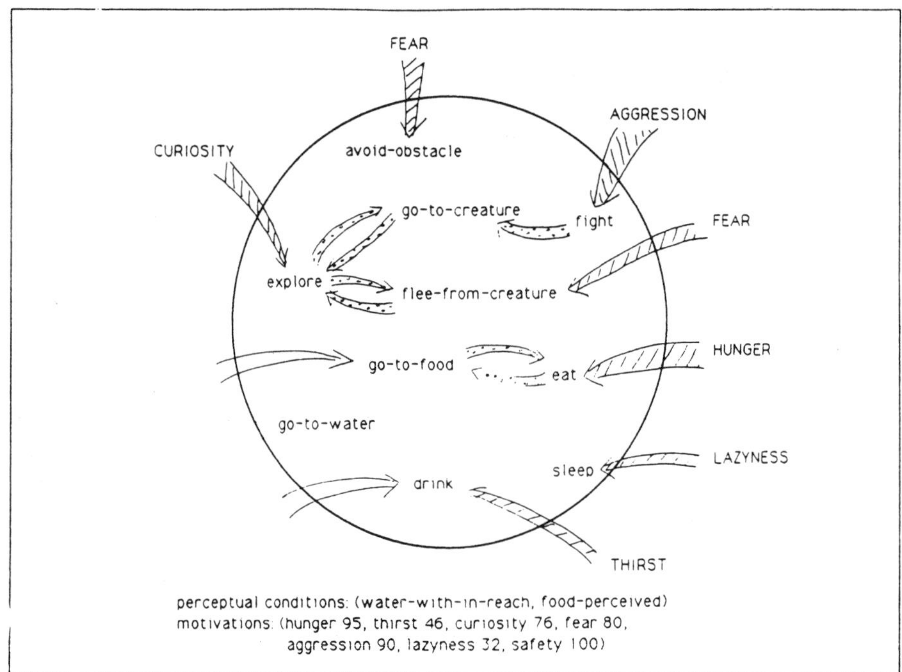

Figure 6: Maes's non-hierarchical, "Bottom-up Mechanism for Behaviour Selection". © acknowledged to MIT Press.

interactions between the nodes and the outside world (see figure 6). Space does not allow for a detailed description of this mechanism but it should be noted that there are no system-level nodes. Maes's mechanism selects between entities which are all assumed to be at the same level, somewhere below the system level.

While Maes's mechanism was reported to cope satisfactorily in a simple simulated environment [Maes, 1991], it is not obvious how well it could cope with the more complicated scenarios of figures 1 and 5 in which it would seem natural to group together actions into different systems and sub-systems. Maes's mechanism has also been tested by the author in a complex simulated environment [Tyrrell & Mayhew, 1991], and shortcomings with it have been uncovered. Some of these problems derive from difficulties in trying to solve what is intrinsically a hierarchical problem with a non-hierarchical architecture. For a detailed account see [Tyrrell, 1993].

1.4. Rosenblatt & Payton

An alternative to a hierarchical decision structure (Tinbergen, Baerends) is what shall be called here a *free-flow hierarchy*, one in which decisions are not taken at every level, but only at the level of the behavioural final common path. The spread of activation between nodes is unrestricted and is able to 'flow down' to all lower nodes via weighted connections.

The idea of a free-flow hierarchy was proposed by Rosenblatt & Payton [1989], who suggested it as an alternative to Brooks' Subsumption Architecture [Brooks, 1986]. In Rosenblatt & Payton's mechanism nodes *express multiple preferences* for each of a set of lower level candidates rather than making a *decision* as to which one is most suitable. This is advantageous because it allows for *combining of evidence* from different nodes and for selection of *compromise candidates* (see figure 7). Each of the nodes in this case (see figure 8) are fairly standard artificial neurons (as used in the field of neural networks), except that their rule for combination of weighted inputs is not necessarily a strict summation.

A hierarchy designed according to these principles will include combination of evidence (rather than winner-take-all) at every level, except at the level of actions (because only one can be executed). The action-level node receiving most activation gets chosen. Any number of nodes can be active to differing degrees at every other level.

Other work relevant to this paper has now been described. Alternative models of action selection, such as Lorenz's 'psycho-hydraulic model' are not relevant to the current discussion and are not considered here. The rest of this paper will consist of a discussion of the relative merits of Tinbergen-like hierarchical decision structures and Rosenblatt & Payton-like free-flow hierarchies. Arguments will then be presented in support of the claim that the latter type of hierarchies are preferable. It is claimed that not only is the problem of action selection intrinsically hierarchical, but, because of the need for combining preferences and selecting compro-

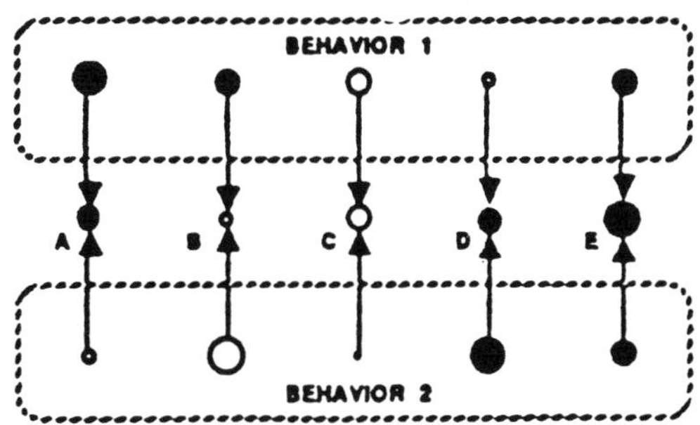

Figure 7: Combining evidence in a Rosenblatt & Payton hierarchy. Filled circles denote excitation, open circles denote inhibition. © acknowledged to IEEE.

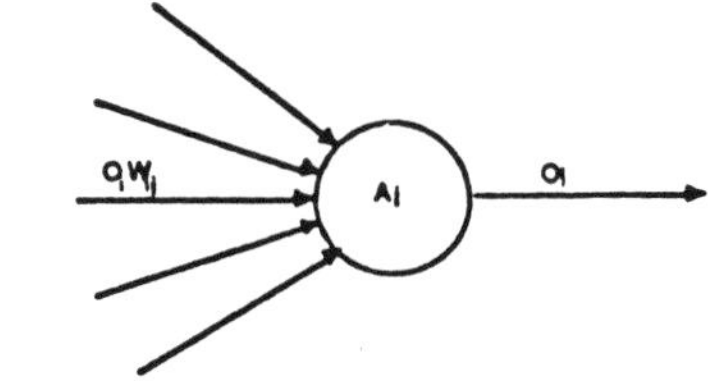

O_i is the output of unit i.
W_{ij} is the weight on the link from unit i to unit j.
$A_j = f_A(O_1W_{1j}, ..., O_nW_{nj})$, is the activation level of unit j with n weighted inputs.
$O_j = f_O(A_j)$, is the output of unit j.

Figure 8: A node from Rosenblatt & Payton's hierarchy. © acknowledged to IEEE.

mise candidates, the solutions should be also. Some evidence from animal behaviour observations will be given in support of these arguments.

2. Hierarchies but not Hierarchical Decision Structures

A list of the shortcomings of Tinbergen and Baerend-like hierarchies is now given, together with a list of the benefits of Rosenblatt & Payton-like structures.

2.1. Some Disadvantages of Hierarchical Decision Structures

1) As mentioned by Maes [1991], top-down control is undesirable. It is brittle and non-robust in the sense that the initial decisions are vitally important and if they are incorrect then the whole performance collapses.

   In order to make correct initial decisions, the top level has to receive and process all of the sensory information relevant to the lower layers, leading to what has been called a 'sensory bottleneck'. For any system of an action selection mechanism there are several relevant internal / external stimuli. Some of these stimuli may be relevant to a whole system or sub-system (e.g. 'perception of partially built nest' to nest building), whereas others will be relevant to only one specific action (e.g. 'perception of egg outside nest' to egg retrieval) [e.g. Hinde, 1953].

   So the desirability of carrying out any specific action will usually depend on several stimuli, some of which are relevant only to that action, and some of which have more widespread relevance. In a hierarchical decision structure the desirability of each system needs to be calculated, so that they can be properly selected between. This desirability for each system will be equal to the maximum of the desirabilities of each of the actions of the system. Therefore, the system-level nodes must each receive all of the relevant stimuli for all of the actions in their system, which produces the 'sensory bottleneck' mentioned above.

   It should be noted that Tinbergen's mechanism does include stimuli which impinge only on the relevant lower-level nodes of the hierarchy and does also select between nodes at each level, but this is sub-optimal. For instance, consider a system which contains a consummatory act for which the appropriate stimulus situation exists (e.g. a 'getting food' system might have a consummatory act 'eat' for which the appropriate stimulus situation is the presence of food). The existence of the stimulus situation appropriate to the consummatory act cannot be taken into account when calculating the likely benefit to the animal of choosing that system as opposed to others.

2) Another consideration is that of the proper treatment of information. By 'shutting off' all parts of the hierarchy, except those beneath nodes winning the competition at their level, there is a *loss of information*, information which might be useful in selecting the most appropriate action. While redundant and irrelevant information can be discarded, relevant information must not be.

3) This loss of information results in an inability to choose *compromise candidates*. This deficit is par-

ticularly apparent in the case of *proscriptive demands* [Tyrrell, 1992] on the animal's actions. A proscriptive demand is 'ruling-out' one, which specifies which action or actions should *not* be performed. If an animal happened to be situated next to a hazard such as a precipitous cliff then the overriding need for it is to avoid that hazard. In a Tinbergen-like system this will cause the 'avoid hazard' system to be chosen and to bring about a movement away from the hazard. In fact there are many actions that would not cause a movement towards the hazard, and some of which would beneficial because of other systems, but these cannot be considered simultaneously with the need to avoid the hazard. Another example occurs when the animal's internal body temperature is dangerously high. In this case it needs to avoid any strenuous actions which will increase its body temperature even further, but that still leaves several different actions that it can undertake. In order to choose usefully between these actions, the preferences of other systems need to be considered simultaneously.

2.2. Some Advantages of Free-Flow Hierarchies

1) In this case there is less top-down *control*, more *influence* from above. System-level nodes receive only motivational stimuli relevant to *all* of the actions in the system. In a free-flow hierarchy of this sort, stimuli impinge on different nodes of the hierarchy. Some stimuli impinge on system nodes, some on sub-system nodes, some on action nodes (dependent on how much of the system they are relevant to). There is no 'sensory bottleneck'.

   Small errors in the calculation or propagation of these stimuli will not significantly affect the performance of the mechanism. The system as a whole is more robust and performance degrades more gracefully as errors increase.

2) Information is treated correctly in a free-flow hierarchy. The preferences of systems and subsystems for all lower-level candidates are always utilised until the level is reached at which a decision has to be made (i.e. the action level). All relevant information is *preserved*.

3) Because of this preservation of relevant information a hierarchy of this sort is able to choose compromise candidates (e.g. see figure 7). In particular, proscriptive demands can be meshed appropriately with preferences from other systems, as shown in figure 9.

The simple Rosenblatt & Payton-type of free-flow hierarchy as sketched here has no propensity for producing sequences (other than that each action tends to produce a stimulus situation appropriate to the next action in the sequence) but it is a simple matter to add this.

A less obvious problem with the basic Rosenblatt & Payton type of structure as outlined above involves nodes which figure in the preferences of many higher-level nodes. For instance, a node for 'explore' which might be relevant to several systems such as 'get food' (when the animal perceives no food sources) and 'get water' (when the animal perceives no water sources), would possess several different sources of activation. When testing this type of hierarchy in the simulated environment of [Tyrrell & Mayhew, 1991] it was found that these nodes tended to regularly dominate others which only figured in one or two preferences. The sum of many slight preferences was usually greater than one strong preference, and consummatory actions relevant to only one system could only rarely obtain enough activation to be chosen. To protect against this shortcoming, the activation for a node should not in most cases be a simple sum of the preferences, but rather should be calculated according to a function of the form

$$A_j = \left(\frac{\max_i(P_{ij}^{+}) + \alpha \sum_{i=0}^{N^{+}} (P_{ij}^{+})}{1+\alpha} \right) + \left(\frac{\min_i(P_{ij}^{-}) + \beta \sum_{i=0}^{N^{-}} (P_{ij}^{-})}{1+\beta} \right)$$

where A_j is the activation of node j, N^+ and N^- are the numbers of higher-level nodes that can express positive and negative preferences (P_{ij}^+ and P_{ij}^- respectively) for that node, and α and β are scaling factors which are greater than 0 but less than 1. The function is the sum of two terms, one for the positive inputs to the node, one for the negative inputs to the node. The first term is a weighted average of the sum of positive preferences and the largest positive preference. The second term is a weighted average of the sum of negative preferences and the most negative negative preference.

Rosenblatt & Payton-type hierarchies, amended to enable contiguous sequences and to protect against dominance by nodes with too many inputs have been tested in the simulated environment mentioned above with good results.

While it is fairly obvious that the problem of action selection is by nature hierarchical, it has not been generally accepted that the best solutions to the problem (i.e. the best action selection mechanisms) should also be hi-

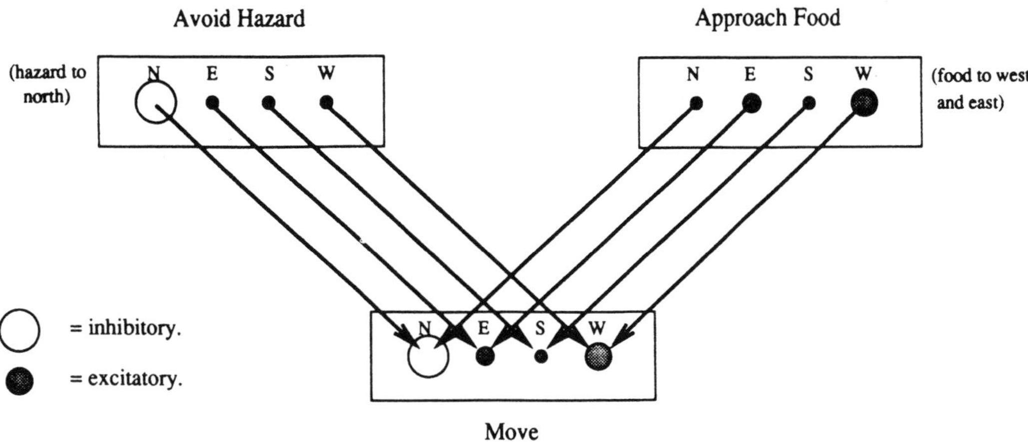

Figure 9: Combining preferences from proscriptive and prescriptive systems (chosen action is 'move west' in a free-flow hierarchy).

erarchical. From a computational viewpoint, it would seem that the need to express and combine preferences between layers means that there *has* to be some kind of hierarchy in any valid action selection mechanism.

The need for combination of preferences has already been appreciated to some extent in robotics, where most of the repertoire of possible actions of a robot usually consists of movements in different directions. Traditionally, action selection mechanisms have been centralised planners with bureaucratic, top-down control. Researchers such as Brooks [1987] have argued against such centralised control and *potential fields* [e.g. Arkin, 1987] have recently become popular. A potential field is a scheme for combining preferences for movements in different directions.

An analogy can be made between the two hierarchical schemas for action selection considered here and the decision-making of a group of ministers or government officials. Imagine that each official is responsible for a particular aspect of policy, such as education, foreign affairs, unemployment or the economy. Imagine further that the group are meeting to decide upon the future political strategy of their nation, and that each official is constrained to evaluate the various strategy options from the standpoint of their individual department only. The prime minister or president resides over the council and makes the ultimate decision as to which of the alternative options gets chosen.

Decision-making with a hierarchical decision structure is equivalent to the prime minister or president listening to each of the various officials in turn and then selecting the one department for which the decision is most crucial. The future policy is then chosen to be that which is most beneficial to the particular department.

By contrast, decision-making with a free-flow hierarchy is analogous to the prime minister or president listening to each official outline the pros and cons of each action for their particular aspect of government, and then coming to a decision which takes into account the views of all officials simultaneously. So, for instance, the official in charge of unemployment might express a strong disapproval of option A because of the number of people who would be put out of work, but be ambivalent as to which of the other options is chosen. The official for foreign affairs could mildly favour option B because it would ease diplomatic relations with another country, but express no preference or dislike for other options. And the various options might each be favoured to differing degrees by the official concerned with the economy, in accordance with the likely effects on the national finances. The preferences of each official for each policy option can be combined to calculate which option is most beneficial when all aspects are taken into consideration.

3. Evidence

Evidence is now presented in support of the claim that the degree of preference for respective alternatives should be maintained throughout each system, rather than the winning system shutting down all the others. The three examples below come from pages 243–245 of [Lorenz, 1985].

1: The simultaneous firing of antagonistic muscles due to simultaneous excitation of conflicting systems:

> Additive superposition is found even in cases in which the two independent motivations ac-

> tivate antagonistic muscles. . . . A conflict between motivations in Anatidae, one demanding a forward extension of the neck, the other a retraction, which can occur in a goose wanting to eat grain offered in a human hand and not quite daring to do so, produces a violent trembling of the neck. . . . The "trembling neck" of the goose probably is effected by conflicting innervation of the antagonistic muscles, but we cannot be certain about this.

2 : The simultaneous operation of opposing sets of fins due to the strong activation of conflicting systems:

> In territory disputed, certain cichlids (*Etroplus maculatus*) position themselves opposite another, threatening across the border separating their territories. As in every threat, aggressive motivation is contending with that for escape. Whenever one of the adversaries moves a short distance forward into enemy territory, it appears as if he were swimming into a current, the speed of which rapidly increases as one proceeds upstream. This effect is produced by the action of the pectoral fins, which are sculling in reverse, and doing so more and more intensely the farther the fish moves into the other's territory. The tail fin is under the control of aggressivity and the pectorals under that of escape, and the observer cannot help feeling – ridiculously – that the pectorals are more afraid than the tail, because they are nearer to the enemy.

3 : The facial expressions of a dog can simultaneously display the intensity of two separate, conflicting motivations, fear and aggression (figure 10).

These three examples all serve to illustrate the point that the activation levels of different nodes in a hierarchy are likely to be maintained, as in a free-flow hierarchy, rather than only one at each level surviving, as in the winner-take-all operation of a Tinbergen-like hierarchical decision structure. As well as the three examples stated above, Lorenz went further to state that

> In nature, behaviour activated by a single motivation is found at least as rarely as hybrids differing in only one gene. A higher animal in its natural habitat must always be ready to undertake a great number of different and – as often as not – mutually exclusive actions, and what it finally does is almost always a compromise made among several necessities.

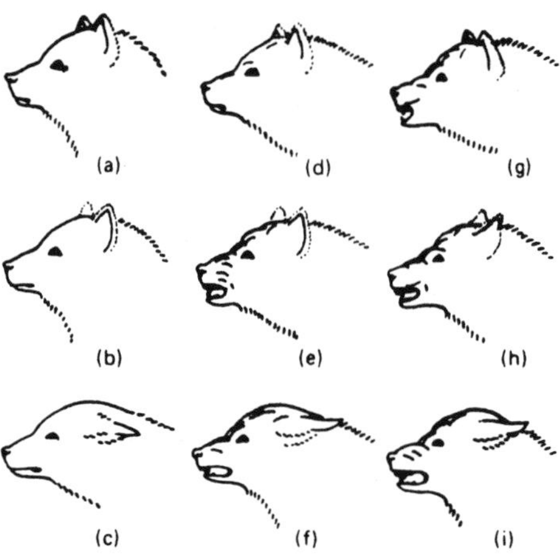

Figure 10: Facial expressions of a dog showing differing degrees of fear and aggression. Readiness to flee increases from top to bottom, aggression increases from left to right. © acknowledged to Springer-Verlag.

4. Conclusion

The answer to the subject of this paper 'how to use hierarchies for action selection?' is therefore that hierarchical decision structures are undesirable but that the use of hierarchies with unrestricted flow of information and combination of evidence (*free-flow hierarchies*) is a valid and sensible approach to action selection. Both computational and ethological arguments point to this same conclusion.

Acknowledgements

I would like to thank David Willshaw and John Hallam for their help and advice during the time I was carrying out this work. I would also like to thank Janet Halperin and Bridget Hallam for commenting on drafts of this paper. This project was supported by SERC (grant no. 89310818).

References

Arkin, Ronald C. 1987. Motor Schema Based Navigation for a Mobile Robot: An Approach to Programming by Behavior. In *Proceedings of the 1987 IEEE International Conference on Robotics and Automation*. Computer Society Press of the IEEE.

Baerends, Gerald P. 1976. The Functional Organization of Behaviour. *Animal Behaviour*. 24:726–738.

Brooks, Rodney A. 1986. A Robust Layered Control System for a Mobile Robot. *IEEE Journal of Robotics and Automation* 2:14–23.

Brooks, Rodney A. 1987. Intelligence Without Representation. In *Proceedings of the Workshop on Foundations of Intelligence*. MIT Press.

Dawkins, Richard. 1976. Hierarchical Organisation: A Candidate Principle for Ethology. In *Growing Points in Ethology*. Bateson P. P. G. & Hinde R. A. eds. Cambridge University Press.

Dawkins, Richard. 1989. *The Selfish Gene* (2nd edition). Oxford University Press.

Hinde, R. A. 1953. Appetitive Behaviour, Consummatory Act, and the Hierarchical Organisation of Behaviour – with Special Reference to the Great Tit (*Parus Major*). *Behaviour* 5:189–224.

Lorenz, Konrad. 1985. *Foundations of Ethology*. Heidelberg: Springer-Verlag.

Maes, Pattie. 1991. Bottom-Up Mechanism for Behaviour Selection In An Artificial Creature. In *Proceedings of the First International Conference on Simulation of Adaptive Behaviour*, (JA Meyer & SW Wilson, eds). MIT Press/Bradford Books.

McFarland, D. & Sibly, R. 1975. The Behavioural Final Common Path. *Phil. Trans. R. Soc. Ser. B*. 270:265–293.

Rosenblatt, Kenneth J & Payton, David W. 1989. A Fine-Grained Alternative to the Subsumption Architecture for Mobile Robot Control. In *Proceedings of the IEEE/INNS International Joint Conference on Neural Networks*.

Tinbergen, Nikko. 1950. The Hierarchical Organisation of Nervous Mechanisms Underlying Instinctive Behaviour. *Sympos. Soc. Exper. Biol.* 4:305–312.

Tinbergen, Nikko. 1951. *The Study of Instinct*. Clarendon Press.

Tyrrell, T. & Mayhew, J. E. W. 1991. Computer Simulation of an Animal Environment. In *Proceedings of the First International Conference on Simulation of Adaptive Behaviour*, (JA Meyer & SW Wilson, eds). MIT Press/Bradford Books.

Tyrrell, T. 1992. Defining the Action Selection Problem. In *Proceedings of the Fourteenth Annual Conference of the Cognitive Science Society*. Lawrence Erlbaum Associates.

Tyrrell, T. 1993. Computational Mechanisms for Action Selection. PhD thesis. Centre for Cognitive Science, University of Edinburgh. In preparation.

Two Methods for Hierarchy Learning in Reinforcement Environments

Mark Ring
Department of Computer Sciences
University of Texas at Austin
Austin, TX 78712
(ring@cs.utexas.edu)

Abstract

This paper describes two methods for hierarchically organizing temporal behaviors. The first is more intuitive: grouping together common sequences of events into single units so that they may be treated as individual behaviors. This system immediately encounters problems, however, because the units are binary, meaning the behaviors must execute completely or not at all, and this hinders the construction of good training algorithms. The system also runs into difficulty when more than one unit is (or should be) active at the same time. The second system is a hierarchy of *transition* values. This hierarchy dynamically modifies the values that specify the degree to which one unit should follow another. These values are continuous, allowing the use of gradient descent during learning. Furthermore, many units are active at the same time as part of the system's normal functionings.

1 Introduction

The importance of hierarchy in adaptive systems that perform temporal tasks has been noted often (Albus, 1979; Wilson, 1989; Roitblat, 1991; Wixson, 1991; Drescher, 1991; Schmidhuber, 1992; Singh, 1992). Dawkins (1976) described the intrinsic importance and variety of hierarchy in animal behavior, and he noted several arguments that demonstrate the merit of hierarchy as a general design principle.

In some systems (Albus, 1979; Roitblat, 1991), hierarchy is developed as an efficient method for modularizing temporal tasks such that they can be accomplished in a general way: in order to perform each task, a sequence of sub-tasks must somehow be performed. In other systems (Wilson, 1989; Drescher, 1991; Schmidhuber, 1992; Singh, 1992), hierarchy is used to organize concept learning. In these cases, sequences or sequential tasks are learned by combining already known sequences or tasks into new ones. In this paper, I will focus on the latter class. Specifically, I will explore two methods for learning *behavior* hierarchies, where a behavior is a sequence of perceptions and/or actions.

The motivation for hierarchy learning is one of efficiency and increased learning potential. As Dawkins pointed out (Dawkins, 1976, p. 16), complex organisms probably evolved from simpler organisms that embodied many of the sub-assemblies required to build the more complex organisms. One might also speculate that organisms capable of performing certain elaborate behaviors may have evolved from simpler organisms that performed less elaborate components of these more complex behaviors. One often finds in the neural network literature the tendency to preprogram into one's learning systems everything that one *can* preprogram easily, because the system might find exactly these aspects of the task very difficult, and it might then learn the remainder of the task—that which is difficult to preprogram—fairly easily (see for example Bachrach, 1983, ch. 5). But even the simplest organisms are often so difficult for artificial systems to simulate, that there is a vast expanse of behavior both too difficult to hard-wire, and too difficult to learn. In these cases, what is needed is a system specifically designed to learn layer after layer of behaviors on top of those that it has already learned, each possibly more complex than the preceding ones (see also Drescher (1991) for a related discussion). With a hierarchical approach such as this in mind, it is conceivable to imagine simulated agents where the foundations necessary for learning a difficult task are not hard-wired into the circuitry of the system, but taught to the continuously evolving adaptive system.

In this paper, I investigate two methods that attempt to capture some aspects of hierarchical learning. In section 2, I will describe a unit devised for learning sequential behavior hierarchies. In section 3, I will describe a continuous version of this unit that overcomes problems encountered with the first method while being simpler to implement.

2 Method I: Behavior Hierarchies

My first attempt at behavior hierarchies was an animat controlled by a system of units.[1] In this system, each unit represents a specific behavior sequence. Some units represent primitive behaviors: a single sensation, or a single action. Other, higher-level units represent a sequence of two primitive units, and still higher-level units represent sequences of any two lower units. The system executes a behavior by choosing the unit that stands for that behavior. If a primitive action is chosen, that action is attempted in an external environment. If a primitive sensation is chosen, the system attempts to perceive that sensation. If a higher-level unit is chosen, it is decomposed into the two units that it represents; then the first unit's behavior is executed, followed by the second unit's. At any time, a new higher-level behavior might be added to the system's abilities by creating a new unit that represents a sequence of two units already in the system.

An example should clarify all this. Suppose the system could sense heat and coldness, light and darkness, and that it could move one step to the north, south, east, or west. Its primitive sensation units would be: SH (sense heat), SC (sense cold), SL (sense light), and SD (sense darkness). Its primitive actions would be: MN (move north), MS (move south), MW (move west), and ME (move East). A new behavior could be created that combined, for example, ME and SC. The new unit would be called: <ME, SC>, and it would represent the behavior, "Move East and see if it's cold". After this unit is created, another new unit might also be formed: <<ME, SC>, MS> (move east and see if it's cold; if it is, move south). As can be seen in the last example, the rest of a sequence is executed only if the part executed so far has been successful. This allows testing the environment and acting on the results: <SD, MW> (see if it's dark, and if it is, move west).

Behaviors are chosen randomly at first in an effort to achieve a reward. When a reward is received, the system learns that the most recently chosen behaviors may be worth repeating. The system must therefore keep track of the choices it has made and the level of reinforcement it has received for these choice-sequences. To do this, the entire system is embedded in a neural network, where the connections between units record this information. The stronger the connection from one unit to another, the more likely execution of the first followed by the second will result in reward. Therefore, in order to determine which behavior the system should execute next, every unit representing a behavior that has just completed votes for a successor with its weights: [2]

$$a_i(t+1) = \sum_j w_{ij} o_j(t), \tag{1}$$

where $o_j(t)$, the output of unit j at time t, is 1.0 if the behavior represented by unit j completed at time t, and is 0.0 otherwise; w_{ij} is the weight of the connection from i to j; and $a_j(t+1)$ is the resulting degree to which the system believes unit j's behavior should occur at the next time-step. When a unit is chosen at the next time-step, $t+1$, the choice is biased by these values: though stochastic, the unit chosen is *probably* the one with the highest activation.

The connection weights are set by use of the delta rule (Widrow and Hoff, 1960), amplified by the reinforcement signal:

$$\Delta w_{ij}(t) = \eta R(t) o_j(t)(T_i(t) - a_i(t)) \tag{2}$$

That is, the weight change at time t of the connection from unit j to unit i is equal to the product of the learning rate, η, the current reward-level $R(t)$, the current output of unit j, and the difference between the activation of unit i and its target, $T_i(t)$. The target of a unit is simply its output at the next time-step, i.e. $T_i(t) = o_i(t+1)$. (They are given different names in equation 1 for the benefit of those already familiar with the delta rule).

This rule states that if some unit B is chosen after another unit A's behavior completes, then wait to see if B's behavior completes. If it does not complete (or if unit B had not been chosen), then the weight from A to B is decreased by an amount proportional to the current reward and unit B's expectation. (So if unit B was highly expected, but it did not complete, the change is large, causing the system to learn not to expect B as much following A.) But if unit B's behavior does complete, then the weight is increased by an amount proportional to the reward received and the amount by which B fell short of its target, 1.0. (The smaller the expectation, the more the weight will be changed, causing the system to increase its expectation of B following A.)

Figure 1 presents a very simple example of how the system could be used. The animat begins at position 1 in the maze. It will receive a reward if it makes it to the asterisk in position 6. From position 5, ME *should* become highly activated because the animat will receive a reward if it moves east. But how does it know it's in position 5? It knows it's in position 5 if it senses a light. Therefore, the sequence SL→ME may frequently be followed by reward, so the connection from SL to ME will become strong. After a while,

[1] I do not have the space here to give all the fine-grained details of this first system. I can however give a general overview and describe the intended behavior of the system from a high-level perspective, depicting the units as something akin to macro-operators. The details of the implementation are somewhat cumbersome, but are given in *slightly* more detail in a previous paper (Ring, 1991).

[2] It is possible for more than one behavior to complete at the same time. For example: SC, <ME,SC>, and <MN,<ME,SC>> would all finish whenever <MN,<ME,SC>> finishes.

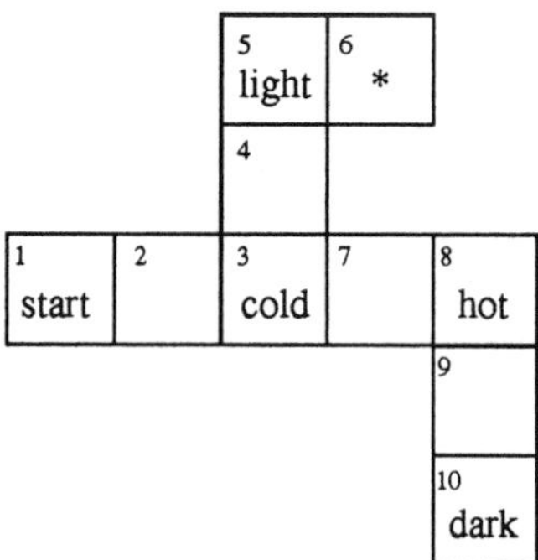

Figure 1: A maze for an animat. The animat would start in position 1 and would receive a reward in position 6. Other labels show what sensations the animat could perceive in different parts of the maze.

a new unit might be formed, <SL, ME>, to encapsulate this behavior. As units are used more and more in the same sequence again and again, the connections between them get stronger, and other new units might be created, such as <SC, <MN, MN>> (useful in position 3), <SH, <MW, MW>> (useful in position 8), and <<<ME, ME>,<SC, <MN, MN>>>, <SL, MR>> (useful in position 1), for example. The units clearly resemble macro-operators, though they are to be used in reinforcement environments with no explicit goals.

Reinforcement, in fact can be done easily: simply reward the last n *choices* made, and even though the behaviors represented by these choices may span a large period of time, reinforcement is spread smoothly across that time span. This is accomplished by slightly modifying equation 2 to:

$$\Delta w_{ij}(t) = o_j(t)(T_i(t) - a_i(t)) + \sigma \Delta w_{ij}(t-1) \quad (3)$$
$$w_{ij}(t) = \eta R(t) \Delta w_{ij}(t) + w_{ij}(t-1)$$

where $0 \leq \sigma \leq 1$ is a decay parameter that discounts previous weight changes in favor of more recent ones. The Δw's are therefore a *trace* of weight changes that decay exponentially—like the eligibility trace presented in (Barto et al., 1983). The trace constantly accrues weight changes over time, biased toward the most recent ones, but the changes are only applied to the weights when a reward is received.

2.1 A Different Approach is Needed

There are problems with this approach. First and most importantly, these units are binary: the behaviors either execute, or they do not. This is a discontinuity that keeps the gradient descent performed by the delta rule from working effectively. Learning tends to be chaotic. Second, it's possible for multiple behaviors to complete simultaneously, as mentioned above, or to *begin* simultaneously. For example, if many sensations are impinging on the system at the same time, the sequence in which they are sensed is irrelevant. In these cases many units could be formed that are functionally identical (grouping together the same sensations), but structurally different (grouping them together in different orders). And third, there may be many ways of achieving the same end. A behavior that takes the animat from home to work, for example, may meet contingencies on the way. A traffic light may be red when a green light was expected. Yet there is no way to encode this contingency within a single unit such that one action is taken when the light is green, and another is taken when the light is red, both ending with the animat arriving at work. If two behaviors could be chosen at the outset, in one of which a green light is expected, and in the other a red light is expected, then the system would merely be inefficient, requiring enormous numbers of units to encode every possible combination of contingencies. But when only one sequence of behaviors can be chosen at a time, encoding contingencies is not just inefficient; it's impossible. A solution to some of these problems is described in the next section.

3 Method II: Transition Hierarchies

The second method of organizing behaviors hierarchically also uses a pool of units in the form of a neural network. This time, however, only the primitive units represent behaviors (as they did with Method I). The higher-level units now represent *transitions* between lower level units. Instead of combining together behaviors as was done with Method I, these units represent the *degree to which one behavior should follow another* at any particular time—they therefore resemble "higher order" units to some extent (c.f. Pollack, 1991; Giles, 1992; and Watrous, 1992).

Take for example Figure 2a. In one case (position 9) the animat should go south when it senses light, while in another case (position 5), it should go north. To decide whether to move north or south after the light, it is sufficient to know whether the animat sensed heat or cold in the previous step. Therefore, a unit can be built, <SL, MN> that causes the connection weight from SL to MN to be strong after sensing heat, but to be weak after sensing coldness. (The connection weight from one unit, A, to another, B, as with Method I, indicates how much the system believes unit B should be chosen directly following unit A.) Another unit, <SL, MS>, can be built to increase the weight from SL to MS after sensing coldness and to decrease it when sensing heat.

The same thing can be done for transitions among higher-level units. For example, in figure 2b, <SL, MN> and <SL, MS> cannot be correctly predicted from the sensation of heat or cold alone, but require knowledge of what happened in the previous step. Thus, a new unit might be built <SH, <SL, MS>> that sets to a high value the weight from SH to <SL, MS> immediately

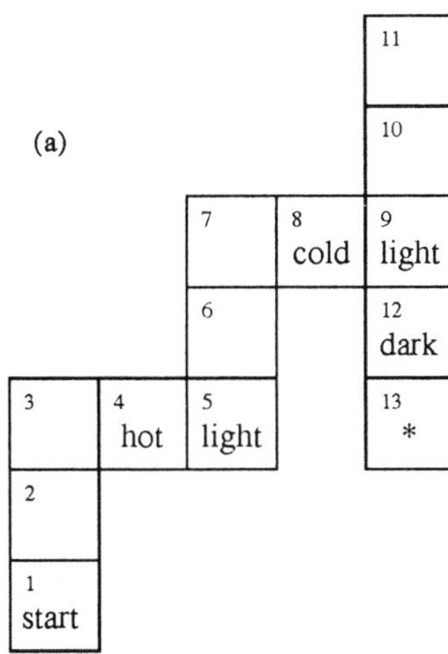

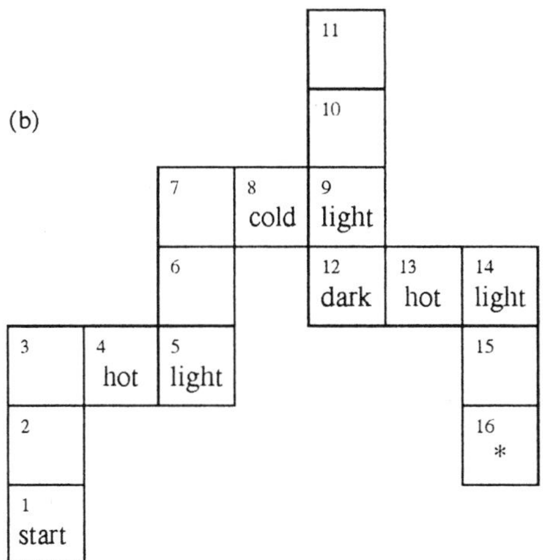

Figure 2: Maze (a) shows the need for two new units: <SL, MS>, to modify the connection from SL (sense light) to MS (move south), and <SL, MN>, to modify the connection from SL (sense light) to MN (move north). In maze (b), new units are needed to modify the connections from SH (sense heat) to <SL, MS> and to <SL, MN>.

following the sensation of darkness (position 12), but sets the weight to a low value otherwise. Clearly, this kind of hierarchy construction can continue indefinitely.

Mathematically, the activation of the units can be expressed as:

$$a_i(t+1) = \sum_j \hat{w}_{ij}(t) o_j(t)$$

$$\hat{w}_{ij}(t) = \begin{cases} w_{ij} + a_{<i,j>}(t-1) & \text{if a unit } <\text{i,j}> \text{ for } w_{ij} \text{ exists} \\ w_{ij} & \text{otherwise} \end{cases}$$

The output of the unit, $o_j(t)$, is the same as its target, $T_i(t)$, and the targets are different for primitive and higher-level units. For a primitive unit, the target is 1.0 if the behavior it represents completes and 0.0 otherwise (as with Method I). For higher-level units, it is given by the learning rule:

$$\begin{aligned} \Delta w_{ij}(t) &= o_j(t-\tau_i)(T_i(t) - a_i(t)) \\ T_{<ij>}(t) &= a_{<ij>}(t) + \Delta w_{ij}(t) \end{aligned} \quad (4)$$

The value τ_i depends on how "high" in the hierarchy unit i is: if i is a primitive unit, τ_i is 1. If i is a higher-level unit, modifying the connection from unit A to unit B, it is $1+\tau_B$. The higher in the hierarchy unit i is, the larger τ_i is, and the longer the time lag is between when the unit is activated and when its target arrives. This learning rule accomplishes actual gradient descent in the error space, unlike the learning rule of the first system.

New units are now created for different reasons from the units of Method I. If one unit is reliably activated after another, there is no reason to interfere with the connection between them. Only when the transition is *unreliable*, that is, when the connection weight should be different in different circumstances, is a unit required to predict the correct value.

In order to decide when a transition is unreliable, a statistical record is kept of each connection. Two long-term averages are maintained: the average change made to the connection, and the average *magnitude* of the change. When the average change is small, but the average magnitude is large, this implies that the learning algorithm is changing the weight of the connection back and forth by a large amount. Therefore, a criteria value, Θ, is chosen arbitrarily, and when

$$\frac{\overline{|\Delta w_{ij}|}}{\epsilon + |\overline{\Delta w_{ij}}|} > \Theta$$

(where ϵ simply keeps the denominator from being zero), a new unit is created for w_{ij}. That is, when the average size of weight-change divided by the size of the average weight-change (plus ϵ) is larger than Θ for some connection w_{ij}, then this connection is judged to be unreliable, and a new unit is created for it. This new unit can now attempt to learn the circumstances under which the connection weight should be one value, and when it should be another. A similar technique for creating new nodes in a non-temporal neural network is given in (Wynn-Jones, 1993).

The resulting system has much in common with the original one, but there are differences. First, this new system has no discontinuities. Higher-level units may come on to a greater or lesser degree, not just completely on or completely off. Second, the behavior hierarchies built by the new system are different from those built by the old system, and these new hierarchies are distributed; execution of a sequence of behaviors, say ME→SC→MS (move east, then if it's cold move south), might require no hierarchy at all! If this sequence always occurs whenever ME is chosen, only ME needs to be chosen, and the rest will follow (since the connection weights from ME to SC and from SC to MS will be large). If, on the other hand, there are *different* sequences that can follow ME, say SC→MS and SD→MW, (where MS always follows SC, and MW always follows SD), then these can be distinguished with new units: <ME, SC> and <ME, SD>. The sequence ME→SC→MS can then be executed by activating *both* ME *and* <ME, SC> at the same time, while *negatively* activating <ME, SD>. Thus, what took only one activation in the first system now takes three simultaneous activations, but they accomplish the same end.

Because of its distributed nature, the new system can handle situations that troubled the first system. Contingencies are a good example. Let's say the desired behavior is: move east, and if it's cold, move south, but if it's hot, move north. This can be done by activating *all* of the following units: ME, <ME, <SC, MS>>, and <ME, <SH, MN>> (while negatively activating any conflicting <ME, ...> units).

3.1 Reinforcement Learning

Reinforcement learning was fairly intuitive in the first system in that it spread reinforcement back over a small number of "choices" while possibly spreading it over an unlimited number of primitive behavior executions. A reinforcement learning scheme in the new system can do nearly the same thing by dynamically modifying the σ of equation 3. This trace can be modified such that unexpected events are remembered strongest at the time of the reward by setting σ equal to a normalized error value for the current time-step.

$$\sigma(t) = (1 - \frac{1}{n}\sum_i |T_i(t) - a_i(t)|)$$

(n is the number of units in the system.) The weight changes are now accumulated in $\Delta' w_{ij}$ (because of the use of $\Delta w_{ij}(t)$ in equation 4).

$$\begin{aligned} \Delta' w_{ij}(t) &= \Delta w_{ij}(t) + \sigma(t)\Delta' w_{ij}(t-1) \\ w_{ij}(t) &= \eta R(t)\Delta' w_{ij}(t) + w_{ij}(t-1) \end{aligned}$$

With this method, if everything in the current time-step is expected exactly as it occurred, the trace of weight changes, $\Delta' w_{ij}(t)$, will remain essentially the same as it was in the previous time-step, but if there is a large error, then the trace is altered significantly. This way, when a reward arrives, it applies the $\Delta' w$'s from the last few time-steps where expectations were not met, no matter how many time-steps have occurred in the mean time.

These methods of reinforcement for both Method I and Method II are really quite old-fashioned. There are many newer and better approaches based on temporal difference (TD) methods (Sutton, 1988) and dynamic programming, for example (Barto et al., 1983; Barto et al., 1989; Sutton, 1990; Barto et al., 1991), that are much more efficient. There is a major obstacle to using these newer, better approaches for reinforcement learning in the hierarchical systems presented here, however: they all depend on accurate knowledge of the state of the environment. It is conceivable that these methods could be used anyway, if one were to allow the hierarchical system to learn also to predict a discounted reinforcement signal, as is used in the TD methods. But despite some work on joining temporal difference methods with hierarchical learning, for example (Singh, 1992; Wixson, 1991), it is not immediately obvious how to tailor the TD approach to the hierarchical systems presented in this paper, (whereas it was relatively straightforward to tailor the reinforcement learning methods given above to these hierarchical systems). I am, however, currently working on doing just this and hope that TD methods allow improvement over the somewhat ad hoc reinforcement learning techniques presented above.

4 Results

It should be noted that the tasks described in the previous sections were presented for explanatory purposes. Certainly there are known techniques, such as recurrent neural networks, that could solve such simple tasks. The important issue that is *not* solved by recurrent neural networks is the implementation of hierarchy. In particular, one would like to have a system that is capable of learning from its environment and using the skills that it has gained so far for the purposes of solving still more difficult tasks and learning even more elaborate skills. Neural networks, on the other hand, are typically renowned for their ability to *forget* when learning something new.

Dawkins (Dawkins, 1976) presented a method of hierarchically reducing the description of symbol sequences without loss of information. This method, similar to the principles exploited here, is also used by Schmidhuber (1992) to build hierarchies within a neural network, though the network is of fixed size and not capable of indefinite extension. The Recurrent Cascade Correlation (RCC) algorithm however is not so limited. This algorithm also learns sequences by adding new units, and it has been shown capable of incremental learning (?). It does not build explicit behavior hierarchies, however, and it cannot be used for reinforcement learning because of the intricacies of its training algorithm.

Despite the fact that it was designed for tasks that required hierarchy learning, Method II has been tested on some traditional sequential tasks that did not require hierarchy learning, and it has compared favorably with other systems. One such task, reported in more detail in (Ring, 1993), was a finite state grammar learning problem that required use of previous sense information to determine the correct output. For this task, reinforce-

Time-step:	0	1	2	3	4	5	6	7	8	9	10	11	12
Sequence 1:	X	A	B	X	C	D	E	F	G	H	I	J	K
Sequence 2:	Y	A	B	Y	C	D	E	F	G	H	I	J	K

Table 1: Training Set for "Gap" task with a gap of two.

	Mean number of Training sets required by:			
gap	Standard recurrent net	Mozer network	Method II	Units created
2	468	328	4	10
4	7406	584	6	15
6	9830	992	8	19
8	> 10000	1312	10	23
10	> 10000	1630	12	27

Table 2: Comparison of Learning Methods on "Gap" Task.

ment learning was *not* used—$R(t)$ was constant for all t. Instead, the task was supervised. That is, the targets were given by a teacher at every time-step. Traditional recurrent networks, including RCC, have been tested on the same task by other researchers (Cleeremans et al., 1989; Fahlman, 1991). The Method II algorithm learned the task approximately 100 times faster than the best results reported by the other researchers. (That is, the other networks needed to see 100 times more training examples before learning the task.) The number of new units in the network after learning completed was, however, between two and twenty times greater than the number of hidden units used in the networks reported by the other researchers.

The finite state grammar task was solvable by keeping track of information from only one time-step into the past. Method II was also tried on (again supervised) tasks that required maintaining information over a much larger time span, and the network quickly learned these tasks as well. For example, tasks of the form given in Table 1 have been given to the network to compare against the recurrent network of Mozer (Mozer, 1992). These two sequences formed a single traning set given to the network. The network was given as sensory input each element in the sequence one at a time until the end of the sequence was reached. At that point, the activations of the higher-level units were reinitialized and the second sequence was given to the network. At each time-step, the network's target output was the item of the sequence that the network would be given as input on the following time-step. Thus, at time-step 1, while experiencing sequence 2, sensory line A would be activated (i.e. set to 1.0), and all others would be quiescent (i.e. set to 0.0). The network's target output would be B. Because the network will always be asked to predict B when its input is A, this part of the task is fairly simple. However, at time-step 2, the network will see B as input and must predict either X or Y, depending upon which sequence it is currently sensing, and this information is contained two steps back in time. Thus, the network must remember what it saw at time-step 0 to correctly predict what it will see at time-step 3.

The difficulty of the task can clearly be increased by lengthening the duration between the initial X or Y stimulus at time-step 0 and its recurrence later on in the sequence. Mozer used sequences generated in this manner to compare his algorithm to traditional recurrent neural networks, which he realized were extremely poor at learning extended time delays. He compared the algorithms on sequences with gaps of between two and ten time-steps from the initial X or Y and its reappearance. The results of his tests, together with the results from Method II, are printed in table 2. Mozer noticed that the number of training sets his architecture required to learn a sequence scaled roughly linearly with the size of the gap. Method II also scaled linearly, but it learned the task approximately 100 times faster than Mozer's network. I tested the network at gaps of up to 24 and found the identical scaling behavior (i.e. 26 training set presentations were required, and 49 new units were built).

It should be noted that the parameters were optimized for these particular tasks and would not necessarily be the best parameters for a different task. Specifically, it is not always beneficial for units to be created as quickly as they were for this task. It should also be noted that Method II learns the precise number of time-steps between when information becomes available and when it will be used. It does so by creating a hierarchy that spans the gap exactly. Mozer's network, on the other hand, maintains more general knowledge and is able to keep information for use over broader periods of time. In the end, one would expect Mozer's network to generalize better than the network of Method II. Part of my current work is to provide the Method II algorithm with the same flexibility that Mozer's network has.

5 Summary and Conclusions

Two methods for hierarchically organizing temporal events have been described. The first is more intuitive: grouping together common sequences of events into single units so that they may be treated as individual behaviors. This system contains discontinuities, however, and it runs into difficulty when more than one unit is (or should be) active at the same time. The second system can dynamically modify the values that specify the degree to which one unit should follow another. These values are continuous, allowing the use of gradient descent during learning. Furthermore, many units are active at the same time as part of the system's normal functionings. The new system is actually more powerful than the first, while being easier to train.

Acknowledgements

This work was supported by NASA Johnson Space Center Graduate Student Researchers Program training grant, NGT 50594. I would like to thank Kadir Liano and my advisor, Robert Simmons, for many helpful discussions. I would also like to thank Pavilion Technologies, Inc. for their generous contribution of computer time and office space required to complete much of this work.

References

Albus, J. S. (1979). Mechanisms of planning and problem solving in the brain. *Mathematical Biosciences*, 45:247–293.

Bachrach, J. R. (1992). *Connectionist Modeling and Control of Finite State Environments*. PhD thesis, Department of Computer and Information Sciences, University of Massachusetts.

Barto, A. G., Bradtke, S. J., and Singh, S. P. (1991). Real-time learning and control using asynchronous dynamic programming. Technical Report 91-57, Computer Science Department, University of Massachusetts at Amherst.

Barto, A. G., Sutton, R. S., and Anderson., C. W. (1983). Neuron-like elements that can solve difficult learning control problems. *IEEE Transactions on Systems, Man, and Cybernetics*, 13:835–846.

Barto, A. G., Sutton, R. S., and Watkins, C. J. C. H. (1989). Learning and sequential decision making. Technical Report COINS Technical Report 89-95, University of Massachusetts at Amherst, Department of Computer and Information Science.

Cleeremans, A., Servan-Schreiber, D., and McClelland, J. L. (1989). Finite state automata and simple recurrent networks. *Neural Computation*, 1(3):372–381.

Dawkins, R. (1976). Hierarchical organisation: a candidate principle for ethology. In Bateson, P. P. G. and Hinde, R. A., editors, *Growing Points in Ethology*, pages 7–54. Cambridge: Cambridge University Press.

Drescher, G. L. (1991). *Made-Up Minds: A Constructivist Approach to Artificial Intelligence*. Cambridge, Massachusetts: MIT Press.

Fahlman, S. E. (1991). The recurrent cascade-correlation architecture. In Lippmann, R. P., Moody, J. E., and Touretzky, D. S., editors, *Advances in Neural Information Processing Systems 3*, pages 190–196. San Mateo, California: Morgan Kaufmann Publishers.

Giles, C. L., Miller, C. B., Chen, D., Sun, G. Z., Chen, H. H., and Lee, Y. C. (1992). Extracting and learning an unknown grammar with recurrent neural networks. In Moody, J. E., Hanson, S. J., and Lippman, R. P., editors, *Advances in Neural Information Processing Systems 4*, pages 317–324. San Mateo, California: Morgan Kaufmann Publishers.

Mozer, M. C. (1992). Induction of multiscale temporal structure. In Moody, J. E., Hanson, S. J., and Lippmann, R. P., editors, *Advances in Neural Information Processing Systems 4*, pages 275–282. San Mateo, California: Morgan Kaufmann Publishers.

Pollack, J. B. (1991). The induction of dynamical recognizers. *Machine Learning*, 7:227–252.

Ring, M. B. (1991). Incremental development of complex behaviors through automatic construction of sensory-motor hierarchies. In Birnbaum, L. A. and Collins, G. C., editors, *Machine Learning: Proceedings of the Eighth International Workshop (ML91)*, pages 343–347. Morgan Kaufmann Publishers.

Ring, M. B. (1993). Learning sequential tasks by incrementally adding higher orders. In Giles, C. L., Hanson, S. J., and Cowan, J. D., editors, *Advances in Neural Information Processing Systems 5*. San Mateo, California: Morgan Kaufmann Publishers.

Roitblat, H. L. (1991). Cognitive action theory as a control architecture. In Meyer, J. A. and Wilson, S. W., editors, *From Animals to Animats: Proceedings of the First International Conference on Simulation of Adaptive Behavior*, pages 444–450. MIT Press.

Schmidhuber, J. (1992). Learning unambiguous reduced sequence descriptions. In Moody, J. E., Hanson, S. J., and Lippman, R. P., editors, *Advances in Neural Information Processing Systems 4*, pages 291–298. San Mateo, California: Morgan Kaufmann Publishers.

Singh, S. P. (1992). Transfer of learning by composing solutions of elemental sequential tasks. *Machine Learning*, 8(3/4).

Sutton, R. S. (1988). Learning to predict by the methods of temporal differences. *Machine Learning*, 3:9–44.

Sutton, R. S. (1990). Integrated architectures for learning, planning, and reacting based on approximating dynamic programming. In Porter, B. W. and Mooney, R. J., editors, *Proceedings of the Seventh International Conference on Machine Learning*, pages 216–224. Morgan Kaufmann Publishers.

Watrous, R. L. and Kuhn, G. M. (1992). Induction of finite-state languages using second-order recurrent networks. In Moody, J. E., Hanson, S. J., and Lippman, R. P., editors, *Advances in Neural Information Processing Systems 4*, pages 309–316. San Mateo, California: Morgan Kaufmann Publishers.

Widrow, B. and Hoff, M. E. (1960). Adaptive switching circuits. In *IRE WESCON Convention Record*, pages 96–104. IRE. New York.

Wilson, S. W. (1989). Hierarchical credit allocation in a classifier system. In Elzas, M. S., Ören, T. I., and Zeigler, B. P., editors, *Modeling and Simulation Methodology*. Elsevier Science Publishers B.V.

Wixson, L. E. (1991). Scaling reinforcement learning techniques via modularity. In Birnbaum, L. A. and Collins, G. C., editors, *Machine Learning: Proceedings of the Eighth International Workshop (ML91)*, pages 368–372. Morgan Kaufmann Publishers.

Wynn-Jones, M. (1993). Node splitting: A constructive algorithm for feed-forward neural networks. *Neural Computing and Applications*, 1(1):17–22.

Should I Stay or Should I Go: Coordinating Biological Needs with Continuously-updated Assessments of the Environment

Liane M. Gabora
Artificial Life Research Group, Dept. of Biology, UCLA
405 Hilgard Ave., Los Angeles, CA
90024-1606
Email: liane@cs.ucla.edu

ABSTRACT

This paper presents *Wanderer,* a model of how autonomous adaptive systems coordinate internal biological needs with moment-by-moment assessments of the probabilities of events in the external world. The extent to which *Wanderer* moves about or explores its environment reflects the relative activations of two competing motivational subsystems: one represents the need to acquire energy and it excites exploration, and the other represents the need to avoid predators and it inhibits exploration. The environment contains food, predators, and neutral stimuli. *Wanderer* responds to these events in a way that is adaptive in the short term, and reassesses the probabilities of these events so that it can modify its long term behaviour appropriately. When food appears, *Wanderer* becomes satiated and exploration temporarily decreases. When a predator appears, *Wanderer* both decreases exploration in the short term, and becomes more "cautious" about exploring in the future. *Wanderer* also forms associations between neutral features and salient ones (food and predators) when they are present at the same time, and uses these associations to guide its behaviour.

1. INTRODUCTION

One approach to modeling animal behaviour is to create an animat that continually assesses its needs, determines which need is most urgent, and implements the behaviour that satisfies that need. However, in the absence of appetitive stimuli such as food or mates, or harmful stimuli such as predators, behaviour is often not directed at the fulfillment of any particular need: an animal either remains still or moves about, and both options have repercussions on *many* aspects of survival. So the question is not "What should I do next?", but rather, "Should I stay where I am, conserving energy and minimizing exposure to predators, or should explore my environment, with the possibility of finding food, mates, or shelter"?

In this paper we present a computational model of how positively or negatively reinforcing stimuli affect an animat's decision whether or not, and if so to what extent, to explore its environment. The model is referred to as *Wanderer*. The architecture of *Wanderer* is an extension of an architecture used to model the mechanisms underlying exploratory behaviour in the absence of positively or negatively reinforcing stimuli (Gabora and Colgan, 1990). The general approach is to consider an autonomous adaptive system as an assemblage of subsystems specialized to take care of different aspects of survival, and what McFarland (1975) refers to as the "final behavioural common path" is the emergent outcome of the continual process of attempting to mutually satisfy these competing subsystems. The relative impact of each subsystem on behaviour reflects the animal's internal state and its assessment of the dynamic affordance probabilities of the environment (for example, how likely it seems that a predator or food will appear). This distributed approach is similar in spirit to that of Braitenburg (1984), Brooks (1986), Maes (1990) and Beer (1990). We make the simplifying assumption that the only possible beneficial outcome of exploration is finding food, and the only possible harmful outcome is an encounter with a predator. The amount of exploration that *Wanderer* engages in at any moment reflects the relative activations of a subsystem that represents the need for food, which has an excitatory effect on exploration, and a subsystem that represents the need to avoid predators, which inhibits exploration.

The earlier version of *Wanderer* exhibited the increase and then decrease in activity shown by animals in a novel environment (Welker, 1956; Dember & Earl, 1957; May, 1963; McCall, 1974; Weisler & McCall, 1976) and all four characteristics that differentiate the pattern of exploration exhibited by animals raised under different levels of predation were reproduced in the model by changing the initial value of one parameter: the decay on the inhibitory subsystem, which represents the animats assessment of the probability that a predator could appear. In the present paper, we first address how salient events such as the appearance of food or predators affect exploration. *Wanderer* does not have direct access to the probabilities that predators and food will appear but it continually reassesses them based on its experiences, and adjusts its behaviour accordingly. This approach merges Gigerenzer and Murray's (1987) notion of cognition as intuitive statistics with Roitblat's (1987) concept of optimal decision making in animals.

We then examine how initially-neutral features can come to excite or inhibit exploration by becoming associated with salient ones (food or predators). It has long been recognized that animals form associations of this kind between simultaneously-occuring stimuli or events (Tolman, 1932; Hull, 1943). This is useful since in the real world features are clustered — for example, predators may dwell in a particular type of cavernous rock, so the presence of rocks of that sort can be a useful indicator that a predator is likely to be near. Thus features of environments that contain a lot of food are responded to with increased exploration (even when there is no food in sight) and features of environments that contain many predators inhibit exploration (even when there are no predators).

2. ARCHITECTURE OF *WANDERER*

Wanderer consists of two motivational subsystems that receive input from five sensory units and direct their output to a motor unit, constructed in Common Lisp (Figure 1). One subsystem represents the need to acquire and maintain energy. It has an excitatory effect on exploration and is linked by a positive weight to the motor unit. Exploration in turn feeds back and inhibits activation of this subsystem: this represents fatigue. Activation of the other subsystem represents the need to avoid predators; it has an inhibitory effect on exploration and is linked by a negative weight to the motor unit. Since every moment that passes without encountering a predator is evidence that there is less need to be cautious, activation of the inhibitory subsystem decreases as a function of time in the absence of predation. In addition, since moving about provides more evidence that there are no predators nearby than does immobility, the inhibitory subsystem, like the excitatory subsystem, receives feedback from the motor unit; its activation decreases by an amount proportional to the amount of exploration that occurred during the previous iteration.

Perception units have binary activations. Activation of unit 0 corresponds to detection of food, activation of unit 1 corresponds to detection of a predator, and activation of units 2, 3, and 4 correspond to detection of rock, tree, and sun respectively. Activation can spread from perception units to subsystems, but not the other way around.

The output for each iteration is either zero, signifying immobility, or a positive number that indicates how much exploration is taking place.

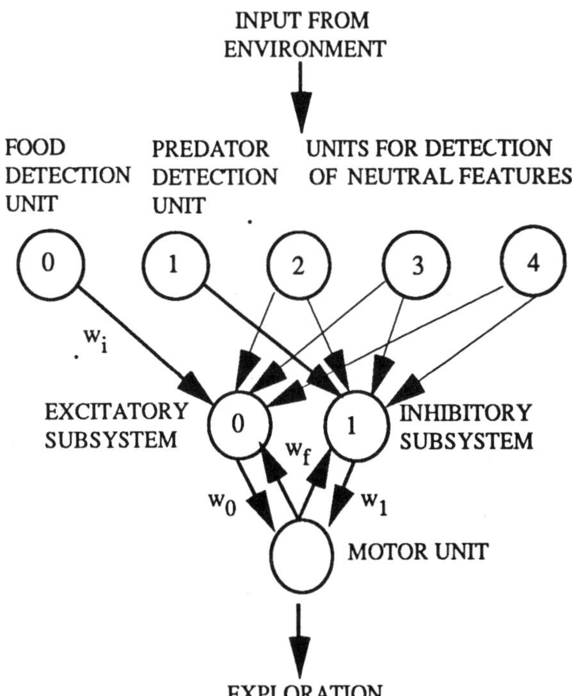

Figure 1. The architecture of *Wanderer*. Dark lines represent fixed connections. Fine lines represent learnable connections.

The relevant variables and their initial values are:

a_i activation of perception unit i = {0, 1}

s0 = activation of excitatory subsystem = 0.9

s1 = activation of inhibitory subsystem = 0.9

E = exploration = activation of motor unit

$w_{i,j}$ = weight from perception unit i to subsystem j;
$w_{0,0} = -0.5$, $w_{1,1} = 0.9$, all others = 0.

w_0 = weight from excitatory subsystem to motor unit = -0.5

w_1 = weight from inhibitatory subsystem to motor unit = 0.5

w_f = feedback weight from motor unit to subsystems = -0.1

k_0 = rate at which hunger increases = 1.05

k_1 = decay on inhibitory subsystem = 0.5

Exploration is calculated using a logistic function as follows:

$$E = 1 / [1 + e^{-(w0s0 + w1s1)}]$$

Thus exploration only occurs if the activation of the excitatory subsystem is greater than that of the inhibitory subsystem. Subsystem activations are then updated:

$$s0_t = \max \{0, k_0 [s0_{t-1} + w_f E + \Sigma_{i=0}^{n-1} w_{i,0}\, a_i]\}$$

$$s1_t = \max \{0, k_1 [s1_{t-1} + w_f E + \Sigma_{i=0}^{n-1} w_{i,1}\, a_i]\}$$

3. *WANDERER'S* ENVIRONMENT

Wanderer's environment contains three kinds of stimuli: food, predators, and features that have no direct effect on survival, which will be referred to as neutral features. The initial presence or absence of neutral features is random. The more exploration *Wanderer* engages in, the greater the probability that a neutral feature will change from present to absent or vice versa in the next iteration:

c_1 = constant = 0.75

$$p(\Delta a)_t = c_1 E_{t-1}$$

Perception unit 2 detects a stimulus that is predictive of the appearance of food. Let us say that Wanderer's primary source of food is a plant that grows on on a certain kind of soil, and that a certain kind of tree also grows only in that soil, so that the presence of that tree is predictive of finding food. Perception unit 2 can only turn on when perception unit 0 is on (that is, food can only be detected when the tree is detected). Also, in accord with the harsh realities of life, Wanderer has to *explore* if it is to find food. The probability of finding food is proportional to the amount of exploration that took place during the previous iteration:

a_0 = activation of food detection unit

c_2 = constant specified at run-time

$$p(a_0 = 1)_t = c_2 a_2 E_{t-1}$$

Perception unit 3 detects a stimulus that is predictive of the appearance of a predator. Let us say that the animal that preys upon Wanderer lives in cavernous rocks, and this unit turns on when rocks of that sort are detected. Perception unit 3 can only turn on when perception unit 1 is on (that is, a predator will only appear when the a rock is present). Since predators can appear even when Wanderer is immobile, it is not necessary that Wanderer explore in order to come across a predator.

a_1 = activation of predator detection unit

c_3 = constant specified at run-time

$$p(a_1 = 1)_t = c_3 a_3$$

Perception unit 4 detects the presence of the sun, such as when it comes out from under a cloud. The sun is predictive of neither food nor predator.

4. EFFECT OF SALIENT STIMULI ON MOTIVATION

4.1 IMPLEMENTATION OF SATIETY

Detection of food is represented by the activation of a single binary unit. Activation of this unit decreases the activation of the excitatory subsystem, which in turn brings a short-term decrease in exploration. This corresponds to satiety; once food has been found, the immediate need for food decreases, thus exploration should decrease.

4.2 IMPLEMENTATION OF CAUTION

Detection of a predator is represented by the activation of a single binary node that is positively linked to the inhibitory subsystem. Activation of this unit has two effects. First, it causes an increase in the activation of the inhibitory subsystem, which results in a pronounced short-term decrease in exploration. Second, it decreases the decay on the inhibitory subsystem. This has the long-term effect of decreasing the rate at which exploration is disinhibited; in other words, every encounter with a predator causes *Wanderer* to be more "cautious". Decay on the inhibitory subsystem is updated each iteration as follows:

$$\partial = 0.2$$

$$k1_{min} = 0.5$$

$$k1_t = \max\ \{ k1_{min},\ (k1_{t-1} + \partial\, [\, s1_t - s1_{t-1}\,])\ \}$$

Since activation of the inhibitory subsystem increases in response to predation, decay increases if a predator appears, and decreases when no predator is present.

5. LEARNING ALGORITHM

If a neutral feature — rock, tree, or sun — is present when a salient feature — food or predator — appears, an association forms between the neutral feature and subsystem that is positively linked with the salient feature. Weights on the lines between neutral features and hidden nodes are initialized to zero, corresponding to the state in which no associations, either positive or negative, have formed. If food or a predator appears in the environment, and if one or more initially-neutral features (p_i) is present, weights on links connecting initially-neutral features to subsystems are updated as follows:

$$\eta = \text{learning rate} = 0.05$$

$$w_t = w_{t-1} + \eta\, |\, s_t - s_{t-1}\, |\, a_i$$

6. RESULTS

Figure 2 plots exploration during a run in which the probability of finding food is high and the probability of predation is zero. Exploration increases quickly initially as activation of the excitatory subsystem increases and the activation of the inhibitory subsystem decreases. It falls sharply whenever food is encountered, and then gradually increases again. Each time food is encountered exploration falls to the same level.

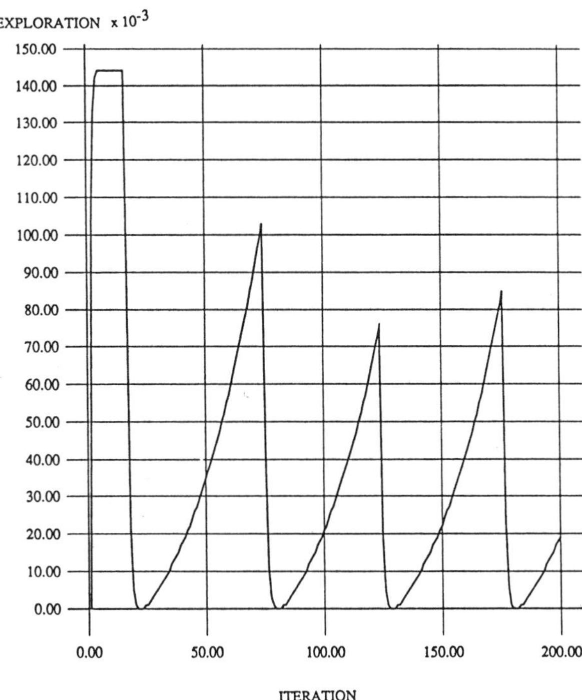

Figure 2. Exploration when p(food) is high and p(predator) = 0.0.

Figure 3 plots exploration during a run in which the probability of finding food is zero and the probability of predation is high. The appearance of a predator causes activation of the inhibitory subsystem to increase, temporarily decreasing exploration. Since no food is present, activation of the excitatory subsystem is high, and exploration quickly resumes. Two more predators are encountered in quick succession. With each encounter, the response is greater, representing an increase in the assessed probability of predation in the current location. Exploration ceases after the third encounter.

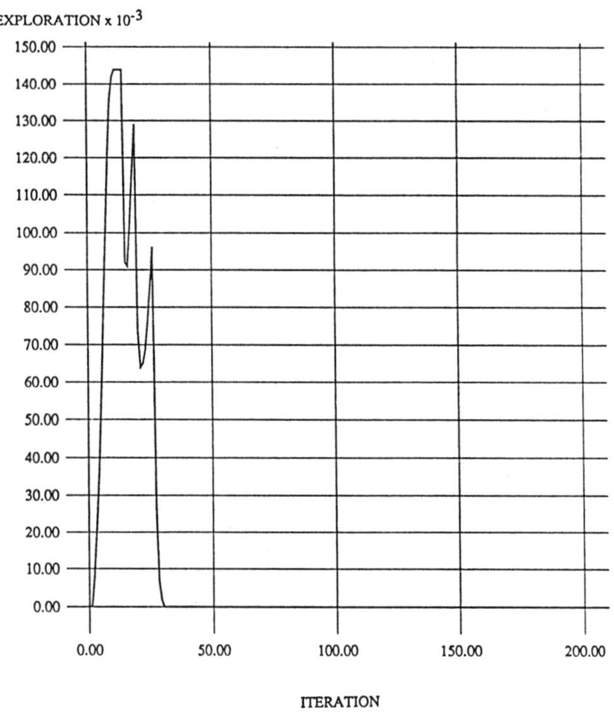

Figure 3. Exploration when p(predator) is high and p(food) = 0.0.

Figure 4 illustrates the effect of associative learning in the presence of food when there are no predators. The exploration curve is less regular. Rocks are present at the beginning of the run, but disappear before food is found. Food never appears unless a tree is present. Food is first found during iteration 24, and exploration drops sharply. At this point associations are formed between food and both the tree and the sun, and the weights on the lines from feature detection units 3 and 4 to subsystem 1 increase (from 0.0 to 0.015). Note that the association between sun and food is spurious; the sun is not actually predictive of food. Exploration increases until until it reaches a plateau. It drops sharply when food is encountered during iteration 80 since at the same time one of the cues predictive of food, the sun, disappears. (Not only is it no longer hungry, but there is indication that there is no food around anyway.) During iteration 84, the tree, the other feature that has been associated with food, disappears as well. Thus exploration increases very slowly. Since little exploration is taking place, features of the environment change little. Rocks appear in iteration 155, but since no association has been formed between rocks and food, this has no effect on exploration. Exploration increases sharply for a brief period between iterations 176 and 183 when the sun comes out, and then again at iteration 193 when trees appear. It plummets once again in iteration 195, with the final appearance of food.

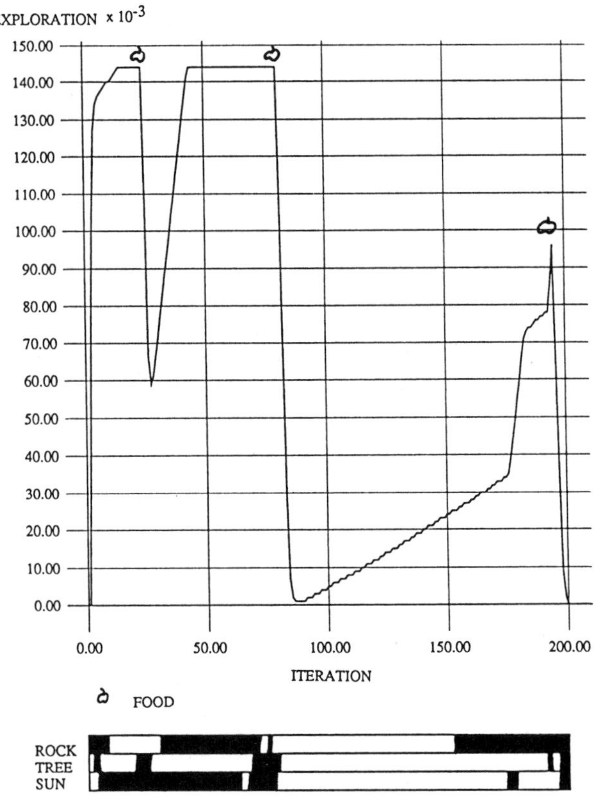

Figure 4. Effect of associative learning when p(food) is high and p(predator) = 0.0. Below: Black bar indicates presence of neutral feature; white bar indicates absence.

The effect of associative learning on response to predation is illustrated in Figure 5. (In this experiment, decay on the inhibitory subsystem is held constant so that exploration does not fall quickly to zero despite the high predation rate.) Response to predation grows increasingly variable throughout the run, reflecting the extent to which features which have become associated with predation are present at the time a predator appears. *Wanderer* eventually associates all three features of its environment with predators, and none with food. Since two of the three features are present, exploration stops at iteration 179 and does not resume by the 200th iteration. Since *Wanderer* is not moving, there is no further change in the neutral features until the end of the run.

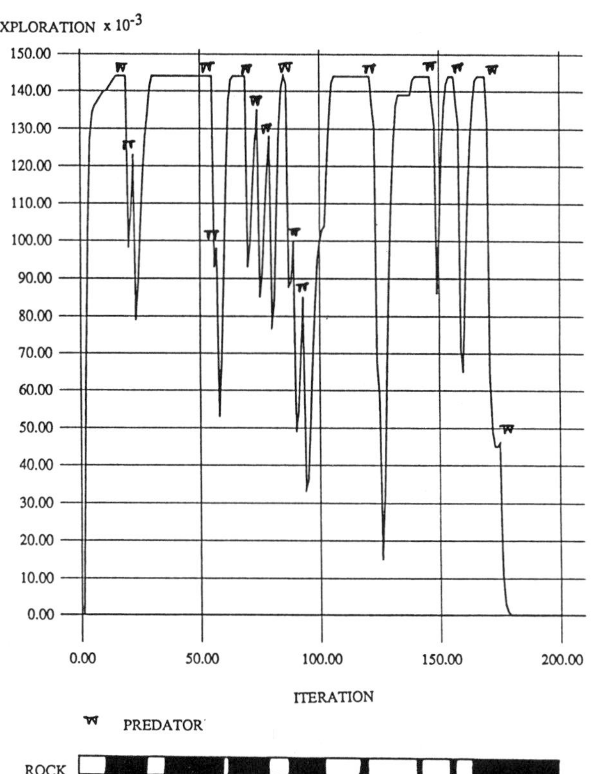

Figure 5. Effect of associative learning when p(food) is high and p(predator) = 0.0. Below: Black bar indicates presence of neutral feature; white bar indicates absence.

The effect of associative learning in the presence of both food and predators is illustrated in Figure 6. Rocks become associated with predators, and trees become associated with food, as expected. (After 200 iterations the weight on the line from Perception Unit 2 to Subsystem 0 is 0.091, and the weight on the line from Perception Unit 3 to Subsystem 1 is 0.170.) However, spurious associations also form between neutral features and salient features (with weights on the relevant lines ranging from 0.046 to 0.112).

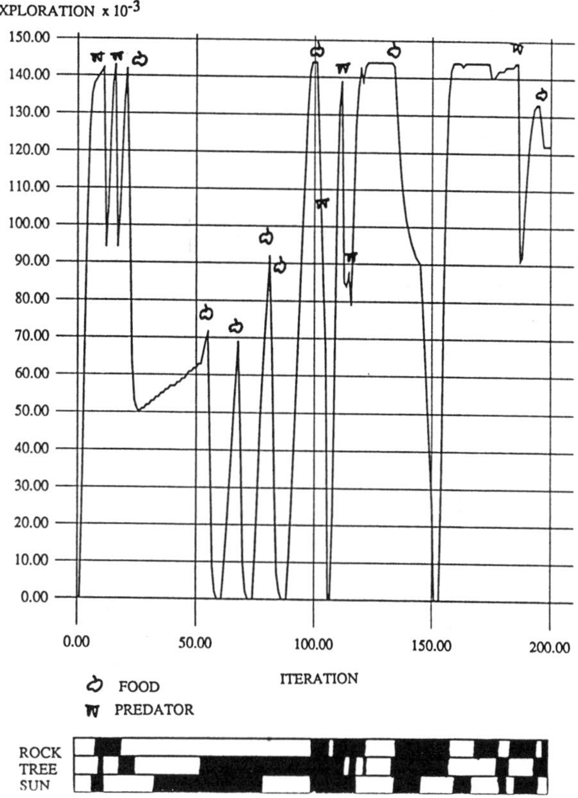

Figure 6. Effect of associative learning when both p(food) and p(predator) are high. Below: Black bar indicates presence of neutral feature; white bar indicates absence.

7. DISCUSSION

Wanderer is a simple qualitative model of the mechanisms underlying underlying how animals coordinate internal needs with external affordances. It does not address a number of real world complexities: the perceptual inputs are ungrounded, and the problems associated with actively moving about in a real environment are bypassed. Since weights never decrease using the delta rule, once associations are formed, they can not be unlearned. However *Wanderer* responds to events in a way that is adaptive in the short term, and reassesses the probabilities of these events so that it can modify its long term behaviour appropriately. When food appears, *Wanderer* becomes satiated and temporarily decreases exploration. When a predator appears, *Wanderer* both temporarily decreases exploration to avoid being caught, and becomes more cautious in the near future. When predators are not encountered, *Wanderer* becomes less cautious. *Wanderer* also forms associations between neutral features of its environment and salient features (predators and food). Since in real environments, features are clustered — neutral features often provide reliable clues regarding the proximity of predators and food — association-forming of this kind can help to optimize behaviour.

In summary, this paper illustrates how an animat can be built using a distributed approach in which subsystems specialized to take care of different needs coordinate internal signals with moment-by-moment assessments of probabilities of events in the external world. The relative activations of these subsystems determines the extent to which the animat moves about or explores its environment.

ACKNOWLEDGEMENTS

I would like to thank Mike Gasser for discussion and Peter Todd for comments on the manuscript. I would also like to thank the Center for the Study of the Evolution and Origin of Life (CSEOL) at UCLA for support.

REFERENCES

Beer, R. D. and H. J. Chiel. (1990). The neural basis of behavioral choice in an artificial insect. In J. A. Meyer and S. W. Wilson (Eds.) *From Animals to Animats: Proceedings of the First International Conference on the Simulation of Adaptive Behaviour, 247-254.*. London: MIT Press.

Braitenburg, V. (1984). *Vehicles: Experiments in synthetic psychology.* Cambridge, MA: MIT Press.

Brooks, R. A. (1986). A robust layered control system for a mobile robot. *IEEE Journal of Robotics and Automation RA-2*, **1**, 253-262.

Dember, W. N. and R. W. Earl. (1957). *Analysis of exploratory, manipulatory, and curiosity behaviours. Psychological Review* **64,** 91-96.

Gabora, L. M. and P. W. Colgan. (1990). A model of the mechanisms underlying exploratory behaviour. In J. A. Meyer and S. W. Wilson (Eds.) *From Animals to Animats: Proceedings of the First International Conference on the Simulation of Adaptive Behaviour, 475-484.* London: MIT Press.

Gigerenzer, G. and D. J. Murray. (1987). *Cognition as Intuitive Statistics.* Hillsdale, NJ: Lawrence Erlbaum Associates.

Hull, C. L. (1943). The problem of intervening variables in molar behavior theory. *Psychological Review*, **50**, 273-291.

Maes, P. (1989). The dynamics of action selection. In *Proceedings of the Eleventh International Joint Conference on AI (IJCAI 89)*, 991-997. Morgan-Kaufmann Publishers.

May, R. B. (1963). Stimulus selection in preschool children under conditions of free choice. *Perceptual and Motor Skills*, **16**, 200-206.

McCall, R. B. (1974). Exploratory manipulation and play in the human infant. *Monographs of the Society for Research in Child Development*, **39** (No. 2).

McFarland, D. J. and R. M. Sibly. (1975). The behavioural final common path. *Philosophical Transactions of the London Royal Society*, **270B**, 265-293.

Roitblat, H. L. (1987). *Introduction to comparative cognition.* New York: Freeman.

Tolman, E. C. (1932). *Purposive behaviour in animals and men.* New York: Century.

Weisler, A. and McCall, R. (1976). Exploration and play: resume and redirection. *American Psychologist* **31**, 492-508.

Welker, W. I. (1956a). Some determinants of play and exploration in chimpanzees. *Journal of Comparative Physiological Psychology* **49,** 84-89.

Welker, W. I. (1956b). Variability of play and exploratory behaviour in chimpanzees. *Journal of Comparative Physiological Psychology* **49,** 181-185.

Wilson, S. W. (1990). The animat path to AI In J. A. Meyer and S. W. Wilson (Eds.) *From Animals to Animats: Proceedings of the First International Conference on the Simulation of Adaptive Behaviour, 247-254.*. London: MIT Press.

Extensions of the Associative Control Process (ACP) Network: Hierarchies and Provable Optimality

Leemon C. Baird III and A. Harry Klopf
Wright Laboratory (Mail stop: AAAT)
Wright-Patterson Air Force Base, Ohio 45433-6543
Telephone: (513) 255-7644
Fax: (513) 476-4302
E-mail: bairdlc@WL.wpafb.af.mil

Abstract

The associative control process (ACP) network is a learning control system that can reproduce a variety of animal learning results from classical and instrumental conditioning experiments (Klopf, Morgan, and Weaver, 1992). We show that the model can be extended so that it is capable of learning to solve optimal control problems, while retaining the ability to reproduce the conditioning results. The modified model is capable of learning to optimally control any Markov sequential decision process, even when given no a priori information about the process. Furthermore, it is possible to simplify the model while retaining these properties, and to combine multiple copies of the simplified model in hierarchies that learn quickly. The proposed models are applied to a standard cart-pole control problem and performance is compared with that of the learning controller developed by Barto, Sutton, and Anderson (1983).

1. INTRODUCTION

The associative control process (ACP) network is a learning control system that can reproduce a variety of animal learning results from classical and instrumental conditioning experiments (Klopf, Morgan, and Weaver, 1992). Section 2 of this paper reviews the ACP network. Section 3 describes modifications to the network, and proves the optimality of the modified system. Section 4 explains how the network can be simplified and Section 5 shows how multiple copies of the simplified network can be arranged in a hierarchy. Section 6 describes simulation results for the modified ACP network and the hierarchical version. Both the modified ACP network and the hierarchical network are used to solve a standard control problem of balancing a pole attached by a hinge to a cart moving on a finite-length track. The proposed model is shown to learn more reliably than previously published learning systems, and is also shown to learn more quickly.

2. THE ACP NETWORK ARCHITECTURE

The ACP network was developed by Klopf, Morgan, and Weaver (1992) and incorporates the drive-reinforcement learning mechanism proposed in Klopf (1988). The ACP network is shown in Figure 1.

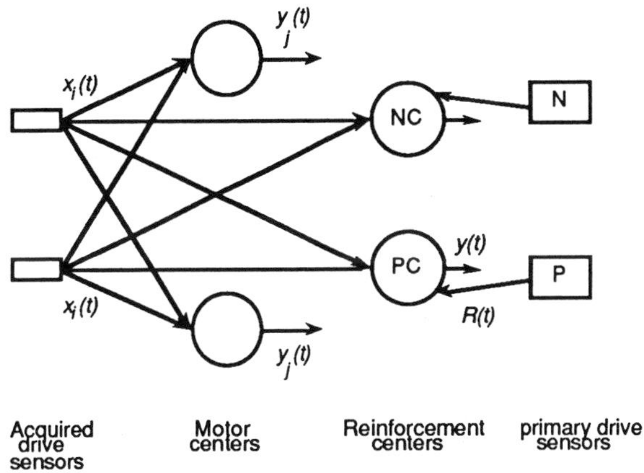

Figure 1. ACP network architecture.

An ACP network receives reinforcement inputs from *primary drive sensors* and initially neutral inputs from *m* state sensors, called *acquired drive sensors*. There are two layers of processing nodes: a layer consisting of *n motor centers*, and a layer consisting of a pair of *reinforcement centers*. The negative reinforcement center (NC) learns to predict the occurrence of primary negative reinforcement (N), and the positive reinforcement center (PC) learns to predict the occurrence of primary positive reinforcement (P). For the optimality proof and simulations in this paper, all reinforcement is assumed to be positive; the negative reinforcement center never receives reinforcement signals. This prevents the weights associated with NC from changing, so it never becomes active and can be ignored here. There are two weights from a given sensor i to a given motor center j: a positive weight W_{ij+} and a negative weight W_{ij-}. For each motor center j, there are two weights from sensor i to the positive reinforcement center that are facilitated by that motor center: W_{0ij+} and W_{0ij-}. Signals pass through these facilitated connections only when the associated motor center is active. The following equations specify the calculation of the outputs of the various centers:

$$y_j(t) = f\left(\sum_{i=1}^{m} \left(W_{ij+}(t) + W_{ij-}(t) \right) x_i(t) \right) \qquad (1)$$

$$y(t) = f\left(R(t) + \sum_{i=1}^{m} \left(W_{0ij_{max}+}(t) + W_{0ij_{max}-}(t) \right) x_i(t) \right) \quad (2)$$

$$f(x) = \begin{cases} 0 & \text{if } x \le \theta \\ 1 & \text{if } x \ge 1 \\ x & \text{otherwise} \end{cases} \quad (3)$$

$$j_{\max} = \text{The index } j \text{ such that } \forall k \ne j \quad y_j(t) > y_k(t) \quad (4)$$

The threshold θ is a small positive constant. If the maximum in Equation 4 is not unique at time t, then j_{max} is not defined, no action is performed, and none of the weights change on that time step. Otherwise, the action associated with motor center j_{max} is performed at time t, and only those weights associated with action j_{max} change. The change in those weights is:

$$\Delta W_{ij_{max}\pm}(t) = \left(c_a + c_b |y(t)|\right) \left| W_{ij_{max}\pm}(t) \right| \left[\Delta x_i(t) \right]^{+} \left(y(t) - y_j(t) \right) \quad (5)$$

$$\Delta W_{0ij_{max}\pm}(t) = \Delta y(t) \sum_{k=1}^{\tau} c_k \left| W_{0ij_{max}\pm}(t-k) \right| \left[\Delta x_i(t-k) \right]^{+} \quad (6)$$

$$\Delta y(t) = y(t) - y(t-1) \quad (7)$$

$$\left[\Delta x_i(t) \right]^{+} = \begin{cases} 1 \text{ if } x_i(t) = 1 \text{ and } x_i(t-1) = 0 \\ 0 \text{ otherwise} \end{cases} \quad (8)$$

The factors c_a, c_b, τ, and $c_1,...,c_\tau$ are all nonnegative constants. The learning process is broken up into periods of time called trials, and weights change only at the end of each trial. The weight change at the end of the trial is simply the sum of all ΔW calculated during the trial.

3. Optimality of Modified Network

Consider a discrete-state, discrete-time Markov sequential decision process with m states and a choice of n possible actions in each state. If action i is performed while the system is in state j, then with probability ${}^iP_{jk}$, on the next time step the system will be in state k and will receive a reward ${}^iR_{jk}$. The reward at time t is $R(t)$. R_{max} and R_{min} are defined to be the maximum and minimum reward value respectively. Costs associated with transitions are represented by negative rewards. A policy vector π gives the action π_i to be performed in each state i. Given all the values of ${}^iP_{jk}$ and ${}^iR_{jk}$, the goal is to find the optimal policy that, starting in any state at time t=0, will maximize the expected value of the total discounted reward:

$$E\left(\sum_{t=0}^{\infty} \gamma^t R(t) \right) \quad (9)$$

The sets of values ${}^iP_{jk}$ and ${}^iR_{jk}$ define a system to be controlled and the policy π defines a controller for that system. The discount factor γ, a real number in the range (0,1), is used to define what is meant by an "optimal" controller. A small value for γ corresponds to greater priority for near term rewards over delayed rewards. The problem is made more difficult if only γ, R_{max}, and R_{min} are given a priori and each ${}^iP_{jk}$ and ${}^iR_{jk}$ must be discovered by the controller through generating actions and observing the results.

A modified form of the ACP network is described here that has the following properties. Given only γ, R_{max}, and R_{min}, it is guaranteed to learn the optimal policy in every state through exploration of the environment. Furthermore, if the environment is deterministic (each ${}^iP_{jk}$ is either zero or one) and it is possible to reach any state from any other, then the modified ACP net will find the optimal policy even if it never explicitly explores.

An ACP network has a set of binary inputs, $\{s_1,...,s_n\}$, a set of binary outputs $\{e_1,...,e_m\}$, and a real-valued input, R, representing the reward signal. There is also an additional input for negative reinforcement signals, but this input is not needed and will be assumed to be zero. The ACP network can therefore be interfaced with the Markov system described above in a natural manner. If the system is in state i at time t, then $s_i(t)$=1 and $s_j(t)$=0 for $i \ne j$. At any point in time, the ACP network has at most one nonzero output. If $e_i(t)$>0 then action i is performed at time t. If all outputs are zero, then the action associated with output e_1 is performed. If performing action i in state j at time $t-1$ causes a transition to state k at time t and yields a reward ${}^iR_{jk}$, then define $R(t)$ as:

$$R(t) = \frac{\left({}^iR_{jk} - R_{\min} \right)(1 - \gamma)}{R_{\max} - R_{\min}} \quad (10)$$

This linear transformation of the network's reinforcement input normalizes it so that the reinforcement input to the controller $R(t)$ always stays in the range $\left[0, \frac{1}{1-\gamma}\right]$. This causes the expected total discounted reward for any policy to be in the range [0,1]. A policy will be optimal for this transformed problem if and only if it is optimal for the original problem. There is a constant scaling weight within the network by which R is multiplied; that factor should be set equal to 1.0.

The proof below requires that the Markov system change state on every time step. If it is possible that the system being controlled does not have this property, then the interface between the network and the Markov process must be modified slightly. The number of inputs to the network, n, will have to be twice the number of states, with two inputs uniquely associated with each state. If the Markov system is in a given state for multiple time steps, then on the first time step in that state one of the two associated inputs will be 1 and the other 0. On the next time step the values will switch, and they will alternate on each time step while in that state. For each state, the same input will start with 1 every time a transition is made into that state from another state. The learning system therefore sees a single Markov process with n states, where the probability of transitioning from any state to itself is zero for all actions.

Given this interface, the ACP network will have $4nm$ parameters, called weights, which can change during learning. For a given state i and an action j, there are four weights associated with that state and action: $W_{ij}+$, $W_{ij}-$, $W_{0ij}+$, and $W_{0ij}-$. Each weight marked "+" is a positive real number, and each weight marked "–" is a negative real number. The sum ($W_{0ij}+$ + $W_{0ij}-$) represents an estimate of the expected total discounted reward received if action j is performed in state i followed by optimal actions being performed in all subsequent states. The other weights are constantly adjusted so that the sum ($W_{ij}+$ + $W_{ij}-$) will tend over time to become equal to ($W_{0ij}+$ + $W_{0ij}-$).

The ACP network is guaranteed to solve Markov sequential decision problems if several modifications are made to it:

1. The definition of $y(t)$ in Equation 2 should not include the $R(t)$ term:

$$y(t) = f\left(\sum_{i=1}^{m} \left(W_{ij_{max}+} + W_{ij_{max}-} \right)(t)\, x_i(t) \right) \quad (11)$$

2. The $\Delta y(t)$ in Equation 6 should be replaced with an expression including $R(t)$ and the discount factor γ.

$$\Delta W_{0ij_{max}\pm}(t) = \left(\gamma y(t) - y(t-1) + R(t) \right) \cdot \sum_{k=1}^{\tau} c_k \left| W_{0ij_{max}\pm}(t-k) \right| \left[\Delta x_i(t-k) \right]^{+} \quad (12)$$

3. The weights should change every time step instead of only at the end of each trial. This change makes the exact timing of the calculations critical. If a $\Delta W(t)$ is calculated that would change the index $j_{max}(t)$, then the weight should change and the calculations should be repeated during that time step. Therefore the order of the calculations should be:

   - Calculate each $y_i(t)$ for all i.
   - Calculate $j_{max} = j$ such that $y_j(t)$ is maximum (the lowest such j in case of tie)
   - Calculate $y(t)$.
   - Calculate each $\Delta W_{ij_{max}}(t)$ and $\Delta W_{0ij_{max}}(t)$.
   - Replace each $W_{ij_{max}}(t)$ with $W_{ij_{max}}(t) + \Delta W_{ij_{max}}(t)$.
   - Recalculate $y_i(t)$, j_{max}, and $y(t)$.
   - Recalculate each $\Delta W(t)$
   - Calculate each $W(t+1)$

4. The network should be able to operate in an exploratory mode and in a controller mode. In controller mode, the index j_{max} should be the index of the highest $y_j(t)$. In exploratory mode, the index j_{max} should be chosen by some other mechanism. The only constraint on the choice of j_{max} is that if the system stays in exploratory mode, it must eventually try every action in every state infinitely often.

5. If the Markov process is nondeterministic, then the learning rate c_1 must slowly decay to zero to ensure weight convergence. If c_1 is monotonically nonincreasing, and if time t_n is the first point in time where every action has been tried in every state at least n times, then $c_1(t)$ should decrease at some rate that satisfies:

$$\lim_{n \to \infty} c_1(t_n) = 0 \quad (13)$$

$$\sum_{n=1}^{\infty} c_1(t_n) = \infty \quad (14)$$

6. The |W| should be removed from Equations 5 and (6), yielding:

$$\Delta W_{ij_{max}\pm}(t) = \left(c_a + c_b |y(t)| \right) \left[\Delta x_i(t) \right]^{+} \left(y(t) - y_j(t) \right) \quad (15)$$

$$\Delta W_{0ij_{max}\pm}(t) = \Delta y(t) \sum c_k \left[\Delta x_{i(t-k)} \right]^{+} \quad (16)$$

Modifications 1 and 2 above are important changes which affect the behavior of the network in significant ways. Modifications 3, 4, and 5 are the obvious properties necessary in almost any learning system if it is to solve infinite horizon Markov decision problems with unknown transition probabilities. Modification 6 is assumed true in the following discussion. Instead of removing the |W| terms from the equation, they can simply be made to have an arbitrarily small effect. This is done by initializing the weights to large values and using correspondingly small learning constants. The weights then change by arbitrarily small percentages during learning, and so have arbitrarily small effects on the rate of learning. Although conditions 4 and 5 are needed for guaranteed optimality, they may not be necessary in practice. Only modifications 1, 2, and 3 were used in the experimental results presented here. It has been verified in simulation that an ACP network with all of these modifications can still replicate the results in Klopf, Morgan, and Weaver (1992). These modifications, therefore, do not adversely affect any of the network's abilities.

Because of the interface with the Markov process described above, any given x_i will never be nonzero for more than one consecutive time step. Therefore, if on any given time step x_i equals 1 then $\Delta x_i(t)$ and $[\Delta x_i(t)]^+$ will both equal 1. If x_i is 0 on a given time step then $\Delta x_i(t)$ will be -1 and $[\Delta x_i(t)]^+$, will be 0. Thus $[\Delta x_i(t)]^+$ is always equal to $x_i(t)$, which is always 0 or 1. Using this fact and choosing values for the arbitrary constants so that $\tau=1$, $c_a=1/2$, and $c_b=c_0=\theta=0$, the equations describing the network reduce to:

$$y_j(t) = \sum_{i=1}^{n} \left(W_{ij+}(t) + W_{ij-}(t)\right) x_i(t) \qquad (17)$$

$$y(t) = \sum_{i=1}^{m} \left(W_{0ij_{max}+}(t) + W_{0ij_{max}-}(t)\right) x_i(t) \qquad (18)$$

$$j_{max} = \text{The index } j \text{ such that } \forall k \neq j \quad y_j(t) \geq y_k(t) \qquad (19)$$

$$\Delta W_{ij_{max}\pm}(t) = \begin{cases} \tfrac{1}{2}\left(y(t) - y_j(t)\right) & \text{if } x_i(t) \neq 0 \\ 0 & \text{otherwise} \end{cases} \qquad (20)$$

$$\Delta W_{0ij_{max}\pm}(t) = \begin{cases} c_1\left(\gamma\, y(t) + R(t) - y(t-1)\right) & \text{if } x_i(t-1) \neq 0 \\ 0 & \text{otherwise} \end{cases} \qquad (21)$$

When the system is initialized, each motor center will give the same output as the reinforcement centers. Equation 20 ensures that on every time step, the excitatory and inhibitory weights to the active motor center will each change so as to eliminate half of the error in its output. Therefore the sum of those weights will change so that the output will perfectly track the output of the reinforcement centers. This ensures that the actions selected are always the actions that maximize the output of the positive reinforcement center. Equation 21 ensures that, when a given action is performed in a given state, the weights associated with that state-action pair are updated to take into account the reinforcement received for that action as well as the reinforcement center output on the next time step.

Given these parameter values and algorithm modifications, the system reduces to Q-learning, a form of dynamic programming developed by Watkins (1989). While performing a given action in a given state, the output of the reinforcement center can be interpreted as the Q-value for that state-action pair: the expected discounted reward for performing that action followed by optimal actions thereafter. The above equations then ensure that the weights are changed in accordance with the equations given in Watkins (1989). Given sufficient exploration, Watkins has proven that a Q-learning system will always converge to the optimal solution; therefore, for these parameter values and modifications, the modified ACP network will also converge to the optimal solution. Thus, the above analysis, together with Watkins' results, constitutes a proof of optimality for the modified ACP network given appropriate choices for the parameter values. [See Williams and Baird (1990) for a discussion of other dynamic programming systems for learning control.]

The parameter values are set differently when reproducing the conditioning results than they are when learning optimal control policies. For example, the parameter τ represents the number of time steps considered during a single update of the weights. Convergence has never been proven for multi-step Q-learning, so τ must be set equal to 1 to ensure optimality. When reproducing conditioning results and when running cart-pole controller simulations in this paper, τ was set equal to 5. Similarly, for large initial values for the weights and correspondingly small initial values for the learning rate, the |W| factor in the learning equation can be made to have an arbitrarily small effect on learning. Classical conditioning results are reproduced when the initial weights are small. Optimality is provable when the |W| factor is removed from Equations 5 and 6, which is the limiting case of large initial weights and small learning rates. A single set of parameter values will not reproduce all the conditioning results while simultaneously remaining provably optimal. It is interesting to note, however, that a single model controlled by a single set of equations can reproduce the conditioning results (given one set of parameter values) and is also equivalent to Q-learning and therefore provably optimal (given another set of parameter values).

4. Single-Layer Model

The above analysis of the two-layer ACP network suggests that it is possible to simplify the network without losing any of the desirable properties. The network in Figure 2 consists of only a single layer of linear components, yet it reproduces all of the results of the two-layer network. Each of the mechanisms in this network are also present in the two-layer ACP network, such as mutual inhibition and global training signals within a layer. Some mechanisms in the two-layer network are absent from this model, such as differing types of learning equations and many of the nonlinearities. On a given time step, each node in the network computes a weighted sum of the inputs. The outputs of these nodes compete in a winner-take-all fashion; the largest output determines actions and learning; all other outputs are ignored. Each node is associated with an action. On a given time step, the action performed by the system is the action associated with the winning node. Learning is driven by reinforcement, which is the sum of the positive reinforcement inputs (rewards) and the negative reinforcement inputs (costs).

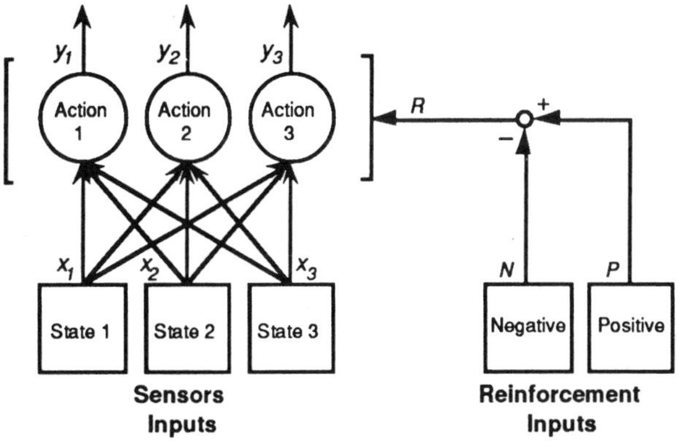

Figure 2. Single layer architecture.

Equations 22 through 26 completely define the operation of the single-layer, simplified model. There is no nonlinearity associated with the outputs. The only nonlinearity associated with the weights is the restriction that the magnitude of a weight cannot fall below 0.1.

$$y_j(t) = \sum_i (W_{ij+}(t) + W_{ij-}(t))x_i \tag{22}$$

$$\begin{aligned} j_{\max}(t) &= \text{largest index } j \text{ such that } \forall i\ y_j(t) \geq y_i(t) \\ &= \text{index of action performed at time } t \end{aligned} \tag{23}$$

$$\begin{aligned} &\Delta W_{ij\pm}(t) = \\ &\quad \left(\gamma\ y_{i_{\max}}(t) - y_{i_{\max}}(t-1) + R(t)\right) \\ &\quad \cdot \sum_{k=1}^{\tau} c_k \left|W_{ij\pm}(t-k)\right| \left[\Delta x_{ij}(t-k)\right]^+ \end{aligned} \tag{24}$$

$$\left[\Delta x_{ij}(t-k)\right]^+ = \begin{cases} x_{ij}(t-k) - x_{ij}(t-k-1) & \\ \quad \text{if } x_{ij}(t-k) - x_{ij}(t-k-1) > 0 & \\ 0 \quad \text{otherwise} & \end{cases} \tag{25}$$

$$x_{ij}(t) = \begin{cases} x_i(t) & \text{if } j = j_{\max}(t) \\ 0 & \text{otherwise} \end{cases} \tag{26}$$

On time step t, the outputs $y_j(t)$ are calculated as linear combinations of the inputs $x_i(t)$. Mutual inhibition among the outputs then selects the largest output, j_{max}. The action associated with that output is performed, leading to a new state with inputs $x_i(t+1)$. Those outputs that were not the largest are then ignored; they do not affect the outputs of the controller and they do not affect learning, so they can be thought of as either set to zero or left unchanged. Only weights associated with winning outputs learn. Learning at time t in Equation 24 is a function of the maximum output at time t and the maximum output at time t–1. Exploration could be implemented by causing an output to win the competition even though it is not the largest.

Each state-action pair has two associated weights: W_{ij+} and W_{ij-}. The weight W_{ij+} is always positive and W_{ij-} is always negative. If W_{ij+} ever falls below 0.1 during learning, then it is set equal to 0.1. If W_{ij-} ever rises above –0.1, then it is set equal to –0.1.

The sum (W_{ij}+ + W_{ij}–), as a result of learning, becomes the expected discounted total return if action i is performed in state j followed by optimal actions from then on. The difference (W_{ij+} – W_{ij-}) affects the speed of learning for a given state-action pair, causing it to learn slowly at first and more quickly after it has gained some experience. This yields the positively accelerating part of the s-shaped learning curve observed in classical conditioning experiments.

The single-layer system reproduces all of the classical conditioning and instrumental conditioning results achieved to date by the two-layer ACP network. By the same procedure used in the discussion of two-layer networks, the one-layer system can be reduced to Q-learning, and is therefore also optimal.

5. Hierarchical Network

The single-layer network described in Section 4 is guaranteed to learn the correct actions eventually. This learning process could be very slow, however, so it may be useful to look at extensions of the architecture to speed learning. This section describes a hierarchy composed of several of these layers. The hierarchy is first described for a standard control problem, and then the application of it to other problems is discussed.

A standard control problem is the cart-pole inverted pendulum problem considered in Michie and Chambers (1968) and Barto, Sutton and Anderson (1983). A cart moves back and forth on a finite-length track. A pole is connected to the top of the cart with a hinge, and the goal is to balance the pole on the cart while avoiding the ends of the track. This is done by applying a 10 newton force to either the left or right side of the cart on each time step. The state of the system is described by four variables:

x: the position of the cart (center of the track is zero, to the right is positive)

$\dot{x}$: the velocity of the cart

θ: the angle of the pole from vertical (to the right is positive)

$\dot{\theta}$: the angular velocity of the pole

Initially, all state variables are set to zero. If the pole exceeds 12° from vertical, or if the cart exceeds 2.4m from the center of the track, that is defined to be failure. The learning system is given no indication of how it is performing until failure occurs. Then, it is informed that a failure occurred, but not whether the failure was due to the pole angle or due to the cart position. After a failure, the cart and pole are returned to the initial state, and the controller is allowed to continue. An error in the controller's output may not result in failure for many time steps. This problem is therefore substantially more difficult than standard model-reference formulations of this problem where performance information is available on every time step.

In Barto, Sutton, and Anderson (1983), each of the elements of the state was divided into intervals having these boundaries:

x: ±.8, ±2.4m

$\dot{x}$: ±.5, ±∞m/s

θ: 0, ±1, ±6, ±12°

$\dot{\theta}$: ±50, ±∞°/s

Using these partitions, the state space is divided into 3 x 3 x 6 x 3 = 162 distinct boxes.

The learning system proposed by Barto, Sutton, and Anderson (1983) was a network composed of an *associative search element* (ASE) and an *adaptive critic element* (ACE). The ASE-ACE was given 162 binary inputs. At each point in time, the input corresponding to the current state of the cart-pole was set to 1 and all other inputs were set to 0. The learning system was given no a priori information about which boxes were adjacent.

For the hierarchical system we implemented , coarser intervals are used:

x: +.8, ±2.4m

$\dot{x}$: ±.5, ±∞m/s

θ: ±1, ±12°

$\dot{\theta}$: ±50, ±∞°/s

Each state variable is partitioned into 3 intervals, except for cart position, which is partitioned into 2 intervals. Instead of combining the four variables into a single number, the hierarchy uses separate sensors for each variable, as shown in Figure 3.

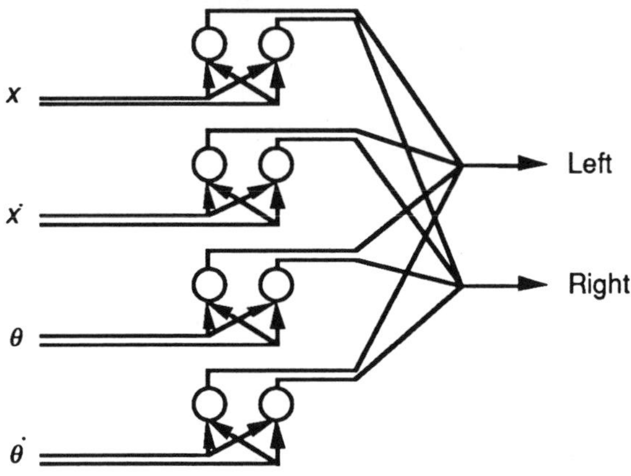

Figure 3. Hierarchical network architecture.

Each state variable provides the inputs to a different layer of the network. Each state variable has three intervals and two binary inputs associated with it. One input is 1 when the variable is in its lowest-valued interval, and the other variable is 1 when it's in its highest-valued interval. Both inputs go to zero when the variable is in the center interval. Cart position, x, has a left and right interval but not a center interval, so it always has one input active. Each of the four layers in the hierarchy is a single-layer controller as described in Section 4. Each layer has two inputs, corresponding to its particular state variable, and two outputs, corresponding to the action of pushing left or pushing right on the cart.

The hierarchy is hard wired such that exactly one layer is active at any given time. When a layer is active it functions consistent with the equations in Section 4. When a layer is not active, it freezes completely. Therefore $t-1$ in the equations in Section 4 does not represent the previous time step, but rather the last time step in which a given layer was active. If either of the $\dot{\theta}$ inputs is set to 1, then the bottom layer becomes active and forces the other three layers to be inactive. If neither $\dot{\theta}$ input is 1, then the bottom layer becomes inactive and control can pass to the θ layer. If either of the θ inputs are 1, then it becomes active and forces the two layers above it to be inactive, and so forth. The output of the active layer on a given time step determines whether the controller applies force to the left or right on that time step. At failure, all of the layers with nonzero inputs become active so they can learn from the failure.

The inputs to the hierarchy are ordered as shown in Figure 3, and are ranked by rate of change. If each variable is divided by the range over which it varies, then it is possible to compare the speed at which the normalized variables change. In the cart-pole system, $\dot{\theta}$ changes much more quickly than any of the other variables. It varies from its lowest value to its highest value in just a few time steps, while x requires hundreds of time steps to go from one end of its range to the other. The input variables are arranged in the hierarchy in order of how rapidly they change. The fastest changing variable is connected so that the network reacts immediately when it reaches extreme values. The network reacts to a slower variable only when all of the faster variables are safely in the center of their ranges. Although the connections were hard wired in this experiment, it would be possible for a network to self-organize so that lower levels connected to faster-changing inputs, and higher levels connected to slower-changing inputs.

This network is given more information than the learning systems described in Michie and Chambers (1968) and Barto, Sutton and Anderson (1983). Essentially, the network is told a priori which boxes are adjacent and which boxes are near zero. This makes the problem easier. On the other hand, the reinforcement signal comes only at failure and the network is not told whether failure was due to the pole angle or the cart position. Thus, this problem still contains the difficult temporal and structural credit assignment problems inherent in the original problem formulation. Success on this problem would suggest the usefulness of this hierarchical architecture.

6. Experimental Results

Simulations were performed with the ASE-ACE controller in Barto, Sutton and Anderson (1983), the modified two-layer ACP described in Section 3, and the hierarchical network described in Section 5. In the ACP networks, initial weights were biased slightly so that in each state it would initially exert force either to the left or to the right. The action to be given the larger weight was chosen randomly, so the behavior of the system on the first trial was dependent on the random number seed. In the ASE-ACE system all weights are initially equal, but the actions are chosen nondeterministically, so the ASE-ACE too is affected by the random number seed.

The cart-pole system was simulated at 50Hz, so each time step represented .02 seconds of simulated time. Each trial started with the cart stationary in the center of the track and the pole stationary and vertical (all state variables set to zero). The trial ended in failure when the cart exceeded ±2.4 m, or the pole angle exceeded ±12°. A controller was considered to have successfully learned if the trial reached 80000 time steps (26.7 minutes of simulated time) without failure. If a controller failed to learn successfully within 100 trials, it was considered unsuccessful. Each controller was tested 10 times, with different random number seeds. Table 1 summarizes the percentage of the 10 runs in which each controller successfully learned, as well as the average time to learn.

Table 1. Comparative assessment of learning reliability and average time to learn.

	% Success	Training Time		
		trials	time steps	simulated time (min)
Two-layer ACP	30	77	75,000	25.0
ASE-ACE	80	70	96,511	32.2
Hierarchical ACP	100	71	4,016	1.3

Out of 10 runs, the two-layer ACP network was successful only 3 times. It often became stuck performing a suboptimal policy. This problem might be overcome by adding an exploration mechanism, but was instead addressed by implementing a four-layer hierarchical architecture. In those cases in which the network did learn, it learned in a reasonable amount of time compared to the ASE-ACE.

The ASE-ACE was more reliable. The time to learn was not reported in Barto, Sutton and Anderson (1983), so the ASE-ACE was reimplemented to obtain this information. The ASE-ACE successfully learned to balance the pole 70% of the time in our sample of 10 runs, with an average of about 50 trials required for learning in successful runs. The average successful run required 96,511 time steps (32.2 minutes of simulated time) to learn. The results in Barto, Sutton and Anderson (1983) seem to indicate that the system learned successfully 80% of the time in their sample of 10 runs, with an average of about 70 trials required for learning in successful runs.

The hierarchical ACP network was the most reliable network for this particular problem. It learned to balance the pole 100% of the time in a sample of ten runs. It required roughly the same number of trials as the other two architectures, but required less than a twentieth of the simulated time for training. It is difficult to make broad generalizations based on the results from a single simulated plant, but it does seem from these simulations that the hierarchical network is a promising approach, improving learning speed by over an order of magnitude for this problem. This architecture might be useful in other regulator problems where the solution involves keeping the state variables near zero. This appears to be a fruitful area for future research.

7. CONCLUSIONS

The original ACP network described in Klopf, Morgan, and Weaver (1992) reproduces a variety of animal learning experimental results. The ACP network modifications proposed here simplify the system, add additional capabilities, and cause the system to be provably optimal, while retaining the ability to reproduce the conditioning results. Although the single-layer network is guaranteed to eventually learn to control any Markov decision process, the simulation results suggest that the learning speed can be improved through the use of a hierarchical architecture. The hierarchical architecture that we have proposed and tested improves the learning speed for the cart-pole problem by more than an order of magnitude, while causing the system to converge to the correct answer more reliably. This hierarchical approach may be general enough to apply to other high-dimensional regulator problems.

ACKNOWLEDGMENTS

This research was supported under Task 2312R1 by the Life and Environmental Sciences Directorate of the United States Air Force Office of Scientific Research. For comments on drafts of this paper, we gratefully acknowledge Steve Atkins, Walt Baker, Gábor Bartha, Andy Barto, Jeff Johnson, Pete Millington, Jim Morgan, and Scott Weaver.

REFERENCES

Baird, L. C., & Baker, W. (1990). A connectionist learning system for nonlinear control. *Proceedings of the AIAA Conference on Guidance, Navigation, and Control*, Portland, Oregon, pp. 1113-1115.

Barto, A. G., Sutton, R. S., & Anderson, C. W. (1983). Neuronlike elements that can solve difficult learning control problems. *IEEE Transactions on Systems, Man, and Cybernetics*, 13, 835-846.

Klopf, A. H. (1988). A neuronal model of classical conditioning. *Psychobiology*, **16** (2), 85-125.

Klopf, A. H., Morgan, J. S., & Weaver, S. E. (1992). Modeling nervous system function with a hierarchical network of control systems that learn. *Proceedings of the Second International Conference on Simulation of Adaptive Behavior*, Honolulu, Hawaii.

Michie, D., & Chambers, R. (1968). Boxes: an experiment in adaptive control. In E. Dale and D. Michie (Eds.), *Machine Intelligence*, Volume 2. Edinburgh, Scotland: Oliver and Boyd Ltd.

Watkins, C. (1989). *Learning from delayed rewards* (Doctoral dissertation, Cambridge University, Cambridge, England).

Williams, R., & Baird, L. C. (1990). A mathematical analysis of actor-critic architectures for learning optimal control through incremental dynamic programming. *Proceedings of the Sixth Yale Workshop on Adaptive and Learning Systems*, New Haven, Connecticut, pp. 96-101.

APPENDIX

The cart-pole equations are identical to the ones used in Barto, Sutton and Anderson (1983) and Baird and Baker (1990). The cart and pole were simulated at 50 Hz by Euler integration of these equations:

$$\ddot{x}_t = \frac{F_t + ml\left[\dot{\theta}_t^2 \sin\theta_t - \ddot{\theta}_t \cos\theta_t\right] - \mu_c sgn(\dot{x}_t)}{m_c + m} \tag{27}$$

$$\ddot{\theta}_t = \frac{\cos\theta_t \left[\dfrac{-F_t - ml\dot{\theta}_t^2 \sin\theta_t + \mu_c \operatorname{sgn}(\dot{x}_t)}{m_c + m}\right]}{l\left[\dfrac{4}{3} - \dfrac{m\cos^2\theta_t}{m_c + m}\right]} + \frac{g\sin\theta_t - \dfrac{\mu_p \dot{\theta}_t}{ml}}{l\left[\dfrac{4}{3} - \dfrac{m\cos^2\theta_t}{m_c + m}\right]} \tag{28}$$

The system was simulated using Euler's method with a time step of 0.02 seconds. The parameters used for the cart-pole system are:

g = 9.8 m/s2, acceleration due to gravity
m_0 = 1.0 Kg, mass of cart
m = 0.1 Kg, mass of pole
l = 0.5 m, half-pole length
m_0 = 0.0005, coefficient of friction of cart on track
m_p = 0.000002, coefficient of friction of pole on cart
F_t = ± 10.0 N, force applied to cart's center of mass at time t

For the two-layer ACP network, the parameters were as follows:

γ=0.95	c_a=0.249	c_b=0.0
c_1=0.033	c_2=0.030	c_3=0.027
c_4=0.024	c_5=0.021	

Positive reinforcement = 0.006
Minimum weight magnitude = 0.1
Initial value of inhibitory weight = –2.0
Initial value of excitatory weight to positive reinforcement center = 2.114

Initial value of excitatory weight to motor centers
= 2.122 (for biased action)
2.121 (for unbiased action)

For the hierarchical network the parameters were:

$c_3 = 0.027$, $c_4 = 0.024$, $c_5 = 0.021$
Positive reinforcement = 0.002
Minimum weight magnitude = 0.1
Initial value of inhibitory weight = –0.7
Initial value of excitatory weight to motor centers
= 0.73000 (for biased action)
0.72999 (for unbiased action)

Behavior networks and force fields for simulating spinal reflex behaviors of the frog

Simon Giszter,
Dept. Brain and Cognitive Sciences
Massachusetts Institute of Technology
77, Massachusetts Avenue,
Cambridge MA
giszter@ai.mit.edu
giszter@18.88.0.79

Abstract

The simulation framework presented here represents a first step towards modelling the behavioral repertoire of the frog spinal cord. This is a biological system exhibiting complex adaptive behaviors. The goal was to obtain a plausible framework within which to represent behavioral effects of components in the frog spinal cord. The target behaviors to be modelled include limb withdrawal, aversive turns, and wiping away of nociceptive stimuli. These behaviors show several phenomena such as switching, blending, kinematic adjustment and searching. The spinal system was modelled using augmented behavior networks (Maes 1989,1991) to drive force field summation. The behavior networks were augmented to include behaviors extended over time, concurrency, variable intensity execution of behaviors, and continuously varying conditions. This augmentation led to several new global variables for tuning network behavior.

1 Introduction:

The goal of the work presented here was to combine two approaches in order to simulate frog spinal behaviors. The model used was a combination of behavior networks (Maes 1989) and force field vector summation (Bizzi, Mussa-Ivaldi and Giszter 1991). The first component of the simulation, the behavior network, 'computes' the most relevant sequences of behavior corresponding to the current situation. The second element, the vector field summation approach, (which the behavior network drives) has been proposed to be a mechanism to generate and control a variety of limb behaviors in vertebrates. The force fields that are summed are considered to constitute 'movement primitives' (Giszter, Mussa-Ivaldi and Bizzi, 1992). The term 'movement primitive' denotes a basic indivisible control element in the spinal cord with a specific force field output. An alternative view is that they represent evolutionarily instantiated or 'bootstrap' schemas. The combination of these two approaches required some augmentation of the original behavior network scheme. The resulting framework of behavior networks driving force field behaviors is quite powerful and t may go a long way towards capturing the capabilities of frog spinal cord.

It may be useful to review these capabilities.

1.1 Spinal Motor Behavior

Autonomous adaptive systems exist in the isolated spinal cord.

After the destruction of the brain the spinal cord of the frog is able to generate complex behaviors. These include limb trajectories for locomotion, scratching/wiping, turning and flexion responses (Berkinblit et al. 1989, Fukson et al. 1980, Giszter et al. 1989, Giszter 1992, Ostry et al. 1991). This demonstrates a remarkable capability for autonomous organization and control of behavior in the cord. Indeed the behavior of the spinal preparation is sufficiently complex to have suggested to early 19th century workers that there was a 'spinal soul'!

Work in spinal frogs has investigated motor equivalence, examined spinal sensory motor transformations, tested notions of equilibrium point control, and examined spinal units of motor control. This work has focussed both on kinematic and force field descriptions of posture and movement. Perhaps most remarkably, it was shown long ago that spinal frogs can make adjusted limb motions to remove irritants: the so-called wiping reflex. Recent investigations of this spinal organization of movement show several interesting features. The spinal cord chooses one of several strategies to wipe depending on the location of the irritant. The kinematic strategies are determined by the constraints of the limb mobility on wiping and reaching. In areas in which two different strategies are possible, the **transition zones**, the

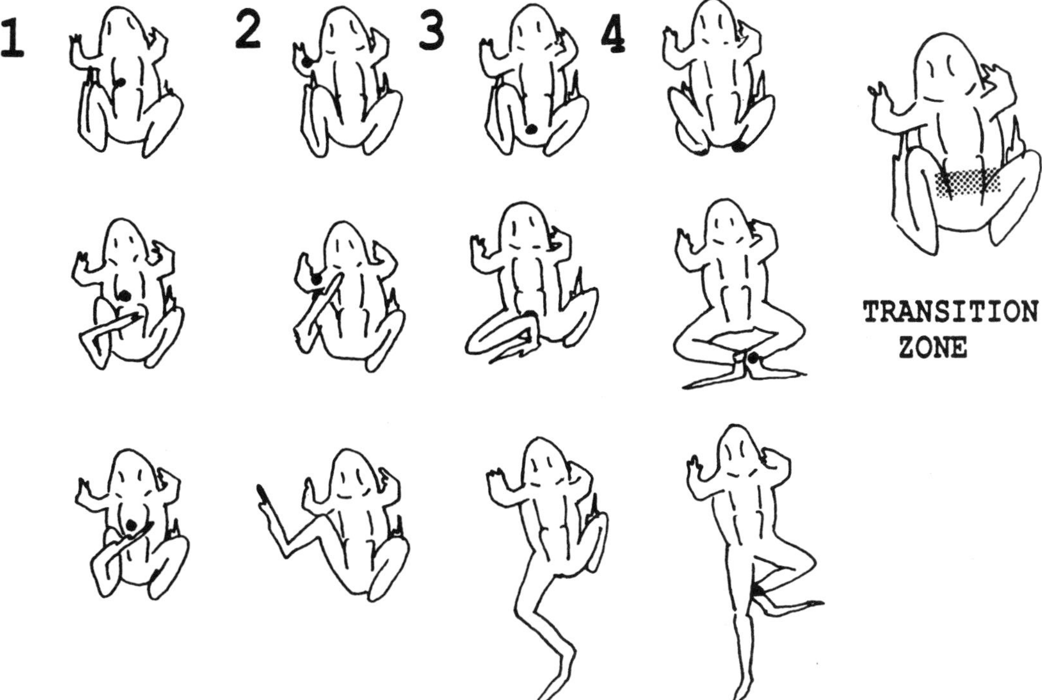

Figure 1 : Types of wiping strategy in spinal frogs. For each wipe strategy three stages of the movements are shown. Each wipe strategy reaches a different target zone. 1: wiping to the back. The foot is placed on the back behind the irritant which is then whisked off. 2: wiping the forelimb. The foot is placed at the shoulder and is either whisked or thrust along the forelimb. 3: wiping the cloacal area. The heel is flexed to rub over the irritant and sometimes to kick it away. 4: wiping the contralateral limb's heel. The two legs are brought together. Depending on irritant location on the lower limb the legs may then scissor over one another or a kick may occur. Wipe types 1 and 2 can be merged into a single smooth response if irritants are placed on both back and forelimb. It is not possible to merge 1 and 3 or 4. Switching between these types occur in dual stimulation. In a transition zone (stippled in diagram to right) either strategy 1 or 3 may occur. Depending on history and the othher irritant sites the spinal frog may do one exclusively or may switch between forms.

strategy chosen can be either of the strategies depending on immediate history and current circumstance. When dual stimulation of 2 areas that require different strategies occurs the spinal cord alternates the two strategies so as to remove both irritants. Finally if two irritants can be removed by a blended strategy the frog spinal cord recognizes and uses this strategy (Berkinblitt et al. 1989). Some examples of these strategies and how they can be combined are shown in figure 1.

Within a zone and strategy the spinal cord adjusts the limb trajectory in relation to the precise stimulus location. To do this the spinal cord controls a redundant manipulator and thus solves an ill-posed problem to choose a trajectory. These movements use simple kinematic strategies to cope with the degrees of freedom problem in the redundant limb. Joint angle adjustments relate linearly to cartesian location of an irritant (Giszter, McIntyre and Bizzi 1989).

1.2 Movement primitives:

More recently we have shown that many postural phases and trajectory fragments of these spinal behaviors can be simply expressed as force fields (Mussa-Ivaldi, Giszter and Bizzi, 1990, Bizzi, Mussa-Ivaldi and Giszter 1991, Giszter, Mussa-Ivaldi and Bizzi, 1991a,b, 992, Giszter 1992). A force field is a continuous function relating a osition to an associated force. A force field thus summarizes the force hat will be generated in the limb at any point in the reachable space. To measure such force fields a six axis force transducer was attached to a spinal frog's leg close to the ankle. The limb was positioned at a location. The spinal cord circuitry or the skin was then stimulated. The result of this was an attempted movement of the leg. The forces generated are recorded by the sensor. The leg is then repositioned at a new location. The procedure is repeated. In this way a set of samples of a 2 or 3 dimensional force field is collected. This

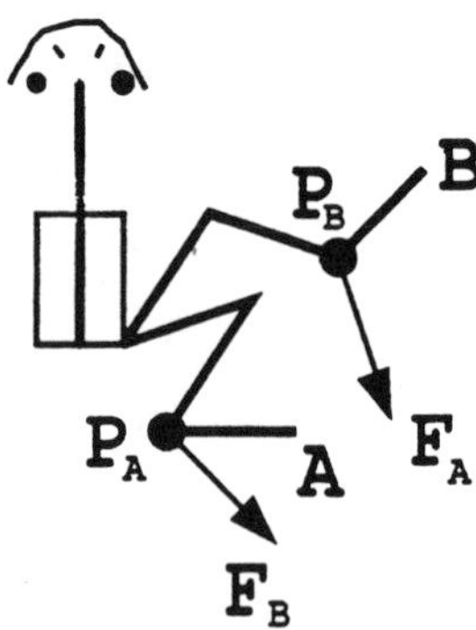

Figure 2: The Construction of Force Field Description. At two configurations of the frog's limb (A and B) the limb is held immobile by a six axis force transducer attached to the ankle (Pa and Pb). On stimulation in an identical manner the animal produces repeatable force responses Fa and Fb respectively. These differ systematically. By repeating this procedure over a grid of positions Pc Pd etc. an estimate of the force field relating a force Fn to a position Pn is built up. These fields show great repeatability between frogs and are often stable convergent patterns with single fixed points (equilibria).

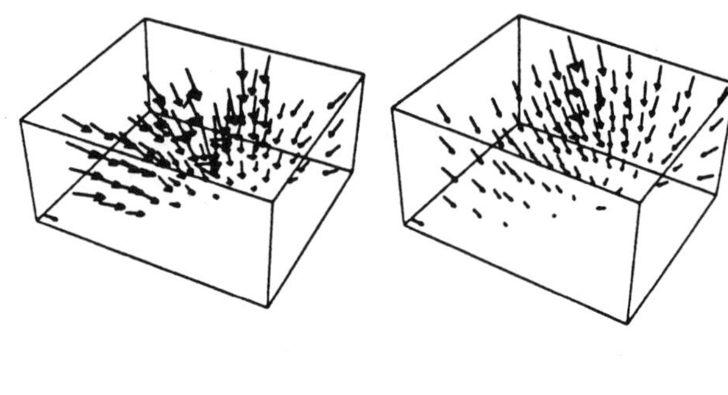

Figure 3: Force field data from two spinal frogs.The forces are associated with a flexion withdrawal. This can be verified from free limb kinematics. The force field predicts limb motion and is clearly repeatable between animals. The actively generated force field remains qualitatively similar through time while the amplitude of forces are modulated up to a peak intensity and down again.

is illustrated in figure 2.

The force fields associated with three different tasks executed by a hind-limb of the spinal frog were examined in detail. It was shown force fields associated with these behaviors had fixed structures. Two examples of 3 dimensional flexion fields from two different spinal frogs are shown in figure 3. The presence of movement primitives generating force fields was therefore hypothesized. Whether movement primitives relate one to one to movement fragments of of the spinal behavior repertoire is an open question. It is conceivable that a movement fragment could utilize several primitives. To date however we have found spinal circuitry microstimulation produces fields that are remarkably similar to the fields underlying behavior or movement fragments generated by skin stimulation. The main finding in the data of interest here was that invariant force field patterns underlay each of these behaviors.

The spinally generated force fields included both position and force control strategies. Spinal systems thus can support both equilibrium point control strategies specifying absolute location and other force field strategies specifying relative movements or contact forces. Even in these latter movements, however, an equilibrium point is defined. This mechanical stability derives from the resting mechanical properties of the leg. The data also showed that total limb stiffness could be largely determined by the resting state of the leg or could be actively controlled. The choice of field type found matched the requirements of each task (Giszter 1992). This work suggests that there may be no explicit path planning in the frog spinal cord but that rather the path emerges from the interaction of limb dynamics with a force field resulting from both the environment and a fixed structure but modulated amplitude force field generated by the spinal cord. It was shown that in several instances these fields may exhibit vector summation when activated in parallel (Bizzi et al, 1991). It thus appears that reflex spinal behaviors of some kinematic complexity are generated using simple fixed force field strategies. These force fields may form the basis for more complex force fields and behaviors, by compounding the underlying movement primitives. (This is a concept described long ago by Sherrington, and by von Holst). These force field or movement primitives might be thought of as permanently instantiated schemas for motor behavior (see Arbib and Cobas, 1991)

1.3 A simulation framework:

To try to capture the manner in which these force field primitives might be assembled and sequenced in the spinal cord I sought a framework with several features. I wanted the model to include physiologically plausible elements and was rich enough to capture a variety of spinal phenomena, and to use the recently described spinal primitives or fixed force fields. Several schemes have been devised to utilize potential functions and vector fields. These have been used to solve planning tasks and guarantee integrable behaviors (Khatib, 1986, Mussa-Ivaldi and Hogan 1990, Mussa-Ivaldi and Giszter, 1992, Arbib and Cobas 1991, Arkin 1991). The simulations presented here sought to avoid any explicit representations or planner to which the design or teaching of a force field structure was delegated.

Rather it was hoped motor equivalent and novel behaviors would be an emergent property of interactions among a few primitives and behavioral nodes. I chose a variant of the behavior networks devised by Maes (1989,1991) using a few biologically reasonable extensions. This behavior selection network was used to drive a system of force field movement primitives which were combined by vectorial summation to move the limb. In this framework it was believed that motor equivalent and novel behaviors could emerge from the interactions on two levels :(1) among behaviors in the behavior network and (2) among their associated force fields in the periphery when activated in various concurrent patterns.

2 The behavior network (Maes 1989)

2.1 The basic network:

The behavior network design used here is built upon the organization originally proposed by Maes 1989. Using this basic design several extensions were used to make the network more biologically plausible. It is worthwhile summarizing relevant aspects of the basic scheme first, which is quite elegant.

The basic behavior network consists of nodes which represent behaviors or 'competence modules'. (In this article I will generally refer to these as 'behavior nodes' but usage of the term is synonymous which 'competence module' throughout). Biologically these nodes might be thought to represent circuits acting as rhythm or sequence generators. These nodes pass activation among themselves. Activation is passed through links which are controlled by the conditions of the environment and the state of the nodes themselves. A node can have one of two states: it can be executable or non-executable.

Associated with each node is a list of conditions in the environment. Conditions may be fulfilled or unfulfilled. Each of these conditions represents a detected state of the environment, thus in a biological analogy the conditions represent relevant afferent inflow. For a node to be executable all of the conditions specified for its execution must be fulfilled.

The overall flow of activation through the network leads to activation rising in those behavior nodes that are executable and also in those nodes that will shortly become executable. Chains of nodes are 'prepared' for action. Thus chains of actions and potential actions emerge from the interaction of the network with the current situation (as specified by the conditions).

2.2 Spread of activation

Behavior nodes receive activation from several sources. These include the conditions, the other nodes and the goals (see below).

Behavior nodes receive activation directly from fulfilled conditions in the current situation (by an amount f). In biologically analogy, fulfilled condition afferents directly excite behavior nodes.

Both executable and non executable nodes can act as sources or sinks for activation. How they do this is determined by the executable/non executable status.

Executable nodes act as sources by passing a fraction of their energy forward to non executable nodes through a collection of successor links in the following manner. There is a successor link activated for each unfulfilled condition of a successor behavior node which the source node's behavior would fulfill. A biologically plausible way of expressing this is that a fulfilled condition afferent inhibits flow in the associated successor links.

Non-executable nodes act as sources by passing a fraction of their energy backward to other nodes through a collection of predecessor links in the following manner. There is a predecessor link activated for each unfulfilled condition of the source node which the receiving predecessor node's behavior would fulfill. A biologically plausible way of thinking about this is that fulfilled conditions of the afference inhibit flow in predecessor links.

The executable to non-executable switch in connectivity is a central mechanism in the network and is diagrammed in a pseudo-biological fashion in figure 4.

As an example of the network operation consider a simulation of a frog spinal cord that has the goal of executing a sequence of movements in which the limb sweeps across an area of the body surface to remove an irritant. This requires a sequence of behaviors : an optional flexion, then a place motion, and a whisk motion. The sequential execution of 'place' and 'whisk' is needed to achieve success. Depending on the situation in which the limb finds itself the behavior network can choose the order of behaviors and 'prepare' the next behavior activations. If 'whisk' and 'place' are not executable they will pass activation back to 'flexion' through predecessor links. Assume 'flexion' is almost always executable. 'Flexion' passes energy forward to 'place' through sucessor links. This positive feedback continues until 'flexion' executes. This causes 'place' to become executable. A positive feedback loop now

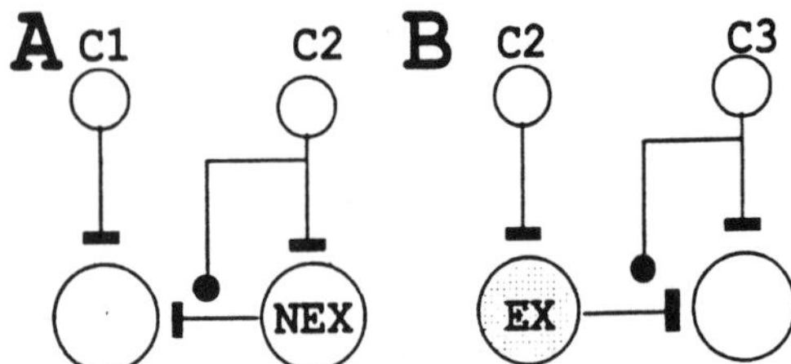

Figure 4: The flow switch which occurs at the non-executable to executable transition. A : a non-executable behavior node sends activity to any nodes likely to make it executable. These channels are turned off should a condition (c2) be fulfilled however (black circle represents inhibition). At the same time as these channels are closed by c2 activity the nonexecutable node is now excited (black oblong) by the c2 condition which is fullfilled. B: When a node becomes executable is begins to send activation forward to nodes which it will help make executable. This is only gated through those pathways not inhibited by fulfilled conditions such as c3.

occurs between 'place' and 'whisk' . This feedback proceeds through the newly activated successor links until the activation exceeds threshold and 'place' executes. This sets the preconditions for 'whisk' which soon occurs.

Any node, executable or non executable can act as a sink for activation through conflictor links. There is an active conflictor link which removes activation from a target node for every fulfilled condition of a behavior node which the actions of the target node would undo.

Goal states can be set, these are desired states for conditions. These act as sources of activation for nodes (g per goal divided among nodes). Similarly goals could be set protected. Definitions of goals and protected goals can be found in Maes 1990. Since these two network mechanisms suppose some overseer for the network they do not figure prominently in the work presented here (but see below).

2.3 Execution

Behaviors are begun when a behavior node is executable, its activation surpasses a threshold (q) and no other behavior is executing. When activation conflicts occur the higher activation behavior gains access to the effector system.

2.4 Tuning the network:

The transfer of activation by incoming links to a node may be weighted so that each node gets equal potential access to activation. This is a 'fan-in' control. Similarly the amount of activation distributed by a goal or condition may be divided among the recipient nodes. This division may be weighted so that conditions or goals have equal influence on the network regardless of the number of recipient nodes (fan-out control). Fan-in and fan-out are parameters resembling synaptic connectivity in the spinal-cord.

Global parameters:

A considerable advantage of this formulation in the present context is that the global behavior patterns can be modulated through a few parameters. These parameters form plausible analogues to effects of neuromodulators and transmitter levels in neurophysiological systems, and connectivity patterns.

Global parameters available in the network are:

1) threshold for commencing execution **q**

2) condition based activation **f**

3) goal based activation **g**

4) protected goal activation removal **d**

5) fan-in control and fan-out control

By judicious tuning of these parameters the overall system behavior can be biased along several different axes. These are: (1) from 'goal-oriented' to 'opportunist' using the ratio of **g** to **f**, (2) from 'thoughtful' to 'speedy' by varying the threshold **q** (Maes 1990) .

2.6 Extensions and additions to the basic network:

In order to use the network to simulate spinal behaviors several extensions were added. Several have been proposed elsewhere and two are novel.

1: Executing behaviors in the present simulation operate over extended time.

2: Behaviors can execute concurrently.

3: Behaviors have intensity. Intensity depends upon the level of activation above a threshold q for an executing behavior.

This factor parameterizes the execution of the behavior. In general in simulation this threshold is the same as the execution threshold. However it is possible that these two thresholds may be modulated separately. Thus selection and intensity can be related but separately controlled global parameters.

4: An exclusion network mediates access to the effectors to prevent conflicting behaviors while allowing activation buildup to proceed.

Concurrent execution is often desirable but can be disastrous for some combinations. For example in the frog the two rostral and caudal wipe types cannot be combined and retain any functional value. The exclusion network used here is very simple. It excludes any behaviors which conflict with a currently executing behavior from access to the effectors. Exclusion occurs on a first come first served basis. There is no pre-empting. It is assumed that the exclusion network design avoids starvation and deadlock problems but this is not dealt with explicitly in this implementation. Thus access to the effector system is separated from the process of activation buildup from which 'planning' emerges. The reason for choosing this scheme over the addition of new 'central' conditions is firstly that this would destroy the analogy of conditions to afferents in the biological system and more importantly that each central condition added would alter the network operation substantially for behaviors that were mutually exclusive. Thus for example adding an exclusion condition to a flexion behavior could have several unforeseen results. A flexion might normally follow extension and thus be a natural candidate for receipt of activation from extension while also being excluded by extension. However using an exclusion condition to suppress the flexion could not allow flexion to promote activation of a third behavior. For example suppose the next behavior were a power stroke: its activation would be uninfluence by an excluded flexion since the flexion would remain non executable so long as it was excluded. In contrast an implementation using a separate exclusion network allows such transfers and thus allows construction of more stable chains and limit cycles. It should also be noted that the separate exclusion 'network' proposed here can be implemented as a simple message scheme passing between the behavior nodes. This method of implementation does not require a proliferation of layers of control or destroy the encapsulation of behavior.

5: Conditions are continuous variables with values between 0 and 2. Switching of executable status of behavior nodes is implemented with a threshold (at 1) rather than by simple boolean conditions as in Maes 1989. The continuously variable conditions allows more precise control of activation patterns while keeping the connectivity patterns within bounds. In the frog spinal behaviors irritants have a graded strength and frogs choose to deal with major irritants prior to minor ones! If we assume behaviors and the environment may increment or decrement conditions

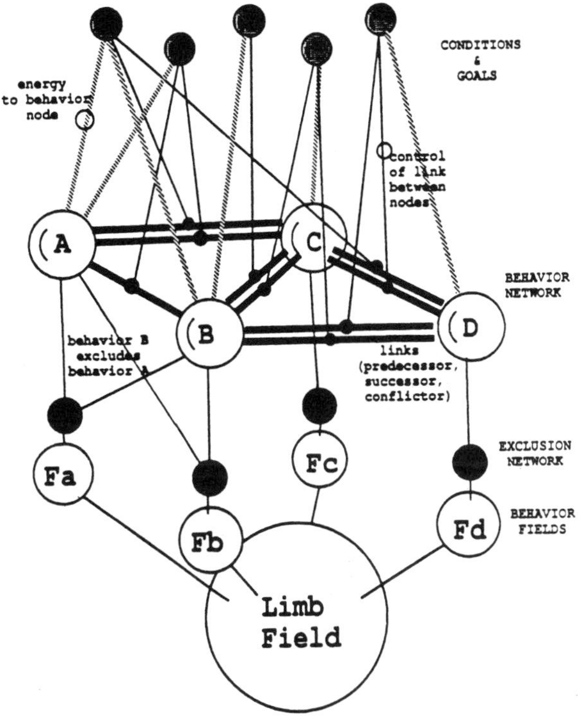

Figure 5: The simulation structure :

Conditions (top) are set by the environment or the action of the network on the environment. Conditions range in the interval 0..2. Conditions which are fulfilled (>1.0) distribute activation to behavior nodes (e.g. A, B, C, D) which have the condition as a prerequisite for execution. Goals are unfulfilled (<1.0) conditions specified to be fulfilled. Goals distribute activation to behavior nodes which will cause them to become fulfilled. Conditions control the direction of activation flow between behavior nodes by determining behavior nodes status (non-executable, or executable) and also modulate the rate of activation flow in the links. Behavior nodes (A,B,C,D) in the network become executable when all preconditions are >1.0. This switches activation outflow from predecessor links to successor links. Execution proceeds when the activation of an executable node is greater than threshold. The level of activation above threshold is then used to parameterize the associated behavior field (Fa-Fd) if access to the field is allowed by the exclusion network. The exclusion network allows only one member of a set of mutually conflicting behaviors access to the limb. In the figure A and B can lock one another out. The activated behavior fields are combined by vector summation to form a limb force field which drives limb behavior.

rather than simply switching them it becomes important to decide how to utilize the information in these continuous variations of conditions. These might represent the probability of achieval of a fulfilled condition, the probable stability of a fulfilled condition or the cost or payoff of the condition.

The continuous condition variation thus allows predecessor, successor and conflictor links to be modulated more smoothly in accordance with the meaning of the value of the condition.

In this scheme the strength (l) of a predecessor or successor link modulated by a condition of value **c** may be given by

$$l = l_0 + k*c \qquad \text{for} \quad 0 < c < 1$$

For **k**= -1 the link decreases activation transfer as a condition is closer to threshold. For **k**= 1 the link increases activation transfer as a condition is closer to threshold.

The strength of a conflictor link is given by

$$l = l_0 + k(c-1) \qquad \text{for } 1 < c < 2$$

For **k**= -1 the link decreases activation removal as a condition is further above threshold. For **k**= 1 the link increases activation removal as a condition is further above threshold. Clearly these condition parameters can also be used with goals and protected goals.

By choosing a value for the parameter **k** for each link type (conflictor, sucessor, predecessor) the network can be tuned with regard to how much it favors easy tasks over hard (**c** close to 0: hard versus **c** close to 1: easy) or how it treats large deviations versus small. Similarly the protected goals and goals can exert differing influence based on the variations of the conditions. These notions are especially useful in modelling spinal reflexes in which stimuli can have very different intensities or noxiousness while being in all other respects similar.

6: Terminator conditions:

Each behavior possessed a set of conditions or propositions terminating execution. These could be as simple as a number of time units, or as complicated as achieval of a payoff of at least 50% of the effects of the behavior node. Final ly termination could be caused by pre-emption by a novel executing behavior. In the simulations shown here a time out terminator was used. In spinal behaviors phases usually proceed to completion or time out.

3 Force fields and Limb response:

The network structure shown in figure 5 was used to model behavior selection and intensity of behavior. The output of the network drove a limb force field simulator which combined 3-dimensional force fields vectorially in order to create a net force field for the limb at the heel. This is shown conceptually in figure 6. The above threshold

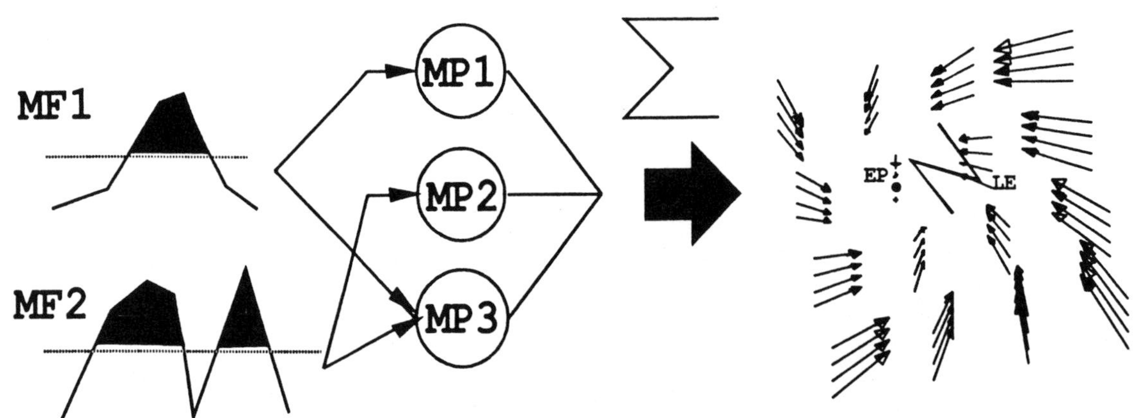

Figure 6: The most general scheme for control of limb force fields in the model. Executable behavior nodes are responsible for generating a fixed structure force field. The above threshold activation is used to set a gain for the movement fragment or force field. In principal this might be composed of several movement primitives (for example different joint controllers) in a fixed balance. The several sets of movement primitives recruited in this way are summed in a near vectorial fashion by the limb mechanism to generate a total limb force field. This force field drives the 'virtual trajectory' and actual limb response. Because the activation provided by the network can vary widely the actual trajectories generated will show great variety.

activation of an executing behavior node is used to set amplitudes for one or more movement primitives. Each movement primitive consists of circuits able to generate a fixed structure force field. The summed movement primitives for a behavior may be treated as a single entity, and, in any case, to date the relation of primitive to behavior is one to one.

Let $\mathbf{F_i(p)}$ be the field relating a position vector **p** to a force vector **f** in the limb (at the ankle) for the behavior node **i**. The total limb field is given by the vector sum of the individual behavior fields modulated by behavior intensity:

$$F_t(p) = S\ \mathbf{a}_i * F_i(p)$$

where $\mathbf{a}_i$ is the intensity of the ith executing behavior

and $F_i(p)$ is the field associated with the ith executing behavior

This equation gives an estimate of the total force field

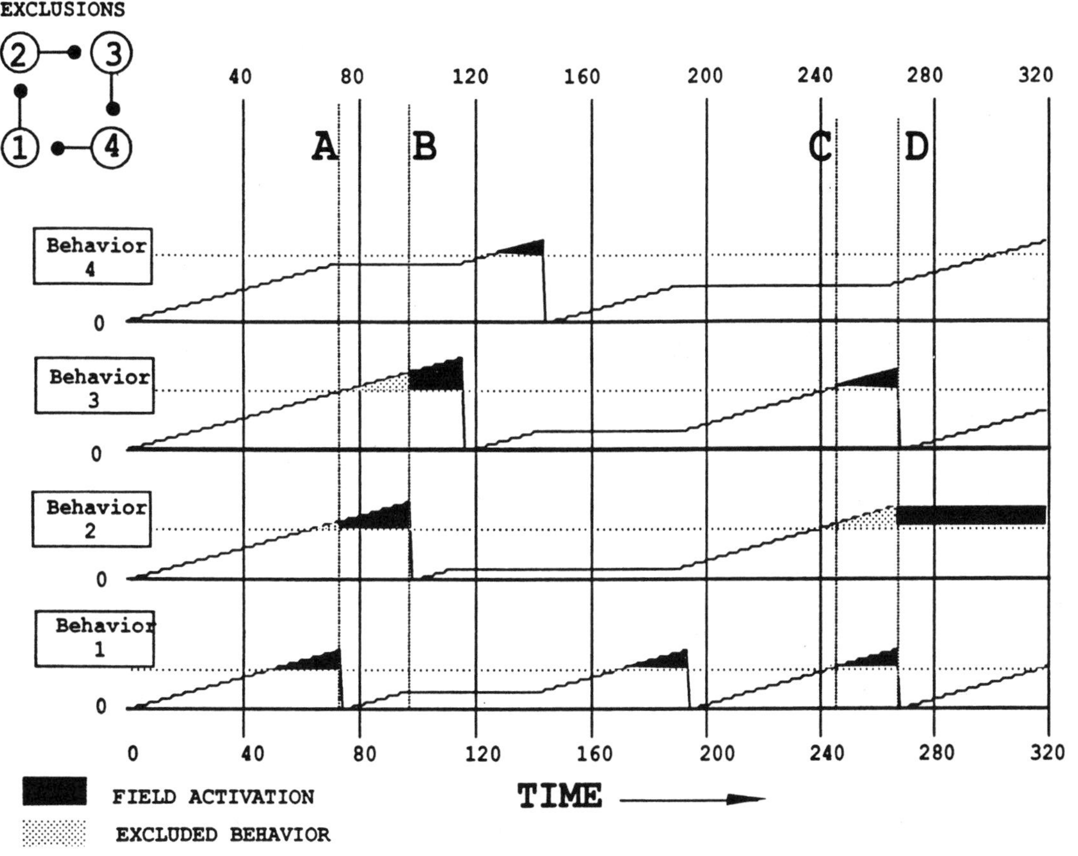

Figure 7: Sample output from a concurrent behavior network. Blending exclusion and switching is seen. Four behaviors exert exclusions in a ring. Thresholds are shown as horizontal dotted lines. Regions in which a behavior is both executable and above threshold but is excluded from access to the limb are shown stippled. Activation of movement primitives is shown in solid black. Note that between A and B behavior 2 suppresses behavior 3 while activation dynamics are unchanged. As a result the onset of behavior 3 is very abrupt at B. Between C and D behavior 2 is excluded for a prolonged period while behaviors 1 and 3 run concurrently. The movement primitives controlled by or represented by behaviors 1 and 3 were combined by vector summation throughout this period.

experienced by the leg when the ankle is at a position in space assuming perfect vector summation is implemented by the limb structure.

The limb itself was modelled as a three link manipulator with kinematics operating in a plane. The plane of operation of the linkage had two degrees of freedom. It could be altered in azimuth and elevation at the hip, but showed no rotation about the hip/heel axis. It was assumed the ankle and knee were strongly coupled. (In the frog this can occur by means of the large double joint muscles of the calf). The knee and ankle were thus assumed to form a planar pantograph. Paths of the linkage were obtained from integration of the vector field at each time instance. The paths shown here thus represent instantaneous estimates of the flow of the time varying vector field. The paths generated incorporate no modelling of physical dynamics.

4 Performance:

Preliminary studies with this simulator demonstrate that it shows behaviors with many features that are reminiscent of the biological systems.

Kinematic variability:

Paths of the limb are quite smooth. As might be expected, the limb may approach the same destination by several different routes, and at different speeds on different trials depending on the stimulus configuration and history of the system. These two factors determine the shape and speed of the rise and fall of the above threshold activation of each movement primitive. This determines the behavior of the total limb force response. The variability of paths thus represents the flow variations of the limb vector fields. These variations are generated as behavioral intensity varies (see Figure 7). The variability of kinematics would be further accentuated in a model incorporating limb dynamics.

Switching and exclusion behaviors:

Different ordering of behaviors, switching and different concurrent patterns of behaviors occur based on conditions and simulation history. This is reminiscent of the switching and blending of kinematics seen in many spinal scratch and wipe behaviors. Two important types of interaction believed to be important in frog spinal behavior are shown in Figure 7. These are exclusion of a behavior while the excluded behavior continues to gain suprathreshold activation, and concurrent blending of two behaviors. The network showing these phenomena in figure 8 settles into periodic limit cycles in the absence of environmental clamping of some conditions. While several key elements of the spinal repertoire can be demonstrated. It remains to be explored how well different arrangements and parameters can generate the full flexibility of spinal repertoire and whether additional types of elements are required.

5 The relation to spinal behaviors

The force fields found in the frog spinal cord and modelled here incorporate potential fields, bias or force control fields and non conservative fields. En masse this variety of fields provide movement primitives or schemas for a wide variety of path plans and interaction with the environment. Thus both equilibrium point and force control can be used to move the limb or to interact with the environment.

A point not focussed upon in this paper is the way in which descending influences might act on the spinal cord. How is supervisory control exerted on the behavior network and/or spinal movement primitives? In the spinal cord control could operate at several different loci. Firstly control could operate through the spinal behaviors by direct activation of them. Secondly descending control could coopt movement primitives independently of behaviors. Thirdly control could circumvent movement primitives and act directly on the motoneuron pools. Finally the wiring diagram of the cord itself could be reorganized by descending control. Clearly these options are not mutually exclusive. It is currently envisioned these control options might be explored in several ways in this model. In keeping with the original behavior net scheme, goals could be set. Alternatively a pre-emptive use of a behavior node might occur in the manner of the subsumption architecture : links, preconditions and activation associated with a node could be controlled directly. This would leave the remaining behavior nodes free to respond to the environment and executing behavior node(s). The network would thus prepare itself and be ready to respond in the event of the release from the pre-emptive control, and might offer assistive behavior in the meantime. Finally, descending pathways could act directly at the effector system and the exclusion network. In order to understand how descending control of spinal-cord structures may operate I believe it is important to grasp the implicit trade-offs of each of these control schemes.

5 Conclusions:

The response patterns of which this framework is capable suggest this framework is a good scheme for modelling the spinal reflex and pattern generating systems.

Several global parameters and connectivity parameters relevant to the function of spinal systems have been discussed. There is a close (but clearly not obligatory) correspondence between the simulation entities used and the spinal entities identified in experiment. Behavior node corresponds to movement primitive/pattern generator; con - ditions correspond to afferent stimuli and the 'body scheme'; spread of activation and integration of afferent stimuli exists in both systems; thresholds exist in both systems; network global parameters in the model might be hypothesized to correspond to neuromodulation, primary afferent depolarization, or habituation. These relatively direct relationships may make aspects of experimental prediction and testing relatively straightforward. The model largely obviates any homunculus or supervisor roles. There is thus the possibility that such modelling efforts may indicate what structural and global factors are most critical to the remarkable abilities of the spinal frog. Pfluger's discussion of 'spinal soul' may perhaps be supplanted by a'Society of Spine' (see Minsky 1986). In summary it is possible that this simulation framework will capture most of the variation, novelty and purpose of behavior exhibited by the isolated spinal-cord of the frog and provide a tool to guide experimental observations.

References

Arbib M Cobas A (1991) In: From Animals to Animats: Proc. First Intl.Conf on Simulation of Adaptive Behavior. ed Meyer J-A and Wilso SW., pp. 142-151

Arkin RC (1991) In: Designing Autonomous Agents ed. Maes P. pp. 105-122 MIT/Elsevier.

Berkinblitt MB, Feldman AG, Fukson OI (1989) In: Visuomotor coordination: amphibians, comparisons, models, and robots (Ewert J-P, Arbib MA, eds), pp. 615-630. New York: Plenum.

Bizzi E, Mussa-Ivaldi FA, Giszter SF (1991) Science 253: 287-291.

Brooks R (1991) In: Designing Autonomous Agents ed. Maes P. pp.3-16 MIT/Elsevier.

Chepelyugina MF (1947) (Ph.D. Thesis) Moscow: University of Moscow.

Fukson OI, Berkinblitt MB, Feldman AG (1980) Science 209: 1261-1263.

Giszter SF (1992) Nature, submitted.

Giszter SF, McIntyre J, Bizzi E (1989) J Neurophysiol 62: 750-767.

Giszter SF, Mussa-Ivaldi FA, Bizzi E (1992a) Neural systems, II (Eeckman FH, ed), in press. Boston, MA: Kluwer.

Giszter SF, Mussa-Ivaldi FA, Bizzi E (1992b) Exp Brain Res Series, in press.

Giszter SF, Mussa-Ivaldi FA, Bizzi E (1992c) J.Neurosci. in press

Giszter SF, Mussa-Ivaldi FA, Bizzi E (1991b) In: Visual structures and integrated functions (Arbib MA Ewert JP, eds), pp. 223-237. New York: Springer-Verlag.

Johnson MB 1990 Build-A-Dude. Master's Thesis MIT Media-Lab.

Khatib O (1986) IJRR 5:1

Maes P (1989) Proc IJCAI -89 Conf Detroit

Maes P (1991) In: Designing Autonomous Agents ed. Maes P. pp.49-70 MIT/Elsevier.

Maes P (1991) In: From Animals to Animats: Proc. First Intl.Conf on Simulation of Adaptive Behavior. ed Meyer J-A and Wilson SW., pp. 238-246

Minsky M (1986) Society of Mind, Simon and Schuster

Mussa-Ivaldi FA, Giszter SF (1992) Biol. Cybern. in press.

Mussa-Ivaldi FA, Giszter SF, Bizzi E (1990) In: Cold Spring Harbor symposium on quantitative biology 55: 827-835. Cold Spring Harbor, NY: Cold Spring Harbor Laboratory Press.

Mussa-Ivaldi FA and Hogan N (1991) Intl J. Robotics Res, 10:481-491.

Ostry DJ, Feldman AG, Flanagan JR (1991) J Neurophysiol 65: 547-562.

Payton DW (1991) In: Designing Autonomous Agents ed. Maes P. pp.89-103 MIT/Elsevier.

Schotland JL, Lee WA, Rymer WZ (1989) Exp Brain Res 78: 649-653.

Shadmehr R, Mussa-Ivaldi FA, Bizzi E (1992) J Neurosci (accepted).

Sherrington C (1961) The integrative action of the nervous system. New Haven, CT: Yale University Press.

von Holst E,(1973) The behavioral physiology of animals and man. Selected papers of Eric von Holst. Coral Gables, Florida: University of Miami Press.

Acknowledgements:

Conversations with Pattie Maes and Michael Johnson were of great help in the design and implementation of these simulations. Extensive comments by Pattie Maes on a first version of the paper were indispensible. Supported by NIH NS09343 and AR26710 and ONRN00014/90/J/1946

The Ariadne's clew algorithm

Emmanuel Mazer, Juan Manuel Ahuactzin
El-Ghazali Talbi, Pierre Bessiere *
Laboratoire d'Informatique Fondamentale et d'Intelligence Artificielle
46 AvenueFélix Viallet, 38031 Grenoble cedex France
manu@lifia.imag.fr

Abstract

We present a general planning strategy to plan the motions of an agent having to explore a continuous state space in order to reach one or several goals. We propose a practical method to implement this technique based on a genetic algorithm and we illustrate the approach on the problem of controlling a mobile robot moving in a maze and looking for several items. Finally, we show that this planning strategy may serve as a possible control structure for an autonomous system.

1 Introduction

This study was motivated by our previous work on robot motion planning using a parallel genetic algorithm [8]. The planner we have design and implemented on a parallel machine is capable of planning collision free paths for a mobile robot placed among obstacles. The main advantage of this planner is its speed, it can plan complex paths such as the two paths represented in figure 1 in less than 0.5 second on a parallel machine with 64 Transputers. As a consequence it can be used to replan on line new paths when the obstacles move. The genetic algorithm is used to minimize a function having a path as argument and returning the distance of the first colliding point of the path with the goal, its value is zero when a valid path to the goal has been found. The nature of the minimization technique implies the possibility of falling into a local minima. In our case a local minima is a path which collides with an obstacle before reaching the goal. For example, figure 2 represents the local minima found by the algorithm when it tries to find a path from A to B. To escape from this frustrating situation we propose the following approach.

*This work has been made possible by: Le Centre National de la Recherche Scientifique (France), Consejo Nacional de Ciencia y Tecnologia (Mexico) and ESPRIT 2, P2528 (EEC)

Instead of using is thread to find the labyrinth's exit as in the legend, Theseus (the robot) will use it to explore the labyrinth in order to find the Minotaur (the goal). One can visualize the proposed algorithm by imagining a robot placing landmarks in the free space starting from its initial position. Each time it places a new landmark it tries to place it as far as possible from landmarks previously placed, the thread is used to connect two landmarks and it is used to move in the space already explored. If the search space is bounded, then the robot will fill the free space connected to its initial position with landmarks. These landmarks will becomes closer and closer as the search time is becoming larger. At a given point in time the goal will necessarily be visible from the last placed landmark and a solution will be found !

First we will describe the "explore" algorithm which places distant landmark in the search space. Then we will define what it does mean to "see" the goal by introducing the pre-image functions. The kernel of the proposed method just consists to run the "explore algorithm" and to evaluate, in parallel, the pre-image function attached to each goal. We will demonstrate how efficient is this strategy on a complex path planning problem. We will argue in favor of the generality and completeness of the proposed method. Finally we will show that the approach can be used to control the behavior of physical autonomous robot.

2 Previous work

2.1 On path planning

Designing a new path planner is a classical exercise in robotic research and it remains a very active field in robotics. A review of the existing approaches can be found in Latombe's book [1]. They are two main ways to tackle this problem: the global and the local approaches.

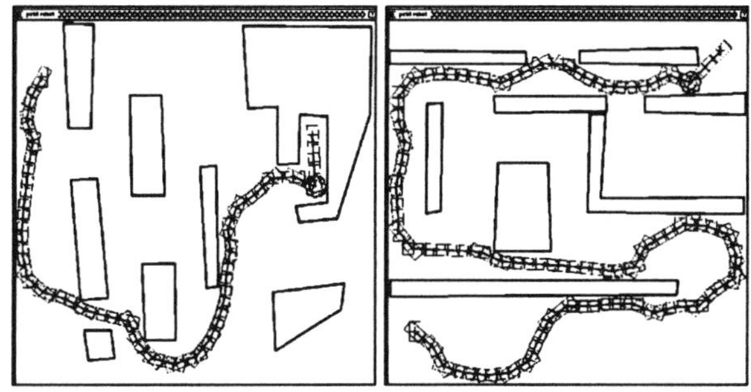

Figure 1: Two complex paths planned by the parallel genetic algorithm.

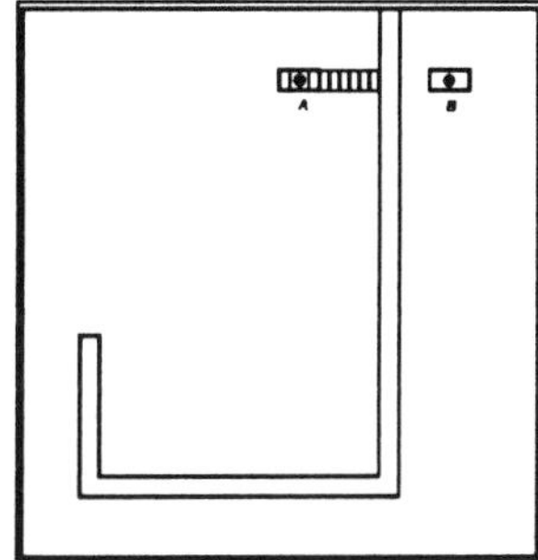

Figure 2: A problem with a local minima.

In the local approach framework, the decisions to move the robot are taken locally, these approaches are generally well suited for robot with many degree of freedom but may lead to local minima (Our initial planner was a local planner). The global methods consist of computing a complete representation of the configuration space before looking for a path, they will find a solution if there is one but are limited to robot with a small number of degree of freedom (not greater than 3). The explore algorithm builds a discreate representation of the configuration which resolution increase with the difficulty of the problem.

2.2 On Genetic algorithms

Genetic algorithms are stochastic search techniques, introduced by Holland [7] twenty years ago, they are inspired by adaptation in evolving natural systems. Development of massively parallel architectures made them very popular in the very last years [10, 9]. They have also been used with success to directly generate robot programs which will drive the robot in a complex environment [14, 15].

2.3 On software architecture for autonomous robot

In the last years a large number of new software architectures have been proposed as a possible alternative to the classical way of controlling robot. The subsumtion architecture developed by Brooks has been used to control a large number of robots placed in "real" situations [17, 16, 18]. Various extension of this approach have since been developed [12, 13]. The proposed "explore function" can be seen as refinment of the *wander* module found in many specifications of dedicated subsumtion architectures.

3 The general case

3.1 The explore algorithm

The goal of the explore algorithm is to successively place a new landmark which will maximize the distance to previously placed landmarks. The process starts from the initial location. We denote by P the set of all *feasible* path starting from the initial location L_1 and by $E(p)$ be the extremity of a particular path $p \in P$. Let p_2 the path of P which maximize the following expression where $\| L_1 - E(p) \|$ denotes the euclidian distance.

$$p_2 : \max_{p \in P} \| L_1 - E(p) \|$$

According to our definitions, the point $L_2 = E(p_2)$ is the most further point of the search space reachable from the initial location L_1, we choose it as the second landmark. Now, we have two landmarks L_1 and L_2. Given a path p we consider the minimum value between $\| E(p) - L_1 \|$ and $\| E(p) - L_2 \|$. To find the third landmark we maximize this value over the set of feasible path P.

$$p_3 : \max_{p \in P} \min\{\| L_0 - E(p) \|, \| L_1 - E(p) \|\}$$

More generally if we have already n landmarks we can find the $n+1$ landmark by maximizing the following expression:

$$p_{n+1} : \max_{p \in P} \min_{j=1,n} \| L_j - E(p) \| \quad (1)$$

By taking $L_{n+1} = E(p_{n+1})$ we get our new $n + 1^{th}$ landmark. Lets consider the function:

$$\forall n \geq 2 : V(n) = \max_{p \in P} \min_{j=1,n-1} \| L_j - E(p) \|$$

If the search space is bounded then:

$$\lim_{n \to \infty} V(n) = 0$$

or

$$\forall \varepsilon \exists n : \forall j > n \quad V(j) < \varepsilon$$

Then, if G is a point of the accessible free space (ie: it exists a path from L_1 to G) then we have:

$$\forall \varepsilon : \exists n \parallel L_n - G \parallel < \varepsilon \qquad (2)$$

We call this property : *epsilon-reachability*. The epsilon-reachability has a strong consequence for planning a path in a continuous space : if one can find ε such that there is a function which solve the path planning problem in any ball of diameter ε, then by combining it with the explore algorithm we get a general method to plan a path between any two points of the configuration space. We call such function a pre-image function [2, 19, 20, 21, 22]. In other words, if there is a mean mean to reach the goal when it is near the robot, then the explore algorithm will lead the robot towards the goal in a finite time from any point. Of course the better th pre-image function is, the less landmarks the robot will have to place.

3.2 The local explore algorithm

At this point, the main problem with the proposed method is: how to maximize the function V over the set P ? We can simplify the problem by considering the sets P_i of all possible paths starting from the landmark L_i and having l as maximum length.

$$V_i = \max_{p_i \in P_i} \min_{j=1,n} \parallel L_j - E(p_i) \parallel$$

$$p_{n+1} : \max_{i=1,n} V_i$$

We consider the function:

$$V'(n) = \max_{i=1,n} V_i$$

We have:

$$\forall n : V'(n) \leq V(n)$$

As a consequence, an algorithm which maximize V' to place a new landmark will also have the epsilon-reachability property. Further, given a ball B_l of center B and of diameter l we define P_B as the set of all possible "feasable" paths in the ball B_l and we define the function V_B ($P_B \stackrel{V_B}{\rightarrow} \Re$) as:

$$V_B = \min_{Lj \in B_l} \parallel L_j - E(p) \parallel$$

If one can find l such that there is an algorithm which maximize V_B over the set P_B for any point B of the search space then one can explore the configuration space with an arbitrary resolution. In other word if there is a way to "locally" explore the configuration space the whole configuration space can be explored. The bigger l is, the fastest the landmarks will be uniformally distributed over the connected free space.

4 Implementation

There is a well known and brute force implementation of the previous theory, it consists of discretizing the search space with an ε resolution and labelling each cell as "free" if it does not contains a C-obstacle[1] and as "occupied" otherwise. The pre-image function is just solving the path planning problem in the free cell containing the goal. The local-explore function can be implemented with a classical A^* algorithm which will search through the connected free cells. This algorithm will decide, in a finite time, if a path can be found at a given resolution ε. The main differences between this brute force algorithm and the algorithm we are about to present are:

- The brute force algorithm uses a given resolution ε, should a lower resolution $\varepsilon' > \varepsilon$ be enought to find a solution the computing time would remain the same. Instead the Ariadne's clew algorithm will select automatically the appropriate resolution. Note that if no solution can be found by the brute force algorithm then our algorithm will miserably take about the same time to discover the cruel truth. This just reflect the intrinsic complexity of the path planning problem [23]

- In practice it is easy to use a partial pre-image function that will define implicitly a much larger pre-image region than the one used by the brute force algorithm. In figure 3, the white region represents all the starting locations from where our local path planner will find a path to the goal G. Should a landmark be placed in this pre-image region then a path will be found. For real robot it is also possible to implicitly define a large pre-image region: think of a beacon and a light seeking behavior.

- In practice it is also easy to define implicitly a set P_i which will scan a much bigger region than the connected cell used by the brute force algorithm, for example, in the figure 4 the black region represent the points reachable from the initial location with our algorithm. The Ariadne's clew algorithm will geometrically jump from distant places to distant places in the configuration space while the brute force algorithm will keep looking locally for a solution, for a randomly placed goal, this increases the chances of placing a landmark into its pre-image. Again, for a real robot it is also possible to implicitly define an explore function which lead the robot to distant places: think of a behavior

[1] Any real obstacle defines a C-obstacle in the search space

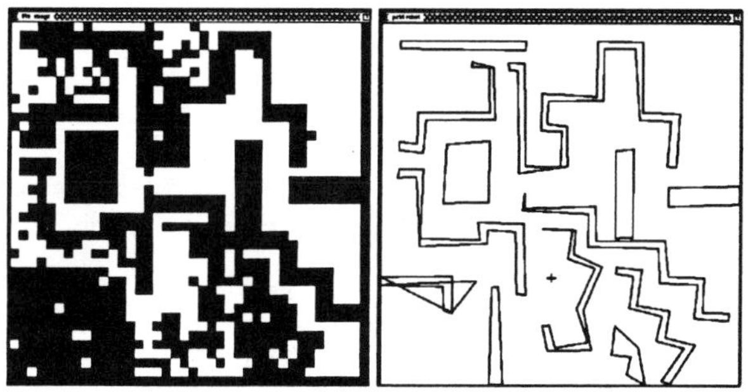

Figure 3: The pre-image region.

which drives the robot away from already placed landmarks.

5 An example: The mobile robot case

In this section we apply the previously defined planning technique to the problem of planning collision free paths for a mobile robot. We will use the genetic algorithm as a general optimization technique for functions which can be evaluated at a given point but which cannot be formally represented.

5.1 The partial pre-image function

We use a modifyed version of our previously developed path planner as our pre-image function. This function implicitly defines a partial pre-image of any point in the configuration space. As we have already seen this pre-image is quite large and looking if a landmark belongs to a pre-image can be readily computed using a parallel implementation.

We consider a discrete subset P'_D of all the *feasible* paths starting from D and having d as maximum length. A path p is coded with k positive integers $\{\theta_i\}_{i=0,k-1}$: each integer as a maximum value M and codes the angle

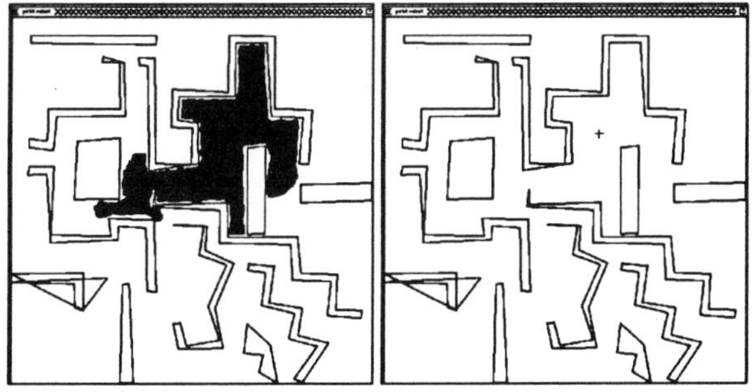

Figure 4: The post-image region of an initial location.

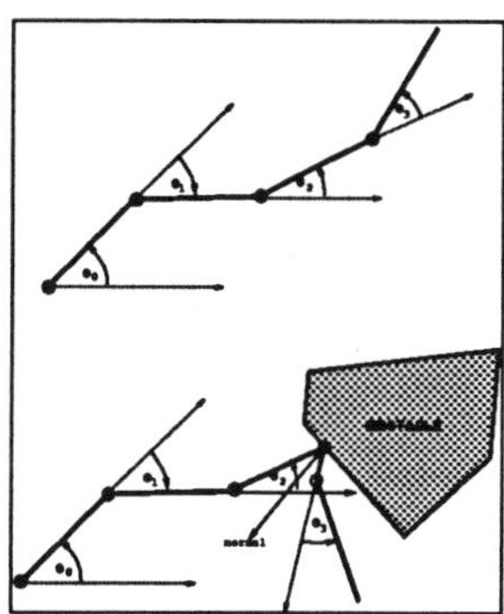

Figure 5: The original path in the free space and its modification by an obstacle.

between two linear segments of trajectory having $\frac{d}{k}$ as maximum length. In a completely free space, a path p is just a set of connected linear segments of length $\frac{d}{k}$. We denote as t_i the initial point of each segment, according to our definition the robot rotate of θ_i at each point t_i and then make a straight move toward t_{i+1}.

In a cumbersome space the code represents the same kind of path excepted when the robot collides with an obstacle. In that case, it "bounces " on the surface of the obstacles (see figure 5). Using this coding technique a code of k integer represents a free path of length l. Note that this coding technique allows us to search only in a subspace of the "feaseable" paths.

We define the function $g(p)$ as follow: $g(p) = 0$ if there exists a "direct" move toward the goal from any point $t_i : i = 0, k$ and $g(p) = \min_{i=0,k} \| t_i - G \|$ otherwise. It is not possible to define an analytical form for g(p), but we can use a genetic algorithm to minimize this function over the set P'_D.

$$\min_{p \in P'_D} g(p)$$

We use a parallel version of the standard genetic algorithm and run it on parallel machine with 128 Transputers. The crossover uses the binary representation of the code defined by the $\{\theta_i\}_{i=0,k-1}$. A typical path, such as the two paths represented figure 1, is found in 15 generations on a 128 population and runs in less than 0.5 second.

5.2 The local explore function

The local explore function is directly inspired from the previous function. Suppose we are trying to place a new landmark L_{n+1}: we use an equivalent set of integers to represent a path and we use the same convention to maintain this path in the free space. Note that the maximum length l of the path can be different as well as the number of segments k. We add a new integer I_n to this set to code the starting position of the path. The value of I_n codes the landmark from which the path is starting.

The genetic algorithm is used to maximize the function $V'(n)$ over a discrete subspace of $\cup_i\{P_i\}$. The figures 6 shows how the explore algorithm successively places new landmarks in the search space.

One interresting improvement of the explore function is to look at the variation of the function $V'(n)$. If $V'(n)$ increases dramatically, it means that a new "room" of the configuration space has been discovered (see figure 7) and it may not be necessarily to consider the previously generated landmarks until the value of $V(n)$ decreases to the previous lower value of $V'(n)$.

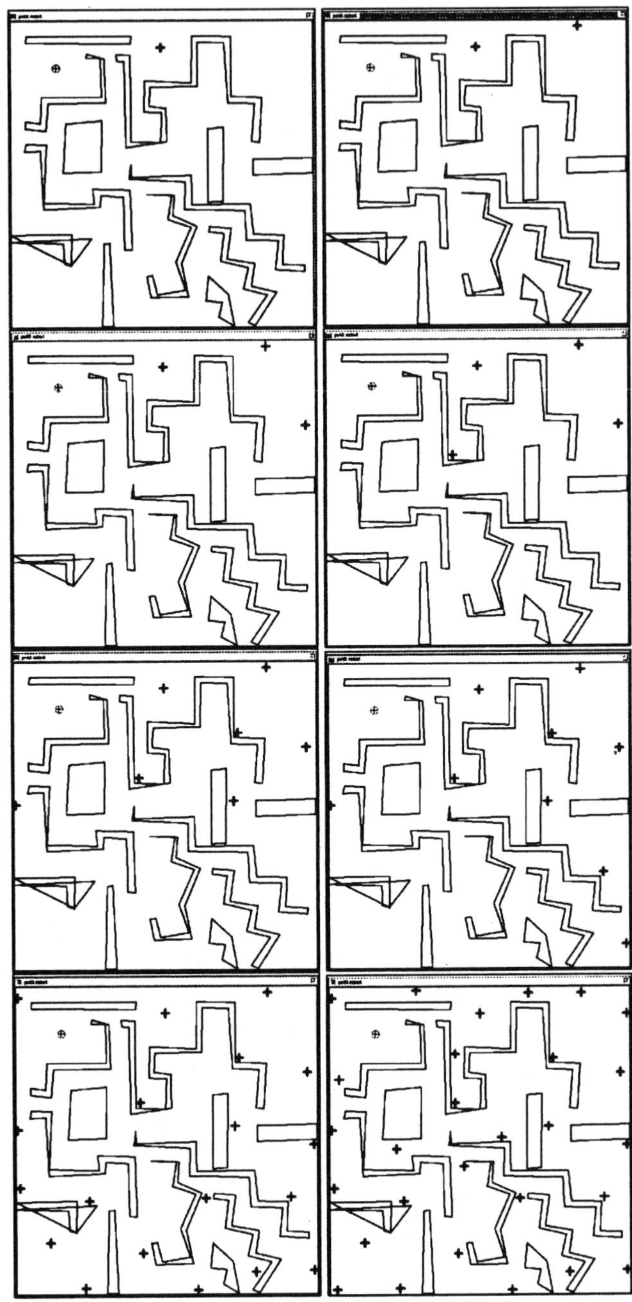

Figure 6: The evolution of landmarks in the search space.

5.3 Combining the functions

The explore function organizes the generated landmarks into a tree. The root of the tree is the initial position of the robot L_1, a new leave is generated each time a new landmark has been found. This leave is connected to the landmark used as the origin of the path which maximize V', the system also save this path (see figure 8). When the pre-image function returns a valid path, the system simply backtrack into the tree towards the origin to find the solution.

The explore function and the pre-image function can run in parallel. The explore function will produce a landmark which will be consumed by the pre-image function while the explore function produces a new landmark. For example, on our machine we could run the explore function in parallel on a torus of 64 transputers and, at the same time, run the pre-image function on the remaining 64 transputers also configured as a torus. This structure has not been implemented yet, the paths presented in figure 9 has been computed on a Sun workstation running the explore and pre-image functions sequentially in about 8 seconds.

5.4 Completeness

There are a number of constants in the planner:

1. M : which define the discretization step for the rotation between two segments.
2. d,l : which define the length of the segments for the explore and pre-image functions.
3. k,k' : which define the number of segments for both functions.

In practice these constants are chosen whithout much care, in the presented examples the length of the paths are chosen so that they could cross half of the search space, the number of segments is arbitrarily set to 20 and the 2π rotation is discretize over 256 values: a gene is represented by a 160 bits string.

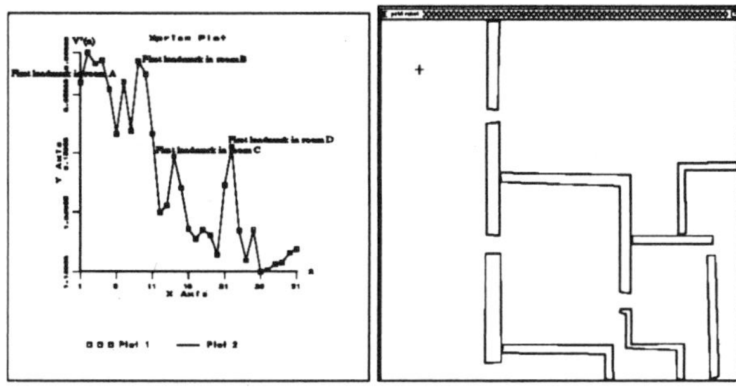

Figure 7: The evolution of V(n) after twenty three landmarks.

The completeness of the proposed algorithm depends on two conditions:

1. The possibility of finding ε such that the pre-image function is guaranteed to define a pre-image region containing a ball of diameter ε centered on any possible goal in the search space.
2. The possibility of finding l such that the explore function is guaranteed to maximize the function V' on any ball of diameter l of the free space.

The first condition can easily be met, simply by restricting the goals to be in a region of the free space where the robot can maneuver in all directions by a given amount ε. Then, the visibility criteria used in our pre-image function will work on this domain.

The second condition is more difficult to obtain since we use a minimization technique based on a genetic algorithm and we have no guarantee that a global maximum will be found with this method. However, our conjecture is that the method will remain valid as long as we are reaching "real" local maxima.

6 Future work

The Ariadne's clew algorithm suggests a simple architecture for an autonomous robot. It gives a robot something to do when there is nothing to achieve : it tell the robot to explore its environement by going to places where it has not been before. New goals can be assign simply by defining new pre-image functions under the form of behaviors triggered by special conditions on the values of the sensors. The most difficult part is to implement an efficient local explore function. Going aways from chemical landmarks will be ideal but technically difficult to realize. A simpler idea is to use the robot odometer to estimate its location and to build [11] a local representation of the real environement using its utlra-sonic sensors. This technique could be used to incrementally build a representation of the real environment similar to the one used in our algorithm. This representation will be use by Ariadne's clew algorithm to suggest a new path to place a new landmark. Should the robot encounter an obstacle when executing this path, it will follow it in order improve the model of the environement, then it will run again the explore algorithm with the updated model to get a new path. We plan to implement these ideas on a real mobile robot in order to find a box placed in a large parking lot.

7 Conclusion

We have presented a general method to search a continuous configuration space. The proposed method evolves two functions: the local exploration function and the partial pre-image function. These functions can efficiently be implemented using a minimization technique based on a genetic algorithm. We have demonstrated the validity of the method on a set of complex path planning problems which can readily be solve on a parallel machine. Finally, we proposed to use our approach as a method to drive the robot in places where it has not been before.

References

[1] Jean-Claude Latombe: *Robot Motion Planning*, Ed. Kluwer Academic Publisher, 1991.

[2] J.C. Latombe, A. Lazanas, S. Shekhar: *Robot motion planning with uncertainty in control and sensing*, Artificial Intelligence 52 pages 1-47, 1991.

[3] David E. Goldberg: *Genetic algorithms in search, optimization and machine learning*, The University of Alabama, Addison-Wesley publishing company, inc. 1989.

[4] Davis Lawrence (Editor): *Genetic algorithms and simulated annealing*, BBN Laboratoires, Cambridge, Massachusetts, 1987.

[5] Davis Lawrence (Editor): *Handbook of genetic algorithms*, VNR Computer Library, Van nostrand Reinhold Pub. New York, 1991.

[6] Davis E. Goldberg: *Genetic algorithms and machine learning*, University of Alabama, Tuscaloosa, University of Michigan, Ann Arbor, in Machine Learning, Kluwer Academic Publishers, 1988.

[7] J.H. Holland: *Adaptation in Natural and Artificial Systems*, Ann Arbor: University of Michigan Pres, 1975.

[8] J.M. Ahuactzin, E. Mazer, P. Bessiere, E.G. Talbi. *Using Genetic Algorithms for Robot Motion Planning*, European Conference on Artificial Intelligence, Vienna, Austria, August 1992.

[9] E.G. Talbi, P. Bessiere: *A parallel Genetic Algorithm for the graph partioning problem*, ACM International Conference on Supercomputing, Cologne, June 1991.

[10] E.G. Talbi, J.M. Ahuactzin, E. Mazer, P. Bessiere. *Parallel Robot Motion Planning*, CONPAR-92 - VAPP V, Lyon France, September 1992.

[11] J. L. Crowley, P. Reignier, O. Causse, F. Wallner: *Action Level Behaviors for Locomotion and Perception*, Preprints of the Second International Symposium on Experimental Robotics, Toulouse France, June 1991

[12] Pattie Maes. *A Bottom-up Mechanism for Behavior Selection in an Artificial Creature* Proceedings of the First International Conference on Simulation of Adaptive Behavior. Paris, France, September 1990.

[13] Pattie Maes. *Learning Behavior Networks from Experience* Proceedings of the First European Conference on Artificial Life, Paris, France, December 1991.

[14] J.R. Koza. *Evolution and Co-Evolution of Computer Programs to Control Independently-Acting Agents* Proceedings of the First International Conference on Simulation of Adaptive Behavior. Paris, France, September 1990.

[15] J.R. Koza. *Evolution of Subsumption Using Genetic Programming* Proceedings of the First European Conference on Artificial Life, Paris, France, December 1991.

[16] R. A. Brooks. *Challenges for Complete Creature Architectures* Proceedings of the First International Conference on Simulation of Adaptive Behavior. Paris, France, September 1990.

[17] R. A. Brooks. *Artificial Life and Real Robots* Proceedings of the First European Conference on Artificial Life, Paris, France, December 1991.

[18] M.J. Mataric *Navigating With a Rat Brain: A Neurobiologically-Inspired Model for Robot Spatial Representation* Proceedings of the First International Conference on Simulation of Adaptive Behavior. Paris, France, September 1990.

[19] A. Lazanas, J.C. Latombe: *Landmark-Based Robot Navigation*, Proceedings of the Tenth National Conference on Artificial Intelligence. San Jose, CA, July 1992.

[20] A. Lazanas, J.C. Latombe: *Landmark-Based Robot Navigation*, Technical Report, Department of Computer Science, Stanford University May 1992.

[21] B.R. Donald: *A Geometric Approach to Error Detection and Recovery for Robot Motion Planning with Uncertainty*, Artificial Intelligence. 37 pages 223-271, 1988.

[22] M.T. Mason, *Automatic Planning to Fine Motions: Correctness and Completeness*, Proceedings IEEE International Conference on Robotic and Automation, Atlanta, GA, 1984.

[23] John Francis Canny. *The complexity of robot motion planning*, PhD Thesis, Massachusetts Institute of Technology, Artificial Intelligence Laboratory, May 1987

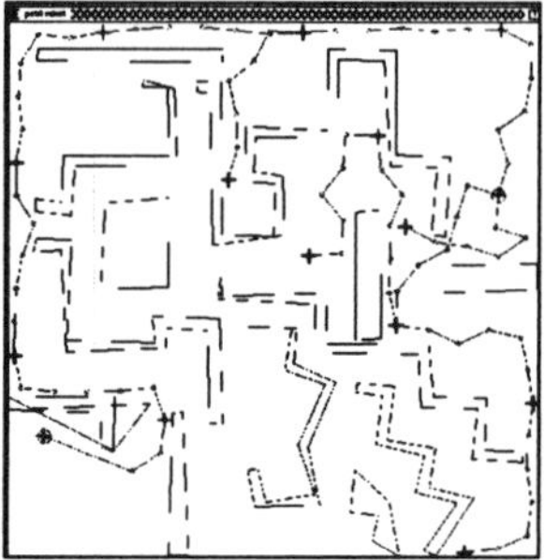

Figure 8: The tree of the landmarks.

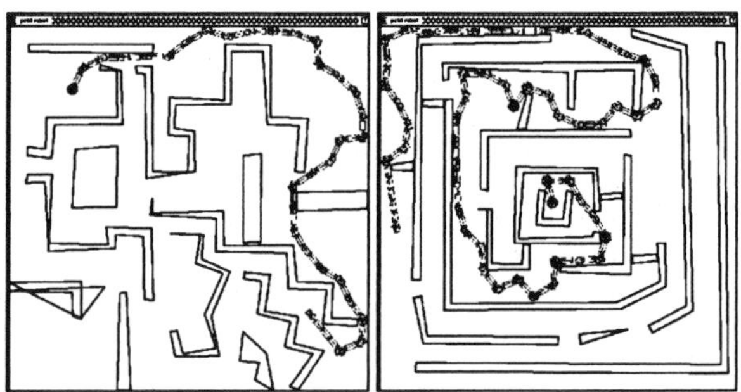

Figure 9: two complex path planned by the Ariadne's clew algorithm.

Dynamic Selection of Action Sequences

Feliz Ribeiro[1], Jean-Paul Barthès[1] and Eugénio Oliveira[2]

[1] Université de Technologie de Compiègne
U.R.A. C.N.R.S. 817 Heudiasyc
B.P. 649 F-60206 Compiègne cédex FRANCE
tel: (+33)44.23.44.23
fax: (+33)44.23.44.77
email: {fribeiro, jpbarthes}@hds.univ-compiegne.fr
[2] Faculdade de Engenharia da Universidade do Porto
D.E.E.C.
P-4099 Porto codex PORTUGAL
tel: (+351-2)27.505
fax: (+351-2)23.192.80
email: eco@garfield.fe.up.pt

Abstract

Planning has been generally considered as a problem-solving activity where it would be possible to search through a state space to find an admissible, and often optimal, solution. Action operators map states to states, modifying accordingly some of the facts known to be true (or false); the decision of which operator to apply at any given step is based on the analysis of what the corresponding plan would look like a few steps ahead. Lately, some authors have been suggesting that planning should, and could, be viewed as the result of the interactions of a group of some sort of computational units (agents)[1]. These units are simple, are strongly interconnected between them and to the external world, and each can be selected to decide on the action to perform at a given moment. What the units can be and what kinds of interactions can take place is what this paper is concerned about. We present here some results we obtained by "wiring" the state and the goals into a network where the nodes are the entities in the world being modeled. They exchange limited information, have simple behaviors, and modify their available interaction links accordingly to their current state. These approaches clearly suggest that decentralised, local forms of control can ensure coherent behavior in changing and unpredictable outcome worlds, while at the same time keeping the units very simple.

1. Introduction

This paper is concerned with planning viewed as the result of interactions between a group of simple units (i.e., presenting restricted cognitive capabilities), each having only local information about the state of the world and having some means of transmitting limited information to the others. Units can be the entities being acted upon (e.g., the blocks in a blocks world), or the actions which can be performed (e.g., instantiated operators). These units are highly reactive to the external environment and to the others, and as a result they increase/decrease some internal measure of the suitability they have to be chosen to perform an action, given the present state of the world. Even if the units are not cognitive by nature (there's neither internal inference nor knowledge representation structures) they are not only purely reactive either. A unit reacting to a changing fact in the environment generally entails a chain of reactions involving other units, which makes that the result of the initial reaction will be "weigthed" over the entire group. As such, these approaches avoid the problems which traditionnal planners generally have to cope with:

- the Sussman anomaly (conjunctive goals[2]).
- the detection and the resolution of conflicts in non-linear plans.
- the exponential growth of the size of the state space to search.

Having no explicit global representation of the world, and since there is no partial plan being built, the group of

1 "This image raises the possibility that we can dispense with the all idea of planning and just focus on competent behavior" — McDermott (1988).

2 cf. p. 112, Waldinger (1977).

units simply ignores these problems. In the remainder of this paper we show how a network of units linked by their local state and their goals "builds" a plan. First, in the next section we describe the algorithm for computing energy. In section 3 we discuss our approach, and section 4 analyses some related work. Finally, in section 5 we expose our concluding remarks. Throughout the paper our examples are taken from the blocks world. The planning problems found in a world simple as it is have been discussed for some time now, even if they were not always solved, or even completely understood. Some examples here and in the related bibliography show difficult cases which are solved in a quite natural way if we look at the effort classical planners do — e.g., in Sacerdoti (1977) the later is proportional to the number of conflicts.

2. How do interacting units plan

Our approach relies on the multi-agent planning paradigm where a group of agents builds collectively a plan. Each agent has a goal, a state, and the task of the group is to satisfy all individual goals; moreover, we want the global solution to be optimal, i.e., the one that minimizes the total number of steps necessary to reach that solution. If we were to characterize our approach inside the planning or action sequencing work, we would say that it is an "attempt to avoid planning" (following McDermott, 1992).

2.1. What units really are

We take here as example the blocks world where cubes must be moved from one place to another. However, we are only interested here in the mechanisms allowing an optimal selection procedure to take place inside a group of agents (whatever they may be) and so we do not care about external elements which could act as resources for these agents — for example, a robot manipulator that could only act as a "transporter", or sensory devices that would act also upon request. In a sense, the agents we consider are aware of these possibilities, although this view can certainly confine our problem to a smaller area of the overall adaptive action selection behavior. Each agent manipulates a crude representation of its current state and that is all that is needed in order to interact with the others — we assume that the means it has to build that representation are available as they do not rely on a complex processing of the data they manipulate.

In our case, agents are the blocks and the table. We say that blocks are *satisfied* if they are both in their final position and the one supporting them is also satisfied; the table is always satisfied (for the moment we deal with an infinite capacity table: there is enough space for all blocks). Blocks have two choices when moving: either their final position is satisfied, in which case they move to it, otherwise they move to the table. When a block is selected to move, it always chooses one of these two options, and so it must be free (i.e., not supporting a block). At each step, the block selected to move, besides being free, must also be the one that minimizes the total number of moves. In other words, with an infinite capacity table, a block has a maximum of two moves: one to the table (if its final position is not satisfied), and another one to its final position.

All the agents are linked by two binary relations: *depends-on* (Don) and *blocked-by* (Bby). The first says that if the goal of **A** is to be on top of **B**, then **A** *depends-on* **B**. The second just reflects the current state of the world: if **A** is on top of **C**, than **C** is *blocked-by* **A**. The inverse relations also exist (i.e., for the above we could say that **B** *is-dependence-of* **A** and that **A** *blocks* **C**); for simplicity we will omit them in what follows, their presence being implicit. The agents and the relations form a network where the nodes (the agents) are going to be assigned numeric values (henceforth called *energy*[3]) which come from other nodes via the links representing the above relations between the entities — see figure 1: the current and final states are shown at the top, and the initial network at the bottom.

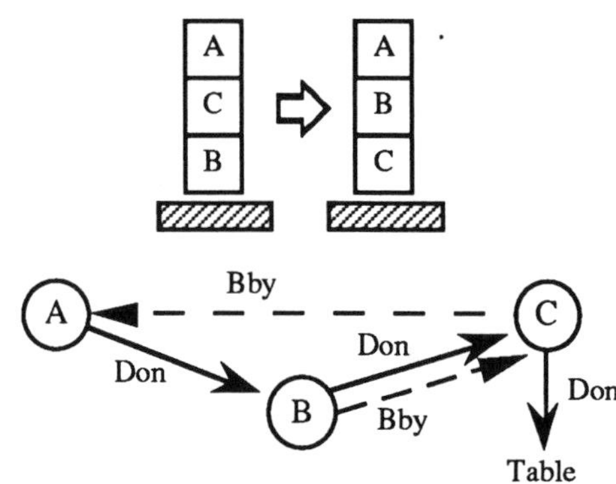

fig. 1. Initial configuration and network.

After a move, the *blocked-by* links are updated according to the new state of the world; unless we allow for changing goals, an agent's *depends-on* link will never be modified. When all agents are satisfied the algorithm stops: the plan executed is then the temporal ordering of all the moves made so far.

Before going further we will highlight two points:

- the energy of a block (which expresses, in a sense, the agent's will of getting satisfaction[4]) is computed based on local information about the node: that is, based on its goal and on its current state, as reflected by the links *blocked-by* and *depends-on* which transmit energy. All decisions

---

3 Given the similarity of the approach, we choosed the term "energy" which plays the same role (albeit computed in a different manner) of the "activation energy" of Maes (1989).

4 As in the Eco-problem-solving approach (Ferber, 1990).

are thus local, although we will see later that blocks propagate also energy: the energy of a block can thus have been modified by some other block.

- the plan is the collection of moves (decisions after each propagation phase). If a move does not produce the desired results (a block falls while being moved by a gripper) only the links between the entities involved — the block being moved and its initial and final positions — are updated. In the next propagation phase there will be no replanning whatsoever (which can be rather complex to deal with, e.g., Drummond and Currie, 1989); the network will just use the new links and again another agent will be chosen. This is quite important when interleaving planning and execution, where there is often the need to modify previous planning sequences that were based on expected outcomes.

Some hypothesis are made concerning the agent's behavior. An agent is commited to retransmit whatever information is to be propagated (see section 2.2). This means that, even if they have some degree of autonomy, they respect the rules governing the action selection mechanism. As they are all engaged in some sort of a cooperative problem-solving process, it is not apparent how they could, for example, hide information so as to benefit from it (e.g., as in Zlotkin and Rosenschein, 1990).

These two remarks will become apparent later. Next we will describe how energy is computed for each agent.

2.2. Computing energy

Planning will be considered here as the collection of choices made by the group of agents at regular time intervals (the time needed to compute the energy terms we will see below). These choices are based on the energy level of each block after all exchanges of energy have been done. It is this mutual exchange, or better, propagation, mechanism which will be described below.

At the beginning of each propagation phase all entities have zero energy; the table besides having no energy is always satisfied — it will never be moved...

Energy is computed as the sum of four components:

E_b is the energy exchanged via the *blocked-by* links.

E_d is the energy coming from the *depends-on* links.

E_{db} is the energy going through the *depends-on* links and propagated via the *blocked-by* links.

E_{bd} is the energy going through the *blocked-by* links and propagated via the *depends-on* links.

Energy values range from $-\infty$ to $+\infty$. E(**X**) denotes one of the above terms for block **X**. Let us first introduce some auxiliary predicates: **sat**, **don** and **bby**. We will say **sat**(**A**) if **A** is satisfied, **don**(**A**, **B**) if **A** *depends-on* **B**, and **bby**(**A**, **B**) if **A** is *blocked-by* **B**. So, if we are computing the energy for block **X**, the following local increments in its energy are made:

- If **bby**(x, y),

$$\Delta E_b(X) = \begin{cases} 0 & \text{if } \mathbf{sat}(X) \\ -1 & \text{otherwise} \end{cases}$$

$$\Delta E_b(Y) = \begin{cases} 0 & \text{if } \mathbf{sat}(X) \\ +1 & \text{otherwise} \end{cases}$$

if $\exists_Z$: **bby**(Z, X) the function **propagate-b**(Z, ΔE_b(X)) is invoked unless X is satisfied.

The function **propagate-b** does the following:

propagate-b(Unit, Value)

E_b(Unit) = E_b(Unit) + Value
If $\exists_X$: **bby**(X, Unit) then
  propagate-b(X, Value)

Intuitively, the energy of a blocked block is decreased while a blocking block sees its energy increased (unless the one below is satisfied) and eventually will be forced (i.e., chosen) to move. This energy by itself would not be able to take into account the goal relations between the nodes; it is only based on the local, and current, state of the blocks. We use then the links *depends-on* so that the blocks' energy will be influenced also by the goal intentions of the agents. It is the introduction of this energy and of the two subsequent propagation phases that will optimize the blocks' moves.

- If **don**(x, y),

$$\Delta E_d(X) = \begin{cases} +1 & \text{if } \mathbf{sat}(Y) \\ E_d(Y)-1 & \text{otherwise} \end{cases}$$

if $\exists_Z$: **don**(Z, X) the function **propagate-d**(Z, ΔE_d(X)) is invoked unless X is satisfied. If X is satisfied, this propagation is useless, because propagated values from satisfied agents are always unitary. The function **propagate-d** does the following:

propagate-d(Unit, Value)

If E_d(Unit) was already computed then
  E_d(Unit) = E_d(Unit) + Value
If $\exists_X$: **don**(X, Unit) then
  propagate-d(X, Value)

This function just takes into account the fact that when we compute the energy for one agent we may be using values that will be updated later. For the example in figure 1 this will happen if we compute E_d(B) before E_d(C); we would find the value –1 for E_d(B) and it should be 0 (see at bottom in figure 2 below). Also, we only update our energy if we have already computed it; otherwise when we compute it later, Value would have been counted twice. As agents are independent and can compute their energy in parallel regardless of the computations going on in the others, these restrictions are compulsory.

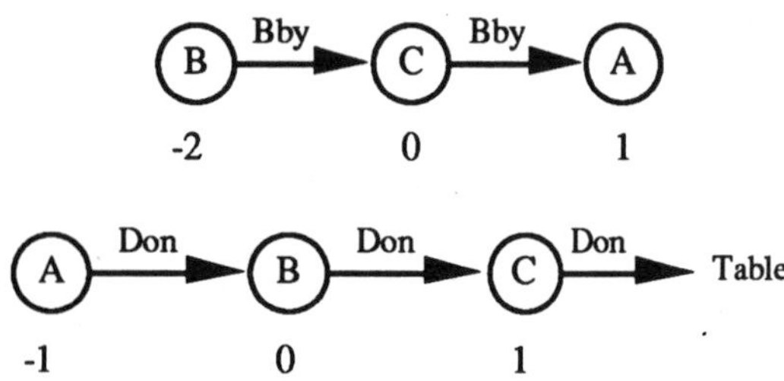

fig. 2. Values of E_b (top) and E_d (bottom) for fig. 1.

After all blocks had their E_b and E_d values computed (as shown in figure 2), we start a phase of forward propagation of energy to compute E_{db} and E_{bd}. This aditional propagation will play the role of an *action at a distance*, and will influence block's energy by those who are only indirectly related to it — that is, not linked by an explicit *depends-on* or *blocked-by* relation. This phase proceeds as described in the next section.

2.3. Propagating mixed energy

We saw before how the current state and the goal intentions of the agents contributed to their internal energy. We now explore the fact that, in order to have a rational, optimal if possible, selection criterion for the agents, there must be some way of weighting their global interaction. That is, given two agents with the same energy why should we prefer one in detriment of the other? We argue that this decision can be made solely by letting the agents exchange information about their local relations to other nodes, this time via both the *blocked-by* and *depends-on* links. This information, which is propagated from agent to agent following some fixed rules, can be though of as a *mixed energy*. For each agent, it will add the contributions of both those who depend on it and of those who are blocked by it.

Propagation and local computation of the remaining two terms go as follows:

• Computing E_{bd}

Take the graph at the top in figure 2. Consider the set **S** of the nodes having a predecessor (**C** and **A**). **B** has no predecessor (incoming **Bby** link). Let **P**(s) be the length of the predecessor chain of s ∈ **S** (including s itself): thus **P**(A)=3 and **P**(C)=2.

∀ s ∈ **S** do:

If ∃x : **don**(s, x) then
  propagate-bd(x, **P**(s))

where **propagate-bd** is defined as follows:

propagate-bd(Unit, Value)

If ∃x : **don**(Unit, x) and not(**sat**(x)) then
  propagate-bd(x,Value)
else
  New-Unit = **blocked?**(Unit)
  E_{bd}(New-Unit) = E_{bd}(New-Unit)+Value

Where **blocked?**(Unit) returns the last in a **Bby** chain starting at Unit, Unit otherwise.

The test on **sat(X)** tells us that if **X** is satisfied that makes no sense to continue propagating energy; its *depends-on* link can only point to another satisfied block, so there's no interest in propagating further. The last remark becomes evident if we recall that an agent is satisfied if it is in its final position, and the one supporting it is also satisfied. We stop the propagation just before the first satisfied agent found. Note also that these functions are simplified from the fact that we do not consider here multiple supporting and supported blocks. If this were the case, then we would have had to consider multiple incoming and outcoming *blocked-by* links for each agent.

• Computing E_{db}

Take the graph at the bottom in figure 2. Consider the set **S** of the nodes having a predecessor (**C** and **B**). As before, we define **P**(s) such that now we have **P**(C)=3 and **P**(B)=2.

∀ s ∈ **S** do:

If ∃x : **bby**(s, x) then
  propagate-db(x, **P**(s))

where **propagate-db** is defined as follows:

propagate-db(Unit, Value)

If ∃x : **bby**(Unit, x) then
  propagate-db(x,Value)
else
  unless ∃y : **don**(Unit, y) and not(**sat**(y)) then
    E_{db}(Unit) = E_{db}(Unit)+Value

This last propagation step is not necessary if the initial agent s is satisfied. Indeed, in this case the agents standing above should not be "forced" to move — it is as if they were standing on the table. From this function we can see that the propagated values are only stored in the end nodes (unless they depend on non-satisfied agents); those along the propagation path do not modify their energy, although this could be useful if certain optimizations to the algorithms were to be done. Specifically, after each propagation cycle energy values are reset. As only one agent is selected to move, only a few links will be modified, having a restricted impact on others' energies which don't need to be recomputed again from the beginning.

If we look at the links in figure 2 it is easily seen that $E_{bd}(A)=2$ and $E_{db}(A)=3$, all the other mixed energies being 0. After all four values have been computed, the non-satisfied agent with the highest energy is chosen to try to achieve its goal; if its final destination is satisfied the block can be moved to it, otherwise it moves to the table. It should be noted that *it is the agent that is chosen, not the action to be performed*; it is then up to the agent to choose which action to take, based on the local information it has.

3. Analysis of the approach

We have presented a model of multi-agent interaction based on two primary relations: agent's dependency and blocking. An agent *depends* on someone (something) to achieve its goal, and it can be *blocked* by someone (something) in its endeavour. These two relations help define the communication channels between the agents. Via these channels, they communicate and propagate received information (essentially numeric values) following a fixed and common set of rules. At the current stage of the research, it is not clear yet how agents can have different behaviors in order to "falsify" (to their own profit) the selection criteria: they just cooperate, and their collaborative effort allows an optimal solution to be found. The latter is indeed the most interesting result of this approach, which means that temporal action sequencing is the optimal. Other recent approaches in other domains make use also of simple (and numeric) information exchange to solve heuristic search-based problems (e.g. Clearwater and Huberman, 1991) which have been traditionnaly viewed as hard state space search problems.

Let alone for efficiency reasons, this result shows some sort of "social" agreement based on two primitive behaviors: know what you want to do and what prevents you from doing it. From that, increase the energy of those who can help you in getting satisfaction, and decrease that of those who prevent you from having it. One notable consequence of this behavior is that no distinction is made between planning and replanning phases. As we said before, only modifying links affects propagation of energy, and this does not rely on the previous states of the group. On the contrary, this is however a question of great concern in traditional planners, which is tackled in a more or less natural way in several experiments (e.g., see Hutchinson and Kak, 1990, Ramos and Oliveira 1991).

There remain several restrictions on a more general application of the approach. When an agent is selected to act, it could only do a move after he decided where to. With more complex situations, with a set of actions to choose from, it could be useful to use the individual components of the energy, or else to have a hard-wired combination of these values directly into each known action — this is what the behavioral approach preconizes (e.g., Brooks 1991, 1991a). It seems however that identifying the *blocked-by* and *depends-on* links should be important when using our approach. Even if they can be related to the classical precondition lists, it is not clear yet how this mapping could be done.

We will discuss next to what extent our approach is inspired from other work in the same, or related, fields.

4. Relation to other work

Essentially, our inspiration comes from the spreading activation network of Maes (1989), and from the eco-problem-solving framework of Ferber (1990)[5]. The first uses a network where the nodes are all the possible actions in the world, and the links between these nodes relate all the facts in the precondition, add, and delete lists of these actions (in the blocks world, actions would be something like put-on-A-B — meaning that A is to be put on top of B — and other facts could be clear-A, on-A-B, etc). Nodes exchange inhibition/activation energy mutualy, weighted by some tuning factors which allow the overall system to be more goal- or situation-oriented.

Besides this later characteristic, which reveals some sort of adaptativity and allows for capabilities such as learning to be introduced, the system presents two drawbacks: first, all possible actions must be explicitly present in the network, even if they are not very important. If the number of possible actions grows, the size (number of nodes and links) of the network grows accordingly. Second, mutual influences must be tuned up prior to using the system. That means the designer must have a pretty good idea of the relative weigths of the links if the system is to behave "as expected". Nevertheless, it is expected that some sort of learning can also be introduced in this case. On the other hand, as the units are all the possible actions, this approach is really more concerned with the action selection problem inside a single agent rather than with viewing the network as a group of agents. Recent experiments (Maes and Brooks, 1990) demonstrated that the activation/inhibition network could be at the basis of an adaptive behavior selection mechanism in a mobile robot.

The second work we consider important to our approach is also based on a simple set of interaction behaviors (Ferber and Jacopin, 1990). MASH (for Multi Agent Satisfaction Handler) is a multi-agent system based on the eco-problem-solving paradigm (Ferber, 1990). Units in MASH are the blocks and the table; a unit can be seen

---

5 The reader is referred to the original papers for detailed descriptions of these works.

as a finite deterministic automaton with a set of simple behaviors: the will to be satisfied, the obligation to move away (when attacked), and the will to be free (which can lead to attack others).

However, there is no mutually agreed upon decision about which unit should be given priority to act. This example could also make use (as in other examples in eco-problem-solving — e.g., Drougoul et al., 1991) of some heuristic function which would allow the system to optimize, choosing the "best" unit to be satisfied first; from the the standpoint of our approach, this would be equivalent to assign to the units more than two "energy" levels, and choose amongst them the highest. Nevertheless, as it is, this approach — simple and conceptually attractive — is well suited to problems where actions are cheap but the time to get to the solution is expensive.

Another source of inspiration has been the "multi-agent planning" work. Although agents in this case are generally considered to be more representation and deduction-oriented (at the expense of an increased decoupling from the external world — but there are exceptions, e.g., Hayes-Roth, 1992), they are also engaged in a global interaction process where global coherence and local consistency are difficult to obtain.

Recent work on new approaches to model cognitive behavior has also provided good and stimulating examples of what non-symbolic techniques can offer (e.g., Real, 1991, Roitblat et al., 1991, and see also Meyer and Guillot, 1990, for a comprehensive review on the attempts to simulate adaptive behavior).

5. Final remarks

We have presented here a model of group interaction based on dependency and blocking relations, which has provided optimal results in the multi-agent planning paradigm. It is based on the assumption that agents are well-behaved, i.e., they respect a fixed set of interaction rules, such as retransmitting information when they are expected to do so, and taking actions when asked to. Moreover, they are commited to update their direct relations to other agents, such as when they are moved to other places. It seems also that more behaviors could be added so as to take into account other characteristics of real-world domains, such as resource constraints, and individuality.

We have seen that the group of agents can adapt itself easily to changing environments: simply by modifying the links between the agents, the system can go on "planning", its internal structure was thus reconfigured to match the state of the environment.

Application to other domains with different characteristics will be necessary to test the validity of this approach. For the moment only well-defined goal relations between agents can be taken into account. We are currently extending our work to domains where these relations are more complex in nature, and involve different types of preconditions.

6. References

Brooks R.A. (1991), "Intelligence without Reason", AI Memo 1293, AI Laboratory, Massachusetts Institute of Technology, Cambridge, MA, april 1991.

Brooks R.A. (1991), "New approaches to Robotics", Science, 253, pp. 1227-1232, september1991.

Clearwater S., and B. Huberman (1991), "Cooperative solution of constraint satisfaction problems", Science, 254, pp. 1181-1183, 1991.

Drogoul A., J. Ferber, and E. Jacopin (1991), "Viewing cognitive modeling as Eco–Problem–Solving: The Pengi experience", Report LAFORIA 2/91, LAFORIA, University Paris 6, Paris, january 1991.

Drummond M. and K. Currie (1989), "Goal ordering in partially ordered plans", *in* Proc. *IJCAI 89*, pp. 960-965, Detroit, MI, august 1989.

Elcock E. & D. Michie, eds. (1977), *Machine Intelligence 8*, Ellis Horwood, Sussex, 1977.

Ferber J. (1990), "Eco–Problem–Solving: How to solve a problem by Interactions", Report LAFORIA 5/90, LAFORIA, University Paris 6, Paris, february 1990.

Ferber J. and E. Jacopin (1990), "A Multi–agent satisfaction planner for building plans as side effects", Report LAFORIA 7/90, LAFORIA, University Paris 6, Paris, july 1990.

Hayes–Roth B. (1992), "Opportunistic control of action in intelligent agents", Technical Report KSL-92-32, Knowledge Systems Laboratory, Stanford University, Stanford, CA, april 1992.

Hutchinson S. and A. Kak (1990), "Spar: A Planner that satisfies operational and geometric goals in uncertain environments", AI Magazine, 11(1), pp. 31-61, 1990.

Maes P. (1989), "How to do the right thing", AI Memo 1180, AI Laboratory, Massachusetts Institute of Technology, Cambridge, MA, december 1989.

Maes P. and R.A. Brooks (1990), "Learning to coordinate behaviors", *in* Proc. *AAAI 90*, pp. 796-802, Boston, MA.

McDermott D. (1988), "Planning and Execution" *in* Swartout (1988).

McDermott D. (1992), "Robot planning", AI Magazine, 13(2), pp. 55-79, 1992.

Meyer J.A. and A. Guillot (1990), "From Animals to Animats: everything you wanted to know about the Simulation of Adaptive Behavior", Report BioInfo-90-1, Groupe de BioInformatique, Ecole Normale Supérieure, Paris, september 1990.

Ramos C. and E. Oliveira (1991), "The generation of efficient high–level plans and the world representation in a cooperative community of robotic agents", *in* Proc. *ICAR 91*, Pisa, 1991.

Real L.A. (1991), "Animal choice behavior and the evolution of cognitive architecture", Science, 253, pp. 980-986, august 1991.

Roitblat H.L., P.W.B Moore, P.E. Natchtigall, and R.H. Penner (1991), "Biomimetic sonar processing: From Dolphin echolocation to artificial neural networks", in J.A. Meyer & S. Wilson, eds, *Simulation of Adaptive Behavior*, pp. 66-67, MIT Press, Cambridge, MA, 1991.

Sacerdoti E. (1977), *A Structure for Plans and Behavior*, American Elsevier, New York, NY, 1977.

Swartout W., ed. (1988), "1987 DARPA Santa Cruz Workshop on Planning", AI Magazine, summer 1988.

Waldinger R. (1977) "Achieving several goals simultaneously", *in* Elcock & Michie (1977).

Zlotkin G. and J. Rosenschein (1990), "Blocks, lies, and postal freight: the nature of deception in negotiation", *in* Proc. *10th AAAI Int'l Workshop on Distributed Artificial Intelligence*, Bandera, TX, october 1990.

PLANNING SIMPLE TRAJECTORIES USING NEURAL SUBGOAL GENERATORS

Jürgen Schmidhuber
Department of Computer Science
University of Colorado
Campus Box 430
Boulder, CO 80309, USA
email: yirgan@cs.colorado.edu

Reiner Wahnsiedler
Institut für Informatik
Technische Universität München
Arcisstr. 21, 8000 München 2
Germany

Abstract

We consider the problem of reaching a given goal state from a given start state by letting an 'animat' produce a sequence of actions in an environment with multiple obstacles. Simple trajectory planning tasks are solved with the help of 'neural' gradient-based algorithms for learning *without a teacher* to generate sequences of appropriate subgoals in response to novel start/goal combinations.

Relevant topic areas: Problem solving and planning, goal-directed behavior, action selection and behavioral sequences, hierarchical and parallel organizations, neural correlates of behavior, perception and motor control.

1 INTRODUCTION

Many researchers in neuro-control and reinforcement learning believe that some 'compositional' method for learning to reach new goals by combining familiar action sequences into more complex new action sequences is necessary to overcome scaling problems associated with non-compositional algorithms.

The few previous ideas for attacking 'compositional neural sequence learning' are inspired by dynamic programming and involve reinforcement learning networks arranged in a hierarchical fashion (e.g. (Watkins, 1989), (Jameson, 1991), (Singh, 1992), see also (Ring, 1991) for alternative ideas).

Our approach is entirely different from previous approaches. It is based on some initial ideas presented in (Schmidhuber, 1991a). We describe *gradient-based* procedures for transforming knowledge about previously learned action sequences into appropriate subgoals for new problems. No external teacher is required. Our approach is limited, however, in the sense that it relies on differentiable (possibly adaptive) models of the costs associated with known action sequences.

2 A TYPICAL TASK

The following task is representative of a variety of analoguous tasks solvable by our method.

Consider figure 1. An 'animat' moves in the real plane defined by the x and y axis, producing a trajectory ω in R^2. There are obstacles in the form of circular swamps. As long as the 'animat' does not cross a swamp, there are no *costs*[1] (= negative reinforcement). The i-th swamp Φ_i with center (x_i, y_i) builds the basis of a cone (growing in the third dimension) with tip $(x_i, y_i, -h_i)$. Crossing Φ_i costs

$$\int_{\omega} g(x, y, \Phi_i)\, dx\, dy, \tag{1}$$

where $g(x, y, \Phi_i) = 0$ if (x, y) lies outside of Φ_i, else $g(x, y, \Phi_i)$ is the distance between (x, y) and Φ_i's cone (measured along the the line through (x, y) perpendicular to the real plane). In figure 1, the grey area indicates the costs associated with a trajectory leading straight through a single swamp.

A problem p is defined by a start state $s^p \in R^m$ and a goal state $g^p \in R^m$. In the above example, $m = 2$ – start states and goal states are simply given by pairs of cartesian coordinates. We are looking for an action sequence leading from s^p to g^p *with minimal costs.*

It is true that in theory such sequences could be learned by conventional reinforcement learning algorithms (e.g. (Barto, 1989), (Barto et al., 1983), (Anderson, 1986), (Schmidhuber, 1991b), (Sutton, 1984), (Lin, 1991), (Williams, 1988), (Watkins, 1989)). For the sake of argument, assume that the maximal step size of the 'animat' is just a tiny fraction of the obstacle diameter. Then all the above algorithms will take nearly forever to find appropriate cost-free trajectories for other than trivial start/goal combinations. One drawback of conventional algorithms is that they will try to learn each new task from scratch, instead of exploiting a possibility

[1] It would be straight-forward, however, to introduce a term penalizing the length of ω.

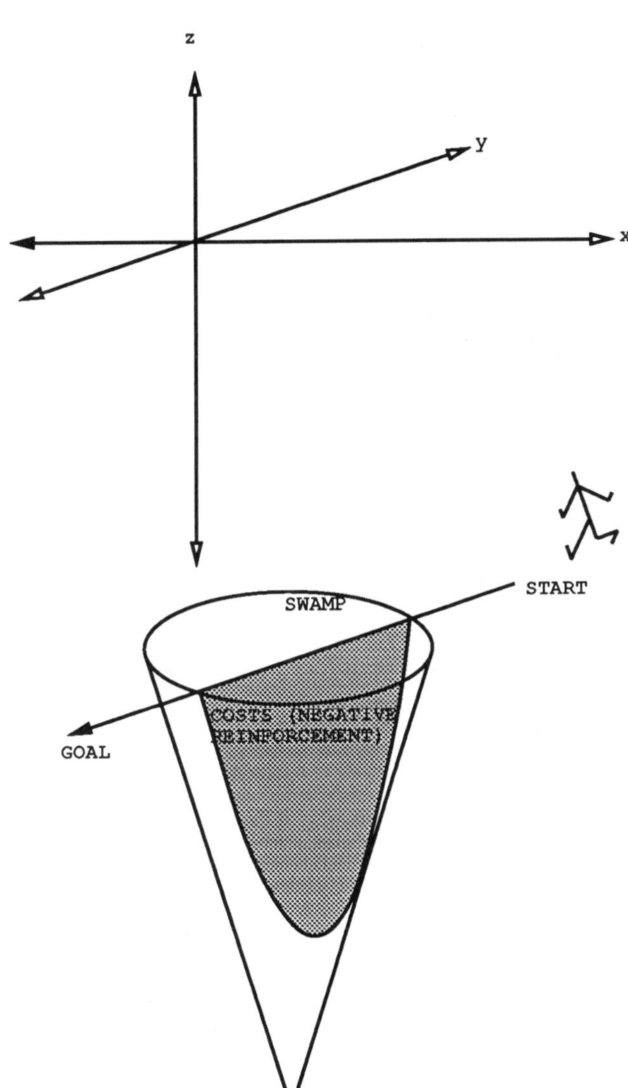

Figure 1: An 'animat' moving in the x, y plane walks through a swamp. The costs are indicated by the grey area.

for speeding up learning and gaining efficiency by solving new tasks through *composition* of solutions for older tasks.

3 BASIC MODULES

Our approach is based on three modules.

The first module is a 'program executer' C, which may be a neural net (but does not have to be one). With a given problem p, C emits a sequence of actions in response to its input vector, the 'problem name' $s^p \circ g^p$. Here '$\circ$' denotes the concatenation operator for vectors. We assume (1) that there are problems for which C does not 'know' solutions with minimal costs but (2) that there also are many problems for which C *does* 'know' appropriate action sequences (otherwise our method will not provide additional efficiency). C may have learned this by a conventional learning algorithm – or possibly even by a recursive application of the principle outlined below.

The second module is the evaluator E. E's input can be the concatenation $s \circ g$ of two states s and g. E's non-negative output $eval(s, g) \in R_0^+$ is interpreted as a prediction of the *costs* (= negative reinforcement) for an action sequence (known by C) leading from s to g. $eval(s, g) = 0$ means minimal expected costs.

E represents a model of C's current abilities. For the purposes of this paper, we need not specify the details of E – it may be an adaptive network (like in (Schmidhuber, 1991a)) as well as any other mapping whose output is differentiable with respect to the input.

The third module is the module of interest: the *adaptive subgoal generator* S. S is supposed to learn to emit a list of appropriate subgoals in response to a novel start/goal combination. Section 4 will present two architectures for S – one for simultaneous generation of all subgoals, the other one for sequential generation of the subgoal list.

The i-th sub-goal of the list ($i = 1 \ldots n$) is denoted by the vector $s^p(i) \in R^m$, its j-th component by $s_j^p(i)$. We set $s^p = s^p(0), g^p = s^p(n+1)$. Ideally, after training the subgoal-list $s^p(1), s^p(2), \ldots, s^p(n)$ should fulfill the following condition:

$$eval(s^p(0), s^p(1)) = eval(s^p(1), s^p(2)) = \ldots$$
$$\ldots = eval(s^p(n), s^p(n+1)) = 0. \quad (2)$$

Not all environments, however, allow to achieve (2). See section 5.

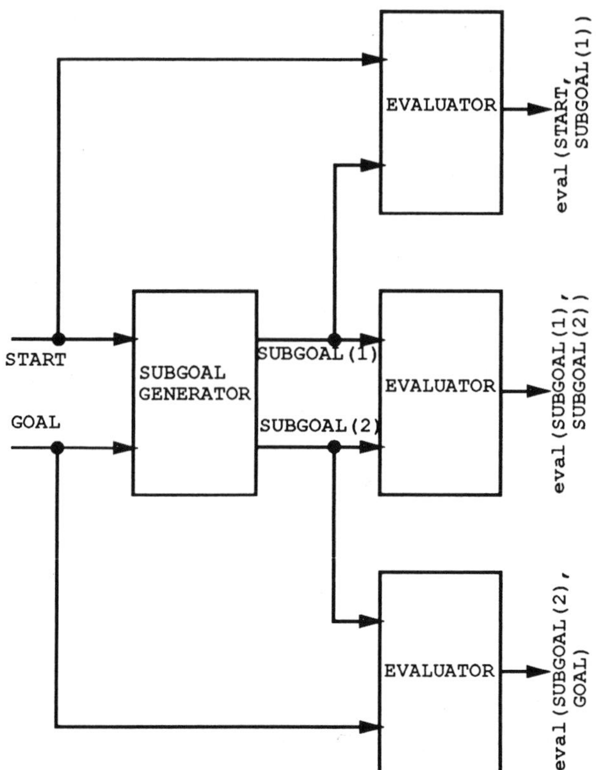

Figure 2: An adaptive non-recurrent subgoal generator emitting two subgoals. Three copies of the differentiable evaluation module are required to compute the proper gradient.

4 TWO SUBGOAL CREATING ARCHITECTURES

4.1 ARCHITECTURE 1

Figure 2 shows a static subgoal generator S (a feed-forward back-prop net, e.g. (Werbos, 1974)). With problem p, the input vector of S is $s^p \circ g^p$.

The output of S is

$$s^p(1) \circ s^p(2) \circ \ldots \circ s^p(n).$$

$n+1$ copies of E need to be connected to S such that the input of the k-th copy of E is equal to $s^p(k-1) \circ s^p(k)$. The output of the k-th copy of E is $eval(s^p(k-1), s^p(k))$.

4.2 ARCHITECTURE 2

Figure 3 shows a *recurrent* subgoal generator S (a back-prop net that feeds its output back to part of its input).

With problem p, the input vector of S at the first 'time step' of the *sequential* subgoal generation process is $s^p \circ g^p$. The output of S is $s^p(1)$.

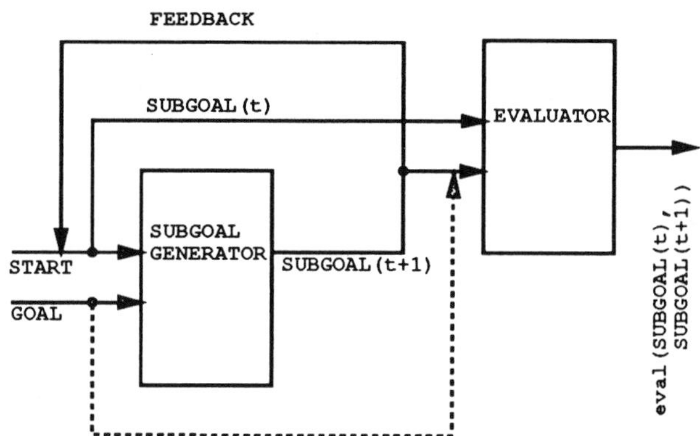

Figure 3: A recurrent subgoal generator emitting an arbitrary number of subgoals in response to a start/goal combination. Each subgoal is fed back to the START-input of the subgoal generator. The dashed line indicates that the evaluator needs to see the GOAL at the last step of the subgoal generation process. See text for details.

At time step $t, 1 < t < n+1$, the input of S is $s^p(t-1) \circ g^p$. Its output is $s^p(t)$.

Again we use E to compute $eval(s^p(k-1), s^p(k)), k = 1, \ldots n+1$, from $s^p(k-1) \circ s^p(k)$.

5 OBJECTIVE FUNCTION

With both architectures we want to minimize

$$E^p = \sum_p \sum_{k=1}^{n+1} \frac{1}{2}(eval(s^p(k-1), s^p(k)))^2. \quad (3)$$

In words, we wish to find a sequence of subgoals such that the sum of the costs of all involved subprograms is minimized. This will be done by using gradient descent techniques to be described in the next section.

6 ALGORITHMS

With both architectures we apply the chain rule to compute the gradient

$$\frac{\partial \sum_{k=1}^{n+1} \frac{1}{2} eval^2(s^p(k-1), s^p(k))}{\partial W_S},$$

where W_S denotes the weight vector of S. During each training iteration, W_S has to be changed in proportion to this gradient.

With architecture 1, this is essentially done by back-propagating error signals (e.g. (Werbos, 1974), (Parker, 1985), (LeCun, 1985), (Rumelhart et al., 1986)) through copies of the evaluator modules down into the subgoal generator. Loosely speaking, each subgoal 'receives error signals from two adjacent copies of E'. These error signals are added and flow down into S, where they cause appropriate weight changes. One might say that in general two 'neighboring' evaluator copies (see figure 2) tend to pull their common subgoal into different directions. The iterative process stops when a local or global minimum of (3) is found. This corresponds to an 'equilibrium' of the partly conflicting forces originating from different evaluator copies.

The derivation of the more complex algorithm for the recurrent architecture 2 is analoguous to the derivation of conventional discrete time recurrent net algorithms (e.g. (Robinson and Fallside, 1987), (Williams, 1989), (Williams and Zipser, in press), (Schmidhuber, 1992)).

7 EXPERIMENTS

(Schmidhuber, 1991a) gives a simple example where the evaluator module E itself is an adaptive back-prop network. In this section, however, we concentrate on the learning process of the subgoal generator S; the *eval* function and its partial derivatives are computed analytically.

For illustration purposes, we assume that C 'knows' all possible action sequences leading to *straight* movements of the 'animat', and that the costs of all these action sequences are already known by E. In that case it is easy to compute (1). The start of the k-th 'sub-program' is $s^p(k) = (s_1^p(k), s_2^p(k))$, its end point is $s^p(k+1) = (s_1^p(k+1), s_2^p(k+1))$. (1) becomes equal to the area

$$F(s_1^p(k), s_2^p(k), s_1^p(k+1), s_2^p(k+1), \Phi_i) \qquad (4)$$

defined by the trajectory of the 'animat' and the corresponding parabola-like projection onto the cone. See again figure 1.

For the k-th 'sub-program', *eval* is defined as

$$eval((s^p(k), s^p(k+1)) =$$
$$\sum_i F(s_1^p(k), s_2^p(k), s_1^p(k+1), s_2^p(k+1), \Phi_i). \qquad (5)$$

Consider figure 4. A single swamp has to be overcome by the 'animat'. With 40 hidden nodes and a learning rate $\eta_S = 0.03$, a recurrent subgoal generator (architecture 2) needed 20 iterations to find a satisfactory solution.

Now consider figure 5. Multiple swamps separate the start from the goal. With 40 hidden nodes and a learning rate $\eta_S = 0.002$, a static subgoal generator (architecture 1) needed 22 iterations to find a satisfactory solution.

Generalization performance. In most non-trivial cases, the system did not generalize very well. After training S on a range of different subgoal generation tasks (various randomly generated start/goal combinations), the subgoals emitted in response to previously unseen problems often were far from being optimal. In such cases the subgoal generator had to be retrained (usually this did not take more than a few iterations, however).

8 LIMITATIONS

One limitation of the approach has just been mentioned – more research needs to be directed towards improving generalization performance.

Another limitation has been mentioned in the introduction: The approach relies on differentiable (although possibly adaptive) models of the costs associated with known action sequences. The domain knowledge resides in these models – from there it is extracted by the subgoal generation process. There are domains, however, where a differentiable evaluator module might be inappropriate or difficult to obtain.

Even in cases where there is a differentiable model at hand the problem of local minima remains. Local minima did not play a major role with the simple experiments described above – with large scale applications, however, some way of dealing with suboptimal solutions needs to be introduced.

ACKNOWLEDGEMENTS

Thanks to Mike Mozer for helpful comments on a draft of this paper. This research was supported in part by a DFG fellowship to J. Schmidhuber, as well as by NSF PYI award IRI–9058450, grant 90–21 from the James S. McDonnell Foundation, and DEC external research grant 1250 to Michael C. Mozer.

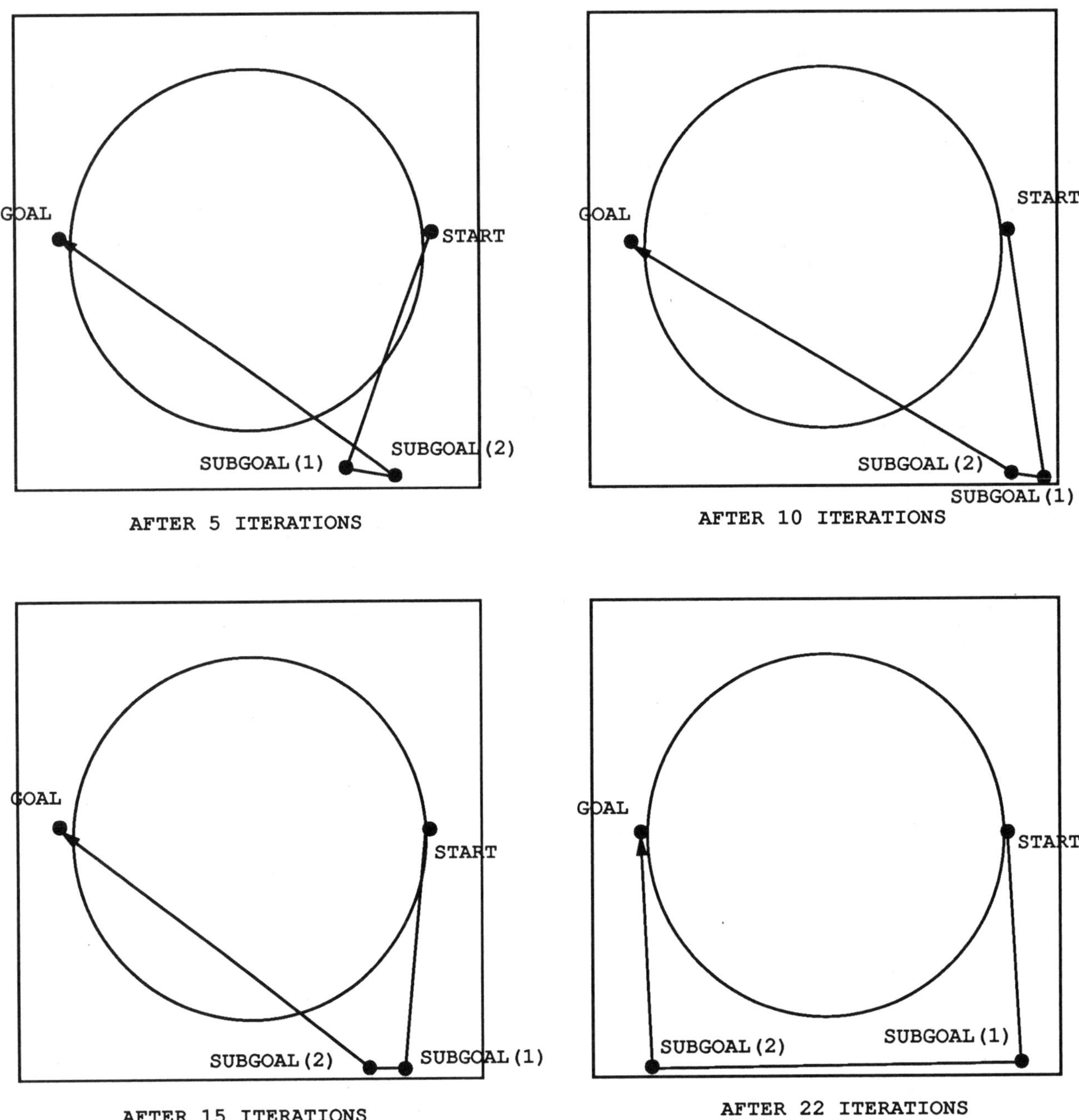

Figure 4: In this example, the task is to find a trajectory (composed of three 'sub-trajectories') leading from START to GOAL. The big circle represents a single swamp. The evolution of two subgoals emitted by an adaptive recurrent subgoal generator is shown.

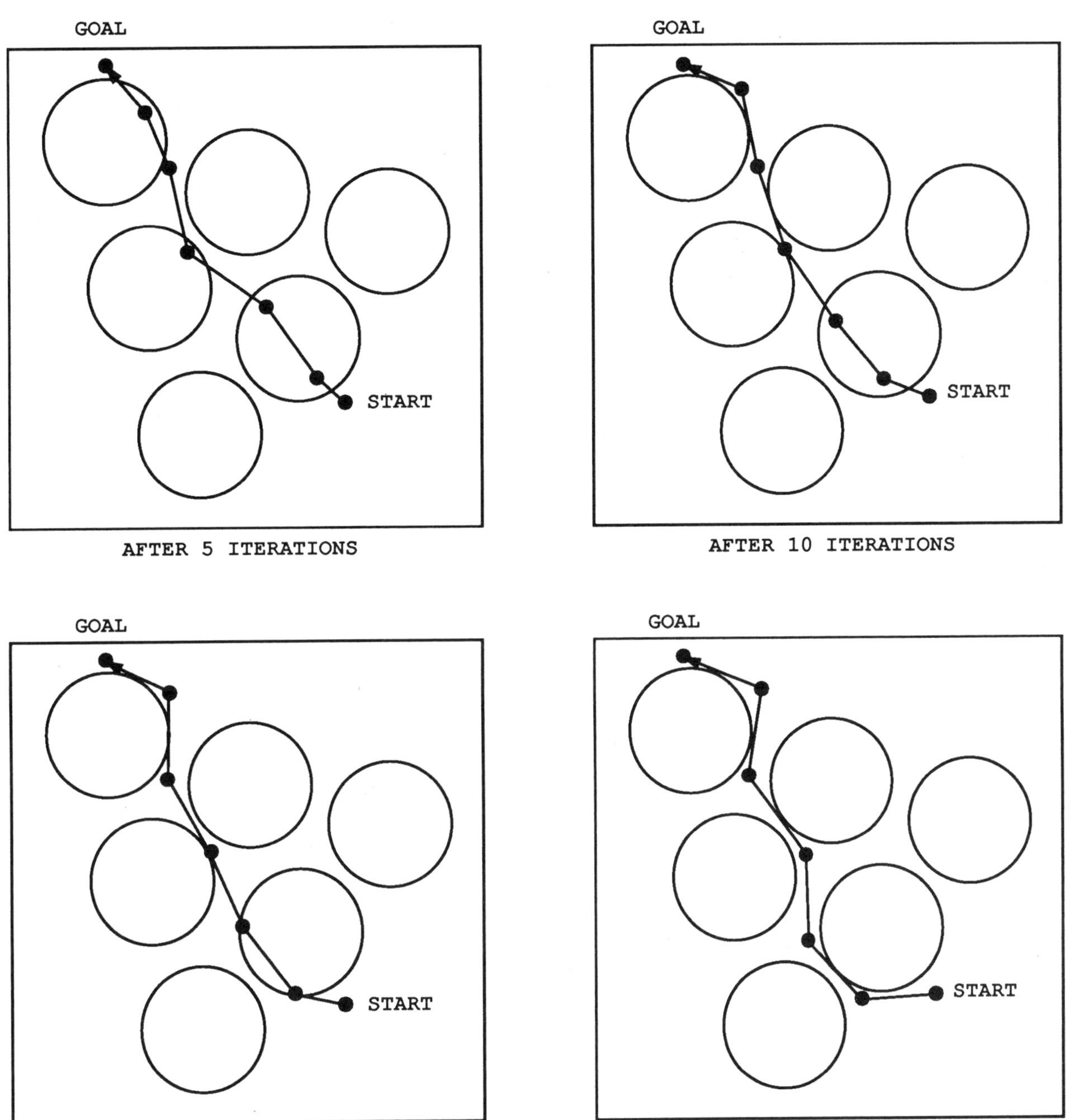

Figure 5: Here many swamps separate the START location from the GOAL location. The evolution of five subgoals (represented by little black dots) emitted by a non-recurrent subgoal generator is shown.

References

Anderson, C. W. (1986). *Learning and Problem Solving with Multilayer Connectionist Systems*. PhD thesis, University of Massachusetts, Dept. of Comp. and Inf. Sci.

Barto, A. G. (1989). Connectionist approaches for control. Technical Report COINS Technical Report 89-89, University of Massachusetts, Amherst MA 01003.

Barto, A. G., Sutton, R. S., and Anderson, C. W. (1983). Neuronlike adaptive elements that can solve difficult learning control problems. *IEEE Transactions on Systems, Man, and Cybernetics*, SMC-13:834–846.

Jameson, J. (1991). Delayed reinforcement learning with multiple time scale hierarchical backpropagated adaptive critics. In *Neural Networks for Control.*

LeCun, Y. (1985). Une procédure d'apprentissage pour réseau à seuil asymétrique. *Proceedings of Cognitiva 85, Paris*, pages 599–604.

Lin, L. (1991). Self-improving reactive agents: Case studies of reinforcement learning frameworks. In Meyer, J. A. and Wilson, S. W., editors, *Proc. of the International Conference on Simulation of Adaptive Behavior: From Animals to Animats*, pages 297–305. MIT Press/Bradford Books.

Parker, D. B. (1985). Learning-logic. Technical Report TR-47, Center for Comp. Research in Economics and Management Sci., MIT.

Ring, M. B. (1991). Incremental development of complex behaviors through automatic construction of sensory-motor hierarchies. In Birnbaum, L. and Collins, G., editors, *Machine Learning: Proceedings of the Eighth International Workshop*, pages 343–347. Morgan Kaufmann.

Robinson, A. J. and Fallside, F. (1987). The utility driven dynamic error propagation network. Technical Report CUED/F-INFENG/TR.1, Cambridge University Engineering Department.

Rumelhart, D. E., Hinton, G. E., and Williams, R. J. (1986). Learning internal representations by error propagation. In *Parallel Distributed Processing*, volume 1, pages 318–362. MIT Press.

Schmidhuber, J. H. (1991a). Learning to generate sub-goals for action sequences. In Kohonen, T., Mäkisara, K., Simula, O., and Kangas, J., editors, *Artificial Neural Networks*, pages 967–972. Elsevier Science Publishers B.V., North-Holland.

Schmidhuber, J. H. (1991b). Reinforcement learning in markovian and non-markovian environments. In Lippman, D. S., Moody, J. E., and Touretzky, D. S., editors, *Advances in Neural Information Processing Systems 3*, pages 500–506. San Mateo, CA: Morgan Kaufmann.

Schmidhuber, J. H. (1992). A fixed size storage $O(n^3)$ time complexity learning algorithm for fully recurrent continually running networks. *Neural Computation*, 4(2):243–248.

Singh, S. (1992). The efficient learning of multiple task sequences. In Moody, J., Hanson, S., and Lippman, R., editors, *Advances in Neural Information Processing Systems 4*, San Mateo, CA. Morgan Kaufmann. To appear.

Sutton, R. S. (1984). *Temporal Credit Assignment in Reinforcement Learning.* PhD thesis, University of Massachusetts, Dept. of Comp. and Inf. Sci.

Watkins, C. (1989). *Learning from Delayed Rewards.* PhD thesis, King's College.

Werbos, P. J. (1974). *Beyond Regression: New Tools for Prediction and Analysis in the Behavioral Sciences.* PhD thesis, Harvard University.

Williams, R. J. (1988). Toward a theory of reinforcement-learning connectionist systems. Technical Report NU-CCS-88-3, College of Comp. Sci., Northeastern University, Boston, MA.

Williams, R. J. (1989). Complexity of exact gradient computation algorithms for recurrent neural networks. Technical Report Technical Report NU-CCS-89-27, Boston: Northeastern University, College of Computer Science.

Williams, R. J. and Zipser, D. (1992, in press). Gradient-based learning algorithms for recurrent networks and their computational complexity. In *Back-propagation: Theory, Architectures and Applications.* Hillsdale, NJ: Erlbaum.

A Note on Rate-Sensitive Habituation

J.E.R. Staddon
Department of Psychology: Experimental
Duke University, Box 90086
Durham, North Carolina 27708-0086
djers@dukemvs.bitnet

ABSTRACT

The responses elicited by many stimuli diminish in strength with repeated stimulus presentation (*habituation*). This property is consistent with a model in which short-term memory for recent stimuli suppresses the current response. Habituation also depends on stimulus spacing: it occurs more rapidly when interstimulus intervals (ISIs) are short than when they are long -- but also recovers more rapidly after short interstimulus intervals. The effect of ISI on habituation rate is consistent with a simple one-stage process, but the effect of ISI on recovery rate seems to require a serial process in which two or more habituating units are cascaded, with earlier (peripheral) units in the series having shorter time constants than later (central) units.

People and rats show distinctive "startle" responses to unexpected loud sounds. Infant rats show distinctive "mouthing" responses to a small squirt of liquid food in their mouths. There are many stimuli that elicit reliable responses like this in most animal species. Unless the stimulus is actually harmful, the vigor and reliability of the response it elicits will eventually decrease as it is presented repeatedly. This waning of a response with repeated stimulus presentation is known as *habituation*[1].

Habituation is a much-studied phenomenon with a number of widely acknowledged properties (see reviews in Groves & Thompson, 1970; and Peeke & Petrinovich, 1984). In this note I describe a very simple process that can mimic several of these properties, most notably the rather puzzling way that habituation, and recovery from habituation, depends on the temporal spacing of stimuli.

The relevant properties are as follows:

1. Rate of habituation varies with the temporal distribution of stimulus presentations: it is slower the lower the rate of presentation of input stimuli. If stimuli are sufficiently infrequent, there is no habituation.

2. Rate of recovery after habituation is related to stimulation rate: when stimuli are presented at a rapid rate, rates of both habituation and recovery from habituation are rapid. When stimulation rate is low, both habituation rate and rate of recovery are slow (e.g., Davis, 1970). A related effect is that with repeated habituation interspersed with recovery periods, the same stimulus sequence produces more habituation each time it is repeated (Petrinovich, 1984).

3. Rate of habituation varies with motivational condition, e.g., a frightened animal will habituate more slowly to a novel sound; feeding-related responses habituate more slowly in hungry animals (Swithers-Mulvey, Miller, & Hall, 1991; Swithers-Mulvey & Hall, submitted).

4. Rates of habituation and recovery may be sensitive to the variance, as well as the mean, of the interstimulus intervals (Davis, 1970).

Note that all these properties are highly adaptive. The first property is consistent with the general truth that the environment is more likely to change as time passes. Hence, the significance (harmful vs. harmless) of a stimulus that is repeated is likely to depend on the time between repetitions. If the stimulus is repeated after a short time, the significance is more likely to be the same than if the stimulus is repeated after a longer time. The second property is consistent with the fact that it takes longer to be sure that a stimulus will not recur if the stimulus has been occurring at long intervals than if it has occurred at short intervals. The fourth property also follows from this argument: it is harder to be sure that a series of stimuli has ceased if the stimuli have been occurring at variable as opposed to fixed intervals (Staddon, 1988). The third property follows from the importance of consequences signaled by the stimuli and their prior probability. Thus, fear responses habituate more slowly in an already frightened animal because the prior expectation of harm is higher; feeding-related responses habituate more slowly in a hungry animal because the possible payoff (should the stimulus signal food) is higher.

[1]Strictly speaking, the effect may also be termed sensory *adaption*, if we can be sure that it takes place peripherally, at the sensory receptor level. The properties I discuss in this note are characteristic of a more central process, for which the term habituation is usually used.

1. Simple Habituation

It is easy to make a model for the basic property of habituation, i.e., for waning in response strength with repeated stimulus presentation. All that is required is negative feedback from the stimulus input to the response via some kind of integrator that accumulates the effects of past stimuli. The idea is that the net response to a stimulus is a function of the *difference* between a direct effect and an average that reflects past stimuli. When the average grows to equal the direct effect, responding ceases.

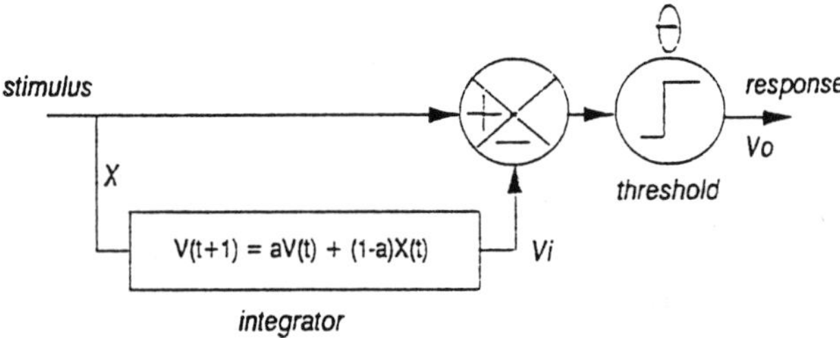

*Figure 1.*Habituation unit (HAB-1). The unit consists of an integrator (with time constant *a*), a summer and a threshold. A response occurs if V_o (= X- V_i) exceeds the threshold. For additional details, see text.

Innis & Staddon (1989) described a simple system along these lines. A slightly modified version, which I will call HAB-1, is shown in Figure 1. A quantity V_i, which is the short-term-memory (STM) of past stimulus inputs, is subtracted from the immediate effect of the current stimulus, denoted by a quantity X. In this version STM is implemented as a "leaky integrator," so that V_i is an exponentially weighted average of all the past inputs. The net output, V_o, is equal to the current input, X, minus integrated negative feedback, V_i. When V_i catches up with X, the net output of the system is zero. Response strength is just the suprathreshold amount of X-V_i. Because of the response threshold, habituation can occur even after responding has ceased ("inhibition below zero").

In discrete-time form, the equations for this system are

$$V_i(t+1) = aV_i(t) + (1-a)X(t), \qquad 0 < a < 1, \tag{1}$$

$$V_o = X - V_i, \text{ if } V_o > \theta \ (0 \le \theta), \tag{2}$$
$$= 0 \text{ otherwise}$$

where V_i is the integrated inhibitory effect of past stimuli, V_o is response strength, θ is a threshold and *a* is a *time constant* that reflects the period over which past stimuli contribute to habituation. If *a* is small, only recent stimuli contribute, and habituation is rapid if the stimulus spacing is short enough. If *a* is large, even stimuli that occurred a while ago contribute, habituation will occur even if stimuli are widely spaced, but habituation is slow.

The properties of this simple system are illustrated in Figure 2. Both panels show the stimulus presentations at the top (the row of "I"s); stimuli are closely spaced in the top panel, more widely spaced in the bottom panel. The filled squares show the response to successive stimulus presentations. Note that the amount of habituation is directly related to stimulus frequency: when stimuli are presented at frequent intervals (top), habituation is rapid and complete. But when they occur less frequently, habituation is much less --

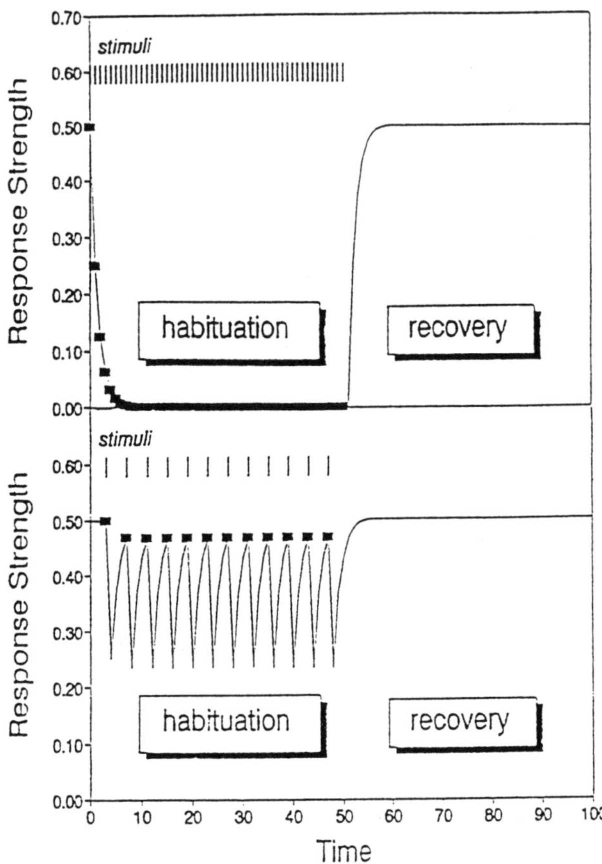

Figure 2. Habituation and recovery as a function of stimulus frequency. Filled squares: suprathreshold response strength, V_o; solid line: recovery envelope; |: stimulus presentations. *a* = 0.5; θ = 0. See text for details.

negligible in the bottom panel when a stimulus is presented only every fourth time unit.

The solid line in each panel shows the *recovery envelope*, that is, the response strength to be expected if a single "probe" stimulus were to be presented at any time. Thus, in the top graph, if a stimulus were to be presented at time 55 during the recovery period, the response strength would be 0.47. In the bottom graph, at time 55, response strength would be 0.498, i.e., almost complete recovery. At any time after about 60 in either graph (i.e., 10 or more time units after the last training stimulus), recovery is complete and a test stimulus yields a response at maximum strength (0.50). The time to complete recovery is short, and shorter after infrequent stimulation than after frequent stimulation.

Thus, a single-stage habituation process shows slower habituation to less frequent stimuli, and negligible habituation if the stimuli are infrequent enough. Slower habituation is consistent with the data, but the very rapid fall-off in habituation as stimulus spacing is increased is greater than what is typically observed. The major discrepancy, however, is that the single-stage model shows faster, rather than slower, recovery after less frequent stimuli.

2. Rate-Sensitive Habituation

In order to for habituation to occur even to intermittent stimuli, and to allow rate of stimulation to have the appropriate effect on recovery rate, it is necessary to have more than one unit, with different time constants. Units might be arranged either in parallel or in series. A parallel arrangement is illustrated in Figure 3. In this arrangement, the stimulus simultaneously affects several units, with different time constants. Thus, if stimuli occur at long interstimulus intervals (ISIs), short-time-constant units will recover completely in between stimulus presentation. Only the units with long time constants will become "charged up" (habituated), so that the level of habituation will be less than with short ISIs. There will nevertheless be some habituation to a range of stimulus spacings determined by the distribution of time constants across units. If there are few large a values, for example, the system will show little habituation at long ISIs.

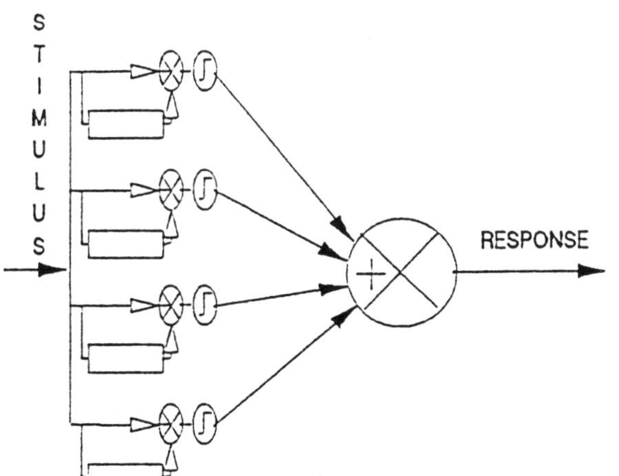

Figure 3. Parallel habituation units. Each unit corresponds to Figure 1; units have different time constants, a , and response strength is the summed output of all units.

The problem with a parallel arrangement is that recovery will be no slower after long-ISI stimulation than after short-ISI stimulation, because the long-time-constant units (which recover slowly) will always show some habituation even at short ISIs. A serial arrangement has properties much closer to the data. Figure 4 shows two units in series, with the more peripheral unit having the shorter time constant. This is a plausible idea: sensory adaptation is more rapid than central habituation, for example, and the idea that dual processes with different time constants are involved in habituation is an old one (e.g., Davis, 1970; Hinde, 1970). In a serial arrangement, the output of peripheral units constitutes the input for central units, but all units are simultaneously active. (McClelland, 1979, in a slightly different context, has discussed the logic of what he calls "cascaded" arrangements like this.) In the arrangement in Figure 4 (HAB-2), the peripheral units act like low-pass filters for the central units. When stimuli occur frequently, the peripheral units soon habituate (see Figure 2, top), thus limiting the input to more central units, which therefore habituate little. Hence, recovery after short-ISI training is determined primarily by the peripheral units. Since the peripheral units have short time constants, recovery after short ISIs is rapid. Conversely, when the ISI is long, the peripheral units have time to recover in between stimuli hence habituate little (see Figure 2, bottom), so that most habituation is attributable to the more central units with longer time constants. Recovery after long ISIs is attributable largely to the central units and is therefore slow.

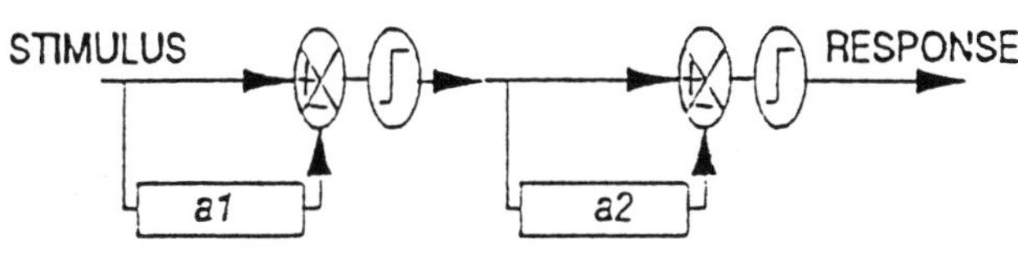

Figure 4. Serial habituation units (HAB-2). Each unit corresponds to Figure 1, and the output of the peripheral unit (time constant a_1,) constitutes the input for the central unit (time constant a_2). The peripheral unit has a smaller time constant that the central unit: $a_1 < a_2$.

These properties are illustrated in Figure 5, which is similar to Figure 2. As before, the stimuli are shown at the top and the output response strength is the filled squares. The solid line indicates the recovery envelope. The open squares show the output of the peripheral unit (the input to the central unit).

Look first at the top panel, where the stimuli occur at short intervals. The open squares show that the peripheral unit habituates rapidly, so that there is no output to the central unit after three or four stimulus presentations. Hence, recovery is rapid, because it is governed by the short-time-constant peripheral unit. Conversely, when ISI is long, as in the bottom panel, the peripheral unit hardly habituates at all (open squares) so that most of the system habituation is attributable to the central unit. Hence, recovery is slow: at time 55 in the top panel, a stimulus would elicit a response with strength 0.442, whereas at the same time in the bottom panel, response strength would be only 0.407. Thus, the effect of ISI on recovery in the two-unit model is exactly the reverse of its effect in the one-unit model: recovery is slower at long ISIs than at short ISIs.

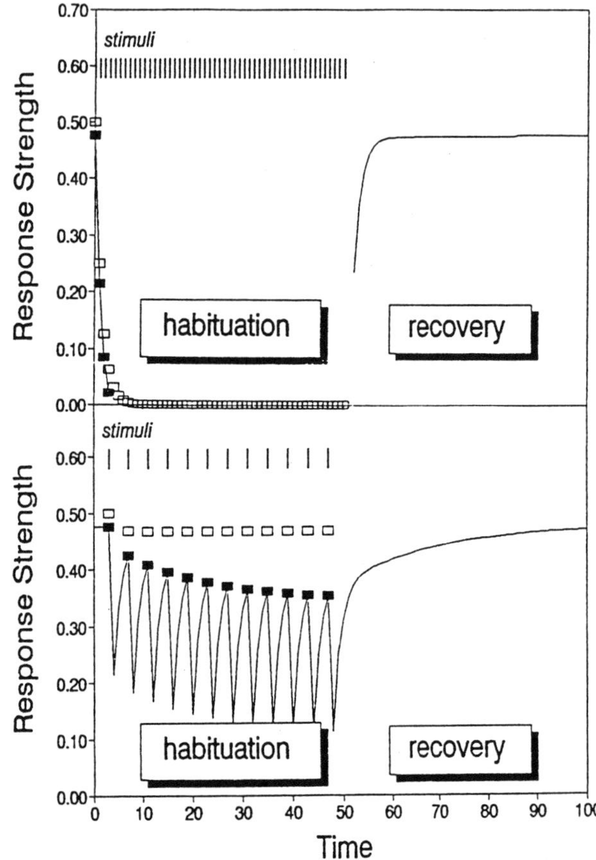

Figure 5. Habituation and recovery as a function of stimulus frequency in the two-unit serial arrangement shown in Figure 4. Open squares: output of the peripheral unit; filled squares: suprathreshold response strength (output of the central unit); |: stimuli; $a_1 = 0.5$, $a_2 = 0.95$, $\theta_1 = \theta_2 = 0$. Solid line: recovery envelope.

Figure 5 shows that this system accounts for properties 1 and 2 in the list I gave at the beginning. Property 4, slower recovery following a series of variable ISIs than following the same number of fixed ISIs with the same mean, is not easily accommodated, however. Simulations show that what is gained on the swings -- greater habituation of the central units after longer ISIs -- is more or less lost on the roundabouts -- less habituation of the central units following shorter ISIs. Thus, sensitivity to ISI variance may require nonlinear integrators -- or a more complex, associative process.

Note that if the stimulus spacing is wide enough to allow the central integrator to discharge fully in between stimulus presentations, the system never habituates (Property 1). Thus, the ability of the system to habituate to widely spaced stimuli is always limited by the time constant of the central unit.

This system suggests several ways for motivation (Property 3) to enter in. Motivational effects could occur via thresholds or via direct effects on time constants. For example, if we are dealing with a hunger-related response, such as the infant-rat "mouthing" behavior studied by Swithers-Mulvey and Hall, hunger, or stomach loading, might raise the output thresholds of all units. In this case most of the habituation will be done by peripheral units, with short time constants, so that overall habituation will be reduced, especially if stimuli are widely spaced (are the effects of hunger on habituation rate increased if stimuli are infrequent?). If hunger directly reduces all time constants, the effect will be similar.

Swithers-Mulvey and Hall (submitted) have recently shown how this system can shed light on the feeding patterns of infant rats. These animals habituate to brief oral infusions of liquid diet, and habituation is rate-sensitive in the way I have described. Swithers-Mulvey and Hall argue that this habituation process is largely responsible for willingness to eat in these animals. They assume that eating will be initiated, during the recovery phase, when the recovery envelope exceeds a threshold. They show that when food is freely available, the model mimics some aspects of the usual pattern of eating in "meals" -- brief episodes that occur at longer and longer time intervals after a period of deprivation.

The mechanism is as follows. As the "animal" eats in the presence of free food, the peripheral unit rapidly habituates, which causes a pause in eating. When the peripheral unit recovers, and eating resumes, the central unit begins to habituate. As this process is repeated, the central unit habituates more and more at the beginning of each eating episode and eventually suppresses eating entirely. Thus, the within- and between-meal spacings are jointly determined by the thresholds and time constants of the units. An example of the eating pattern produced in the presence of ad lib. food is shown in Figure 6.

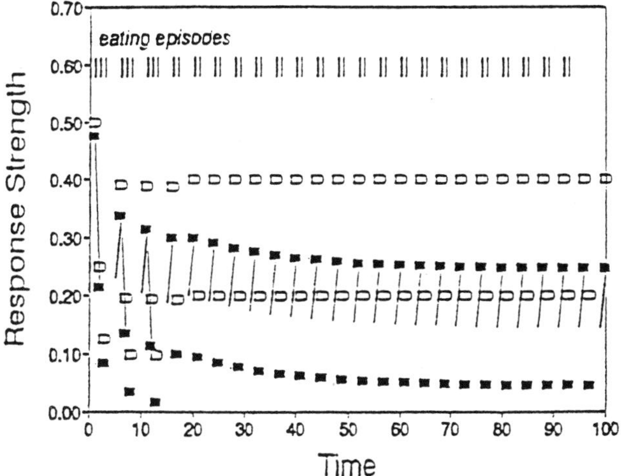

Figure 6. Eating in bouts explained by two-stage habituation (after Swithers-Mulvey & Hall, submitted). Food is continuously available; eating occurs when the recovery function (solid ine) exceeds a threshold. $\theta_2 = 0.1$. Other details as in Figure 5. See text for explanation.

It is easy to see that this same process will produce greater and greater habituation to the same training sequence as the sequence is repeatedly presented at intervals long enough to allow for some recovery (Property 2). At the beginning of each new training series, the slow, central units receive an additional "charge" which (if the central time constant is large enough) can accumulate from one training series to the next and produce progressively greater habituation each time.

The system described here can be modified in a number of ways if this particular version fails to match quantitative features of data. For example, habituation at long ISIs is more complete if the second-stage unit receives input even when no stimulus is present; I have not explored this possibility in detail. I have also described only two units, in series. Such a simple system shows a discernible "break point" in its recovery curve (see Figure 5). But it is obvious that given normal variability, such a break point might be hard to discover in practice -- and three or more units in series might well give smooth, apparently exponential, curves with no measurable break point. The main point of this note is to argue that the rate-sensitive property of habituation seems to require a serial process that involves at least two sets of concatenated units with time constants ordered such that the more rapidly habituating units are peripheral and provide the inputs to slower central units.

Acknowledgments

This work was first presented in the Biological Psychology Group at Duke University in April 1990. I am grateful to Ted Hall and Jennifer Higa for comments on earlier versions. Research supported by grants from the NSF and NIMH to Duke University. Correspondence should be addressed to J. E. R. Staddon, Department of Psychology: Experimental, Duke University, Durham, NC 27707 USA.

References

Davis, M. (1970) Effects of interstimulus interval length and variability on startle-response habituation in the rat. *Journal of Comparative and Physiological Psycholo gy*, 72, 177-192.

Groves, P. M., & Thompson, R. F. (1970) Habituation: A dual-process theory. *Psychological Review, 77*, 419-440.

Hinde, R. A. (1970) Behavioural habituation. In G. Horne & R. A. Hinde (Eds.) *Short-term changes in neural activity and behaviour.* Cambridge: Cambridge University Press.

Innis, N. K., & Staddon, J. E. R. (1989) What should comparative psychology compare? *International Journal of Comparative Psychology, 2*, 145-156.

McClelland, J. L. (1979) On the time relations of mental processes: An examination of systems of processes in cascade. *Psychological Review, 86*, 287-330.

Peeke, H. V. S., & Petronovich, L. Eds. (1984) *Habituation, sensitization and behavior.* New York: Academic Press.

Petrinovich, L. (1984) A theory of habituation and sensitiza tion. In Peeke, H. V. S., & Petronovich, L. Eds. *Habituation, sensitization and behavior.* New York: Academic Press. Pp. 17-55.

Staddon, J. E. R. (1988) Learning as inference. In R. C. Bolles, & M.D. Beecher (Eds.) *Evolution and learning*. Hillsdale, NJ: Erlbaum. Pp. 59- 77.

Swithers-Mulvey, S. E., & Hall, W. G. (1992) Oral experience as the source of satiety. Submitted

Swithers-Mulvey, S. E., Miller, G. L., & Hall, W. G. (1991) Habituation of oromotor responding to oral infusions in rat pups. *Appetite, 17*, 55-67.

COGNITIVE MAPS
AND INTERNAL WORLD MODELS

Categorization, Representations, and the Dynamics of System-Environment Interaction: a case study in autonomous systems

Paul F.M.J. Verschure, Rolf Pfeifer.
AI lab, Institute for Informatics, University of Zürich,
Winterthurerstrasse 190, CH- 8057 Zürich,
Switzerland.
e-mail: verschur/pfeifer@ifi.unizh.ch

Abstract

Since the world is partly an unpredictable place the agents that have to function in it have to rely on learning to adjust to it. To understand the adaptive properties of autonomous agents, that are related to their learning capacities, it is necessary to explore what they exactly learn. In order to do this we will further analyse an autonomous agent designed according to the methodology of distributed adaptive control. It is shown by means of a simulation study that the mappings between sensing and acting the system acquires through its interaction with the environment are topology preserving. Moreover, on the basis of these results it is shown that these mappings implement action related prototypes. This is demonstrated by translating the mapping back into world coordinates. Based on these results an extension of the model is proposed that illustrates another aspect of our methodology; stretching a model. To overcome some limitations of Hebbian learning, which is crucial for the self-organizing properties of the model, an expectancy mechanism is included in the control architecture. This allows the development of mechanisms that influence the categorization process independently of immediate sensory states. This can be seen as a necessary next step to come to a closer definition of the concept of representation in the context of autonomous agents.

1. Introduction

In Verschure et al. (1992) and Pfeifer and Verschure (1992a) we have presented a methodology for developing control architectures for autonomous agents, distributed adaptive control. It was shown how a system based on this methodology could develop adaptive behavior in simple navigation tasks involving target approach and obstacle avoidance. Moreover, the system showed emergent behaviors that resulted from the system-environment interaction, e.g. 'anticipation' and 'wall following'. Moreover, in Almassy and Verschure (1992) it was demonstrated that this model is robust over a large parameter domain. In contrast to other reinforcement learning schemes this approach is based on a local association mechanism which displays topology preserving mappings of the system-environment interaction. In this paper we will analyse the mappings the system develops in order to understand the behavior it generates. This will allow us to develop a further understanding of the concept of "representation". We want to illustrate that a mapping is on one hand an expression of a sense-act coupling and on the other not a static but a dynamic entity whose formation is action dependent. Representations, that are build up out of these mappings, must be taken as properties of a system that are independent of immediate sensory states. We will explore this property of representations by introducing an "expectancy" loop into the control structure.

2. Learning and categorization

Our approach is based on several assumptions: 1) The real world is only partially knowable and only partially predictable. Therefore, there cannot be a predefined body of knowledge that approximates the relevant properties of the real world. 2) The world does not consist of a collection of objects and events. These notions can only be defined in connection to the interaction between a system and the world. 3) The input to the system does not consist of discretely changing input vectors, but of gradually varying sensory states. 4) There is a *need to act*. The system is under time pressure to act in the world (see Verschure, 1992, and Pfeifer and Verschure (1992b) for a more elaborate treatment and a comparison to other approaches).

From these assumptions it follows that we have to conceive of autonomous agents as learning systems. This raises the question *when* and *why* a system should learn. Assumption 1) answers the why question. It does not imply, however, that *nothing* can be foreseen in advance. For instance, what the food looks like that a specific animal feeds on can be foreseen from the phylogenetic perspective of its genetic setup. Where it is exactly located in the environment, however, cannot be predefined. From this perspective it is reasonable to assume that, roughly speaking, the sensors are "prespecified", they determine the potential sensory states. How this space is filled in, how categorization takes place, depends on the experience at run time. The empirical fact that the genetic code has only a limited coding capacity and can therefore not be expected to code a complete body of knowledge might therefore imply that instead of being 'short on memory' the genetic code only predefines what can be predefined and will leave dealing with uncertainty in the real world to ontogenetic mechanisms for adaptation and learning (see also Harley, 1981; Verschure, 1992).

3. Distributed adaptive control

The agent we will consider is developed according to the design methodology of distributed adaptive control (Verschure et al., 1992) which is related to a distributed self-organizing model of the behavioral phenomenon of classical conditioning (Verschure and Coolen, 1991). We will base our example on a simulated agent that has to learn to avoid obstacles and locate food sources in an environment.The basic setup of the agent is given by its value scheme (Edelman, 1989, McFarland, 1992) which can be seen as genetically predefined. The value scheme defines the properties of the sensors and effectors, the morphology of the system, the structure of the control architecture, and the mechanisms for changing the properties of this structure. Moreover, it defines some basic reflexes, like if the system collides to the right it will reverse and turn to the left. This provides the system with a coarse adaptation to the environment. These reflexes consist of prewired relationships between primitive sensors of the system and its actions. The way in which they are activated by the system environment interaction will initially completely determine the actions the agent will take. To enable the system to adapt to the exact properties of its interaction with the environment it is equipped with a sophisticated sensor which responds to properties of the environment extended beyond the morphology of the system. The integration of this sensor in the actions of the system will lead to a finetuned adaptation to the system-environment interaction. This integration process can be seen as the development of a specific categorization of this interaction. The value scheme constrains this categorization process as will be further explained below. It is important to note that the control architecture defined by the value scheme must be seen as a structure with specific spatial properties. Before elaborating on the nature of this categorization process the properties of the agent used in the present simulation study will be described (Figure 1).

Sensors: The agent has three sensors: range finder (the sophisticated sensor), collision sensors, and target sensors (the primitive sensors). The range finder spans over -90° and 90° from the centre of the robot. It consists of 37 elements that each cover a part of this receptive field. The receptive fields of each of these elements, their angular resolution, decrease when they get closer to the centre of the agent. Each element of the range finder represents the average distance detected in its visual field. The system has 37 collision sensors that cover the same region as the range finder. The two target sensors are placed at -90° and 90° degrees from the centre of the robot. They can be seen as being sensitive to a gradient of a specific quality, like a sound or odour diffused through the environment by a target. The difference between the states of the two target sensors indicates the direction of the target from the center of the agent.

Actions: The agent can perform 4 actions: "turn left", "turn right", "reverse", and "advance". The avoidance actions consist of a "reverse" action followed by a turn. The approach actions consist of only a turn. The default action of

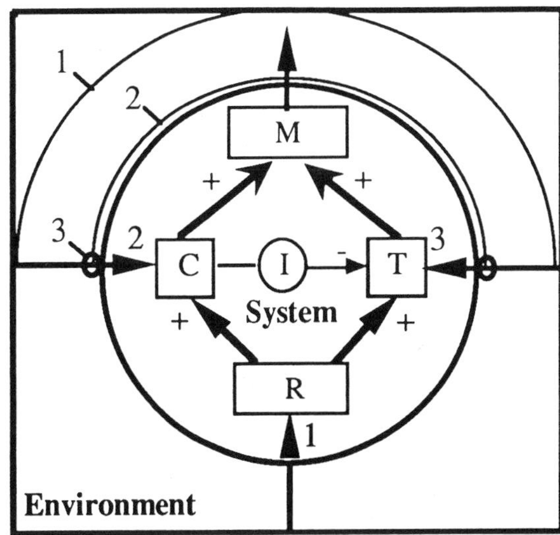

Figure 1: The sensors, morphology, and the control architecture of the agent: 1, receptive field of the range finder. 2, area covered by collision sensors. 3, target sensors. RF receives input from the range finder. C receives input from the collision sensors. T receives input from the target sensors. M is the group of command units. I is the inhibitory unit. + indicates an excitatory connection, - represents an inhibitory connection.

the system is to advance. The system can only make turns over 9°.

Control: The control architecture consists of four neural groups and one inhibitory unit. The first group (RF) which consists of 37 units receives its input from the elements of the range finder. The continuous activation a_i of each unit i is determined by the inverse value of a corresponding unit r_i in the range finder. In this way these units code a measure for 'time to contact' (Lee, 1976). The transduction function that transforms range finder states into RF states is given by:

$$s_j = f(r_j) = \frac{1}{e^{x(r_j - d^{max})}} \tag{1}$$

Where d^{max} determines at what distance from the sensor a maximal response will be given and x is a scaling factor. In the presented experiments d^{max} was set to 30 while x was set to 0.1.

The second group (C), which consists of 37 units, receives its input from the collision sensors. As in the case of RF there is a one to one mapping between units of C and collision sensors. If one collision sensor is triggered the corresponding unit of C will receive an input of 1. The third group (T), consisting of two units, relates to the difference between the intensities detected by the two target sensors. If the value of the right target sensor is lower then the value of the left one the first unit will receive an input of 1 and vice versa. Next to the input from a specific primitive sensor the units of both these groups also receive input from RF. This

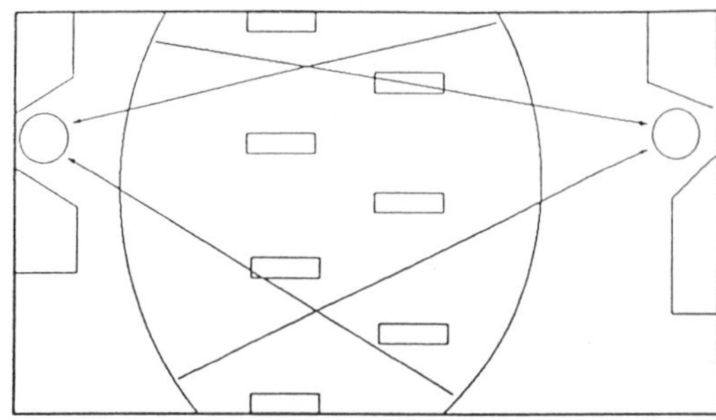

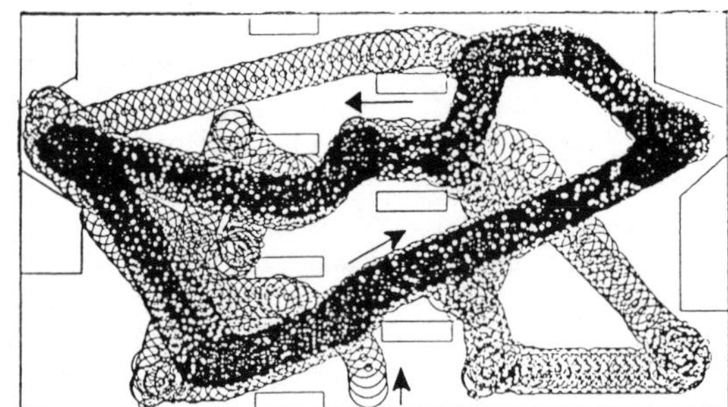

Figure 2: a: The environment, see text for explanation. b: Trace of the behavior during 5000 steps, arrows indicate the direction of movement.

input is modulated by the weights of the projections from RF to C and T. The input or local field, h_i^λ, to the units of C and T is defined as:

$$(2) \quad h_i^\lambda = c_i^\lambda + \sum_{j=1}^{N} K_{ij}^\lambda s_j$$

Here λ indexes the groups C and T, c_i^λ denotes the input from the related specialized sensor, c_i^λ {0, 1}, s_j the activation of the units in RF, s_j [0, 1], and K_{ij}^λ the weight of the projections of RF to T and C. These weights are updated according to:

$$(3) \quad \Delta K_{ij}^\lambda = \frac{1}{N}\left[\eta\ s_i^\lambda s_j - \varepsilon \bar{s}^\lambda K_{ij}^\lambda\right]$$

Where N defines the number of units in RF, η the learning rate, ε the decay rate, and $\bar{s}^C$ the average activation in group λ. $\bar{s}^C$ introduces an active decay: decay will only take place when other connections increase in strength.

Next there is a special unit I that regulates the relation between C and T. This unit will inhibit the output of T. It will not inhibit the activity of this group. Activation in C will increase the activation, a, of I.

$$(4) \quad a(t+1) = \alpha a(t) + \beta\left(\frac{1}{N^c}\sum_{i=1}^{N^c} S_i(t)\right)$$

α denotes the decay rate, β the excitation rate, N^C the number of elements of C, and s_i^C the activity of element i of C. The output function of the inhibitory element is binary, i.e. inhibition of T only takes place if the activation value of the inhibitory unit exceeds a threshold.

The actions are coded by a set of command units in group M which consists of 5 elements.

The relations between the T, C and M are prewired. A collision to the left will automatically trigger a "reverse-and-turn-right" action (and symmetrically for collisions to the right). If the target is detected to the left of the system a "turn-left" action will be executed. If the target is detected to the right the system will turn to the right. One unit in C or T can trigger a unit in M. The groups C and T can be defined in two clusters of units each dependent on the unit in M to which they project: e.g. all units of C that are connected to collision sensor located at 90° to 0° from the center of the agent project to the "reverse-turn-left" command unit.

Since the activations of all units in the system can only have positive values learning is expressed in the development of excitatory connections between RF and C and T. Also the connections between C and T and M are excitatory. The inhibitory unit, however, implements a specialized inhibitory circuit.

4. An experiment

In the experiment we consider the system is supposed to find food in the environment depicted in Figure 2a. The size and location of the targets is indicated by a circle. The system can sense the targets at the distance indicated with the large circles. A target is found by the agent when it touches it. If a target is found it will disappear from the environment. It will reappear if the target at the other side of the environment is found. In the experiment the agent has 5000 steps to find as many targets as possible with the parameter settings η = 0.1, ε = 0.9 and all thresholds, except for I, set to 0.5. The threshold of the inhibitory unit is set to 0.15. In this case the agent found a total of 32 targets while colliding

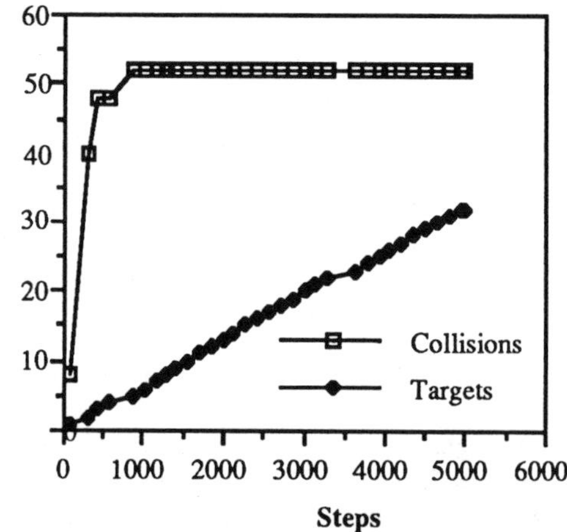

Figure 3: The cumulative number of collisions and targets found over time.

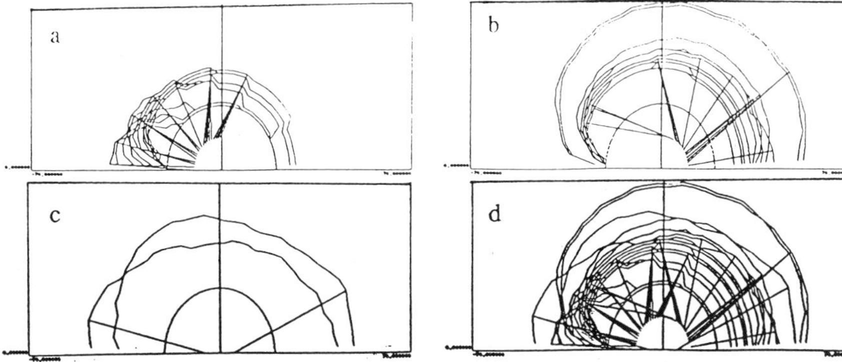

Figure 4: Profiles after 700 steps: see text for explanation. a: profiles related to "avoid-turn-right-actions". b: profiles related to "avoid-turn-left-actions". c: profiles related to "approach". d: all profiles.

52 times. The complete trace of the trajectory followed by the agent is depicted in Figure 2b (arrows indicate the direction of movement). Figure 3 lists the number of collisions and targets found over time.

5. Explaining the behavior

We will now try to explain the behavior of the agent by focusing on the mapping that resulted from the integration of RF into the actions of the system. This mapping expresses the history of the interaction with the environment. To do this the distance profiles detected by the range finder will be determined that trigger the units of C and T given a particular matrix K^{λ}. These profiles are calculated as follows. As described earlier each unit in C and T can on its own trigger the command neuron to which it is connected. The prototypical patterns of RF leading to activation of the units of C and T are estimated by assuming a uniform contribution of all units of RF to h^{λ}. Since the threshold of each of the units of C and T was set to 0.5 the contribution of each unit of RF to the local fields of the units of C and T is, given the assumption of uniform contributions, 0.0135 (0.5 \ 37). Using (2) we can now determine the activation of the units of RF where we take h_i as given, 0.0135, and determine s_j according to: $s_j = h_i/K_{ij}^{\lambda}$. With the activation of unit j of RF known we can determine the distance, d_j, that due to the transduction function (1) will lead to this activation level in j by $d_j = \ln(s_j)/-x + d^{max}$. In this way a set of distance profiles can be generated that relate to the distances that must be perceived by the elements of the range finder to trigger the units of C and T.

In Figure 4 the profiles related to the weights as developed after 700 steps are depicted. Here a distinction is made between the distance profiles related to the cluster of C units for avoid turn right (Figure 4A) and avoid turn left (Figure 4B), and between the T units for approach turn left and approach turn right (Figure 4C), and for the complete collection of distance profiles (Figure 4D).

The half circle in the lower middle part of the figures indicates the morphology of the agent. The lines surrounding it represent the distance profiles. Each of these profiles is connected to the unit of C or T to which it is related through K^C or K^T respectively. For each unit a line is drawn to the related profile at the point where the distance is maximal. Some profiles related to the C units fall back to the surface of the agent. This indicates that the distance detected by the units of RF at those locations should be smaller than the size of the agent (which is 20) to lead to the uniform input to the related unit of C. This implies that these profiles will not be able to trigger these units of C with a uniform contribution of all units of RF. These units of C can, however, become activated when the distances detected fall within the profile (i.e. are closer to the agent) since this will, due to (1), give rise to a higher activation in RF.

The figures indicate that the projections of RF to C and T are topology preserving. Given the one to one mapping between the primitive sensors and C and T described earlier this property is conserved in the development of the weights. For instance, the left most unit of C receives its primitive input for the left most collision sensor. Initially an association between this unit and RF can, given (2), only be established when the input from the related collision sensor, c_i, is 1. Since this collision sensor is the outmost left one the profile on RF that will be associated with this unit of C will be related to situations where a collision is detected at this location; where physical contact to an obstacle is established. This property of the system will be discussed further in the next section.

To get an impression of the dynamics of the mapping the agent forms Figure 5 depicts the same projections but now after 5000 steps.

When we compare Figure 5A to 4A it becomes clear that between steps 700 and 5000 the profiles related to the cluster of units of C that trigger "avoid-turn-right-actions" have decreased in strength. These profiles are less extended to the right of the agent and fall back earlier. Comparing 5B and 4B indicates that the profiles relating to "avoid-turn-left-

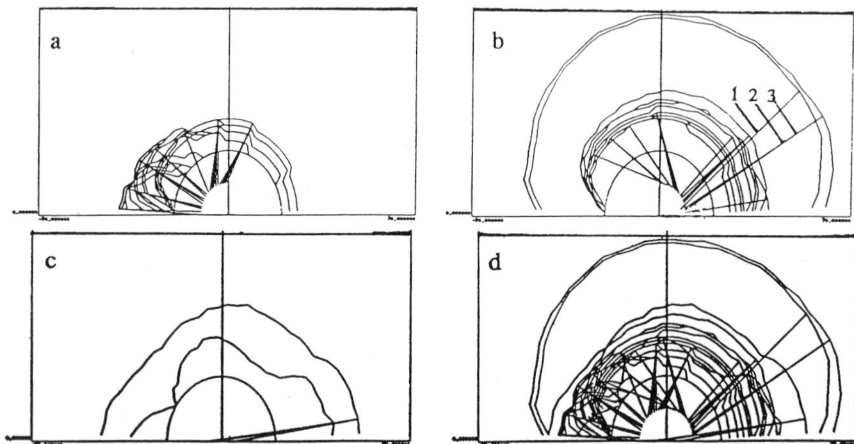

Figure 5: Profiles after 5000 steps: see text for explanation. a: profiles related to "avoid-turn-right-actions". b: profiles related to "avoid-turn-left-actions". c: profiles related to "approach". d: all profiles.

actions" increased their dominance. Especially, the three units of this cluster of units of C, indicated in Figure 3B with 1, 2, and 3, have strongly extended profiles, which dominate all others (see also 4D and 5D).

Comparing 4C and 5C indicates that the same trend holds for both the units that relate to approach actions. This trend implies that the avoidance behavior is dominated by "avoid-turn-left" actions, while approach is dominated by "turn-left" actions.

The competition of the profiles to dominate the actions of the system can be explained by the dynamics of the learning rule (2) and the interaction with the environment. If a specific association develops the actual states of RF and the learned distance profile can become less and less similar to activate the relevant units of C or T. This can be seen as a generalization process. If a unit of C or T is activated solely by a state of RF this will lead to a self-reinforcement of the underlying weights. This implies that mappings that relate to structural properties of the system-environment interaction and that are developed relatively early will tend to dominate the actions of the system due to self-reinforcement. This self-reinforcement is an direct result of the Hebbian learning rule (3) used.

To further illustrate the generalization capability of the agent Figure 6a and b depicts the profiles that relate to one of the dominant units (unit 3) of C after 700 and 5000 steps. In these projections the profiles are calculated for a decreasing number of contributing units.

The outer profile represents the distances that must be detected to get a uniform non-zero contribution of 34 of the 37 RF units to trigger this C unit (in this case 3 units of RF are not active). The inner profile relates to a non-zero contribution of only 1 unit of RF. The small lines on the profiles indicate the minimal number of units of RF that must be activated by the distance profile to lift this C unit above threshold.

6. Action prototypes and topology preservation

The mappings formed between RF and C and T are topology preserving. This is an interesting property because the network itself does not contain any topological information (i.e. there is no distance metric expressed in lateral connections encoding neighbourhood relations like in a Kohonen network, Kohonen, 1987). It is due to the fact that there is a one-to-one mapping between the primitive sensors and C and T. More important, collision sensors and RF units are morphologically arranged such that when a collision sensor fires there is typically activation in the physical vicinity of this C unit in RF. Since this occurs when learning is taking place the mapping preserves the topology. In other words the topology is preserved not because there is topological information in the network but because of the morphology of the robot, i.e. the physical arrangement of the sensors and the structure of the control architecture.

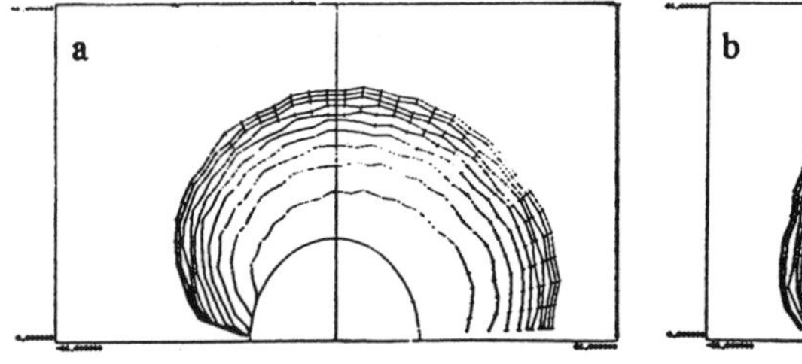

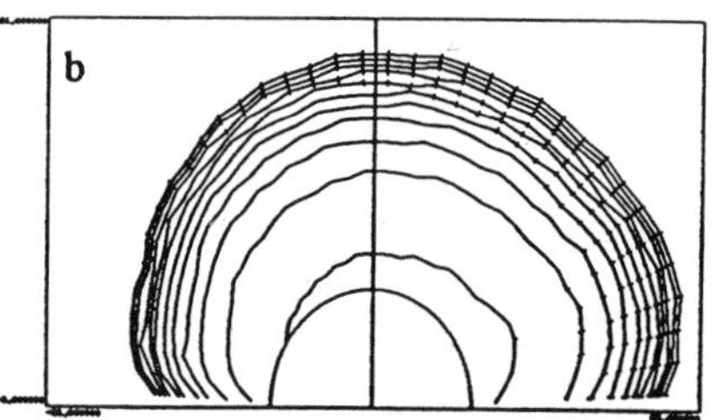

Figure 6: Profiles for dominant C unit for varying contributions from RF after 700 and 5000 steps: See text for explanation.

The mappings formed by the system of the interaction with the environment consists of two elements. On one hand there is an action component which is initially automatically triggered by specific clusters of C and T related to the primitive sensors. On the other, due to learning this action component will be transferred to states of RF that systematically relate to states of the primitive sensors. These mappings encode the set of distance profiles that through the units of C and T connect to a specific action. Two aspects of the mappings of the system can be distinguished. First, a meaning component (action) and second, a content component (the sets of distance profiles). The first component is given by the value scheme. The exact properties of the second component are dependent on the specifics of the system environment interaction. The coupling of these two components leads to a set of action prototypes. On the basis of these prototypes sensory states are classified. This implies that from the perspective of the agent an event or stimulus is defined as a sense-act coupling expressed in the action prototypes. This implies that we can only speak of an "event" or "stimulus" from the perspective of the dynamics of the interaction between the agent and its environment.

It is important to note that the depicted profiles only give an estimate of the content of the action prototypes. On the one hand the assumption of uniform input from RF to C and T will seldom be satisfied in the interaction with the environment. At some points the distance might be higher while at others it can be smaller. The profiles, in this respect, represent an average over a set of possible configurations. Moreover, also the units of the range finder determine the average distance in their receptive field. Again a larger set of environmental conditions can be expressed in this average value. As an estimate of the size of the set of environmental configurations we can calculate the binomial coefficient for the profiles depicted in Figure 6. To give an impression of the number of different configurations of environmental conditions expressed in the profiles this coefficient is depicted in Figure 7 for the profiles depicted in Figure 6b. The contributing units expresses the number of units participating in the profile (which is dependent on their capability to deliver the uniform input to C). The units needed express the number of units that must be active in RF to trigger the C unit.

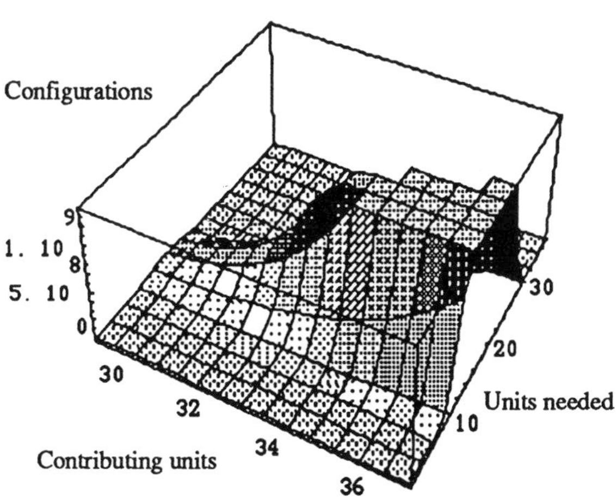

Figure 7: The number of configurations of environmental conditions expressed in the prototypes: see text for explanation.

Figure 7 indicates that the class of stimulus configurations encoded in the mapping the agent develops is very large.

7. Representations

To be able to talk about representations the relevant mappings must be independent of the immediate sensory states. As a first step towards developing representations in the presented control architecture an expectancy mechanism is introduced. The introduction of this mechanism is based on the observation that the system needs a mechanism that allows it to develop a flexibility in its behavior and counteract the strong dominance that can be the result of the earlier described self-reinforcement of a subset of the action prototypes.

This step is an example of the evolutionary design strategy that we try to adopt: a system with a specific behavioral potential is defined by a value scheme and translated into a structure. Next, this system is put in an environment and its behavior is evaluated in a systematic way (e.g. Almassy and Verschure, 1992). On the basis of these observations an additional property is added to the structure in order to improve its adaptive behavior. The structure that is added, however, must be designed in relation to the already existing structures and be embedded in it. We could say that the model is *stretched* and not extended with a new module (as would be the case in, for instance, subsumption based architectures, Brooks, 1986).

The mechanism embedded in the existing structure implements an "expectancy" loop. The mechanism used is based on a reentrant mapping (Edelman, 1989) were the activation in C and T is projected back onto RF modulated by K^{λ}. This projection, however, has an inhibitory effect on RF: units of RF are inhibited by the input they receive from C and T. This introduces a matching process that results in a state of RF that is the difference between the immediate sensory input, coming from the range finder elements, and the action prototype related to the executed action which is expressed in the interconnectivity of RF with C and T. The dynamics of this matching process has the following elements. First, the state of RF is projected onto C and T, which after sufficient learning experiences will result in activation in these groups. Second, this activation in C and T is projected onto M and results in an action. Concurrently the state of C and T is projected back onto RF and is matched against the state of RF. Only mismatching states remain. Figure 8 depicts the dynamics of this reentrant mapping.

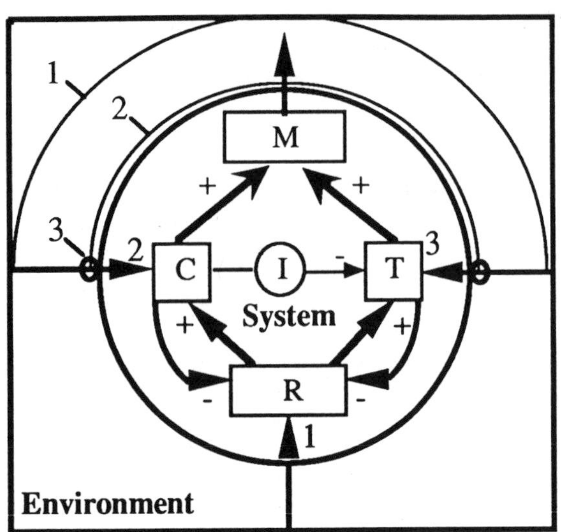

Figure 8: Dynamics of the expectancy loop: See Figure 1 and text for explanation.

Matching mechanisms are well known in the neural network literature (e.g. Grossberg, 1980). An important distinction between the present proposal and others is that in this case the constraint of acting in real time is taken seriously. This implies that in our case, opposed to for instance Grossberg's proposal, the matching process is not used to cycle through a set of "representations" in order to find the rightone. This matching process, proposed in adaptive resonance theory, will lead to a system that is not able to act in real time. A lot of processing time is invested in a matching process which must be completely finished before the system can classify the stimulus. The matching process we propose influences the association process, and not the immediate classification necessary to act.

The matching process is implemented as follows. The input to unit j of RF, h^-_j, projected back form units i of C and T is defined by:

$$(5) \qquad h_j^- = \sum_{i=1}^{N^\lambda} K_{ij}^\lambda s_i^\lambda$$

The activation, s_j, of unit j in RF now becomes:

$$(6) \qquad s_j = s_j - h_j^-$$

In the case that h^-_j is bigger than s_j, s_j will be reset to 0. When the activation of RF is reset according to (6) the learning rule, (3), is applied.

Figure 9 shows the behavior of an agent based on this stretched architecture in the same task and with the same parameters as described earlier.

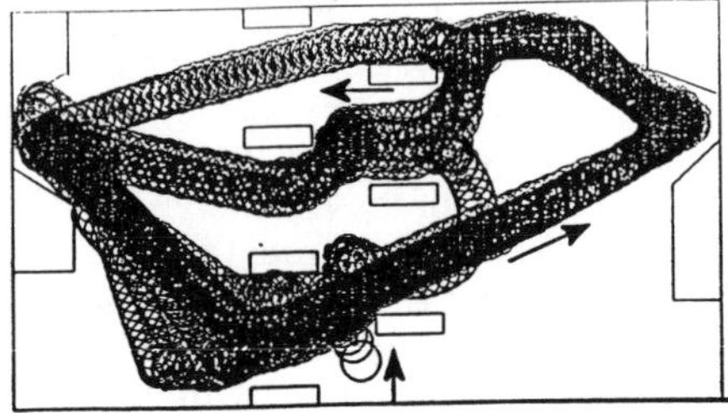

Figure 9: The expectancy loop, trace of the behavior during 5000 steps.

In this case the agent collided 45 times and found 45 targets (without expectancy these results were 52 and 32 respectively, see Figure 3).

To understand the improvement in behavior of the agent Figure 10 lists the distance profiles after 5000 steps.

In this case there is a clear symmetry is displayed in the profiles. Both avoid actions as well as approach actions have a significant specificity. Whereas, the model before stretching would loose its flexibility and limit its behavioral repertoire to a subset of its initial action the stretched model maintains its complete behavioral potential.

8. Discussion

In this paper we develop a further definition of the notions "categorization" and "representation" in the context of distributed adaptive control. This exploration was based on concrete examples. Although some might argue that simulations are not concrete enough we consider these

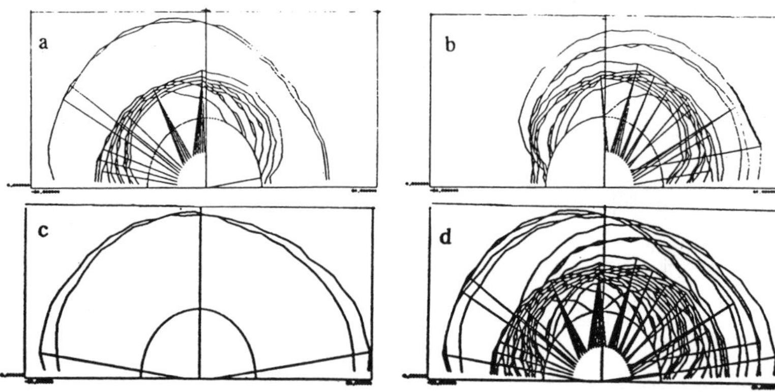

Figure 10: The expectancy loop, profiles after 5000 steps: see text for explanation. a: profiles related to "avoid-turn-right-actions". b: profiles related to "avoid-turn-left-actions". c: profiles related to "approach". d: all profiles.

studies sufficient to explore the properties of mechanisms that control the behavior autonomous agents. These explorations must of course be complemented with experiments with real robots. Some preliminary explorations with distributed adaptive control have been successfully performed (Van Aeken and Sinnaeve, 1992).

Several conclusions can be drawn. First, topology preserving maps of the system-environment interaction develop due to the morphological properties of an agent. Second, These mappings, or action prototypes, express a sense-act relationship. This implies that the notion "stimulus" or "event" can only be understood from the perspective of this acquired sense-act relationship: the history of the system-environment interaction expressed in the interconnectivity of RF and C and T. We could say that without actions there are no events. Third, representations can only be understood if the physical properties of the agent, its morphology and the properties of its sensors, are taken into account. Fourth, by introducing adaptive mechanisms that are independent of immediate sensory states, but express the learning history of the system, a self-organizing learning mechanism can be stabilized: self-reinforcement of connections is counteracted and the agent maintains its full action repertoire. Further, the described models form an illustration of an evolutionary design methodology where a model is stretched instead of modules added.

The proposed expectancy mechanism needs to be further explored. It can, however, be seen as a first step towards autonomous agents that develop representations of their interaction with the environment as a result of a bootstrapping process (see also Edelman, 1989). This property, from our perspective, is necessary, contrary to other suggestions (e.g. Brooks, 1991), in order to reach a point where autonomous agents can make the leap to new domains of behavior beyond obstacle-avoidance and target-approach.

Acknowledgements

This research was partly sponsored by grant #21-34119.92 of the Swiss National Science Foundation to Rolf Pfeifer.

References

Almassy, N., & Verschure, P.F.M.J. (1992) Optimizing self-organizing control architectures with genetic algorithms: The interaction between natural selection and ontogenesis. R. Männer and B. Manderick (Eds.)*Proceedings of the Second Conference on Parallel Problem Solving from Nature*. 451-460. Amsterdam, Holland: Elsevier.

Brooks, R.A. (1986) A robust layered control system for a mobile Robot. *IEEE: Journal on Robotics and Automation*, **ra.2**, 14-23.

Brooks, R.A. (1991). Intelligence without reason. *IJCAI-91, Proceedings of the Twelfth International Conference on Artificial Intelligence, vol 1*, 569-595.

Edelman, G.M. (1989) *The Remembered Present: A Biological Theory of Consciousness.* New York: Basic Books.

Grossberg, S. (1980) How does a brain build a cognitive code, *Psychological Review*, **87**, 1-51.

Harley, C.B. (1981) Learning the evolutionary stable strategy. *Journal of Theoretical Biology*, 89, 611-633.

Kohonen, T. (1987) *Self-Organization and Associative Memory* (2nd ed.). Berlin: Springer.

McFarland, D. (1992) Animals as cost-based robots. *International Studies in the Philosophy of Science*, 6, 133-153.

Pfeifer, R., and Verschure, P.F.M.J. (1992a) Distributed adaptive control: a paradigm for designing autonomous agents. In *First European Artificial Life Conference Proceedings*. Cambridge, Mass.: MIT Press. pp. 21-31.

Pfeifer, R., and Verschure, P.F.M.J. (1992b) Beyond rationalism: Symbols, patterns, and behavior. *Connection Science*, 4, 313-325.

Van Aeken, F., & Sinnaeve, G. (1992) Applying classical conditioning to a real robot: experiments in reinforcement learning. AI memo, AI lab, Free University Brussels.

Verschure, P.F.M.J. (1992). Taking connectionism seriously: The vague promise of subsymbolism and an alternative. *Proceedings of the Fourteenth Annual Conference of the Cognitive Science Society*, 653-658. Hillsdale, N.J.: Erlbaum.

Verschure, P.F.M.J., & Coolen, A.C.C. (1991) Adaptive Fields: Distributed representations of classically conditioned associations. *Network*, 2, 189-206.

Verschure, P.F.M.J, Kröse, B.J.A., & Pfeifer, R.(1992). Distributed Adaptive Control: The self-organization of structured behavior. *Robotics and Autonomous Agents*, 9, 181-196.

A directional spreading activation network for mobile robot navigation.*

David Kortenkamp and Eric Chown
The University of Michigan
Artificial Intelligence Laboratory
1101 Beal Avenue
Ann Arbor, MI 48109
korten@engin.umich.edu

Abstract

Spreading activation networks are attractive for compactly representing and searching a topological map of places. However, a traditional spreading activation network that links distinctive places lacks potentially useful information, such as directions, one-way routes and safe routes that are not optimal. This paper describes a spreading activation network that can represent such information without departing from the simple mechanisms that underlie spreading activation networks. The starting point of this research is the NAPS connectionist cognitive mapping model. This research is part of a larger framework for a complete theory of cognitive mapping in humans and a related project in developing cognitive maps for mobile robots.

1 Introduction

Topological or route maps have become increasingly popular in mobile robotics research [Brooks, 1985; Kuipers and Byun, 1987]. Such maps are attractive because they encode an environment very compactly by only storing distinctive places much as humans do [Byrne, 1979]. A common representation for such maps is as a spreading activation network, where each node in the network is a distinctive place and each connection is a path between two places. An example of such an implementation is the robot Toto [Mataric, 1990]. Aside from the compactness issue, spreading activation is attractive because it allows for efficient search, potentially in parallel, in a fashion that happens to be analogous to human processing. However, a simple network linking distinctive places lacks some potentially useful information that we shall show can be encoded simply and efficiently. First, differentiating connections according to experience can be helpful because not all paths are created equal; some are safer, more familiar, etc. Second, spreading activation relies on passing activity in both directions along a path which intrinsically assumes that all paths are bi-directional. Finally, a connection does not capture spatial relationships between nodes, only the fact that they are connected. Networks that do not incorporate such information essentially perform breadth-first searches and return the shortest sequence possible. Networks which do incorporate this information can focus search in terms of preferred routes, exchanging the optimality of minimum distance for a smaller chance of getting lost or getting into dangerous areas.

While the aim of the system presented in this paper is for use on mobile robots, many of the ideas are inspired by human and animal cognitive mapping. The optimality we strive for is not necessarily mathematical, but instead is more practical, recognizing that the real world is too complex to be perfectly encoded. Our implementation recognizes that errors can occur, but works to minimize their impact. In turn we argue that these goals can be accomplished within the spreading activation framework and don't require an arsenal of additions such as marker passing or labeled connections. Our implementation, an extension of the NAPS (Network Activity Passing Simulation) system [Levenick, 1991], extends the node and path concept to better reflect experience, but does so without fundamentally changing their character. In this paper we show how to construct a directional spreading activation network of routes and how to search such a network. We also present some preliminary results using a simulated network and look at the issues involved in moving the implementation to an actual mobile robot.

*This work is partially sponsored by the Department of Energy Grant No. DE-FG02-86NE37969

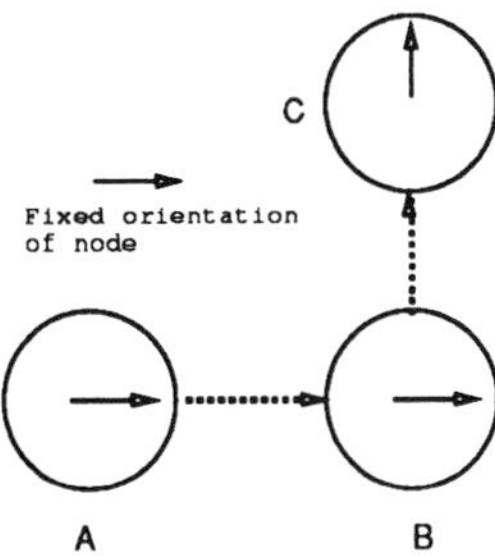

Figure 1: A route containing three nodes, each with a fixed direction. The route had the robot start at A proceed to B, turn left and move to C.

2 Constructing the network

The critical difference between our perspective and that of most researchers in mobile robotics is that we emphasize experience whereas most research emphasizes the finished representation. For example, in Toto, all routes are considered equal in desirability and bi-directional (i.e., if the robot can travel one way down it route in can travel the other way). However, not all routes have these properties. Some routes, although less optimal, may be desirable because they pass by landmarks that the robot can used to orient itself. Other routes can only be traversed in a single direction, maybe because the robot can only push a door open and it cannot pull a door open. Our representation is fundamentally driven by the robot's experiences in the environment.

Another critical difference between our representation and that of other researchers using topological networks is that our network explicitly encodes direction. Thus, constructing our network is slightly more difficult than constructing a traditional topological map. First, each node in the network has a fixed forward direction and any other directions from that node are referenced to the fixed forward. Forward for each node is defined as the direction *away from* the previous node (or, in the case of the first node, the direction in which the robot was started). For example, Figure 1 shows a route with three places, A, B and C. Let's assume that a robot starts at A and is facing B (i.e., it doesn't need to turn in order to reach place B). When the robot reaches B, the previous place (A) is directly behind it, so the direction of B is the same as A. Then the robot turns 90 degrees to the left and approaches place C. The forward of place C is directly away from the previous place (B). The fixed forward direction is shown as an arrow in Figure 1. In this representation the robot only needs to keep track of its orientation with respect to the place it just left, not with respect to any other place or to a world coordinate system. This means that dead reckoning errors will not accumulate over the entire representation, but will be confined to travel between places.

A problem with fixing the orientation of nodes is that the same node can be approached from several different directions. In Figure 1 for example, if the robot goes from A to B to C then the nodes are oriented one way, but if the robot goes from C to B to A the nodes are oriented a different way. We solve this problem by fixing the orientation of a node during the first traversal of a route containing that node. Any other traversal of routes containing that node are referenced to this fixed orientation, which never changes. This is not ideal, as one can imagine a node having several different "forwards" depending on the route that is currently being traversed. Easing this restriction is a current research topic.

Once the orientation of a node is fixed, it is relatively easy to represent directions to and from neighboring nodes. We let each node contain a collection of sub-nodes, each of which correspond to a direction to or from that node. There are two kinds of sub-nodes: out-nodes and in-nodes. Out-nodes represent the direction in which the next place along a route lies. In-nodes represent the direction in which the previous place along a route lies. Appropriate connections are formed between in-nodes and out-nodes to create routes. In simple terms a node represents "I am here", an out-node represents "I am on my way to there" and the in-node represents "I have just left from there" along with directions to the latter two places. This is a significant increase of information in the network, but, of course, the network is also more complex than a traditional spreading activation network.

Figure 2 shows how the in-nodes and out-nodes along a route are connected. In-nodes are filled circles and out-nodes are open circles. Connections between nodes are represented by the arrows. However, the arrows are only for clarity of presenting the construction of the network; during activity passing, activation flows in both directions along a connection. This does not mean that routes are bi-directional as the in-nodes and out-nodes explicitly represent direction as will be shown later.

In this example, the robot starts at place A and moves forward to place B. The forward directions of node A and node B are fixed, as is shown by the arrows in the nodes. Then, an out-node and an in-node are created in the forward direction of A (in-nodes and out-nodes are always created in pairs, the reason for this will be stated later) and an out-node and an in-node are created in the backward direction of B. Then the out-node of A and the in-node of B are connected, representing the fact that the robot moved from A to B (see Figure 2a). Since the out-

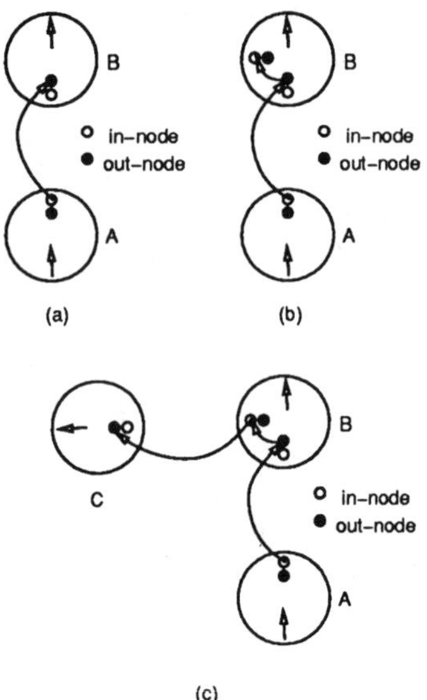

Figure 2: (a) Connections for the first move. (b) Connections for the turn. (c) Connections for the second move. The fixed, ego-centric orientation of each node is represented by an arrow.

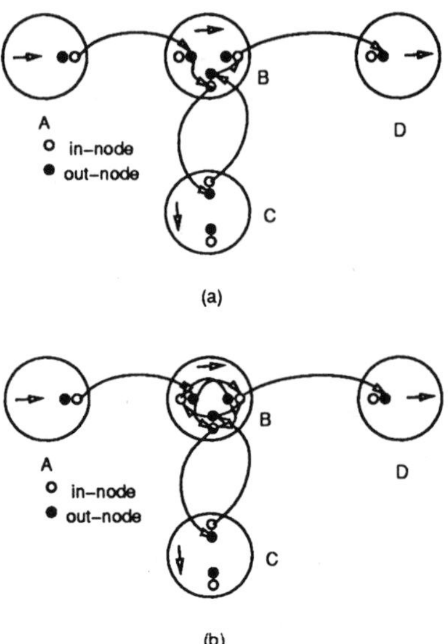

Figure 3: (a) Two routes from A to B to C and from C to B to D. (b) The same representation with internal connections to allow for discovery of novel routes. Arrows show the ego-centric, forward direction of each node.

node of A is connected to the in-node of B, the path between A and B is uni-directional (if the path where from B to A then the out-node of B would be connected to the in-node of A). This represents the fact that routes are not bi-directional.

Now the robot turns 90 degrees left at B. A new pair of in-nodes and out-nodes is created and placed at the 90 degree left direction of the node. Now the backwards in-node of B is connected to the 90 degree left out-node of B (see Figure 2b). Finally, the robot proceeds to place C and the backwards in-node of place C is connected to the 90 degree left out-node of place B, creating an entire route from A to B to C (see Figure 2c).

2.1 Multiple routes

The previous section showed how a single route through a series of nodes is connected. If two different routes share a common node the same procedure can be repeated to represent the second route, as is shown in Figure 3a for a route from A to B to C and from C to B to D. However, this structure lacks one of the biggest features of a spreading activation network – the ability to combine pieces of different route to create a new route that has never been traversed in its entirety. For example, given the network in Figure 3a, if we ask the robot to find a route from place A to place D it will fail as the connections do not meet at any single node. The solution is to add internal connections between all of the in-nodes and all of the out-nodes within a single node (Figure 3b). This will allow for retrieval of new routes that are constructed out of pieces of previously traversed routes. This is also the reason that in-nodes and out-nodes are constructed in pairs.

With these new internal connections, the spreading activation network will act like a true network and not like a collection of single routes. There is considerable adaptive advantages in having a true network, the most important advantage is that the robot is not limited to traversing routes that it has already experiences, but can find and traverse novel routes.

2.2 Adaptation

As routes are traversed, the network adapts so that more frequently traversed routes will be stronger than less frequently traversed routes. This has two consequences. First, frequently traversed routes will be extracted from the network more quickly, since they are more easily activated. Since routes that were traversed frequently in the past will likely be traversed often in the future, extracting them more quickly is an advantage. Second, if the robot has traversed two different routes from one place to another, the one that has been traversed more frequently will be preferred. This is not the case in many systems, such as Toto, where the shorter route will be preferred. There is significant adaptive advantage in biasing toward the familiar, as the familiar route will usually be the safer route since it has been traversed repeatedly in the past and, therefore it is more likely that future traversals will be successful.

Route are made stronger by incrementing the strengths on the connections between nodes with each traversal of a route. The equation for incrementing is taken from NAPS and is:

$$S(l) = S(l) + (1 - S(l))^2 * LR,$$

where S is the strength of connection l, and LR was the learning rate (set to 0.20 for most of our experiments).

In addition, when a node is repeatedly visited, it gets more resources, making it more resistant to fatigue (fatigue is discussed in the next section). Resources are increased by the following equation:

$$R(n) = R(n) + (1 - R(n))^2 * LR,$$

where R is the resources of node n and LR is again the learning rate.

3 Searching the network

Searching a directional network is similar to that of many spreading activation networks, such as NAPS, except it is much more directed. First, all of the out-nodes of the start node are activated (in this implementation their activation is set to the maximum level of 1.0). Similarly, all of the in-nodes of the goal node are activated. The simulation then iteratively propagates activation across each connection. The input activity of a node is determined by the following equation (similar to the equation used in NAPS):

$$I_i(n) = \sum_{l_{m,n}} A_i(m) * S(l_{m,n}),$$

where A_i is the activation level of a node at time i, $l_{m,n}$ is a connection between node n and node m and S is the strength of the connection.

After activity is propagated through one generation of connections (i.e., activation is spread to the immediate neighbors of each node), each node in the network is fatigued. Fatigue is a control mechanism that is used in NAPS to prevent the network from becoming too active. As a node is activated it consumes resources; the more highly activated it is, the more resources it consumes. As a node consumes more resources it fatigues and its activation level is reduced until its resources can be replenished. Thus, fatigue is dependent upon the activation level of the node and the resources that it has. These combine to produce a fatigue level, which is a value between 0 and 1 with 0 meaning no fatigue and 1 meaning completely fatigued. Thus, activation of a node n is updated accordingly by the following equation (similar to the equation used in NAPS):

$$A_{i+1}(n) = (1 - F(n)) * (A_i(n) + (I_i(n) * (1 - A_i(n)))),$$

where F is the fatigue level of a node and I_i is the net input activation to the node at time i (calculated above).

After each generation of activation, the network is searched for a node that has one, and only one, in-node above a threshold (in the experiments, the threshold was an activation level above 0.75) ***and*** one, and only one, out-node above a threshold. Such a node is called a subgoal. The sub-goal becomes the new goal and the process is repeated, with one significant difference, since the active in-node of the subgoal represents the direction of the previous node, activation only needs to be spread in that direction. So only the in-node in that direction is activated for the new search. However, all out-nodes of the start place have to be re-activated since no information about direction from the start is yet available. The network is not cleared of activity between each search as the previous search should have primed the activation of the route between the start and the goal allowing for quicker activation of other subgoals.

At the end of the search, the next place in the route will be known, as will its direction from the current place. The robot can move to this place and searching for the next place along the route can begin, On this next search, the direction to the goal is known (it is the active out-node of the subgoal) so activity can be concentrated in this direction. This procedure continues until an entire route is traversed.

3.1 Advantages of direction

A directional network has several advantages over a network that does not code direction, such as the network used by Toto. The first advantage is that the robot now has a simple, spreading activation means for representing the direction in which it should turn at each node. At each node the robot knows where to turn to move to the next node. In many other spreading activation networks, such as NAPS or Toto, the robot would have to rely on external cues, such as landmarks, in order to determine where to turn to move to the next node if there were several options.

A second advantage of a directional spreading activation network is that activation can be more focused. If the robot knows what direction (in the network) the goal is, then it can focus its activation in that direction,

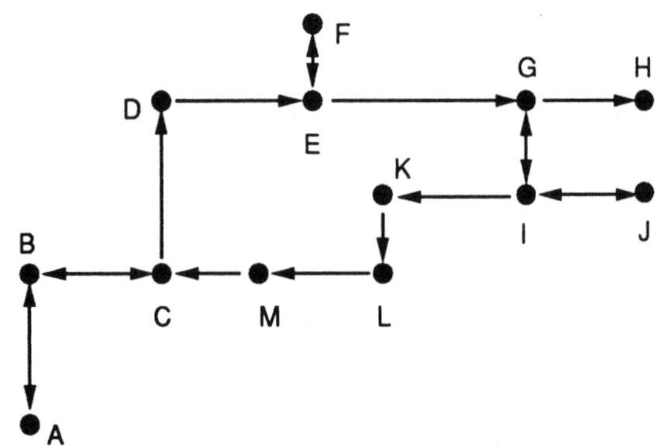

Figure 4: An experimental network with 13 nodes, 32 in-nodes, 32 out-nodes and 33 links.

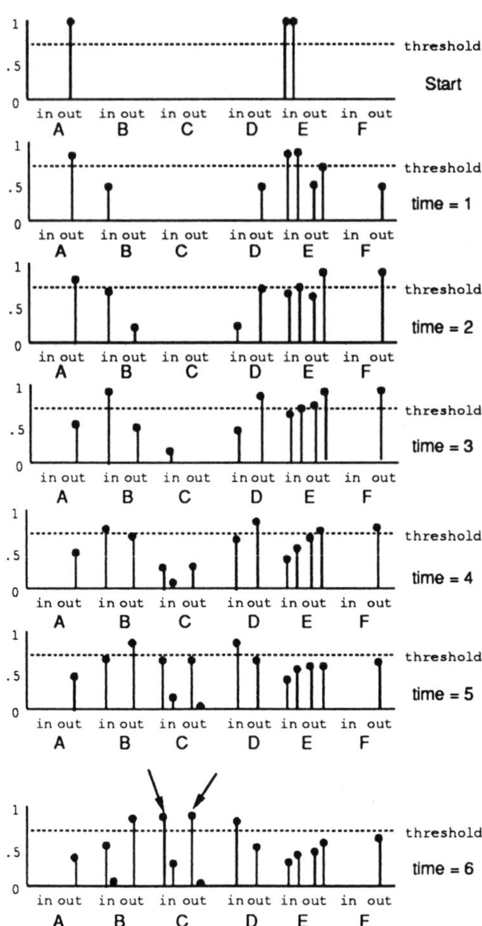

Figure 5: The spread of activation from start node A to goal node E of the network in Figure 4 is shown. Each node has in-nodes and out-nodes, some have several of both as multiple routes pass through. Each node that was activated above 0.0 is shown. The threshold is at 0.75. A sub-goal node is decided when both an in-node and an out-node of a node are above threshold, as is shown with arrows for node C.

rather then spreading the activation through the entire network. This can result in less confusion for the robot and more clarity in its route extraction.

A final advantage of directional spreading activation networks is that they can serve as a stepping stone to larger, more spatial representations that represent the overall spatial structure of the environment. Directional networks still only represent directions between neighboring places; directions between distant places would require an additional level of representation. We are actively working on mechanisms and representations for this level, both in a complete theory of human cognitive mapping and a related project on cognitive mapping for mobile robots [Chown *et al.*, 1992].

4 Preliminary results

We have constructed (in simulation) a large, directional network of places and tested its ability to extract routes. The network is pictured in Figure 4. It corresponds to a series of hallways and rooms in the basement of our laboratory. The nodes correspond to places that have been experimentally determined to match those places that our actual robot recognizes as distinctive with its sonar sensors (see the next section for details on this process). Thus, while all results are in simulation since it would have taken too long to conduct extensive experiments with a real robot, the network corresponds to a network that an actual robot would construct.

The network was formed by traversing four routes: A-B-C-D-E-F, F-E-G-H, F-E-G-I-J, and J-I-K-L-M-C-B-A. The first and last routes where traversed four times and the middle two routes where traversed three times. After the network was formed, it was tested using 26 pairs of start and goal nodes and seeing if a correct subgoal node was found. A subgoal is considered correct if it lies on a path between the start and the goal and the correct in-nodes and out-nodes corresponding to the start and goal direction are activated. Of the 26 pairs of start and goal locations, 23 were processed correctly. Considering the small amount of time we have been experimenting with this network, the results are heartening. Even well-tuned systems, such as NAPS, only get success rates in the low 90 percent range.

Figure 5 shows how activity spreads through the network during a typical search. Notice how fatigue causes activity to slowly move through the network, almost as two waves from the start and the goal, until the activity

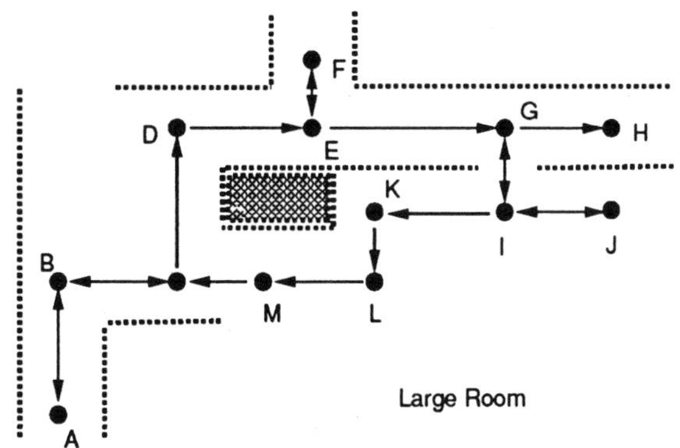

Figure 6: The network of Figure 4 is superimposed on the hallways and rooms of the basement of our laboratory, showing the detection of gateways. The distance from D to H is about 12m.

coalesces at a central sub-goal. Also important is that many of the nodes in the network had zero activity during the search (only active nodes are represented in the figure). The directionality of the search causes whole areas of the network to be excluded from the search space. This reduces confusion in the system.

The three failures in the test cases were caused by a common problem in spreading activation networks. When links between nodes are very strong, a subgoal can be found when activation comes from only a single direction. For example, the start node can activate a tightly connected neighboring node above threshold without any activation from the goal node. A number of these errors can be solved by tediously tweaking the network's learning rate and its subgoal threshold. We didn't have enough experience with the parameters of this network to successfully eliminate some errors. However, even the best networks will fall prey to this problem.

5 Mobile robot issues

We have begun implementing a mobile robot navigation system that will have the directional spreading activation network outlined in this paper at its heart. However, before we could get to the stage of traversing and remembering routes using an actual robot, several issues needed to be addressed. While these issues are not the thrust of this paper, a brief overview of how we are approaching them will allow for the directional spreading activation network to be put into context (see [Kortenkamp *et al.*, 1992b] for more details on the mobile robot implementation).

5.1 Detecting nodes

The first issue that needed to be addressed is where the robot detects nodes. We have defined certain places in the environment as gateways. Gateways mark the transition from one space to another. In an indoor environment, gateways can be entrances to rooms, intersections of hallways or turns. Gateways are detected by using sonar sensors on the robot. The sonar sensors search for openings that are large enough to pass through. Once the robot passes through the opening it calls it a gateway and creates a node. The direction through which the robot passed is the forward direction of the node. Our gateway detection algorithm has been shown to be reliable and repeatable on an actual mobile robot in an actual indoor environment [Kortenkamp *et al.*, 1992a]. Figure 6 superimposes the hallways and rooms in the basement of our laboratory on the network constructed in Figure 4 and shows the gateways between them. All of the gateways shown can be detected by our sonar algorithm.

5.2 Recognizing nodes

While we have a reliable algorithm for detecting gateways, this algorithm, using only sonar sensors, cannot detect a specific gateway. Gateways, in and of themselves are not very distinguishable. To help us distinguish individual gateways we do two things. First, we classify each gateway as a certain type (e.g., intersection, entrance to room, etc.). Second, we use a camera to store visual cues that are available at the gateway. Currently, only vertical edges are used as visual cues. By matching the type of gateway, the vertical edges and by knowing the expected gateway given the robot's previous location, we have shown that the robot will be able to distinguish where it is (see [Kortenkamp *et al.*, 1992b]).

One significant problem that using a real robot presents over the simulation used in this paper is recognizing the same place when it is approached from different directions. If this is not done, there will be no network, only a collection of routes and, thus, no way of combining pieces of several routes to create new ones. We are still examining how to use various geometric and environmental constraints to overcome this problem.

6 Conclusions

The major limitation of the network discussed in this paper is that it is far more complex than an ordinary network, because it is encoding much more information. This limits the lengths of routes that can be extracted. However, as is demonstrated in NAPS, hierarchy can be used to overcome this limitation by representing long routes with nodes at a higher level. We have not yet implemented hierarchies in our direction network.

Several extensions will have to be made for this network to scale-up. As routes get stronger, activity may get out of control if inhibitory links are not added. For example, as one direction out of a node gets activated, this could inhibit activation of other directions. Also, we would like to add a compensatory learning rule so that the network can adapt to large-scale changes in the environment. In compensatory learning, links are weakened as well as strengthened. For example, if the robot has frequently traversed a route from A to B to C and then is forced to begin traversing a route from A to B to D, the link from B to C would weaken as the link from B to D strengthens. Adding a compensatory learning rule to our system would be a minor next step. Finally, we are interested in applying directional spreading activation networks to non-spatial domains. We hope that the focus of activity and the directionality of sequences that this network representation gives us will be helpful in solving other, non-spatial problems.

In summary, we have extended the traditional spreading activation concept as it applies to navigation such that more spatial information can be encoded while still using the original tools. This approach enhances traditional networks by reducing their reliance on external cues for orientation and by further focusing the search for routes. In addition the routes that are returned are automatically encoded with spatial information. Such capabilities are especially critical for mobile robots giving their limited perceptual abilities to date. By making the robot's representations better reflect its experiences and usage of those representations we can shift some of the burden of navigation from the robot's perceptual system to the representations themselves hence bestowing the ability to take advantage of the robot's strengths while minimizing its weaknesses.

References

[Brooks, 1985] Rodney A. Brooks. Visual map making for a mobile robot. In *Proceedings IEEE Conference on Robotics and Automation*, 1985.

[Byrne, 1979] R. W. Byrne. Memory for urban geography. *Quarterly Journal of Experimental Psychology*, 31(1), 1979.

[Chown *et al.*, 1992] Eric Chown, Stephen Kaplan, and David Kortenkamp. Prototypes, location and associative networks (PLAN): Towards an unified theory of cognitive mapping. Submitted to *Cognitive Science*, 1992.

[Kortenkamp *et al.*, 1992a] David Kortenkamp, L. Douglas Baker, and Terry Weymouth. Using gateways to build a route map. In *Proceedings of the IEEE/RSJ International Conference on Intelligent Robots and Systems*, 1992.

[Kortenkamp *et al.*, 1992b] David Kortenkamp, Terry Weymouth, Eric Chown, and Stephen Kaplan. A scene-based, multi-level representation for mobile robot spatial mapping and navigation. Technical Report CSE-TR-119-92, The University of Michigan, 1992.

[Kuipers and Byun, 1987] Benjamin J. Kuipers and Y.T. Byun. A qualitative approach to robot exploration and map-learning. In *Proceedings IEEE Workshop on Spatial Reasoning and Multi-Sensor Fusion*, 1987.

[Levenick, 1991] James R. Levenick. NAPS: A connectionist implementation of cognitive maps. *Connection Science*, 3(2), 1991.

[Mataric, 1990] Maja K. Mataric. A distributed model for mobile robot environment-learning and navigation. Technical Report AI-TR 1228, MIT Artificial Intelligence Laboratory, 1990.

Memorizing and Representing Route Scenes

Saburo Tsuji and Shigang Li
Department of Systems Engineering
Osaka University
Toyonaka, Osaka 560, Japan
Email tsuji@ce.osaka-u.ac.jp

Abstract

How can a robot autonomously represent and memorize the route it has passed ? As a step toward the solution, we have studied quantitative/qualitative representations of scenes along the route, which guide autonomous navigation. A robot continuously scans the side-view and yields an intermediate representation, called *Panoramic Representation*. The robot can locate itself in the route by matching the memorized *Panoramic Representation* against that of the incoming scenes. The matching of entire scenes, however, wastes both memory and computing time. We, thereby, explore making of a more abstract and qualitative map represented by landmarks which are extracted as distinctive patterns along the route.

1. Introduction

Much research on vision-based navigation has been focused on road-following and obstacle-avoidance. Long distance navigation of a robot, however, needs also global information on the route both to judge whether it is following a correct path and to locate itself in the route. We have been exploring how an intelligent robot acquires the route information in a wide outdoor environment. Scenario of our project is as follows: A robot moves along a certain route and autonomously memorizes the route by observing scenes continuously. When the robot is commanded to pursue the same route, it keeps observing the scene and verifies the correctness of the route and instructs the road-following module, by referring to the memorized route representation, where it should make a turn or stop.

This paper presents ideas how the robot autonomously represents scenes along the route the robot has passed. Rather than building a world model from a set of images taken at discrete points [Ayache 87, Elefes 87, Moravec 83, Yeap 88], our robot continuously views the environment and arranges its essential information into a Panoramic Representation, which provides rich information along the route as a path-centered 2(1/2)-D sketch [Zheng 90A]. The Panoramic Representation is an intermediate representation, as Marr proposed [Marr 78], from which we can build more abstract and compact route representations.

A natural method for locating the robot in the route is to establish correspondences between two Panoramic Representations obtained through different moves along the same route. Experiment results have shown robust pattern matching is possible by a DP-based method [Zheng 90A].

Memorizing and matching features over the entire route, however, seem inefficient and less intelligent, particularly for a long route. Humans memorize objects or patterns with distinctive features along the route as landmarks and move along the route guided by them. Autonomous extraction of landmarks along a route is, thus, important, but such tasks have been done primarily with the assistance by human operators in identifying objects in specific environments [Lawton 86]. Since a mobile robot should be able to move in various environments, our landmarks are not defined as any specific type of objects. We explore what are distinctive patterns over a wide range and present a method for extracting them in the Panoramic Representation and building a qualitative map with them.

It is well known that computer analysis of outdoor scenes is very difficult and often fails in acquiring reliable scene/image information. Iconic properties such as brightness and color in the outdoor scenes vary significantly with weather. Noise-free range data, if available, provide useful information to find the environment structure [Yeap 88], but we cannot expect precise 2(1/2)D vision data are available in the outdoor environment, in particular for far objects. This paper investigates ideas and methods for analyzing, in a qualitative way, the structure and iconic features of a wide outdoor world from continuous observations by a moving perceiver in order to select the landmarks.

2. Representation of Scenes along a Route

2.1 Symbolic vs. Iconic Representation

Let us consider how a human represents the route he/she has moved along. The following is some examples.

[1] I walked the street about 1 km and ....
[2] I turned to the right at the third corner and ......
[3] I walked along an avenue and entered in a shopping district .....
[4] I turned to the left at the corner next to an old Gothic church .....

The first example is a geometrical representation of the route by metric. The second is another geometrical representation in terms of its topology instead of the metric. In the third example, the patterns along the route are used as descriptors and the fourth uses a landmark, an old Gothic church, to represent the route. Note that all of these representations are symbolic. Humans, however, use also iconic representations to memorize the scenes along the route. We sometimes say "I am sure I have been here before because I memorize this scene". We cannot tell the detail of the memorized scene before viewing it again, but we can match an incoming scene against the memorized representation and find their differences. This indicates that humans use both symbolic and iconic representations of the environment.

2.2 Panoramic Representation of Environment

The environment is a large scale space, a space which is too large to be perceived in a view at a point and, therefore, the perceiver should move about it in order to develop its model or Cognitive Map [Yeap 88]. Rather than building a world model from a set of images taken at discrete points by finding their correspondences, our robot continuously views the environment and arranges its essential information into a *Panoramic Representation*, a path-centered 2(1/2)-D sketch, from which we can build more abstract and compact route representations.

A method for getting a wide view of the environment is to look around at an observation point. Suppose a camera swivels at point C at a constant angular velocity and continuously takes pictures through a vertical slit, as Fig. 1 (a) shows. By arranging the slit imagery along the horizontal axis, we get a panoramic view which contains all objects visible from point C. Since the temporal image data are arranged into a spatial 2-D image, we call this type of image formation a *2-D dynamic projection* [Zheng 90B]. Since the camera focus coincides with C, the camera motion is pure rotation, and therefore, we cannot acquire the range information by this scheme.

Modify slightly the scheme so as for the camera to move along a circle with a radius R at a constant speed, keeping its optical axis orthogonal to the motion direction, as Fig. 1 (b) shows. If we extract a vertical image line at the center of each image and arrange them into an image, we get an almost same image as one obtained by swiveling the camera. The camera motion, however, contains a translational component and we can acquire omnidirectional range information by this imaging [Ishiguro 90].

More generally, the camera moves along a smooth curve on a horizontal plane, as shown in Fig. 1 (c), to obtain a generalized panoramic view by arranging the slit imagery. We can estimate distance to each object in the scene from its image velocity moving across the slit. Mathematical foundations of the depth estimation from paths with different shapes are given in [Zheng 90A].

Now we call all the images generated by the schemes illustrated in Fig. 1 *Panoramic Views*. The images yielded

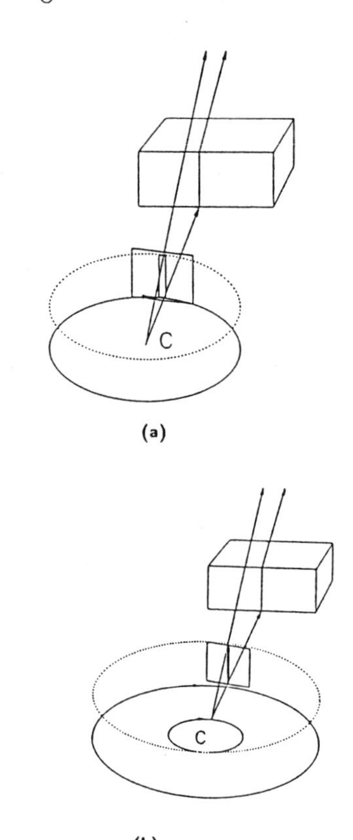

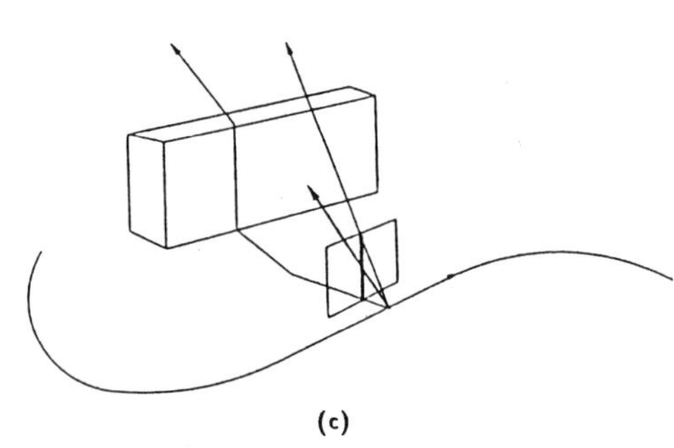

Figure 1: Generating *Panoramic Views* by taking slit imagery by a camera (a) swiveling, (b) moving along a circle or (c) moving along a smooth path.

Figure 2: A memorized *Panoramic View* (upper) is matched with a new *Panoramic View* (lower) generated from the incoming scenes by a DP-based method.

by Fig. 1 (a) and (b) are wide but local, thus they are called *Local Panoramic Views*, while those by Fig. 1 (c) are called *Route Panoramic Views* which contain image data along the route.

We consider both types of *Panoramic Views* are useful for autonomous map making. For example, a robot looks around at a start point if it knows little about the world. Finding a coarse environment structure around the point, it plans a path to wander and then moves and observes the environment by viewing the side scenes continuously. At a junction of paths, it looks around again to memorize the scenes and moves along a selected path. As mentioned before, this paper discusses mainly how the robot memorizes the scenes along a specified route and we use the *Route Panoramic View* as input of the map making process.

Integrating a *Panoramic View* with the range estimates and camera motion, we get a *Panoramic Representation*, a 2(1/2)D representation of scenes along the camera path. Note that a 2(1/2)D representation proposed so far [Marr 78] is camera-centered in the sense that a local scene is represented with reference to a static camera, while our *Panoramic Representation* is path-centered; it integrates scene data in a wide area into a compact representation with reference to a 1D camera path. The Panoramic Representation provides iconic properties, such as color, texture and shape, of objects along the route and their spatial information, such as their arrangement and sizes, as well.

2.3 Matching of Panoramic Views

A simple and straightforward application of the *Panoramic Representation* is to memorize 2D iconic properties viewed from the route. Suppose a robot moved along a route and memorized a *Panoramic Representation* of scenes along the route. If the robot moves along the same route again, it can match, by a DP matching method, a new *Panoramic View* generated from incoming scenes against the memorized *Panoramic View* , although the actual path in the road and the camera velocity may change significantly from time to time [Zheng 90A]. Fig. 2 shows results of matching two *Panoramic Views*, memorized and new incoming ones, acquired through two navigation along a same route in the campus of Osaka University. In spite of significant differences between their camera velocities, the method succeeds in correct matching.

3. Qualitative Representation of Route

3.1 Qualitative Map

Cognitive science claims a key function of the human visual memory is selectivity [Cohen 89]. If a human walks along a new route, what he/she memorizes on the route is probably the most remarkable and impressive objects or scenes in certain ranges. Usually, we call them landmarks.

The method described in the preceding section memorizes all views, although data are compressed, through the navigation, and as a result, works only for short routes; it wastes too much memory and computing power. We, thereby, explore making of a qualitative map on the route. Since humans can recognize objects selected as landmarks, a compact symbolic representation of route such as "Turn right at the corner next to an old Gothic church." is possible. Conventional computer vision systems, however, have difficulties in recognizing a wide variety of objects along the route. Thus, we study an easier approach to autonomous making of a qualitative map. Our system does not find identities of objects, such as a church or a bridge, but examines 3D and iconic properties in *Panoramic Representation*, finds objects which are distinctive in some attributes over a wide range, and uses them as landmarks.

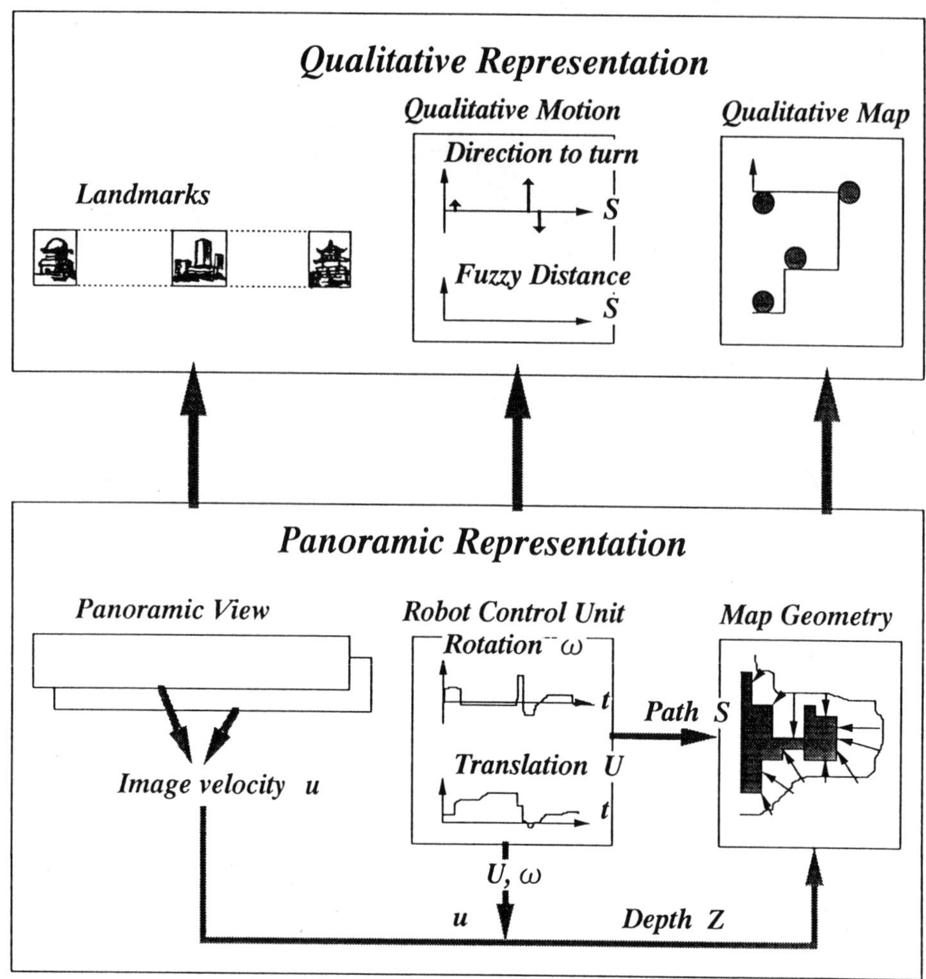

Figure 3: Qualitative Map and *Panoramic View*

Fig. 3 shows structures of the qualitative map and *Panoramic Representation*. The *Panoramic View* is replaced with a compact representation by the distinctive objects or patterns selected as landmarks. Qualitative motion representation in terms of turn directions and fuzzy distance descriptions, such as *very long* or *short*, is used instead of quantitative records of linear and angular velocities. The numerical map geometry is converted into a topological route representation.

3.2 How Landmarks Are Found ?

What are the distinctive patterns along the route ? They depend upon the environment. Objects remarkable in some attributes, such as height, shape or color, in one area may be not salient in other areas. The robot, thus, should examine distribution of image/scene features along the route and select distinctive ones in each part of the route. If an object or pattern in a *Panoramic View* is distinctive in some attributes over a wide range, we register it as a landmark in the area.

A method for finding distinctive iconic properties in the *Panoramic Views* has been presented [Zheng 91]. Dividing a wide *Panoramic View* into regions with almost homogeneous attributes, we map all parameters of image/scene attributes, such as color, edge density, minimum range and maximum height, of each region onto a multi-parameter space. We analyze the space to evaluate which attribute or combination of attributes is remarkable. The results, however, highly rely on success in finding and/or measuring such attributes. In the outdoor scenes, color attributes such as hue and saturation significantly change with the spectral distribution of illuminant. Determining of shape properties, such as areas and perimeters of texture elements, in natural scenes is often unreliable. Thus, we need more robust methods for finding landmarks.

3.3 Scene Features Guides Finding and Selection of Landmarks

Here we present a new idea to select distinctive scene features for landmarks. We use spatial information in the *Panoramic Representation* as a robust qualitative cue.

Although the range estimates by the moving camera are non-precise and vary with the camera velocity, the spatial and size relations between objects are invariant. The environment structure is characterized by ground and objects standing upon it. The objects are segmented from the ground by height information, and then, they

Figure 4: A *Panoramic View* generated from an image sequence with 1016 frames

Figure 5: Disparity map

are segmented each other by their ranges. The results are arranged into a structure map that represents their spatial relationships as well as their iconic properties. By examining the structural map, we can find distinctive 3D objects which can be used as landmarks for guiding the long distance navigation.

4. Structure Map

4.1 Range Map and Scene Segmentation

We can estimate the distance of feature points in a *Panoramic View* by measuring their image velocities [Zheng 90A]. Image points appeared in the sampling slit are tracked in the consecutive frames and their disparities are estimated. We yield a disparity map by assigning the disparities to the corresponding feature points in the *Panoramic View*. Fig. 4 shows a 1016 by 240 *Panoramic View* generated from an image sequence of 1016 frames taken while the camera is moving linearly. Fig. 5 displays its disparity map in which farther points from the camera path are shown as darker.

Now, let us consider how we can find suitable landmarks in the disparity map. A human often describes a route by 3D objects above the ground such as a post office or a tower; the ground provides little information as landmarks. We compute the heights of the feature points in the disparity map using the motion parameters, measured by the internal sensors of the robot, and filter out the low 3D points, so as to segment the object points in the *Panoramic View* from the ground.

Next, we segment these object points into each object by a simple one-pass cluster analysis [Li 92A]. Since the disparity map contains only feature points, the segmented results are also sparse. We, thereby, determine each object in the *Panoramic View* by fusing the segmented results by range with its color patches [Li 92A].

4.2 Structure Map

Using the segmented results, we build a map representing the environment structure, called *Structure Map*, by arranging the objects along the path of which direction is horizontal in the map. Fig. 6 displays a perspective view of the structure map generated from Fig. 4. Forty objects are found in the scene and each is assigned an identity number. We use the disparity as the distance from the path, rather than the estimated Euclidean distance, for setting an equal scale in estimation reliability. Fig. 7 is a top view of the structure map shown in Fig. 6. Visible points on each object exist within the corresponding rectangle in the top view.

The structure map contains the spatial information such as distances of objects from and their arrangements along the path. It also provides both the geometry of each object, such as its height and width, and its orthogonal view which provides color and shape. Note that although the disparities and the widths of the objects vary with the change of the perceiver's motion, their relative distances, relative sizes and order appearing along the path are invariant.

4.3 Finding Landmark

Based upon the spatial/size relations and iconic property of objects in the structure map, landmarks can be

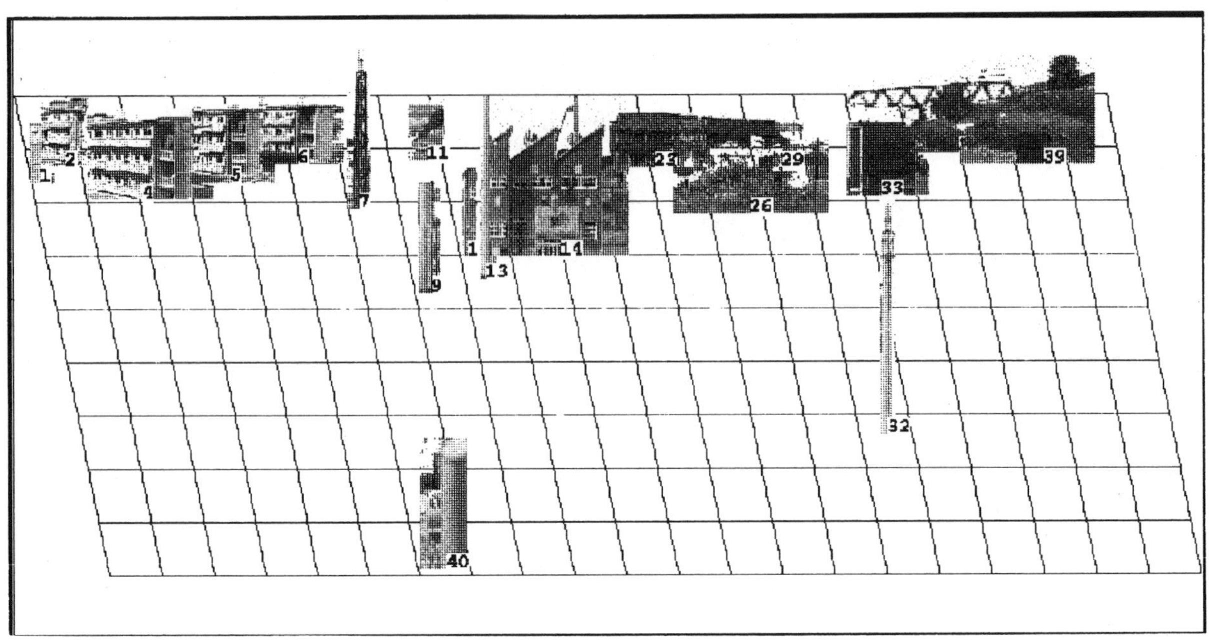

Figure 6: A perspective view of *Structure Map*

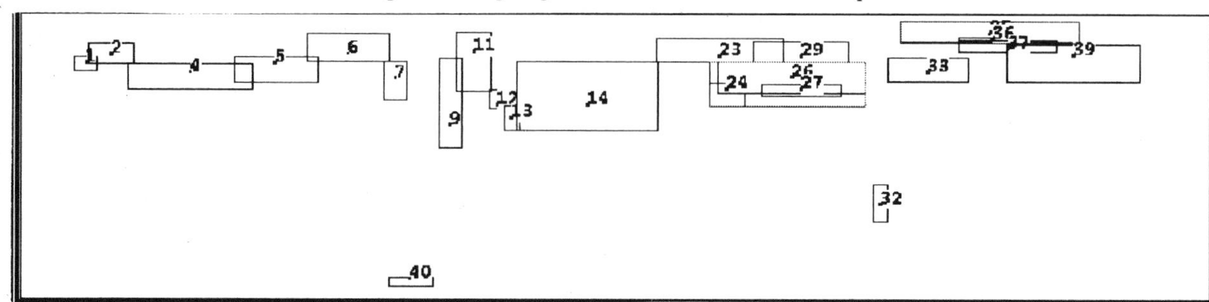

Figure 7: Object arrangement in *Structure Map*

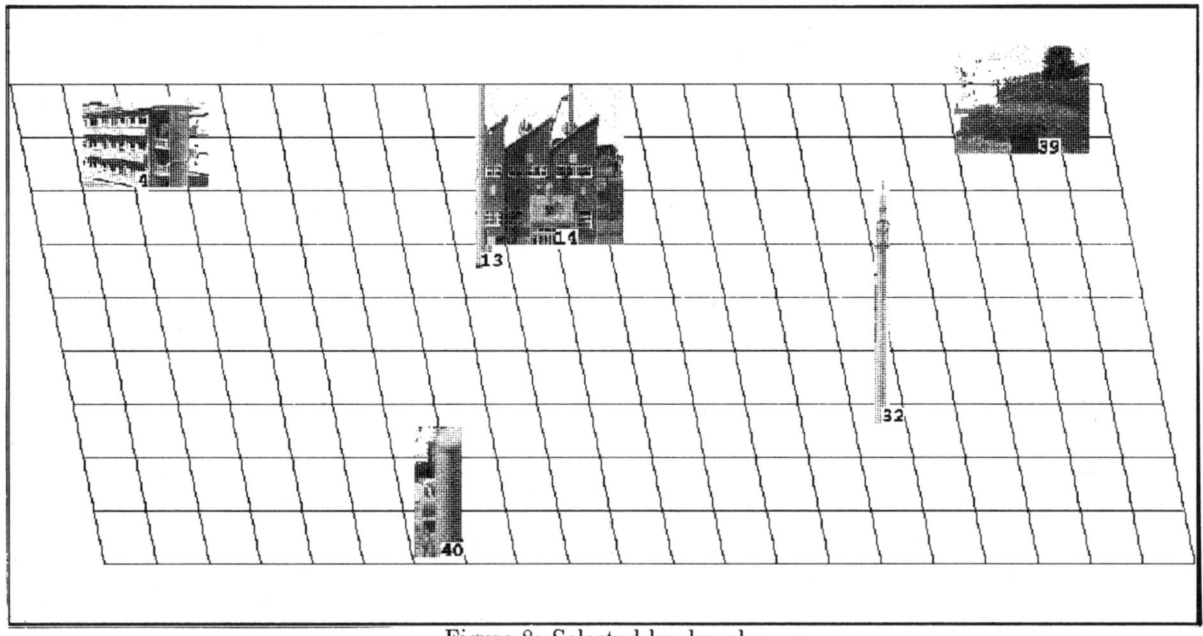

Figure 8: Selected landmarks

Figure 9: A *Panoramic View* acquired from observations from the same route of Figure 4 under different camera speed and illumination

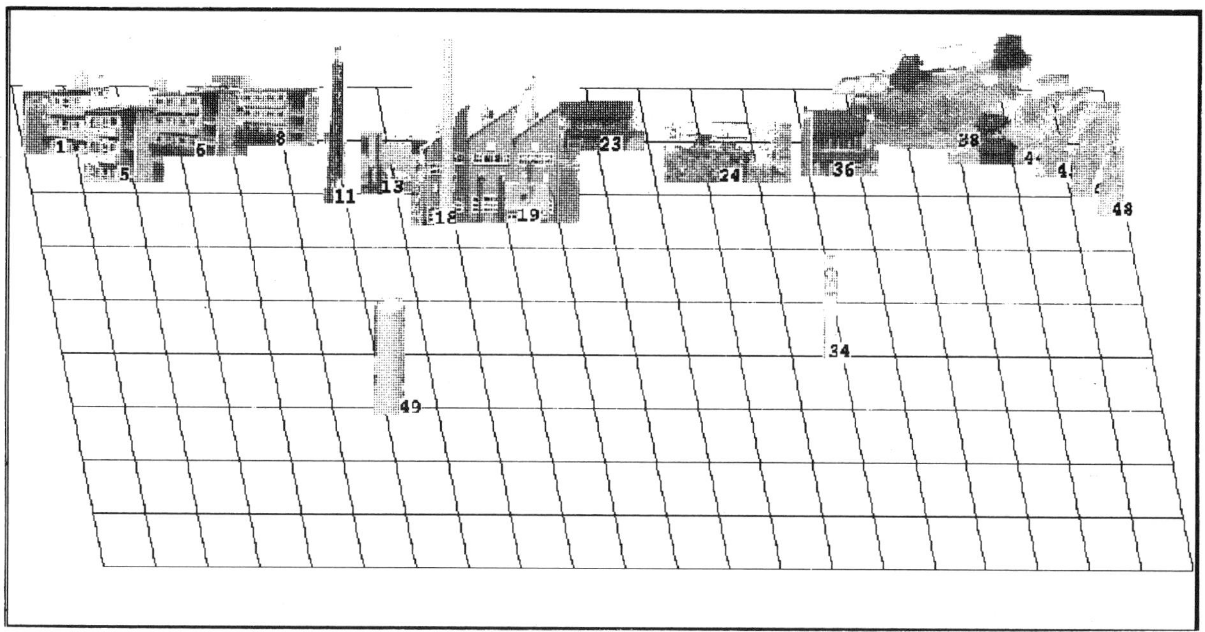

Figure 10: A perspective view of *Structure Map yielded from Figure 9*

selected. We measure the distinctive range of segmented objects in the *Structure Map* [Zheng 91]. The object with a long distinctive range along the *t-axis* has a high priority in selecting candidates for landmarks.

At present, we use a simple evaluation function, the object size weighed by its average disparity, for selecting landmarks. Thus, large regions near the camera are likely to be selected as landmarks. We set two levels to select and memorize the landmarks. The higher level consists of landmarks with higher distinctive values while the low level memorizes those with lower distinctive values. Merit of this representation is that the patterns on the lower level provide supplementary information when the robot falls into confusion as a result of the failure in finding patterns memorized on the higher level. Fig. 8 shows the landmarks selected for the higher level from the objects in the *Structure Map* of Fig. 6.

4.4 Route Recognition by Matching Selected Landmarks

Based upon the selected landmarks, the route is recognized by the perceiver when it pursues the same route. Since the object sequence selected as landmarks is memorized, the route recognition is equivalent to search the new input scenes for each landmark.

Although the perceiver moves along the same route, change of its speed causes variations in the estimates of the distance, height and width of the object. New occlusion may occur as a result of change in viewing direction. Change in the spectral distribution of the illuminant influences on the perceived color. Fig. 9 shows a *Panoramic View* acquired while the robot moves along the same route as Fig. 4, but with a slower speed and different illumination. As results, the widths of objects increase and color shifts toward red. The dark steel tower becomes occluded partly by the grey tank standing close to the camera path in Fig. 12.

Fig. 9 is also transformed into a new structure map shown in Fig. 10. A model-based matching method, which examines the differences of the distance from the path, shape, and color distributions, succeeds in reliable matching of the memorized landmarks to the corresponding objects in the new structure map by allowing a certain amount of color shift and estimating the color similarity.

5. Conclusion

We have explored how a robot can autonomously build representations of the route it has passed, from continuous observation of the side views. Panoramic Representation provides path-centered 2(1/2)-D sketch by which the robot can locate itself in the route. Ideas for building more a qualitative map from *Panoramic Representation* are discussed.

References

[Ayache 87] Ayache, N. and Faugeras, O. D., Building, registrating and fusing noisy visual maps, *Proc. 1st ICCV*, pp. 73-82 (1987).

[Bolles 87] Bolles, R. C. et al., Epipolar-plane image analysis: An approach to determining structure from motion, *Int. J. Comput. Vision*, 1, 1, pp. 7-56 (1987)

[Cohen 89] Cohen, G., *Memory in the Real World*, Lawrence Erlbaum Associates, Hove (1989).

[Elefes 87] Elefes, A.: Sonar-based real-world mapping and navigation, IEEE J. Robotics & Automation, **RA-3**, No. 3, pp. 249-265.

[Ishiguro 90] Ishiguro, H., Yamamoto, M. and Tsuji, S., Omni-directional stereo for making global map, *Proc. 3rd ICCV*, pp. 540-547 (1990).

[Li 92A] Li, S. and Tsuji, S., Selecting distinctive scene features for landmarks, *Proc. IEEE Int. Conf. Robotics and Automation* pp. 53-59 (1992).

[Li 92B] Li, S. and Tsuji, S., Finding landmarks autonomously along a route,, *Proc. 11th ICPR*, pp. 316-319 (1992).

[Marr 78] Marr, D., Representing visual information, in Hanson, A. and Riseman, E.M. (eds.) *Computer Vision Systems*, Academic Press, New York (1978).

[Moravec 83] Moravec, H. P., The Stanford Cart and CMU Rover, *Proc. IEEE*, 71, 7, pp. 872-884 (1983).

[Yeap 88] Yeap, W.K.: Toward a computational theory of cognitive maps, *Artificial Intelligence*, **34**, pp. 297-360.

[Zheng 90A] Zheng, J.Y. and Tsuji, S., Panoramic representation of scenes for route understanding, *Proc. 10th ICPR*, pp. 161-167, 1990.

[Zheng 90B] Zheng, J.Y. and Tsuji, S., From anorthoscope perception to dynamic vision, *Proc. IEEE Int. Conf. robotics & Automation*, pp. 1154-1160 (1990).

[Zheng 91] Zheng, J.Y., Barth, M. and Tsuji, S., Autonomous landmark selection for route recognition by a mobile robot,*Proc. IEEE Int. Conf. Robotics & Automation*, pp. 2004-2009, 1991.

Building Long-range Cognitive Maps using Local Landmarks

Tony J. Prescott and John E. W. Mayhew

Artificial Intelligence Vision Research Unit,
Sheffield University,
Sheffield S10 2TN,
United Kingdom.

Telephone +44 742 768555 ext. 6546/6554
Fax +44 742 766515

Email: tony@aivru.sheffield.ac.uk jewm@aivru.sheffield.ac.uk

Abstract

Cognitive maps can be built using only information about the relative positions of locally visible landmarks. We describe a system that can compute paths between any two locations, irrespective of whether they share common visible landmarks, without using 'compass' senses or dead reckoning abilities. This is achieved by encoding the position of each landmark in the *barycentric* co-ordinate frames defined by groups of neighbouring cues. Paths between distant points are computed by calculating, using these frames, the positions relative to the agent of landmarks further and further away from the immediate scene. Once the relative positions of landmarks local to the goal are known a vector giving its position in the agent's egocentric frame can be found. This implicit map allows the agent to compute the overall distance and direction to distant targets; find and follow paths to goal locations; generate explicitly the layout of the whole environment relative to its own position; and discriminate between perceptually similar landmarks. The system is robust to noise, its calculations require only linear mathematics, and its memory requirements are proportional to the total number of landmarks.

1 Introduction

There is substantial evidence (see O'Keefe and Nadel (1978); Gallistel (1990); O'Keefe (1990) for reviews) that birds and mammals are able to find novel or straight-line routes to distant positions outside the current visible scene. The spatial knowledge underlying this navigation competence appears to be *declarative* rather than *procedural* in nature in that it describes the relations between places rather than encoding specific instructions of how to travel from one place to another. It also represents *metric* (rather than merely topological) information since both the distance and direction to important locations can be found. These observations can be summarised by saying that animals construct *cognitive maps* of their environments that code the locations of salient places in allocentric (i.e. non egocentric) co-ordinate frames.

There is some controversy, however, over how perceptual data is used to construct the cognitive map. Several researchers (Gallistel 1990; McNaughton, Chen et al. 1991) have argued that the principal sources of position information are dead-reckoning skills (integrating changes in position from sensory signals) and 'compass' senses (determining orientation by using non-local cues such as the sun, or by sensing physical gradients such as geomagnetism). These skills are used to maintain an estimate of the animal's current position and heading relative to the origin (e.g. the nest) of a global allocentric frame. Places are coded in terms of the distance and direction from this origin or from single landmarks whose position in the global frame are already stored. Following McNaughton et al. (1991) such a mapping scheme is here called a *vector coding* system. An alternative view, proposed for instance by O'Keefe (1990), is that a place is encoded in terms of the array of local landmarks visible from that position. In other words, that the cognitive map stores the locations of potential goals in the *local allocentric co-ordinate frames* determined by groups of (two or more) salient cues. Such a system is called a *relational coding*.

This paper is not concerned with the empirical question of which coding method is used in animal cognitive maps. Indeed, there seems no particular reason to believe that any one method will be relied upon to the exclusion others. Rather, since robust navigation skills are critical to survival, multiple coding systems may be employed. In other words, for any specific navigation task, both vector and relational solutions may be computed and behaviour chosen to be as consistent as possible with all available constraints.

The goal of this paper, is instead to consider some of the computational issues involved in using relational codes. McNaughton et al. base their preference for vector encoding over relational methods partly on the grounds that the former is computationally simpler and substantially more economical in memory use. We describe here a model of a relational map that encodes spatial knowledge and calculates paths over a wide environment yet requires memory and processing time proportional only to the number of landmarks. The system performs parallel computations using linear mathematics that can be implemented by a simple associative neural network. It is therefore not significantly more complex or demanding of memory than a vector coding. This encourages the view that similar mechanisms could be employed in animal navigation.

2 Using relational maps

The task of navigating a large-scale environment using relational methods divides into three problems: identification and re-identification of salient landmarks; encoding, and later remembering, goal locations in terms of sets of visible local cues; and finally, calculating routes between positions that share no common view. The first task, landmark identification, has been considered elsewhere both from the point of view of animal and robot navigation systems (Zipser (1983a,b); Levitt and Lawton (1990); O'Keefe (1990)). In this paper landmarks are taken to be prominent, visually distinct objects that have point-based locations in egocentric space. We assume the agent is able to select suitable landmarks from the visual scene and determine their positions relative to itself. Our primary concerns are therefore with the problems of encoding and remembering goals in local landmark frames, and extending these methods to long-range navigation tasks. The problems arising from inaccurate perceptual data and visually ambiguous landmarks are also briefly discussed.

3 Local allocentric frames

O'Keefe (1990) has proposed an interesting model of a local relational coding inspired by empirical studies of 'place' cells in the hippocampus of the rat. He suggests that the rat brain computes the origin and orientation of a polar co-ordinate frame from the vectors giving the egocentric locations of the set of salient visible cues. Specifically, he proposes that these location vectors are averaged to compute the origin (or *centroid*) of the polar frame, and that the gradients of vectors between each pair of cues are averaged to compute its orientation (or *slope*). Goal positions can then be recorded in the co-ordinate system of this allocentric frame in a form that will be invariant regardless of the position and orientation of the animal. However, there are problems with this hypothesis. Firstly, the computation of the slope is such that the resulting angle will differ if the cues are taken in different orders[1]. Since any ordering is essentially arbitrary, a specific sequence will have to be remembered in order to generate the same allocentric frame from all positions within sight of the landmark set. Secondly, as landmarks move out of sight, are occluded by each other, or new ones come into view, the values of the slope and centroid will change. Rather than changing the global frame each time a landmark appears or disappears it seems to us more judicious to maintain multiple local frames based on subsets of the available cues. These would supply several mutually-consistent encodings making the mapping system robust to changes in individual landmarks.

The use of multiple local frames has been proposed by Levitt and Lawton (1990). They observe that the minimum number of landmarks required to generate a co-ordinate frame is two (in two-dimensions, three in 3D). They also provide a useful analysis of how the constraints generated by multiple local frames can be combined, even in the presence of very poor distance information, to provide robust location estimates. To calculate, from a novel position, a goal location that has been encoded in a two landmark frame

[1] This arises because the gradient of a line is a scalar function with a singularity at infinity when the line is parallel to the y axis. Hence in order to average gradients this must be done in terms of angles or vectors, in which case the order in which the points are compared is important.

requires non-linear computations (trigonometric functions and square roots). It also requires that an arbitrary ordering of the two landmarks is remembered in order to specify a unique co-ordinate system.

Zipser (1986), who also considered a landmark pair method (Zipser 1983b), points out that if one more landmark is used to compute the local frame then all the calculations required become linear. In fact, all that is required to encode a goal location using three landmarks (in 2D, four in 3D) is that one constant is associated with each cue. Zipser called these constants "β-coefficients", they are, however, identical to the *barycentric*[2] co-ordinates that have been known to mathematicians since Moebius (see for instance Farina, 1988). Since the system for long-range navigation described below uses this three landmark method the following section considers it in more detail. The remainder of the paper treats the navigation problem as two-dimensional, however, the extension of these methods to three dimensions is straightforward.

4 Barycentric co-ordinates

Figure One shows the relative locations of a group of three landmarks (hereafter termed an *L-trie*) labelled A, B, and C, seen from two different viewing positions V and V'. A goal site G is assumed to be visible only from the first viewpoint.

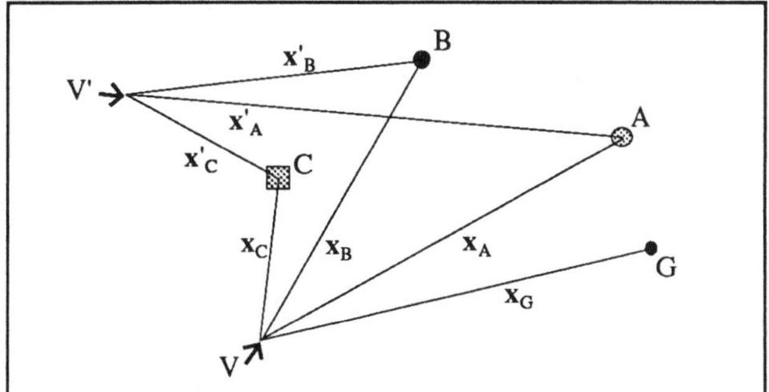

Figure One: relative positions of three landmarks and a goal from two viewpoints V and V'.

The column vectors $\mathbf{x}_i = (x_i, y_i, 1)^{\mathrm{T}}$ and $\mathbf{x}'_i = (x'_i, y'_i, 1)^{\mathrm{T}}$ give the location in homogeneous co-ordinates of object i in the egocentric frames centred at V and V' respectively. The two frames can therefore be described by the matrices

$$\mathbf{X} = [\mathbf{x}_A \quad \mathbf{x}_B \quad \mathbf{x}_C],\ \mathbf{X}' = [\mathbf{x}'_A \quad \mathbf{x}'_B \quad \mathbf{x}'_C]$$

If the three landmarks are distinct and not collinear then there exists an unique vector $\beta = (\beta_A, \beta_B, B_C)^{\mathrm{T}}$ such that

$$\mathbf{X}\beta = \mathbf{x}_G \text{ and } \mathbf{X}'\beta = \mathbf{x}'_G.$$

In others words, by remembering the invariant β the egocentric goal position from any new viewing position V' can be determined by the linear sums

$$\begin{aligned} x'_G &= \beta_A x'_A + \beta_B x'_B + \beta_C x'_C, \\ y'_G &= \beta_A y'_A + \beta_B y'_B + \beta_C y'_C, \\ (1 \ &= \beta_A + \beta_B + \beta_C). \end{aligned}$$

Note that since each constant is tied to a specific cue the ordering of the landmarks is irrelevant.

The β vector can be determined directly by computing the inverse matrix $\mathbf{X}^{-1}$ since

$$\beta = \mathbf{X}^{-1}\mathbf{X}\beta = \mathbf{X}^{-1}\mathbf{x}_G.$$

Though this inverse calculation uses only linear maths, the value of the β-encoding as a possible biological model has been questioned on the grounds of its apparent mathematical complexity (Worden 1992). However, Zipser (1986) points out that an even simpler computational mechanism is possible by allowing the β values to converge to a solution under feedback. This can be viewed as adapting the connection strengths of a linear perceptron-like (Rosenblatt 1961) learning unit. A network architecture that instantiates this mechanism is as follows. The network consists of two types of simple processing unit. The first are object-position units (*object-units* hereafter) whose activation represents the locations in egocentric space of specific goal-sites and salient landmarks. These units receive their primary input from high-level perceptual processing systems that identify goals and landmarks and determine their positions relative to the self. The second type of processor is termed a *β-coding unit.* This receives input from three object-units and adapts its connection strengths (the β values) to match its output vector to the activation of a fourth.

An example of this architecture is illustrated in Figure Two which shows a β-coding unit G/ABC that receives the positions of the landmarks A, B, and C as its inputs. The unit adapts its weights (β_A, β_B, B_C) till the output (x, y, z) matches the goal vector $(x_G, y_G, 1)$. The unit is assumed to be triggered whenever all three input nodes are active. Gradient-descent learning is used to adapt the

[2]This term, originally used in physics, is derive from "barycentre" meaning "centre of gravity" .

connection strengths. For the weight β_i from the ith object unit this gives the update rule at each iteration

$$\Delta\beta_i = \eta[(x_G - x)x_i + (y_G - y)y_i + (1 - z)]$$

where the parameter η is the learning rate. The network rapidly converges to an accurate estimate of the β values.

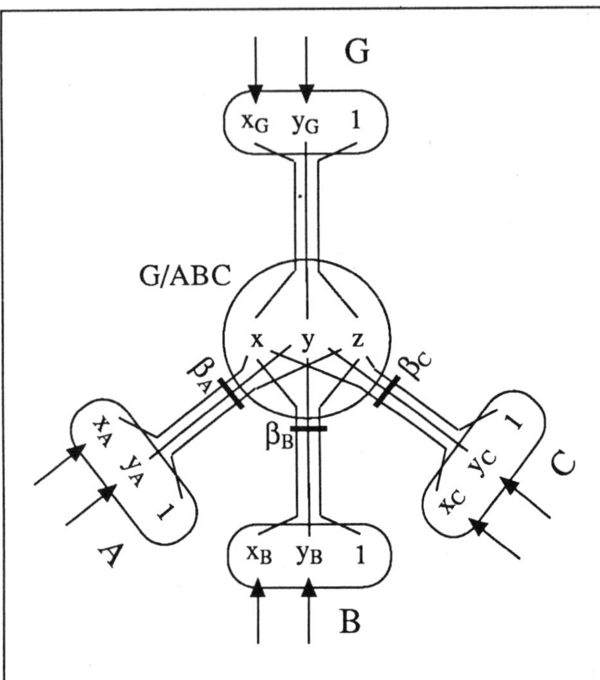

Figure Two: The β-coding unit. A perceptron model of the β-coefficient calculation.

In order to provide a further understanding of the β-encoding a geometrical interpretation can be given. The coefficient associated with each landmark is the ratio of the perpendiculars from the goal and that landmark to the line between the other two cues. For example, consider landmark *A* in Figure Three. The coefficient β_A defines an axis that is perpendicular to the line BC and scaled according to the ratio of the two perpendiculars h_G/h_A (this can also be thought of as the ratio of the areas of the triangles GBC and ABC). Taken together the three β coefficients define a *barycentric* co-ordinate frame.

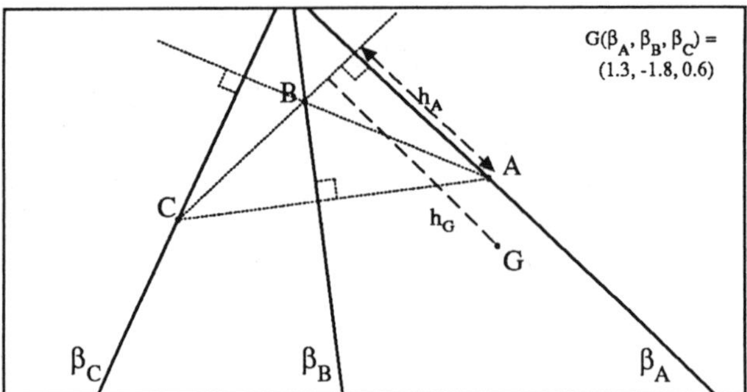

Figure Three: Coding a goal position (G) relative to the three landmarks A, B, and C using barycentric co-ordinates.

5 Long-range navigation

We now describe how this coding method can be extended to navigate between points over a wide environment that share no common landmarks. The essence of the method is to build a two-layer *relational network* of object and β-coding units that stores the positions of landmarks in the local frames defined by neighbouring L-trie groups. The resulting structure will therefore record the relationships between multiple local frames. Thereafter, the locations of distant landmarks (and goal sites) can be found by propagating local view information through this network. Zipser (1983b) and Levitt and Lawton (1990) have both discussed methods of this type for long-range navigation using landmark-pair co-ordinate frames. The advantage of using the three landmark method, however, is that following a sequence of transformations through the network is significantly simpler. Since all calculations are linear and independent of landmark order the process can be carried out by spreading activation through the relational network. In contrast, a landmark-pair method would require networks of local processing units of considerably greater complexity in order to perform the necessary non-linear transformations.

6 Encoding the cognitive map

The relational network that encodes the cognitive map is constructed whilst exploring the environment. The specific method investigated here is as follows. Each time the agent moves the egocentric positions of all visible landmarks are computed. If there are any new landmarks in this set then new object-units are recruited to the lower layer of the network to represent landmark locations. Then, for each L-trie combination in the set a test is made to see if a β-coding unit (with this local frame) already exists for each of the remaining visible cues. If not, new β-units are recruited to the network's upper layer and linked appropriately with the object-nodes. The β-coefficients are then calculated either directly (using matrix inversion) or gradually (via the perceptron learning mechanism) as the agent moves within sight of the relevant cues.

Figure Four shows an example of this process for a simple environment of five landmarks. From the current view position four landmarks A, B, C, and D are visible (as a simplification we assume 360° vision) for which the agent generates β–coding units A/BCD, B/ACD, C/ABD, D/ABC. Following adequate exploration the network illustrated in Figure Five will have been generated.

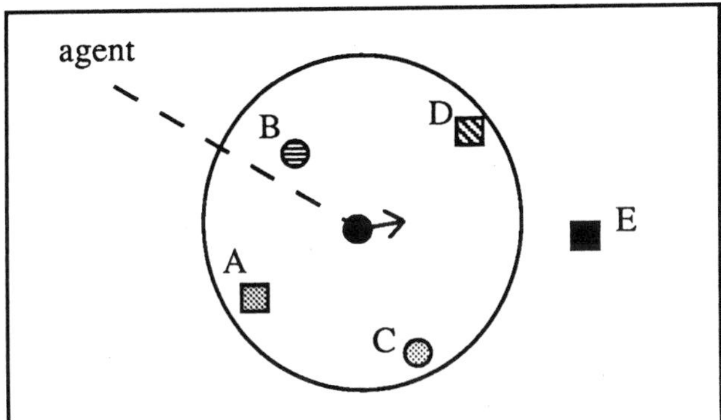

Figure Four: An environment with five landmarks, the agent is oriented towards the right with field of view as indicated by the circle .

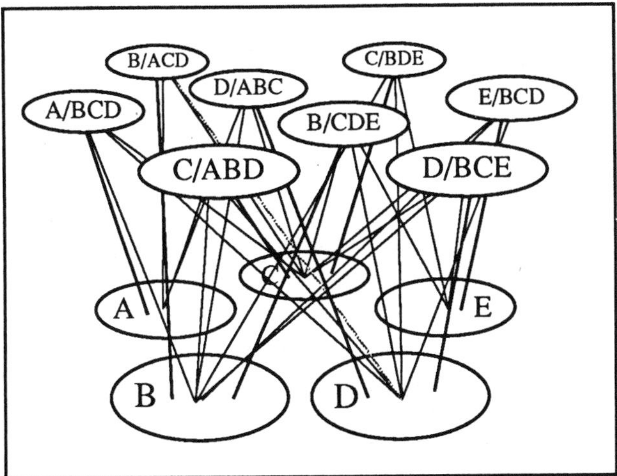

Figure Five: A relational network for the five landmark environment. The network consists of an input/output layer of object-units and a hidden layer of β-coding units that encode landmark transformations in specific local frames. The thin lines indicate input of known landmark positions to the hidden layer, thick lines show the output of newly calculated cue locations.

Given this network the agent can determine the location of any target landmark when it is within sight of any group of three others. For instance if cues A, B, and C are visible and E is required, then the active object units will trigger D/ABC (activating unit D) and hence E/BCD to give the egocentric location of the target. The method clearly generalises to allow the position of any goal site that is encoded within an L-trie frame to be found.

7 The topology of the relational net

The connectivity of the relational network defines a graph of the topological arrangement of local landmark frames. For instance, the network shown above instantiates the L-trie graph shown in Figure Six.

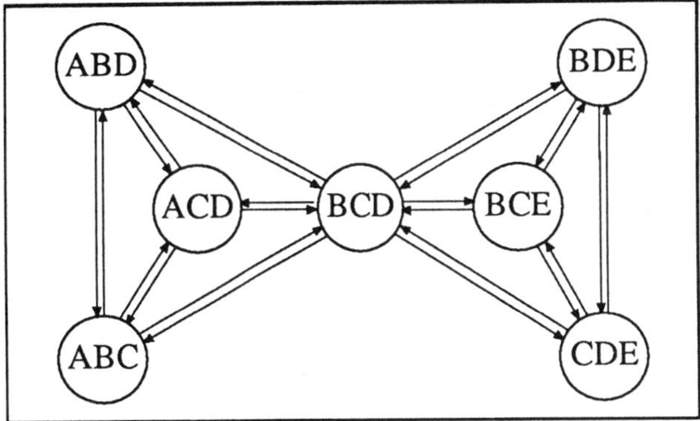

Figure Six: the L-trie adjacency graph for the five landmark environment.

The links between nodes in this graph correspond to the β–coding units. Although the graph shown here has entirely bilateral connections, there is nothing intrinsically symmetrical about the coding method. For instance, it would be quite possible to encode the relationship D/ABC and not the reverse A/BCD. This could plausibly happen if the agent, whilst moving through its environment, encodes the positions of landmarks in front with respect to those it is already passing but not vice versa. This property of the mapping mechanism accords with observations of non-reflexive navigation behaviour and spatial knowledge in humans (for a review of this evidence see Kuipers, 1982).

Figures Seven and Eight show respectively an environment of twenty-four landmarks and the adjacency graph generated after exploration by random walk. In learning this environment the system was restricted to encoding the relative locations of only the four closest landmarks at any time. This reduces the connectivity of the graph and the memory requirements of the network substantially. However, even without this restriction, the memory requirements of the system are O(N) (i.e. proportional to the number of landmarks) rather than $O(N^2)$ since only local landmark relations are stored.

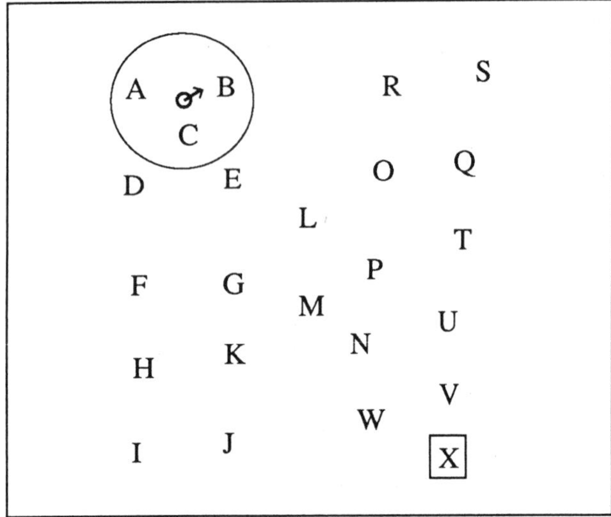

Figure Seven: Landmark locations for a sample environment. The circle indicates the range of the simulated perceptual system. The box indicates a target landmark (see below).

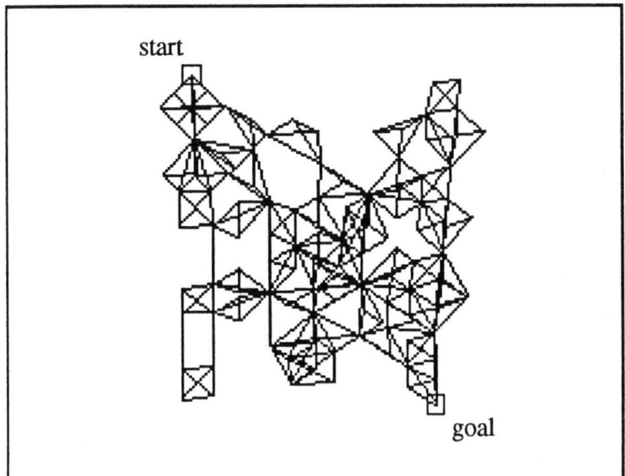

Figure Eight: An L-trie graph. Each vertice represents an L-trie node and is place in the position corresponding to the centre of the triangle formed by its three landmarks (in the previous figure). The boxes enclose the L-trie nodes local to the agent's position and the target landmark 'X'.

8 Target finding: estimating the distance and direction to desired goals

From Figure Eight it is evident that there are multiple possible paths through the network that will connect any two landmark groups. Hence the system represents a highly redundant coding of landmark locations. As described in the previous section the (external) activation of the object units for any group of three landmarks triggers the firing of all associated β-coding units which in turn activate further object units. This 'domino' effect will eventually propagate egocentric position estimates of all landmarks throughout the graph. Indeed, due to the redundancy of the paths through the graph many estimates will be computed for each landmark, each arriving at the object node after differing periods of delay. For any specific goal or landmark the delay (between the initial activation and the arrival of the first estimate) will be proportional to the length of the shortest sequence of frames linking the two positions.

Assuming noise in the perceptual mechanisms that determine the relative positions of visible cues (and hence noise in the stored β-coefficients) the position estimates arriving via different routes through the graph will vary. The question then arises as to how the relative accuracy of these different estimates can be judge. The simplest heuristic to adopt is to treat the first estimate that arrives at each node as the best approximation to that landmark's true position. This is motivated by the observation that each transition in a sequence of frames can only add noise to a position estimate, hence better estimates will (on average) be provided by sequences with a minimal number of frames (whose outputs will arrive first). We call this accordingly the *minimal sequence* heuristic. However, there is a second important factor that effects the accuracy of propagated location estimates which is the spatial arrangement of the cues in each L-trie group. The worst case is if all the landmarks in a given group lie along a line, in this situation the β-coefficients for an encoded point will be undefined. In general, landmarks groups that are near collinear will also give large errors when computing cue positions in the presence of noise. One possibility, not explored here, is for the system to calculate estimates of the size of these errors and propagate these together with the computed landmark positions. Each computed location would then arrive with a label indicating how accurate an estimate it is judged to be.

In the following examples landmark positions were calculated simply by rejecting information from L-trie frames that were near-collinear (i.e. within some margin of error) and otherwise using the minimal-sequence heuristic, that is, adopting the first location estimate to arrive at each node. The issue of combining multiple estimates to obtain greater accuracy is considered further below.

Finding the direction and distance to a specific goal by propagating landmark positions is here called *target finding*. This competence is sufficient to support behaviours such as orienting toward distant locations, and moving in the direction of a goal with the hope of finding a direct route. However, this mechanism will not always be appropriate as a method of navigation for two reasons. First, the direct line to a goal location is clearly not always a viable path. Secondly, the target finding system is susceptible to cumulative noise. We have simulated the effect of 0, 5, 10 and 20% gaussian relative noise[3] in the measurement of all egocentric position vectors that occurs during map learning and navigation. Figure Nine shows an example of the effect of this noise on estimates for the position of landmark X (in the environment shown in Figure Seven) relative to the agent's starting location. The figure demonstrates that with the less accurate perceptual data only a rough approximation to a desired goal vector can be obtained. Of course it is would be possible for the agent to move in the direction indicated by target finding and then hope to use landmarks that are recognised en route to gradually correct the initial error and so home in on the goal. However, this will often be a risky strategy as a direct line will not necessarily cross known territory. The following section describes a method which exploits a heuristic of this sort but in a form that is more likely to generate a successful path to the goal.

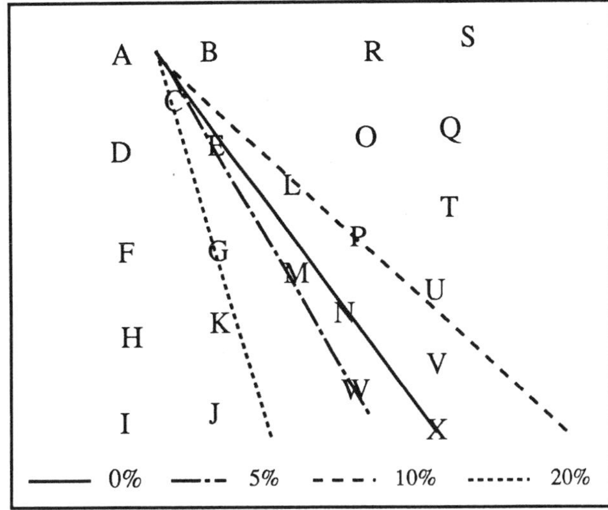

Figure Nine: *Target finding* in the presence of 0, 5, 10 and 20% relative noise in perceived landmark positions.

9 Path following: a robust method for moving to a goal location.

An alternative strategy is to move, not in the direction of the goal itself, but towards landmarks that are known to lie along a possible path to the goal. This method, here called *path following,* involves determining a sequence of adjacent local frames that link start and goal positions prior to setting out, then navigating by moving from frame to frame through this topological sequence. Because perceptual information about known landmarks will (very likely) become available as each frame is crossed, the agent will be able to replace estimates of cue positions with 'hard' data, thus avoiding the build-up of noise encountered by the target finding system. There is however, some computational overhead to be incurred through the need to calculate a suitable sequence of adjoining frames. Since, again, there are multiple sequences to choose from some heuristics are required to determine which should be preferred. The *minimal sequence* heuristic is again appropriate though on the slightly different grounds that shorter sequences should (on average) give more direct routes. Other heuristics are possible, for instance, estimates of the actual distances covered by alternate routes could be calculated allowing a more informed judgement as to which is the shortest path.

To find the minimal sequence we simply reverse the process of propagating information through the relational network. In other words, we perform a spreading activation search from the goal back toward the start position. This is easiest to imagine in the context of the L-trie graph (Figure Eight) however it could be implemented directly in the relational network by backward connections between units.

[3] If n_x and n_y are samples from the gaussian noise distribution, the vector (x,y) is perceived as $(x + n_x x, y + n_y y)$.

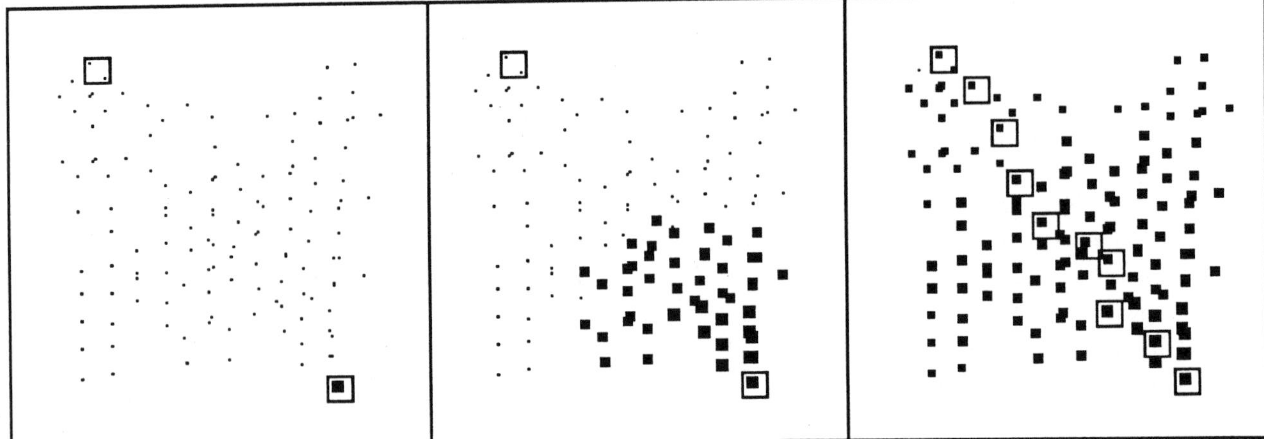

Figure Ten: Spread of activation through the L-trie graph (Figure Eight) after 0, 4, and 9 time steps ($\lambda = 0.95$). The points in the figures represent the vertices in the L-trie graph. The size of each point shows the level of activation of that L-trie node. The boxes indicate that a minimal sequence ABC BCE CEL EGL GLM LMN MNP MNW NVW VWX was found.

Our simulations model this parallel search process through a series of discrete time-steps. This occurs as follows. The L-trie node closest to the goal is activated and clamped on (i.e. its activity is fixed throughout the search) while all other nodes are initialised with zero activity. The signal at the goal is then allowed to diffuse through the adjacency graph decaying by a constant factor λ for each link that is traversed[4]. Once the activation reaches the L-trie node local to the agent the minimal sequence can be found. Beginning with the start node this sequence is traced through the network simply by connecting each node to its most active neighbour.

This spread of activation is illustrated in Figure Ten. The three frames show the activity after 0,4, and 9 time-steps, after which time the activity has filtered through to the start node. The path found is indicated by the boxes enclosing the winning nodes.

Having found a minimal sequence the *path following* method proceeds as follows. The agent moves toward the average position of the landmarks vectors for the first L-trie in the path. Once that position is reached (it will be near the centre of the three cues), the position of the next L-trie is generated (using direct perceptual data as far as possible) and so on till the goal is reached. Figure Eleven illustrates this mechanism for the noise-free case, and Figure Twelve for noise levels of 5, 10 and 20%. The second figure demonstrates that path following is extremely robust to noise as the error in the final goal estimate is independent of total path-length.

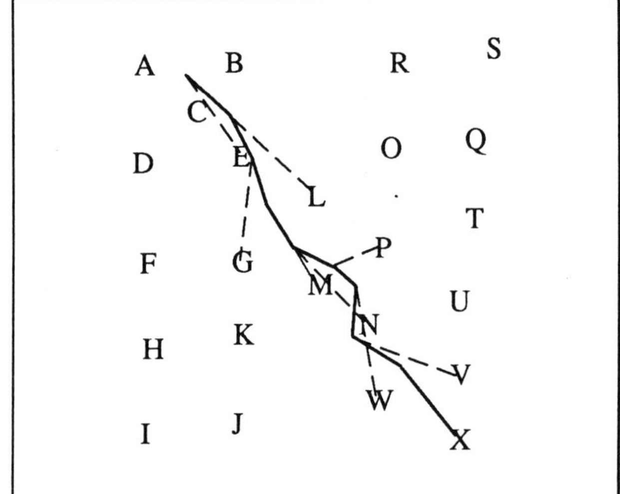

Figure Eleven: Moving to the goal by *path following*. The dotted lines indicate additional landmark locations that were utilised en route.

[4]This is achieved by, at each time-step, updating the acticity of each L-trie node to be equal to the maximum of its own activation and that of any of its immediate neighbours (multiplied by the decay factor) at the previous time-step.

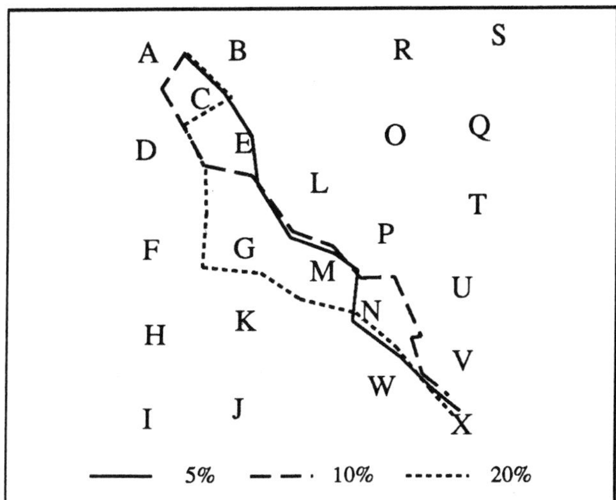

Figure Twelve: Performance of the *path following* system in the presence of 5, 10 and 20% relative noise in perceived landmark positions. (Different L-trie sequences were followed in each case as networks with different connectivity were acquired during exploration).

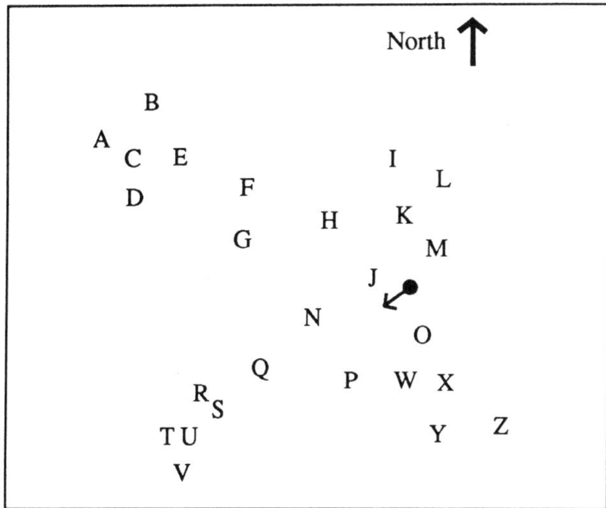

Figure Thirteen: An environment of twenty-six landmarks with the agent positioned and oriented as shown.

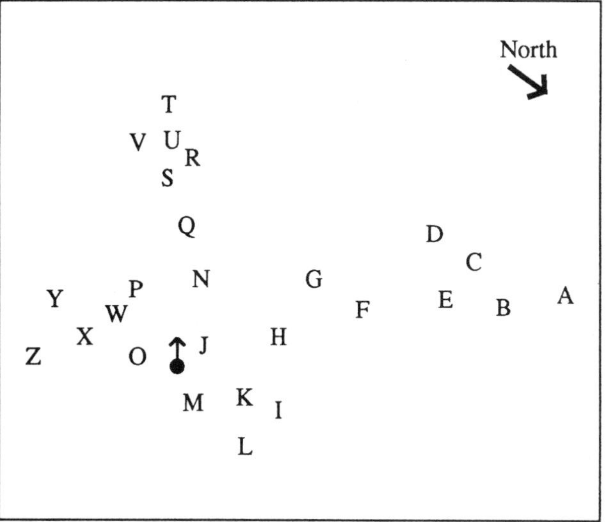

Figure Fourteen: The cognitive map in the agent's egocentric co-ordinate frame generated from the viewing position shown in the previous figure.

10 Building a predictive map

The 'domino' effect that propagates local landmark positions through the relational net will eventually generate egocentric location estimates for all landmarks (with connections to the L-trie graph). The resulting activity can be thought of as a dynamic map of the environment which could update itself as the agent moves and is automatically arranged with the agent at the centre and oriented towards its current heading. Figures Thirteen and Fourteen show this egocentric map computed (with 20% noise) for an environment of twenty-six landmarks.

As a result of cumulative error the exact layout of landmarks is more accurately judged close at hand than further away, however, the topological relations between landmarks are reproduced throughout. One use to which such a map might be put is to disambiguate perceptually similar landmarks by calculating predictions of upcoming scenes. In other words, if agent moves sees a landmark which appears identical to one it already knows, then it can judge whether the two cues actually arise from the same object from the extent to which the place where the landmark appears agrees with the location predicted for it by the mapping system. If there is a large discrepancy between actual and predicted locations then the new landmark could be judged to be a distinct object. On the other hand, if there is a good match the agent could conclude that it is observing the original cue.

11 Future Work

An examination of the error tolerance of the computation of β values reveals several interesting facts. One is that the error in encoding the position of an arbitrary goal relative to an L-trie is minimised if the three landmarks form an equilateral triangle. This arises because the size of the error in the β-coefficients is proportional to the variance (due to noise) in the area of this triangle. This variance is lowest when the ratio of the area to the total length of the sides is maximal. By the same argument, when encoding each of four landmarks relative to the other three the optimal configuration is for the landmarks to form a square. This suggests that certain landmark configurations should be given greater weight during path computation. A second factor affecting the size of the error in location estimates is the viewing position at which the β computation is made. Through a monte carlo simulation we have found that the error is generally lower when the agent is within the area enclosed by the four positions and has a minimum near to the centroid of the L-trie. The difference in error due to viewing position also becomes more exaggerated as the landmark configuration becomes less optimal. We hope to use these findings to determine better methods for coping with noise in the map computations. Both in encoding the β-coefficients during exploration and in combining multiple estimates of landmark positions during navigation.

12 Conclusion

We have described a system for way-finding between places that share no common views. The system works by encoding landmark locations in the local co-ordinate frames defined by groups of three nearby cues. These relations can be stored in a simple linear network of perceptron-like units. The system can orient towards distant targets, find and follow a path to a goal, form an overall map, and disambiguate perceptually similar landmarks. The robust and economical character of this system makes it a feasible mechanism for implementing a large-scale cognitive map.

Acknowledgements

The authors are grateful to John Porrill, John Frisby, Neil Thacker, Pete Coffey, and Mark Blades for advice and discussion. This research was funded by the Science and Engineering Research Council.

References

Farin, G. (1988). *Curves and Surfaces for Computer Aided Geometric Design: A Practical Guide.* Boston, Academic Press.

Gallistel, C. R. (1990). *The Organisation of Learning.* Cambridge, MA, MIT Press.

Kuipers, B. (1982). "The "map in the head" metaphor." *Environment and behaviour* **14**: 202-220.

Levitt, T. S. and D. T. Lawton (1990). "Qualitative navigation for mobile robots." *Artificial Intelligence* **44**: 305-360.

McNaughton, B. L., Chen, L. L. and E.J. Markus (1991). "Landmark learning and the sense of direction - a neurophysiological and computational hypothesis." *Journal of Cognitive Neuroscience* **3**(2): 192-202.

O'Keefe, J. (1990). The hippocampal cognitive map and navigational strategies. *Brain and Space.* Oxford, Oxford University Press.

O'Keefe, J. A. and L. Nadel (1978). *The Hippocampus as a Cognitive Map.* Oxford University Press.

Rosenblatt, F. (1961). *Principles of Neurodynamics: Perceptrons and the Theory of Brain Mechanisms.* Washington, DC, Spartan Books.

Worden, R. (1992). "Navigation by fragment fitting: a theory of hippocampal function." *Hippocampus* **2**(2): 165-188.

Zipser (1983a). *The representation of location.* Institute for Cognitive Science, UCSD, ICS 8301.

Zipser, D. (1983b). *The representation of maps.* Institute of Cognitive Science, UCSD, ICS 8304.

Zipser, D. (1986). Biologically plausible models of place recognition and place location. *Parallel Distributed Processing: Explorations in the Micro-structure of Cognition, Volume 2.* Cambridge, MA, Bradford. 432-70.

DYNAMICS OF SPATIAL NAVIGATION: AN ADAPTIVE NEURAL NETWORK

Nestor A. Schmajuk and H. T. Blair
Northwestern University
Department of Psychology
Evanston, IL 60208-2710
U.S.A.

ABSTRACT

This study presents a real-time neural network capable of describing the dynamics of spatial navigation. The network incorporates detectors that can be tuned to the values of visual angles of different spatial landmarks, as they are perceived from the location where a reinforcing event is encountered. After a detector has been tuned, its output generates an "effective stimulus" which peaks at the distance from the landmark where positive or negative reinforcement was encountered before. The outputs of the tuned detectors become associated with the reinforcing event. The network generates spatial generalization surfaces that can guide navigation from any starting location that is within view of familiar landmark cues, even if the starting location has never been visited before. Spatial navigation is described by adopting a "stimulus-approach" principle, that is, by approaching appetitive places and avoiding aversive places. When generalization surfaces are assumed to represent forces driving an animal's behavior, the dynamics of spatial movements can be described. Computer simulations were carried out for appetitive and aversive place learning. The paper shows that the network correctly describes the navigational trajectories and dynamics of several spatial learning tasks.

1. INTRODUCTION

Spatial navigation is a major area of inquiry in animal behavior, as well as in modern robotics. Schmajuk (1990) described spatial navigation using a neural network that assumes animals perceive the visual angles of different spatial landmarks. These visual angles are used to build a spatial *generalization surface* around the location of an appetitive stimulus. Based on this generalization surface, and making use of a "stimulus-approach" principle, the network is able to describe place learning independently of the responses used to approach the goal. However, Schmajuk (1990) applied his model only to appetitive spatial learning, omitting tasks in which animals move away from aversive locations or approach appetitive stimuli while detouring around aversive places. Furthermore, Schmajuk's (1990) model does not describe the dynamics of spatial navigation. Therefore, in order to offer a more exhaustive neural network account of spatial learning, the present paper extends Schmajuk's (1990) model to the depiction of aversive place learning and describes the physical dynamics (acceleration, velocity, and position as a function of time) of spatial navigation.

2. THE NEURAL NETWORK

Figure 1 shows a neural network, based on Schmajuk's (1990) model, that accomplishes place discrimination. Briefly, the first stage of the network is a layer of detectors, each of which receives a signal proportional to the visual angle of a spatial landmark; the second stage is a neural element that associates the output of the detectors with another event (e.g., an unconditioned stimulus or US, denoted S^k in Figure 1), and generates the output of the system. An additional neural element compares S^k to the system's output, in order to control the formation of associations between the detectors and the US.

In the first stage of the network shown in Figure 1, a detector D_i^k can be tuned to the value of the visual angle, Ω_i, of spatial landmark L_i at the spatial location where unconditioned stimulus S^k is encountered. When landmark L_i is viewed after the detector has been tuned, the output of the detector, effective stimulus E_i^k, peaks at the distance from L_i where S^k was encountered before. In the second stage of the network shown in Figure 1, the outputs of the tuned detectors, E_i^k, become associated with S^k. The association between E_i^k and S^k is designated V_i^k. According to Figure 1, each E_i^k activates the output unit in proportion to V_i^k, thereby generating an output G^k equal to $\Sigma_i V_i^k(t) E_i^k$. The signal G^k is also fed back to a neural unit where it is compared with S^k, in order to control associative learning. Each E_i^k may increase its association V_i^k until G^k equals the intensity of stimulus S^k, λ^k.

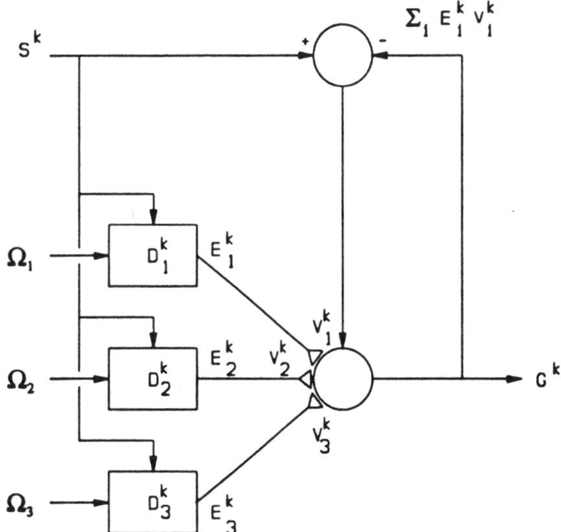

Figure 1. Diagram of the adaptive neural network. Effective stimuli E_i^k generated by different tuned detectors D_i^k are connected to a minimum square error network. Visual angles Ω_i are the inputs to detectors D_i^k. S^k is the tuning signal for detectors D_i^k. V_i^k are modifiable synaptic weights. G^k is the output of the network. Arrows represent nonmodifiable connections and triangles represent plastic synapses.

The visual angle hypothesis

Zipser (1985, 1986) proposed a neural model capable of recognizing a given spatial location. The model consists of two layers of neural elements. Each unit in the first layer is specific for a given spatial landmark, and fires maximally when the current visual angle of the landmark equals a previously stored visual angle. The second layer in Zipser's model generates an output proportional to the sum of the outputs of all units in the first layer. Following Zipser, Schmajuk (1990) assumed that animals use the visual angle subtended by spatial landmarks in order to define spatial locations. A landmark L_i of size O_i at a distance d_i subtends a unique visual angle $\Omega_i\ (d_i)$. Formally, the visual angle $\Omega_i\ (d_i)$ of spatial landmark L_i is defined by

$$\Omega_i\ (d_i) = \arctan\ (\ O_i\ /\ d_i), \qquad [1]$$

where O_i is the size of landmark L_i, and d_i denotes the distance to L_i. The visual angle $\Omega_i(d_i)$ of L_i is equal to 90 degrees when $d_i = 0$. $\Omega_i(d_i)$ gradually decays to zero degrees as distance d_i from L_i increases. As Zipser (1985) pointed out, visual angle $\Omega_i(d_i)$ remains constant if both distance d_i and size O_i "dilate" simultaneously.

Tuned detectors

Detectors D_i^k are tuned by S^k to the value of the visual angle Ω_i of landmark L_i. When L_i is encountered after the detector has been tuned, effective stimulus $E_i^k(d_i)$ peaks at the place where S^k was encountered before. The tuning of a detector is accomplished by storing the value of the visual angle Ω_i at the place where S^k is encountered. For example, consider the case of stimulus S^k encountered in the spatial vicinity of landmark L_i. T_i^k represents the memory of the value of the visual angle Ω_i, stored at the place where S^k has been encountered. Memory T_i^k is updated according to

$$\Delta\ T_i^k\ (t) = B\ X_i(d_i)\ S^k\ [\ \Omega_i(d_i) - T_i^k(t)\ X_i(d_i)\ ], \qquad [2]$$

where B is the learning rate and $X_i(d_i)$ is a representation of L_i that, unlike the visual angle $\Omega_i(d_i)$, does not decrease over distance. $X_i(d_i)$ is 1 whenever $\Omega_i(d_i) > \varepsilon$ (where ε is arbitrarily small) and 0 otherwise. S^k equals 1 when stimulus k is encountered, and 0 when it is absent. By Equation 2, changes in $T_i^k(t)$ occur only when $S^k(d_i)$ is present, $X_i(d_i)$ is 1, and $T_i^k(t)\ X_i(d_i)$ differs from $\Omega_i(d_i^k)$. Therefore, $T_i^k(t)$ stores the value of the visual angle $\Omega_i(d_i^k)$, subtended by L_i at the place where S^k is encountered. A neural architecture for tuned detectors D_i^k, which incorporates the associative value T_i^k, was proposed by Schmajuk (1990).

Effective stimuli

When the L_i is encountered after detector D_i^k has been tuned according to Equation 2, the detector generates an output which peaks at the distance from the landmark L_i where S^k was previously encountered. This distance is denoted d_i^k, and therefore detector D_i^k peaks when $d_i = d_i^k$. The effective spatial stimulus, $E_i^k(d_i)$, for S^k based on L_i, is given by the equation

$$E_i^k(d_i) = f\{\ X_i(d_i) - C^k\ [\ T_i^k(t)\ X_i(d_i) - \Omega_i(d_i)\ ]^2\ \}, \qquad [3]$$

where $f[x] = x$ if $f[x] > 0$ and $f[x] = 0$ otherwise. By Equation 3, $E_i^k(d_i)$ assumes its maximum value of 1 at a given distance from L_i where $T_i^k(t)\ X_i(d_i) = \Omega_i(d_i)$. After tuning, this is the distance d_i^k where S^k has previously been encountered. At distances greater than or less than d_i^k, output of the detector becomes smaller, so that Equation 3 describes spatial generalization with a peak at the distance d_i^k. Notice that the parameter C^k determines the slope of the generalization gradient. In agreement with Miller's (1944, 1959) suggestion that the slope of generalization for an aversive stimulus is steeper than the generalization of an appetitive stimulus, $C^{aversive}$ is assumed to be greater than $C^{appetitive}$.

Associations between effective stimuli and S^k

Once spatial effective stimuli E_i^k are available from tuned detectors, they can be associated with stimulus S^k. Changes in the associative value between effective stimulus $E_i^k(d_i)$ and S^k, V_i^k, are defined by

$$\Delta\ V_i^k(t) = D\ E_i^k(d_i)\ [\ \lambda^k - \ \Sigma_j\ V_j^k(t)\ E_j^k(d_i)\ ], \qquad [4]$$

where $E_i^k(d_i)$ is the magnitude of the effective stimulus of L_i for S^k, D is the learning rate parameter ($0 < D \leq 1$), λ^k is the intensity of S^k, and $\Sigma_j\ V_j^k(t)\ E_j^k(d_i)$ is the combined prediction of S^k made upon all spatial effective stimuli. In order to have a net positive V_i^k on a given trial, $D = D'$ whenever $\lambda^k > \Sigma_j\ V_j^k(t)\ E_j^k(d_i)$, and $D = D''$ otherwise. It is important to notice that in Equation 4, whereas $E_i^k(d_i)$ is a function of the distance d_i from a given location to landmarks L_i, $V_i^k(t)$ is a function of time. That is, $E_i^k(d_i)$ changes only when the animal moves, but $V_i^k(t)$ changes continuously even in the absence of movement.

For simplicity, Equation 4 allows V_i^k to assume both positive and negative values (for a description of a system which learns using only positive weights, see Schmajuk & DiCarlo, 1992). As in the case of Widrow and Hoff's (1960), Rescorla and Wagner's (1972), Sutton and Barto's (1981), and Pearce and Hall's (1980) learning algorithms, Equation 4 implies that each E_i^k competes with all other E_i^ks in order to gain association with S^k, and the best predictor of S^k becomes most associated with it. In associative learning, the best predictor is a stimulus highly correlated with S^k, i.e., a stimulus that is present every time S^k is present and absent every time S^k is absent. In the case of effective stimuli, the best predicting E_i^k is the one most precisely predicting S^k, i.e., other things being equal, the E_i^k that peaks nearest to S^k with the least generalization to other locations. In addition, use of Equation 4 implies that when equally good predictors are used, all of them should be present in order to predict the full intensity of S^k, $\lambda^k(t)$.

Generalization surfaces

As shown in Figure 1, each E_i^k activates the network's output unit in proportion to V_i^k, thereby generating an output G^k equal to $\Sigma_i\ V_i^k(t)\ E_i^k(d_i)$. The output of the network at all points in a spatial environment yields a *generalization surface*--an internal representation of the spatial environment. The height of the generalization surface peaks at the location of stimulus S^k, and gradually decreases at points further from the stimulus. As will be explained, we assume that animals can approach or avoid a discriminated place by following the gradient of this generalization surface.

Equation 3 defines the value of effective stimulus $E_i^k(d_i)$ as a function of the Euclidian distance d_i to landmark L_i. If landmark L_i is stationary, then d_i itself is a function of the Cartesian coordinates x and y, which specify the animal's location. Thus $E_i^k(d_i)$ may also be expressed as $E_i^k(x,y)$. Therefore, the output of the neural network at a spatial position (x,y), $G^k(x,y)$, can be expressed as

$$G^k(x,y) = \Sigma_i V_i^k(t) E_i^k(x,y). \quad [5]$$

$G^k(x,y)$ represents the height of a generalization surface at a point (x,y).

In the case of combined appetitive and aversive generalization surfaces, the net generalization surface is given by

$$G^{US\ net}(x,y) = G^{US\ appetitive}(x,y) - G^{US\ aversive}(x,y). \quad [6]$$

Different appetitive USs (food, water, etc.) are assumed to have different generalization surfaces, that the animal will use to approach the alternative goals according to their motivational states. We adopt the convention that generalization surfaces of appetitive stimuli increase downwards whereas generalization surfaces of aversive stimuli increase upwards.

Performance rules

The next section introduces performance rules that define how spatial generalization surfaces are related to (a) navigational trajectories and (b) navigational dynamics.

Navigational trajectories

We adopt a "stimulus-approach" view of behavioral control, by which animals approach appetitive stimuli and avoid aversive stimuli. Different appetitive stimuli will be approached according to the animal's motivational state (hunger, thirst, etc.). At each point in space, the animal should move from less to more appetitive regions of the motivationally selected generalization surface. In order to accomplish this result, we assume that the animal is able to produce small movements around a given point, staying in the next point if it is more appetitive than the previous one, and going back to the previous one in the other case. This behavior is similar to Tolman's (1932) *vicarious trial-and-error behavior*. According to Tolman, at choice points in a maze, animals sample different stimuli before making a decision. This active scanning of alternative next places reflects the animal's generation and comparison of the appetitiveness of different places.

When the *net generalization surface is appetitive*, i.e., $G^{US\ appetitive}(x,y) > G^{US\ aversive}(x,y)$, animals will move from a point defined by coordinates (x_o, y_o) to a point defined by coordinates $(x_o + \Delta x, y_o + \Delta y)$ if

$$G^{US\ appetitive}(x_o+\Delta x, y_o+\Delta y) > G^{US\ appetitive}(x_o, y_o). \quad [7]$$

When the *net generalization surface is aversive*, i.e., $G^{US\ appetitive}(x,y) < G^{US\ aversive}(x,y)$, animals will move from a point defined by coordinates (x_o, y_o) to a point defined by coordinates $(x_o + \Delta x, y_o + \Delta y)$ if

$$G^{US\ aversive}(x_o+\Delta x, y_o+\Delta y) < G^{US\ aversive}(x_o, y_o). \quad [8]$$

Movement continues until the net generalization surface equals zero, $G^{US\ net}(x,y) = 0$. Under the adopted convention that generalization surfaces of appetitive goals increase downwards whereas generalization surfaces of aversive goals increase upwards, animals always move in the direction of the steepest descent on the generalization surface. As in any gradient traversal method, movement along the generalization surfaces might be halted by local minima. However, because $V_i^k(t)$ changes if the animal does not find the US (see Equation 4), generalization surfaces $G^k(x,y)$ undergo modifications over time, and these variations usually permit escape from local minima.

Navigational dynamics: retarding forces

As explained in the previous section, animals move on either the appetitive or aversive generalization surface, depending on the value of the net surface $G^{US\ net}$. In addition to determining which surface the animal moves on, the net generalization surface also determines the dynamics of the movement. In order to derive the dynamics of spatial navigation, the behavioral meaning of generalization curve $G^k(x,y)$ needs to be specified. According to Brown (1942), the magnitude of the approach tendency to a goal can be measured by the force with which rats pull against a restraining harness at different distances from the rewarded place. Therefore, a possible behavioral interpretation of a generalization surface $G^k(x,y)$ is that it represents the force which drives the animal's movements towards or away from point (x,y). This view is coherent with the "stimulus-approach" position adopted in the previous section, and assumes that appetitive stimuli "pull" the animal toward them, and aversive stimuli "push" the animal away from them.

Equations 7 and 8 define the trajectory an animal will follow when navigating in an environment with aversive and appetitive locations. We assume that (a) animals move from a point defined by coordinates (x_o, y_o) to a point defined by coordinates $(x_o + \Delta x, y_o + \Delta y)$, driven by a motivational force that is determined by the value of the net generalization surface at the next point $G^{US\ net}(x_o + \Delta x, y_o + \Delta y)$, and (b) that animals are subject to a retarding force, $R\ v(t)^2$, that tends to oppose their movement as velocity increases. Whereas the motivational driving force may be understood as the appetitiveness or aversiveness of different environmental locations, the retarding force may be interpreted as a resistance to movement linked to physical factors (muscle and joint friction, terrain in which the animal is moving). For instance, the retarding force will be larger when the animal is swimming in the water than when the animal is walking or running on the ground.

Applying Newtons' second law, we obtain

$$a(t)\ M = G^{US\ net}(x_o + \Delta x,\ y_o + \Delta y) - R\ v(t)^2, \quad [9]$$

where M represents the animal's mass and R is a retarding coefficient.

By Equation 9, as velocity increases, a(t) will gradually decrease and the animal will move at a constant velocity, called *terminal velocity*, v_t. The value of the animal's terminal velocity is obtained by setting a(t) equal to zero in Equation 9. Thus, terminal velocity at the location (x_o, y_o) is given by

$$v_t(x_o,\ y_o) = (\ G^{US\ net}(x_o{+}\Delta x,\ y_o{+}\Delta y)\ /\ R\ )^{1/2}. \quad [10]$$

By Equation 10, terminal velocity increases with increasing driving forces (e.g., a more appetitive location) and decreasing retarding coefficient R (e.g., running versus swimming). If the initial velocity exceeds the value of the terminal velocity, the velocity will decrease. When the initial velocity is much smaller or much larger than the value of the final velocity computed by Equation 10, the animal might not be capable of reaching terminal velocity between points (x_o, y_o) and ($x_o + \Delta x$, $y_o + \Delta y$). In this case, Equation 9 must be used to describe the transition from initial to terminal velocity. However, when the difference between initial and terminal velocity is small enough, the animal is capable of reaching terminal velocity between points (x_o, y_o) and ($x_o + \Delta x$, $y_o + \Delta y$), and Equation 10 may be used to approximate the actual velocity at each point. For a simple treatment of motion with a retarding velocity-dependent force the reader is referred to Tipler (1982, page 144).

Navigation toward a goal: decelerating forces

Hull (1932) argued that, in order to obtain reward at an appetitive location, animals should reach the place where reward is encountered at an appropriate final velocity. This final velocity should be small in order to apprehend the reward without colliding with the rewarding object. In order to combine a fast movement toward the goal with a slow final velocity, animals should decelerate as they near the goal. The dynamics of this combined accelerated-decelerated movement is readily captured by the assumption that in addition to its appetitive association $V_i^k(t)$ (Equation 4), *an appetitive location also accrues a decelerating association that prevents collisions with the rewarding object.* This assumption reflects the fact that any object can be aversive if it hits the animal hard enough.

Therefore, at the location of the goal, an *appetitive and a decelerating detector are tuned by the appetitive US*, according to Equation 2, yielding

$$\Delta\ T_i^{appetitive}(t) = B\ X_i(d_i)\ S^{US\ appetitive}\ [\ \Omega_i(d_i) - T_i^{appetitive}(t)\ X_i(d_i)\ ], \quad [11]$$

and

$$\Delta\ T_i^{decelerating}(t) = B\ X_i(d_i)\ S^{US\ appetitive}\ [\ \Omega_i(d_i) - T_i^{decelerating}(t)\ X_i(d_i)\ ]. \quad [12]$$

Each detector will provide an effective stimulus given by

$$E_i^{appetitive}(d_i) = f\{\ X_i(d_i) - C^{appetitive}[\ T_i^{appetitive}(t)\ X_i(d_i) - \Omega_i(d_i)\ ]^2\ \}, \quad [13]$$

and

$$E_i^{decelerating}(d_i) = f\{\ X_i(d_i) - C^{decelerating}[\ T_i^{decelerating}(t)\ X_i(d_i) - \Omega_i(d_i)\ ]^2\ \}. \quad [14]$$

Since parameter C in Equations 13 and 14 is generally considered to be larger for aversive stimuli than for appetitive stimuli (see Equation 3), $C^{decelerating}$ is assumed to be larger than $C^{appetitive}$. The result of this difference is that the decelerating generalization surface has a steeper gradient than the appetitive generalization surface, and thus falls to zero faster (closer to the goal). Therefore, the net generalization surface is only affected by the decelerating force within a certain distance from the goal. The points in space where the animal comes under the influence of the decelerating force are called *brakepoints*, since that is where the animal begins slowing down to avoid collision with the goal.

In order to obtain a near-zero velocity at the goal, we assume that the decelerating effective stimulus, $E_i^{decelerating}$, which has been tuned by $S^{US\ appetitive}$, is also associated with $S^{US\ appetitive}$. That is, we assume that the decelerative force preventing the collision with the goal increases together with the appetitiveness of the goal. Changes in the associative value between effective stimulus $E_i^{appetitive}(x,y)$ or $E_i^{decelerating}(x,y)$ and $S^{US\ appetitive}$, are defined by

$$\Delta\ V_i^{appetitive}(t) = D\ E_i^{appetitive}\ [\ \lambda^{appetitive} - \Sigma_j\ V_j^{appetitive}(t)\ E_j^{appetitive}(x,y)\ ], \quad [15]$$

and

$$\Delta\ V_i^{decelerating}(t) = D\ E_i^{decelerating}\ [\ \lambda^{appetitive} - \Sigma_j\ V_j^{decelerating}(t)\ E_j^{decelerating}(x,y)\ ]. \quad [16]$$

As explained before, $G^{appetitive}(x,y)$ represents the motivational force driving the animal towards the goal, and the final force driving the animal is equal to the motivational force minus a retarding force. In addition to the retarding force introduced in Equation 9, a decelerative force must now be added, yielding

$$a(t)\ M = G^{US\ appetitive}(x_o + \Delta x,\ y_o + \Delta y) - K\ G^{decelerating}(x_o,\ y_o)\ v(t) - R\ v(t)^2. \quad [17]$$

The term K $G^{decelerating}(x_o,\ y_o)\ v(t)$, where K is a deceleration coefficient, represents the *decelerating* force opposing the accelerating force in proportion the velocity of the animal, where $G^{decelerating}(x,y) = V_i^{decelerating}(t)\ E_i^{decelerating}$. As the retarding force, the decelerative force is also a function of velocity. This is to be expected, because the animal only needs to decelerate when moving too fast in the direction of the goal. However, unlike the frictional force, the decelerative force is also a function of the direction of movement. The value of the animal's terminal velocity in the vicinity of the goal is now given by

$$v_t(x_o, y_o) = (1/2R)\ \{-K\ G^{decelerating}(x_o, y_o) + [\ (K\ G^{decelerating}(x_o, y_o))^2 + 4R\ (G^{US\ appetitive}(x_o+\Delta x, y_o+\Delta y))\ ]^{1/2}\ \}. \quad [18]$$

By Equation 18, the terminal velocity in the vicinity of the goal increases with increasing appetitive values and decreases with increasing decelerating forces and retarding coefficient R. Outside of the braking region, where $G^{decelerating}(x_o, y_o) = 0$, Equation 18 is identical to Equation 10.

In summary, in order to obtain reward at an appetitive location, animals should reach the place where reward is encountered at an appropriately small final velocity. This condition can be achieved by assuming that the dynamics of movement toward the goal are controlled by a learned decelerating force, which opposes the learned accelerating force that drives the animal toward the goal.

Aversive stimulation at the goal

As described, any appetitive goal location acquires a decelerating aversive association, which is proportionate to its accelerating appetitive association. If the goal location is negatively reinforced by an additional aversive stimulus, then an added aversive association will be developed. When the appetitive generalization curve is replaced by the net generalization curve, $G^{US\ net}$, the terminal velocity is given by

$$v_t(x_o, y_o) = (1/2R)\ \{-K\ G^{decelerating}(x_o, y_o) + \ [\ (K\ G^{decelerating}(x_o, y_o))^2 + 4R\ (\ G^{US\ net}(x_o+\Delta x, y_o+\Delta y))\ ]^{1/2}\ \}. \quad [19]$$

When the initial velocity is large compared to the value of the final velocity computed by Equation 19, the animal might not be capable of reaching terminal velocity between points (x_o, y_o) and $(x_o + \Delta x, y_o + \Delta y)$. In this case, Equation 17 must be used to describe the transition from initial to terminal velocity. However, when the difference between initial and terminal velocity is small, and therefore the animal is capable of reaching terminal velocity between points (x_o, y_o) and $(x_o + \Delta x, y_o + \Delta y)$, Equation 19 may be used to approximate the actual velocity at each point.

From a physical standpoint, the problem of deceleration involves determining the proper strength of the decelerative force and the proper place to apply it (the brakepoint) in order to stop a moving object at the goal. The strength of the decelerative force increases with increasing with increasing accelerating force, $G^{US\ net}$, and decreases with increasing resistance coefficient, R, and decreasing distance from the brakepoint to the goal. In our model, the brakepoint is predetermined by the value of the parameter $C^{decelerating}$.

Summary

Navigational trajectories and dynamics are defined by the following performance rules: (a) When the net generalization curve is appetitive, animals will move toward the most appetitive adjacent location (Equation 7); (b) When the net generalization curve is aversive, animals will move toward the least aversive adjacent location (Equation 8); (c) At locations removed from the goal, the velocity of the approach to the most appetitive adjacent place, or the least aversive adjacent place, is a function of the value of the net generalization surface at the adjacent place and a retarding factor (Equation 10); (d) Appetitive goal locations accrue decelerative associations that prevent collisions with the rewarding objects (Equations 15 and 16).

3. COMPUTER SIMULATIONS

This section presents computer simulations obtained with the tuned network for different spatial learning paradigms: appetitive place learning, aversive place learning, and appetitive-aversive interactions. In every case, similar results were obtained by assuming that the simulated animal (a) is free to navigate through the training environment and to find appetitive and aversive locations, (b) is forcedly exposed to every spatial position including appetitive and aversive locations, and (c) is forcedly exposed only to the appetitive and aversive locations.

Parameter values

Computer simulations generate values of the relevant variables only at discrete spatial distances. Simulation parameters were $B = 1$, $D^{appetitive'} = .1$, $D^{appetitive''} = .0013$ $D^{aversive'} = .1$, $D^{aversive''} = .0013$, $R = .5$, $K = 2.5$, $C^{appetitive} = 160{,}000$, $C^{aversive} = C^{decelerative} = 400{,}000$.

Appetitive place learning

Experimental data. Morris (1981) trained rats to escape cool water by locating a hidden platform in a tank filled with opaque water (Morris' tank). He found that if rats were trained to navigate to the invisible platform from a given starting point, they could swim directly to the goal from any other starting location in the pool during testing. During a place task, the room is usually well-lighted, and a number of distinctive extramaze cues (table, door, blackboard, fluorescent lights, rack of cages) are visible.

Brown (1942) trained a group of hungry rats to obtain food reward at the end of an alley. After the rats were trained, Brown measured the magnitude of the approach tendency by the force with which rats pulled against a restraining harness. He found that rats pulled harder as the distance to the rewarded place decreased.

Computer simulations. Figure 2a shows an appetitive place learning simulation. The simulated environment consisted of a rectangular matrix (20 x 20), representing the pool. In an environment like Morris' water tank, the animal is motivated to escape the water, and therefore, the platform becomes an appetitive US. Simulated acquisition consisted of 10 trials, during which the animal was exposed to 36 equally spaced points in the pool and rewarded only at the goal (indicated by the asterisk). During training, the animal perceives three distal landmarks (indicated by rectangles) from every point in the field, which are used to build a generalization surface around the appetitive location. In agreement with Morris' (1981) data, the trained animal can find the goal from any starting point

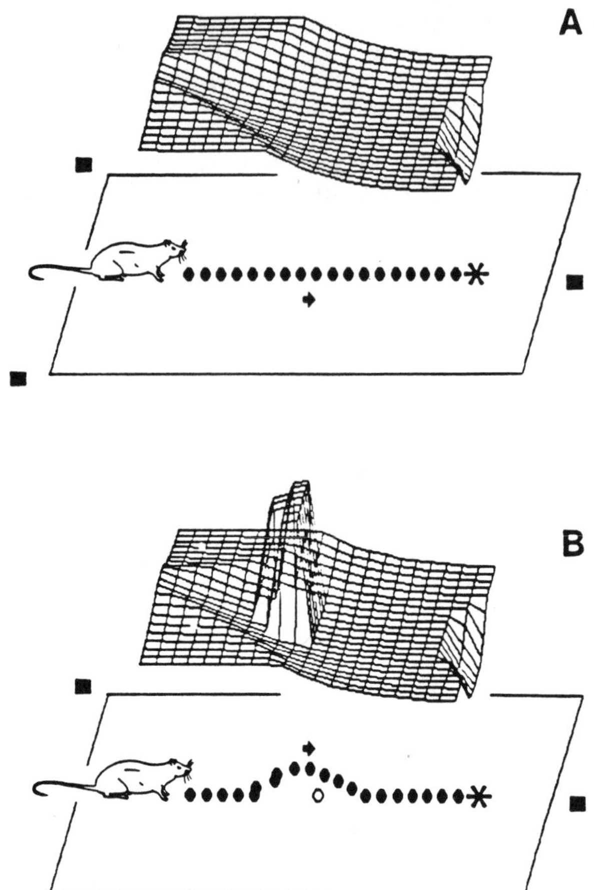

Figure 2. Appetitive generalization surface for combined appetitive and aversive place learning. A: Appetitive generalization surface, $G^{appetitive}(x,y)$, for an appetitive US encountered at the point indicated with the asterisk. B: Composite generalization surface for an appetitive US encountered at the point indicated with the asterisk and an aversive US encountered at the point indicated with the open circle. Squares indicate the location of the spatial landmarks. Solid circles indicate different routes to the goal from different starting places. Arrows indicate the direction of movement.

(see also Schmajuk, 1990). In agreement with Brown (1942), the appetitive force is greatest at the rewarded place, and decreases at locations farther from the rewarded place.

Aversive place learning

Experimental data. Brown (1942) also studied the avoidance gradient from an aversive place in an alley. He gave a group of rats two brief electric shocks at the end of an alley. After receiving the shocks, when animals were placed at that end of the alley without shock, they showed a tendency to avoid the place. Brown measured the magnitude of the avoidance tendency by the force with which rats pulled against a restraining harness at different distances from the place where they had received the shock. The rats pulled harder as the distance from the shocked place decreased. In addition to aversive stimuli, barriers, walls, and objects may also be regarded as mildly aversive objects, since animals avoid colliding with them.

Computer simulations. Figure 2b shows a simulation of combined appetitive-aversive place learning. The simulated animal was trained and rewarded exactly as in Figure 2a, but with an aversive stimulus introduced at the center of the field. The animal builds two generalization surfaces: one around the appetitive location, and another around the aversive location. The surface shown in Figure 2b is composed of both the appetitive and aversive generalization surfaces. At locations where the appetitive surface is greater than the aversive surface (i.e., $G^{US\ appetitive}(x,y) > G^{US\ aversive}(x,y)$), Figure 2b shows the height of the appetitive surface. At places where the aversive surface is greater than the appetitive surface (i.e., $G^{US\ appetitive}(x,y) < G^{US\ aversive}(x,y)$), the height of the aversive surface is shown. Using these generalization surfaces, the simulated animal finds the goal from any starting point, while also avoiding the aversive place. It should be noted that, because velocity is defined by the net generalization surface according to Equation 10, the animal slows down as it approaches and detours around the aversive location.

Navigational dynamics in a runway

Experimental data. Wagner (1961) and Amsel, Rashotte, and MacKinnon (1966) recorded the running speed of animals at different points in a runway. Wagner (1961) and Amsel, et al. (1966) found that under continuous reinforcement, animals accelerate in the start box, reach peak velocity in the alley, and decelerate in the goal box. Velocities at all points in the runway increase over acquisition trials.

Computer simulations. In order to evaluate the performance of the model, we computed velocity at different positions in the runway using Equation 19. A point at one end of the alley was chosen as the location of an appetitive US. Because a narrow alley is essentially a unidimensional environment, one landmark suffices for spatial generalization. Therefore, we assumed that a single landmark (the rear wall of the alley) is located behind the rewarded place. Navigation under the guidance of a single landmark has been called "cue" learning (Jarrard, 1983).

In a unidimensional environment, generalization surfaces become generalization curves. As explained in the previous section, we assume that a rewarded place acquires both appetitive and decelerating generalization curves. Whereas the appetitive curve represents the accelerating force driving the animal toward the goal, the decelerating curve represents a decelerating force (that opposes the accelerating force) which ensures that the goal is reached with a small velocity; that is, without colliding with the rewarding object.

As with generalization surfaces, we adopt the convention that appetitive generalization curves increase downwards, whereas aversive curves increase upwards. Figure 3 shows aversive (decelerative), appetitive, and net generalization curves, together with velocity, as a function of trials and position in the runway. Positive values of the net generalization curve represent the force driving the animal in the direction of the goal. Positive values of the velocity curve represent the velocity with which the animal moves toward the goal. Positive values of the aversive (decelerating) curve represent the decelerating force when the animal is moving at the velocity shown by the velocity curve. Both the appetitive accelerating curve and the aversive decelerating curve peak at the position of the goal, and increase in amplitude over trials. Both net driving force and velocity increase at the start point, peak midway down the runway, and decrease toward the goal. Although peak net driving force and velocity increase over trials, the net driving force and final velocity remain relatively constant at the goal. Figure 3 shows that the appetitive curve generalizes over the whole runway, and therefore is able to guide the animal from the start box to the goal. The aversive curve generalizes over half of the runway, thereby decelerating the animal from the middle of the runway, starting at the brakepoint, until it reaches the goal with a small velocity. In agreement with Wagner's (1961) results, Figure 3 shows that velocities at different points in the runway increase over acquisition trials. In agreement with Brown's (1942) results (see previous simulation), Equation 21 shows that the force measured by the harness equals $G^{US\ appetitive}(x_o + \Delta x, y_o + \Delta y)$, which increases as the animal is located closer to the goal.

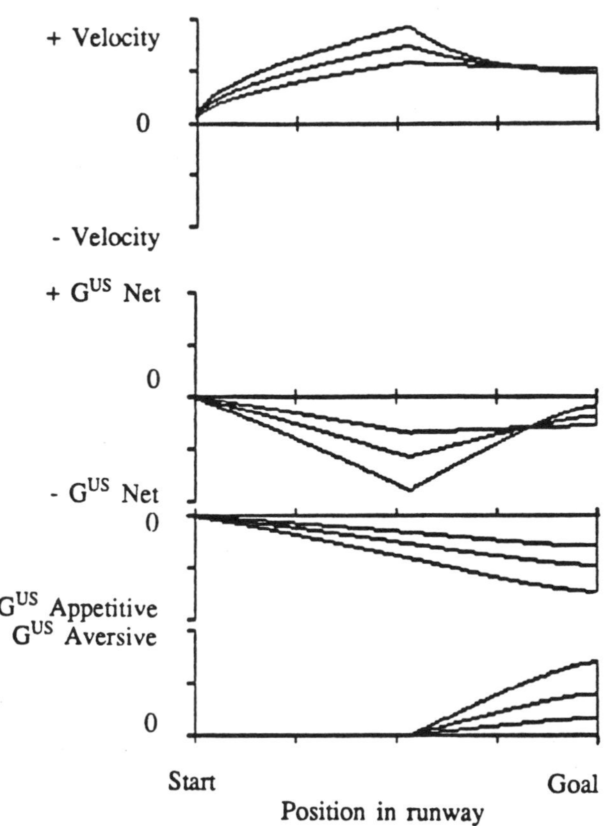

Figure 3. Navigational dynamics in a runway. Simulated velocity, net generalization curve, appetitive generalization curve, and aversive (decelerating) generalization curve at different places in a runway, for acquisition trials 2, 4, and 10. The goal acquires both appetitive and aversive generalization curves. Whereas the appetitive generalization curve accelerates the animal toward the goal, the aversive generalization curve decelerates the animal and ensures a smooth arrival at the goal.

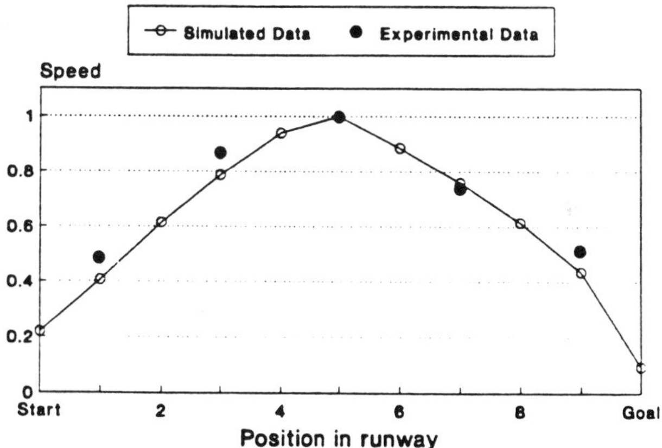

Figure 4. Velocity profile in a runway. Experimental and simulated velocity as a percentage of peak velocity, at different places in a runway. Experimental data from Amsel, Rashotte, and MacKinnon (1966).

Notice that although a decelerating force prevents the animal from colliding with or overshooting the goal, this force is not measured by the harness in Brown's (1942) experiment because the harness keeps the animal at rest. Applying Newtons' second law when the animal is restrained by the harness with force F_h in the vicinity of the goal, we have

$$a(x_o, y_o)\ M = G^{US\ appetitive}(x_o + \Delta x, y_o + \Delta y) - F_h - G^{decelerating}(x_o, y_o)\ v(x_o, y_o) - R\ v(x_o,y_o)^2. \quad [20]$$

When the animal does not move, $a(x_o, y_o) = 0$ and $v(x_o,y_o) = 0$, and therefore

$$F_h = G^{US\ appetitive}(x_o + \Delta x, y_o + \Delta y). \quad [21]$$

Figure 4 shows the simulated velocity profile in a runway after 10 simulated trials. As shown in Figure 4, simulation results are in close agreement with Amsel, et al.'s (1966) empirical data.

Appetitive-aversive interactions in a runway

Experimental data. Miller, Brown, and Lipovsky (1943) studied the behavior of albino rats in situations in which different intensities of avoidance and approach tendencies were in conflict. Miller, et al. trained hungry rats to run down an alley to obtain food, and afterwards they gave the rats a brief shock while they were eating. After training in different combinations of shock intensity and hunger level, the rats were placed at the start of the alley and their behavior was observed. Figure 5 (drawn after Miller, 1944) shows that the place at which animals stop is determined by the relative strength of the two drives. Under both strongly appetitive and aversive drives, the animals stop close to the goal (point A). With both weakly appetitive and aversive drives, animals stop close to the goal (point B). With a weakly appetitive and a strongly aversive drive, animals stop far from the goal

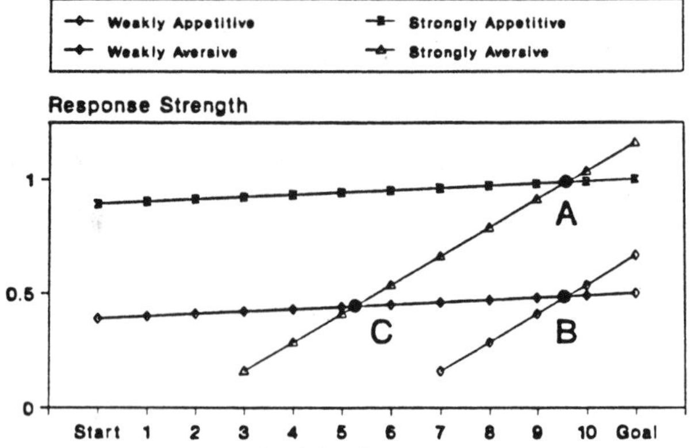

Figure 5. Appetitive-aversive interactions in a runway (after Miller, 1944). Tendencies to approach and avoid the goal box as a function of the distance to the goal box, when the goal box is made strongly or weakly appetitive and strongly or weakly aversive. Notice the steeper slope of the aversive tendencies.

(point C). Although response strength is represented by a straight line in Figure 5, Miller (1944) observed that it might be represented, as in our model, by a curvilinear function.

Computer simulations. In order to evaluate the performance of the model, we computed the final position in a runway under different combinations of appetitive and aversive reinforcements at the goal box. Simulated animals were trained to run down an alley to obtain either a strong or a weak reward for 10 trials. Subsequently, animals received several trials with either strong or weak punishment at the goal box, in addition to appetitive reinforcement. After training in different combinations of punishment and reward intensities, the simulated rats were placed at the start of the alley and their behavior was observed. Movement proceeded in the direction of the goal until a certain point was reached, where navigation stopped. From the start of the alley up to the point where movement stops, simulated results were computed in real time as the animal moves towards the goal. Because velocity becomes negative beyond the stop point, curves plotted beyond the stop point in Figure 6 represent the force and velocity of movement away from the goal.

As in Miller, et al's (1944) experiment, Figure 6 shows that the place where animals stop is determined by the relative strength of the appetitive and aversive stimuli. Panels A, B, and C in Figure 6 correspond to points A, B, and C in Figure 5. In panel A, after 4 trials with both strongly appetitive and aversive stimuli, the animals stop close to the goal. In panel B, after 4 trials with both weakly appetitive and aversive stimuli, animals stop close to the goal. Finally, in panel C, after only one trial with a strongly aversive stimulus and a weakly appetitive stimulus, animals stop far from the goal. Figures 5 and 6 show that simulations accurately reflect Miller, et al.'s results.

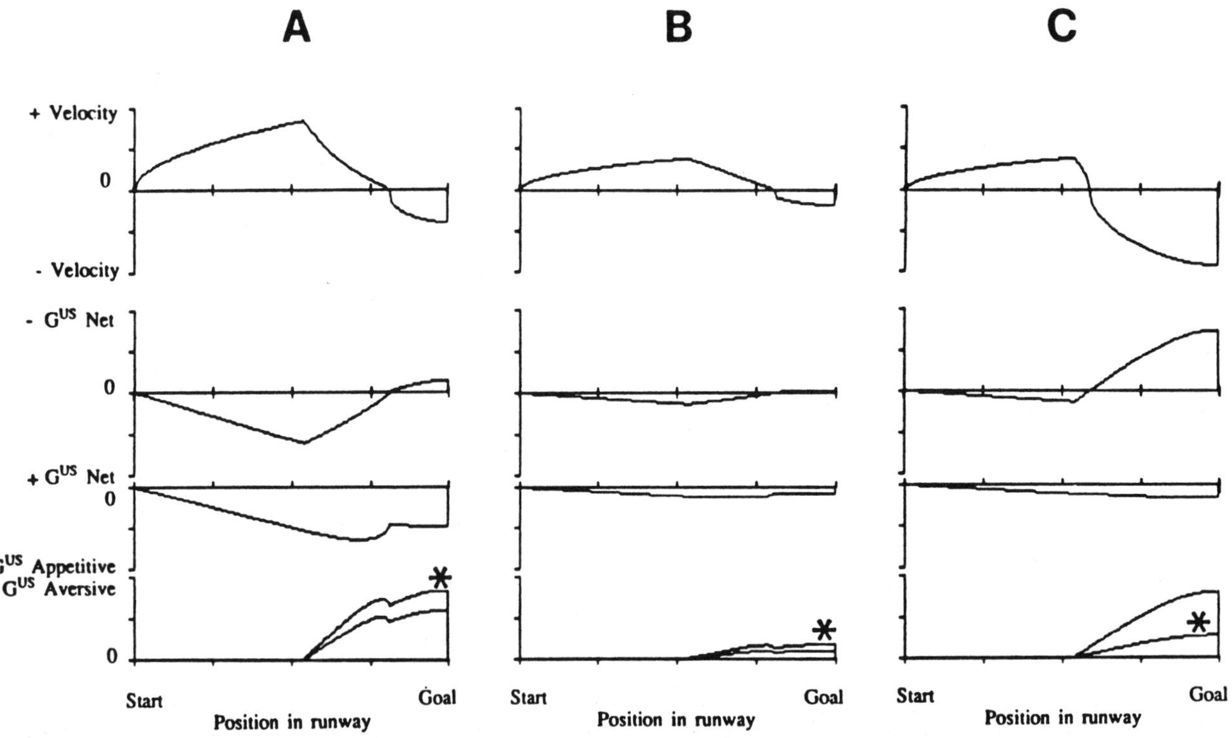

Figure 6. Appetitive-aversive interactions in a runway. Velocity, net, appetitive, decelerating, and aversive generalization curves for: (A) a strong appetitive US and a strong aversive US, (B) a weak appetitive US and a weak aversive US, and (C) for a weak appetitive US and a strong aversive US, encountered at the goal. Decelerating curves are graphed as an aversive force and indicated by asterisks.

4. DISCUSSION

Schmajuk (1990) introduced a real-time neural network capable of describing both temporal discrimination and spatial learning in a unified fashion. When applied to place discrimination in the spatial domain, the neural network tunes detectors to respond to the values of the visual angles of different landmarks as they are perceived from the spatial location where a reinforcing event is encountered. The pattern recognition mechanism that provides each detector with information concerning a specific landmark is not described in the present rendition of the model. After a detector has been tuned, its output generates an effective stimulus which peaks at the distance from the landmark where positive or negative reinforcement was encountered before. The outputs of the tuned detectors become associated with the reinforcing event. This feature allows the network to generate appropriate spatial generalization surfaces that are used to guide spatial navigation in situations where appetitive places are approached and aversive places are avoided. Schmajuk (1990) carried out computer simulations for appetitive place and cue learning tasks. Under the assumption that appetitive generalization gradients are less steep than aversive generalization gradients, the present paper shows that the model successfully depicts appetitive-aversive place and cue learning.

When generalization surfaces are assumed to represent forces driving animal's behavior, the model allows the description of the dynamics of navigation toward the goal. We assume that animals are subject to a retarding force that opposes the movement of the animal. At locations removed from the goal, velocity is a function of the value of the net generalization surface and the retarding factor. We propose that appetitive places accrue both appetitive (accelerating) and decelerating associations. Whereas appetitive associations accelerate the animal toward the goal, decelerating associations slow the animal down to ensure proper velocity upon arrival at the goal.

In an appetitive place learning task, computer simulations show that the animal can find the goal from any start point, a result that is in agreement with Morris' (1981) data. In addition, as in Brown (1942), simulations demonstrate that appetitive forces show a maximum at the rewarded place and decrease with increasing distances from the rewarded location. Also in agreement with Brown (1942), computer simulations show that aversive forces show a maximum at the punished place and decrease with increasing distances from the punished location. When combined appetitive and aversive place learning was simulated, results show that animals are able to move toward the goal and detour around aversive places. When the model was applied to the computation of the velocity at different positions in a runway, simulation results offered a proper quantitative description of Amsel, et al.'s (1966) data. Finally, computer simulations of the final position in a runway under different combinations of appetitive and aversive reinforcement at the goal box are in close agreement with Miller, et al.'s (1943) results.

In summary, the model provides (a) accurate qualititative descriptions of appetitive and aversive place learning and (b) good quantitative characterizations of speed profiles in a runway.

ACKNOWLEDGEMENTS

The authors are thankful to Peter Killeen, William Revelle, and Aaron Thieme for their helpful comments on a previous version of the manuscript. This project was supported in part by Grant BRSG SO7 RR07028-22 awarded by the Biomedical Research Support Grant Program, Division of Research Resources, National Institutes of Health, and Grant N00014-91-J-1764 from the Office of Naval Research.

REFERENCES

Amsel, A., Rashotte, M.E., & MacKinnon, J.R. (1966). Partial reinforcement effects within subjects and between subjects. *Psychological Monograph: General and Applied, 80*, (20, Whole # 628).

Barto, A.G., & Sutton, R.S. (1981). Landmark learning: an illustration of associative search. *Biological Cybernetics, 42*, 1-8.

Brown, J.S. (1942). The generalization of approach responses as a function of stimulus intensity and strength of motivation. *Journal of Comparative Psychology, 33*, 209-226.

Hull, C.L. (1932). The goal gradient hypothesis and maze learning. *Psychological Review, 42*, 117-121.

Jarrard, L.E. (1983). Selective hippocampal lesions and behavior: effects of kainic acid lesions on performance of place and cue tasks. *Behavioral Neuroscience, 97*, 873-889.

Miller, N.E. (1944). Experimental studies in conflict. In J.McV. Hunt (Ed.), *Personality and the behavior disorders*. New York: Ronald Press.

Miller, N.E. (1959). Liberalization of basic S-R concepts: Extensions to conflict behavior, motivation, and social learning. In S. Koch (Ed.), *Psychology: A study of a science, Vol 2*. New York: McGraw Hill.

Miller, N.E., Brown, J.S., & Lipofsky, H. (1943). A theoretical and experimental analysis of conflict behavior: III. Approach-avoidance conflict as a function of strength of drive and strength of shock. Cited in Miller (1944).

Morris, R.G.M. (1981). Spatial location does not require the presence of local cues. *Learning and Motivation, 12*, 239-260.

Pearce, J.M., & Hall, G. (1980). A model for Pavlovian learning: Variations in the effectiveness of conditioned but not of unconditioned stimuli. *Psychological Review, 87*, 532-552.

Rescorla, R.A., & Wagner, A.R. (1972). A theory of Pavlovian conditioning : Variations in the effectiveness of reinforcement and non-reinforcement. In A.H. Black and W.F. Prokasy (Eds.), *Classical Conditioning II: Theory and Research*, (pp 64-99). New York: Appleton-Century-Crofts.

Schmajuk, N.A. (1990). Role of the hippocampus in temporal and spatial navigation: An adaptive neural network. *Behavioral Brain Research, 39*, 205-229.

Schmajuk, N.A. and DiCarlo, J.J. (1992). Stimulus configuration, classical conditioning, and the hippocampus. *Psychological Review, 99*, 269-305.

Sutton, R.S., & Barto, A.G. (1981). Toward a modern theory of adaptive networks: Expectation and prediction. *Psychological Review*, *88*, 135-170.

Tipler, P.A. (1982). *Physics*. New York: Worth Publishers.

Tolman, E.C. (1932). Cognitive maps in rats and men. *Psychological Review*, *55*, 189-208.

Wagner, A.R. (1961). Effects of amount and percentage of reinforcement and number of acquisition trials on conditioning and extinction. *Journal of Experimental Psychology*, *62*, 234-242.

Widrow, B., & Hoff, M.E. (1960). Adaptive switching circuits. IRE WESCON Convention Record, Part 4, 96-104.

Zipser, D. (1985). A computational model of hippocampal place fields. *Behavioral Neuroscience*, *99*, 1006-1018.

Zipser, D. (1986) Biologically plausible models of place recognition and goal location. In J.L. McClelland, D.E. Rumelhart and the PDP Research Group, *Parallel Distributed Processing. Explorations in the Microstructure of Cognition. Volume 2: Psychological and Biological Models*, pp. 432-470. Cambridge, MA: MIT Press.

LEARNING

Modeling Nervous System Function with a Hierarchical Network of Control Systems that Learn

A. Harry Klopf, James S. Morgan, and Scott E. Weaver
Wright Laboratory (Mail stop: AAAT), Wright-Patterson Air Force Base, Ohio 45433-6543
Telephone: (513) 255-7649; Fax: (513) 476-4302; E-mail: klopfah%avlab.dnet@aa.wpafb.af.mil

Abstract

A computational model of nervous system function during classical and instrumental conditioning is proposed. The model assumes the form of a hierarchical network of control systems. Each control system is capable of learning and is referred to as an *associative control process* (ACP). Learning systems consisting of ACP networks, employing the drive-reinforcement learning mechanism (Klopf, 1988) and engaging in real-time, closed-loop, goal-seeking interactions with environments, are capable of being classically and instrumentally conditioned, as demonstrated by means of computer simulations. In multiple-T mazes, the systems learn to chain responses that avoid punishment and that lead eventually to reward. The temporal order in which the responses are learned and extinguished during instrumental conditioning is consistent with that observed in animal learning. Also consistent with animal learning experimental evidence, the ACP network model accounts for a wide range of classical conditioning phenomena. ACP networks, at their current stage of development, are intended to model limbic system, hypothalamic, and sensorimotor function, suggesting a relationship between classical and instrumental conditioning that extends Mowrer's (1956, 1960/1973) two-factor theory of learning. ACP networks constitute solutions to temporal and structural credit assignment problems, suggesting a theoretical approach for the synthesis of machine intelligence.

1.0 INTRODUCTION

Currently, two theoretical paradigms prevail in attempts to model and emulate the biological mechanisms of memory, learning, and intelligence. In the *artificial intelligence (or cognitive science) paradigm*, it is assumed that symbolic or cognitive relationships having the character of IF-THEN statements can serve as building blocks for the analysis and synthesis of intelligent information processing systems. Alternatively, in the *pattern recognition paradigm* which has been favored by neural network modelers, a central question is that of how to construct networks of neuron-like elements that can be trained to recognize spatial patterns. We suggest that a fundamental and possibly crucial aspect of natural intelligence has been left out of both of these paradigms. That aspect is real-time, closed-loop, goal-seeking interactions between a (biological or synthesized) learning system and its environment (e.g., see Wiener, 1948/1961; Ashby, 1952/1960; Mowrer, 1960/1973; Klopf, 1972, 1982, 1986, 1988, 1989; Sutton and Barto, 1981, 1990; Wilson, 1986; Bitterman, 1988; Roitblat, 1988; Baird and Baker, 1990; Cliff, 1990; Klopf and Morgan, 1990; Moore, Berthier, and Blazis, 1990; Morgan, Patterson, and Klopf, 1990a, 1990b; Williams and Baird, 1990; Johnson, 1991; Meyer and Wilson, 1991).

In modeling nervous system function, we find that we can incorporate the temporal dimension, closed-loop processes, and goal-seeking mechanisms by drawing upon two paradigms that were favored in the 1940s and 1950s, namely, *animal learning psychology* and *control theory*, the latter paradigm relating to what was referred to, especially a few decades ago, as cybernetics (Wiener, 1948/1961; Ashby, 1952/1960). One reason that the approaches of animal learning psychologists and control theorists can be more readily combined and extended now is that the theory of what is called real-time or time-dependent learning mechanisms (Klopf, 1972, 1982, 1986, 1988, 1989; Sutton and Barto, 1981, 1990; Kosko, 1986; Moore et al., 1986; Tesauro, 1986; Gluck, Parker, and Reifsnider, 1988; Sutton, 1988; Brown, Kairiss, and Keenan, 1990; Klopf and Morgan, 1990; Moore, Berthier, and Blazis, 1990; Morgan, Patterson, and Klopf, 1990b) has advanced in recent years. We will show that real-time or time-dependent learning mechanisms are well suited for use in control systems that are interacting in networks. Furthermore, as we have demonstrated by means of computer simulations, networks of trainable control systems, as models of nervous system function, can exhibit a variety of classical and instrumental conditioning behaviors seen in animal learning.

Each control system in our network model is capable of learning. We have investigated the forms that such control systems may take if they are to interact in networks in neurobiologically and psychologically plausible ways. We refer to a control system that is capable of learning as an *associative control process* or ACP. Thus, we are investigating learning systems consisting of ACP networks as theoretical models of nervous system function, using the experimental results of neurobiological and animal learning research as constraints.

In the laboratory, animal learning is investigated by means of two experimental procedures: classical conditioning and instrumental conditioning. The distinction between these two procedures is a simple one. Classical conditioning is an open-loop experimental procedure; controlled stimuli delivered by the experimenter are not contingent on the animal's behavior. Instrumental conditioning is a closed-loop experimental procedure;

stimuli received by the animal are contingent on its behavior.

The question arises of how the experimental results of an open-loop analysis of animal learning relate to the experimental results of a closed-loop analysis. This has been a central question of animal learning research for decades (Wise, 1989; Roitblat, 1987; Mackintosh, 1983; Dickinson, 1980; Gray, 1975; Rescorla and Solomon, 1967). We suggest an answer in the form of an ACP network model of nervous system function. In proposing the model, we are motivated by a desire to create a theoretical framework within which animal learning psychology, physiological psychology, neurobiology, neural network theory, control theory, and machine learning can be related. We see our efforts as being part of what is sometimes referred to as computational neuroethology.

The model we propose relates to a model due to Mowrer (1956, 1960/1973), who proposed a two-factor theory of learning in which it was suggested that animals learn instrumental responses in two phases. First they acquire the appropriate emotional response, such as hope, fear, relief, or disappointment, to name four emotions that Mowrer judged to be fundamental. Then, in a second phase of conditioning, the appropriate motor response or behavior is learned, this learning being guided by the emotional responses learned in the first phase. Actually, these two phases or aspects of learning may, in general, be occurring in parallel as is the case for the learning system we describe below.

Consistent with Mowrer's (1956, 1960/1973) two-factor theory of learning, we have synthesized networks made up of two kinds of ACPs, *reinforcement centers* and *motor centers*. Reinforcement centers learn to anticipate or predict reinforcement and are intended to model the limbic system and hypothalamus. Fonberg (1986, p. 310) states that "reward and punishment sites, both in man and animals, are mostly localized within the structures of the limbic system." Motor centers directly generate behavior and are intended to model sensorimotor function. The reinforcement centers utilize the drive-reinforcement learning mechanism (Klopf, 1988). The motor centers utilize a learning mechanism that adjusts connection strengths so as to cause the motor center outputs to track reinforcement center outputs in such a way that appropriate behavior comes to be generated. The ACP networks we have investigated consist of four ACPs: two reinforcement centers and two motor centers.

The ACP network-controlled learning systems we synthesized were evaluated by means of computer simulations of classical and instrumental conditioning tests. The classical conditioning tests measured the ability of the learning system to model or predict seventeen categories of Pavlovian animal learning phenomena. Fifteen instrumental conditioning tests measured the ability of an ACP network-controlled system to learn to navigate multiple-T mazes in order to obtain primary positive reinforcement and avoid primary negative reinforcement, the former being defined to be synonymous with reward and the latter with punishment. Learning occurred during real-time, closed loop interactions between the simulated system and a simulated multiple-T maze. The seventeen classical conditioning tests and the fifteen instrumental conditioning tests yielded behavior consistent with experimental results from animal learning research

A terminological point should be noted. Our definition of primary negative reinforcement as being synonymous with punishment is consistent with Mowrer's (1973) and Rolls' (1986a) definitions of negative reinforcement but differs from another definition often employed in animal learning psychology. In the alternative definition (e.g., see Hall, 1989, p. 115), negative reinforcers increase responding by reason of their removal.

During instrumental conditioning, the learning system accomplished *self-supervised* (Morgan, Patterson, and Klopf, 1990a) or *reinforcement* (e.g., see Sutton, 1991) learning in that no teacher or trainer provided feedback in the form of desired responses, as is done in *supervised* learning. The system, as a consequence of its initial apparently random behavior in the multiple-T maze, would occasionally encounter primary positive or negative reinforcement. On the basis of these infrequent experiences, the system was able to develop an internal model of its world and come to successfully navigate the maze, beginning in a "start box" and chaining a series of turns in order to proceed directly to the primary positive reinforcement while, at each step along the way, avoiding primary negative reinforcement. *Internal* as distinguished from *primary* (external) positive and negative reinforcement was generated by the reinforcement centers within the system. In a three-intersection multiple-T maze, sixty trials or less were required for the system to learn to successfully navigate the maze.

As far as we know, ACP networks represent the first computational model of nervous system function that accounts for a wide range of classical conditioning phenomena as well as instrumental conditioning phenomena including chaining. ACP networks constitute solutions to temporal and structural credit assignment problems, suggesting a theoretical approach for the synthesis of machine intelligence. ACP networks lend themselves to analysis in control theoretic terms.

2.0 ASSOCIATIVE CONTROL PROCESS NETWORKS

A diagram of an ACP network is shown in Figure 1. The network consists of sensors, ACPs, and effectors. As noted above, the ACPs are of two types: reinforcement centers and motor centers. The function of the reinforcement centers is to anticipate or predict future primary reinforcement. The function of the motor centers is to generate behavior such that primary positive reinforcement is obtained and primary negative reinforcement is avoided. Reinforcement center activity and motor center activity may be innate or learned. While the innate component in biological systems is not discounted, in this study we have focused on the learned component.

Reinforcement centers are of two types: positive and negative. Positive reinforcement centers support and promote approach behavior (Vaccarino, Schiff, and Glickman, 1989). Negative reinforcement centers support and promote avoidance behavior (Gray, 1987). In animals and humans, activity in positive reinforcement centers is associated with pleasurable experiences and activity in negative reinforcement centers is associated with painful experiences (Heath, 1986). Consistent with Young (1955), Fonberg (1986, p. 308) states that "in spite of the enormous differentiation of emotions in humans, it is still possible to divide them into two hedonically separate classes: positive and negative." In conjunction with the observation that all affective processes may be classified as positive or negative, it should be noted that, ultimately, all animal and human behavior may be directed at two objectives: approach or avoidance [See Spence (1960) and, in particular, chapters 21 and 22, pp. 359-392]. In the ACP network model, learning is accomplished in the reinforcement centers by means of the drive-reinforcement learning mechanism (Klopf, 1988).

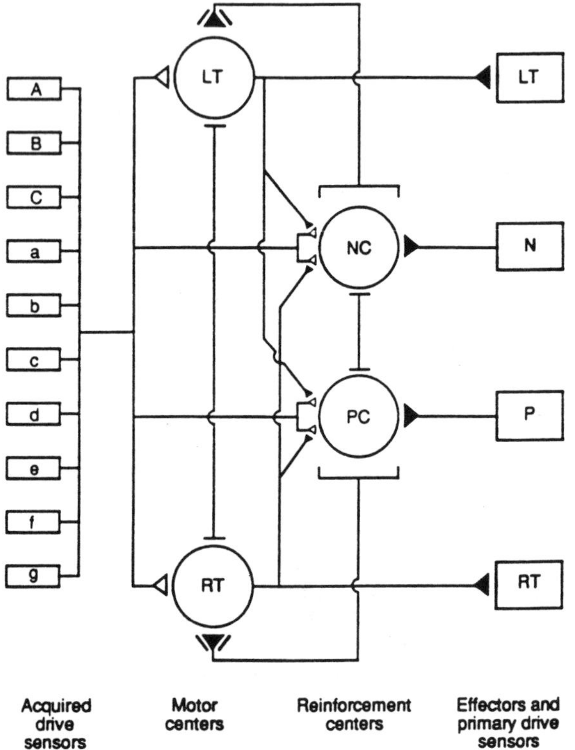

Figure 1. An associative control process (ACP) network diagrammed to illustrate the interconnect pattern for sensors, motor centers, reinforcement centers, and effectors. Solid connections are hard-wired and open connections are plastic. Hard-wired connections that synapse on plastic connections indicate that the plastic connection is functional (enabled) only in time steps in which the hard-wired connection has a positive signal on it. Solid synapses with adjacent lines indicate *reinforcing* connections, meaning that the signals affect the learning mechanism, but do not directly affect the input-output relationship of the postsynaptic ACP. All other connections are *regular* connections meaning that the signals directly affect the input-output relationship of the receiving node. Reinforcing connections signal the output of PC minus the output of NC. LT and RT motor centers are reciprocally inhibitory, as are NC and PC. LT: left-turning; RT: right-turning; NC: negative reinforcement center; PC: positive reinforcement center; N: primary negative reinforcement sensor; P: primary positive reinforcement sensor.

In the ACP network, the reinforcement centers are *reciprocally inhibitory*, as are the motor centers. When a pair of centers is reciprocally inhibitory, only one of the two centers can be active at any given time. The center that is active is the one that is driven more strongly by the weighted inputs. The other center's output is forced to zero. If the two centers are equally driven, neither is active.

2.1 Drive-Reinforcement Learning

Reinforcement centers employ the drive-reinforcement (D-R) learning mechanism which has been demonstrated to model or predict a wide range of classical conditioning phenomena (Klopf, 1988). The D-R learning mechanism, like other temporal difference learning mechanisms (Sutton and Barto, 1981, 1990; Sutton, 1988), provides a means of learning to anticipate or predict primary reinforcement which, in the ACP network, is the responsibility of the reinforcement centers.

The D-R learning mechanism achieves its capability for predicting primary reinforcement by correlating earlier changes in input signals with later changes in output signals and then changing eligible connection weights as a function of these correlations. Connection weights are said to be *eligible* (Klopf, 1972, 1982, 1988; Sutton and Barto, 1981, 1990) for modification by the D-R learning mechanism when the connection has experienced an increase in signal level within the past τ time steps. Primary reinforcement, by definition, always reaches the ACP network reinforcement centers via hard-wired connections with relatively large associated weights. If changes in output signals occasionally reflect primary reinforcement as is the case with the reinforcement centers, then by correlating earlier changes in input signals with later changes in output signals, the connection weights changed by the D-R learning mechanism come to encode links in a cause-effect chain that leads to primary reinforcement. Exactly how this happens will be explained later when a control theoretic representation of the the D-R learning mechanism is discussed.

Two equations specify the D-R learning mechanism. The first is termed the *input-output (I/O) equation*. A network component using the D-R learning mechanism computes its output by forming a sum of its weighted inputs and then thresholding the sum. This type of I/O relationship has often been used by neural network researchers. The specific form of I/O relationship we use in conjunction with the D-R learning mechanism is as follows:

$$y(t) = L\left[\sum_{i=1}^{m} w_i(t)x_i(t)\right] \quad (1)$$

$$\text{where } L[v] = \begin{cases} 0 & \text{if } v < \Theta; \\ 1 & \text{if } v > 1; \\ v & \text{otherwise;} \end{cases}$$

$y(t)$ = output at time t,
$w_i(t)$ = efficacy (weight or gain) of ith connection,
$x_i(t)$ = signal amplitude on i^{th} connection,
Θ = threshold,
m = number of connections or inputs.

The *learning mechanism equation* completes the specification of the D-R learning mechanism:

$$\Delta w_i(t) = \Delta y(t) \sum_{j=1}^{\tau} c_j \left| w_i(t-j) \right| [\Delta x_i(t-j)]^+ \quad (2)$$

where $\Delta w_i(t) = w_i(t+1) - w_i(t)$, $\Delta y(t) = y(t) - y(t-1)$, $\Delta x_i(t-j) = x_i(t-j) - x_i(t-j-1)$, and $[\Delta x_i(t-j)]^+ = \max(\Delta x_i(t-j),0)$. $\Delta w_i(t)$ represents the change in the efficacy of the ith connection at time t, yielding the adjusted or new efficacy of the connection at time $t+1$. $\Delta x_i(t-j)$ represents a change in the input signal level at time $t-j$ and $\Delta y(t)$ represents a change in the output signal level at time t. τ is the longest interstimulus interval, measured in discrete time steps, over which delay conditioning is effective, and c_j is an empirically established learning-rate constant that is proportional to the efficacy of conditioning when the interstimulus interval is j. [In delay conditioning, conditioned stimulus onset precedes unconditioned stimulus onset and the conditioned stimulus continues at least up to the time of unconditioned stimulus onset (Flaherty, 1985).] The remaining symbols are defined as in Equation 1. It is in Equation 2 that earlier changes in inputs are being correlated with later changes in outputs to yield changes in eligible connection weights that encode links in causal chains.

2.2 Motor Learning

Motor centers employ a *motor learning mechanism.* Initially, in evolving the ACP network architecture, we assumed that the D-R learning mechanism could be used in both the reinforcement and motor centers. As our investigation progressed, we concluded that the role of the motor centers is so different from the role of the reinforcement centers that the motor centers required a different class of learning mechanisms. In seeking to account for both classical and instrumental conditioning phenomena with the ACP network model, we arrived at the motor learning mechanism specified below. The drive-reinforcement learning mechanism used in the reinforcement centers provides a means of learning to anticipate or predict primary reinforcement. The function of the motor learning mechanism, as noted earlier, is to adjust motor center connection weights so as to cause the motor center outputs to track reinforcement center outputs in such a way that appropriate behavior comes to be generated. How the motor center learning process achieves this objective will be discussed in control theoretic terms in the next section. In this section, we will specify the motor learning mechanism in mathematical terms.

The input-output equation for the motor learning mechanism is identical to that used with the drive-reinforcement learning mechanism and is, therefore, specified by Equation 1. The motor learning mechanism equation is as follows:

$$\Delta w_i(t) = [c][\left| w_i(t) \right|][\Delta x_i(t)]^+[y_p(t) - y_n(t) - y(t)][\text{sgn}[y(t)]] \quad (3)$$

where c = learning rate factor = $c_a + (|y_p(t) - y_n(t)|)c_b$,
c_a, c_b = positive constants,
$y_p(t)$ = positive reinforcement center output,
$y_n(t)$ = negative reinforcement center output,
$y(t)$ = motor center output,
$\text{sgn}[y(t)]$ = 1.0 if $y(t) > 0.0$, 0.0 otherwise.

The remaining symbols are defined as in Equations 1 and 2. Next, the D-R and motor learning mechanisms, along with the ACP network architecture, are explained in functional terms within a control theoretic framework.

2.3 Control Theoretic Representation of ACP Networks

Functionally, an ACP network can be understood as a hierarchical network of control systems, with each control system in the network being capable of learning. An ACP consists of an error detector, a learning mechanism, and an input-output relationship that can be modified by the learning mechanism. Reinforcement centers and motor centers can be seen to be ACPs if the input-output relationship is identified with Equation 1 and the error detector combined with the learning mechanism is identified with Equation 2 or 3 for reinforcement or motor centers, respectively.

The ACP network architecture shown in Figure 1 assumes the form of a hierarchical network in which the reinforcement centers are at the top of the hierarchy. The reinforcement centers function as learning control systems that minimize the error in the predicted reinforcement. Their output constitutes the reference level for the motor centers which function as learning control systems for the effectors that are interfaced to the environment. [For a detailed description and explanation of this hierarchical network architecture, along with additional performance data for classical and instrumental conditioning tests, Klopf, Morgan, and Weaver (1992) should be consulted.]

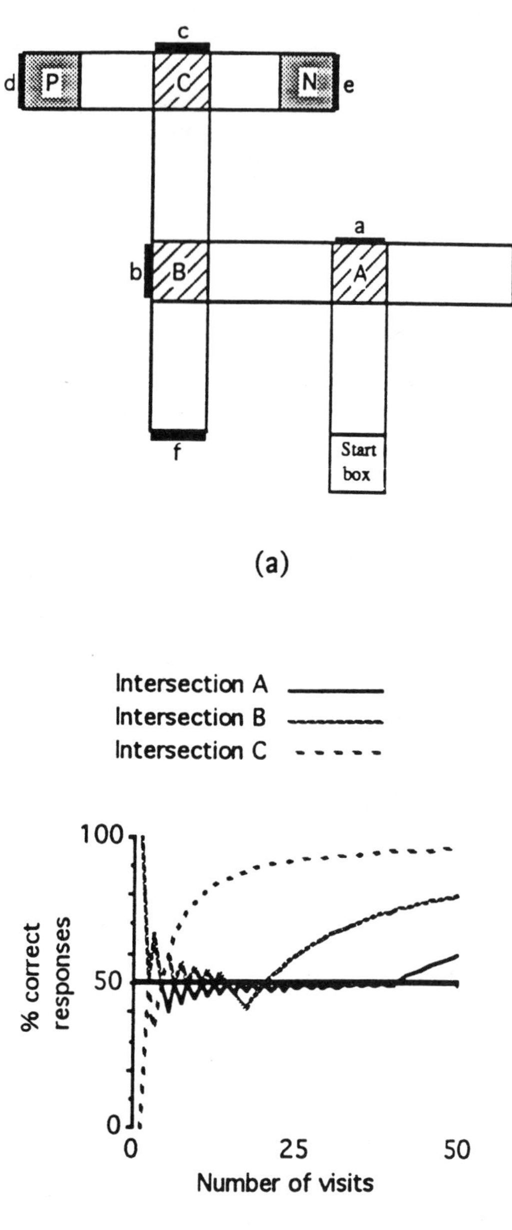

Figure 2. (a) Multiple-T maze used to instrumentally condition a learning system controlled by an ACP network. Upper-case letters represent tactile stimuli and lower-case letters represent visual stimuli. P and N represent stimuli that provide primary positive and negative reinforcement, respectively. (b) Performance of the learning system that was tested in the multiple-T maze, demonstrating the chaining of learned responses. Plotted is the percentage of correct responses in an intersection versus the number of times the learning system visited that intersection.

3.0 INSTRUMENTAL CONDITIONING

For the purpose of determining whether an ACP network could account for instrumental conditioning effects including the chaining of responses, we designed a learning system controlled by an ACP network and also designed an environment with which the system could engage in real-time, closed loop interactions. By means of computer simulations of the learning system, the environment, and their interactions, we observed and measured the performance of the system during a series of trials in which the system had the opportunity to learn to navigate in a multiple-T maze.

In order to demonstrate that the ACP network could learn to chain a series of decisions and actions leading eventually to reward while, along the way, avoiding punishment, the network was tested in the maze shown in Figure 2(a). The network used internal reinforcement signals from the positive reinforcement center to chain the effects of primary positive reinforcement back to earlier and earlier stimuli during learning. The behavior of the learning system during the first 50 trials is graphed in Figure 2(b) in terms of the percentage of correct responses in an intersection versus the number of times the system visited that intersection. The system is seen to have successfully learned to navigate the multiple-T maze such that, after training, when the system is placed in the start box, it proceeds directly to the reward by turning left at A, right at B, and left at C. In Figure 2(b), it can be seen that the number of visits to an intersection before the correct response in that intersection was learned increased with increasing distance of the intersection from the primary positive reinforcement. This is evidence that the ACP network is having to use internal reinforcement signals to learn correct responses in intersections not proximal to the reward. First, the positive reinforcement center, PC, has to learn to anticipate the reward when stimuli associated with the C-intersection are experienced. Then, using that knowledge, PC acquires the ability to anticipate the reward when stimuli associated with the B-intersection are experienced and, finally, PC chains its anticipation of reward back to the A-intersection. This kind of temporal and spatial chaining of learned behavior from C back to B back to A is consistent with that observed in instrumental conditioning experiments with animals (Hill, 1939; Hull, 1952; Rescorla, 1977; Hampson, 1990). When the primary reinforcement is removed, animals extinguish their behavior in the same order (Hill, 1939; Hull, 1952; Rescorla, 1977; Hampson, 1990), that is, the learned behavior first extinguishes at C, then B, then A. The simulated ACP network-controlled learning system behaved in the same way.

4.0 CLASSICAL CONDITIONING

A series of classical conditioning tests were administered to the ACP network to determine if the same model that yielded instrumental conditioning effects in multiple-T mazes would account for classical conditioning effects consistent with the results of animal learning experiments.

Positive results were anticipated because the drive-reinforcement learning mechanism had been demonstrated to account for a wide range of classical conditioning phenomena (Klopf, 1988) and, in the ACP network, motor centers learn by tracking reinforcement center outputs which, themselves, are products of drive-reinforcement learning.

To determine if the ACP network model could account for the effects of classical conditioning, we utilized the positive reinforcement center and one motor center shown in Figure 1. Only the positive reinforcement center was needed because the unconditioned stimulus (US) in our classical conditioning tests functioned as a reward. Only one motor center was needed because the motor center functioned in a manner analogous to, for example, the center controlling the musculature of the salivary gland. There was no need for an opposing motor center, unlike the case of right- and left-turning motor centers for instrumental conditioning in multiple-T mazes. The primary positive reinforcement sensor, P, was connected to both the reinforcement center and the motor center, the regular hard-wired connection to the motor center being added to cause the motor center to generate an unconditioned response (UR) that is an integral part of classical conditioning. In the instrumental conditioning tests, connections between primary reinforcement sensors and motor centers were unnecessary but such connections could have been added to reflect, for example, innate consummatory or fleeing responses that animals might exhibit in reaction to rewards and punishments, respectively.

The computer-simulated classical conditioning tests that were administered to the ACP network were identical to those administered to the drive-reinforcement theoretical neuron, as reported in Klopf (1988). In every case, the form of the response of the ACP network was similar to that of the drive-reinforcement neuron, establishing that the ACP network, as does the drive-reinforcement neuron, predicts or models a wide range of experimentally observed classical conditioning phenomena including delay and trace conditioning, conditioned and unconditioned stimulus duration and amplitude effects, partial reinforcement effects, interstimulus interval effects, second-order conditioning, conditioned inhibition, extinction, reacquisition effects, backward conditioning, blocking, overshadowing, compound conditioning, and discriminative stimulus effects.

5.0 SUMMARY AND CONCLUDING REMARKS

At this point in their theoretical development, associative control process networks consist of two kinds of ACPs: reinforcement centers that learn to predict primary reinforcement and motor centers that learn to generate behavior appropriate to the pursuit of primary positive reinforcement and the avoidance of primary negative reinforcement. Reinforcement centers are of two kinds: positive reinforcement centers that support approach behavior and negative reinforcement centers that support avoidance behavior. ACP networks employ two kinds of learning mechanisms: drive-reinforcement learning in reinforcement centers and motor learning in motor centers. After learning occurs, reinforcement centers model the world by anticipating the consequences of actions and motor centers generate behavior consistent with reinforcement center assessments. ACP networks account for a wide range of classical conditioning phenomena and some instrumental conditioning phenomena including the chaining of learned responses across time and space.

Regarding future research, a number of questions present themselves. Can internal drives and an attention mechanism be modeled within the theoretical framework of ACP networks? Should each internal drive have a pair of reinforcement centers, one positive and one negative, associated with the drive? In order to account for animal behavior, in general, can ACP network models be extended so that a number of pairs of reinforcement centers interact with a hierarchy of motor centers with, perhaps, the reference levels of the motor centers being determined by the reinforcement center outputs and the outputs from higher-level motor centers? Behind all of these questions, a more fundamental question is this: In the case of biological systems, when we understand motor control, and when we understand learning in relationship to motor control, will we then have the prerequisites for understanding memory, learning, and intelligence, in general?

The computational model that we have proposed emphasizes the emotional and control theoretic aspects of nervous system function. These two aspects appear to be logically related. Emotions have to do with goals and goal-seeking. Consideration of goal-seeking leads quite naturally to control theoretic formulations. In this way, we are confronting what we see to be an interesting possibility: Emotional and control theoretic aspects may form the foundation of natural intelligence.

ACKNOWLEDGMENTS

This research was supported under Task 2312 R1 by the Life and Environmental Sciences Directorate of the United States Air Force Office of Scientific Research. For comments on drafts of this paper, we gratefully acknowledge Steve Atkins, Leemon Baird, Walt Baker, Gábor Bartha, Andy Barto, Jeff Johnson, Joan Klopf, Pete Millington, John Moore, and Larry Stein.

REFERENCES

Ashby, W. R. (1952/1960). *Design for a brain.* New York: Wiley.

Baird, L. C., & Baker, W. L. (1990). A connectionist system for nonlinear control. *Proceedings of the American Institute of Aeronautics and Astronautics Conference on Guidance, Navigation, and Control* (pp. 1113-1119), Boston, Massachusetts.

Bitterman, M. E. (1988). Vertebrate-invertebrate comparisons. In H. J. Jerison & I. Jerison (Eds.), *The evolutionary biology of intelligence* (pp. 251-276). Berlin: Springer.

Brown, T. H., Kairiss, E. W., & Keenan, C. L. (1990). Hebbian synapses: Biophysical mechanisms and algorithms. *Annual Review of Neuroscience*, **13**, 475-511.

Cliff, D. T. (1990). *Computational neuroethology: A provisional manifesto* (Cognitive Science Research Paper 162). Brighton, England: School of Cognitive and Computing Sciences, The University of Sussex.

Dickinson, A. (1980). *Contemporary animal learning theory*. Cambridge: Cambridge University Press.

Fonberg, E. (1986). Amygdala, emotions, motivation, and depressive states. In R. Plutchik & H. Kellerman (Eds.), *Emotion: Theory, research, and experience*, Volume 3, *Biological foundations of emotion* (pp. 301-331). New York: Academic Press.

Gluck, M. A., Parker, D. B., & Reifsnider, E. (1988). Some biological implications of a differential-Hebbian learning rule. *Psychobiology*, **16**(3), 298-302.

Gray, J. A. (1975). *Elements of a two-process theory of learning*. New York: Academic Press.

Gray, J. A. (1987). *The psychology of fear and stress* (Second edition). Cambridge: Cambridge University Press.

Hall, J. F. (1989). *Learning and memory* (Second edition). Boston: Allyn and Bacon.

Hampson, S. E. (1990). *Connectionistic problem solving: Computational aspects of biological learning*. Boston: Birkhauser.

Heath, R. G. (1986). The neural substrate for emotion. In R. Plutchik & H. Kellerman (Eds.), *Emotion: Theory, research, and experience*, Volume 3, *Biological foundations of emotion* (pp. 3- 36). New York: Academic Press.

Hill, J. H. (1939). Goal gradient, anticipation, and perseveration in compound trial-and-error learning. *Journal of Experimental Psychology*, **25**, 566-585.

Hull, C. L. (1943). *Principles of behavior*. New York: Appleton-Century-Crofts.

Hull, C. L. (1952). *A behavior system: An introduction to behavior theory concerning the individual organism*. New Haven: Yale University Press.

Ito, M. (1989). Long-term depression. *Annual Review of Neuroscience*, **12**, 85-102.

Johnson, J. D. (1991). *The selectively attentive environmental learning system* (Doctoral dissertation, University of Cincinnati).

Klopf, A. H. (1972). *Brain function and adaptive systems - A heterostatic theory* (Rep. No. 133 [AFCRL-72-0164]). L.G. Hanscom Field, Bedford, Massachusetts: Air Force Cambridge Research Laboratories. (DTIC Report AD 742259, available from the Defense Technical Information Center, Cameron Station, Alexandria, Virginia 22304-6145)

Klopf, A. H. (1982). *The hedonistic neuron: A theory of memory, learning, and intelligence*. New York: Hemisphere/ Taylor and Francis.

Klopf, A. H. (1986). A drive-reinforcement model of single neuron function: An alternative to the Hebbian neuronal model. In J. S. Denker (Ed.), *AIP Conference Proceedings 151: Neural networks for computing* (pp. 265-270). New York: American Institute of Physics.

Klopf, A. H. (1988). A neuronal model of classical conditioning. *Psychobiology*, **16**(2), 85-125.

Klopf, A. H. (1989). Classical conditioning phenomena predicted by a drive-reinforcement model of neuronal function. In J. H. Byrne & W. O. Berry (Eds.), *Neural models of plasticity: Experimental and theoretical approaches* (pp. 104-132). New York: Academic Press.

Klopf, A. H., & Morgan, J. S. (1990). The role of time in natural intelligence: Implications of classical and instrumental conditioning for neuronal and neural network modeling. In M. Gabriel & J. Moore (Eds.), *Learning and computational neuroscience: Foundations of adaptive networks* (pp. 463-495). Cambridge, MA: MIT Press.

Klopf, A. H., Morgan, J. S., & Weaver, S. E. (1992). A hierarchical network of control systems that learn: Modeling nervous system function during classical and instrumental conditioning. To be published as a United States Air Force technical report.

Kosko, B. (1986). Differential Hebbian learning. In J. S. Denker (Ed.), *AIP Conference Proceedings 151: Neural networks for computing* (pp. 277-282). New York: American Institute of Physics.

Mackintosh, N. J. (1983). *Conditioning and associative learning*. Oxford: Clarendon Press.

Meyer, J., & Wilson, S. W. (Eds.) (1991). *Proceedings of the International Workshop on the Simulation of Adaptive Behavior: From Animals to Animats*. Cambridge, MA: MIT Press.

Moore, J. W., Berthier, N. E., & Blazis, D. E. J. (1990). Classical eye-blink conditioning: Brain systems and implementation of a computational model. In M. Gabriel & J. Moore (Eds.), *Learning and computational neuroscience: Foundations of adaptive networks* (pp. 359-387). Cambridge, MA: MIT Press.

Moore, J. W., Desmond, J. E., Berthier, N. E., Blazis, D. E. J., Sutton, R. S., & Barto, A. G. (1986). Simulation of the classically conditioned nictitating membrane response by a neuron-like adaptive element: Response topography, neuronal firing, and interstimulus intervals. *Behavioral Brain Research*, **21**, 143-154.

Morgan, J. S., Patterson, E. C., & Klopf, A. H. (1990a). Drive-reinforcement learning: A self-supervised model for adaptive control. *Network: Computation in Neural Systems*, **1**, 439-448.

Morgan, J. S., Patterson, E. C., & Klopf, A. H. (1990b). A drive-reinforcement model of simple instrumental conditioning. *Proceedings of the International Joint Conference on Neural Networks*, Volume II, San Diego, California, pp. 227-232.

Mowrer, O. H. (1956). Two-factor learning theory reconsidered, with special reference to secondary reinforcement and the concept of habit. *Psychological Review*, **63**, 114-128.

Mowrer, O. H. (1960). *Learning theory and behavior*. New York: Wiley. (Krieger Edition, 1973)

Rescorla, R. A. (1977). Pavlovian second-order conditioning: Some implications for instrumental behavior. In H. Davis & H. M. B. Hurwitz (Eds.),

Operant Pavlovian interactions (pp. 133-164). Hillsdale, NJ: Lawrence Erlbaum.

Rescorla, R. A., & Solomon, R. L. (1967). Two process learning theory: Relationships between Pavlovian conditioning and instrumental learning. *Psychological Review*, **74**(3), 151-182.

Roitblat, H. L. (1987). *Introduction to comparative cognition*. New York: W. L. Freeman.

Roitblat, H. L. (1988). A cognitive action theory of learning. In J. Delacour & J. C. S. Levy (Eds.), *Systems with learning and memory abilities* (pp. 13-26). New York: Elsevier.

Spence, K. W. (1960). *Behavior theory and learning: Selected papers*. Englewood Cliffs, NJ: Prentice-Hall.

Sutton, R. S. (1988). Learning to predict by the methods of temporal differences. *Machine Learning*, **3**, 9-44.

Sutton, R. S. (1991). Reinforcement learning architectures for animats. *Proceedings of the International Workshop on the Simulation of Adaptive Behavior: From Animals to Animats* (pp. 288-296). Cambridge, MA: MIT Press.

Sutton, R. S., & Barto, A. G. (1981). Toward a modern theory of adaptive networks: Expectation and prediction. *Psychological Review*, **88**, 135-170.

Sutton, R. S., & Barto, A. G. (1990). Time-derivative models of Pavlovian reinforcement. In M. Gabriel & J. Moore (Eds.), *Learning and computational neuroscience: Foundations of adaptive networks* (pp. 497-537). Cambridge, MA: MIT Press.

Tesauro, G. (1986). Simple neural models of classical conditioning. *Biological Cybernetics*, **55**, 187-200.

Vaccarino, F. J., Schiff, B. B., & Glickman, S. E. (1989). Biological view of reinforcement. In S. B. Klien & R. R. Mowrer (Eds.), *Contemporary learning theories: Instrumental conditioning theory and the impact of biological constraints on learning* (pp. 111-142). Hillsdale, NJ: Lawrence Erlbaum.

Wiener, N. (1948/1961). *Cybernetics or control and communication in the animal and the machine*. Cambridge, MA: MIT Press.

Williams, R. J., & Baird, L. C. (1990). A mathematical analysis of actor-critic architectures for learning optimal control through incremental dynamic programming. *Proceedings of the Sixth Yale Workshop on Adaptive and Learning Systems* (pp. 96-102). New Haven, CN: Yale University.

Wilson, S. W. (1986). Knowledge growth in an artificial animal. In K. S. Narendra (Ed.), *Adaptive and learning systems* (pp.255-266). New York: Plenum.

Wise, R. A. (1989). The brain and reward. In J. M. Liebman & S. J. Cooper (Eds.), *The neuropharmacological basis of reward* (pp. 377-424). Oxford: Clarendon Press.

Young, P. T. (1955). The role of hedonic processes in motivation. In M. R. Jones (Ed.), *Nebraska symposium on motivation* (pp. 193-238). Lincoln: University of Nebraska Press.

An optimization-based categorization of reinforcement learning environments

Michael L. Littman

Bellcore / Carnegie Mellon University
mlittman@cs.cmu.edu

Abstract

This paper proposes a categorization of reinforcement learning environments based on the optimization of a reinforcement signal over time. Environments are classified by the simplest agent that can possibly achieve optimal reinforcement. Two parameters, h and β, abstractly characterize the complexity of an agent: the ideal (h,β)-agent uses the input information provided by the environment and at most h bits of local storage to choose an action that maximizes the discounted sum of the next β reinforcements. In an (h,β)-environment, an ideal (h,β)-agent achieves the maximum possible expected reinforcement for that environment. The paper discusses the special cases when either $h = 0$ or $\beta = 1$ in detail, describes some theoretical bounds on h and β and re-explores a well-known reinforcement learning environment with this new notation.

1 Introduction

Studying adaptive agents without considering their environments is a lot like looking at a fish out of water. A successful agent extracts, exploits, and depends upon regularities in its environment. Wouldn't fish be different if water were solid?

Wilson (1990) created a scheme for cataloging artificial environments based on the indeterminacy of an environment with respect to the sensory capabilities of its agents. Agents in Class 0 and Class 1 environments can completely determine the state of their environments whereas agents in Class 2 environments have only partial information about the state. In a Class 2 environment, an agent cannot know from instantaneous sensory input alone the state of the whole world. Although natural agents always find themselves in indeterminate environments such as this, Wilson's scheme is very useful for understanding and designing artificial agents and reinforcement learning environments. Researchers creating new adaptive algorithms have found that different architectural features are necessary depending on the class of the environment.

In the categorization scheme presented here, environments are classified by the simplest agent that can possibly achieve optimal reinforcement. Two parameters, h and β, abstractly characterize the complexity of an agent: the ideal (h,β)-agent uses the input information provided by the environment and at most h bits of local storage to choose an action that maximizes the discounted sum of the next β reinforcements. In an (h,β)-environment, an ideal (h,β)-agent achieves the maximum possible expected reinforcement for that environment. This description gives a formal footing to Wilson's (1990) basic types: Class 0 corresponds to ($h = 0$, $\beta = 1$)-environments, Class 1 to ($h = 0$, $\beta > 1$)-environments, and Class 2 to ($h > 0$, $\beta > 1$)-environments. The ($h > 0$, $\beta = 1$)-environments also form an interesting special case referred to as Class 1b in this work.

2 Definitions and Notation

In the environments considered here, the agent or algorithm is presented with discrete *inputs* (or stimuli), one after another. The agent uses these inputs, numbers or vectors of numbers from a finite set, to produce *actions* (or outputs), also numbers or vectors of numbers from a finite set. The action is evaluated by the environment and a *reinforcement signal* is returned— a measure of worth of the agent's last action and its current situation (a result of past actions). It is a single number (at each point in time) and larger values are more desirable than smaller ones.

A distinction can be drawn between this *reinforcement learning paradigm* and well-known *supervised learning* — supervised learning requires a training signal: output the learner *could have* produced to maximize its reinforcement, whereas reinforcement learning requires only a scalar reinforcement signal. The categorization described in this work applies to the reinforcement learning case.

2.1 The environment

Following Wilson (1990), an environment is a finite-state machine (FSM) whose state is indirectly accessible to the agent as input patterns. The agent's actions (outputs) cause state transitions which generate new inputs. The environment's state, s, at any time is an element of the finite set S of all possible states. The agent's action, a, is drawn from the finite set A of all possible actions and its input, x, comes from the finite set X of all possible inputs.

Three functions define the environment. The transition function $F(s,a,s')$ gives the probability that executing action a in state s will lead to state s'. The function F must have the property that all its values are between 0 and 1 and for all $s \in S$ and $a \in A$, $\sum_{s' \in S} F(s,a,s') = 1$; that is, the sum of the probability of all possible transitions from s (given action a) is 1.

The perception function, G, controls the inputs an agent perceives as a function of the environment's underlying state. In particular, $G(s,x)$ is the probability that a state s will appear to the agent as input x where every value of G must be between 0 and 1 and $\sum_{x \in X} G(s,x) = 1$ for all states $s \in S$.

While moving through the environment, the agent is presented with reinforcement signals, r, from the finite set R. The reinforcement function, $H(s,a,r)$, is another probabilistic function of the environment's state and the agent's action that defines the likelihood that a given reinforcement value, r, is returned to the agent for performing action a in state s. Every value is between 0 and 1 and for all $s \in S$ and $a \in A$, $\sum_{r \in R} H(s,a,r) = 1$— some reinforcement is returned no matter what. It is sometimes convenient to express this function in terms of the expected (or average) reinforcement for performing a given action in a state: $\hat{H}(s,a) = \sum_{r \in R} H(s,a,r) \cdot r$.

A discounting parameter, γ (between 0 and 1), indicates the fraction of its value that a reinforcement signal retains after a single timestep. Values of γ close to 0 indicate that an agent should consider a greedy strategy since reinforcement is not worth much if deferred. Values closer to 1 allow an agent to be more methodical since it can still get close to full credit for a delayed reinforcement. In this paper, the discount parameter is considered part of the environment— that is, out of the agent's control, but in practice, many researchers choose values for γ that encourage their agents to exhibit a particular style of behavior. See Sutton (1991) for a justification of the use of the γ parameter in defining reinforcement learning environments.

Two functions specify the agent's behavior in an environment. Both take as input the current sensory input, x, provided by the environment and combine it with m, a string of h 1's and 0's representing the contents of an agent's short term memory or internal state. The function $a = B(x,m)$ is a deterministic function specifying the agent's chosen action given a particular input and internal state and the deterministic function $m' = L(x,m,r)$ provides the next internal state given the current input, internal state, and the reinforcement value returned to the agent after executing the most recent action.

Definition 1 *An* environment *is specified by the functions $F(s,a,s')$ (transition), $G(s,x)$ (perception) and $H(s,a,r)$ (reinforcement) and the discount parameter γ. An* agent *is specified by the functions $B(x,m)$ (behavioral policy) and $L(x,m,r)$ (short term memory) and the number of internal storage bits, h.*

These functions and values are the crucial building blocks used in this paper to concretely define reinforcement learning environments. There is a wide range of alternate definitions that would not substantially affect the analyses presented later— for instance, the agent's previous action could be presented as part of its input. There are other changes that might have a more significant impact, for example defining agents with randomized behaviors. Nonetheless, these definitions were chosen to apply to a significant number of artificial reinforcement learning environments in the literature while at the same time providing a convenient form for formal manipulation.

2.2 The adaptive objective

For the purposes of this paper, the goal of an agent in a reinforcement learning environment is to choose a sequence of actions that maximizes its expected discounted future reinforcement.

For a formal definition of expected discounted future reinforcement, it is helpful to define $F_0(s)$ as the probability distribution of initial states of the environment and m_0 as the agent's initial internal state.

Definition 2 *The* value *of a state/internal state pair for a given agent is:*

$$V(s,m) = \sum_{x\in X}(G(s,x)\cdot(\sum_{r\in R} H(s,a,r)\cdot r + \gamma\sum_{s'\in S} F(s,a,s')\cdot V(s',m')))$$

(where $a = B(x,m)$ and $m' = L(x,m,r)$).

This (recursive) definition expresses the value (expected discounted reinforcement) of a state/internal state pair by summing over all possible inputs (x) the probability of the agent seeing that input ($G(s,x)$) times the value of the agent's response. The value of the agent's response has an immediate and a delayed component where the immediate value of the agent's response is the weighted average of all possible reinforcements the agent might receive (r) times their probabilities ($H(s,a,r)$) given the agent's chosen action ($a = B(x,m)$). The delayed value of the state/internal state pair is added in by considering all possible successor states (s'), and multiplying their probability ($F(s,a,s')$) times their value ($V(s',m')$) given the agent's successor internal state ($m' = L(x,m,r)$). This value is then discounted by γ since it takes place one step in the future.

The equation is intended to define, for any environmental state and any of the agent's internal states, the expected discounted future reinforcement for that agent. The recursive nature of the definition is intended as a notational convenience— the equation could be expressed equally well using some sort of looping construct. The value does not diverge as long as $\gamma < 1$ (if $\gamma = 1$ the sum can grow infinitely large).

Clearly, for any moderately complex environment, it is impractical to compute this function. Nevertheless, the definition creates a concrete basis for comparison between different behavioral strategies.

Definition 3 *The weighted sum of the value of all possible initial states:*

$$V^{\text{agent}} = \sum_{s\in S} F_0(s)V(s,m_0)$$

represents the expected discounted reinforcement *for a given agent.*

The optimal agent for an environment, then, is one for which no other agent has a larger value of V^{agent}. An agent *solves* an environment if it achieves the maximum possible value of V^{agent} for that environment.

2.3 Inadequacies of FSM's for classification

There are many ways in which the FSM formalism described above might usefully distinguish between environments: the size of the state space S, the degree of randomness in the reinforcement function H, the minimum size of a program that implements the transition function F, can all be used as measures of environmental complexity. However, from the perspective that an agent's objective is to maximize reinforcement, it becomes more important to consider the attributes of environments that relate to reinforcement optimization.

Wilson (1990) observes a connection between an agent's ability to achieve goals in an environment and whether the environment's state is "indeterminate" with respect to the agents' perceptual stimuli. The perception function, G, relates the state of the environment, s, to an input stimulus, x.

Definition 4 *If there is no input x for which $G(s,x) > 0$ and $G(s',x) > 0$ and $s \neq s'$ (no input can be a result of two different underlying states), then the environment is* determinate— *the input uniquely determines the state.*

In an indeterminate environment, different environmental states might appear to the agent as identical— a situation known as "perceptual aliasing" (Whitehead, 1991) since a single input (percept) is an alias for multiple environmental states. Perceptual aliasing can make it difficult for an agent to find actions which optimize reinforcement.

Unfortunately, classifying environments by whether or not they are determinate provides minimal leverage for making important distinctions. Two environmental states can map to the same input and not be *functionally* distinct— the states might be the same with respect to the actions needed to maximize reinforcement. This situation is addressed in Section 5.1.

For this reason, this paper categorizes environments only after looking at them through the agent's eyes. Two environments are categorized differently only if there is some important distinction between the agents that can achieve maximum reinforcement in them. The next section details a classification of agents that makes such a categorization possible.

2.4 The agents

A great deal of the interest in examining artificial environments and agents is in creating adaptive algorithms that change an agent's behavior to improve the expected discounted reinforcement through "learning" or "evolution" or some other adaptive algorithm. The interactions and dynamics of learning algorithms and environments are fascinating (see Thrun (1992), for example) but this paper addresses only the classification of environments— differences between agents are factored out by considering only those that are perfectly adapted.

Certainly an arbitrary perfectly adapted agent does not serve to distinguish between classes of environments. However, by selectively limiting the computational or representational power of an agent and considering only those that are ideally adapted given their limitations, we can identify an environment with the weakest agent that is able to attain maximum reinforcement.

Concretely, agents are parameterized by two values: h is the size (in bits) of the agent's internal state (as described before), and β is a number which roughly measures the number of steps ahead an agent considers when choosing an action. To define β more precisely, it is necessary to extend the definition of a value of a state.

Definition 5 *The* expected discounted β-step reinforcement *for a state/internal state pair is*

$$V_\beta(s,m) = \sum_{x\in X}(G(s,x) \cdot (\sum_{r\in R} H(s,a,r) \cdot r + \gamma \sum_{s'\in S} F(s,a,s') \cdot V_{\beta-1}(s',m')))$$

(where $a = B(x,m)$, $m' = L(x,m,r)$, *and* $V_0(s,m) = 0$*).*

This is identical to the definition of $V(s,m)$ given earlier (Definition 2) except values are summed only β steps into the future. For $\beta = 1$, the equation reduces to $V_\beta(s,m) = \sum_{x\in X} G(s,x) \cdot \hat{H}(s,a)$ where $a = B(x,m)$ and $\hat{H}(s,a)$ is the expected reinforcement.

Definition 6 *An* (h, β)-agent *is one that uses no more than* h *bits of internal storage and, for every state/internal state it encounters, chooses an action which maximizes its discounted* β*-step reinforcement.*

There are a number of properties that make this definition peculiar. For one, why is it useful to consider an agent that is perfectly adapted to optimize a function (β-step discounted reinforcement) that is different from its true objective function (average discounted reinforcement)? Essentially, optimizing β-step reinforcement is a more localized objective and it is feasible to imagine an agent adapting its behavior over time to meet it. Further, at least in the case of a determinate environment, it is known that the behaviors that achieve optimal average discounted reinforcement and optimal $\beta = \infty$ step reinforcement are identical (see Section 5.1).

Another peculiar aspect of the definition is the apparently circular definition of the agent's behavior. The value of a state/internal state pair, $V_\beta(s,m)$ is clearly dependent on the strategy an agent employs. However, the strategy of the optimal (h, β)-agent is defined as one which always chooses actions that optimize $V_\beta(s,m)$. The circularity is removed by thinking of the definition as specifying a property that the behavior and value functions must have instead of as a constructive definition of these functions. A behavior function that satisfies this property can be called a *behavioral fixed point* as it represents a fixed point of the obvious adaptation function.

Definition 7 *A behavior function, B, is a* behavioral fixed point *if the actions chosen are exactly those which maximize expected discounted* β*-step reinforcement.*

It is extremely important to note that there is no guarantee that a behavioral fixed point will exist for a given h and β. Indeed, it is easy to construct indeterminate environments that will have no optimal (h,β)-agent for certain values of h and β. It is not known whether, for a given environment, there is always some finite values h and β such that any $h' \geq h$ and $\beta' \geq \beta$ are guaranteed to have behavioral fixed points.

3 Agent classification

As defined above, an (h,β)-agent is an agent that generates actions that maximize the expected β-step discounted reinforcement, given h bits of local storage. Four special cases are worthy of further description.

The $(h > 0, \beta > 1)$-agents (Class 2), form the most general class of agents. They use some number of bits of storage and maximize discounted reinforcement potentially well into the future. It is probable that every environment has some agent in this class that performs optimally. Since this class of agents is so general, it can be used as the standard by which the other classes are judged.

An $(h = 0, \beta > 1)$-agent (Class 1) chooses the best course of action given only a single input— no past history is used in decision making. Although the underlying state, s, may be impossible to determine from a single input, the agent will choose the action which, on average, leads to the best possible future reinforcement.

Using some encoding of its history, an $(h > 0, \beta = 1)$-agent (Class 1b) computes an action which maximizes only the current reinforcement. This agent seeks out "instant gratification" and ignores delayed reinforcement. It will choose the short term best move instead of the move which might put it in good stead later on whenever the short term move is more attractive.

The most limited agent is the ($h = 0$, $\beta = 1$)-agent (Class 0) which encodes no information about its past and maximizes reinforcement only for the present situation. It makes local decisions as to the best course of action for now given what it senses now. Simple as it is, such an agent can still perform well in benign environments.

4 Environmental classification

There is likely some ideal Class 2 agent which maximizes the expected discounted future reinforcement for any environment— no agent in any other class can do better. Environments can be easily constructed, however, in which simpler agents perform just as well— it is possible to construct an environment in which the performance of an ($h = 0$, $\beta = 1$)-agent (Class 0) is optimal for that environment. The categorization of agents becomes a categorization of environments with the realization that environments differ as to the capabilities an agent needs to achieve the optimal performance.

Definition 8 *In an* (h,β)-environment, *the performance of an (h,β)-agent is optimal for any agent in that environment.*

The classification scheme that results closely echoes Wilson (1990). A Class 0 environment, for Wilson, is a determinate environment with at least one a for every possible s producing a positive expected reinforcement: $\hat{H}(s, a) > 0$. This is roughly an ($h = 0$, $\beta = 1$)-environment— it can be optimized by maximizing the immediate expected reinforcement, $\hat{H}(s, a)$, given only x, the current input. This new definition agrees in spirit with Wilson's and may actually be a better description of his intention. An agent should maximize average future reinforcement, not just seek positive reinforcement. Adaptation in this type of environment is called simple "reinforcement learning" (Ackley, Littman, 1990).

Wilson's Class 1 environments are ($h = 0$, $\beta > 1$)-environments— maximum expected discounted reinforcement can only be attained by choosing actions with concern for future reinforcement. In these environments the agent needs to look more than one step forward to know the true consequences of a given action. Tic-tac-toe, for instance, is an ($h = 0$, $\beta = 5$)-environment because the value of a given move is known by the end of a game and perhaps not before and only the current input is needed to choose optimal actions. Adaptive agents in this type of environment solve the "temporal reinforcement learning" (Sutton, 1984) problem since effective learning must cope with the temporal delay of the reinforcement signal.

Wilson's Class 2 environments are general ($h > 0$, $\beta > 1$)-environments: those that require encoding of past experience and deliver delayed reinforcement. Any moderately complex environment falls into this category.

Wilson does not consider ($h > 0$, $\beta = 1$)-environments as a separate type, though from an architectural standpoint, there is a useful distinction to be made. In these "Class 1b" environments, there is no difference between maximizing current reinforcement and maximizing average future reinforcement, so no complicated "temporal credit assignment" problems need to be solved. Instead, difficulty lies in the fact that there is insufficient information in a single stimulus to choose the best action.

Discovering the right short-term experience to record is referred to as the problem of "hidden state" or "perceptual aliasing," and researchers have begun to focus on algorithms for solving these problems (Bachrach (1992), Lin (1992), also, work by Allen (1989), Ghahramani and Allen (1991) and others in the related supervised recurrent network case). The "Little Prince" world Wilson mentions is in Class 1b since there is incomplete state information in the input signals but a reinforcement signal is made available at every step.

5 Examples

5.1 Observations on h and β

Throughout this paper, the notion of determinate vs. indeterminate perception functions is used as a rough division between "simpler" and "less simple" environments. A host of theoretical results exist for determinate environments that cannot be applied to general indeterminate environments. This section attempts to broaden the set of environments for which bounds on the optimal values of h and β are known.

Recall the definition of a determinate environment: there is no input x for which $G(s, x) > 0$ and $G(s', x) > 0$ and $s \neq s'$ (no input can be a result of two different underlying states).

Proposition 1 *Determinate environments can be solved with $h = 0$.*

A proof of this proposition, as well as later ones, depends on reduction to a dynamic programming problem. Imagine an *omniscient* agent— one which has exact knowledge of the environment's underlying state at all times, independent of what the perception function tells it. Clearly no agent with partial knowledge of the underlying state can do better than an omniscient agent. Consider the equation (after Watkins, 1989):

$$Q(s,a) = \sum_{r\in R}(H(s,a,r)\cdot r + \gamma \sum_{s'\in S} F(s,a,s') \cdot \max_{a'\in A} Q(s',a'))$$

A basic result from the theory of dynamic programming (in the terminology of this paper) is that the value $\max_{a\in A} Q(s,a)$ represents the maximum achievable discounted reinforcement an omniscient agent could achieve from a given state, s, of the environment (see Bertesekas, 1987, for instance).

For a class of environments, agents can be built that perform identically to the omniscient agent and therefore optimally.

Definition 9 *The* omniscient agent's *behavior is defined by a set of optimal actions from each environmental state:* $\mathcal{B}(s) = \{a \mid Q(s,a) = \max_{a'\in A} Q(s,a')\}$.

It is known from the theory of dynamic programming that $\mathcal{B}(s)$ is non-empty for all s. This set is well-defined for any environment regardless of whether or not there is some agent that can actually implement such a behavior.

Observe that in a determinate environment, an agent is functionally omniscient— from an input alone, the agent can infer the underlying environmental state, s.

Definition 10 *The* state set *for an input, x, is:*

$$W(x) = \{s \mid s \in S \text{ and } G(s,x) > 0\}$$

which represents all the states, s, that can appear to the agent as x.

In a determinate environment, $W(x)$ contains no more than one element for all inputs x, so clearly the function $B(x,m) = \mathcal{B}(s)$ such that $s \in W(x)$ defines an optimal behavior. It is straightforward to show that this is also the behavior of an $(h = 0, \beta = \infty)$-agent in this environment.

Proposition 2 *Literal environments can be solved with $h = 0$.*

The above proof can easily be extended to a slightly wider class of environments.

Definition 11 *A* literal *environment is one that satisfies the relation:*

$$\forall_{x\in X} s \in W(x) \text{ and } s' \in W(x) \Rightarrow \forall_{a\in A}\ a \in calB(s) \Leftrightarrow a \in \mathcal{B}(s')$$

This says: any two states that can have identical appearances have exactly the same set of optimal actions. For a literal environment, $B(x,m) = \mathcal{B}(s)$ such that $s \in W(x)$ defines an optimal behavior because any of the optimal actions for any of the possible states, s, underlying the input x are guaranteed to be identical to an action that an omniscient agent might have taken. Determinate environments form an important subclass of literal environments because they trivially satisfy the above condition.

As long as all the states, s, that could possibly appear as input x have at least *one* optimal action in common, the same argument holds. These environments might be called *monotonically literal* since they can be turned into a literal environment by removing some optimal actions.

Definition 12 *A* monotonically literal *environment is one that satisfies:*

$$\forall_{x\in X} s \in W(x) \text{ and } s' \in W(x) \Rightarrow \exists_{a\in A}\ a \in \mathcal{B}(s) \text{ and } a \in \mathcal{B}(s')$$

Proposition 3
Monotonically literal environments can be solved with $h = 0$.

The argument is that a behavior function can be constructed so that the action taken upon encountering input x is the action which is optimal for all possible states which can appear as x.

Proposition 4 *Any environment represented by a deterministic transition function, F, and initial state distribution F_0, can be solved with $h = \log_2(|S|)$.*

For identifying minimal values of h and β, it is convenient to think of an algorithm that takes a known environment (in terms of its transition, perception, and reinforcement functions) and creates behavioral and short term memory functions for that environment. This differs from the typical learning case because a learning agent must usually discover details of the environmental functions on its own. The results discussed in this section apply to the case in which a learning agent has had significant experience with the environment to have discovered its underlying structure and now must specify its behavior in terms of fixed behavioral (B) and short term memory (L) functions.

In this case, $\log_2(|S|)$ bits (where $|S|$ represents the size of the state set— i.e. the number of distinct states) is enough to uniquely specify any state in the environment so an internal state m can be used as an alias for for a state. By defining, $B(x,m) = a$ such that $a \in calB(m)$, $L(x,m,r) = m'$ such that $F(m, B(x,m), m') = 1$ and $m_0 = m$ such that $F_0(m) = 1$, the agent is essentially mimicking the actions of an omniscient agent and therefore achieves optimal performance.

Proposition 5 *Any environment that can be solved by presenting the agent with a moving time window of the most recent w inputs can be solved with $h = w \cdot \log_2(|S|)$.*

This follows from the fact that $w \cdot \log_2(|S|)$ bits is enough to encode the value of w distinct states. The short term memory function, $L(x,m,r)$, needs to be constructed so that at each time step, the new input x is encoded and the input from w time steps in the past is deleted from the representation.

There is not much known to bound h and β for an arbitrary non-deterministic environment. If the optimal solution can be represented as some length l repeating sequence of actions, then $h = log_2(l)$ bits will suffice but it is difficult to define the environments in which such a solution is optimal. When non-deterministic action selection is required on the part of the agent, short term memory might be used to generate pseudo-random numbers but the exact value of h would seem to depend on the required accuracy of the generator.

5.2 The Woods 7 environment

Although the categorization in this paper is defined in terms of optimal performance, the definitions of h and β are useful for examining how optimal performance falls off with an agent's decreasing capabilities. The degree to which an environment can be partially solved by a simpler agent is perhaps a more telling measure of environmental difficulty than the capabilities of the *optimal* agent.

This section details a particular reinforcement learning environment and describes its exploration in terms of the categorization scheme presented here. The example is a Class 2 environment known as WOODS7 (Wilson, 1985) (see Figure 1) which consists of an eighteen by fifty-eight cell toroidal grid on which an agent can wander to any of its eight neighboring cells in a single time step. Non-empty cells contain "trees" which block motion and "food" which serves as a positive reinforcement. An omniscient agent with perfect knowledge of the world and its position averages 0.46 foods per step.

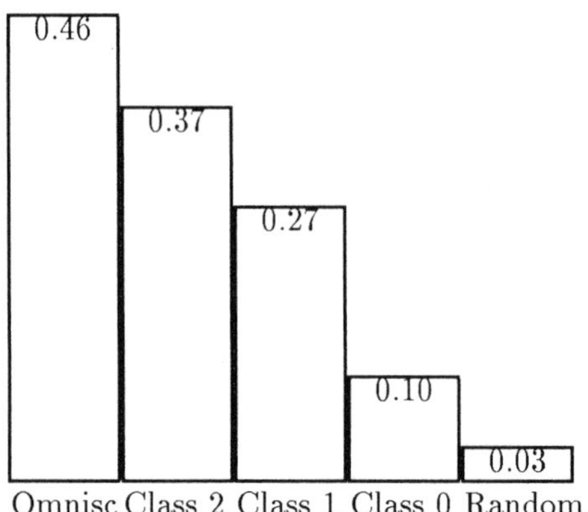

Figure 2: Performance (foods per step) for various agents in Woods 7.

However, agents are not given information about their position— they only see the contents of the eight cells surrounding them.

Using a greedy optimization technique it was possible to find a Class 2 ($h \leq 9\log_2(91) \approx 58.6$, $\beta = 9$)-agent which averages 0.37 foods per step. Wilson's learning experiments involved placing a Class 1 agent, implemented by a simplified classifier system, into this world which achieved a mean performance of between 0.20 and 0.25 foods per step. Q-learning (Watkins, 1989) identified a Class 1 agent that averages 0.27 foods per steps. Dynamic programming found the optimal Class 0 (and Class 1b) agent which encounters 0.10 foods per step and also determined that an agent which ignores its input and moves at random encounters fewer than 0.03 foods per step (for summary, see Figure 2).

The WOODS7 environment is provably Class 2, but this designation alone is incomplete. For learning experiments, it is useful to know that there are Class 1 agents with performance close to 73% of that of the best known Class 2 agent. A researcher could then consider the tradeoffs of working with a more complex agent given the potential performance gain.

5.3 Non-stationary environments

Up until now, the classes in this paper have applied only to environments in which the underlying FSM is static. Is it possible to say something concrete about non-stationary environments? On the face of it, non-stationary environments must be Class 2 or Class 1b ($h > 0$): How can an agent conquer a changing en-

```
...........T.........................TT.........T.........
.TFT.......F........F.........T.......F.........FT........
...........T........TT.......F............................
............................T......T.........F......T.....
...F.......TFT........TFT..........F.........TT......F....
...TT..............................T..................T...
..........TT.......T........TT....................T.......
.TFT.......F.......TF........F.........TFT........F.......
..................................................T.......
...TT.......T.................T........TT.......T.........
...F.......F.......T.........FT........F........TF....TFT.
...........T.......TF.....................................
..T......................T............T......T.......T....
..F.......F...............F..........FT.......F......TF...
..T.......TT...............T...................T..........
.....................T.....................T..............
...F........TFT......F..........F.........F......TF.......
...TT................T..........TT.......T.......T........
```

Figure 1: Bird's-eye view of the complete Woods 7 world.

vironment without having the capability of tracking these changes? Even though the environment might have changed its underlying FSM, it still may not be *functionally* different from an optimization perspective. It is even possible to construct cases in which non-stationarity actually *simplifies* an environment.

Consider a Class 0 environment in which the optimal behavior is $B(x,m) = x + w$. The input stimulus, x, and the action, a, represent integers and the best output is the sum of the input stimulus and some number w. A mildly non-stationary version of this environment is made by choosing a new w every once in awhile, say from a mean 0 normal distribution. This environment is Class 1b because it is possible for an agent to improve its performance by changing its policy to reflect the slowly changing value of w. Now imagine that the environment is wildly non-stationary: A new value for w is chosen at *every* time step. The environment has become Class 0 once again— since w cannot be tracked, a Class 1b agent that tries to track these changes has no advantages over one which simply assumes $w = 0$ and behaves accordingly. Indeed, it is possible to show that such a Class 0 agent achieves the highest expected reinforcement.

Some work has been done to understand non-stationary environments in a reinforcement learning setting. See Littman, Ackley (1991), for an example of a Class 1b non-stationary environment, and Sutton (1990) for a look at several Class 2 non-stationary environments.

A special kind of non-stationary environment adapts specifically *against* the agent, minimizing its expected return. Multi-player games are a natural example of this type of environment. Almost all formal work on reinforcement learning has assumed a single adaptive agent, so much of the developed theory does not hold for multi-player games. Economists studying game theory are now considering computational limitations in their models (eg., Kalai and Stanford, 1988)— this literature might be useful for reinforcement learning theorists.

6 Conclusions

This paper describes a crisp, formal categorization scheme for artificial environments which sorts out interactions between environments and agents by considering only optimally adapted agents of different designs. Though this work extends and improves existing classifications (Wilson, 1990), more work can be done to better understand the effects of regularity in environments and the capabilities of particular classes of agents. This paper details some theoretical observations and gives an example of a particular environment, Wilson's (1985) Woods 7 to show how the new classification can be used to disclose structure in a well-known artificial environment.

By placing environments beside agents as a topic worthy of study, and by giving some informal observations a more theoretical grounding, this work strives to further the understanding of adaptive systems in general.

Acknowledgments

Thanks to Stewart Wilson, Peter Todd, and David Ackley for support and guidance.

References

[1] [Ackley, Littman, 1990] Ackley, D.H., Littman, M.L. Generalization and scaling in reinforcement learning. In *Advances in Neural Information Processing Systems*, 2:550-557. Morgan Kaufmann, San Mateo, CA. Touretsky, D.S., Ed.

[2] [Ackley, Littman, 1991] Ackley, D.H., Littman, M.L., Interactions between learning and evolution. In *Artificial Life II*, 10:487-509. Santa Fe Institute Studies in the Sciences of Complexity. Addison-Wesley. Redwood City, CA. Langton, C., Taylor, C., Farmer, J.D., Ramussen, S., Eds.

[3] [Allen, 1989] Allen, R.B. Adaptive training and connectionist state machines. In *ACM Computer Science Conference.* 428. Louisville.

[4] [Bachrach, 1992] Bachrach, J.R. *Connectionist Modeling and Control of Finite State Environments.* Ph.D. diss., Dept. of Computer and Information Science, University of Massachusetts.

[5] [Bertsekas, 1987] Bertsekas, D.P, Dynamic Programming: Deterministic and Stochastic Models, Prentice-Hall.

[6] [Ghahramani, Allen, 1991] Ghahramani, Z., Allen, R.B., Temporal Processing with Connectionist Networks. In *International Joint Conference on Neural Networks.* Seattle.

[7] [Kalai, Stanford, 1988] Kalai, E., Stanford, W. Finite Rationality and Interpersonal Complexity in Repeated Games. *Econometrica* 56: 397-410.

[8] [Lin, 1992] Lin, L.J., Reinforcement learning in non-Markovian domains. CMU Tech report CMU-CS-92-138.

[9] [Littman, Ackley, 1991] Littman, M.L., Ackley, D.H. Adaptation in constant utility non-stationary environments. in *Proceedings of the Fourth International Conference on Genetic Algorithms*, 136-142. Morgan Kaufmann, San Mateo, CA. Belew, R. K., Ed.

[10] [Sutton, 1984] Sutton, R.S. *Temporal Credit Assignment in Reinforcement Learning.* Ph.D. diss., Dept. of Computer and Information Science, University of Massachusetts.

[11] [Sutton, 1990] Sutton, R.S. Integrated architectures for learning, planning, and reacting based on approximating dynamic programming. In *International Machine Learning Conference.*

[12] [Sutton, 1991] Sutton, R.S. Planning by Incremental Dynamic Programming. 1991 Machine Learning Workshop.

[13] [Thrun, 1992] Thrun, S. Efficient exploration in reinforcement learning. CMU Tech Report, CMU-CS-92-102, Pittsburgh, PA.

[14] [Todd, Wilson, 1992] Todd, P.M., Wilson, S. Studying behavior through environmental variation. To appear in *Proceedings of the Second International Conference on Simulation of Adaptive Behavior: From Animats to Animals.*

[15] [Watkins, 1989] Watkins, C.J.C.H. *Learning with Delayed Rewards.* Ph.D. diss., Psychology Department, Cambridge University.

[16] [Whitehead, 1991] Whitehead, S. Learning to perceive and act by trial and error. In *Machine Learning*, 7:45-83.

[17] [Wilson, 1985] Wilson, S.W. Knowledge Growth in an artificial animal. In *Proceedings of the First International Conference on Genetic Algorithms and Their Applications.* 16-23. Hillsdale, NJ: Lawrence Erlbaum Associates.

[18] [Wilson, 1990] Wilson, S. W. The Animat Path to AI. In *From Animals to Animats: Proceedings of the First International Conference on the Simulation of Adaptive Behavior*, Cambridge, MA: The MIT Press/Bradford Books.

Reinforcement Learning With Hidden States

Long-Ji Lin
School of Computer Science
Carnegie Mellon University
Pittsburgh, PA 15213
e-mail: ljl@cs.cmu.edu

Tom M. Mitchell
School of Computer Science
Carnegie Mellon University
Pittsburgh, PA 15213
e-mail: mitchell@cs.cmu.edu

Abstract

Reinforcement learning is an unsupervised learning technique for sequential decision making. *Q-learning* is a widely-used reinforcement learning method. The convergence of Q-learning relies on the Markovian environment assumption, meaning that any information needed to determine the optimal action is reflected in the agent's state representation. If some important state features are missing (or hidden) from the state representation, the true world states cannot be directly identified and optimal decisions cannot be made based on this state representation. This problem is known as the *hidden state problem.* A possible solution to the problem is to use history information to help uncover the hidden features. This paper studies three reinforcement learning architectures that learn to use history to handle hidden states: *window-Q*, *recurrent-Q*, and *recurrent-model.* Empirical study of these architectures is presented. Their relative strengths and weaknesses are also discussed.

1 Introduction

In the reinforcement learning paradigm, a learning agent continually receives inputs from its sensors, determines its action based on the inputs and its *control policy*, executes that action, and receives a scalar *reinforcement* or *payoff.* The goal of the agent is to construct an optimal policy so as to maximize its performance, which is often measured by the *discounted cumulative reinforcement* in the future or, for short, *utility*:

$$V_t = \sum_{k=0}^{\infty} \gamma^k \, r_{t+k} \tag{1}$$

where V_t is the discounted cumulative reinforcement starting from time t throughout the future, r_t is the reinforcement received after the transition from time t to $t+1$, and $0 \le \gamma \le 1$ is a *discount factor*, which adjusts the importance of long-term consequences of actions.

Q-learning is a widely-used reinforcement learning method [20, 10, 9]. The idea of Q-learning is to construct an evaluation function called *Q-function*:

$$Q(state, action) \rightarrow utility \tag{2}$$

The Q-function is used to predict the discounted cumulative reinforcement (i.e., utility) for each state-action pair given that the agent is in that state and executes that action. Given an optimal Q-function and a state x, the optimal control policy is simply to choose the action a for which $Q(x, a)$ is maximal over all actions.

The optimal Q-function can be incrementally constructed based on *temporal difference* (TD) *methods* [17], which are a type of dynamic programming [4]. For deterministic domains [1], the utility of an action a in response to a state x is equal to the immediate payoff r plus the best utility that can be obtained from the next state y, discounted by γ. Therefore, the optimal Q-function must satisfy Equation (3):

$$Q(x, a) = r + \gamma \cdot Max\{Q(y, k) \mid k \in actions\} \tag{3}$$

During learning, the equation may not hold true, and the difference between the two sides of the equation is what to be minimized. The Q-function thus can be updated in the following way:

$$Q(x, a) \leftarrow Q(x, a) + \eta \cdot (r + \gamma \cdot \max_k Q(y, k) - Q(x, a)) \tag{4}$$

where η is the learning rate. The update rule used in this work was in fact more sophisticated and efficient than (4). For further details, see [11, 9].

Q-learning converges and finds the optimal policy under two primary conditions (along with a few weak ones): the Q-function is represented by a lookup table, and the environment is Markovian [21]. The latter means that

[1] It is straightforward to extend the discussion here to handle nondeterministic worlds [20, 4].

at any given time, the next state of the environment is determined only by the current state and the action taken. In such environments, all information needed to determine the current optimal action is reflected in the current state representation. Although the first condition disallows generalization, when the state space is large and the lookup table representation is unacceptable, some generalization method is often used to approximate the Q-function. For example, Lin [8, 10, 9] has successfully combined the connectionist error back-propagation algorithm and Q-learning to solve several nontrivial learning problems. In essence, the Q-function is represented by neural networks called *Q-nets*, and the network weights are adjusted by the back-propagation algorithm to reduce the difference between the two sides of Equation (3).

Consider a reinforcement learning agent whose state representation is based on only its immediate sensation. When its sensors are not able to make essential distinctions among world states, the Markov assumption mentioned above is violated. Consider a packing task which involves 4 steps: open a box, put a gift into it, close it, and seal it. An agent driven only by its current visual percepts cannot accomplish this task, because when facing a closed box, the agent does not know if a gift is already in the box and therefore cannot decide whether to seal or to open the box. This problem is known as the *hidden state problem*, because some state features (in this example, *whether there is a gift in the box*) are hidden from the agent's sensory inputs. One possible solution to this problem is to use history information, such as whether a gift was ever put in the box, to help determine the current world state.

In this paper we study three connectionist architectures that learn to use history information to control a non-Markovian environment. An OAON network architecture is also proposed for learning recurrent action models and recurrent Q-functions. Empirical study of these architectures is presented, and their relative strengths and weaknesses are also discussed.

2 Three Memory Architectures

Figure 1 depicts three memory architectures for reinforcement learning in environments with hidden states. These architectures all use temporal difference methods to incrementally learn a Q-function, which is represented by artificial neural networks called Q-nets.

Instead of using just the current sensation as state representation, the *window-Q architecture* uses the current sensation, the N most recent sensations, and the N most recent actions taken all together as state representation. In other words, the window-Q architecture allows a direct access to the information in the past through a sliding window. N is called the *window size.* The window-Q architecture is simple and straightforward, but the problem is that we may not know the right window size in advance. If the window size is chosen to be not large enough, there will be not enough history information to construct an optimal Q-function. Moreover, if the window size needs to be large, the large number of units in the input layer will require a lot of training patterns for successful learning and generalization. In spite of these problems, it is still worth study, since this kind of *time-delay neural networks* has been found quite successful in speech recognition [19] and several other domains.

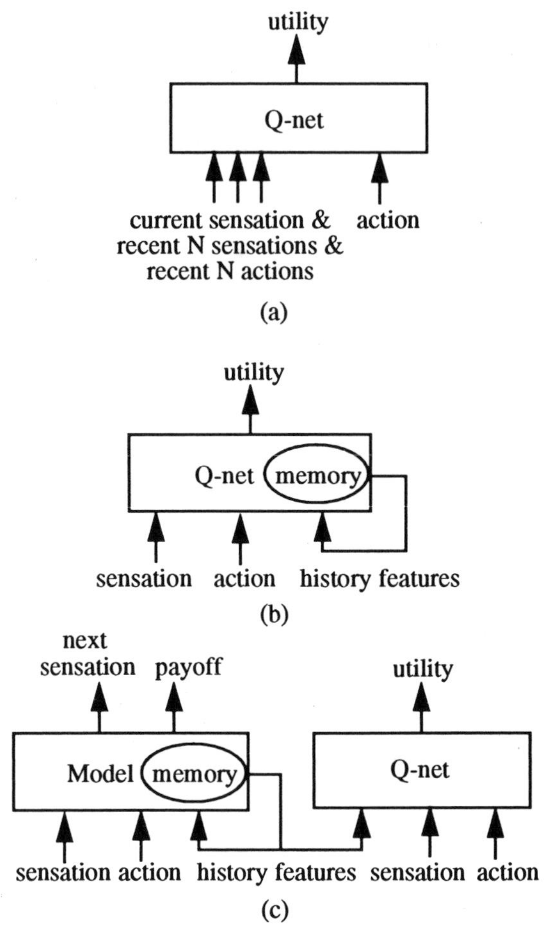

Figure 1: Three memory architectures for reinforcement learning in environments with hidden states: (a) window-Q, (b) recurrent-Q, and (c) recurrent-model.

The window-Q architecture is sort of a brute force approach to using history information. An alternative is to distill a (small) set of *history features* out of the large

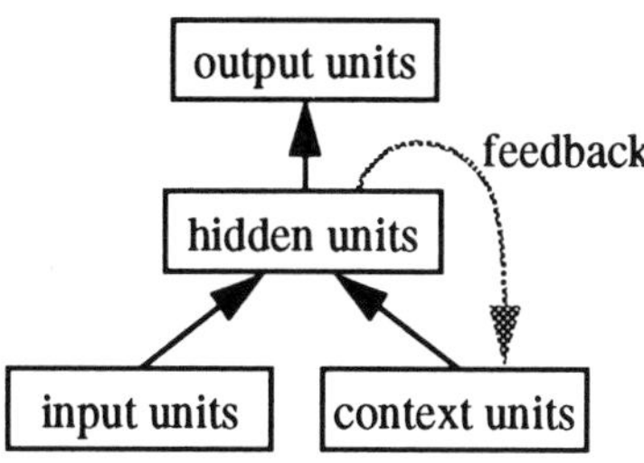

Figure 2: An Elman Network.

amount of information in the past. This set of features together with the current sensation become the agent's state representation. The optimal control actions then can be determined based on just this new state representation, if the set of history features reflects the information needed for optimal control. The *recurrent-Q* and *recurrent-model* architectures illustrated in Figure 1 are based on this same idea, but the ways they construct history features are different. Unlike the window-Q architecture, both architectures in principle can discover and utilize history features that depend on sensations arbitrarily deep in the past, although in practice it is difficult to achieve this.

Recurrent neural networks, such as Elman networks [7], provide a way to construct useful history features. As illustrated in Figure 2, the input layer of an Elman network is divided into two parts: the true input units and the *context units*. The operation of the network is clocked. The context units hold feedback activations coming from the network state at a previous clock time. The context units, which function as the memory in Figure 1, remember an aggregate of previous network states, so the output of the network depends on the past as well as on the current input.

The recurrent-Q architecture uses a recurrent network to model the Q-function. To predict utility values correctly, the recurrent network (called recurrent *Q-net*) will be forced to develop history features which enable the network to properly assign different utility values to states with the same sensation.

The recurrent-model architecture consists of two concurrent learning components: learning an *action model* and Q-learning. An action model is a function which maps a sensation and an action to the next sensation and the immediate payoff. To predict the behavior of the environment, the recurrent action model will be forced to develop a set of history features. Using the current sensation and this set of history features as state representation, we can in effect turn a non-Markovian task into Markovian one and solve it using the conventional Q-learning, if the action model is perfect. This is simply because at any given time, the next state of the environment now can be completely determined by this new state representation and the action taken. This idea of learning an action model for controlling a non-Markovian environment has also been studied by other researchers [16, 18, 3, 5].

Both the recurrent-Q and recurrent-model architectures learn history features using a gradient descent method (i.e., error back-propagation), but they differ in an important way. For model learning, the goal is to minimize the errors between actual and predicted sensations and payoffs. In essence, the environment provides all the needed training information, which is consistent over time as long as the environment does not change. For recurrent Q-learning, the goal is to minimize the errors between temporally successive predictions of utility values. The error signals here are computed based partly on information from the environment and partly on the current approximation to the true Q-function. The latter (i.e., the learned Q-function) changes over time and carries no information at all in the beginning of learning. In other words, these error signals are in general weak, noisy and even inconsistent over time. Because of this, whether the recurrent-Q architecture will ever work in practice may be questioned.

In general the action model must be trained to predict not only the new sensation but also the immediate payoff. Consider another packing task which involves 3 steps: put a gift into an open box, seal the box so that it cannot be opened again, place the box in the proper bucket depending on the color of the gift in the box. A reward is given only when the box is placed in the right bucket. Note that the agent is never required to know the gift color in order to predict future sensations, since the box cannot be opened once sealed. Therefore a model which only predicts sensations will not have the right features which are needed to accomplish this task. However, for each of the tasks described in Section 4, the action model does not need to predict the immediate payoff in order to discover history features needed for optimal control.

It is worthwhile to note that combinations of the three architectures are possible. For example, we can combine the first two architectures: the inputs to the recurrent Q-net could include not just the current sensation but also recent sensations. We can also combine the last two architectures: the memory is shared between a recurrent model and a recurrent Q-net, and history features are developed using the error signals coming from both the model and the Q-net. This paper is only concerned with the three basic architectures. Further investigation is needed to see if these kinds of combination will result in better performance than the basic versions.

3 The OAON Architectures

Both the Q-function and action model take two kinds of inputs: sensation and action. There are two alternative network structures to realize them. One is a monolithic network whose input units encode both the sensation and the action. For domains with discrete actions, this structure is often undesirable, because the monolithic network is to be trained to model a highly nonlinear function— given the same sensation (and same history features), different actions may demand very different outputs of the network.

An alternative is what we call the OAON (*One Action One Network*) architectures. We use multiple networks, one for each action, to represent the Q-function and the model. Figure 3 illustrates two types of recurrent OAON architectures: linear and nonlinear. The linear OAON consists of single-layer perceptrons, and the nonlinear one consists of multilayer networks of units with a nonlinear squashing function. At any given time, only the network corresponding to the selected action is used to compute the next values of the output and context units, while the others can be ignored. It is important to note that we also have to ensure that the multiple networks will use the same (distributed) representation of history features. This is achieved by having the networks share activations of context units, and can be further reinforced (in the case of the nonlinear one) by having the networks share all connections emitting from the hidden layer. As found empirically, the sharing of connections does not seem necessary but tends to help.

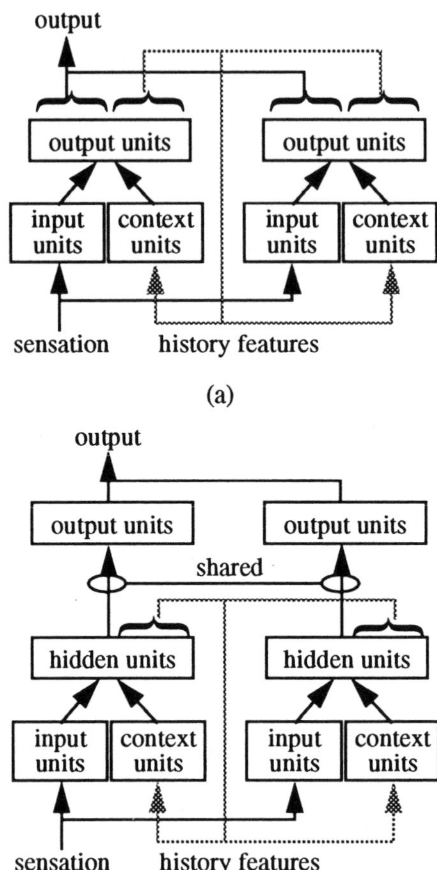

Figure 3: Two OAON architectures for recurrent models and recurrent Q-nets: (a) linear and (b) nonlinear. At any given time, only the network corresponding to the selected action is used to compute the next values of the output and context units.

As shown in Figure 3, the input layer of each network (either linear or nonlinear) is divided into two parts: the true input units and the context units, as we have seen in the Elman network (Figure 2). Note that each of the recurrent networks in Figure 3.b is a modified Elman network. In the "standard" Elman network, the whole hidden layer is fed back to the input layer, but here only a portion of hidden units is fed back. Consider an environment with just one hidden feature that needs to be discovered. In such a case, it makes sense to have many hidden units but just one context unit.

The linear OAON architecture shown in Figure 3.a is in fact the SLUG architecture proposed by Mozer and Bachrach [13], who have applied SLUG to learn to model finite state automata (FSA) and demonstrated its success in several domains. (They did not use SLUG to model a Q-function, however). They also found that the conventional recurrent networks, such as the Elman network, were "spectacularly unsuccessful" at modeling FSA's. This may be explained by the fact that their experiments took the monolithic approach (one network for all actions). In contrast, our experiments using the nonlinear OAON architecture were quite successful. It always learned perfectly the FSA's that SLUG was able to learn.

To model FSA's, we probably do not need a nonlinear OAON; linear OAONs (SLUG) may suffice and outperform nonlinear OAONs. But for many applications, a nonlinear OAON is necessary and cannot be replaced by the linear one. For example, Q-functions are in general nonlinear. For a pole balancer to be discussed later, its action model is also nonlinear. For the sake of comparing simulation results, we used nonlinear OAONs for all the recurrent Q-nets and models in all the experiments to be presented below.

Back-propagation through time (BPTT) [15] was used to train the recurrent networks. To apply BPTT, the recurrent networks were completely unfolded in time, errors were then back-propagated through the whole chain of networks, and finally the weights were modified according to the cumulative gradients. To restrict the influence of output errors at time t on the gradients computed at times much earlier than t, we applied a decay to the errors when they were propagated from the context units at time t to the hidden layer at time $t-1$. Better performance was found with this decay than without it. The decay we used here was 0.9. The context units were initialized to 0 at the start of each task instance.

4 Experimental Results

This section presents a study of the three architectures for solving various learning problems with different characteristics. Through the study, we expect to gain more insights into these architectures, such as whether these architectures work and which one may work best for which types of problems. Each of the following experiments consisted of two interleaved phases: a learning phase and a test phase. In the learning phase, the agent chose actions randomly but tended to chose actions with high utilities. This randomness in action selection ensured sufficient exploration by the agent during learning. In the test phase, the agent always took the best actions according to its current policy. All of the experiments were repeated 5 times. The learning curves shown below describe the mean performance in the test phase. See [11] for detailed descriptions of the training algorithm and parameter settings.

4.1 Task 1: 2-Cup Collection

We started with a simple 2-cup collection task (Figure 4). This task requires the learning agent to pick up two cups located in a 1-D space. The agent has 3 actions: walking right one cell, walking left one cell, and pick-up. When the agent executes the pick-up action, it will pick up a cup if and only if the cup is located at the agent's current cell. The agent's sensation includes 4 binary bits: 2 bits indicating if there is a cup in the immediate left or right cell, and 2 bits indicating if the previous action results in a collision from the left or the right. An action attempting to move the agent out of the space will cause a collision.

The cup-collection problem is restricted such that there are only two possible initial states (Figure 4). In each trial, the agent starts with one of the two initial states. Because the agent can only see one of the two cups at the beginning of each trial, the location of the other cup can only be learned from previous trials. To collect the cups optimally, the agent must use history information, such as which initial state it starts with, to decide which way to go after picking up the first cup. Note that the reason for restricting the number of initial states is to simplify the task and to avoid ambiguities in the very beginning where no history information is available. This task is not trivial for several reasons: (1) The agent cannot sense the cup right in its current cell, (2) it gets no reward until both cups are picked up, and (3) it often operates with no cup in sight especially after picking up the first cup. The optimal policy requires 7 steps to pick up the 2 cups in each situation.

2 possible initial states:

Figure 4: Task 1: A 2-cup collection task.

Figure 5 shows the learning curves for the three architectures. These curves show the mean performance over 5 runs. The Y axis indicates the number of steps to pick up the four cups in both task instances shown in Figure 4 before time out (i.e., 30 steps). The X axis indicates the number of trials the agent had attempted so far. In each trial the agent started with one of the two possible initial states, and stopped either when both cups were picked up, or else after time out. It is obvious from the learning curves that all of these architectures successfully learned the optimal control policy. The following are some additional observations, which are not shown in Figure 5:

The window size N. The performance in Figure 5.a was obtained with $N = 5$. As a matter of fact, the optimal policy could be learned (but only occasionally) with $N = 2$. Imagine that the agent has picked up the first cup and is walking towards the second cup. For a few steps, the most recent 3 sensations (including the current one) in fact do not provide the agent any information at all (namely, all sensation bits are off). How could the agent ever learn the optimal policy with $N = 2$? The way it worked is the following: After picking up the first cup, the agent determines the right direction to move. Later on, the agent simply follows the general direction the previous actions has been headed for. In other words, *the agent's action choices are themselves used as a medium for passing information from the past to the present.*

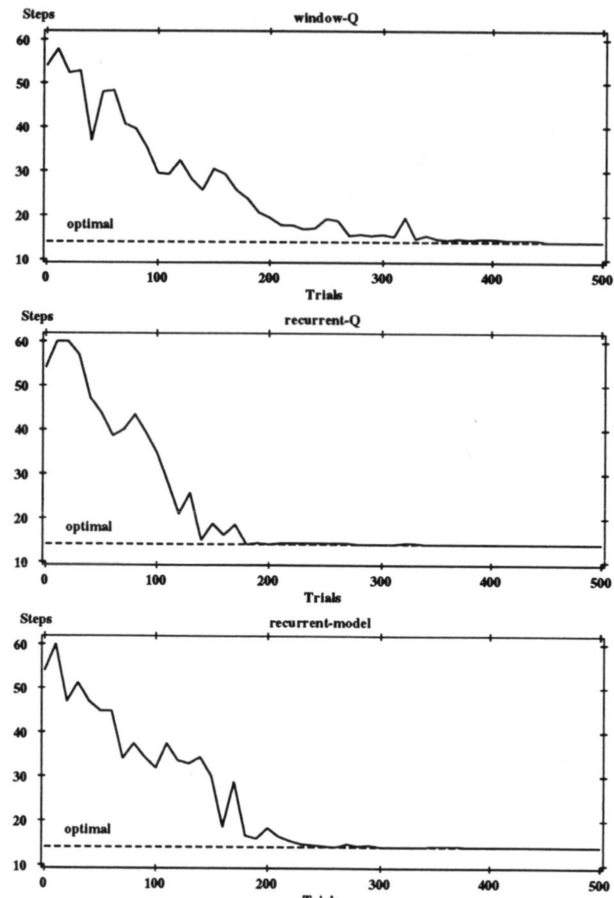

Figure 5: Performance for Task 1: (a) window-Q, (b) recurrent-Q, and (c) recurrent-model.

Imperfect model. The agent never learned a perfect action model within 500 trials. For instance, if the agent had not seen a cup for 10 steps or more, the model normally was unable to predict the appearance of the cup. But this imperfect model did not prevent Q-learning from learning an optimal policy.

This experiment revealed two lessons: (1) All of the three architectures worked for this simple cup-collection problem. (2) For the recurrent-model architecture, just a partially correct model may provide sufficient history features for optimal control. This is good news, since a perfect model is often difficult to obtain.

4.2 Task 2: Task 1 With Random Features

Task 2 is simply Task 1 with two random bits in the agent's sensation. The random bits simulate two difficult-to-predict and irrelevant features accessible to the learning agent. In the real world, there are often many features which are difficult to predict but fortunately not relevant to the task to be solved. For example, predicting whether it is going to rain outside might be difficult, but it does not matter if the task is to pick up cups inside. The ability to handle difficult-to-predict but irrelevant features is important for a learning system to be practical.

The learning curves for this task were found similar to those for Task 1, except that the curve of the recurrent-model architecture displayed some instability— once in a while, it unlearned the optimal policy that was once acquired. The explanation for this instability is as follows: Because the activations of the context units are shared between the model network and Q-net, a change to the representation of history features on the model part can simply destabilize a well-trained Q-net, if the change is significant. Since the model could never reduce the prediction errors on the two random bits, significant changes to the network weights might occur even after a long period of training. To test this explanation, we fixed the model at some point of learning and allowed only changes to the Q-net. In such a setup, the instability was no longer observed.

This experiment revealed two lessons: (1) The recurrent-Q architecture is more economic than the recurrent-model architecture in the sense that the former will not try to learn a history feature if it does not appear to be relevant to predicting utilities. (2) A potential problem with the recurrent-model architecture is that changes to the representation of history features on the model part may cause instability on the Q-net part.

4.3 Task 3: Task 1 With Control Errors

Noise and uncertainty prevail in the real world. To study the capability of these architectures to handle noise, we added 15% control errors to the agent's actuators, so that 15% of the time the executed action would not have any effect on the environment. (The 2 random bits were removed.) Figure 6 shows the mean performance of these architectures over 5 runs. Note that we turned off the control errors when we tested the performance of the agent, so the optimal number of steps in the figure is still 14.

In 3 out of the 5 runs, the window-Q architecture successfully found the optimal policy, while in the other two runs, it only found suboptimal policies. In spite of the control errors, the recurrent-Q architecture always learned the optimal policy (with little instability). The recurrent-model architecture always found the optimal policy after 500 trials, but again its policy oscillated between the optimal one and some sub-optimal ones due to the changing representation of history features, much as happened in Task 2. If we can find some way to stablize the model (for example, by gradually decreasing the learning rate to 0 at the end), we should be able to

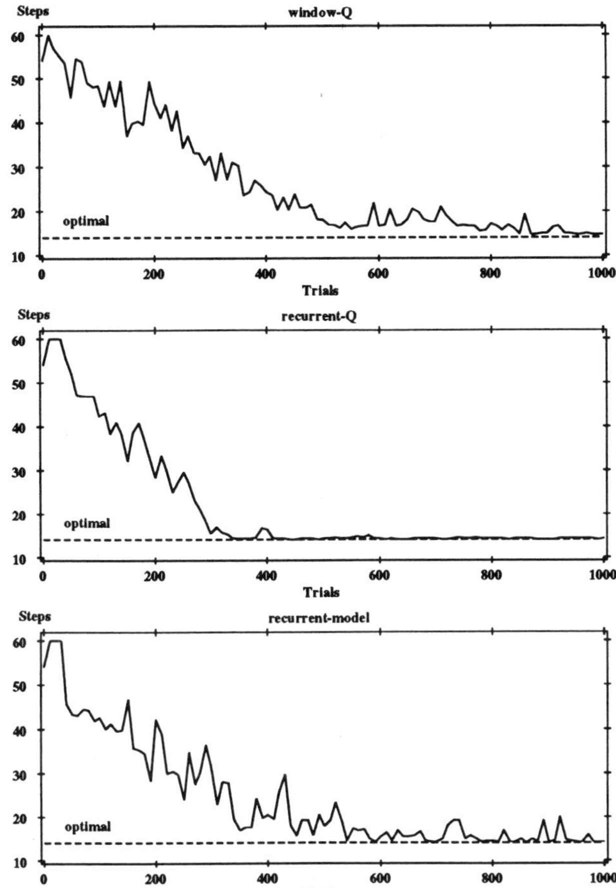

Figure 6: Performance for Task 3: (a) window-Q, (b) recurrent-Q, and (c) recurrent-model.

obtain a stable and optimal policy.

We learned two lessons from this experiment: (1) All of the three architectures can handle small control errors to some degree. (2) Among the architectures, recurrent-Q seems to scale best in the presence of control errors.

4.4 Task 4: Pole Balancing

The traditional pole balancing problem is to balance a pole on a cart given the cart position, pole angle, cart velocity, and pole angular velocity (Figure 7). This problem has been studied many times (e.g., [1]) as a nontrivial control problem due to sparse reinforcement signals, which are -1 when the pole falls past 12 degrees and 0 elsewhere. Task 4 is the same problem except that only the cart position and pole angle are given to the learning agent. To balance the pole, the agent must learn features like velocity. In this experiment, a policy was considered satisfactory whenever the pole could be balanced for over 5000 steps in each of the 7 test trials where the pole starts with an angle of 0, ± 1, ± 2, or ± 3

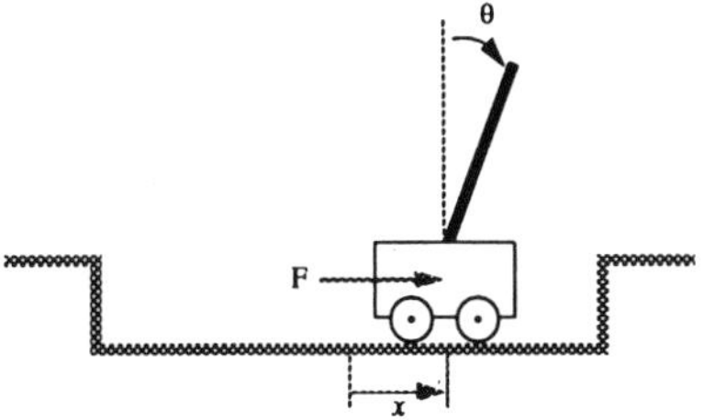

Figure 7: The pole balancing problem.

degrees. The initial cart velocity and pole velocity are always set to 0. (The maximum initial pole angle with which the pole can be balanced indefinitely is about 3.3 degrees.) We used $N = 1$ in this experiment.

The input representation used here was straightforward: one real-valued input unit for each of the pole angle and cart position. The following table shows the number of trials taken by each architecture before a satisfactory policy was learned. While the recurrent-Q architecture was the most suitable architecture for the cup collection tasks, it was outperformed by the other two architectures for the pole balancing task.

window-Q	recurrent-Q	recurrent-model
206	552	247

5 Discussion

The above experiments provide some insight into the performance of the three memory architectures. This section considers problem characteristics that determine which architecture is most appropriate to which task environments. The three architectures exhibit different advantages whose relative importance varies with task parameters such as:

- **Memory depth.** One important problem parameter is the length of time over which the agent must remember previous inputs in order to represent an optimal control policy. For example, the memory depth for Task 1 is 2, as evidenced by the fact that the window-Q agent was able to obtain the optimal control based only on a window of size 2. The memory depth for the pole balancing task is 1. Note that learning an optimal policy may require a larger memory depth than that needed to represent the policy.

- **Payoff delay.** In cases where the payoff is zero except for the goal state, we define the payoff delay of a problem to be the length of the optimal action sequence leading to the goal. This parameter is important because it influences the overall difficulty of Q-learning. As the payoff delay increases, learning an accurate Q-function becomes increasingly difficult due to the increasing difficulty of credit assignment.

- **Number of history features to be learned.** In general, the more hidden states an agent faces, the more history features the agent has to discover, and the more difficult the task becomes. In general, predicting sensations (i.e., a model) requires more history features than predicting utilities (i.e., a Q-net), which in turn requires more history features than representing optimal policies. Consider Task 1 for example. Only two binary history features are required to determine the optimal actions: "*is there a cup in front?*" and "*is the second cup on the right-hand side or left-hand side?*". But a perfect Q-function requires more features such as "*how many cups have been picked up so far?*" and "*how far is the second cup from here?*". A perfect model for this task requires the same features as the perfect Q-function. But a perfect model for Task 2 requires even more features such as "*what is the current state of the random number generator?*", while a perfect Q-function for Task 2 requires no extra features.

  It is important to note that we do not need a perfect Q-function or a perfect model in order to obtain an optimal policy. A Q-function just needs to assign a value to each action in response to a given situation such that their relative values are in the right order, and a model just needs to provide sufficient features for constructing a good Q-function.

5.1 Architecture Characteristics

Given the above problem parameters, we would like to understand which of the three architectures is best suited to which types of problems. Here we consider the key advantages and disadvantages of each architecture, along with the problem parameters which influence the importance of these characteristics.

- **Recurrent-model architecture.** The key difference between this architecture and the recurrent-Q architecture is that its learning of history features is driven by learning an action model rather than the Q-function. One strength of this approach is that the agent can obtain better training data for the action model than it can for the Q-function, making this learning more reliable and efficient. In particular, training examples of the action model (<sensation, action, next-sensation, payoff> quadruples) are directly observable with each step the agent takes in its environment. In contrast, training examples of the Q-function (<sensation, action, utility> triples) are not directly observable since the agent must estimate the training utility values based on its own changing approximation to the true Q-function.

  The second strength of this approach is that the learned features are dependent on the environment and independent of the reward function (even though the action model may be trained to predict rewards as well as sensations), and therefore can be reused if the agent has several different reward functions, or goals, to learn to achieve.

- **Recurrent-Q architecture.** While this architecture suffers the relative disadvantage that it must learn from indirectly observable training examples, it has the offsetting advantage that it need only learn those history features that are *relevant* to the control problem. The history features needed to represent the optimal action model are a superset of those needed to represent the optimal Q-function. This is easily seen by noticing that the optimal control action can in principle be computed from the action model (by using look ahead search). Thus, in cases where only a few features are necessary for predicting utilities but many are needed to predict completely the next state, the number of history features that must be learned by the recurrent-Q architecture can be much smaller than the number needed by the recurrent-model architecture.

- **Window-Q architecture.** The primary advantage of this architecture is that it does not have to learn the state representation recursively (as do the other two recurrent network architectures). Recurrent networks typically take much longer to train than non-recurrent networks. This advantage is offset by the disadvantage that the history information it can use are limited to those features directly observable in its fixed window which captures only a bounded history. In contrast, the two recurrent network approaches can in principle represent history features that depend on sensations that are arbitrarily deep in the agent's history.

Given these competing advantages for the three architectures, one would imagine that each will be the preferred architecture for different types of problems:

- One would expect the advantage of the window-Q architecture to be greatest in tasks where the memory depths are the smallest (for example, the pole balancing task).

- One would expect the recurrent-model architecture's advantage of directly available training examples to be most important in tasks for which the payoff delay is the longest (for example, the pole balancing task). It is in these situations that the indirect estimation of training Q-nets is most problematic for the recurrent-Q architecture.

- One would expect the advantage of the recurrent-Q architecture — that it need only learn those features relevant to control — to be most pronounced in tasks where the ratio between relevant and irrelevant history features is the lowest (for example, the cup collection task with two random features). Although the recurrent-model architecture can acquire the optimal policy as long as just the relevant features are learned, the drive to learning the irrelevant features may cause problems. First of all, representing the irrelevant features may use up many of the limited context units at the sacrifice of learning good relevant features. Secondly, as we have seen in the experiments, the recurrent-model architecture is also subject to instability due to changing representation of the history features— a change which improves the model is also likely to deteriorate the Q-function, which then needs to be re-learned.

The tapped delay line scheme, which the window-Q architecture uses, has been widely applied to speech recognition [19] and turned out to be quite a useful technique. However, we do not expect it to work as well for control tasks as it does for speech recognition, because of an important difference between these tasks. A major task of speech recognition is to find the temporal patterns that already exist in a given sequence of speech phonemes. While learning to control, the agent must look for the temporal patterns generated by its own actions. If the actions are generated randomly as it is often the case during early learning, it is unlikely to find sensible temporal patterns within the action sequence so as to improve its action selection policy.

6 Summary

This paper presents three memory architectures for reinforcement learning in non-Markovian domains: window-Q, recurrent-Q, and recurrent-model. These architectures are all based on the idea of using history information to discriminate situations that are indistinguishable from immediate sensations. As we have shown, these architectures are all capable of learning some non-Markovian tasks. They are also able to handle irrelevant features and small control errors to some degree. We also have discussed strengths and weaknesses of these architectures in solving tasks with various characteristics. The following is our general summary on each of these architectures:

1. Surprisingly, the recurrent-Q architecture seems to be much more promising than we thought before this study. We (as well as several other researchers) in fact did not expect this architecture to work at all. As long as the memory depth and payoff delay required by a task are not too large, this architecture appears to work effectively.

2. For tasks where a small window size N is sufficient to uncover hidden states, the window-Q architecture should work well. However, it is unable to represent an optimal control policy if the memory depth of the problem is greater than N.

3. The recurrent-model approach seems quite costly to apply, because model learning often takes a lot more effort than what seems to be necessary. The difficulty of the general problem of model learning is well recognized. There are few methods that are truly successful. For example, the *diversity-based inference procedure* proposed by Rivest and Schapire [14] is restricted to deterministic, discrete domains. Instance-based approaches, such as the work by Moore [12], Atkeson [2], and Christiansen [6], are suitable for nondeterministic, continuous domains, but cannot learn history features. Chrisman [5] studied a model learning method based on maximum likelihood estimation. That method can handle nondeterminism and history features, but does not seem to scale well. We also do not think the architectures proposed here scale well to handle problems with very large memory depths. On the other hand, once a model is learned for a task, it may be re-usable for other tasks.

Finally, as mentioned before, combinations of these architectures are possible and may give better performance than the basic versions. Further study of this remains to be done.

Acknowledgements

We thank Chris Atkeson, Ronald Williams, Rich Sutton, and Sebastian Thrun for fruitful discussions on issues related to this work. We also thank Lonnie Chrisman and Sebastian Thrun for helpful comments on a draft of this paper.

References

[1] C.W. Anderson. Strategy learning with multilayer connectionist representations. In *Proceedings of the*

Fourth International Workshop on Machine Learning, pages 103–114, Ann Arbor, Michigan, 1987. Morgan Kaufmann.

[2] C.G. Atkeson. Using locally weighted regression for robot learning. In *Proceedings of the 1991 IEEE International Conference on Robotics and Automation*, pages 958–963, Sacramento, California, 1991.

[3] J.R. Bachrach. *Connectionist Modeling and Control of Finite State Environments.* PhD thesis, University of Massachusetts, Department of Computer and Information Sciences, 1992.

[4] A.G. Barto, S.J. Bradtke, and S.P. Singh. Real-time learning and control using asynchronous dynamic programming. Technical Report 91-57, Computer Science Department, University of Massachusetts, 1991.

[5] L Chrisman. Reinforcement learning with perceptual aliasing: The predictive distinctions approach. In *Proceedings of the Tenth National Conference on Artificial Intelligence*, pages 183–188. AAAI Press/The MIT Press, 1992.

[6] A.D. Christiansen. *Automatic Acquisition of Task Theories for Robotic Manipulation.* PhD thesis, Carnegie Mellon University, School of Computer Science, 1992. Technical Report CMU-CS-92-111.

[7] J.L. Elman. Finding structure in time. *Cognitive Science*, 14:179–211, 1990.

[8] Long-Ji Lin. Programming robots using reinforcement learning and teaching. In *Proceedings of the Ninth National Conference on Artificial Intelligence*, pages 781–786. AAAI Press/The MIT Press, 1991.

[9] Long-Ji Lin. *Reinforcement Learning for Robots Using Neural Networks.* PhD thesis, Carnegie Mellon University, School of Computer Science, 1992. (To appear).

[10] Long-Ji Lin. Self-improving reactive agents based on reinforcement learning, planning and teaching. *Machine Learning*, 8:293–321, 1992.

[11] Long-Ji Lin and T.M. Mitchell. Memory approaches to reinforcement learning in non-Markovian domains. Technical Report CMU-CS-92-138, School of Computer Science, Carnegie Mellon University, 1992.

[12] A.W. Moore. *Efficient Memory-Based Learning for Robot Control.* PhD thesis, University of Cambridge, Computer Laboratory, 1990. Technical Report No. 209.

[13] M.C Mozer and J.R. Bachrach. SLUG: A connectionist architecture for inferring the structure of finite-state environments. *Machine Learning*, 7:139–160, 1991.

[14] R.L. Rivest and R.E. Schapire. Diversity-based inference of finite automata. In *Proceedings of the Twenty-Eighth Annual Symposium on Foundations of Computer Science*, pages 78–87, 1987.

[15] D.E. Rumelhart, G.E. Hinton, and R.J. Williams. Learning internal representations by error propagation. In D.E. Rumelhart and J.L. McClelland, editors, *Parallel Distributed Processing: Explorations in the Microstructure of Cognition*, volume 1, chapter 8. The MIT press, 1986.

[16] J. Schmidhuber. Reinforcement learning in Markovian and non-Markovian environments. In D.S. Touretzky, editor, *Advances in Neural Information Processing Systems 3*, pages 500–506. Morgan Kaufmann, 1991.

[17] R.S. Sutton. Learning to predict by the methods of temporal differences. *Machine Learning*, 3:9–44, 1988.

[18] S.B. Thrun, K. Möller, and A. Linden. Planning with an adaptive world model. In D.S. Touretzky, editor, *Advances in Neural Information Processing Systems 3.* Morgan Kaufmann, 1991.

[19] A. Waibel. Modular construction of time-delay neural networks for speech recognition. *Neural Computation*, 1:39–46, 1989.

[20] C.J.C.H. Watkins. *Learning from Delayed Rewards.* PhD thesis, King's College, Cambridge, 1989.

[21] C.J.C.H. Watkins and P. Dayan. Technical note: Q-learning. *Machine Learning*, 8:279–292, 1992.

Efficient Learning and Planning Within the Dyna Framework *

Jing Peng and Ronald J. Williams
College of Computer Science
Northeastern University
Boston, MA 02115
jp@corwin.ccs.northeastern.edu
rjw@corwin.ccs.northeastern.edu

Abstract

Sutton's Dyna framework provides a novel and computationally appealing way to integrate learning, planning, and reacting in autonomous agents. Examined here is a class of strategies designed to enhance the learning and planning power of Dyna systems by increasing their computational efficiency. The benefit of using these strategies is demonstrated on some simple abstract learning tasks.

1 Introduction

Many problems faced by an autonomous agent in an unknown environment can be cast in the form of *reinforcement learning* tasks. Recent work in this area has led to a clearer understanding of the relationship between algorithms found useful for such tasks and asynchronous approaches to dynamic programming (Bertsekas & Tsitsiklis, 1989), and this understanding has led in turn to both new results relevant to the theory of dynamic programming (Barto, Bradtke, & Singh, 1991; Watkins & Dayan, 1991; Williams & Baird, 1990) and the creation of new reinforcement learning algorithms, such as *Q-learning* (Watkins, 1989) and *Dyna* (Sutton, 1990; 1991). Dyna was proposed as a simple but principled way to achieve more efficient reinforcement learning in autonomous agents, and this paper proposes enhancements designed to improve this learning efficiency still further.

After first providing a concrete illustration of the kind of task any of these reinforcement learning methods are designed to handle, we then outline the formal framework and existing techniques that serve as a backdrop for the new methods examined here.

*We wish to thank Rich Sutton for his many valuable suggestions and continuing encouragement. This work was supported by Grant IRI-8921275 from the National Science Foundation.

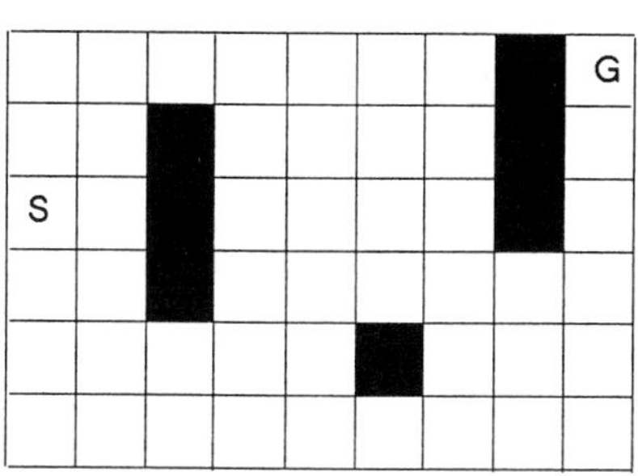

Figure 1: A maze navigation task.

2 An Illustrative Task

Suppose a learning agent is placed in the discretized 2-dimensional maze shown in Figure 1. Shaded cells in this maze represent barriers, and the agent can occupy any other cell within this maze and can move about by choosing one of four actions at each discrete time tick. Each of these actions has the effect of moving the agent to an adjacent cell in one of the four compass directions, north, east, south, or west, except that any action that would ostensibly move the agent into a barrier cell or outside the maze has the actual effect of keeping the agent at its current location. The agent initially has no knowledge of the effect of its actions on what state (i.e., cell) it will occupy next, although it always knows its current state.

We also assume that this environment provides rewards to the agent and that this reward structure is also initially unknown to the agent. For example, the agent may get a high reward any time it occupies the state marked G (for *goal*) in the maze. Loosely stated, the objective is for the learning agent to discover a policy, or assignment of choice of action to each state, which enables it to obtain the maximum rate of reward received over time. More specifically, every time the agent occupies the goal state we may place it back at S (for *start*). In this case, the agent's objective is simply to discover a shortest path from the start state to the goal state.

We use variations on this basic task to provide concrete illustrations of the different methods described here, and these also serve as test problems on which to demonstrate the improvement obtained from use of the specific strategies we propose. We stress that all of these methods apply more generally to a much wider range of learning control tasks, in which case the 2-dimensional maze is simply a conceptual stand-in for the appropriate abstract state space for the actual problem and the compass direction moves used here represent the various control actions available.

3 Task Formalization: Markov Decision Problem

This maze task can be viewed as a special case of a *Markov decision problem*, which has the following general form. At each discrete time step, the agent observes its current state x, uses this information to select action a, receives an immediate reward r and then observes the resulting next state y, which becomes the current state at the next time step. In general, r and y may be random, but their probability distributions are assumed to depend only on x and a. For the maze task, we can give the agent an immediate reward of 1 for any state transition into the goal state and 0 for all other state transitions. Both the immediate reward and state transition functions are deterministic for this maze task, but later we will consider stochastic variants.

Informally, an agent can be considered to perform well in such a task if it can choose actions that tend to give it high rewards over the long run. A little more formally, at each time step k we would like the agent to select action $a(k)$ so that the *expected total discounted reward*

$$E\left\{\sum_{j=0}^{\infty}\gamma^j r(k+j)\right\}$$

is maximized, where $r(l)$ represents the reward received at time step l and γ is a fixed discount factor between 0 and 1. In the above maze task it is not hard to see that optimal performance according to this criterion amounts to always being able to get to the goal state in as few moves as possible since a reward of 1 received j time steps in the future is only worth γ^j at the current time. A function that assigns to each state an action maximizing the expected total discounted reward is called an *optimal policy*.

4 Q-Learning and Dynamic Programming

One set of methods for determining an optimal policy is given by the theory of *dynamic programming* (Bertsekas, 1987). These methods entail first determining the *optimal state-value function* V, which assigns to each state the expected total discounted reward obtained when an optimal policy is followed starting in that state. Following Watkins (1989), we can define a closely related function that assigns to each state-action pair a value measuring the expected total discounted reward obtained when the given action is taken in the given state and the optimal policy is followed thereafter. That is, using the notation given above, with x the current state, a the current action, r the resulting immediate reward, and y the resulting next state,

$$\begin{aligned} Q(x,a) &= E\{r+\gamma V(y)|x,a\} \qquad (1)\\ &= R(x,a)+\gamma\sum_y P_{xy}(a)V(y), \end{aligned}$$

where $R(x,a) = E\{r|x,a\}$, $V(x) = \max_a Q(x,a)$, and $P_{xy}(a)$ is the probability of making a state transition from x to y as a result of applying action a. Note that once we have this Q-function it is straightforward to determine the optimal policy. For any state x the optimal action is simply $\arg\max_a Q(x,a)$.

Watkins's *Q-learning* algorithm is based on maintaining an estimate $\hat{Q}$ of the Q-function and updating it so that (1), with estimated values substituted for the unknown actual values, comes to be more nearly satisfied for each state-action pair encountered. More precisely, the algorithm is as follows: At each transition from one time step to the next, the learning system observes the current state x, takes action a, receives immediate reward r, and observes the next state y. Assuming a tabular representation of these estimates, $\hat{Q}(x,a)$ is left unchanged for all state-action pairs not equal to (x,a) and

$$\hat{Q}(x,a) \leftarrow \hat{Q}(x,a)+\alpha\left[r+\gamma\hat{V}(y)-\hat{Q}(x,a)\right], \qquad (2)$$

where $\alpha \in (0,1]$ is a learning rate parameter and $\hat{V}(y) = \max_b \hat{Q}(y,b)$. An estimate of the optimal action at any state x is obtained in the obvious way as $\arg\max_a \hat{Q}(x,a)$.

This algorithm is an example of what Sutton (1988) has called a *temporal difference* method because the quantity $r+\gamma\hat{V}(y)-\hat{Q}(x,a)$ can be interpreted as the difference between two successive predictions of an appropriate expected total discounted reward. The general effect of such algorithms is to correct earlier predictions to more closely match later ones. Sutton has pointed out that the learning checkers playing program of Samuel (1959) and Holland's (1986) bucket brigade algorithm are also of this general type. The relationship of this framework to the use of static evaluation functions in game-playing programs is particularly direct, and Tesauro (1992) has recently applied a version of these learning techniques in conjunction with neural network methods to obtain a highly successful and entirely self-taught backgammon playing program.

Throughout this paper we will usually use the term *backup* to refer to a single application of equation (2). Each backup leads to updating of the Q-estimate for a single state-action pair. There are other related reinforcement learning algorithms in which a corresponding set of estimates of state values or state-action values are maintained and updated in a similar fashion, and it is common to apply the term *backup* in these cases as well. Here we use the more self-explanatory term *value function estimate update* when referring generically to the corresponding step of any such algorithm.

5 Dyna

A key feature of the Q-learning algorithm is that when combined with sufficient exploration it can be guaranteed to eventually converge to an optimal policy without ever having to learn and use an internal model of the environment (Watkins, 1989; Watkins & Dayan, 1992), In adaptive control theoretic parlance, this qualifies it as a *direct* rather than an *indirect* method (Sutton, Barto, & Williams, 1992). From an AI point of view, what is interesting about this is that the eventual behavior of the system is as good as might be obtained if the system had carried out explicit *planning*, which can be thought of as simulation of possible future agent-environment interactions in an internal model to determine long-range consequences.

However, the cost of not using an internal model is that convergence to the optimal policy can be very slow. In a large state space, many backups may be required before the necessary information is propagated to where it is important. In our maze example, it is clear that the optimal state value function is highest near the goal and declines exponentially as the number of steps required to reach the goal increases. Thus correct values must propagate from the goal state outward. Since Q-learning only performs backups for transitions as they are experienced, it is clear that many steps must be taken in the real world before the values are even close to correct near the start state. Even if the same path were taken on every trip from the start state to the goal state, the number of such trips required before Q-learning brings information about the goal state back to the start state is equal to the length of this path. In the maze example, this problem means that an agent using Q-learning will not perform well even after having arrived at the goal many hundreds of times.

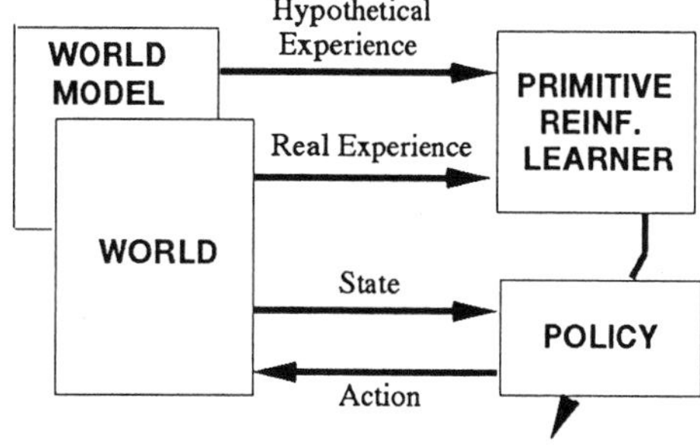

Figure 2: Overview of the Dyna architecture. The primitive reinforcement learner represents an algorithm like Q-learning. Not shown is the data path allowing the world model to learn to mimic the world.

To correct this weakness, Sutton (1990; 1991) has introduced the *Dyna* class of reinforcement learning architectures, in which a form of planning is performed in addition to learning. This means that such an architecture includes an internal world model along with mechanisms for learning it. But the novel aspect of this approach is that planning is treated as being virtually identical to reinforcement learning except that while learning updates the appropriate value function estimates according to experience as it actually occurs, planning differs only in that it updates these same value function estimates for simulated transitions chosen from the world model. It is assumed that there is computation time for several such updates during each actual step taken in the world, and the algorithm involves performing some fixed number of total updates during each actual time step. Figure 2 depicts the organization of a Dyna system.

In this paper we focus on a version (called *Dyna-Q* by Sutton) whose underlying reinforcement learning algorithm is Q-learning. By performing several backups at each time step and avoiding the restriction that these backups occur only at current state transitions, such a system can perform much more effectively than simple Q-learning on tasks like the maze example. In Sutton's work the learned world model was simply a suitably indexed record of (state, action, next-state, immediate-reward) 4-tuples actually

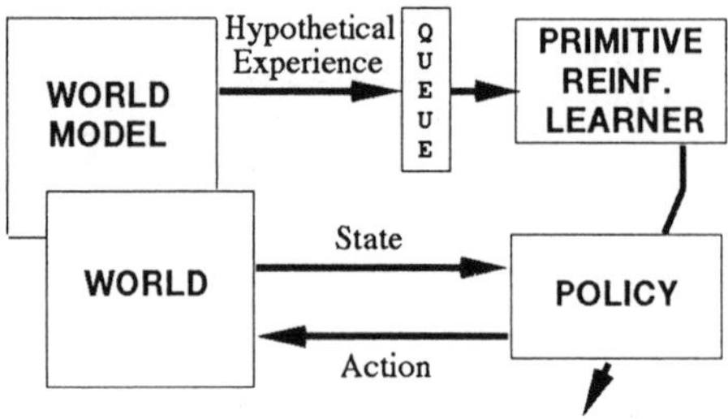

Figure 3: Overview of the queue-Dyna architecture. The primitive reinforcement learner represents an algorithm like Q-learning. Not shown is the data path allowing the world model to learn to mimic the world.

encountered in the past, and simulated experiences were obtained for planning purposes by selecting uniformly randomly from this record. His simulations demonstrated that such a system improves its performance much faster than a simple Q-learning system.

6 Queue-Dyna

Although Sutton's (1990; 1991) demonstrations of Dyna showed that use of several randomly chosen past experiences along with the current experience for value function estimate updates outperforms the use of current experience only, it is natural to ask whether a more focused use of simulated experiences could lead to even better performance. The main contribution of this paper is to introduce and study *queue-Dyna*, a version of Dyna in which value function estimate updates are prioritized and only those having the highest priority are performed at each time step. Figure 3 depicts the organization of a queue-Dyna system.

Here we examine two specific versions of this strategy employing slightly different criteria for prioritizing the potential updates. One of these applies to both deterministic and stochastic tasks, although the details of the respective algorithms differ somewhat, and the other currently applies only to deterministic tasks.

In all cases, an important aspect of the algorithm is the identification of places where the value function estimates may require updating, as will be more fully explained below. We call these places *update candidates*. In the Q-learning version we use here, these are state-action pairs for which a resulting next state and immediate reward prediction can be made. As in the work of Sutton, we take these to be simply state-action pairs that have been experienced at least once in the world.

6.1 Deterministic Environment

For any state-action pair (x, a) under consideration, define the *prediction difference* to be

$$r + \gamma\hat{V}(y) - \hat{Q}(x, a),$$

where r is the immediate reward and y the next state known from the model to result from state-action pair (x, a). Each update candidate is first checked to see if there is any significant prediction difference (based on comparison with an appropriate threshold). If there is, then its priority is determined and it is placed on the queue for eventual updating. The top several update candidates are then removed from the queue on each time step and the backup

$$\hat{Q}(x, a) \leftarrow r + \gamma\hat{V}(y) \tag{3}$$

actually performed for each. Note that this is the same as equation (2) with $\alpha = 1$.

New update candidates are obtained from two main sources on each time step. For any backup actually performed, if the state-value estimate for the corresponding predecessor changes, then all transitions into that state become update candidates. The current transition is also made an update candidate, and this represents a further subtle difference between this approach and that investigated by Sutton. While one of the several backups performed during a single time step was always reserved for the current state-action pair in his system, in our approach it is given no special priority.

One other interesting source of update candidates that can be used effectively in this approach is externally provided information about changes in the environmental reward or transition structure, as we examine later.

6.1.1 Priority Based on Prediction Difference Magnitude

One straightforward way to assign priority to an update candidate, also recently explored extensively in independent work of Moore and Atkeson (1992), is to simply use the magnitude of the prediction difference. The larger the difference, the higher the priority. Figure 4 outlines the main steps of the queue-Dyna algorithm using this method for determining update priority. If, as is typical, all initial Q-estimates are taken equal to 0, then in the maze example the following behavior is observed when this algorithm is used. First, the queue is empty for every time step until the goal is discovered,[1] so no backups will occur

[1] It is assumed that some form of exploratory behavior is generally available (especially when there is no clear-cut su-

1. Initialize $\hat{Q}(x, a)$ to 0 for all x and a and the priority queue *PQueue* to empty.
2. Do Forever:
   (a) $x \leftarrow$ the current state.
   (b) Choose an action a that maximizes $\hat{Q}(x, a)$ over all a.
   (c) Carry out action a in the world. Let the next state be y and immediate reward be r.
   (d) Update world model from x,a,y, and r.
   (e) Compute $e = \left|r + \gamma\hat{V}(y) - \hat{Q}(x, a)\right|$. If $e \geq \delta$, insert (x, a, y, r) into *PQueue* with key e.
   (f) If *PQueue* is not empty, do planning:
      i. $(x', a', y', r') \leftarrow$ **first**(*PQueue*).
      ii. Update:
      $$\hat{Q}(x', a') = \hat{Q}(x', a') + \alpha(r' + \gamma\hat{V}(y') - \hat{Q}(x', a'))$$
      iii. For each predecessor x'' of x' do:
      - Compute $e = \left|r_{x''x'} + \gamma\hat{V}(x') - \hat{Q}(x'', a_{x''x'})\right|$. If $e \geq \delta$, insert $(x'', a_{x''x'}, x', r_{x''x'})$ into *PQueue* with key e.

Figure 4: Main steps of a queue-Dyna algorithm using prediction difference magnitude as priority.

during this initial exploration. Then, once the reward of 1 is obtained at the goal state, a prediction difference will occur at the Q-value for the state-action pair leading to the goal state, which will cause this transition to be placed on the queue as its only item. When this backup is performed, this predecessor state will have its state-value changed from 0 to 1, which will cause any state-action pairs known to lead to it to be placed on the queue, and so forth. Because of the discount factor, it is clear that prediction differences will be smaller as distance from the goal increases, so the effect of this strategy is a breadth-first spread of value estimate updates outward from the recently discovered high-reward goal state.

6.1.2 Priority Based on Effect on Start-State Value

Another interesting strategy that is appropriate for problems having a well-defined start state S is to try to estimate what the effect of any update would be on the estimated long-term reward at this start state. Our efforts at developing a general approach for this are preliminary at this point, so we sketch the details here only for one useful subclass of problem where we have identified a sensible algorithm for this: deterministic environments having a single terminal positive reward, with all other rewards being zero. The maze task given above is an example. If we also assume that all initial value estimates are overly pessimistic, it then makes sense to use

$$\gamma^{d(x)}[r + \gamma\hat{V}(y)]$$

as the priority for updating $\hat{Q}(x, a)$, where $d(x)$ is an estimate of the minimum number of time steps required to go from S to x. There are various choices for $d(x)$ that one might sensibly use. For example, if the state space is equipped with a metric, one might choose $d(x)$ to be proportional to the metric distance between S and x. An even more interesting choice is to try to maintain an estimate of the length of the shortest path from S to x in a manner that is entirely analogous to the manner in which discounted total rewards are estimated. In particular, we can use another priority queue for the necessary updates and thereby maintain fairly accurate estimates of the actual proximity of states visited to the start state very efficiently.

The overall effect of a priority scheme of this type is that backups are directed in a more focused way. For example, in the maze task, once the goal is discovered backups essentially proceed directly back to the start state before being done anywhere else. In fact, with Q-values initialized to 0, upon discovery of the high-reward goal state G the algorithm performs value estimate updates in the same order as an A^* search (Nilsson, 1980) would proceed from G backwards toward S, with the d function serving as the heuristic estimate of remaining path length (backward) to S.

perior action, as when all Q-estimates are equal) so that the high-reward goal state is eventually discovered.

6.2 Stochastic Environment

Starting from equation (1) we can write

$$\begin{aligned} Q(x,a) &= E\{r+\gamma V(y)|x,a\} \\ &= \sum_y P_{xy}(a)E\{r+\gamma V(y)|x,a,y\} \\ &= \sum_y P_{xy}(a)\left[E\{r|x,a,y\}+\gamma V(y)\right]. \quad (4) \end{aligned}$$

For an environment which may be stochastic, it then makes sense to form a learned model by storing all past experiences together with appropriate counters and using this to compute estimates $\hat{P}_{xy}(a)$ of the relevant transition probabilities as well as estimates $\hat{R}_y(x,a)$ of $E\{r|x,a,y\}$, the expected immediate rewards conditioned on next state. We can then maintain estimates $\hat{Q}_y(x,a)$ of the bracketed expression on the right-hand side of (4) and update them using

$$\hat{Q}_y(x,a) \leftarrow \hat{R}_y(x,a) + \gamma\hat{V}(y), \quad (5)$$

with Q-value estimates computed using

$$\hat{Q}(x,a) = \sum_y \hat{P}_{xy}(a)\hat{Q}_y(x,a).$$

In this case a natural choice of prediction difference is

$$\hat{P}_{xy}(a)\left[\hat{R}_y(x,a)+\gamma\hat{V}(y)-\hat{Q}_y(x,a)\right],$$

and it is appropriate to count a single application of (5) as one backup.

Just as in the deterministic case, one useful way to assign priority to any update candidate (x,a) is to set it equal to the magnitude of this prediction difference and this is used in one of the experiments described below. However, it is not straightforward to generalize the more focused method described earlier for tasks with a single starting state to stochastic environments, since both the probability of landing at a state and the number of actions taken must be taken into account in general.

7 Experimental Demonstrations

Here we describe the results of several experiments designed to test the performance of the methods proposed. In particular, the following three algorithms were used in these experiments: (1) Dyna with updating along randomly chosen transitions, together with the current transition, as in Sutton's (1990; 1991) work; (2) queue-Dyna with priority determined by prediction difference magnitude; and (3) queue-Dyna with priority determined by estimated value of the start state. For this last algorithm, estimates of minimum distance from the starting state were maintained using an additional queue, as outlined above. In the interest of brevity, henceforth we refer to these algorithms as *random-update Dyna*, *largest-first Dyna*, and *focused Dyna*, respectively.

All tasks studied involved variants on the maze task of Figure 1, as described earlier, with the agent having four possible actions at each state. In each case there was a well-defined start state and a single goal state, with all rewards equal to 0 except upon arrival at the goal state, when a reward of 100 was delivered. Arrival at the goal state was always followed by placing the agent back at the start state.

In every experiment, the agent's efficiency at negotiating the maze from the start state to a goal state at various points in the learning process was measured by interspersing test trials with the normal activities of the agent. Each such test trial consisted of placing the agent at the start state and letting it execute its currently best action for each state visited until a goal state was reached (or until an upper limit on number of moves allowed was reached). At the end of such a test trial the agent resumed its usual activities from the state it had been in before the test trial began. These test trials were performed solely to obtain this data and no learning took place during them. Also, the normal activity of the agent included some random overriding of its current policy in order to foster exploration, and this was shut off during testing.

In all cases each system was allowed 5 updates for every action taken in the world (excluding actions taken during test trials). The discount parameter used throughout was $\gamma = 0.95$, and the queue-Dyna threshold parameter δ was set to 0.0001. The learning rate parameter for Dyna was set at $\alpha = 0.5$, which was found experimentally to optimize its performance across tasks. All Q-values were initialized to 0 at the start of each experiment.

One set of experiments was performed on a series of related tasks, each using essentially the same deterministic maze environment shown in Figure 1 and described earlier except for the coarseness of representation of the states and actions. The number of states ranged from 47 for the coarsest partitioning to 6016 for the finest. Two of these state spaces are shown in Figures 5 and 6.

Figure 7 shows the solution time (measured in number of backups) as a function of problem size for the 3 systems. These numbers represent averages over 10 runs. Both forms of queue-Dyna clearly show slower growth with respect to state space size than random-

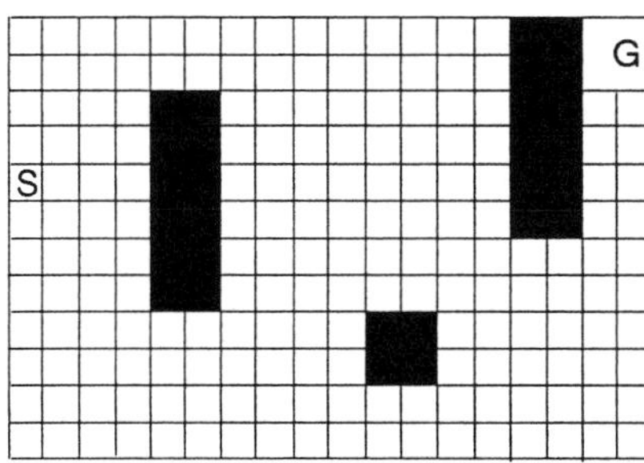

Figure 5: A more finely partitioned version of the maze of Figure 1.

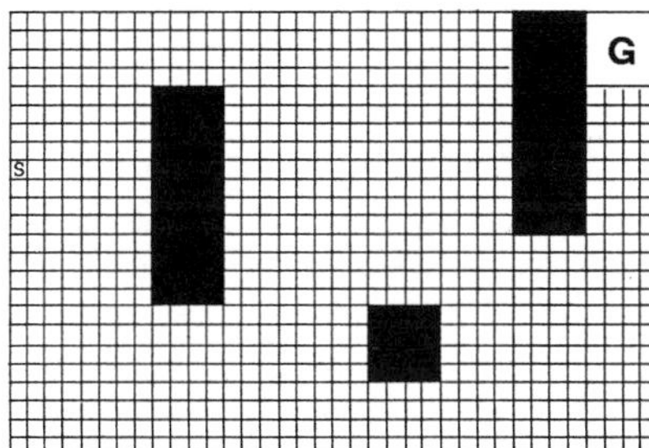

Figure 6: An even more finely partitioned version of the maze of Figure 1.

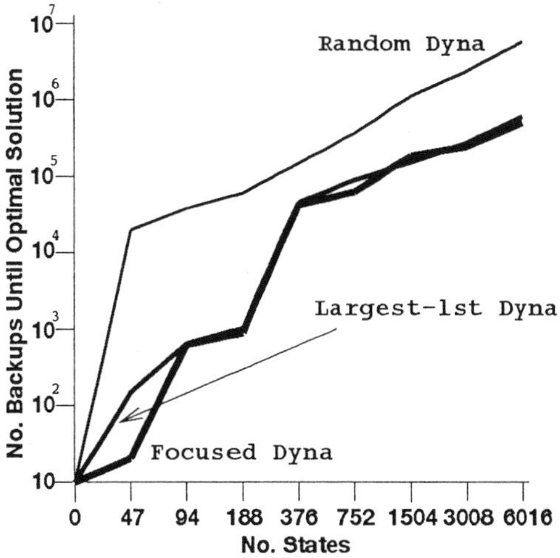

Figure 7: Growth of number of backups required until optimal performance with state space size.

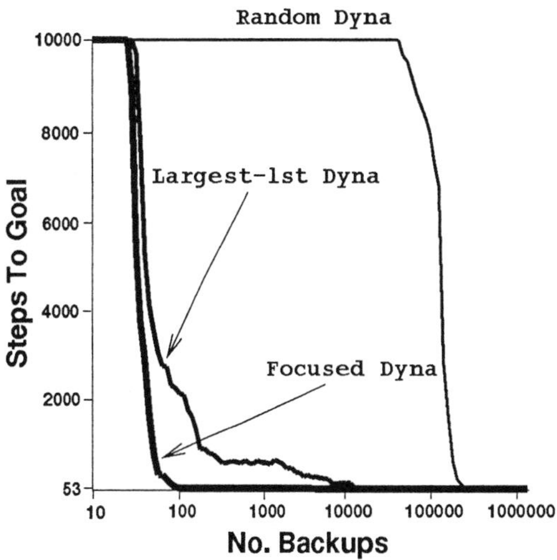

Figure 8: Performance on the maze of Figure 6.

update Dyna. Figure 8 shows learning curves for the 3 systems, each an average over 100 runs, for the 752-state maze shown in Figure 6. While Figure 7 does not show any clear difference between focused Dyna and largest-first Dyna in their ability to discover an optimal path, Figure 8 suggests that focused Dyna generally gives much more rapid improvement in the early stages of learning. The nature of the exploration strategy used may play a role in the specific results obtained, but this is an issue we have not addressed systematically in this work.

It is also possible in any Dyna system to make use of externally provided information about changes in the environmental reward or transition structure. In one interesting experiment along these lines, we first let an agent learn to find the shortest path to the goal state in the maze of Figure 9, with the cross-hatched cell occupied by a barrier. Then we opened up this cell and "told" the agent about it. More precisely, we updated its model to correctly reflect the effects of the 3 actions that could now move the agent into this cell and the 4 actions that could be taken from inside this cell. For queue-Dyna, we also placed these on the priority queue as if these actions had just been taken by the agent itself, and for the version that focuses backups toward the start state, we also placed these on the queue for updating of the minimum distance from the start state. Performance results for the 3 algorithms are shown in Figure 10.

We also performed an experiment with a stochastic environment based on the maze of Figure 5 but with actions that have a somewhat random effect. In particular, the direction of actual movement matched

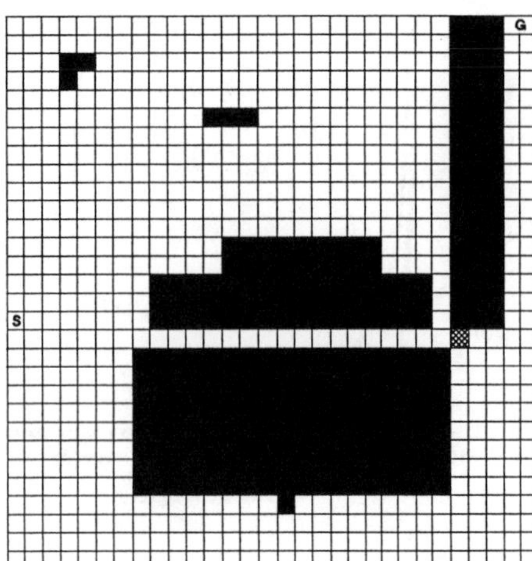

Figure 9: Maze used in one experiment. The agent first learned the shortest path to the goal with the cross-hatched block in place. This path, of length 66, goes along the bottom. Then this block was removed and the agent "told" about it.

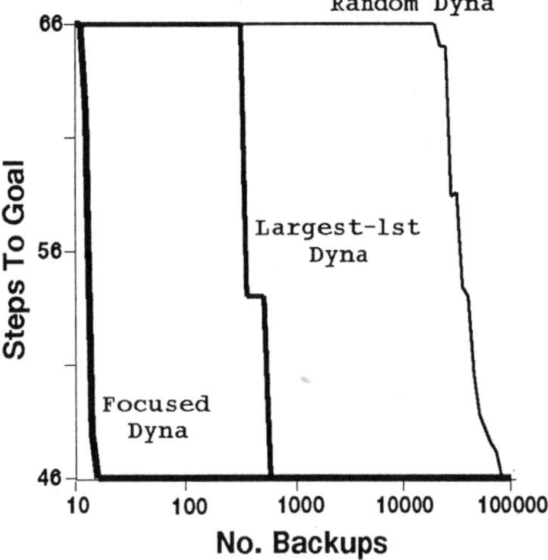

Figure 10: Performance on the task of Figure 9 after the agent was made aware of the removal of the cross-hatched block.

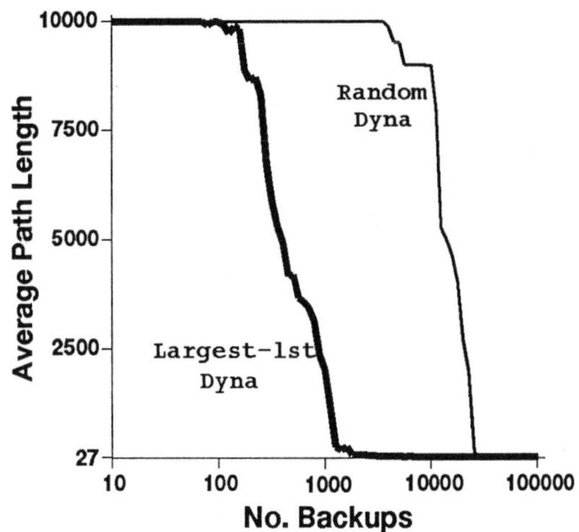

Figure 11: Performance on the stochastic maze task.

that of the action selected with a $\frac{2}{3}$ probability but there was a $\frac{1}{3}$ probability that the actual motion would be in one of the two adjacent compass directions instead, with the two "noisy" results being equally likely. For example, if the agent picked the action corresponding to the northward direction, its actual movement would be northward with probability $\frac{2}{3}$, westward with probability $\frac{1}{6}$, and eastward with probability $\frac{1}{6}$ (where these represent "virtual" directions in the sense that they result in no movement at all whenever such movement is illegal). Figure 11 shows the results obtained when the largest-first and random-update Dyna systems were used on this task. The numbers obtained were averages over 10 runs.

8 Issues and Further Directions

There are a number of relevant issues that we have not addressed here. Of substantial importance in realistic environments is the need for generalization in the world model. This presents some interesting challenges for the techniques investigated here, at least in their current form. One of the reasons that the queue-Dyna approach works well with the form of model we have used here is that the environmental transition and reward structure are assumed to be revealed one state-action pair at a time, and the model we have used is thus affected in a correspondingly simple and circumscribed way. If each state transition in the world could lead to model changes for many state-action pairs, it would generally be inappropriate to specifically identify them all. Instead, there needs to be a way to identify more concisely what direct consequences this may have on the estimated value function and compute value function updates accordingly. A similar difficulty occurs if we imagine providing external information that is relevant in many parts of the state or state-action space.[2]

An additional aspect considered in some depth by Moore and Atkeson (1992) in their work with this approach is the issue of efficient exploration. While we have highlighted the efficiency of queue-Dyna in terms of number of backups required and have emphasized its relationship to backwards search from the goal, it is worth noting that a somewhat different behavior emerges when the initial value function estimates are overly optimistic when compared with the actual reward structure. For example, consider the variant of the maze task where Q-values are once again initialized to 0, but the reward is 0 for any transition into the goal state and -1 for any other transition, Using priority based on prediction difference magnitude, one finds that more backups are required but exploration occurs automatically as a result of following the current policy. As Moore and Atkeson have emphasized, the efficiency with which queue-Dyna propagates value function updates leads to much more purposeful exploration in such cases, and the agent can thus much more rapidly discover high-reward states.

9 Conclusion

The combination of dynamic-programming-based planning strategies with learned world models represents a promising approach to effective learning control (Moore, 1991), and the computational expense of more conventional planning makes incremental approaches like Dyna (Sutton, 1990; 1991) especially appealing in this context. Here we have proposed that a prioritizing scheme be used to order the value function estimate updates in Dyna in order to improve its efficiency, and we have suggested two specific natural ways of setting this priority. In one, the largest known changes are made first, with predecessors of the corresponding states becoming the next candidates for consideration. In the other, the changes are prioritized based on what is effectively an estimate of the likelihood that the update is relevant for determining actions to be taken when starting from a given start state. We have demonstrated on simple tasks that use of such prioritizing schemes do indeed lead to drastic reductions in computational effort and corresponding dramatic improvements in performance of the learning agent.

Thus we argue that not only does the Dyna framework represent a useful conceptual basis for integrated learning, planning, and reacting systems, but we are also optimistic that simple improvements like those we have examined here can help give it sufficient power to allow it to serve as the basis for creating artificial autonomous agents that can adapt quickly to more complex and realistic environments.

[2]For example, suppose we tell the agent traversing the maze of Figure 6 at some point that any step in a southward direction taken from a state in the western half of the maze will henceforth incur a reward of -5.

References

Barto, A. G., Bradtke, S. J., & Singh, S. P. (1991). *Real-time learning and control using asynchronous dynamic programming* (COINS Technical Report 91-57). Department of Computer Science, University of Massachusetts, Amherst, MA.

Barto, A. G., Sutton, R. S., & Watkins, C. J. C. H. (1989). *Learning and sequential decision making* (COINS Technical Report 89-95). Department of Computer and Information Science, University of Massachusetts, Amherst, MA.

Bertsekas, D. P. (1987). *Dynamic Programming: Deterministic and Stochastic Models.* Englewood Cliffs, NJ: Prentice Hall.

Bertsekas, D. P. & Tsitsiklis, J. N. (1989). *Parallel and Distributed Computation: Numerical Methods.* Englewood Cliffs, NJ: Prentice Hall.

Holland, J. H. (1986). Escaping brittleness: The possibility of general-purpose learning algorithms applied to rule-based systems. In: R. S. Michalski, J. G. Carbonell, & T. M. Mitchell (Eds.) *Machine Learning: An Artificial Intelligence Approach, Volume II.* Los Altos, CA: Morgan Kaufmann.

Moore, A. W. (1991). Variable resolution dynamic programming: Efficiently learning action maps in multivariate real-valued state-spaces. *Proceedings of the 8th International Machine Learning Workshop.*

Moore, A. W. & Atkeson, C. G., (1992) Memory-based reinforcement learning: Converging with less data and less real time, *Proceedings of NIPS*92.*

Nilsson, N. J. (1980) *Principles of Artificial Intelligence*, San Mateo, CA: Morgan Kaufmann.

Samuel, A. L. (1957). Some studies in machine learning using the game of checkers. *IBM Journal of Research and Development, 3*, 210-229. Reprinted in: E. A. Feigenbaum and J. Feldman (Eds.) (1963). *Computers and Thought.* New York: McGraw-Hill.

Sutton, R. S. (1988). Learning to predict by the methods of temporal differences. *Machine Learning, 3*, 9-44.

Sutton, R. S. (1990). Integrated architectures for learning, planning, and reacting based on approximating dynamic programming. *Proceedings of the Seventh International Conference in Machine Learning*, 216-224.

Sutton, R. S. (1991). Planning by incremental dynamic programming. *Proceedings of the 8th International Machine Learning Workshop.*

Sutton, R. S., Barto, A. G., & Williams, R. J. (1992). Reinforcement learning is direct adaptive optimal control. *IEEE Control Systems Magazine, 12*, 19-22.

Tesauro, G. (1992). Practical issues in temporal difference learning. In: J. E. Moody, S. J. Hanson, & R. P. Lippmann (Eds.), *Advances in Neural Information Processing Systems 4*, 259-266.

Watkins, C. J. C. H. (1989). *Learning from delayed rewards.* Ph.D. Dissertation, Cambridge University, Cambridge, England.

Watkins, C. J. C. H. & Dayan, P. (1992). Q-learning. *Machine Learning, 8*, 279-292.

Williams, R. J. & Baird, L. C., III (1990). A mathematical analysis of actor-critic architectures for learning optimal controls through incremental dynamic programming. *Proceedings of the Sixth Yale Workshop on Adaptive and Learning Systems*, August 15-17, New Haven, CT, 96-101.

Increasing Behavioural Repertoire in a Mobile Robot*

Ulrich Nehmzow*, Tim Smithers‡ and Brendan McGonigle*

*Laboratory for Cognitive Neuroscience at the Department of Psychology
University of Edinburgh
Appleton Tower
GB - Edinburgh EH8 9LE
Telephone +4431 - 650 8449 Fax +4431 - 650 6512
E-mail:ulrich@castle.ed.ac.uk, B.O.McGonigle@ed.ac.uk

‡Artificial Intelligence Laboratory
Vrije Universiteit Brussel
Pleinlaan 2
B - 1050 Brussel
Tel +322 - 641 2965 Fax +322 - 641 3582
E-mail:tim@arti1.vub.ac.be

Abstract

This paper presents an investigation of the the suitability of the robot controller presented in [Nehmzow *et al.* 89] and [Nehmzow *et al.* 90] for a computationally cheap expansion of the behavioural repertoire of a mobile robot.

Experiments with mobile robots are presented that show that this is possible by simply adding further so-called *instinct-rules* without altering the controller itself: through the robot's interaction with its environment effective associations between sensors and actuators arise in an artificial neural network which serves as an associative memory.

1 Introduction

Designing intelligent controllers for autonomous mobile robots is a task often underestimated by the designer. Sensor signals turn out to differ from what is expected in theory, and actuators produce different effects than anticipated. Whilst many of these differences between expected and observed behaviour can be overcome by building actual robots, there remain uncertainties and variations that are due to temperature conditions, wear, battery charge etc., as well as more drastic changes in agent (failure of components) task or environment (changed external conditions). To deal with these through *a priori* defined strategies is (in practice) impossible.

One possible solution to the problem of coping with such unforeseen situations is the use of self-organising controllers that determine the effective wiring between sensors and actuators autonomously. Such an approach is described in [Nehmzow 92], for example. An additional property of the proposed architecture is discussed in *this* paper: that it allows an easy expansion of the robot's behavioural repertoire by adding so-called *instinct-rules*, without necessitating changes to the controller architecture itself. This increases the robot's flexibility to accomplish new tasks.

1.1 Related Work

Some work has been done on the acquisition of single competences in autonomous mobile robots, for example by [Mahadevan & Connell 91], [Maes & Brooks 90] and [Kaelbling 91]. Mahadevan and Connell and Kaelbling use reinforcement learning to control robots acquiring the competences of box pushing and phototaxis (moving towards a light source) respectively. Maes and Brooks use the correlation between a particular robot behaviour and positive reinforcement to establish 'relevant' behaviours; the likelihood of a behaviour being invoked then is proportional to its relevance. All of these architectures are designed particularly to facilitate the acquisition of *one* particular motor-sensory skill only (box-pushing, moving towards a light, and walking, respectively). Contrary to this, the experiments described here aim to accomplish the acquisition of *various* motor-sensory skills, using the same controller architecture throughout.[1]

Addressing the question of automatic acquisition of behaviours, Brooks discusses first results of John Koza's genetic programming implementation ([Koza 90]) for the determination of computer programs. Here, LISP programs are determined by a genetic algorithm. This approach is promising, however the resulting programs are not yet complex enough to actually control robots (see [Brooks 91]).

2 The Controller Architecture

For all experiments described in this paper the same controller architecture was used. New behaviours are acquired by the robot by autonomously determining the effective wiring between sensory input and motor actions in a trial and error process.

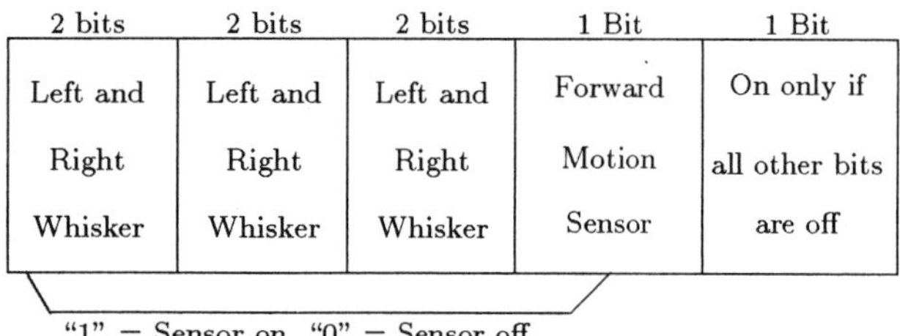

Figure 1: The input vector.

The experiments presented here were conducted with the mobile robots Alder (shown in figure 2) and Cairngorm (shown in figure 8). Both are completely autonomous, Alder is controlled by an on-board ARC 52 controller (based on the Intel 8052 microprocessor) and uses two tactile sensors (whiskers) mounted at the front for the experiments discussed below, as well as a forward motion sensor. Controller card and whiskers are clearly visible in the photograph. Cairngorm is controlled by a Flight 68 k controller card, based on the Motorola 68000 processor; like Alder it is equipped with tactile sensors.

The controller architecture used in the experiments reported here is shown in figure 3. Its central element is a connectionist associative memory (Perceptron-like) which stores the effective associations between input signals and motor actions.

The performance of the robot is assessed through *instinct-rules*, which are fixed, predefined rules such as "Keep whiskers straight"[2]. Each instinct-rule is monitored by a dedicated sensor. The control mechanism is as follows[3]: as soon as the violation of an instinct-rule is detected by the monitor[4], an input vector (see figure 1) is generated and presented to the associative memory.

In this associative memory—a Perceptron-like, two-layer network—associations between the input signals and the four output units of the network are stored. These output units of the artificial neural network stand for four possible motor actions of the robot (left and right turn, forward and backward movement). The motor action associated with the output node responding most strongly to a particular input vector is then performed for about three seconds[5]. If, within this period, the violated instinct-rule is resolved again, the association between the original input vector and the respective motor action is confirmed to the network, if not, the action associated with the second strongest output node[6] is performed for a slightly longer period of time (the increment is two seconds). This process continues until appropriate responses by the robot are found and stored in the associative memory: effective associations between input signals and motor responses thus arise through the interaction of the robot with its environment.

[1] Investigations into reinforcement learning architectures that might be used for robot control are presented by many researchers, for example by [Kaelbling 90, Sutton 91, Prescott & Mayhew], but these have not been conducted using real robots.

[2] Strictly speaking, the robot only monitors the signals coming from the whiskers, the whiskers being off when they are straight and on when they are bent. There is no notion of a bent whisker being identical with an obstacle, for instance.

[3] For more details see [Nehmzow 92].

[4] If more than one instinct-rule is used instinct-rules are tested for violation beginning at the latest (the newest) and ending at the first instinct-rule.

[5] This value is mostly dependent on the velocity of the robot.

[6] At the beginning of the learning phase, when no associations are stored yet, motor actions are tried in turn, beginning with the first output node of the network and ending with the fourth.

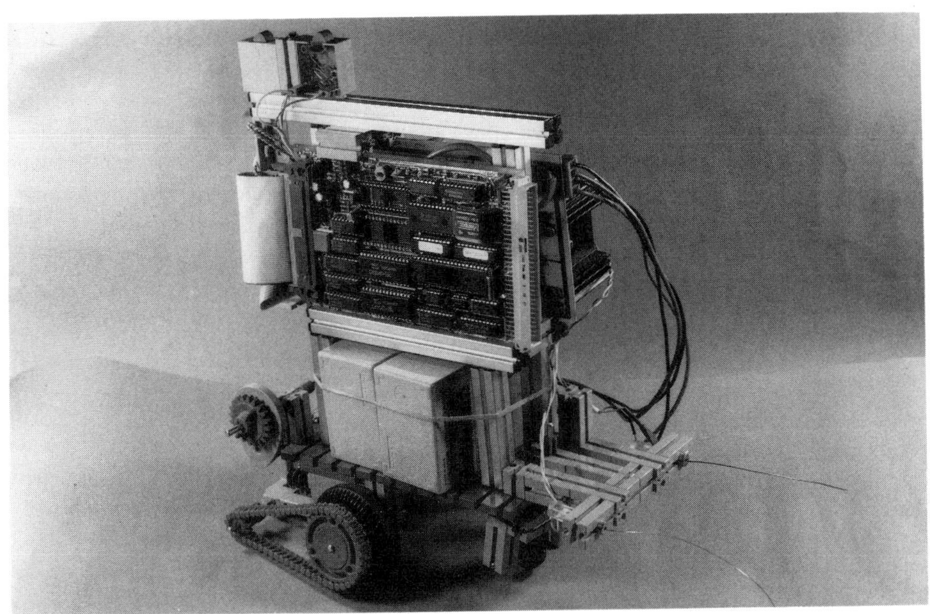

Figure 2: Alder.

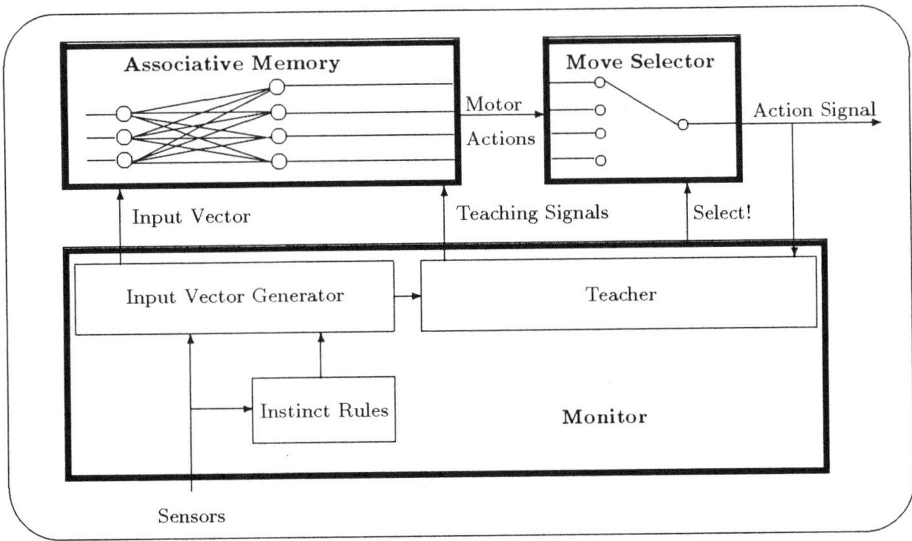

Figure 3: The controller architecture.

3 Experimental Results

3.1 Learning to Move Forward

Using the controller architecture presented in the previous section and one instinct-rule, the one shown in figure 4, Alder is able to determine the motor action that will make its forward motion sensor turn on.

1. Keep forward motion sensor on

Figure 4: The instinct-rule for learning forward motion.

A schematic diagram of the forward motion sensor of Alder is shown in figure 5. It is a pushbutton switch, operated by a cam that is attached to the caster wheel of the robot. If the caster wheel is aligned with the central axis of the robot (this happens after the robot has been moving forward for at least three seconds) the pushbutton switch is pressed, thus indicating that the robot is performing a forward motion.

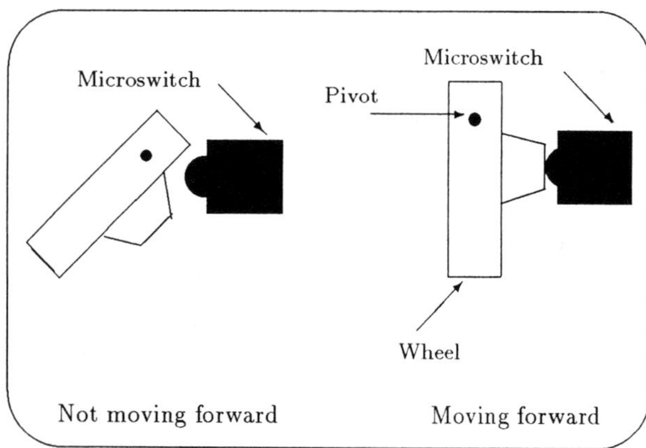

Figure 5: The forward motion sensor of Alder.

Independently from the initial wiring of the motors, Alder learns the "correct" output node of the network (the one that results in forward motion) after having found the correct node for the first time (one learning step). This takes between five and twenty seconds, dependent on how many other motor actions have to be tried until the forward motion node is found.

3.2 Additional Learning of Obstacle Avoidance Behaviour

The previous experiment resulted in a robot determining the effective wiring between its motors and its forward motion sensor in order to move forward, independently from the initial wiring of the motors.

It is possible to increase the behavioural repertoire by simply adding a further instinct-rule to the already existing one, without altering anything else in the controller architecture. Figure 6 shows the set of two instinct-rules that lets Alder learn how to move forward, and how to move away from obstacles.

1. Keep forward motion sensor on 2. Keep whiskers straight

Figure 6: The instinct-rules for learning forward motion and obstacle avoidance.

When started, the robot determines the correct motor action to move forward, as before. It will then start moving forward. As soon as any of the two whiskers emits a signal, instinct-rule 2 is violated and Alder will initiate motor actions to stop the whiskers signalling (that this coincides with the robot moving away from obstacles is not represented inside the controller; no symbolic representation of the world is used). Learning the wiring that accomplishes both forward motion and appropriate turn actions when an obstacle is encountered is achieved in approximately ten learning steps, requiring one to two minutes, dependent on the amount of perturbance from bouncing or caught whiskers, i.e., the consistency of sensor readings.

3.3 Additional Learning of Wall Following Behaviour

Again without changing anything but the set of instinct-rules, Alder is able to learn also to follow walls, as well as to maintain the two previously mentioned skills. The set of instinct-rules used for this experiment is shown in figure 7.

When Alder is started, it acquires the forward movement competence as before. After this, if a whisker gives a signal (i.e., touches something) Alder learns which way to turn in order to release the whisker. If no whisker signal is received within four seconds, the third instinct-rule initiates a wall-seeking movement. Provided the robot is near a wall it will eventually find it and thus learn which way to turn in order to satisfy the third

1. Keep forward motion sensor on
2. Keep whiskers straight
3. Make whiskers signal after 4 seconds

Figure 7: Instinct-rules for learning forward motion, obstacle avoidance and wall following.

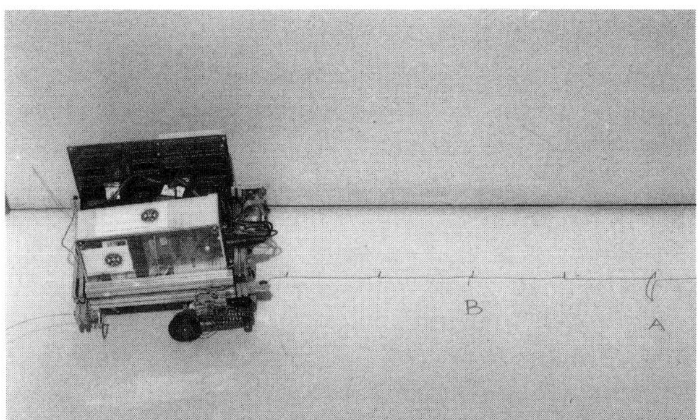

Figure 8: Cairngorm, learning to follow a wall.

instinct-rule. As soon as the wall is touched, of course, instinct-rule number 2 is violated and the robot will turn away again. The resulting behaviour is a movement along a wall, performing zig-zag motions towards and away from the wall every four seconds (see figure 8).

To acquire all three skills takes about ten to fifteen learning steps (which take one to two minutes), however it can take longer if, in the course of acquiring the obstacle-avoidance competence the robot moves so far away from the wall that instinct-rule number 3 can no longer be satisfied straight away. This occasionally happens.

3.4 Additional Learning of Corridor Following Behaviour

Figure 9 shows the set of instinct-rules that make the robot learn how to follow a corridor, touching alternate sides of the corridor as it goes along. Again, the only component changed in this experiment, compared to the previous ones, is the fourth instinct-rule.

To acquire the corridor following competence (as well as the three previously discussed competences) requires approximately five minutes. It turns out that the robot is more dependent on reliable sensor signals in this experiment than in the previous ones. The forward motion sensor, for example, only signals if the robot *has been moving forward* for at least three seconds, because

1. Keep forward motion sensor on
2. Keep whiskers straight
3. Make whiskers signal after 4 seconds
4. Make *alternate* whiskers signal

Figure 9: Instinct-rules for learning forward motion, obstacle avoidance and corridor following.

of the way it is built. Therefore, for example, pushing against one wall of the corridor—which can easily happen in the early learning phases—will result in the forward motion sensor not signalling, even if the robot is issuing the correct motor commands. This of course will lead to some 'confusion' which can (and often does) affect the rate of learning. Eventually, however, the correct corridor following behaviour *is* acquired, even under adverse conditions.

4 Discussion

4.1 How to devise Instinct-Rules

The expansion of Alder's behavioural repertoire was achieved through adding instinct-rules. How these can be determined is an interesting question, especially because it is conceivable that the determination of instinct-rules could be automated. An algorithm for finding instinct-rules has not been established yet, however some general guidelines can be identified:

- The violation of instinct-rules is detected by sensors dedicated to a particular instinct-rule. Sensors in this sense can be physical sensors (e.g., whiskers), internal sensors (e.g., timer), or values in memory locations ("Make alternate whiskers signal").
- Instinct-rules are not behaviours, but sensory conditions that have to be maintained. It would therefore be wrong to have an instinct-rule "Move towards the light", the correct rule would be "Increase the reading from a light sensor", or "Keep the light sensor on".
- As instinct-rules generate the desired behaviour, one question to be asked is "Which sensor signal can be associated with the desired behaviour?". The answer to this question is a guideline for deriving instinct-rules.
- It should be borne in mind that instinct-rules are checked for violation beginning at the newest rule

and ending at the first instinct-rule. This ordering therefor defines priorities between instinct-rules.

4.2 Advantages

A number of properties make the self-organising controller presented in this paper interesting for robotics applications.

- The algorithm learns fast: effective connections between sensors and actuators are established within a few tens of learning steps, rather than several hundred or thousand as can be found in controllers using other kinds of reinforcement learning, see ([Prescott & Mayhew, Kaelbling 90, Sutton 91], for example. This is an important property, not so much because the operational period of a robot is short (batteries), but more because certain functions (like obstacle avoidance) *have* to be learned quickly in order to keep the robot operational at all.

- Because the effective wiring between sensors and actuators is determined by the robot, not the designer, setting up of a robot becomes less prone to error: sensors and actuators may initially be connected arbitrarily.

- Whereas acquired knowledge in reinforcement learning is often compartmentalised ([Kaelbling 91]), i.e., the robot is not able to generalise from experience, a benefitial side effect of using a connectionist associative memory is that such a generalisation does take place. For example will the robot turn left if *both* whiskers are on, even if it has only ever experienced the *right* whisker to be on.

- If the learning process has to be guided by the experimenter in the early stages, as is the case for some implementations ([Kaelbling 90]), this can diminish the robot's ability to cope with new situations. Here such initial guiding helps, but is not required.

- Because the controller is self-organising, it can not only determine the effective connections between sensors and actuators in the first place, it can also reestablish them in the event of unforeseen situations (swapped whiskers, swapped motor connections, change of environment etc., see also [Nehmzow 92]).

4.3 Comparision to Biological Systems

The system described thus far is certainly based on the designer's interpretation of a given niche within which the robot is supposed to work (office or laboratory environment with smooth, level floors, containing walls and box-like obstacles). This limitation is, we believe, an essential one: a general purpose robot does not exist.

In biological systems such behaviours as are described in this paper, based on taxes and tropisms, and selected over many generations, work robustly within the confines of well specified contexts. *Salmon* fry, for example, are positively phototropic when young and stay in bright (i.e., shallow) water, later they become negatively phototropic and seek dark (i.e., deep) water (the sea). As in the robot described here, the actual behaviour need not be specified in advance: behaviour selection can readily occur, ensuring the successful maintenance of the tropistic values set (the instinct-rules). Furthermore, in both cases the knowledge of the world is analogous and indirect: just as the wall is a whisker signal to the robot, so is the water route towards the sea associated with decreasing light intensity. In the salmon, a biological clock determines when the time is right to change the response to light and head for darker waters, which means that the overall behaviour is purposeful without requiring the agent to acquire any long term plan or represent a specific objective. One last similarity to the robot described is that the details of the behaviour are not specified: the agent can select those actions which best support the tropism.

Selecting specific behaviours from the total response set (as described here) is an example of procedural learning, an 'old' competence from an evolutionary perspective. Such competences can be dissociated both in phylogeny and in human clinical conditions (such as amnesia) from episodic, semantic and explicit forms of knowledge. There is no evidence, moreover, that declarative types of knowledge based on episodic or semantic forms of memory derive from a procedural motor (sub) system. On the contrary, as [Sherry & Shacter 87] have argued, separate multiple memory systems have evolved to cater for different types of achievement. It would be somewhat unwise, therefore, to propose a motor (based) learning system to support a general purpose kind of knowledge acquisition. The system presented here is designed to achieve a specific action-related 'representation' of an environment as in 'when to go', 'when to stop', 'when to turn' etc. Specifying *descriptive/declarative* systems in ways which yield actual robot implementations *remains* one of the major problem areas. To do this, we shall need complex biological agents as a model, for it is only in these that such competences are well developed — if they exist at all in simpler systems remains in doubt.

5 Conclusions

We have presented a controller architecture for mobile robots, using plastic components (connectionist associative memory) and fixed components (instinct-rules) that allows an easy expansion of the behavioural repertoire of a robot by merely adding further instinct-rules, leaving the controller itself unchanged.

Experiments with the mobile robots Alder (see figure 2) and Cairngorm (see figure 8) are presented: the robots autonomously determine the effective wiring between their sensors and actuators to achieve forward movement, obstacle avoidance, wall following and corridor following.

Besides offering an easy expansion of the behavioural repertoire of a mobile robot, as described in this paper, the architecture presented gives a higher degree of flexibility in unforeseen circumstances: the robot becomes able to cope with changes in its own morphology, changes of the task and changes in the environment (see [Nehmzow 92]).

Acknowledgements

The work reported here was supported by grant GR/F/5852.3 from the Science and Engineering Research Council. Other facilities and technical support were provided by the Department of Artificial Intelligence at Edinburgh University. John Hallam and Peter Forster were also involved in the funded project and we acknowledge their contribution. We thank Douglas Howie for producing the photographs of Alder and Cairngorm. Tim Smithers currently holds a visiting chair at the VUB AI Lab, Brussels.

References

[Brooks 91] Rodney Brooks, *Artificial Life and Real Robots*, Proceedings of 1st European Conference on Artificial Life, Paris 1991, published by MIT Press 1992

[Kaelbling 90] Leslie Kaelbling, Learning in Embedded Systems, PhD Thesis, Stanford Technical Report TR-90-04, 1990

[Kaelbling 91] Leslie Kaelbling, *An Adaptable Mobile Robot*, Proceedings of 1st European Conference on Artificial Life, Paris 1991, published by MIT Press 1992

[Koza 90] John Koza, *Evolution and Co-Evolution of Computer Programs to Control Independently Acting Agents*, From Animals to Animats, MIT Press 1991

[Maes & Brooks 90] Pattie Maes and Rodney Brooks, *Learning to Coordinate Behaviours*, National Conference on Artificial Intelligence 1990

[Mahadevan & Connell 91] Sridhar Mahadevan and Jonathan Connell, *Automatic Programming of Behavior-based Robots using Reinforcement Learning*, 9th National Conference on Artificial Intelligence 1991

[Nehmzow *et al.* 89] Ulrich Nehmzow, John Hallam and Tim Smithers, *Really Useful Robots*, in T. Kanade, F.C.A. Groen and L.O. Hertzberger (eds.), *Intelligent Autonomous Systems 2*, Amsterdam 1989

[Nehmzow *et al.* 90] Ulrich Nehmzow, Tim Smithers and John Hallam, *Steps towards Intelligent Robots*, DAI Research Paper No. 502, Department of Artificial Intelligence, Edinburgh University, 1990

[Nehmzow 92] Ulrich Nehmzow, *Experiments in Competence Acquisition for Autonomous Mobile Robots*, PhD Thesis, University of Edinburgh 1992

[Prescott & Mayhew] Tony Prescott and John Mayhew, *Obstacle Avoidance through Reinforcement Learning*, to appear in J.E. Moody, S.J. Hanson and R.P. Lippmann (eds.), *Advances in Neural Information Processing Systems 4*, Sam Mateo, Morgan Kaufman, no year

[Sherry & Shacter 87] D.F. Sherry and D.L. Shacter, *The Development of Multiple Memory Systems*, Psychological Review, Vol 94, pp. 439-454, 1987

[Sutton 91] Richard Sutton, *Reinforcement Learning Architectures for Animats*, From Animals to Animats, MIT Press 1991

Learning Biped Robot Obstacle Crossing

Thomas Ulrich Vogel
Computer Laboratory
University of Cambridge
Cambridge CB2
England
tuv@cl.cam.ac.uk

Abstract

A robot has learned to walk on an obstacle-free horizontal surface, and it now derives obstacle crossing gaits from existing gaits. A strategy based on the qualitative equivalence between two behaviours is introduced to derive new behavioural patterns from previous ones. This enables the robot to reason about its actions at a higher level of abstraction, and facilitates the transfer and adaptation of existing knowledge to new situations. As a result, the robot is able to derive stepping over an obstacle from stepping on a horizontal surface.

The robot analyses its successful obstacle crossings in order to generate a generic obstacle crossing strategy. This is done by comparing how the successful obstacle crossing of the robot differs from its normal behaviour. By analysing and operationalising these differences, the robot acquires the capability to overcome previously unencountered obstacles. The robot's obstacle crossing capabilities are demonstrated by letting the robot walk across randomly generated obstacle combinations.

1 Introduction

This paper presents some algorithms which address the problem of how a robot can generate new, complex behavioural patterns from previously acquired simple ones. It is assumed that a dynamic biped robot has already learned a gait that enables it to walk over a horizontal, obstacle free surface (further details in [Vog91]). It is now the task of the robot to develop new gaits which enable it to cross obstacles like fences or steps. To do this the robot can use its previously acquired knowledge of how to walk over a horizontal surface and use it to generate new, related obstacle crossing gaits.

These new gaits are produced by using a generate and test strategy which systematically modifies previously successful gaits and tries to cross the obstacle using this new modified gait. Successful obstacle crossing gaits are stored. These obstacle crossings represent a behaviour which the robot is not able to obtain from scratch, such complex behaviours are the result of incremental searches over increasingly complex problem spaces. However, these obstacle crossing gaits proved to be relatively brittle. Hence in a second step the robot uses the previously acquired obstacle crossing examples and operationalizes them to a generic obstacle crossing strategy. In this step the robot investigates how the obstacle crossing behaviour differs from a behaviour which would be displayed if the obstacle wasn't there. Describing how the behaviours differ and where in the state space these differences occur allows the robot to generalize and reconstruct an obstacle crossing.

The algorithms are documented using a simulated dynamic biped robot based on the Biper3 robot (built by H. Miura and I. Shimoyama [MS84]). Biper3 is essentially a pair of stiff (kneeless) legs, linked by a hip. Biper3 walks like a person on stilts, a little bit like *Charlie Chaplin.* The robot weighs about 1 kg, and it is about 30 cm high and 7 cm wide. Figure 1 shows a view of Biper3 from the front and from the side. The view from the front is also called the view along the ***roll axis***, whereas a view from the side corresponds to a view along the ***pitch*** axis. The biped can move along the pitch and roll axes (forwards and sideways), but it can not turn (no moves around the ***yaw*** axis).

2 Modifying Gaits

We assume the robot is at a point where it has learned to execute and control gaits. The latter were developed in order to enable it to cross an obstacle-free horizontal plane. However the robot is unable to cross obstacles by relying on these gaits alone. Even so the sequence of actions needed to step forward is not very different from the stepping over a small obstacle. It is therefore interesting to see how the original ability of the robot to walk on a horizontal plane can be ***adapted*** in order to cross

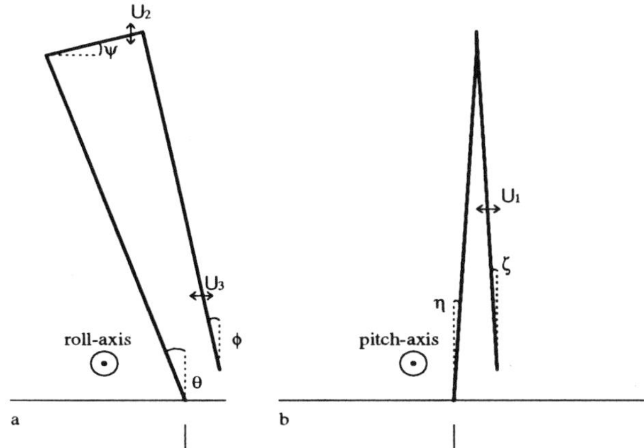

Figure 1: The biped. Position (a) shows the biped robot from the front (along the roll axis), position (b) shows the biped from the side (along the pitch axis). The robot's behaviour is described by the 5 angles θ, ψ, ϕ, η,and ζ, and their respective velocities. Motor1 moves the free leg with torque u_1 around the pitch axis, Motor2 moves the hip with torque u_2 around the roll axis, and Motor3 moves the free leg with torque u_3 around the roll axis.

an obstacle. This adaptation is based on modifications of the *entire gait.* Thus the robot changes its bias from the search for motor commands to the search for gaits and gait modifications. This provides it with a powerful mechanism to speed up and improve the search process. In this section the term *behaviour* will be used to describe a sequence of movements made by the biped robot such as a step forward. These behaviours usually correspond to the motion patterns which the robot learnt to control.

Research on biological motor control [Bro86] suggests that motion is organised in the form of activity templates. Any activity learnt by an animal or a human is stored as a pattern of muscular activities. For example we have a pattern stored away somewhere that describes how to write the letter "a". If we want to write the letter a bit larger or a bit faster, then we will still use the same pattern, but the frequency of the pattern and the amplitude of the pattern will change [VT80]. However, this theory is not undisputed, and little is known about the transition between different motion patterns[Sch82].

Related recent work has focussed on the generation of trajectory modifications. Y.F. Zheng [Zhe90] proposes to use the van der Pol oscillator to (manually) generate gaits for biped walking. These gaits are then changed by using a neural network to modify the constants of the van der Pol oscillator. As a result he generated gait *trajectories*, which are then used to servo the robot joints.

2.1 Qualitative Equivalence

This section defines various gait modifications which preserve the qualitative equivalence between the original gait and the resultant modified gait. These modifications have to meet several criteria:

- The definition of qualitative equivalence has to be operational. Once a qualitatively equivalent gait has been identified its execution should be easy.
- Many locomotive patterns can be regarded as periodic functions. A gait modification should exist that modifies the amplitude of this periodic function. A definition of qualitative output equivalence ($\approx_o$) is given which is aimed at generating such a modification. Output equivalence results in a gait which achieves the same goal in a different way.
- The robot needs the ability to generate gaits which allow it to achieve new goal states. A definition of qualitative input equivalence ($\approx_i$) is given which is aimed at generating new trajectories while attempting to preserve some properties of the old gait.

The resulting gait modifications can be derived as follows: a gait is defined as a start position P followed by a sequence of motor commands. For example gait G can be defined as

$$G = (P, u_1, u_2, ..u_n)$$

where each motor command u_i is a triplet of torques

$$u_i = m_{i1}, m_{i2}, m_{i3}.$$

Various gait modification heuristics are defined to preserve the input equivalence between two gaits: one (*add*) that uniformly increases the torque used in the motor commands, one (*sub*) which uniformly decreases it, one (*lengthen*) which adds an additional motor command to the gait, and one (*shorten*) which cuts the last command. Another heuristic (*amplify*) is defined which aims at the preservation of output equivalence. This heuristic splits the motor commands in half and increases the first half and decreases the second half or vice versa.

Assuming the original gait is defined as above, and the torque $m_i, 1 \leq i \leq 3$ refers to the i-th torque in a motor command, then the gait modifications can be defined as follows:

$$\mathbf{add(G, i)} : G = (P, \text{plus}(u_1, i), \ldots \text{plus}(u_n, i))$$

where $\text{plus}(u_j, i)$ is defined as increasing the i-th torque m_i in the motor command u_j by one unit.

$$\mathbf{sub(G, i)} : G = (P, \text{minus}(u_1, i), \ldots \text{minus}(u_n, i))$$

where minus(u_j, i) is defined as decreasing the i-th component of u_j by one unit. The modification

$$\textbf{shorten(G)} : G = (P, u_1, u_2, ..u_{n-1}).$$

shortens the gait by one time-slice.

$$\textbf{lengthen(G)} : G = (P, u_1, u_2, ...u_n, u_{n+1})$$

adds a further motor command to the gait. The value of u_{n+1} is computed from the average of the previous commands:

$$m_{n+1,i} = \sum_{k=1}^{n} m_{k,i}/n.$$

These heuristics preserve most of the properties of the original gait. Since only the torques applied to one joint are effected, most parameters of the robot will remain uneffected. These heuristics also preserve the qualitative input properties $\approx_i$ of the gait since they introduce constant change of the input torques in one direction.

The only gait transformation of $\mathbf{B}_1$ which produces an output equivalent gait $\mathbf{B}_2$ where $\mathbf{B}_1 \approx_o \mathbf{B}_2$ is the *amplify* heuristic.

amplify1(G,i):

$$G = (P, \text{plus}(u_1, i), \ldots \text{plus}(u_{\frac{n}{2}}, i), \text{minus}(u_{\frac{n}{2}+1}, i), \ldots \text{minus}(u_n, i)).$$

amplify2(G,i):

$$G = (P, \text{minus}(u_1, i), \ldots \text{minus}(u_{\frac{n}{2}}, i), \text{plus}(u_{\frac{n}{2}+1}, i), \ldots \text{plus}(u_n, i)).$$

In this case the first half of the gait is increased and the second half is decreased (or vice versa). The reason for the inclusion of this gait transformation heuristic is that by increasing and then decreasing the torque applied to the system it is hoped to produce an amplification of the underlying periodic behaviour of the system only, and therefore to preserve the qualitative output equivalence $\approx_o$.

Using these qualitative equivalence heuristics the robot managed to cross obstacles like fences and steps, provided it started the obstacle crossing with the right distance to the obstacle. The efficiency of the obstacle crossing could be enhanced by presenting the robot with a training series of obstacles of increasing height. Figure 2 shows such a training series. However, the search space of possible gait modifications proved to be very large and hence it was interesting to see whether a successful obstacle crossing could be generalized to improve further performance.

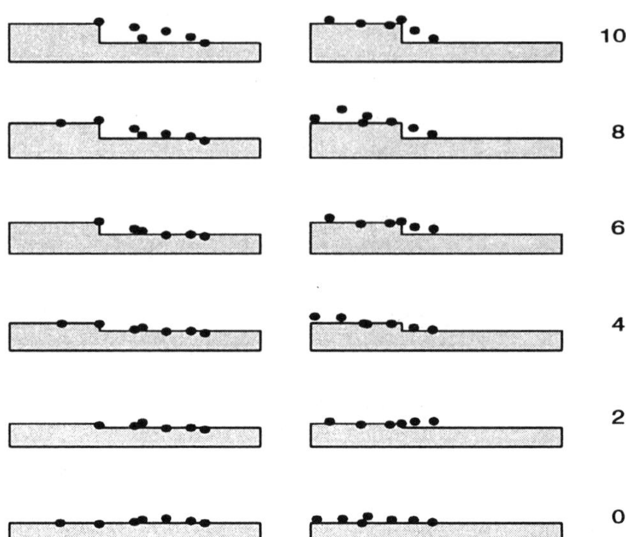

Figure 2: Using the qualitative equivalence heuristic to cross a step upstairs. The biped is trained with obstacles of increasing height (the number on the right indicates the step height in millimeters). In each row we see on the left the trajectory of the free foot during the first step (lifting the first leg over the step), sampled at intervals of 0.02 sec. On the right we see the movement of the free foot during the second step, finishing with the robot standing with both legs on the step. The biped walks from the right to the left.

3 Learning from Examples

Originally the robot developed a gait which enabled it to walk on an obstacle free horizontal plane. The robot found this gait by searching for a sequence of motor commands which brings its position close to the desired goal position. The function which tells the robot which motor command is preferable over another motor command is called the evaluation function. Whenever the robot is unable to use this gait we assume that the robot is in an *obstacle space*. The obstacle space is defined as a hyperrectangle inside the state space where the robot is unable to execute its standard gaits.

Imagine the robot in some posture P in the obstacle space of some obstacle O. Because the robot is *inside* the obstacle space of O it will at least once take an action that is different from the action that it would have taken if it were in the same posture P *outside* the obstacle space O. The aim is to compare the actual action of the robot in some posture P inside the obstacle space with the action in the same posture P in some state away from any obstacle.

Assume the obstacle crossing gait is a sequence $\mathcal{C}$ of motor commands $u_1, u_2, \ldots, u_n$ and a starting state $\mathcal{S}_0$. This leads the robot through a series of states $\mathcal{S}_0..\mathcal{S}_n$: $u_1 \circ \mathcal{S}_0 \rightarrow \mathcal{S}_1, u_2 \circ \mathcal{S}_1 \rightarrow \mathcal{S}_2, \ldots u_n \circ \mathcal{S}_{n-1} \rightarrow \mathcal{S}_n$

If the robot searched for steps as if the obstacle were not present, then it would choose for any state $\mathcal{S}_i$ a motor-command u'_{i+1}, resulting in a state $\mathcal{S}'_{i+1}$. It would select a motor command which brings the robot as close as possible to some goal state, and the distance to the goal would be measured by the original evaluation function.

Provided the robot is given some goal state, then for each state $\mathcal{S}_i$ there will always be exactly one best successor state $\mathcal{S}'_{i+1}$ with respect to the original evaluation function and the goal state. This state transition $\mathcal{S}_i \rightarrow \mathcal{S}'_{i+1}$ will be called the ***standard state transition*** of $\mathcal{S}_i$. Now each state transition inside the obstacle space $\mathcal{S}_i \rightarrow \mathcal{S}_{i+1}$ will be compared with the result of the standard state transition of $\mathcal{S}_i$, namely $\mathcal{S}'_{i+1}$. Assuming each state is defined as a tuple of parameters

$$\mathcal{S'}_{i+1} : x'^{i+1}_1, x'^{i+1}_2, \ldots x'^{i+1}_n$$

$$\mathcal{S}_{i+1} : x^{i+1}_1, x^{i+1}_2, \ldots x^{i+1}_n,$$

then the qualitative difference $\mathcal{S}_{i+1} \ominus \mathcal{S'}_{i+1}$ can be expressed as the difference per parameter filtered by some threshold θ:

$$\mathcal{S}_{i+1} \ominus \mathcal{S'}_{i+1} = \Delta_\theta(x^{i+1}_1, x'^{i+1}_1), \Delta_\theta(x^{i+1}_2, x'^{i+1}_2), \ldots \Delta_\theta(x^{i+1}_n, x'^{i+1}_n)$$

where Δ_θ is defined as the qualitative difference between the two parameters filtered through the threshold θ:

$$\Delta_\theta(a, b) = \begin{cases} 0 & \text{if } |a-b| < \theta \\ + & \text{if } a-b > \theta \\ - & \text{if } a-b < -\theta \end{cases}$$

This qualitative difference $\mathcal{S}_{i+1} \ominus \mathcal{S'}_{i+1}$ describes how the state transition chosen by the robot in state $\mathcal{S}_i$ differs depending on whether or not there is an obstacle. If state $\mathcal{S}_i$ is inside the obstacle space then the next state will be state $\mathcal{S}_{i+1}$. Otherwise, if state $\mathcal{S}_i$ is outside the obstacle space, then the state transition will be from $\mathcal{S}_i$ to $\mathcal{S'}_{i+1}$. The qualitative difference $\mathcal{S}_{i+1} \ominus \mathcal{S}'_{i+1}$ describes whether the individual parameter values in $\mathcal{S}_{i+1}$ are greater or less than their respective values in $\mathcal{S}'_{i+1}$.

The qualitative difference $\mathcal{S}_{i+1} \ominus \mathcal{S}'_{i+1}$ is however dependent on the state $\mathcal{S}_i$, with the state $\mathcal{S}_{i+1}$ being taken from the obstacle crossing example, and the state $\mathcal{S}'_{i+1}$ being computed on the assumption that state $\mathcal{S}_i$ isn't close to any obstacle. It is important to note that once a state $\mathcal{S}_i$ has been annotated with such a qualitative difference list, it is possible to *approximate* the successor state $\mathcal{S}_{i+1}$. Therefore the qualitative difference between $\mathcal{S}_i$'s actual successor $\mathcal{S}_{i+1}$ and its successor using the standard state transition $\mathcal{S}'_{i+1}$ will be called the *virtual evaluation function* used at state $\mathcal{S}_i$. The robot originally doesn't know why the successor state $\mathcal{S}_{i+1}$ was chosen, but it assumes that some evaluation function was used in order to select the best of all possible successor states of $\mathcal{S}_i$. Since it doesn't know much about this evaluation function the term *virtual* will be used. Figure 3 shows the virtual evaluation functions identified during the crossing of the step upstairs. Note that only one type of virtual evaluation function is needed.

The biped lifts the first leg up the step.
In every position the biped uses UP as virtual evaluation function, which is equivalent to lifting the hip around the roll axis.

The biped lifts the second leg up the step by using normal search. Thus in every position the biped uses the normal evaluation function.

○ support foot position

● free foot position using normal evaluation function

■ free foot position using virtual evaluation function UP

Figure 3: Identifying the virtual evaluation functions of a step upstairs. We see the first and the second step at a step height of 10mm, taken directly from Figure 2.

In other words: ***the virtual evaluation function of state S_i is the qualitative difference between state S_i's standard successor S'_{i+1} and its actual successor S_{i+1}.*** The virtual evaluation function is basically a labeling of the state space which will be used in order to compute the best possible successor state. In order to generalise from the obstacle crossing examples, the robot analyses the successful obstacle crossings and annotates each state $\mathcal{S}_i$ in the successful crossings with the virtual evaluation function which was used to get to its successor state $\mathcal{S}_{i+1}$. *Whenever in the future the robot finds itself in a state similar to $\mathcal{S}_i$ it will use this virtual evaluation function for its next state transition.*

A state transition from a state S_i based on a virtual evaluation function v_i is computed as follows: we assume the robot has m operators $u_1, .., u_m$ available to generate the successor states of S_i. Applying these operators to state S_i

$$u_1 \circ S_i \xrightarrow{u_1} S^1_{i+1}, u_2 \circ S_i \xrightarrow{u_2} S^2_{i+1}, ..., u_m \circ S_i \xrightarrow{u_m} S^m_{i+1}$$

results in a set of possible successor states $S^k_{i+1}, k : 1..m$. Furthermore the standard transition from S_i can be computed, let this state be S'_{i+1}. For each state $S^k_{i+1}, k : 1..m$ the qualitative difference v_k

$$v_k = S^k_{i+1} \ominus S'_{i+1}$$

is computed. Let S_{v_i} be the set of all those states S^k_{i+1} with a qualitative difference equal to v_i.

$$S_{v_i} = \{S^k_{i+1} | S^k_{i+1} \ominus S'_{i+1} = v_i\}.$$

For each state in S_{v_i} the Euclidean distance to the state S'_{i+1} is computed, and the state furthest away from state S'_{i+1} is selected as successor state of state S_i. This state has been chosen since the idea is to make the robot behave *differently* from its normal behaviour. By choosing the state furthest away from state S'_{i+1} the robot chooses an action which maximises this difference.

4 Identifying the Obstacle Space

Once the set of virtual evaluation functions is identified, the corresponding hyper-rectangles of the state space are identified. Several algorithms have been proposed [Sal88, Moo90], and in the case of dynamic biped walking the division of the state space into a disjoint set of labeled hyper-rectangles proved to be a straight forward task: let there be n dimensions in the obstacle space of the robot. Let S be the set of all states of all successful obstacle crossing exemplars. Let $\mathcal{V} : v_1, .., v_m$ be the set of all virtual evaluation functions annotated to states in S except for the virtual evaluation function consisting only of zeros (ie. where the robot follows its standard transition). For each virtual evaluation function v_i in $\mathcal{V}$, inspect each state in S that has been annotated with v_i. Let the set of these states be S_{v_i}. For each dimension j of the n dimensions of the obstacle space find the maximum and minimum value of the corresponding parameter in S_{v_i}, and call them $\max_{v_i}(j)$ and $\min_{v_i}(j)$.

Assuming a state S is described as

$$S = (x_1, x_2, .., x_n),$$

then the hyperrectangle $\mathcal{P}(v_i)$ identified with the virtual evaluation function v_i will be described by the set of all states for which the following holds:

$$\mathcal{P}(v_i) = \{S \mid S = (x_1, x_2, .., x_n), \\ x_j < \max_{v_i}(j) \wedge x_j > \min_{v_i}(j), j : 1..n\}$$

Once the hyperrectangles for each virtual evaluation function have been identified it is possible that two such hyperrectangles overlap: this would in effect mean that the robot could be required to carry out two contradictory activities like lower and lift the leg. The conflict resolution heuristic is to test whether the obstacle crossing capabilities of the robot remain uneffected if the overlapping region is removed from one of the two hyperrectangles.

5 Adjusting Step Length for Obstacle Crossings

Obstacle crossing requires that the robot stands with the correct distance to the obstacle before initiating the obstacle crossing gait. If the robot is too close to the obstacle then it will not be able to lift its foot quick enough over the obstacle, and as a result it will crash into the obstacle. Similar problems occur if the robot is initiating the obstacle crossing behaviour too far away from the obstacle. Very recently Hodgkins and Raibert [HR91] discuss control algorithms to manage step length adjustments for a dynamic biped robot. Pal and Jayarajan [PJ91] use the A^* algorithm to search for foot placements for a planar quadruped robot.

The approach taken here is a combination of backtracking and step length adjustment. We recall that the biped searches for new motor commands until it reaches a local minimum with respect to its goal position. It then finishes the current step and starts again. If the biped has to find a step with a different step length then it simply ignores the first local minimum which it encounters. Thus the new step becomes slightly longer and should provide the robot with the necessary displacement. Whenever the robot fails to cross an obstacle it backtracks to the last position in which it executed a normal gait for planar surfaces. This time it will execute a step with different step length as just described.

6 Some Results and Discussion

Figure 5 presents some random examples of the successfully crossed obstacle combinations. We can see that the robot could cope with combinations of steps, fences and slopes. Each dot in the picture represents the position of the foot every 0.2 seconds. The obstacle height is 1cm.

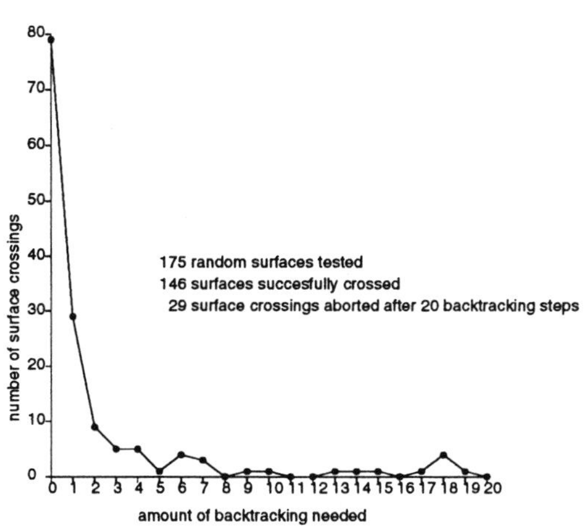

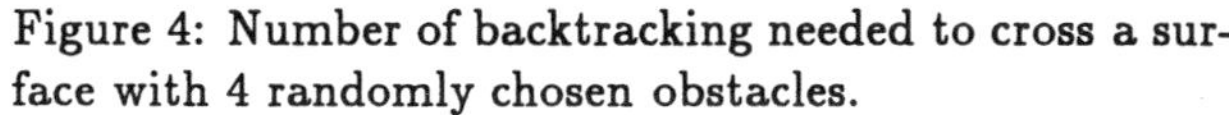
Figure 4: Number of backtracking needed to cross a surface with 4 randomly chosen obstacles.

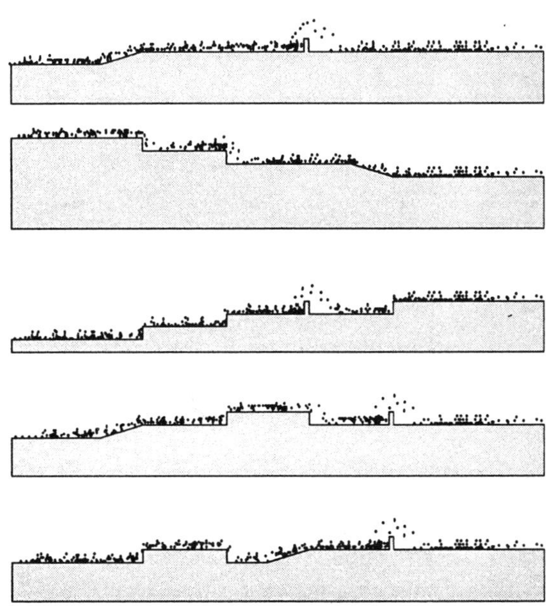

Figure 5: The robot crosses a sequence of random obstacles. The robot walks from the right to the left. Small black dots indicate the position of the free foot.

Figure 4 shows the amount of backtracking used in a complex test series of crossing 175 randomly created test surfaces (Figure 5 shows in fact some examples of such surfaces). The distance between each obstacle was 90mm. 79 test surfaces could be crossed without backtracking, and another 29 could be crossed with only one backtracking step. Backtracking occurred twice on 9 test surfaces, and three times on 5 test-surfaces. 29 test surfaces could not be crossed with less than 20 backtracking steps. This indicates the high reliability of the virtual evaluation function concept.

These results demonstrate that the strategy of incremental learning of gait modifications (qualitative equivalence heuristic) combined with a later analysis of the reasons for their success (virtual evaluation function) enables the robot to cross successfully previously not encountered obstacles. This represents an advantage over previous work[HR91] concerning dynamic biped obstacle crossing, which required the explicit computation of the relevant control laws.

Work in robotic learning has been concerned with the acquisition of a world model based on which the robot then searched for actions leading to its goal [Moo90], alternatively a control law was learned by the robot [BAS83], or in a subsumption architecture a stimulus response pattern was learned [MB90]. Progress was limited to relatively small dimensional search spaces. The approach presented here provides a way to integrate these previous results into the search of large, regular, and incremental state spaces. It now becomes possible to use these previous approaches in order to establish a first set of behaviours, and then to search over the space of behavioural modifications. The presented algorithms allow the robot to start to learn behaviours based on a small, manageable search space, and then to expand these behaviours into a larger dimensional, obstacle cluttered search spaces, and the results therefore provide a possibility to remove the curse of high dimensionality.

Acknowledgments

This paper is based on research carried out while the author was supported by the German Academic Exchange Service, the British Council, Wolfson College, and the Computer Laboratory of the University of Cambridge.

Thanks to Andrew Moore and Thomas Clarke who helped me to clarify my thoughts in numerous discussions.

References

[BAS83] A.G. Barto, C.W. Anderson, and R.S. Sutton. Neuron like adaptive elements that can solve difficult learning control problems. *IEEE Transactions on Systems, Man and Cybernetics 13*, 13:835–846, 1983.

[Bro86] V.B. Brooks. *The Neural Basis of Motor Control.* Oxford University Press, Oxford, 1986.

[HR91] J.K. Hodgins and M.H. Raibert. Adjusting step length for rough terrain locomotion. *IEEE Transactions on Robotics and Automation*, 7(3):289–298, 1991.

[MB90] P. Maes and R.A. Brooks. Learning to coordinate behaviors. In *AAAI 90*, pages 796–802, Boston, Ma, 1990.

[Moo90] A.W. Moore. Efficient memory-based learning for robot control. Technical Report No.209, Computer Laboratory, University of Cambridge, 1990.

[MS84] H. Miura and I. Shimoyama. Dynamical walk of biped locomotion. In M. Brady and R. Paul, editors, *Robotics Research, the First International Symposium*, pages 303–325. MIT Press, Cambridge,Ma., 1984.

[PJ91] P.K. Pal and K. Jayarajan. Generation of free gait – a graph search approach. *IEEE Transactions on Robotics and Automation*, 7(3):299–305, 1991.

[Sal88] S. Salzberg. Exemplar based learning: Theory and implementation. Technical Report TR–10–88, Harvard University, 1988.

[Sch82] R.A. Schmidt. *Motor Control and Learning.* Human Kinetics Publishers, Inc., Champaign, Il., 1982.

[Vog91] T.U. Vogel. *Learning in Large State Spaces with an Application to Biped Robot Walking.* PhD thesis, University of Cambridge, 1991. Technical Report No. 241, Computer Laboratory, University of Cambridge.

[VT80] P. Viviani and C. Terzuolo. Space-time invariance in learned motor skills. *Adv. Psychol.*, 1:525–533, 1980.

[Zhe90] Y.F. Zheng. A neural gait synthesiser for autonomous biped robots. In *IEEE International Workshop on Intelligent Robots and Systems IROS'90*, pages 601–608, 1990.

LEARNING TO CONTROL AN AUTONOMOUS ROBOT BY DISTRIBUTED GENETIC ALGORITHMS

Marco Colombetti
Progetto di Intelligenza Artificiale e Robotica
Dipartimento di Elettronica e Informazione
Politecnico di Milano
Piazza Leonardo da Vinci, 32
20133 Milano, Italy
colombet@ipmel2.elet.polimi.it

Marco Dorigo
International Computer Science Institute
1947 Center Street
Suite 600
Berkeley, California 94704-1105
USA
dorigo@icsi.berkeley.edu

Abstract

Machine learning shows promise as a method for developing autonomous robots. In this paper, we report the results of a few experiments carried out both in simulated environments and with a real moving robot. A parallel implementation of a learning classifier system, ALECSYS, is used to shape an agent to perform Animat-type tasks, like chasing a prey or escaping a predator. In particular, we concentrate on the role of innate architecture for scaling up the size of learnable tasks. We show how a relatively complex behavior pattern can be learned as the composition of basic behaviors. A coordination behavior controls the interactions between the basic behaviors.

1. Introduction

Machine learning and autonomous robotics are becoming more and more tightly coupled. People from the machine learning community find the autonomous robot problem – or its version known as the Animat problem (Wilson, 1987) – a challenging issue to test new algorithms and methodologies. On the other hand, many researchers in "traditional AI" robot planning believe that learning is going to be necessary to program robots, and also scientists like Brooks (1991b, 1992), who proposed an engineering approach to robot building, recognize the importance of learning to give robots adaptive capabilities.

Our long term research goal is the design of autonomous systems with learning capacities. Even if many different machine learning schemes are known today, learning complex robot control programs is still a very difficult task. In Dorigo & Schnepf (1993), we proposed the use of a straightforward engineering approach to reduce the complexity of learning tasks: we designed modules dedicated to the solution of very simple learning problems; each module had access to a limited amount of sensorial information and learned to propose actions according to its local goals. Such organization can be viewed as a possible implementation of a theoretical model of behavior organization like the one proposed by Tinbergen (1966); or, it can be regarded as a mere engineering approach aiming at the construction of complex learning systems by an appropriate composition of simpler modules, as proposed in Colombetti & Dorigo (1992).

In order to have a flexible tool to build such learning systems, we designed and implemented ALECSYS, a distributed learning classifier system (for a technical description see Dorigo, 1992c). ALECSYS is designed to permit machine learning researchers to carry out experiments in rather complex domains, building hierarchies of classifier systems (CSs). In our approach, each of the learning modules is a CS working on a rule base acquired by interaction with the environment. The learning algorithms, based on genetic rule-discovery, allow the rule base to improve incrementally, guided by feedback received as a result of interaction with the environment.

In fact, we are using ALECSYS to devise new ways of using the learning classifier system, proposed by Holland & Reitman (1978), as a framework for "shaping" an agent to survive in a given environment. Some experiments using ALECSYS to build a simple hierarchical learning system were presented in Dorigo & Sirtori (1991) and in Dorigo & Schnepf (1993). Further results in that direction can be found in Colombetti & Dorigo (1992). In this paper we are interested in the application of ALECSYS to controlling the *AutonoMouse*, an autonomous mouse-shaped robot.

The paper is organized as follows. Section 2 briefly illustrates related work, both in autonomous robotics and in reinforcement learning. In Section 3 we sketch our approach to building adaptive systems. In Section 4 we illustrate the experimental setting in a simulated environment and report results obtained by the learning agent. Section 5 is devoted to the discussion of results obtained by a real robot in a simpler, but real, environment. Finally, in Section 6 we draw some conclusions and indicate the future directions of our research.

2. Related work

Recently, much work has been carried out in *reinforcement learning*. Reinforcement learning is a kind of machine learning in which all the feedback information the learning system receives is in the form of positive or negative numbers, respectively called *rewards* and *punishments*. This means that only a minimal amount of domain knowledge is given to the system[1]. Reinforcement learning is generally *unsupervised*, i.e. new examples are created by the explorative activity of the learning agent, and are not chosen *a priori* by a teacher. Nevertheless, a teacher is sometimes used, either to give rewards, or to help through the presentation of a feasible (or optimal) solution (see for example reinforcement learning with teaching in Lin, 1991, 1992).

Reinforcement learning has been studied in different algorithmic frameworks. Notably, we have connectionist reinforcement learning (e.g., Barto, Sutton & Anderson, 1983; Williams, 1992); classifier systems reinforcement learning (e.g., Holland & Reitman, 1978; Robertson & Riolo, 1988; Booker, 1988; Dorigo, 1992b); temporal differences reinforcement learning and related algorithms, like the adaptive critic heuristics (Sutton, 1984) and Q-learning (Watkins, 1989, 1992). Often, adaptive critic heuristics and Q-learning are implemented by means of a connectionist system (e.g., Lin, 1992).

Most of the applications used to illustrate and compare the proposed algorithms are taken from the realm of autonomous robotics. A few of them deal with real robots, most with simulated ones. In many cases, the application problem is a subset of the Animat problem, that is the issue of realizing an artificial system able to adapt and survive in a natural environment.

In our work we define a number of *basic* and *coordination* behavioral modules, we combine them in a hierarchical architecture, and then we make the system learn basic behavioral patterns and coordination policies. To guide the learning process, we use a *shaping procedure*, which is reminiscent of the procedures used by laboratory psychologists to shape experimental subjects. We use reinforcement to shape basic behaviors first, and then the coordination behavior.

Many researchers have advocated some kind of architecture (see for example Brooks's subsumption, 1991a). Some of them do not rely on learning (Brooks), others use learning only for basic behaviors (Mahadevan & Connell, 1992; Mahadevan, 1992). Still other researchers (see for example Lin's application of Q-learning, Lin, 1992) do not face the problem of task factorization, and learn by some "flat" system – that is, systems with no explicitly built-in architecture. At the authors' knowledge, our project is the only one using learning to coordinate learned behavioral modules, and also the only one exploiting classifier systems to shape real robots.

1 It is impossible to provide no knowledge at all about the problem domain. The learning system designer has at least to define the interface with the environment, which is itself determined by the problem structure. It is also the case that, in systems like ours, a certain amount of information is put into the learning system architecture. This means that we solve the problem of the system architecture, that in nature was solved by evolution.

3. Our framework

In our learning system there are basically two learning entities: *basic behaviors* and *coordination behaviors*. They are implemented and composed to build a hierarchical architecture using ALECSYS. ALECSYS, introduced in Dorigo & Sirtori (1991) and in Dorigo (1992c), is a tool that allows one to distribute classifier systems on a net of transputers. Through ALECSYS, a transputer net can host many CSs, and each CS can in turn be distributed on a subnet of the transputer net.

In our work we have been influenced by Wilson's Animat problem. This accounts for our interest in behavioral patterns that are the artificial counterparts of basic natural responses, like feeding and escaping from predators. Our experiments are therefore to be seen as possible solutions to fragments of the Animat problem. Moreover, we are also interested in applying to real robots the results obtained with simulated Animats. Although we believe that experiments should be carried out in the real world to be truly significant, such experiments are in general costly and time-consuming; therefore, we use simulations to preselect a small number of potentially relevant experiments to be performed with the real robot.

One of the hypotheses we explore is that relatively complex behavioral patterns can be built bottom-up from a set of simple responses. In this paper we consider three kinds of basic responses:

- the *approaching behavior*, i.e. approaching an (almost) steady object with given features; in the natural world, this response is a fundamental component of feeding and sexual behavior;
- the *chasing behavior*, i.e. following and trying to catch a moving object with given features; as the preceding approaching behavior, this response is important for feeding and reproduction;
- the *escaping behavior*, i.e. moving as far as possible from an object with given features; the object can be viewed as a predator.

Other kinds of behaviors have been the subject of previous work (Dorigo & Sirtori, 1991; Dorigo, 1992a); in particular:

- the *mimetic behavior*, i.e. entering a well-defined physical state which is a function of a feature of the environment; this is inspired by the natural behavior of a chameleon, changing its color according to the color of the environment;
- the *avoidance behavior*, i.e. avoiding physical contact with an object of a given kind; this can be seen as the artificial counterpart of a behavioral pattern which allows an organisms to avoid hurting objects.

More complex behavioral patterns can be built from these simple responses in many different ways. So far, we have studied the following building mechanisms (composition rules):

- *Independent sum*: two or more independent responses are produced at the same time; for example, an agent may assume a mimetic color while chasing a prey.
- *Combination*: two or more homogeneous responses are combined into a resulting behavior; consider the movement of an agent which is following a prey and trying to avoid an obstacle at the same time.
- *Suppression*: a response suppresses a competing one; for example, the agent may give up chasing a prey in order to escape from a predator (suppression is similar to subsumption, as studied by Brooks, 1991a, and by Mahadevan & Connell, 1992).
- *Sequence*: a behavioral pattern is built as a sequence of simpler responses; for example, fetching an object involves reaching the object, grasping it, and coming back (sequences have been extensively studied by Singh, 1992a,b).

In general, more than one mechanism can be at work. Consider an agent trying to avoid steady hurting objects while chasing a moving prey and being ready to escape if a predator is perceived. In this case, the chasing behavior will be combined with obstacle avoidance; at times, the escaping behavior will suppress the chasing behavior (but still combine with obstacle avoidance!).

4. Experiments in the simulated environment

Given the framework of Section 3, a number of different experiments can be carried out. Some experiments regarding the learnability of basic behaviors and of coordination behaviors have been discussed in Dorigo & Sirtori (1991), in Dorigo & Schnepf (1993), and in Colombetti & Dorigo (1992). In this paper, we start to investigate the scalability of our approach, when the whole behavior increases in complexity. Below we report on the following experiment.

Consider an agent who should learn the following behavior:

```
If there is a predator
   then Escape
   else if hungry
           then Feed
           else Chase the moving object
```

In the previously cited papers we showed that the correct behavior can be easily learned by a hierarchical structure in which basic modules learn basic behavioral patterns and coordination modules learn the coordination policy. Reinforcement is given to the learning system by a program that implements the above described behavior (for example, there is a positive reward if the Animat moves in such a way that causes its distance from a predator to increase, etc.). In Figure 1 we report an example of the input-output interface for the chasing behavior[2] (CS-Chase). The input pattern, i.e. a message the learning system receives from its sensors, gives a coarse code of the chased object position. (The Animat has four on/off eyes, one on each side of its square shape. Each eye is set to 1 when the object is seen, to 0 when it is not seen.) The output pattern is made up of two components; the first one is a proposed action (in which direction to move, and whether to move or not; it is sent to the effectors), while the second one is a message sent to the coordinator, to let it know that CS-Chase was proposing an action.

The architecture we used to combine the three behaviors is sketched in Figure 2. This is only one of a set of possible choices which are described in detail in Colombetti & Dorigo (1992). Essentially we have three basic CSs, whose task is to learn the basic behavioral responses. We also have a coordinator CS, whose task is to learn to coordinate basic CSs. Basic modules send to the coordinator a bit string (in this application a single bit) whose meaning is learned. This means that, when the system has learned, each basic module will set the bit sent to the coordinator to a particular value when it wants to do something. For example, CS-Escape could learn to set the bit to 1 whenever it sees a predator. CS-coordinator then learns some kind of composition rule, which gives different weights to the actions proposed by basic CSs. In our example the composition rule learned is *suppression*, meaning that only one out of the three basic behaviors has the right to control the learning system effectors.

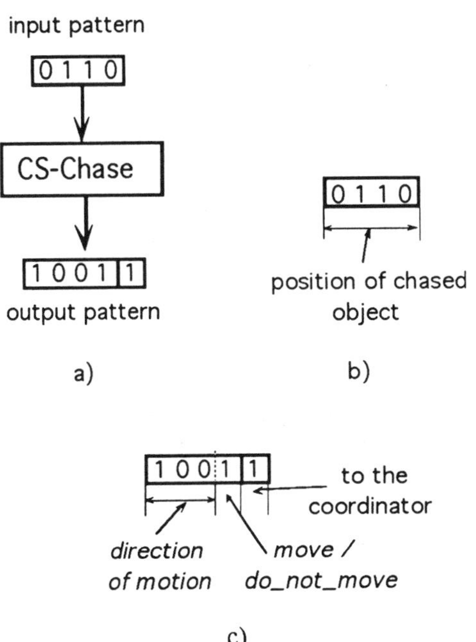

Figure 1. a) Example of input-output interface for the CS-Chase behavior;
b) Example of input message;
c) Example of output message.

2 CS-Feed and CS-Escape have a very similar structure.

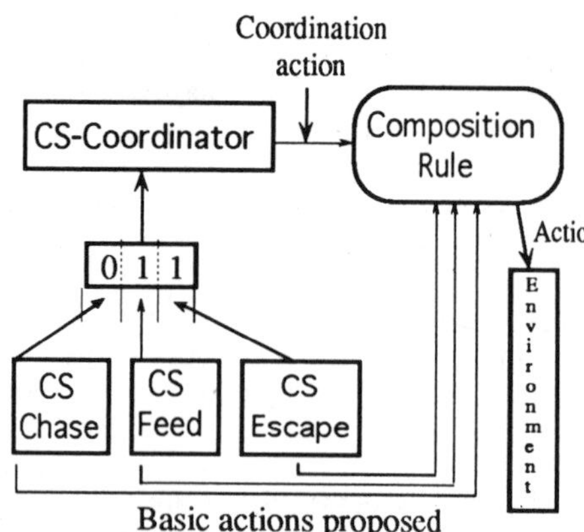

Figure 2. Example of hierarchical architecture for a three behaviors learning task.

We now make the problem more difficult by composing the coordination learning problem with a discrimination learning problem. In Dorigo (1992a), we showed that CSs can be used to discriminate between input patterns. They can be used for example to discriminate between similar objects, to learn which of them are food and which are not. In this new experiment we let the learning agent perceive many different objects for each class; besides learning to do the right thing, the agent must also learn to choose which, among the different objects in a class, is the relevant one. We label each class of objects with names that remind the role they play in our example: *possibly-dangerous-animals*, *food-like-objects* and *possibly-interesting-moving-objects*. The behavior to be learned becomes:

```
If there is a predator in possibly-dangerous-
   animals
   then Escape
   else if there is food in food-like-objects
          then Feed
          else Chase a particular object in
               possibly-interesting-moving-
               objects
```

The two simulated environments in which our Animat lives are sketched in Figure 3. In the next section we present some results obtained with our system in both the coordination task and in the coordination task with discrimination. Experiments were run in both environments. The resulting performance of experiments run in the environments of Figures 3a and 3b are reported respectively in Figures 4a and 4b. Performance is measured as the ratio of the number of correct responses to the total number of responses produced from the beginning of the simulation. Clearly the performance is always ≤ 1. In both experiments we shaped the robot in three phases. In the first phase, we shaped the basic behaviors; in the second phase, we froze the basic behaviors (i.e., we deactivated the learning algorithms), and started to shape the coordination behavior[3]. Finally, in the last phase we let all the system free to go on learning. Results show that the first phase was more difficult in the case of the environment of Figure 3b. This is clearly due to the discrimination task, which made the search space much larger. Nevertheless, if we give enough time to the system to learn the basic behaviors, the following phases lead to comparable overall performance.

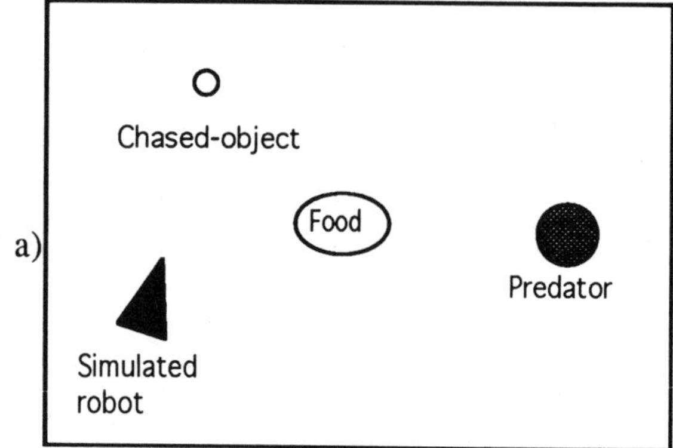

Figure 3. a) Simulation environments: One object in each class (no discrimination is necessary).

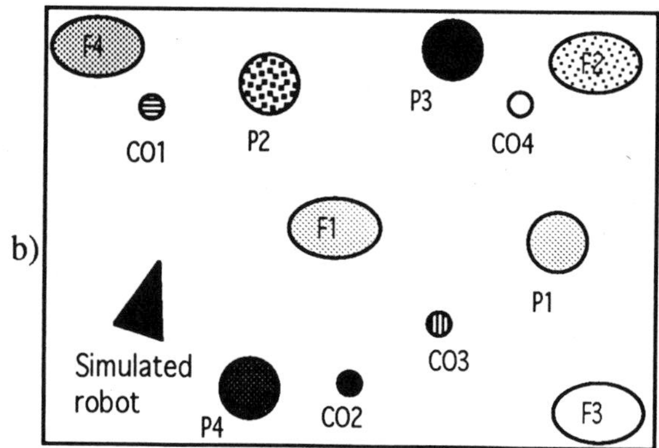

Figure 3. b) Simulation environments: Four objects in each class (discrimination becomes necessary).

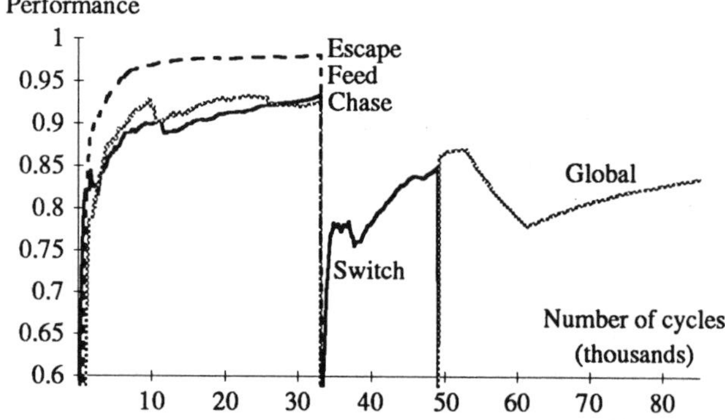

Figure 4. a) Performance of the typical experiment with environment of Figure 3a. Between cycles 0 and 33,000 basic behaviors were shaped; between 33,000 and 49,000 basic behaviors were frozen and the coordinator (switch) was shaped; after cycle 49,000 the system was free to go on learning.

3 In this experiment the coordination module is also called *switch* because its task is to choose one of the basic behaviors.

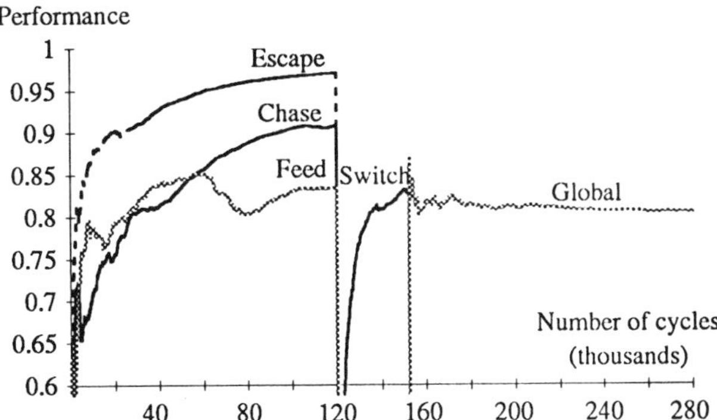

Figure 4. b) Performance of the typical experiment with environment of Figure 3b. Between cycles 0 and 120,000 basic behaviors were shaped; between 120,000 and 152,000 basic behaviors were frozen and the coordinator (switch) was shaped; after cycle 152,000 the system was free to go on learning.

5. Some experiments with the real robot

As it is often the case, experiments with the real robot are not so sophisticated as the ones in the simulated environment. This is mainly due to scheduling constraints: we had first to evaluate simulations results, and then to apply the best performing algorithms to the real robots (we call our robot *AutonoMouse*, due to its autonomous nature and mouse size). So, up to now, experiments with the AutonoMouse have been run only for a single behavior environment. The task we chose for our experiments is the *light chasing* task. The AutonoMouse can perceive a light source and should learn to approach (or follow) it. Light is sensed by means of two on/off eyes which are positioned on the front of the AutonoMouse (see Figure 5). Each eye senses the light within a cone of about 60 degrees. There can therefore be situations in which the light is on, but the AutonoMouse must turn to see it. In this and in the following experiments the performance was evaluated through light intensity, detected by a central light sensor positioned on the robot. This sensor could discriminate 256 levels of light intensity. Inherent uncertainty associated with sensors is not modeled.

In the graphs of Figures 6 and 7 we also plot the average reward over intervals of 20 cycles, multiplied by 25 to ease visual comparison. Figure 6 shows the result of the light approaching experiment. The drop in performance at cycle 225 is due to a sudden change in light position caused by the experimenter moving the light far away from the robot. The big difference in the number of cycles required to reach the light in this experiment and that required to rich a high performance in the experiments of Figure 4 is easily explained if you think that the correct behavior is more frequent than the wrong one as soon as performance is higher than 50%. The AutonoMouse starts therefore to approach the light source much before it has reached a high frequency of correct moves. In this and in the following experiments, 100 cycles were run in about 60 seconds.

Figure 5. The AutonoMouse

Figure 7 shows the result of the same experiment after we inverted the AutonoMouse's eyes. (We made "hardware surgery" on the robot, connecting the previous right eye input to the left eye and vice versa.) Also in this experiment the light was moved away as soon as it was reached by the AutonoMouse (at cycle 150). The results of the experiments are qualitatively similar and show that the AutonoMouse was capable of adapting to the new situation with inverted eyes.

The comparison between the graphs of Figures 6 and 7 brings in the problem of the instrument to use to compare performance. In fact, as an experiment depends on variables like the randomly generated initial knowledge-base of the robot, the stochastic processes guiding the learning algorithms and, most important, the dynamics of the real environment, it cannot be exactly replicated. This means that, even if we make repetitive experiments with the same initial knowledge base and with equal pseudo-random sequences of numbers for the stochastic algorithms, still we would get different results. So, we are forced to give qualitative assessments of the results obtained, especially when comparing different runs. Most of the time, it turns out that it is very easy for a human observer to judge the quality of the results of an experiment through videorecordings; however, it is much more difficult to translate this qualitative assessment into numbers (or graphs). For the same reasons explained before, it is not interesting or not even possible to present "average graphs", i.e. graphs of results averaged on a number of experiments. All our graphs are relative to a single run. Different runs generated qualitatively similar graphs.

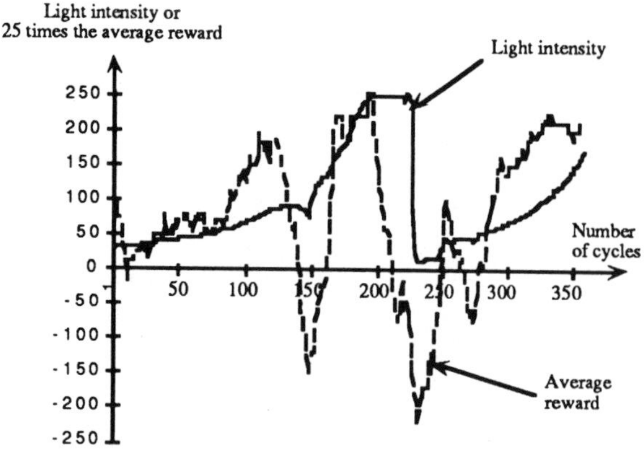

Figure 6. The robot learns to approach a stationary light source.

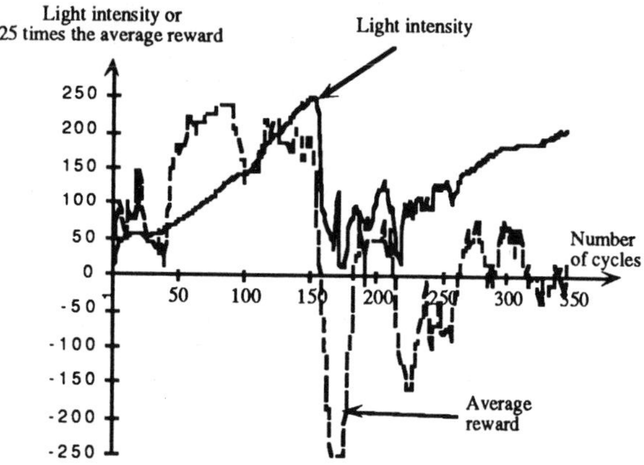

Figure 7. The robot learns to approach a stationary light source using inverted eyes.

In Figure 8 we show the result of an experiment in which one eye (the left one) of the AutonoMouse was disconnected. Again, the AutonoMouse was capable of reaching the light source, although with a somewhat degraded performance: it took 300 cycles to reach the light instead of the 150-200 of previous experiments. The drop in performance observed at cycle 135 is due to the fact that the AutonoMouse lost sight of the light and turned right until it saw the light source again.

Figure 9 shows the results of the last experiment of this paper. Here the task was to learn to follow a moving light source. In this experiment we faced a major dilemma; the reward function cannot use distance (or light intensity) changes to decide whether or not to give a reward. In fact, there are situations in which the AutonoMouse goes towards the light source, but at the same time the light source moves in the same direction. If the light source speed is higher than the AutonoMouse's, then the distance increases although the AutonoMouse made the right move. A possible solution is to let the AutonoMouse learn to approach a stationary light, then to freeze the rule set (i.e., stop the learning algorithm) and use it to follow the light. With this procedure one should be aware that, after learning has been stopped, the AutonoMouse can use only rules developed during the learning phase; this must therefore be as complete as possible. To ensure complete learning we need to give the AutonoMouse the opportunity to learn the right behavior in every possible environmental situation (in our case, every possible relative position of the light source).

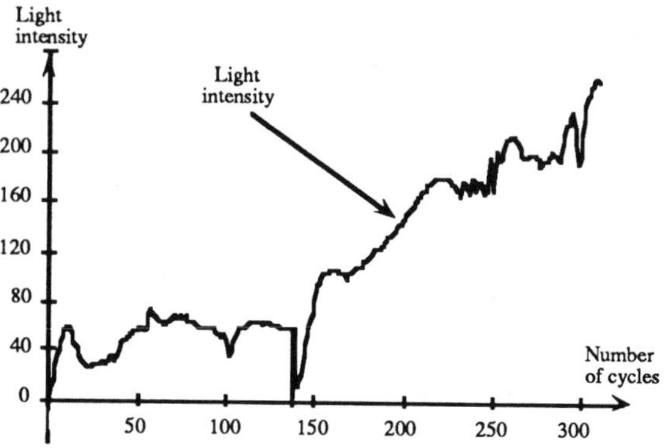

Figure 8. The robot learns to approach a stationary light source using only one eye (blind robot).

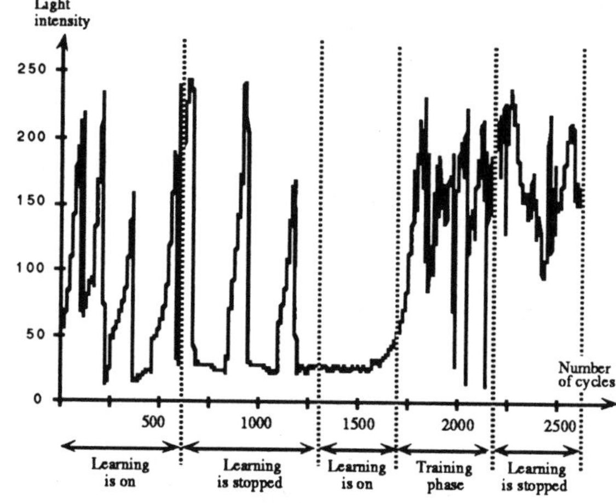

Figure 9. The robot learns to follow a moving light source.

In Figure 9 we report the results of the following experiment. At first the AutonoMouse is left free to move and to learn the approaching behavior. After 600 cycles we stop the learning algorithm, start to move the light source and let the AutonoMouse follow it. It appears that during the first learning phase the AutonoMouse did not learn all the relevant rules (in particular: it did not learn to turn right when the light was seen by the right eye) and therefore the resulting performance was not satisfactory. At cycle 1300 we therefore started the learning algorithm again and performed a new training phase from cycle 1700 to 2200. During this training phase we presented the lamp to the AutonoMouse on one side, and waited until the AutonoMouse started to do the right thing. This procedure was repeated many times, presenting the light alternately in front, on the right, on the left and behind, until direct observation told us that ALECSYS had learned (i.e., the AutonoMouse was following the light). After this training phase, learning was stopped again (at cycle 2200) and the light source was steadily moved. Figure 9 shows that this time the observed behavior was much better (performance is far from maximum, however, because the light source is moving and the AutonoMouse therefore never reaches it).

6. Conclusions

In this paper we report a few results of an experimental activity in robot learning, carried out with the ALECSYS system in both the real and simulated worlds. The main goal of our research is to develop an autonomous robot through learning; in particular, we are interested in the use of learning classifier systems endowed with a hierarchical architecture.

Reinforcement learning appears to be suitable for shaping robots. Its main virtue is that the trainer need not present examples of correct behavior, and can rely on the robot's own exploration activity. As soon as the learning task becomes nontrivial, unfortunately, known learning algorithms tend to become slow and cumbersome. Naturally, we can hope to discover more powerful algorithms in the future; but many past experiences, like the ones of traditional Artificial Intelligence, warn us that magic algorithm may well not exist. In our opinion, the key issue for scaling up learning applications is "innate" architecture, that is the built-in structure of the learning agent.

Another problem with reinforcement learning is that the feedback information that guides learning is strongly local. This means that many behaviors are difficult to describe in terms of rewards and punishments. Take for example the light-following behavior, intuitively defined as "keep as close as possible to the moving light". In fact, such a description implicitly refers to a *global* property of the robot's behavior, which could be made explicit, for example, as the mean-squared distance of the robot from the light over a generic interval of time. However, to be translated into a program that gives rewards and punishments, the description of the desired behavior has to be transformed into a *local* criterion, for example: "reward the robot if it gets closer to the light, punish it if it gets farther". But this translation does not completely capture the original description.

We have a similar problem when we try to measure the robot's performance. Clearly, to provide sensible results such a measure must be strictly coupled with the reward program: the responses that are positively rewarded must count as good performance, and the ones that are punished must count as bad performance. However, it has constantly been clear to us during experiments that there is more in the robot's behavior than what can be plotted in a graph. In other words, there are *qualitative* aspects emerging from the robot's behavior, that are not described by performance graphs.

It appears that we need to set up the conceptual apparatus and the technical terminology of a new discipline, that might well be dubbed *ethology of the artificial*, in order to describe the qualitative aspects of emerging behavior of artificial agents. Such a discipline would be concerned with the classification and description of different kinds of behavior and environments, with the design of experimental protocols, and with the choice of reliable criteria for evaluating performance.

Acknowledgements

This research was supported in part by a grant from CNR - Progetto finalizzato sistemi informatici e calcolo parallelo - Sottoprogetto 2 - Tema: Processori dedicati and from CNR - Progetto finalizzato robotica - Sottoobiettivo 2 - Tema: ALPI.

References

Barto, A. G., R. S. Sutton & C. W. Anderson, 1983. Neuronlike elements that can solve difficult learning control problems. *IEEE Transactions on Systems, Man and Cybernetics*, **13**, 834-846.

Booker, L., 1988. Classifier Systems that Learn Internal World Models. Machine Learning, **3**, 2-3, 161–192.

Brooks, R. A., 1991a. Intelligence without representation. *Artificial Intelligence*, **47**, 1-3, 139–159.

Brooks, R. A., 1991b. Artificial Life and Real Robots. *Proceedings of the 1st European Conference on Artificial Life (ECAL)*, Elsevier Publisher, Paris, France.

Brooks, R. A., 1992. Artificial life outside the computer. *Presented at Artificial Life III*, Santa Fe, NM.

Colombetti, M., & M. Dorigo, 1992. Robot Shaping: Developing Situated Agents through Learning. Technical Report 92-040, International Computer Science Institute, Berkeley, CA.

Dorigo, M., 1992a. *Optimization, learning and natural algorithms*, Ph.D. Thesis, Politecnico di Milano, Milano, Italy.

Dorigo, M., 1992b. ALECSYS and the AutonoMouse: Learning to control a real robot by distributed classifier systems. Technical Report 92–011, Dipartimento di Elettronica e Informazione, Politecnico di Milano, Milano, Italy.

Dorigo, M., 1992c. Using Transputers to Increase Speed and Flexibility of Genetics-based Machine Learning Systems. *Microprocessing and Microprogramming Journal*, 34, 147-152.

Dorigo, M., & U. Schnepf, 1993. Genetics-based machine learning and behavior-based robotics: A New Synthesis. *IEEE Transactions on Systems, Man, and Cybernetics*, **23**, 1.

Dorigo, M., & E. Sirtori, 1991. ALECSYS: A parallel laboratory for learning Classifier systems, *Proceedings of Fourth International Conference on Genetic Algorithms*, Morgan Kaufmann, San Diego, CA.

Holland, J. H., & J. S. Reitman, 1978. Cognitive systems based on adaptive algorithms. In D.A. Waterman & F. Hayes-Roth (Eds.), *Pattern-directed inference systems.* Academic Press, New York.

Lin, L-J., 1991. Programming robots using reinforcement learning and teaching. *Proceedings of the Ninth National Conference on Artificial Intelligence, AAAI-91,* 781-786.

Lin, L-J., 1992. Self-improving reactive agents based on reinforcement learning, planning and teaching. *Machine Learning*, **8**, 3, 293-322.

Mahadevan, S., 1992. Enhancing transfer in reinforcement learning by building stochastic models of robots actions. *To appear in the Proceedings of the Ninth Conference on Machine Learning* , Aberdeen, Scotland.

Mahadevan, S., & J. Connell, 1992. Automatic programming of behavior-based robots using reinforcement learning, *Artificial Intelligence*, **55**, 2.

Robertson, G.G., & R. L. Riolo, 1988. A tale of two classifier systems. *Machine Learning*, **3**, 2-3, 139–160.

Singh, S., 1992a. Transfer of learning by composing solutions of elemental sequential tasks. *Machine Learning*, **8**, 3/4, 323–339.

Singh S., 1992b. Reinforcement learning with a hierarchy of abstract models. *Proceedings of the Tenth National Conference on Artificial Intelligence, AAAI-92*, 202–207.

Sutton, R.S., 1984. Temporal credit assignment in reinforcement learning. Ph.D. dissertation, Dep. of computer and information science, University of Massachusetts, Amherst, MA.

Tinbergen, N., 1966. *The Study of Instincts.* Oxford University Press, 1966.

Watkins, C. J. C. H., 1989. *Learning with delayed rewards.* Ph.D. dissertation, Psychology Department, University of Cambridge, England.

Watkins, C. J. C. H., & P. Dayan, 1992. Technical Note: Q-learning. *Machine Learning*, **8**, 3-4, 279–292.

Williams, R. J., 1992. Simple statistical gradient-following algorithms for connectionist reinforcement learning. *Machine Learning*, **8**, 3-4, 229–256.

Wilson, S., 1987. Classifier systems and the Animat problem. *Machine Learning*, **2**, 3, 199–228.

Temporary Memory for Examples Can Speed Learning in a Simple Adaptive System

Lawrence Davis
Tica Associates
36 Hampshire Street
Cambridge, MA 02139 USA
(617) 864 2292
FAX (617) 494 4850
Email: 70461.1552@compuserve.com

Stewart Wilson
The Rowland Institute For Science
100 Cambridge Parkway
Cambridge, MA 02142 USA
(617) 497 4650
FAX (617) 497 4627
Email: wilson@smith. rowland.org

David Orvosh
Tica Associates
36 Hampshire Street
Cambridge, MA 02139 USA
(617) 864 2292
FAX (617) 494 4850
Email: 70461.1552@compuserve.com

Abstract

A temporary memory for recently experienced examples was coupled with BOOLE, a previously developed one-step classifier system that learns incrementally. Regimes were found in which the performance of the combination was superior to that of BOOLE alone, whether the task was to maximize average performance with respect to number of external trials, or the sum of external plus internal trials. The results suggest that storing and periodically reviewing a limited number of recent examples may enhance learning rates in otherwise strictly incremental adaptive systems.

1. Introduction

Many artificial autonomous learning systems, whether based on networks or classifier systems, are *incremental*--that is, they may learn something from each trial, example, or experience when it occurs, but they do not store raw experience for possible later study and processing. On the other hand, a number of important techniques from the AI domain of concept learning [9-10] collect and store large numbers of examples before processing them as a batch to derive the concepts. These latter techniques are distinctly *non*-incremental and differ from those of the incremental systems, but they can often learn faster in terms of the total number of examples that must be processed.

Despite this, incremental techniques are usually regarded as more realistic for autonomous adaptive systems, which may have limited leisure for off-line processing and whose environments are often noisy and non-stationary. We wondered, however, whether there might be ways in which small amounts of temporary memory for recent examples could be beneficial to incremental systems. Higher animals appear to have temporary memory, and people sometimes review and rehearse recent situations which had, e.g., unexpected outcomes. In this paper we present some very simple experiments in which temporary memory added to an existing incremental learning system gave performance superior to that of the incremental system alone. In our view, these results may be related to the psychological phenomenon of rehearsal [4].

In the next section we describe the *multiplexer* problem--a Boolean concept learning domain in which the experiments were carried out. In Section 3 we describe the incremental learning system BOOLE to which we attached the temporary example memory. In Section 4 we describe our first procedure for using memory with BOOLE, and show that this procedure greatly improves BOOLE's performance when one measures only the number of presentations of examples from an external source. In Section 5 we describe a second procedure and show that this improves BOOLE's performance versus the sum of the number of external and internal presentations. Finally in Section 6 we present our conclusions.

2. The Multiplexer Problem

Our problem domain was one in which randomly generated bit strings of length L were presented to the system and it had to learn to reply with the correct value, 1 or 0, of a Boolean function F of the bits of the string. The function F used was the so-called Boolean multiplexer in which a subset of the bits address one of the remaining bits, the value of which gives the value of F for that string. For example, in the 6-bit multiplexer, F(011011) = 0. The first two bits are the addressing bits. They form the number "1" in binary, thus addressing the second of the remaining four "data" bits, i.e., data bit 1, whose value is 0. Similarly, F(110001) = 1, where the last bit, data bit 3, is the one addressed by the first two bits. A larger problem, the 11-multiplexer, can be constructed the same way, except that in it the first three bits address the remaining eight bits of an 11-bit string.

The multiplexers form a family of relatively intricate Boolean functions that have served as task domains and have permitted comparisons in studies of several learning systems, including connectionist networks, classifier systems, and decision trees [1-3,10-11]. We chose the multiplexers here especially because they formed the task domain for earlier research with the incremental classifier system BOOLE to which, in this work, we coupled temporary memory. The multiplexer problem's high level of difficulty makes it a good stand-in for more realistic problems that may also require the use of memory.

3. BOOLE

The program BOOLE is a specialization of the general classifier system model [8] to one-step, or "stimulus-response", problems in which the system simply sees an environmental input, produces an output, and collects a reinforcement or payoff from the environment. The basic system is presented in [11], to which the reader is referred for details. The system was extended in [3], which showed that its performance could be significantly improved by large increases in the intensity of reinforcement; because of this new reinforcement scheme, the modified system was called NEWBOOLE. For the present paper, however, we used BOOLE in its original guise, taking, for the 6-multiplexer experiments, exactly the parameter settings of Figure 1 of [11], and for the 11-multiplexer experiments, the parameter settings of the dotted curve of Figure 4 of that paper.

Very briefly, BOOLE contains an initially random population (a set) of condition-action rules called classifiers, in which the condition part of the classifier (a string of length L formed from 1, 0, and the "don't care" symbol #) may match an input string, and the action says in what way (1 or 0) that classifier would have the system respond. On a particular trial, the input string will be matched by a subset [M] of the population: in general, some matchers advocate the response 1, the rest advocate 0. The system's decision occurs as follows.

Associated with each classifier is a scalar value called *strength* which is adjusted by the system's reinforcement algorithm and estimates that classifier's worth to the system. Given, as above, a particular input string and the resulting set [M] of matching classifiers, the system decides its output by selecting a single classifier from [M] using a probability distribution over the strengths of the classifiers in that set. (That is, the probability of being selected equals a classifier's strength divided by the sum of the strengths of all classifiers in [M]--a sort of "roulette wheel" but with wheel sectors sized according to strength.) The system output is then simply the value of the action (1 or 0) of the selected classifier.

For the experiments in this paper, BOOLE was reinforced according to the following regime. Let the *action set* [A] consist of the classifiers in [M] that advocated the selected output. Then, if the output was *correct*, the strengths of classifiers in [A] were incremented by the quantity 1000 divided by the number of members of [A]. If the output was *wrong*, the strengths of [A] were reduced by 80 percent of their current values. In addition, in both cases, and prior to the above adjustments, the strengths of [A] were reduced by 10 percent (see [11] for further details). The effect of reinforcement is to increase the likelihood that previously correct classifiers control future decisions.

Finally, BOOLE employs a periodic *genetic algorithm* (GA) step (see [6] and [7] for introductions to genetic algorithms) in which *new* classifiers are produced by selecting a pair of high-strength classifiers, copying them to form offspring, and then recombining or mutating the offspring strings before inserting them into the population (two low-strength classifiers are deleted).

1. Run BOOLE as usual on an external example.

2. Add this ordered triple to the head of the *memory-examples* list: <100 stimulus response>, where 100 is the example's initial weight, stimulus is the example's bit string, and response is the correct response to that stimulus.

3. Sort *memory-examples* by decreasing order of the weight of its members.

4. If the length of *memory-examples* is greater than *memory-size*, remove the last member of *memory-examples*.

5. If the length of *memory-examples* is less than *memory-size*, go to step 1. Otherwise, execute step 6 and then go to step 1.

6. Memory Cycle: Perform a-d *number-of-examples-to-run* times:
   a. Select an example randomly from *memory-examples*, where each example's chance of being selected is proportional to its weight.

   b. Present the example to BOOLE and reward BOOLE using the example's answer as the correct response.

   c. Decrement the weight of the example by 1.

   d. Run BOOLE's genetic algorithm step.

Figure 1: Temporary memory regime for reducing the number of external presentations.

The rate at which the GA step occurs is keyed stochastically to the rate of input trials (e.g., one new offspring for every two input trials, on average.) Through the GA, the system searches the space of potential classifiers. In general, BOOLE evolves a population consisting primarily of classifiers whose conditions map straightforwardly to the terms (conjuncts) of the disjunctive normal form of the function being learned [11].

4. Storing Examples in Memory

In the results reported here we implemented the temporary memory as a self-contained adjunct to BOOLE, making no attempt to integrate the two (a point discussed further in [5]). We represented the memory simply as a fixed-length list of examples.

Our intuition in adding memory was that by maintaining a list of examples whose classification is known and by presenting those examples to BOOLE between presentations of external examples, the performance of BOOLE with respect to the number of external presentations could be substantially increased. The components of our memory module were as follows:

memory-examples, a list of triples of the form <weight stimulus response>. This list contains the temporary memory. The three elements associated with each example are: a *weight* measuring the example's prominence in memory; a copy of the *stimulus* from an externally-presented example; and a copy of the correct *response* for that stimulus.

memory-size, a variable determining the maximum length of *memory-examples*. The value of this variable was held constant at 40 in the experiments reported in the next section, and was varied from experiment to experiment in the experiments reported in this section.

number-of-examples-to-run, a variable set to the desired number of examples from memory to present to BOOLE after each presentation of an external example. This value varied from experiment to experiment.

MEMORY SIZE		TRIALS PER MEMORY CYCLE 1	4	10	30	50	100
1	external	598	325	272	624	*	
	total	1195	1620	2978	19302		
4	external	661	384	290	582	**	
	total	1318	1902	3150	17910		
10	external	645	388	338	604	1446	
	total	1280	1902	3618	18429	72922	
30	external	672	392	325	314	315	510
	total	1314	1840	3279	8839	14586	48049
50	external	592	417	318	267	235	257
	total	1134	1885	3001	6767	9506	20935
100	external	647	416	342	283	235	222
	total	1194	1679	2763	5761	6998	12389

Table 1: Trials to 90% performance for BOOLE with memory on the 6 multiplexer problem. Results are averaged over 24 runs. Without memory BOOLE requires ~1088 external presentations to achieve a performance level of 90%. * indicates runs that were halted at 3930 external, 197,000 internal presentations with performance level < 80%. ** indicates runs that were halted with performance < 90% at 200,000 total presentations.

Our first algorithm for employing memory in the context of a run of BOOLE on a multiplexer problem uses these variables, and is detailed in figure 1.

The algorithm described in Figure 1 is a simple procedure for storing examples after they have been presented externally, and for running them between external presentations. We used a roulette wheel technique for selecting examples rather than cycling through the examples in order because cycling produced diminished performance. We hypothesize that this occurred because examples that are similar and that are grouped together may cause BOOLE to focus too much on them while deleting classifiers that are good for other classes of examples. A single occurrence of such a cluster of examples may not cause BOOLE to suffer, but repeated presentation of such clusters does. Use of probabilistic example choice reduces this effect. Note that step 6d involves the *probabilistic* running of BOOLE's GA step. A classifier is produced in this step with the same probability that it would be produced after the presentation of an external example.

The size of the memory and the number of examples to run after each external presentation are variables that had interesting effects on the performance of the system. Table 1 shows the number of external trials and number of total trials (external plus internal trials) for runs of BOOLE on the 6-multiplexer problem, with the size of memory held constant in each row and the number of internal presentations held constant in each column. The value in each cell of the table is based on the average of 24 runs, where the run was terminated when the average performance of BOOLE over the last 50 external examples was greater than or equal to 90 percent correct, or when the number of total presentations exceeded our limit. Note that the average number of external trials required by BOOLE to achieve this level of performance without memory was 1088.

There are several interesting features of the data in Table 1. The first is that the row showing results with memory size held constant at 1 displays significant performance enhancements. But this column represents the effect of re-presenting the most recent external example *number-of-examples-to-run* times. In the cell for memory size 1 and 1 trial, we see that BOOLE achieves 90% performance in nearly half the number of trials required without memory. But this is very little memory at all. In particular, it only requires "remembering" an example until the next external example is presented. Repeating the example just given doubles BOOLE's speed. Repeating it four or ten times makes BOOLE three times as fast. Repeating it thirty times is worse than repeating it 10 times.

The results for memory size 1 with 10 trials are comparable to those gained with NEWBOOLE. This fact leads us to hypothesize that the gains derived from NEWBOOLE's strategy of greatly

MEMORY SIZE		TRIALS PER MEMORY CYCLE					
		1	4	10	30	50	100
1	external	4557	3242	3966	*		
	total	9113	16206	43618			
4	external	5143	2958	3986	*		
	total	10282	14772	43808			
10	external	5040	3684	4228	*		
	total	10070	18379	46407			
30	external	4940	3328	3306	5580	*	
	total	9850	16519	36063	172080		
50	external	4203	2619	2680	**	**	
	total	8356	12896	28984			
100	external	4108	2721	2220	1191	1052	**
	total	8116	13204	23416	33930	48661	

TABLE 2: Trials to 90% performance for BOOLE with memory on the 11 multiplexer problem. Results are averaged over 24 runs. Without memory BOOLE requires ~7598 external presentations to achieve a performance level of 90%. * indicates runs that were halted at 30,000 external, 871,000 total presentations with performance level < 77%. ** indicates runs that were halted with performance < 90% at 100,000 total presentations.

increasing negative reinforcement when an example is gotten wrong can also be achieved by repeating the example multiple times, allowing BOOLE to get the example wrong if there is a significant chance of doing so.

Note that, counter to what one might expect, the results do not get better as one goes down each column. We believe that the beneficial effects of selecting mixed examples from a larger memory are offset in the 6-multiplexer data by the fact that runs terminate quite quickly. A run with memory size 50 does not begin to use memory until 50 examples are in memory. This means that BOOLE with a smaller memory begins to use memory sooner, and is therefore likely to terminate more quickly.

The results do not get uniformly better as the number of trials increases in rows with small memory sizes. We hypothesize that the use of a great many trials from a small memory degrades BOOLE's performance because the examples being seen by BOOLE are not representative of the complete distribution of examples, and BOOLE focuses too much on the examples currently in memory when the ratio of memory trials to memory size is large. Once memory is size 50 and up, increasing the number of trials appears to increase performance.

Table 2 shows the algorithm's performance on the 11-multiplexer problem. Runs were executed as described above, except that the window over which we measured average performance was increased from 50 to 100 external presentations. Note that the average number of trials required by BOOLE without memory on this problem was 7598. The observations we have just made apply to these results as well.

These data are not, in general, surprising. We conclude that if one uses the traditional measure of classifier system performance for problems like the multiplexer problem--average performance with respect to external presentations--then one can significantly increase BOOLE's speed in attaining high performance levels by storing examples in memory and by executing cycles of internal example presentation, reinforcement, and genetic algorithm triggering after each presentation of an example from the environment. The use of memory in this way could be quite useful to natural organisms, in situations in which the acquisition of external example data is costly, compared to the use of such data under a simulated regime. Of course, a great deal of internal processing is required in order to produce the greatest improvements in performance. In the next section we discuss techniques for minimizing the processing of examples from internal or external sources.

5. Estimating the Value of Memory Examples

It is not always the case that the processing of examples from memory is inexpensive compared to the processing of examples from the environment. Perhaps there is little time in which to process examples internally. Perhaps it is just as costly to process such an example as it is to acquire an example from the environment. Can memory be of assistance in such cases? In particular, if the cost of executing an example from memory equals the cost of executing an example from the environment, can memory be of assistance to BOOLE?

It is clear from the data presented in Tables 1 and 2 that the algorithm in Figure 1 will degrade BOOLE's performance when memory processing is as expensive as processing examples from the environment, since in every cell of Tables 1 and 2 the total number of examples processed by BOOLE exceeds the number processed by BOOLE without memory. In this section we describe two memory-based algorithms that decrease the total number of trials required by BOOLE. The algorithm described in Figure 1 adjusted the weight of examples based on the number of times they had been presented to BOOLE. The algorithms introduced here adjust the weight of the examples in memory based on the relative strengths of the classifiers matching the example's stimulus. These two algorithms, BALANCE and WRONG, are calculated in the following way. Let r denote the total strength of the correct classifiers matching an example's stimulus, and let w denote the total strength of the incorrect classifiers matching the example's stimulus. Then the weight of an example under the BALANCE regime is:

$1 - \left(\frac{|r-w|}{(r+w)}\right)$, while the weight of an example under the WRONG regime is $\frac{w}{(r+w)}$.

BALANCE, the first algorithm described above, sets the weight of an example in memory to the degree to which the strengths of the correct and incorrect classifiers for that example are equal. The intuition here is that an example is valuable to BOOLE if BOOLE has something to say about it, if the things BOOLE says are about equally strong, and if the things BOOLE says conflict. Running such an example will help settle the conflict for BOOLE, either by causing the correct classifiers to receive additional reinforcement, or by causing the incorrect ones to lose strength.

WRONG, the second algorithm described above, sets the weight of an example in memory to the ratio of the total strength of the classifiers that matched it and were incorrect to the sum of the strengths of all classifiers that matched it. The intuition behind this algorithm is that an example is valuable to BOOLE if BOOLE gets it wrong– the more wrong, the more valuable. Examples matched only by classifiers that classify them incorrectly get the highest weight.

We discovered early on that the use of examples under the BALANCE or WRONG regimes must be sparing at best if one is to improve BOOLE's performance on total presentations, and we modified our algorithm for running memory accordingly. The modified algorithm is given in Figure 3, where the variable *memory-ratio* is used in place of the variable *number-of-examples-to-run*.

The difference between this algorithm and the previous one, aside from the replacement of techniques for computing example weight, lies in the way the algorithm selects memory examples. We initially expected that a roulette wheel approach to example selection would be best. However, while selection based on weight worked well early in a run, late in a run a single example sometimes dominated in memory, and is then presented every time. This seemed to cause BOOLE to concentrate too much on a single example, and degraded performance. The regime described in Figure 3 uses weight to decide which examples to maintain in memory, but not to decide which examples to run.

Tables 3 and 4 show the results of using this algorithm on the 6-multiplexer and the 11-multiplexer, based on variation in the value of the *memory-ratio* parameter. The data show that for all the values of *memory-ratio* less than 1.0 for BALANCE, and for all the values for WRONG, the performance of BOOLE is improved, if one's criterion is based on the number of examples presented to BOOLE either from the environment or from memory. The optimal values of *memory-ratio* lie near 0.25, suggesting that if one wishes to reduce total trials, one should maintain a list of hard examples in memory and process one of them for each four examples processed from the environment.

1. Run BOOLE as usual on an external example.

2. Compute the weight of the external example using BALANCE or WRONG.

3. Place at the head of the *memory-examples* list the ordered triple consisting of the external example's weight, stimulus pattern, and correct response.

4. Remove from the *memory-examples* list any example with weight less than or equal to .00000000000001.

5. Sort *memory-examples* by decreasing order of the weight of its members.

6. If the length of *memory-examples* is greater than *memory-length*, remove the last member of *memory-examples*.

7. If fewer than 10 examples have been presented to BOOLE, go to step 1. Otherwise, run memory examples as described in step 8 and go to step 1.

8. Where the length of *memory-examples* is N, cycle through each example on the *memory-examples* list using a probability level = *memory-ratio* / N.
Carry out the following procedure on each example:

   A. If a random test of the probability level fails, do nothing with the example.

   B. Otherwise,

      a. Present the example to BOOLE and reward BOOLE using the example's answer as the correct response.

      b. Replace the example's weight with the weight computed by BALANCE or WRONG.

      c. Run BOOLE's genetic algorithm procedure.

Figure 3: Temporary memory regime for reducing the total number of external and internal presentations.

METHOD	***MEMORY-RATIO***			
	.1	.25	.5	1.0
BALANCE	980	913	945	1131
WRONG	998	959	1025	1041

TABLE 3: Total trials to 90% performance for BOOLE with memory on the 6 multiplexer, averaged over 22 runs. Without memory BOOLE requires ~1088 external presentations to achieve 90% performance.

METHOD	***MEMORY-RATIO***			
	.1	.25	.5	1.0
BALANCE	7502	6703	6854	7877
WRONG	7337	6985	7659	6680

TABLE 4: Total trials to 90% performance for BOOLE with memory on the 11 multiplexer, averaged over 21 runs. Without memory BOOLE requires ~7598 external presentations to achieve 90% performance.

A point of interest to us in future work is understanding the effects of BALANCE and WRONG on adaptive systems. These two regimes maintain quite different lists of examples--in fact, once the use of memory has gotten under way, systems using BALANCE and WRONG on the 11-multiplexer problem contain non-intersecting memory lists. Investigation of the conditions under which these regimes perform poorly and well is one of our future goals.

6. Conclusions

We have shown that the idea of adding rudimentary memory capabilities to a stimulus-response classifier system can improve its performance under either of two natural performance measurements. The most dramatic improvements are obtained, as one might expect, when the system is not penalized for processing examples in memory. However, clear improvements may be obtained as well when the use of memory incurs a penalty equal to that for processing examples originating in the system's environment.

The sort of memory we have introduced here--a simple fixed-length list of examples that have been experienced--is not the only sort of memory one can envision combining with adaptive systems, and other types should be explored. We believe that investigation of those other types, and continued investigation of the memory regimes detailed here, is likely to produce interesting results.

References

[1] Anderson, C. W. (1986). Learning and Problem Solving with Multilayer Connectionist Systems. Ph.D. Dissertation (Computer and Information Science). The University of Massachusetts.

[2] Barto, A. G. (1985). Learning by statistical cooperation of self-interested neuron-like computing elements. Human Neurobiology 4, 229-256.

[3] Bonelli, P., Parodi, A., Sen, S., and Wilson, S. (1990). NEWBOOLE: a fast GBML system. Machine Learning: Proceedings of the Seventh International Conference (pp. 153-159). San Mateo, CA: Morgan Kaufmann.

[4] Bower, Gordon H. and Hilgard, Ernest R. (1981). *Theories of Learning.* Englewood Cliffs, NJ. Prentice-Hall.

[5] Davis, L. (forthcoming). Covering and memory in classifier systems. To appear in proceedings of the October 1992 Workshop on Classifier Systems, Houston, Texas.

[6] Davis, L. (1991). Handbook of genetic algorithms. New York: Van Nostrand Reinhold.

[7] Goldberg, D. E. (1989). Genetic algorithms in search, optimization, and machine learning. Reading, MA: Addison-Wesley.

[8] Holland, J. H. (1986). Escaping brittleness: the possibilities of general-purpose learning algorithms applied to parallel rule-based systems. In R. S. Michalski, J. G. Carbonell & T. M. Mitchell (eds.), Machine learning, an artificial intelligence approach. Volume II. Los Altos, California: Morgan Kaufmann.

[9] Michalski, R. S. (1986). Understanding the nature of learning: issues and research directions. In R. S. Michalski, J. G. Carbonell & T. M. Mitchell (eds.), Machine learning, an artificial intelligence approach. Volume II. Los Altos, California: Morgan Kaufmann.

[10] Quinlan, J. R. (1988). An empirical comparison of genetic and decision-tree classifiers. Proceedings of the Fifth Internation Conference on Machine Learning (pp. 135-141). San Mateo, CA: Morgan Kaufmann.

[11] Wilson, S. W. (1987). Classifier systems and the animat problem. Machine Learning 2, 199-228.

Implementing Inner Drive Through Competence Reflection

Alexander Linden and Frank Weber
AI Research Division
German National Research Center for Computer Science (GMD)
D-5205 Sankt Augustin 1, FRG
email: Alexander.Linden@gmd.de, Frank.Weber@gmd.de

Abstract

We present a neural network architecture which combines the method of gradient search in input space of multilayer perceptrons [4, 15] with modeling their error [8, 13]. This architecture is used to implement an inner drive to have a computational agent explore its environment autonomously through reflection on its own capabilities. We compared this architecture to a standard supervised training scheme. The application task was to learn the kinematics of a robot arm in order to enable it to reach goals in workspace. Our experiments show that the proposed architecture needs a lot fewer physical experiences in terms of arm movements to solve the reaching task with sufficient accuracy.

1. Introduction

An autonomous agent that has to perform certain tasks in an unknown environment needs to acquire knowledge about it. This process is called exploration. Experiences gained during exploration are often not suited for direct construction of a good policy for the agent. Instead indirect methods offer greater appeal in their generality and flexibility. Here experiences are stored incrementally in world models such as a *(state) transition model*, which models the dynamics of the environment, or a *kinematic model*, which models (some aspects of) the geometric relationship between the physical part of the agent and its environment. To this collection also belong evaluative world models, which model the utility of a state w.r.t. to the task at hand. Reinforcement learning relies on those kinds of world models.

In a second step, the policy may be derived from the world model(s). Jordan [3] and many others constructed policy mappings (he calls it controller) indirectly from a transition model.

Munro [10] adapted the same indirect technique for reinforcement learning. It is also possible to dispense with an explicit controller and to generate suitable control signals by inverting the world model [2, 14].

Considering the desire to minimize the costs of the exploration, two aspects are important in learning world models: A high degree of autonomy reduces costly human intervention, and the number of physical experiences should be minimal for obtaining near optimal policies while limiting consumption of the physical agent. The latter requirement is very difficult to meet since, in general, it is not known which and how many experiences are sufficient. This depends heavily on the functional properties of the agent and its environment, and on the learning capabilities of the agent.

In this paper we propose an architecture which takes these aspects into account. The following section discusses general aspects of exploration. Section 3 introduces the idea of competence reflection on an abstract level. In section 4.1 the robot arm task for our autonomous system is described. The standard solution from supervised control is presented and its disadvantages are discussed. Then we describe the detailed exploration architecture with competence reflection for our application. The *competence model* can be considered as an evaluative meta world model, which predicts the error of the corresponding world model. It is used to drive the physical agent into those regions where it is assumed that the computational agent performs badly. Our experiments indicated that the proposed exploration heuristic works far better than the standard approach of supervised control [9] (see section 4.5).

2. Exploration

2.1. Online- vs. Offline-Exploration

If an agent needs knowledge about its environment to carry out its tasks, it has to explore it. If early fulfillment of the tasks is important, a trade-off between these and the exploration activities arise: In exploring its environment, the agent may detect better ways to perform its tasks, but extensive exploration may lead to possibly expensive delays in actual performance. Exploration that is intertwined with early exploitation of a possibly bad world model (we call it *online exploration*) has already been studied [12, 13]. If the agent is not deemed to carry out tasks in the beginning of learning, it is more convenient to have it perform *offline exploration*. It gains knowledge about the environment without being disturbed by the obligation to fulfill tasks. In addition, offline exploration offers a better framework for comparisons than online exploration.

2.2. A General Architecture for Offline Exploration

Let us assume that the agent has to construct a world model by means of the experiences that it collects during exploration. Such a world model is an approximation of some function f that holds for the environment. Figure 1 shows a general architecture for acquiring a world model through offline exploration.

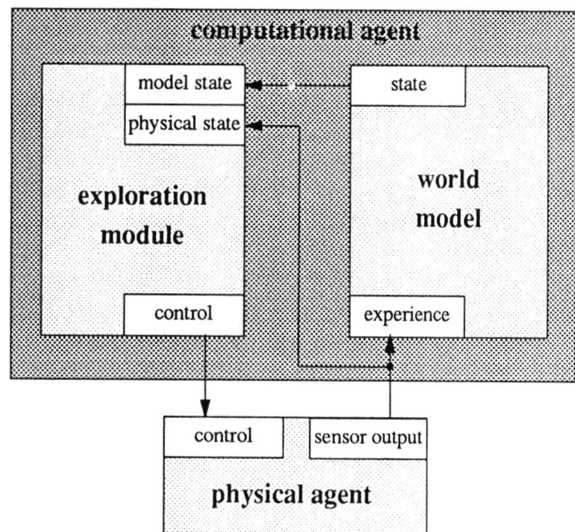

Figure 1: General offline exploration architecture

The overall structure of our computational agent consists of the world model and an exploration module. The exploration module may implement any kind of exploration strategy. For any given state it generates new control signals based on its own experiences. Through its sensors, the agent observes the new resulting state (internal as well as in relation to the environment) and refines both its world model and its exploration module. This implements an exploration loop.

3. Competence Modeling

If time or consumption of the physical agent is the decisive cost factor, exploration should need as few steps as possible to construct a policy or indirectly a world model. This means that the world model should get by with few experiences, hence it must show good generalization. Since for most classes of models this depends on the kind of experiences, it is important to find such experiences that make the model approximate f quickly. If the world model is implemented by a multilayer perceptron that is trained by backpropagation, a good heuristic approach is to choose such experiences as training examples, for which the approximation is still bad. Of course, the quality of the approximation for an x that has not yet been observed cannot be known but it can be estimated from the current approximation accuracy on the collected experiences. If the estimation is good enough, it should be worthwile to put the physical agent into a state where the computational agent can collect the experience $(x_0, f(x_0))$ with x_0 being the point where the estimated error of the world model is the highest. A way to generate the estimates is to use a second multilayer perceptron that is trained with the x values from the experience set and the corresponding errors of the world model. Thus the perceptron models the competence of the world model. x_0 can be found through gradient search in the input space of the network. In the next section, we describe experiments that demonstrate a successful application of this method to a robotics task. We also discuss competence modeling in more detail.

4. An Application: Learning the Kinematics of a Robot Arm

4.1. The kinematics of the robot arm

A multilayer perceptron is to learn the kinematics K of a simulated planar robot arm with two revolute joints (see fig. 2). Abstracting from reality, we made the following assumptions:

- The arm is static, it can be led to new positions by control signals in the form of joint angle changes; inertia and dynamics are not modeled.
- The arm reacts deterministically to received control signals.
- The sensors of the arm always work correctly.

A configuration q is defined by a pair of angles $(\varphi_1, \varphi_2) \in [-\pi, +\pi[\times [-\varphi_2^{\max}, \varphi_2^{\max}]$ with $\varphi_2^{\max} < \pi$. So, there is no limitation to the rotation of the first joint, while the set of possible positions for the second one is restricted such that collisions between the arm segments are avoided. In our experiments, we chose $\varphi_2^{\max} = \frac{9}{10}\pi \approx$

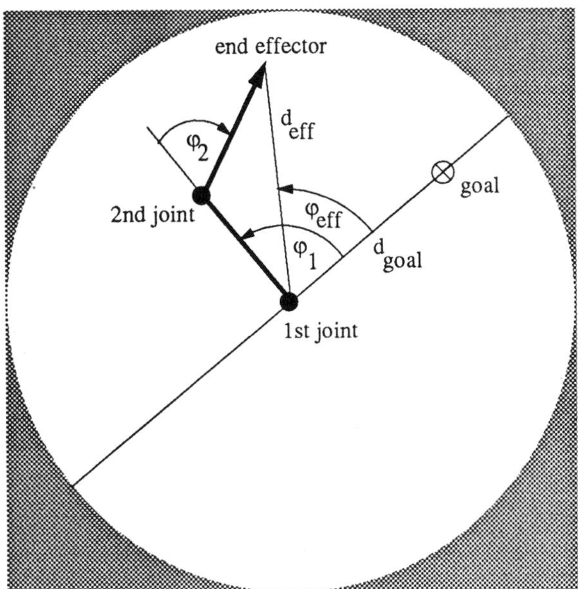

Figure 2: Simulated robot arm.

2.8274. The end effector position (EEP) is given in polar coordinates by $(d_{\text{eff}}, \varphi_{\text{eff}})$. As shown in the figure, φ_1 and φ_{eff} are defined relative to the line running through the arm base and the goal. Thus the descriptions of configurations and EEPs are invariant to rotations of the goal around the base. The advantage of this will become apparent below. Actions are limited joint transitions, thus the transition model is trivial and can be disregarded. The kinematics K maps every configuration to the EEP in workspace: $K(\varphi_1, \varphi_2) = (d_{\text{eff}}, \varphi_{\text{eff}})$.

During exploration, the arm is transferred into various configurations. Through its sensors, it can determine the current configuration and EEP. These data form a kinematic experience, which is put into the training set of the multilayer perceptron. This device realizes a mapping $\hat{K}$, which eventually should approximately equal K. It is trained with the well-known backpropagation technique [11].

4.2. Inverting the forward kinematics to reach goals

A central control task for a robot arm is to move its end effector to a given goal point with a certain accuracy. Here this task can be reduced to finding a configuration q which minimizes $(K(q) - (d_{\text{goal}}, 0))^2$ since, due to the relative formulation, the EEP at the goal is $(d_{\text{goal}}, 0)$, with d_{goal} being the distance between goal and arm base. The minimum can be approximated by inversion of $\hat{K}$ [15, 4, 2]. This method works by reducing the error measure $E_{\text{Inversion}} = (\hat{K}(\varphi_1, \varphi_2) - (d_{\text{goal}}, 0))^2$ through gradient descent in input space (here: configuration space) with

$$\Delta\varphi_i = -\eta \frac{\partial E_{\text{Inversion}}}{\partial \varphi_i},$$

where η is the inversion rate, analogous to the learning rate of the generalized delta rule. This process is already implemented by backpropagation, with the difference that only input unit activations are changed instead of weights. If $\hat{K}$ is accurate enough, we get activations that represent a goal configuration with sufficient precision. By subtracting the current configuration from the computed one, an action or a sequence of actions can be derived that drives the end effector to the goal.

The inversion method is particularly useful here because it gets rid of redundancies in a natural way. We find such redundancies in K as there are two configurations for most EEPs so that the inverse kinematics is not well-defined. With the inversion method, the input activations converge to one inverse solution near to the starting configuration.

Thanks to the relative view, the set of potential goal configurations is a 1-dimensional subspace of the 2-dimensional configuration space. For determining goal configurations by inversion, it is only in the vicinity of this subspace that $\hat{K}$ has to be accurate. For other configurations q, it suffices that the gradient search ultimately reaches this region.

4.3. The Grid Method for Modeling Kinematics

The standard method in neurocontrol [9] of acquiring a kinematic model $\hat{K}$ (or world model in general) is to collect experiences along a predefined grid. Fig. 3 shows a trajectory along which the arm can move and visit all 380 grid points of the configuration space. Each point together with the corresponding EEP constitutes an element of the training set.

We found that the number of points of this grid was near to the minimum to approximate K sufficiently well, i.e. the error of $\hat{K}$ remained too high for the coarser grids we tried. We obtained best results with standard backpropagation using two hidden layers (4 hidden units in each layer).

We defined the precision of $\hat{K}$ to be sufficiently good if for 25 different, evenly distributed distances of the goal from the arm base and with each of the 380 grid configurations as start input, inversion of $\hat{K}$ delivers a configuration in which the EEP is near the goal within the given tolerance.

Other methods make the arm perform a random walk or head for randomly chosen configurations [2] in-

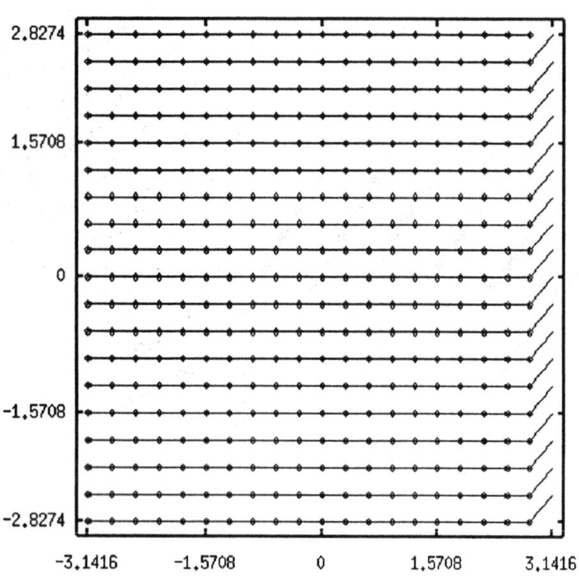

Figure 3: Trajectory through grid in configuration space.

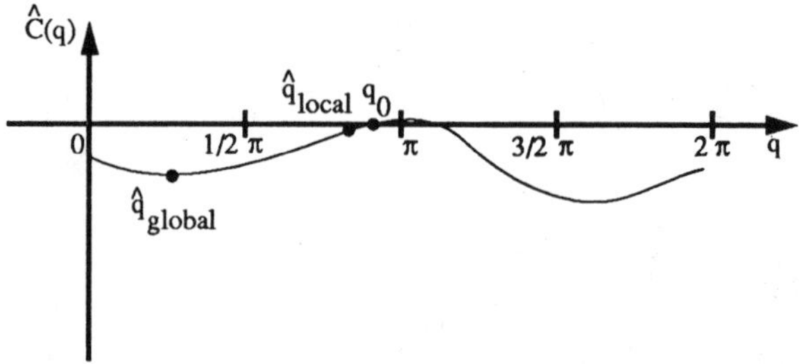

Figure 4: A possible competence graph for a 1-joint arm.

stead of making it traverse a fixed grid. Nevertheless this whole class of procedures suffers from several drawbacks: The approximation capabilities of the multilayer perceptron w.r.t. the kinematics are not considered, it is not a priori clear how fine the grid must be to let $\hat{K}$ perform sufficiently well, and it is inflexible because in more complex configuration spaces a traversion is not trivial.

4.4. Reflective Exploration

Consider an imperfect $\hat{K}$ at the beginning. There always exists q for which the deviation $(\hat{K}(q) - K(q))^2$ is maximal. We assume this q as a very promising exploration point to improve $\hat{K}$ quite rapidly. Because we do not know where $(\hat{K}(q) - K(q))^2$ is maximal, we introduce a competence model similar to Thrun and Möller [13] with $C(q) := -(\hat{K}(q) - K(q))^2$. This competence model is implemented with a second (two-hidden-layer) net $\hat{C}$ and is used to generate promising exploration points for $\hat{K}$. Figure 4 shows a sample graph of $\hat{C}$ in the case of a 1-joint arm. Since $\hat{C}$ is only an estimation, it may be positive for some angles. These positive regions indicate unknown areas of the configuration space and should be visited. Therefore not simple gradient descent is performed but it is tried to determine an angle whose $\hat{C}$-value is as far as possible from 0. This is realised by gradient ascent in input space for $\hat{C}^2$. The angle found by this technique may be only a local extremum, of course (as is $\hat{q}_{\text{global}}$ in the figure).

Figure 4 also indicates a further particular feature of the algorithm: Gradient search is aborted when a configuration is reached that cannot be entered through a single action from the current configuration q_0. $\hat{q}_{\text{local}}$ is such a configuration. The arm then performs a maximal step in the direction of this configuration. The reason for the abortion is illustrated in Figure 5. If we performed the gradient search thoroughly arriving at some configuration $\hat{q}_{\text{global}}$, we might unnecessarily visit well-learned configurations on our way to the new configuration.

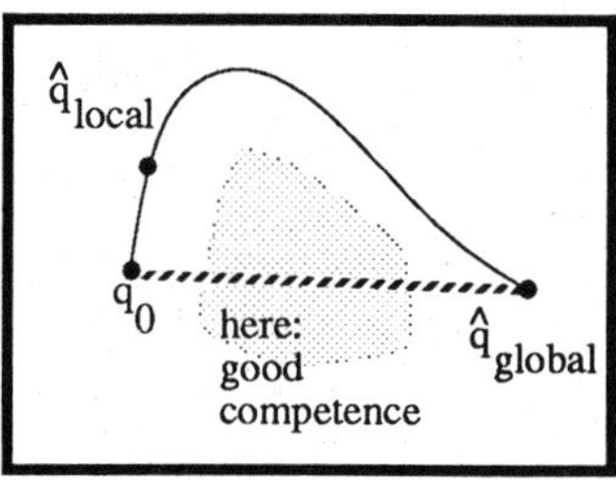

Figure 5: While starting at q_0 it is not in any case meaningful to drive directly to the estimated (global or local) minimum of competence. On the way there might be regions (shaded area) at which the agent is very good. Our experiments performed better when the agents iteratively descended the competence (error) surface.

4.4.1. Algorithm

(See also figure 6)

1. Store new kinematic experience: The arm sends its current configuration q_i with corresponding EEP to T.
2. Experiences so far in T are used to improve $\hat{K}$.
3. If $\hat{K}$ performs sufficiently well, stop!
4. Because $\hat{K}$ changed, also $\hat{C}$ must be updated: $\forall q_i \in T$ train $\hat{C}$ with target $-(\hat{K}(q_i) - \text{EEP}_i)^2$
5. Shadowing (see next subsection): Decrease $\hat{C}(q)$ for some random q. This will decrease the assumed competence for unseen configurations.

6. Determine some "interesting" q with minimal $\hat{C}(q)$ by gradient descent in input space, similar to the inversion method, using q_i as starting configuration.
7. The action generator computes an action leading from q_i to q.
8. The robot arm executes the action. Its new state is q_{i+1}. Increase i and goto 1.

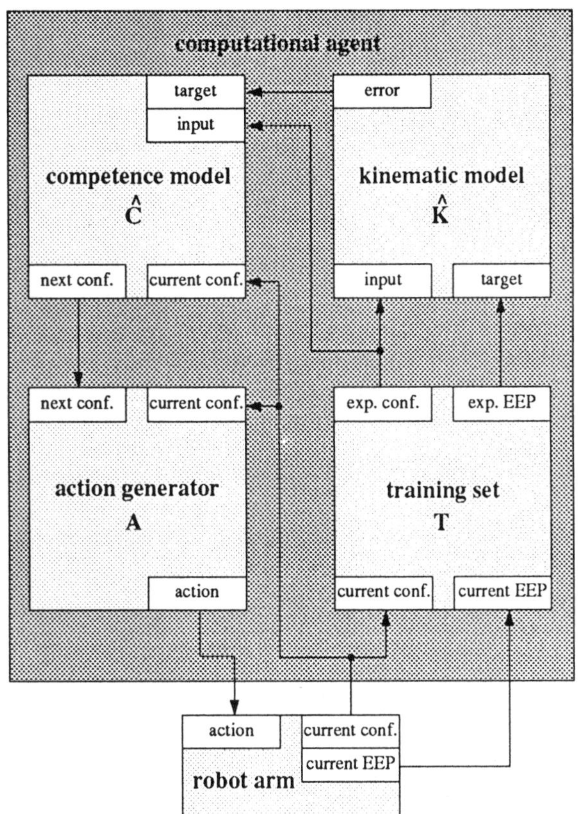

Figure 6: The architecture with competence modeling is explained in detail in the algorithmic section. (conf. = configuration, exp. = experienced).

4.4.2. Shadowing

The shadowing method provides negative examples randomly. The method is probably used by many other researchers in other contexts; one example can be found in character recognition, where random patterns were added to the normal training process [4] to increase reliability of classification. The term has been coined in a similar context by Atlas et al. [1].

Reflective exploration as proposed in this paper needs shadowing to avoid that backpropagation trains the competence model only on positive (already seen) examples. In that case, after a while, the competence model would predict zero error for any configuration of the robot arm, leading to unguided and hence less useful exploration. Technically speaking, the competence surface converges towards zero. Shadowing pushes the competence surface at random points to lower values. In a sense these are negative examples. The agent will therefore assume lower competence within unseen regions. The training set prevents the competence surface from escaping to $-\infty$.

4.5. Experiments with Reflective Exploration

The proposed method is able to choose its own path through the configuration space in order to collect kinematic experiences. Compared to figure 3, figure 7 shows a much shorter exploration path using only 160 arm movements instead of 380. One experiment run with training of $\hat{K}$ and $\hat{C}$ took 15 minutes on a SUN-Sparc2-workstation.

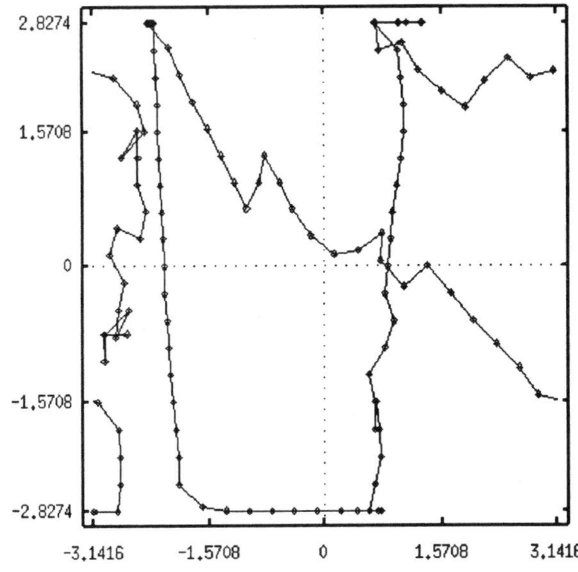

Figure 7: Trajectory generated by reflective exploration.

5. Conclusions

We have presented a method for learning the kinematics of a robot arm by exploring the configuration space. By modeling the competence of the kinematic model it is possible to select "interesting" training elements that lead to faster convergence of the model, thus reducing the required number of arm movements, as compared to traversing a grid. It seems promising to apply this reflective method also to exploring constrained kinematics, if more complicated robots are used or if obstacles are present in workspace, and to other classes of world models. We are currently investigating in this direction.

Acknowledgements

We would like to thank Jörg Kindermann, Heinz Mühlenbein, Frank Smieja and Christoph Tietz for comments on draft versions. This work is supported by the federal ministry of research under grant 01 IN 111 A/4 of the joint project REFLEX.

All experiments were performed using the multipurpose simulator environment SESAME [7, 5, 6].

References

[1] L. Atlas, D. Cohn, and R. Ladner. Training connectionist networks with queries and selective sampling. In *Advances in Neural Information Processing Systems Book 2, Proceedings of the NIPS Conference 1989*, pages 566–573, 1990.

[2] D. A. Hoskins, J. N. Hwang, and J. Vagners. Iterative inversion of neural networks and its application to adaptive control. *IEEE Transactions on Neural Networks*, 3(2):292 - 301, 1992.

[3] M. I. Jordan. Generic constraints on underspecified target trajectories. In *Proc. of the First Int. Joint Conf. on Neural Networks, Washington, DC.* IEEE, 1989.

[4] A. Linden and J. Kindermann. Inversion of multilayer nets. In *Proceedings of the First International Joint Conference on Neural Networks, Washington DC*, San Diego, 1989. IEEE.

[5] A. Linden and C. Tietz. SESAME — a software environment for combining multiple neural network paradigms and applications. In I. Aleksander and J. Taylor, editors, *Artificial Neural Networks II: Proceedings of the International Conference on Artificial Neural Networks - ICANN 92 -*, Brighton, United Kingdom, 1992. Elsevier Science Publishers.

[6] A. Linden and C. Tietz. An object-oriented framework and its implementation for the simulation of neural nets. In *Advances in Neural Information Processing Systems 6, Proceedings of the IEEE Conference in Denver (to appear)*, 1993.

[7] A. Linden and Ch. Tietz. Eine Softwareumgebung für Design und Analyse komplexer neuronaler Systeme. *Wirtschaftsinformatik*, 33(5):386–397, 1991.

[8] A. Linden and F. Weber. Exploring the kinematics of a robot arm by competence modelling. In B. Becker and T. Gordon, editors, *AI-Reader*. Erscheint als Arbeitspapier der GMD, 1992.

[9] W. T. Miller, R. S. Sutton, and P. J. Werbos, editors. *Neural Networks for Control*. MIT Press, Cambridge, 1990.

[10] P. Munro. A dual backpropagation scheme for scalar-reward learning. In *Ninth Annual Conference of the Cognitive Science Society*, pages 165–176, Hillsdale, NJ, 1987. Cognitive Science Society, Lawrence Erlbaum.

[11] D. E. Rumelhart, G. E. Hinton, and R. J. Williams. Learning internal representations by error propagation. In D. E. Rumelhart and J. L. McClelland, editors, *Parallel Distributed Processing. Vol. I + II.* MIT Press, 1986.

[12] J.H. Schmidhuber. Making the world differentiable: On using supervised learning fully recurrent neural networks for dynamic reinforcement learning and planning in non-stationary environments. Technical report, Technische Universität München, München, West Germany, 1990.

[13] S. Thrun and K. Möller. Active exploration in dynamic environments. In J. E. Moody, S. J. Hanson, and R. P. Lippmann, editors, *Advances in Neural Information Processing Systems 4*. Morgan Kaufmann, 1992.

[14] S. Thrun, K. Möller, and A. Linden. Planning with an adaptive world model. In D. S. Touretzky and R. Lippmann, editors, *Advances in Neural Information Processing Systems 3*, San Mateo, 1991. Morgan Kaufmann.

[15] R. J. Williams. Inverting a connectionist network mapping by backpropagation of error. In *8th Annual Conference of the Cognitive Science Society*, Hillsdale, NJ, 1986. Lawrence Erlbaum.

Dynamic Flight Control with Adaptive Coarse Coding

Bruce E. Rosen
Div. of Mathematics, Computer Science and Statistics
The University of Texas at San Antonio
San Antonio, TX, 78249
rosen@ringer.cs.utsa.edu

James M. Goodwin
Computer Science Department
University of California, Los Angeles
Los Angeles, CA, 90024
jmg@oahu.cs.ucla.edu

Abstract

This paper describes a new adaptive algorithm for autonomous control based on adaptive coarse coding. We present dynamic aircraft control as an example of its use and as a demonstration of its applicability. We show that combining reinforcement learning algorithms with adaptive neuron-like range coders can increase a autonomous system's ability to learn. Using adaptive region coding, initial state space range codings need not be optimal and resolution can remain coarse, reducing computational resources and facilitating generalization. Flight control experiments illustrate how an autonomous system with variable paritionings is capable of autonomous learning, and show superior flight performances over learning algorithms using with fixed regions shapes and sizes.

1. Introduction

This paper describes a new adaptive algorithm for autonomous control based on adaptive coarse coding. We present dynamic aircraft control as an example of its use and as a demonstration of its applicability. However the algorithm is most applicable to systems with limited asynchronous feedback, whose dynamics are unknown and are difficult to analyze by traditional control theory.

As systems become more complex they can become less understandable and harder to control. In general, autonomous control can be a difficult problem, further complicated when 1) little is known about the characteristics of the process being controlled, and 2) feedback or reinforcement is infrequent and limited in its information. Our adaptive algorithm, when incorporated into autonomous systems, can learn to operate difficult control tasks. It is robust and is designed to run on parallel computers.

Our connectionist approach has been motivated by stochastic reinforcement learning algorithms and their parallel implementations. These algorithms map input states to actions with a goal of maximizing reinforcement. They either develop a single global associative functional map, or create multiple piecewise associative functions that, when combined, locally map selected inputs to control actions. Coarse coding, often referred to as range coding, is one method of creating local maps which simplify learning by partitioning the input states into a finite set of discrete regions. The system need only learn a single control strategy for each region, rather than one for each state in the input space. Even though fine grain information in the original state is discarded, coarse coding has the advantages of compact implementation and efficient execution.

In general the performance of coarse coding algorithms is highly dependent on the quality of the partitioning. In earlier efforts, *a priori* knowledge of the control task has been needed to choose the regions effectively, requiring hand tooling of partitions. A significant weakness of that approach was that optimal partitioning could not be achieved automatically. The adaptive coarse coding algorithm presented here addresses this fundamental issue. This learning algorithm performs dynamic partitioning automatically. Furthermore, since learning occurs "on the fly", the algorithm has an additional advantage of enabling the near optimal tracking of time-varying system dynamics.

This research demonstrates that combining reinforcement learning algorithms with adaptive neuron-like range coders can increase a system's learning ability. By adaptation, regions equalize their activation frequency. (A region is deemed active when the current input is mapped to it.) Frequently active regions contract, thus they reduce their probability of reactivation and increase the chances that neighboring regions will receive input. This procedure creates a neural-like focusing mechanism, akin to foveation, allowing concentrated activity in specific regions to be finely discriminated.

2. Biological Range Coding

The algorithm, Adaptive Coarse Coding (ACC), is based on biological aspects of learning, particularly the adaptation of neural receptive fields and on operant conditioning. Biological neurons show adaptive variation of their connectivity, a form of biological adaptive range coding. Axons show complex branching during ontogenesis, and mature neurons exhibit sprouting of nerve fibers and the creation of new synapses, altering their receptive fields.

Significant reorganization in the development of visual system of the hamster neural network after injuries occurred have been reported by Schneider (Schneider 1973). He hypothesized that two effects are involved in neural self-organization: "pruning" and competition for available space. *Pruning* is exhibited in two situations: in damaged yet active areas, and in areas where synapse formation by a neuron is impossible. In these cases neighboring neurons extend and grow into the available area. *Competition* occurs when nerve fibers compete with each other to obtain space for synapse formation.

Lynch and Baudry (Lynch 1984) described a growth or enlargement of dendritic nodes that facilitated reception of neurotransmitters by the dendrites. They suggested that during high frequency stimulation of neurons, a proteinase was released that brought about an alteration in the size and structure of the dendritic nodes. This corresponded to Hebb's conjecture (Hebb 1949) that "some growth process or metabolic change" resulting from neuronal activity.

Observations by Alkon (Alkon 1989) suggest a focusing effect during reinforcement learning, and found physiological evidence in animals that associative reinforcement learning causes structural changes in neurons. Alkon found that the normal axonal terminals of the Hermissenda (an alabaster sea slug) fan out like a river delta while in the associatively conditioned animals, the axon fanned out over a 50 percent smaller region. The animals that learned to respond most strongly had the most tightly focused axon terminals.

3. Modeling Operant Learning for Control

A learning system (human or artificial) must discover which action works best in each circumstance, by producing actions and observing the resulting information, e.g. by *operant conditioning,* learning based on delayed rewards. Klopf (Klopf 1972, 1982, 1987) developed an extensive theory based on the hypothesis that neurons are adaptive heterostats, i.e., they use feedback information to seek or maintain some *maximal* condition of their inputs. Klopf proposed that neurons are independent goal seeking "hedonists" that attempt to maximize their level of excitation (frequency and amplitude of firings). The internal goal of each neuron firing decision was to maximize subsequent excitation while minimizing inhibition. One practical instantiation of Klopf's theory was Barto's Adaptive Critic Element (Barto 1983), used to learn control tasks.

4. Adaptive coarse coding: Focusing for control

We hypothesize that combining reinforcement learning algorithms with adaptive coarse coders, in which a neuron-like decision element's receptive field region changes, can increase the performances of an autonomous learning system. Adaptive Coarse Coding builds approximate control rules that maximize performance by emulating *operant conditioning*, implemented by incorporating reinforcement learning into the control process in the form of punishment and reward learning. Adaptive Coarse Coding is specifically designed to reduce the problems caused by the *a priori* fixed state space partitioning. From a given initial configuration, regions are progressively reshaped by the environmental dynamics. Regions self-organize, reflecting the dynamics of the controlled system and the environment. Frequently active regions can reduce their probability of activation by shrinking, thereby increasing the chances that *neighboring* regions will receive input, making *them* more frequently active. The self-organization emulates the neural focusing mechanism concentrating state activity in specific regions, allowing more finely discriminated decisions to be made.

When used as part of a search strategy, Adaptive Coarse Coding allows the control system to explore its environment. A controller can progressively learn the relationship between its actions and the resulting changes in its environment, insofar as they can be detected by its sensors. The result is the development within the controller of an internal model of the environment and its effective control laws.

5. The Problem of Autonomous Control

Controlling an unknown system by learning its operating characteristics is difficult problem. Control processes for high performance systems must handle large amounts of information at high speeds. Control must often be delegated to automated systems because real time human control is either economically inefficient, too slow, unreliable, or unfeasible. For instance, if the information delay time is lengthy (such as the control of a deep space probe), the delay may make remote control by humans impossible. Even in manned systems, unanticipated situations may occur. Thus highly parallel adaptive connectiosit system have been considered.

5.1 The BOXES Algorithm

Michie and Chambers (Michie 1968) "BOXES" algorithm is an *unsupervised* "bang-bang" control program that learned to balance a pole hinged to a cart moving on a bounded track. At the beginning of the algorithm, the state space is partitioned into several statically ranged states which divide the space into *boxes* (regions). A *demon* is placed in each box who can push the cart left or right. The demon counts clock pulses (one for each action), from the time of the box's last action, until the reception of a global feedback signal indicating failure and the end of a trial. In each box, the algorithm selected the action decision (e.g., the direction to a fixed impulse i.e., the bang), having the highest average number of steps before failing. Hence, box decisions were punished after a system failure by reducing their tendency to be repeated. The magnitude of the punishment depended on the recency of the box's action to a failure; decisions made immediately preceding a system failure were primarily punished most.

5.2 ASE/ACE Algorithm

Barto, Sutton and Anderson (Barto 1983), proposed a pair of stochastic neuron-like elements for unsupervised control. They first approximated the BOXES's strategy with an element, called the Associative Search Element (ASE), that chose the desired action having the longest time until failure. Influenced by Klopf (Klopf 82), another processing unit was added, called the Adaptive Critic Element (ACE), and was used to estimate an action's desirability based on its expected time weighted sum of future reinforcements. The algorithm would then choose the most desirable the actions (i.e., those having the largest sums).

Using the same task as Michie, the ACE algorithm kept the pole balanced for over 60,000 steps after 100 learning trials, a great improvement over BOXES. In several runs the system managed to keep the pole balanced for over 500,000 steps.

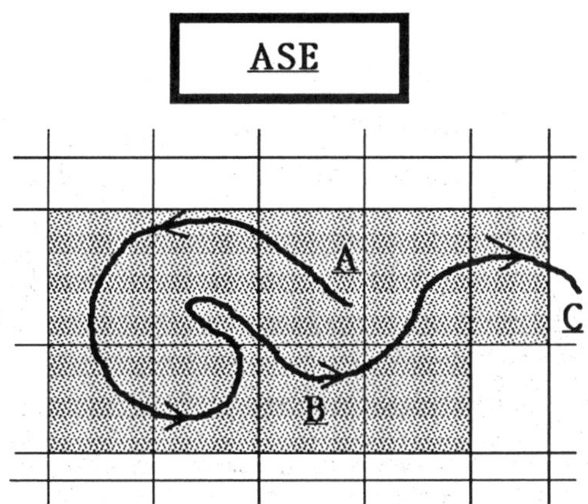

Figure 1. The ASE (BOXES) Algorithm.

Figure 1, (above) illustrates the ASE (and BOXES) learning paradigm. When the control system enters a failure region (e.g., failure states are those at the edges of the diagram), the local actions in the regions traversed (shaded rectangles), are punished by reducing their desirability values. The magnitude of these changes depends on the length of time from the last region action to the time of failure (e.g., after a failure in State C, the desirability values of actions executed in Region B are reduced more than those in Region A).

In the more advanced ACE algorithm, the system first estimates action desirabilities while simultaneously using the ASE algorithm to choose its control actions. Later, if a region action's accumulated reinforcement is smaller than expected, actions taken in it are punished by reducing their desirability. Conversely, if a region accumulated more reinforcement than expected, its action desirabilities are increased. Whenever actions result in transfer into a region whose actions are less desirable, they are punished. On the other hand, if the new region's actions have higher desirability values, the actions leading to the transfer are rewarded, (though they may still lead to failure). Thus, inter-trial decisions become optimized.

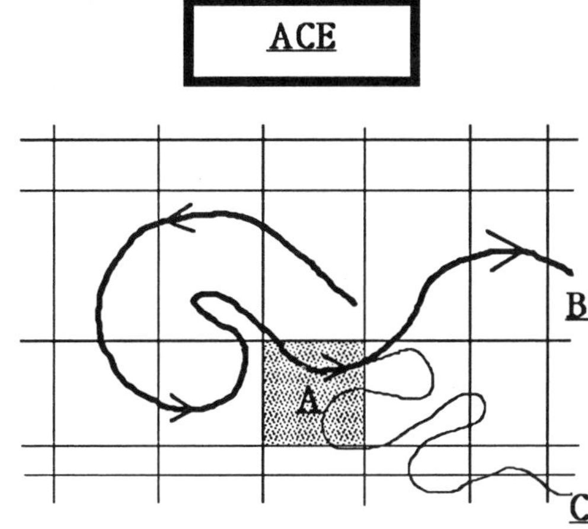

Figure 2. The ASE/ACE (Associative Search Element - Adaptive Critic Element) Algorithms.

Figure 2 illustrates the ACE algorithm. Actions executed in Region A are punished if they lead to a failure at B. Later, the same control actions executed in Region A would be rewarded if they caused a failure at C, since the actual time until failure (and hence accumulated time weighted reinforcement), was greater than previously estimated. A modified version is referred to as the Adaptive Heuristic Critic (AHC).

5.3 Topological Feature Maps

Kohonen (Kohon 1984), developed a general approach that would detect, model, and respond to the salient features and patterns in the system's inputs. His unsupervised algorithm allowed a *network* of processing units to self organize, and create a "feature map" of the inputs that preserved the data's topological relationship. The processing units self organized solely based on the input data and, after reorganization, the distribution of each unit's weights approximated the distribution of the inputs.

6. The Adaptive Coarse Coding Algorithm

Adaptive Coarse Coding automates the partition selection process for unsupervised control problems by combining delayed reinforcement learning with self organizing regions. It contrast and expands the regions in the processes of learning. Figure 3 illustrates a mapping from the input space into just such an adaptively encoded set of regions. The size and shape of the regions have been determined by the distribution of past activity in the input space. In the figure below, only the currently active region is shaded.

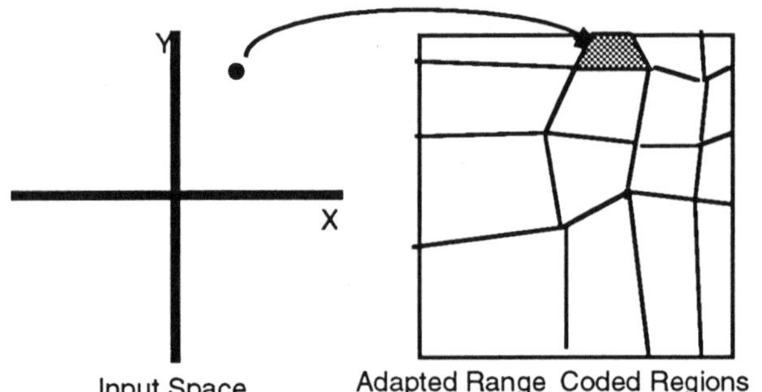

Figure 3. Adaptive Encoding, (Showing the new mapping of the input state space).

The adaptive coder makes the vertices of more frequently active regions contract toward the current state, thereby reducing their activation probability and increasing the chances that neighboring regions will receive input.

Consider the state space shown in Figures 4a and 4b, partitioned into three regions by the vertical lines. The heavy curve shows the (unknown) theoretical optimal control surface of the state space that should be approximated by the weight in each region. The dashed horizontal lines show the learned weight values. In Figure 4a, the state space is partitioned evenly and the weights approximate the mean value of the true control surface in each of the regions. Figure 4b shows the regions after the boundaries have been adjusted. Both 4a and 4b reflect the mean of the true control surface, but the new partitioning much more accurately represents the surface (i.e. with a smaller mean squared error). With a fixed partition size, weights are constrained to be constant even in areas where the control surface varies rapidly. With adaptable partitioning, region boundaries can be located in areas of rapid variation of the control surface.

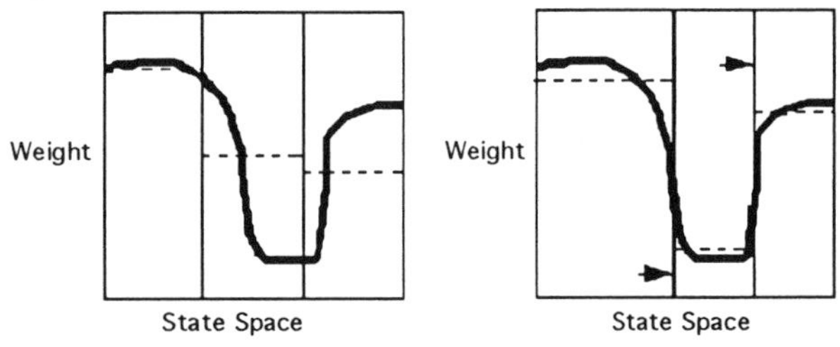

Figure 4a and b. Fixed and Adaptive Partitioned Regions.

Adaptive encoding has several advantages over static encoding techniques. First, the initial ranges and region specifications need not be optimal. Next, resolution can remain coarse, reducing computational resources and facilitating generalization. Lastly, fewer regions imply fewer weights to adjust, thus decreasing processing time. Dynamic shaping of the region boundaries allows for more appropriate region shapes and positions without sacrificing memory or learning speed.

6.1. Adaptive Coarse Coding Equations

When the constraint of *fixed* vertices is removed, the shape of each region can change from an n-dimensional hyper-parallelepiped to an n dimensional polygon, i.e. polytope. In ACC, the polytope shape is determined by the current activation state and its average activity. Adaptive Coarse Coding *moves each polytope vertex toward or away from the current environmental state.* The reinforcement signal governs the rate of region contraction and expansion. When there is no reinforcement, no change in the boundaries occur. Figure 5 shows the environment-learning controller interaction.

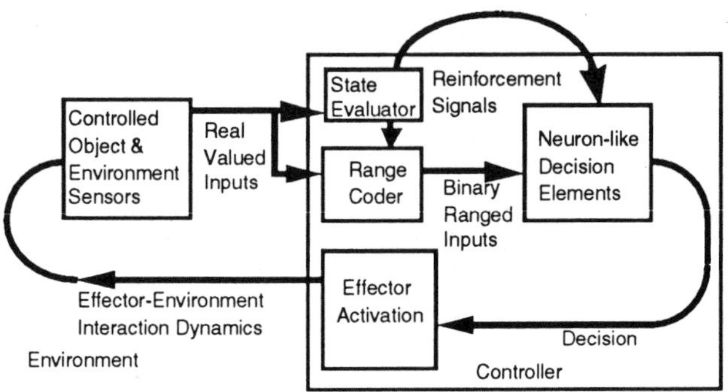

Figure 5. Environment-Controller Interaction Adaptive Coarse Coding. The controller incorporates range coding and neuron-like decision elements into the decision process. Reinforcement is sent to the decision elements, and also to the range coder.

The equation used to adjust each region boundary stems, in part, from Kohonen's topological mapping algorithm (Kohon 1984) previously described. Each region (box) (B_i) consists of 2^d vertices, $B_{ij}(t)$, that describe that region's boundaries. Each vertex is moved toward the current state activity E(t),

$$B_{ij}(t+1) = B_{ij}(t) + \kappa g(\hat{r}) h(B_{ij}(t) - E(t)) \qquad (1)$$

where h(x) is the contraction/expansion function, e.g. a Gaussian function with mean 0 and standard deviation σ. The reinforcement, $\hat{r}$, reflects the desirability of the current state, and is generated by a temporal learning algorithm such as the Adaptive Heuristic Critic. The reinforcement magnification function is g(x), which might even be the identity function. The gain determining the magnitude of the polytope expansion or contraction is κ.

Figure 6 illustrates the ACC algorithm's region alteration method, and figure 7 shows the parallel pseudo code of the ACC algorithm.

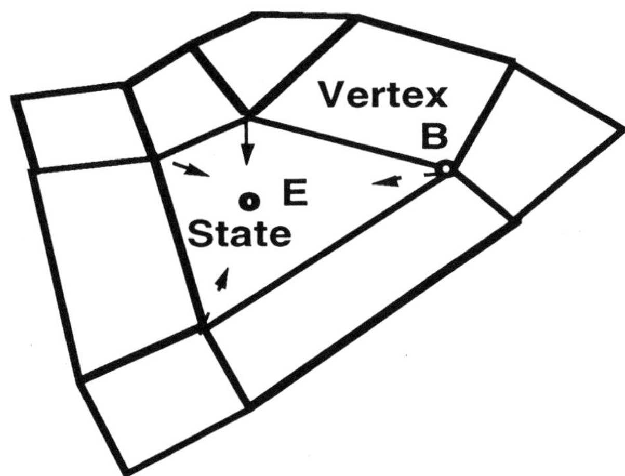

Figure 6. Adaptive Alteration of Regions. Current system State E and positive reinforcement r cause Region Vertex B to contract toward E. Other region vertices also move toward E, causing the region to contract.

Parallel Real

W_k,	Weight(s) for region k, vertex j
B_{kji},	Region k, vertex j, coordinate i
E_i,	System state vector, coordinate i
ι.	Expansion/Contraction gain

Real

$\hat{r}$;	Scalar reinforcement

```
While controlling the system Do
  {
  Find region Bk, ∋ E ∈ Bk
  Choose control action f(Bk, Wk)
  Observe or estimate r̂
  Update learning weights Wk

  Update Region Boundaries
  Parallel: ∀ region Bk
    Parallel: ∀ vertex j ∈ Bk
      if (Bkj is not fixed),
        Parallel: ∀ coordinate i ∈ Bkj
          Bkji += κ*g(r̂)* h(Bkji- Ei);
  }
```

Figure 7. Parallel pseudo code description of the Adaptive Coarse Coding Algorithm.

Although Adaptive Coarse Coding incorporates ideas from Kohonen topological feature maps, there are three major differences between the ACC equations and Kohonen's algorithm. First, Kohonen's equations describe a weight change procedure, whereas ACC determines the region of the state space where the system input are accepted or ignored. In a neural analogy, Kohonen presents a procedure for changing the synaptic efficacies of an artificial neuron, while ACC is a procedure for changing the receptive field size of an artificial neuron. Second, Kohonen's equations converge due to a time decay term, 1/kt, guaranteeing that the weights will stabilize if given enough time. Equation (1), guarantees stability only when the weights in the regions are stable and the reinforcement is zero. Thus if a region's weight converges, so do its boundaries. Should the environment become nonstationary, the boundaries will adjust until appropriate weights are found. Lastly, in Kohonen's algorithm, weights are adjusted by moving them towards the current input, while in ACC, vertices can move towards or away from the input.

7. NASA F-15 Flight Simulation

7.1 The F-15 Flight Control Problem

A full-scale aerodynamic simulation of the F-15 fighter plane was used to investigate the possibilities of autonomous reinforcement learning of flight control. An aerodynamic model originally developed at NASA Langley, has been ported to our laboratory workstations. It is a "full envelope," six degree of freedom aerodynamic model that included a Control Augmentation System (CAS). The simulated model permits an aircraft angle of attack from -10 to +40 degrees, and allows speeds up to Mach 2.5. The simulator contains approximately 6000 lines of FORTRAN code. It iteratively updates the aircraft state every 0.02 seconds, and can simulate aircraft flight in real time[1]. While simplifying assumptions often separate an aircraft simulation from real control, flight simulators do provide an important testbed for research in adaptive control.

7.2 Task Description

The task posed for ACC in the following experiments was to control a fully simulated F-15 aircraft to fly, under constant thrust, a straight and level course within 100 feet of a preassigned altitude,. The task required the aircraft to begin flying at an assigned altitude of 20,000 feet, with its wings level (no roll or yaw), and with an initial attitude of 3 degrees. The initial aircraft velocity was 600 mph and the aircraft accelerated at 80% of full thrust. Its initial elevator position was 2 degrees below the plane of the aircraft. These aircraft parameters were initially fixed for 20 seconds of real time, allowing all other dependent flight variables to stabilize. The aircraft elevator could vary, but all other control surfaces were fixed. From the initial aircraft state with no elevator control, the aircraft quickly

---

1 When run on a Sun 4/380 Sparcstation or HP9000 workstation, with a light load.

descended below 100 feet of its assigned altitude.

7.2.1 F-15 State Space Partitioning

Sensory signals consisting of the aircraft's attitude (att), altitude (alt), vertical velocity ($\dot{alt}$), and vertical acceleration ($\ddot{alt}$) were received by ACC. The algorithm controlled the elevator position.

The state space was divided into four dimensions, each dimension representing an attribute. Each attribute was evenly divided into six ranges as follows:

alt = {19900, 19933, 19966, 20000, 20033, 20066, 20100} feet

$\dot{alt}$ = {-∞, -100, -50, 0,50, 100, ∞} ft/sec

$\ddot{alt}$ = {-∞, -1, -0.5, 0, 0.5, 1, ∞} ft/sec^2

att = {-.16, -0.027, 0.11, 0.25, 0.38, 0.52, 0.66} rad.

Thus, the initial 6x6x6x6 partitions divided the state space into 1296 separate regions. The controllers output value ranged from -1 to 1 and controlled the elevator position. The controller output multiplied by 7.5, set the actual aircraft elevator position. The associated control dynamics were of a considerably higher complexity than those previously discussed in (Barto 1983) and (Rosen 1992).

7.2.2 Performance Criteria

Each flight experiment consisted of fifty runs. Each run consisted of 100 learning trials. The trial length was the number of time steps that the aircraft flew within acceptable flying limits.

The aircraft performance was determined by the number of time steps (in each trial) in which the aircraft was within acceptable flying conditions. These conditions were:

19,900 ft < aircraft alt < 20,100 ft, and

-0.166 rad < attitude < 0.66 rad.

7.2.3 Parameter Search

Although optimal control parameters for the cart pole task are listed in (Sutton 1984), appropriate learning parameters for the more complex F-15 control task had to be determined. As the F-15 control tasks were considerably different from the cart pole balancing tasks, one would expect that the learning parameters also would be different. There is an order of magnitude difference in minimum task failure times.

We searched to find suitable values for the AHC and ACC parameters α, β, γ, δ, and λ. In the searches, all parameters were fixed, except for the parameter under study, which took values from its range (shown below). Different parameter values were tested, each on a single run.

Values tested in this parameter search were:

α = (1024, 2048, 4096, 8192, 16384),

β = (1.0, 0.75, 0.5, 0.25),

γ = (1.0, 0.75, 0.5, 0.25, 0.125, 0.95),

δ = (1.0, 0.75, 0.5, 0.25, 0.125, 0.9),

λ = (1.0, 0.75, 0.5, 0.25, 0.125, 0.8)

TRANSFER FUNCTION= (SIGMOID, IDENTITY),

OUTPUT = (PROBABILISTIC BINARY, REAL).

After testing a set of values, each variable was set to its best performing parameter value. Results of the 31 tested values are not shown, but the best combination values found were α = 4096, β = 0.5, γ = 0.95, δ = 0.9, and λ = 0.8, with identity function as the transfer function producing real output. All of the following experiments used these values. The ACC runs then used additional values κ=512, and σ=8.

7.3 Reinforcement in Flight Control

In our simulation experiments, the controller received delayed feedback in the form of negative reinforcement, *only when the aircraft ascended above, or descended below, 100 feet from the preassigned altitude.* This is a more difficult and general problem than flight control with immediate reinforcement.

A delayed reinforcement function was chosen over an immediate reinforcement function for two reasons. First, delaying the reinforcement signal forces a learning system to explore many different control combinations and large areas of the state space. Immediate reinforcement learning systems explored fewer control combinations and smaller state space areas. Although an expanded search can prevent a learning system from falling into suboptimal and local minima, yielding poor solutions, it unfortunately can increase the learning time and inhibits convergence to a good control strategy.

The second reason for using a delayed reinforcement function, is that it can be difficult to find an appropriate *immediate* reinforcement function, even using intuition or *a priori* knowledge of the system dynamics. We did consider two immediate reinforcement functions $r_1()$ and $r_2()$, shown in equations (2) and (3) below.

$$r_1() = - (\text{desired altitude - current alt})^2 \quad (2)$$

$$r_2() = - (\text{desired altitude - current alt})^2 - (\text{current vertical velocity})^2 \quad (3)$$

Performance was poor when using either immediate reinforcement function. With immediate reinforcement, short term tactics dominated the behavior of the controller. The controller had difficulty learning an effective control strategy because of the lag between the control decision and its later effect (several time steps later). The control lag led to increasingly large oscillations about the assigned altitude, resulting in large weight changes.

In simulations with delayed reinforcement, using a single delayed feedback signal, the controller often developed a viable control strategy that predicted the delay between action and effect. Thus the controller could learn the causal relationship between the current state, the proposed control action, and long term task reinforcement.

7.3.1 The Control Decision Process

The control decision output y, is based the weighted sum of regional inputs x_i plus some stochastic noise[2]. When the outputs are discrete actions, the output is then thresholded.

$$y(t) = f\left(\sum_{i=1}^{n} w_i(t)\, x_i(t) + noise(t)\right) \quad (4)$$

where f(z) is

$$f(z) = \begin{bmatrix} +1 \text{ if } z \geq 0 \\ -1 \text{ if } z < 0 \end{bmatrix} \quad (5)$$

for bivalued outputs. For real valued outputs

$$f(z) = z \quad \text{or} \quad f(z) = \frac{1}{1+e^{-z}}$$

Here, $x_i(t)$ represents the activation value of region i at time t, and y(t) represents the output decision made at time t. $w_i(t)$ is the efficacy of the *i* th pathway at time t, and *noise* is a real randomly (Gaussian) distributed value, with some mean μ and variance σ^2.

The region decision weight is a sum of its previous weight, and the product of the learning rate (α), the actual or estimated reinforcement ($\hat{r}$), and the region's eligibility (e). Equation (6) shows that future weight changes are dependent on eligibility and reinforcement.

$$w_i(t+1) = w_i(t) + \alpha\hat{r}(t)e_i(t) \quad (6)$$

The eligibility index $e_i(t)$, determines how eligible a weight is to the weight change process.

Equation (7) shows how the recency and frequency can be incorporated as part of the eligibility index. The index $e_i(t)$ in (6) is an exponentially decaying function, indicating the relative activity of an element via a moving average. The first term in (7), applies the recency heuristic. Eligibility exponentially decreases with time or, stated another way, increases with recency of activation. The second term in (7) incorporates the frequency heuristic. Each time the system state is within a region it becomes active, and its eligibility index is increased (decreased when y is negative).

$$e_i(t+1) = \lambda_w e_i(t) + (1-\lambda_w)y(t)x_i(t) \quad (7a)$$

or (as suggested by Sutton (Sutton 1987),

$$e_i(t+1) = \lambda_w e_i(t) + (1-\lambda_w)(y(t) - \bar{y})x_i(t) \quad (7b)$$

Here λ_w is the weight eligibility decay gain, $0 <= \lambda_w <= 1$, $x_i \in \{0,1\}$, and $y \in \{-1,1\}$. The output value y is the last output decision (for a binary output control function). $\bar{y}$ is the average output, and λ_w determines the decay rate. The terms y(t) and $x_i(t)$, refer to the input and output activation levels of the element and their product ultimately determines the weight change. The direction (increase or decrease), of the weight change (efficacy), due to the final term in (7), is that of the last action taken, y(t).

Finally, the reinforcement function in the system is given as:

$$\hat{r}(t) = \begin{cases} -1 & \text{when the system fails} \\ p.r. & \text{otherwise} \end{cases} \quad (8)$$

Where p.r. is the predicted reinforcement.

We the Adaptive Heuristic Critic to generate the predicted reinforcement. Sutton (Sutton 1984) provides a more detailed description of the weight change process along with the method for predicting future reinforcement values.

8. Parallel Simulations

A motivation for the design of the ACC algorithm, was the desire to exploit massively parallel computing during learning. Of particular interest was the concept of data-level parallelism, whereby a problem is decomposed into fine-grain identical operations executing on multiple data. If a large number of processors are available, then each one could execute these operations on its local data elements. The ACC algorithm naturally decomposes into this form of parallelism.

The F-15 experiments were conducted on UCLA's Connection Machine (CM-2) (Hillis 1985), which offered a unique platform for simulating and testing neural networks. Its fine granularity (16k message passing processors), can quickly and effectively simulate large scale artificial neural networks. Parallel processing programs running on the CM can be executed much more rapidly than on sequential computers.

To achieve high performance with data level parallelism, our simulations required large numbers of processors that could operate concurrently on multiple copies of the data. The CM has 65,536 processing elements.

The ACC algorithm is naturally parallel. Porting the code from its original sequential implementation to the CM required minimal coding changes. During execution, the CM's SIMD architecture eliminated many of the bottlenecks involved in sequential computing. Its fine grain parallelism also enabled larger numbers of regions to be accessed simultaneously. Parallel debugging, however, was more difficult and time consuming than serial debugging.

---

[2] For convenience, we will use the same notation as in (Barto 1983) and (Sutton 1984) to describe the decision making process.

9. Results

Figure 8 below shows the average performance of 50 runs of each algorithm. As in the cart pole experiments, eligibility values were determined by Equation (7b). The superiority of the ACC algorithm over the AHC algorithm is clearly shown.

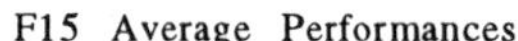

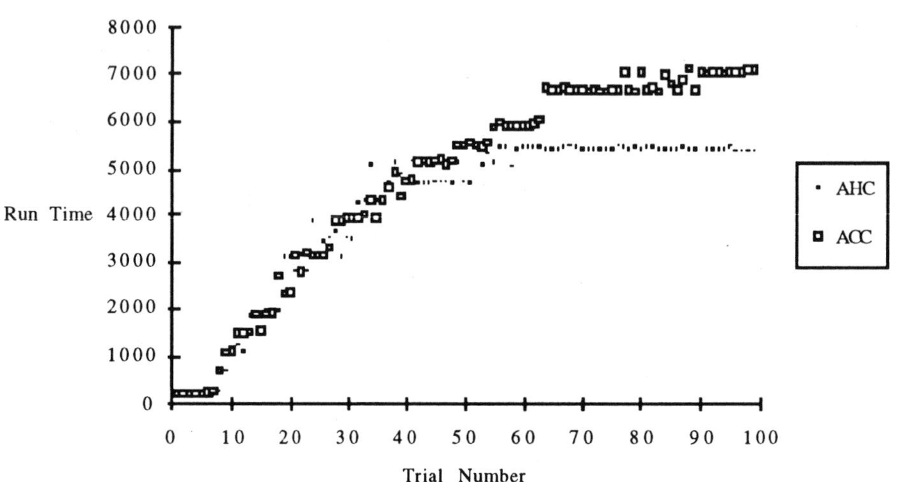

Figure 8. Comparison of the AHC, and ACC Learning Rates on the F-15 Flight Task. The F-15's initial altitude was 20,000 feet. Successful flight time is shown as function of learning trials.

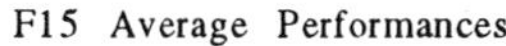

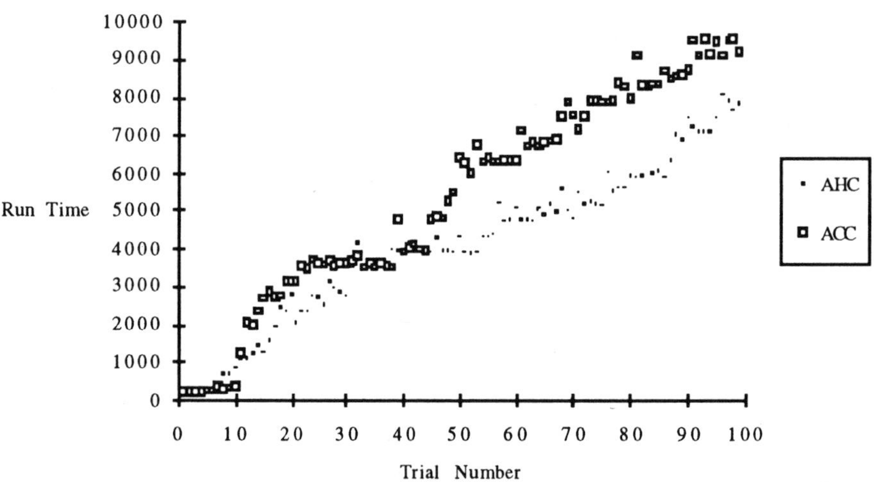

Figure 9. Comparison of the AHC, and ACC Learning Rates on the F-15 Flight Task (Using Equation (7a)). The F-15 was initialized with an altitude of 20,000 feet. Successful flight time is shown as a function of the learning trials.

The performance divergence was due primarily to the increased number of successful ACC flights, compared with the AHC flights. Of the fifty ACC runs, only 17 were successful, although in 24 of the runs the aircraft flew the maximum flight time. In the AHC runs, there were only 14 successful runs, and only 22 runs lasted for the maximum flight time.

The second aircraft experiment used Equation (7a) instead of (7b) to improve performance. Figure 9 shows the superiority of the ACC algorithm over the AHC algorithm.

Twenty-two of the ACC experiments were successful, and 31 of the runs flew for the maximum flight time. In the AHC experiments, there were only 18 successful runs, and only 23 runs flew for the maximum flight time.

In the two flight experiments, the Adaptive Coarse Coding Algorithm outperformed the Adaptive Heuristic Critic by an average of 20%. Flight performances in the second aircraft experiment improved when Sutton's new weight adjustment formula (7b) was replaced with a more traditional equation (7b). The two algorithms were statistically different at the 90% confidence level.

9.1 Performance with Skewed Partitions

In the next set of experiments, the initial state space partitions were changed; new nonsymmetrical skewed ranges for alt and $\dot{\text{alt}}$ were used:

alt = {19900, 19928, 19956, 19985, 20013, 20041, 20100}

(One partition every 28 feet, with the last partition 59 feet)

$\dot{\text{alt}}$ = {-∞, -107.5, -65, -22.5, 20, 62.5, ∞}

(One partition every 42.4 feet)

The alt and $\dot{\text{alt}}$ partitions were skewed, although there were still six ranges.

Figure 10 below shows the average performances of 50 runs of both algorithms using skewed partitionings.

F15 Average Performances-Alternate Partitioning

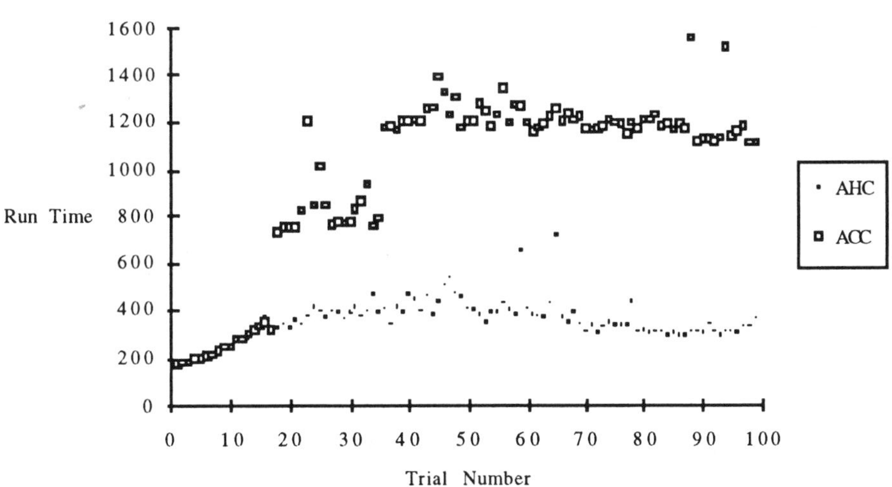

Figure 10. Comparison of the AHC, and ACC Learning Rates on the F-15 Flight Task with Skewed Partitions.

The alternative partitioning significantly influenced the learning ability of the system. Both algorithms performed worse than in previous experiments. However, the Adaptive Coarse Coding Algorithm again performed better than the Adaptive Heuristic Critic.

9.1.1 Discussion

Table 1 summarizes the results of the F-15 aircraft flight experiments. The initial partitioning had a significant effect on the aircraft flight task. Performance results were markedly inferior when the initial partitioning was poorly chosen. The initial partitioning in the previous experiments was clearly far from optimal.

Algorithm	Partitioning	Average Failure Time
AHC	Regular	7831
ACC	Regular	9224
AHC	Skewed	364
ACC	Skewed	1108

Table 1. F-15 Aircraft Flight Results.

The solution to this problem is to form a more appropriate partitioning. Although Adaptive Coarse Coding could mitigate these effects, it was clearly not a panacea. To improve the partitioning, the system must adjust the regions before learning their control actions. Possible improvements might be to decrease the weight adjustment learning gain while simultaneously increasing the region contraction parameter κ.

The small number of regions most certainly influenced the performances of both algorithms. The initial partitioning defined the number of regions. More regions would have increased each algorithm's performance. However, this increase would have been at the expense of their learning time.

The most significant reason for the relatively poor success rates of both algorithms was that the reinforcement was delayed until the aircraft flew beyond its stated bounds. Using immediate reinforcement would have improved performance levels, although doing so would have required an *a priori* knowledge of an evaluation function.

10. Conclusion

The two major premises underlying the experiments were that: 1) A minimum of *a priori* knowledge is incorporated into the learning system, and 2) Only a delayed binary failure signal indicates a task failure. The two algorithm performances in the F-15 tasks should not be taken out of context. Flight performances should be compared with systems using similar knowledge bases and evaluative functions. The experiments presented here serve mainly to illustrate that autonomous systems with variable paritionings are capable of autonomous learning, and can be superior to those learning system with fixed regions shapes and sizes.

The experiments presented here illustrate that a reinforcement learning system can acquire, through experience, knowledge of how to perform a difficult control task. The experiments also illustrated that altering the initial state space partitioning enabled significant learning increases. Although the current demonstrations involved somewhat restricted control tasks, using small numbers of inputs and outputs, this method can be extended to more complex problems of higher dimensionality.

The implementation of this system on parallel computers like the CM, allowed rapid execution and testing of a learning algorithm's effectiveness. It also demonstrates the viability of implementing parallel learning algorithms, such as Adaptive Coarse Coding, on parallel hardware for faster real time performance.

References

D. L. Alkon (1989) "Memory Storage and Neural Systems", in *Scientific American,* **261**, No. 1.

A. G. Barto, R. S. Sutton, and C. W. Anderson (1983) "Neuron-like Elements That Can Solve Difficult Learning Control Problems", in *IEEE Transactions on Systems, Man, and Cybernetics,* **13**, No. 5, pp. 834-846.

D. Hebb (1949)*The Organization of Behavior* New York: Wiley.

W. D. Hillis, (1985)*The Connection Machine,* MIT Press, Cambridge MA.

H. Klopf (1972) *Brain Function and Adaptive Systems: A Heterostatic Theory,* Air Force Cambridge Research Laboratories Special Report No. 133 (AFCRL-72-0164). Also DTIC Report AD 742259 available from the Defense Technical Information Center, Cameron Station, Alexandria, VA 22304.

H. Klopf (1982) *The Hedonistic Neuron: A Theory of Memory, Learning, and Intelligence,* New York: Harper & Row/ Hemisphere.

H. Klopf (1987) *Drive Reinforcement Learning: A Real-time Learning Mechanism for Unsupervised Learning,* in Proceedings of the First Annual International Conference on Neural Networks.

T. Kohonen (1984) *Self-Organization and Associative Memory,* Springer-Verlag, New York.

G. Lynch, and M. Baudry (1984) "The Biochemistry of Memory: A New and Specific Hypothesis." in *Science,* **224**, p. 1057-1063.

D. Michie and R. Chambers (1968) *Machine Intelligence,* E. Dale and D. Michie (eds.), Oliver and Boyd, Edinburgh, p. 137.

B. E. Rosen, J. M. Goodwin, and J. J. Vidal, (1992) "Process Control with Adaptive Coarse Coding" in *Biological Cybernetics,* **6**, No. 4.

G. E. Schneider (1973), "Early Lesions of the Superior Colliculus: Factors Affecting the Formation of Abnormal Retinal Projections," in *Brain, Behavior and Evolution,* **8**, pp 73-109.

R. S. Sutton, (1984) "Temporal Credit Assignment in Reinforcement Learning", Doctoral Dissertation, University of Massachusetts.

R. S. Sutton, and A. G. Barto (1987),*A Temporal-Difference Model of Classical Conditioning,* GTE Tech Report TR87-509.2, GTE Laboratories Incorporated.

Learning via Task Decomposition

Josh Tenenberg *, **Jonas Karlsson, and Steven Whitehead** †‡
Department of Computer Science
University of Rochester
Rochester New York 14627-0226
FAX: (716) 461-2018
{josh,jonas,white}@cs.rochester.edu

Abstract

Reinforcement learning is applied to agents encountering multiple, time-varying goals. We extend the standard formalism by decomposing the learning task into a set of separate control modules, one for each goal that the agent might encounter. Learning is facilitated since each module learns the optimal policy associated with its goal without respect to other current goals, greatly simplifying the state representation and speeding the learning time compared to a single, monolithic controller. When the robot is faced with a single goal, the module associated with that goal is used to determine the overall control policy. When faced with multiple goals, information from each associated module is merged to determine the policy for the combined task. In general, these merged strategies yield good, but suboptimal performance, so that the modular agent is trading off performance that is optimal in the limit but prohibitively costly to learn, for good initial performance and tractable learning costs. We consider several merging strategies, and demonstrate that their use results in significant performance improvements over the single monolithic controller.

1 Introduction

Reinforcement learning has recently been receiving attention among researchers interested in developing autonomous systems. As a method for learning sequential decision and control tasks, it has several appealing properties, including that little or no *a priori* domain knowledge is required, the behavior is both highly reactive and adaptable to change, and the techniques rest upon a sound mathematical foundation. While reinforcement learning is almost certain to play a role in future autonomous systems, the prominence of that role will be largely determined by the extent to which reinforcement learning can be scaled to larger and more complex control tasks.

A class of such complex control tasks that we have been exploring involves an agent pursing multiple, time-varying goals. For example, a rat must sustain itself with food and water, groom itself to protect against parasites and infection, avoid predators, locate a mate, nest, procreate, and tend its young. Similarly, an autonomous robot in an office environment would likely be called on to perform a variety of useful functions, such as delivering a number of documents to different locations, keeping a photocopier supplied with paper, while avoiding collisions with both people and other objects.

In this paper, we consider the application of reinforcement learning to agents whose desired behavior involves achieving such multiple, time-varying goals. Consider the example of Figure 1, which shows a "creature" at a particular location, which has the goal of having both food and water, shown at other locations in the figure. We begin by describing how single, time-invariant problems (e.g., getting just food) can be expressed within the reinforcement learning framework, and in particular how these problems can be formalized using the language of Markov decision processes. Recent results by Watkins [Watkins, 1989] demonstrate that given a sufficient number of trials, an agent can learn an optimal policy for this problem using the simplest of computational capabilities (essentially table look-up and simple update rules). This policy tells the agent what action to choose in each state in order to maximize its long-run return.

Although this formalism is sufficiently expressive to encode multiple, time-varying problems, such as getting *both* food and water, doing so requires an exponential growth in the size of the creature's memory requirements as a function of the number of distinct tasks it will be faced with. This *monolithic* approach, then, is clearly infeasible in all but the simplest of domains.

To avoid this *curse of dimensionality* [Bellman, 1957], we propose a modular architecture wherein the overall

*Currently at Department of Mathematics and Computer Science, Indiana University at South Bend,P.O. Box 7111,South Bend, Indiana 46634, (219) 237-4335, josh@natasha.iusb.indiana.edu, FAX (219) 237-4538

†Currently at GTE Laboratories Incorporated, 40 Sylvan Road, Walthan, MA 02254

‡This material is based on work supported by the National Science Foundation under grants IRI-9003841 and IRI-8903582. This work was also supported by ONR research grant N00014-90-J-1811, Air Force - Rome Air Development Center research contract F30602-91-C-0010, and Air Force research grant AFOSR-91-0108. The Government has certain rights in this material.

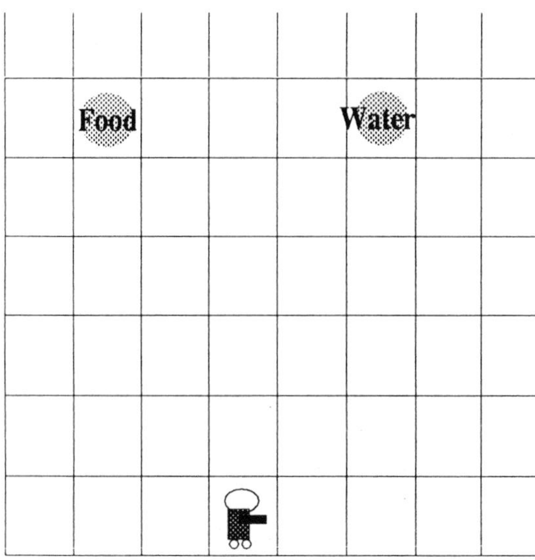

Figure 1: Example multi-goal problem

learning task is decomposed into its constituent pieces. Following this approach, each individual goal (or activity) is associated with a control module whose objective is to learn only that goal. Decomposing the task in this way facilitates the learning of individual activities, since information about goal priorities, which is relevant only to coordinating multi-purpose activity, is eliminated from each module's state space representation. Instead of learning over a single, monolithic state space, whose size is exponential in the number of goals, the modular architecture learns over a linear number of of constant sized state spaces.

When the robot is faced with a single task, the module associated with that task is used to determine the overall control policy. When faced with multiple tasks, information from each associated module is merged to determine the policy for the combined task. Since policies for individual goals can be learned much more quickly than a monolithic, global policy, enhanced multi-purpose performance can be attained if good policy merging strategies can be found.

Several policy merging strategies are considered. One simple strategy is to select the action associated with the highest utility module. This *greedy* strategy is easily seen to be non-optimal; however, it yields significant performance improvement over the monolithic architecture. More sophisticated merging strategies that involve lookahead search are also considered. Overall, our formalism suggests that, even though monolithic architectures do not scale well to multi-goal tasks due to their exponential growth as a function of the number of tasks, modular architectures that decompose the task by goal learn at a linear rate and often learn near-optimal decision policies.

The remainder of the paper is organized as follows. Section 2 reviews the basics of reinforcement learning. Section 3 discusses multiple goal tasks and considers the learning complexity of the monolithic approach. In Section 4, a modular architecture is presented and shown to significantly outperform the monolithic approach, even when simple strategies are used for policy merging. Section 5 considers search-based merging strategies, and conclusions are drawn in Section 6.

2 Reinforcement Learning

Q-learning is a class of algorithms for incremental dynamic programming, which can be used to learn optimal policies for multi-stage decision problems modeled as Markov decision processes (MDP's) [Watkins, 1989]. A discrete, finite MDP is formalized as a four-tuple, (S, A, T, R), where S is a finite set of states, A is a finite set of actions, T is a (possibly stochastic) transition function mapping state-action pairs to states, and R is a (possibly stochastic) reward function mapping states to real numbers. In Q-learning, the system's objective is to learn a control policy f, which maps states into actions such that the cumulative discounted reward is maximized. This cumulative reward, called the *return*, is defined as

$$return(t) = \sum_{n=0}^{\infty} \gamma^n r_{t+n} \qquad (1)$$

where γ is the temporal discount factor ($0 \leq \gamma \leq 1$), and r_{t+n} is the reward received at time $t+n$. Because the process may be stochastic, the robot's objective is to find a policy that maximizes the *expected return*.

The decision system maintains an *action-value* function, Q, that maps state-action pairs into expected returns. That is, $Q(x, a)$ is the decision system's *estimate* of the return that it expects to receive given that it executes action a in state x and follows an optimal policy thereafter. Given Q the decision system's policy f is determined by the rule:

$$f(x) = a \quad \text{such that} \quad Q(x, a) = \max_{b \in A}[Q(x, b),] \qquad (2)$$

where A is the set of possible actions.

The estimates represented by the action-value function are incrementally improved through trial and error by using updating rules based on temporal difference (TD) methods [Sutton, 1988]. In 1-step Q-learning only the action-value of the most recent state-action pair is updated. The rule used is

$$Q_{t+1}(x_t, a_t) \leftarrow (1-\alpha)Q_t(x_t, a_t) + \alpha[r_t + \gamma U_t(x_{t+1})], \qquad (3)$$

where

$$U_t(x) = \max_{b \in A}[Q_t(x, b)],$$

and α is the learning rate. Finally, the robot's control policy is updated using Equation 2, and the cycle repeats.

3 Multiple goal tasks

In this section we present an MDP-based approach to modeling multiple goal tasks, by augmenting the MDP model by including in the agent's state representation a bit for each goal denoting which goals are currently active. We then show that the most straightforward application of Q-learning, the *monolithic* approach, suffers from intractably slow learning due to state space growth that is exponential in the number of possible goals. A modular architecture that avoids this combinatoric explosion is presented in Section 4.1.

Suppose the robot has n goals, $\Gamma^1, \Gamma^2, \ldots, \Gamma^n$. Associate with each goal Γ^i a set of satisfying states $G^i \subset S$ and a reward function R^i such that

$$R^i(x) = \begin{cases} c^i & \text{if } x \in G^i \\ 0 & \text{otherwise.} \end{cases} \tag{4}$$

where c^i is a scalar constant reward associated with each goal Γ^i. Each goal also has associated with it a time dependent activation, which we denote by ${g^i}_t$. For simplicity we assume that activations are binary valued processes, where ${g^i}_t = 1$ indicates that, at time t, Γ^i is active, and ${g^i}_t = 0$ indicates Γ^i is inactive. At each time point, then, we view each g^i as a bit, and the vector of all such bits we call the activation vector:

$$\bar{g} = g^1 \cdot g^2 \cdot g^3 \cdots g^n. \tag{5}$$

Intuitively, a goal's activation encodes its current importance. Functionally, activation values are used to modulate the reward received by the robot. In particular, we assume that the robot only receives a reward upon entering a goal state for an active goal. Under this new scheme, the overall reward function R depends on both the current world state and the current activation vector:

$$R(x, \bar{g}) = \sum_{i=1}^{n} R^i(x) g^i. \tag{6}$$

We assume that the dynamics of goal activations are described by the following transition rules:
If ${g^i}_t = 1$, then

$${g^i}_{t+1} = \begin{cases} 0 & \text{if } x_t \in G^i \\ 1 & \text{otherwise.} \end{cases} \tag{7}$$

If ${g^i}_t = 0$, then

$${g^i}_{t+1} = \begin{cases} 1 & \text{with probability } p \\ 0 & \text{with probability } 1 - p. \end{cases} \tag{8}$$

Using these transition rules, a goal, once activated, persists until it is achieved. Inactive goals on the other hand, spontaneously become active according to a Bernoulli process.

Multiple goal tasks can be modeled as Markov decision processes by extending the state space to include both the state of the external world and state of the activation vector. Formally, a multiple goal task is defined by the MDP (S_m, A_m, T_m, R_m), where

- $S_m = S \times \bar{G}$, where S is the set of possible world states and $\bar{G}$ is the set of possible goal activation vectors,
- A_m is the set of actions available to the robot,
- T_m is the composite transition function on $S \times \bar{G} \times A_m$ into $S \times \bar{G}$, and
- R_m is the composite reward function given by Equation 6.

We shall use f^*_m and Q^*_m, respectively, to denote the optimal policy and optimal action-value function for a given multi-goal task. Considering the example shown in Figure 1, the states encode not only position, but also the set of goals that are currently active (i.e., whether the robot needs to get food, water, or both). The robot's need for food or water will arise according to a Bernoulli process, and once the food or water is obtained, the robot receives a reward, and the associated goal activation is set to 0. The robot then turns its efforts toward achieving its remaining active goals.

Our definition of multiple goal task is somewhat different than others found in the literature (e.g., [Singh, 1992; Mahadevan and Connell, 1991]). In [Singh, 1992] a *composite* task is defined by sequentially concatenating multiple *elemental* tasks. In a composite task, rewards are generated only when the system achieves a subtask (goal) in a prescribed order. In effect, in a composite task only one goal is active at a time. Although related, Singh's objective is substantially different from ours. Singh's objective is to develop systems that can efficiently learn long, complex sequences of behavior by first learning simpler elemental sequences, and then learning to compose them. Our objective is to study system that coordinate behavior in order to pursue multiple, independent goals in parallel. In our model, we assume active goals can be achieved in any order that is convenient. Similarly, the work described in [Mahadevan and Connell, 1991] is more closely related to that of Singh, in that Mahadevan and Connell describe a system that decomposes a single complex activity into a series of subactivities, each of which is learned by an individual module. This sequential decomposition substantially improves the learnability of such complex sequential tasks. However, it does not address the issue of coordinating behavior between parallel competing goals.

3.1 Learning Multiple Goal Tasks

Because multiple goal tasks, (as we have defined them), are MDPs, we know that Q-learning can be used to construct robots that are guaranteed to eventually learn an optimal control policy. However, the straightforward application of Q-learning, in a *monolithic* controller, leads to prohibitively slow learning. In particular, scaling from a single goal task to a n-goal task leads to an exponential growth in the state space. Instead of having to learn action-values for $|S| \cdot |A|$ state-action pairs, $|S| \cdot 2^n \cdot |A|$ action-values must be learned. In general, if goal activations are allowed to take on a range of values, say m (where value encodes priority) the size of the state space scales as m^n. Without any means of generalizing (or interpolating) action-value estimates across problem instances, the learning time can be expected to scale exponentially in the number of goals. Generalization techniques such as CMACs or neural networks are unlikely to be effective since they do not take into account how small changes in the activation vector (e.g., the activation/deactivation of a single goal) can profoundly affect the action-value. However, our decomposition approach allows agents to generalize what they have learned, since any expertise obtained relative to a particular goal that was active in previous multi-goal tasks can be applied to any other multi-goal task involving this same goal, regardless of the other active goals.

To evaluate the performance of the monolithic architecture (and later, our merging strategies), we tested it on a series of tasks on a 20x20 grid. Since the optimal policy is in general intractable to compute, and for all practical purposes is impossible to learn absolutely, we have adopted a performance criterion based on "reasonably good performance." This level of performance is achieved when the robot can consistently obtain reward at a rate equivalent to 90% of that obtained by a robot using an "optimal-greedy strategy" — that is a robot that at each point in time takes an action that is optimal with respect to achieving the nearest goal. This strategy is suboptimal with respect to the overall multiple goal task, but yields reasonably good performance. We ran experiments where the number of goals ranged from 1 to 9 in increments of 2, and measured the time needed to reach our criterion. The poor performance prediction for the monolithic agent is verified in Figure 2, which shows the time needed by a monolithic Q-learning robot (the dark line, labeled **Monolithic**) to reach criterion. The other curves are for our two simple merging strategies applied to the decomposition architecture, which we describe in the following section.

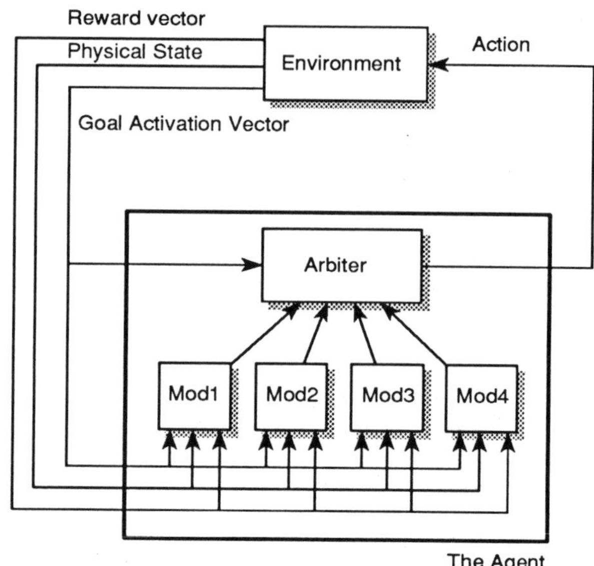

Figure 3: The modular architecture. Each module is responsible for learning to achieve a single goal. The arbiter is responsible for merging information from the individual modules in order to derive the single action performed by the robot at each time step.

4 A Decomposition Approach

4.1 The modular architecture

In the modular architecture, pictured in Figure 3, a set of independent, fixed sized Q-learning modules are used. Each module is itself an adaptive controller and is responsible for learning to achieve a single goal. A module is considered active if its associated goal is active. The state space of each module encodes only information about the external world (goal activation information is not represented). The set of states, actions, and the transition function for each module are taken to be the same, so that the modules differ in their reward function[1], and hence in their action-values and their policies.

Modules learn to achieve their respective goals in parallel. A *reward vector* is generated after each time step, where each component in the vector corresponds to the reward value of a single goal. Thus, when a goal is achieved and a reward is generated, that goal's reward is routed directly and only to the module responsible for learning that goal. Also, when a module updates its action-values it uses goal specific utility estimates derived from its local action-value function. To facilitate the propagation of utility information, each active module is updated at each time step, regardless of the reward it receives and whether or not it was responsible for generating the current action.

Since individual modules may specify conflicting actions, an arbitration module is used to mediate global control. This arbiter receives as input both the world state and the global activation vector. At each time step, it generates the single action performed by the robot. There are a variety of algorithms that can be used to implement the arbiter. We have focussed on algorithms that construct estimates for the global action-value function, Q^*_m, by merging action-values from the individual modules. A range of merging strategies can be defined by trading off solution quality for computational efficiency.

4.2 Simple Merging Strategies

The most elementary strategies combine and compare the modular action-values for the current state only, taking time that is linear in the number of goals, whereas more sophisticated strategies use a predictive model and lookahead search using more computational resource to construct better estimates. One simple merging strategy that we have explored is the *nearest neighbor* strategy, whose global policy we denote by f_{nn}. When using nearest neighbor, the arbiter chooses the action among all active modules that has the maximal action value. If all active goals have the same reward, the active goal clos-

[1] Actually, all of our algorithms only assume that there is a common set of actions defined across all modules, allowing for differences in state spaces and transition functions between modules. This might occur, for example, if there are inputs encoding features of the domain that are only relevant to particular goals.

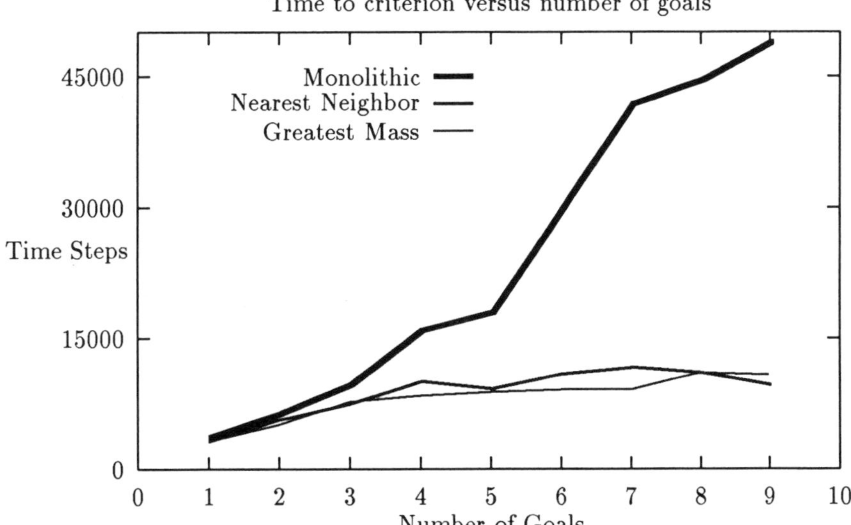

Figure 2: The time needed to reach the "reasonable-performance" criterion as a function of the number of goals in a multi-goal task for two modular systems and a monolithic system. The learning time required by the modular systems is largely independent of the number of goals.

est to the agent's current position (it's nearest neighbor) will be chosen. This is formally defined as:

$$f_{nn}(x, \bar{g}) = \arg\max_{a \in A} Q_{nn}(x, \bar{g}, a), \quad (9)$$

where

$$Q_{nn}(x, \bar{g}, a) = \max_{i \in [1 \ldots n]} \left[Q^i(x, a) \cdot g^i\right]. \quad (10)$$

and where Q^i denotes the action-value function maintained by the ith module. Returning to the situation illustrated in Figure 1, the robot must choose between going to water and going to food. Assume each module has learned an accurate action value function for its goal, and that the reward for food is 60 units and for water 50 units. Since the goals are equidistant but the food has a higher value, the policy action associated with the *get-food* module will have the highest action-value, and hence this action will be chosen by f_{nn}. Once food is obtained, the robot will move toward the water, since this is the only remaining active goal. Because each module's policy corresponds to performing a gradient ascent in the utility space, a robot using the nearest neighbor strategy will tend to complete its current goal, using the policy from a single module, before switching to another goal and a different module.

Nearest neighbor may perform poorly because it considers goals individually. In the case where a cluster of small valued goals has a higher cumulative value than a single large-valued goal, nearest neighbor will prefer the single larger valued goal over the cluster, even when the optimal strategy is to pursue the cluster.

An alternative strategy, which we call *greatest mass*, accounts for goal clustering. Using this strategy, the next action chosen by the arbiter is the one that maximizes the sum of the expected values across all modules. That is,

$$f_{gm}(x, \bar{g}) = \arg\max_{a \in A} \left[Q_{gm}(x, \bar{g}, a)\right], \quad (11)$$

where

$$Q_{gm}(x, \bar{g}, a) = \sum_{i=1}^{n} \left[Q^i(x, a) \cdot g^i\right]. \quad (12)$$

The intuition behind the greatest mass strategy is for the robot to move toward regions of the state space with the most reward. Methods analogous to it have been used in several path planning systems. In [Arbib and House, 1987], a frog's trajectory planning is modeled by letting obstacles and targets (a fly) rate different directions of travel, and chosing the direction with the highest combined rating. Similarly, [Khatib, 1986] assigns positive and negative potentials to obstacles and goals, which combine to form a potential field that the robot traverses using a gradient descent.

With greatest mass, the robot may forgo a large nearby reward in favor of multiple smaller rewards in the future. Generally, the trade off depends upon the number, magnitude, and distance to the rewards and upon the strength of the temporal discount. The less future reward is discounted, the more likely closer goals will be abandoned in favor of a distant cluster. However, for heavily discounted rewards ($\gamma \ll 1$), the greatest mass strategy, like nearest neighbor, will tend to pursue nearby goals first.

These simple strategies have the following desirable characteristics:

1. In each state, arbitration takes time linear in the number of goals.
2. Since only local action values are used for arbitration, simple strategies are appropriate in domains

where prediction is difficult (e.g., non-deterministic domains).

3. Under conditions of high temporal discount ($\gamma \ll 1$), both strategies closely approximate the optimal policy (assuming the individual goal modules have accurate action-value functions).

Figure 2 shows performance curves for two modular systems, one using the nearest neighbor merging strategy and the other using the greatest mass strategy. The figure shows that, unlike the monolithic system, the time needed to reach criterion for the modular system is largely independent of the number of goals.

In general, the modular architecture trades off optimal performance in the limit, for faster learning up front, when compared to the monolithic architecture. This follows since, even if each goal module learns to achieve its goal optimally, global performance is limited by sub-optimal arbitration. On the other hand, decomposing the system into goal-achieving modules, substantially reduces the learning time needed to reliably achieve each goal. In addition, these simple merging strategies yield good performance in domains analogous to those we have tested, and near optimal performance under high temporal discount. For applications in which satisficing behavior is sufficient, the trade off seems justified.

5 Search-based merging

There are many common tasks, for instance those involving ordered subgoals, in which the modular agent would benefit from reasoning about the future before it acted. For example, suppose that the agent of Figure 1 had the combined goal of getting both water and food back to its starting position (home), where a policy for solving each goal separately (get food home, get water home) was encoded in separate modules. The simple merging strategies would solve these goals in sequence (get food, go home, get water, go home), whereas an optimal strategy would interleave the subgoals (get food, get water, go home). An agent that could reason about what would happen if it were to perform certain sequences of action would more closely approximate optimal behavior than an agent using the simple merging strategies.

In deterministic domains – those having deterministic rather than probabilistic transitions and rewards – the agent could apply standard search techniques [Pearl, 1974] to improve its return. Under this view, the states and actions generate a tree of possible action sequences that the agent can execute, where the root of the tree is the current state, the other nodes denote accessible states, and the arcs denote actions from state to state. What this demands of the agent representationally is that it possess an explicit model of the states and transitions so that it is able to mentally generate and search this tree.

Unfortunately, such trees grow as an exponent of the number of steps into the future that the agent reasons about. Thus, exhaustive search methods are intractable for all but the most trivial problems. It is common in such cases that agents use heuristic methods for significantly reducing the size of the search tree, such as placing fixed bounds on search depth, or using domain-specific estimators to determine which arc to traverse next.

We are currently exploring a number of such search-based heuristic methods for improving the arbiter's selection strategy for choosing the next action. One such strategy is for the agent to compare the predicted results, for each of its action choices a_i, of executing in sequence a_i and those actions specified by the nearest neighbor strategy (or greatest mass) thereafter (or up to some fixed search depth bound). Using this strategy, a step toward the closest goal (or region of greatest mass) will be pursued next unless it is shown that pursuing another goal will eventually lead to a better return. Search-based strategies are described in more detail in [Whitehead *et al.*, 1993]

With all search-based methods, however, one must balance the increase in solution quality with the added cost of prediction. These costs primarily involve the need to learn, store, and maintain an explicit predictive model, and the time required to compute the search paths. Thus, not only are we evaluating increases in reward that the agent obtains from using more sophisticated search strategies, we are comparing this to the added computation time required to obtain the marginal benefits.

6 Summary

Reinforcement learning is almost certain to play a role in the future development of autonomous robotic systems. However, the prominence of that role depends upon the extent to which it can be scaled to complex robot learning tasks. In this paper, we have considered control tasks that require the robot to coordinate behavior in order to accomplish a series of independent time varying goals. We have shown how these tasks can be formulated as Markov Decision Processes by augmenting the state space description with a set of goal activation inputs. Formulating the problem in this way leads to an exponential growth in the state space size, and makes the straightforward application of Q-learning intractable. To overcome this scaling problem, we have proposed a modular architecture, which decomposes the task by goals. Each goal is associated with a control module, whose objective is to learn to achieve that goal. Learning is facilitated by reducing the state space from a single monolithic one, whose size is exponential in the number of goals, to a set of fixed sized state spaces (one per goal). Overall control in the modular architecture is the responsibility of an arbiter, who uses information encoded in the individual goal-modules as a resource for decision making. In general, computationally feasible arbitration strategies yield sub-optimal (but good) performance. Thus, in comparison with the monolithic architecture, the modular architecture trades off optimal performance in the limit for faster learning, while still achieving reasonable performance over a large class of problems.

References

[Arbib and House, 1987] Arbib, Michael A. and House, Donald H. 1987. Depth and detours:an essay on visually guided behavior. In Arbib, M. and Hanson, A., editors 1987, *Vision, Brain, and Cooperative Computation.* MIT Press, Cambridge, MA.

[Bellman, 1957] Bellman, R. E. 1957. *Dynamic Programming.* Princeton University Press, Princeton, NJ.

[Khatib, 1986] Khatib, O. 1986. Real-time obstacle avoidance for manipulators and mobile robots. *International Journal of Robotics Research* 5(1).

[Mahadevan and Connell, 1991] Mahadevan, Sridhar and Connell, Jonathan 1991. Scaling reinforcement learning to robotics by exploiting the subsumption architecture. In *Proceedings of the Eighth International Workshop on Machine Learning.*

[Pearl, 1974] Pearl, Judea 1974. *Heuristics.* Addison-Wesley.

[Singh, 1992] Singh, Satinder 1992. Transfer of learning by composing solutions of elemental sequential tasks. *Machine Learning* 8:323–339.

[Sutton, 1988] Sutton, Richard S. 1988. Learning to predict by the method of temporal differences. *Machine Learning* 3(1):9–44.

[Watkins, 1989] Watkins, Chris 1989. *Learning from delayed rewards.* Ph.D. Dissertation, Cambridge University.

[Whitehead *et al.*, 1993] Whitehead, Steven; Karlsson, Jonas; and Tenenberg, Josh 1993. Learning multiple goal behavior via task decomposition and dynamic policy merging. In Connell, Jonathan and Mahadevan, Sridhar, editors 1993, *Robot Learning.* Kluwer Academic Press.

EVOLUTION

Neural networks with motivational units

Federico Cecconi Domenico Parisi

Institute of Psychology
National Research Council
15, Viale Marx, 00137 Rome, Italy
tel.: +39.6.86894596
fax: +39.6.824737
e-mail: cecconi at irmkant.bitnet
domenico at irmkant.bitnet

Abstract

Organisms with multiple goals exibit behavior which is more autonomous with respect to the environment because the same environmental input can be responded to with different behaviors as a function of the currently active goal. We present simulations of the evolution of populations of neural networks with motivational units, i.e. units which contribute to the network's output but are not activated by environmental events. Different activation states of these units mean "hunger" or "thirst". Organisms endowed with these units evolve a behavior that seeks food when the motivational state is "hunger" and water when it is "thirst", thereby exibiting multiple goals. A final simulation shows that organisms will spontaneously evolve such motivational units to control their behavior.

1. Towards more autonomous artificial organisms

An important aspect of the autonomy of organisms with respect to the environment in which they live is revealed by the goal-directedness of their behavior. Behavior which is goal-directed is behavior that is only partially determined by environmental stimuli. The goal the organism is trying to attain is another, internal, determinant of the behavior. Consider an organism that at one particular instant is exposed to stimulus S. The response of the organism to the stimulus will be a function of S but also of the state of the organism, more specifically of the goal which is driving the organism at that time or, as we might also say, of the organism's motivational state.

The goal-directedness of behavior is a very basic and primitive property of organisms. Goal-directedness does not necessarily imply that goals are "represented" in the organism in any explicit sense (McFarland, 1989). In fact, behavior which appears to be goal-directed can be demonstrated in very simple simulated organisms living in an environment. The goal-directed behavior results from the evolution of populations of such organisms based on selective reproduction and random mutation.

Consider a simple organism whose nervous system is modeled by a feedforward neural network. The input units of the network encode sensory information from the environment about food position and the output units encode motor behavior which allows the organism to displace itself in space (Nolfi, Elman, and Parisi, 1990; Parisi, Cecconi, and Nolfi, 1990). An initial population of these organisms is generated initially by assigning to each individual network a randomly chosen weight matrix. Since what output (movement in space) is generated given a certain input (sensory information about food position) depends on the connection weights of the network and since these weights are initially assigned on a random basis, these organisms will move randomly in the environment, i.e. their behavior will look "goal-less". Through an evolutionary process of selective reproduction (based on number of food elements "eaten") and mutation we observe an increase in the average fitness of successive generations of organisms (Figure 1). In other words, organisms become increasingly capable of moving in the environment in such a manner that they approach and eat food efficiently. If we look at the trajectories (sequences of movements) generated by individual organisms belonging to the first and to the last generation, we can see how behavior has become goal-directed from being "goal-less" initially (Figure 2). One typical feature of goal-directedness can be observed in the behavior of evolved organisms: equifinality. If we put an organism belonging to one of the later generations in a new location in space, the organism will equally move toward its goal (food). Evolved organisms can reach food from any starting position.

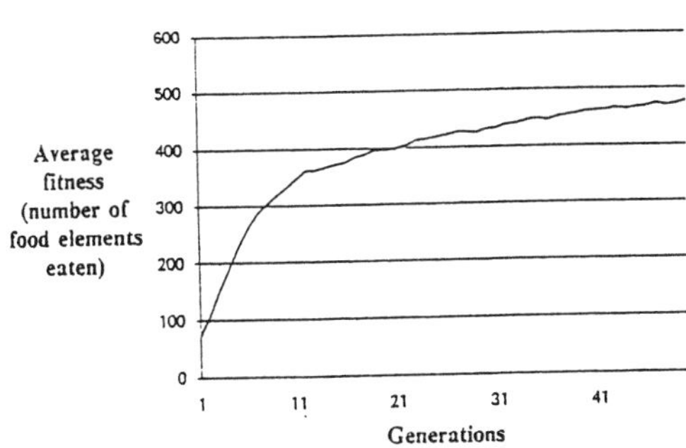

Fig. 1 Increase of food getting capacity in a population of organisms across 50 generations.

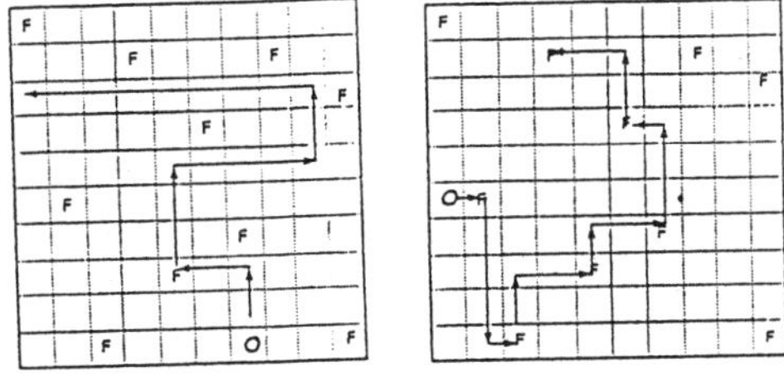

Fig. 2 Goal-less trajectory of an individual belonging to the first generation (a) and goal-directed trajectory of an individual belonging to the last generation (b).O = organism;F = food

Of course, as we said, no representation of goals must be supposed in these organisms, i.e. in their neural networks. The goal-directed behavior that is obtained is a result of a careful search by the selection and mutation process through the multidimensional space that contains all possible weight matrices. This search succeeds in identifying weight matrices (points in the multidimensional space) that generate sequences of responses to sensory input which have a goal-directed character.

One significant limitation of these simulations from the point of the autonomy of organisms is that our organisms have only one single goal: approaching food. It makes no sense to ask which goal an individual is pursuing at any given time since we already know that it must be approaching food. Furthermore, the autonomy of these organisms is limited because given a certain sensory information there is only one type of behavior which an organism can generate in response to this information: approaching the food element which is presently stimulating the organism. A more fully autonomous organism has more than a single goal or a single motivational state, so that it makes sense to try to determine which particular goal the organism is pursuing at any given time by observing the organism's behavior. (The importance of having multiple goals in order to be an 'autonomous agent' is also being recognized in classical, symbol-manipulation, artificial intelligence. See Bobrow, 1991; Covrigaru and Lindsay, 1991.) An organism with multiple goals will respond to the same sensory information from the environment in different ways as a function of the particular goal which is active in the organism in that particular moment. Consider an organism which is currently seeing both a piece of food and some water in front of itself. If the organism is hungry it will approach and eat the food. If it is thirsty it will approach and drink water. The environmental stimuli's influence on the organism becomes less strong because the effects of the stimuli on the organism's behavior are manifestly mediated by the organism's currently active goal or motivational state.

If we want to construct these more complex organisms we must endow them with motivations, that is, with information that in a certain moment they have some specific need. And the organisms must be able to respond to this motivational information by selecting goal-directed behavior which is appropriate to the particular motivation.

Our objective in the simulations to be described below is therefore to construct artificial organisms that have multiple motivational states and whose behavior is influenced by the particular motivational state which is currently driving their behavior. The basic novelty of these organisms with motivational state concerns the architecture of the neural network which simulates their nervous system. The network architecture of our basic organisms includes a layer of input units, a layer of hidden units, and a layer of output units. The input units encode sensory information about location of food, and the output units encode motor actions. The new architecture has an additional layer of "motivational" units. These units share with the input units the property of sending activation to the hidden units, thereby contributing together with the input units to determining the activation state of the hidden units and therefore the activation state of the output units (motor behavior). However, unlike the input units, the motivational units are not activated (only) by sensory information about the environment. Therefore, motivational units are, in some sense, "internal" input units. It remains to be seen what determines the activation state of these motivational units. We will describe various simulations that try to answer this question.

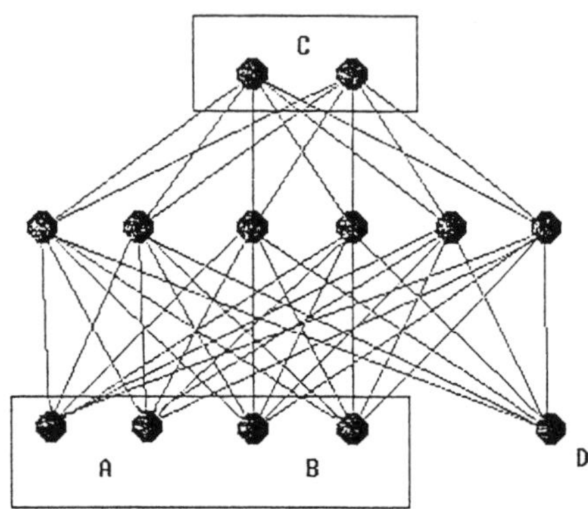

Fig. 3 Neural network with motivational unit
A: Angle and distance of nearest food element
B: Angle and distance of nearest water spot
C: Motor output
D: Motivational unit

2. Neural networks with motivational units

Our organisms live in a bi-dimensional environment that contains an approximately equal number of randomly distributed food elements and water spots. The environment is a square of 10x10 square cells 40% of which are occupied by either food or water. The organism and each food element or water spot occupy a single cell.

The nervous system of the organisms is a neural network with 4 input units, 2 output units, 9 hidden units, and a single motivational unit (see Figure 3). Two input units encode angle (direction) and distance of the nearest food element. The other two input units encode angle and distance of the nearest water spot. In both cases the angle is measured clockwise from the organism's facing direction and is mapped in the interval 0 to 1. The distance is the Euclidean distance of an object from the organism and is also mapped in the interval 0 to 1, with 1 being the maximum possible distance. At any given instant the network "sees" two objects, one food element and one water spot, although the nearest two objects may be both food elements or both water spots.

The two output units encode one of four possibile motor actions which are binarily encoded: to go one step forward in the facing direction (11), to turn 90 degrees right (01) or left (10), and to do nothing (00).

What is special about the present networks is that they include an additional "motivational" unit. This motivational unit encodes the motivational state of the organism. If the motivational unit has an activation level which is greater than .5, the organism is hungry, if the activation level of the unit is less than .5, the organism is thirsty. The motivational unit sends its activation to the hidden units; hence, from this point of view, the motivational unit functions as an additional input unit contributing to the activation state of the output units and therefore influencing the motor output of the organism. However this motivational unit is different from a standard input unit since its activation state is not externally determined by the environment. As we will see below, the motivational unit's activation state could be partially influenced by environmental stimuli. However, what is essential in the definition of a motivational unit is that its activation state is never completely determined by the environment, but it must be at least partially internally determined. In this sense, motivational units are distinct from input units. They are internal input units. We will see in a moment how the activation state of the motivational units of our networks is determined.

An initial population of 100 networks with the architecture we have described and an individually different random assignment of connection weights (between +1 and -1) lives for a total of 2,500 activation cycles or actions. Each individual network lives alone in its environment. The total lifespan of 2,500 actions is made up of 10 epochs of 50 actions each in 5 different environments. Each environment is characterized by a different random distribution of food and water. Each epoch of 50 cycles begins with a different random initial positioning of the organism in the same environment.

At the end of life each individual network is evaluated on the basis of a fitness criterion. The 20 best individuals reproduces by generating 5 offspring with the same weight matrix as their parent. However, a little less than 10% of the connection weights (6 out of

63) are mutated by adding a quantity randomly chosen between +1 and -1 to the original weight. The best individuals are selected on the basis of a criterion of fitness. The fitness formula for all the simulations described below is the following:

$$\text{fitness} = (A - B)$$
where:
$$A = (\text{food} + \text{water})$$
$$B = \frac{|\text{food} - \text{water}|}{k}$$
$$k = 2$$

In other words, to determine the fitness value of any individual organism we count number of food elements eaten plus number of water spots drunk minus the absolute difference of these two numbers divided by two. It is clear from this fitness formula that, to increase biological plausibility, we want to reward the organisms for their ability to reach food and water but we also want them to have a "balanced diet", that is, we want them to eat about the same number of food elements as they drink water spots. Therefore, organisms are penalized if the difference between food eaten and water drunk, in one direction or the other, is too large. However, we want the "balancing" component of the fitness to be less important than the ability to approach food or water. Hence, we subtract only half of the difference between food and water from their sum.

Furthermore, since the fitness of an organism is increased if the organism ingests food only when its body needs food and ingests water only when its body needs water, but not viceversa, we increase the fitness score of an organism if the organism eats when it is hungry but not when it is thirsty, and viceversa for water. In summary, the kind of behavior that should evolve given our fitness formula, is an ability to approach efficiently food elements when the organism is hungry and water spots when it is thirsty, and a capacity to ingest a roughly equivalent quantity of food and water. We will call the first component of the fitness formula "approaching" and the second component "balancing".

The 20x5 = 100 offspring of the 20 best individuals of generation 0 make up the next generation 1. The process of selective reproduction and mutation is applied to them and then to successive generations for a total of 50 generations.

3. Simulations

Simulation #1: No motivational state

A first simulation was run to determine a baseline of performance for organisms that do not have an internal motivational state. These organisms have bodily needs which alternate (need for food/need for water) but they don't know anything about them. In other words, they never feel hungry or thirsty. To this purpose the activation level of the motivational unit was set at a fixed value of .5, which implies that these organisms were unaware of the changing nature of their bodily needs. Although their body needed both food and water, and in equal proportions, as implied by the fitness criterion for reproduction, nothing in their nervous system (neural network) signaled to them that they were hungry or thirsty. The algorithm which computes the fitness value for each individual assumes that the body of an organism has a bodily need for food (or water) at the beginning of an epoch and stays in this "physiological" state for half an epoch (25 spreadings of activation). Then the body shifts to the alternative bodily need for the rest of the epoch (25 more spreadings). The obtainment of a food element (water spot) by the organism translates into a unit increase in its fitness only if the organism's body needed food (water) at that time.

In these circumstances the behavior that emerges evolutionarily is not very efficient. Figure 4 shows the changes in average fitness for a population of such organisms across 50 generations. The limited increase in fitness which is observed in this population appears to be due to two factors which are not specifically relevant for the present purposes. Through selective reproduction and mutation organisms become more sensitive to input conditions (initial random weights tend to generate stereotypical behavior which is completely insensitive to changes in input) and they evolve a limited tendency to approach sources of stimulation, whether food or water. But not all food eaten or water drunk leads to a fitness increase, and these organisms are unable to eat when their body needs food or to drink when it needs water since their nervous system is simply not informed about these bodily needs.

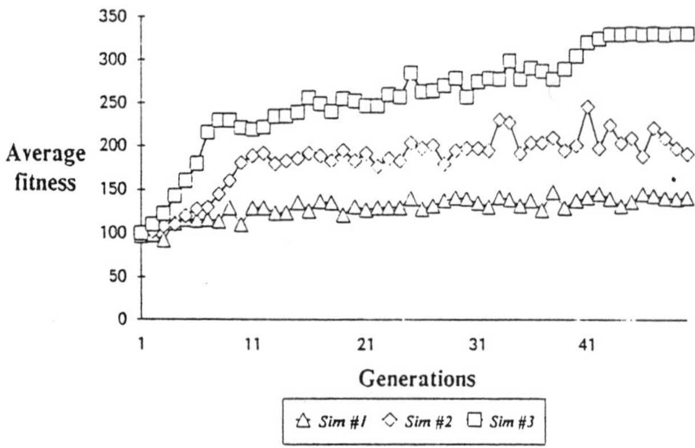

Fig. 4 Evolutionary change of average fitness in three different populations:without motivational state (Sim #1); with motivational state externally manipulated (Sim #2); with motivational state under control of behavior of organism (Sim #3).

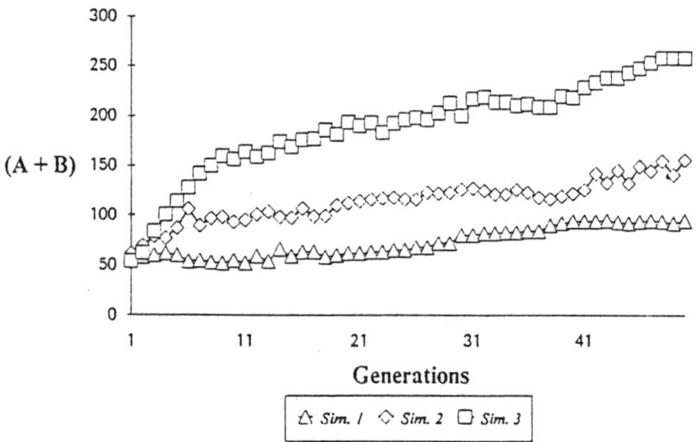

Fig. 5 Evolutionary change in the "approaching" component of fitness in the 3 simulations.

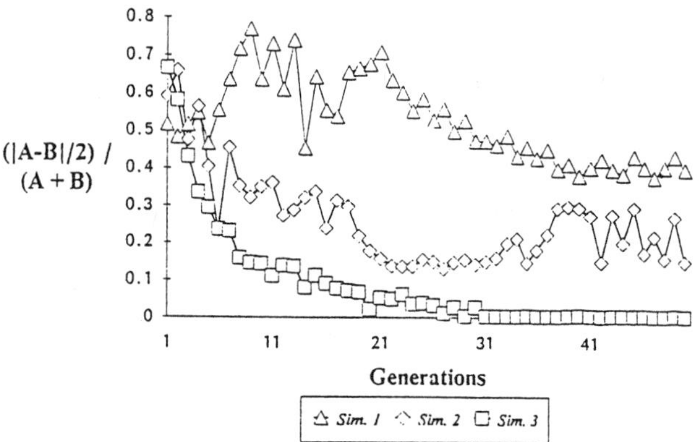

Fig. 6 Evolutionary change in the "balancing" component of fitness in the 3 simulations. Better balancing corresponds to lower values in the ordinate.

It is possible to analyze the fitness of our organisms by separating the portion of fitness which is due to the ability to approach food or water from the portion of fitness which is due to the ability to keep a balanced "diet". If we analyze the evolution of fitness in our population in this way, we observe that the slight increase in total fitness is due to the first component (see Figure 5), for the reasons we have described, whereas the capacity to ingest the same amount of food and water does not increase at all (Figure 6). For these organisms it is impossibile to keep a balanced diet since they don't know at any given time how much they have eaten or drunk.

Simulation #2: Motivational state externally manipulated

In this simulation the organisms have a motivational state that can be either hunger or thirst but this motivational state is externally manipulated and is not dependent on the organisms's own behavior. The motivational unit can take either a value of 1 or a value of 0. A value of 1 means "hunger", and a value of 0 "thirst". From the point of view of the calculation of fitness, the fitness is increased of one unit if a food element is eaten when the organism is hungry (1) but not when it is thirsty (0), and viceversa if a water spot is drunk. Furthermore, the difference between food eaten and water drunk (divided by two) is subtracted from the sum of food elements and water spots. However, the motivational states of hunger and thirst are not under the control of the organism itself. It is as if somebody from outside, e.g. a researcher, manipulates the nervous system of the organism and makes it hungry or thirsty at his/her will. More concretely, in each epoch (50 spreadings of activation) the first 25 spreadings have the motivational unit set to a value of 1 (hunger) or 0 (thirst), randomly selected, while for the remaining 25 spreadings the activation value is reversed.

The results (Figure 4) show that in these conditions the average fitness of the population increases more than when organisms are not informed of their bodily needs (Simulation #1) but it does not increase very much. For some reason if organisms are aware of their bodily needs but have no control on these needs, this hinders the attainment of a satisfactory performance level (Figure 5 and Figure 6). One possible explanation is that an externally imposed motivational state may favour evolution of the following strategy: evolve an ability to find food (but not water) and wait until the appropriate motivational state (hunger) is on, or viceversa, for water and thirst. The strategy is clearly sub-optimal and causes a lower level of fitness.

We conclude that up to this point we haven't been able to construct organisms which respond to hunger by looking for food and to thirst by looking for water. If organisms are informed about their bodily needs but have no control on these needs, a population of such organisms is unable to evolve a type of behavior which can be said to be pursuing a goal at a certain time and another goal at another time.

Simulation #3: Motivational state under the control of the behavior of the organism

In this third simulation we designed a more realistic condition in which the behavior of the organism regulates its motivational state. In other words, eating made the organism less hungry and drinking made it less thirsty. The activation level of the motivational unit becomes a function of how much the organism had been eating or drinking recently. To be more specific, at the beginning of an epoch an organism is either maximally hungry (activation level of the motivational unit = 1) or maximally thirsty (acivation level = 0). If it is hungry, the activation level of the motivational unit is decreased of a certain amount for each food element eaten until it reaches .5. It is necessary to eat 5 pieces of food to cease to be hungry. When hunger is satiated the organism becomes thirsty. The activation level of the motivational unit is changed to 0, i.e. to maximum thirst. Through drinking thirst is gradually eliminated until it ceases (at .5) and the organism becomes hungry again, restarting the cycle. Of course, in contrast to Simulation #2, in which hunger and thirst were externally manipulated and they changed in a fixed manner independently of the organism's behavior, now the organism can remain in a given motivational state for a variable time length. However, an evolutionarily adaptive strategy (greater reproductive success) is dependent on efficient eating and drinking at the right time, i.e. it is based on an ability to reach food and water in as little time as possible and on an appropriate sensitivity to the organism's current motivational state.

Organisms that have motivational units which inform them of their changing bodily needs and that can control these bodily needs with their behavior, evolve a type of behavior which is more adapted to the fitness criterion and which appears to be pursuing different goals in different circumstances. Figure 4 shows the evolutionary increase in average fitness for this population, which clearly surpasses that of our previous populations. Furthermore, this increase appears clearly to be due to both components of fitness: approaching and balancing. In other words, these organisms have developed not only an ability to approach food or water efficiently but also an ability to so regulate their behavior that approximately equal amounts of food and water are ingested during their life.

The reason for this success becomes clear if one observes the actual behavior of these organisms. While the organisms of the first generation are equally likely to step on a food element or on a water spot whether they are hungry or thirsty, the behavior of the evolved organisms of the last generation clearly reflects their motivational state. When they are hungry, they look for food and ignore water, while when they are thirsty they look for water and ignore food. Figure 7 shows the number of food elements and of water spots reached by the first generation of organisms when they were hungry and when they were thirsty, respectively. There are no significant differences between these numbers. There is no preference for food when the animal is hungry or for water when it is thirsty. Figure 8 presents the same results for the organisms of the last generation. As it is clear, the evolved organisms seek and find food when they are hungry, and they seek and find water when they are thirsty.

More direct evidence on the nature of the behavior that we have succeeded in creating is presented in Figure 9. The figure shows two movement trajectories (50 successive actions) by an organism belonging to the last generation when the organism is hungry and, respectively, thirsty. When hungry the organism is attracted by food elements and it ignores water although its trajectory passes nearby water spots. The opposite is true when the organism is thirsty. It goes to water spots and ignores food.

Simulation #4: Evolution of motivation

If an organism can increase its reproductive success through behavior which satisfies its current bodily needs, it is clearly useful for the organism to evolve motivational units that at any given time can signal to the organism's nervous system what the organism's bodily needs are. In this way the nervous system can select motor behavior, in response to sensory information, which is appropriate to the known motivational state and therefore to the bodily needs. The preceding simulations have in fact shown that if an organism's fitness depends on the organism's capacity to satisfy its currently active bodily needs (cf. our fitness formula) it is better for the organism to have motivational units than not to have them (Simulation #1 vs. Simulation #2). Furthermore, it is better to have the activation state of these units dependent on the organism's behavior rather than externally imposed (Simulation #2 vs. Simulation #3).

The transition from Simulation #1 through Simulation #2 to Simulation #3 can be viewed as reflecting an evolutionary sequence. If there is a population of organisms in which the possession of efficient motivational units is a trait which (a) varies among individuals, (b) is inherited, and (c) is subject to mutation, then we can expect such population to evolve efficient motivational units. In other words, if individuals are selected for reproduction on the basis of their ability to obtain food when hungry and water when thirsty, and of their capacity to eat and drink in equivalent quantities, individuals which do not have motivational units or have inefficient motivational units will be gradually eliminated from the population, and the whole population will be progressively colonized by individuals with an efficient motivational system and an ability to utilize it.

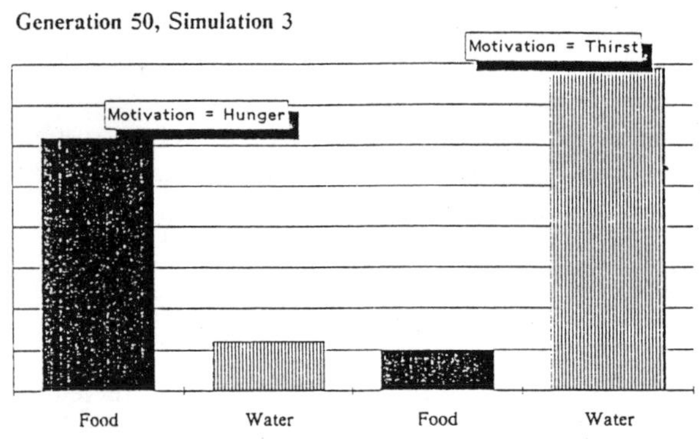

Fig. 8 Average quantity of food and water reached when the motivational stateis hunger and when it is thirst in the last generation.

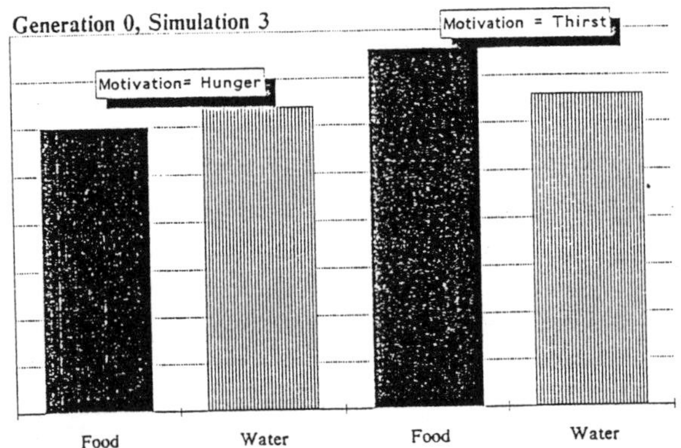

Fig. 7 Average quantity of food and water reached when the motivational stateis hunger and when it is thirst in the first generation.

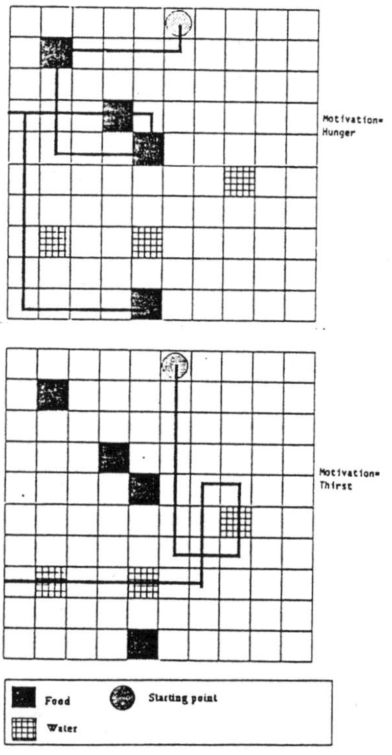

Fig 9 Two trajectories, in the same environment, of an organism belonging to the last generation when the organism is hungry and thirsty, respectively.

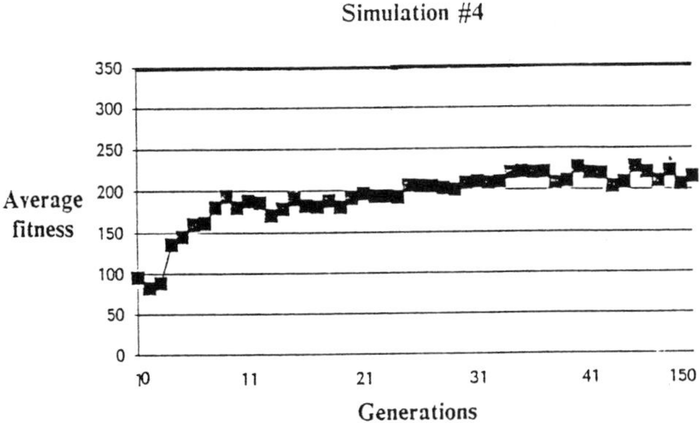

Fig. 10 Evolutionary change of average fitness in a population with evolving motivational units.

To demonstrate this point we have run a further simulation (Simulation #4) in which all networks have a functioning motivational unit which signals to the organism whether the motivational state is hunger or thirst. Furthermore, the activation level of this unit is influenced by the behavior of the organism in that eating reduces hunger and drinking thirst. Hence, from this point of view the organisms of Simulation #4 are identical to those of Simulation #3. The only difference is that the activation level of the motivational unit at any given time has some amount of random noise added to it and this noise varies from individual to individual. In other words, the information channel from the body (bodily needs) to the nervous system can be more or less efficient as a function of the particular individual considered. In this simulation the organisms belonging to the first generation are assigned a noise parameter which varies from individual to individual with a uniform distribution. This noise parameter is part of the genotype of the individual, which means that it is inherited by the offspring of the individual (if the individual reproduces) and it is subject to mutation. In other words, the initial generation includes both individuals which have a more efficient motivational system (i.e. motivational units that inform faithfully the nervous system of the needs of the body - small noise) and individuals with a less efficient motivational system (larger noise).

We have run a simulation of the evolution of this type of population using the same general parameters of the other simulations: 100 individuals per generation, the 20 best individuals reproduce, etc. Individuals are selected for their capacity to eat and drink efficiently and in a balanced way. However, another trait of an individual which may indirectly influence the individual's reproductive chances is the amount of noise in its motivational system. There are individuals with no noise and individuals with an increasing amount of noise. Noise is a positive or negative number randomly selected within a given range that is added to the current activity value of the individual's motivational unit. The range varies from zero to .4. A particular range, e.g. +.25 to -.25, characterizes each individual. If the individual is one of the 20 reproducing individuals, its range is slightly mutated when copied into the range of its offspring. The objective of the simulation was to determine whether the direction of evolution of the population was towards individuals with an efficient motivational system, i.e. with little noise disturbing the motivational units' activation level.

The results show that this is the case. The evolutionary increase in fitness for this population is presented in Figure 10. It was necessary to run 150 generations instead of the 50 generations of the preceding simulations to reach comparable results. This appears to be due to the necessity for this population to free itself of the initial excessive noise in the organisms' motivational system. But the more interesting result is that if organisms are left free to evolve efficient motivational systems, they will evolve them. Figure 11 shows how average noise in the organisms' motivational systems decreases across generations. Evolved organisms have developed motivational systems that efficiently inform their nervous systems of current bodily needs. At the same time, nervous systems evolve a capacity to use this information to generate behavior which increases reproductive success. It is also interesting to observe that the average noise affecting the motivational system of the individuals of the last generations is very low but it is not zero. This is agreement with many results reported in the literature showing that an appropriate level of noise is an asset, not a liability, for the optimal functioning of neural networks (Hanson, 1991; Nolfi,Pedone, and Parisi, 1991).

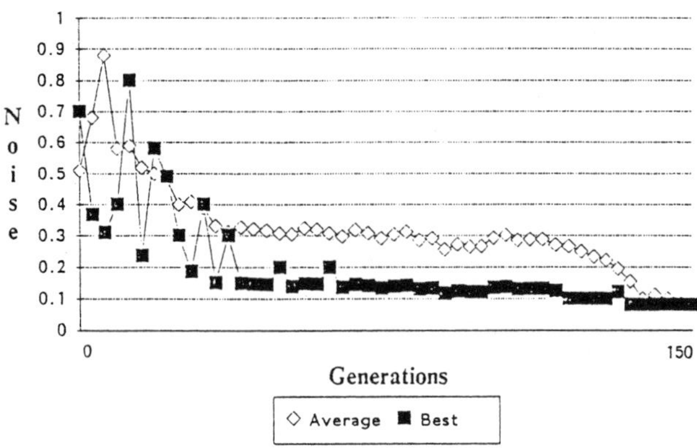

Fig. 11 Decreasing noise on motivational unit for average and best individual across 150 generations.

4. Discussion

If organisms have multiple bodily needs it is useful for them to evolve motivational units which contribute to determining the organisms' behavior together with sensory information from the environment. The activation level of these motivational units represents the organisms' motivational state. The motivational state informs the nervous system of current bodily needs so that the nervous system can generate behavior which is appropriate to these needs, thereby increasing the organism's probability of leaving offspring. However, motivational units turn out to be really useful if behavior can change bodily needs and therefore the organism can control its bodily needs with its behavior. This creates a circular causal relation between behavior and bodily needs (bodily needs influence behavior through the motivational system and behavior influences bodily needs) which makes an organism more autonomous with respect to the environment and more capable to reach a dynamic equilibrium with the environment.

This greater autonomy of organisms with motivational units is apparent in their behavior. The current state of the external environment, as reflected in the sensory input to the organisms' nervous system (neural network), is not the only determinant of the organisms' behavior. If an individual is currently sensing a food element and a water spot in two different locations in the environment, the resulting behavior is not uniquely determined by such sensory information but it depends on the organism's current internal state, i.e. on the activation level of the organism's motivational units (motivational state). This activation level in turn is a function of the current bodily needs of the organism, although it can additionally be sensitive to sensory information (cf. the notion of "incentive" in the literature on motivation; see, e.g., Toates, 1986). For example, the seeing of food (=incentive) can activate hunger (motivational state), although motivational states appear to be always more or less dependent on bodily needs.

The behavior of organisms with motivational units appears to be more goal-directed than the behavior of organisms without motivational units. As a matter of fact, only with the former organisms it is appropriate and meaningful to ask which goal is currently being pursued by a particular organism since these organisms can pursue different goals at different times. And determining which particular goal an organism is pursuing at any given time is the only way to make sense of the behavior of these organisms. Considering the stimuli currently impinging on the organism would not be enough.

The cause of a motivational state (level of activation of motivational units) is internal but is not in the nervous system of the organism. The body can be viewed as a distinct system which, as a function of the organism's behaviors (eating and drinking) which lead to changes in the body, stimulates the nervous system through internal receptors - our motivational units. In real animals internal receptors are placed in the stomach and in the blood for hunger and in the mouth and elsewhere for thirst (Toates, 1986). It remains an open question whether motivational systems can be purely neural, i.e. if the nervous system can generate motivational states by itself without the intervention of the body. It might be that these purely neural motivations appear in more sophisticated animals while simpler animals are restricted to physiological motivations like hunger, thirst, fear, and physical pain. The distinction may be related to whether a motivation is sensorily felt or not. Hunger and thirst are states that are sensorily felt and this may involve the existence of internal receptors as channels from the body to the nervous system. On the other hand, purely neural motivations such as many human motivations may influence behavior as physiological motivations do but, unlike physiological motivations, they are not sensorily felt because they do not involve internal body receptors.

Systems with evolved motivational states of the type we have described in this paper can have multiple goals and can react to the environment in more autonomous ways. One and the same environmental stimulus can elicit different responses from the system as a function of the currently active goals. Furthemore, the system can control with its behavior its currently active goals. Future research should be directed to simulation of more complex systems with motivational states, for example systems with many simultaneously active goals, with potential conflict, coordination, and decision among these goals, and systems which are capable to delay action required to satisfy a currently active goal.

References

Bobrow, D.G. Dimensions of interaction. AI Magazine, 1991, Fall 1991, pp. 64-80.

Covrigaru, A.A. and Lindsay, R.K. Deterministic autonomous systems. AI Magazine, Fall 1991, pp.110-117.

Hanson,S.J. A stochastic version of the delta rule. In Forest, S. (Ed.) Emergent computation. Cambridge, MIT Press, 1991.

McFarland. In Montefiore, A. and Noble, D. (Eds.) Goals, no-goals, and own goals. London, Unwin Hyman, 1989.

Nolfi, S., Elman, J.L., and Parisi, D. Learning and evolution in neural networks. Technical Report, Center for Research in Language, University of California, San Diego, 1990.

Nolfi, S., Parisi, D., Pedone R. How noise helps generalization in feedforward networks. In E. Caianiello (Ed), Singapore, World Scientific, in press.

Parisi, D., Cecconi, F. and Nolfi, S. ECONETS: neural networks that live in an environment. Network, 1990, 1, pp.

Toates, F. Motivational systems. Cambridge, Cambridge University Press, 1986.

Evolutionary Learning of Predatory Behaviors Based on Structured Classifiers

Hitoshi IBA[1] **Hugo de GARIS**[2] **Tetsuya HIGUCHI**[2]
1)Machine Inference Section, 2)Computational Models Section,
Electrotechnical Laboratory
1-1-4 Umezono, Tsukuba-city, Ibaraki, 305, Japan
{iba,degaris,higuchi}@etl.go.jp, +81-298-58-5918

Abstract

This paper introduces an adaptive learning model of foraging behavior. Foraging is essential for animals confronted with a choice of food types in the sense that reproductive success depends heavily upon the efficiency of their predatory behavior. Foraging can be regarded as an optimization problem, in which certain mathematical biological formulae can be analyzed in a manner similar to techniques taken from optimal control theory or game theory. Our predatory learning model is based on an extended version of classifier systems. Simulations of our model produce results which correspond with the predictions of a well-known foraging theory. The extension of our model to give it more realistic biological properties is then discussed.

1 Introduction

Animals do not necessarily eat everything which is nutritious for them. We observe that they eat a restricted range of kinds of foods when they are in ample supply, yet eat a wider range of foods when these food is scarce. Searching for food, i.e. foraging, is vital to the survival of animals, which spend most of their day in this pursuit. If an animal has the ability to gather food efficiently in a limited time, it is able to grow faster, and to store surplus food in the form of fat. Its chances of survival and reproduction are then improved. Changing preferences depending upon the richness of the food supply can be regarded as an efficient strategy.

It is a common biological principle that organisms are designed so as to behave efficiently. Recently, researchers in the field of "evolutionary ecology" have regarded biological behaviors as adaptive strategies, with a view to maximizing lifetime reproductive success. They have made mathematical models which make use of techniques taken from optimal control theories, statistical decision theories or game theories, e.g.[Iwasa90].

This paper introduces an adaptive learning model of optimal foraging behavior for animals confronted with a varieties of food types. The learning mechanism is based on an extended version of classifier systems, "Structured Classifiers". The effectiveness of this learning model is shown by the fact that its simulated behavior agrees with predictions from mathematical biology. More biologically realistic extensions to the model are also discussed, e.g. non uniform food supplies and internal energy status.

2 Foraging as optimization

Foraging can be considered as a kind of adaptive strategy, in which the optimal predatory behavior can be established through evolution [Krebs87]. Following the formulation of [Iwasa81], this section describes an optimization model of foraging, i.e. searching for a specific type of food when confronted with an ample choice of different foods.

Consider n different kinds of food $(f_1, \cdots, f_n)$. The predators of our model can choose to eat one kind or several kinds of food, from amongst the range of foods they are confronted with, by deciding whether they eat whatever they hit upon or not. We assume the following characteristics for each kind of food.

Kind of food	f_i
frequency	λ_i
energy	g_i
digestion cost	h_i

Table 1 Food characteristics

In our model the predators are expected to come across food f_i at a frequency of λ_i times for a unit time clock. If they eat this kind of food f_i, they gain g_i energy units, while it takes h_i units of time to eat (or digest) it before searching for further food. Our predators eat i-th food f_i with the probability of p_i when they meet with it. The average "predatory velocity" (i.e. the average energy absorption rate), which depends on $(p_1, \cdots, p_n)$, can be shown to be:-

$$r(p_1, \cdots, p_n) = \frac{\frac{\sum_i \lambda_i p_i g_i}{\sum_i \lambda_i}}{\frac{1}{\sum_i \lambda_i} + \frac{\sum_i \lambda_i p_i h_i}{\sum_i \lambda_i}} \qquad (1)$$

Where the first term in the denominator is the expected waiting time to come across any kind of food, because $\sum_i \lambda_i$ is equal to the probability of an encounter with any food at a unit time. The numerator represents the averaged energy gain and the second term in the denominator is the average digestion time cost, since $\frac{\lambda_i}{\sum_i \lambda_i}$ is the probability that the found food is the i-th kind. In order to maximize the predatory velocity r, we differentiate the above equation:-

$$\frac{\partial r}{\partial p_k} = \{\frac{\lambda_k h_k}{1+\sum_i \lambda_i h_i p_i}\}\{\frac{g_k}{h_k} - r\} \qquad (2)$$

Since $0 \leq p_i \leq 1$ $(i = 1, \cdots, n)$, it follows that the animal can increase its predatory velocity by eating food f_k whose $\frac{g_k}{h_k} > r$ with probability $p_k = 1$. Foods with $\frac{g_k}{h_k} < r$ should be discarded. Thus if n kinds of food are ordered according to $\frac{g_i}{h_i}$ (energy gain over digestion cost) with the average predatory velocity r^* as follows:-

$$\frac{g_1}{h_1} > \frac{g_2}{h_2} > \cdots > \frac{g_k}{h_k} > r^* > \frac{g_{k+1}}{h_{k+1}} > \cdots \frac{g_n}{h_n}, \qquad (3)$$

then the k greatest kinds of food $(i = 1, \cdots, k)$ are eaten and the others are ignored. Note that r^* is independent of the quantitative information of the ignored foods. In other words, whether the (j+1)-th food is used or ignored is decided by $\frac{g_{j+1}}{h_{j+1}}$ and j kinds of preferred food quantities $(\lambda_1, \cdots, \lambda_j)$, but not by λ_{j+1} itself. This foraging optimization model is the basis of various predatory behaviors of wild animals, which have been observed outdoors and tested indoors statistically [Krebs87]. This model relies on the evolutionary assumption that efficient foraging behavior improves an animal's reproductive success, i.e. its fitness.

3 Structured Classifier Systems

The learning mechanism of our model is based on an extended version of Classifier System [Smith80]. This section describes the fundamental ideas of "Structured Classifiers".

3.1 Structured Representation for Genetic Algorithms

[Koza90] introduced the hierarchical GA (HGA) approach and proposed genetic programming paradigm, which tree-like expressions are manipulated as gene

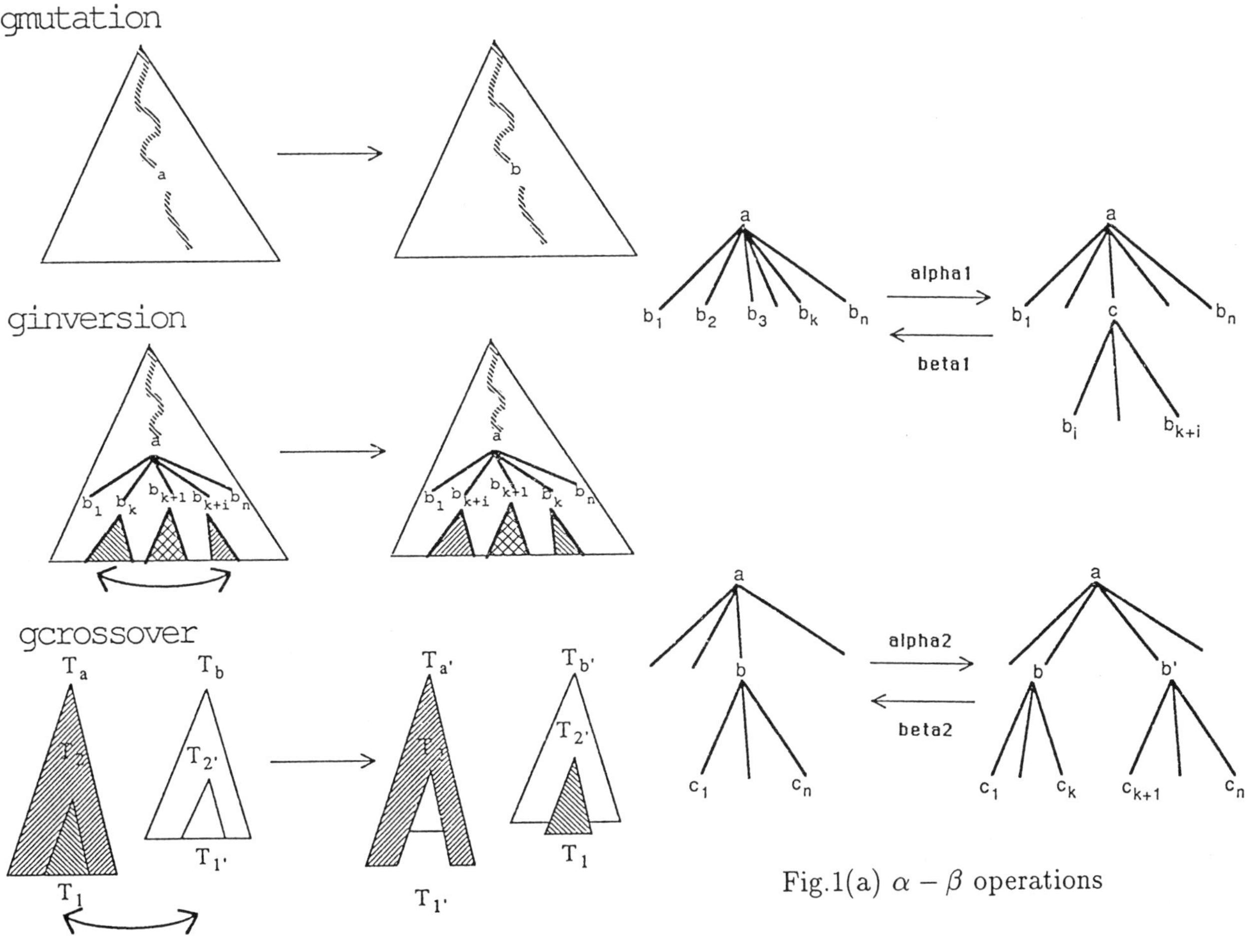

Fig.1(b) GA operators on trees

Fig.1(a) $\alpha - \beta$ operations

codes for recombination. We extend this method in order to efficiently realize graph-theoretical manipulations. The following graph-theoretic manipulations ($\alpha - \beta$ operations, [Lu78]) are introduced as primitive operators (Fig.1(a)).

1. α_1 father-son splitting
2. β_1 father-son merging
3. α_2 brother-brother splitting
4. β_2 brother-brother merging

We further realize the following tree-manipulations (G-operations) as recombination methods (Fig.1(b)).

5. **Gmutation** changing the node label
6. **Ginversion** reordering siblings
7. **Gcrossover** swapping subtrees

These operations are natural extensions of string-based GA operators. For example, the Gmutation works by avoiding the local-extrema trap, just as does the mutation operator in string-based GAs. As can be seen in later experiments, G-operators play a role in the speed-up of convergence times. This is partly because G-operations are constructed of $\alpha - \beta$ operations as shown below.

The distance between trees T_1 and T_2 is defined to be:-

$$d(T_1, T_2) := min\{\#(M) \mid M \in \{\alpha_1, \alpha_2, \beta_1, \beta_2\}^* \wedge M(T_1) = T_2\}, \quad (4)$$

where $\#(M)$ means the length of sequence of M. $M(T)$ is the tree transformed by the operations of M. Thus the distance of T_1 and T_2 is the minimum length of sequences of $\alpha - \beta$ operators, which transform T_1 into T_2. Obviously this definition satisfies the axiom of distance (i.e. $d(T,T) = 0$, $d(T_1,T_2) = d(T_2,T_1)$, $d(T_1,T_2) + d(T_2,T_3) \geq d(T_1,T_3)$). This tree distance can be derived with complexity of $O(n^3)$ and where n is the number of tree nodes [Lu89]. The effect of G-operations can be described in terms of this tree distance. For instance, in the case of Gcrossover, the following relations are satisfied.

$$d(T_a, T_a') = d(T_b, T_b') = d(T_1, T_1') \quad (5)$$

$$d(T_a, T_b') = d(T_b, T_a') = d(T_2, T_2'), \quad (6)$$

where T_a and T_b are the parents for the Gcrossover, and T_a' and T_b' are their children. Fig.1(b) shows the subtrees T_1, T_1', T_2 and T_2' as operands of the Gcrossover operator. Thus, G-operations are expected to work as useful subroutines composed of $\alpha - \beta$ operations.

Since the genetic algorithms for structured representations are straightforward, we omit the details. In order to confirm our approach, we conducted several experiments by solving some problems in graph theory. There are many invariants known for graphical features, such as Ramsey numbers, independent numbers and connectedness (See [von Laszewski91] for details of graph theory). We attempted to construct a desired graph, given a set of specified invariants [Iba92b]. Some of theses problems are known to be difficult and remain unsolved. Moreover, we further experimented in higher-level knowledge acquisition, such as functional synthesis or rule-based plan generations. The results of these experiments were encouraging and we felt the effectiveness of structured representations has been confirmed.

3.2 Structured Classifiers

To simulate our foraging model, we used Classifier Systems [Smith80]. We chose to use Pitt approach, in which a single chromosome contains a set of rules. Our representation was based on "Structured Classifiers". We have several reasons for this choice.

1. In the Pitt approach, the competition of matched rules is difficult to solve. LS-1, for instance, uses a multiple-firing method, which may cause an explosion of working memories [Smith80]. As described later, by using a structured representation, we can avoid this problem by traversing trees.
2. A reinforcement mechanism for each rule is not required with a structured approach.
3. By pruning unnecessary or useless rule nodes, efficiency is improved for learning with tree structures.
4. Genetic operations work well for substructures of rules since structured representations express useful rule clusters as subtrees.

An example of our structured classifier is as follows:-

```
(NODE3  (RULE1)
        (NODE2  (RULE2)
                (NODE2  (RULE3)   (RULE4)))
        (NODE2  (RULE5)   (RULE6)))
```

We have two types of nodes, terminal nodes (T) and non-terminal (functional) nodes (F).

$$F = \{NODE_1, NODE_2, \cdots, NODE_n\} \quad (7)$$

Where $NODE_i$ takes i arguments to bind i subtrees (See Fig.2).

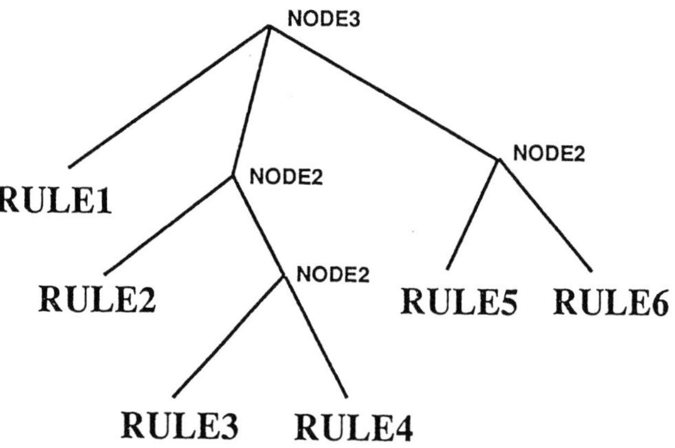

Fig.2 Structured classifier

Terminal nodes are classifiers. For example,

RULE1	#10#	:	$action_1$
RULE2	#11#	:	$action_2$
RULE3	#1#1	:	$action_3$
RULE4	1###	:	$action_4$
RULE5	#0#0	:	$action_5$
RULE6	#1#1	:	$action_6$

The competition of matched rules for a given message is solved by breadth first search. For instance, suppose 0111 is given as a message. Although both RULE2 and RULE6 are matched, RULE2 is fired because it is met first by the breadth-first search of the tree (Fig.2).

We have three types of genetic operators.

1. **Gcrossover**
   Replacing subtrees (see Fig.1(b)).
2. **Gmutation**
   Pick up a node N from a parent tree.
   (a) If N is terminal, change N:-
      i. into another terminal node.
      ii. into a non-terminal node to make a new subtree.
   (b) If N is non-terminal, change N:-
      i. into a terminal node and remove the underlying subtree.
      ii. into another non-terminal node to make a new subtree.
3. **Rmutation**
   Change one bit of the conditional part of a terminal classifier.

For instance, the Rmutation of RULE1 above may result in

RULE1' #00# : $action_1$

We also have several pruning heuristics for efficient evolutionary learning which help prevent structured classifiers from growing too large, e.g.

1. Prune terminal nodes whose classifiers rarely match messages.
2. Prune duplicated terminal nodes, etc.

4 Experimental Results

We undertook some experiment in the evolution of predatory behavior; i.e. the evolution of an optimal choice of foraging for food. In these simulations, we used 5 kinds of foods, as shown:-

Kind of food	1	2	3	4	5
energy g_i	5	3	4	2	1
digestion cost h_i	1	1	2	2	2

Table 2 Food example

Since $\frac{g_1}{h_1} > \frac{g_2}{h_2} > \cdots > \frac{f_5}{f_5}$, the optimal order in food choice is $f_1 > f_2 > \cdots > f_5$ from (3). To estimate λ_i (frequency of food f_i), we introduce the concepts of a food distance, e.g. distance of 1, 2, 3. We assume that it takes d_i units of time to reach the food of distance d_i. Since any distance value is randomly taken from 1,2 and 3, the averaged distance is 2. Thus $\lambda_i = \frac{1}{2}$ for all i.

Our classifier used here is as follows:-

Classifier	0 # #	# # #	# # 0	0 1 #	1 # #	: 3
distance	1 2 3	1 2 3	1 2 3	1 2 3	1 2 3	
food	f_1	f_2	f_3	f_4	f_5	

The condition part is a 15-length string (3 kinds of distance values × 5 kinds of food), where 0 is the non-existence of the food, 1 is existence, and # is a wild card. The action part is an integer which indicates the kind of food to eat.

As discussed in the previous section, the chromosome is a tree whose terminal nodes are classifiers. The fitness for each tree is calculated by generating a sequence of random inputs and computing cumulative statistics that estimate the ratio of $\frac{g}{h}$ of energy gained to total cost. More formally, assuming that we use *lfood* kinds of food and that their distance values range from 1 to *ldist*, the fitness of the chromosome (i.e. rule set) is defined according to the following algorithms:-

Step1 $i := 1.\ h := 0.\ g := 0.$ (for a rule set value) $h^* := 0.\ g^* := 0.$ (for an pseudo-optimal value)

Step2 Generate a message $M = m_1 \cdots m_l$ ($l = lfood \times ldist$, $m_i \in \{1, 0\}$). If there are no 1's in $\{m_i\}$ then $h^* := h^* + penalty$. Else let $p := \min_j\{j | m_j = 1\}$, $h^* := h^* + mod(p, ldist) + h_{rem(p,ldist)}$ and $g^* := g^* + g_{rem(p,ldist)}$.

Step3 Find a terminal node C, (a classifier) whose condition part matches M by breadth-first search. If there is no matched classifier, then $h := h + penalty$ and go to STEP6.

Step4 If the action part of C is k, get the k-th food description of the message M; i.e. $m_{(k-1)\times ldist+1} m_{(k-1)\times ldist+2} \cdots m_{(k-1)\times ldist+ldist}$. Let this part be $d_1 d_2 \cdots d_{ldist}$.

Step5 If there is a 1 in $\{d_i\}$ then $h := h + \min_j\{j | d_j = 1\} + h_k$ and $g := g + g_k$.

Step6 $i := i + 1$.

Step7 If $i <$ **cycle − step** then go to STEP2.

Step8 Return $\frac{g}{h} / \frac{g^*}{h^*}$ as fitness.

Where $rem(x, y)$ and $div(x, y)$ represent the remainder and the quotient of x divided by y respectively. The above routine calculates an estimation of g (i.e. the energy gained) and h (the total time cost) for **cycle − step** messages randomly generated. Note that $\frac{g^*}{h^*}$ is pseudo-optimal value according to (3). "Pseudo" means that fitness 1.0 is approached in the case of the optimal predatory behavior (not exactly 1.0 because of the randomized distance distribution). The penalty should be paid for digestion cost in case of non-existence of designated food or no matching rules (Step2, Step3).

We use the following parameters for the simulation. As shown in the function symbols, each tree node is restricted to having at most 3 daughter nodes for the simplicity of experiments.

Population size	60
Gcrossover prob.	0.6000
Gmutation prob.	0.0333
Rmutation prob.	0.0020
function symbols	(NODE1 NODE2 NODE3)
No. of food	5
Max. distance	3
step / cycle	500

Table 3 Parameters

Fig.3 shows the result of the experiment. As can be seen, the best fitness approaches 1.0 (i.e. optimal behavior) over the generations. One acquired rule set (at generation 1003) is as follows:-

```
(NODE2
 (NODE2
  (RULE3468)
  (NODE2 (RULE3473) (RULE3590)))
   (NODE3
    (RULE2753)
    (NODE2
     (RULE3357)
     (NODE2
      (RULE3589)
      (NODE2
       (NODE2
        (RULE3654)
        (NODE2
         (RULE3633)
         (NODE3
          (NODE3
           (RULE3593)
           (NODE2
            (RULE3585)
            (RULE3051))
           (RULE2989))
          (RULE3616)
          (RULE3503))))
       (NODE2
        (NODE2
         (NODE3
          (NODE2
           (RULE3306)
           (NODE2
            (RULE3634)
            (NODE2
             (RULE3447)
             (NODE2
              (RULE3515)
              (RULE3665)))))
          (RULE3647)
          (RULE3622))
         (RULE3608))
        (RULE3344)))))
  (NODE3
   (NODE2
    (RULE3572)
    (NODE2 (RULE3338) (RULE2330)))
   (RULE3499)
   (RULE3284))))
```

name	cond.		act.	#*match*
*RULE*3665	#0 1 0 #####0 0 ##1 #	:	1	5
*RULE*3654	#0 0 ####0 #0 #0 ##1	:	2	26
*RULE*3647	#0 ##0 #1 #0 #0 ####	:	3	56
*RULE*3634	0 #1 #####0 ####0 #	:	2	80
*RULE*3633	####0 0 0 ########	:	1	135
*RULE*3622	#1 1 ###########0	:	1	10
*RULE*3616	##1 #########0 #0	:	1	54
*RULE*3608	##0 ##0 0 ########	:	1	136
*RULE*3593	######0 #0 1 #0 ###	:	1	36
*RULE*3590	#0 #0 0 #1 #######0	:	3	53
*RULE*3589	##1 ##1 ###0 ####0	:	1	7
*RULE*3585	####1 0 #######0 0	:	1	65
*RULE*3572	1 #####0 #0 #####0	:	1	24
*RULE*3515	0 #####0 #1 1 #0 ###	:	1	10
*RULE*3503	#0 ######0 ######	:	1	447
*RULE*3499	#0 ######0 #####0	:	1	275
*RULE*3473	####0 0 0 ########	:	1	1418
*RULE*3468	#0 ##0 #1 ###0 ####	:	3	856
*RULE*3447	#0 ####0 #0 0 #####	:	1	49
*RULE*3357	###########0 #0 1	:	2	169
*RULE*3344	0 ##0 ##########0	:	1	211
*RULE*3338	#0 ##0 #########0	:	1	186
*RULE*3308	#0 ##0 ###0 #####1	:	2	0
*RULE*3306	####1 ########0 0	:	1	311
*RULE*3284	############0 #0	:	1	1758
*RULE*3051	#0 ###0 0 ##0 #####	:	1	57
*RULE*2989	##########0 ###0	:	1	386
*RULE*2753	##0 ####0 #0 #0 ###	:	2	521
*RULE*2330	##0 0 0 ######0 ###	:	2	335

The fitness of this rule is about 1.0. Notice that two kinds of effective classifiers are included in the above tree.

(1) Choose the appropriate existent food, i.e. never take the non-existent food choice. For instance, $RULE3572, RULE3622$.

(2) Choose the better choice among two or more kinds of food, e.g. $RULE3665, RULE3589$.

Since most of the actions in the above classifiers designate either food f_1 or f_2, the simulation is successful in learning the optimal food choice based on equation (3).

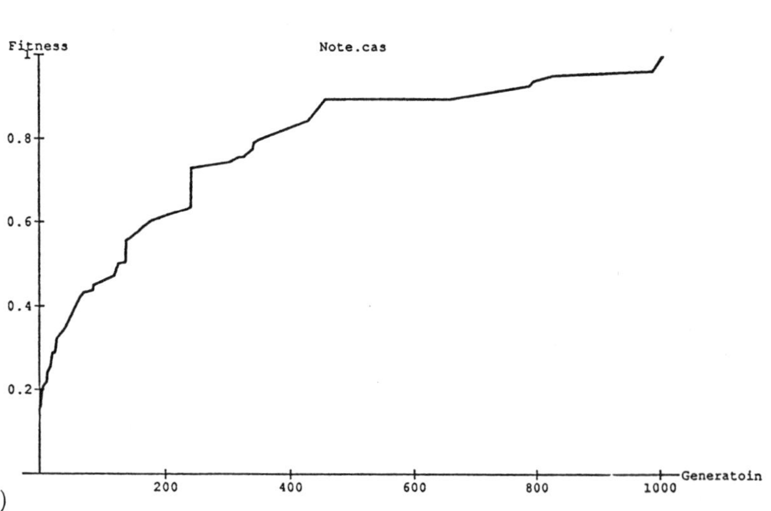

Fig.3 Fitness changes with generations

In the second experiment, we tested the influence of food quantities, i.e. λ_i. In this simulation, learning environments are extended in the following way:-

(1) *Multiple-food choice*
In order to designate multiple kinds of food, *lfood* bits are used for the action part. For instance, the classifier
001##########0## : 01001
shows the choice of both f_2 and f_5.

(2) *Message generation according to λ_i distribution*
We used uniform distribution in the previous experiment and $\lambda_i = \frac{1}{2}$. In order to generate differences between the λ_i's, we used a (non-uniform) distribution for setting the distance of food in the message generations. For instance, if we use a distribution in which $p(d_1 = 1) = \frac{1}{4}$, $p(d_2 = 2) = \frac{1}{4}$, $p(d_3 = 3) = \frac{1}{2}$, then the new $\lambda'_i = 1/\{\frac{1}{4} \times 1 + \frac{1}{4} \times 2 + \frac{1}{2} \times 3\} = \frac{4}{9}$. Therefore, we can realize $\lambda'_i < \lambda_i$ relation.

(3) *Choice of abandoning food*
The action part whose bits are all 0's represents the choice of abandoning food. We changed the fitness evaluations for estimating this case so that our predators can continue searching instead of imposing a "penalty".

To illustrate the above extensions, suppose that the following message is given.

Message	001	001	001	000	000
food	f_1	f_2	f_3	f_4	f_5

The following classifier

Classifier ##1 ##1 ### 000 ### : 11000

results in

$$g := g + g_1 + g_2 = g + 5 + 3, \text{ and} \tag{8}$$

$$h := h + d_3 + h_1 + d_3 + h_2 = h + 3 + 1 + 3 + 1. \tag{9}$$

On the other hand, the classifier

Classifier ##1 ##1 ### 000 ### : 00000

results in

$$g := g \text{ and } h := h + 1. \tag{10}$$

and the next message is generated.

In a second experiment the same parameters as in the first experiment was used with different λ_i relations. The λ values used are shown in Table 4 (Case 1) and Table 5 (Case 2). Fig.4 and Fig.5 show the results of experiments for Case 1 and Case 2. The fitness is normalized by the optimal value ($\frac{g^*}{h^*}$) as before. However in these cases, the optimal values are underestimated because of introducing the non-uniform of distribution and the choice of abandoning food as mentioned above ((2) and (3)). Thus the fitness exceeds the value 1.0 in both cases. As can be seen in Fig.5, this excess is more remarkable for Case 2, which is caused by the ample supply of the most nutritious food f_1 (compare λ values of f_1 in Table 4 and Table 5).

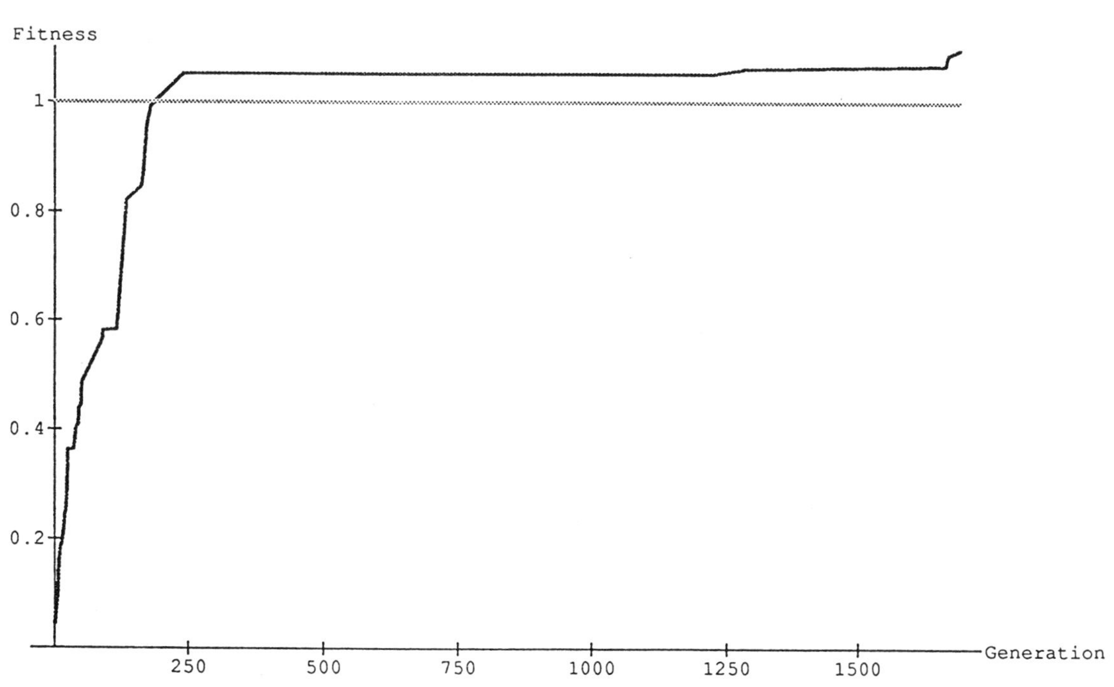

Fig.4 Fitness changes with generations (Case 1)

Kind of food	Case 1 d_1	d_2	d_3	λ
f_1	0.25	0.25	0.5	0.444
f_2	0.6	0.2	0.2	0.625
f_3	0.1	0.1	0.8	0.370
f_4	0.1	0.1	0.8	0.370
f_5	0.1	0.1	0.8	0.370

Table 4 λ values for foods (1)

Kind of food	Case 2 d_1	d_2	d_3	λ
f_1	0.5	0.25	0.25	0.571
f_2	0.25	0.25	0.5	0.444
f_3	0.1	0.1	0.8	0.370
f_4	0.1	0.1	0.8	0.370
f_5	0.1	0.1	0.8	0.370

Table 5 λ values for foods (2)

Examples of the acquired classifiers are as follows:-

food	f_1	f_2	f_3	f_4	f_5		
Case1	1#0	000	###	###	##0	:	10000
	0##	000	0##	###	###	:	00000
	##0	000	###	###	###	:	00000
	###	##1	###	###	###	:	11000
Case2	000	##1	###	###	###	:	00000
	000	###	###	1##	###	:	00000
	1#1	###	###	###	###	:	10000
	00#	###	###	###	###	:	00000

The results confirmed the predictions of the foraging theory of Section 2. That is, if the favorite food f_1 is in ample supply, then all other kinds are ignored (Case 2). If f_1 is scanty, f_2 is used, but f_3 is ignored if f_2 is ample (Case 1). If both f_1 and f_2 are scanty, f_3 is also used. Thus it is concluded from the experiments that whether the (k+1)-th food is used or ignored is decided by $\frac{g_{k+1}}{h_{k+1}}$ and the k kinds of preferred food quantities $(\lambda_1, \cdots, \lambda_k)$, but not by λ_{k+1} itself.

5 Discussion

The results of foraging theory [Krebs87] suggest the following:-

(1) If the preferred food (g/h is large) is in ample supply, then predators should eat only it.

(2) The decision of whether to eat a preferred food is independent of the richness of the supply of less preferred foods.

(3) As the supply of a preferred food becomes ample, a sudden change occurs from the "non-selective" state (i.e. predators eat mixed kinds of food) to the "selective" state (i.e. predators always eat a preferred kind of food and ignore other kinds).

We have confirmed the first two claims with our experimental results. In the first experiment, where all foods are in equally amply supply, the classifier rules (such as RULE3665) were evolved which claim that an animal should ignore less preferred foods if it can obtain a more nutritious kind. In the second experiment, the evolved

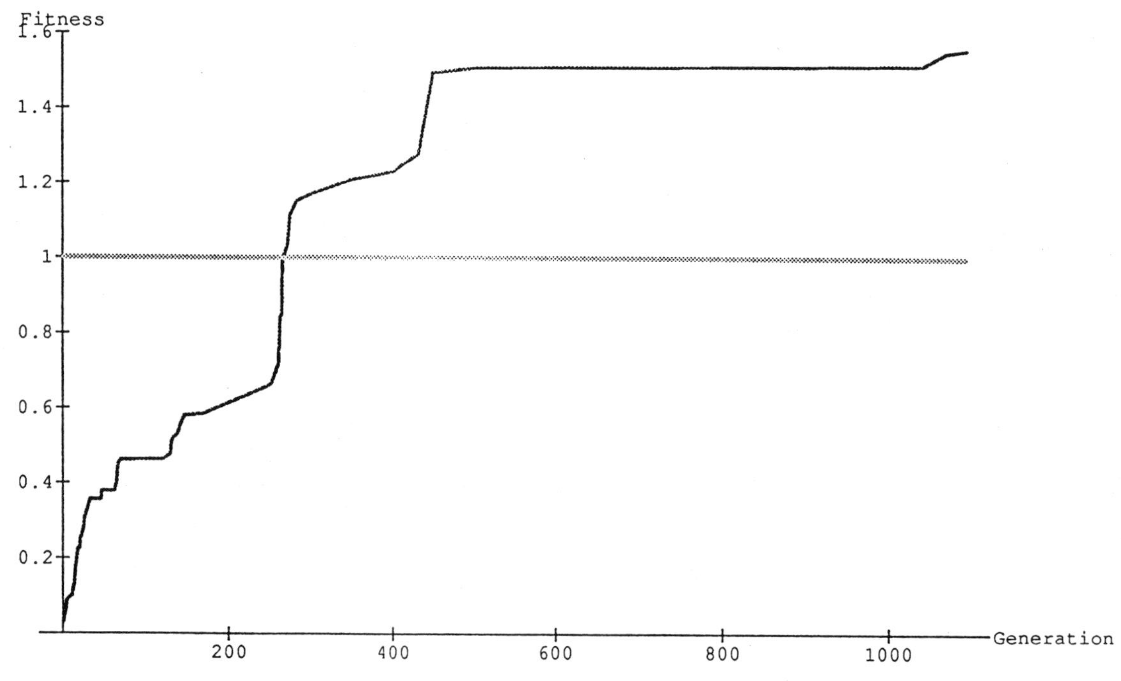

Fig.5 Fitness changes with generations (Case 2)

classifiers expressed the idea that an animal should not have high digestion costs on less preferred food, despite its large amount if the λ of the preferred food is high. The third claim is not yet confirmed by our simulation. We intend to extend our learning mechanism for the purpose of confirming the third claim with our simulation.

One of the authors has tried to realize an evolutionary learning system based on an adaptive predatory theory similar to that described in this paper. As a preliminary study, we experimented with a "bug searcher" program in which bugs adaptively hunt for bacteria [Iba92c]. The extension of this idea led to implementing BUGS (a bug-based search strategy based on genetic algorithms) for practical applications such as computer vision [Iba92a].

6 Conclusion

This paper has described an adaptive learning model for predatory behavior. We presented a fundamental theory of foraging using a formulation from mathematical biology. Our learning mechanism is based on an extended version of Classifier Systems. The simulated behavior agreed with predictions from this theory, which shows the validity of our approach. We believe that our model can be applied to more biologically realistic predatory behaviors. Further research on these ideas is currently under way.

References

[Iba *et al.*92a] Iba, H. Akiba, S. Higuchi, T. and Sato, T. BUGS : A bug-based search strategy using genetic algorithms, In *Proc. of 2nd Parallel Problem Solving from Nature*, North-Holland, 1992

[Iba *et al.*92b] Iba, H. and Sato, T. Meta-level strategy learning for GA based on structured representation, In *Proc. of 2nd Pacific Rim International Conference on Artificial Intelligence*, 1992

[Iba *et al.*92c] Iba, H., deGaris, H. and Sato, T. A bug-based search strategy for problem solving, ETL-TR92-24, 1992

[Iwasa *et al.*81] Iwasa,Y., Higashi, M. and Yamamura, N. Prey distribution as a factor determining the choice of optimal foraging strategy, *American Naturalist*, 117, 1981

[Iwasa 90] Iwasa,Y. An introduction to mathematical biology, HBJ publisher, in Japanese, 1990

[Koza90] Koza, J. Genetic programming: A paradigm for genetically breeding populations of computer programs to solve problems, Report No. STAN-CS-90-1314, Dept. of Computer Science, Stanford Univ., 1990

[Krebs *et al.*87] Krebs, J.R. and Davies, N.B. An introduction to behavioral ecology, (2nd ed.), Blackwell scientific publications, 1987

[Lu78] Lu, S. and Fu, K. Error-correcting tree automata for syntactic recognition, In *IEEE Tr. on computers*, vol.c-27, no.11, 1978

[Lu84] Lu, S. A tree-matching algorithm based on node splitting and merging, In *IEEE Tr. on pattern analysis and machine intelligence*, vol.PAMI-6, no.2, 1984

[Smith80] Smith, S.F. A learning system based on genetic adaptive algorithms, Ph.D thesis, University of Pittsburgh, 1980

[von Laszewski91] von Laszewski, G. Intelligent structural operators for the k-way graph partitioning problem, In *Proc. of International Conference on Genetic Algorithms*, 1991

Issues in Evolutionary Robotics

Inman Harvey[1] and Philip Husbands[1] and Dave Cliff[1,2]
[1]School of Cognitive and Computing Sciences
[2]IRC, School of Biological Sciences
University of Sussex, BRIGHTON BN1 9QH, U.K.
inmanh or philh or davec, all @cogs.susx.ac.uk

Abstract

In this paper we propose and justify a methodology for the development of the control systems, or 'cognitive architectures', of autonomous mobile robots. We argue that the design by hand of such control systems becomes prohibitively difficult as complexity increases.

We discuss an alternative approach, involving artificial evolution, where the basic building blocks for cognitive architectures are adaptive noise-tolerant dynamical neural networks, rather than programs. These networks may be recurrent, and should operate in real time. Evolution should be incremental, using an extended and modified version of genetic algorithms. We finally propose that, sooner rather than later, visual processing will be required in order for robots to engage in non-trivial navigation behaviours.

Time constraints suggest that initial architecture evaluations should be largely done in simulation. The pitfalls of simulations compared with reality are discussed, together with the importance of incorporating noise. To support our claims and proposals, we present results from some preliminary experiments where robots which roam office-like environments are evolved.

1 Introduction

This paper firstly gives an analysis which proposes that an evolutionary approach to the design of robots can be expected to supercede design by hand; it then explores issues arising from this, and presents results from some preliminary experiments: using an extended genetic algorithm, we have evolved control architectures for a simulated version of a physical robot constructed at Sussex.

An evolutionary approach to real robotics was discussed at a 1987 workshop (3), and in the context of subsumption architecture by a student of Brooks (27); but no practical results have been reported. A number of researchers have shown the method to be viable for simulated robots in highly simplified simulated worlds (1), but have not had to face the exponential increase in complexity that follows with progress from toy worlds into the real world.

Independently in 1991, we (as members of the PRANCE consortium) made a research proposal to use an evolutionary approach in developing real autonomous robots (24); and Brooks proposed at ECAL-91 in Paris a different evolutionary approach, using genetic programming (9).

Straightforward Genetic Algorithms (GAs) use evolutionary ideas for function optimisation, and are not immediately applicable to robotics. Necessary adaptations to GAs are discussed in (14). This paper concentrates on other issues, in particular whether the cognitive architecture of a robot should be evolved in the form of a Behavioural Language, as advocated by Brooks, or in the form of artificial neural networks. We argue that there are good reasons for the latter approach.

After setting the stage with these theoretical considerations we go on to report on preliminary simulation experiments in evolving control networks for simple robots equipped with a few touch sensors. The simulations are not naive – they are based on observations of a real robot and attempt to model the physics of its interactions with the world.

2 Interesting robots are too difficult to design

Traditional approaches to the development of autonomous robot control systems have made only modest progress, with fragile and computationally very expensive methods. This is largely because of the traditional implicit assumption of functional decomposition — the assumption that perception, planning and action can be analysed independently of each other.

In contrast, recent work at MIT bases robot control architectures around *behavioural decomposition* (6, 8). In theory, this involves analysing independent behaviours of a robot or *animat*,[1] such that each behaviour can be 'wired in' all the way from sensor input to motor output. Simple behaviours are wired in at first, and then more complex behaviours are added as separate layers, affecting earlier layers only by means of suppression or inhibition mechanisms.

It is extremely difficult to foresee all possible interac-

[1] *Animat*: simulated animal or autonomous robot (28).

tions with the environment, and between separate parts of the robot itself (8, 22). Designing appropriate cognitive architectures is a task with inherently explosive complexity. Complexity is likely to scale much faster than the number of layers or modules within the architecture — it can scale with the number of possible interactions between modules.

To design cognitive architectures for robots with emergent behaviours hence requires either (a) a computationally intractable planning problem (10) or (b) a creative act on the part of the designer — which is to be greatly admired, though impossible to formalise. In both cases it seems likely that the limits of feasibility for real robots doing useful things are currently being reached.

3 Let's evolve robots instead

If, however, some objective fitness function can be derived for any given architecture, there is the possibility of automatic evolution of the architecture without explicit design. Natural evolution is the existence proof for the viability of this approach, given appropriate resources. Genetic Algorithms (GAs) (12) use ideas borrowed from evolution in order to solve problems in highly complex search spaces, and it is here suggested that GAs, suitably extended in their application, are a means of evading the problems mentioned in the previous section.

The artificial evolution approach will maintain a population of viable genotypes (chromosomes), coding for cognitive architectures, which will be inter-bred and mutated according to a selection pressure. This pressure will be controlled by a task-oriented evaluation function: the better the robot performs its task the more evolutionarily favoured is its cognitive architecture. Rather than attempting to hand-design a system to perform a particular task or range of tasks well, the evolutionary approach will allow their gradual emergence.

There is no need for any assumptions about means to achieve a particular kind of behaviour, as long as this behaviour is directly or implicitly included in the evaluation function. Brooks' subsumption approach was mentioned above as a contrast to the dogmatic assumptions of functional decomposition implicit in much of traditional robotics. Nevertheless, it is similarly not necessary to be dogmatically committed to an exclusively behavioural decomposition. By allowing either type of decomposition, the evolutionary process will determine whether in practice either one, or neither, should characterise the robots' cognitive architecture.

4 An incremental, species approach

An animal should not be considered as a solution to a problem posed 4 billion years ago. Nevertheless, in the short term, adaptations in a species may be usefully interpreted as solving particular problems for that species. So when using the evolution of animals as a source of ideas for the evolution of *animats*, GAs should be used as a method for searching the space of possible adaptations of an existing *animat*, not as a search through the complete space of *animats*. The basis for extending standard GAs to cope with this has been worked out in (14). The implications are that the population being evolved is always a genetically-converged *species*; and that increases in genotype length, associated with increases in complexity, can only happen very gradually.

This of course has strong resemblances to Brooks' incremental approach, wherein 'low-level' behaviours are wired in and thoroughly debugged, before the next layer of behaviour is carefully designed on top of them. The difference with the approach we advocate is that of substituting evolution for design.

5 The use of simulation

Artificial evolution requires that the members of a sizeable population must be evaluated over the course of many generations. In the case of the evolution of autonomous robot control systems, to date it has been assumed it would take far too long to do all of these evaluation in the real world (15, 9, 24, 3). Instead it is suggested that most evaluations should be done in simulation. In the short to medium term this seems a sensible strategy but we have strong doubts about its long term viability.

Assuming the use of simulation for the time being, it is crucial that it is kept as closely in step with reality as possible. A number of techniques can be used to this end. Firstly, the simulation can be calibrated at regular intervals by carefully testing the architectures evolved in the real robot. Serious discrepancies should be ironed out. Secondly, accurate simulations of the inputs to the robot sensors and the reactions of the actuators should be based on carefully collected empirical data. Thirdly, and above all, noise must be taken into account at all levels. In order to acquire the desired level of accuracy it may be necessary to use a mixed hardware/software simulation in which simulated signals are fed into hardware sensors or actuators and the response is read directly. The use of low resolution sensing makes this approach feasible. It is important to remember that it is not our world that is being simulated, but the robot's.

A range of unstructured dynamic environments should be used in the simulation. A cognitive architecture that has evolved to cope with a range of such environments is much more likely to be robust than one evolved to operate in a single well structured world.

If adaptive noise-tolerant units, such as neural nets, are used as the key elements of the control system, then 100% accuracy is not required. Discrepancies between the simulations and the real world, as long as they are not too big, can be treated as noise; the system can adapt to cope with this.

In the long term, as the robots become more sophisticated and their worlds more dynamic, will the simulation run out of steam? The simulation of a medium resolution visual system with, for instance, motion detection preprocessing is painfully slow on today's hardware. Techniques to test many generations of control systems in real worlds will have to be developed. We are currently pursuing the development of one such technique: see (11) for further details.

6 What should we evolve?

So far we have not addressed the question of what exactly it is that is being evolved. There are at least three useful ways to implement the control system of an autonomous robot:

- An explicit control program, in some high level language;
- A mathematical expression mapping inputs to outputs, e.g. a polynomial transfer function;
- A blue-print for a *processing structure*, a network of simple processing elements.

6.1 High Level Programs

In (9), following a suggestion by Langton, Brooks proposes using an extension of Koza's genetic programming techniques (18) as the method for evolving a physical or simulated robot.

One potential problem with evolving a programming language is that, if it supports partial recursion, programs to be evaluated may never halt, unless some arbitrary 'time-out' is imposed. Brooks' Behaviour Language (7) does not use partial recursion, and hence can be evolved without this problem. Subject to the qualification that Genetic Programming should have genotype length changes restricted to small steps his approach at first sight seems reasonable, but we have two broad objections.

The first is that any such programming approach treats the 'brain' as a computational system, producing a set of motor outputs for any given set of sensor inputs. This snapshot view of cognition has been the main paradigm in AI, but we support an alternative view of agents as dynamical systems rather than computational systems, which are perturbed by their interactions with the environment, which is also a dynamical system. This view is expressed in (19, 5, 26), and will not be developed further here.

The second objection, which is supported by our simulation results, is that the primitives manipulated in the evolutionary process should be at the lowest level possible, and this is in contrast to Brooks' use of higher level languages. The Behavior Language, BL, is in effect a blueprint for a network of Finite State Automata, and the target language Brooks proposes for Genetic Programming is an even higher level language, GEN, which can be compiled into BL.

Our intuitions are based on the notion that any high level semantic groupings necessarily restricts the possibilities available to the evolutionary process, compared to the alternative of letting the lowest level of primitives be manipulated by genetic operators. The human designer's prejudices are incorporated within their choice of high-level semantics, and these restrictions give rise to a much more coarse-grained fitness landscape, with steeper precipices. It might be thought that the use of low-level primitives necessitates enormously many generations of evolution with vast populations before any interesting high-level behaviour emerges, but our simulations show that this is not the case at all.

A further factor concerning high-level languages is that the injection of noise into anything other than the lowest levels becomes difficult to justify. For a network considered to be modelled at a physical level it is easier to justify the insertion of noise at many points within the system, and as will be seen this appears to have valuable effects, not least in making the fitness landscape more blurred and hence less rugged for evolution.

6.2 Polynomial Transfer Functions

There are a number of close relationships, in this context, between polynomial transfer functions and artificial neural networks, not least that the input-output associations of most neural networks can be arbitrarily closely approximated by a polynomial function and vice versa. Clearly the problem of brittleness and halting is not an issue, yet neither scheme is computationally restricted.

Even for modest numbers of inputs and outputs, the most useful transfer function may be a highly complex non-linear expression with many terms; the search space is potentially very large. Simulation results suggest that the search space, except for low dimensions, lacks structure, resulting in the GA degenerating into random search. Similar results for the related problem of system identification have also been reported (16).

The robustness required for useful behaviour in the real world is almost certainly going to demand either some degree of adaptation or an expression complicated enough to cover a wide enough range of situations. The latter leads to the problems described above. The former will require auxiliary systems identification algorithms which will seriously complicate matters by being computationally expensive (25) and requiring error measures.

6.3 Neural Nets

Evolutionary approaches to designing connectionist network architectures are manifold, e.g. (17, 13, 21, 23); All these have used some form of genetic algorithm to search through a pre-defined finite space of possible network architectures. In other words, at a more or less sophisticated level, the basic architecture has been defined with some parameters left as variables, and the GA has been used to tweak the parameters to optimal values. It is argued in (14) that for the equivalent of robot evolution it will be necessary to extend this to open-ended evolution instead, with significant implications. Nevertheless, the evolvability of connectionist networks in general is clearly established.

It might be argued that in practice connectionist networks are simulated on a serial computer; and in turn that a serial Turing machine can be simulated with a connectionist network. This does not mean that their evolvability is the same. To build a connectionist network as a virtual machine on top of a conventionally programmed computer does not alter the fact that the virtual machine may be suitable for evolutionary development whereas the underlying real machine is not — the mutations of structure are at the virtual machine level only. The price paid for this, however, is the computational inefficiency of simulating one type of computation with another.

Concise specification on the genotype of sub-networks or modules which may be repeatedly used is possible, provided that there is a mechanism to interpret such specifications several times analogously to the way subroutines are called within a program. The desirability of adaptation has been mentioned above, and obviously artificial neural networks allow for this. The massively parallel nature of neural nets enables very fast implementation in the appropriate hardware, in contrast to the necessarily (locally) serial interpretation of a behaviour language.

What sort of network?

There are good grounds for thinking that a generalised form of connectionist network could be one very appropriate class. Let us start with three basic axioms:

1. The 'brain' should be a physical system, occupying a physical volume with a finite number of input and output points on its surface.

2. Interactions within the brain should be mediated by physical signals travelling with finite velocities through its volume, from the inputs, and to the outputs.

3. Subject to some lower limit of an undecomposable 'atom' or node, these three axioms apply to any physical subvolume of the whole brain.

A justification for the third axiom is that of the incremental development of the whole by alterations and additions over evolutionary timescales. The consequence of these axioms, as can be seen by shrinking in any fashion the surface containing the original volume, is a network model where internal nodes are the undecomposable atoms, and connections between inputs, internal nodes and outputs are through directed arcs by signals taking finite times. Such a network can be arbitrarily recurrent. The assumption of only a finite number of input/output points on any surface means that this is not a field theory. It rules out of this model such more general methods of physical interaction as might be assumed to be involved with, e.g. diffuse chemical neurotransmitters in the human brain.

No assumptions about the operations of the nodes have yet been made. The simplest assumptions would be those of standard connectionist models. Input signals are weighted by a scalar quantity; all output signals are identical when they leave the node, being calculated from the weighted sum of the inputs. If this weighted sum is passed through a sigmoid or thresholding function, then we have the non-linear behaviour we have learnt to know and love. So far the only generalisation this model has when compared with the picture given in (20) is that timelags between nodes need to be specified. But a whole new universe of possible dynamical behaviours is opened up by this extension.

Such networks are more difficult to analyse than standard feedforward ones. However with an evolutionary approach it may not be necessary to analyse *how it works*, but rather one should be able to assess *how good is the behaviour it elicits*. This is no short-cut recipe, but requires that the internal complexity of the 'brain' (of an organism or a machine) be dependent on the history of interactions with its world; the more the complexity that is required, the longer the history that is needed to mould it.

A particular type of network falling under this general classification, and used in the experiments described in this paper, is described in more detail in section 9.1.

7 Timing issues

The practical problems of timing should be taken note of. The robot will have timing circuitry to synchronise sensing, control and motor activities. This should not cause any undue problems for the implementation of evolved neural networks. As long as they operate using discrete time intervals, then even complex recurrent networks can be handled in a straightforward manner. The more general and possibly more powerful class of asynchronous continuous time networks are a little more difficult but create no significant problems. Arbitrarily complex polynomial transfer functions, which may involve a lengthy computation, are certainly more difficult to handle than discrete time networks. Potentially non-halting high level programs with many conditional

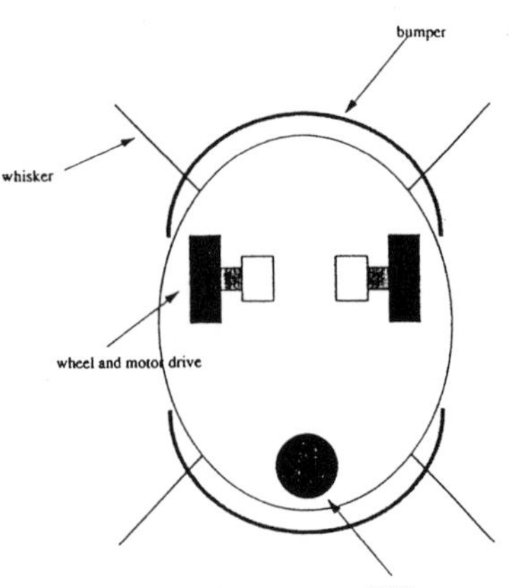

Figure 1: Plan view of simple six-sensor robot.

branches are harder still.

8 Robots need vision

In autonomous robot navigation, a number of sensor technologies are commonly employed to enable the task of navigation. For the purposes of the discussion that follows, it is useful to employ the distinction found in the biology literature between *exteroceptors* and *interoceptors*. An exteroceptor is a receptor (i.e. sensor) which detects stimuli external to an animal, e.g. light or sound; an interoceptor senses or detects stimuli that arise inside the animal, e.g. blood pressure.

The development of a successful navigating robot depends on finding a satisfactory combination of exteroceptors and interoceptors. Here the discussion focusses on the exteroceptors we envisage necessary for our robot.

The majority of recent projects in autonomous behavioural[2] robotics have not employed vision as a primary exteroception mechanism. Most commonly, mechanosensory "whiskers" and "bumpers", or active ranging devices (such as ultrasound depth sensors or laser light-stripers) have been employed. Such sensors are essentially *proximal* sensing devices. That is, they only provide reliable data for the immediate surroundings of the robot. Such robots are thus forced to employ primitive navigation strategies. The most common such strategy is "wall following", where the robot must always maintain sensory contact with a sizeable static external surface, such as a wall of the robotics lab. Wall-following robots that lose sensory contact with all external surfaces often suffer from sensor-blindness, the chief symptom of which is a significant degradation, or total loss, of navigation ability.

In some restricted behavioural or ecological niches, wall-following is a satisfactory navigation strategy, and sensor-blindness can be overcome by wandering until sensory contact is re-established. The need for more sophisticated navigation competences, which we take as manifest, is only likely to be overcome fully by an increased reliance on *distal* sensors — in particular, vision.

[2] I.e., subsumption-based or reactive-systems robotics.

There is growing research in the field of mounting computer vision systems on mobile robotic platforms – an approach referred to as *animate vision* (2). While many projects are underway in developing animate vision systems, we are not aware of any where evolution is employed in preference to design.

Although using vision does not *eliminate* problems such as sensor-blindness, it does provide a rich source of information concerning an agent's external environment. Whether designing or evolving a visual system, a number of factors have to be taken into account. Significant factors include:

- The discretization of the sampling of the optic array, i.e. how many pixels do we want in the images our robot samples, and what sort of geometry should the image have (a square raster is not necessarily convenient). The number of pixels in the image has a manifest effect on the bandwidth of the visual processing channels.
- The angular extent of the vision system's field of view – should the robot be equipped with 360° vision or will a more restricted field of view suffice?
- The visual angular resolution of the robot's optics. Should the vision system employ a uniform resolution, or have some sort of spatially variant "foveal" (nonuniform) vision system? Many animals have resolution which varies across the visual field. Typically this is a result of the need for high-resolution vision for certain tasks (predation or identifying mates) coupled with a need for a wide field of view, sampled at a lower resolution.

That many animals, particularly insects, successfully occupy their ecological niches using low-resolution low-bandwidth vision as a primary source of exteroception information indicates that such an approach (as opposed to high resolution and bandwidth) is worth exploring within an evolutionary robotics context, in the first instance at least.

Simulation vs. Reality in Vision

For the evolutionary approach to be successful, methods of varying the details of the visual sampling and the subsequent processing of the visual signal are imperative.

Evolutionary learning can be accelerated if the populations undergoing evolution exist within a simulated system. The problem here is in ensuring that the simulated visual systems correspond in a useful manner to the physical visual systems with which the robot will be equipped. While such simulations are possible in principle, the computational demands soon become considerable and, unless the necessary processing hardware (e.g.

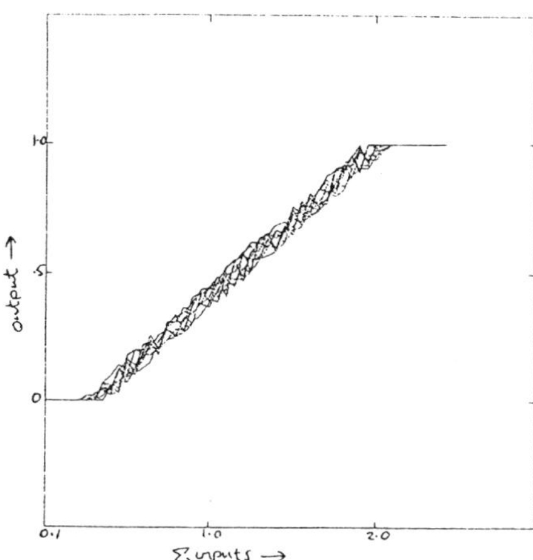

Figure 2: Noisy neuron transfer function.

specialised graphics pipeline processors) is readily available, it is envisaged that physical instantiation of the visual systems would be required at an early stage.

For a physical robot to be equipped with a vision system that has variable sampling bandwidth, geometry, visual extent, and angular resolution, requires that the camera(s) mounted on the robot are capable of offering performance at the upper limits of what is envisaged necessary. For example, a high-resolution image can be subsampled (with averaging or smoothing) to provide a lower-resolution image. This could be done under genetic control, which is a very crude first step towards evolving sensors.

Whether the image-capture mechanism is real or virtual, the image-processing scheme can be simulated (i.e. the parallelism can be simulated rather than embodied in truly parallel hardware). But as the imaging bandwidth increases, or if the robot's speed of reaction is critical, specialised image processing hardware (with suitably adjustable parameters) would be required.

Envisaging what is necessary for the robot is likely only to be possible after some experience with it: a circularity which reveals that some iteration is required between the simulation work and the building of real robots – a pluralist approach will be the most fruitful.

9 Preliminary Experiments

A real robot assembled in the Engineering Department at Sussex has been simulated using the methodology established above. The behaviour of the motors propelling the wheels has been modelled for the outputs, as have inputs from whisker and bumper touch sensors. Simulation of a low resolution insect-type visual system has been added and results using that are described in another paper (11). This is part of an ongoing project at Sussex to develop an evolutionary approach to robotics, with increasingly sophisticated tasks leading to navigation using learnt visual landmarks.

The first phase of the work explored the methodology using careful simulations. Results from this are presented here. We are now into the second phase of the work which will directly calibrate the simulations using the real robot. A further phase, described in (11), also just begun, will look at the evolution of visually guided behaviours without using simulations at all.

A plan view of the robot used in the simulation experiments is shown in Figure 1. The robot is cylindrical in shape with two wheels towards the front and a trailing rear castor.

The wheels have independent drives allowing turning on the spot and fairly unrestricted movement across a flat floor. The signals to the motor can be represented as a real value in the range $[-1.0, 1.0]$. This range is divided up into five more or less equal segments, depending on which segment the signal falls into, the wheel will either: remain stationary; rotate full speed forward; full speed backward; half speed forward; or half speed backward.

The aim of the experiments was to evolve 'neural-style' networks to control the robot in a variety of environments. Before going on to describe the experiments in detail, the particular type of neural networks used, and their genetic encoding, will be described.

9.1 The neural networks

As explained in Section 6.3 we advocate the use of continuous real-valued networks with unrestricted connections and time delays between units. These can be thought of as something like analogue circuits with real-valued signals continuously propagating through the connections. Our experience, and also that of others (4), is that this sort of network can support a range of behaviours, depending on its exact couplings with the world, and so is highly adaptive without using Hebbian-type weight changes or the like.

The particular networks used in the experiments have a fixed number of input nodes, one for each sensor, and a fixed number of output units, two for each motor. As all the units are linear threshold devices with outputs in the range $[0.0, 1.0] \subset \mathbf{R}$, two units are needed to give the motors a signal in the range $[-1.0, 1.0] \subset \mathbf{R}$. If the output signals from these four output units are labelled S_{o1}, to S_{o4} then, the left motor signal is given by $S_{o1} - S_{o2}$, and the right motor signal is given by $S_{o3} - S_{o4}$.

Each unit is a noisy linear threshold device. Internal noise was added because we felt it would provide further useful and interesting dynamical properties. Any physical implementation of our nets would be likely to include naturally occurring noise anyway. The input-output relationship for such a node is shown in Figure 2, which was generated by plotting the output for a fixed set of inputs ten times and overlaying them.

Within the networks two types of connection are al-

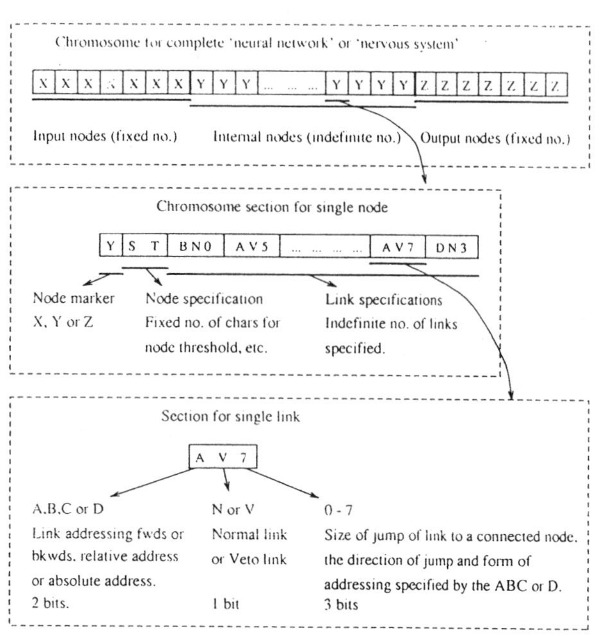

Figure 3: The genetic encoding scheme

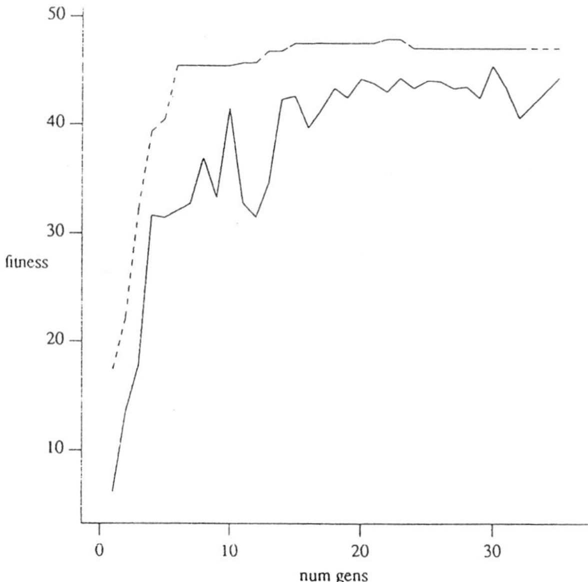

Figure 4: Results of simple experiment. See text for further explanation.

lowed: normal and veto. A normal connection is a weighted link joining the output of one unit to the input of another. A veto connection is a special infinitely inhibitory connection between two units. If there is a veto connection between units a and b, and a's output exceeds its veto threshold, then all normal connection outputs from b are turned off (though in the current implementation, further veto outputs are not affected). The veto threshold is always much higher than the lower threshold for the normal signal. The veto mechanism is a crude but effective model of phenomena found in invertebrate nervous systems.[3]

As well as the input and output units, each network will have some number of 'hidden' units. This number is not prespecified – the genotypes can be a variable length. The genetic encoding specifies properties of the units and the connections and connection-types emanating from them. It is now described in more detail.

9.2 *The genetic encoding*

The genetic encoding used is illustrated in Figure 3.

The genotype is interpreted sequentially. Firstly the input units are coded for, each preceded by a marker. For each node, the first part of its gene can encode node properties such as threshold values; there then follows a variable number of groups each representing a connection from that node. Each group specifies whether it is a normal or veto connection, and then the target node indicated by jump-type and jump-size. The jump-type allows for both relative and absolute addressing. Relative addressing is provided by jumps forwards or backwards along the genotype order; absolute addressing is relative to the start or end of the genotype. These modes of addressing mean that offspring produced by crossover will always be legal.

The internal nodes and output nodes are handled similarly with their own identifying genetic markers. Clearly this scheme allows for any number of internal nodes. The variable length of the resulting genotypes necessitates a careful crossover operator which exchanges homologous segments. In keeping with SAGA principles, when a crossover between two parents results in an offspring of different length, such changes in length (although allowed) are restricted to a minimum.

9.3 *The physics: simulating movement*

In the experiments described next the continuous nature of the system was modelled by using a fine-time-slice simulation. At each time step the sensor readings are fed into the neural network. The continuous nature of the networks is simulated by running them (synchronously updating all units inputs and outputs for a number of iterations (about 100), with a variance to counter distorting periodic effects) and then converting the outputs to motor signals. The new position of the robot is then calculated by using the appropriate kinematic equations. Using the wheel velocities, the motion is resolved into a rotation about one wheel plus a translation parallel to

[3]For example, feed-forward inhibition of the locust LGMD visual interneuron acts as a veto to prevent the LGMD from producing transient responses caused by delays in earlier processing. See e.g. (29, pp.77-78).

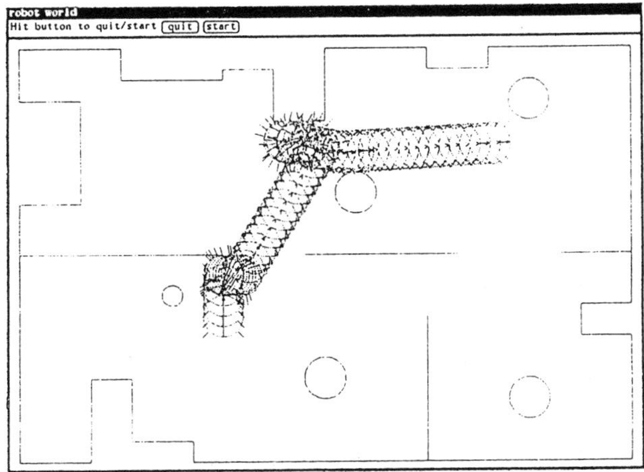

Figure 5: Motion of a single robot controlled by an evolved network.

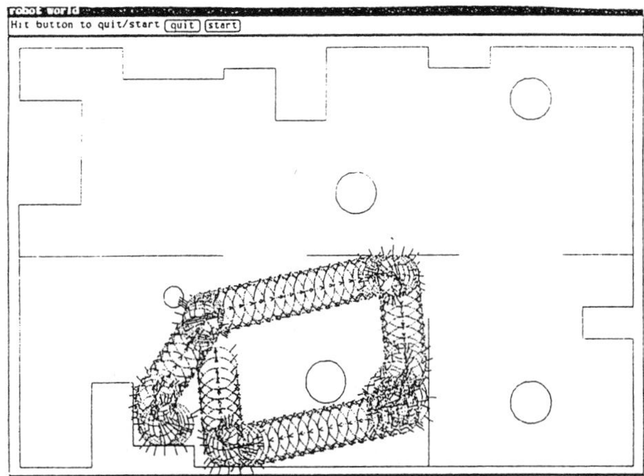

Figure 6: Motion of a robot evolved to maximise the area of the bounding polygon of its path over a limited time period.

the velocity vector of the other. Standard Newtonian mechanics are used. However, the motion is not modelled as being wholly deterministic: noise is injected into the calculations. Collisions are handled as accurately as possible — using observations of the real system. The nature of the collision depends on speed and angle of incidence as well as the shape of the obstacle.

This type of simulation is not perfect, it can and will be made more accurate, but we feel it is realistic enough to take our results seriously.

9.4 The experiments

Each of the following experiments was run for 50 generations, each with a population size of 40. The crossover rate was set at 1.0, while the mutation rate was of the order of 1 bit per genotype.

Figure 4 shows the results for an experiment in which a control network was evolved using an evaluation function which encouraged wandering in a cluttered office-type environment containing walls, pillars and doorways (see Figure 5). Robust control networks were favoured by scoring each genotype several times for a single fitness evaluation. The robot was always started from the same position in the same orientation, and was scored on how far away from its starting position it moved in a fixed time period. On each scoring run the robot faced a different set of situations because of the noise in the system. The *minimum* of the scores achieved was taken as the fitness value for the genotype. The robots were started from rest with no initialising signals; internal noise was sufficient to allow fitter nets to settle into useful initial states. The bottom line on the graph shows the fitness of the best individual in each generation. The top line shows the best score achieved by any member of the population for any of the runs making up its evaluation set. The fact that these two lines converge indicates that more and more robust networks began to appear. Clearly very good control networks have evolved for this simple specific task. Figure 5 shows a short run by a robot controlled by one of these networks. As a matter of convenience, the robot's whiskers are shown moving through objects.

It can be seen that the network generates a 'move in a straight line at full speed' behaviour when in free space, and various rotational movements when presented with obstacles. Members of earlier generations had far more random behaviours, spending most of their time in messy collisions or just sitting still.

Figure 6 shows a typical behaviour generated by a network evolved under a evaluation function describing a much more difficult task. The evaluation function measured the area of the enclosed polygon formed by the robot's path over a finite time period. This time the robot was always started at random locations with a random orientation. Note the robot turns fairly smoothly on encountering obstacles. In earlier generations collisions were much more messy.

Figure 7 gives interesting comparative results for different fitness functions based on the above evaluation function. It shows the best, average and worst scores of the best individuals per generation scored over its evaluation set as in the previous experiment.

The upper graph was obtained by taking the fitness to be the *average* of the small number of runs in the evaluation set; the lower graph was obtained by taking the fitness to be the *worst* of the runs. Each run started from a random position with a random orientation. The results clearly show that evaluating from the average gives a better average performance but a very poor noisy worst performance. Evaluating from the worst pushes the worst and average much closer together, providing a far more

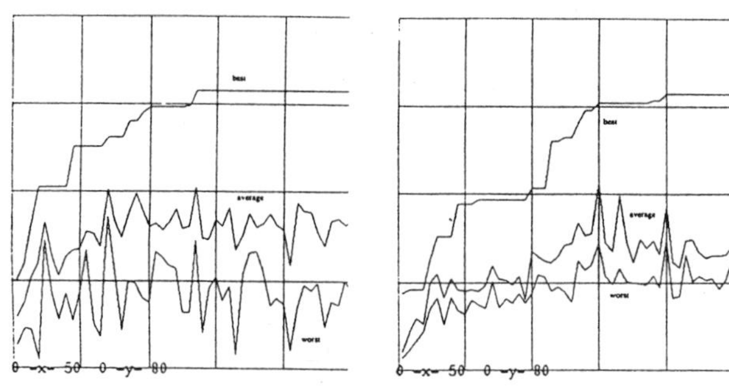

Figure 7: Comparative results for different fitness functions. Left-hand graph is where fitness is measured by the *average* of a series of tests; right-hand graph where fitness is measured as the *worst* performance in a series of tests. Abscissa is generation number; ordinate is fitness value. See text for further explanation.

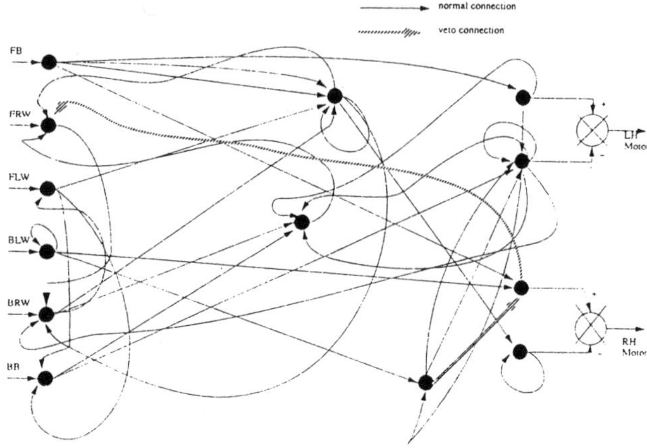

Figure 8: An evolved network: no work of art, but a working robot controller.

robust solution.

Figure 8 shows a network evolved in this second experiment. It is fairly complex with many feedback loops, but it is interpretable in terms of generated behaviours. If it reminds you of a bowl of spaghetti without the bolognese sauce and chianti, this is probably partly due to the fact that there is no term in the evaluation functions that penalises unnecessary links. However, initial populations are started with individuals having (randomly) one or zero internal nodes; the number can only grow gradually if that promotes greater fitness. We expect that more concise networks will result if we introduce a cost for link creation in the evaluation function, and allow for the possibility of non-unity time delays and/or weights on connections.

These early experiments with primitive behaviours have clearly been successful: we have built on them by evolving networks for sighted robots; further details of the work involving vision are given in (11).

10 Conclusions

There is no evidence to suggest that humans are good at designing systems which involve many emergent interactions between many constituent parts. But robust control systems for robots may well fall under this classification. Artificial evolution seems a good way forward, and it has been advocated in this paper.

Results from realistic simulation experiments have been presented. They lend weight to our claim that an incremental artificial evolution is a viable methodology.

Acknowledgements

Many thanks to Tony Simpson for the engineering design work on the robot, and to Linda Thompson for her help in the preparation of this paper. Inman Harvey has been supported by the SERC. This work is currently supported by a University of Sussex research development grant.

References

[1] D. H. Ackley and M. L. Littman. Interactions between learning and evolution. In C. G. Langton, J. D. Farmer, S. Rasmussen, and C. Taylor, editors, *Artificial Life II: Proceedings Volume of Santa Fe Conference Feb. 1990*. Addison Wesley: volume XI in the series of the Santa Fe Institute Studies in the Sciences of Complexity, 1991.

[2] D. H. Ballard. Animate vision. *Artificial Intelligence*, 48:57–86, 1991.

[3] J. Barhen, W.B. Dress, and C.C. Jorgensen. Applications of concurrent neuromorphic algorithms for autonomous robots. In R. Eckmiller and C.v.d. Malsburg, editors, *Neural Computers*, pages 321–333. Springer-Verlag, 1987.

[4] R. D. Beer and J. C. Gallagher. Evolving dynamical neural networks for adaptive behaviour. Technical Report CES 91–17, Department of Computer Engineering and Science, Case Western Reserve University, Cleveland, Ohio, 1991.

[5] R.D. Beer. A dynamical systems perspective on autonomous agents. Technical Report CES-92-11, Case Western Reserve University, Cleveland, Ohio, 1992.

[6] R. A. Brooks. Achieving artificial intelligence through building robots. A.I. Memo 899, M.I.T. A.I. Lab, May 1986.

[7] R. A. Brooks. The behavior language. A.I. Memo 1227, MIT AI Lab, 1990.

[8] R.A. Brooks. Intelligence without representation. *Artificial Intelligence*, 47:139–159, 1991.

[9] Rodney A. Brooks. Artificial life and real robots. In F.J. Varela and P. Bourgine, editors, *Toward a Practice of Autonomous Systems, Proceedings of the First European Conference on Artificial Life*. MIT Press/Bradford Books, Cambridge, MA, 1992.

[10] David Chapman. Planning for conjuctive goals. *Artificial Intelligence*, 32(3):333–377, 1987.

[11] D. T. Cliff, P. Husbands, and I. Harvey. Evolving visually guided robots, 1992. Elsewhere in this volume.

[12] David E. Goldberg. *Genetic Algorithms in Search, Optimization and Machine Learning*. Addison-Wesley, Reading, Massachusetts, USA, 1989.

[13] Steven A. Harp, T. Samad, and A. Guha. Towards the genetic synthesis of neural networks. In J. D. Schaffer, editor, *Proceedings of the Third International Conference on Genetic Algorithms*, San Mateo, California, 1989. Morgan Kaufmann.

[14] Inman Harvey. Species adaptation genetic algorithms: The basis for a continuing SAGA. In F.J. Varela and P. Bourgine, editors, *Toward a Practice of Autonomous Systems, Proceedings of the First European Conference on Artificial Life*. MIT Press/Bradford Books, Cambridge, MA, 1992.

[15] P. Husbands and I. Harvey. Evolution versus design: Controlling autonomous robots. In *Integrating Perception, Planning and Action, Proceedings of 3rd Annual Conference on Artificial Intelligence, Simulation and Planning*, pages 139–146. IEEE Press, 1992.

[16] Timothy Johnson and Philip Husbands. System identification using genetic algorithms. In H.-P. Schwefel and R. Männer, editors, *Parallel Problem Solving from Nature*. Springer-Verlag, Lecture Notes in Computer Science Vol. 496, 1991.

[17] Michel Kerszberg and Aviv Bergman. The evolution of data processing abilities in competing automata. In Rodney M. J. Cotterill, editor, *Computer Simulation in Brain Science*, pages 249–259. Cambridge University Press, 1988.

[18] John R. Koza. Genetic programming: A paradigm for genetically breeding populations of computer programs to solve problems. Technical Report STAN-CS-90-1314, Department of Computer Science, Stanford University, 1990.

[19] H.R. Maturana and F.J. Varela. *The Tree of Knowledge: The Biological Roots of Human Understanding*. Shambhala Press, Boston, 1987.

[20] J. L. McClelland and D. E. Rumelhart, editors. *Explorations in Parallel Distributed Processing*. MIT Press/Bradford Books, Cambridge Massachusetts, 1986.

[21] Geoffrey F. Miller, P. M. Todd, and S. U. Hegde. Designing neural networks using genetic algorithms. In J. D. Schaffer, editor, *Proceedings of the Third International Conference on Genetic Algorithms*, San Mateo, California, 1989. Morgan Kaufmann.

[22] H.P. Moravec. The Stanford Cart and the CMU Rover. In *Proc. of IEEE*, volume 71, pages 872–884, 1983.

[23] H. Muhlenbein and J. Kindermann. The dynamics of evolution and learning - towards genetic neural networks. In R. Pfeifer, Z. Schreter, F. Fogelman-Soulie, and L. Steels, editors, *Connectionism in Perspective*, pages 173–197. Elsevier Science Publishers B.V. (North-Holland), 1989.

[24] PRANCE. Perceptive robots: Autonomous navigation and cooperation through evolution. Unpublished research proposal, PRANCE consortium: Univ. of Sussex, Cap Gemini Innovation, École Normale Supérieure (Paris) and Université Libre de Bruxelles, 1991.

[25] T. Soderstrom and P. Stoica. *System Identification*. Prentice Hall, 1989.

[26] Tim van Gelder. What might Cognition be if not Computation? Technical Report 75, Indiana University Cognitive Sciences, 1992.

[27] P. Viola. Mobile robot evolution. Bachelors thesis, M.I.T., 1988.

[28] S.W. Wilson. Knowledge growth in an artificial animal. In J. Grefenstette, editor, *Proceedings of the First International Conference on Genetic Algorithms and their applications*. Lawrence Erlbaum Assoc., 1985.

[29] D. Young. *Nerve Cells and Animal Behaviour*. Cambridge University Press, Cambridge, 1989.

Evolving Visually Guided Robots

Dave Cliff[1,2] **and Philip Husbands**[1] **and Inman Harvey**[1]
[1]School of Cognitive and Computing Sciences
[2]IRC, School of Biological Sciences
University of Sussex, BRIGHTON BN1 9QH, U.K.
davec or philh or inmanh, all @cogs.susx.ac.uk

Abstract

We have developed a methodology grounded in two beliefs: that autonomous agents need visual processing capabilities, and that the approach of *hand-designing* control architectures for autonomous agents is likely to be superseded by methods involving the *artificial evolution* of comparable architectures.

In this paper we present results which demonstrate that neural-network control architectures can be evolved for an accurate simulation model of a visually guided robot. The simulation system involves detailed models of the physics of a real robot built at Sussex; and the simulated vision involves ray-tracing computer graphics, using models of optical systems which could readily be constructed from discrete components.

The control-network architecture is entirely under genetic control, as are parameters governing the optical system. Significantly, we demonstrate that robust visually-guided control systems evolve from evaluation functions which do not explicitly involve monitoring visual input.

The latter part of the paper discusses work now under development, which allows us to engage in long-term fundamental experiments aimed at thoroughly exploring the possibilities of concurrently evolving control networks and visual sensors for navigational tasks. This involves the construction of specialised visual-robotic equipment which eliminates the need for simulated sensing.

1 Introduction

Designing control architectures for visually guided mobile autonomous robots that exhibit adaptive behaviour is likely to be a very difficult task. So difficult, in fact, that we advocate the abandonment of approaches to the problem which involve solution by manual design.

In place of design-by-hand, we propose using evolutionary techniques. Focus then shifts from specifying *how* the robot is to generate adaptive behaviours, to specifying *what* adaptive behaviours are generated. By creating an initial varied population of control architectures, and rating each according to whether desired behaviours are exhibited, evolutionary pressure can be exerted on the population. Using a suitably extended form of genetic algorithm, viable architectures may result.

In this paper we present results which validate our proposals. We employed the SAGA evolutionary principle [6] to develop neural-network control architectures for a simulation model of a real robot under construction at Sussex. The simulation system incorporates accurate physics, based on empirical observations of the real system, with added noise and uncertainty. The visual sensor capabilities are simulated using a ray-tracing computer graphics system [2]. Parameters governing the robot's sampling of its visual field are under genetic control, and the resultant specifications could readily be constructed from discrete components.

Our results demonstrate that it is possible to evolve control architectures for visual guidance, using high-level evaluation functions which make *no explicit reference* to vision.

The results presented here are all for robots operating in relatively simple environments, comparable to those used for testing some real visually guided robots (e.g. [4]); but not as visually complex as a typical cluttered office environment. The computational costs of providing appropriately accurate simulation data scales very poorly as the complexity of the environment increases. In order to fully explore the possibilities of our methodology with more challenging tasks in increasingly complex environments, we have developed an approach which allows us to eliminate much of the computationally expensive simulation work. This involves using specially designed robotic equipment which allows for the use of 'real' (optical) vision, while facilitating exploration of issues in the concurrent evolution of visual sensors and control networks for navigation tasks. Section 6 describes this work, which we have only recently commenced.

This paper deals largely with practical issues: our methodological position is expressed in more depth in a separate paper [7]. For the sake of completeness, it is summarised briefly in the next section.

2 Background

In another paper [7], we have presented arguments supporting the notion that an evolutionary approach to the design of robot control systems can be expected to supersede design by hand. In that paper we also explored issues arising from the adoption of an evolutionary approach and gave results of preliminary simulation experiments in evolving control architectures for simple robots equipped with a few touch-sensors: four 'whiskers' and two 'bumpers'. For reasons explained in [7], the control architectures were based on a particular kind of 'neural' network, and central to the evolutionary mechanisms is the notion of a gradual incremental development, building on already existing capabilities.

The results of the experiments with purely tactile sensors are highly encouraging: for certain types of evaluation function, the robot population can evolve to the point where genuinely useful behaviours emerge. Nevertheless, the proximal nature (and low dimensionality) of the robot's sensors forever constrain it as unable to go beyond primitive 'bumping and feeling' strategies in navigating around its environment. For more sophisticated navigation strategies, based on distal information, the addition of visual sensing capabilities is required. Briefly, the rationale for adding vision is that it allows for much more sophisticated behaviour patterns (e.g. location recognition in navigation). The remainder of this paper discusses our experiences in adding visual processing capabilities to the simulated robot.

3 And Then There Was Light

Rather than imposing on the robot some visual sensors with fixed properties, it seemed much more sensible, and in keeping with our incremental evolutionary approach, to investigate the concurrent evolution of visual sensors and control networks. In essence we have started with simple very low resolution devices coupled to small networks, and will work towards higher resolution devices made useful by more complex networks generating more sophisticated behaviours. Major factors affecting how this occurs are under evolutionary control.

3.1 Preliminaries

Because the simulated robot is based on a physical robot under development, it is necessary to sufficiently constrain the visual processing capabilities available under evolutionary control, so that whatever designs evolved are (at least in principle) capable of being built using available hardware. In essence, this meant opting for very low visual resolution. The total number of pixels had to be at least two or three orders of magnitude lower than that used in conventional computational vision research.[1]

A cursory survey of some biology literature indicated that, for creatures such as insects or other arthropods which have very few photoreceptor units, the photoreceptors often have large angles of acceptance,[2] and are distributed around the body so as to sample a wide visual field. These simple photoreceptor units are perhaps best not thought of as pixels in an image (or 'tiles' in a retinal 'mosaic'): a more appropriate approach is to consider the photoreceptors as simple local brightness detectors. For example, if the portion of the optic array directly above an animal suddenly goes dark while the rest of the optic array remains constant, it seems likely that something is about to drop on the animal from above, and rapid evasive action is probably a sensible adaptive behaviour in such situations. Of course, the animal doesn't have to construct any internal representations or reason about the cause of the darkness; it just has to do something useful.

For this reason, our work to date on evolving visually guided robots has concentrated on ultra-low-resolution vision, close in spirit to Braitenberg's *Vehicles* [1]. The simulated robot has been given a few photoreceptor units, which could realistically be added to the physical robot. This could be done using discrete components (e.g. photodiodes, phototransistors, or LDR's) with individual lenses, thereby creating an electronic compound eye, cf. [4]; or by using conventional CCD cameras but impairing their optics by mounting sand-blasted glass screens in front of the lens so as to generate input images with focus-independent blur, prior to some coarse sub-sampling scheme.

The simulated robot was equipped with vision by embedding it within the SyCo vision simulator system described in [2]. The SyCo simulator was developed for studying issues in visual processing for control of an airborne insect, but only minor alterations were required: the 'altitude' was clamped at a constant value, because the robot is a wheeled vehicle travelling on a flat floor; and the visual sampling pattern, which is fixed in SyCo had to be placed under genetic control.

The SyCo simulator synthesizes vision by means of a computer graphics technique called *ray-tracing* (see e.g. [5]). This is a method which involves instantaneous point-sample estimates ('rays') of the relevant projection integrals, and so *aliasing* is a common problem. Put most simply, aliasing is a problem where insufficient samples are taken to give an accurate impression of the (visual) signal being sampled.

[1] In 'conventional' computer vision, image sizes of 512×512 (i.e. 262144 pixels) are not considered large.

[2] The acceptance angle of a photoreceptor can be defined as twice its maximum incidence angle, where the maximum incidence angle is the largest angle, measured as eccentricity off the 'receptor's visual axis ("direction of view"), at which an incoming ray of light can still have a significant effect.

To limit the effects of aliasing, the SyCo code was configured to determine each photoreceptor's activity by averaging the readings from several rays per simulated receptor, distributed across that receptor's visual field. This provides more accurate estimates of image brightness in the receptor's field of view. However, it is important to keep the number of rays per receptor relatively low. This is for two reasons: one pragmatic, the other theoretical. First, ray-tracing is a computationally expensive process, so using fewer rays per receptor saves processing time. Second, real vision is not an arbitrary-precision process. In vision, noise is inescapable, and noise effectively reduces a continuum of brightness levels to a limited-precision signal. By limiting the number of rays per receptor, the precision of the brightness-value estimate is correspondingly reduced. The simulated robot must be able to cope with noisy limited precision perception, because that is all the real world has to offer.

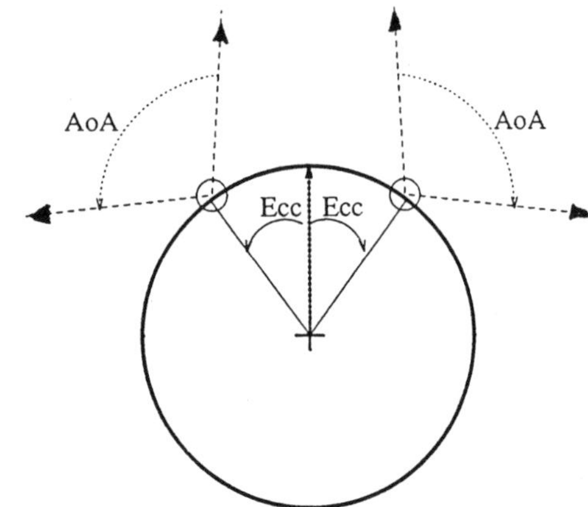

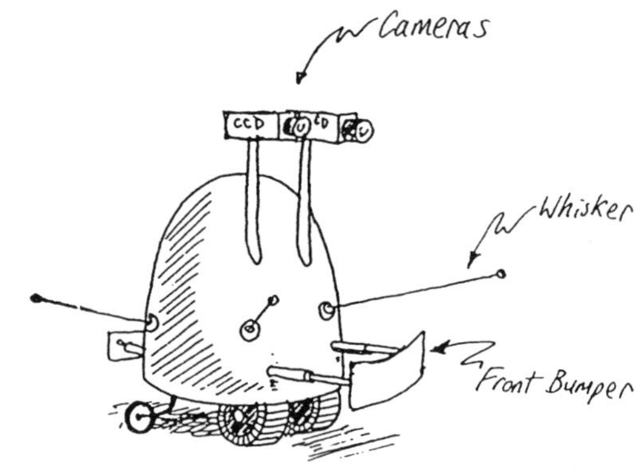

Figure 1: Angle of acceptance and eccentricity for the two-photoreceptor robot. Upper diagram shows top-down view of the robot, and the relevant angles. Lower diagram shows a cartoon of an appropriate robot: the angle of acceptance can be altered using zoom lenses. The eccentricity can be altered by rotating the cameras on their stalks.

3.2 Particulars

3.2.1 Vision

In keeping with the minimal incremental approach advocated in [7], we have commenced our studies by exploring the effects of adding just two photoreceptors to the sensor suite (bumpers and whiskers) described above. Taking a cue from biological vision, the sensors are situated in positions which are bilaterally symmetric about the robot's longitudinal midline.

Having only two receptors introduces manifest limitations on the classes of behaviours that can be expected to evolve in the robot. Assuming that the receptors sample largely distinct portions of the optic array, the only information the robot can access concerning its visual surroundings is likely to be limited to the raw data (the brightness levels recorded by the photoreceptors) and summary statistics such as the average brightness, or the difference between the two signals.

Nevertheless, the acceptance angles of the photoreceptors, and their positions relative to the longitudinal axis, can be varied under genetic control. The two receptors are constrained to have the same angle of acceptance, which is coded as a binary number represented as a bit-vector field in the robot's genome. A second bit-vector field in the genome governs the eccentricity of the photoreceptors, measured off the robot's longitudinal axis. Figure 1 illustrates these two angles.

The details of the genetic coding of the acceptance angle α and the eccentricity β of the two photoreceptors is straightforward. In principle, the angles are constrained to the ranges $\alpha \in (0, \pi] \subset \mathbf{R}$ and $\beta \in [0, \pi/2] \subset \mathbf{R}$, but the use of a bit-vector genome forces a discretization of these ranges. Both angles are represented by four bits in the genome, giving a choice of $2^4 = 16$ discrete values for each angle, i.e. a total of $2^8 = 256$ configurations of α and β. If the integer values represented by the genome fields for α and β are i_α and i_β respectively (i_α, i_β both $\in \{0, 1, \ldots, 15\} \subset \mathbf{N}$), then $\alpha = (1+i_\alpha)\pi/16$, and $\beta = i_\beta \pi/15$.

The genome is currently being extended to allow the number of photoreceptors to be placed under genetic control. In the current two-receptor model, each receptor has a square cross-section to its receptive field. As an anti-aliasing measure, sixteen rays, arranged on a regular 4×4 grid, are traced for each pixel.

All experiments to date have involved evolving architectures which enable the robot to guide itself within a closed cylindrical room. The curved walls of the room are black, while the floor and ceiling are white. Figure 2 illustrates output from the ray-tracing system in this en-

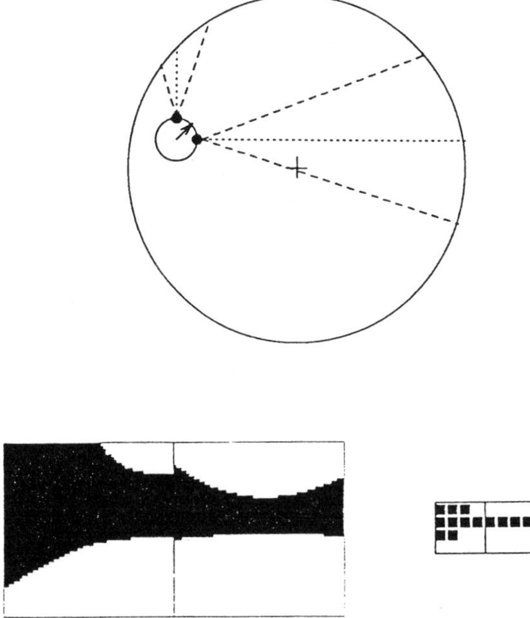

Figure 2: Illustration of the ray-tracing system. The top figure shows the robot's position and orientation within the cylinder, which has black walls and white floor and ceiling. Below that is a pair of relatively high-resolution images, traced from the robot's position inside the cylinder. The next figure shows the two 4×4 images traced prior to averaging, with $\alpha = 1.571$ and $\beta = 0.628$. The final two photoreceptor brightness levels are derived by averaging the 4×4 images.

vironment; Figure 3 illustrates the effects of varying α and β.

3.2.2 Physics

The simulation involves a realistic physics for determining the effects of the robot moving across the floor and colliding with the walls. As described in more detail in [7], the simulated robot is cylindrical in shape with two wheels towards the front and a single trailing rear castor. The wheels have independent drives allowing turning on the spot and fairly unrestricted movement across a flat floor. Outputs from the robot's control networks feed direct to the wheel drives. Depending on the strength and sign of their signal, the wheels rotate at one of five rates: full speed forward; full speed backward; half speed forward; half speed backward; and stationary. The continuous movement of the robot is simulated by polling the network outputs at an appropriate rate. At each step of the simulation the next position and orientation of the robot is calculated using the appropriate kinematic equations (with a suitable amount of noise added). Collisions are handled as accurately as possible, based on

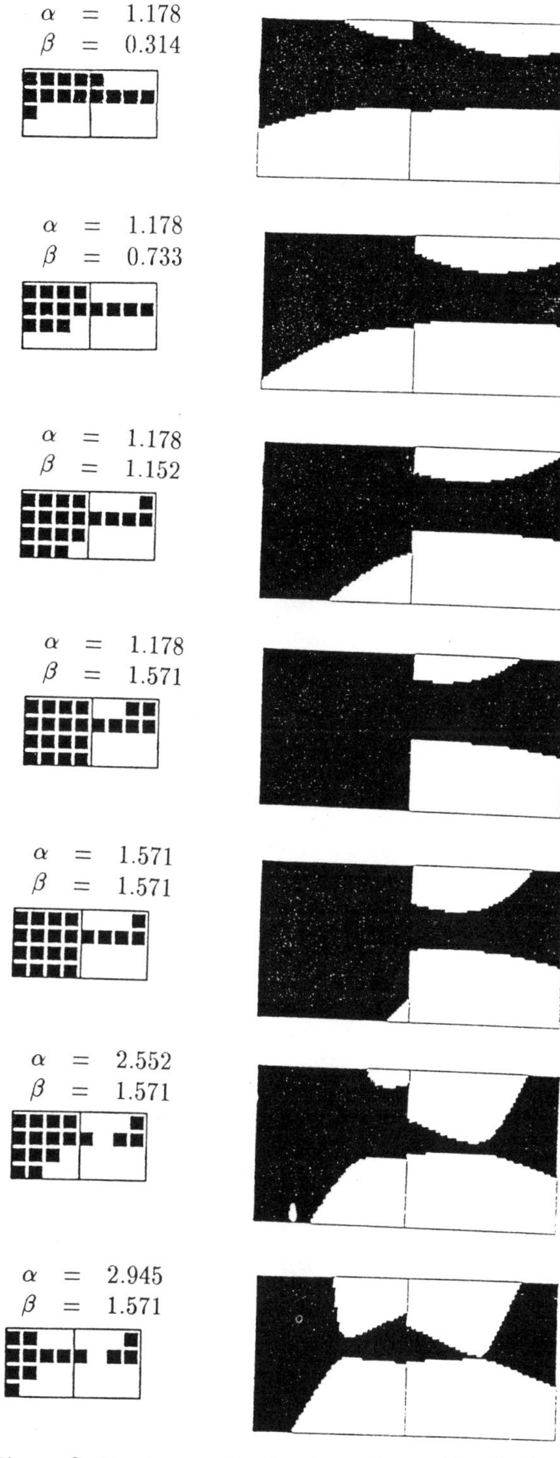

Figure 3: Varying α and β. For all the figures, the robot's position is the same as in Figure 2; the left-hand column shows the pair of 4×4 images, while the right-hand column shows the respective higher-resolution images.

observations of the physical system. Briefly, if the robot

collides with a high velocity normal to the surface it undergoes a noisy reflection with a rotation determined by its original direction of motion; if it collides at low speed its behaviour depends on the angle of incidence – it may rotate until normal to the obstacle or it may skid around until it is parallel.

4 Experiments

Results from earlier experiments discussed in [7] demonstrated that our methods could be used to evolve robots which could engage in primitive tactile-based navigation patterns such as wall-following. The primary goal in the experiments described below was to explore the possibility of evolving robots which could use their visual perception capabilities to avoid collisions with the walls prior to making physical contact with the wall via one of their tactile sensors. Using intentional language, we can say that the robot learns to predict, from visual data alone, that a collision is likely in the near future, and takes appropriate evasive action. We felt this was a suitably low-level task for preliminary experiments. More complex behaviours are currently being evolved from this one.

So, the first task set for our robots was to roam around an empty cylindrical room without hitting the walls. The two-photoreceptor robot has, in theory, sufficient sensory data to avoid the dark walls. Examination of the visual data shown in Figures 2 and 3 confirms this. For example, a useful strategy would be: if the difference between the brightness levels of the two receptors is greater than some threshold, dependent on the values of α and β, then the robot should turn in the direction of the brighter receptor.

The evolutionary process requires an evaluation function $\mathcal{E}$ by which the fitness of individuals in the population can be rated. We have found three evaluation functions useful:

$$\begin{aligned}
\mathcal{E}_1 &= \sum_{\forall t} \mathcal{D}(t) \\
\mathcal{E}_2 &= \left(\sum_{\forall t} \mathcal{D}(t)\right) \cdot \left(\sum_{\forall t} \mathcal{B}(t)\right) \\
\mathcal{E}_3 &= \left(\sum_{\forall t} \mathcal{D}(t)\right) \cdot \left(\sum_{\forall t} \mathcal{G}(t)\right)
\end{aligned}$$

where:

$\forall t$ denotes all time, i.e. the lifetime of the individual;

$\mathcal{D}(t)$ denotes the distance travelled on timestep t

$\mathcal{B}(t)$ denotes the average brightness of the two photoreceptors at time t

$\mathcal{G}(t)$ denotes a Gaussian function of the robot's distance from the centre of the cylinder at time t

The reasons behind choosing these evaluation functions were straightforward. The function $\mathcal{D}$, used in all the evaluation functions, encourages the robots to move (otherwise the best way of avoiding bumping into walls is simply to remain stationary).

$\mathcal{E}_1$ only employs $\mathcal{D}$, so the robots which travel furthest in their lifetimes are rated as the fittest: nevertheless, the mechanics of the collision simulation still penalises robots which collide with the walls at all often.

$\mathcal{E}_2$ is an extension of $\mathcal{E}_1$: the inclusion of the sum of brightness $\mathcal{B}$ introduces a selection pressure which is explicitly vision-oriented. As a robot approaches a wall, the value of $\mathcal{B}$ drops because the wall will tend to occupy more of the visual field of the two receptors. So, robots which over their lifetime have a high value of $\sum \mathcal{B}$ are ones which have tended to avoid approaching walls, and are hence rated as fitter than those which spend a lot of time moving close up to walls.

$\mathcal{E}_3$ is a more subtle version of $\mathcal{E}_2$. Rather than explicitly rate the fitness according to total brightness over a lifetime, we rate the robots on the basis of how much of their time is spent near the centre of the cylinder's floor disk. This is done by measuring the robot's distance d from the floor-centre at time t, and then weighting the distance by a Gaussian $\mathcal{G}$ of the form:

$$\mathcal{G} = \exp(-d^2/c)$$

for some constant c, which ensures that $\mathcal{G} \approx 0$ for $d >\sim 2r/3$, where r is the cylinder's radius. So, while there is no explicit mention of vision in $\mathcal{E}_3$, it is hoped that the robots will evolve to the point where they use their visual input to ensure they are always some distance away from the walls.

Section 5 discusses the results from using these evaluation functions. Before that, we describe some details of the evolutionary mechanisms used.

4.1 *Evolutionary Mechanisms*

Populations of robot genotypes underwent evolution guided by selective pressures based on the evaluation functions given above. The genotype of each robot consists of two chromosomes: one codes for the neural architecture and the other for properties of its visual sensors. As was described in Section 3.2.1, the visual sensor chromosome is a simple fixed length bit string which decodes into a set of parameters giving angle of acceptance and eccentricity of the robot's two photoreceptors. The neural architecture chromosome is more complex, needing a fairly involved process of decoding. The coding and its interpretation are described briefly below, but further details can be found in [7].

The robots 'neural-style' control networks have a fixed number of input units: one for each sensor. In this case there are eight: front and back bumper, two whiskers toward the front and two whiskers toward the back, and the two photoreceptors, or 'eyes' (cf. Figure 1).

The networks also have a fixed number of outputs; two for each of the motor drives. As all of the units are noisy linear threshold devices (as described in [7]) with outputs in the range $[0.0, 1.0] \subset \mathbf{R}$, two units are needed to give the motors a signal in the range $[-1.0, 1.0] \subset \mathbf{R}$, so that forwards and backwards motion is possible. If the output signals from these four output units are labelled S_{o1} to S_{o4}, then the left motor signal is the difference between S_{o1} and S_{o2}, while the right motor signal is the difference between S_{o3} and S_{o4}.

As well as these units these network chromosome codes for a number of 'hidden' units. The number is not pre-specified - the chromosomes are of variable length. The bulk of the chromosome codes for the connections between the units. These are unrestricted; complex recurrent nets are quite possible, as will be seen below.

The networks are real-valued and continuous – think of them as analogue circuits with real-valued signals continuously propagating – which gives them many desirable dynamical adaptive properties. A link may be one of two types: normal or veto; this property is under genetic control. A normal connection joins the output from one unit to the input of another, with unity weight. A veto connection is a special infinitely inhibitory connection between two units. If there is a veto connection between units a and b, and a's output exceeds its veto threshold then all normal connection outputs from b are switched to zero. The veto threshold is always significantly higher than the lower threshold for a neuron's sigmoid transfer function.

The genetic algorithm used is in accordance with the SAGA principles [6]: crossover allows only gradual changes in genotype length. Although we only present results here from simple preliminary experiments, we are currently evolving more complex nets from those developed here, still in keeping with the incremental SAGA approach.

Within this framework, the aims of our first set of simulation experiments was to try and evolve coupled networks and visual sensors capable of generating interesting behaviours.

5 Results

All of the following results were achieved with population size 40, a crossover probability of 1 and a mutation rate of the order of one bit per genotype. The visual sensor and network chromosomes are crossed and mutated separately, but both contribute to the resultant phenotype: the sighted robot. Rank based selection was used with the fittest individual being twice as likely to breed as the median individual. So far the experiments have only been run for a relatively small number of generations, given the expense of the ray tracing and the fact that

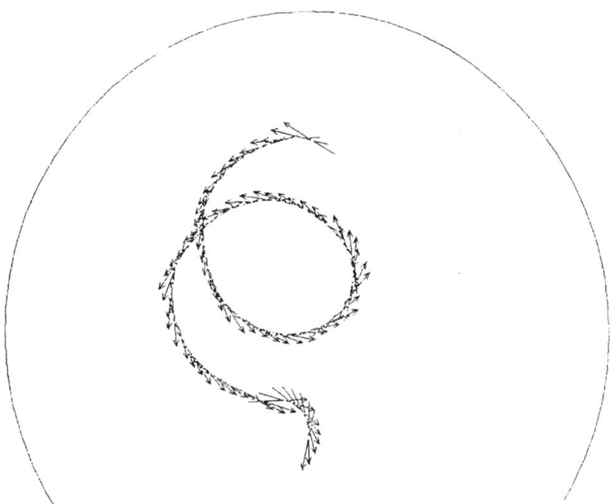

Figure 4: Typical path of blind robot under evaluation function $\mathcal{E}_1$. The arrows show the orientation of the robot at each time step, and their length is equal to the diameter of the robot.

each individual is evaluated multiple times, as described below.

Each individual in each generation was run four times from random starting positions and orientations. Each run was for a fixed number of time steps. The fitness of the individual was taken as the *worst* score from their four runs. This strategy is used to encourage robustness, remembering that there is noise at all levels in the system. A fine-time-slice simulation was used as a close approximation to a continuous system. At each time step the sensor readings are fed into the neural network. The continuous nature of the networks was simulated by running them (synchronously updating all unit inputs and outputs) for a number of iterations (about 100, but with a variance to counter distorting periodic effects) and then converting the outputs to motor signals. The new position of the robot is then calculated, using the model physics described in Section 3.2.2.

By using suitably fine time-slices, this mode of simulation is more than adequate; although we are working on more subtle techniques to allow fully asynchronous event-based simulations.

The first set of experiments used evaluation function $\mathcal{E}_1$, a simple integration of distance moved. Comparisons were made between sighted and blind robots (which used only the six touch sensors). Both did well although the evolved behaviours were quite different in the two cases. The blind robots evolved to make looping elliptical movements like that shown in Figure 4.

The strategy seems sensible as it tends to keep the robot away from the walls. The networks quickly evolved to the state where sensory inputs triggered changes in directions which sped the robot away from the wall. See Figure 8, later, for an example of such behaviour.

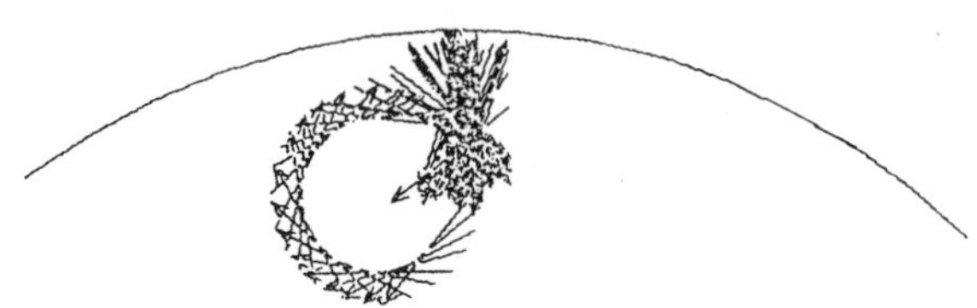

Figure 5: Evolved behaviour of sighted robot under evaluation function $\mathcal{E}_2$.

The sighted robots did better, tending to keep moving by staying away from the walls using visually guided behaviours like those shown in Figure 7, described in more detail later.

The second set of experiments use $\mathcal{E}_2$. This evaluation function makes explicit use of the visual signal, so a comparison with blind robots was not sensible. The behaviours which evolved were unexpectedly simple but made perfect sense. A very fit and robust behaviour which rapidly dominated is shown in Figure 5.

The robot evolved to have photoreceptors with high angle of acceptance and high eccentricity, and it turns in a tight circle by jamming one motor full on and one off. Turning in a circle at full speed rapidly moves the robot away from the wall if it collides, as shown in Figure 5. So this strategy tends to maximise $\sum \mathcal{D}(t)$, but it also gives a very high value for $\sum \mathcal{B}(t)$ given that this visual signal is high except if a photoreceptor is close to and pointing towards a wall. The graphs of visual signals against time look like those shown in Figure 6.

The third set of experiments, using $\mathcal{E}_3$, produced the most interesting behaviours. Remember the Gaussian function, $\mathcal{G}(t)$, drops off sharply towards the walls. Early on, the circular motion behaviour predominated as shown in Figure 6. It can be seen that there is no correlation between visual signal and motor output; vision is not yet being used.

This behaviour is not very robust as it scores poorly on $\sum \mathcal{G}(t)$ if the robot starts off near a wall. But within a few generations the much more robust behaviour of Figure 7 appeared. Here the robot is making clear use of vision to keep it away from the walls and so score well on the Gaussian function.

The graphs in Figure 7 show the visual signals and the motor signals (with noise removed for easier interpretation) plotted against time. The basic strategy is to jam one motor on full speed and one on half speed (in this case it is moving backwards) [3] to move in a circle. But

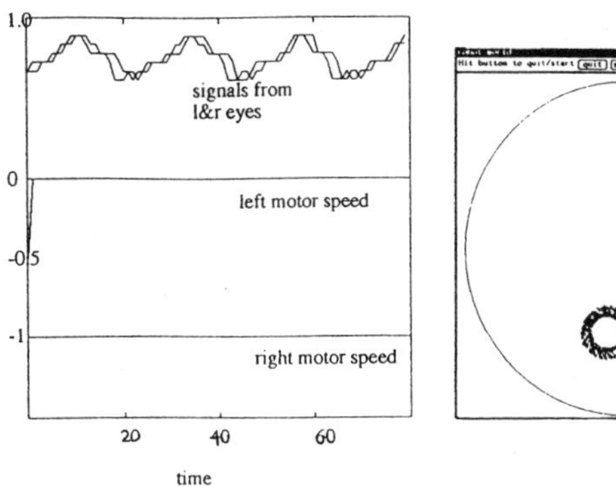

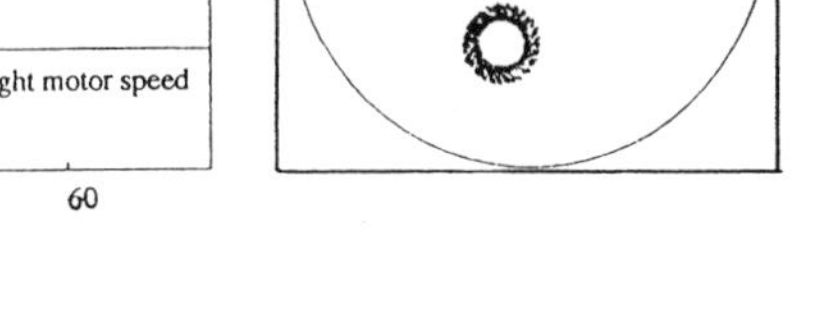

Figure 6: Fittest behaviour of sighted robot in very early generations under evaluation function $\mathcal{E}_3$.

when the visual signal drops, one of the motors is turned off, causing the tight turns shown in the figure. The sensors evolved to have a fairly high angle of acceptance but a low eccentricity (both 'eyes' clearly pointing forward) which makes sense in the context of this behaviour. So here we see a clear correlation between visual signal and motor output; vision is being used to great effect.

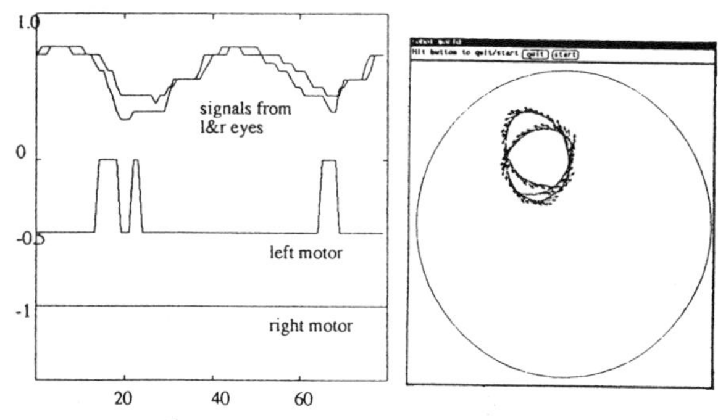

Figure 7: Later evolved behaviours under $\mathcal{E}_3$.

Examination of the evolved network (see [3] for illustration) that generates the behaviour in Figure 7 reveals a complicated connectivity with many indirect feedback loops and subtle uses of veto connections. The jammed-on right motor is achieved by the relevant output unit feeding back into itself and having no other inputs. Once internal noise generates an input to the unit it will amplify and then circulate forever (at the moment signals do not attenuate in time, although of course veto connections can turn parts of the net on and off). Visual signals feeding into the left motor outputs provide its visually

[3] We, as experimenters, have designated a particular mode of movement as 'forward' (motor signals positive), but clearly in this simple environment there is a duality between forwards and backwards movement. 'Running towards light' and 'running away from dark' are equivalent behaviours.

correlated behaviour.

In earlier generations, the tactile sensors seem to have been used much more. By the later stage at which the behaviour shown was produced, vision is dominant. Examination of the wiring strongly suggests that many of the tactile sensor input nodes are essentially being used as 'internal' nodes: vision keeps the robot away from the walls and hence avoids the possibility of turning the sensors on, thereby rendering the tactile input units virtually redundant; later, over a number of generations, the 'input' units are employed for other uses. This is a good example of the strongly opportunistic nature of evolution: it pays no regard to the initial characterisations given to the nodes.

One of the most remarkable phenomena we observed was the emergence of networks involving oscillatory circuits built up from complicated loops of veto and normal connections. Under certain initial conditions, when the robot's visual signals became high these circuits would periodically turn the motors on and off so that the robot moved slowly through the bright area of the room. Although this reduces the score on the $\sum \mathcal{D}(t)$ component of $\mathcal{E}_3$ it is effective in increasing the score on the $\sum \mathcal{G}(t)$ component.

The mature evolved networks typically appeared rather complex for their given tasks. We are currently exploring methods of exerting an evolutionary pressure towards simpler networks, by introducing costs for link creation in the evaluation functions, and by employing neuron models with more flexibility (e.g. variations in time delays and/or connection strengths).

Blind robots did fairly well on the $\mathcal{E}_3$ evaluation function too; directly evolving strategies to move well away from the wall, such as reversing, as shown in Figure 8. The change in direction of the robot in the middle of its path (this one is moving forwards) is a clear case of reversing.

In each of the experiments the networks were capable of generating a wide range of behaviours. This was due to their dynamical properties and gave important advantages. Although Hebbian-style learning is on our agenda, we can probably delay its use for a while given the power of these continuous dynamical nets.

6 Discussion and Further Work

The results show quite clearly that, in all three cases, the robot design evolved to satisfy the evaluation function. Furthermore, there was a clear behavioural difference between those robots which used vision, and those which were unsighted. Interesting results have been achieved with relatively small populations and after relatively few generations. We think this is largely due to the particular type of networks we have chosen to use. They have properties which appear to result in a search space highly suited to evolutionary techniques. The SAGA principles

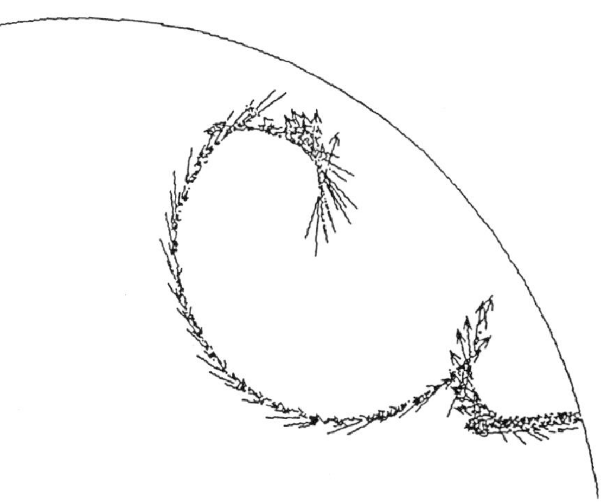

Figure 8: Evolved behaviour of blind robot under $\mathcal{E}_3$.

of gradual and incremental evolution should help to keep the search space constrained so that small to medium sized populations can be used throughout our work.

Our work to date has involved evolving robots which move around an empty cylindrical room without hitting the walls. Work is currently in progress on extending the robot's behaviour so it can move in cluttered environments without collisions. However, the computational costs of the ray-tracing system scales roughly in proportion with the number of objects in the robot's environment: simulating vision in cluttered environments soon imposes deeply problematic computational burdens on the overall system.

Nevertheless, the results so far have been sufficiently successful that our approach bears further exploration in increasingly complex environments and with more challenging tasks. But there is a severe limitation on how much further the work can be taken in its current form: the computational costs of simulating vision and realistic physics mean that vast quantities of computer time are taken up with providing an accurate 'virtual reality' for the simulated robots. For this reason, we are moving into a second phase in our work. This reduces our reliance on simulation, by using an accurately controllable real-world robot linked to off-board processing. We call this system 'toytown'.

The toytown experimental setup described below is now under development and we expect our first results in the near future. The apparatus has been designed to allow us to engage in long term fundamental experiments aimed at thoroughly exploring the possibilities of our evolutionary methodology. In particular, we aim to explore the concurrent evolution of control networks and visual sensors for navigational tasks. As in the experiments described earlier, details of the visual sensing and neural architecture are under genetic control.

6.1 Toytown

Our experiences to date have confirmed earlier intuitive notions that simulation of visual inputs is computationally horrendous — this is directly associated with the usefulness of vision, in that it gives inputs from a vast range of the environment both far and near. So the incentives for working with real rather than simulated vision are even higher than with the other senses. Active vision for a robot in a real world requires something like a camera moving with the robot through that world, which for experimental purposes normally requires a decision to be made between having computational processing of visual inputs done onboard the robot, or offboard via some link to more powerful stationary computers. Both of these choices have negative factors associated, either the size and weight of onboard computation, or the problems of radio links and tangled umbilical cables.

So for experimental purposes we have devised a third method, which allows a miniature robot with active vision, with the robot size effectively only a few cms across, to roam freely through an environment set up by the experimenters. The environment could be a 'toytown', although the word 'toy' here only refers to the size. It is a real world that the robot is in, with real-world vision problems.

A gantry is set up above a flat surface, with a horizontal girder able to move west and east by means of a stepper motor, providing the X-coordinates of the robot. Along the girder another stepper motor allows movement of a platform north and south (the Y-coordinates). From the platform a CCD camera is fixed pointing vertically downwards. A mirror is fixed some cms below the lens and occupying its field of view. The mirror can be rotated independent of the camera. The camera and mirror can be moved together with its supporting platform in the X and Y dimensions. Vertical movement relative to the platform can also be provided to give the Z dimension. The mirror itself can be considered as the body of the sighted artificial creature which can move through the environment provided for experimental purposes. A sketch of the toytown system is shown in Figure 9.

Direction of view is changed by rotating the mirror. Any number of strategies for sampling the visual field can be effected in software, and software sampling (under 'genetic' control) can provide the required number of virtual pixels or photoreceptors facing in (genetically specified) different directions. A system of servo motors, racks and pinions can provide an accuracy of movement of plus or minus one millimetre. Touch sensors around the mirror complete the 'body' of the robot. The robot's control network is simulated off-board on a computer. The sensory inputs are fed into the controller via an umbilical cable and interfacing cards. In a similar way the controller sends motor commands to the various actuators.

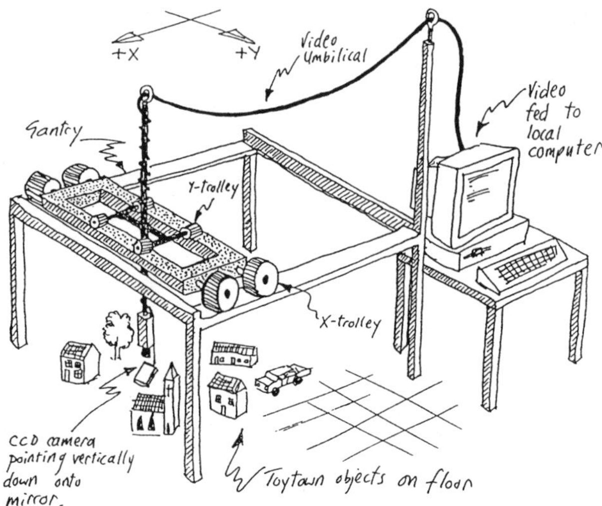

Figure 9: The toytown gantry system. See text for further details.

The 'body' of the robot is only the size of the mirror plus touch sensors, and subject only to its attachment to the camera above, and hence to the gantry, can be moved anywhere in an experimental setup. This setup can be suitably small, and easily altered. In this way all of the real world characteristics of moving around in a noisy visual environment are retained, with a number of advantages for experimental purposes over a wheeled ground-based autonomous robot:

- There are no problems with tangled umbilicals, and on-board power supplies and computers are not an issue.
- The environment is easily changed - it can be made less structured or more dynamic or whatever suits the current level of evolution.
- Time can be slowed down to a rate appropriate to computational resources. As cognitive processing becomes more computationally demanding the speed of movement of the creature and other dynamic objects in the environment can be made as slow as is desired.
- The highly controllable nature of the apparatus means that experiments are repeatable and very long runs can be achieved without any human intervention. This means that, for each generation, each member of the population can be evaluated without recourse to simulation.

A succession of tasks of increasing complexity can be set for such a robot. Automatic evaluations for each task allow a succession of tests, and the evolutionary process, to continue without immediate human intervention. A possible succession of tasks would be:

- Movement towards an 'object' (a prominent dark mark, perhaps).
- Rotation (virtual rotation via software resampling of camera input) to face a moving object.
- Avoidance of obstacles.
- Movement between two objects.
- Movement centrally along a striped corridor.
- Identification of, and movement through, 'doorways'.
- Exploratory movement within a simple maze.
- Identification of particular 'situations' within such a maze or environment, and return to them after exploration.
- Development of 'place recognition' by navigation through the environment between specified points via self-selected intermediary places.
- Navigation and interaction with a dynamic world.
- Performance of previous tasks but subject to arbitrary polarity reversal of the motor outputs.

The outputs from the controller provide signals to the motor drives (with the deliberate addition of noise if desired) which effectively allow the robot to move continuously and freely in this world. The robot is to all intents and purposes autonomous. However, although it does not 'know' its absolute position and orientation, this information is always available to the experimenters. This is extremely useful for automatic fitness evaluation, repeatability, repositioning and so on.

The 'Toytown' environment has some similarities with the 'Tinytown' environment at Rochester [8]. However the latter has a camera pointing down that can move only in two dimensions, giving the equivalent of 'low-flying aerial photographs'. In contrast, the toytown robot has a (virtual) rotational degree of freedom, and can travel in and amongst the objects of a 3-D world, with a horizontal field of view manipulable between $0°$ to $360°$.

7 Summary and Conclusions

As further support of our claims in [7], we have presented early results from experiments in evolving network processing architectures for mobile robots. Using networks of relatively constrained processing units ('neurons'), and simple evaluation functions, we have been able to evolve visual control architectures, even when the evaluation function is not defined in terms of monitoring visual inputs.

The results have demonstrated the feasibility of the approach, but the computational costs of simulating vision have lead us to develop a method which allows for a mix of 'real' vision and evolutionary methods, using readily available hardware. The 'toytown' project is at an early stage, but our current results are sufficiently promising that we are confident of future success. Watch this space.

Acknowledgements

Many thanks to Linda Thompson, and to staff at the Kings Ambassador Hotel, Perth, Australia, for help in the preparation of this paper. Ongoing research is supported by a grant from the University of Sussex Research Development Fund.

References

[1] V. Braitenberg. *Vehicles: Experiments in Synthetic Psychology.* M.I.T. Press — Bradford Books, Cambridge MA, 1984.

[2] D. T. Cliff. The computational hoverfly; a study in computational neuroethology. In J.-A. Meyer and S. W. Wilson, editors, *From Animals to Animats: Proceedings of the First International Conference on Simulation of Adaptive Behavior (SAB90)*, pages 87–96, Cambridge MA, 1991. M.I.T. Press — Bradford Books.

[3] D. T. Cliff, P. Husbands, and I. Harvey. Evolving visually guided robots. Technical Report CSRP 220, University of Sussex School of Cognitive and Computing Sciences, 1992.

[4] N. Franceschini, J.-M. Pichon, and C. Blanes. Real time visuomotor control: from flies to robots. In *Proceedings of the 1991 International Conference on Advanced Robotics, Pisa*, 1991.

[5] A. S. Glassner, editor. *An Introduction to Ray Tracing.* Academic Press, London, 1989.

[6] I. Harvey. Species adaptation genetic algorithms: A basis for a continuing SAGA. In F.J. Varela and P. Bourgine, editors, *Towards a Practice of Autonomous Systems: Proceedings of the First European Conference on Artificial Life (ECAL91)*, pages 346–354. M.I.T. Press — Bradford Books, Cambridge MA, 1992.

[7] I. Harvey, P. Husbands, and D. T. Cliff. Issues in evolutionary robotics. Technical Report CSRP 219, University of Sussex School of Cognitive and Computing Sciences, 1922.

[8] R. C. Nelson. Visual homing using an associative memory. *Biological Cybernetics*, 65:281–291, 1991.

An Evolved, Vision-Based Behavioral Model of Coordinated Group Motion

Craig W. Reynolds

cwr@red.com

Electronic Arts / 1450 Fashion Island Boulevard / San Mateo, CA 94404 / USA

Abstract

Coordinated motion in a group of simulated *critters* can evolve under selection pressure from an appropriate fitness criteria. Evolution is modeled with the Genetic Programming paradigm. The simulated environment consists of a group of critters, some static obstacles, and a predator. In order to survive, the critters must avoid collisions (with obstacles as well as with each other) and must avoid predation. They must steer a safe path through the dynamic environment using only information received through their visual sensors. The arrangement of visual sensors, as well as the mapping from sensor data to motor action is determined by the evolved controller program. The motor model assumes an innate constant forward velocity and limited steering. The predator preferentially targets isolated "stragglers" and so encourages aggregation. Fitness is based on the sum of all critter lifetimes.

1 Introduction

In the work described here, a behavioral controller for a 2d *critter* (animat, artificial animal, autonomous agent, robot, or what-have-you) is obtained through simulated evolution. A stimulus-response controller for a type of *coordinated group motion* begins to emerge under selection pressure from an appropriate fitness measure. The evolutionary process starts with primitive computational elements that provide simulated perception and motor control, as well as the connections between them. The fitness of an individual controller is determined by installing it in a group of simulated critters, placing them in a simulated world and judging their collective performance.

The critters move forward at a constant rate and the controller must "steer" to avoid collisions with static obstacles, moving critters, and a pursuing predator. All collisions are considered fatal. A controller's fitness is based on the total number of simulation steps taken by all of the critters prior to their demise. Over time, under the patient guidance of fitness testing, the evolutionary process constructs an increasingly effective mapping from perception to motor control which allows the critters to get increasingly effective at avoiding the dangers in their simulated world.

This work is not intended to be a realistic model of the evolution of coordinated group motion in natural animals. Instead it provides an abstract example of how such behavior *can* arise in an evolutionary process. It provides a computational model for examining theories about how specific selection pressures and various environmental factors affect the evolution of coordinated group motion. This model provides a framework which can be used to investigate more sophisticated forms of coordinated group motion. The experiments reported here are a first step towards an eventual goal of evolving behavior reminiscent of the fluid, graceful, and visually fascinating motion seen in large groups of natural animals.

In nature, here are many reasons why animals congregate in groups, such as increased access to mates and the group's ability to forage over larger areas. This work focuses on simulating just one aspect of herding: the highly aligned, tightly packed, closely synchronized motion seen when a herd is exposed to a predator. The aim is to have this behavior emerge through artificial evolution given the conflicting selection pressures to: evade predators, avoid obstacles, and coordinate with herd-mates. At one extreme a critter could attempt to avoid everything in its world since all collisions are fatal. Predation pressure confers a survival advantage on those that cluster together. As a result the critters will tend to move close to their herd-mates while collectively avoiding obstacles and collectively evading the predator. Since all critters have the same behavior, coordinating motion is based on the principle that "if I don't run into my herd-mates, they won't run into me". This cooperation is a form of evolved altruism.

While admittedly unconnected to natural evolution of corresponding behaviors in real animals, this work aspires to a certain level of plausibility by the *closed* nature of its simulated world. The controller's action is fully determined by the information it obtains about the simulated world through its simulated perceptions. The fitness of a controller is fully determined by the performance of its simulated behavior in the simulated world. The critter's behavior is *grounded* in its perception of the world, and its perception directly reflect the consequences of its behavior.

2 Previous Work

Coordinated group motion exists in many forms in the natural world: flocks of birds, schools of fish, herds of mammals, and colonies of social insects. These behaviors presumably arose through the process of evolution. The work presented here seeks to investigate aspects of the relationship between various selection pressures and the evolution of coordinated group motion.

Zoologists and other scientists have studied coordinated group motion in nature for a long time, see for example [Partridge 1982] and [Potts 1984]. These phenomena are very difficult to study in an objective yet non-invasive way. In recent years, as computer modeling and simulation has provided a concrete way to test theories, many researchers have implemented models of certain aspects of natural coordinated group motion: [Amkraut 1985], [Meyers 1985], [Reynolds 1987], [Girard 1990], [Heppner 1990], [Drake 1991], and [Durkin 1991]. These behavior models were "written by hand" (not evolved) and were based on some type of global knowledge about the environment which is an unnatural model for an autonomous agent.

In contrast, Olivier Renault developed a vision-based behavioral model for obstacle avoidance in [Renault 1990]. Lawrence Dill described a model of coordinated animal motion based on abstracted visual signals in [Dill 1991]. And Helmut Lorek created a vision-based model of flocking that ran on a large parallel computer in real time [Lorek 1992]. These three were non-evolved vision-based implementations.

An evolved, vision-based approach similar to the work described in this paper was used to address the single-critter obstacle avoidance problem in [Reynolds 1993?]. Larry Yaeger's PolyWorld [Yaeger 1993?] is a conceptually vast Artificial Life simulator based (in part) on visual perception and non-goal-directed evolution. In some PolyWorld runs, species have evolved which display locomotion behavior similar to coordinated herding.

Maja Mataric has investigated (non-evolved) coordinated group motion in a group of 20 small robots based on the subsumption architecture [Mataric 1992]. Ronald Arkin has researched strategies for collective robotic action inspired by cooperation in ant colonies [Arkin 1992].

Evolved collective behavior for "central place foraging" in a type of grid-based artificial ant, has been investigated by Robert Collins and David Jefferson [Collins 1991] and by John Koza (see chapter 12 in [Koza 1992]).

A classical work in behavioral modeling is [Braitenberg 1984] which touched on many of the ideas here, but as thought experiments whose implementation was somewhat fanciful. The behavioral controllers described in this paper are very much in the spirit of the *subsumption architecture* described by Rodney Brooks [Brooks 1986]. These *reactive agents* base their behavior directly on the world as perceived through their sensors. They have little or no higher cognition and do not bother with complex mental models of their environment, preferring to use "the world is its own map" [Brooks 1991]. The work reported here is strongly influenced by Dave Cliff's manifesto on *computational neuroethology* [Cliff 1991a] as well as his hoverfly simulation [Cliff 1991b]. While the models described here are not based on neurons, the principles of using a closed, grounded simulation to test behavioral models are fundamental to this project.

This work grew out of conversations the author had with Andy Kopra at the Artificial Life II meeting in Santa Fe in February 1990. Many of the basic ideas presented here (evolved coordinated motion, using the 2d case, vision basing, the predator, evaluation in closed and grounded simulation) came directly from those talks. At almost the same time (or perhaps a little earlier) Stephen Smith and Johnny Ornelas of Thinking Machines Inc. were having amazing similar conversations, and had envisioned strikingly similar experiments. Unfortunately neither groups was able to pursue the project back then due to more immediately pressing matters.

3 Genetic Algorithms, Genetic Programming and the Steady State

At the heart of the work described here is the notion of simulated evolution. The basic evolution model used here is the venerable Genetic Algorithms ("GA"), originally developed by Holland [Holland 1975]. The Genetic Algorithm has been widely studied by many authors and applied to a myriad of practical problems in many different fields [Holland 1992]. Over the years many variations on the basic Genetic Algorithms have been proposed. A hybrid of two such variations are used to implement the simulated evolution described in this paper.

John Koza forged a link between the Genetic Algorithm and computer programming technology with his Genetic Programming paradigm [Koza 1989], [Koza 1992]. Genetic Programming ("GP") is a technique for automatically creating computer programs (traditionally, but not necessarily, in the Lisp language) that satisfy a specified fitness criteria. There is a very strong analogy between the operation of the Genetic Algorithm and Genetic Programming. The main difference is in the representation of genetic information: bit strings in GA, fragments of Lisp code in GP. The use of fitness-proportionate selection, reproduction, crossover, and mutation are all directly analogous. One significant difference is that while classic Genetic Algorithms work on fixed length bit strings, Genetic Programming deals with objects of inherently varying size. The complexity of programs created by GP tend to correspond to the complexity of the problem being solved. If simple programs do not satisfy the fitness function, the Genetic Programming paradigm creates larger programs that do. As a result, Genetic Programming does not require that the user know, or even estimate, the complexity of the problem at hand. This was an important consideration for the goal of coevolving sensor arrays and coordinated group motion. We did not want to specify how many sensors should be used. Genetic Programming did not require such a specification, instead that implicit parameter could be left to evolve its own preferred value.

(Karl Sims independently developed the idea of using Lisp code as genetic material. He used the concept in combination with a system much like *The Blind Watchmaker* ("BW") [Dawkins 1986]. An apt analogy might be to say that GP is to GA as Sims work is to BW. A discussion of crossover and mutation operations can be found in [Sims 1991]. These mutation operations were incorporated into the GP system described in this paper, but the experiments described here did not use mutation.)

Gilbert Syswerda described a variation on traditional GA he called *Steady State Genetic Algorithms* ("SSGA") in Appendix A of [Syswerda 1989], an analysis of their performance can be found in [Syswerda 1991] and [Davis 1991]. A similar technique had previously used in classifier systems and is described on pages 147-148 of [Holland 1975]. Darrell Whitley independently discovered this variation and described it in [Whitley 1989]. While the term "steady state" has apparently become accepted, the comparison of "traditional GA" versus "steady state GA" suggests terms like "batch" versus "continuous" to this author. In any case, the basic idea is to do away with the synchronized *generations* of traditional GAs. Instead there is a continuously updated population ("gene pool") of evolved individuals. Each step of the SSGA consists of fitness proportionate selection of two parents from the population, creation of new individual(s) through crossover and (occasional) mutation, removal of individual(s) from the population to make room, and finally insertion of the new individual(s) back into the population. An additional requirement is that all individuals in the population are required to be unique. (The step of creating new individuals loops until unique offspring are found.) The general observation is that SSGAs are more *efficient* than traditional GAs in terms of the number of fitness tests required before a given problem is solved. There seems to be some evidence that SSGAs are less prone to premature convergence on suboptimal solutions. In the work reported here, the concept of SSGA was applied to GP to produce a system for "Steady State Genetic Programming".

4 Coordinated Group Motion as Genetic Programming

In order to solve a problem with Genetic Programming we must restate the problem in a canonical form. We must specify a list of *functions,* a list of *terminals*, and a *fitness function*. The Genetic Programming paradigm will evolve programs according to the judgment of the fitness function. The programs themselves are nested Lisp expressions: a function applied to subexpressions. The subexpressions are either one of the terminals or (recursively) another such expression. (These hierarchies are known variously as "s-expressions", "lists", "Lisp fragments", "parse trees" and so on.)

The terminals used in the evolved group motion problem are just an assortment of numerical constants: 0, 0.01, 0.1, 0.5, and 2. The list of functions is:

```
+
-
*
%
abs
iflte
turn
look-for-friend
look-for-obstacle
look-for-predator
```

The functions **+**, **-**, and ***** are the standard Common Lisp [Steel 1990] arithmetic functions for addition, subtraction, and multiplication. Each of them take an arbitrary number of arguments. The function **abs** is the standard Common Lisp absolute value function which take one argument. The functions **%** and **iflte** are suggested in [Koza 1992]. Koza calls **%** "protected divide", a function of two arguments (A and B) which returns 1 if B=0 and A/B otherwise. The conditional **iflte** combines the standard Common Lisp functions **if** and **<=** into "if less than or equal". In the implementation described here, **iflte** is a Lisp *macro* which makes this source-level transformation:

```
(iflte a b c d) → (if (<= a b) c d)
```

Using **iflte** instead of **if** and **<=** produces a set of functions which are easily interchangeable: all of the values being passed around are numeric. The Boolean value returned by <= would cause an error if supplied where a number was expected. These "nonviable" programs would not survive to reproduce. Evolution could eventually discover how to plug **<=** into **if** by itself, but by smoothing off this rough edge beforehand, we can get GP to focus its effort more directly on the problem at hand. We want survival to be based on increases in fitness rather than details of syntax.

The functions **turn**, **look-for-obstacle**, **look-for-friend**, and **look-for-predator** are specific to the coordinated group motion problem. (Note that "friend" refers to another critter.) Each of them take a single argument, an angle relative to the current heading. Angles are specified in units of *revolutions*, a normalized angle measure: 1 revolution equals 360 degrees or 2π radians. These functions will be explained more fully below, but basically: **turn** steers the critter by altering its heading by the specified angle (which is returned as the function's value). The **look-for-...** functions "look" in the given direction and return a measure of how strongly (if at all) a friend, obstacle, or predator is "seen through the fog".

We must also provide the *fitness function* that the Genetic Programming paradigm will use to judge the quality of the programs it creates. The fitness function takes one argument, an evolved program, and returns a numerical fitness value. In the implementation described here, fitness values are normalized to lie in the range between zero and one inclusively. A fitness of zero means "totally unfit", a category that can include programs that get errors during execution. A fitness of one signifies a perfect solution to the problem at hand. For more details see the "Fitness" section below.

Finally there are a few other parameters required to specify a Genetic Programming run. The maximum size of programs in the initial random generation is set to 50. The size of the "steady-state gene pool" (which is roughly comparable to the population in a traditional "batch" generation GA) was set to various values for different runs, but ranged between 20 and 200 individual programs. The mutation rate is zero.

5 The Critter and its World

The critter model used in these experiments is a computer simulation based on widely-used principles of computational geometry and computer graphics. Its simplicity and abstraction make it an equally good (or by the same token, equally bad) model of a living creature, a physical robot, or simply an abstract synthetic creature.

The critter moves on a two dimensional surface. It is essentially equivalent to the LOGO *turtle* [Abelson 1981]. Its state consists of a position and an orientation. In the accompanying illustrations, the critter's body is depicted as a triangle to indicate its heading. For purposes of collision detection, however, its body is modeled as a disk of unit diameter.

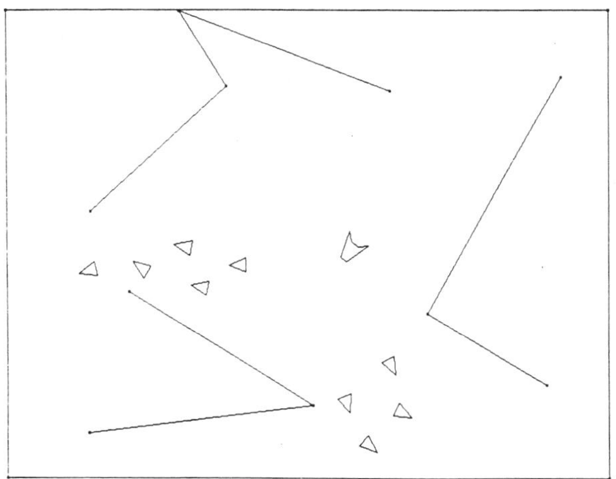

Figure 1: the critter's world

The simulated world consists of a group of critters, some static *obstacles*, and a *predator*. A critter will die if it *collides* with another critter, an obstacle, or the predator. Collision is defined by a simple distance criteria. In the case of critter/critter or critter/predator collisions, the criteria is overlap of the two bounding disks. In the case of critter/obstacle collisions, the criteria is overlap of the critter's bounding disk with any of the line segments that make up an obstacle. Figure 1 shows some critters, the predator, and the obstacle course (named "Box-and-Fences") which was used in all of the experiments described here.

There are two kinds of motor actions in the critter's repertoire: *move forward* and *turn*. In the particular problem being studied here, we will assume that forward motion is constant and innate. The critter will always move forward (that is, along its own heading) by one half of its body length each simulation step.

Beyond these fixed innate properties, the critter's *volition* comes from its evolved control program. Typically the controller will use the perception primitives (**look-for-obstacle**, **look-for-friend**, and **look-for-predator**) to get information about the environment, do some conditional and arithmetic processing, and then a **turn** based on the result.

Various schemes have been used in these experiments to enforce the idea of a non-zero turning radius. In some cases, turning too much is considered fatal. In other cases, large turning angles are allowed but are truncated to a "reasonable" range. Hybrids of these two approaches have also been tried. The maximum per-step turning angle threshold used in these runs is ±0.08 revolutions (29 degrees or 0.50 radians). Both of these approaches will ensure that turning rates are bounded, but the more forgiving "truncation" approach seems less likely to block evolutionary progress by ruthlessly killing off promising new variations which happen to turn a little too much.

The predator is controlled by a hand-crafted program which does not evolve. In general, the predator will select the nearest critter as its prey. The "targeting criteria" is actually a combination of three factors: distance, relative heading, and isolation. Critters that are heading away from the predator are harder to catch and so are considered less desirable. Similarly, the predator prefers isolated "stragglers" and so considers critters in close proximity to others to be less desirable. The predator chases its prey trying to get close enough to "kill" it. Because the predator is only 95% as fast as the critters, they can escape by running directly away from the predator. Rather than heading towards its prey's current location, the predator uses a simple linear predictor and heads to where it "thinks" the prey will be at the time of capture, based on the prey's current heading.

6 Perception

The **look-for-obstacle**, **look-for-friend**, and **look-for-predator** functions simulates the critter's perception and so are the controller's only source of information about its world. All adaptive, time-varying behavior must be derived somehow from the variations of these perceptions as the critter moves through the world. When (for example) **look-for-obstacle** is called, a *ray-tracing* operation is performed. That is, a geometric ray ("half line") is constructed from the critter's position in the direction specified by the sum of the critter's heading and the argument to **look-for-obstacle**. The intersection (if any) of that ray with each object in the environment is calculated. The object whose ray intersection is closest to the critter's center is deemed the *visible object*. Note that all objects are treated as *opaque* and so for example, a critter can "hide" from the predator by moving behind an obstacle. Similarly, a critter that is surrounded by other critters can see only them and not any obstacles or predators that lie beyond them.

In order to provide the controller with an indirect clue about distances, we have postulated that the critter's world is a very foggy place. Visual stimuli are attenuated by distance. Certainly this aspect of the simulation can be criticized as being *ad hoc*. But the alternatives are daunting: without attenuation, a critter surrounded by obstacles is in a featureless environment, whatever direction it looks it sees an obstacle. Postulating more complicated sensory mechanisms (such as stereo vision or texture recognition) seemed too complex and would have introduced a new crop of *ad hoc* details to be explained away. The "foggy world" model is somewhat plausible: real fish in murky water face a similar perceptual realm, and the phenomenon known as "aerial perspective" refers to attenuation in air caused by dust and water vapor. If desired, say for robotic experimentation, technology exists (in the special effects industry) for filling rooms with "smoke" of precisely controlled density. The last rationalization for the foggy world model is that it is only slightly different in effect from perception based on active sonar as used by bats and dolphins.

It has been assumed that the critter's visual system can immediately distinguish between the three kinds of object (obstacles, friends, and predators) in its world. While this provides a vast simplification, one plausible explanation is to assume that critters have a form of *color vision* and that obstacles, friends, and predators all have unique primary hues. The implementation described here glosses over these details, but we can imagine that perceived color is decomposed into hue (indicating the type of object) and saturation (indicating distance through the fog).

The value returned from (for example) **look-for-obstacle** is a number between zero and one. A value of one would indicate that the obstacle is coincident with the critter, but this does not occur in practice since this would imply a collision had occurred. As the distance between the critter and the obstacle increases, the visual signal drops off quadratically in strength. At a certain threshold value (15 body lengths in these experiments) the signal will have reached zero. Hence a value of zero returned from **look-for-obstacle** indicates that the closest obstacle in the given direction (if any) is at least 15 units away.

Note that the argument to the **look-for-...** functions are not restricted to be constants and so the process of evolution will often derive bizarre formulations that calculate a dynamic value and use that to specify the direction in which to look. Originally the author had assumed that evolution would create a sort of *retina*, with fixed sensors pointed in the directions of interest. In hindsight it becomes clear that a better model is a simple form of *animate vision* [Cliff 1991b] where the controller "aims" its visual fovea at the area of interest.

7 Fitness

In order to test the fitness of a newly evolved control program we place the critters in the world, start them running and measure how long they can avoid collisions and predation. Specifically, the critters are told to take 200 steps. The number of steps taken by each critter (before it dies) is divided by 200 and those values are averaged together to produce the controller's normalized raw score.

The raw score is modified by multiplication by some "style points" (less objective criteria). In order to encourage critters to use generally smooth paths they are penalized for "excessive turning". In order to encourage symmetrical behavior and discourage looping paths, the critters are penalized for "unbalanced turning". Statistics on turning are accumulated during the run, a sum of all turn angle magnitudes, a sum of signed turn angles, and a count of left-versus-right steps. A controller that made the maximum legal turn each time step would receive the "most harsh" excessive turn penalty of 0.5, whereas a controller that never turned would get value of 1.0 (i.e.: no penalty). The penalty for "unbalanced turning" is analogous.

Using a single fitness test will produce a controller for solving the one exact situation represented by the fitness test. However this solution may turn out to be very fragile and opportunistic. It may well have incorporated expectations of incidental properties of the specific fitness test.

To strive for *robust* behavior we need an alternative to a single fitness test. One solution would be to randomize some aspect of the world. This is an appealing approach since fitness trials in nature are effectively randomized. When randomization was attempted in these experiments, it became clear that the noise injected into the fitness values made it very hard for both the human experimenter and for the evolution software to determine if progress was actually being made. Instead each controller was tested on two sets of initial conditions, the starting positions and orientations of the critters and predator are "randomized" using a restartable pseudo-random number generator which is reset for each new controller being tested. This has the effect of discouraging fragile solutions, without introducing uncorrelated noise into the fitness measure.

8 Results

The results of two runs of cooperative group motion evolution are discussed below. Note that these runs were in progress when these summaries were prepared, in fact the simulation are proceeding in the background as this paper is being prepared for submission. Note also that the fitness values specified below are normalized to the size of the herd and so are not directly comparable except for identical herd sizes.

In the run called Herd-D there were 20 critters in the herd. The SSGP "gene pool" had a population of 200 programs. Minimum turn radius was enforced by the strict method: critters died if the turned too much. After about 6600 new individuals were created and fitness tested, the program that had attained the best fitness of 12% was:

```
(- (look-for-obstacle 0.01)
   (look-for-predator (turn (look-for-obstacle 0.01)))
   (iflte (turn (look-for-friend 0.1))
        (look-for-predator 0)
        (- (look-for-friend (turn (look-for-obstacle 0.1)))
           (look-for-obstacle 0.1)
           (look-for-friend 0.5))
       0))
```

Astonishingly this program has not been "cleaned up" to make it more readable as is often done when using the Genetic Programming paradigm. This is the unretouched program exactly as evolved. Despite this program's apparent simplicity, analyzing its operation is challenging. Its is apparently trying to avoid collisions with obstacles and friends, based somehow on its relative perception of friends and predators. Figures 2 and 3 show the "trail" of all simulation steps for this program for the two sets of initial conditions.

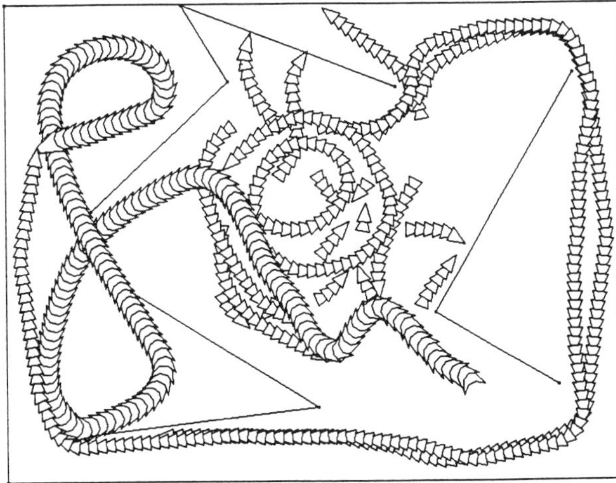

Figure 2: Herd-D, after 6600 runs, first of two trials

The opaque symbols are laid down sequentially, so when two paths cross the one that appears to be on top happened later in time. The wider path is the predator. Sharp turns in the predator's path generally correspond to a "prey capture and retarget" event. Wide, smooth turn usually indicate it is in "prowl mode".

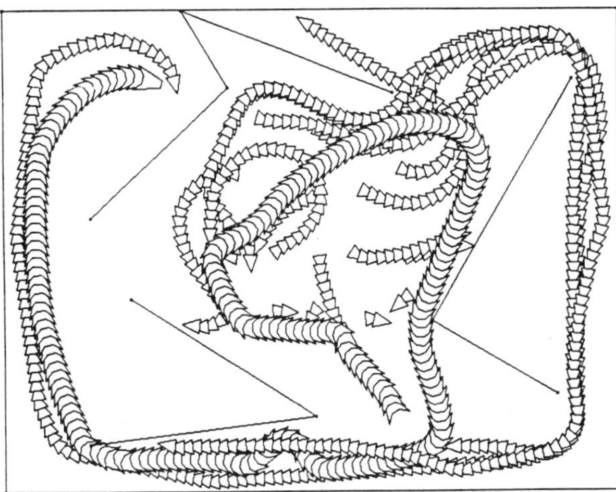

Figure 3: Herd-D, after 6600 runs, second of two trials

It can be seen (in animation if not in these static diagrams) that most of the critters parish early due to collisions or predation while two or three survivors manage to escape into the upper right hand corner and swoop around out of sight of the predator. Figure 4 shows a plot of best-of-run fitness and population-average fitness after every 200 individuals.

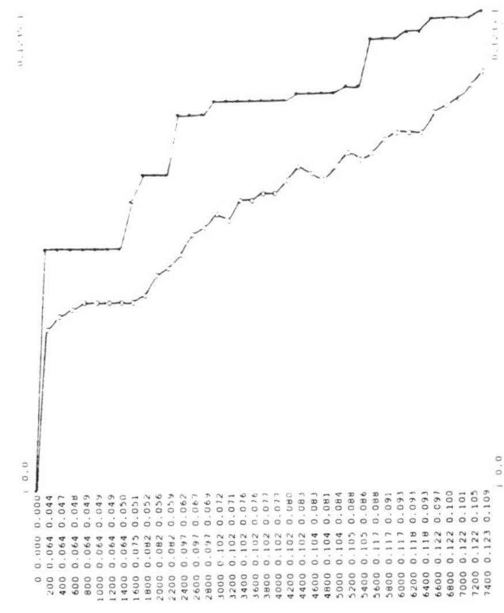

Figure 4: Herd-D, fitness versus time

In the run called Herd-G there were 16 critters in the herd. The SSGP "gene pool" had a population of 30 programs which is quite small. Minimum turn radius was enforced by the permissive method: critters could "ask" for any amount of turn angle, but they would be allowed only a certain amount each simulation step. After about 2000 new individuals were created and fitness tested, the program that had attained the best fitness of 13% was:

```
(iflte (look-for-obstacle (iflte (look-for-obstacle 0.1) (look-for-friend (look-for-friend 0)) (turn (look-for-friend (+ (iflte (look-for-friend 0.1) (look-for-obstacle (look-for-friend 0)) (look-for-predator (look-for-obstacle (turn (+ 0.01 (look-for-obstacle 0.1)))) ) (turn (turn 0))) (look-for-predator (look-for-obstacle 0.1))))) 0)) (* 0.001 (look-for-friend 0.01)) (+ 1 (iflte (look-for-obstacle (iflte (look-for-obstacle 0.1) (look-for-friend (look-for-friend 0)) (turn (look-for-friend (+ (iflte (look-for-friend 0.1) (look-for-obstacle (look-for-friend 0)) (look-for-predator (look-for-obstacle (turn (+ 0.01 (look-for-obstacle 0.1) )))) (turn (turn 0))) (look-for-predator 0)))) 0)) (* 0.001 (look-for-friend 0.01)) 0 (turn (look-for-obstacle 0.1)))) (turn (look-for-obstacle 0.1)))
```

This code is pretty convoluted and essentially impossible to understand. It was not clear to the author that it could be simplified significantly. Worth noting perhaps is that it contains several small "core" strategies such as:

```
(turn (look-for-obstacle 0.1))
(turn (+ 0.01 (look-for-obstacle 0.1)))
(turn (look-for-friend ...))
```

These fragments implement interacting obstacle and critter avoidance. (For example, the first fragment causes turning in the positive direction based on how strongly an obstacle is perceived at an angle of 0.1 revolutions from the current heading. The closer the obstacle is, the sharper the turn will be.) It is not immediately clear if this controller implements predator evasion at all. Figures 5 and 6 show the "trail" of all simulation steps for this program for the two sets of initial conditions.

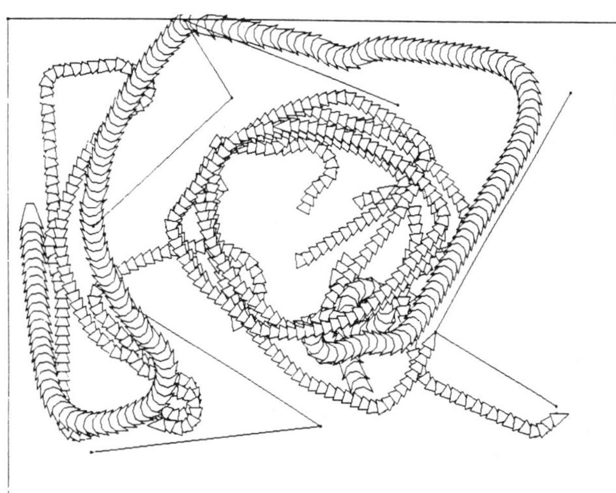

Figure 5: Herd-G, after 2000 runs, first of two trials

Note that in Figure 5 the predator becomes wedged in the concavity at the top center. Since the predator does not die when it collides with an obstacle, it continues to "tunnel through" to the other side of the obstacle. This is not an evolution problem, it is just a bug in the author's design of the predator's control program.

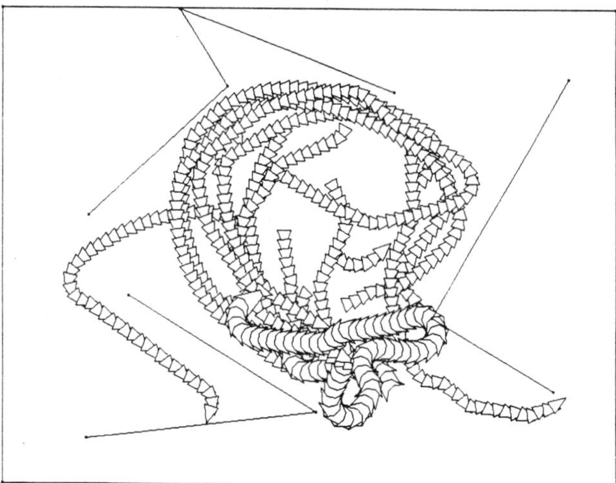

Figure 6: Herd-G, after 2000 runs, second of two trials

Figure 7 shows a plot of best-of-run fitness and population-average fitness after every 30 individuals.

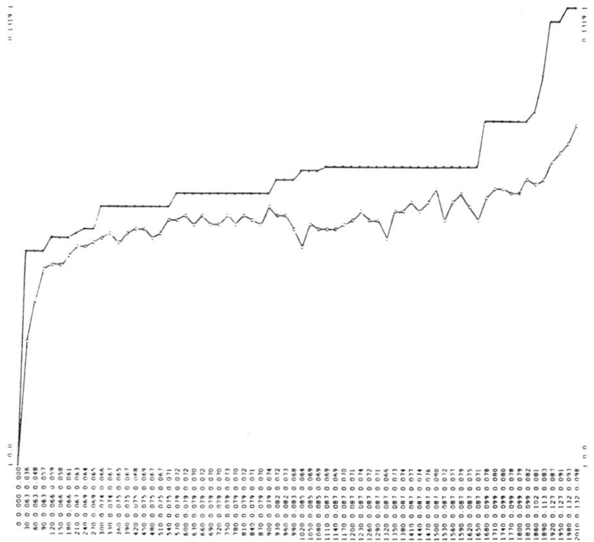

Figure 7: Herd-G, fitness versus time

9 Conclusions

The preliminary results reported here represent only partial solutions to the problem of robust coordinated group motion in the presence of obstacles and under threat of predation. None of the behaviors evolved in this work are anywhere near as robust and general purpose as herding behaviors seen in natural animals. Thoughts about how to proceed beyond these limitations are given in the next section.

On the other hand, there is no question that vision-based

coordinated group motion strategies have begun to emerge, given only the requisite primitives, an appropriate fitness measure, and the action of Darwinian evolution through natural selection and survival of the fittest.

10 Future Work

Generally the future goals of this work are to find increasingly competent, robust, and graceful coordinated group motion. In the current model, where the predator is slower than the prey, a herd of really skillful critters should be able to evade the predator indefinitely. We would like to see critters that can form into groups (and so discourage predation) while coordinating their motion to avoid collisions with each others. In the results presented here we can see the beginnings of these behaviors, but they are not nearly as vivid and graceful as the examples seen in natural herds.

One problem with the current model is that while critters can perceive the position of herd-mates and the predator, they can not sense the other's orientation. Presumably this would be very significant information. One simple way to provide this cue would be to consider the "front" and "rear" of the critters (and predator) to have distinct colors. This would allow critters to evolve a different reaction to seeing a herd-mate directly ahead based on its orientation. If a critter sees another critter's "front" directly ahead, it indicates a potential collision which must be avoided. Whereas seeing another critter's "back" directly ahead is normal while herding and requires no reaction.

It is anticipated that better, more robust, coordinated group motion could be be obtained by pitting the critters sequence of ever more sophisticated predators. But that approach puts a significant burden on the human designer of the predators. As the critters become proficient at predator avoidance, it would become increasingly difficult to come up with predators that would challenge them. These considerations suggest that perhaps the predator should *coevolve* with the critters. This kind of coevolution of problem-solvers and problem-poser has been examined in [Hillis 1990]. The fitness of an evolved predator would be judged by how well it could catch the critters. In the confrontation between a given critter and predator, a capture early in the simulation would reflect poorly on the critter and well on the predator. Conversely, a capture late in the simulation (or an escape) reflects well on the critter and poorly on the obstacle.

Acknowledgments

The research reported here was pure amateur science. It was not an officially sanctioned project of any corporation, university, or other funding agency. The individuals and companies listed below helped the author out of the goodness of their hearts and their interest in the subject matter. For generous grants of computer facilities, I am deeply indebted to Tom McMahon and Bart Gawboy of Information International Incorporated, Koichi Kobayashi of Nichimen Graphics Incorporated, and Richard Hollander of Video Image Associates. Special thanks go to Andrea Lackey whose workstation I repeatedly commandeered. Heartfelt thanks to Andy Kopra who cheerfully put up with my intrusions to his busy production schedule, and who helped brainstorm many of these ideas back at ALife II. Thanks to: Larry Malone, Dave Dyer, Jay Sloat, Dave Aronson, Joseph Goldstone, Glen Neufeld, DJ, Antoine Durr, and whoever else I forgot. And finally, this work would probably not have happened without John Koza's trail-blazing work on the Genetic Programming paradigm. Many thanks to John and to James Rice for their helpful and encouraging comments during this project.

I'd also like to thank Electronic Arts for ending that stint of "unsupported research" by hiring me recently.

References

Harold Abelson and Andrea diSessa (1981) *Turtle Geometry: The Computer as a Medium for Exploring Mathematics*, MIT Press, Cambridge, Massachusetts.

Susan Amkraut, Michael Girard, and G. Karl (1985) "Motion studies for a work in progress entitled *Eurhythmy*" in SIGGRAPH Video Review, Issue 21.

Ronald C. Arkin (1992) Cooperation Without Communication: Multi-Agent Schema Based Robot Navigation, in Journal of Robotic Systems, 9(3), pages 351-364.

Valentino Braitenberg (1984) *Vehicles: Experiments in Synthetic Psychology*, MIT Press, Cambridge, Massachusetts.

Rodney Brooks (1986) A Robust Layered Control System for a Mobile Robot, in *IEEE Journal of Robotics and Automation*, 2(1).

Rodney A. Brooks (1991) Intelligence Without Representation, in *Artificial Intelligence* 47, pages 139-160.

Dave Cliff (1991a) Computational Neuroethology: A Provisional Manifesto, in *From Animals To Animats* proceedings of SAB90, Meyer and Wilson editors, MIT Press, Cambridge, Massachusetts.

Dave Cliff (1991b) The Computational Hoverfly; a Study in Computational Neuroethology, in *From Animals To Animats* proceedings of SAB90, Meyer and Wilson editors, MIT Press, Cambridge, Massachusetts.

Robert Collins and David Jefferson (1991) AntFarm: Towards Simulated Evolution, in *Artificial Life II*, Langton *et al.* editors, Addison-Wesley.

Lawrence Davis, editor (1991) *Handbook of Genetic Algorithms* Van Nostrand Reinhold.

Richard Dawkins (1986) *The Blind Watchmaker*, Harlow

Logman.

Lawrence Dill (1991) Predicting the 3D Structure of Animal Aggregations from Function Considerations: the Role of Information, (not yet published) presented at the NSF workshop on *Animal Aggregations: 3D Measurement and Modeling*, Monterey Bay Aquarium, October 1991.

Tom Drake and Julia Parrish (1991) Computer Simulation of Fish Schooling, (not yet published) presented at the NSF workshop on *Animal Aggregations: 3D Measurement and Modeling*, Monterey Bay Aquarium, October 1991.

James Durkin (1991) An Implementation of a Behavioral Model of Aggregate Animal Motion, (not yet published) presented at the NSF workshop on *Animal Aggregations: 3D Measurement and Modeling*, Monterey Bay Aquarium, October 1991.

Michael Girard and Susan Amkraut (1990) Eurhythmy: Concept and Process, *The Journal of Visualization and Computer Animation*, 1:15-17.

Frank Heppner and Ulf Grenander (1990) A Stochastic Non-Linear Model for Coordinated Bird Flocks, in the *Ubiquity of Chaos* (Saul Krasner editor), AAAS Publications, Washington, pages 233-238.

W. Daniel Hillis (1990) Co-Evolving Parasites Improve Simulated Evolution as an Optimization Procedure, in *Emergent Computation*, Stephanie Forrest editor (a special issue of *Physica D* 42) pages 228-234, MIT Press/North-Holland.

John Holland (1975) *Adaptation in Natural and Artificial Systems*, The University of Michigan Press, Ann Arbor, Michigan.

John Holland (1992) Genetic Algorithms, in *Scientific American*, July 1992.

John R. Koza (1989) Hierarchical Genetic Algorithms Operating on Populations of Computer Programs, in *Proceedings of the 11th International Joint Conference on Artificial Intelligence*, Morgan Kaufmann, San Mateo, California.

John R. Koza (1992) *Genetic Programming*, MIT Press, Cambridge, Massachusetts.

Helmut Lorek (1992) personal communication, publication anticipated, contact lorek@informatik.uni-oldenburg.de for details.

Maja J. Mataric (1992) Minimizing Complexity in Controlling a Mobile Robot Population, *Proceedings, IEEE International Conference on Robotics and Automation*, pages 830-835.

Rob Meyers, Peter Broadwell, and R. Schaufler (1985) PLASM: Fish Sample, an installation piece at the acm SIGGRAPH 1985 Art Show.

Brian L. Partridge (1982) The Structure and Function of Fish Schools, in *Scientific American*, June 1982, pages 114-123.

Wayne K. Potts (1984) The Chorus-Line Hypothesis of Maneuver Coordination in Avian Flocks, letter in *Nature*, volume 30, pages 344-345.

Olivier Renault, Nadia Magnenat Thalmann, and Daniel Thalmann (1990) A Vision-Based Approach to Behavioral Animation, *The Journal of Visualization and Computer Animation*, 1:18-21.

Craig W. Reynolds (1987) Flocks, Herds, and Schools: A Distributed Behavioral Model, in *Computer Graphics*, 21(4) (SIGGRAPH '87 Conference Proceedings) pages 25-34.

Craig W. Reynolds (1993?) An Evolved, Vision-Based Model of Obstacle Avoidance Behavior, submitted to *Artificial Life III*, forthcoming.

Karl Sims (1991) Artificial Evolution for Computer Graphics, in *Computer Graphics*, 25(4) (SIGGRAPH '91 Conference Proceedings) pages 319-328.

Guy L. Steele Jr. (1990) *Common Lisp the Language*, second edition, ISBN 1-55558-042-4, Digital press.

Gilbert Syswerda (1989) Uniform Crossover in Genetic Algorithms, in *Proceedings of the Third International Conference on Genetic Algorithms*, pages 2-9, Morgan Kaufmann Publishers.

Gilbert Syswerda (1991) A Study of Reproduction in Generational and Steady-State Genetic Algorithms, in *Foundations of Genetic Algorithms*, pages 94-101, Morgan Kaufmann Publishers.

Darrell Whitley (1989) The GENITOR Algorithm and Selection Pressure: Why Rank Based Allocation of Reproductive Trials is Best, in *Proceedings of the Third International Conference on Genetic Algorithms*, pages 116-121, Morgan Kaufmann Publishers.

Larry Yaeger (1993?) Computational Genetics, Physiology, Metabolism, Neural Systems, Learning, Vision, and Behavior or PolyWorld: Life in a New Context, submitted to *Artificial Life III*, forthcoming.

Evolution of Herding Behavior in Artificial Animals

Gregory M. Werner
Michael G. Dyer
AI Lab/Computer Science Department
University of California
Los Angeles, CA, 90024

Abstract

We have created a simulated world ("BioLand") designed to support experiments on the evolution of cooperation, competition, and communication.

In this particular experiment we have simulated the evolution of herding behavior in prey animals. We placed a population of simulated prey animals into an environment with a population of their predators. The behavior of each of the animals is controlled by a neural network architecture specified by its individual genome. We have allowed these populations to evolve through interaction over time and have observed the evolution of neural networks that produce herding behavior. The prey animals evolve to congregate in herds, for the protection it provides from predators, as well as the help it provides in finding food and mates. An interesting evolutionary pathway is seen to this herding, from aggregation, to staying nearby other animals for mating opportunities, to using herding for safety and food finding.

1 Introduction

We are pursuing a bottom-up exploration of the evolution of cooperative behavior and communication.

Our work has involved building a simple model of the world ("BioLand") that contains information relevant to the day-to-day life of simple animals (termed "biots"). This environment is then populated with biots whose behavior evolves to best survive in interaction in the environment. If the relevant features of the real world are included in the simulation, the biots should evolve cooperative skills similar to those seen in nature.

Each biot is controlled by a neural network, specified by its own genome. By examining those neural networks that evolve, we might be able to gain some insights into how animal brains might accomplish similar cooperation tasks. In addition, we believe that the task of constructing BioLand simulations will reveal aspects of what the actual constraints, goals, etc. of cooperation might be like in the real world.

2 Herding, Flocking, and Schooling

Many types of animals seek the company of others. There are several benefits to be gained by gathering into groups with others of the same species, including safety from predators, access to mates, and help in finding food. The advantages discussed here for animals that herd are true in large part, for example, with flocking birds and schooling fish.

Above all, herding provides safety for the individual. It increases the effective vigilance of the individual, can confuse or intimidate a predator, and can be used to provide cover where none exists. It also makes it less likely for predators to find prey, perhaps limiting the predators' numbers.

When animals are feeding, they must occasionally stop and look around to avoid being eaten by a predator. If an animal can tell if another in the herd senses danger, it no longer has to spend as much time looking around.

In addition, simply having more individuals looking makes it less likely that danger will be overlooked. More eyes and noses working together increase the chance that a predator will be located before it is within striking distance.

If a predator approaches the herd, the large numbers of animals in the herd can be used to fight off the predator. Circular defensive formations are used by some animals, and others may attack or mob the predator together. Musk oxen form a circle with their horns pointed out to deter predators, and baboons will mob leopards to chase them off [7].

The numbers of similar appearing possible targets also can confuse a predator. Once the predator tries to attack an individual, other animals moving around nearby can distract the predator, perhaps making it change its target animal repeatedly instead of pursuing one animal.

Finally, each animal may attempt to hide behind another, less fortunate herd-mate. This is known as selfish herding. Basically it is using another animal as a shield. Each animal in a herd may struggle to stay in the relatively safe center of the herd at the expense of the others. This hiding behind other animals clearly can keep a herd together. This desire to remain in the center of the herd must be balanced with the greater access to resources often found at the periphery of the herd.

Herding also provides increased feeding opportunities. Just as many animals watching for danger is better than one, a parallel search for food is better for each individual involved, given some kinds of food clustering.

If food is found in patches that can be shared, but where the patches themselves are somewhat difficult to find, there is pressure to cooperate in finding the patches.

Herding also brings together prospective mates, allows copying of behavior, and aids navigation.

action	cost for deer
move	$(speed/maximumspeed)^2$
mate successfully	-200
mate unsuccessfully	-1
eat succesfully	+100
eat unsuccesfully	-1
make sound	-1
exist	-1
be born	+400

Table 1: Costs and gains for deer actions.

action	cost for wolves
move	$(speed/maximumspeed)^2$
mate successfully	-200
mate unsuccessfully	-1
eat succesfully	+energy of prey
eat unsuccesfully	-1
make sound	-1
exist	-1
be born	+400

Table 2: Costs and gains for wolf actions.

3 Design and Goals

We hope to recreate an evolutionary orgin of herding. We are trying to simulate the evolution of herding behavior in animals that do not originally herd.

We hope to evolve herding in simulated prey animals, possibly with danger and food signals to help coordinate the herd. This could illustrate a possible evolutionary path to this cooperative behavior.

We also hope to evolve group hunting in simulated predators.

To these ends, we have set up an initial 2-D environment with 2 species of animals, which we call "deer", and "wolves." There are 2 kinds of non-animal objects in the environment as well: "plants", and "trees."

Deer increase their energy level by eating plants. Wolves increase their energy level by eating deer. This energy is used up by the animals' baseline metabolism, and there is an energy cost for each action a biot makes. Mating, eating, and producing sounds all have specific costs, and movement uses more energy the faster a biot moves. Each of these values is a parameter that must be set reasonably to evolve interesting behavior (Tables 1 and 2).

New plants are added to the environment at a constant rate to provide energy for the animals. They are placed near other existing plants so that clumps of plants grow. Trees are positioned at the beginning of the simulation, and cannot be eaten or moved. They are obstacles in this environment and can allow the possibility of more complex future biots forming simple maps of the environment.

To reproduce, an animal has to have a high enough energy level to be fertile, and must find another animal willing to mate.

Each type of object has a specific (non-volitional) sound or smell associated with it that diffuses away from its location, and can potentially be sensed by a biot. The strength of this smell decays exponentially with distance. The (non-volitional) sound produced by animals is proportional to their speed. Non-animal entities (e.g. trees) produce smells of constant strength (Figure 1).

Mating and eating behaviors also have characteristic (non-volitional) sounds that can be heard by other animals. This allow other biots to make use of the information about what another biot is doing.

In addition, animals can voluntarily produce sounds of varying "frequency" and "loudness." Louder sounds propagate farther than do softer sounds. Different frequencies allow different sounds and sound combinations to be used and discriminated. These sounds can be used as signals to other animals.

This environment should contain enough features of the real world to allow herding to evolve.

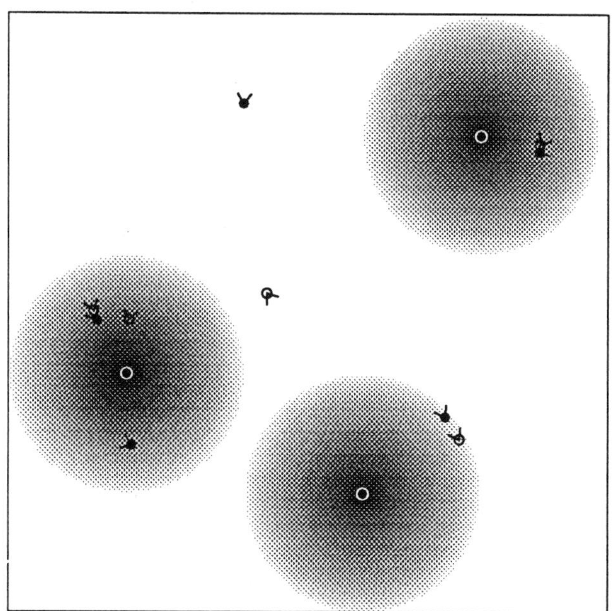

Figure 1: Each object in BioLand produces a number of gradients. Only plant smell gradients are shown here. Sensory neurons on the ends of the animals' "antenae" fire proportionally to the log of the gradient strength for which they are sensitive.

4 Modeling Biots

The behavior of each biot is determined by a neural network. Each biot perceives its environment in a species-specific way, then performs an action in response to its inputs. Biots have sensors on both sides of their bodies which sense the strength of each of the smell and sound gradients. There are specific sensory neurons for each smell and for each sound "frequency." The activation of these sensory neurons is proportional to the logarithm of the gradient strength. This is important because the exponential decay of sounds and smells creates gradient strengths over several orders of magnitude. In addition to sensory and motor neurons, each biot contains hidden neurons (3 in the current model) and higher order gating (axoaxonal) connections (Figure 3).

The neural networks that determine the behavior of the animals are themselves evolved. The sensory neurons and motor neurons of each species are predetermined before the experiment, and connections, hidden units, and axoaxonal connections are allowed to evolve. This allows arbitrary internal architectures to be specified given specific inputs and output capabilities.

Each animal has a genome that encodes the architecture of the neural network for that particular

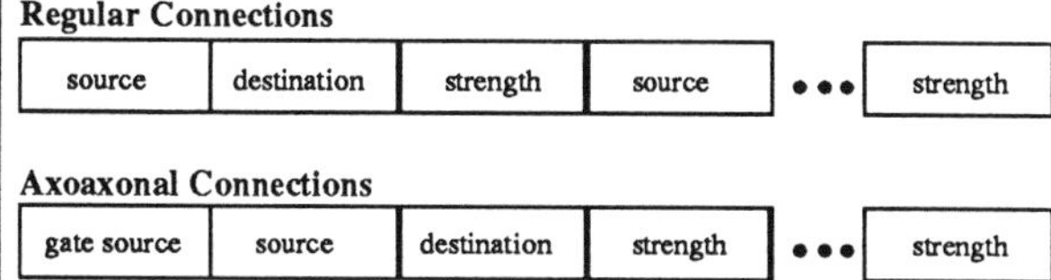

Figure 2: The genome for a biot is split into 2 parts. The first part encodes the regular connections made between two neurons. Bits along the string encode first the source neuron (where the connection originates), then the destination, and finally the strength of that connection. The second part of the genome encodes axoaxonal connections. The first several bits here encode which neuron is the source of the gating connection. The next bits encode which connection is actually gated. Finally the gating strength is encoded.

animal. When animals mate, the genomes of the two parents are combined using crossover and mutation operations at the bit level [5] [6] and a new genome for the offspring is produced. This genome is then translated into the neural network that controls the new animal. Parameters are set so that each animal has one crossover on average, and has a 10 percent chance of having a mututation. Because of the coding used, each biot can effectively have a genome of any length between zero and 400 bits.

The scheme we use for encoding a neural network on a genome is a modification of that proposed by Collins [4] who represents a genome as containing a list of triples. Each triple encodes a single connection between 2 neurons. The triple contains the identification (ID) of the source neuron, the ID of the target neuron, and the strength of the connection between them. We have found that this scheme rarely evolves a hidden layer of neurons in between the input and output neurons. Since resulting networks are only 2 layers, and such networks are limited in their functionality, there are many behaviors that are not achievable.

To get around this problem, we have added a separate genome that encodes axoaxonal connections in the network. These are multiplicative connections that gate normal neuron-to-neuron connections, thus adding considerable computational power to a 2 layer network [3]. We encode each axoaxonal connection as a tuple with 4 elements. Each 4-tuple contains the ID of the source (gating) neuron, the IDs of the two neurons whose connection is being gated, and the strength of the gating synapse (Figure 2).

This gating can be used a number of ways to improve biots' behavior. A neuron detecting the presence of a predator can gate the connection between food and eating, for example. This would keep the biot from stopping to eat when it was in danger.

5 Experiment

We placed 8,000 prey animals and 8,000 predator animals into a 1000 by 1000 biot-length, toroidal environment.

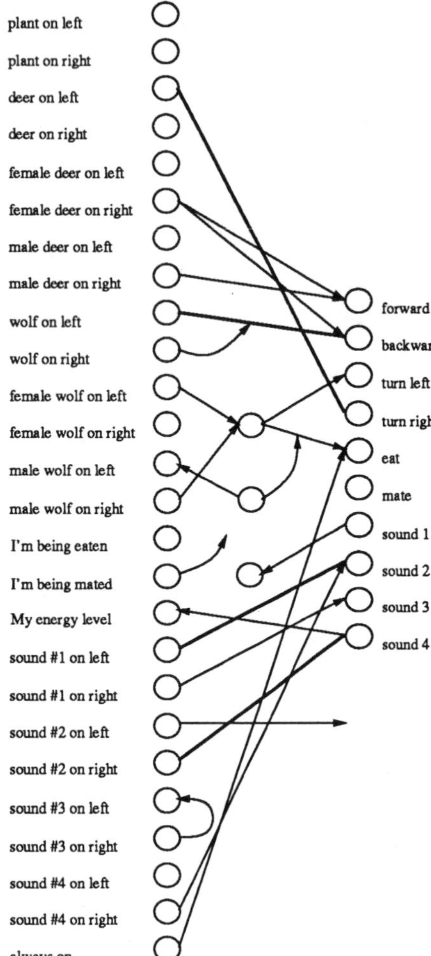

Figure 3: A random neural network from the initial population. Thickness indicates strength of the connection. Axoaxonal connections (curved arrows) act to gate other connections. Note that some connections are "junk" in the sense that they are fragmentary or not interpretable (e.g. connections from input to input layer).

Each animal had a random beginning genome. Each genome can encode up to 25 regular, and 25 axoaxonal connections. The total number of bits in the genome was 400, so that there are 2^{400} total possible biot neural architectures.

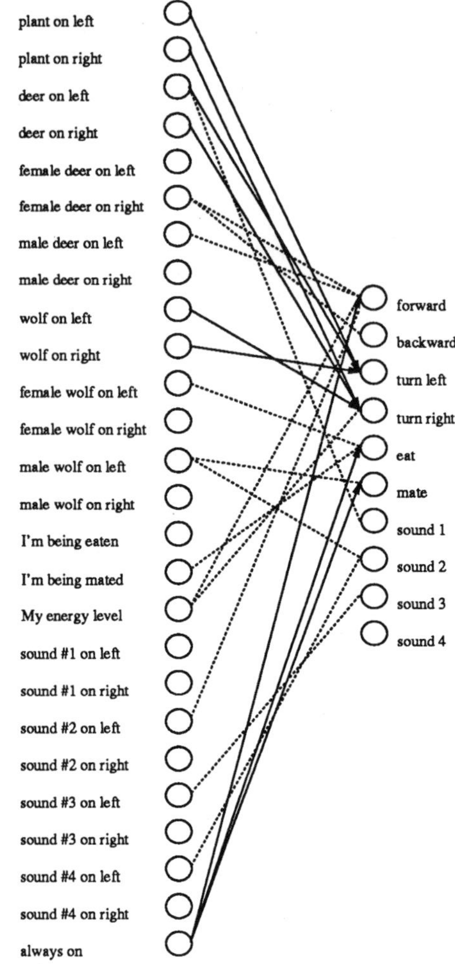

Figure 4: The neural network of an evolved female deer after 80 generations. Axoaxonal connections have been ommitted for clarity. Solid lines are shown for connections which are common in female deer and clearly useful. Dotted lines indicate connections that are less common and presumably less useful.

The behavior of the populations was checked occasionally throughout the run, and after approximately every 20 generations, a sample of the current genomes was taken. This sample was then analyzed to determine how the animals were implementing the behavior seen. Since there are not explicit generations in the simulation (because the animals mate and produce offspring at different times), the "generation length" is somewhat inexact. Every time the population produced a number of offspring equal to its average population size, we considered it another generation. Initial generations have a large number of sense/move cycles. Subsequent generation times shorten as biots become better at finding mates.

6 Results and Analysis

Early in the run, the behavior of the biots is random. Most of the biots die off because they cannot find food. The population shrinks down to about 400 biots. These have enough capability to eat and mate. Viable biots appear within the very first generation because all that is needed for eating/mating is that there exist some connection from the appropriate olfactory neurons to the appropriate motor neurons. For example, if a male biot moves toward the scent of a female biot and continuously executes the mating motor neuron (and the female does the same) then mating will occur. This behavior only requires the existence of a few connections. Later evolutionary pressures can then operate on these genotypes to improve mating efficiency (e.g. only firing the mating motor neuron when right next to a mate).

After about 30 generations, the predators have evolved to home in on the smell of prey, and the prey have evolved to move away from predators. This is accomplished by simply turning toward the side of the body in which the smell gradient is stronger in the case of the predators. Prey animals simply turn away from the stronger predator smell. In addition, the prey animals have evolved to home in on plants.

Once these behaviors are common in the population, we see that the animals tend to clump together. While they move in groups, this is not yet herding, but aggregation, because the animals are not seeking each other's company. They are simply pushed together by environmental features (i.e. food sources, places away from predators). Since the food is clumped together, the animals tend to clump together.

After 80-100 generations, we see that there evolves a tendency to move toward other animals of the same species. We can tell this by noting that neural connections that produce this behavior have arisen in the biots' neural networks (Figures 4 and 5).

At this point we see that most of the animals converge into small herds which are constantly splitting up and reforming as the groups interact with each other (Figures 6, 7, and 8).

Herding probably starts as a way of locating a mate. However, in this simulation there are at least 3 distinct pressures on the animals to do this. Once it occurs, the grouping of animals is true herding, because they are seeking to be in groups.

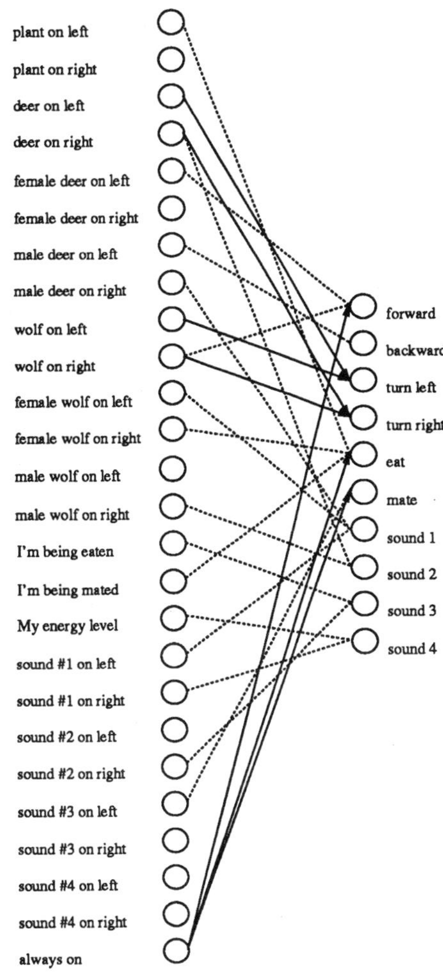

Figure 5: The neural network of a male wolf after 80 generations. Axoaxonal connections have been ommitted for clarity.

The first environmental pressure to herd is the pressure to find a mate. While aggregation provides mating opportunities, a biot that actually moves toward prospective mates clearly has an advantage over those who do not.

Second, there is pressure from predators. The prey "confusion effect" [7] is seen in these animals. A predator has a more difficult time in homing in on one prey animal than it does on more than one. We tested this case by placing a single predator animal into a test environment with one or more prey animals. We found that the predator animal took longer to capture a prey animal when the predator was in a group of prey than it did for a single animal. This was because the smell gradients produced by the prey interfered with each other so that there was not a single gradient to follow directly. The slope of the gradient

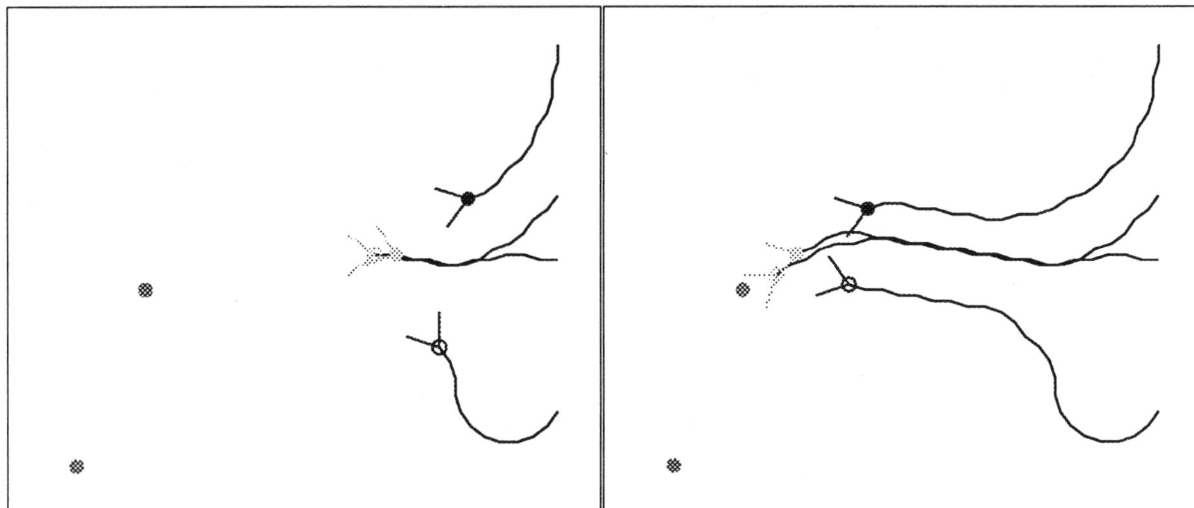

Figure 6: Actual graphical output of lifelines of four biots in Bioland. Deer are shown in gray, wolves in black. Males are filled circles, females outlined. The "antennae" on the biots indicate where their sensors are located. Plants are black circles without antennae. Lines trailing the biots show their path. Note that the two deer have moved together, their paths intertwined and two wolves have begun to pursue them. Elapsed time here is 12 steps.

Figure 7: The wolves have gained on the deer over the past 12 time steps. The deer are moving toward the plant to eat it, while at the same time avoiding the wolves.

was smaller, causing the predator to turn less quickly toward any one of the animals.

Third, there is pressure to find food. A group of animals can sense a larger area of the environment than can one.

If a animal senses food that the others cannot, it will move towards the food, slightly drawing the group with it. The rest of the group will then get to the point where they can sense the food as well, and the whole group will move to the food source. Because we made the food in this environment grow in patches, there is an advantage to cooperatively finding food.

Why is this model as successful as it is? We think there are several reasons:

1. There is plenty of food in the environment to begin with (8000 plants). Furthermore, the massive death of the initial biot population leaves plenty of food for those who have survived.

2. Biots do not die through aging. Therefore, any biot who has evolved to eat can live almost indefinitely, thus increasing the likelihood of mating.

3. The input neuron, termed "always on," represents a kind of internal "drive." Without this neuron, biots are completely reactive which is not realistic. A biot who only moves when it senses food, for example, will become immobile and therefore trapped if there is no gradient around it of sufficient intensity.

4. The neural net evolutionary space for this task is rather smooth. That is, biots don't have to have perfect connections to survive. For example, even if the "always on" neuron is not connected, there may be enough connections from other sensors to successfully move the biot toward food and mates.

7 Current Implementation and Future Work

BioLand is implemented on a 16k processor CM2 Connection Machine whose massive SIMD style parallelism is well suited for such tasks. It is written in C* and it took several days to run the experiment described here. Simulating the gradients in the environment is the major bottleneck.

Just as herding among predators has evolved, we would like to evolve group hunting by predators. We hypothesize that the following circumstances will need to be in effect: (a) prey must be able to outrun predators, (b) prey must be able to metabolically outlast predators, and (c) prey must provide more food than a single predator can consume. Currently, prey and predators move within the same velocity ranges and when a predator "kills" a prey, the predator's metabolism is increased by an amount equal

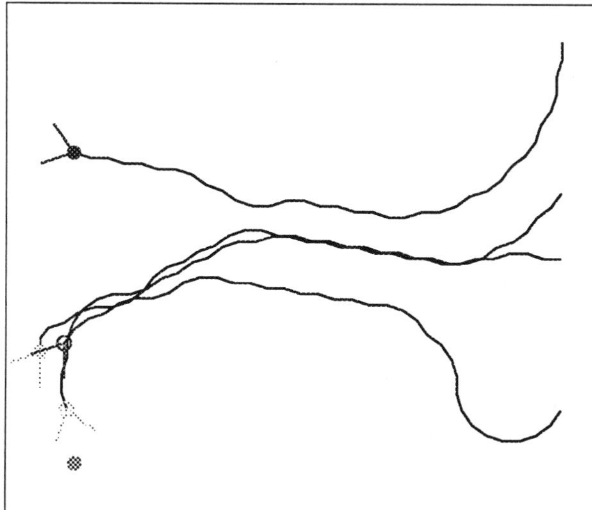

Figure 8: In the next 12 time steps, several things have happened. One of the deer has eaten the plant along their path. The male wolf has moved off to pursue something off-screen. The female wolf is about to consume the male deer. And the female deer has broken away to consume a meal of a nearby plant.

to the prey's metabolism. There is nothing like a "carcass" being left as additional food in the environment. If prey are larger and faster than predators, then predators who hunt together should evolve. Group hunting, for example, allows one hunter to rest while the others continually force the prey to "burn" metabolism and thus tire out. The resulting kill can then supply food for the entire "pack".

An interesting additional direction is to explore under what circumstance volitional signaling might evolve among predators who hunt in groups. If predators have weak olfaction but good audition, then they might evolve to signal to each other the location of the prey as it runs out of sensory range.

8 Conclusions

We have shown how herding behavior could have arisen in previously non-herding animals. Pressure to locate a mate and the clustering of food sources could have originally brought animals together simply as a side-effect of the environment. Subsequent advantages for prey would then arise, namely: (a) confusing predators by remaining in groups and (b) increasing the likelihood of finding more distant food clumps by following members who have already sensed the food and are following its gradient. These advantages would generate selection pressures for explicit herding to have spread throughout the evolving population. Once herding is in place, more coordinated group behaviors could then evolve (e.g. group defense formations and explicit signaling between herd members).

9 Acknowledgments

This research is supported in part by NSF grant IRI-910730 to the second author.

The CM-2 Connection Machine was acquired through NSF equipment centers grant BBS-87-14206, maintained through NSF grant DIR-90-24251. The CM-2 is managed by the UCLA Cognitive Science Research Program.

Thanks also to Liane Gabora and Adam King for insightful comments.

References

[1] John A. Alcock. *Animal Behavior: An Evolutionary Approach.* Sinauer Associates, Inc., Sunderland, MA, 1984.

[2] John T. Bonner. *The Evolution of Culture in Animals.* Princeton University Press, Princeton, New Jersey, 1980.

[3] Valentino Braitenburg. *Vehicles.* The MIT Press, Cambridge MA, 1984.

[4] Robert J. Collins. *Studies in Artificial Evolution.* PhD thesis, UCLA, 1992.

[5] D. E. Goldberg. *Genetic Algorithms in Search, Optimization, and Machine Learning.* Addison-Welsey, 1989.

[6] J. H. Holland, K. J. Holyoak, R. E. Nisbett, and P. A. Thagard. *Induction. Processes of Inference, Learning, and Discovery.* The MIT Press, Cambridge, MA, 1986.

[7] D. McFarland, editor. *The Oxford Companion to Animal Behavior.* Oxford University Press, Oxford, 1987.

[8] C. W. Reynolds. Flocks, herds, and schools: A distributed behavioral model. In *Procedings of SIGGRAPH*, 1987.

[9] Gregory M. Werner and Michael G. Dyer. Evolution of communication in artificial organisms. In *Artificial Life II*, 1991.

An Evolutionary Approach to Cognition

Dwight Deugo and Franz Oppacher
Intelligent Systems Research Group
School of Computer Science, Carleton University
Ottawa, Canada, K1S 5B6
E-mail: dwightdeugo@scs.carleton.ca, oppacher@scs.carleton.ca

Abstract

In contrast to the 'evolutionary' species learning studied in Animats and Artificial Life, individual learning is the learning that an organism does in its lifetime. Recent models combining these two forms of learning have only examined the effects of individual learning on the species, and not how individual learning could evolve and function in an organism. Work in Evolutionary Epistemology offers many ideas on the topics of the evolution of knowledge, learning, and behavior. Our computational approach to Evolutionary Epistemology applies various 'genetic operators' to the sorts of symbolic structures that are used in traditional AI systems, and thus gives rise to an evolutionary variant of Case-Based Reasoning called Evolution-Based Reasoning. Computational Evolutionary Epistemology is ultimately interested in thinking construed as evolution that takes place on a time scale of milliseconds in an organism's brain.

1 Introduction

Since knowledge is a product of our biology, and since our biology is a product of evolution, knowledge must be explained in terms of evolution. Our approach to this conception of evolutionary epistemology is called Computational Evolutionary Epistemology (CompEE). CompEE is the computational study of the evolution of individual learning using abstractions of known biological mechanisms and simplified Darwinian processes.

CompEE follows the holistic, bottom-up, approaches, of Animats and Artificial Life (AL), to intelligence. CompEE uses the process of evolution, used in Genetic Algorithms (GAs) and Classifier Systems (CSs), on the symbolic structures of traditional artificial intelligence (AI) systems. CompEE is ultimately interested in evolution that takes place on a time scale of milliseconds in a being's brain. CompEE asks questions like the following: is the very process of thinking an evolutionary one, i.e. is the perceived sequential train of thoughts the outcome of Darwinian selection, where pieces of thoughts are put together and compared with memories as to their appropriateness in the current situation, and the best 'fitting' one, i.e. the one with the best 'match', selected as the next part of the 'train of thought? *Does the brain operate as an Evolutionary Machine?*

1.1 Motivation

Traditional AI has proposed many different models of specific human abilities, such as planning [Hammond, 1989], searching [Nilsson, 1980], inductive learning [Holland *et al.*, 1986], and natural language processing [Winograd, 1983] to name but a few. Although powerful and transparent within specific domains, 'symbolic' AI systems suffer from brittleness outside narrowly defined domains [Holland, 1986; Holland, *et al.*, 1986]. As Wilson points out [Wilson, 1991], the brittleness of many AI systems results from their addressing only 'isolated competences':

- AI systems often ignore the fact that they must work in sensory environments and satisfy multiple conflicting goals.

- AI systems are often more concerned with algorithmic processes like search and exact reasoning than with natural abilities like adaptation and categorization.

One notable symbolic AI system that attempts to be more flexible is a case-based reasoning (CBR) system. A CBR system is designed to learn from experience and to reuse what has been learned instead of constructing new solutions from scratch [Hammond, 1989; Kolodner, 1988, 1987]. A CBR system uses the description of a problem to look for a matching case in its memory. The solution of the best matching case is adapted to meet the current problem and stored for future use.

CBR systems compare favorably with other 'symbolic' approaches such as rule-based expert systems or planners that always work from first principles. But their potential as a general approach to machine learning (ML) is diminished by their reliance on unchanging adaptation rules which tend to produce repetitive solutions, and by their current inability to maintain a library of nonredundant cases. These shortcomings are exacerbated when CBR is not just used in situations, such as expert systems tasks, in which occasional learning is treated as a welcome side effect, but when learning itself becomes the primary goal.

'Subsymbolic' systems such as neural networks [Hinton, 1990a, 1990b; Judd, 1990] and GAs [De Jong, 1990; Goldberg, 1989; Davis, 1987; Holland, 1975; Grefenstette, 1988; Wilson, 1989], show some characteristic advantages such as robustness, capability of handling contradictions, and fault tolerance, but, because of their lack of transparency and inability to handle chains of inferences, are not yet convincing in traditional AI applications like expert systems or planners.

'Subsymbolic' approaches other than GAs, e.g. connectionist systems, have so far proven weak in domains requiring high level knowledge processing. In cognitively complex domains, it is important to be able to use previously acquired domain knowledge. The use of such knowledge may not just improve performance but may actually make the difference between satisfactory and unacceptable results [Fogelmann-Soulie, *et al.*, 1990]. GAs naturally represent and profit from previously acquired knowledge ('building block hypothesis', [Goldberg 1989, 41ff.]), and the introduction of rules into a CS by a knowledge engineer is straightforward. This contrasts sharply with connectionist systems, in which the introduction of domain knowledge requires ad-hoc 'connections engineering', i.e. the careful wiring of the network architecture.

In contrast to the top down approaches to AI, the Animats [Wilson, 1991] and AL [Langton, *et al.*, 1992] approaches to intelligence assemble simple, often subcognitive units. 'The animat approach advocates maintaining the holism of the situation of real animals in real environments, while progressively but efficiently increasing animat complexity only as necessary' [Wilson, 1991, 20ff.]. 'Artificial Life involves the realization of lifelike behavior on the part of man-made systems consisting of populations of semi-autonomous entities whose local interactions with one another are governed by a set of simple rules' [Langton, 1989, xxiiff.]. Both approaches begin with minimal ad hoc machinery and work upward synthetically from there, building larger complex machinery in order to support life and intelligence. Rather than focusing on the production of intelligent solutions, these approaches focus on the production of intelligent behavior. The force driving the changes in behavior is evolution.

In AL, "evolutionary adaptation can be viewed as a kind of 'learning' that takes place on time scales much longer than the lifetimes of individual organisms" [Langton, *et al.*, 1992, 13ff.]. This class of learning is a product of the AL model: a population of organisms introducing changes by constructing (reproducing) other organisms, and natural selection providing the feedback as to how good, or how bad, the changes were by allowing only the strongest organisms to reproduce. The result is that over many generations, organisms evolve that are better suited for their environment. Even though individual organisms change between, and during, generations, this form of 'evolutionary species learning' is concerned with only those changes that are useful to, and maintained by, the species.

In contrast to evolutionary species learning, 'individual learning' is learning that an organism does in its lifetime. AL, when considering individual learning, has combined the traditional methods of learning studied by the ML community, such as back-propagation, with evolutionary learning. For example, [Ackley and Littman, 1992] found that a combination of evolutionary species learning and individual learning (as implemented with neural networks and back-propagation) worked well. Similarly, [Belew, *et al.*, 1992] found that this particular hybrid worked well because of the combined effects of the global searching performed by the population and the local searching performed by the individuals. These models, however, examine only the effects of individual learning on the species, and do not examine how individual learning could evolve and function in an organism!

Unlike the AL approach, the Animats approach is concerned with the development of individual learning. However, with the notable exception of [Sutton, 1991], most of the Animat learning architectures are only effective at trial-and-error learning. What is missing from these architectures is the ability to plan or reason.

The approaches of GAs, CSs, AL, and Animats all take adaptation seriously. However, GAs and CSs usually adapt only structures of fixed length bit strings (for two exceptions, see [Koza, 1989; Oppacher and Deugo, 1991]). These structures make for easy application of genetic operators but their expressive power is insufficient for typical symbolic problem solving tasks required of many expert systems today. Knowledge in symbolic AI systems is often couched in a rich symbolic notation, for example, frames. A frame can represent many more values than a single binary gene.

CompEE combines the advantages of the approaches mentioned above into a cognitive model that uses evolution as the primary source of information gain.

1.2 Approach

CompEE is a theory of individual learning that treats cognition as a biological phenomenon by extending biological evolution to those traits of animals and humans that are the biological substrates of cognition.

Our theory of individual learning has three fundamental canons:

> A living thing is a hierarchically organized system, each level of which is defined by the presence of an evolutionary process.

> All knowledge is gained by a process of evolution.

> Learning and reasoning are evolved traits and are themselves treated as evolutionary processes.

Our model for individual learning has two primary components:

1. *A Being* implemented as an evolutionary machine, and consisting of a collection of sensors, and of a hierarchy of three dependent levels: the genetic level, the development level, and the cognitive level. Each of these levels is subjected to greatly simplified simulations of the Darwinian Theory of

Evolution by Natural Selection: 1) fitness proportional reproduction, and 2) variation through the application of genetic operators such as crossover and mutation.

2. *A Class 2 Environment* [Wilson, 1991] in which the optimal action for a being to take in any situation is no longer knowable from the immediate sensor stimuli, and in which behavior reinforcement is not immediate.

CompEE demonstrates that learning - changes to a being's internal structures - occurs at many different levels. Knowledge that must be obtained immediately in order to survive is determined at the cognitive level. New physical structures enabling a being to perform better in its environment are determined at the development level. The description of the physical structures is determined at the genetic level. Each level also acquires information that is important for the next one - without a brain, there would be no theories, and without genes there would be no brain.

CompEE also demonstrates that evolution is a universal process for knowledge gain. Each of its three levels relies on a process of evolution for the acquisition of that level's knowledge.

In particular, by showing that the growth of symbolic knowledge can be achieved with evolution, CompEE proposes a new model of reasoning: **Evolution-Based Reasoning** (EBR). Similar to CBR, EBR attempts to reuse past knowledge. However, in contrast to CBR, EBR takes learning and adaptation to be integral components of the reasoning method. The construction of knowledge is construed as a process of differential selection on variation, similar to the one that governs the evolution of beings.

CompEE also shows that hierarchies can be used to evolve complex structures. GAs derive most of their power from the implicit processing of schemata. Schemata can be viewed as stable subsystems that are continually combined, forming larger stable subsystems. It is important to note, however, that schemata, as described in the literature, function only as theoretic constructs: they are not processed explicitly. We have already described [Deugo and Oppacher, 1992] the benefits of exploiting the power of schemata directly, not just by using them to analyze the performance of a GA, but by using them as explicit components of the representation.

We treat strong hierarchies as stable, nondisruptable schemata. These hierarchies are combined, in turn, into higher-level hierarchies. Using this view 'the time required for a complex system to evolve by a process of natural selection is very much shorter if the system is itself comprised of one or more layers of stable component subsystems than if its elementary parts are its only stable components' [Simon, 1973].

CompEE provides an approach to managing the 'preprogramming' problem of Machine Learning - the hand-coding of knowledge and control parameters. Determining the parameter values of a genetic algorithm is as arbitrary as defining its fitness function. Similarly, how can one know, a priori, what adaptation rules a CBR system will require, or what knowledge an explanation-based learning system will need? Only the system and the environment are capable of determining the parameters, rules, and background knowledge.

In the following sections, we describe CompEE in more detail. However, before getting to specific details, the next section is provided to give the reader an introduction to evolutionary epistemology, from which the idea for CompEE emerged. Later sections include descriptions of a being, its levels, and its environment, and a discussion of our preliminary results. The final section concludes.

2 Evolutionary Epistemology

Evolutionary epistemology (EE) is a theory of knowledge development analogous to evolutionary theory. EE takes seriously the fact that evolution can be seen as a knowledge gaining process, and that knowledge must be explained in terms of evolution

In general, EE applies the mechanism of differential selection on variation to bring about the growth of knowledge. 'In this sense knowledge is seen to be a function of success in a field of alternative ideas' [Thompson, 1988]. EE maintains that this mechanism can be generalized to other activities such as learning and science [Plotkin, 1986]. While some proposals simply evoke randomness as a source of novelty, as may be the case with Thorndike's 'method of trial, error, and accidental success' [Thorndike, 1987], and as seems the case with Monte Carlo simulation and the AI paradigm of 'generate and test', many others are based on a clear understanding that randomization alone is not powerful enough: only repeated rounds of random variation followed by nonrandom selection suffice to produce complex new structures. These versions of EE all have this in common: they attempt to explain the cognitive capacities of humans in terms of biological evolution. For a recent large (600 items) bibliography of evolutionary epistemology, see Campbell [Campbell *et al.*, 1987].

The implications of an evolutionary theory for epistemology have been studied by many, e.g. Toulmin [Toulmin, 1981], Popper [Popper, 1972], Ruse [Ruse, 1986], and Campbell [Campbell, 1987]. Typically, these authors have tried to account for theory growth by appealing to a mechanism of differential selection on variation, operating in a field of competing theories. Theories with higher confirmation, or greater explanatory power (or other, often pragmatic, features indicative of 'epistemic success', 'strength' or 'fitness') win the struggle for incorporation into the body of accepted scientific knowledge.

There are essentially two strands of EE, both of which start with the fact of evolution. The first version studies the evolution of cognitive mechanisms, structures and processes - such as nervous systems, brains, and sensory organs - that support cognitive capacities, with the aim to learn something about the limits of cognition from an understanding of these underlying biological mechanisms and their development - *the literal extension of biological evolution*. Indeed, Lorenz [Lorenz, 1973] holds that life itself is a cognitive process because the structures of living things encode properties of the world they live in.

The second version of EE studies the development of culture - the growth of science and other forms of rational knowledge - using models analogous to evolutionary biology - *an analogous, metaphorical extension of biological evolution.* This form of EE sometimes takes the form of a methodology or metatheory [Popper, 1974, 1972, 1963], or a sociobiological theory [Dawkins, 1982].

While this second version is concerned with, for the most part, the historical evolution of science - the phylogenetic development of knowledge by humans, and the first version with the phylogenetic development of cognitive mechanisms, our approach concentrates instead on the ontogenetic development of knowledge in an individual rather than in a species. Apart from this difference, our approach - CompEE - is also computational in nature, i.e., we demonstrate the viability of our ideas by providing a computational model. One problem in accepting the other versions of EE is that their current arguments are merely verbal. For researchers in the Animat, AL, AI, ML and cognitive science communities, a computational approach seems clearly preferable.

3 A Being

In CompEE evolution operates on a being that is represented as a multi-leveled control hierarchy. There are three levels in the hierarchy: the genetic level, the development level, and the cognitive level. At each level of the hierarchy, there exists a population of entities: genomes, somatic structures, and knowledge. Each entity is in turn represented as a hierarchy. A genome is composed of genes, a being is composed of somatic structures, and knowledge is composed of plans, hypotheses, analogies, and concepts. Although each level in the control hierarchy is independent (with respect to the evolution of each level's entities), each level depends on the others for its operation.

3.1 Genetic Level

We believe that it is impossible a priori to determine the exact format of the chromosome and to determine what genes should be placed close to one another to form meaningful building blocks. Recognizing the problems of fixed location and binary chromosomes, we propose the following genome model:

- Genes may use different binary or non-binary alphabets.
- Genes are arranged into a hierarchy so that they can form dependencies and epistatic interactions with one another.
- Genes are used to define the structure of a being.
- Genes are used for the control of evolution within the genome.

This model is a large departure from the simple notion of a genome presented by the GA community. First, because genes are hierarchically organized, when evolution works with a part of the hierarchy it is directly manipulating a building block. Next, genes control the adaptation process! Together, these two aspects of our model are a first step towards a parameterless system. We are not proposing that the system create its own parameters, but it will identify the values for the ones we give it.

3.2 Development Level

A being is composed of four systems: a Motivational System, a Stimulus System, a Memory System, and a Problem Solving System. A being's genome defines all of the parameters for each of these systems, making a being a parameterless system.

3.2.1 Motivational System

The Motivational System organizes a being's drives and helps it to determine which behavior it is to engage in next. A being has the following drives: thirst, hunger, sex, existence, pleasure, curiosity, and an external drive defined by an external source, for example a math problem. A drive behaves like a thermostat. Each drive has a current value, a threshold value that indicates at what value the drive becomes activated, and a shutoff value that indicates at what value the drive becomes deactivated.

Many drives may be active at any moment. To identify the priorities of the drives, they are arranged into a hierarchy, called the Motivational Drive Hierarchy, which is part of the genome. The highest priority drive is found at the root node of the hierarchy. The closer a drive is to the root drive, the greater its priority. The drive with the greatest priority is chosen as the active drive.

We do not presume to know the exact level at which to place each drive in the hierarchy. Therefore, initially drives are placed randomly in a being's Motivational Drive Hierarchy. Subsequent evolution of the species' genes determines the placement of drives in the hierarchy that best suits the environment.

3.2.2 Stimulus System

The Stimulus System controls a being's five senses. Each sense has a sensitivity value. For the senses of sight, smell, and hearing, sensitivity refers to from how far away a stimulus can be detected by the sense. For the senses of taste and touch, sensitivity refers to the amount of stimulus that must be present for the sense to detect it.

The Stimulus System's major responsibility is to return a list of stimuli perceived from a being's current position in the environment. A being may not, however, have all five senses at its disposal.

When a being senses an environmental object (such as another being, a rock, a hole, some food, poisonous food, or water) it forms a conjunction of the features that it can sense about the object. For example, if a being can only feel and smell things and runs into food, it would form the conjunction (smells(good), feels(soft)); but if it could see, it would form the conjunction (smells(good), feels(soft), looks(green)). The problem with this conjunction is that it may be the same as one formed by a being running into another being, if beings in this environment also smell good, feel soft, and look green. A being must determine what is and what is not food given that many objects can have overlapping features.

3.2.3 Memory System

The Memory System controls a being's long and short term memories. A being's short term memory consists of a limited stream of contexts, formed from its sensations, and actions. A being's sensations are conjunctions returned by its Stimulus System. A being's actions in the current implementation include the following: drink, eat, mate, reproduce, moveNorth, moveSouth, moveWest, moveEast, stayPut. A being performs one of these actions either in response to its current context, its active drive, or both.

A being's fixed sized short term memory stream appears as follows:

$A_t\, C_t\, A_{t-1}\, C_{t-1}\, A_{t-2}\, C_{t-2}$........

where A is action, C is context, and *t* is time.

A being's fixed size long term memory consists of a stream of schemata. A schema is a tripartite structure, consisting of a conditional context, an action, and an expected context. There are four types of schemata, described in detail in section 3.3.1, that represent plans or hypotheses, analogies, concepts, and complex schemata.

Schemata are created by two different types of methods:

- By the application of schema templates to short term memory, looking for repetitive patterns of sensations and actions.

- By the Problem-Solving System (described in section 3.2.4).

The first method is based on three assumptions: 1) beings have 'built-in' templates for forming schemata; 2) such templates are genetically hard wired and imposed on nature to break the unending sequence of events into law-like chunks; 3) many templates are reasonable, trustworthy and often confirmed; and, 4) these schema-forming templates result from evolution and their presence in a being is controlled by its genome.

The templates are based on extensions of Mill's methods of experimental inquiry aimed at the discovery of causes [Skyrms, 1975]. Since the templates form the knowledge of the cognitive level, the specific templates and their application are described in detail in the cognitive level section (section 3.3).

The second method of creating schemata is performed by the Problem-Solving System and is described in the next section.

3.2.4 Problem-Solving System

Using long term memory, the Problem-Solving System returns an action to decrease a being's currently active drive, given its external environment[1]. However, a being's knowledge is not preprogrammed, it must be learned.

In the last section, we showed that schemata are found in short term memory using templates. These schemata are valuable to the Problem-Solving System in two ways. First, if a schema exactly matches the current external environment and active drive, its action is returned as a solution to the problem. Second, when none of them match exactly, they are used as the raw material from which the solution is built. This solution, a complex schema, may in turn be a building block in future solutions.

Complex schemata are formed by a process called Evolution-Based Reasoning. Similar to CBR, EBR attempts to reuse past knowledge. However, in contrast to CBR, EBR takes learning and adaptation of knowledge as integral components of the reasoning method. The construction of knowledge is seen as the process of differential selection on variation - evolution. Knowledge evolves in a manner similar to the evolution of a being: the survival of the fittest.

Since EBR forms the spine of the Cognitive level, we discuss its details and the precise format of the different types of schemata it manipulates in section 3.3.1.

If the Problem-Solving System's EBR process cannot find or produce a suitable schema for the current problem, a new one is created with the current context and a randomly selected action. Therefore, when a being does not know what to do, it at least does something. Even a random action might be correct. The current situation and action are recorded in short term memory and form the raw data for future pattern learning.

3.3 Cognitive Level

A being can acquire knowledge in one of two ways. The first way, as described in section 3.2.3, is by observing repetitive patterns in short term memory. In its primitive form, learning by observation associates particular stimuli with responses. For example, a being can learn what a wall is by running into it, or it can learn to avoid heat by moving away from it. This is a very costly learning method that uses a lot of memory. A being that does not encode its repetitive experiences as general hypotheses, must record all its particular experiences.

The second way a being can acquire knowledge is by adapting its existing knowledge. The process of adapting old solutions to new problems is not only cognitively plausible [Riesbeck and Schank, 1989; Ross, 1989] but also rests on the well supported assumption of CBR [Kolodner, 1987],

---

1 For example, if the being is hungry and there is food beside him, an appropriate action would be to eat the food.

i.e., that small changes to existing knowledge will often result in further useful knowledge.

This form of learning has close parallels to evolution. Initially, variations occur in a being's knowledge, either voluntary (the 'what happens if?' question) or involuntary (errors in memory or in the copying process). Some variations benefit the being, and constitute new 'knowledge', others do not. Natural selection prefers the former, resulting in a reproduction differential in the knowledge for the next generation. Therefore, evolution can and does occur at the cognitive level.

Both forms of learning take place in the cognitive level. Pattern learning plays an important initial role. Tissue needs present a being with its first problems as well as with a specific criterion for judging the adequacy of its solutions. For example, hunger forces a being to move around to find food. The immediate result of finding food is a successful outcome to an action taken as part of the proposed solution. Initially tentative solutions are proposed, based on the acquired schema templates. Some of these schemata are discarded immediately by using existing knowledge to rule them out, while others must be tried out to determine their appropriateness. Next, more complex schemata are built from the simple ones. The more knowledge a being has, the more knowledge it can generate.

In the next two sections we describe how simple schemata are found in short term memory and then describe how the EBR process uses them to produce new, complex schemata.

3.3.1 Schema Types

The only unit of knowledge in long term memory is a schema. A schema is a tripartite structure, similar to Drescher's schema [Drescher, 1991], consisting of a conditional context, an action, and an expected context. An action is an event that can affect the state of a being's environment. A context is collection of propositions about the state of the world, that include a being's sensations, its active drive, and its position.

A schema is the primary building block for complex knowledge and is interpreted both declaratively and procedurally. Declaratively, a schema makes factual assertions about the environment. Procedurally, a schema states how a decrease in a drive can be achieved.

There are four types of schemata: plan or hypothesis, analogy, concept, and complex. The first three simple schemata are created by applying the built-in schema templates, described in section 3.2.3, to a short term memory that is structured as follows:

$$A_t\, C_t\, A_{t-1}\, C_{t-1}\, A_{t-2}\, C_{t-2}\ldots\ldots$$

where A is action, C is context, and *t* is time.

A plan or hypothesis schema is formed using a template based on the *presumption of redundancy and regularity* and *enumerative induction.* The former principle states that whatever happens, expect it to happen again; and the latter one states that the more often something occurs, the more likely it is true. For example, if in short term memory the sequence:

$$C_t\, A_{t-1}\, C_{t-1} \ldots\ldots\ldots\, C_{t-x}\, A_{t-x-1}\, C_{t-x-1}$$

is found, where $C_t = C_{t-x}$, $A_{t-1} = A_{t-x-1}$, and $C_{t-1} = C_{t-x1}$, applying the template would create a plan schema with the following structure: $C_t\, A_{t-1}\, C_{t-1}$. If a being is able to generalize (controlled by its genome), the new context includes only those features that match in the source and destination contexts. A plan schema asserts that if the action is taken when its source context's conditions are all satisfied, then the new expected context will be obtained.

An analogy schema is formed using a template based on *simple analogy.* This principle states that if two things match partially - along features previously involved in successful hypotheses, and thus 'entrenched' as relevant features - infer a full match. For example, if in short term memory the sequence:

$$C_1\, A_2\, C_2 \ldots\ldots\ldots\, C_3\, A_2\, C_2$$

is found, applying the template would create an analogy schema with the following structure: $C_1 \leftrightarrow C_3$. An analogy schema asserts that the two contexts can be interchanged with one another.

A concept schema is formed using a template based on the principle of *simple causal laws.* This principle states that if one event occurs followed by another one in many confirmed cases, then infer that the first event causes the second.

For example, if in short term memory the sequence:

$$C_1 \ldots\ldots\ldots\, C_2$$

is found, where C_1 and C_2 share common features, a concept schema with these common features is created. A concept schema implies that its component features are causally related to one another.

Complex schemata are formed by combining other schemata (complex or simple) into schemata hierarchies. For example, using the simple plan schema in figure 1, we wish to build a schema that can be used given the current environmental context C_c and desired expected environmental context C_e.

Obviously the schema in figure 1 will not solve the problem. However, if we add the plan schema ($C_c\, A_2\, C_1$), the resulting schema, shown in figure 2, is closer to solving the problem, but it still does not have the desired expected context.

Then, if we add the analogy schema ($C_2 \leftrightarrow C_e$), the resulting schema, shown in figure 3, is a solution to the problem.

The complex schema, shown in figure 3, demonstrates that to get from context C_c to C_e two actions must be performed: A_2 and A_1, and that when the context C_2 is reached it can be considered the same as context C_e. After each action there is an expectation of what environmental context will be present. This makes it easy to check if a proposed complex schema is making good predictions about its behavior.

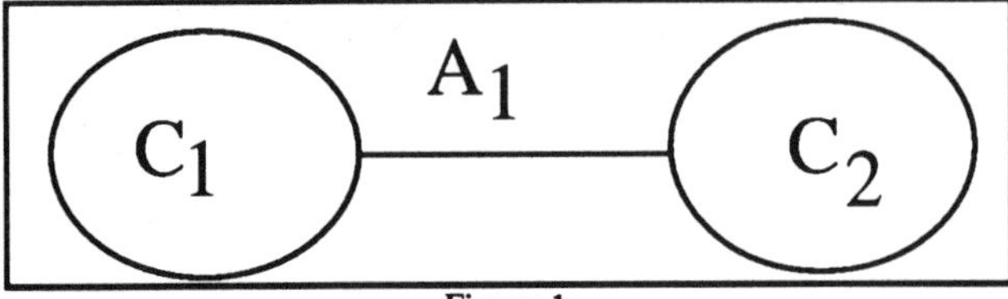

Figure 1.

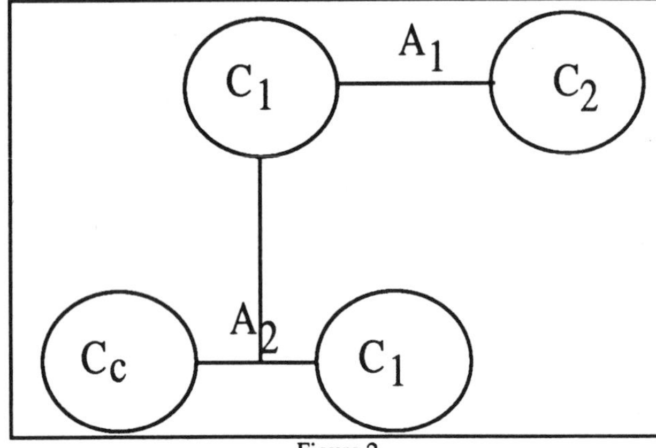

Figure 2.

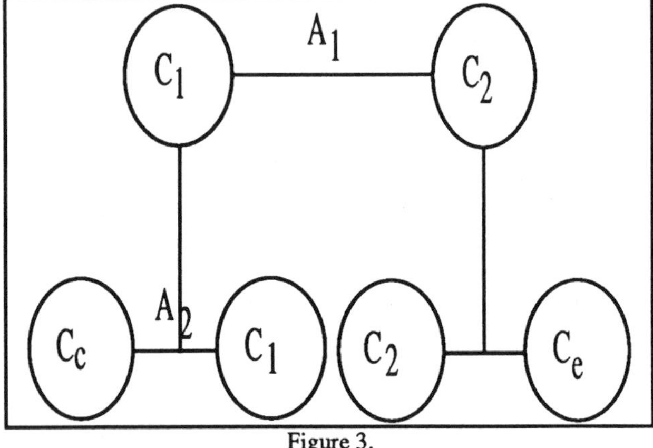

Figure 3.

How are these complex schemata built? This is the topic of the next section.

3.3.2 Evolution-Based Reasoning

If no schema is available to answer a being's problem, it must make a new complex solution schema out of existing schemata. To do this, a being uses EBR, an evolution-based reasoning method.

EBR can be summarized as the following steps: retrieve a population of the best schemata from memory for solving the current problem; with the available genetic operators, form a new population by combining the existing schemata; choose the new focus contexts for the next iteration of the process; and repeat the process until a schema that solves the current problem is found or the maximum number of generations is reached. On the second, and subsequent, iterations, other schemata are retrieved, based on the focus contexts, and added to the population produced by the last iteration.

The focusing mechanism changes back and forth between the contexts of the problem and the contexts of the fittest schema in the population. This is an attempt at combining exploitation and exploration. During exploitation, EBR attempts to build schemata that solve the problem. During exploration, EBR attempts to build schemata that use the best schemata in the population. It may be better to explore more and exploit less, or vice-versa. However, by simply changing back and forth, the end effect is the same.

The initial retrieval process finds the best (fittest) schemata for the current problem. The current problem consists of reducing a being's current drive in the given context. A schema's fitness value represents its past success and how well it matches the current problem's contexts.

It is calculated as follows:

$$\frac{relativeFrequencyOfSuccess \ + \ contextMatch}{2}$$

The schema's context match value is calculated as follows:

$$\frac{MFICC \ + \ MFIEC}{(\ TFICC \ + \ TFIEC\ )}$$

where MFICC is the number of features in the schema's conditional context that match with the given conditional context, MFIEC is the number of features in the schema's expected context that match with the given expected context, TFICC is the total number of features in the given conditional context, and TFIEC is the total number of features in the given expected context.

A schema's relative frequency of success is calculated as follows:

$$\frac{positive}{positive \ + \ negative}$$

A schema's relativeFrequencyOfSuccess is the ratio of the number of times it has been used successfully to the total number of times it has been used. Since a schema's relativeFrequencyOfSuccess and contextMatch values are less than or equal to one, a denominator value of 2 for the fitness calculation, produces a fitness value between 0 and 1.

After the selection of the best schemata for EBR's working population, genetic operators are randomly applied to produce a new population of complex schemata. There are four genetic operators: mutation, crossover, split, and join. The mutation operator can add, remove, or change any context's feature to another value. The crossover operator breaks the two mating schemata into two parts and joins the first part of one with the second part of the other. The split operator can either break one complex schema into two smaller schemata, or split the contexts of a simple schema in two, forming two simple schemata with smaller contexts. The join operator joins two schemata together.

After producing a new population, a conditional and expected context are chosen for the focus of the next iteration. Focusing allows EBR to explore new alternatives and then exploit them to solve the problem. To achieve this, EBR changes back and forth between focusing on the current problem contexts and the contexts of the best schema in the genetically produced population.

After setting the focus contexts, the fitness values of all schemata in memory are adjusted to reflect the new contexts. Then, the best schemata are taken and added into the population, replacing the weak ones. EBR is repeated on this new population.

After producing a good schema, or running out of generations, the current best schema is checked to ensure that it meets a minimum fitness criterion, and is returned as the solution to the problem. If the schema's fitness falls below the criterion, no solution is returned. In this case a random schema will be generated and used as the answer.

Ultimately it is the performance of a schema that determines whether it will be used in the future. Since memory is of a fixed size, only the best schemata are kept.

4 Discussion

A being's environment consists of a square grid of cells, the middle cell of the grid found at the position (0, 0). Beings or other environmental objects can position themselves on any cell, and duplicate objects on the same cell are permitted.

There are six different environmental objects: beings, rocks, water, holes, nonpoisonous food, and poisonous food. Each object has the following features: color, smell, taste, loudness, and texture, which correspond to the features that a fully functional being could sense.

One important point about the environment is that the features of the environmental objects overlap for different objects. This means that a being will have to sort out what features are representative of a particular object.

Another important point about the environment is that, from the point of view of a being, the optimal action for it to take in any situation is not knowable from its immediate sensor data; therefore, behavior reinforcement is not immediate.

A being can perform any one of its actions with, or on, each of the environmental objects. Tables are used to describe how a being's performance of an action affects its drives. The way a drive changes depends on both the action and the object of the action.

Using the above environment, out preliminary results indicate that the model meets its objectives. Beings manage to produce and maintain useful, non-redundant schemata in their memories using the four simple genetic adaptation rules of mutation, crossover, split, and join. A being generates many schemata in its lifetime. It is important for it to be able to distinguish the good ones from the bad ones, especially when memory capacity is limited. The bad schemata must be removed to make room for new ones, while the old, good schemata should remain until they too have outlived their usefulness. Figure 4 shows the average number of successes and failures accumulated in the knowledge of the population of beings over time. It is easy to see that the knowledge of the population is improving - EBR is doing its job! In the early generations, random actions are generated. However, after a being has constructed an initial population of beliefs, we see that it relies more and more on it and EBR to generate its actions. For example, figure 5 shows that the beings use evolved actions far more often than random ones.

After simple schemata are formed, EBR begins producing complex schemata from the simple ones. In one experiment, an environment was generated with instances of water always placed just east of two instances of rocks. After a being had discovered that to satisfy its thirst it must drink water and that by heading east after seeing two rocks it would find water, it was able to produce the complex schema, using EBR, of heading east when it saw two rocks and then, when finding water, drinking the water in order to satisfy its thirst. At one point the being overgeneralized the schema, heading east when it saw only one rock. This schema did not work and was removed from memory. However, the simple schema of heading east when seeing two rocks, which resulted in the sight of water, was still in memory, and was quickly used to rebuild the original complex schema.

We are currently increasing the complexity of the environment by adding predators, more types of food and hazards, and giving a being more available actions. These additions should provide more problems for a being and force it to think more, stressing its EBR process, its body and its genes.

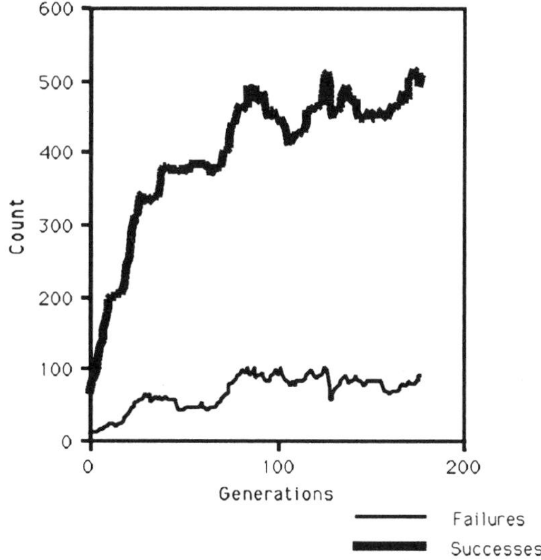

Figure 4. Knowledge Success and Failure Counts

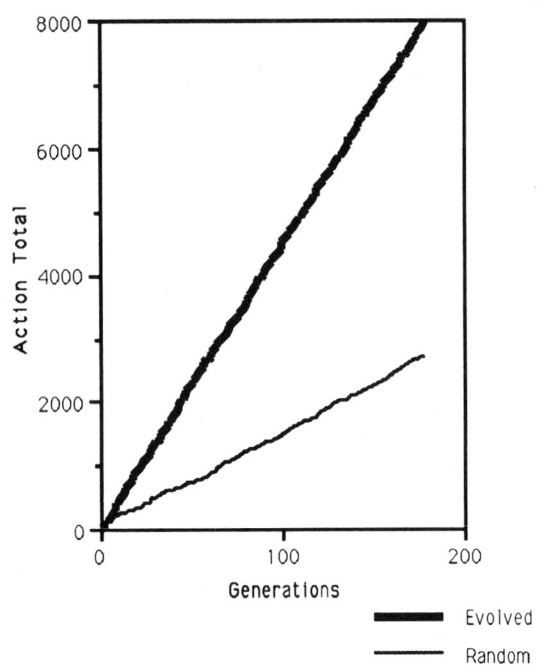

Figure 5. Evolved and Random Action Totals

5 Summary

CompEE is a new, biologically motivated approach to cognitive modeling and machine learning that uses abstractions of known biological mechanisms and simplified Darwinian processes, and is developed for computational study of the evolution of individual learning and knowledge on a computer.

CompEE holds that: 1) evolution is a knowledge gaining process at many levels; 2) scientific knowledge grows and develops in the same way as the embedded knowledge found in beings; and, 3) a being increases its fitness, through adaptation, by internally modeling stable features of the environment at many different levels.

To represent a being, CompEE uses a hierarchy containing three distinct evolutionary levels: 1) the genetic level, 2) the development level, and, 3) the cognitive level. Each level has an influence on the other levels. Associated with each level is a population of entities: the genetic level has a population of genomes; the development level has a population of beings; and, the cognitive level has a population of beliefs. While each level depends on the others for its operation, its population evolves independently of the others, i.e., mechanisms of variation, selection, and reproduction exist at each level.

Hierarchies are used to represent different structures: a gene hierarchy for the genome; a motivational hierarchy for a being's drives, and a schema hierarchy for complex schema beliefs.

In CompEE, the growth of knowledge is evolutionary. To solve problems, EBR assembles existing schemata and compares them with memories as to their appropriateness. If no 'good' schema is found to solve a problem, existing schemata are adapted to fit the problem. Schemata are never blindly assembled, they are always guided by background knowledge that limits their range of variability. The best 'fitting' knowledge, i.e. the one with the best match to the problem, is selected as the solution. The solution, however, may not appear right away. It may take several generations and variations of competing schemata to determine one for the current situation.

CompEE's genetic and development levels correspond to Animat's and AL's genotype and phenotype levels. These levels fix parameters and 'knowledge' that cannot be learned at the cognitive level. However, it is the cognitive level that can make better use of the traits provided by the other two levels.

CompEE is related to CBR, especially by the way EBR manipulates previously used schemata in constructing and proposing new solutions. The main difference between EBR and CBR is rather than just 'tweaking' past solutions with hand-coded rules or methods as CBR does, EBR defines knowledge structures - schemata - and operators for the explicit purpose of adapting knowledge. CompEE, using evolution, takes adaptation seriously.

CompEE is related to GAs, but manipulates hierarchical structures, rather than fixed size linear bit strings.

CompEE is also related to EE. The work in EE has gone virtually unnoticed by the GA, AL and Animat communities. This is an omission that we wish to correct. EE offers many ideas on the topics of the evolution of knowledge, learning, and behavior, and should not be overlooked. Although EE has failed to advance detailed, empirically testable ideas, CompEE does just that.

CompEE attempts to understand learning 'by abstracting the fundamental dynamic principles underlying biological phenomena' [Langton *et al.*, 1992, pp. *xv*ff] and synthesizing these dynamics on a computer. It allows us to study *learning-and-knowledge-as-we-know-it* as well as *learning-and-knowledge-as-it-could-be*.

References

Ackley, D. and Littman, M., Interactions Between Learning and Evolution, In [Langton, *et al.*, 1992], 487-509, 1992.

Belew, R. K., McInerney, J., and Schraudolph, N. N., Evolving Networks, In [Langton, *et al.*, 1992], 511-547, 1992.

Campbell, Donald. T., Evolutionary Epistemology, In W.W. Bartley (Ed.) Evolutionary Epistemology, Rationality, and the Sociology of Knowledge, Open Court, 47-90, 1987.

Campbell Donald. T., Heyes, C.M., and Callebaut, W., Evolutionary Epistemology Bibliography, In Callebaut, Pinxten, 405-431, 1987.

Collins, R.J., and Jefferson, D.R., AntFarm: Towards Simulated Evolution, In [Langton, *et. al., 1992*], 579-601, 1992.

Davis, L., Genetic Algorithms and Simulated Annealing, Pitman , London, 1987.

Dawkins, R., The Selfish Gene, Oxford University Press, 1976.
Dawkins, R., The Extended Phenotype, W.H. Freeman, Oxford, 1982.
De Jong, K., Genetic Algorithm-based Learning, In [Kodratoff and Michalski, 1990], 611-638, 1990.
Deugo, D.L., and Oppacher, F., Explicitly Schema-Based Genetic Algorithms, Proceedings of the Ninth Biennial Conference of the Canadian Society for Computational Studies of Intelligence, 46-53, 1992.
Drescher, G.L., Made-Up Minds: A Constructivist Approach to Artificial Intelligence, The MIT Press, 1991.
Fogelmann-Soulie, F., Gallinari, P., and Thiria, S., Network Learning, unpublished manuscript, 1990.
Goldberg, D.E., Genetic Algorithms in Search, Optimization, and Machine Learning, Addison-Wesley, 1989.
Grefenstette, J.J., Credit Assignment in Genetic Learning Systems, Proceedings of the Seventh National Conference on Artificial Intelligence, Morgan Kaufmann Publishers, 596-600, 1988.
Hammond, K.J., Case-Based Planning: Viewing Planning as a Memory Task, Academic Press, 1989.
Hinton, G.E., Connectionist Learning Procedures, In J. Carbonell (Ed.) Machine Learning, Paradigms and Methods, MIT Press, 185-234, 1990a
Hinton, G.E., Connectionist Learning Procedures, In [Kodratoff and Michalski, 1990], 555-610, 1990b.
Holland, J.H., Adaptation in Natural and Artificial Systems, University of Michigan Press, 1975.
Holland, J.H., Escaping Brittleness: The Possibilities of General-Purpose Learning Algorithms Applied to Parallel Rule-Based Systems, In R.S. Michalski, J.G. Carbonell, and T.M. Mitchell (Eds.) Machine Learning: An Artificial Intelligence Approach, Vol II, Morgan Kaufmann Publishers Inc., 593-624, 1986.
Holland, J.H., Holyoak, K.H., Nisbett, R.E., and Thagard, P.R., INDUCTION: Processes of Inference, Learning, and Discovery, The MIT Press, 1986.
Judd, J.S., Neural Network Design and the Complexity of Learning, The MIT Press, 1990.
Kodratoff, Y., and Michalski, R., Machine Learning: An Artificial Intelligence Approach, Vol: III, Morgan Kaufmann, 1990.
Kolodner, J.L., Simpson, K., and Sycara-Cryanski, K., A Process Model of Case-Based Reasoning in Problem Solving, Proceedings of the Sixth National Conference of Artificial Intelligence, Morgan Kaufmann, 284-290, 1987.
Kolodner, J.L., Extending Problem Solver Capabilities Through Case-Base Inference, Proceedings: Case-Based Reasoning Workshop, Morgan Kaufmann, 21-30, 1988.
Koza, J., Genetic Evolution and Co-Evolution of Computer Programs, In [Langton, *et al.*, 1992], 603-630, 1992.
Langton, Christopher, Artificial Life, Addison Wesley, 1989.
Langton, C., Taylor, C., Farmer, J., and Rasmussen, S., Artificial Life II, Addison Wesley, 1992.
Lorenz, K., Behind the Mirror, Harcourt Brace Jovanovich, New York, 1973.
Meyer, J., and Wilson, S.W., Proceedings of the First International Conference on Simulation of Adaptive Behavior, The MIT Press, 1991.
Nilsson, N.J., Principles of Artificial Intelligence, Tioga, 1980.
Oppacher, F., and Deugo, D.L., Integrating Case-Based Reasoning with Genetic Algorithms, In N. Cercone and G. Gardin (Eds.) Computational Intelligence, III, North-Holland, 103-114, 1991.
Plotkin, H.C., An Evolutionary Epistemological Approach to the Evolution of Intelligence, In Harry J. Jerison and Irene Jerison, (Eds.) Intelligence and Evolutionary Biology, Springer-Verlag, 73-92, 1986.
Popper, K.R., Conjectures and Refutations, Routledge & Kegan Paul, 1963.
Popper, K.R., Objective Knowledge: An Evolutionary Approach, Oxford Univ. Press, Oxford, 261, 1972.
Popper, K.R., Replies to My Critics, In P.A. Schilpp (Ed.) The Philosophy of Karl Popper, La Salle: Open Court, 1061, 1974.
Ruse, M., Talking Darwin Seriously, Basil Blackwell, 1986.
Schilpp, P.A., The Philosophy of Karl Popper, Open Court, LaSalle, Ill., 1974.
Simon, Herbert, A., The Organization of Complex Systems, In H.H. Pattee (Ed.) Hierarchy Theory, New York: Braziller, 1973.
Skyrms, Brian, Mill's Methods of Experimental Inquiry and the Nature of Causality, In Choice and Chance: An Introduction to Inductive Logic, Dickenson Publishing Company, Ch. 4, 1975.
Sutton, S.S., Reinforcement Learning Architectures for Animats, In [Wilson, 1991], 288-296, 1991.
Thagard, P., Computational Philosophy of Science, The MIT Press, 1988.
Thompson, P., Conceptual and Logical Aspects of the New Evolutionary Epistemology, Canadian Journal of Philosophy, V14, The University of Calgary Press, 235-253,1988.
Thorndike, In R.J. Richards (Ed.) Darwin and The Emergence of Evolutionary Theories of Mind and Behavior, University of Chicago Press, 440, 1987.
Toulmin, S., Evolution, Adaptation, and Human Understanding. In M.B. Brewer & B.E. Collins (Eds.), Scientific Inquiry and the Social Sciences: A Volume in Honor of Donald T. Campbell, San Fancisco: Josssey-Bass, 18-36, 1981.
Wilson, S. W., The Genetic Algorithm and Simulated Evolution, In [Langton, 1989], 157-166, 1989.
Wilson, S. W., The Animate Path to AI, Proceedings of the First International Conference on Simulation of Adaptive Behavior, The MIT Press, 15-21, 1991.
Winograd, T., Language as a Cognitive Process, Addison-Wesley, 1983.

Emergence of Nest-Based Foraging Strategies in Ecosystems of Neural Networks

Dario Floreano
Department of Psychology
University of Trieste
Via dell'Universita', 7
34123 Trieste, Italy
E-mail: floreano@univ.trieste.it

Abstract

This research studies the emergence of nest-based foraging behaviours in organisms whose nervous system is simulated by a neural network. The paper stresses the importance of the interaction between the characteristics of the environment and the actions of the organisms for the development of internal maps of the environment, different behavioural strategies and efficient adaptation to difficult environmental conditions. Two different single case studies are analyzed in more detail to understand the evolutionary history of the development of nest-based foraging strategies. It is found that a gradual impoverishment of the environmental conditions drastically improves the capacity of the organisms to survive and facilitates the emergence of new behavioural abilities.

1.0 Introduction

This research studies the evolution of an ecosystem of sensory-motor neural networks. An ecosystem defines some relationship between a physical environment and the organisms living in it; this relationship is often bidirectional, in that the actions of the organisms can modify some characteristics of the environment, which in turn affect the organisms' behaviour (Rizki & Conrad, 1986). Even a highly simplified ecosystem represents a rich source of potentially complex phenomena (Floreano, Miglino & Parisi, 1991).

Most of the biological dynamics can be generally described in the above terms, and a relatively new field of research called Artificial Life has arisen in order to study them in a new perspective. Artificial Life attempts to understand such biological phenomena as life, evolution, intelligence and other ecological issues by means of simulated reproduction. Artificial reproduction of biological facts gives the experimenter evident advantages, such as the control of some important variables, the ability to go back in time to observe the emergence of complex structures, and the possibility to replicate a phenomenon many times from the same initial conditions (Taylor, 1991). This "synthetic" approach (Braitenberg, 1984) -as opposed to the more common analytic method- finds a fruitful methodological tool in the combination of evolutionary techniques and the connectionist paradigm. More specifically, evolutionary algorithms (Rechenberg, 1973; Holland, 1975) can be used for evolving populations of neural networks that simulate the nervous system of organisms living in an environment.

2.0 Nest-Based Foraging Strategies

The following set of simulations have attempted to study the evolution of nest-based foraging strategies in static and changing environments. Many living organisms possess a nest at some time in their life. The nest is very important because it provides a safe shelter from predators, atmospheric factors and other sort of dangers. In some species a nest is only a precise location where the eggs are deposited, in other species it is also a place to meet the partner or eat the food, and again in other species (eg, the ants) the nest is a food store, the centre of the social and reproductive life and it has a very complicated structure. Rather than studying the nesting behaviour (ie, the choice of the physical zone and the construction of the nest), the research considers the aspects related to the return to the nest after foraging. Despite all the various degrees of complexity of what a nest affords, it is generally true that every living organism can locate its own nest and go back to it when required. If the food can be eaten only within the nest, then the organism can be said to use a rudimentary plan which grossly specifies a sequence of actions to leave the nest, locate and approach the nearest food token, and carry it back to the nest.

This research aims to study the evolutionary development of nest-based foraging strategies in a simple ecosystem, and to understand the structure of the emerging behaviours. Also, it attempts to understand how these strategies are affected in a changing environment, such as a world where there is a gradual impoverishment of the food resources during the evolutionary process.

In these simulations the environment is an infinite grid with some food tokens distributed within a 40*40 area around a 6*6 central nest. The food tokens are never placed inside the nest. Given these initial conditions, the organism must pick up one food token at a time and carry it back to the nest, where it will eventually be able to eat it and increment its fitness. Once a food token has been grasped, the organism will not be able to pick up any other token before it has reached the nest and eaten it. Grasping and eating food tokens is easy: once the organism has reached a food location, the token is automatically loaded in its hand (provided that it has not already another token), and as soon as it reaches the nest, the food is automatically passed from its hand to its mouth. There are at least three non-trivial abilities involved in this task: approaching the food, approaching the nest, and switching the goal of the actions (food search or return to the nest). In this set of simulations the second requirement is slightly eased because the nest is always in the same position and the organism receives direct sensory information about where its centre is (angle and distance); nevertheless, the network must form an internal map of the environment in order to coordinate its own actions for the goal to be reached.

2.1 Related Studies.

This research stems from previous simulations of foraging strategies in various conditions (Parisi, Cecconi & Nolfi, 1990; Miglino & Parisi, 1991; Floreano, Miglino & Parisi, 1991). The task studied here has also been tackled by Collins & Jefferson (1991) who have attempted to artificially reproduce the cooperative (social) behaviour of colonies of ants. Their simulated environment is a 16*16 toroidal grid; each cell can contain many food tokens and more than one ant, and the nest occupies the central cell. 76.5% of the cells are filled with food, i.e. all the cells except those in the straight line from the nest (horizontal, vertical and diagonal). Each environment contains a colony of 128 ants which have all the same genetic code and share the available resources. 16,384 colonies, each in its own environment, contemporaneously live on a Connection Machine parallel computer. The colony's task consists of picking up a food token and bringing it back to the nest in order to increment the colony's fitness. The Authors have run various simulations with different network architectures. They have obtained poor performances both with simple multilayer feedforward networks; very good results have instead been obtained when two recurrent networks are used together (one for food approaching and another for the return to the nest, with a built-in rule to switch from one network to the other) or when the network architectures are designed by the genetic algorithm itself. In the last case -the most interesting- nearly every successful network presented some recurrent connection. However, they have never observed the emergence of social behaviours, that is a cooperative search for food by means of the communication chemicals (pheromone units).

3.0 The Simulation Schema

In most of the simulations reported below the environment contains 160 food token randomly distributed in a 40*40 area (however, remember that the environment is infinite, or -better- as wide as the number of steps each network is allowed to take), that is about 10% density (compared to 76.5% in Collins & Jefferson), and there are no food tokens in the nest.

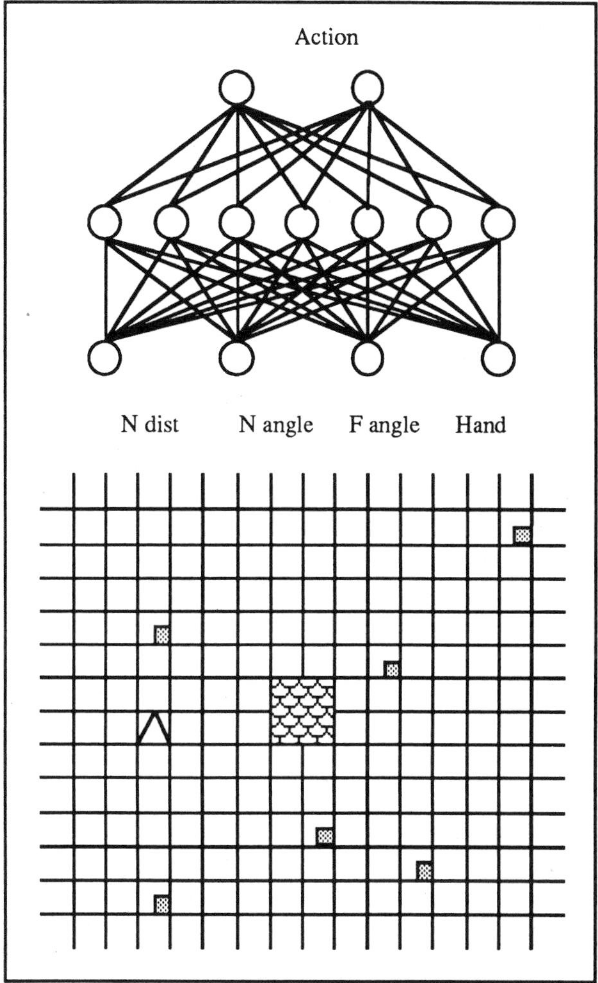

Figure 1: Environment and network architecture. The small triangle represents the organism facing a food token. The structure at the centre is the nest. The network receives sensory information about the distance of the nest (N dist), the direction of the nest (N angle), the direction of the nearest food token (F angle), and whether the hand is empty or not (Hand). The output units code the motor action (go forward, turn right, turn left, stay still).

A three-layered feedforward neural network simulates the nervous system of a very simple organism, which has only one hand and a small repertoire of actions (go forward, turn left, turn right, stay still; they are coded in two output units); as I have mentioned above, a food token is automatically grasped when the organism reaches its location (provided that the hand is empty) and it is eaten as the nest is entered. The sensory system receives information about the direction of the nearest food token, the direction and the distance of the centre of the nest and whether the hand is empty or not. The distance from the centre of the nest has been provided so that the network can understand how far away is from it and develop an internal map of the environment. The network is provided with 7 hidden units (experimental studies on the minimal number required have been previously carried out) and its architecture cannot be modified by the genetic algorithm. Each organism lives alone in its environment and is not a member of a colony[1].

The evolutionary technique used is a version of Evolution Strategies (Rechenberg, 1973); it does not make use of crossover, it operates on continuous valued strings and it relies on a high mutation rate (however, the strategy parameters are not evolved). Each neural network is directly mapped into the chromosome where each gene represents the strength of a synaptic connection. The probability of mutation p_m is 0.098 and the range of mutation r is a random number between -1.0 and +1.0. The population size is 100 and is fixed along generations. The initial weight values of the networks are initialized to a random value between -0.5 and +0.5. The evolutionary system works as follows.

a) An initial random population of 100 neural networks is created (generation 0).

b) Each organism lives for five "years" (epochs); in each epoch it visits three different environments (with a different random food distribution), and it is free to move for 500 steps in each of them. The total number of steps in an organism's life is therefore [5*(3*500)]=4500. Every time an organism visits a new environment, it is placed at a new random location within the 40*40 grid and the hand status in not updated. Its fitness value is incremented for each food token grasped and carried back to the nest.

c) All the organisms are then ranked by fitness and the best 20 individuals are allowed to reproduce. Each individual produces 5 offspring by copying its weight matrix and thus a new population of 100 individuals is obtained (generation 1).

d) Each weight value of the new population is then mutated ("biased mutation", Montana & Davis, 1989) with probability p_m and range r. The algorithm repeats from step b).

4.0 The Simulations

Given the stochastic nature of genetic algorithms, the results reported below are the average of three different runs, each starting from a different random weight initialization and lasting 50 generations each. The statistics collected during the simulations and reported in the graphs show the best individual fitness, the average fitness and the standard deviation of the fitness values within each generation. The last is a measure of diversity of the phenotype. The networks readily learn to maximize their fitness, as shown in Graph 1. The standard deviation values show a possible division between the exploration and the exploitation phase. In the exploration phase (corresponding to the first 30 generations where the SD values keep increasing) the genetic algorithm maintains diversity exploring different zones of the landscape. In the exploitation phase (the second half of the evolutionary process, where the SD values become stable) the low performance individuals gradually disappear and the average performance increases while the best individuals do not further improve: the genetic algorithm has found a minimum.

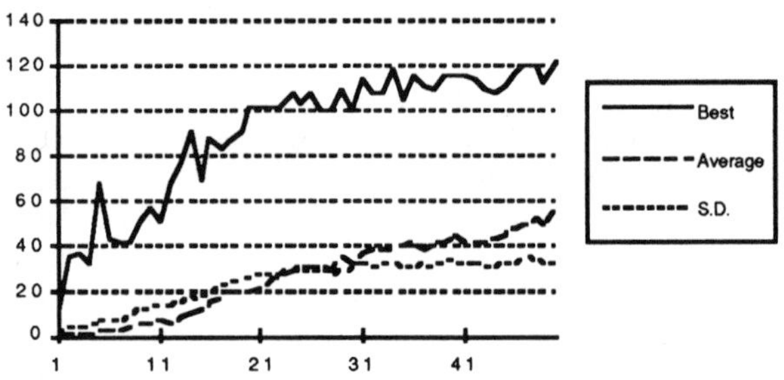

Graph 1: Fitness values. Each value is the average over three runs (Best and Average are the average values; SD is the square root of the averaged SD^2).

However, a closer look at the networks behaviour will better explain what the networks have actually learned. The selected individuals of the initial generation are usually organisms who are "exploratory", i.e. they move in straight lines (this gives them higher probability to walk through a food token and then go across the nest), but they are not sensitive to the sensory input. The straight walk strategy is kept by the best individuals of the first 10 generations; additionally, they gradually learn to move always in the nest direction (eg, southward if they are in the upper portion of the environment, but they do not change their trajectories to enter the nest) from any starting position and they turn back when they get too far away from the nest location.

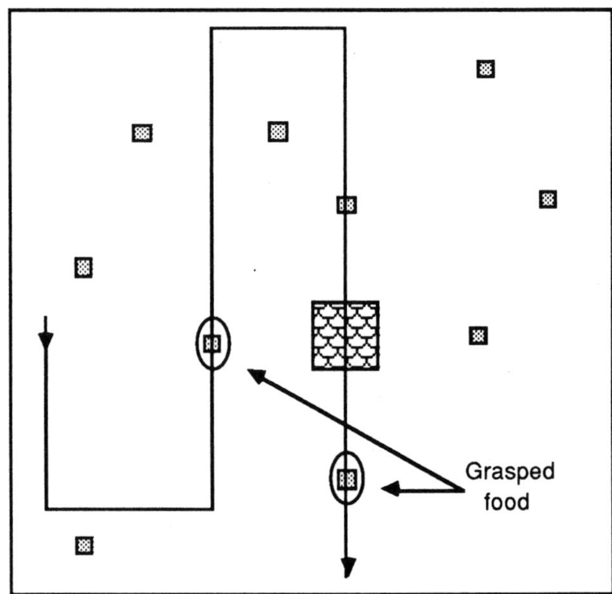

Figure 2: Typical strategy of the best individual of the 50th generation evolved in a static environment. The neural network is not very sensitive to the food position. The nest is entered through preferential paths (the "north path" depicted in the illustration is the most frequent) which are genetic memory of the evolutionary history.

[1] Foraging in a shared environment has been analyzed in [Floreano, 1992]. In that study also the architecture of the neural network can be modified by the genetic algorithm.

In the remaining generations the networks gradually refine their internal map of the environment. The best individuals of the last generation have learned to move in the surroundings of the nest (within the area where the food is distributed). Their trajectories are more articulated, but still are formed of straight lines (Figure 2). The nest is entered through preferential paths (eg, there is often a "main" entrance from north, whose path is at least 5 or 8 steps long). Nevertheless it is not yet possible to observe efficient food approaching strategies, nor an evident "switching behaviour" once the food token has been grasped.

4.1 Single Case Studies.

If on one side it is necessary to run the same simulation many times in order to draw robust conclusions, on the other side it is difficult and odd to average behaviours. A better way to understand what and how the networks learn is to describe and display the strategies used by individual networks (as done above), or to do single case studies. Single case studies have been introduced and justified by Ackley & Littman (1991). A single case is simply a single run of the evolutionary system. Individual networks can then be observed in their learning environment and tested in new conditions, but it must be remembered that the features displayed might not always be generalizable: they are the result of certain starting conditions and of the succession of certain events specific to that run. Something like real life. Two single case studies have been performed on two different environments.

4.1.1 Static Environment.

One of the runs of the simulations described in the previous section has been carried on until the 600th generation. In that case, 10% of the locations are occupied by a food token along the whole evolutionary process. As shown in Graph 2, the networks have continued to improve their performance until the 200th generation (the remaining generations are not plotted here because the curves become fairly flat). The temporary stabilization of the standard deviation around the 50th generation has turned to be only a local feature. The improvement in fitness is accompanied by an increment in the population diversity.

When observed, the best individual of the last generation is apparently very efficient. Its behaviour is much more articulated (the long straight lines are not dominant anymore) and it has learned to stay in the vicinity of the nest. The food approaching strategies are not yet perfect, but since the environment is rich enough, perhaps it is not worth learning to be accurate in grasping the nearest food, but rather learning to return to the nest once that a food has been grasped. The achievement of this behavioural "switch" is the most notable feature: once that the hand is full, the network is rather fast in finding its way back to the nest. In order to further test the abilities of this network, it has been placed in a new very sparse environment (food density = 1.125%). Now it becomes evident that the food-approaching phase consists of a -more or less- random walk with a high degree of exploration. It is also more apparent that the nest is still entered through some preferential paths (a very evident one is still from north, and another is from the south). Furthermore the nest is nearly always left from the side opposite to the entrance (see Figure 2). These features are the inheritance (genetic memory) of ancient strategies used in the first generations, when long straight walks cutting across the nest were used.

4.1.2 Environmental Change.

It may be the case that the environment must contain less food tokens for the networks to develop efficient food approaching strategies. But, training the networks on a sparse environment could have catastrophic effects. The fitness landscape would present few narrow minima that could be difficult to find by evolution. It makes more sense to start with a rich environment and then gradually decrease its food density during the evolutionary process. This stretches out the fitness landscape, causing a gentle slope toward the global minimum: instead of approaching the hard situation rapidly, we make it easier at the beginning and we gradually add constraints as the networks develop more efficient strategies. Decreasing the food density is also a way to increase the selection pressure: only the really better fit individuals will survive in a new impoverished environment. This situation does seem to take place in nature. The environment is not static. It changes according both to physical rules (seasons, climate, biological growth and death, etc.) and to active intervention of the agents living in it. These mutations take place at various time scales and may affect in different ways the life of the organisms. For example, on the long run the food resources of a local environment may decrease when many populations of individuals exploit the same territory. To approximate this change, a new simulation has been run where the networks start evolving in the standard environment (10% food density); every 30 generations the food density is decreased by 10% of the previous density. The simulation has been carried on for 600 generations, until the last environment contained only 18 food tokens (1.25% food density).

In a changing environment the absolute measure of the

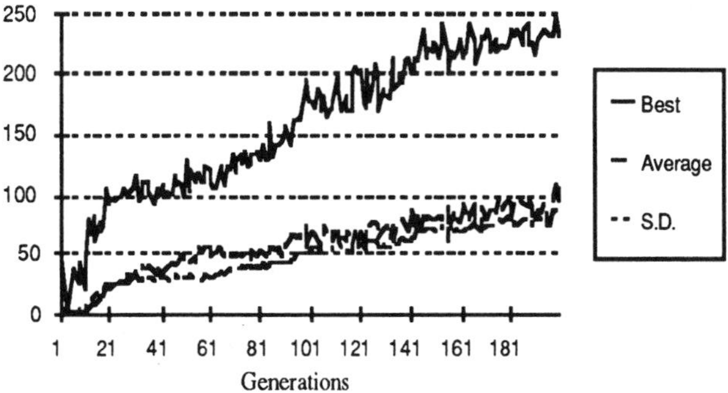

Graph 2: The fitness values of the first 200 generations of organisms evolved in a static environment. The data for the remaining 400 generations have not been plotted because they are fairly invariate.

fitness is not a reliable measure of the organisms performance. In fact, given a fixed life span, it is much harder to grasp and carry back to the nest 7 food tokens in an environment with 18 tokens (best individual in generation 600) than to take back 11 food tokens in an environment with 79 tokens (best individual in generation 220). A fitness measure that takes into account the food density of the environment would be a better index of performance. In general, it is difficult to compute the maximum expected fitness for these organisms; there is no fixed optimum value that applies to different starting positions and different food distributions. A possible solution would be to compute the maximum fitness that is obtained if any food token (not necessarily the nearest) is approached and carried back to the nest: this would be a *benchmark fitness*. In this case the environment can be thought of as a long array with a random distribution of food tokens (Figure 3).

Figure 3: Representation of the environment as an array of cells; filled cells contain a food token.

If the food distribution is truly random, then a food token will be placed on average every x cells. It is assumed that each time that an individual exits the nest and approaches a food token, it must step x times on average before reaching it (far tokens require more steps, near tokens less). In order to gain one fitness point the organism must carry it back to the nest, stepping back x times again. Each fitness point is therefore achieved in 2x steps. In order to compute the maximum number of eaten food tokens, this value must be weighted by the number of steps allowed in each environment, the number of environments visited in each epoch, and the number of epochs. This procedure gives a standard measure of the expected fitness for each organism, but it is very rough and does not take into account the fact that nearest food tokens should be approached first. Given a finite number of steps, if the networks learn to approach efficiently the food tokens, the fitness values reported should be larger than the benchmark fitness. The benchmark fitness is computed as follows:

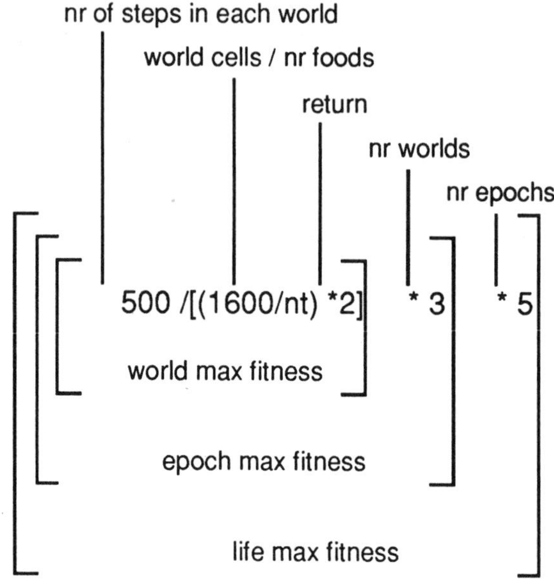

In order to get a normalized fitness measure, the individual fitness is divided by the benchmark fitness.

Graph 3 displays the performance of the organisms evolved in the changing environment using this "normalized" fitness measure. As it can be seen, the plot shows a continuous growth in the networks' performance.

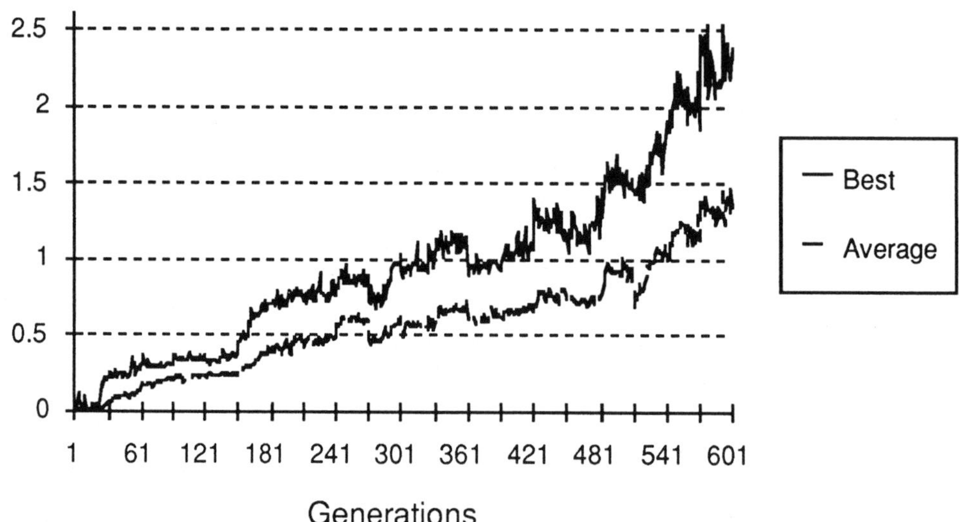

Graph 3: Normalized fitness values reported by organisms that are evolved in a changing environment.

After the 300th generation, the best individuals obtain a fitness value higher than the benchmark value (fitness > 1). This means that they begin to approach the nearest food token rather than following preferential paths. The best individual of the 600th generation displays a fairly good set of strategies to approach the nearest food in the very sparse environment, even though the tokens must still be in a certain position with respect to its frontal direction in order to be "detected". Better results could be achieved with further evolutionary training because the normalized fitness values show a steep growth rate. The dramatic improvement in the foraging behaviour can be observed when the same individual is placed in a richer environment. The return to the nest is not achieved by stepping on the same way back (as in earlier generations), but through shorter paths, even though sometimes the organism enters the nest following a specific path. The nest centre is not necessarily always reached or cut across; sometimes the organism reaches only one of the nest corners and soon exits it to approach another food token. Furthermore, the food search takes place in the near surroundings of the nest. The latter two observations are a strong evidence for the development and use of an internal map of the environment.

5.0 Discussion

All the simulations reported above share some common emergent features for what concerns the evolution of nest-based foraging strategies. In the first phase of the evolution, the networks gradually learn a rudimentary map of the environment telling that the nest is the centre of the environment and that the food tokens are scattered in its neighbourhood. In this phase the most economical strategy employed consists in long straight walk that cut across the centre of the environment (where the nest is located) without stepping too far away from it. In the second phase they learn to return quickly to the nest once that a food token has been grasped. This means that the repertoire of actions used is more complex than simple straight walks. In the last phase, only achieved with the gradual shrinking of the food density, the networks become more sensitive to the food location and perform more efficient food-approaching strategies. In this latest case the search for food takes place in the immediate surrounding of the nest. The difficult and late achievement of efficient food-approaching strategies shows that there is not a unique sensory-motor mechanism underlying both the reaching for food and the reaching for the nest. The presence of two different sensory-motor systems (but not necessarily coded in completely separate neurons and synaptic weights) is also stressed by the different features of the behavioural strategies.

These results are only partially due to the sensory information provided to the organisms. Despite the fact that real organisms do not have always information about the position of the nest, it may be assumed that they locate it by means of some stable landmark. What really matters is that the nest represents a stable reference point that usually does not change position, whereas the food sources are more likely to do it. Learning first to find the nest and using it as a reference point to build the internal map of the environment, may be an emergent strategy that these organisms share with biological organisms.

A common characteristic of all the simulations has been the genetic memory of ancient strategies for the return to the nest; the preferential paths to the nest are what remained of the old straight vertical (or horizontal) lines traced across the centre of the environment. For many generations, the networks have been looking for these paths, rather than for the nest itself; once they were into a path, they automatically reached the nest. The occurence of non-optimal neural structures in biological organisms has been recently the focus of attentive study (Stork, Jackson & Walker, 1991). The preferential paths to the nest can be seen as non-optimality at the behavioral level, the expression of old strategies upon which evolution has built more economical and efficient solutions.

The environmental change has caused a drastic improvement in the quality and efficiency of the foraging strategies. In fact, the random walks for foraging employed in rich environments are not useful when the food is sparse. In this case, approaching efficiently the food tokens is as important as returning to the nest through the shortest path. Graph 4 shows the comparison of the best individuals evolved in the two environmental conditions (with the static and dense food distribution, and with the gradual shrinking of the food density), using the normalized fitness measure. After the 150th generation the best networks evolved in the dense environment do not improve their fitness anymore, whereas the networks living in a poorer environment rapidly become more efficient. The fact that the behavioural strategies of the networks living in the rich environment do not change in the last 450 generations supports the hypothesis that a stable minimum has been reached. The artificial environmental change roughly simulates what happens in nature when an environmental niche is gradually exploited by generations of organisms. This is only a rough approximation of what happens in nature, but it reveals the importance of considering also the mutations that take place in the physical environment. The modification of the environment, even though it consists just of a change of its parameters, puts a harder selection pressure on the organisms living in it and facilitates the emergence of new and better fitted behaviours.

In conclusion, this research has tackled some of the aspects related to the development of nest-based foraging behaviours. The most notable feature has been the great improvement in the set of behavioural abilities developed when the environment undergoes a change, stressing the importance of the co-evolution of the physical environmnent and of the organisms living in it. The evolutionary study has shown the existence of two separate sensory-motor mechanisms employed by the organisms which are developed in successive stages: the first one achieves a map of the environment centered on the nest, the second develops strategies to reach efficiently the nearest food tokens. Also, the occurrence of non-optimal strategies has been explained as a genetic memory of solutions (pre-adaptation) to a different earlier set of interactions between the organisms and the environment.

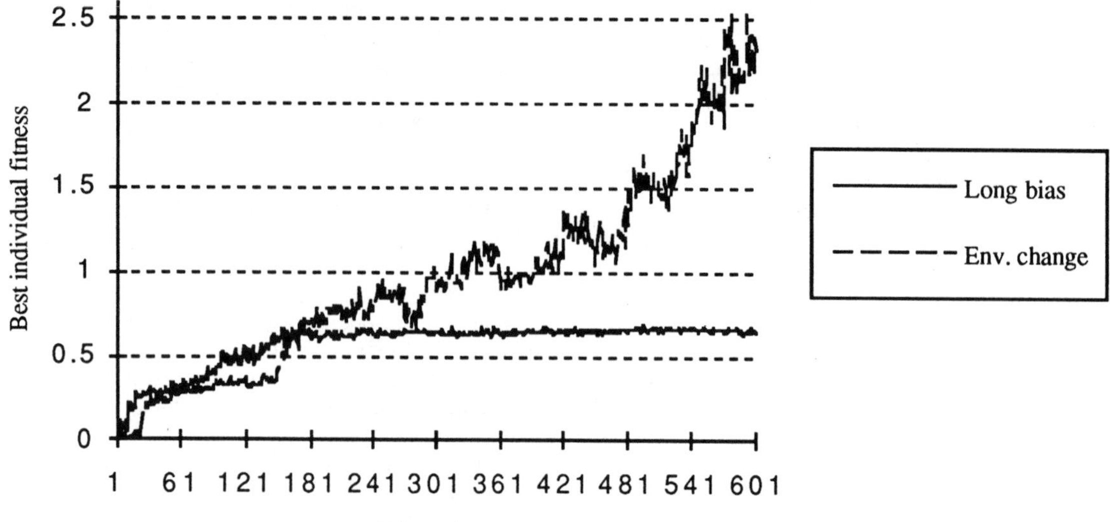

Graph 4: The normalized fitness of the best individuals for 600 generations in the two single case studies (Long bias = rich and static environment; Env. change = gradual impoverishment of the food density).

Acknowledgments

I wish to thank Leslie S. Smith for his help in setting up some simulations and commenting this paper, Domenico Parisi and Federico Cecconi for the discussions, and the Centre for Cognitive and Computational Neuroscience at the University of Stirling (Scotland) for the facilities offered.

References

Ackley, D. & Littman, M. (1991). Interactions Between Learning and Evolution. In Langton et al., (Eds), *Artificial Life II*, Addison-Wesley, Redwood, CA.

Braitenberg, V. (1984). *Vehicles: Experiments in Synthetic Psychology.* MIT Press, Cambridge, MA.

Collins, R.J. & Jefferson, D.R. (1991). AntFarm: Towards Simulated Evolution. In Langton et al., (Eds), *Artificial Life II*, Addison-Wesley, Redwood, CA.

Floreano, D. (1992). Patterns of Interactions in Ecosystems of Neural Networks. M.Sc. Thesis, Centre for Cognitive and Computational Neuroscience, University of Stirling, Scotland.

Floreano, D., Miglino, O. & Parisi, D. (1991). Emergent complex behaviours in ecosystems of neural networks. In Caianiello, E.R. (Ed), *Parallel Architectures and Neural Networks.* World Scientific Press, Singapore.

Holland, J.H. (1975). *Adaptation in natural and artificial systems.* The University of Michigan Press, Ann Arbor.

Miglino, O. & Parisi, D. (1991). Topographic map formation in Econets. TR 09-91, Institute of Psychology, CNR, Rome (Italy).

Montana, D.J. & Davis, L. (1989). Training Feedforward Neural Networks Using Genetic Algorithms. In *Proceedings of the Eleventh IJCAI.*

Parisi, D., Cecconi, F. & Nolfi, S. (1990). Econets: Neural networks that learn in an environment. *Network*, **1**, 149-168.

Rizki, M.M. & Conrad, M. (1986). Computing the Theory of Evolution. *Physica*, **22D**, 83-99.

Rechenberg, I. (1973). *Evolutionstrategie: Optimierung technischer Systeme nach Prinzipien der biologischen Evolution.* Friedrich Frommann Verlag, Stuttgart.

Stork, D.G, Jackson, B. & Walker, S. (1991). "Non-optimality" via Pre-adaptation in Simple Neural Systems. In Langton et al. (Eds), *Artificial Life II*, Addison-Wesley, Redwood, CA.

Taylor, C.E. (1991). "Fleshing Out" Artificial Life II. In Langton et al., (Eds), *Artificial Life II*, Addison-Wesley, Redwood, CA.

Evolving Hardware with Genetic Learning: A First Step Towards Building a Darwin Machine

Tetsuya HIGUCHI[1] Tatsuya NIWA[1] Toshio TANAKA[1]
Hitoshi IBA[2] Hugo de GARIS[1] Tatsumi FURUYA[1]
1) Computational Models Section, 2) Machine Inference Section,
Electrotechnical Laboratory (ETL),
1-1-4 Umezono, Tsukuba, Ibaraki, 305, Japan.
higuchi@etl.go.jp, tel +81-298-58-5868, fax +81-298-58-5871

Abstract

This paper introduces an idea which the authors hope and believe will create not only a new branch of Artificial Life, but may also serve as the basis for a radically new approach to electronic and computer design. The idea can be expressed in two words, "evolvable hardware". Software configurable hardware, such as programmable logic arrays, are on the market which accept a bit string instruction which is used to configure or "wire up" a hardware circuit to give it a desired architecture. This can be done a large number of times. By treating the bit string instruction as a Genetic Algorithm "chromosome", one has the means to evolve hardware. This paper reports on a successful experiment to simulate the evolution of a GAL16Z8 hardware chip, which solves the 6-multiplexor problem. The concept of evolvable hardware can be used to build "Darwin Machines", i.e. special devices which are capable of adapting to their environment by modifying their own hardware architecture using genetic learning techniques.

Keywords: Evolvable Hardware, Programmable Logic Arrays, Software Configurable Hardware, Genetic Algorithms (GAs), Genetic Programing (GP), Animats, Biots (Biological Robots), Artificial Life, Generic Array Logic, GAL16Z8 chip, Darwin Machines, Multiplexor Problem, Boole.

1 Introduction

One of the major aims of Artificial Life is to build autonomous artificial creatures (animats or biots (biological robots)) which can adapt themselves to their environment using such techniques as reinforcement learning. This paper introduces an initial step towards building a biot which is capable of adapting its own architecture, i.e. its own hardware, according to rewards received from the environment. More specifically, this paper shows how the hardware architecture of an electronic circuit can be evolved directly, using genetic learning techniques. The concept of evolvable hardware was proposed by one of the authors and was given the label "Darwin Machine" [de Garis 91, 92, 93]. Initially, the concept of a Darwin Machine probably sounds like a dream, but recent hardware technologies (e.g. programmable logic devices) offer excellent capabilities which make it feasible to build evolvable hardware.

Programmable logic gate arrays consist of *logic cells* and their *interconnections*. A logic cell performs some logical function using flip-flops, and combinations of AND and OR gates. Its logic function can be selected by specifying special bits in the device. The interconnections are also specified in this way. Thus, application specific gate arrays are easily produced in a field-programmable manner, i.e. the user, and not the manufacturer, determines the architecture and hence the behavior of the device. This flexibility has made programmable logic gate arrays very popular.

The programmable bits of these devices are referred to as *architecture bits* in this paper. Once they are specified, the Boolean functions of the logic cells, their interconnections, and thus the total logical behavior of the gate array is determined. Therefore, in order to evolve a gate array chip which adapts to a given environment, we only have to find the desirable architecture bits. The hardware is given environmental inputs which determine its output according to the current architecture bits. By receiving rewards from the environment, the architecture bits can be evolved.

This paper reports on the first experiment conducted toward the longer term aim of building Darwin Machines, using a programmable logic chip, GAL16Z8, manufactured by Lattice Corporation (Hillsboro, Oregon). Initially we deal only with simpler combinatorial (rather than sequential) circuits. A software simulation of the evolution of the GAL16Z8 chip is presented, which solves the 6-multiplexor problem.

2 The "Darwin Machine" Concept

This section provides a brief introduction to the concept of a Darwin Machine (or DM). As mentioned earlier, the work presented in this paper introduces the idea of evolvable hardware, and takes a first step towards achieving the longer term goal of building Darwin Machines. *A Darwin Machine is a device which evolves its own architecture directly in hardware.*

Darwin Machines may be useful because,

1. The execution speed of the evolved system will be extremely fast (at least three orders of magnitude faster than a software implementation) because the result of adaptation is the hardware structure itself.
2. Fault tolerant design is realized because evolvable hardware can change its own structure in the case of hardware error or environmental change.

The Darwin Machine concept is a very broad one, which may be applicable to the evolution of virtually any form of hardware. It is also a very powerful concept, because evolved systems can be very complex, yet be functional, if they are evolved successfully. It may be possible in the future to evolve circuits more complex than are humanly designable. If so, Darwin Machines may eventually form the basis of a new electronics and computer industry. They may also provide the means to build biots with a greater behavioral repertoire than is possible today. DMs may end up playing a vital role in the field of biotics (i.e. artificial creature construction).

Since the Darwin Machine concept is very broad, it is likely that many different options will emerge on how DMs can be implemented. For example, two of the authors of this paper, Higuchi and de Garis, have diverse conceptions on possible DM architectures and application areas.

Higuchi's conception, for example, involves the application of reinforcement learning ideas to teach a biot's evolving hardware circuits to behave appropriately in an unknown environment. Signals coming from the environment would serve as reinforcers to reward or punish the biot's actions. These reinforcers would act directly upon the hardware by changing its architecture. This would enable the biot to respond in real time to its environmental signals, because its response would be implemented directly in hardware, not software.

de Garis's conception of a Darwin Machine is to implement a Genetic Algorithm [Goldberg 89] directly in hardware, and to use the DM to build/evolve useful electronic circuits, for example, fully connected neural networks, or (on a longer term basis) artificial nervous systems for biots. de Garis has helped establish a new "Brain Builder Group", which intends (starting 1993 in another lab) to use Darwin Machines to evolve neural circuit modules (and their connections) for biots with 10, 100, 1000,... behaviors.

3 Genetic Learning for Evolvable Hardware

Wilson's *Boole* is a classifier system which learns difficult multiplexor problems [Wilson 87]. He solved a 6-multiplexor problem with Boole.

Figure 1 shows a 6-multiplexor. One of 4 binary input channels is selected by the 2 address bits, to become the output channel. For example, if the input 4-vector (I1,I2,I3,I4) is (0,0,1,0), and the address bits (A1,A2) are (1,0), then I3(=1) is connected to the output OUT.

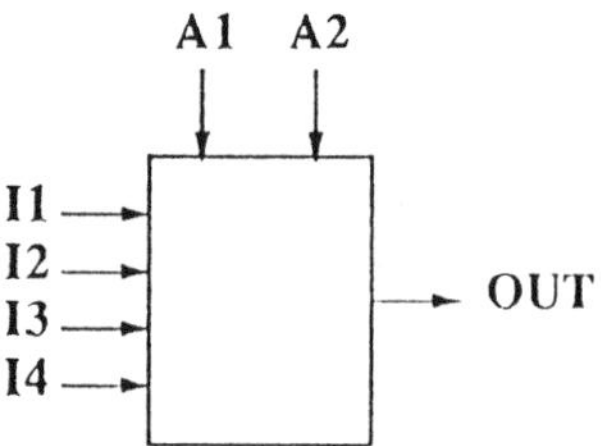

Figure 1: A 6-multiplexor

In *Boole*, rules necessary to construct the multiplexor are learned in the form of IF-THEN rules. The experiment in this paper also deals with multiplexor functions. However, in contrast with *Boole*, the knowledge acquired through adaptation is not IF-THEN rules, but a hardware design (as specified by its architecture bits). This section describes the basic hardware of the GAL16Z8 chip, and the genetic learning scheme employed for its evolution.

3.1 The Architecture of the GAL16Z8 Chip

The GAL16Z8 chip is a programmable logic device manufactured by Lattice Corporation. Earlier programmable logic chips were bipolar devices called PLAs (Programmable Logic Arrays), and were widely used in hardware systems. PLAs, however, can only be programmed once, because the logical functions are "burned in", and unchangable.

To address this weakness of the bipolar approach, PLAs based on UVCMOS (ultra violet CMOS) technology were introduced to enable reprogramming. However, ultra violet reprogramming took 20 minutes. This made it an expensive step in the manufacturing process. This delay would also make hardware evolution inefficient.

Although the GAL16Z8 chip is also a CMOS device, its erase (or reprogramming) time is only 50 milliseconds (24,000 times faster than a UVCMOS PLA). In addition to this, the GAL16Z8 chip can be reprogrammed a large number of times. Its logical functions are also more versatile than earlier programmable chips. Therefore, the GAL16Z8 chip is a promising tool to test the concept of evolvable hardware.

Figure 2 shows a logic diagram of the GAL16Z8 chip. It consists of a fuse array and 8 logic cells (called OLMCs, i.e. Output Logic Macro Cells). Pins 1 to 9 usually serve as inputs to the device, and pins 12 to 19 are the outputs of the 8 logic cells.

The fuse array is used to determine the interconnections between device inputs and logic cells, as well as to specify the logic cells' AND-term inputs. If a link on a particular row of a fuse array is set to "connected" (shown as a dot in Figure 2), then the corresponding (vertical) input signal is connected to the row. The input signal then becomes one of the AND-term members.

For example, Figure 2 shows the product-term input pattern to the logic cell, OLMC 19. The input signals

P2 and P3 are connected to the first row because the corresponding fuse links are "connected". These inputs generate the product-term, P2*P3 (i.e. P2 AND P3). Similarly, the input signals P4 and P5 are connected to the 8th row and generate the product-term, P4*P5. These product terms are then gated with "product term disable" bits, one bit for each row. If the bit is off, the product term is allowed to enter into the logic cell. In Figure 2, the two "product term disable" bits are off for the logic cell OLMC 19. Therefore, P2*P3 and P4*P5 are entered into the OLMC19 cell.

The logic cell has the structure shown in Figure 3. It contains a flip-flop, an OR gate, various multiplexors, etc. The function of a logic cell is selected from 5 possible operational modes, such as "registered device" or "combinatorial output device", by specifying 3 special bits (SYN, AC1, AC0). The polarity of the output is also selected by an XOR bit. By setting these bits at SYN=1, AC0=0, AC1=0 and XOR=1, the function of OLMC 19 in Figure 2 is determined to be "P2*P3 + P4*P5". The internal structure is selected as shown in Figure 4.

Thus, an arbitrary Boolean function can be specified by determining both the links of the fuse array pattern, and the logic cell function.

3.2 Genetic Learning Scheme

We now describe how we simulated the evolution of the GAL16Z8 chip. Firstly, the representation of the bit string chromosome used to configure the chip is described. This is followed by a description of the genetic learning algorithm that was used to perform the simulation.

3.2.1 Chromosome Representation

We simulated the hardware evolution of the solution to the 6-multiplexor problem. The solution takes the form of a Boolean function, and is evolved with one logic cell

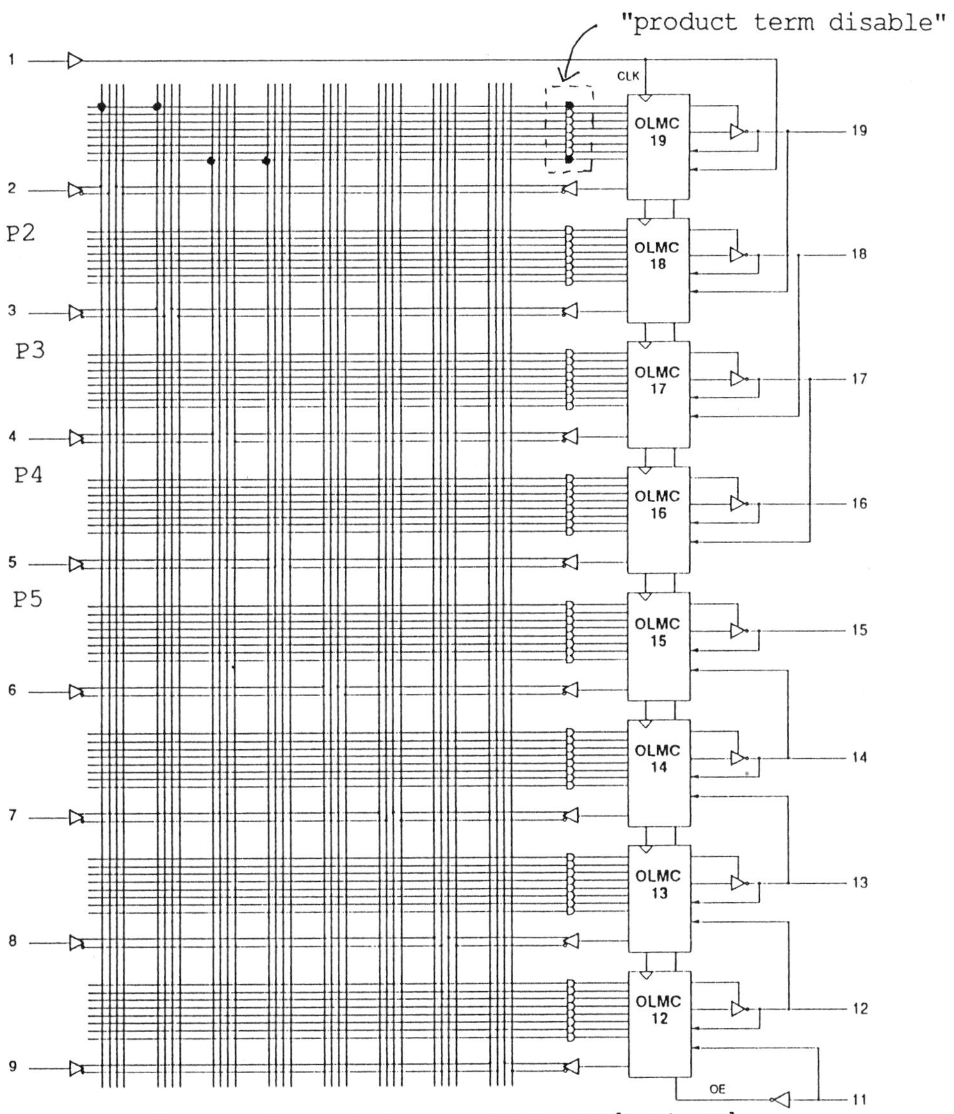

Figure 2: The block diagram of GAL16Z8 [Lattice 90]

of the GAL16Z8 chip. This boolean function only requires 6 input bits. Therefore, we do not need to use all the chip's logic cells. Only one logic cell and its corresponding fuse array were evolved, by representing them in one chromosome.

The resulting chromosome had 108 bits. Its representation is explained as follows. The fuse array uses 8 rows and 12 columns (as shown in Figure 2). The twelve columns correspond to the 6 input signals, because each input signal has both a positive and negative input. There are 8 rows as inputs to a logic macro cell. Therefore, the fuse array representation needs 96 bits (12*8).

In addition to this, 12 bits are needed for the logic cell definition, i.e. 8 bits are needed to specify the product term disables, and 4 bits are needed to specify the selection of the logic cell behavioral mode. Thus, the length of the chromosome is 108 bits.

Given this chromosome and a 6-bit input pattern, we can configure the GAL16Z8 chip's structure and then produce the output corresponding to the 6-bit input. The output is then examined to see whether the software configured chip gives the desired output or not.

3.2.2 Learning Algorithm

The genetic learning scheme employed in our experiments is shown in Figure 5. In practice, we simulated the evolution of the GAL chip using software. Instead of rewriting the GAL chip repeatedly, it is written only once, i.e. after the most desirable chromosome is found. We employed this policy at this stage because the current version of GAL chips do not guarantee an indefinite number of reprogrammings. This is one of the weaknesses of current PLGAs (Programmable Logic Gate Arrays) as a vehicle for evolvable hardware.

The GAL simulator in Figure 5 accepts inputs to the GAL, one chromosome at a time, and generates the output according to the structure specified by the chromosome. (The execution time of the GAL simulater is 100 micro seconds. If a GAL chip is actually used, the execution time is 10 nano seconds, i.e. 10,000 times faster) Next, the GAL output enters the fitness evaluation module for the 6-multiplexor problem. Once the fitness values have been determined, the conventional genetic algorithm operators (selection, mutation, crossover) are applied to the chromosome population as shown below.

Step 1 Calculate the fitness of each chromosome. The 6-multiplexor problem uses all 64 possible input patterns as the training set. To measure the fitness of a chromosome, all 64 6-bit input vectors are presented to the 6-multiplexor that it codes for. If the actual output bit from the circuit is the same as the desired bit, then the fitness score is incremented. The maximum raw fitness score is 64. The final fitness was defined to be the percentage of the 64 actual output bits which were correct.

Step 2 Select two chromosomes with a probability in proportion to their fitness values

Step 3 GA operations. Crossover and mutate the chromosomes selected in Step 2. Uniform crossover is executed.

Step 4 Replacement. Replace the entire old population with the new chromosome selected in Step 3.

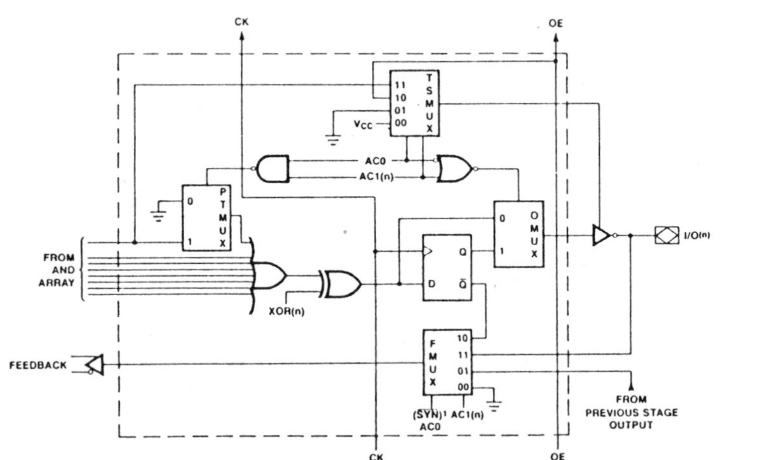

Figure 3: The structure of a logic macro cell [Lattice 90]

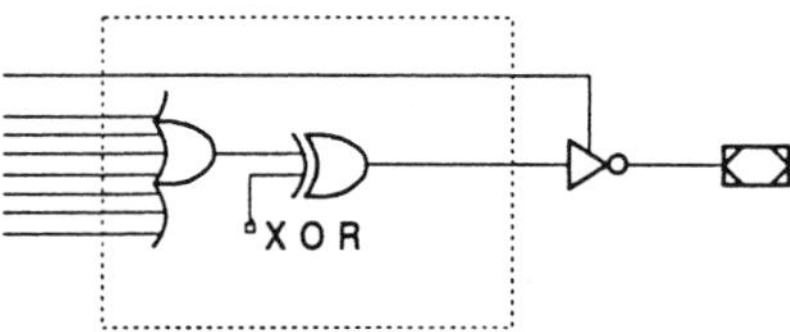

The operational mode: "dedicated combinatorial output with programmable polarity"

Figure 4: The selected structure of OLMC19 [Lattice 90]

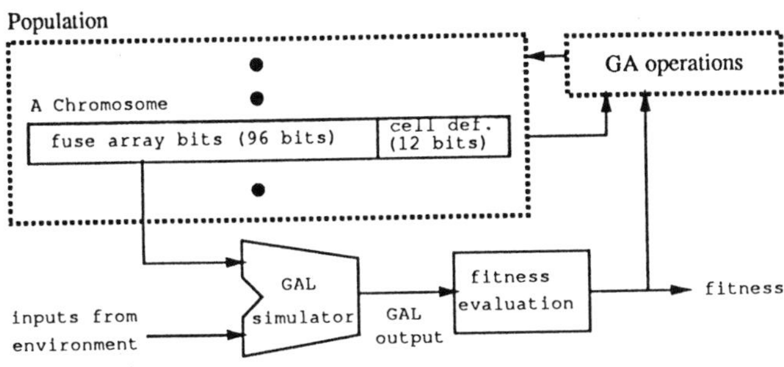

Figure 5: The genetic learning scheme for the experiment

4 Experimental Results

The experiment was conducted with a population of 100 chromosomes. The probability of uniform crossover was 20%. The probability of mutation was 0.1% per bit.

Figure 6 shows an example of the evolution, where the best and the average fitness of 100 chromosomes are shown. It attains the fitness of 100 % in about 2,000 learning cycles.

Figure 7 shows the on-line and off-line performance. Each is the average of 10 runs with different seeds for random number generation.

Figure 8(a) is a chromosome obtained as the result of the evolution. As mentioned earlier, a chromosome consists of fuse array bits, product term disable bits, and logic cell behavioral mode bits. Figure 8(b) explains what the chromosome of Figure 8(a) means. The first eight rows of the chromosome in Figure 8(a) represent the fuse pattern which corresponds to Figure 8(b). The bottom row of Figure 8(a) represents the product term disable bits and logic cell behavioral mode bits (i.e. XOR, AC0, AC1 and SYN).

With these specifications contained in the chromosome, the functions of each row of a logic macro cell is defined as shown in Figure 8(c). The first value of each row (i.e. 0 or 1) is that of the product term disable bits. If 0, the function is invalidated. The seventh row of Figure 8(c) is $1*(p2*\tilde{p}3*\tilde{p}4*p5*\tilde{p}5*p7)$ is also invalidated because the p5 inputs with both polarities are contradictory. Thus, the total function of a 6-multiplexor is represented as,

$out=\tilde{}((p2*p3*\tilde{p}4)+(p2*\tilde{p}3*\tilde{p}5)+(\tilde{p}2*p3*\tilde{p}6)+(\tilde{p}2*\tilde{p}3*\tilde{p}7))$

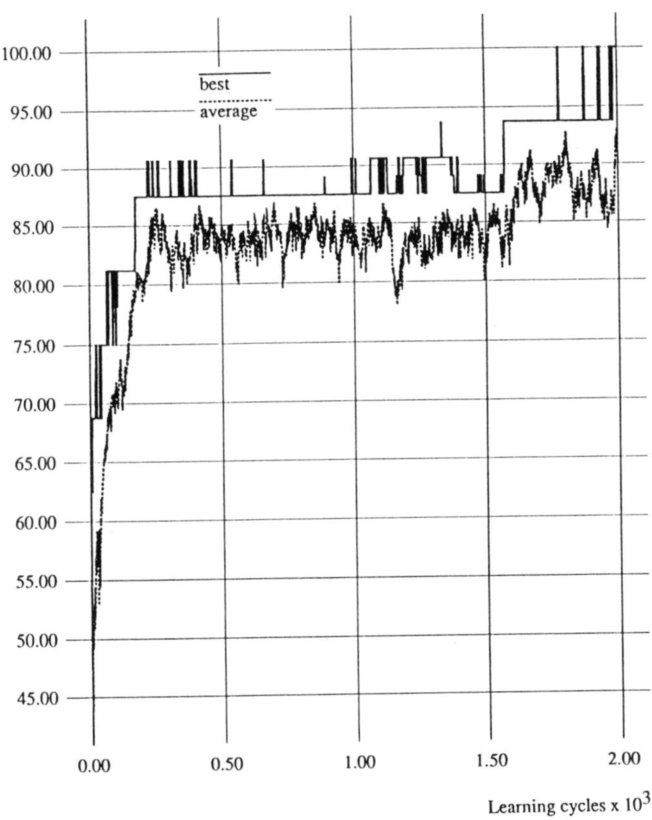

Figure 6: Learning of the 6-multiplexor problem

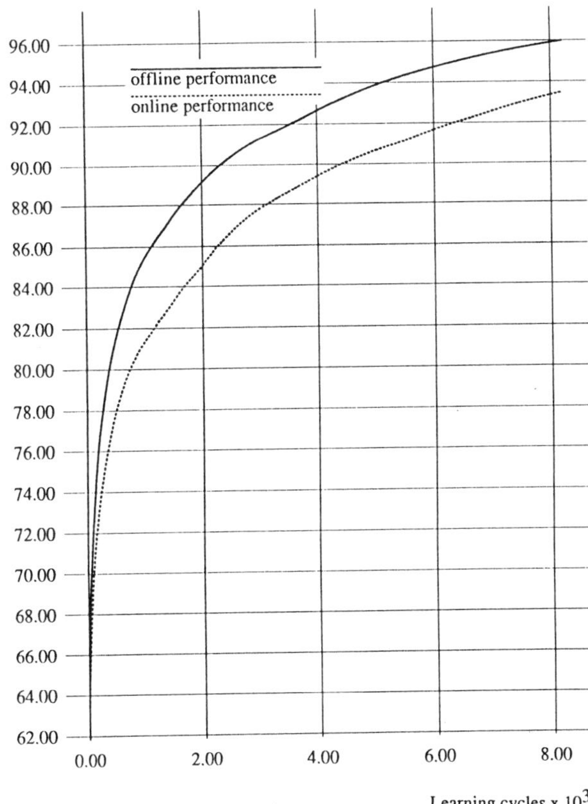

Figure 7: The on-line and off-line performance

The evolved circuit is shown in Figure 9.

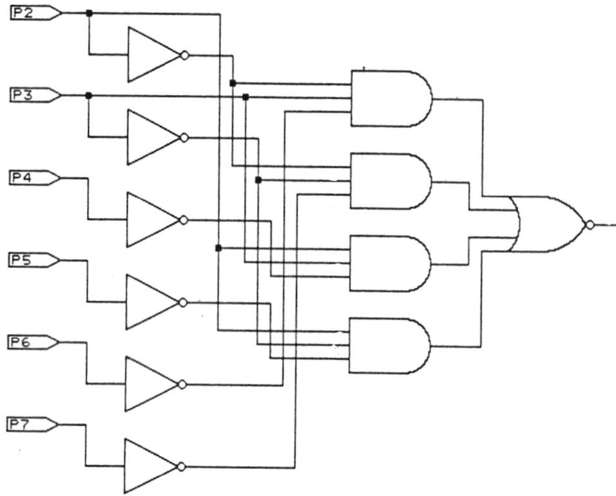

Figure 9: The circuit obtained by evolution

5 Discussion

The experiment in the previous section showed very promising results. In order to evolve more "intelligent"(or complex) hardware, however, two problems should be addressed.

The first is to deal with larger programmable logic devices. In the above experiment, we used only one of the eight logic cells contained in the GAL16Z8 chip. We need to evolve an entire GAL and much larger programmable devices called FPGAs (Field Programmable Gate Arrays), which can contain up to 20,000 gates. Even though FPGAs contain many more gates than a GAL chip, their hardware can still be configured by "programming". Therefore, it is expected that the genetic learning algorithms proposed in this paper can be extended to FPGAs.

It is necessary to process a large number of architecture bits, in order to evolve large devices. FPGAs require from 2000 to 30000 architecture bits to configure their circuits, while this experiment dealt with only 108 architecture bits. The current representation scheme of 108 bits is rather naive, and it is not confirmed yet that this representation scheme works well for a larger number of architecture bits. To evolve an entire GAL device, for example, roughly 2000 architecture bits are required. An experiment to do just this is currently under way. It may be necessary to devise a more precise representation for the architecture bits.

The second problem to be addressed is to evolve sequential logic circuits. The multiplexor function implemented on the GAL16Z8 chip is a combinatorial circuit, where no internal states exist, i.e. the output is a function of the input only. In order to evolve more intelligent hardware, sequential circuits become essential. Because GAL chips contain flip-flops and clock inputs to strobe states, sequential circuits can be implemented on GAL devices.

If the sequential circuit evolution succeeds, it may serve as a new learning paradigm for problems which have internal states. Those problems are very difficult for neural networks to handle, because neural networks can not express "states" effectively.

What the authors would like to do with sequential circuit evolution is the learning of finite state machines which could be used as the control structure for robots such as subsumption architecture [Brooks 89]. Adaptation with evolvable hardware may provide real-time control for animats.

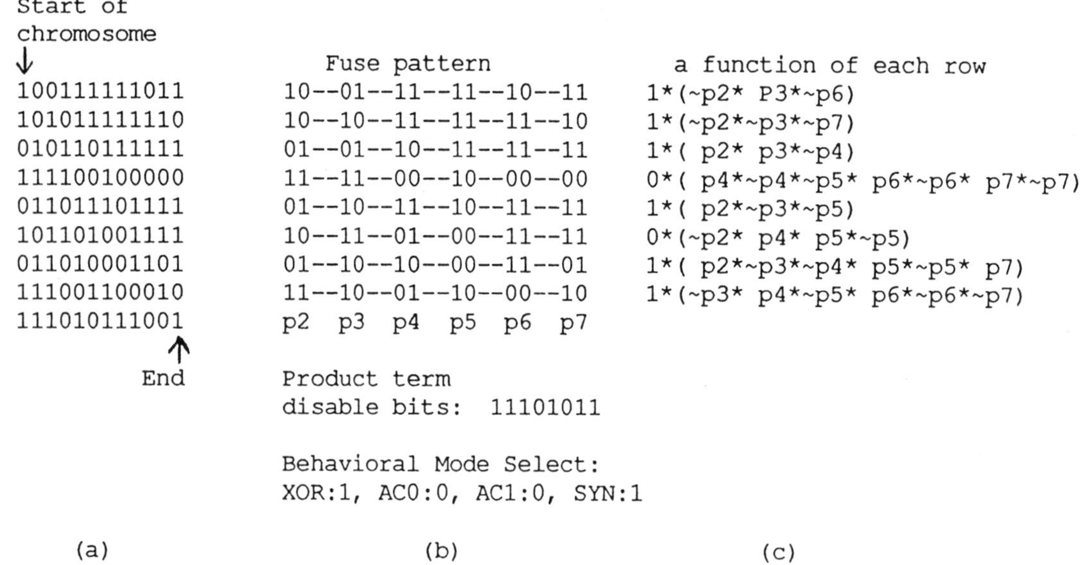

Figure 8: A chromosome bit pattern for the 6-multiplexor

6 Conclusions and Future Research

This paper has shown that programmable logic devices can be evolved using genetic learning. This paper has described a first step towards building Darwin Machines. Using only inputs to the device from the environment, and rewards resulting from the device's output, the architecture of the device can be reconfigured repeatedly to evolve desirable behaviours. This approach is the opposite of traditional hardware design, where the logical behaviours of the system are given first, and then the corresponding circuit design follows.

To give some ideas on possible DM architectures in the near future, two brief descriptions are given here.

Higuchi intends to extend the ideas of this paper by evolving more complex hardware circuits than the rather simple combinatorial circuits discussed in this paper. One such development Higuchi has just started, is to use GAL chips and Transputers to build a simple Darwin Machine which evolves such circuits as finite state machines, where the evolving chip is a GAL, and Transputers are used to measure the fitness of the evolving GAL chip, all done directly in hardware. The demonstration that evolvable hardware can be used to generate a finite-state machine in unknown environments, will have a significant impact on control design for animats.

For example, computer control of simple actions in animats may be implemented in Darwin Machine hardware, not by software. Before microprocessors became widely available, such control was implemented with sequential circuits in the form of finite state machines. With evolvable hardware, such finite state machines may be learned adaptively and replace the control programs. Current effort on learning finite state machines using evolvable hardware is reported in [Higuchi 92].

On the other hand, de Garis is thinking of using VLSI techniques to create new chips which are specifically designed with evolvable hardware concepts in mind. GAL chips for example, were not designed to be evolved, because the designers of GAL chips had no inkling of the concept of evolvable hardware. Figure 10 shows a tentative high level VLSI "evolvable chip" design, and how such chips could be linked in a two dimensional grid to implement a distributed (i.e. parallel) version of a Genetic Algorithm [e.g. Muhlenbein 91]. The electronic circuits being evolved would be fully connected neural network modules (GenNets) [de Garis 1993].

Building a Darwin Machine will require a lot of hard thinking and probably a lot of trial and error. For example, it is possible that the current candidate of FPGAs as the building block for Darwin Machines, may prove to be unsuitable. The manufacturers of FPGAs did not have the notion of evolvable hardware in their heads when their designers dreamed up the chips. Hopefully, a new generation of VLSI chip designers will be inspired by the notion of evolvable hardware and Darwin Machines, by creating new chips which are a lot more "genetically programmable".

Acknowledgement Authors thank Dr. Toshitugu Yuba for providing us opportunities to pursue this research.

References

[Brooks 89] Brooks, R. "A robot that works: Emergent behavior from a carefully evolved network" Neural Computation, 1989.

[de Garis 91] Hugo de Garis "Genetic Programming", Chapter 8 in book "Neural and intelligent system integration,"(ed. Branco Soucek) Wiley, 1991.

[de Garis 92] Hugo de Garis "Genetic Programming: Evolutionary Approach to Multistrategy Learning",

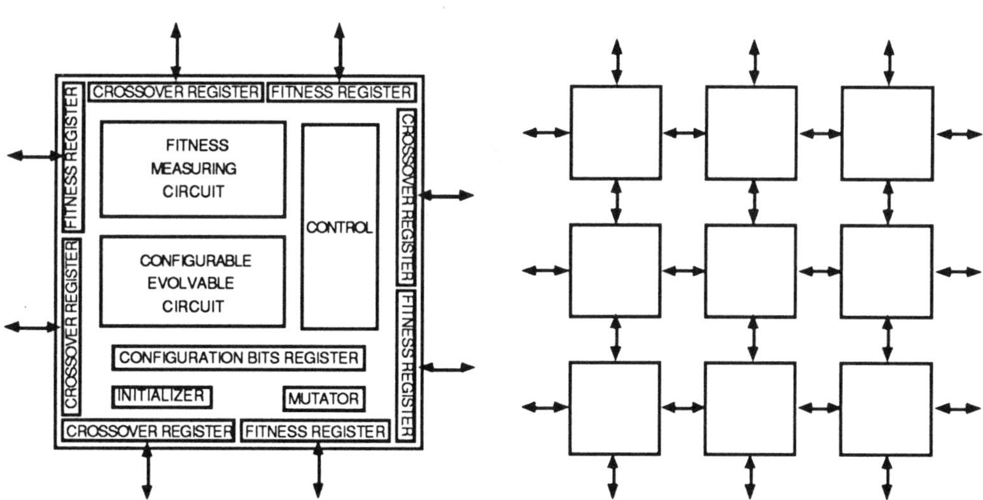

Figure 10: A distributed Darwin Machine architecture

Chapter 21 in book "Machine Learning: A Multistrategy Approach Vol.4"(ed. R.S. Michalski) Morgan Kauffman, 1992.

[de Garis 93] Hugo de Garis "Genetic Programming: GenNets, Artifificial Nervous System, Artificial Embryon", Wiley manuscript.

[Goldberg 89] Goldberg, D. Genetic Algorithms in Search, Optimization, and Machine Learning, Addison Wesley, 1989.

[Higuchi 92] Higuchi, T. et al. Genetic Based Hardware Evolution, Electrotechnical Lab. Tech. Report, Nov. 1992.

[Lattice 90] Lattice Semiconductor Corporation "GAL Data Book", 1990.

[Muhlenbein 91] Muhlenbein, H. "Evolution in time and space – the parallel genetic algorithm", in "Foundations of Genetic Algorithms", Morgan Kaufmann, 1991.

[Wilson 87] Wison,S. "Classifier Systemss and the animat problem" Machine Learning 2, 199-228, 1987.

Evolving Artificial Insect Brains for Artificial Compound Eye Robotics

Luis R. Lopez[a] and Robert E. Smith[b]

[a]Computer Resources Hardware Division, U.S. Army Space and Strategic Defense Command, Huntsville AL, 35807-3801, ubu@tecnet1.jcte.jcs.mil

[b]Engineering Mechanics Department, University of Alabama, Tuscaloosa AL, 35487, rob@comec4.mh.ua.edu

Abstract

This paper reports on a machine for experimenting with genetic learning of adaptive robotic control rules using a recently developed electro-optic compound-eye sensor. We discuss a newly constructed compound-eye robotic learning system along with results from earlier experiments using an all-analog non-learning compound eye. Compound-eye robotics offers a new, yet unexplored, possibility for robotic vision. We have observed that very simple rules can lead to surprisingly complex behavior when presented with highly selective information from compound-eye sensors. In a previous experiment, a single rule using compound-eye hardware surpassed human opponents in a game of pendulum ping-pong. These developments in theory and practice of artificial compound-eye systems have resulted in an eye that "sees" only designed-for information (i.e., it sees only motion). Our analog compound-eye hardware mimics the initial optical and neural processing layers found in compound-eyes of insects. By design, the eye provides only information of interest to the learning system allowing emergent complex behavior using very simple rules.

1.0 Introduction

This paper develops an application of genetic learning to evolve artificial "brains" for recently developed robotic compound eyes [1]. We report on the machine learning system Lopez has constructed and overview the genetic learning methods that will be explored to develop adaptive real-time robotic problem solving behavior. Behavior of a robot that uses compound vision is expected to evolve towards the behavior of insects. (As in Cliff's hoverfly [2].) Genetic learning gives the system an ability to self-organize meaningful input patterns into acceptable behavioral actions. This is accomplished by a set of adaptive control rules. Our goal is to develop both hard-wired rules and flexible real-time modifiable rules that allow the system to learn how to solve problems during operation.

Simple rules can produce complex behavior when using highly selective sensor information. This phenomenon was observed by Lopez for an all analog 8-omatidia eye [1]. There is a trade-off between generality of robotic tasks and the apparently complex emergent behavior of a simple set of rules. Robotic devices using compound-eyes must necessarily be designed as highly task-specific. This is due to the highly selective information gathering requirements of compound sight. Much like the specialized shapes and functions of insect species, compound eyes are physically designed "in tune" with the information they gather. We can only state the importance of this concept for compound-eye sensor design. The physics and non-linear dynamics of *how* compound-eye systems are designed for detecting *task-specific* information is far beyond the scope of this paper. A basic overview on the engineering of our first all-analog compound-eye system is given by Lopez [1].

We begin by touching on the architecture and qualitative results of the early one-dimensional, motion-sensitive, compound-eye experiment. We then proceed to discuss the experimental robotic eye system we have built and report on the adaptive problem solving behavior we are after. Unfortunately, at the time of this writing only preliminary robotic hardware was in place so no learning results could be included here. Within this context, a discussion of genetic learning classifier systems follows to provide some basic details on how the learning algorithm will be implemented.

2.0 Emergent Complex Behavior from Simple Rules

One of us (Lopez) has developed a process for building artificial omatidia of given geometric optical and electrical properties. A one-dimensional 8-omatidia eye connected to a motion sensitive electric analog processing layer was built. The device was successfully demonstrated to have robust motion tracking capability [1]. We demonstrated this functionality using a lighted pendulum for a target. In a simple experiment the eye controls a paddle with a single hard-wired rule, while a human opponent controls another paddle. The human subject is used to test the dynamical behavior of the eye by playing pendulum ping-pong against it. In tests and demonstrations the eye plays the game relentlessly. It continuously adapts its rate of hitting to counter the human. Fast hits are countered by fast hits from the eye. Against human opponents, the eye typically wins. This is a dramatic example of how "adaptive" a single rule can be when it works with the proper information. It is the inherent dynamic processing of this electro-optic system that is responsible for providing the rule with *highly selective information* [1,3]. Neural and optical computations preprocess the information so that discovery of a simple rule will lead to emergent complex behavior. Inspired by the performance of the one-dimensional 8-omatidia eye we have constructed a two-dimensional 37-omatidia device for learning experiments.

3.0 A One-Dimensional Artificial Compound Eye

Here we review the non-learning 8-omatidia system and its behavior. The first stages in opto-electric transduction are accomplished by the simple circuit shown in Figure 1.

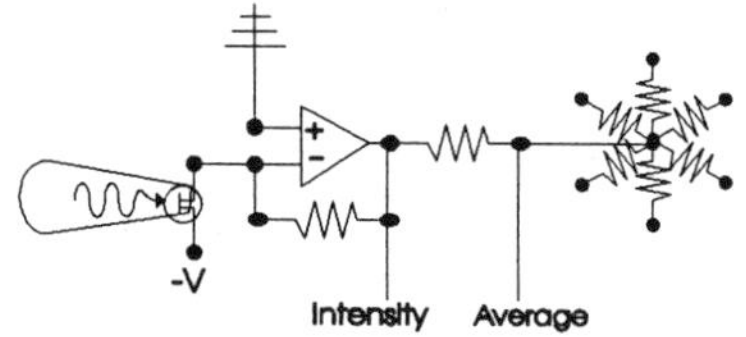

Figure 1. Artificial omatidium device showing the photo detection circuit and spatial averaging resistive network.

The omatidium optics are coupled to a photo transistor operated in a photo conductive mode. This provides a sensitive optical transducer that will increase output voltage with increased light. A good introduction to photo detector electronics is left to [4,5,6]. Also in Figure 1 is a resistive network that allows for automatic adjustment to variable background intensities as described in Carver Mead's artificial retina [4,6]. Stages for motion computation are critical to the functioning of this eye but are not shown here for brevity. Franceschini et al have developed motion tracking electronics based on the neural motion detector of a fly's eye [7]. The analog motion neurons discussed here are implemented using non-linear dynamics of a simple second-order neural motion detector [8] and off-the-shelf analog electronic parts [1].

We built an 8-element eye that proved to be very robust and capable of tracking one-dimensional motion in a variety of lighting conditions. Part of its robustness is due to the spatial averaging resistive network. The other part comes from the feed forward shunt neurons [1,8] that compute motion. These neurons are designed to "see" only moving patterns. The basic architecture of the 8-element eye is shown in Figure 2.

An Analog/Digital (A/D) converter and computer are used to view the omatidial and neural response on a computer screen. The computer connection is passive and not required for operation of the eye. We can plug the computer into the various layers of the eye to observe neural response. This is required when initially calibrating the omatidia photo transistor response and neuron weights. Figure 3 shows the omatidial outputs for a moving light *before* they reach the neural motion layer. Response is identical as the light moves in either direction.

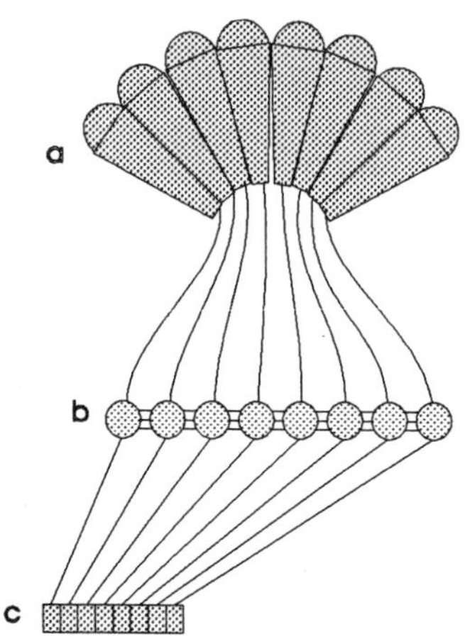

Figure 2. Architecture of the all-analog 8-omatidia eye. a) Optics; b) Motion detection neurons; c) Output right to left motion field.

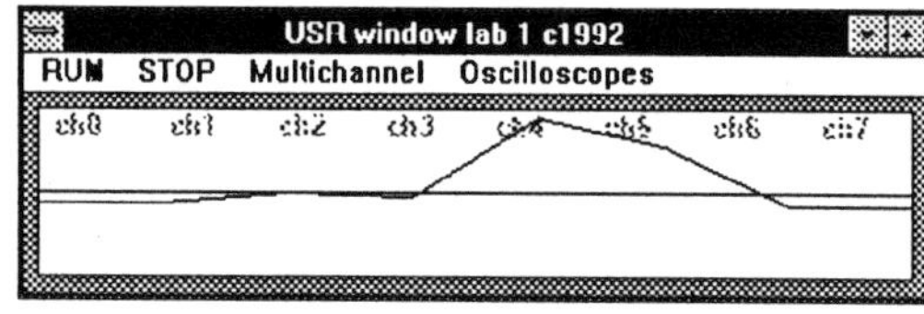

Figure 3. A/D snapshot of 8-omatidia response to a lighted pendulum.

Response of the *motion detectors* will be only right-to-left for this 8 neuron system. A/D snapshots of the motion neuron outputs for each direction are given in Figures 4 and 5.

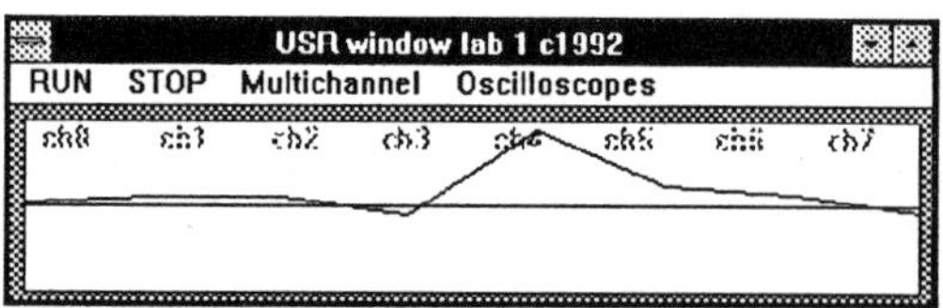

Figure 4. A/D converter snapshot of the 8-omatidia eye motion neurons while it views the lighted pendulum swinging in the preferred direction of motion -- right to left.

We see confirmation of the expected neural output in these data. Motion in the preferred direction stimulates the feed forward shunting layer many times more than motion in the non-preferred direction. The small amount of neural response in the non-preferred direction (Figure 5) can be predicted by feed forward shunting theory [1,8].

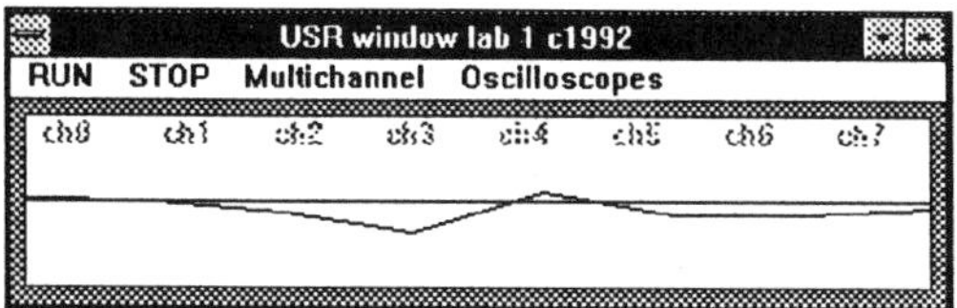

Figure 5. Snapshot of A/D converter sampled output from the 8-omatidia eye while it views a lighted pendulum swinging in the non-preferred direction of motion -- left to right.

To test and demonstrate the functionality of the 8-element eye, a single simple rule was developed so it could keep a lighted pendulum in motion[1]. The rule is implemented by connecting a wire from motion neuron number 6 to a paddle controller. (See Figure 6.) When the voltage exceeds a threshold, indicating motion in the preferred direction, the paddle controller fires. The paddle will strike only when the pendulum moves towards it, thus keeping it in motion and providing competition against gravity and/or a human. This experiment worked quite well. The eye paddled non-stop for 8 hours in one test, stopping only because the battery in the paddle ran down. A schematic of the experimental setup and rule are shown below.

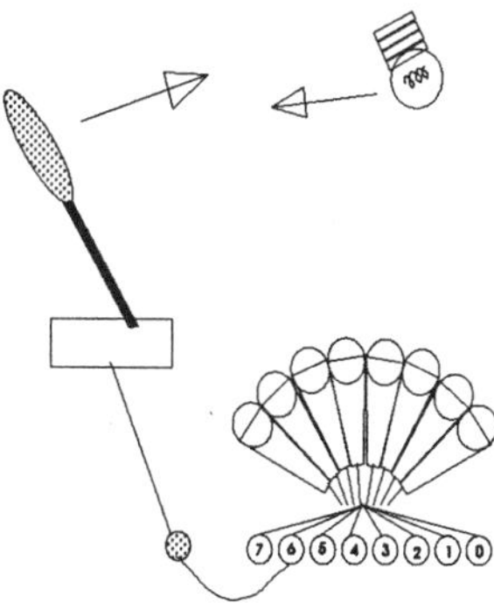

Figure 6. Experimental setup used to allow the eye to play pendulum ping-pong with a single wire rule. The numbered circles represent motion neurons.

To test the eye's dynamical response a second, human-controlled, paddle was constructed. A game of pendulum ping-pong was played by a variety of subjects. The striking frequency of the eye varied continuously with the frequency of the human. Fast hits by the human were always countered with fast hits by the eye. In other experiments a human was given the task of keeping the pendulum in motion as the eye had initially done for 8 hours. In most trials the human subject kept the pendulum in motion for only a few minutes. In all cases the eye was able to out hit the human.

This observed high-level behavior was accomplished by a *single,* remarkably simple, rule. This is possible because the information used by the rule was highly selective -- *compound eyes provide highly selective information*. Rule learning systems using compound eye vision appear very promising in light of these results. To further explore this concept we have developed a 37-omatidia analog-digital "bug-eye" robot system.

4.0 A Two-Dimensional Compound-Eye Robot for Machine Learning

A two-dimensional 37-omatidia eye and servo powered multiple degree-of-freedom robot was built for control experiments. Figure 7 shows the intensity map of a desk lamp, before and after thresholding, as detected by the 37-omatidia eye. As of this writing; the eye circuitry for simple intensity detection and servo control of the eye's gaze was complete, interface electronics and software were also finished, integration of the genetic learning software was in progress. The system is very flexible and has been designed to accommodate our proposed adaptive genetic control experiments. This system is shown in Figure 8. The lead author has also designed the necessary neural systems for motion and moving edge detection, although motion is not currently computed in the eye presented here.

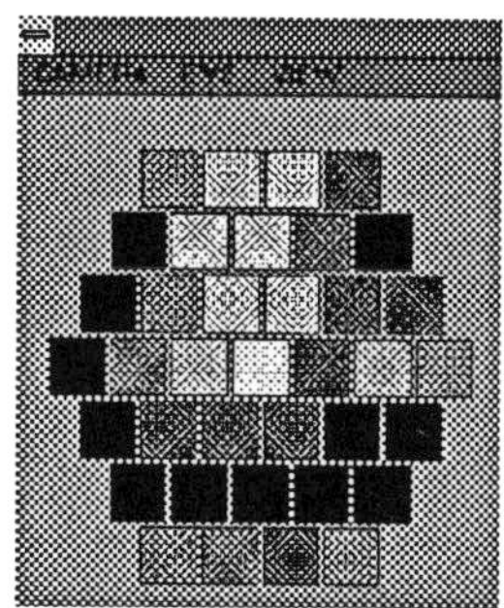

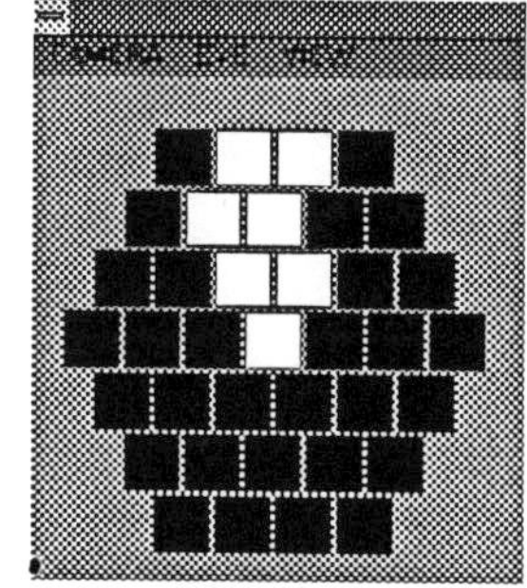

Gray Level Image *Threshold Image*

Figure 7. Typical raw, or gray level, input image of a desk lamp and the corresponding binary threshold image.

In addition to the "bug-eye" camera, we developed a multiple degree-of-freedom robot. The robot consists of modular servo-powered segments with the compound-eye mounted on the end. This allows servo action to control

[1] The target has to be lighted since the phototransitors used were of very low quality - and price. Hence, a high signal-to-noise ratio is required for reliable operation. More sensitive detectors are available -- at higher cost.

gaze. A stream of image snapshots at a rate of 10 to 50 frames per second are used for input. Likewise a stream of servo commands are output at the same rate for dynamic gaze control. Servo controls are actually digital pulse trains that can be easily coded in the genetic classifier system discussed in section 5.0. It is possible to code servo commands that specify velocity, acceleration and position of each servo joint as functions of time.

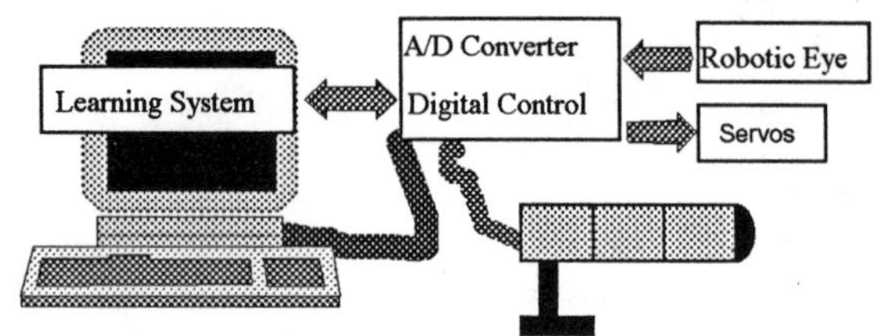

Figure 8. A system for genetic learning of servo control rules for a robotic 37-omatidia compound-eye.

Initially we have constructed a two degree-of-freedom "snake" to use in our learning experiments. Since the design is modular, it can be expanded to many degrees-of-freedom when we wish to increase problem complexity. The basic architecture of this compound-eye robot is illustrated in Figure 9.

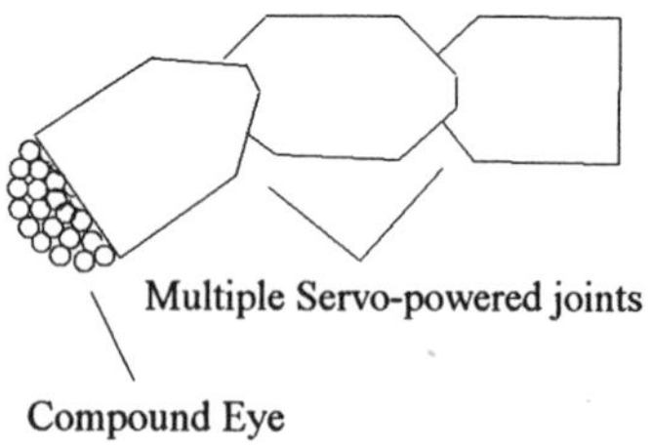

Figure 9. The compound-eye sensor on the end of a multiple degree-of-freedom robotic arm resembles a segmented "snake". Each joint is servo-powered and new joints can be added to increase problem complexity. Our current system has two segments and a 37-omatidia eye.

To affect learning, we make a few system-level assumptions. The main assumption in this learning system is that the robot knows how to compute the "goodness" of a given view. For example, the robot may be given the *goal* of "pointing" at a light. This will require the eye to center its gaze on a lighted object. A goodness of the current view may be computed by the intensity centroid's distance from the central omatidium. This type of measure of goodness will drive the genetic learning system to always adapt servo commands in order to maintain a gaze on the lighted target -- *in spite of obstructions*. Progress of a given command will be measured by a change in the goodness before and after the servo commands are sent. This will be used to affect genetic learning of control rules. Our goal is to develop genetic learning concepts for adaptive real-time robotic control using compound-eye hardware. We are working to demonstrate adaptive real-time problem solving behavior in this system and the robot will operate in a continuous learning mode.

In these experiments, genetic condition rules will be *raster* coded from the compound-eye view as in Figure 10. This will create an input pattern to be used by the learning system. Several options exist for developing codings of eye views that have various degrees of geometrical invariance and pattern matching capacity. Wilson suggests the use of adaptive cortical mappings for genetic based self-organizing pattern matching [9]. The response portion of each genetic rule will code for a servo command pulse train.

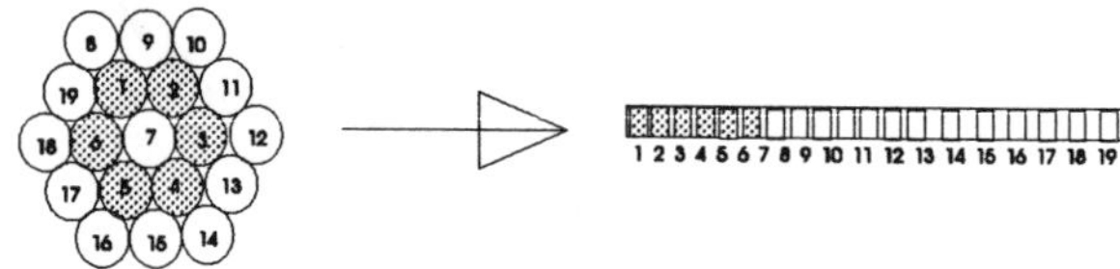

Figure 10. A raster code for compound eye inputs suitable for genetic learning.

The initial experiments with this system are aimed at measuring how long it takes to learn to accomplish a simple task, like pointing at a light, and how long it takes it to adapt to an unfamiliar obstruction placed in its path. On the basis of our experiences with genetic rule learning and compound eye systems, the results from these experiments should be interesting. Figure 11 illustrates how we expect the system to adapt to an obstruction.

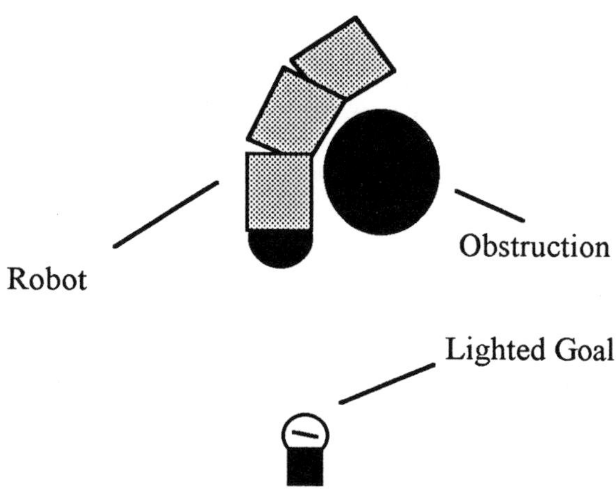

Figure 11. A possible solution to achieve a light gazing goal with an obstruction present.

The following section provides some basic details of the genetic learning system we will be using.

5.0 Basic Details of the Genetic Learning System

The configuration proposed for the genetic learning experiments is a ***learning classifier system*** (LCS). An LCS is a production system that uses a ***genetic algorithm*** (GA) as its primary rule discovery mechanism [10,11]. In the LCS, one assumes a set of *detectors* that code environmental conditions into binary messages *(environmental messages).* In the system suggested here, the *detectors* are the physical omatidia and the *environmental messages* are the thresholded, mapped, rasterized views from the eye. (See Figure 10.) Environmental messages are matched against LCS rules. The set of matching rules are selected to post internal messages. Some internal messages are used as memory, while others are matched by fixed rules that cause actions through a set of *effectors*. In the context of our "bug-eyed snake" robot the *effectors* are just the digital pulse coded servo commands.

In the most common LCS syntax, rule conditions are taken from the alphabet {0,1,#}, where a 1 or 0 matches the associated bits in messages, and the #, matches either 1 or 0 in messages. A nomenclature that includes the symbols '&' for AND and '/' for THEN is also used. Rule actions are internal messages. For instance, the rule;

0 0 # & 1 0 0 / 1 1 1

reads:

"IF (message 0 0 0 OR message 0 0 1) AND (message 1 0 0) appear on the message list, THEN (post message 1 1 1)."

This is not the only possible syntax for an LCS. An interesting alternative strategy is suggested by Valenzuela [12]. This approach uses rules that match "fuzzified" messages from detectors incorporating aspects of fuzzy logic. Actions are defuzzified at the effectors. This approach offers the ability to perform more continuous mappings from state messages to actions. Wilson [13] also suggests an LCS syntax that allows for continuous mappings. Smith [14] shows how the LCS framework can be seen as a method of searching for connectivity in a neural network. This work suggests other learning implementations that incorporate connectionist training techniques along with genetic learning.

There are a wide variety of ways to implement the specific details of the LCS. However, the most significant feature of its operation is the nature of the underlying search problem. Note that the goal of the search is a diverse, cooperative set of rules: a sort of computational ecology. The number of distinct "species" of rules need not be known beforehand. This is simply a function of the requirements of the environment.

Given its ecological basis, the GA is especially well suited to the task of finding cooperative rules. Specialized techniques exist for preserving diversity in a GA [15,16]. Smith, Forrest, and Perelson [15] suggest an immune system framework for developing co-adapted species. They consider the evolution of simple antibodies to match a limited list of simulated antigens. Analytical and experimental [17] results show that a process of sampling the list of antibodies, determining a "best" antibody from the sample, assigning a score, and iterating a simple GA yields a stable, effective set of antibodies. Moreover, the generality of the antibodies can be controlled by the sample size.

These results have direct implications for the LCS applied to insect eye robotic control. The "antigens" in this case can be thought of as inputs from the eye, and the produced "antibodies" are internal rule conditions. These internal conditions can function as memory and or drive external actions via *effectors* which would simply be pulse coded servo commands. Given this analogy a sampling and scoring procedure similar to that used in the experiments by Smith, Forrest and Perelson [15] should yield an effective set of goal directed behavioral responses to light stimulus. The GA must find an appropriate set of actions (i.e. moves) in order to successfully to interact with environmental light patterns. This approach should allow real-time adaptation to changes in the effectiveness of particular servo command sequences when obstructions are encountered. More advanced intelligent control schemes can build on these concepts. Such types of methods have been discussed by Lopez and Smith [18].

6.0 Summary

We have reported on our development of a compound eye robotic system for machine learning. Machine learning for compound eye robotics is expected to produce emergent complex behavior based on the results of [1]. We have discussed some basic assumptions and methods for genetic compound eye learning and provided basic details of the learning system we are using.

Acknowledgments

The second author wishes to acknowledge support provided by the National Science Foundation under grant ECS-9212066 and by NASA under grant NAG 9-625.

References

[1] Lopez, L. R., "Building biology: Electro-optic compound eyes," Unpublished Manuscript, July, 1992.

[2] Cliff, D. T., "The computational hoverfly; a study in computational neuroethology," Proc. First International Conference on Simulation of Adaptive Behavior (SAB'90), 1991, M.I.T. Press -- Bradford Books.

[3] Veldkamp, W., "Binary optics," Scientific American, May, 1992.

[4] Mead, C., *Analog VLSI and Neural Systems*, Addison-Wesley, 1989.

[5] Mims, F. M., "A sensor roundup," (column) Computer Craft, February, 1992.

[6] Mead, C., "The silicon retina," Scientific American, May, 1991.

[7] Franceschini, N., Pichon, J.-M., Blanes, C., "Real time visuomotor control: from flies to robots," Proc. International Conference on Advanced Robotics, Pisa, 1991.

[8] Lopez, L. R., "Feed forward shunting: A simple second-order neural motion detector," SPIE Proc. vol.1297, 1990.

[9] Wilson, S. W., "Adaptive 'cortical' pattern recognition," Proc. of An International Conference on Genetic Algorithms and Their Applications, July, 1985.

[10] Goldberg D., (1989), *Genetic Algorithms in Search, Optimization and Machine Learning*, Addison-Wesley, 1989.

[11] Holland, J.H., "Genetic algorithms," Scientific American, July, 1992.

[12] Valenzuela-Rendon, M., "The fuzzy classifier system: A classifier system for continuously varying variables," Proc. Fourth International Conference on Genetic Algorithms, Morgan Kaufman, 1991.

[13] Wilson, S. W., "Classifier System Mapping of Real Vectors," Paper Presented at the First International Workshop on Learning Classifier Systems, Houston, Texas, October, 1992.

[14] Smith, R. E., "Is a classifier system a type of neural network?," Paper presented at The First International Conference on Learning Classifier Systems, Houston, Texas, October, 1992.

[15] Smith, R.E., Forrest, S., and Perelson, A.S., "Searching for diverse, cooperative populations with genetic algorithms," TCGA Report No. 92002, University of Alabama, Tuscaloosa, 1992.

[16] Deb, K., "Genetic algorithms in multimodal function optimization," Master's Thesis, University of Alabama, Tuscaloosa, The Clearinghouse for Genetic Algorithms (TCGA) Report No 89002, 1989.

[17] Forrest, S., Javornik, B., Smith, R. E., & Perelson, A. S., "Using genetic algorithms to explore pattern recognition in the immune system," Unpublished Manuscript, 1992.

[18] Lopez, L. R., Smith, R. E., "A genetic fuzzy expert for compound eye robotic control," Proc. of First IEEE Invited Workshop on Emerging Technologies and Factory Automation, Elsevier (in press), August, 1992.

COLLECTIVE BEHAVIOR

Designing Emergent Behaviors: From Local Interactions to Collective Intelligence

Maja J Mataric
MIT Artificial Intelligence Laboratory
545 Technology Square #721
Cambridge, MA 02139
phone: (617) 253-8839
fax: (617) 253-0039
email: maja@ai.mit.edu

Abstract

This paper describes a research program for studying social interactions leading to group behavior. The goal of the research is to understand the types of simple local interactions which produce complex and purposive group behaviors. We describe a synthetic, bottom–up approach to studying group behavior, consisting of designing and testing a variety of social interactions and cultural scenarios with artificial agents situated in the physical world. We propose a set of basic interactions which can be used to structure and simplify the process of both designing and analyzing emergent group behaviors. The presented behavior repertoire was developed and tested on a herd of physical mobile robots. The paper presents the experimental results.

1 Introduction

Intelligence is a social phenomenon. Most intelligent animals live, obey the rules, and reap the benefits of a society of kin. Societies vary in size and complexity, but have a key common property: they provide and maintain a shared culture.

In order to be understood, individual intelligence must be observed and analyzed within its social and therefore cultural environment. In contrast to traditional AI, which addresses intelligence as an isolated phenomenon, this work is based on the belief that intelligent behavior is inextricably tied to its cultural context and cannot be understood in isolation. This emphasis is similar to the founding principles of ethology, the study of animal behavior. In contrast to the behaviorism branch of biology, ethology studies animals in their natural habitats. Similarly, this research attempts to understand intelligent behavior in its natural habitat: situated within a culture.

The complexity of culture results from the local interactions among individuals. This research will focus on exploring simple local social interactions which result in purposive group behaviors.

Nature abounds with systems whose complex global behaviors emerge from simple local interactions. Such behaviors can be found in many domains and at all scales, from the subatomic (Gutzwiller 1992), to the semantic (Minsky 1986), to the social (Deneubourg, Goss, Franks, Sendova-Franks, Detrain & Chretien 1990). In contrast to these bottom–up effects, most of AI relies on top–down modularity. As expressed by Simon (1969), a system is well designed if it is analyzable through *decomposition* into non–interacting modules.

However, imposing such modularity minimizes precisely the type of interactions that seem to generate complexity in nature. The global behavior of complex systems, such as groups of social agents, is determined by the local interactions of their constituent parts. These interactions merit careful study in order to understand the global behavior of the society. In natural systems, such interactions resulted in the evolution of complex and stable behaviors that do not lend themselves to traditional, top–down style of analysis. In order to reach that level of complexity synthetically, such behaviors must be generated through a similar, interaction–driven, incrementally refined process. In this paper we describe such an approach, a combination of bottom–up experiments and theory with the purpose of of designing, observing, and formalizing emergent behaviors.

In particular, our work deals with the problem of controlling a group of autonomous agents, such as a colony of robots foraging and collecting objects, or a group of agents learning from each other. Beni & Wang (1989) refer to such "swarm intelligence" as "the interplay of computation and dynamics." The goal of our work is to explore that interplay and determine how to best, and most simply, design the computational component in order to take advantage of the dynamics.

2 Related Work

Interactions between artificial agents have been studied almost entirely in simulation. Steels (1989) describes a simulation of simple robots using the principles of self organization to perform a gathering task. Brooks, Maes, Mataric & Moore (1990) report a set of simulations in a similar domain, with a fully decentralized collection of non-communicating robots. Arkin (1992) describes a schema-based approach to designing simple navigation behaviors to be extended to multiple physical agents.

The field of Artificial Life (Alife) focuses on bottom-up modeling of biological complex systems. In particular, Alife features much work on simulating ant colonies (Colorni, Dorigo & Maniezzo 1992, Beni & Hackwood 1992, Drogous, Ferber, Corbara & Fresneau 1992, Travers 1988) and many others. Deneubourg et al. (1990), Deneubourg & Goss (1989), and their other work describes experiments with real and simulated ant colonies and examined the role of simple control rules and limited communication in producing trail formation and task division. Deneubourg, Theraulax & Beckers (1992) define some key terms in swarm intelligence and discuss issues of relating local and global behavior of a distributed system. Assad & Packard (1992), Hogeweg & Hesper (1985) and other related work also report on a variety of simulations of simple organisms collectively producing complex behaviors emerging from simple interactions.

In contrast to the majority of Alife research, this work is concerned with fewer, but individually more intelligent agents, and the behavior emerging from their interactions.

3 Emergent Behavior

Emergent behavior is one of the main topics of research in the field of swarm intelligence. Such behavior is characterized by the following properties: 1) it is manifested by global states or time-extended patterns which are not explicitly programmed in, but result from local interactions among a system's components, and 2) it is considered interesting based on some observer-established metric. Emergent behavior can be observed in any sufficiently complex system, i.e. a system which contains local interactions with spatial and/or temporal consequences.

Emergent phenomena are appealing to some researchers because they appear to provide something for nothing, such as interesting collective behaviors emerging without *a priori* design or analysis of the system. In reality, any purposive behavior must be obtained either analytically or empirically. In this paper we will describe how a particular type of emergent collective behavior can be reliably obtained empirically, then analyzed and used as a tool. The next section addresses the difficulties of the alternative, analytical approach.

3.1 Analyzing Complex Behavior

Analyzing and predicting the behavior of a single situated agent is an unsolved problem in robotics and AI. Even highly constrained domains are intractable, and realistic worlds usually do not contain the structure, determinism and predictability necessary for strict formal analysis (Canny 1988, Brooks 1990*b*, Brooks 1991).

Predicting the behavior of a multi-agent system is even more complex than the single-agent case. In general, no satisfactory solution exists for predicting the behavior of a system with nontrivial interacting components. Statistical methods used for analyzing particle systems do not apply as they require minimal interactions among the components (Weisbuch 1991). While systems with large numbers of simple and simply interacting components can be analyzed this way (Wiggins 1990), no tools are available for systems consisting of comparatively few but more complex components with more complex interactions.

Instead of attempting to analyze arbitrary complex behaviors, this work focuses on providing a set of behavior primitives that can be used for synthesizing and analyzing a particular type of complex multi-agent systems. We will describe a set of local interactions which produce cohesive collective behaviors in this domain, and can be combined into variety of more complex global behaviors. The behaviors we describe emerge from local interactions, but rather than being unexpected, are repeatable and well understood.

4 Basic Principles

The following principles form the basis for the methodology used in this work.

- Agents are homogeneous in terms of hardware and software. No *a priori* leaders or followers are designated.

- Agents do not use any explicit one-to-one communication. Instead, all communication is based only on sensing the external state of nearby agents. This type of stigmergic[1] communication is ubiquitous in social insects. In particular, it is analogous to cues bees use to indirectly exchange information. In contrast to signals, such as bee dance, which

[1] Stigmergic communication uses modifications to the environment rather than direct message passing.

are behaviors with the sole purpose of transmitting information, cues are by-products of all other behaviors (Seeley 1989).

- Agents do not engage in any explicit cooperation. Instead, cooperation is implicit, and occurs through the world rather than through directed communication. Agents affect one another by means of their distribution and external state only.

- Agents have no hidden goals. This work does not deal with the agents' underlying motivations, the possibility of cheating, competition, and ulterior motives. Agents are assumed to have a set of common, similar, or at least overlapping goals.

- Agents are able to detect other agents of the same kind. The ability to categorize the perceptible objects in the world into at least two classes: "others like me" and "everything else" is a necessary condition for intelligent collective behavior. With this ability, which is innate and ubiquitous in nature, even the simplest of interactions can produce purposive collective behavior, as we will demonstrate in the following sections.

5 Basic Interactions

Interactions between individual agents need not be complex to produce complex global consequences. Here we describe some of the simplest, most basic yet useful types of interaction.

Table 1 defines the interaction primitives we have discovered so far. These interactions serve as building blocks for designing more complex behaviors. In this work, a primitive is not an atomic behavior. Rather, it is any group behavior constructed with simple local interactions that can be used as a building block. For example, *herding*, a group behavior involving collective motion guided by a subset of the agents, could be constructed with a combination of flocking and homing. The agents on the fringes and at the front of the herd would engage in the homing behavior while the others would simply flock. Similarly, *foraging*, which involves finding and collecting food in an open area, can be constructed from dispersion and homing, with the use of following and flocking in areas of high density. This example is described in more detail in a latter section.

The enumerated interactions are sufficient for producing a variety of goal-driven group behaviors involving motion, navigation and object (i.e. food) manipulation. Our continuing work attempts to formalize what basic interactions are necessary for achieving particular types of collective behaviors.

In order for the interaction primitives to be useful, they must be able to be combined without producing further higher-level interactive effects. In particular, since the behaviors cannot be strictly temporally isolated, they may overlap. The discussion section explains our approach to solving this problem.

6 Methodology

Since complex interactive behavior depends strongly on the particular parameters of the system, in order to duplicate the behavior it is necessary to either construct a very accurate model of the system or to build the system and experimentally reproduce the behavior. Our work relies on the latter approach, a bottom-up experimental methodology, which drives and refines our theories. Although there is a great tendency to design behaviors around solving a problem, or simulating a naturally system, it is necessary to go beyond finding a working solution to evaluating the effects of various possibilities.

Rather than attempt to to simulate biological systems, the goal of this work is to elucidate the phenomena of social interaction by synthesizing, observing, and analyzing similar phenomena. Consequently, our evaluation criteria are based on performing and analyzing a variety of experiments in our synthetic domain.

Our group behavior experiments are implemented and tested on a collection of twenty physically identical mobile robots. Each robot is a 12"-long four-wheeled vehicle, equipped with one piezo-electric bump sensor on each side and two on the rear of the chassis. Each robot has a two-pronged forklift for picking up, carrying, and stacking pucks. For this purpose, the forklift contains six infra-red sensors: two pointing forward and used for detecting objects, two break-beam sensors for detecting a puck within the "jaw" and "throat", and two down-pointing sensors for aligning the fork over an object (figure 1).

The robots are equipped with radio transceivers, which use two radio base stations to triangulate the robots' position, and transmit and receive one byte of data per robot per second. The radio system is used for data gathering and for simulating additional sensors. In particular, radios are used to distinguish robots from other objects in the environment, an ability which cannot be implemented with the on-board IR sensors. the flexibility of the radio system allows for testing a variety of sensing parameters.

The robot experiments are run fully autonomously with all of the processing and power on board. The robots are programmed in the Behavior Language, a parallel programming language based on the Subsumption Architecture (Brooks 1990*a*, Brooks 1987). Their control systems consist of a collection of parallel, concurrently active behaviors. Some of the behaviors implement basic

Collision Avoidance	the ability of an agent to avoid colliding with anything in the world. Two distinct strategies can be devised; one for other agents of the same kind, and another for everything else that the robot might perceive.
Following	the ability to stay behind or along side of another agent without colliding.
Dispersion	the ability of a group of agents to spread out over an area in order to establish and locally maintain some predetermined separation.
Aggregation	the ability of a group of agents to gather in order to establish and maintain some predetermined distance. This behavior is an inverse of dispersion.
Homing	the ability of one or a group of agents to reach a goal region or location.
Flocking	the ability of a group of agents to move as a coherent aggregate without prespecified leaders and followers. Flocking includes components of collision avoidance, following, dispersion and aggregation.

Table 1: The basic interaction primitives.

survival instincts while others implement more complex social interactions.

7 Experimental Results

This section describes the robot implementation of the basic interaction primitives, and illustrates their performance. The data presented in this section plots the robot position over time, based on radio data, displayed from a top view, and showing the time history with trails. The sizes of the robots and the testing area shown in the display are scaled to the exact dimensions of the physical environment. The robots are shown as black rectangles aligned in the direction of their heading, with the ID numbers in the back, and white arrows indicating the front. The corner display shows actual elapsed time, in seconds, for each snapshot of the experiment. The data is also available on video tape.

7.1 Collision Avoidance

Finding a guaranteed general-purpose collision avoidance strategy for an agent situated in a dynamic world is difficult. In a multi-agent world the problem can become intractable. Observation of biological systems indicates that insects and animals do not have precise avoidance routines. Instead, they are equipped with a simple basic avoiding behavior which is effective most of the time, and a small number of special-purpose behaviors for the few important specific cases (Wehner 1987).

Inspired by such simple strategies, and based on the robots' infra-red sensor capability to detect obstacle presence in two regions in front, we devised the following avoidance behavior:

```
Avoiding Other Agents:
If another robot is on the right
   turn left
   otherwise turn right.
```

The *Avoid-Other-Agents* behavior takes advantage of the fact that agents are homogeneous. The spatial symmetry on which this behavior is based works because all of the robots execute the same program. In case a robot fails to recognize another, it will subsequently detect it with its IRs, and treat it as a generic obstacle, using the *Avoid-Everything-Else* behavior:

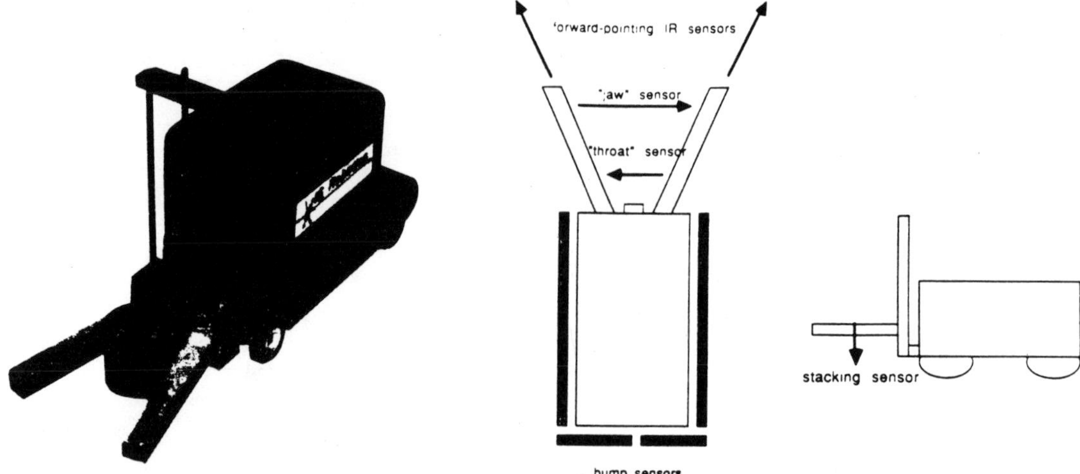

Figure 1: Each of the robots is a 12"-long four-wheeled base with a two-pronged forklift for picking up, carrying, and stacking pucks, and a radio transceiver for inter-robot communication and data collection. The robots are equipped with bump sensors on each side and the rear of the chassis, and six infra-red (IR) sensors on the forklift. Two forward-pointing IRs are located at the ends of the forks, two break-beam IRs in the jaw and throat of the fork, and one down-pointing IR for stacking pucks is in the middle of each of the forklift arms.

```
Avoiding Everything Else:
If an obstacle is on the right only
    turn left, go.
If an obstacle is on the left only
    turn right, go.
After tree consecutive identical turns
    backup and turn.
If an obstacle is on both sides
    stop and wait.
If an obstacle persists on both sides
    turn randomly and backup.
```

Although not a guaranteed strategy, this simple avoidance protocol has been effective in the majority of typical collision modes we have observed.

7.2 Following

Following can be implemented as an inverse of the collision avoidance behavior, since both are based on the same sensory inputs:

```
If an object is on the right only,
    turn right.
If an object is on the left only,
    turn left.
If an object is on the left and right,
    keep going and count time.
If an object is on the left and right,
and has been there for a while,
    stop.
```

All but the last condition-action pair above are a direct complement of those implementing the *Avoiding-Everything-Else* behavior. The last pair is needed to prevent collisions. It converts a binary IR sensor into a range sensor through the use of time. Distance from the object being followed in terms of time to collision is estimated from the time an object has continuously remained within the IR sensor range. Figure 2 illustrates *following* on 3 robots.

Following is analogous to osmotropotaxis exhibited by ants (Calenbuhr & Deneubourg 1992). While ants use the differential in pheromone intensity perceived by the left and right antennae to decide in which direction to turn, our agents turn based on the binary state of the front two IR sensors.

Under conditions of sufficient density, *collision avoidance* and *following* can produce more complex global behaviors. For instance, chemotropotaxic ants exhibit emergence of unidirectional traffic lanes. The same lane-forming effect could be demonstrated with robots executing *following* and *avoiding* behaviors. However, more complex sensors than IRs must be used in order to determine which direction to follow. If using only IRs, the robots cannot distinguish between other robots heading toward and away from them, and are thus unable to select whom to follow.

7.3 Dispersion

In order to balance goal-directed behavior against interference, the agents must be able to not only avoid but also escape congested situations. A robust *dispersion* behavior can be designed as an extension of the existing collision avoidance. While collision avoidance relies on the presence of a single agent, *dispersion* uses the local distribution (i.e. the locations of other agents within the range of the agent's sensors) in order to decide in which direction to move. The algorithm computes the local centroid to determine where most of the nearby agents are, and then moves away from that direction.

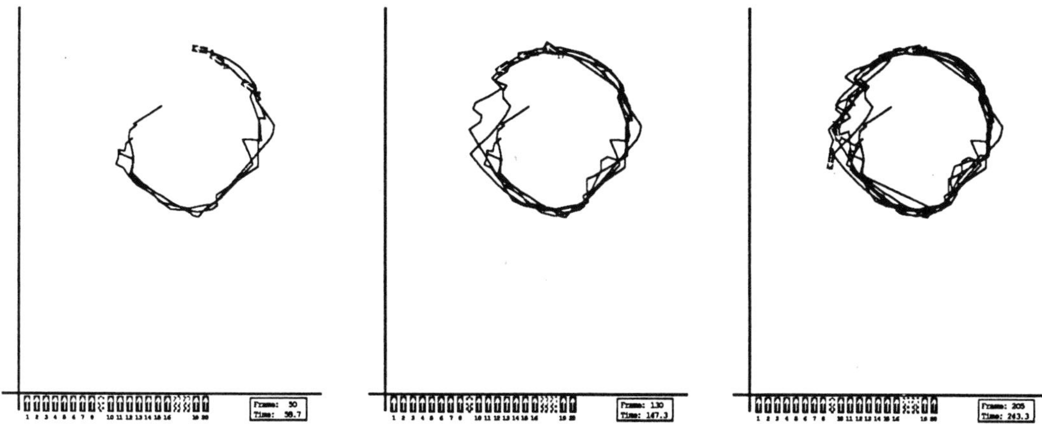

Figure 2: This figure shows continuous *following* behavior of 3 robots over a four minute period. Due to sensor inaccuracies, one of the robots diverged after two minutes. The other two stayed together for the duration of the shown run (243.3 seconds).

```
If another robot is sensed
within the ''personal space''
   turn to avoid it
   then go forward for a fixed time.
If multiple robots are sensed
   move away from the local centroid,
   then go forward for a fixed time.
Otherwise, stop.
```

In situations of high density, the system can take a long time to achieve a dispersed state since local interactions propagate far, and the motion of an individual can disturb the state of many others. Thus, *dispersion* is best viewed as an ongoing process that maintains a desired distance between agents while they are engaging in other behaviors.

7.4 Aggregation

Aggregation is the inverse of dispersion. Its goal is to bring all of the agents within a determined distance from each other.

```
If no robot is found
within a predetermined ''comfort zone''
   turn toward the local centroid,
   then go forward for a fixed time.
Otherwise, stop.
```

Dispersion and *aggregation* are similar to behaviors exhibited by army ants in the process of stabilizing the temperature of a bivouac. Individual ants aggregate and disperse by following the local temperature gradient (Franks 1989). Temperature control is a side-effect of these two interactions. Similarly, density control could be used as a means of collecting and distributing objects in the environment, as in the foraging and sorting behaviors described earlier.

7.5 Homing

The simplest *homing* strategy is a greedy local one:

```
Turn toward the direction of the goal,
   go forward.
If at home, stop.
```

Figure 3 illustrates the homing behavior of five robots. The data illustrates that the actual trajectories are far from optimal, due to mechanical and sensory limitations, in particular due to the error in the sensed position.

Individual *homing* is effective as long as the density of agents is sufficiently low. If enough agents are trying to home, they begin to interfere with each other. Interference worsens if the agents have non-zero turning radii, unequal velocities, or are subject to sensor and control errors. All of the above conditions are common in robots, suggesting the need for some form of group navigation.

7.6 Flocking

Flocking is an essential means for a group[2] of agents to move together. It can be viewed as a combination of avoidance, following, aggregation, and dispersion. Each of these constituent behaviors produces an effector command either telling the agent to stop, go, or turn. *Flocking* weights and combines these outputs.

[2] A group is defined to be a collection of size three or more.

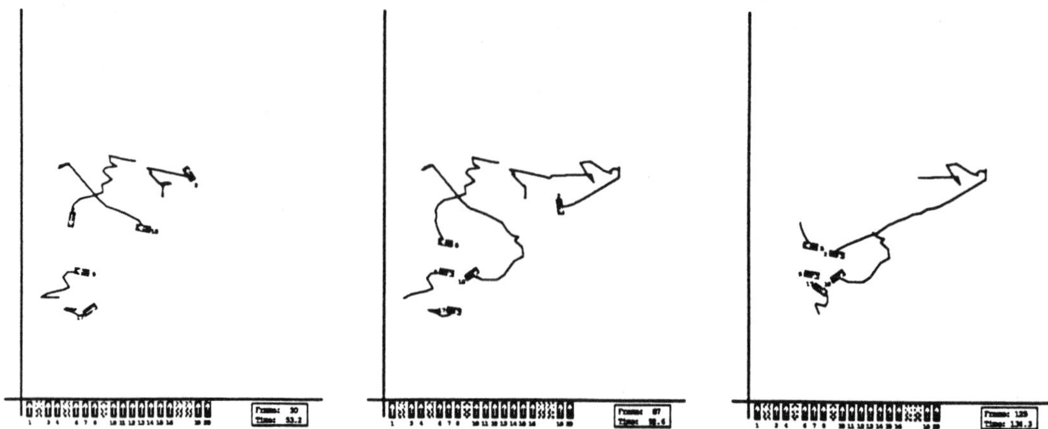

Figure 3: This figure illustrates the *homing* behavior of 5 robots. Started in an arbitrary initial configuration, four of the robots reached the home region within 100 seconds, and the fifth joined them 30 seconds later.

```
Weight the inputs from
  avoid, follow, aggregate, disperse
  then compute a turning vector.
If in the front of the flock,
  slow down.
If in the back of the flock,
  speed up.
```

The choice of weights on the behavior outputs depends on the dynamics and mechanics of the agents, and the ranges of the sensors. Due to the number of tunable parameters involved, *flocking* is the most complex basic interaction implemented in this work so far. It consisted of a combination of *avoidance* and *aggregation* only. *Following* and *dispersion* resulted from the the combination. *Avoidance* had the highest priority; the strength of *aggregation* was proportionate to the agent's distance from the computed centroid.

The flocking algorithm was inspired by an elegant simulation of bird flocking by Reynolds (1987). However, the robot implementation required many more details than the simulation, due to the more complex dynamics. Figure 4 demonstrates two runs of the flocking behavior with five robots.

8 Discussion

8.1 Hardware Implications

The types of experiments that can be implemented on robots are strongly constrained by the sensory, mechanical, and computational limitations of the hardware. In addition to the expected sensory and mechanical error, our robots suffer from extremely inaccurate steering and radio transmission. Further, the infra-red sensors have very long and varying ranges. Consequently, not only do different robots have different sensing regions, but the sensitivity between the two sensors on a single robot varies as well.

Hardware variability between robots is reflected in their group behavior. Although programmed with identical software, the robots behave differently due to their varied sensory and actuator properties. Small differences between individuals become amplified as many robots interact over extended time. As in nature, individual variability creates a demand for more robust and adaptive behavior. The described interaction primitives were designed to be general enough to span a variety of mechanical and sensory variations. As with any physical system, the particular parameter values were tuned to the specifics of the system. The resulting interaction primitives were robust and repeatable within the allowable margins of the hardware.

8.2 Combining Interactions

In order to test the sufficiency and the additive properties of the basic interactions, we are currently implementing a number of more complex behaviors including foraging and puck sorting. These compound behaviors emerge as temporal sequences of basic interactions, each triggered by the appropriate conditions in the environment. For instance, a foraging task is initiated by a dispersing behavior. The agents disperse until they find food (pucks). Once an agent is holding a puck, it starts for home. If it encounters an agent with a different external state (e.g. not carrying food), it avoids it. Conversely, whenever an agent is close to another of the same state (e.g. carrying food) it follows it. More than two following same-state agents form a flock. Depending on the other goals and the built-in terminating condition, robots either continue to indefinitely search for pucks, or eventually, after not finding any, time out and go home.

Combining interactions temporally relies on the agents' ability to perceive both the state that triggers

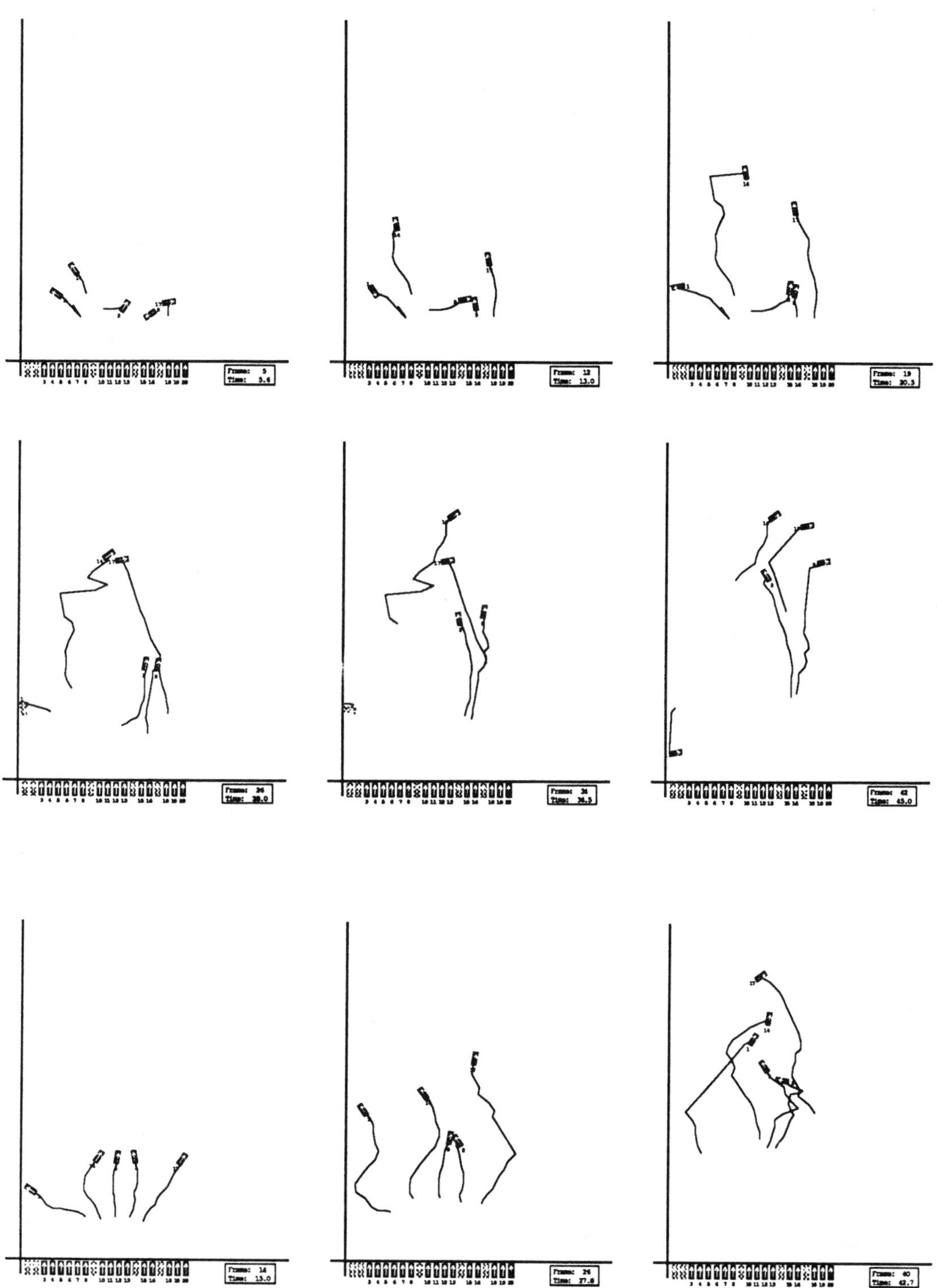

Figure 4: This figure shows the *flocking* behavior of 5 robots in two different trials. In the first experiment, shown in the top two rows, one of the robots diverges, without affecting the behavior of the others. It loses sight of the flock before it is able to recover and rejoin it. In the second experiment, shown in the bottom row, the robots maintain a coherent flock. The data illustrates that the flock moves and stays together in spite of the variance in the spacing between the robots.

a behavior change and the external state of other agents to interact appropriately. Combining interactions spatially is more challenging. While two behaviors cannot overlap in time, they can do so in space. For example, some of the agents may be following, while others may be trying to disperse. If the two groups come into contact, they must not create an unexpected higher–order behavior.

In theory, there is no full-proof method for eliminating the possibility of such emergent behaviors. In practice, however, it is possible to orthogonalize the behavior trigger states so as to make them mutually exclusive (Mataric 1992). Consequently, when two groups come into contact, one must take precedence over the other. This is implemented by ordering the behaviors into a fixed precedence hierarchy, the structure of which is determined by the group goal. We are currently experimenting with this and other combination methods for designing compound, higher-level behaviors.

8.3 Imitation

In our work described so far, the culture of the society consisted of local rules of interaction. Specifically, an agent's immediate behavior is influenced by that of the agents around it. In most cases, the agent perceives the relevant external states and actions of the surrounding agents. An extension to this behavior would allow for detecting sequences of states and actions, and storing the observed information. This ability to **imitate** can be used to propagate local interactions globally, both spatially and temporally. We call the latter ability *social learning*.

Learning through imitation is ubiquitous in nature (McFarland 1985). Animals imprint and imitate adults of their own kind instinctively, often without primary reinforcement (McFarland 1985, Gould 1982). The propensity for imitation appears to be innate. Our continuing work utilizes the described interaction primitives as the basis for social interactions learnable through imitation.

9 Summary

This paper has described a research program for studying social interactions leading to group behavior. The goal of the research is to understand the types of simple local interactions which produce complex and purposive group behaviors. We described a synthetic, bottom-up approach to studying group behavior, consisting of designing and testing a variety of social interactions and cultural scenarios with artificial agents situated in the physical world. Specifically, we have described a set of basic interactions which can be used to structure and simplify the process of both designing and analyzing emergent group behaviors.

Synthesizing and observing group behavior will offer insights into understanding social interactions in biology, as well as help derive methods for principled behavior control in robotics and AI.

Acknowledgements

Many thanks to Matt Marjanovic and Owen Wessling for making the unruly robot herd behave, and helping its collective intelligence emerge in spite of many hardware problems. Matt wrote and debugged the flocking software as well as the tools for recording and displaying robot data. Thanks to Mike Bolotski for comments on an earlier draft of this paper.

The research reported here was done at the MIT Artificial Intelligence Laboratory. Support for this research was provided in part by the Jet Propulsion Laboratory contract 959333 and in part by the Advanced Research Projects Agency under Office of Naval Research grant N00014-91-J-4038.

References

Arkin, R. C. (1992), 'Cooperation without communication: Multiagent schema based robot navigation', *Journal of Robotic Systems*.

Assad, A. & Packard, N. (1992), Emergent colonization in an artificial ecology, *in* F. Varela & P. Bourgine, eds, 'Toward A Practice of Autonomous Systems: Proceedings of the First European Conference on Artificial Life', The MIT Press, pp. 143–152.

Beni, G. & Hackwood, S. (1992), The maximum entropy principle and sensing in swarm intelligence, *in* F. Varela & P. Bourgine, eds, 'Toward A Practice of Autonomous Systems: Proceedings of the First European Conference on Artificial Life', The MIT Press, pp. 153–160.

Beni, G. & Wang, U. (1989), Swarm intelligence in cellular robotic systems, *in* 'NATO Advanced Workshop on Robots and Biological Systems', Il Ciocco, Tuscany, Italy.

Brooks, R. A. (1987), A hardware retargetable distributed layered architecture for mobile robot control, *in* 'IEEE International Conference on Robotics and Automation', Raleigh, NC, pp. 106–110.

Brooks, R. A. (1990*a*), The behavior language; user's guide, Technical Report AIM-1127, MIT Artificial Intelligence Lab.

Brooks, R. A. (1990*b*), Challenges for complete creature architectures, *in* J. A. Meyer & S. Wilson, eds, 'From Animals to Animats: International Conference on Simulation of Adaptive Behavior', The MIT Press.

Brooks, R. A. (1991), Intelligence without reason, *in* 'Proceedings, IJCAI-91'.

Brooks, R. A., Maes, P., Mataric, M. J. & Moore, G. (1990), Lunar base construction robots, *in* 'IROS 90, IEEE Int. Workshop on Intelligent Robots and Systems', Tokyo.

Calenbuhr, V. & Deneubourg, J. L. (1992), 'A model for osmotropotactic orientation (i)', *Journal of Theoretical Biology.*

Canny, J. F. (1988), *The Complexity of Robot Motion Planning*, The MIT Press, Cambridge, Massachusetts.

Colorni, A., Dorigo, M. & Maniezzo, V. (1992), Distributed optimization by ant colonies, *in* F. Varela & P. Bourgine, eds, 'Toward A Practice of Autonomous Systems: Proceedings of the First European Conference on Artificial Life', The MIT Press, pp. 134–142.

Deneubourg, J.-L. & Goss, S. (1989), Collective patterns and decision-making, *in* 'Ethology, Ecology and Evolution 1', pp. 295–311.

Deneubourg, J. L., Goss, S., Franks, N., Sendova-Franks, A., Detrain, C. & Chretien, L. (1990), The dynamics of collective sorting, *in* 'From Animals to Animats: International Conference on Simulation of Adaptive Behavior', The MIT Press, pp. 356–363.

Deneubourg, J. L., Theraulax, G. & Beckers, R. (1992), Swarm-made architectures, *in* F. Varela & P. Bourgine, eds, 'Toward A Practice of Autonomous Systems: Proceedings of the First European Conference on Artificial Life', The MIT Press, pp. 123–133.

Drogous, A., Ferber, J., Corbara, B. & Fresneau, D. (1992), A behavioral simulation model for the study of emergent social strucutres, *in* F. Varela & P. Bourgine, eds, 'Toward A Practice of Autonomous Systems: Proceedings of the First European Conference on Artificial Life', The MIT Press, pp. 161–170.

Franks, N. R. (1989), 'Army ants: A collective intelligence', *American Scientist* **77**, 139–145.

Gould, J. L. (1982), *Ethology; The Mechanisms and Evolution of Behavior*, W. W. Norton & Co., New York.

Gutzwiller, M. (1992), 'Quantum chaos', *Scientific American.*

Hogeweg, P. & Hesper, B. (1985), 'Socioinformatic processes: Mirror modelling methodology', *Journal of Theoretical Biology* **113**, 311–330.

Mataric, M. J. (1992), 'Integration of representation into goal-driven behavior-based robots', *IEEE Transactions on Robotics and Automation* **8**(3), 304–312.

McFarland, D. (1985), *Animal Behavior*, Benjamin Cummings.

Minsky, M. L. (1986), *The Society of Mind*, Simon and Schuster, New York.

Reynolds, C. W. (1987), 'Flocks, herds, and schools: A distributed behavioral model', *Computer Graphics* **21**(4), 25–34.

Seeley, T. D. (1989), 'The honey bee colony as a superorganism', *American Scientist* **77**, 546–553.

Simon, H. (1969), *The Sciences of the Artificial*, The MIT Press.

Steels, L. (1989), Cooperation between distributed agents through self-organization, *in* 'Workshop on Multi-Agent Cooperation', North Holland, Cambridge, UK.

Travers, M. (1988), Animal construction kits, *in* C. Langton, ed., 'Artificial Life', Addison-Wesley.

Wehner, R. (1987), 'Matched filters – neural models of the external world', *Journal of Computational Physiology* **A**(161), 511–531.

Weisbuch, G. (1991), Complex system dynamics, *in* 'Lecture Notes Vol. II, Santa Fe Institute Studies in the Sciences of Complexity', Addison-Wesley, New York.

Wiggins, S. (1990), *Introduction to Applied Nonlinear Dynamical Systems and Chaos*, Springer-Verlag, New York.

Adaptive Action Selection for Cooperative Agent Teams

Lynne E. Parker
MIT Artificial Intelligence Laboratory
545 Technology Square, Room 709
Cambridge, MA 02139
phone: (617) 253-8827
fax: (617) 253-0039
email: parkerl@ai.mit.edu

Abstract

This paper discusses two types of animal societies — differentiating and integrative — and their parallels to cooperative mobile robot work. The paper then presents an architecture for adaptive action selection in teams of cooperative agents of the second, integrative, type of society. In this architecture, task allocation is achieved through the selfish interests of individual agents, modified by the current and previous actions of other team members. Agents need not have *a priori* knowledge of the abilities of other agents, thus allowing previously "unfamiliar" agents to be easily brought together to customize a team responsible for a specified mission. The architecture utilizes two mechanisms for achieving adaptive cooperation — motivational behaviors and sensory filters — which are described in some detail. The results of simulation experiments are presented which show this architecture to be successful in allowing agents to adapt their actions both to a dynamic environment and to the actions of other agents.

1 Introduction

The behavioristic approach to autonomous robot control that has gained popularity in recent years has its roots in the observations of animal behavior. Animals, particularly the lower animals, are existence proofs that interesting results can be achieved without the need for a complex, human-level architecture. Many animals appear to be "hard-wired" for certain behaviors, producing very stereotypical reactions to particular stimuli. For instance, a robin begins defending its territory when it sees the red breast of another robin, or even a bunch of red feathers [Etkin, 1964]. A pregnant Three-spined Stickleback fish approaches a male Stickleback with a red belly, or even a crude model of a Stickleback, as long as it is painted red underneath [Tinbergen, 1953]. A male grayling butterfly flies up to mate rather large, dark, close, dancing objects, which could include not only female graylings, but also birds, falling leaves, and shadows [Tinbergen, 1965].

Applying animal observations to the realm of autonomous robotics, interesting and seemingly intelligent activities can be obtained by layering behaviors which react to stimuli from the world according to the robot's current internal state [Brooks, 1986]. Rather than decomposing the robot control system based on information processing functions, the behavioristic approach decomposes the control into task achieving behaviors, such as obstacle avoidance, exploration, and map building. The result has been a series of autonomous robots that can survive in a dynamic world, avoiding obstacles, exploring the environment, following walls, building maps, climbing over uneven terrain, and so forth [Brooks, 1990].

But this same approach — the observation of animal behavior — that has been used for inspiration in the development of individual robots is just as easily used to gain insight into the creation of groups of robots that cooperate toward attaining some goal. By learning how various species of animals function as groups, we can develop ideas for building a cooperating team of autonomous robots.

1.1 Two Types of Animal Societies

Since there are so many varieties of social behavior in the animal kingdom, a classification of animal societies is useful. One such classification, proposed by Tinbergen [Tinbergen, 1953], is of particular interest for current robotics research in cooperative systems, as it parallels two possible approaches to cooperating robot development. According to Tinbergen, animal societies can be grouped into two broad categories: those that differentiate, and those that integrate.

Societies that differentiate are realized in a dramatic way in the social insect colonies [Wilson, 1971]. These colonies arise due to an innate differentiation of blood relatives that creates a strict division of work and a system of social interactions among the members. Members are formed within the group according to the needs of the society. In this case, the individual exists for the good of the society, and is totally dependent upon the society for its existence. As a group, accomplishments are made that are impossible to achieve except as a whole.

On the other hand, societies that integrate depend upon the attraction of individual, independent animals to each other. Such groups do not consist of blood relatives that "stay together", but instead consist of individuals of the same species that "come together" by integrating ways of behavior [Portmann, 1961]. These individuals are driven by a selfish motivation which leads them to seek group life because it is in their own best interests. Interesting examples of this type of society are wolves, or the breeding colonies of many species of birds, in which hundreds or even thousands of birds congregate to find nesting partners. Such birds do not come together due to any blood relationship; instead, the individuals forming this type of society thrive on the support provided by the group. Rather than the individual existing for the good of the society, we find that the society exists for the good of the individual.

1.2 Parallels in Cooperative Robotics

In analyzing the research underway in cooperative autonomous robots, a parallel can be drawn with the classifications of animal societies discussed above. A large body of work in robotics [Deneubourg *et al.*, 1990, Steels, 1990, Wang and Beni, 1990, for example] involves the study of emergent cooperation in colonies of robots — an approach comparable to differentiating animal societies. This research emphasizes the use of large numbers of identical robots that individually have very little capability, but when combined with others can generate seemingly intelligent, cooperative behavior. Cooperation is achieved as a side-effect of individual behaviors.

A second approach parallels the integrative societies in the animal kingdom. Not yet studied extensively, this research aims to achieve higher-level, "intentional" cooperation amongst robots. Rather than beginning with robots having very low-level behaviors, individual robots that have a higher degree of "intelligence" and capabilities are combined to achieve purposeful cooperation. The goal is to use robots that can accomplish meaningful tasks individually, and yet can be combined with other robots with additional skills to complement one another in solving tasks that no single robot can perform alone. To be purely analogous to the integrative animal societies, robots in this type of cooperation would have individual, selfish, motivations which lead them to seek cooperation [McFarland, 1991]. Such cooperation would be sought because it is in the best interests of each robot to do so to achieve its mission. Of course, the possession of a selfish motivation to cooperate does not necessarily imply consciousness on the part of the robot. It is doubtful that we would attribute consciousness to all the integrative societies in the animal kingdom; thus, some mechanism must exist for achieving this cooperation without the need for higher-level cognition.

The type of approach one should use for the cooperative robot solution is dependent upon the applications envisioned for the robot team. The differentiating cooperation approach is useful for tasks requiring numerous repetitions of the same activity over a relatively large area (relative to the robot size), such as waxing a floor, cleaning barnacles off of ships, collecting rock samples on a distant planet, and so forth. Such applications would require the availability of an appropriate number of robots to effectively cover the work area while continuing to maintain the critical distance separation.

On the other hand, the intentional cooperation approach would be required in applications requiring several distinct tasks to be performed, perhaps in synchrony with one another. Throwing more robots at such problems would be useless, since the individual tasks to be performed cannot be broken into smaller, independent subtasks. Examples of this type of application include automated manufacturing, industrial/household maintenance, search and rescue, and security, surveillance, or reconnaissance tasks,

Of course, there is overlap in the relevance of these approaches to various applications, and in some instances the differences are a matter of degree. For instance, if large numbers of robots are too expensive or are not available to be applied to, say, planet exploration, then more purposive cooperation is required to achieve the goal of the mission. Combinations of the approaches are also possible by using intentionally cooperating robots to guide the activities of smaller groups of swarm robots in a coordinated way.

1.3 Integrative Autonomous Robot Approach

This paper addresses the development of autonomous robot teams that parallel the integrative type of social animals. This type of cooperation requires achieving coordinated and coherent solutions to problems involving a few (say, 2 to 10) possibly heterogeneous agents, each of which is able to perform meaningful tasks alone, but which requires the presence of other agents to fully complete its mission. The agents operate in dynamic, unstructured environments, and must respond appropriately to their sensory feedback, the actions of other agents, and the priorities of the tasks in the mission, adapting their actions as necessary as these inputs change.

A fully distributed architecture is presented which utilizes adaptive action selection to achieve cooperative control. In this architecture, task allocation is achieved through the selfish interests of individual agents, modified by their analyses of the current and previous performance of other team members. The *performance* of an agent is determined solely by how that agent affects the world, and is not dependent upon explicit, often artificial skill metrics. Since agents need not have *a priori* knowledge of the effect of other agents on the world, previously "unfamiliar" agents can be easily brought together to customize a team responsible for a specified mission. Simulation results will show this approach to result in very robust, reactive, opportunistic, and efficient cooperative teams of autonomous agents.

Section 2 describes an example cooperation task we would like a group of autonomous robots to perform, followed by a presentation of the cooperative architecture in section 3. Section 4 describes the results of our simulation studies utilizing this architecture. The paper closes in section 5 with some directions for continuing research.

2 Example Cooperative Task

As an illustrative example of the type of cooperation an integrative collection of robots must accomplish, consider a Janitorial Service team of robots. Such a robot team must clean a room in an office building that is unfamiliar to the agents at the beginning of the task, and may change dynamically due to people occupying the room. The overall mission consists of three high-level tasks: emptying the garbage, dusting the furniture, and cleaning the floors. The robots assigned to this mission are not familiar with the capabilities of the other agents in the team, which may change dynamically due to mechanical failure or environmental change. Each agent has a different mixture of capabilities which allows them to complete a portion of the mission on their own. However, since no single agent has all the capabilities necessary to accomplish the task alone, the agents must work as a team to accomplish the mission. Due to limited time and energy, we would also like the agents to accomplish their mission efficiently, minimizing redundant actions as much as possible.

The efficiency requirements and the dynamic environment of this mission require the agents to adapt their activities over time due to the current and previous actions of other agents, and to the sensory feedback received from the environment. The following section describes the architecture that allows the agents to accomplish such a mission. The simulation results of this particular application are described in section 4.1.

3 Cooperative Agent Architecture

Under this architecture, group cooperation emerges as a side-effect of the actions of the individual agents. These agents possess a variety of high-level functions that they can perform during a mission, and must at all times select an appropriate action based on the requirements of the mission, the activities of other agents, the current environmental conditions, and their own internal states. Adaptive action selection is facilitated in this architecture by designing the agents to be somewhat selfish and lazy. They are selfish in that they only do what they "want" to do and what they "think" is in their own best interests, as determined by their motivations and the environment[1]. The purpose of this approach is to maintain a purely distributed cooperative control scheme which affords an increased degree of robustness; since individual agents are always fully autonomous, they have the ability to perform useful actions even amidst the failure of other agents.

The agents in this architecture are lazy in the sense that, although they want certain tasks to be accomplished, they do not care if some other agent performs those tasks for them. For example, a baggage-handling robot may want both (1) the baggage to be removed from the airplane, and (2) the removed baggage placed on a cart. However, it is fine with this robot if another robot does one of these tasks, as long as the task gets done.

In this architecture, the individual agents are designed using a behavior-based approach [Brooks, 1986]. Under this construction, a number of task-achieving behaviors are active simultaneously, each receiving sensory input and controlling some aspect of the actuator output. The lower-level behaviors correspond to primitive survival behaviors, such as obstacle avoidance, while the higher-level behaviors correspond to higher goals, such as map building and exploring. This approach has been used successfully in a number of robotic applications [Brooks, 1990].

Extensions to this approach are necessary, however, when an agent must select among a number of competing actions — actions which cannot be pursued in parallel. Figure 1 shows the architecture we have developed which enables adaptive action selection in a cooperative robot team. Unlike typical behavior-based approaches, this architecture delineates several "behavior sets" that are either active as a group or are hibernating. Each behavior set corresponds to those levels of competence

[1]The *best interests* of an agent, for the purposes of this paper, are determined from the local point of view of that agent, not from some omnicient onlooker with a global view. These interests are defined very simply as the action(s) the agent is most motivated to perform at each point in time.

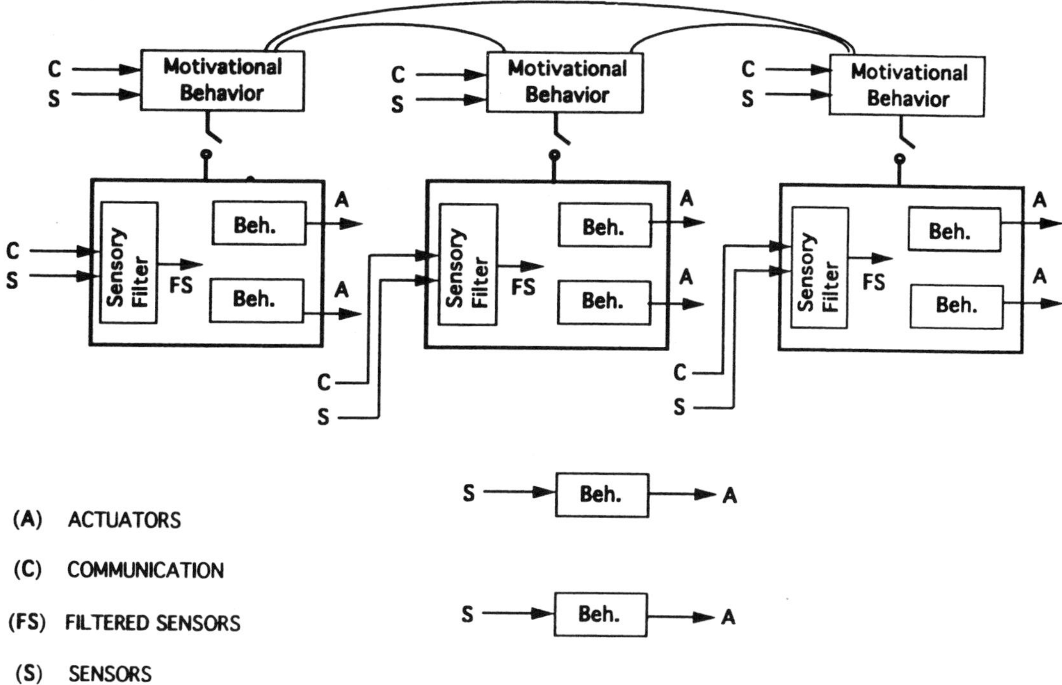

Figure 1: Reactive architecture for cooperative agents.

required to perform some high-level task, such as cleaning the floor or emptying the garbage. Due to conflicting goals, only one of these behavior sets are active at any point in time. However, other lower-level competences, such as collision avoidance, may be continually active regardless of the high level goal the agent is currently pursuing. Because of the alternative goals that may be pursued by the agents, they must have some means of selecting the appropriate behavior set to activate. Two primary mechanisms for achieving this adaptive action selection are utilized in this architecture: motivational behaviors and sensory filters. These mechanisms can be shown to result in a provably terminating allocation of tasks to agents, thus guaranteeing that this architecture will allow a team of agents to successfully complete their mission (if the mission is achievable at all). The proof is omitted here, however, due to space restrictions. The following subsections describe these mechanisms in more detail.

3.1 Motivational Behaviors

Controlling the activation of each behavior set is a *motivational behavior*. Each motivational behavior receives input from a number of sources, including sensory feedback, inter-agent communication, inhibitory feedback from other active behaviors, and internal motivations (such as impatience). The output of a motivational behavior is the activation level of its corresponding behavior set, represented as a non-negative number. When this activation level exceeds a given threshold, the behavior set becomes active; once a behavior set is activated, other behavior sets are suppressed, so that only one behavior set is active in an individual agent at a time.

Intuitively, a motivational behavior works as follows. The motivation to perform a given behavior set is initialized to some number reflecting the priority of that behavior set. This priority indicates the relative importance of the behavior set among all behavior sets of the agent. Then, over time, the motivation for performing a behavior set increases as long as the corresponding task is not being accomplished, as determined from sensory feedback. For example, a robot with the ability to clean floors should have an increasing motivation to clean the floors as long as the floors are not getting clean, as detected through that robot's dust sensor. On the other hand, if the sensory feedback indicates that the behavior set is not applicable, then the motivation to perform that behavior set should go to zero. Thus, our floor-cleaning robot should not be motivated to clean an already-clean floor, as evidenced through its sensors.

Additionally, we want our robots to be responsive to the actions of other agents, adapting their task selection to the activities of team members. Thus, if an agent is aware that another agent is performing a particular task, the first agent should be satisfied for a time that that task is going to be performed even without its own participation in the task, and thus go on to some other applicable action. Of course, detecting and interpreting the actions of other agents is not a trivial problem for robots, and often requires perceptual abilities that are not yet possible with current sensing technology. As it stands today, the sensory capabilities of even the lower animals far exceeds the present robotic capabilities. Thus, to enhance the robots' perceptual abilities, this architecture utilizes a simple form of broadcast communication to allow agents to inform other team members of their current activities, rather than relying totally on sensing through the world. Each agent broadcasts a statement of its current actions at a pre-specified rate, which other agents may use or ignore as they wish. No two-way conversations are employed in this architecture.

Each agent is designed to be somewhat impatient, however, in that it is only willing for a certain period of time to allow the communicated messages of other agents to affect its motivation to activate a behavior set. Continued sensory feedback indicating that a task is not getting accomplished thus overrides the statements of another agent that it is performing that task. This characteristic allows agents to adapt to failures of other agents, causing them to ignore the activities of an agent that is not successfully completing its task. As an example of this feature, consider two robots, $R1$ and $R2$, that want to empty a garbage can in a room. By chance, $R1$ responds first to the sensory feedback indicating the presence of a full garbage can, and begins broadcasting its actions of garbage emptying. $R2$ is then satisfied that the garbage will be emptied, and sits patiently with nothing to do. However, assume that $R1$ experiences a mechanical failure that prevents it from emptying the can, although it is not aware that it has a problem. In the meantime, $R2$'s impatience to empty the garbage has been increasing because its sensory feedback indicates the task still needs to be performed. Initially, this impatience was dulled by the communication from $R1$, but over time, it has steadily increased. Eventually $R2$'s motivation to activate the empty-garbage behavior set passes the threshold of activation, and it proceeds to empty the garbage itself. In this manner, impatience allows agents to adapt to dynamic changes in the environment or in the actions of other agents.

A complementary characteristic in these agents is that of acquiescence. This characteristic allows an agent to give up its current activity after a certain period of time if another agent has begun performing the same task. Just as the impatience characteristic reflects the fact that other agents may fail, the acquiescence characteristic indicates the recognition that an agent itself may fail. As an agent performs a task, its willingness to give up the task increases over time as long as the sensory feedback indicates the task is not being accomplished. As soon as some other agent indicates it has begun that same task, the unsuccessful agent will give up that task in an attempt to find an action at which it is more productive. In this way, an agent adapts its actions to its own failures. This is illustrated by continuing the previous example — once $R2$ announces its garbage-emptying activity, $R1$ acquiesces that task to $R2$ if $R1$ has attempted the task for a sufficient length of time.

The design of the motivational behaviors also allows the agents to adapt to unexpected environmental changes which alter the sensory feedback. The need for additional tasks can suddenly occur, requiring the agents to perform additional work, or existing environmental conditions can disappear, and thus relieve the agents of certain tasks. In either case, the motivations fluidly adapt to these situations, causing agents to respond appropriately to the current environmental circumstances.

3.1.1 Formal Definition

This section provides a more formal definition of the activation level calculations performed by the motivational behaviors. Given:

θ_i^j = Threshold of activity of behavior set i for agent j

Six sources of input affect the motivation to perform a particular behavior set. These inputs are defined as:

Behavior set priority:
α_i^j = Initial priority of behavior set i for agent j

Sensory feedback:
$sensory\_feedback(j, i, t) =$

$$\begin{cases} 1 & \text{if the sensory feedback for behavior } i \text{ at time } t \text{ in agent } j \text{ indicates that behavior } i \text{ is applicable} \\ 0 & \text{otherwise} \end{cases}$$

Inter-agent communication:

ρ_i^j = Rate of messages per unit time that agent j sends concerning behavior set i

$communicate(j, agent\_set, i, \rho_i^j) \Rightarrow$
Agent j sends activity message concerning behavior set i to agents in $agent\_set$ at a rate of ρ_i^j
$communication\_received(j, a, i, t) =$

$$\begin{cases} 1 & \text{if agent } j \text{ has received message related to behavior set } i \text{ in the last } t \text{ time units, } t \neq 0 \text{ (returns agent id in } a) \\ 0 & \text{otherwise} \end{cases}$$

Agent impatience:

ϕ_i^j = Time agent j is willing to allow another agent's communication message to affect the motivation of behavior set i

$\delta\_fast_i^j$ = Rate of impatience of agent j concerning behavior set i in the absence of other agents performing a similar behavior set

$\delta\_slow_i^j$ = Rate of impatience of agent j concerning behavior set i after discovering other agents performing a similar behavior set

$impatience(j,i,t) =$

$$\begin{cases} \delta\_slow_i^j & \text{if } communication\_received(j,x,i,\phi_i^j) \\ \delta\_fast_i^j & \text{otherwise} \end{cases}$$

Agent acquiescence:

ψ_i^j = Time agent j wants to maintain behavior set i's activity before yielding to another agent

$$override\_OK(j,i,t) = \begin{cases} 1 & \text{if behavior set } i \text{ of agent } j \text{ has been active for more than } \psi_i^j \text{ time units at time } t \\ 0 & \text{otherwise} \end{cases}$$

$acquiescence(j,i,t) =$
$\neg(override\_OK(j,i,t)$
$*communication\_received(j,x,i,\phi_i^j))$

Suppression from active behavior sets: $activity\_suppression(j,i,t) =$

$$\begin{cases} 0 & \text{if another behavior set } k \text{ is active, } k \neq i, \text{ on agent } j \text{ at time } t \\ 1 & \text{otherwise} \end{cases}$$

Motivation Calculation:
The motivation of agent j to perform behavior set i at time t is calculated as:

$$\begin{aligned} m_i^j(0) &= \alpha_i^j \cdot sensory\_feedback(j,i,0) \\ m_i^j(t) &= [m_i^j(t-1) + impatience(j,i,t)] \\ &\quad *activity\_suppression(j,i,t) \\ &\quad *sensory\_feedback(j,i,t) \\ &\quad *acquiescence(j,i,t) \end{aligned}$$

Behavior set i of agent j is active at time t when $m_i^j(t) > \theta_i^j$; whenever behavior set i is active, optionally broadcast this robot's current activity to other agents:

$$m_i^j(t) > \theta_i^j \Rightarrow communicate(j, agent\_set, i, \rho_i^j)$$

3.2 Sensory Filters

The second mechanism facilitating adaptive action selection is the sensory filter. Similar to the motivational behavior, which determines whether a behavior set will be active, the sensory filter influences the activities of a behavior set once it has been activated. A sensory filter serves as an attention focusing mechanism that allows the agent to be more reactive to the actions of other agents. These filters allow agents to minimize duplication of, or wasted, effort when more than one agent has comparable behavior sets active. The sensory filter converts communication about actions of other agents into altered sensory readings so that the agent ignores certain sensory readings or "hallucinates" other sensory readings, and acts on the altered sensory feedback as if it were real. The inputs that influence the sensory filters are the same as those controlling the motivational behaviors: task priorities, actions of other agents, sensory feedback, and internal state (including impatience and acquiescence rates). As with motivational behaviors, sensory information is only allowed to be filtered as long as other agents demonstrate "through the world" their ability to perform those actions. If an agent communicates that it is performing a particular task, and yet does not successfully alter the environment, other agents will adapt to the failed agent, ignoring its communication and possibly taking over that portion of the task.

As an example of the operation of the sensory filter, consider two robots, $R3$ and $R4$, which both have activated "dust furniture" behavior sets, and are working in an office that has a number of pieces of furniture to dust (the robots dust any non-moving object shorter than a given height). Ideally, we would like each piece of furniture to be dusted successfully by exactly one robot, to assure full coverage and minimum redundancy of action. Thus, when $R3$'s dust furniture sensory filter receives communication from $R4$ that it is dusting a particular piece of furniture, it "blinds" $R3$'s dust furniture behavior to the presence of that piece of furniture, causing $R3$ to react to some other furniture in the room that needs dusting. However, $R3$ is only blinded to the sensory feedback as long as $R4$ is successful in its task. Just as in the case of the motivational behaviors, impatience characteristics cause the true sensory feedback to be transmitted to $R3$'s dust furniture behavior if $R4$ is not successful.

Of course, in this simple example, ignoring certain sensory feedback based on the actions of other agents does not mandate the use of a sensory filter, since the same function could be performed within the dust furniture behavior set. However, in more complex tasks, when several sensors provide information that is distributed across a number of behaviors within the dust furniture behavior set, the centralized alteration of all applicable sensory readings serves as a more efficient and reliable mechanism for achieving behavior that is reactive to the actions of other agents.

The formal model of the sensory filters parallels that of the motivational behaviors. Therefore, due to space limitations, it is not included here.

4 Results from Simulation Studies

This architecture has been successfully demonstrated in a number of application domains in simulation. The simulation experiments were conducted on a Macintosh-II using a multi-agent simulator, written in Lisp, developed in the MIT Mobot Laboratory. The robot control programs were written in the Behavior Language[Brooks *et al.*, 1990] — an extension to the subsumption architecture. Two of these applications are described here.

4.1 Janitorial Service

Snapshots of the janitorial service robot team simulation, which was introduced in section 2, are shown in figure 2. Using this architecture, the agents were able to successfully divide tasks among themselves in a reactive and dynamic fashion to accomplish the mission without duplicating the actions of other agents. As an example of the adaptation of action selection due to the actions of other agents, consider the first 4 frames of figure 2. Initially, robots 1 and 2 (numbering robots left to right in the first snapshot) both select the action of emptying the garbage, and both head north toward the closest garbage can (garbage cans are modeled in the simulator as small square objects). However, upon hearing that robot 2 is also headed to empty the same garbage can, robot 1 is satisfied that that garbage can will be emptied, and thus selects another garbage can to empty (in this case, the one to the southeast, as shown in the second snapshot). After emptying its garbage can, robot 2 then heads toward the third garbage can to the east (as seen in the third and fourth snapshots), bypassing the garbage can that robot 1 has emptied. Robot 1 is then satisfied that all garbage cans will be emptied, even though robot 2 has not yet reached the third garbage can, and proceeds to select another action — that of dusting furniture — as seen in the fourth snapshot.

Many unexpected events have been modeled in these experiments to illustrate the true adaptiveness of the architecture to the dynamic environment and the actions of other agents. For example, in the discussion above, if either of the robots 1 or 2 were unsuccessful in emptying one of the garbage cans, the other agent would become impatient with the lack of progress and proceed to empty that can regardless of the fact that the other agent had selected that action earlier. If additional garbage cans are added, the robots react fluidly to the environmental change and empty the new cans as if they were always present. If an existing garbage can is suddenly empty, the robots again react immediately by pursuing some other task. New team members can be added to the group and are allowed by the existing team members to help with the mission. Many other such changes to the environment and the abilities of the agents were simulated and handled successfully by this architecture.

4.2 Bounding Overwatch

An additional, quite different, simulation application also studied is the bounding overwatch problem, which requires a team of agents to dynamically divide themselves into two subgroups, and then to travel to the initial assembly points of their respective subgroups and determine a subgroup leader. Next, one team must head out for the next waypoint (i.e., they *bound*) while the other team monitors their progress and remains alert for danger (i.e., they *overwatch*). Once the first team reaches its waypoint, the roles of the teams switch, so that the first team overwatches while the second team bounds. Figure 3 shows several snapshots of this simulation in progress. The utilization of the architecture put forth in this paper resulted in a very robust cooperative team that successfully accomplished its mission.

5 Conclusions and Continuing Work

This paper has presented a distributed architecture for cooperating, integrative, agents that facilitates adaptive action selection. This architecture allows robotic teams to achieve high-level group goals without the need for cooperative planning or conversations. Team members easily adapt to the current actions of other agents and to a dynamically changing environment.

Implementation of this architecture will soon be extended to teams of physical mobile robots. Additionally, work is continuing on the addition of a learning capability that will allow agents to improve their performance over a number of trials. With this ability, agents will react not only to the current performance of other agents on certain tasks, but also to their previous performances of those tasks. Agents should then be able to select appropriate actions based merely on the presence of certain agents with which they have previously worked. Thus, over time, a team will be able to learn to work together at an even higher level of efficiency and adaptability.

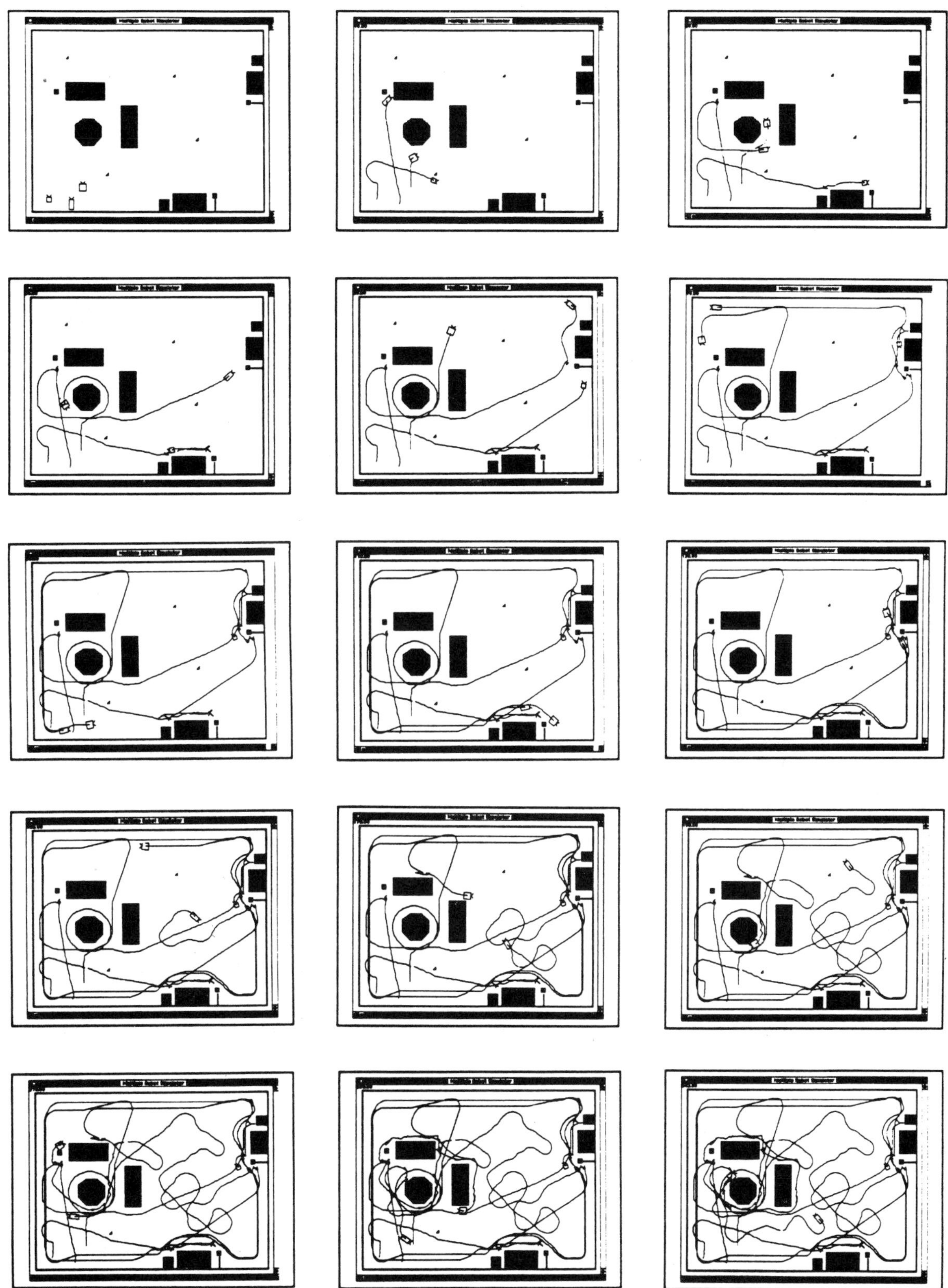

Figure 2: Janitorial Service Simulation (read left to right, top to bottom).

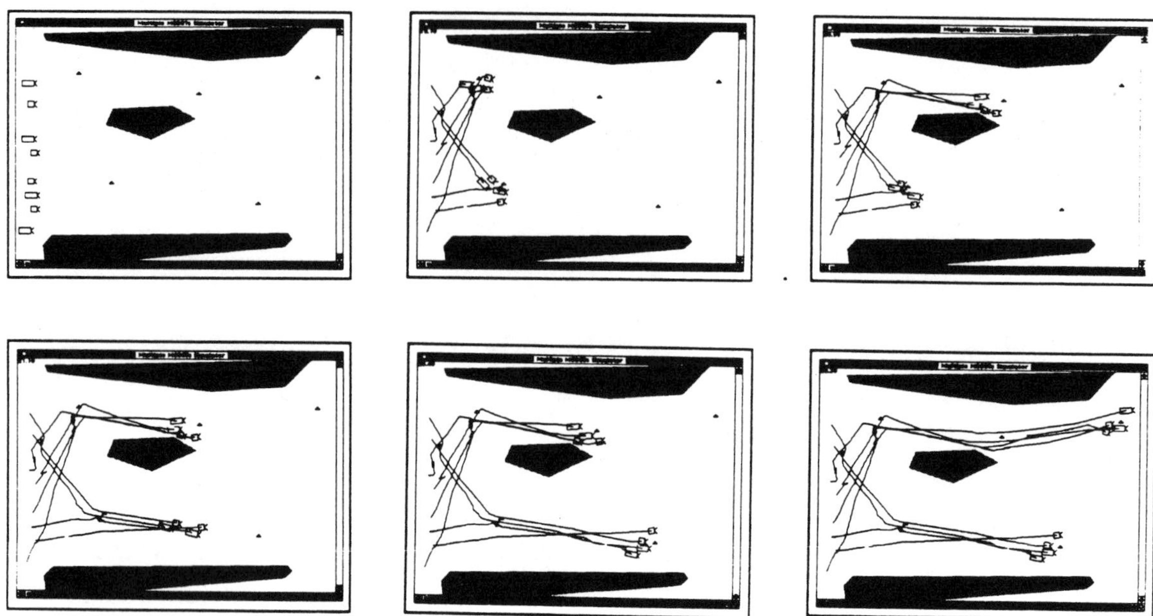

Figure 3: Bounding Overwatch Simulation.

Acknowledgements

I am grateful to Rodney Brooks for many intriguing discussions on this research. Thanks also to Yasuo Kagawa, a visiting scientist from the Mazda Corporation, for developing the first version of the multi-agent simulator used in this research.

Support for this research was provided in part by the University Research Initiative under Office of Naval Research contract N00014-86-K-0685, in part by the Advanced Research Projects Agency under Office of Naval Research contract N00014-85-K-0124, and in part by the Mazda Corporation.

References

[Brooks *et al.*, 1990] Rodney A. Brooks, Pattie Maes, and Maja Mataric. Lunar base construction robots. In *Proceedings of the IEEE International Workshop on Intelligent Robots and Systems*, pages 389–392, Tsuchiura, Japan, 1990.

[Brooks, 1986] Rodney A. Brooks. A robust layered control system for a mobile robot. *IEEE Journal of Robotics and Automation*, RA-2(1):14–23, March 1986.

[Brooks, 1990] Rodney A. Brooks. The behavior language: User's guide. Memo 1227, MIT A.I. Lab, Cambridge, MA, April 1990.

[Deneubourg *et al.*, 1990] J. Deneubourg, S. Goss, G. Sandini, F. Ferrari, and P. Dario. Self-organizing collection and transport of objects in unpredictable environments. In *Japan-U.S.A. Symposium on Flexible Automation*, pages 1093–1098, 1990.

[Etkin, 1964] W. Etkin. *Social Behavior from Fish to Man*. The University of Chicago Press, Chicago, 1964.

[McFarland, 1991] David McFarland. personal communication, March 1991.

[Portmann, 1961] A. Portmann. *Animals as Social Beings*. The Viking Press, New York, 1961.

[Steels, 1990] Luc Steels. Cooperation between distributed agents through self-organization. In Yves Demazeau and Jean-Pierre Muller, editors, *Decentralized A.I.* Elsevier Science, 1990.

[Tinbergen, 1953] N. Tinbergen. *Social Behavior in Animals*. Chapman and Holl LTD, Great Britain, 1953.

[Tinbergen, 1965] N. Tinbergen. *Animal Behavior*. Time-Life Books, New York, 1965.

[Wang and Beni, 1990] Jing Wang and Gerardo Beni. Distributed computing problems in cellular robotic systems. In *Proceedings of the IEEE International Workshop on Intelligent Robots and Systems*, pages 819–826, Tsuchiura, Japan, 1990.

[Wilson, 1971] E. Wilson. *The Insect Societies*. The Belknap Press, Cambridge, 1971.

From Tom Thumb to the Dockers: Some Experiments with Foraging Robots

Alexis Drogoul, Jacques Ferber

LAFORIA, Boîte 169,Université Paris VI,
75252 PARIS CEDEX O5 FRANCE
drogoul@laforia.ibp.fr,
ferber@laforia.ibp.fr

Abstract

In this paper, we experiment, from the point of view of their efficiency, different implementations of the "explorer robots application". Three types of "Tom Thumb robots", whose behavior is based on the foraging behaviors of ants are proposed and their results are critically examined. We then introduce chain-making robots (the "dockers"), governed by local perceptions and interactions. This helps us to show that only a few changes in the robots' behavior may greatly improve the efficiency of the population.

Introduction

In the research conducted in the field of swarm intelligence, the "explorer robots application" appears to be one of the most common examples found to illustrate the capacity of a population of poorly intelligent creatures to handle with a global goal.

In this case study, the goal is to make a team of robots find and collect samples in an unpredictable environment and take them back to a home base.

These robots usually operate independently and behave in a quite simple way. They can sense the samples, the home base and some other environmental signs (possibly left by other robots) and, of course, pick up and put down samples.

This application appears to be very popular because of its use in the three most influent fields of Artificial Life, namely the simulation of animal's behaviour, with the works of (Deneubourg & al. 1986), GA's and genetic programming (see e.g., (Koza 1990) with the Santa-Fe trail) and robotics, where it has been used to introduce the idea of using small cheap robots for exploring planets or dangerous locations (Brooks 1990). Furthermore, it is now widely accepted as the best illustration of "swarm intelligence", along with the collective sorting example (Deneubourg & al. 1991).

Recent papers have explored the ability of these multi-robot systems to have useful behaviors, but none has emphasized on their efficiency. Moreover, although all the individual mechanisms of the robots are accounted for, still there is no understanding and explanation of how the overall patterns of foraging results from the interactions between these mechanisms. Consequently, even if the general idea is appealing, it is still difficult to choose between all the proposed solutions when one wants to use them in a real application. That is why we are interested in the comparisons between these systems in terms of efficiency. We hope that such comparison would significantly advance the understanding of these systems and the design of new ones.

In this paper, we then intend to review some of the frameworks used so far for the implementation of this example. All the choices will be discussed and their results compared with respect to the needs of robustness, adaptivity and efficiency required. We will also compare them to our new system of "chain-making" robots.

The plan of the paper is as follows: in Section 1, we introduce the application and the framework shared by all the robots. We then provide in Section 2 experimental results obtained with non-social robots, namely robots that do not interact directly with each other. Section 3 presents our "chain-making" robots and contains some numerical results and a few comparisons with the previous ones. We close in Section 4 by comparing all the systems presented so far and discussing some perspectives in swarm intelligence.

1 General Framework

The first report about the "collecting samples" application has been made in (Steels 89). The key idea is to make a set of little robots collect rock samples in an unknown environment.

In all the experiments we describe in the next sections, our world (see Fig. 1) will be constituted by a variable population of robots, a home base that emits a signal decreasing with the distance and three heaps of one hundred samples each.

The distance between the heaps and the base is 40 meters and the speed of the robots is 1 meter/cycle. The robots can sense samples from a short distance (2 meters). The field created by the home's signal defines an area some 80 meters in diameter.

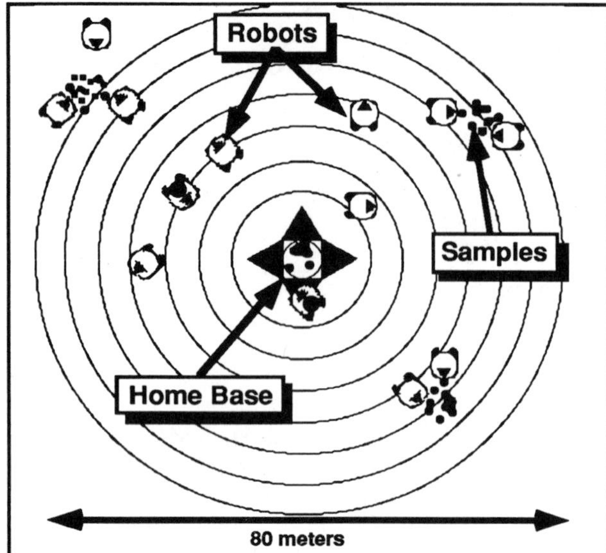

Figure 1 - The case study

The robots are simulated using the EthoModelling Framework previously described in (Drogoul & al. 1992). They are built out of simple primitive behaviors that basically include:

- obstacle and other robots avoidance
- following of the home's gradient field
- picking up and laying samples
- random move

These primitive behaviors are combined into concurrent tasks (see e.g. Drogoul & Ferber 1992), each of them being triggered by an internal or environmental stimulus. For more convenience, the behaviors of the robots will be described in the next sections with diagrams that represent the decision-making process performed by them at each step. Note that these diagrams do not exactly correspond to the way the robots are implemented. However, they simplify the understanding and the comparison of their behaviors.

An example of such a diagram is shown on Fig. 2. It represents the behavior of the silliest foraging robot one can imagine: it simply searches randomly for samples, pick up one when it finds some, come back to the base, lay the sample and then returns to its random search.

Whatever their lack of ability, these silly robots will be used as a basis for the next generations of robots. As a matter of fact, they are provided with the necessary autonomy and basic behaviors needed for completing the global task. We will see in the next sections that minor transformations at the individual level may lead to very important changes at the population level and to the emergence of cooperating processes.

2 Tom Thumb Robots

This kind of robots was inspired by the foraging behavior of ants. The basic idea is to make the robots that have found samples put down "crumbs" on their way back from the samples to the base. It is assumed that the other robots are attracted by the crumbs when they move onto them and then able to locate more quickly the samples. Roughly similar robots can be found in several papers including, but not limited to (Steels 1989, Deneubourg 1990). We decided to call them Tom Thumb, because of the resemblance their behavior shows with that of Charles Perrault's character.

To provide the previous silly robots with this behavior, we only have to change one node and add one action (as shown in light-grey on Fig. 3). What is interesting is that this simple change now enables the robots to cooperate, even if it is a kind of non-intentional cooperation. They do not interact directly with one another, but they do transmit information that allow the other ones to minimize their search.

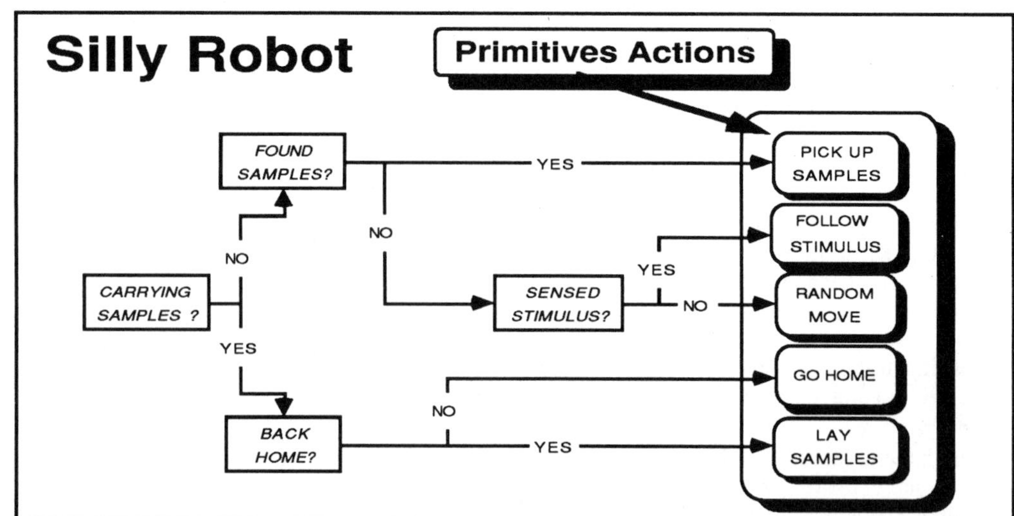

Figure 2 - The behavioral diagram of a silly foraging robot

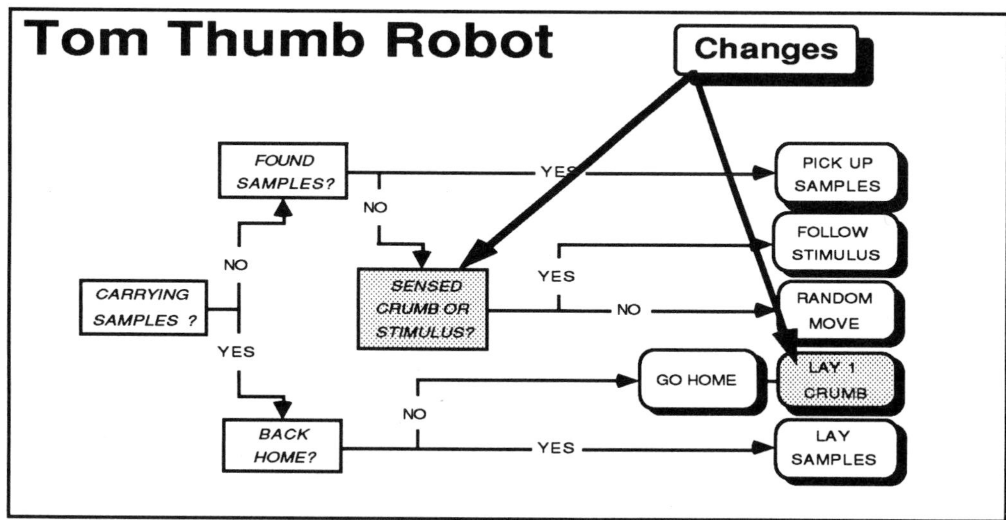

Figure 3 - The behavioral diagram of the first Tom Thumb robots

Let us now introduce the experimental results obtained with these robots. The case study has been described in Section 1. We measure the efficiency of populations of Tom Thumb robots, by plotting the number of cycles needed to pick up all the samples against the number of robots in the population. As shown on the log plot on Fig. 4, the curve dramatically decreases in the first steps, downto a minimum of 1113 cycles (for 63 robots) and then regularly increases (up to a maximum, not shown here, of approximately 3500 cycles, where it stabilizes).

What do these results mean ? First point, the increase in performance of the populations (from one to 63 robots) is clearly due to the crumb laying and following. This helps to focus the population on the task it has to accomplish. Yet, and that is the second point, the positive feedback supplied by this behavior is not counterbalanced by any negative feedback that could depend on the amount of samples available on each site. That is, an empty heap of samples will continue to attract robots because the path between this heap and the base will remain stable. This explains the brutal variations of the curve, due to the random choice made by each robot between the three paths. If several robots chose a path leading to an empty heap, the overall efficiency of the population clearly decreases.

We will see below that we need another factor to explain the decrease of efficiency observed for the most numerous populations. However, let us firstly try to implement a negative feedback at the population level by modifying the robots behaviors.

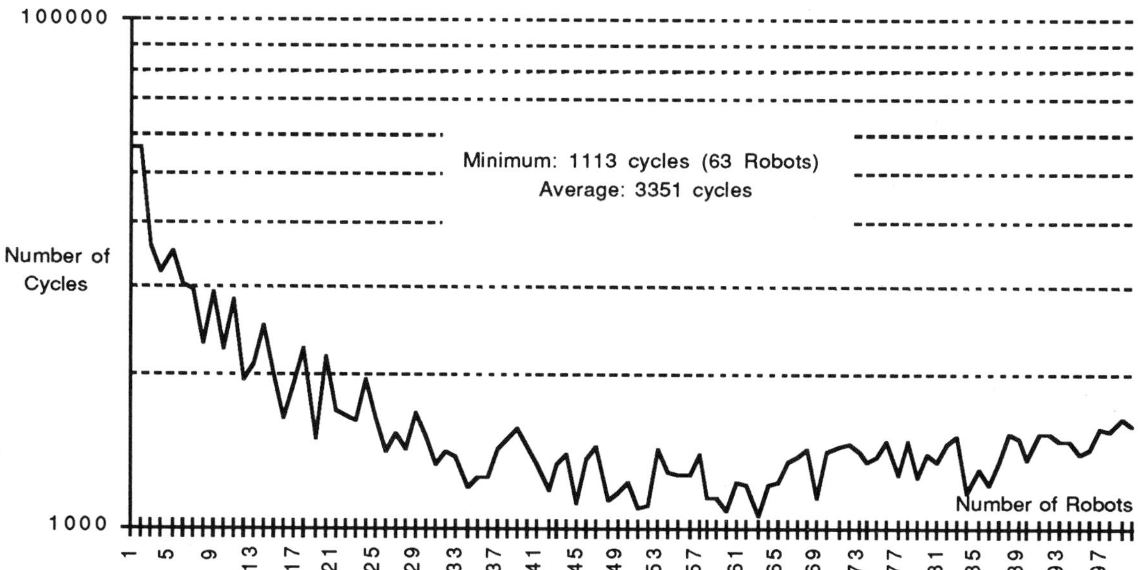

Figure 4 - Results obtained with 100 populations of Tom Thumb robots

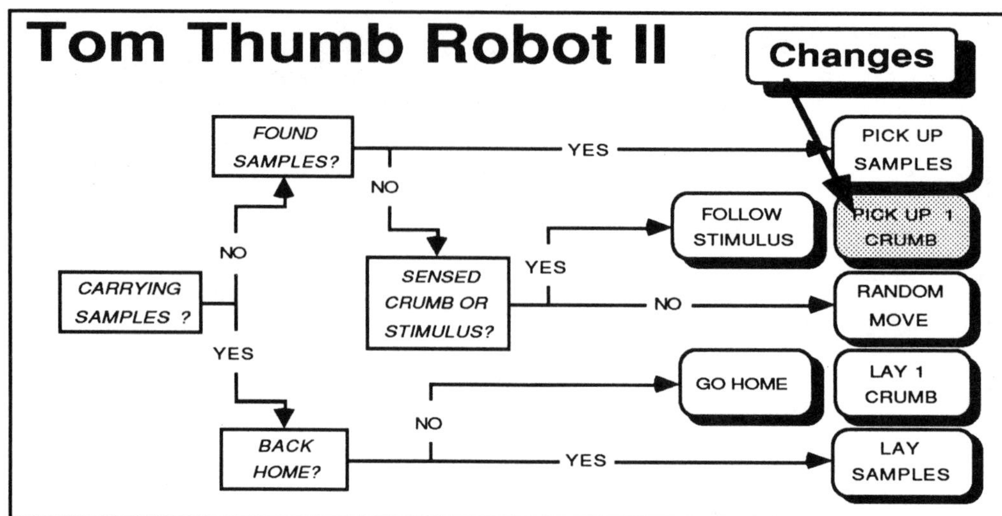

Figure 5 - The behavioral diagram of the second Tom Thumb robots

Once again, the idea can be found in Charles Perrault's novel, where the path established by Tom Thumb is being destroyed by birds that pick up the crumbs. If we make robots pick up crumbs, too, when they are following a path, we enable them to build dynamical trails and to cancel them when they lead to an empty heap (as a matter of fact, a robot following the trail will erase it. If it does not find samples, it will not rebuild it by coming back to the base).

This new behavior only induces a minor change in the Tom Thumb robots, as shown on Fig. 5.

The experimental results obtained with the robots are plotted on Fig. 6. The dashed lines show the previous results and the solid lines the new ones. We see that the new behavior has suppressed the brutal variations of the curve and that the performance of a given population can be roughly predicted from the performance of the previous one.

However, the evolution of this efficiency is not really satisfactory with respect to the previous results. For small populations (less than 60 robots), we have clearly lost in efficiency what we have gained in stability and predictability. Why is it so ? In fact, it seems that we have introduced too much dynamics in the system. Letting one robot destroy a path means that it hides a lot of information to the others during its trip, until it comes back to the base. On one hand, robots are no more attracted towards useless crumb paths, but on the other hand, they often temporarily lose already made paths.

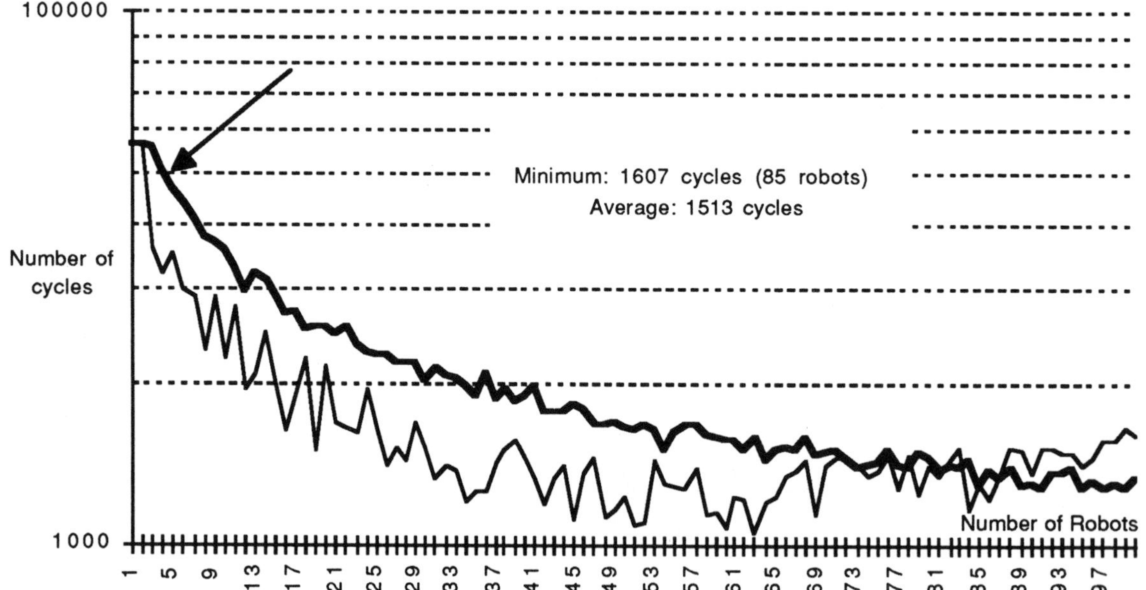

Figure 6 - Results obtained with 100 populations of Tom Thumb II robots

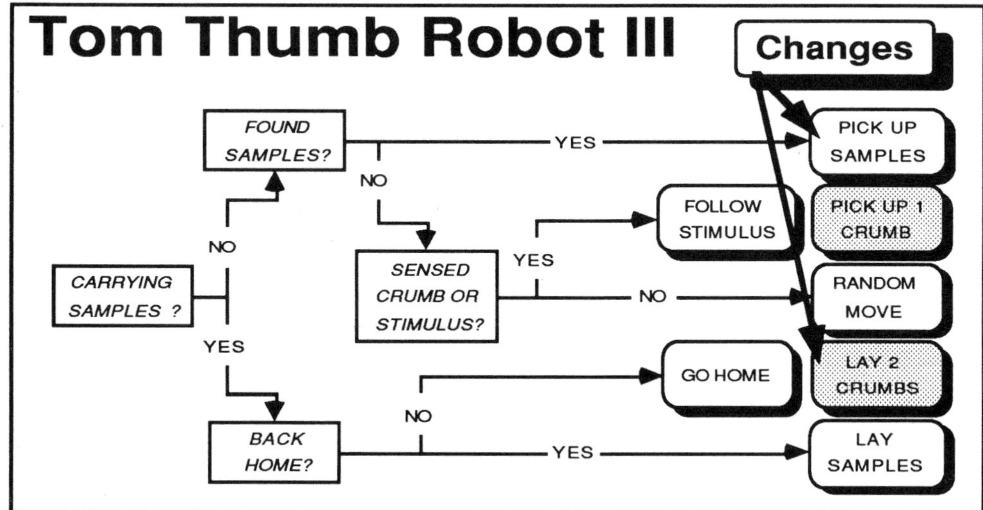

Figure 7 - The behavioral diagram of the third Tom Thumb robots

So the solution, already proposed in (Steels 1991), is to provide them with a mixed behavior. We need the robots to build paths that they can erase, but slower. Then, we just tell them to put down two crumbs when coming back to the base and to pick up one when following the path (see Fig. 7).

The results, plotted on Fig. 8, clearly show two things. Firstly, the efficiency of this robot is much better than that of the previous one. Secondly, the curve remains very regular until the population reaches 85 robots. For most of the cases, this solution seems to be a good compromise between the two previous Tom Thumb robots, combining efficiency with regularity.

Still a question has yet to be answered. Why is there an increase in the number of cycles in the last 15 results ? In fact, the answer is pretty simple. The 15 last populations of robots are facing important **traffic jams**. And, though it might be funny to imagine robots stuck in traffic jams, this raises a major problem. If we look more closely to the results, we can see that a population of 25 robots is as efficient as a population of 100 robots, and that a population of 60 robots is twice as efficient. So the cooperation, which emerges quite quickly for small populations, is counterbalanced in bigger populations by the competition between the robots.

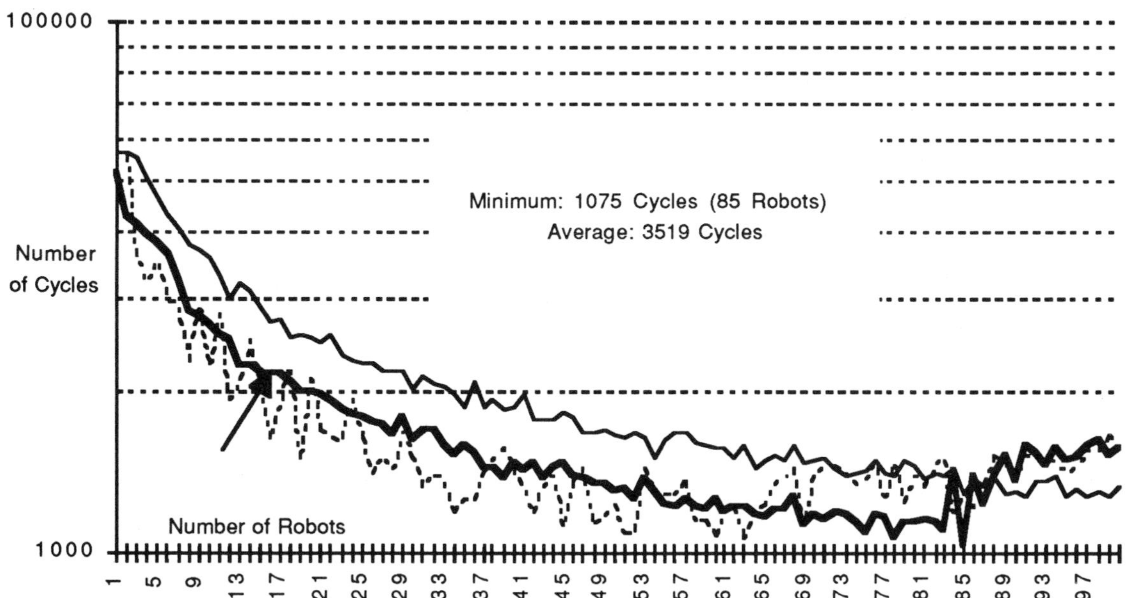

Figure 8 - Results obtained with 100 populations of Tom Thumb III robots

Fig 9a - Unorganized dockers

Fig 9b - Chain-making dockers

3 Chain-Making Robots

The problem to solve is then to make the robots cooperate more deeply without competing too much. In fact, the previous robots were only cooperating by sharing information (namely the location of samples) but they were not able to cooperate by coordinating their actions.

Let us take an example borrowed from everyday life. When a ship enters a harbor in order to be discharged, the dockers do not run all together towards the ship, competing for the access to the gangway (like in Fig. 9a). Instead, they organize themselves, making a chain from the ship to the wharves and thus minimizing their waste of energy and maximizing their efficacy (Fig. 9b).

Why did we take this example? In fact, the first situation peculiarly looks like the situations created by our last robots: a huge crowd around the samples with everybody trying to escape the place to come back to the base. And, of course, we would evidently like to obtain something like the second situation.

The differences between these two situations are quite obvious. In the first one, the dockers act as if they were alone, without paying attention to the others. In the second one, they coordinate their actions. They have then to be aware of the behaviors of other dockers. If we want this global behavior to emerge in our application, the challenge is to implement these relationships in robots that cannot communicate.

In which way do we have to modify the behavior of Tom Thumb to let it become a docker?

The first idea is to transform our robots in order to make them detect the samples carried by other robots (as if these samples were on the floor). A robot carrying a sample can, for example, switch on a light on its head. This signal will trigger in the other robots the same behavior than the samples detection. In that way, robots will be able to react upon the state of others.

The second idea is to let the robots be able to pick up samples carried by others . Several solutions can be conceived and we will not get into further details about it. We just assume that they are provided with an arm and a skip and that their arm can pick up things from the skip of other robots (see Fig. 10).

Figure 10 - A possible design for the chain-making robots

With these two primitive actions, correctly arranged within the framework of the previous robots (see Fig. 11), we claim that it is possible to obtain chains from the samples to the base, whatever the number of robots.

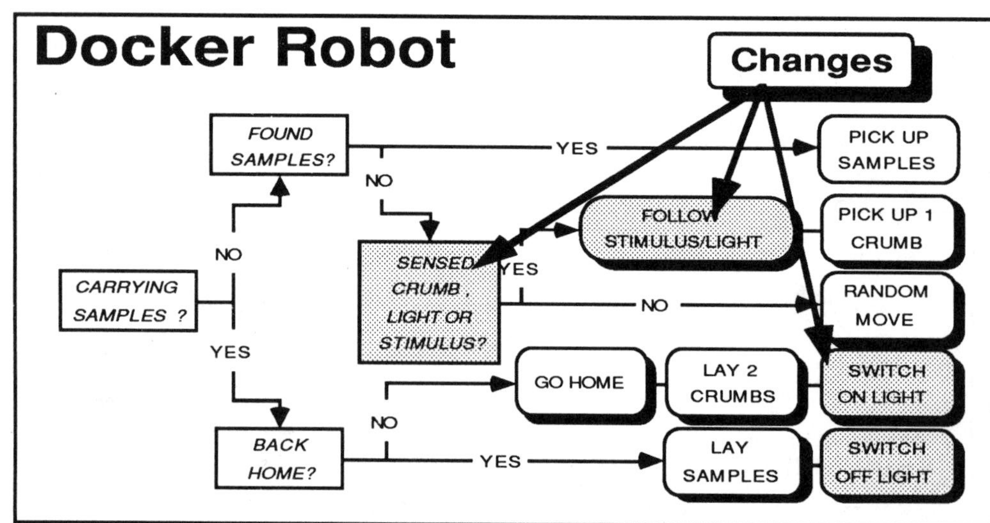

Figure 11 - The behavioral diagram of the docker (or chain-making robots)

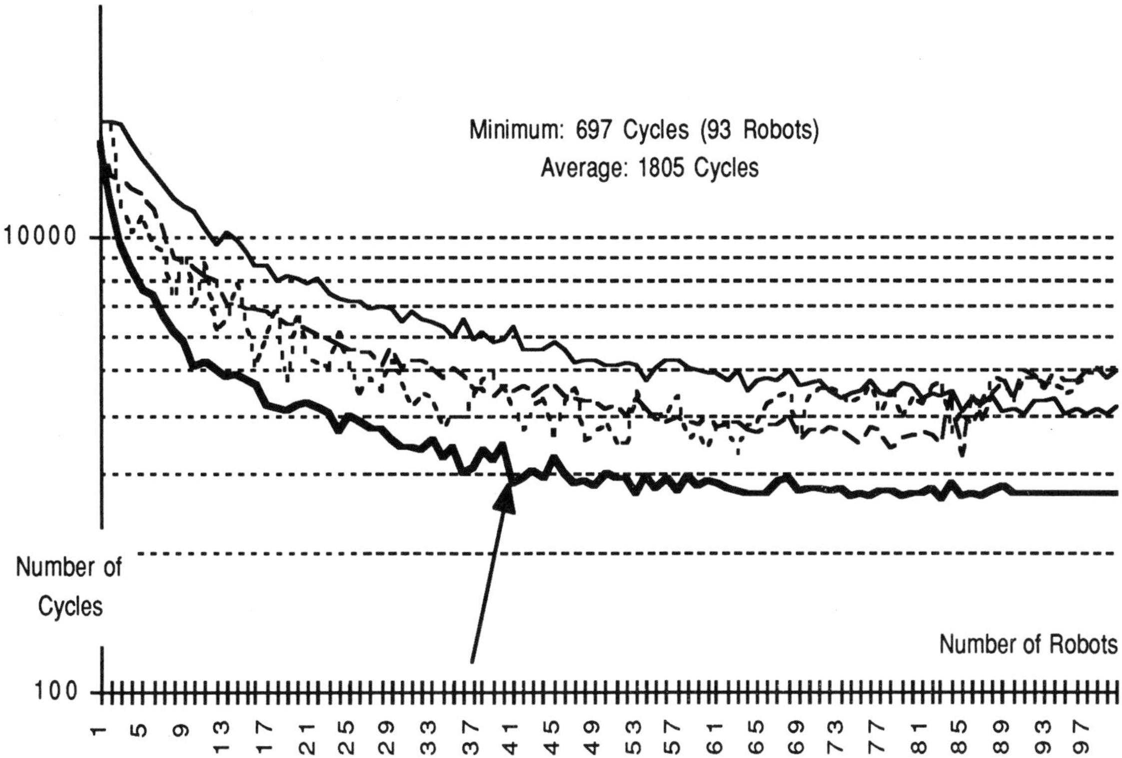

Figure 12 - Results obtained with 100 populations of docker (chain-making) robots

This emergent functionality is illustrated on Fig. 13, which contains two snapshots of the simulation in progress. One can see, on the right-hand window, the three chains being build from the three heaps of samples to the base. The robots that make up these chains do not move all the way from the samples to the base, but only between one location where they pick up samples (a robot or a heap) and one location where they are discharged of them (by themselves in the nest or elsewhere by another robot).

The consequence of this double cooperation (information sharing and action coordination) is a real improvement in the efficiency of the populations, from the first (one robot) to the last one (a hundred robots).

The curve, plotted on Fig. 12, is very regular (at least with respect to the previous ones) and evolves towards the asymptotic direction Y = 700. In most cases, the results are twice as best as any of the results obtained with the former Tom Thumb robots.

The explanation appears to be twofold:

(1) From the robot's point of view, once it is involved in a chain, it has less distance to cover (to pick up samples and to put them down) than any of the Tom Thumbs robots. Those were actually obliged, at each time, to cover the whole distance between the nest and the heaps. In the best cases, the chain-making robots do not even need to move to get and give samples. This explains the very impressive efficiency observed in almost any of the populations.

(2) This reduction of the number of moves appears to prevent the robots from going and disturbing the others, and thus avoids traffic jams around the nest and the samples. And when the number of robots is very important compared to the size of the environment, samples can of course be conveyed without difficulty, from robot to robot, without needing the robots that carry them to escape the jams. This is especially interesting for populations of great size, where the brutal decrease of performance does not arise as in the previous cases.

Of course, one can argue that these chain-making robots are a little more complex than the Tom Thumb robots and perhaps, physically speaking, a little harder to build. So it could be difficult to rely on their behavior, which needs direct interactions between them. But the chain appears to be very robust and fault-tolerant. Even if some robots miss their goal, the chain will continue to work, evolving dynamically towards stable states.

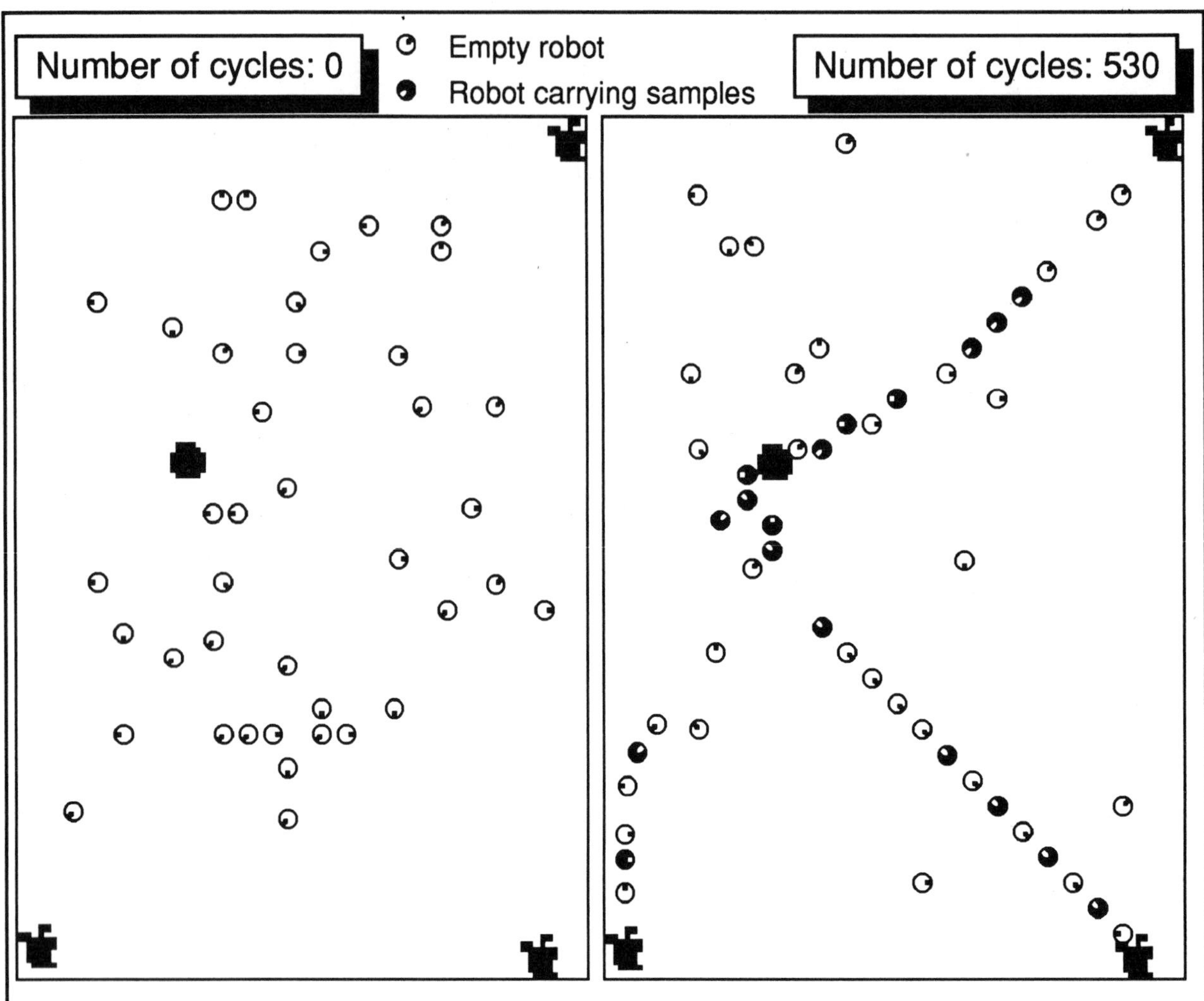

Figure 13 - Two snapshots of a simulation in progress

4 Conclusion

What we have learned in these four experiments can be summarized in the two following points:

(1) In these dynamical systems, small changes at the individual level can greatly modify the global behavior of the population. If we look at the three Tom Thumb robots, the differences between them are not really important (in term of capabilities). But the results at the population level are quite substantial. This implies to be very careful when designing a swarm intelligence based system or any distributed system in which intelligence is collectively exhibited by non-intelligent entities. The methodology we followed here is that of the "increasing complexity". The key idea is to firstly experiment solitary entities that do not have any social behavior and to progressively increase their capabilities in terms of communication and interaction. The first robots were only able to indicate something (namely the location of samples) to the others. The second generation added the ability to manipulate this information, by simply cancelling it. The third one implemented a more advanced manipulation of this information, giving the robots the faculty to change it. And, finally, the chain-making robots were provided with direct interactions. A very interesting challenge would then be to supply these robots with means of (limited) communication in order to test the efficiency of the chain-making robots proposed by (Deneubourg & al. 92).

(2) This application of chain-making robots is still on its early stages and it is somewhat difficult to foresee what is going to be done and experimented with it. However, some perspectives may be drawn. First, we are extending the application to cope with several bases that may move. It is easy to see the interest of such an application, for example in agriculture (where harvesting could be performed by dispatching many robots in the fields) or in the military domain (for managing the supply lines between different corps). Secondly, we are interested in the emergence of topological structures and the chains obtained

between different corps). Secondly, we are interested in the emergence of topological structures and the chains obtained here are nothing else but structures dynamically created that stay stable as long as the flow of energy that has created them (from the samples to the nest) remains. We hypothetize that more complex geometrical structures could be observed by multiplying the number of heaps and the number of bases. We hope to have soon results on this subject.

Acknowledgements

We wish to acknowledge the contribution of Steffen Lalande in programming most of the applications described here during his first year of doctorate. We are deeply grateful to him for his wise advices and stimulating discussions.

Bibliography

R. Brooks (1990) "Elephants Don't Play Chess" *in* "Journal of Robotics and Autonomous Systems", Volume 6, p. 3-15.

J.L. Deneubourg, S. Aron, S. Goss, J.M. Pasteels, G. Duerinck (1986) "Random Behaviour, Amplification Processes and Number of Participants: How they Contribute to the Foraging Properties of Ants" *in* Physica 22D, North-Holland, Amsterdam, p. 176-186.

J.L.Deneubourg, S.Goss, N.Franks, A.Sendova-Franks, C.Detrain, L.Chretien (1991) "The dynamics of collective sorting Robot-like Ants and Ant-like Robots" *in* "From Animals to Animats", MIT Press, p. 356.

A. Drogoul, J. Ferber, B. Corbara, D. Fresneau (1992), "A Behavioral Simulation Model for the Study of Emergent Social Structures" *in* "Towards a Practice of Autonomous Systems, Proceedings of ECAL'91", MIT Press.

A. Drogoul, J. Ferber (1992), "Multi-Agent Simulation as a Tool for Modeling Societies: Application to Social Differentiation in Ant Colonies", *in* Proceedings of MAAMAW'92 (forthcoming "Decentralized AI IV").

J.R. Koza (1990) "Evolution and Co-Evolution of Computer Programs to Control Independent-Acting Agents" *in* "From Animals to Animats", MIT Press.

L. Steels (1989) "Cooperation between distributed agents Through self-organisation" *in* "Journal on robotics and autonomous systems", North Holland, Amsterdam.

L. Steels (1991) "Towards a Theory of Emergent Functionality" *in* "From Animals to Animats", MIT Press, p. 451.

Collective Robotic Intelligence

C. Ronald Kube and Hong Zhang
Department of Computing Science
University of Alberta
Edmonton, Alberta CANADA T6G 2J9
kube@cs.ualberta.ca zhang@cs.ualberta.ca

Abstract

In this paper, we examine the problem of controlling multiple behaviour-based autonomous robots. Based on observations made from the study of social insects, we propose five simple mechanisms used to invoke group behaviour in simple sensor-based mobile robots. The proposed mechanisms allow populations of behaviour-based robots to perform tasks without centralized control or use of explicit communication. We have verified our collective control strategies by designing a robot population simulator called *SimbotCity*. We have also constructed a system of five homogeneous sensor-based mobile robots, capable of achieving simple collective tasks, to demonstrate the feasibility of some of the control mechanisms.

1 Introduction

Can simple behaviour-based mobile robots achieve tasks collectively? The behaviour-based approach, characterized by a direct coupling of perception to action, has been demonstrated by a number of researchers on situated and embodied mobile robots (see[16] for several papers). The majority of research projects have concentrated on designing *single* autonomous robots, capable of functioning in a dynamic world. Taking behaviour-based robotics towards more sophisticated capabilities has resulted in the interest, by a number of researchers, in collective task-achieving behaviour [5, 7, 30]. By organizing multiple robots into collections of task-achieving populations, we conjecture that useful tasks can be accomplished with simple behaviour-based control mechanisms. In this paper, we describe our approach to real-time multiple robot control motivated by several observations of collective behaviour made from the study of social insects.

Recent interest in multiple robot systems has produced several interesting ideas [2, 10, 17]. Brooks and Flynn [7] propose sending a colony of small robots to explore the surface of the Moon. Dario *et al.* [8] propose a social organization of *societies* of cellular mobile robots where useful tasks are carried out through collaboration rather than individual effort. Additionally, Yuta and Premvuti [30] describe an approach to cooperation of multiple mobile robots using environmental resources while working toward a common goal.

Brooks [5] has outlined several issues raised in controlling multiple autonomous mobile robots to generate a global behaviour. Our own efforts to address the problem of real-time multiple robot control have led to a simple strategy involving *group behaviours* and five mechanisms with which to invoke them. The mechanisms proposed do not represent a comprehensive set, but rather strategies we have found based on observations from the study of social insects. The proposed mechanisms may be used individually or in combination to achieve a desired collective behaviour. Our method is fundamentally different from the approach taken in Distributed Robotic Systems[3] in that we do not use any centralized coordination; subsequently, the complexity of the system does not increase with the number of robots. In addition, no explicit communication is used to control the robots, but rather a form of implicit communication is used through passive sensing. Although the proposed mechanisms are not restricted to behaviour-based control architectures, we have found the approach is better suited for this style of implementation.

The five mechanisms presented here represent our initial exploration into multiple robot control. The first mechanism makes use of a common task and a simple cooperation strategy of non-interference. The second mechanism produces a *follow* behaviour that keeps a group of robots together in herds. The third mechanism uses environmental cues to invoke the group behaviour. The fourth mechanism allows the robot to invoke its group behaviour once it senses it is within a group. The fifth mechanism invokes group behaviour through *autostimulation*, a method in which an individual robot may invoke a behaviour within the group.

In order to test our proposed control mechanisms for collective behaviour, we have constructed a simulator. Simulation allows one to test the feasibility of a given control mechanism. We have tested the first two control mechanisms in simulation. However, given the importance of *situatedness* in this style of work and that we ultimately build these robots, it is very important to simulate only what we can build. To do otherwise would leave us open to the simplifications so often criticized of simulation work. A series of experiments in simulation, using our Robot Population Simulator *SimbotCity*, led to the refinement of our strategy which we then implemented in a system of physical robots consisting of five homogeneous behaviour-based mobile robots capable of achieving simple collective tasks.

The ultimate test of the validity of the control strategy requires the physical contruction of the robots. The robots are each equipped with two photovoltaic goal sensors, two near-infrared robot-avoidance sensors and one stagnation sensor used to provide positive achievement feedback. As a demonstration, the robots form a homogeneous group of task-achieving autonomous agents capable of collectively locating and moving a box otherwise unmovable by a single robot. They accomplish this simple task without any central coordination or explicit communication between the robots. All communication is implicit and in the form of passive sensing and avoidance of other robots. The experimental result demonstrates the feasibility of constructing a simple homogeneous group of autonomous mobile robots to achieve tasks collectively.

The remainder of this paper is organized as follows. The next section describes several interesting examples of collective behaviour found in the literature on social insects. Based on these examples, we then present in section 3 our approach to controlling multiple mobile robots using *group behaviours* and the five mechanisms used to invoke them. Section 4 discusses our initial exploration of this biologically-inspired control strategy for autonomous behaviour-based mobile robots which we call the Collective Robotic Intelligence Project (CRIP). We then discuss our simulation results used to verify the first two mechanisms. Section 5 discusses a system of five homogeneous sensor-based mobile robots, capable of achieving simple collective tasks, which we constructed in order to test the feasibilty of the first mechanism. Finally, section 6 provides a summary and discusses the advantages and disadvantages of this approach to controlling multiple mobile robots and suggests some directions for future research.

2 Collective Behaviour in Social Insects

Life provides us with countless examples of collective task achieving societies. Bees, ants and termites all function collectively in groups, efficiently accomplishing tasks with, seemingly simple, insect intelligence. Can the study of collective behaviour in social insects lead to a viable control strategy for autonomous robots? [9, 23, 27, 1] have proposed various cooperative strategies for autonomous robots inspired by social insects. By examining several specific examples of collective behaviour, we have found that the vast array of task achieving behaviours displayed by social insects are a result of the diverse assortment of sensing capabilities. Moreover, it is this sensor array that serves to trigger the behavioural patterns which result in the emergent collective behaviour [28, 18]. It would appear that evolution has made up for a lack of higher level reasoning, in insects, by increasing the number of behaviour producing sensors. Whereas man has made up for a lack of sensors by developing higher level reasoning.

For behavioural biologists one of the main problems in understanding how an insect society functions, is to be able to deduce collective activity from individual behaviour. Some believe that collective behaviour is not simply the sum of each participant's behaviour, as others emerge at the society level[20]. This they claim creates a paradox—how can individual ants appear so inefficient and disorganized, for example in their nest building activity, while at the same time build highly elaborate nest structures?

To answer such a question, Pasteels *et al.* [20] feel researchers adopt one of several attitudes. The first is to consider that their behaviour is far less random than it appears. This is the viewpoint taken by the majority of communication or division of labour studies. Ants are not random particles, they do communicate and subtle forms of division of labour are often observed.

A second attitude is to consider the behavioural variance as being irrelevant to the society's functioning. Descriptions of behavioural sequences are reported in deterministic terms, with only the functional acts being reported as the observations of the society are filtered.

Another view is to admit randomness at the individual level could be part of the society's functioning[20]. Due to their great number, Oster and Wilson [19] have suggested that social insects can well afford behavioural variance. This variance, they claim, could increase the probability that a social activity will eventually be performed. Their collective reliability more than compensates for the individual inefficiency.

In the absence of a stochastic theory, our attention has been focused on several specific examples of collective behaviour[14]. Using a common task, [29] described nest construction by weaver ants. Weaver ants construct the walls of their nest by folding leaves. They begin by spreading over its surface and randomly tug at any edge they can grasp. One part is turned more easily than the others, and the initial success causes other ants to aid the effort and abandon their own.

A second example of collective behaviour, we found

interesting, involves invoking a *follow behaviour* used in such activities as *swarming*. Several different sensor modalities are used to invoke the behaviour. Tandem running, which uses tactile sensing, rapid running, which uses visual sensing and odour trails are all examples of a *follow behaviour* which cause the insects to move as a group[28].

A third example involves invoking collective behaviour by a stimulus in the environment. These *environmental cues* invoke the same behaviour in the insects almost simultaneously. For example, bees use light intensity to govern the amount of time used for food collecting behaviours [22]. Similarly, some ants begin their daily foraging activity upon the detection of the light of dawn[21]. Thus, in these cases events in the environment (i.e. dawn or dusk) serve to activate the collective behaviour.

Another example suggests that ants alter their behaviour when found in large groups. For example, worker ants were found to excavate the soil and attend larvae at a higher rate when found in large groups[11]. Wilson [28] found that when workers of *Acanthomyops claviger* are kept in solitude, they are nearly insensitive to the natural alarm substances of the species. In contrast, those placed in the same nest with a few hundred nestmates respond normally to the alarm substances.

The last example, which motivated our mechanisms, is called *autostimulation* and involves an individual insect invoking the collective behaviour using an alarm substance. In Stuart's nest reparation experiments [25, 26], termites used chemical odour to attract additional workers to the site of repair activity. Foraging workers were found to communicate with themselves when they dispense orientation pheromones in their odour trails and then follow the traces during the return journey to the target areas[12]. These examples demonstrate how an insect can invoke a collective behaviour (i.e. nest-building or trail-following) within its own colony.

Although the field of behavioral biology lacks a common theory that adequately explains the collective behaviour of social insects, it does provide many well researched observations that can be used in our quest for a theory to control multiple autonomous mobile robots. In the next section we outline our proposed mechanisms for invoking group behaviour in mobile robots.

3 Collective Behaviour in Autonomous Robots

The collective behaviour which we seek for our autonomous robots is in the same vein as emergent behaviour, a key concept, in Artificial Life [15]. Collective behaviour can be viewed as an emergent property[1] of a self-organizing system with a few simple rules of interaction. This emergent property results from the system interacting with its dynamic environment. Collective tasks must therefore be designed with an interaction loop comprising of the system and the environment, ultimately converging towards the desired performance. In order to achieve collective behaviour[2] we must first learn to control groups of autonomous robots. Our approach is to design robots with group behaviours. From the examples of the previous section we propose five mechanisms with which to invoke a group behaviour, resulting in the collective behaviour of the system.

The first mechanism used to invoke the group behaviour makes use of a *common goal* and *non-interference* as a simple form of cooperation. For example, if we design a group of robots to locate and converge upon a single object and while doing so the robots do not interfere with one another, we have then successfully controlled the movement of the group as a whole. Non-interference as suggested by Yuta and Premvuti [30] is a simple form of cooperation in which the robots do not interfere with the operation of other robots in the group. In our implementation (described in section 5) non-interference simply becomes *robot-avoidance*. Collective tasks can be designed in which the common task invokes the group behaviour. For example, robots equipped with heat and fire sensors roam an area until a fire causes them to converge and extinguish the flame.

The second mechanism creates a 'herd' of robots by using a *follow* behaviour. The collective task may require that groups of robots remain together. Consider grass cutting by a group of small robots who travel in herds. The control of the group is accomplished using a behaviour designed to keep them together; the task is accomplished by having all the robots execute a function (i.e. cutting) while the group is moved through its environment.

The third mechanism uses *environmental cues* to invoke group behaviour. Both dawn and dusk provide ants with a visual cue to begin or end food collecting behaviours and are an example of an environmental cue. Collective tasks can be designed to allow the environment, in which the robots work, to provide the cue that invokes the group behaviour. For example, a group of building cleaning robots, designed to keep the outside surface of buildings clean, would begin their activity at dusk by depositing photosensitive chemicals on the outside surface. Cleaning action would begin the next day when the chemical reacted with sunlight.

The fourth mechanism relies on the ability of the robot to detect if it is within a group before invoking its group behaviour. Sensors would be placed around

[1] See[24] for an excellent discussion of emergent properties.

[2] A precursor to Collective Intelligence.

the periphery of the robot, enabling it to detect other robots both in front and behind as well as to the left and right. The group behaviour is then executed once the robot finds itself surrounded by other robots. For example, bulldozer robots designed to level the ground would only be effective once a large group was formed travelling in the same direction. The robots in the center of the group would execute the group behaviour while those on the periphery would be responsible for navigating the group over the surface to be leveled. This mechanism to control multiple robots would be useful if the group behaviour required the robots to be in a certain formation, for example, when cleaning a hockey rink of snow.

The fifth mechanism invokes group behaviour through autostimulation. For example, suppose we are using a group of robots to search an area for a particular substance; once a single robot finds the substance it broadcasts a signal which in turn invokes a group behaviour in all robots receiving the signal. This method of control is different from the above mechanisms because it is a form of *self-facilitation*[3].

The above mechanisms, taken from examples of collective behaviour in social insects, are designed to control groups of mobile robots. In doing so we hope to achieve tasks unsuitable or impossible for a single robot. In this respect, this work shares in the goals of the Distributed Robotic Systems [3] which are suited for such tasks as distributed actuation or distributed perception. The mechanisms proposed do not represent a comprehensive set, but rather strategies we have found based on observations from the study of social insects. In the next section we discuss the verification of the first two mechanisms by simulation.

4 Verification by Simulation

The ultimate goal of this work is to design and build a number of real physical robots capable of achieving simple tasks collectively. In this section we present our robot population simulator *SimbotCity* and discuss its use as a tool for investigating control mechanisms used to control populations of mobile robots. We have verified by simulation the first two control mechanisms of the previous section. We have found it is possible to control a group of mobile robots using a common task and a simple non-interference cooperation strategy and that groups of mobile robots could be kept together in herds, and therefore controlled, using a simple *follow* behaviour. Other control mechanisms can be similarly examined with simple modifications.

[3] A term taken from the psychological literature meaning communication that promotes rather than inhibits activity.

4.1 Simulation Objectives

When multiple robots start to interact a whole series of new issues begin to surface. Brooks[6] outlined several of these issues, a subset of which we shall consider here.

Emergence Each robot's control system consists of a set of behaviours, we would like to see what the collective behaviour of a group of homogeneous robots will be. Further, if an incremental modification to the individual robot is made, we would like to determine its effect on the collective behaviour of the group.

Cooperation In achieving collective tasks, some form of cooperation will be necessary. This may simply take the form of not interfering with other robots, as they progress towards a common goal, as [30] have suggested or may involve some other form of cooperation requiring more explicit communication.

Allocation We would like to know the minimum number of robots necessary to accomplish a collective task. Brooks[6] refers to this as 'density-dependence'. Also, should we decide to use more than the minimum number, at what point does the system cease to be functional due to the glut of robots? For example, a task requiring the spatial distribution of robots along one side of an object can eventually have too many robots to perform the task effectively.

Herding There are advantages in keeping a group of robots together. Collectively they can respond much more quickly to a given stimulus than if they are more spatially distributed. An example might be a group of fire fighting robots whose *extinguish* behaviour activates upon fire detection. A group would respond quicker to the blaze and gain control easier than just one robot. Given the limited local perceptive abilities of the robots, what are the suitable behaviours needed for herding?

These are the issues we wish to investigate with simulation; and the lessons learned in the process, have served as a guide in building the physical system.

4.2 SimbotCity: A Robot Population Simulator

SimbotCity is our simulator used to model robot populations (see Figure 1). A robot model consists of a set of sensor and actuator resources as well as a set of behaviour modules that map sensor inputs to actuator outputs. Behavior arbitration is currently handled with a modified fixed priority ***subsumption*** architecture[4].

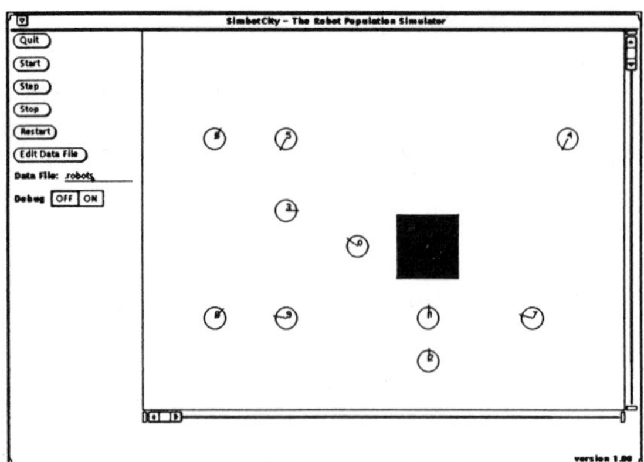

Figure 1: Initial robot configuration. Robots must locate and collectively push the black box.

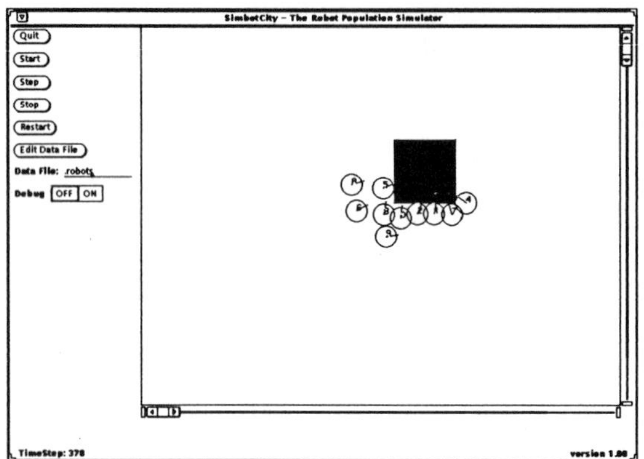

Figure 2: Robot configuration after 378 simulation steps; box is being pushed upwards.

4.3 Control Mechanism 1: *common task*

In order to verify the feasibility of the first control mechanism, we created a simple common task requiring the collective efforts of at least two robots to accomplish. The task involved locating and pushing an object in the robots' environment, a task otherwise unaccomplishable by a single robot due to the weight of the object.

A simple form of cooperation called *non-interference*[30] was employed which successfully kept the robots from colliding with one another as they converged on the goal (see Figure 1 and Figure 2).

Since the task required the robots to spatially distribute themselves along the sides of the object, we found that any number of robots greater than the number that could fit on the surface of the object was redundant for this particular task.

Once an object was located, the robots collectively pushed the object off an edge of their world. Should a robot find itself pushing on the opposite side of a group, a progress behaviour which monitors progress towards the goal invokes an avoidance response allowing the robot to assume a new position on the object. Behaviours used to implement an individual robot's control are explained in[14].

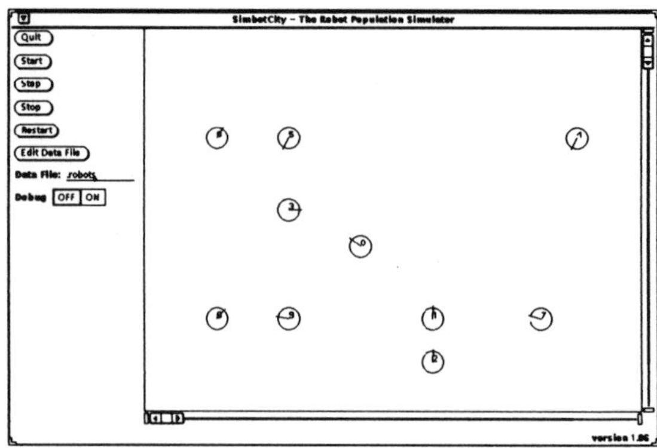

Figure 3: Initial robot configuration. Robots must locate and follow another robot.

By combining a common task and non-interference as a cooperation strategy a group of simulated robots could be successfully controlled to execute a collective task otherwise unaccomplishable by a single robot. The first mechanism is further verified in Section 5. Next we consider the second mechanism for group control.

4.4 Control Mechanism 2: *follow behaviours*

To test *follow* behaviours as a means of controlling a group of mobile robots, we equipped each simulated robot with sensors to detect other robots. The idea is based on equipping our physical robots with near-infrared transmitter-receiver pairs for robot detection.

A follow behaviour was designed which caused the robot to move towards a detected neighbouring robot. Robots begin by executing a random walk until a robot is detected, at which point the follow behaviour is invoked. Avoidance behaviours keep the forward moving robots from colliding. Herds begin to form with robots executing a random walk leading the herd (see Figure 3). Once formed, the herd remains intact by adapting the follow behaviour using a *behaviour preference*.

Behavior preferences are methods by which a behaviour module narrows its focus on sensor inputs. For example, the follow behaviour receives sensor input with an initial *sensor-view-angle* of 180 degrees, allowing the robot to 'see' in a very wide forward-looking direction. As the robot joins a herd by following a neighbouring robot its behaviour preference narrows the sensor's view angle to 45 degrees, ensuring the robot is not distracted from its group by another herd passing in close proximity. In this way the robot is able to adapt its behaviour to suit the task at hand. This method is similar to

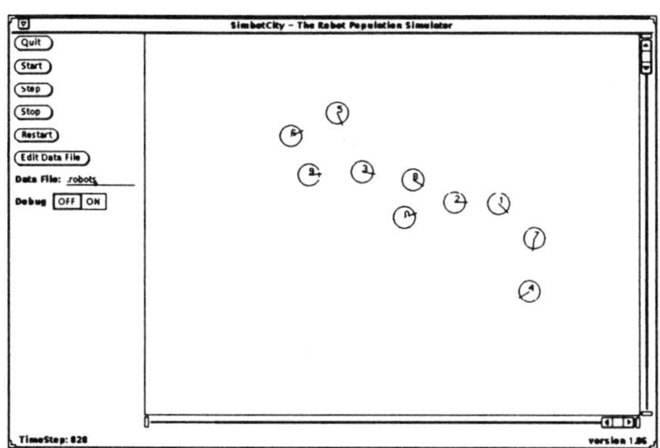

Figure 4: Robot configuration after 828 simulation steps; robots have formed a herd using a follow behaviour.

the way humans adjust their focus-of-attention in visual tasks.

The follow behaviour coupled with behaviour preferences successfully controls a group of simulated robots and allows them to form a variety of 'herd' configurations (see Figure 4). This control mechanism can be combined with the first mechanism to allow groups of robots to roam in herds searching for objects to push. By keeping robots together in a herd the system of robots responds more quickly to the task at hand due to the simultaneous sensing of an object by several robots. We found this increases the likelihood that the distribution of robots around the perimeter of the object will be asymmetrical, causing the object to move in one direction quicker than if a symmetrical distribution occurred simultaneously. In the next section we discuss a system of five homogeneous mobile robots designed and constructed to further verify the first control mechanism.

5 Verification by Implementation

In order to test the *common task* control mechanism, verified by simulation, in the real world we have constructed a system of five identical behaviour-based mobile robots capable of achieving simple collective tasks without centralized coordination or use of explicit communication. Control of the group of robots is accomplished by having each robot work toward a common goal. A simple form of cooperation among the robots is achieved through non-interference as they progress towards the common task. This is accomplished with a simple robot-avoidance behaviour. Each robot is autonomous and equipped with sensors for detecting both the goal (a brightly lit object) and obstacles in their environment.

In this section we present a simple collective task implementation and discuss its use in verifying the first control mechanism. We found it was possible to control a group of robots without the need for explicit communication or centralized coordination using simple reflexive behaviours and a common task control mechanism. We begin by outlining our objectives in constructing robots and present the collective task we have demonstrated.

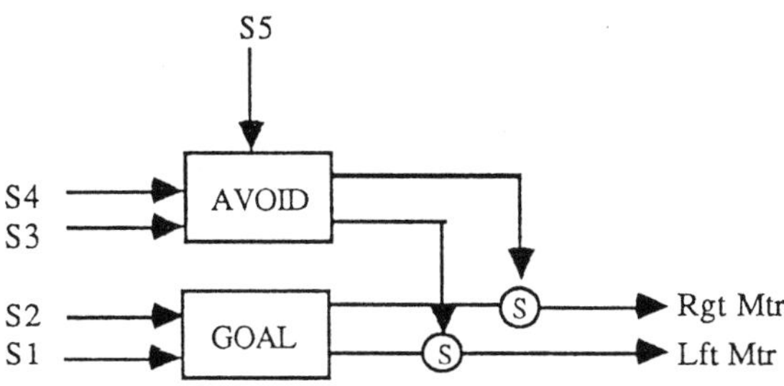

Figure 5: The box-pushing robot's control model used to control two wheel motors.

5.1 Implementation Objectives

Building physical robots and testing their performance and dynamic interaction in the real world is the ultimate test for any *proposed* system. In doing so, we hoped to discover how well the proposed control mechanism did or did not work. By having already tested the control strategy in simulation we have lessened the burden and increased the likelihood for success.

The collective task we chose to implement was *box-pushing*. The task is such that it cannot be accomplished by one robot due to the weight of the box; therefore, the collective effort of several robots is necessary. To accomplish this task the robots must locate the box; move toward it while avoiding collisions with other robots; distribute themselves along a side and push. In doing so, we hoped to test the first control mechanism, namely, control of the group can result by executing a common goal oriented collective task. We also hoped to test the simple cooperative strategy of non-interference thereby verifying its usefulness in collective behaviour.

5.2 A Simple Collective Task

The box-pushing robot's architecture consists of GOAL and AVOID behaviour modules implemented in simple combinational logic circuits. The GOAL behaviour functions to locate and guide the robot toward the box, while the AVOID behaviour handles obstacle avoidance including other robots. The control model is illustrated in Figure 5.

Each robot is equipped with five sensors. Sensors *S1* and *S2* are used by the GOAL behaviour to locate the box. Sensors *S3* and *S4* provide forward looking

Figure 6: Initial configuration of three box-pushing robots before sensing the box at the top of the picture.

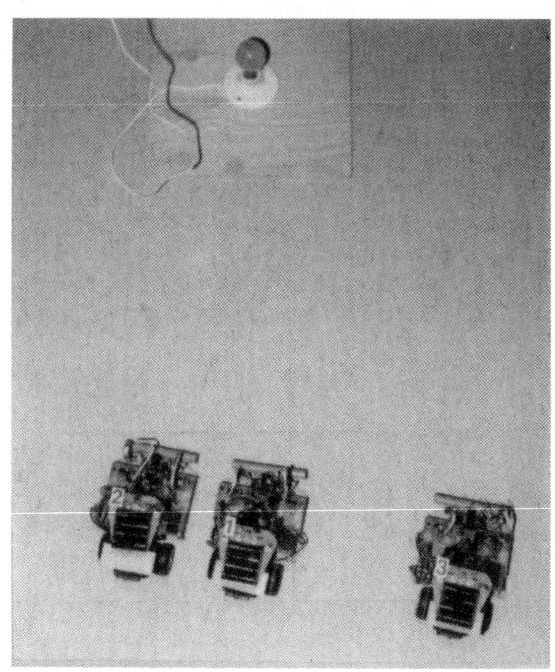

Figure 7: Robots 1 and 2 about to collide before avoid behaviour activated.

obstacle detection and sensor *S5* is used to detect lack of progress toward the goal. A simple fixed priority between the behaviours controls arbitration with the AVOID behaviour having the highest priority.

All demonstrations designed to test the system were video recorded. The robots were placed in an initial configuration, much the same way as in simulation. By adjusting the goal sensors to respond to the light on the box only, the system could be started and stopped by turning the box light on and off. Video recordings were useful in that it allowed us to review test runs, making corrective adjustments in between.

The system was tested with a variety of initial configurations. The robots converged on the goal and pushed the box in a number of directions depending on how many robots were on a given side (see Figure 6, Figure 7, and Figure 8). In the event that a robot began pushing on a side opposite a group of robots, and subsequently was pushed backwards along with the box, a progress sensor invoked the avoidance behaviour allowing the robot to find a new spot on the box. As the robots progressed toward the box the AVOID behaviour kept the robots from colliding for the majority of the time. Collisions occurred whenever the sensors missed an oncom-

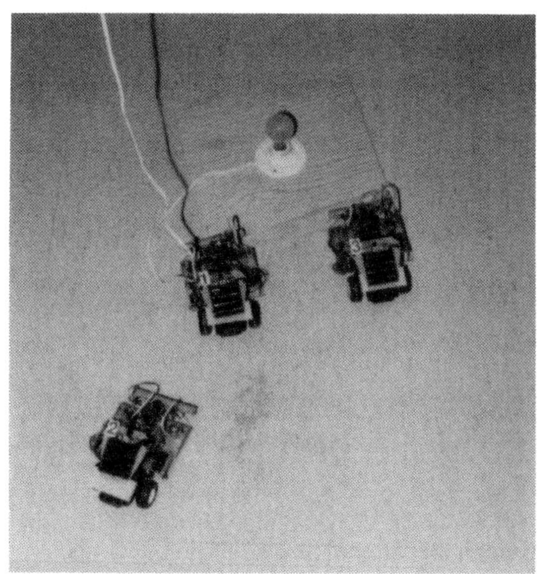

Figure 8: Robot 1 overtakes robot 2 to avoid a collision, while progressing towards the box. Robots 1 and 3 pushing the box forward

ing robot. Reliability of the AVOID behaviour could be increased by adding additional obstacle sensors.

We also observed that stagnation could occur in the system if the robots approached the box from all sides resulting in an equal distribution and force applied to the sides of the box. In this case the robots did not move the box. This could be solved with a *stagnation detection* behaviour, to be implemented, which would have as input a sensor monitoring constant wheel motion.

The system demonstrated that the common task control mechanism was a feasible approach to controlling a small group of robots using a non-interference cooperation strategy. In the next section we present our conclusions and discuss future work.

6 Conclusions and Future Work

Research in behaviour-based robotics has led to radically different architectures for controlling autonomous robots. These new architectures emphasize a more direct coupling of perception to action and a dynamic interaction with the environment resulting in systems with emergent properties. Systems that choose to employ this methodology must be designed in a way that makes use of an interaction loop between the system and the environment which ultimately converges towards the desired performance. Most research projects have concentrated on designing *single* autonomous robots capable of achieving a simple insect-like intelligence. Useful tasks may be accomplished with these simple behaviour-based control mechanisms provided multiple robots are organized into collections of task achieving populations.

The research described in this paper attempts as a first step to propose five control mechanisms suitable for controlling populations of behaviour-based robots. Our approach to controlling multiple robots involves the use of group behaviours which may be invoked using several sensory-based mechanisms. The mechanisms proposed have resulted from the study of social insects which exhibit collective task achieving behaviours. To test our control mechanisms we created a simulator, called *SimbotCity*, which allowed us to create configurations of multiple robots designed to achieve simple collective tasks. Once satisfied the control strategies were feasible, we then constructed a system of five physical robots designed to accomplish a simple collective task, without any centralized coordination or use of explicit communication. The approach, employed to control the group of five robots, involved having the robots work toward a common goal. Using non-interference as a simple form of cooperation, the robots were able to collectively locate and push a brightly lit box in their environment.

An important feature of the system is that simple reflexive behaviours can be used to control the individual robot in a goal directed manner using equally simple binary sensors. The behaviours and their arbitration mechanism are constructed using simple combinational logic. An important implication of this simplicity is that the control architecture could be scaled down to fit on a small silicon chip. This would allow for the creation of a large number of small cost effective robots to be used in areas too small for more traditional robots.

What is lacking in this approach to collective behaviour is a formal mathematics on which to base control models designed to solve tasks requiring multiple robots. Kiss[13] suggests using process dynamics, or Chaos Theory, with its well established mathematical theory, as a tool with which to study the behaviour of autonomous intelligent systems. If successfully applied, process dynamics could aid in the understanding of collective behaviour and its control models. A structured methodology for designing collective tasks is needed. Currently this is more of an 'art' than science. How should a control strategy be synthesized in terms of simple mechanisms? And what is their relationship in both time and space? Some of these questions could be answered if a formal theory can be established to analyze and design the control strategy.

The remaining three control mechanisms need to be verified in simulation as well as implementation. The research described is intended to be an initial exploration into achieving tasks collectively using a system of multiple robots. As such, its primary goal was to examine the feasibility of the approach we have outlined in this paper. Achieving collective behaviour with multiple robots is the first step in achieving Collective Robotic Intelligence.

References

[1] Ronald C. Arkin. Cooperation without communication: Multiagent schema-based robot navigation. *Journal of Robotic Systems*, 9(3):351–364, 1992.

[2] Hajime Asama, Maki K. Habib, Isao Endo, Koichi Ozaki, Akihiro Matsumoto, and Yoshiki Ishida. Functional distribution among multiple mobile robots in an autonomous and decentralized robot system. In *1991 IEEE International Conference on Robotics and Automation*, pages 1921–1926, 1991.

[3] Gerardo Beni and Jing Wang. Theoretical problems for the realization of distributed robotic systems. In *1991 IEEE International Conference on Robotics and Automation*, pages 1914–1920, 1991.

[4] Rodney A. Brooks. A robust layered control system for a mobile robot. *IEEE Journal of Robotics and Automation*, RA-2(1):14–23, March 1986.

[5] Rodney A. Brooks. Challenges for complete creature architectures. In *First International Conference on Simulation of Adaptive Behavior*, pages 434–443, Cambridge, MA, 1990. MIT Press.

[6] Rodney A. Brooks. Intelligence without reason. AI Memo 1293, MIT, 1991.

[7] Rodney A. Brooks and Anita M. Flynn. Fast, cheap and out of control. AI Memo 1182, MIT, 1989.

[8] P. Dario, F. Ribechini, V. Genovese, and G. Sandini. Instinctive behaviors and personalities in societies of cellular robots. In *1991 IEEE International Conference on Robotics and Automation*, pages 1927–1932, 1991.

[9] J-L. Deneubourg, S. Goss, N. Franks, A. Sendova-Franks, C. Detrain, and L. Chretien. The dynamics of collective sorting robot-like ants and ant-like robots. In *First International Conference on Simulation of Adaptive Behavior*, pages 356–363, Cambridge, MA, 1990. MIT Press.

[10] Toshio Fukuda, Tsuyoshi Ueyama, and Fumihito Arai. Control strategy for a network of cellular robots. In *1991 IEEE International Conference on Robotics and Automation*, pages 1616–1621, 1991.

[11] W. Hangartner. Carbon dioxide, a releaser for digging behavior in solenopis geminata. *Psyche*, 76:58–67, 1969.

[12] B. Holldobler, M. Moglich, and U. Maschwitz. Communication by tandem running in the ant camponotus sericeus. *Journal of Comparative Physiology*, 90:105–127, 1974.

[13] George Kiss. Autonomous agents, AI and chaos theory. In *First International Conference on Simulation of Adaptive Behavior*, pages 518–524, Cambridge, MA, 1990. MIT Press.

[14] C. Ronald Kube. Collective robotic intelligence: A control theory for robot populations. Master's thesis, University of Alberta, Edmonton, Alberta, 1992.

[15] C. Langton. Artificial life. In *Proceeding of the First Conference on Artificial Life*, pages 1–47, 1987.

[16] Pattie Maes, editor. *Designing Autonomous Agents: Theory and Practice from Biology to Engineering and Back.* MIT Press, Cambridge, MA, 1990.

[17] Maja J. Mataric. Minimizing complexity in controlling a mobile robot robotic population. In *1992 IEEE International Conference on Robotics and Automation*, pages 830–835, 1992.

[18] J.C. Moser. Pheromones of social insects. In D. Wood, R. Silverstein, and M. Nakajima, editors, *Control of Insect Behavior by Natural Products*, pages 161–178. Academic Press, 1970.

[19] G.F. Oster and E.O. Wilson. *Caste and Ecology in Social Insects.* Princeton University Press, 1978.

[20] J.M. Pasteels, J. Deneubourg, and S. Gross. Self-organization mechanisms in ant societies: Trail recruitment to newly discovered food sources. In J.M. Pasteels and J. Deneubourg, editors, *From Individual to Collective Behavior in Social Insects*, pages 155–175, 1987.

[21] T.C. Schneirla. The army ants. In *Report of The Smithsonian Institution for 1955*, pages 379–406, 1955.

[22] B. Schricker. Die orientierung der honigbiene in der dammerung zugleich ein beitrag zur frage der ocellenfunktion bei bienen. *Zeitschrift fur Vergleichende Physiologie*, 49:420–458, 1965.

[23] Luc Steels. Cooperation between distributed agents through self-organisation. In Yves Demazeau and Jean-Pierre Muller, editors, *Decentralized A.I.*, pages 175–196, Amsterdam, 1990. North-Holland.

[24] Luc Steels. Towards a theory of emergent functionality. In *First International Conference on Simulation of Adaptive Behavior*, pages 451–461, Cambridge, MA, 1990. MIT Press.

[25] A.M. Stuart. Alarm, defence, and construction behavior relationships in termites (*isoptera*). *Science*, 156:1123–1125, 1967.

[26] A.M. Stuart. Social behavior and communication. *Biology of Termites*, 1:193–232, 1969.

[27] G. Theraulaz, S. Goss, J. Gervet, and J-L. Deneubourg. Task differentiation in polistes wasp colonies: a model for self-organizing groups of robots. In *First International Conference on Simulation of Adaptive Behavior*, pages 346–355, Cambridge, MA, 1990. MIT Press.

[28] E.O. Wilson. *The Insect Societies.* The Belkap Press of Harvard University Press, 1971.

[29] E.O. Wilson and B. Holldobler. *The Ants.* The Belkap Press of Harvard University Press, 1990.

[30] S. Yuta and S. Premvuti. Consideration on cooperation of multiple autonomous mobile robots. *IEEE/RSJ International Workshop on Intelligent Robots and Systems*, pages 545–549, 1991.

Collective Choice of Strategic Type

Chisato Numaoka and Akikazu Takeuchi

Sony Computer Science Laboratory Inc.
Takanawa Muse Building, 3-14-13 Higashi-gotanda,
Shinagawa-ku, Tokyo, 141 JAPAN
chisato@csl.sony.co.jp
takeuchi@csl.sony.co.jp

Abstract

This paper proposes a computational model for an emergent collective behavior that collectively changes strategic type, such as from attack to defence, as seen in any kind of battle. This paper describes the result of an experimental simulation with multiple autonomous robots based on the proposed model. Our model first defines payoff functions that create multiple equilibrium states, each of which corresponds to one strategic type. Subsequently, we attempt to model the dynamics that cause the robots to change their choice of strategic type collectively when a small number of robots change their chosen type. In these dynamics, we pay particular attention to how many robots, called *instigators*, are required to make all robots eventually change their strategic type. In addition, to make it easy for all robots to change their strategic type, we provide a mechanism by which the robots themselves reduce the utility of strategies.

1 Introduction

Probably the most important advantage of autonomous robots is, in contrast to non-autonomous robots, their robustness; even without a complete description of their possible working environment, the robots can dynamically adapt their behavior by gathering information directly from their surroundings. Robots with robustness are expected to work well in unpredictable circumstance (e.g. on other planets). This advantage has been pointed out by many researchers (e.g. [Brooks 86, Maes 90, Steels 91]). Autonomous robots would thus be able to take full advantage of their ability when used for exploring other planets.

There are, nevertheless, limits to the capability of a single robot. Suppose we have only one autonomous robot acting as a mine detector and we are going to detect a mine laid in the sand. The robot has to follow this mission itself. However, the robot may, if unlucky, be damaged as a result of not having detected a mine, or go wrong because of severe weather conditions.

The use of multiple robots is one possibility. In this case, we gain the advantage of having many workers engaged in a single task. If the task can be divided into many fine-grained sub-tasks performed independently of other sub-tasks, the efficiency of achieving the task will increase linearly as the number of robots increases. Nevertheless, having multiple autonomous robots is somewhat troublesome. This is because most of the tasks to be achieved by multiple robots require coordination.

Controlling multiple robots without losing their autonomy is not so easy. Control and autonomy are intrinsically opposite notions. We want to control multiple autonomous robots as little as possible. Rather, we want to give robots a tendency to cooperatively work together toward one team goal while letting them act autonomously. The problem here is how to give such a cooperative nature to autonomous robots. Here we are interested in autonomous robots that can dynamically find their role and decide the action they are to take. Their decision must be appropriate not only from each individual's viewpoint but also from their group's viewpoint. The collective behavior described here is an example of "teamwork." Teamwork is collective behavior appropriate to the situation where there is a task to be carried out by multiple participants but there is no control structure overseeing them. In a teamwork, members must decide their behavior autonomously with consideration to tasks performed by other members so that they can create a cooperative collective behavior. The feature of teamwork is the robustness of the collective behavior. Two critical issues of teamwork for robustness must be considered.

First, it is required that robots be able to consistently choose one strategic type. Suppose that a number of robots are fighting a fire and they are basically of two strategic types: attack and defence. The strategies of the attack type are to fight with chemicals, bombs, and so on. Those of the defence type concentrate on trying to escape, find shelter, and so on. When a fire is weak, attack strategies are expected. When it is strong, defence strategies are recommended for the robots to protect themselves. Note that defence strategies among attack strategies are inefficient, conversely attack strategies among defence ones are dangerous. Therefore it is desirable for robots, as a whole, to choose one strategic type to reflect the situation.

Second, according to a change in the situation, robots may be required to change their strategic types. Whenever this requirement happens, even among a small number of robots, and the number is continuously increasing, it is desired that all robots collectively change their strategic type. Suppose that a group of robots is again fighting a fire. If a fire were strong, some robots would suffer relatively heavy damage and others would have only light damage. Because of the accumulated heavy damage, eventually a robot may make a "serious" change in its strategic type from *attack* to *defence*. Here, by the term "serious" we mean a long-standing decision. The number of such robots depends on the strength of the fire. Even a robot with light damage may think that the current strategic type is not so effective. In this situation, we often observe the phenomenon of "collective change of strategies."

To date, Huberman, Hogg et al. have published many articles describing various aspects of collective behavior in relation to non-linear dynamics causing a variety of oscillations including chaos [Huberman and Hogg 88]. Team-like behavior, however, has not been considered well where, under a multi-stable system, robots are collectively changing from one strategic type to another, where one strategic type forms one stable state.

In this paper, we describe non-linear dynamics that bring forth this sort of team-like collective behavior on autonomous robots, where we assume global communication with the restricted purpose of knowing the population of robots choosing a strategy. The rest of this paper is organized as follows: Section 2 describes a model of the emergence of team-like collective behavior and analyses the properties of non-linear dynamics exhibited as the result of the autonomous decision making behavior of multiple robots. We propose the methodology of a strategic type alteration guided by a relatively small number of robots, called *instigators*, that act as the trigger for all other robots to change a set of strategies. Section 3 shows the result of computer simulations that realize an example of a world of multiple autonomous robots. In Section 4, we discuss remaining issues and related work. Finally, we conclude this paper in Section 5.

2 The Model

2.1 A game-theoretical model of autonomous robots

We consider a collection of mutually interacting autonomous robots, all of which are functionally equal. The behavior of each robot is ruled by a game-theoretical model developed by Huberman et al. [Huberman and Hogg 88]. First we overview their model.

The model consists of a number of robots. They make their decisions asynchronously. Whenever they make a decision, they are free to choose a strategy from among a number of strategies, according to the perceived payoff. The payoff function for the i-th strategy, taking account of cooperation with finite capacity is defined as follows:

$$P_i(n_i) = (U - \Gamma n_i)(P_0 + Cn_i) \tag{1}$$

where n_i is the number of robots taking the i-th strategy, and U, Γ, P_0, C are positive parameters. U, Γ, P_0, C are the capacity, the positive amount by which the payoff decreases as each additional robot adopts the strategy, payoff accrued in the absence of any cooperation, and extra benefit due to cooperation, respectively. In the real world, it is impossible to obtain exact information about the environment, including the states of other robots. Even when appropriate knowledge is obtained, a certain amount of time delay is inevitable. In their model, imperfect knowledge is modeled by introducing error into the perceived payoffs, and time delay is modeled by delay in perceiving payoffs.

Huberman et al. showed that the asymptotic behavior of a collection of robots consists of complicated oscillations, chaotic behavior and intermittent oscillations.

2.2 Model of collective adaptive behavior

Let us consider the case in which strategies are grouped into types. Within the same type, robots can choose any strategy, but strategies of different types may interfere with each other.

We propose the following payoff function to satisfy the above characteristics:

$$P_i(\mathbf{n}) = (U - \Gamma n_i)(P_0 + Cn_i) - Dn_i \sum_{j \notin type(i)} n_j \tag{2}$$

where $\mathbf{n}$ is a vector of n_i's, U, Γ, P_0, C, D are positive parameters, the first four having the same meanings as before. *type(i)* is a function that returns the same set of strategies as the i-th strategy. Compared with Equation (1), the second term is introduced to represent the loss incurred in mixing different strategic types. For simplicity, we neglect the negative payoff yielded by Equation (2). Thus, instead of Equation (2), the following payoff function, which replaces a negative payoff with a small positive constant value, is used:

$$P_i(\mathbf{n}) = \max((U - \Gamma n_i)(P_0 + C n_i) \\ -D n_i \sum_{j \notin type(i)} n_j, \quad P_{min}) \qquad (3)$$

Proposition 2.1 *The payoff function defined in Equation (3) has multiple equilibrium states. Each equilibrium corresponds to one strategic type that is the only strategic type chosen in the equilibrium.*

2.3 Collective change of strategic types

Our primary goal is to show that a group of robots having multiple strategic types has such dynamics that a change in the strategic type in a small number of robots, which we henceforth call *instigators*, causes the same change throughout the whole group. This implies in the underlying dynamics that a group of robots moves from one equilibrium to another by being triggered by the migration of a small number of robots. Such dynamics give powerful adaptability to a group of robots since even a small change in an environment, recognized by a small number of robots, can cause a global change in the strategic type.

Now we can see two important phenomena in the case of collective change of strategies. They are:

1. serious change in the strategic types of instigators, and
2. the widely acknowledged perception of the ineffectiveness of the current strategic type.

Neither of these can be a reason for causing global change of strategic type, but if these two are perceived simultaneously then they constitute a good reason for the global change.

With the following slight modification, our model can cover the above situation. Phenomenon (1) can be modeled by instigators that keep choosing a specific strategy no matter what payoffs they receive. Phenomenon (2) can be captured in the model by the reinterpretation of the parameter U in Equation (3) as the utility of i-th strategy, which is generally a function of an environment such that it may change in response to the environmental change.

It will be shown by simulation that even when one strategic type is dominant, if the utility of that strategic type is decreasing and a certain number of robots make a long-standing decision to discard the current strategic type and choose another, this partial change causes a global change such that all robots discard their current strategic type and adopt a new one. Mathematically speaking, this corresponds to the movement from one stable equilibrium to another, as triggered by a small displacement. If the utility U is large enough ($\geq \Gamma N$, where N is the total number of robots), it is difficult to break the stable state by the term $-n_i(t)(\sum_{j \notin type(i)} n_j(t))$. As long as the variation from the stable state is relatively small, a restoration force will act to preserve the stable state. Therefore, a decrease in the current utility has the effect of making the current state less stable. The minimum size of a subgroup of robots that causes the global change is of great interest. The ratio of this subgroup size to the whole size is called the "critical ratio."

There are many equilibrium states in this system, each of which corresponds to one strategic type. For simplicity, we assume that the number of strategic types is two, i.e., type 1 and type 2. Also we assume that type 1 and type 2 have three (i.e. 1, 2, 3) and two (i.e. 4, 5) strategies, respectively. Let us consider the case of the strategic type changing from type 1 to type 2. Let N be the total number of robots, M be the total number of strategies, and m be the number of strategies that the instigators choose. A critical ratio λ can be computed from the following consideration:

1. *calculates the ideal bifurcation state where a payoff of a strategy of type 1 is the same as the payoff of a strategy of type 2.* Note that, with respect to one strategic type, payoff functions have the same form. If we equate the payoffs of two types, we obtain the following equation:

   $$(U - \Gamma\frac{N-x}{m})(P_0 + C\frac{N-x}{m}) - D\frac{N-x}{m}x \\ = (U - \Gamma\frac{x}{M-m})(P_0 + C\frac{x}{M-m}) \\ -D\frac{x}{M-m}(N-x) \qquad (4)$$

   where x robots choose strategies of different types from those chosen by the instigators.

   When we solve this equation under the conditions that $C = 0.1$, $\Gamma = 1.0$, $P_0 = 0.2$, $U = 200.0$, $D = 0.1$, $N = 200$, $M = 5$, and $m = 2$, the value of x is 102.673.

2. *takes a strategic type that the maximal number of robots are choosing and gets the number of robots to each strategy, by way of dividing the number of robots by the number of strategies of the type.* In the example given in step 1, the number of robots choosing a type that instigators are also choosing is less than the number of robots choosing another type. Thus, the other type is the maximal type. By dividing 102.673 by 3, we get 34.224.

3. *multiplies the number of robots calculated in step 2 by the number of strategies of a type that instigators are choosing.* By multiplying 34.224 by 2, we get 68.448.

4. *calculates the number of instigators by subtracting the value calculated in step 3 from the number of*

robots of the type that instigators are choosing, as is calculated in step 1. The number of robots choosing a type that instigators are choosing is 97.327. Thus, the number of instigators is 28.879, the difference between 97.327 and 68.448. As a result, critical ratio λ is, in this case, 14.44 (%).

Since the ideal bifurcation state is hard to realize when all robots are choosing one strategic type, instead we attempt to realize an equivalent state with some instigators and reduced utility. Steps 2 to 4 are allocated for the calculation of the equivalent state where step 1 performs a calculation of the ideal state.

Readers may think that this mechanism is very similar to the technique of simulated annealing [Kirkpatrick *et al.* 83] or that adopted by the Bolzmann Machine [Ackley *et al.* 85]. In fact, the effect of reducing utility seems to correspond to that of temperature rise in simulated annealing or the Bolzmann Machine. We are now investigating this relationship in detail.

3 Experiments

Based on the model described above, we simulated what happens in real settings. Our purpose was to investigate the dynamics of the collective behavior of autonomous robots where multiple equilibrium states exist. Especially, we were interested in the case where partial behavior of the system eventually influences and changes the behavior of the total system.

For all simulations, we provided 200 robots in a rectangular region of 500×450. Figure 1 shows a sample snapshot of this simulation environment. In each simulation time, a robot gets from all other robots their chosen strategy and tries to change its strategy at rate α, called the *decision rate.* In the case of changing strategy, robots choose the i-th strategy with probability:

$$\rho_i = \frac{P_i}{\sum_{j=1}^{M} P_j} \qquad (5)$$

Through simulations, for simplicity, we use $C \times \Gamma$ as D in the payoff function described in Equation (3).

We provided three attacking strategies and two defending strategies. In terms of reducing utility, for simplicity, all robots were assumed to simultaneously reduce and fix their utility 20 time units after when instigators choose another strategic type. In the simulation of changing a strategic type to defence, we assumed that more than 50 time units have passed since all robots converged to attack type strategies.

3.1 Stabilizing a collective behavior

We first examine whether Equation (3) really represents multiple stable points, each of which corresponds to a situation in which all robots choose one strategic type. It is interesting to observe how the number of robots

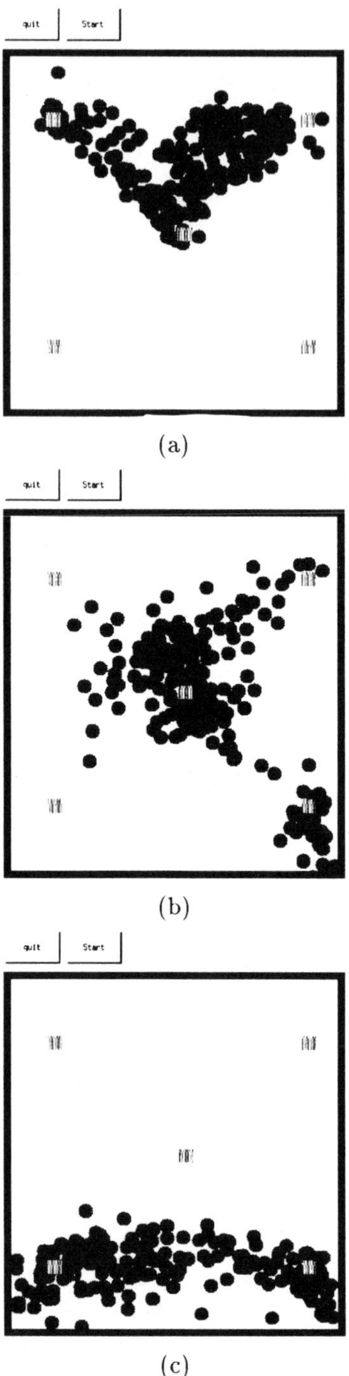

Figure 1: Snapshots of a Simulation: The black circles correspond to autonomous robots. Grey squares correspond to targets of a strategy: The upper three are attacking positions and the lower two are defending positions. Figure (a) shows a snapshot where 200 robots are choosing attacking type strategies, (b) shows a snapshot where 200 robots are in transient states, and (c) shows a snapshot where 200 robots are choosing defending type strategies.

choosing one particular strategy changes. In this simulation, we begin the simulation with initial distribution of populations of 34, 33, 33, 50, and 50 over five strategies.

The results of simulation for three sets of parameters and special conditions are shown in Figure 2. If both C and Γ are greater than the order of 0.001, we can obtain the expected effect regardless of the utility of strategies; multiple autonomous robots dynamically, asymptotically and rather rapidly choose one strategic type and then distribute to m strategies of that type in the ratio of $\frac{1}{m}$ (see Figure 2 (a)). If we consider communication delay, as Huberman and Hogg have pointed out [Huberman and Hogg 88], we can observe oscillations. Figure 2 (b) illustrates oscillation when the communication delay is τ=50 (time units, henceforth tu). Note that the number of robots choosing the 4th strategy exhibits an oscillation that eventually converges. By reducing the decision rate α to $\frac{1}{3}$, the effect of oscillation is weakened (See Figure 2 (c)).

On the contrary, if both C and Γ are fairly small, say less than the order of 0.0001, we never observe the expected effect in our simulation; multiple autonomous robots, irrespective of strategic types, distribute to M strategies in the ratio of $\frac{1}{M}$.

3.2 Transferring between stable states

To examine the dynamics by which all robots collectively change their strategic type followed by instigators, we begin simulations with an initial distribution of 67, 67, 66, 0, and 0 to five strategies. This state is assumed to have continued for at least 50 time units. This is because we introduce a communication delay of 50 time units. The values of parameters C, Γ, and P_0 are 0.1, 1.0, and 0.2, respectively. At the beginning of the simulation, λ percent of robots are supposed to change their strategy to the 5th strategy. Utility U is originally set to 200.0, changed at time t_1 to 80, and then restored at time t_2. Namely, U is defined as the following step function of time t:

$$U(t) = \begin{cases} 80 & \text{if } t_1 \leq t \leq t_2; \\ 200 & \text{otherwise.} \end{cases} \qquad (6)$$

Various simulations were performed, considering the following viewpoints:

1. What is the minimum number of instigators required?

2. With the necessary number of instigators, is it always possible to converge to the desired state unless communication delay exists?

3. What happens in a case with communication delay?

4. When there are no instigators, can it be guaranteed that no robots change their strategic type even if U is reduced to 80.0?

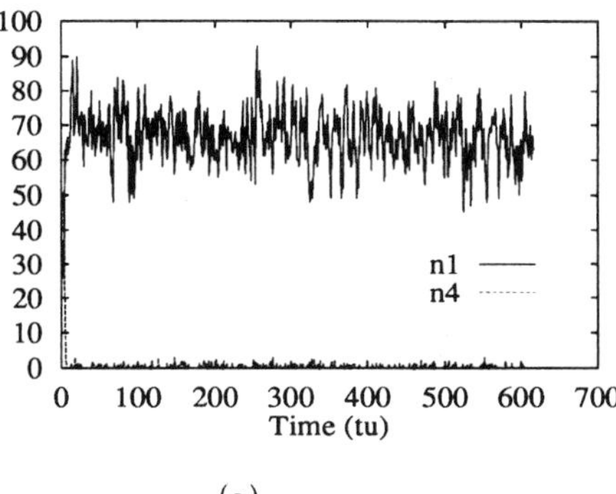

(a)

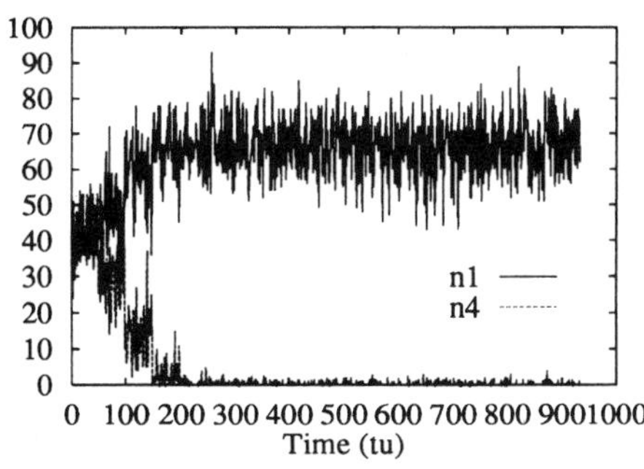

(b)

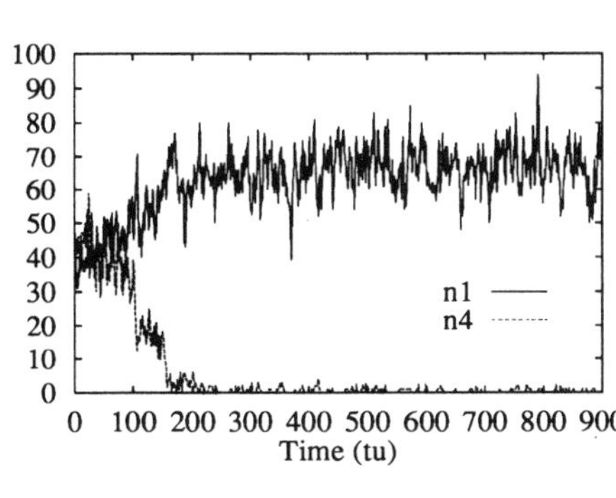

(c)

Figure 2: Experiment-1: The transient behavior of robots choosing the 1st (upper, solid line) and the 4th (lower, dotted line) strategies under the condition that C = 0.1, Γ = 1.0, P_0/C = 0.2, P_{min} = 0.0001, and U/Γ=200. (a) no delay and α = 1.0 (b) τ = 50 (tu) and α = 1.0 (c) τ = 50 (tu) and α = 1/3.

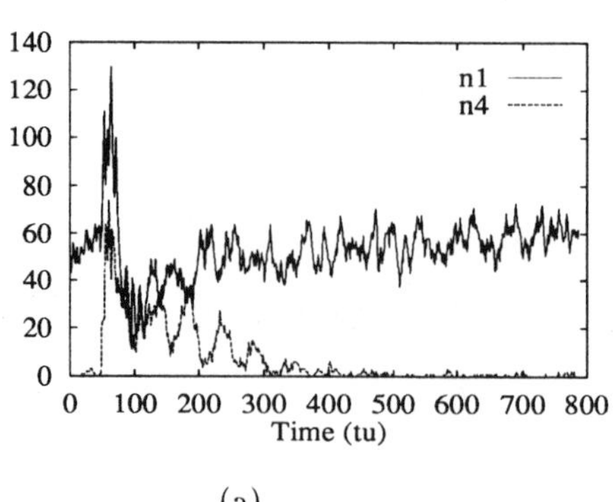

(a)

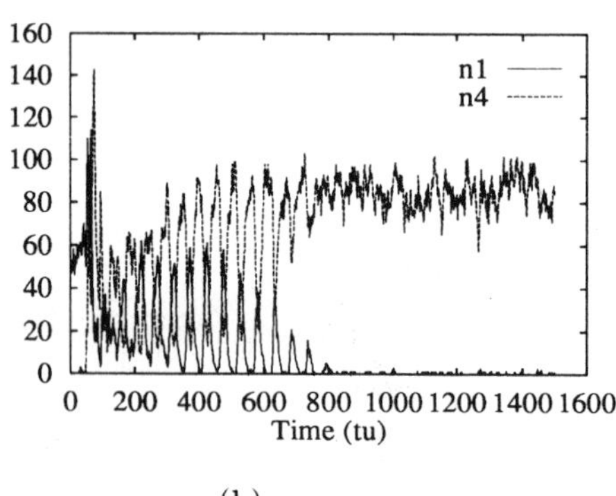

(b)

Figure 3: Experiment-2: The transient behavior of robots choosing the 1st (solid line) and the 4th (dotted line) strategies under the condition that $C = 0.1$, $\Gamma = 1.0$, $P_0/C = 0.2$, $P_{min} = 0.0001$, $U/\Gamma = 200$, $\tau = 50.0$(tu), and $\alpha = 1/6$ with (a) 27 instigators or (b) 28 instigators.

The last one is important. Although U is reduced for the purpose of finding a new possible strategic type, we do not want this to affect the stability of the system when no instigators change their strategy. In the following, we show the results obtained through computer simulations.

Number of instigators. We estimated in the previous section that at least 28 instigators are required. This has been confirmed by our simulation. Figures 3 (a) and (b) show the cases for 27 and 28 instigators, respectively, where the communication delay is 50 time units, α is $\frac{1}{6}$, and t_1 and t_2 are 20 and 120 time units (tu). It is clear from these figures that 28 instigators indicate the boundary if global transition is to take place. The oscillation observed in Figure 3 (b) becomes sluggish and converges quickly as the number of instigators increases. [1]

[1] In our simulation, with 34 instigators, the transition converges about 250 time units from the beginning.

Converging behavior without communication delay. Except for some irregular cases, most robots converge on strategies of the type that instigators have not chosen. Besides, this convergence is extremely rapid and happens soon after U is restored at t_2. One example is shown in Figure 4 (a).

The effect of communication delay and decision rate. Once a communication delay is introduced, oscillations occurs. In the case of Figure 4 (b), a communication delay of 50 time units causes never-converging oscillation. This oscillation, fortunately, can be converged by reducing decision rate α. Figures 4 (c) and (d) illustrate these dynamics.

In every simulation, if we set α to $\frac{1}{6}$, all robots will choose one of the 4th and 5th strategies of the defending type. However, with shorter intervals, e.g. (20, 70), the convergence is not successful when the decision rate is less than $\frac{1}{8}$. Namely, in this case, the initial distribution of populations is preserved.

The case of no instigators changing strategy. Our purpose for this simulation was to examine whether all robots can collectively change their strategic types to a particular type that a small number of robots choose. Since every robot is deciding their strategy based on payoff functions, no robots are commanded to choose a particular strategic type. Every decision is strictly the robot's own responsibility. Therefore, we introduce dynamics to control such masses indirectly. This can be done by both instigators and reduced utility.

The problem here, however, is when robots should decide to reduce the amount of utility. One possibility is to give robots a mechanism to enable them to change the amount of utility periodically by defining a cyclic step function or to change it individually depending on the internal or external states. When they are in equilibrium and utility U is 200.0, provided instigators do not change their strategic type, all robots can stay at the equilibrium state. However, if robots make use of such a cyclic step function, they periodically reduce the utility to 80.0. Therefore, we must examine whether all robots can remain in the equilibrium state even if the utility is reduced to 80.0, as long as instigators never change their strategic type.

Despite whether there is a communication delay, if decision rate α is 1.0, while utility is reduced, a transient behavior oscillates even though it rapidly converges to the original state after the utility is restored, except for the case in which the length of the interval is 10 or 50 time units. This oscillation can be suppressed by reducing decision rate α. Figures 5 (a) and (b) illustrate, with 50 time units' communication delay, two cases of $\alpha = 1$ and $\alpha = \frac{1}{3}$, respectively.

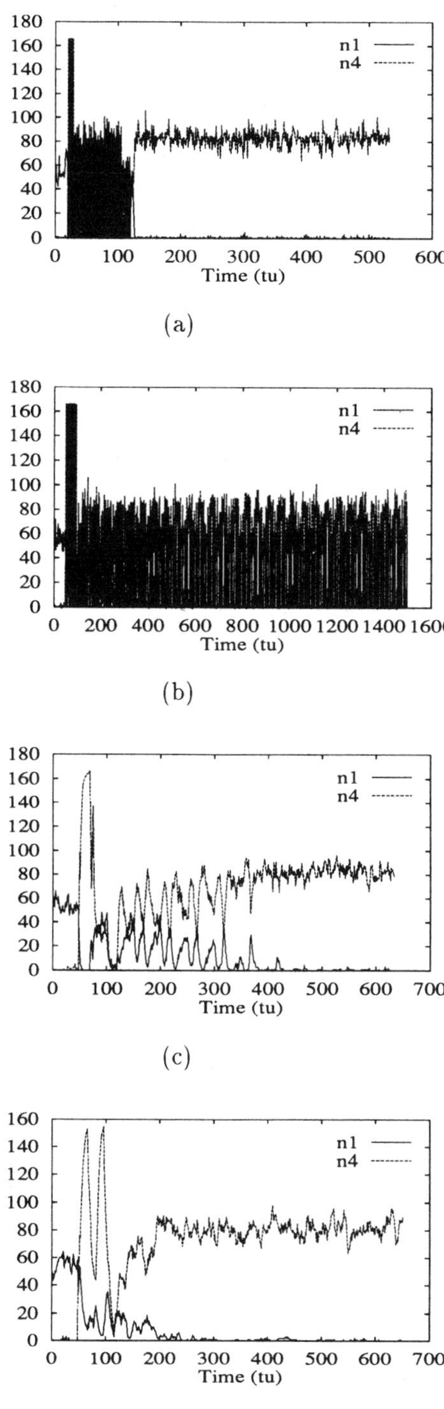

Figure 4: Experiment-3: The transient behavior of robots choosing the 1st (solid line) and the 4th (dotted line) strategies under the condition that C = 0.1, Γ = 1.0, P_0/C = 0.2, P_{min} = 0.0001, and U/Γ=200 with 34 instigators. t_1 and t_2 are 20 and 120 (tu) from the beginning. (a) no delay and α = 1.0 (b) τ = 50 (tu) and α = 1.0 (c) τ = 50 (tu) and α = 1/3 (d) τ = 50 (tu) and α = 1/6.

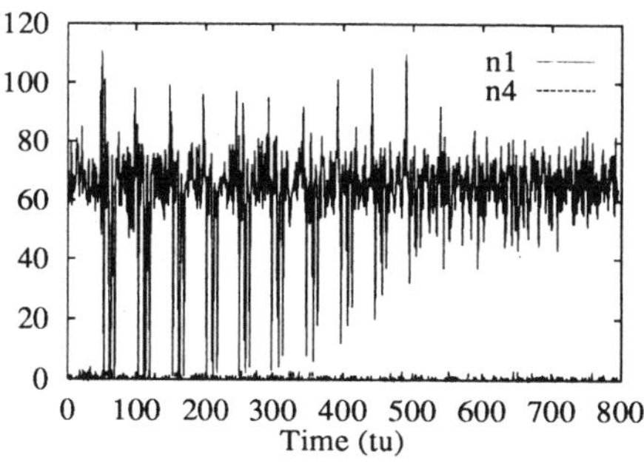

(a)

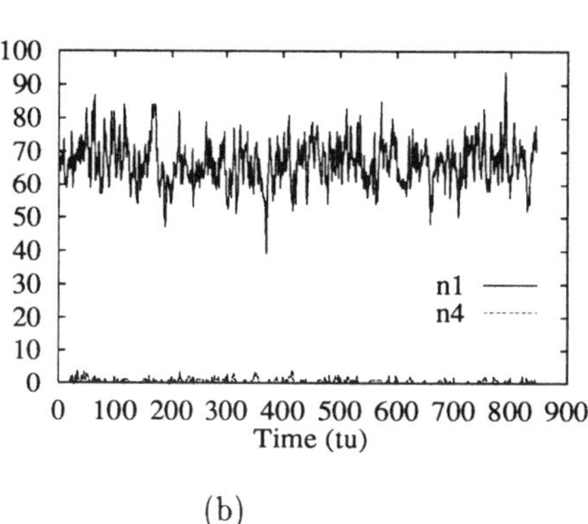

(b)

Figure 5: Experiment-4: The transient behavior of robots choosing the 1st (upper, solid line) and the 4th (lower, dotted line) strategies under the condition that C = 0.1, Γ = 1.0, P_0/C = 0.2, P_{min} = 0.0001, U/Γ=200 and τ = 50 (tu) with no instigator. t_1 and t_2 are 20 and 70 (tu) from the beginning. (a) α = 1.0 (b) α = 1/3.

3.3 Total evaluation

To evaluate the performance, we use both the time required to converge to some equilibrium state and the result of transition that is either success (following the instigators) or failure (otherwise). Through simulations with 34 instigators, with respect to communication delay τ, decision rate α, and the length of interval reducing utility $ivl = t_2 - t_1$, we obtain the result shown in Table 1. In this table, S and F correspond to success and failure, respectively. NC indicates "no convergence."

Every item shows time units from the beginning required to converge to some equilibrium state. One evaluation we obtain from this table is that, to achieve the desired goal despite there being a communication delay, one preferable combination of *alpha* and *ivl* is α = 1/6 and ivl = 50 (tu).

Another fact discovered from this evaluation is that communication delay plays an important role in causing drastic changes in a system. As shown in Table 1,

Table 1: Simulation results

	No delay		
Interval (tu)	1	50	120
$\alpha = 1$	21 (S)	70 (F)	140 (S)
$\alpha = 1/3$	50 (F)	90 (S)	140 (F)
$\alpha = 1/6$	55 (F)	120 (S)	210 (F)
$\alpha = 1/10$	21 (F)	120 (F)	280 (F)
	delay = 50 (tu)		
Interval (tu)	1	50	120
$\alpha = 1$	45 (F)	NC	NC
$\alpha = 1/3$	50 (F)	1850 (S)	480 (S)
$\alpha = 1/6$	50 (F)	950 (S)	290 (S)
$\alpha = 1/10$	50 (F)	520 (F)	450 (S)

although there are some exceptions, it seems to be generally difficult for a change to succeed when there is no communication delay. On the other hand, when there is a communication delay, most simulations succeed.

Of course, it may be too early to conclude that communication delay is necessary for this sort of experiment. However, as a general tendency in our experiments, communication delay seems to have a functionality to promote a drastic change with small fluctuations in transient behavior.

4 Related Work

Deneubourg, Goss et al. have been pursuing the dynamics of emergent collective behavior in their research on social insects. They reported on an idea to develop ant-like robots to sort objects according to their types [Deneubourg *et al.* 91]. Every ant-like robot decides its action with a probability calculated by a function due to estimation of the fraction of nearby points occupied by objects of the same type. According to their paper, we can observe that a collection of robots exhibiting this simple behavior results in a meaningful output in which objects are clustered in every type.

In addition, they report very interesting collective behavior that they call *recruitment* [Beckers *et al.* 90]. It is known that in a typical ant trail recruitment, a scout discovers a food source and returns to the nest, laying a chemical trail and, at the nest, other foragers detect the trail and follow it to the source. Their work gives us a mathematical model to explain why most ants tend to choose the richer source when there is more than one sucrose solution. In terms of the research direction to get a consistent and useful output by multiple robots pursuing self-interest, their work is very similar to ours. Perhaps, the main difference between ours and theirs is that our payoff functions consider not only positive feedback but also negative feedback, whereas their functions consider only positive feedback.

Huberman's group has been continuing their studies on computational ecosystems. With relation to collective alteration, Ceccatto and Huberman's work on a thermodynamic-like formalism is of particular interest [Ceccatto and Huberman 89]. In our experiments, every robot chooses its next strategy with a probability having a normal distribution in proportion to payoffs. On the other hand, in Ceccatto and Huberman's work, the probability of choosing the next strategy involves a temperature-like parameter β, which actually corresponds to *certainty-ness*; perfect knowledge implies $\beta = \infty$ and maximal uncertainty is denoted by $\beta = 0$.

They proved that, only in the case of imperfect knowledge (i.e. wrong evaluation of the payoffs), many robots can change from one strategy to other. Using such a thermodynamic-like formalism may make it possible for us to realize dynamics where robots alter their strategic type without instigators. We have to know, however, as Ceccatto and Huberman pointed out, "a large collection of computational agents in an open system will not spontaneously generate adaptive behavior when the introduction of novel constraints produces metastable configurations." Thus, if global communication is available, the idea of instigators and reducing utility works better for the adaptability of a collection of robots.

5 Discussion and Conclusion

We have shown that if we give autonomous robots a particular form of payoff function to decide a strategy, a collective behavior will emerge from the multiple robots. It was shown that the resultant collective behavior is mathematically a stable equilibrium. The strategies correspond to a variable which Luc Steels calls the *emergent property* [Steels 91]. The collective behavior with this emergent property is robust for small fluctuations and thus is desired for robots working in an ever-changing environment.

The purpose of this paper was to model the dynamics of a group of robots such that robots collectively choose one type of strategies reflecting the situation. In the case of robots fighting a fire, either an attack or defence strategic type should collectively be chosen. Consistent choice of strategic type is desired for their behavioral efficiency. We have modeled robots to decide a strategy, considering how many robots chose each strategy. As a result, the type of a strategy that robots will choose depends fully on the population of robots choosing each strategy.

Next we analyzed the number of robots required as instigators to invoke a global transition from one strategic type to another. Our model can predict the critical ratio of instigators by considering an equal balance over some types of strategies.

In addition, to enlarge the effect of instigators changing and fixing a strategy, we propose a technique of reducing utility. This resembles our losing interest in a particular matter, despite our concentrating on the matter. Although in our experiment, reducing utility is defined as a stepping function, we may find a more interesting phenomena if we think of utility as a function of time. We will report on this in the future.

Through computer simulation, we confirmed that our model succeeds in showing the desired dynamics, at least where every robot has global information, when we give an appropriate set of parameters that can be defined regardless of the environment. With our results, we were able to realize a team of multiple robots that collectively change a strategic type, say from attack to defence, depending on the situation. Especially, the number of instigators completely agrees with the prediction made with our model.

There are reasonable criticisms of the payoff functions: 1) the payoff function we use is too far from reality and 2) it would be difficult to embody it, in advance, into each robot. In this paper, we thus concentrated on looking for a fundamental model for the computation of team-like collective behavior and investigating the general nature of the model. For this purpose, we took Huberman and Hogg's approach as the basis of the model since they have clarified some aspects of collective behavior where every robot calculates its next strategy, based on a payoff function. In future work, we would need to set up parameters and/or payoff functions with consideration to some real applications. In response to the second criticism, we are thinking that reinforcement learning (e.g. [Lin 91, Kaelbling 92]) would be an aid.

The following issue may also be raised: global communication is too idealistic in the real world whereas local communication is rather practical. In fact, our next goal is to investigate the local communication case. In investigating the local communication case, our experiments of the global communication case provide good samples for comparison.

Another issue that requires more detailed investigation is the effect of communication delay. As seen in Table 1, without communication delay, it is difficult to achieve the desired goal. Nevertheless, we cannot control communication delay completely. Therefore, we would have to find a solution to get the same effect as communication delay, even when there is no communication delay. This may also important topic for the future.

Acknowledgment

We would like to express our gratitude to Dr. Mario Tokoro (Keio University and Sony CSL) for encouraging our research. We would like to thank to Dr. Scott Clearwater, who read our earlier draft and gave us fruitful comments including the suggestion of the relationship between Ceccatto and Huberman's work on multistable systems and our work. We are grateful to Prof. Simon Goss for giving us access to his related work on social insects. The referees have been very helpful in providing insightful comments that have resulted in substantial improvements.

References

[Ackley *et al.* 85] David H. Ackley, Geoffrey E. Hinton, and Terrence J. Sejnowski. A Learning Algorith, for Bolzmann Machines. *Cognitive Science*, Vol. 9, pp.147–169, 1985.

[Beckers *et al.* 90] R. Beckers, J. L. Deneubourg, S. Goss, and J. M. Pasteels. Collective Decision Making Through Food Recruitment. *Insectes Sociaux, Paris*, Vol. 37, No. 3, pp.258–267, 1990.

[Brooks 86] Rodney A. Brooks. A Robust Layered Control System for a Mobile Robot. *IEEE Journal of Robotics and Automation*, Vol. RA-2, No. 1, March 1986.

[Ceccatto and Huberman 89] H. A. Ceccatto and B. A. Huberman. Persistence of nonoptimal strategies. *Proc. of National Academy of Science, USA*, Vol. 86, pp.3443–3446, 1989.

[Deneubourg *et al.* 91] J. L. Deneubourg, S. Goss, N. Franks, A. Sendova-Franks, C. Detrain, and L. Chretien. The Dynamics of Collective Sorting Robot-like Ants and Ant-like Robots. In Jean-Arcady Meyer and Stewart W. Wilson, editors, *Proceedings of the First International Conference on Simulation of Adaptive Behavior: From animals to animats*, pp. 356–263. The MIT Press/Elsevier, 1991.

[Huberman and Hogg 88] Bernardo A. Huberman and Tad Hogg. The Behavior of Computational Ecologies. In Bernardo A. Huberman, editor, *The Ecology of Computation*, pp. 77–115. Elsevier Science Publishers B.V. (North Holland), 1988.

[Kaelbling 92] Leslie Pack Kaelbling. An Adaptable Mobile Robot. In Francisco J. Varela and Paul Bourgine, editors, *Proceedings of the First European Conference on Artificial Life: Toward a Practice of Autonomous Systems*, pp. 41–47. The MIT Press/Elsevier, 1992.

[Kirkpatrick *et al.* 83] S. Kirkpatrick, C. D. Gelatt, and M. P. Vecchi. Optimization by simulated annealing. *Science*, Vol. 220, pp.671–680, 1983.

[Lin 91] Long-Jin Lin. Self-improving Reactive Agents: Case Studies of Reinforcement Learning Frameworks. In Jean-Arcady Meyer and Stewart W. Wilson, editors, *Proceedings of the First International Conference on Simulation of Adaptive Behavior: From animals to animats*, pp. 297–305. The MIT Press/Elsevier, 1991.

[Maes 90] Pattie Maes. Situated Agents Can Have Goals. In Pattie Maes, editor, *Designing Autonomous Agents*, pp. 49–70. The MIT Press/Elsevier, 1990.

[Steels 91] Luc Steels. Towards a Theory of Emergent Functionality. In Jean-Arcady Meyer and Stewart W. Wilson, editors, *Proceedings of the First International Conference on Simulation of Adaptive Behavior: From animals to animats*, pp. 451–461. The MIT Press/Elsevier, 1991.

An Adaptive Communication Protocol for Cooperating Mobile Robots

Holly Yanco and **Lynn Andrea Stein***
Artificial Intelligence Laboratory
Massachusetts Institute of Technology
545 Technology Square
Cambridge, MA 02139
email: holly@ai.mit.edu, las@ai.mit.edu

Abstract

We describe mobile robots engaged in a cooperative task that requires communication. The robots are initially given a fixed but uninterpreted vocabulary for communication. In attempting to perform their task, the robots learn a private communication language. Different meanings for vocabulary elements are learned in different runs of the experiment. As circumstances change, the robots adapt their language to allow continued success at their task.

1 Introduction

In this paper, we investigate the evolution of simple communication protocols among nonverbal subjects engaged in cooperative tasks. Gregarious animals, small children, and even adult humans lacking common language engage in such activity routinely. Grunts, gestures, and other nonverbal signals take on mutually agreed-upon meanings in the context of cooperative tasks. "Follow me," "Look out!" and "Raise your end of the table higher" can all be conveyed without previously agreed-upon language. Satisfactory completion of cooperative tasks such as table-carrying, hunting, or tribal survival often depends on making effective use of such communications.

This paper describes an example of a cooperative task—coordinated movement—achieved by a troupe of mobile robots. Depending on circumstances, different actions are required. One robot, in the role of the leader, has access to this information and learns to act appropriately. In addition, the leader must communicate to the troupe what actions are required on their parts. The communication language is not fixed at the outset; instead the troupe must learn to associate appropriate actions with the commands issued by the leader. As circumstances evolve, the meanings of the leader's commands may change; the troupe must adjust their actions accordingly. The goal is for the entire troupe to act appropriately and to adapt those actions and the underlying language over time.

When a task requires cooperation, there is often a need for some form of communication between the participating agents. Cooperative work requires communication whenever one agent's actions depend critically on knowledge that is accessible only to another agent. It is often an expedient even when one agent can accomplish the task on its own or when all agents have access to the requisite information. Previous work on cooperative behavior among mobile robots has largely assumed a fixed communication language. (See, for example, [Fukuda and Kawauchi, 1990], [Matsumoto *et al.*, 1990], or [Shin and Epstein, 1985].) However, a language created for the robots may not provide the optimal solution. The language itself may not be natural either to the robots or to the task at hand. In addition, in a changing world, a hard coded language may make it difficult for the agents to adapt to novel situations. Fixed communication languages are less able to handle circumstances in which changing environments dictate changing communications, just as agents that cannot adapt to new environments are at an evolutionary disadvantage relative to those that are able to learn.

The research described in this paper is aimed towards giving autonomous agents the ability to develop their own language. Our initial work was inspired by that of [Shewchuk, 1991]. His Ph.D. thesis addresses the design of appropriate reinforcement learning algorithms to learn languages for internal representation as well as for communication. He has implemented a simple simulation of a language learning task similar to the basic experiment we describe below (two robots, two language elements) as a part of his symbolic test suite for reinforcement learning algorithms. Work on the development of communication between groups of autonomous agents has also been done

*This report describes research done at the Artificial Intelligence Laboratory of the Massachusetts Institute of Technology. Support for the laboratory's artificial intelligence research is provided in part by the Advanced Research Projects Agency of the Department of Defense under Office of Naval Research contract N00014-85-K-0124. The first author is supported in part by a scholarship from Digital Equipment Corporation. The second author is supported in part by the Class of 1957 Career Development Chair and in part by a General Electric Junior Faculty Career Award. Support for this research was also provided by the Gordon S. Brown Fund of the Department of Electrical Engineering and Computer Science at MIT.

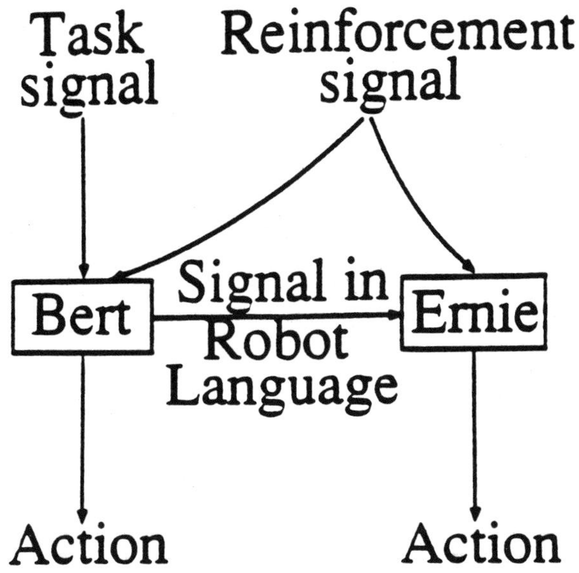


```
Leader:

   loop:  on valid input signal from environment
             choose an action to perform
             choose a signal to send to follower via
                the radio boards
          wait for reinforcement signal
          on reinforcement signal
             increment variables for action and signal
          goto loop

Follower:

   loop:  on valid input signal from leader
             choose an action to perform
          wait for reinforcement signal
          on reinforcement signal
             increment variables for action
          goto loop
```

Figure 1: Information flow in the coordinated movement task. The diagram on the left is for the two robot paradigm; for larger troupes, the additional followers would have the same inputs and outputs as Ernie.

by [MacLennan, 1990] and [Werner and Dyer, 1990]. Their research addresses the problem of language learning with genetic algorithms. Language evolves over many generations of the community. Within an individual agent, however, language is fixed over its lifetime. In all of these cases, implementation is limited to simulation; only the work of Shewchuk addresses the problem of task-based reinforcement (see below).

2 The task

The cooperative task that we have chosen is coordinated movement. Groups of animals engage in such activity when hunting, escaping predators, herding, flocking, migrating, or supervising their young. Environmental cues inform the leader (or leaders) of the troupe as to appropriate troupe movements; a successful leader learns to interpret these cues. Further, the leader learns to communicate to the rest of the troupe the tasks that they are to execute. For example, upon hearing predatory noises, a mother may shepherd her young in the opposite direction or encourage them to remain motionless to avoid detection. The followers may be unaware of or unable to interpret the environmental cues.

We have implemented this task with troupes with two and three members and with a variable number of vocabulary elements on robots and in simulation. A troupe of two robots made up of one leader, Bert, and one follower, Ernie, was used for the robot experiments. The simulator was used to gather data for the three agent experiments and for the larger vocabulary experiments with two agents. Because we are particularly interested in the development of language, we assume that the followers do not have access to the task specification (i.e. the environmental cues) and must rely completely on the communication signals emitted by the leader. In future experiments, we expect to allow the follower robot(s) to use some environmental input to modulate the communication signals from the troupe leader.

Since this is a cooperative task, successful performance depends on the actions of the troupe as a whole. Analogously, the mother animal succeeds in hiding her young only if all remain motionless; one disobedient cub can give away the hiding place and cause the whole troupe to be eaten. Environmental reinforcement is therefore positive only if all agents perform the appropriate actions. Since the followers cannot correctly interpret the environmental cues, this performance can be achieved reliably only when the leader and follower robots mutually agree on the development and interpretation of a private communication protocol.

Thus, the learning tasks are as follows:

- For the leader robot, the interpretation of the environmentally supplied signal, the execution of an appropriate action, and the transmission of an appropriate signal to the follower robot.

- For the follower robots, the execution of an appropriate action based on the signal received from the leader robot.

The "appropriateness" of an action is determined by the environmentally supplied signal. The "appropriateness" of the leader robot's signal, however, is constrained not by the environment but by the leader and follower robot's adapted internal state. That is, the signal is appropriate if and only if the follower robot takes the (environmentally constrained) appropriate action when that signal is received. (The algorithm is summarized in figure 1.)

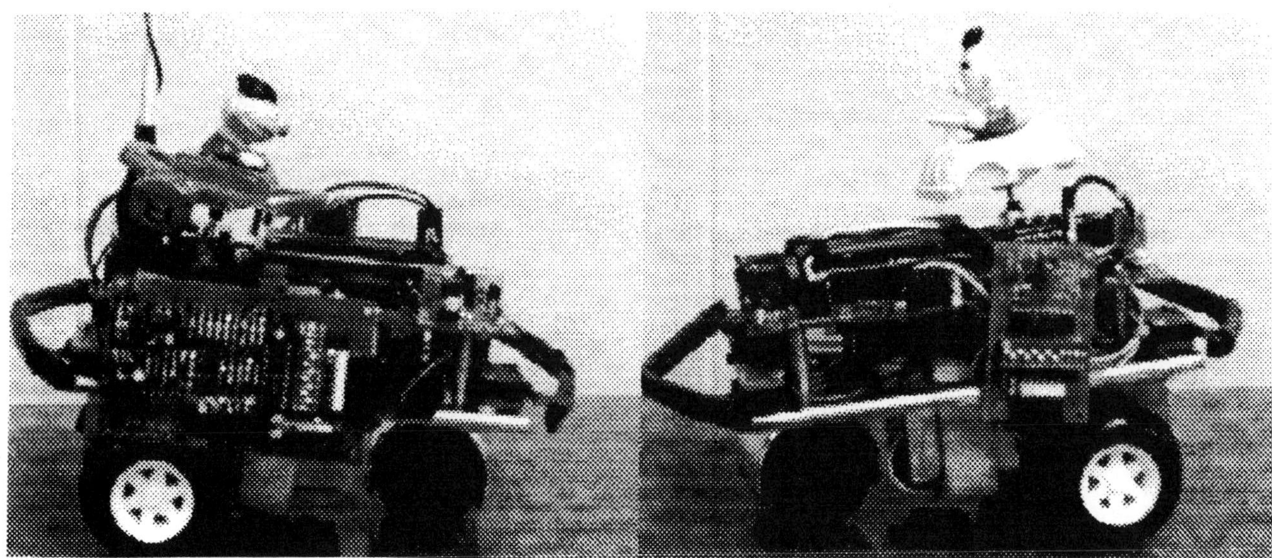

Figure 2: Ernie and Bert

3 The robots

Bert and Ernie, the two robots used in this research, are Sensor Robots designed by Fred Martin at the Media Laboratory at the Massachusetts Institute of Technology [Martin and Sargent, 1991]. Each robot is approximately $9''l \times 6''w \times 4''h$, with a single circuit board containing most of the computational and sensory resources of the robot. A 6v battery strapped to the underside of the chassis supplies the power for the robot. The robots are shown in figure 2.

The primary computational resource is an onboard Motorola 6811 microprocessor. The programming environment is IC, a multi-tasking interactive C compiler and interpreter developed by Randy Sargent [Sargent and Martin, 1991]. IC allows a Sensor Robot to be addressed through a serial line from a host computer as well as the downloading of programs for autonomous activity. The work described in this paper was implemented with the robots under autonomous control.

Locomotion is controlled by a dual geared-wheel drive stripped from a Radio Shack Red Fox Racer. The direction of the robot is controlled by varying the speeds of the left and right motors (with negative speed moving the motor backwards). The two motorized wheels are at the rear of the robot chassis and a caster is on the front.

Communication from human to Bert is through an infra-red remote control transmitter. Bert uses infra-red receivers similar to those found in televisions and VCRs. (While Ernie also has infra-red receivers on board, they are not being used in this work – only Bert hears signals from humans.) The robots communicate between themselves using a pair of radio transmitter and receiver boards similar to those used in garage door openers. (The transmitter and receiver each run off of a separate 9v battery.) Additionally, each robot has a speaker and a 16-character LCD, both used primarily for debugging and monitoring of the robot's activity.

In addition to the infra-red and radio receivers, the sensor robots contain four (front and rear, left and right) bump sensors, left and right shaft encoders, an inclination sensor, photosensitive cells, a microphone, and infra-red emitters. These additional sensory abilities of the robots were not substantively used in the experiments described here.

4 The implementation

In our experiments, the environment is represented by a human "instructor" who issues one of a number of signals to indicate the desired action. Currently, the number of signals is equal to the size of the language. The leader robot performs an action and also signals the follower robot. Upon receipt of the leader's signal, the follower robot selects and performs an action. If both robots have performed correctly, positive reinforcement (+) is issued. If either robot performs incorrectly, negative reinforcement (−) is issued. Based on this environmental feedback, the robots learn to select appropriate actions and communication signals. This algorithm is summarized in figure 1.

Both the action selection and the signal selection are learned using standard reinforcement learning techniques. (See, e.g., [Kaelbling, 1990] or [Sutton, 1992] for overviews of reinforcement learning.) The particular algorithm that we use is adapted from Kaelbling's interval estimation method [1990]. Interval estimation is a relatively simple form of reinforcement: A table of inputs × actions is maintained. Each time an input is received, the expected "best" action is taken and the counter for that input/action pair is incremented. If positive reinforcement is received, a second counter for that input/action pair is also incremented. The "best" action given some input is selected by an optimization function. If no one particular action is the "best", an action is selected randomly. (The algorithm for interval estimation

The initial state, s_0, consists of the integer variables x_0, n_0, x_1, and n_1, each initialized to 0.

```
u(s,a,r) = if a = 0 then begin
                  x0 := x0 + r
                  n0 := n0 + 1
           end else begin
                  x1 := x1 + r
                  n1 := n1 + 1
           end

e(s)   =   if ub(x0,n0) > ub(x1,n1) then
                  return 0
           else
                  return 1
```

where

$$ub(x,n) = \frac{\frac{x}{n} + \frac{z^2_{\alpha/2}}{2n} + \frac{z_{\alpha/2}}{\sqrt{n}}\sqrt{(\frac{x}{n})(1-\frac{x}{n}) + \frac{z^2_{\alpha/2}}{4n}}}{1 + \frac{z^2_{\alpha/2}}{2n}}$$

and $z_{\alpha/2} > 0$.

Figure 3: Kaelbling's interval estimation algorithm [Kaelbling, 1990, Figure 21].

is given in figure 3.)

In our initial experiments, we allow each of the robots two possible actions. At each iteration, each robot chooses either *go straight* or *spin*. Further, the communication protocol contains only two vocabulary elements—high and low—so that the learning problem remains tractable. The leader robot must thus learn to select one of four possible action/communication pairs; the follower robot must learn to associate each of the vocabulary items with one of its two possible actions. Convergence on the robots is easily verified by testing each environmental input; if all behaviors are as expected, the protocol will not change further without environmental adaptation.

We have also implemented the identical learning algorithms in simulation in C running under UNIX on SUN SPARCstations. The simulation is used primarily for ease of data collection over large numbers of runs and in scaling up the experiments to larger language and troupe sizes. To assess convergence, we wait until all of the instructor's signals (i.e. all distinct environmental cues) have been completed three times consecutively without negative reinforcement. At that point, each input is tested to verify that convergence has truly been reached. (This leads to slightly inflated convergence times in simulation over experiments on the robots.)

In the case of a two-element language, convergence times vary wildly when a true random function is used. Extended series of a single environmental cue cause oscillations in the agents' state variables, leading to protracted convergence times in a substantial fraction of the runs. (The simulation took an average of 12006.25 iterations to converge for a two element language using two agents, with a minimum of 10 iterations and a maximum of 235109 iterations. In 100 tests of this case, the simulation took over 100 iterations to converge in one quarter of the tests.) To avoid this problem, we used a biased random function that prevented extended series of similar environmental inputs. The data given in the results section of this paper was collected using the biased random function. Data was also collected with an unbiased random function; in all but the two-element case, the results are comparable.

In the implementation on our robots, communication noise is dwarfed by human error and by the complexity of the task-based learning problem; we therefore omit it from our simulation.

5 Task-based reinforcement.

Our experiment is unusual in that reinforcement—positive environmental feedback—is received only when both robots succeed in performing the appropriate actions. This sort of *task-based* reinforcement contrasts with the usual individually based reinforcement typical in the literature. Because robots receive reinforcement only when the troupe as a whole performs the task correctly, it is possible for an individual to perform correctly but receive negative feedback. In addition, none of the robots can sense the action taken by the others; thus, the environmental reinforcement cannot be interpreted in that light. This further complicates the reinforcement learning task.

Reinforcement learning algorithms typically generate action policies for individual agents given some environmental constraints. The adaptation that we describe here is no exception. The leader robot, for example, learns policies for what action to take and what signal to send the follower on a given input signal. However, what is reinforced—what the environment rewards—is not the policy of the individual robot but the successful performance of the total cooperative task.

For example, if the environmental constraints make *both spin* the appropriate course of action, the leader robot may spin and send the follower robot the signal that the leader believes to mean *spin*. If the follower has not yet learned the communication protocol, it may incorrectly interpret the leader's signal to mean *go straight*. In this case, the leader has performed correctly—both its action and its signal were appropriate—but receives negative reinforcement. Similarly, if the leader issues an inappropriate signal—*go straight*—but the follower interprets that signal to mean *spin*, the environment provides positive reinforcement (for a correctly executed task) in spite of the incorrect internal communication. Further, neither robot is aware of the action taken by the other and so cannot use that knowledge to assess the environmental feedback.

The choice of this form of *task-based reinforcement* is motivated by biological analogy. The world does not generally reinforce inappropriate action, no matter how well meant. Similarly, fortuitously apt actions are rewarded even though the underlying intention is flawed.

	Appropriate action	Leader's action	Leader's signal	Follower's action	Reinforcement
1.	↑↑	*spin*	low	*spin*	−
2.	○○	*spin*	low	*straight*	−
3.	↑↑	*straight*	high	*spin*	−
4.	○○	*straight*	high	*straight*	−
5.	○○	*spin*	low	*spin*	+
6.	↑↑	*straight*	high	*spin*	−
7.	○○	*spin*	low	*spin*	+
8.	○○	*spin*	low	*spin*	+
9.	○○	*spin*	low	*spin*	+
10.	↑↑	*spin*	low	*spin*	−
11.	↑↑	*straight*	high	*straight*	+
12.	↑↑	*straight*	high	*straight*	+
13.	○○	*spin*	low	*spin*	+

Table 1: A sample run. The desired behavior is ***both spin*** on input ○○, ***both go straight*** on input ↑↑. After thirteen iterations, convergence is reached.

(This is the root of serendipity and the sentiment underlying the saw, "Necessity is the mother of invention.") Because the robots' communication protocol is private and not interpreted by the external environment (or human "instructor"), it is not relevant to the reinforcement received. If the robots can succeed in taking appropriate actions in spite of miscommunication, they continue to receive positive feedback. In principle and in practice, the task is designed so that only successful learning of the private language allows continued successful execution of the cooperative task.

Size of Language	Number of Iterations to Convergence: Average	Minimum	Maximum
2	15.34	10	24
3	110.30	33	501
4	340.38	53	990
5	906.62	255	2472
10	15011.61	2868	51031
20	232267.82	44196	1241767

Table 2: Learning times for a two member troupe. Experiments for each language size were run 100 times.

6 Results

6.1 Developing a Shared Language

Bert and Ernie are able to learn both synchronous action—both performing the same action in the same interval—and divergent action—e.g., leader *spins*, follower *goes straight*. Convergence times typically range from five to twenty iterations. A sample run of the experiment is given in table 1. In this run, the appropriate actions are for both robots to *spin* on input ○○ and for both robots to *go straight* on input ↑↑. The robots converge on a mutually agreeable language—a low signal means that the follower should *spin*, while a high signal means to *go straight*—after thirteen iterations.

Size of Language	Number of Iterations to Convergence: Average	Minimum	Maximum
2	27.21	10	80
3	327.71	35	1211
4	1530.12	340	6666
5	4415.60	652	17533
10	163530.62	37130	705029

Table 3: Data above is for a three member troupe and was collected over 100 runs for each language size.

6.2 Adaptability of language

Once the robots converge on a particular dialect, they continue to receive positive reinforcement as long as the environmental constraints do not change. If circumstances change, however, the robots may find that their previously successful actions no longer earn them positive feedback. For example, after the run in figure 1, we might change the "appropriateness" of the robots' actions by giving positive reinforcement to *leader spin, follower go straight* on ↑↑. Under such circumstances, the robots can adapt their behavior—and, when necessary, their communication protocol—to the changing environment. Convergence times for the new task (i.e., to unlearn portions of the old task and relearn the newly appropriate behavior) range from roughly comparable to the initial learning task to roughly double the time, depending on the difficulty of the new task, the differences between the old and the new, and how firmly the previous behavior is entrenched.

Dialect	Two robots	Three agents
low = spin high = straight	45	52
low = straight high = spin	55	48

Table 4: The agents can agree on differing dialects in each run. Totals for each dialect are based on 100 runs of the two element language experiment.

Dialect	Two robots	Three agents
low = right med = straight high = left	19	14
low = right med = left high = straight	14	20
low = straight med = right high = left	16	15
low = straight med = left high = right	9	14
low = left med = right high = straight	13	17
low = left med = straight high = right	29	20

Table 5: In 100 runs, agents develop all of the six possible dialects in a three element language. The number of times each dialect was developed is given.

6.3 Scaling Up the Language

The simulator has been used to collect statistics on languages ranging in size from two to twenty elements using troupes of two and three agents. For each language size, 100 experiments were run to convergence. Mean, minimum, and maximum convergence times (number of iterations) are given in table 2 and table 3. Time to learn a language grows exponentially in the number of vocabulary elements in the language.

6.4 Variation over Dialects

In order to achieve convergence on any of these tasks, a particular language must be agreed upon. However, the language varies from run to run. For example, in the run in figure 1, the robots agree that a low signal means that the follower should *spin*. In another run of the same experiment (○○ means *both spin*, ↑↑ means *both go straight*), a high signal may be interpreted as *spin* and a low signal as *go straight*. Such dialect differences depend partly on the random selection of vocabulary elements; however, it is critical to the success of the task that the leader and the followers all agree on the same dialect.

Using the simulator, we have counted the numbers of times that particular dialects appear over 100 runs of a particular experiment. In table 4, data is given for the two element language using both two and three agents; table 5 shows data for the three elements language using two and three agents. These percentages are variable and we expect that the agents' selection between dialects would be evenly distributed in a large number of runs.

6.5 Increasing Troupe Size

When the troupe size is increased to three, the amount of time necessary to converge upon a language increases due to the additional learning that is required. (See table 3.) For the twenty element language using three agents, the agents required 12,105,480 iterations to agree upon a dialect. (The experiment was only run once since it required more than 24 hours of processing time on a SUN Sparc2.)

The learning time might be reduced by having a subset of the agents (in this case, two of the agents) agree on a dialect, then have these robots bootstrap the other members of the troupe. This is similar to the way humans learn language; every person who speaks a particular language does not need to relearn the language when other people are learning it. This learning method will be explored in future work.

7 Scaling up

As the number of possible actions and signals increase, the time necessary for convergence increases exponentially. This is due to the reinforcement learning algorithm. For every signal, a table needs to maintained that contains each of the actions that could be performed. In the experiments, we are usually looking for a one–to–one correspondence between signals and actions; however, this fact is not exploited to speed up the learning process since it would make the algorithm too specific.

If we rely on learning a new signal for every action, the learning task quickly becomes intractable. Currently, we are exploring alternate directions for language development.

The language that we have described here maps single vocabulary items onto single actions. Human language gains power by virtue of its compositional nature. That is, because vocabulary elements can be combined into sentences, a vocabulary of fixed size can generate an exponential number of utterances. Further, the interpretation of the sentence depends on the interpretation of the vocabulary elements in isolation, allowing a word learned in one context to be correctly understood in a novel utterance. The next phase of our experimentation will address the task of learning a compositional language.

For example, the robots might have a language with one set of signals for direction of motion and another set for speed. The leader's communications might then be utterances such as "go left slowly" or "spin quickly." Because the learning problem is per word rather than per utterance, the complete language can be approximated by a sublinear number of vocabulary elements. Even allowing for the exponential blowup in space and time of current reinforcement learning methods, the problem remains in the realm of computational feasibility.

8 Discussion

Implications of task-based reinforcement. Task-based reinforcement poses particular challenges for reinforcement learning algorithms. The robots are learning individual action policy but receiving reinforcement based on the global performance of the cooperative task. As a result, task-based reinforcement behaves somewhat like noise in the reinforcement signal. Because most reinforcement learning algorithms are designed to function in the presence of some amount of noise, they are adequate for this situation. However, task-based reinforcement is not random noise, and some algorithms will be better suited to the job than others. Experiments such as ours provide a useful testbed for learning algorithms. [Shewchuk, 1991] describes efforts to design reinforcement learning algorithms more suited to this sort of problem.

Complex tasks. The selected task—coordinated movement—is one in which reinforcement is received at every iteration. In more complex tasks, reinforcement may be received only after completion of a sequence of actions. This *delayed reinforcement* complicates the learning problem and necessitates the use of more sophisticated learning techniques, such as Sutton's temporal differencing (TD) methods [1988]. By replacing the interval estimation algorithm that we have used with an appropriate variant on TD, it should be possible to extend our adaptive communication protocol to tasks in which the cooperative task requires several sequential steps. This will of course slow down the learning phase considerably.

Taking the human out of the loop. One shortcoming of the current work is that a human "instructor" is currently needed to observe the robot's behavior and provide positive or negative reinforcement. In a more natural task, the environment itself should be able to provide that feedback. [Maes and Brooks, 1990] describe such an experiment with an individual legged robot that self-reinforces to learn a balanced gait. Because our robots are somewhat fragile and because their effective ability is largely limited to wheeled locomotion, we have not yet attempted such autonomic reinforcement. The design of a cooperative task that does not pose undue hazard to the hardware but allows for repeated experimentation and miscommunication remains an open challenge.

Acknowledgements

The work described in this paper was inspired by a simulation experiment described by John Shewchuk. The hardware and software that we used were originally developed for the 6.270 course and 6.915 Robot Design Seminar at MIT. The course staff and students of that class spent innumerable hours working on what ultimately became the substrate for our research. We are particularly indebted to Fred Martin, who masterminded the Sensor Robots; to Randy Sargent, who designed and implemented the IC programming language; to Philip Alvelda, who built the prototype radio system; to Tim Tang, who helped to build and debug Bert and Ernie, and who implemented their radio communications; to Anne Wright, who implemented the IR communications; and to Scott Willcox, who helped debug the radio boards in a pinch. Last, but certainly not least, Ian Horswill, Jeanne Speckman, Nancy Pollard, Mark Torrance, and Rod Brooks listened to our ideas and offered support and encouragement for our work. We thank them.

References

[Fukuda and Kawauchi, 1990] T. Fukuda and Y. Kawauchi. Communication and distributed intelligence for cellular robotic system CEBOT. In *1990 Japan-USA Symposium on Flexible Automation*, pages 1085–1092, July 1990.

[Kaelbling, 1990] Leslie Pack Kaelbling. Learning in embedded systems. Technical Report TR–90–04, Teleos Research, Palo Alto, California, June 1990.

[MacLennan, 1990] Bruce MacLennan. Evolution of communication in a population of simple machines. Technical Report CS–90–99, University of Tennessee, Knoxville, Tennessee, January 1990.

[Maes and Brooks, 1990] Pattie Maes and Rodney A. Brooks. Learning to coordinate behaviors. In *Proceedings of the Eighth National Conference on Artificial Intelligence*, pages 796–802, Boston, Massachusetts, July 1990. MIT Press.

[Martin and Sargent, 1991] Fred Martin and Randy Sargent. The MIT sensor robot: User's guide and technical reference. October 1991.

[Matsumoto *et al.*, 1990] A. Matsumoto, H. Asama, and Y. Ishida. Communication in the autonomous and decentralized robot system ACTRESS. In *Proceedings of the IEEE International Workshop on Intelligent Robots and Systems*, pages 835–840, Tsuchura, Japan, July 1990.

[Sargent and Martin, 1991] Randy Sargent and Fred Martin. IC: Multi-tasking interactive C for the 6811. IC Version 2.5, October 1991.

[Shewchuk, 1991] John P. Shewchuk. Ph.D. thesis proposal. Department of Computer Science, Brown University, Providence, Rhode Island, 1991.

[Shin and Epstein, 1985] K. Shin and M. Epstein. Communication primitives for a distributed multi-robot system. In *Proceedings of the IEEE Robotics and Automation Conference*, pages 910–917, 1985.

[Sutton, 1988] Richard S. Sutton. Learning to predict by the methods of temporal differences. *Machine Learning*, 3:9–44, 1988.

[Sutton, 1992] Richard S. Sutton. Special issue on reinforcement learning. *Machine Learning*, 8(3–4), May 1992.

[Werner and Dyer, 1990] Gregory M. Werner and Michael G. Dyer. Evolution of communication in artificial organisms. Technical Report UCLA–AI–90–06, University of California, Los Angles, California, November 1990.

Dimensions of Communication and Social Organization in Multi-agent Robotic Systems

Ronald C. Arkin and J. David Hobbs
College of Computing
Georgia Institute of Technology
Atlanta, Georgia 30332-0280

Abstract

Communication, social organization, task type and complexity are defining characteristics of a multi-agent system. In this paper, extensions of schema-based reactive navigation are presented as a basis for constructing multi-robot societies. As has been our tradition, ethological studies provide significant insights into the way in which robotic systems can be structured. An analysis of relevant animal behavior, a delineation of the dimensions of multi-agent systems, a description of the overall project and simulation results to date constitute the body of this paper. The multi-robot testbed on which the results of this study will be deployed is also described.

1 Introduction

Multi-agent robotic systems hold tremendous potential for applications in hazardous and dynamic environments, especially in partially modeled or unmodeled worlds. Situations found in space exploration, undersea construction, nuclear waste management and reactor maintenance, all could benefit from the development of effective teams of robots coordinating their efforts towards a common goal. Typical problems would include such things as retrieval, simple construction tasks, routine cleaning and finishing, etc.

We have previously demonstrated [3] that cooperation between robotic agents is possible even in the absence of communication. Although teaming can occur under these conditions, it does not mean that the resultant work is necessarily efficient. There are many dimensions to the teaming of multi-agents that require significant additional study. These include the role and structure of communication in these systems, social structure and organization among the agents, the nature of the task to be accomplished, and the dynamics of the target environment.

This paper describes an on-going research project funded by the National Science Foundation on cooperation and communication in multi-agent reactive robotic systems. Our research has long been influenced by psychological, neuroscientific and ethological considerations [5,6,7]. This trend continues in our multi-agent study. Studies in animal behavior and communication provide models and insights that are being used to formulate implementations on real robotic hardware. It should be recognized that the goal of our research is to produce intelligent autonomous agents and not necessarily to be faithful to the biological models upon which much of our strategies are based [6,7]. To that end, we are less concerned with the biological fidelity of ethological models than their potential usefulness for extrapolation to robotic systems. We do not attempt to reproduce actual animal behavioral patterns, but rather look towards those systems for design inspiration (not replication) in our robotic systems.

This paper is structured as follows. Section 2 provides a brief review of related work in robotic multi-agent systems, followed by an overview of our schema-based (behavioral) methodology for robot control. Section 3 surveys relevant animal social behaviors and communication systems in this context. Section 4 describes the research effort and results to date and discusses the target hardware testbed using 3 Denning Mobile Robots. A Summary and Conclusions section completes this paper.

2 Related Robotics Research

The field of robotics is still largely concentrating on the issues of single agent performance. A limited number of researchers have performed some work in the area of multiple coordinated agents; this section reviews some of their progress to date.

Fukuda's pioneering work on multi-agent systems led to the development of the CEBOT system [17], a collection of heterogeneous agents capable of assembling themselves at run-time. A more recent paper [32] describes a hierarchical communication network between the disparate agents.

Mataric [23] is studying task performance in a population of twenty homogeneous mobile robots. Tasks such as homing, flocking, and puck gathering are being examined. This system is constructed within the context of the subsumption architecture, a behaviorally-oriented reactive system.

Beni and Hackwood [20] describe a multi-agent system which possesses the ability to redistribute sensing elements within a colony. Although not ported to a real robotic system yet, they indicate that future work regarding communication would enhance performance in their circulating swarm model.

Noreils has developed an architecture capable of supporting multiple mobile robots in hazardous environments [26] which has been implemented on two indoor mobile robots. The Gofer project at Stanford University [12] involves a more traditional planner using A^* search to coordinate three indoor mobile robots over a road network. Sugihara and Suzuki [31] describe a simulation method for multiple mobile robots to achieve various formations. Miller [24] describes a potential application of multiple reactive robots for use in planetary surface missions.

This research area is progressing rapidly on many different fronts. The examples above are merely representative of the large body of on-going work in this field.

The schema-based approach for mobile robot behavior, developed in our laboratory, is reviewed below prior to its discussion in the context of multi-agent systems.

2.1 Schema-based Reactive Control

Schema theory [2] provides a fruitful methodology for implementing a behavior-based robotic system. This methodology, strongly influenced by work in cognitive psychology [28,29], has been developed into a modular behavior-based control system for mobile robots [4].

Motor schemas form the basis for all activity of the robot: each motor schema corresponds to a primitive behavior. A wide range of schemas has been developed including **move-to-goal**, **move-ahead**, **stay-on-path**, **docking**, **noise**, **avoid-static-obstacle**, **dodge**, **escape**, and so on. These and other behaviors are described in more detail in [4,8,9,10].

Each behavior is concurrently active, producing a single velocity vector in response to its perception of the environment. Perceptual schemas channel the requisite perceptual information for each motor schema to perform its task. This partitioning of perceptual activity on the basis of motor behavioral need is referred to as *action-oriented perception* [5]. Each individual vector is summed and normalized and the result transmitted to the robot for execution. This stimulus-response reaction ensures timely response to changing environmental conditions. Effective robot navigation has been demonstrated in a wide-range of domains including indoor office buildings, outdoor campus settings, manufacturing environments, and in simulation for undersea and aerospace applications and rough terrain [4,8,9,5].

For the sake of completeness, formulations for several of the motor schemas used in the simulation studies follow:

- **Move-to-goal**: Move towards a perceptually discernible goal.

  $V_{magnitude}$ = fixed gain value
  $V_{direction}$ = in direction towards perceived goal

- **Noise**: a random vector used for exploration and to circumvent certain problems associated with potential fields methods [4,14].

  $V_{magnitude}$ = fixed gain value
  $V_{direction}$ = random direction for a given time persistence

- **Avoid-static-obstacle**: A repulsion is generated by a detected barrier to motion:

$$V_{magnitude} = \begin{array}{l} 0 \quad for \quad d > S \\ \frac{S-d}{S-R} * G for \quad R < d \leq S \\ \infty \quad for \quad d \leq R \end{array}$$

where:
S = Sphere of influence (radial extent of force from the center of the obstacle)
R = Radius of obstacle
G = Gain
d = Distance of robot to center of obstacle

$V_{direction}$ = along a line from robot to center of obstacle moving away from obstacle

Each active schema, at each point in time, generates a single velocity vector which is combined with the outputs of the other active schemas to yield the gross motion of the robot. No memory of the environment is involved at this level - the robot reacts to its immediate perceptions in a manner consistent with its goals. The net result is intelligent emergent navigational behavior.

3 Behavioral Aspects Relevant to Multi-Agent Systems

In order to produce effective multi-agent robotic systems we feel that it is important to study biological systems first. Insights gained through these studies can often be applied to robotic systems [5,6,7]. In particular, we look to ethological studies of communication and social organization in animal groups as potential models for multi-robot systems. Five particular areas are studied: system reliability, social organization, communication, multi-agent searching and coordination.

The intent of this study is to provide an understanding of both the dimensions of the solution space for task-achieving robotic societies, and indications of potential feasible solutions within that space. It is necessary to understand the variables which affect multi-agent performance. As has been our tradition, we first look towards biological system to provide a basis for our system development. The insights gained from these studies can assist in an efficient search of the multi-dimensional space involved in constructing efficient and effective multi-agent societies. This section, thus, details aspects of animal behavior which we believe to have potential utility in the design of multi-agent systems. This material is of necessity terse, and it should be recognized that it is presented from the viewpoint of a roboticist and not that of an ethologist. From a biological perspective, much has been boiled away or overlooked, but to a roboticist, these sample points can provide useful information as existence proofs of functioning multi-agent systems and to serve, to a degree, as design guidelines and avenues for experimental exploration in multi-agent robotics.

An overview of several different dimensions which can affect the design of multi-agent robotic systems follows.

3.1 System Reliability

System reliability, defined as the probability that the system can act correctly, is discussed by Wilson [34] regarding groups of ants. He draws the analogy between the design of parallel-series systems from engineering to the reliability of animal social systems. When a component fails in a series system, then the whole system fails. On the other hand, if a component fails in a parallel-series system, another component can take over. Wilson proposes a theorem that redundancy should be at low levels rather than at higher organizational levels. For instance, a more reliable system will emerge when individual robots rather than whole teams of robots are redundant.

Wilson also argues that the agents must perform above a certain competence level for working in groups to be beneficial. Basically, the agents must have a certain aptitude at working together for the teamwork to pay off. A trivial example is two robots which are trying to move the same item in two different directions. A more plausible problem would be two robots which are programmed to retrieve objects in mutually harmful ways, such as one robot lifting an object while the other attempts to drag it. If they do not have a certain competence at working together, then the overall reliability of accomplishing the task will be lower than if they were working individually.

3.2 Social Organization

A natural design decision involves how the agents should be organized. Animal societies are organized in many ways (Wilson has established 10 "qualities of sociality" and Deegener has defined over 40 categories of animal societies [33]). Social networks are one of the most natural ways for humans to think of social structures. The assignment of castes or types of agents is also a natural consideration.

There are several types of social structures in animals, including the multi-level, hierarchical structure of baboons [33], the uni-level structure of a fish school [33], and the loosely structured Whiptail Wallaby mob [21].[1] Animals without multi-level hierarchies are able to conduct activities of potential application for robotics. For instance, ants are able to build complicated structures, grow food, capture slaves, wage war, transport queens, and weave leaves without a strict and complicated hierarchy. The ants utilize a heterarchical structure where there are many castes but communication between the castes is unstructured. This heterarchy allows information to flow quickly, without having the information flow up and down chains of command [16,34].

Another issue is how many different types of agents exist within the social system. Wilson [33] states that if a contingency occurs regularly, that there should be a class of agents to handle this contingency. For instance, when building a lunar base, it may be better to have separate classes of builders and retrievers of appropriate materials. On the other hand, there must be a certain redundancy within each class for reliability to be high (Sec. 3.1).

Mode	*Directionality*	*Distance*	*Relevant Uses*
Audition	Low-Medium[5]	Far[6]	Alarm, Individuality
Luminescense	High[7]	Medium	
Chemical	Low[8]	Low[9]	Mass Communication
Reflected Light[10]	Medium	Medium	Social Distance [11]
Tactile	High	Low	
Electric	Low	Low	

TABLE I
SIMPLE COMMUNICATION

3.3 Communication

One of the most important measures of human's artificial communication systems is bandwidth (roughly, the amount of information conveyed). It appears that animals do not use a bandwidth anywhere near the range of modern day communication systems.[2] Mammals, birds, and fish have a very small range of "major displays" [27] (approximately[3] between 15 and 35). Typical ant colonies have between 10 and 20 signals [34].

Another important issue is the mode of communication. Animals use chemical, bioluminescence, reflected light, tactile, acoustic, echolocation, IR, and electric communication. Robotics and AI sensing research often stresses vision, but many animals are able to do several things with relatively simple visual systems. Table I summarizes the characteristics of some of these modalities, which can help designers choose a less expensive and more appropriate communication medium than vision.[4]

[1]Many prominent social structures are actually dominance systems ("pecking orders") which do not directly apply to robotic systems. In dominance systems, the more dominant agents have easier access to food, nesting sites, estrus females, freedom of movement, or roosting places. An example dominance system is among lions, where the dominant lions eat before the other lions. Lion cubs often die from this (by having weaker lions not reproduce, the overall strength of the species increases); robots need not compete at this level. Since the robots are not directly competing amongst themselves, these dominance systems are unnecessary.

[2]Vision may be a high bandwidth medium, but the amount of information conveyed is often small, e.g., flashing a red card may only convey one bit. Our visual system may have evolved so that we can extract information from the world when we do not share an active protocol with the world.

[3]Although the exact number of bits of communication may be inexact, the bandwidth is still extremely low. Each major display may be "graded", that is, an analog signal.

[4]For more complete information on the different modes and communication information on particular animals, see [30].

[5]The directionality depends on the frequency.

[6]There are design reasons for limiting the broadcast range. In animal systems, predators may hear the broadcast. In friendly environments, there may be a problem with noise.

[7]The receiver may know exactly where the sender is, but it may be more difficult for the sender to direct the message to the receiver.

[8]Except in constant wind conditions (where the scent can be followed), or where the scent is left on an object.

[9]Except in wind.

[10]One of the reasons that reflected light may be used by animals is because of "ritualization". Ritualization occurs when a normal animal activity, such as tugging at grass with teeth, is exaggerated in form to communicate something.

3.4 Multi-agent searching

It is a well-accepted fact that animals working in groups are more effective at foraging or hunting in certain circumstances. The relationship that seems most prevalent in animals and most applicable to robots is that between the distribution of the resource and the social structure of the animals. Some of the possible social animal configurations for food-seeking involve small versus large groups and overlapping versus non-overlapping foraging ranges. There appears to be a relationship between the density of the resource and the group size (more abundant resources correspond with larger group sizes) and the distribution of the resource and the searching range (the more restricted the more overlap) [1,13]. A group of agents would not necessarily have to forage together. For instance, according to Horn's principle of group foraging, if a resource is evenly distributed it may be better for birds to form individual partitioned territories rather than roost and forage together [33]. Useful models for ant foraging have also been developed [15,18].

In robotics, for any exploration task, the distribution of what needs to be located should be considered first to determine the search space and search groups. For instance, assume a robotic system is given the task to clean the hull of a ship. If the barnacles are uniformly distributed, it may be best first to have the robots distribute themselves evenly and then start cleaning. If the barnacles are dispersed and abundant, then larger teams should search disjoint spaces. In fact it may be best to have a different caste of robots determine what the distribution should be based on the species and age of the barnacles.

3.5 Multi-agent Coordination

Animals participate in many activities, sometimes alone, sometimes in groups, and sometimes in subgroups. These activities must be coordinated. An example is the whiptail wallaby [21], which belongs to a mob of 30-40 individuals, but grazes with dynamically changing sub-groups. Robots should also show a wide range of behaviors.

Finding each other becomes an issue when robots participate in a wide range of behaviors alone or in sub-groups. An obvious method of finding one another is to have a central meeting place. In animals, this becomes desirable for certain foraging strategies and for better defense. Lekking is a another method where a number of individuals of the same sex get together in a group and all make noise at the same time. This increases the chance of an agent hearing the location. Table II depicts these and other strategies. (The information center hypothesis referred to in the table states that colonizing birds use information from the incoming birds about where they will go next for food. The hypothesis is not universally accepted [19]).

The remainder of this paper discusses the framework in which many of these insights are being tested and developed.

Method	*When Useful*
Colony	Group Defense Information Center Hypothesis
Lekking	Multiple Agents looking for widely dispersed individual agents
Distinctive Call	Only certain agents can respond to find lost
Assembly Calls	Collect widely dispersed agents

TABLE II
SIMPLE COORDINATION

4 Project overview

The overall goal of this research is to develop a design theory for multi-agent robotic systems. Through the specification of a societal task and a particular environment, design recommendations should be available as to the number of agents that are required, the modes of communication necessary for reliable task achievement, and the social structure of the individual agents. By using an understanding of biological social systems, we expect to be able to converge on such a design theory more rapidly than would be attainable otherwise.

This section describes the first phase of an on-going NSF funded research effort in multi-agent robotics. Simulation results are presented below. The research underway involves an investigation of multi-robot systems along several different dimensions. These dimensions include the nature of communication between agents, the amount of communication between agents (bandwidth), the inter-relationships of agents (teaming effects), the nature of tasks (both simple and more complex), and the migration of the simulation results onto a working robotic system. Although these dimensions will be discussed separately in the sections below, it should be recognized that a holistic and/or synergistic effect is quite possible and the multi-dimensional space is being analyzed for such trends. The results are being evaluated in terms of task completion time, computational cost, efficiency in terms of overall utilization of resources, etc.

The simulation testbed described below provides the basis for expanding and enhancing these preliminary results prior to their migration onto working robotic systems. This testbed is an extension of the motor schema simulator system within which we test our research prior to actual robotic experimentation. It is a well developed and highly modular system that can support new schemas and communication mechanisms readily with little development overhead.

4.1 Dimensions of the Study

The project involves an analysis of the effects of communication, social organization, and task type and complexity for multi-agent robotic systems. Data points discovered in biological systems, such as discussed in Section 3, can facilitate the discovery of efficient solutions in this very complex solution space. Quantitative measures of system performance, in terms of time for completion, efficiency of completion, and other metrics (e.g., safety) are being applied to produce substantive evaluations between candidate systems.

4.1.1 Effects of Communication

It is perhaps most important to understand the impact of adding communication ability to these multi-agent units. It is crucial to determine the effects of the nature of information flow on task accomplishment. The variables include simplex or duplex communication, simple positional reports with or without acknowledgment of receipt, dynamic teaming arrangements via polling, and other more complex arrangements. The analysis is being conducted along the dimensions of direction of communication, quantity of information transmitted, broadcast or direct inter-agent communication, and specific inter-agent communication protocols.

4.1.2 Effects of Organization

Both inter-robot and intra-robot effects of organization are being studied. Intra-robot organization involves an assessment of the impact of non-symmetrical robotic agents. In the most severe case this includes pure master/slave relationships. Additionally, an analysis of how robots that possess different functional attributes (as with drones, workers, etc.) can cooperate and subdivide difficult tasks effectively forms an integral part of the overall project.

Inter-robot organization involves the impact of teaming: coordinated effort and communication between groups of multiple agents. These agents can be both symmetric and non-symmetric. The effect of team size is being assessed as well.

4.1.3 Effects of Task Type and Complexity

Thus far we have studied a simple retrieval task (below). Adding goal sequencing, something required for assembly-type tasks, is one simple extension being developed. More complex tasks such as maintenance of material flow throughout an organization, surveying, and simple construction also will serve as test scenarios for multi-agent robotics.

Other factors such as coordinated servicing (where two or more robots are required to complete a task such as a complex assembly), are also to be studied. The effects of such a *critical mass* of robots on task completion is to be analyzed in light of alternate control and communication regimes.

4.2 Simulation Results for Multi-agent Retrieval

Results have already been obtained showing multi-agent systems cooperating both in the absence of any inter-agent communication [3] and with simple communication mechanisms [25]. Three different schema assemblages have been developed representing forage, acquire, and deliver states (Fig. 1) for a simple target gathering task. Schema assemblages are aggregations of motor schemas that are parameterized to manifest an emergent behavior that is consistent with the particular state that the agent happens to be in. Much of our inspiration is derived from studies in ant behavior [15,16,18,34], although there is no attempt to simulate ant societies through this work.

An individual robot agent initially starts in a forage state, which consists of an assemblage of high-gain noise, moderate obstacle avoidance, and inter-agent repulsion. This assemblage of behaviors produces wide coverage of an area during search for an attractor object while avoiding collisions with

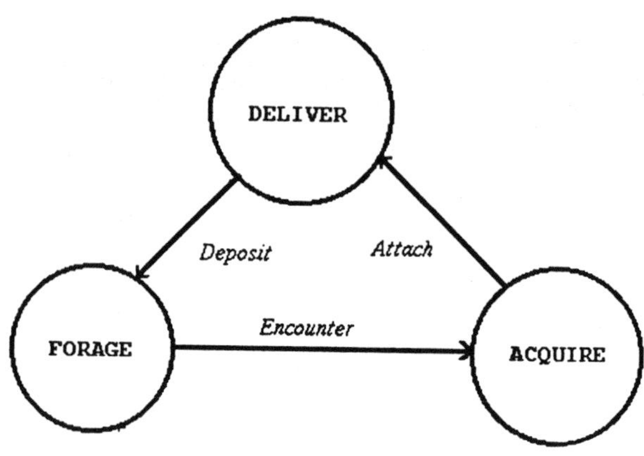

Fig. 1. Schema-assemblages for retrieval task

sensed obstacles. When an attractor is sensed within some arbitrary range of the robot, it transitions to the acquire state. This state assemblage consists of a very low-gain **noise**, a **move-to-goal** schema directed toward the attractor object, and an **avoid-static-obstacle** schema (Section 2.1). Additionally the inter-agent repulsion is turned down significantly, allowing multiple agents to congregate in a small area. After acquiring the attractor object, the system transitions to the deliver state, which redirects the **move-to-goal** to the deposit location, leaving the other schemas in the assemblage the same as in the acquire state. The specific parameterizations for these assemblages appears in [3].

4.2.1 Retrieval in the Absence of Communication

The first phase of the study, involved developing an understanding of what could be accomplished in the absence of any inter-agent communication. Ants leave chemical trails to denote where they have been, which is an indirect communication mechanism. No such information was provided here - only what was immediately perceivable to the agent (nearby goals, close obstacles, and the presence of other robots) was available. Each agent had no knowledge of what the other agent was doing and operated completely independently.

It was observed, that even in the absence of communication, coordinated completion of the task of object retrieval is possible and surprisingly efficient. The phenomena of recruitment is observed as well, something often associated with communicating agents. Recruitment refers to the collective behavior of multiple agents working together to accomplish a common task. Figure 2 depicts one example where the robots collaborate in returning a target object. In this Figure, two independent agents start near the center, both in foraging mode. After a bit of wandering, the leftmost agent senses the attractor (light disk) behind the obstacle (dark disk). It proceeds towards it and starts to retrieve it. In the meantime,

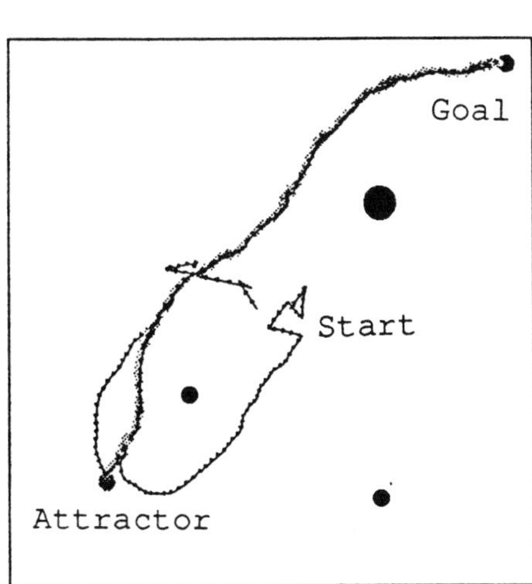

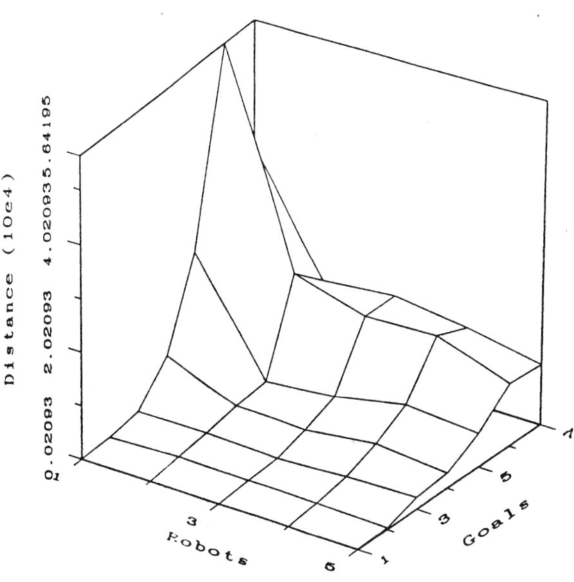

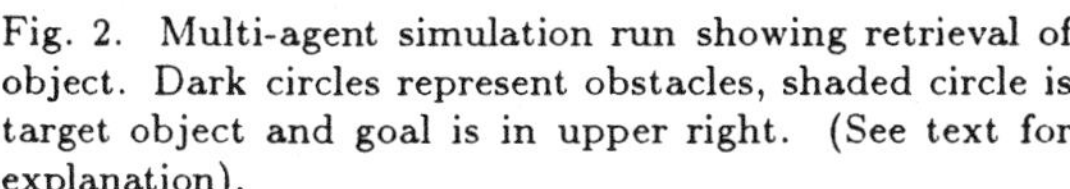

Fig. 2. Multi-agent simulation run showing retrieval of object. Dark circles represent obstacles, shaded circle is target object and goal is in upper right. (See text for explanation).

Fig. 3. Total Foraging Distance - No Communication, 10% Obstacles.

the other agent also senses the attractor. It joins the other agent in retrieving it, speeding up the return rate twofold.

Extensive simulation studies were performed to develop an understanding of the relationships between numbers of agents, numbers of goals, and system efficiency for particular environments. Several metrics have been developed reflecting speed, safety and efficiency. Figure 3 presents the total distance spent by the robots seeking out goals (foraging) for 1-5 robots retrieving 1-7 goals. This is one measure used to determine system efficiency. The more time spent foraging, the less efficient the system. The reader is referred to [3,25] for additional simulation studies.

4.2.2 Retrieval with State Communication

As discussed in Section 3.3, there are many ways in which agents can communicate with one other. The amount of information transmitted is an important consideration. As most of our research is geared for developing robots that can function in dynamic and hazardous environments, our studies have begun by exploring minimal communication methods and assessing the impact on system performance.

In the instance described here, communication between agents consisted merely of transmission of the state of the agent if it was in either retrieval or acquire mode. Under these circumstances, if an agent that was in forage state learned that a nearby agent was in acquire or retrieve state, it moved directly towards that agent. This was a more direct elicitation of recruitment. No knowledge of where the goal was given however, only the information that the communicating agent had discovered a target object. More efficient methods can be imagined such as the transmission of the coordinates of the attractor (e.g., bees), but that is not the case here.

Figures 4 shows simulation results acquired for various numbers of robots and various numbers of attractor objects when this form of communication is permitted. It can be seen that the simple communication mechanisms described above facilitate societal task accomplishment (this is the expected result). Although Figures 3 and 4 may look similar, the scales to which they are drawn are different, with the maximum value for Figure 4 being about 25% that of Figure 3, clearly illustrating the impact of even this minimal form of communication. These and other results are discussed in more detail in [25].

We intend to continue to explore alternate communication strategies including:

- Transmission of attractor coordinates when they are discovered.
- Directional versus non-directional communication.
- Communication strength.
- Distinctive signals for different actions.
- Certain types of robots being attracted to one another, and when a certain critical threshold is exceeded they call for all the other agents (assembly calls or lekking).

Reiterating, the goal of this project is to ultimately provide design guidelines for those developing multi-agent robotic systems in terms of numbers of agents, social organizations, and modes of communication. We are especially concerned with systems operating in hazardous environments where individual agents can be considered expendable. The biological studies discussed in Section 3 provide guidance for efficiently exploring the very large space of potential solutions.

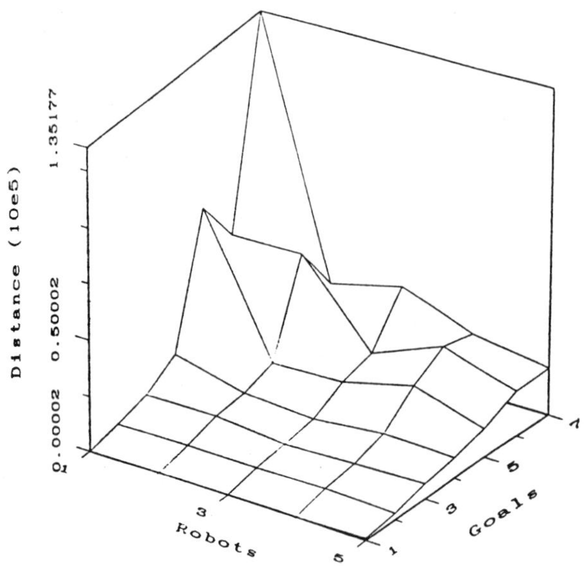

Fig. 4. Total Foraging Distance - State Communication, 10% Obstacles. Note change in scale of vertical axis from previous figure.

4.3 Hardware Configuration

The simulation work is in the process of being ported to 3 Denning Mobile Robots: two MRV-2's and 1 DRV-1. Each robot is connected to a Sun Sparc 4/40. In addition to the 24 ultrasonic sensors and shaft encoders mounted on each robot, a monochrome CCD Pulnix camera will be mounted on-board each. The cameras are to be mounted upwards and have a conic located immediately above the lens to provide a full 360 degree field of view for each robot [22]. A 19.2 kilobaud serial link using Lawn transmitters is used to maintain communication with the offboard hosts. A video link transmits the data for digitization by a Sun videopix board. Communication between the agents is conducted over ethernet.

5 Summary and Conclusions

This paper presents preliminary results from an on-going research project in multi-agent robotic systems. The relevance of ethological studies for application in this domain has been stressed and will be utilized as a guide for the development of a schema-based reactive system.

Preliminary simulation results are promising and provide solid ground for continuing work in exploring the dimensions of communication, social order, and task complexity for this work. Guidelines for the development of multi-agent robotic systems in terms of communication protocols, numbers of agents, and their structure will be a major product of this research. The system is being ported to real mobile robots for testing.

It must be remembered, that the perspective and goals of this paper are those of a roboticist, not an ethologist. No claims are made for the completeness of the ethological material presented. Nonetheless, these data points have been very helpful in determining our approach to designing multi-agent robotic systems. It is hoped that continued studies and additional interactions with colleagues in the biological sciences will provide further insights and models for potential application in robotic systems such as these.

Acknowledgments

The Mobile Robot Laboratory is supported in part by the National Science Foundation under grants #IRI-9113747 and #IRI-9100149, and the CIMS program and Materials Handling Research Center of Georgia Tech. The authors would like to thank Elizabeth Nitz for her generation of some of the simulation results used in this paper.

References

[1] Altmann, S.A., "Baboons, space, time, and energy", *American Zoologist*, 14:221-248, 1974.

[2] Arbib, M.A., "Schema Theory", article to appear in *Second Edition of Encyclopedia of Artificial Intelligence*, 1992.

[3] Arkin, R.C., "Cooperation without Communication: Multi-agent Schema Based Robot Navigation", *Journal of Robotic Systems*, Vol. 9(3), April 1992, pp. 351-364.

[4] Arkin, R.C., "Motor Schema-Based Mobile Robot Navigation", *International Journal of Robotics Research*, Vol. 8, No. 4, August 1989, pp. 92-112.

[5] Arkin, R.C., "The Impact of Cybernetics on the Design of a Mobile Robot System: A Case Study", *IEEE Transactions on Systems, Man, and Cybernetics*, Vol. 20, No. 6, Nov/Dec 1990, pp. 1245-1257.

[6] Arkin, R.C., "Neuroscience in Motion: The Application of Schema Theory to Mobile Robotics", chapter in *Visuomotor Coordination: Amphibians, Comparisons, Models, and Robots*, ed. P. Evert and M. Arbib, Plenum Publishing Co., pp. 649-672, 1989.

[7] Arkin, R.C., "Modeling Neural Function at the Schema Level: Implications and Results for Robotic Control", chapter to appear in *Biological Neural Networks in Invertebrate Neuroethology and Robotics*, ed. R. Beer et al, Academic Press.

[8] Arkin, R.C. and Murphy, R.R., "Autonomous Navigation in a Manufacturing Environment", *IEEE Transactions on Robotics and Automation*, Vol. 6, No. 4, August 1990, pp. 445-454.

[9] Arkin, R.C. and Gardner, W., "Reactive Inclinometer-Based Mobile Robot Navigation", *Proc. of 1990 IEEE International Conference on Robotics and Automation*, Cincinnati, OH, pp. 936-941.

[10] Arkin, R.C. and Carter, W.C., "Active Avoidance: Escape and Dodging Behaviors for Reactive Control", *Proc. Applications of Artificial Intelligence X*, Orlando, FL, April 1992, pp. 676-688.

[11] Box, H.O., *Organisation in Animal Communities*, Butterworth, 1973.

[12] Caloud, P., Choi, W., Latombe, J., LePape, C., and Yim, M., "Indoor Automation with Many Mobile Robots", *1990 IEEE International Workshop on Intelligent Robots and Systems (IROS90)*, pp. 67-72.

[13] Carr, G.M. and MacDonald, D., "The Sociality of Solitary Foragers: a Model Based on Resource Dispersion", *Animal Behavior*, 34:1540-1549.

[14] Clark, R.J., Arkin, R.C., and Ram, A., "Learning Momentum: On-line Performance Enhancement for Reactive Systems", *Proc. 1992 IEEE International Conference on Robotics and Automation*, Nice, France, May 1992, pp. 111-116.

[15] Deneubourg, J.L. and Goss, S., "Collective Patterns and Decision-making", *Ethology Ecology and Evolution* 1: 295-311, 1989.

[16] Franks, N., "Teams in Social Insects: Group Retrieval of prey by army ants", *Behavioral Ecology and Sociobiology*, 18:425-429, 1986.

[17] Fukuda, T., Nakagawa, S., Kawauchi, Y., and Buss, M., "Structure Decision for Self Organising Robots Based on Cell Structures - CEBOT", *IEEE International Conference on Robotics and Automation*, Scottsdale Arizona, pp. 695-700, 1989.

[18] Goss, S., Beckers, R., Deneubourg, J., Aron, S., and Pasteels, "How Trail Laying and Trail Following Can Solve Foraging Problems for Ant Colonies", *Behavioral Mechanisms of Food Selection*, ed. Hughes, R., NATO ASI Series, Vol. G20, Springer-Verlag, 1990.

[19] Gotmark, F., "A Test of Information-centre hypothesis in a colony of sandwich terns *sterna sandvicensis*". *Animal Behavior*, 39:487-495, 1990.

[20] Hackwood, S. and Beni, S., "Self-organization of Sensors for Swarm Intelligence", *1992 IEEE International Conference on Robotics and Automation*, Nice, pp. 819-829.

[21] Kaufmann, J.H., "Social Ethology of the Whiptail wallaby, *macropus parryi*, in northeastern New South Wales", *Animal Behavior*, 22:281-369, 1974.

[22] MacKenzie, D. and Arkin, R.C., "Autonomous Helicopter Position Determination using an On-board Integrated Vision System", *Proc. SME/MVA Applied Machine Vision Conference '92* Vol. I, Atlanta, GA, June 1992.

[23] Mataric, M., "Minimizing Complexity in Controlling a Mobile Robot Population", *1992 IEEE International Conference on Robotics and Automation*, Nice, pp. 830-835.

[24] Miller, D.P., "Multiple Behavior-Controlled Micro-Robots for Planetary Surface Missions", *Proc. 1990 IEEE SMC Conference*, Anaheim, CA.

[25] Nitz, E. and Arkin, R.C., "Communication of Behavioral State in Multi-Agent Retrieval Tasks", submitted to *1993 IEEE International Conference on Robotics and Automation*, Atlanta, GA, May 1993.

[26] Noreils, F.R., "Multi-Robot Coordination for Battlefield Strategies", pre-publication manuscript from author.

[27] Moynihan, M., "Control, suppression, decay, disappearance, and replacement of displays", *Journal of Theoretical Biology*, 29:85-112, 1970.

[28] Norman, D. and Shallice, T., "Attention to Action: Willed and Automatic Control of Behavior", from *Consciousness and self-regulation: Advances in research and theory*, **4**, p. 1, (R. Davidson, G. Schwartz, and D. Shapiro, eds.), Plenum Press, New York, 1986.

[29] Neisser, U., *Cognition and Reality: Principles and Implications of Cognitive Psychology*, Freeman, 1976.

[30] Sebeok, T., Ed., *How Animals Communicate*, Indiana University Press, 1977.

[31] Sugihara, K. and Suzuki, I., "Distributed Motion Coordination of Multiple Mobile Robots", *1990 IEEE International Conference on Robotics and Automation*, pp. 138-143.

[32] Ueyama, T., Fukuda, T., and Arai, F., "Configuration of Communication Structure for Distributed Intelligent Robotic System", *1992 IEEE International Conference on Robotics and Automation*, Nice, pp. 807-812.

[33] Wilson, E.O., *Sociobiology: The New Synthesis*, Belknap Press, 1975.

[34] Wilson, E.O., *The Ants*, Belknap Press, 1990.

Evolution of Trading Strategies Among Heterogeneous Artificial Economic Agents

Andrea Beltratti* and Sergio Margarita**

* Istituto di Economia Politica G. Prato
Università di Torino
Via della Cittadella 10/E, 10122 Torino, Italia
Tel. +39 11 540900; Fax +39 11 541497

** Istituto di Matematica Finanziaria
Università di Torino
Via Assarotti 3, 10122 Torino, Italia
Tel. +39 11 546805; Fax +39 11 544004

Abstract

We consider an artificial stock market populated by three types of neural network-based agents, which we call smart (S), dumb (D) and naive (N), differing as to information sets and procedures to process such sets. We interpret the various procedures as different trading strategies in the sense that, given a specific information set, the action of the agent depends on such procedures. Agents can switch probabilistically from one strategy to the other, choosing among the best performing strategies. It is shown that D-agents disappear from the market after a few periods of time, so that two types remain to interact in the long run. S-agents use a sophisticated methodology to make predictions of market prices, but to achieve this they have to pay a fixed cost every period; N-agents only look at the most recent market price for their forecasts. In the long run the market endogenously determines whether it is more effective to be of type S or N. It turns out that the proportion of the two types depends on the history of market prices: in periods of turbulence the more complicated machinery used by S-agents is worth the cost, while in tranquil times N-agents do not have a comparative disadvantage and take-over the market. It is noticeable that times become tranquil or turbulent as a result of the proportion of S-agents in the market: S-agents learn the model very quickly and stabilize the market, in this way preparing the ground for the expansion of N-agents. In the long run however the type taking over the market depends on the value of the cost of information.

1. Introduction

One remarkable feature of the new literature on Artificial Life and complex systems lies in the effort of trying to understand the aggregate dynamics of a system in terms of interactions of many simple units. This research programme is well described by Langton (1989):

> Nonlinear interactions between the objects specified by the GTYPE (generalized genotype) provide the basis for an extremely rich variety of possible PTYPES (generalized phenotypes). PTYPES draw on the full combinatorial potential implicit in the set of possible interactions between low-level rules.

This idea seems to be very important for understanding many social phenomena which are not easily explained on the basis of standard models. In economics for example there is a tradition, especially popularized during the seventies, of analyzing aggregate dynamics by means of representative agent models; this however is not convincing for some situations, for example when a large number of traders interact in a market (see for example Shiller, 1989). The problem is how to examine the aggregate consequences of heterogeneity without losing analytical tractability. In a previous paper (Beltratti and Margarita, 1992, from now on BM) we have argued that an artificial neural network (from now on ANN)-based methodology can take into account diversity of agents and on-line learning of the environment preserving tractability of the model (at least at the level of computer simulations).

This paper elaborates the model presented in BM (1992), where there are 100 different agents (100 different ANNs) interacting in an artificial stock market, trying to outperform each other by improving their ability to *forecast the forecasts of others*. Each agent forecasts future prices and interacts with other agents by buying or selling assets, modifying her model of the world as information accumulates over time. Prices are endogenously determined. This paper presents two substantial improvements of that basic framework, suggested to us by the literatures on Artificial Life and Genetic Algorithms (from now on GAs) (Holland, 1992): (i) we consider agents differing from each other not only in their elaboration of the information set but also in their trading strategies (ii) we consider both ANNs and GAs as interacting learning devices. This extended model is used to analyze the evolution of strategies of the different traders; we are interested in examining under which conditions agents switch from one strategy to the other, when (and in what proportion) agents with different strategies coexist, and which strategy is more profitable in the long run.

The paper is organized as follows: section 2 describes the model, section 3 describes agents as ANNs, section 4 considers learning, while evolution of strategies is discussed in section 5. Section 6 presents the results of the simulations and section 7 concludes.

2. The model

2.1 Notation

The notation is the following:

J	denotes the number of agents;
π_t	the stock market price in terms of money;
$E_{i,t}P_{t+1}$	the output of network i at time t, to be interpreted as i-th agent's forecast of the price at which a transaction will be executed at t+1;
$I_{i,t}$	the information set available at the beginning of period t, used to form the expectation;
$P_{ij,t}$	the price at which the actual transaction between agents i and j is executed during period t;
$M_{i,t}$	the stock of money of agent i available at the beginning of day t, equal to the stock available at the end of t-1, after the markets closed;
$S_{i,t}$	the number of shares held at the beginning of day t by agent i, equal to those at the end of t-1;
$W_{i,t}$	the stock of wealth of agent i at the beginning of t;
c	information cost;

2.2 The behavior of the agents

Agent i enters the early morning of day t with a given amount of money $M_{i,t}$, a stock of shares $S_{i,t}$ and an information set $I_{i,t}$. We will shortly be more specific about the content of the latter. She has two choices for carrying her wealth to the following morning: money and shares, about which she will have to make a decision at noon of day t. Each day t shares can be bought or sold against money in a stock market opening at noon, at a price $P_{ij,t}$ which depends on the value assigned to shares by the agent j who will be (randomly) met in the marketplace (see section 2.3). We also assume that: (i) agents buy the asset which pays a higher expected return (this is equivalent to assuming risk-neutrality) (ii) each transaction involves buying or selling 1 share (iii) actions of day t are based on expectations formed in the morning of time t before the market opens. The relevant expectation is the price at which the share may be sold in period t+1, denoted (for agent i), by $E_{i,t}P_{t+1}$ (for the way expectations are formed see the next section). Given these assumptions the optimal action is to buy (sell) 1 share if $P_{ij,t}$ is such that $(E_{i,t}P_{t+1} - P_{ij,t}) > 0$ (<0).

The behavior of the agent is simple to interpret: the anticipation of a growth in prices induces the agent to demand shares since this is more convenient than holding money. This behavioral rule can be easily related to actual stock market activity, where professional traders buy or sell every day with the hope of making a short-run profit. In the expectation of a future increase (drop) in the price traders are willing to buy (sell) a quantity that depends on their demand function, so that the larger the expected increase (drop) the larger the amount they are willing to buy (sell). The simplification we adopt in our model is to make the demand independent of the size of the expected change in the price; however we maintain the flavor of agents that act in order to increase their wealth on the basis of their forecasts. In fact an agent who on average makes few mistakes on the change in prices will tend to buy low and sell high, and to increase her total amount of wealth more than an agent who on average make mistakes by buying high and selling low.

2.3 The marketplace

After forming their expectations agents meet randomly in a marketplace. From the sample of J agents we randomly select two agents and match them. Given the assumptions we have made about the demand schedule, a transaction always occurs at a price:

$$P_{ij,t} = 0.5\,(E_{i,t}P_{t+1} + E_{j,t}P_{t+1}) \qquad (1)$$

$$\text{if } E_{i,t}P_{t+1} < E_{j,t}P_{t+1}, \text{ j buys 1 share at } P_{ij,t}$$

$$\text{if } E_{i,t}P_{t+1} > E_{j,t}P_{t+1}, \text{ i buys 1 share at } P_{ij,t}$$

which means that we arbitrarily decide that each transaction takes place at a price which is the simple average of the two expectations. After the transaction is completed we exclude agents i and j and sample from the remaining agents, obtaining another transaction and another price. When all the agents have been selected and all the transactions have been performed we have J/2 prices, whose simple average is considered for determining the market price at time t, π_t. Note that the market price π_t is not directly relevant to any of the transactions which took place during day t, since they were carried out at a price which is the simple average of the two expected prices. The market price is however a useful piece of information, being a signal of the average opinion of the agents.

All the transactions take place because agents differ in their expectation of the future. The interest of this simple model lies precisely in the fact that we can analyze a complex environment where each agent is trying to forecast the forecast of others. There is no *objective* centre of attraction in this system, since the different evaluations depend on differences in the information set and on different ways to interpret a given set of signals.

3. Agents as artificial neural networks

To model the expectations of the agents we use ANNs, which can be described as biologically inspired devices used for mapping a set of inputs into a set of outputs (Wasserman, 1989). The mapping is carried out by the processing elements, called artificial neurons, that are interconnected to form a network divided into some (usually three) layers: the input layer receiving inputs from outside (for example, as in our work, from the environment in which it operates), the output layer sending outputs to the outside and one or more hidden layers connecting the input and output layers. In what follows we consider two different architectures, to model agents with different abilities to discover non-linear relations in the variables in the information set.

3.1 Smart agents

To describe smart agents (from now on S-agents) we use (Figure 1) a standard architecture, known as three-layer, fully interconnected, feed-forward network with back-propagation learning (Rumelhart-McClelland, 1986).

The information set $I_{i,t}$ is a vector composed of the following inputs: π_{t-1}, $\Delta\pi_{t-1}$, $P_{ij,t-1}$, $\Delta P_{ij,t-1}$. In general we can therefore write:

$$E_{i,t}P_{t+1} = g^i(I_{i,t}) = f[B_{i,t}f(A_{i,t}I_{i,t})] \qquad (2a)$$

where the functional form is equal for each network, but the weights vary from one to the other, as shown by the last expression on the right of (2a), where f does not depend on i, being a logistic for all the ANNs, but the matrices A and B of weights and the information set I are both agent-specific and time-varying. On the basis of the weights connecting the three layers (about the training of which we will say more later on) the network forecasts the price at t+1.

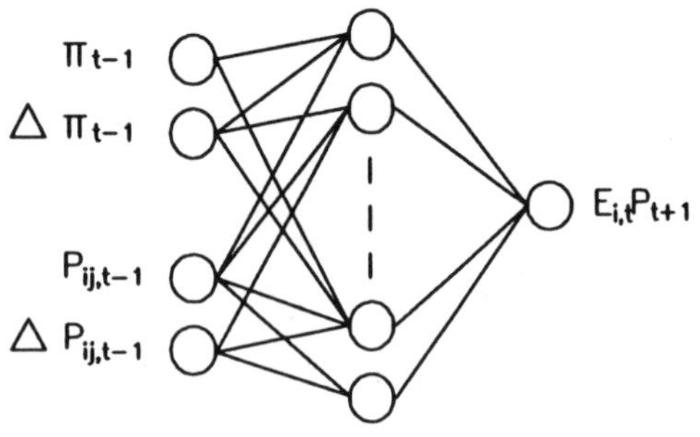

Figure 1. The structure of S- and D-agents.

Of course the weights of an ANN are not fixed, but vary over time in order to improve the forecasting performance. Learning must be done in real time, since agents have to forecast prices at each time t, and cannot wait for a complete time series before estimating the weights. They in fact use an on-line algorithm, common in the ANN literature, known as back-propagation (BP). White (1991) shows that BP is a sort of nonlinear least squares, following the standard rule of minimizing the square of the forecast error. The derivation of the proper term of comparison to calculate such error is however not a trivial task, as will be shown in section 4.

3.2 Dumb agents

Dumb agents (from now on D-agents) are structurally equal to S-agents, apart from one peculiarity, described in detail in BM (1992): they do not take the information provided from the outside world seriously, and always forecast an extreme value of the price, equal to either 0 or 1. This is due to the particular configuration of their weights, which induces them both to forecast extreme values and not to change their weights very much when comparing realizations and expectations.

To see this we need to consider again the learning process: there are cases in which BP does not allow agents to enter the morning of day t+1 with a better way of interpreting the information set and of using it to predict the price at time t+2. The intuition is the following: the logistic function which processes the information coming to the output node produces a number between 0 and 1. If this information is a large negative (positive) number the output will be 0 (1). BM (1992) show that in these circumstances BP does not modify the weights which gave rise to the previous forecast. We are in the presence of networks which do not learn, and maintain a definite opinion about the evolution of the variable, always forecasting either 0 or 1.

Including such agents might seem useless, since it may seem obvious a priori that agents that can't adapt have no hope of competing when circumstances change. This intuition is however not completely exact, as shown by the results of Beltratti and Margarita (1992), since it may happen that under some circumstances some dumb agents are not the worst performers in the market. Suppose in fact that the market price has a positive trend with few fluctuations, it will then be true that there are roughly equal probabilities that after a few periods the richest agent will be smart or dumb, since in this case the dumb agent is already born with the right reaction to the information set. This is however not true when the dynamics of the market is complicated by many ups and downs, since in this case the ability to learn is very important in determining the forecast of the future price.

3.3 Naive agents

Finally, to describe *naive* agents (from now on N-agents) we use a very simplified structure. The information set is restricted to the last value of the market price; there is one input node, no hidden layer and one output node. This structure should be less efficient than the other one to uncover nonlinear regularities in the data.

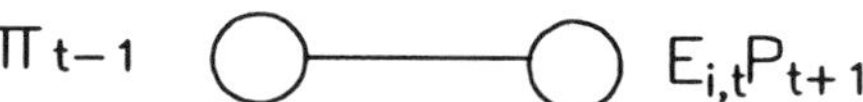

Figure 2. The structure of N-agents.

The analytical formulation is simpler than (2a):

$$E_{i,t}P_{t+1} = g^i(I_{i,t}) = f(A_{i,t}I_{i,t}) = f(a_{i,t}\pi_{t-1}) \qquad (2b)$$

where $a_{i,t}$ is a time-varying parameter.

3.4 Cost and computational complexity

The difference between the first two and the third types of agents is justified by different abilities and possibilities to analyze market data. S-agents (for example money managers) look at a wide information set, and elaborate the information with a complicated structure. N-agents (for example households investing in financial markets) do not have the time and ability for this and just look in a very naive way at the most recent market price.

Such different abilities are accounted for by a cost c, which is paid every period by S-agents to maintain their computational ability. The combination of information processing complexity, cost and differences in parameters due to different learning paths are the elements which make agents heterogeneous, and induce them to assign different values to the assets they can trade. From now on we refer to a complexity/cost combination as a trading strategy followed by the agent. In section 5 we describe how our agents choose long-run forecasting strategies, in the sense of selecting an appropriate combination of complexity and cost.

4. Learning and evolution

What is the mechanism which induces the agents to forecast in a more precise way? To answer this question, note that at the end of the day agents know the market price π_t, and can therefore spend the night doing two things:

(i) calculate the market value of their wealth; for an agent i who bought during the day, wealth is equal to:

$$W_{i,t+1} = (M_{i,t} - P_{ij,t}) + \pi_t(S_{i,t} + 1) - c$$

If the agent was instead a seller we have:

$$W_{i,t+1} = (M_{i,t} + P_{ij,t}) + \pi_t(S_{i,t} - 1) - c$$

where c is equal to 0 for N-agents.

(ii) update their *view of the world* (the weights of the network). The forecast made at the beginning of day t cannot be compared to anything known at the end of period t, since the forecast is about variables which will become known during period t+1. What the network can do at the end of day t is to compare the forecast which was made at time t-1 with the new information available on day t. In order to find the proper term of comparison note that the transaction at time t was executed at price given by equation (1), and this price was exactly what the network was trying to forecast at t-1. Therefore, conditional on transacting with agent j, the output of network i at t-1 is the simple average between the forecast of the output of the same network i at t and the forecast of the output of network j at t. But the network does not know which agent will be met in the marketplace at t. Given our random matching procedure it is equally likely that any of the remaining J-1 agents will be met, so that the network should assign equal probability to meeting any of them. Therefore we can write:

$$E_{i,t-1}P_t = 0.5\,[E_{i,t}P_{t+1} + (J-1)^{-1} \sum_{\substack{j=1 \\ j\neq i}}^{J} E_{j,t}P_{t+1}] \qquad (3)$$

which can be rewritten in a more interpretable way by noting that:

$$\pi_t = J^{-1} \sum_{j=1}^{J} E_{j,t}P_{t+1} \qquad (4)$$

so that the second term in the right-hand-side of (3) becomes:

$$(J-1)^{-1} (\sum_{\substack{j=1 \\ j\neq i}}^{J} E_{j,t}P_{t+1} + E_{i,t}P_{t+1} - E_{i,t}P_{t+1}) =$$

$$= (J-1)^{-1} (J\pi_t - E_{i,t}P_{t+1}) \qquad (5)$$

Substituting (5) in (3), we can see that the forecast of the network should be compared with:

$$E_{i,t-1}P_t = 0.5\,[E_{i,t}P_{t+1}+(J-1)^{-1}(J\pi_t-E_{i,t}P_{t+1})] =$$

$$= 0.5\,(J-1)^{-1}[(J-2)E_{i,t}P_{t+1} + J\pi_t] \qquad (6)$$

A network learning from her mistakes should modify her

weights after comparing her output at t-1 with the expression in (6), i.e. the simple average between her output at t and a function of the market price. To an economist this reminds the Keynesian *beauty context* interpretation of the stock market, reformulated by Townsend (1983) as *forecasting the forecasts of others*.

We can now describe, for given proportions of S-, D- and N-agents, the dynamics of the model from the analytical point of view:

$$\pi_t = J^{-1} \sum_{j=1}^{J} E_{j,t}P_{t+1}$$

$$E_{i,t}P_{t+1} = \begin{cases} g^i(\pi_{t-1}, \Delta p_{t-1}, P_{ij,t-1}, \Delta P_{ij,t-1}) & \text{if i is S or D} \\ g^i(\pi_{t-1}) & \text{if i is N} \end{cases}$$

$$P_{ij,t} = 0.5\,(E_{i,t}P_{t+1} + E_{j,t}P_{t+1}) \qquad (7)$$

Note the importance of the proportions of the types (S, D and N) in determining the dynamics of prices, due to the fact that the formation of expectations is type-specific. The larger the proportion of agents belonging to a type the larger the impact of this type on the market price. Our model is however more complicated than what is described by (7), since proportions themselves are endogenous to the model, as we describe in the next section.

5. Evolution of trading strategies

The last important feature of our model is that agents choose their type: is it worth paying the cost c to have more information and to process it in a more sophisticated way? To answer this question strategies have to be endogenous in the long run. In the model in fact agents are not stuck with a certain strategy, but periodically have an opportunity to switch to a different one. What we do is the following:

(i) every T periods, by using GAs (Goldberg, 1989), we randomly select in the population, with a probability directly proportional to the market value of wealth of the agents, some strategies.

(ii) We reproduce the chosen strategies subject to some random mutations that depend on a fitness index defined in terms of accumulated wealth. The modifications are random since the new strategies are picked up according to the probability density function defined in terms of wealth: strategies which were more effective in the past have a higher probability of being selected by the traders.

(iii) We randomly assign the new strategies to the old traders, who begin a new race starting from the same amount of wealth which was disposable right before the reshuffling of strategies.

Note that in (iii) we dissociate the strategy from the amount of wealth that was accumulated as a result of the application of the trading strategy itself. In a certain sense this may be interpreted as breaking the connection between genotypes and fitness. But in our economic model this is justified by the fact that we interpret the times at which the genetic algorithms are applied as moments in which traders revise their strategy, by randomly choosing, according to some probabilities that are determined by the fitness in terms of accumulated wealth, among the set of possible strategies. The simple revision of strategy in fact does not have any effect on the amount of wealth of the trader, who simply starts a new race with her competitors with a new strategy and the old wealth. Of course by picking up with a high probability the best performing strategies the trader hopes to improve her future performance. However also the other traders are choosing new strategies, and it may well turn out that a strategy that was highly effective given the previous set of strategies is not effective anymore, conditional on the new constellation of strategies. The interpretation of GAs in this context is somewhat different from the standard one: here GAs do not perform a maximization over the space of strategies, but over the space simultaneously defined by both traders and strategies.

In this way the strategies which work better (allow accumulation of more wealth) get more diffusion among the agents, while those performing poorly are abandoned. Note that one agent can therefore vary her strategy according to the general evolution of the environment. Under some conditions, depending on the strategies adopted by the majority of the other agents, it may be worth paying a cost for computational complexity, while in other circumstances, for example when prices are easy to forecast and most of the other agents adopt the no-cost strategy, it may be more profitable to be naive. The choice of a strategy is not a once-for-all decision, but has to be revised every T period, as a function of the environment, that is of the trading strategies adopted by the other agents.

6. Results

The population is composed of 100 networks, divided at the beginning of the simulation into 50 N-agents and 50 between S- and D-agents. Share prices are normalized between 0 and 1. The learning rate of S- and D- (N-) agents is 0.6 (0.3), and the momentum is 0.9 (0.0), in order to take into account different learning abilities of the various types. We perform simulations with 3 values of the cost parameter c (equal to 0.004, 0.01, 0.02) in order to modify the comparative advantage (in terms of wealth) of S- with respect to N-agents.

Figures 3, 4 and 5 show the proportions of the types of agents over 3000 periods, for the 3 values of c. In each case the proportion of D-agents goes to 0 after few iterations because of the low learning ability we have discussed in section 4. The proportions of S- and N-agents are time-varying and depend crucially on the value of c. In the long run, if c is low (figure 3), S-agents take over the market very quickly, while N-agents disappear. At the opposite (figure

5), if the cost is too high it is more convenient to be of type N. When c=0.01 no type can drive the other out of the market during the 3000 periods we consider, even if the proportion path shows some definite trend against S-agents.

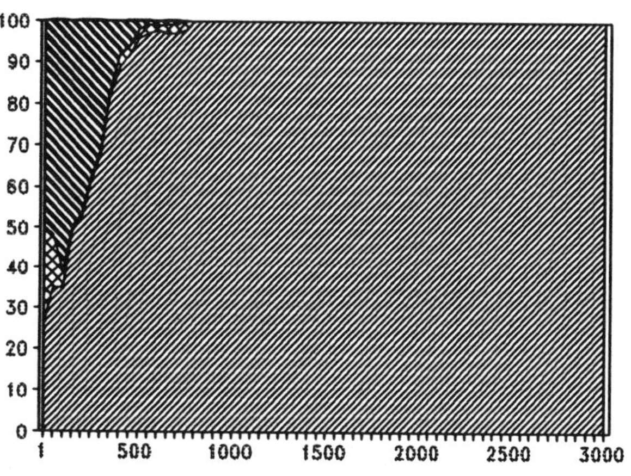

Figure 3. Evolution of S- D- and N-agents, c=0.004

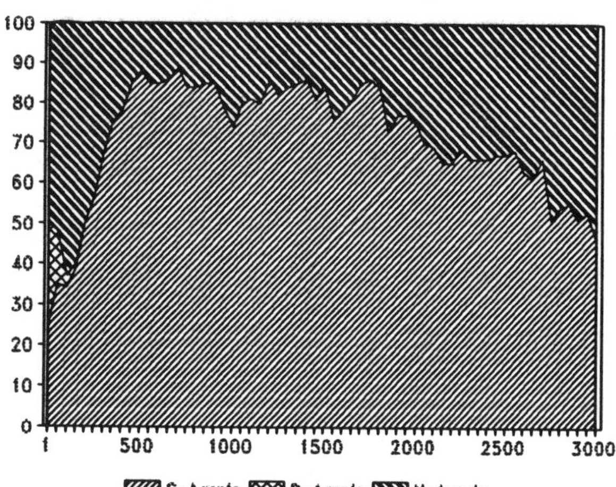

Figure 4. Evolution of S- D- and N-agents, c=0.01

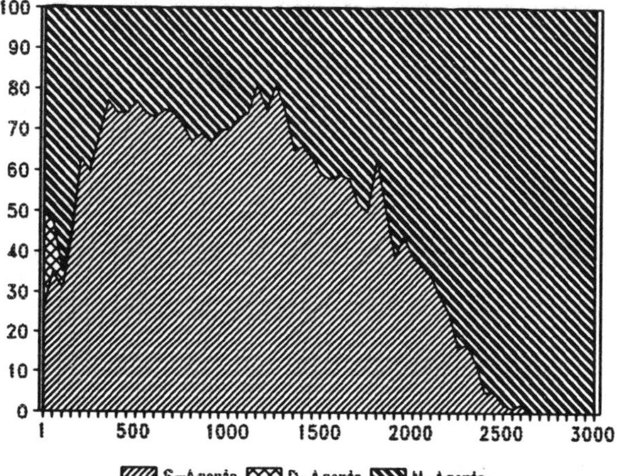

Figure 5. Evolution of S- D- and N-agents, c=0.02

These different results can be understood by considering the effects on market prices of the strategies of the two types. At first the market price moves a lot (figure 6 reports a very typical plot, see also BM, 1992), so that being a sophisticated analyst is very helpful to improve predictions. The endogenous increase in the proportion of N-agents however brings about a stabilizing effect on the price, which makes the (computational) comparative advantage less and less relevant. In fact figure 7 shows that the standard deviation of the forecasts of the various agents decreases over time, especially in the case of S-agents; agents come to agree on a (conventional) valuation. When the price is stable it is not worth paying a (high) cost for processing information more efficiently, since under these circumstances a naive forecasting rule works as efficiently as a more complicated one. When the price is stable, the combination of cost c and the equalization of the forecasting rules across agents starts to deteriorate the wealth of S-agents, as shown in figures 8, 9 and 10.

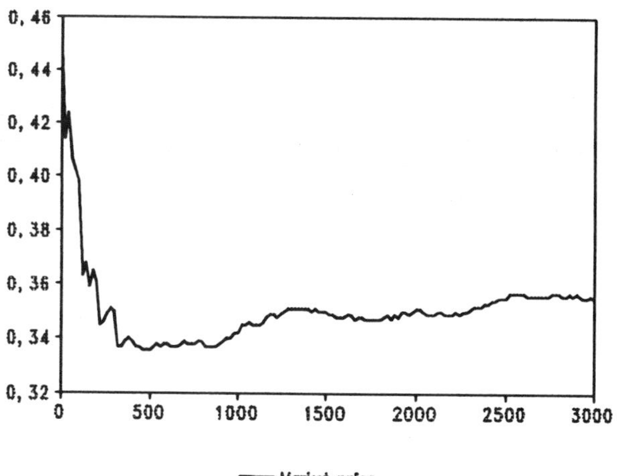

Figure 6. Market price, c=0.01

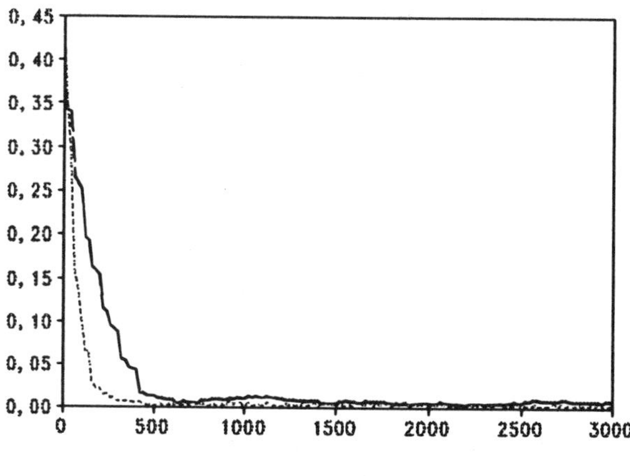

Figure 7. Dispersion of forecasts, c=0.01

The fact that the long-run price is stable regardless of

(but at a value depending on) the history of the process gives us few chances to observe more frequent changes in the type of agent dominating the market. It is likely that in a market hit by continuous exogenous shocks (unlike the model we are considering, where evolution is totally endogenous) the resulting volatility of the market price would make S-agents *useful* even for a high cost c, since N-agents by themselves would not be able to understand and stabilize the price process. In fact in our last simulation (figure 11) we start up the market with a proportion equal to 20% of S-agents and a relatively high cost of 0.01 (which according to figure 5 would drive S-agents out of the market). The initial variability of price makes S-agents more apt to understand the environment, which increases their proportion beyond 90% before the cost c drives down their wealth with respect to the wealth of N-agents (figure 12). The rise of S-agents stabilizes the price, and their decadence is due to their own performance.

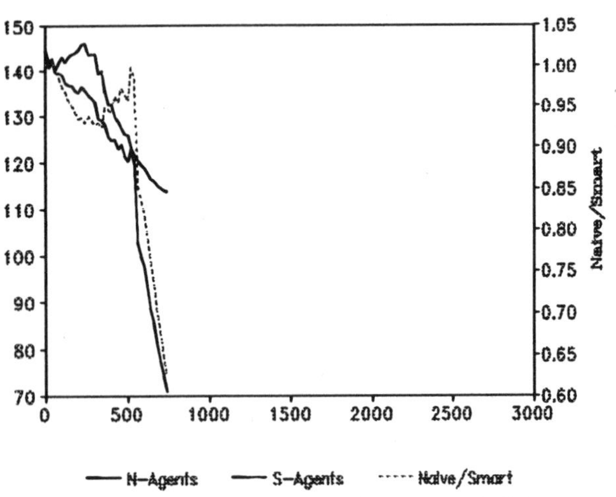

Figure 8. Wealth of S- D- and N-agents, c=0.004

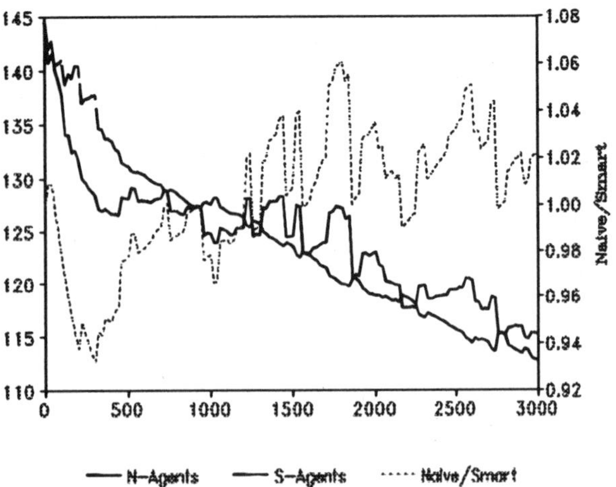

Figure 9. Wealth of S- D- and N-Agents, c=0.01

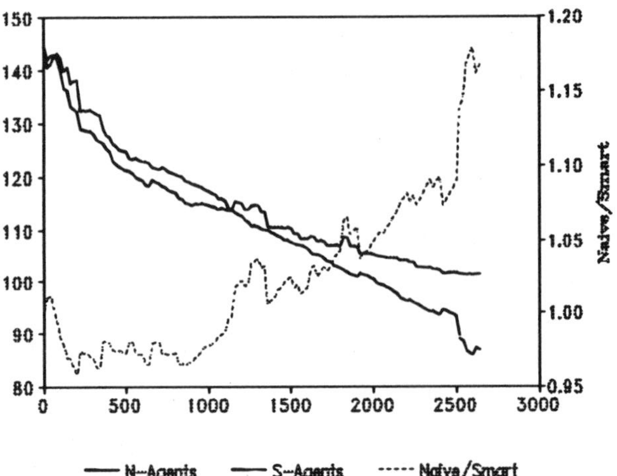

Figure 10. Wealth of S- D- and N-agents, c=0.02

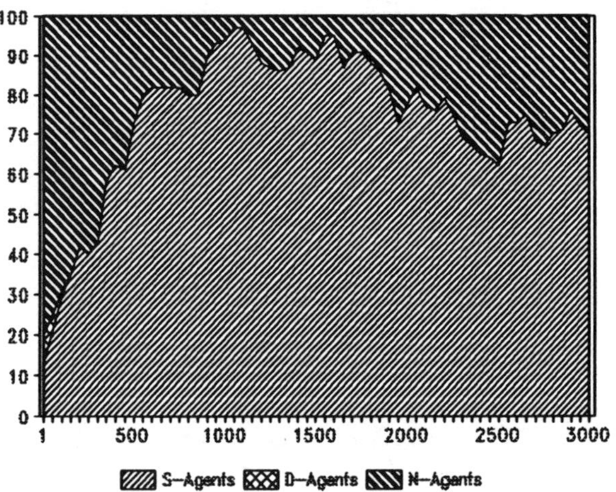

Figure 11. Evolution of S- D- and N-agents, c=0.01
Initial proportions: 20 S- and D-agents, 80 N-agents

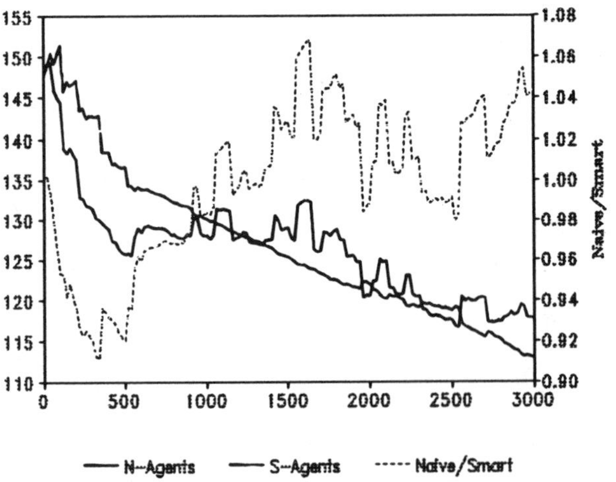

Figure 12. Wealth of S- D- and N-agents, c=0.01
Initial proportions: 20 S- and D-agents, 80 N-agents

7. Conclusions

Our model has studied the endogenous evolution of a market with 3 types of agents. The perturbed initial situation quickly eliminates agents who are not able to learn; after that there is a race between the remaining 2 types. As long as general conditions are unstable it is worth paying a cost for being able to process information more efficiently. But the very effects of these smart agents is to stabilize the market and make life easier to naive agents who do not pay any processing cost and just look at the most recent market behavior. The absence of exogenous shocks does not move the price away from the stable path, even in the case that naive agents dominate the market. It is likely that the introduction of such exogenous shocks would continuously change the relative advantage of the various types, shifting the proportions of the agents in the population.

We hope that the simple model we have proposed is however useful for two reasons: (i) it calls for analyzing markets with models based on heterogeneous agents. This may be particularly important when the long-run equilibrium of the market depends on the type of agents that dominates. Abrupt changes that are difficult to interpret in representative agent models may be more understandable in the context of models with different populations, that may explain structural changes as a consequence of take-overs on the part of some specific subset of agents (ii) it provides an example of an adaptive simulation model that endogenously determines the market price. Future research will proceed in the effort of making the model more detailed, that is based on the interaction of many agents differing as to trading strategies and other individual characteristics.

Acknowledgements

We thank two anonymous referees for useful suggestions on a previous version of this paper.

This research was partly financed by the FEEM, Fondazione Eni Enrico Mattei, Milan.

References

Arthur W.B., 1991, Designing economic agents that act like human agents: a behavioral approach to bounded rationality, *American Economic Review*, vol. 81, n.2, 353-359.

Beltratti A. and Margarita S., 1992, *An artificial adaptive speculative stock market*, Working Paper, Rome, LUISS University.

Goldberg D.E., 1989, *Genetic algorithms in search, optimization and machine learning*, Reading, MA, Addison-Wesley,.

Holland J.H., 1992, *Adaption in natural and artificial systems*, Cambridge, MA, MIT Press.

Holland J.H. and Miller J.H., 1991, Artificial adaptive agents in economic theory, *American Economic Review*, vol. 81, n.2, 365-370.

Keynes J.M., 1936, *The general theory of employment, Interest and Money*, London, MacMillan.

Langton C.G., 1992, Life at the edge of chaos, in Langton et al., *Artificial Life II*, Redwood City, Addison-Wesley.

Langton C.G., Taylor C., Farmer J.D. and Rasmussen S., 1992, *Artificial Life II*, Redwood City, Addison-Wesley.

Margarita S., 1992, Interacting neural networks: an artificial life approach to stock markets, in I. Aleksander, J. Taylor (Eds.), *Artificial Neural Networks 2*, Amsterdam, North-Holland, .

Nottola C., Leroy F. and Davalo F., 1991, Dynamics of artificial markets, *Proceedings of the 1st European Conference on Artificial Life*, Cambridge, MA, MIT Press.

Rumelhart D.E., McClelland J.L., 1986, *Parallel distributed processing, explorations in the microstructure of cognition*, Cambridge, MA, MIT Press.

Shiller R.J., 1987, Investor behavior in the October 1987 stock market crash: survey evidence, in Shiller, 1989 *Market volatility*, Cambridge, MA, MIT Press.

Shiller R.J., 1989, *Market volatility*, Cambridge, MA, MIT Press.

Townsend R., 1983, Forecasting the forecasts of others, *Journal of Political Economy*, vol. 91, n. 4, 546-588.

Wasserman P.D., 1989, *Neural computation - Theory and practice*, New York, Van Nostrand Reinhold.

White A., 1991, Learning in artificial neural networks: a statistical perspective, *Neural Computation*, vol. 1, 425-464.

Action Selection and Learning in Multi–Agent Environments

Gerhard Weiß
Institut für Informatik, Technische Universität München
Arcisstr. 21, 8000 München 2, Germany
weissg@informatik.tu-muenchen.de

Abstract. This paper focusses on reactive multi–agent systems in which *(i)* each agent only knows a specific part of the environment, *(ii)* each agent is specialized in a specific action, and *(iii)* actions of different agents can be incompatible. The central problem addressed is how several agents can collectively adapt to their environment by learning to generate a sequence of action sets that solves an environmental task.

The contents and organization of the paper are as follows. Section 1 briefly motivates the topic of action selection and learning in multi–agent systems. Section 2 introduces a new algorithm called DFG (for "Dissolution and Formation of Groups") for the reinforcement learning of appropriate sequences of groups of concurrently active agents. Section 3 provides theoretical and experimental results on the the DFG algorithm. Section 4 concludes with a brief summary and an outlook on future work.

Keywords. Multi–agent systems, collective learning, action selection, group development.

1. Motivation

The last several years have witnessed a rapidly growing interest in multi–agent systems, that is, in systems that are composed of a number of agents being able to interact and differing from each other in their skills and their knowledge about the environment. Nowadays these systems establish a major research subject in Distributed Artificial Intelligence (e.g. Bond & Gasser, 1988; Huhns, 1987; Gasser & Huhns, 1989; Brauer & Hernandez, 1991). The growing interest is largely founded on the insight that many real–world problems are best modelled using a set of interacting agents instead of a single agent. In particular, multi–agent modelling allows to cope with natural constraints like the limited processing power of a single agent and to profit from inherent properties of distributed systems like robustness, parallelism and scalability.

A great part of the research on multi–agent systems has focussed on the issues of cooperation and communication in the context of distributed problem solving (see e.g. Decker, 1987; Durfee, Lesser & Corkill, 1989). Against that, only little work has been done on learning and adaptation; see (Weiß, 1992b) for an overview of actual literature. This is in contradiction to the common agreement that there are two important reasons for studying learning and adaptation processes in multi–agent systems:

- to be able to endow artificial multi–agent systems (e.g. a system of interacting robots) with the ability to learn and to improve their performance, and
- to get a better understanding of the learning and adaptation processes in natural multi–agent systems (e.g. human groups or societies).

There is a great variety in the multi–agent systems studied in the field of Distributed Artificial Intelligence; see (Huhns, 1987, foreword) for a classifying overview. This paper deals with reactive multi–agent systems in which

- each agent has only local information about the environment (i.e. no agent is "omniscient"),
- each agent can only carry out a specific action (i.e. no agent is "omnipotent"), and
- the actions of different agents can be incompatible.

("Reactive" means that the behavior and the environment of the system are strongly coupled, i.e. that there is a continuous interaction between the system and its environment.)

The central problem addressed is how multiple agents can collectively learn to coordinate their actions such that they solve a given environmental task. In multi–agent systems action coordination and action selection brings up the following two questions:

- Which actions have to be carried out concurrently, and
- which sets of concurrent actions have to be carried out in sequence?

Answering these questions is problematic. On the one side, the search space of all possible sequences of action sets is extremely large. This is because in each environmental state in which the agents can carry out N compatible actions there are $2^N - 1$ different action sets. On the other side, this search space is hard to sample. This is because the usefulness of an action in achieving a goal (solving a task) greatly depends on the environmental state and on other actions carried out. As a consequence, from the fact that an action set is useful or useless in one environmental state, it does not follow that it is also useful or useless, respectively, in another state. Similarly, from the fact that an action set is useless or useful (in some state) it does not follow that a subset or a superset of this action set is also useless or useful, respectively. Because of these difficulties in multi–agent action coordination and selection it would be desirable if the agents themselves are able to collectively learn appropriate sequences of sets of concurrent actions. In the following sections an algorithm called DFG (for "Dissolution and Formation of Groups") is described which aims at endowing multiple agents with this ability.

2. The DFG Algorithm

2.1. The Basic Working Method

The DFG algorithm (DFG stands for "Dissolution and Formation of Groups") is designed to solve the problem of learning appropriate sequences of action sets in reactive multi–agent systems. Its basic working method can be described as follows. The DFG algorithm distinguishes between single agents and groups of compatible agents as the acting units in a multi–agent system. Collective learning and adaptation encompasses two interrelated processes. First, *credit assignment*, that is, the process of estimating or approximating the goal relevance of the agents and the groups in different environmental states. Second, *group development*, that is, the process of dissolving and forming groups in dependence on their goal relevance. In each environmental state *action selection* is realized by arranging a competition between the agents and groups on the basis of their estimated goal relevance. The winner of this competition is allowed to become active and to change the environment. All together, an appropriate sequence of action sets is learnt by the repeated execution of the following *working cycle* of the DFG algorithm:

1. [Check for activity] The agents and groups check whether they could become active in the actual environmental state.[1]
2. [Group development] Existing groups that have not contributed to the goal attainment dissolve, and agents and groups that are willing to cooperate form new groups.
3. [Action selection] Based on their estimated goal relevance in the actual state, the agents and groups compete with each other for the right to carry out their actions. Only the winner becomes active and transforms the actual into a new environmental state.
4. [Credit assignment] The agents and groups adjust the estimates of their goal relevances by assigning credit or blame to each other.

The next subsections describe the steps of this working cycle in detail.

2.2. Agents, Groups, and Activity

The DFG algorithm distinguishes between two types of acting **units** in a multi–agent system: single agents and groups of compatible agents. An **agent** is composed of a *sensor component*, a *motor component*, a *knowledge base*, and a *learning element*. The sensor and the motor component enable the agent to interact with other agents and its environment (e.g. by communicating with other agents, by receiving visual information about the current environmental state, or by carrying out an action that changes the environment). The knowledge base contains the agent's knowledge (e.g. about other agents or the environment). The learning element is responsible for the modifications in the knowledge base that improve the agent's interaction abilities (e.g. by refining its motor skills or by increasing the efficiency of its cooperation with other agents). Figure 1 illustrates this view of a single agent. An agent is restricted in a twofold manner. First, because of limitations imposed on its sensor abilities, an agent knows only a part of the environment; and second, because of limitations imposed on its motor component, an agent is specialized in a specific action. As a consequence of these restrictions, different agents may know different aspects of the environment, and they may be specialized in different actions.

[1]The DFG algorithm as it is described in this paper requires that each agent is specialized in only one action; however, it can be easily extended to systems in which each agent can carry out several actions.

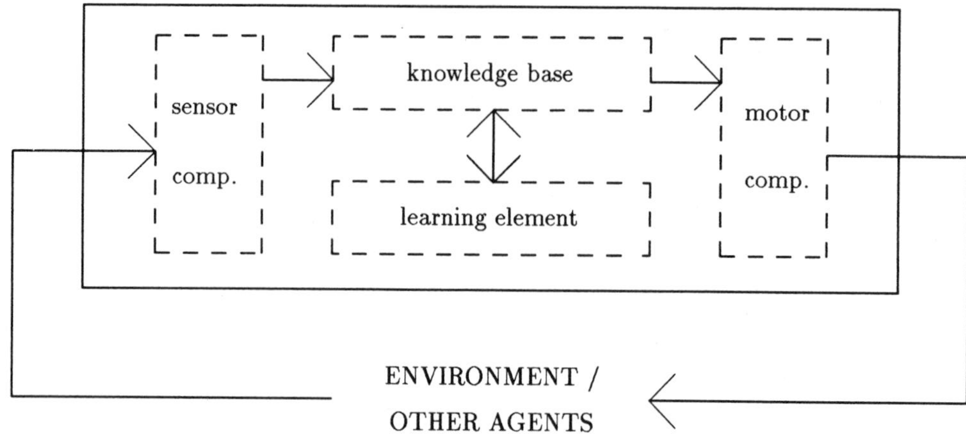

Figure 1: An agent and its components. (See text for details.)

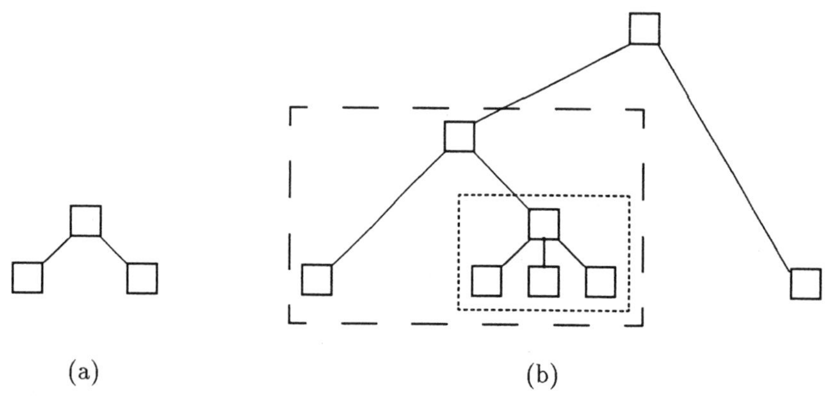

Figure 2: Structural organization of groups. A group is defined as a set of agents (□) that is structured by leader–member relations (/ , \). *(a)* shows the most simple group consisting of a leader and two members each being a single agent. *(b)* shows a a more complicated group having two members, one being a group (dashed box) and the other being a single agent. The "dashed group" again has a group (dotted box) and a single agent as its members, where the "dotted group" has three members each being a single agent.

A **group** consists of a *group leader* and several compatible *group members*, where a group leader is a single agent and a group member is either a single agent or another group. This recursive definition is rather general and covers both low and high structured groups; see figure 2 for an illustration. The task of a group leader is to represent the group's interests; this includes, for instance, to decide whether the group should persist as an autonomous acting unit, cooperate with another acting unit, or dissolve. The group members have to be *compatible* in the sense that the activity of no member leads to environmental changes that prevent the activity of another member.

There are three concepts that are elementary to the learning and adaptation processes induced by the DFG algorithm: the **(potential) activity**, the **activity context**, and the **autonomy** of a unit. An agent is said to be active (potentially active) simply if it carries out (could carry out) its action. The activity of a group results from the concerted activity of the group members, and a group is said to be active (potentially active) if all its members are so. The activity context of an agent in an environmental state is given by the agent's knowledge about this state, and the activity context of a group is given by the activity contexts of all group members. Finally, an agent as well as a group is said to be autonomous, if it is not a member of a potentially active group. The next sections describe the roles of these concepts in detail.

The following **notation** is used throughout the rest of this paper. S_j refers to an environmental state. U_i refers to a unit of the multi–agent system, where a unit is either an agent A_i or a group G_i. If a unit U_i is a member of a group G_k then this is symbolized by $U_i \in G_k$. $[S_j]_i$ refers to the part of S_j that is known to the agent A_i.

$[U_i, S_j]$ denotes the activity context of the unit U_i in the environmental state S_j; this context can be formally described by

$$[U_i, S_j] = \begin{cases} [S_j]_i & \text{if} \quad U_i = A_i \\ \bigcup_{U_l \in G_i} [U_l, S_j] & \text{if} \quad U_i = G_i \end{cases} .$$

(Note that $[U_i, S_j] \cap [U_k, S_j]$ may but need not be empty, and that $\bigcup_i [U_i, S_j]$ is not necessarily equal to S_j. Similarly, $[U_i, S_j] \cap [U_i, S_k]$ may but need not be empty; in particular, it may be the case that $[U_i, S_j] = [U_i, S_k]$, which means that a unit may be unable to distinguish between different environmental states.) Finally, $\overline{U_i}$ is defined as

$$\overline{U_i} = \begin{cases} A_i & \text{if} \quad U_i = A_i \\ \text{the leader of } G_i & \text{if} \quad U_i = G_i \end{cases} .$$

This is only a "technical definition" that allows to give an efficient description of the DFG algorithm.

2.3. Action Selection and Credit Assignment

Action selection and credit assignment base on the action–oriented variant (Weiß, 1991, 1992a) of Holland's (1985, 1986) *bucket brigade model* of learning in classifier systems. Informally, the DFG algorithm realizes action selection and credit assignment as follows. In each actual environmental state, a competition runs between the units. Each unit makes a bid for its right to become active, where this bid depends on the estimate of the unit's state–specific goal relevance. Only the unit making the highest bid is allowed to become active and, in this way, transforms the actual into a new environmental state. This selection of the actual winning unit corresponds to the selection of the actions that are carried out in the actual state. The actual winner then reduces the estimate of its goal relevance by the amount of its bid and hands this amount back to the preceding winner. The preceding winner, in turn, adds the received amount to the estimate of its goal relevance. (The actual winner pays for the previlege of being active and rewards the preceding winner for appropriately setting up the environment.) Additionally, if a reward is received from the environment, this reward is added to the estimate of the actual winner's goal relevance. The effects of this bucket–brigade–type action selection and credit assignment are as follows. In a sequence of winning units, each unit pays a certain amount to its direct predecessor and receives a certain amount from its direct successor or from the environment. This has two major effects. First, the estimate of a unit's goal relevance increases (decreases), if the unit pays less (more) than it receives. Second, a change (i.e. an increase or decrease) in an estimate of an unit's goal relevance is propagated, over time, from this unit backwards through the chain of its predecessors. All together, this results in a *stabilization* of a sequence of active units, if the last unit of the sequence regularly attains payoff, and in a *disintegration* of a sequence, if its last unit does not.

Formally, action selection and credit assignment are realized as follows.

Action Selection. For each unit U_i that is potentially active and autonomous in the actual environmental state S_j, $\overline{U_i}$ makes a bid B_i^j for U_i's right to become active. (The autonomy condition ensures that there is no competition between a group and its members; see below.) This bid is calculated by

$$B_i^j = \alpha \cdot E_i^j + \beta \cdot E_i^j \quad , \tag{1}$$

where α is a small constant called *risk factor*, β is a small random number called *noise factor*, and E_i^j is a scalar value called *estimate*. The $\alpha \cdot E_i^j$ is called the *deterministic part* and the $\beta \cdot E_i^j$ is called the *stochastic part* of B_i^j. The deterministic part of B_i^j is the fraction of E_i^j that $\overline{U_i}$ is willing to risk for U_i's right to become active in S_j. The stochastic part of B_i^j introduces noise into the bidding process in order to avoid getting stuck into local learning minima.[2] The E_i^j is $\overline{U_i}$'s estimate of U_i's goal relevance in the activity context $[U_i, S_j]$. (The first time a unit U_i is potentially active in a state S_j, $\overline{U_i}$ initializes E_i^j with a predefined value E^{init}; E^{init} is called the *initialization value* of the estimates.) On the basis of their bids, a competition runs between the potentially active units and the unit U_i^j with

$$B_i^j = \max_k \{B_k^j\} \tag{2}$$

is allowed to become active.

Credit Assignment. Credit assignment happens by means of a collective adjustment of the estimates E_i^j. Let U_i be the winning unit in the actual state S_j, and let U_k be the winning unit in the preceding state S_l (i.e. U_k transforms S_l to S_j). Then $\overline{U_i}$ reduces its estimate E_i^j by the amount of the deterministic part of its bid B_i^j, i.e.

$$E_i^j = E_i^j - \alpha \cdot E_i^j \quad , \tag{3}$$

and hands this amount back to $\overline{U_k}$. $\overline{U_k}$, in turn, adds the received amount to its estimate E_k^l of U_k's goal relevance in the context $[U_k, S_l]$, i.e.

$$E_k^l = E_k^l + \alpha \cdot E_i^j \quad . \tag{4}$$

Additionally, if the activity of U_i leads to a new state in which a reinforcement is received from the environment, then $\overline{U_i}$ adds this reinforcement to its estimate E_i^j.

[2]In the literature on classifier systems different methods for introducing noise in the bidding process have been proposed; see e.g. (Goldberg, 1989; Riolo, 1989).

2.4. Group Development

According to the DFG algorithm, group development includes two contrary processes: group formation and group dissolution. Both processes largely depend on the past relevance of the agents' and the groups' actions to goal attainment. Informally, group development bases on the following *developmental principles*:

- Initially each agent and each newly created group is "egoistic" and is not willing to cooperate.
- An agent as well as a group is not willing to cooperate, if the estimate of its goal relevance tends to increase.
- An agent as well as a group is willing to cooperate, if the estimate of its goal relevance tends to increase too slowly, to stagnate, or even to decrease.
- Compatible agents and groups that are willing to cooperate form new groups.
- A group dissolves in its members, if the estimate of its goal relevance tends to fall below a certain minimum level.

These principles are formally realized as follows. In order to be able to decide about the formation of new groups and the dissolution of existing ones, each $\overline{U_i}$ calculates the mean values of its estimates over the previous episodes, where an episode is defined as the time interval between the receipts of two successive environmental reinforcements.[3] These mean values serve as measures of the actions' past relevance to goal attainment. More exactly, during each episode $\tau+1$, $\overline{U_i}$ calculates the *gliding mean value* $M_i^j[\tau+1]$ of its estimate E_i^j as

$$M_i^j[\tau+1] = \frac{1}{\nu} \cdot \sum_{T=\tau-\nu+1}^{\tau} E_i^j[T] \quad , \tag{5}$$

where ν is a constant called *window size* and $E_i^j[T]$ is E_i^j at the end of episode T. Both group formation and group dissolution proceed in dependence on the gliding mean values of the estimates.

Group Formation. Let S_j be the actual environmental state and let $\tau+1$ be the actual episode. For each unit U_i that is potentially active and autonomous in S_j, $\overline{U_i}$ decides that U_i is ready to cooperate and to form a new group with other units in the context $[U_i, S_j]$ if

$$M_i^j[\tau+1] \leq \sigma \cdot E_i^j[\tau-\nu] \quad , \tag{6}$$

where σ is a constant called *cooperation factor* which influences the units' readiness to form new groups. (The autonomy condition ensures that a unit does not cooperate if it is already a member of a potentially active group.) The units that are ready to cooperate in their activity contexts form new groups as follows. Let $\mathcal{U}$ be the set of all units that are ready to cooperate:

until $\mathcal{U} = \emptyset$ do

- Let $U_i \in \mathcal{U}$ be the unit with $E_i^j = \max_l\{E_l^j : U_l \in \mathcal{U}\}$. Then $\overline{U_i}$ announces a "cooperation offer" to the other units.
- For each unit $U_l \in \mathcal{U}$ that is compatible with U_i, $\overline{U_l}$ sends a "cooperation response" to $\overline{U_i}$.
- Let $\mathcal{U}^{resp} \subseteq \mathcal{U}$ be the set of all responding units. Then $\overline{U_i}$ chooses the unit $U_k \in \mathcal{U}^{resp}$ with $E_k^j = \max_l\{E_l^j : U_l \in \mathcal{U}^{resp}\}$ as the cooperation partner of U_i. $\overline{U_i}$ and $\overline{U_k}$ form a new group G that has U_i and U_k as its members and either $\overline{U_i}$ or $\overline{U_k}$ as its leader. The leader of G initializes its estimate of G's goal relevance in the context $[G, S_j]$ with a predefined value E^{init}.
- $\mathcal{U} = \mathcal{U} \setminus \{U_i, U_k\}$.

(Note that each group has exactly two members; this could be easily extended towards multi-member groups by allowing $\overline{U_i}$ to chose several cooperation partners.) There are two things that have to be stressed. First, the process of group formation does not require an exchange of environmental information — neither among group members, nor among group members and leaders, nor among leaders of different groups. Second, the formation of each new group occurs within the frame of the group members' activity contexts. If $\overline{U_i}$ and $\overline{U_k}$ form a new group G in the state S_j, then they do so because they are ready to cooperate *in their activity contexts* $[U_i, S_j]$ and $[U_k, S_j]$, respectively. The group G is potentially active in every state S_l with $[U_i, S_l] = [U_i, S_j]$ and $[U_k, S_l] = [U_k, S_j]$. (In each such state $\overline{U_i}$ and $\overline{U_k}$ inform the leader of G that they are potentially active, and then the leader for its part declares G as being potentially active.) With that, cooperation and group formation is a highly context-sensitive process (each group is attached to a specific activity context), but does not require an exchange of environmental information among the units.

Group Dissolution. Again let S_j be the actual environmental state and $\tau+1$ the actual episode. For each group G_i that is potentially active and autonomous in S_j, $\overline{G_i}$ decides that G_i has to dissolve in its members if

$$M_i^j[\tau+1] \leq \rho \cdot E^{init} \quad , \tag{7}$$

where ρ is a constant called *dissolution factor* which influences the robustness of the existing groups, and E^{init}

[3] Compared with a cycle-based calculation, an episode-based calculation enables a more balanced group development.

is the initialization value of the estimates (see 2.3). (Here the autonomy condition ensures that a group does not dissolve as long as it is a member of another group.)

3. Analysis

3.1. Learning Convergence

The DFG algorithm aims at generating appropriate sequences of action sets. Therefore an important question is how this algorithm changes the estimates of the goal relevances of units that are successively active. An answer to this question can be found by extending Grefenstette's (1988) convergence result on the bucket brigade algorithm to the DFG algorithm. This leads to the following

Proposition. Consider a collection of units $U_{i_1}, \ldots, U_{i_n}$ in which

(i) each unit U_{i_k}, $1 \leq k < n$, is coupled with unit $U_{i_{k+1}}$ in the sense that each activity of U_{i_k} in the context $[U_{i_k}, S_{j_k}]$ is followed (in the next cycle) by the activity of $U_{i_{k+1}}$ in the context $[U_{i_{k+1}}, S_{j_{k+1}}]$, and

(ii) the only external reward (if any) is received by U_{i_n}.

If $E_{i_n}^{j_n}$ converges to a constant value E^*, then $E_{i_k}^{j_k}$, $1 \leq k < n$, also converges to E^*.

Proof. If U_{i_k}, $1 \leq k < n$, is active during the cycle t and $U_{i_{k+1}}$ is active during the cycle $t+1$, then

$$E_{i_k}^{j_k}[t+2] = E_{i_k}^{j_k}[t] - \alpha \cdot E_{i_k}^{j_k}[t] + \alpha \cdot E_{i_{k+1}}^{j_{k+1}}[t+1] \quad ,$$

where $E_{i_k}^{j_k}[t+2]$ is $E_{i_k}^{j_k}$ at the beginning of cycle $t+2$. This yields

$$E_{i_k}^{j_k}[\overline{s}+2] = (1-\alpha)^n \cdot E^{init} + \\ + \sum_{r=1}^{s} \alpha \cdot (1-\alpha)^{s-r} \cdot E_{i_{k+1}}^{j_{k+1}}[\overline{r}+1] \quad ,$$

where $s \in \mathsf{N}$ and $\overline{s}$ is defined as $\overline{s} = t$ iff the sth activity of U_{i_k} in the context $[U_{i_k}, S_{j_k}]$ occurred during the cycle t. Now suppose that $E_{i_{k+1}}^{j_{k+1}}$ converges to E^*. Then

$$\lim_{t\to\infty} E_{i_k}^{j_k}[t] = lim_{s\to\infty} E_{i_k}^{j_k}[\overline{s}+2] = E^* \quad ,$$

i.e. $E_{i_k}^{j_k}[t]$ also converges to E^*. ■

This result shows that under the DFG algorithm the estimates of the goal relevance of successively active units tend to converge to an equilibrium level. Under equilibrium conditions, a unit pays to its predecessor the same amount than it receives from its successor. With that, the estimates serve to predict the internal rewards.

3.2. Experimental Results

The blocks world is chosen as a task domain. This domain is well known in Artificial Intelligence and has been intensively studied in the fields of problem solving and planning, and it is clear enough for experimental studies in the unknown field of multi-agent learning. What has to be learnt by a given set of agents is to transform a start constellation of blocks into a goal constellation within a limited time interval. This paper summarizes the results on the task shown in figure 3. In this task, each agent is *specialized* in a specific action; for instance, agent A_1 is able to put block A on the bottom (symbolized by a $\perp$) and agent A_6 is able to put block D on block A. The precondition for applying an action $put(x,y)$ is that no other blocks are placed on x and y, i.e. x and y have to be empty. Each agent is assumed to have only *minimal information* about the environment: it only knows ("sees") whether the precondition of its action $put(x,y)$ is fulfilled. Because of this information constraint, an agent is unable to distinguish between all different environmental states.[4] In particular, an agent may be unable to distinguish between a state in which its action is relevant and a state in which its action is not relevant to goal attainment. For instance, agent A_2 cannot distinguish between a "relevant state" in which block B is placed on the bottom and an "irrelevant state" in which block B is placed on block F; similarly, A_5 cannot distinguish between a state in which block D is placed on the bottom and a state in which D is placed on A. (The fact that an action may be relevant in one state but irrelevant in another is sometimes called the *Sussman's anomaly*; see e.g. (Ginsberg, 1986).) Two actions are considered to be *incompatible* if their concurrent execution is not possible. Formally, two actions, $put(x,y)$ and $put(u,v)$, are incompatible if $x \in \{u,v\}$ or $u \in \{x,y\}$ or $y = v \neq \perp$. Examples of sets of incompatible actions are $\{put(A,\perp), put(A,B)\}$ (i.e. a block cannot be placed on different positions at the same time), $\{put(B,F), put(E,F)\}$ (i.e. different blocks cannot be put on the same block), and $\{put(C,D), put(D,A)\}$ (i.e. a block cannot be put on a block which, at the same time, is put on another block). The transformation from the start into the goal constellation has to be done in *at most four cycles*.

An analysis of the search space of this task shows that there is one solution sequence (i.e. a sequence of action sets that transforms the start into the goal constellation) of length 2, 24 solution sequences of length 3, and 210 solution sequences of length 4. The solution sequence of length 2 is given by $\langle\{put(A,\perp), put(C,\perp), put(F,\perp)\}, \{put(A,B), put(C,D), put(E,F)\}\rangle$. There is no solution sequence containing less than 5 actions; consequently, a sequential "one-action-per-cycle" approach would require at least 5 cy-

[4] Instead, each agent only distinguishes between the class of states in which its action is applicable and the class of states in which its action is not applicable. A less strong restriction is used in (Weiß, 1992c).

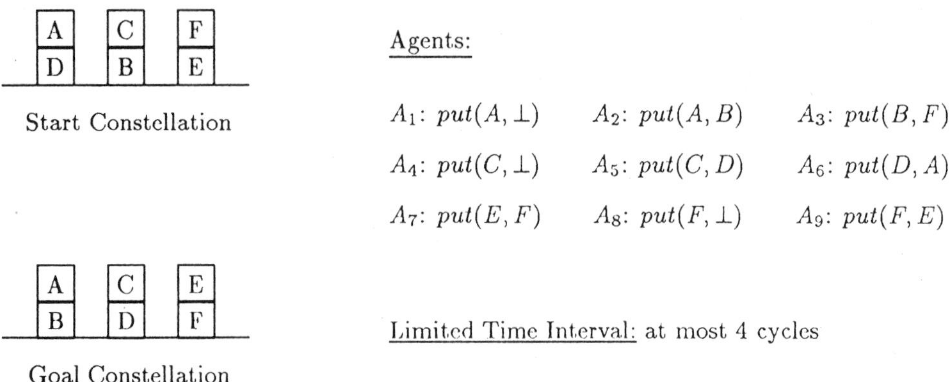

Figure 3: Blocks world task. (See text for details.)

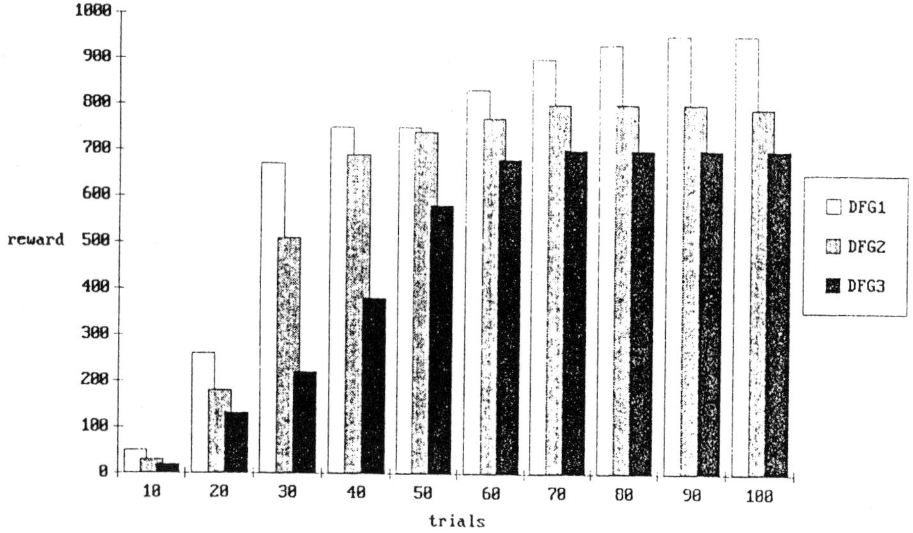

Figure 4: Learning performance of the DFG algorithm. (See text for details.)

cles to solve the task. In the case of a random walk through the search space (i.e. in the case of randomly choosing, in each environmental state, an applicable set of compatible actions), the probability of finding the solution sequence of length 2 is less than 1 percent, the probability of finding a solution sequence of length 3 is less than 4 percent, and the probability of finding a solution sequence of length 4 is less than 5 percent. With that, the probability that a random sequence of at most four action sets transforms the start into the goal constellation is less than 10 percent.

The experimental setting was as follows. A *trial* is defined as any sequence of at most four cycles that transforms the start into the goal constellation (successful trial), as well as any other sequence of exactly four cycles that transforms a start into a non-goal constellation. Learning proceeds by the repeated execution of trials. At the end of each trial the start constellation is restored, and the agents again try to solve the task. Additionally, only at the end of each successful trial a non-zero external reward R^{ext} is provided. Parameter setting: $E^{init} = R^{ext} = 1000$, $\alpha = 0.15$, $\beta \in [-\alpha/5 \ldots + \alpha/5]$ (randomly chosen for every bid), and $\nu = 4$.

Figure 4 shows the learning results of the DFG algorithm for $\sigma = 1 + 3\alpha$ and $\rho = 1 - \alpha$ (*DFG1*), $\sigma = 1 + \alpha$ and $\rho = 1 - \alpha$ (*DFG2*), and for $\sigma = 1 + \alpha$ and $\rho = 1 - 3\alpha$ (*DFG3*).[5] Each data value reflects the mean environmental reward per trial obtained during the previous 10 trials, averaged over 10 runs started with different

[5]Similar results have been obtained in the experiments that we carried out with various other agent and block constellations; additionally, in all these experiments the DFG algorithm turned out to be robust over a broad range of parameter settings.

random-number-generator seeds. The learning performance of both the DFG1, the DFG2 and the DFG3 variant is clearly above the random performance level (which is less than 100, see above). The highest performance level of the DFG1, the DFG2 and the DFG3 variant was 950, 800, and 700, respectively. The DFG1 performed better than the DFG2 which performed better than the DFG3 variant. The reason for these performance differences is that the DFG1 uses a less strict criterion for the formation of groups than the DFG2, and the DFG2 uses a less strict criterion for the dissolution of groups than the DFG3 (cf. the σ and ρ values). As a consequence, under the DFG1 more groups were created than under the DFG2, and under the DFG2 more groups dissolved than under the DFG3. In other words, the DFG1 turned out to be more flexible than the DFG2, and the DFG2 turned out to be more flexible than the DFG1. This is illustrated by table 1 which shows, for the three variants, the number of created and dissolved groups per run, averaged over the ten runs. (Note that the ratio of created and dissolved groups under the DFG2 is smaller than under the DFG1 and the DFG3.)

Avg. number per run	DFG1	DFG2	DFG3
created groups	27.5	19.1	20.2
dissolved groups	5.7	6.0	3.8

<u>Table 1:</u> *Group development.* (See text for details.)

Additional experiments are required in order to make these results conclusive. However, the results described in this paper demonstrate the ability of the DFG algorithm to produce both useful and stable sequences of active units, although the individual agents do only have local information about their environment.

4. Conclusion

This paper took the first steps towards a better understanding of the relations between action selection and learning in reactive multi-agent systems. An algorithm called DFG was presented that implements multi-agent reinforcement learning of appropriate sequences of concurrent actions on the basis of credit assignment and group development. Theoretical and experimental results were provided that show the learning abilities of this algorithm.

A limitation of the DFG algorithm is that its success relies on an explicit exploration of a sufficient number of environmental states and actions. This leads to an impractical amount of time required for learning, if the state and action spaces are too large and complex. There are two basic methods which can be used in order to cope with this kind of limitation and which have been intensively studied in the field of Artificial Intelligence. First, to endow the agents with the ability to generalize over the search space. And second, to endow the agents with the ability to built up an internal world model which can be used for look-ahead and planning activities. Both methods, generalization and planning, can be applied within the frame of the DFG algorithm.

Additional investigations are needed for a deeper understanding of the learning approach described in this paper. Important research topics are, for instance, an analysis of the mutual influence of the critical learning parameters (e.g. window size, cooperation and dissolution factor), the extension of the concept of a group (e.g. towards multi-member groups with different bindings between the members, or towards groups of successively active agents), and the development of alternative criteria and strategies for group dissolution and group formation.

Acknowledgements

I am indebted to Martin Eldracher for many fruitful discussions on learning and group development in multi-agent systems. I also would like to thank the reviewers for their useful comments.

References

Bond, A. H., & Gasser, L. (Eds.). (1988). *Readings in distributed artificial intelligence.* San Mateo, CA: Morgan Kaufmann.

Brauer, W., & Hernández, D. (Eds.). (1991). *Verteilte Künstliche Intelligenz und kooperatives Arbeiten.* Springer.

Decker, K. S. (1987). Distributed problem-solving techniques: a survey. *IEEE Trans. on Systems, Man, and Cybernetics, SMC-17(5),* 729–740.

Durfee, E. H., Lesser, V. R., & Corkill, D. D. (1989). Trends in cooperative distributed problem solving. *IEEE Trans. on Knowledge and Data Engineering, 1(1),* 63–83.

Gasser, L., & Huhns, M. N. (Eds.). (1989). *Distributed artificial intelligence* (Vol. 2). Pitman.

Ginsberg, M. L. (1986). Possible worlds planning. In M. P. Georgeff, & A. L. Lansley (Eds.), *Reasoning about actions and plans - Proceedings of the 1986 workshop* (pp. 213–243). Timberline, Oregon: Morgan Kaufmann.

Goldberg, D. E. (1989). *Genetic algorithms in search, optimization, and machine learning.* Reading, MA: Addison–Wesley.

Grefenstette, J. J. (1988). Credit assignment in rule discovery systems based on genetic algorithms. In *Machine Learning,* 3, 225–245.

Holland, J. H. (1985). Properties of the bucket brigade algorithm. In J. J. Grefenstette (Ed.), *Proceedings of the First International Conference on Genetic Algorithms and Their Applications* (pp. 1–7). Pittsburgh, PA: Lawrence Erlbaum.

Holland, J. H. (1986). Escaping brittleness: The possibilities of general–purpose learning algorithms to parallel rule–based systems. In R. S. Michalski, J. G. Carbonell, & T. M. Mitchell (Eds.), *Machine learning: An artificial intelligence approach* (Vol. 2, pp. 593–632). Los Altos, CA: Morgan Kaufmann.

Huhns, M. N. (Ed.). (1987). *Distributed artificial intelligence.* Pitman.

Riolo, R. L. (1989). The emergence of coupled sequences of classifiers. In *Proceedings of the Third International Conference on Genetic Algorithms* (pp. 256–264). Fairfax, VA: Morgan Kaufmann.

Weiß, G. (1991). *The action–oriented bucket brigade.* Technical Report FKI–156–91. Institut für Informatik, Technische Universität München.

Weiß, G. (1992a). Learning the goal relevance of actions in classifier systems. In B. Neumann (Ed.), *Proceedings of the 10th European Conference on Artificial Intelligence* (pp. 430–434). Vienna, Austria: Wiley.

Weiß, G. (1992b). *Collective learning and action coordination.* Technical Report FKI–166–92. Institut für Informatik, Technische Universität München.

Weiß, G. (1992c). *Learning to coordinate actions in multi–agent systems.* Internal Working Paper (available from the author).

ONE-PAGE SUMMARIES

Structure from Associative Learning

John H. Andreae, Shaun W. Ryan and Mark L. Tomlinson

Department of Electrical & Electronic Engineering,
University of Canterbury, Christchurch, New Zealand.
Email: andreae@elec.canterbury.ac.nz

Summary

Our distant aim is to design a robot that can learn like a human child. Because of the infinity of structures that can be inferred from any finite sequence, it is not possible for unique knowledge structures to be extracted from a child's (or a robot's) input-output or stimulus-action sequence without additional constraints. Some of these constraints will be innate (built-in) and some may be environmental. We are attempting to find out what innate constraints are necessary by teaching our multiple context robot learning system (called PURR-PUSS or just PP) [Andreae, 1977; Andreae & MacDonald, 1991] structured tasks with the minimum of built-in constraints.

PP is a *tabula rasa* system in which learned experience is stored as associations of events (actions and stimuli) in the form of productions. The types of events which can be associated in these productions are prescribed by a fixed, built-in set of production templates. These templates represent the built-in constraints of the system. We see them as corresponding to the many well-known areas of the cerebral cortex in which afferents from particular sensory or motor areas, or from other association areas, converge to associate.

Some of the constraints on human behaviour can be seen in the selective way we react to various emotional expressions and gestures of other humans. This sensitivity to the emotional signals of others enables us to join in cooperative activity and to acquire the goals and aversions of the community in which we live. PP only needs to be pushed around or activated by reflexes for rapid learning and novelty-driven exploration to occur. However, something like a reaction to "smiles" and "frowns" is needed to facilitate cooperative or aversive behaviour.

In the last two decades, developmental psychologists have been showing how mothers and other caretakers influence the infant's acquisition of behaviours by systematic intervention. It has been suggested that babies learn turn-taking from mothers intervening in the baby's burst-pause pattern during suckling [Kaye, 1982]. In this case, the intervention interacts with an innate tendency.

The experiment described in the paper being summarized shows that PP can learn a structured task, comprising 5 levels of subtask, when PP's "teacher" intervenes with a single "auxiliary" action the first time each subtask begins. The action is auxiliary in the sense that it is not needed for the performance of the task. It is called "raise-eyebrows" to emphasise its irrelevance to the task.

The task in question is a cut-down version of the well-known 15- and 8-puzzles, called the 5-puzzle, in which 5 tiles are moved around a 2 x 3 grid by moving one tile at a time into the one empty grid space. The hierarchical solution of the task being taught to PP uses robot hand movements at the bottom level, sequences of hand movements called shifts at the next level, rotations of subpatterns of tiles at the next level, Korf's [1985] macro-operators at the 4th level, and finding the next tile positions at the 5th level. After the teacher's initial intervention, PP uses the auxiliary action to handle the subtasks at each level of the structured task. A collection of 3 production templates, which are not task or domain specific, allow PP to store the items of temporary information needed for handling subtasks.

Gleitman & Wanner [1984] have suggested that the open/closed class structure of natural language is learned by infants from adults' use of stressed and unstressed words. In a second experiment with PP, templates specific to the stressing of sounds have enabled it to learn the changing positions of O's and X's on a tictactoe board. We are now in the process of designing a simple language task, on which to try out this method of intervention with stressed and unstressed speech.

References

Andreae,J.H. (1977) *Thinking with the Teachable Machine.* Academic Press.

Andreae,J.H. & MacDonald,B.A. (1991) Expert Control for a Robot Body. *Kybernetes* 20(4) 28-54.

Chomsky,N. (1980) Rules and Representations. *Behavioral and Brain Sciences* 3(1) 1-61.

Gleitman,L.R. & Wanner,E. (1984) Richly Specified Input to Language Learning. In Selfridge et al *Adaptive Control of Ill-defined Systems.* Plenum.

Kaye,K. (1982) *The Mental and Social Life of Babies.* Harvester Press.

Korf,R.E. (1985) *Learning to Solve Problems by Searching for Macro-Operators.* Pitman.

The Roots of Motivation

Christian Balkenius
Lund University Cognitive Science
Kungshuset, Lundagård, S-223 50 LUND, Sweden
Christian.Balkenius@fil.lu.se

Summary

I want to propose that a motivational system is a prerequisite for any cognitive system. The role of the motivational system is to direct the animal towards one of its different engagements. Without it, a complex animal could not evolve. An animal must necessarily engage in a number of different activities. If all these activities were controlled by one large system, any change to it during evolution would inevitably prove to be fatal. A much more robust system consists of a number of autonomous modules that control the different activities. Changes can be made to one module without affecting the other modules. This implies that there exists an evolutionary pressure towards such an architecture. This type of architecture requires a control system that allows exclusive control of behaviour to one of the modules at a time. This is the origin of the motivational system.

It is possible to find three architectural principles that superimpose on each other during evolution. Based on their underlying architectural principle they can be divided into three classes: (0) Subsumption Architecture, (1) Centralized Control Architecture, and (2) Layered Architecture.

The class 0 system will consist of sensors and effectors. The sensors are connected directly to the effectors and either activates or inhibits them (cf. Braitenberg, 1984). In a larger creature, the need arises for a connecting inter-neuron between the sensor and effector. This step does not change the behavioural abilities of the creature but is a requirement for its greater physical size. It is also essential to the future development of the species, as it is the origin of the nervous system. The inter-neurons make it possible for the sensory signals to interact before they reach the effectors. For example, two sensory signals can converge on a single inter-neuron that will then detect the conjunction of two sensory events. A parallel development is the introduction of both external and internal sensors. This is the result of a bodily change that places some sensors inside the organism. For example, the internal sensor of the feeding system could react on hunger and the external system could react on food being present. If both sensors where signalling, an eating behaviour would be triggered. Each system is governed by its own sensory signals that control its behaviour regardless of the other systems. The robots presented in (Brooks, 1991) are essentially of class 0 complexity.

The class 0 creatures are characterized by the lack of central control. This is changed in the class 1 creatures which exhibit the simplest possible architecture capable of centralized decisions. This is a necessary step towards a cognitive system, and the origin of the motivational system. When the organism develop more complex behaviours, they will inevitably disturb each other. When this happens it is essential that the different systems inhibit each other in order to produce *one behaviour at a time*. (cf. Gulz, 1991) At this stage, the system can develop in a new way. While the basic subsumption architecture keeps the creature alive, evolution can experiment on the next layer of the architecture.

In class 2 creatures, a learning mechanism is introduced that makes it useful for the animal to develop a more advanced perceptual system that can supply the learning system with more advanced perceptual cues. Mechanisms for categorisation and classification will now give the animal an adaptive advantage. A reduplication of the entire motivational system can construct two opposing systems that are able to compute the signal necessary for drive reduction driven learning. They may also be responsible for the rebound effects observed in animal learning (Solomon, 1980). Computer simulations of the different architectures are presented in Balkenius (1992).

References

Balkenius, C. (1992). *On motivation*. Lund University Cognitive Science, in preparation.

Braitenberg, V. (1984). *Vehicles: Experiments in synthetic psychology*. Cambridge, MA: MIT Press.

Brooks, R. A. (1991). "How to build complete creatures rather than isolated cognitive simulators". In VanLehn, K. ed. *Architectures for intelligence*. Hillsdale, NJ: Lawrence Erlbaum Associates. 225-239.

Gulz, A. (1991). *The planning of action as a cognitive and biological phenomenon*. Lund University Cognitive Studies, 2.

Solomon, R. L. (1980). "The opponent process theory of acquired motivation". *American Psychologist, 35*. 691-712.

Learning Continuous-Space Navigation Heuristics in Real Time

Gregory D. Benson and Armand Prieditis
Department of Computer Science, University of California, Davis, California 95616
email: prieditis@cs.ucdavis.edu, tel: (916)752-6958, fax: (916)752-4767

Summary

Navigating a robot from an initial position to a goal position in an environment with unknown obstacles is a fundamental problem. Reinforcement learning is one approach that involves learning a table of suggested actions for each state of the robot; this table then helps the robot navigate based on a reward function. An alternative approach relies on the shortest path algorithm, but this method requires complete or nearly complete map which is unreasonable to obtain for large spaces.

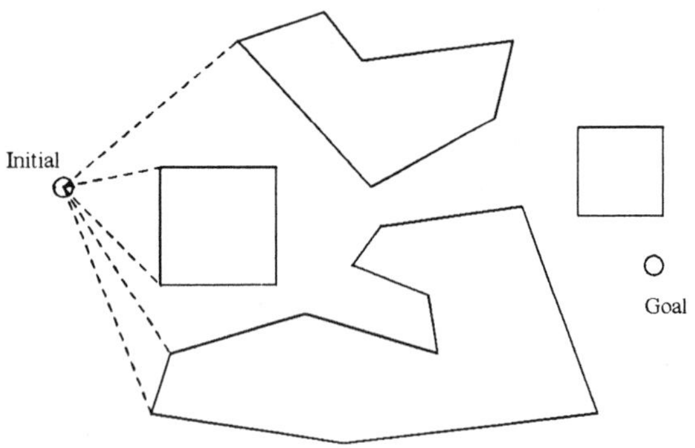

Figure 1: A Polygonal World

In [1] we have developed a method to learn continuous-space heuristics (distance estimators) in real time for real-time decision making. In terms of reinforcement learning our heuristics represent the reward function. Our model assumes a point robot that travels through a continuous two-dimensional world which is occupied by both convex and concave polygonal obstacles (see Figure 1). The robot is equipped with an ideal sensor that can identify decision points in the world, which in our polygonal world are the line-of-sight vertices. The robot also knows the location of the goal at any given time.

For training data, the robot is randomly placed at a point v somewhere in the world. It then proceeds to "find" the goal. The robot determines it next move by acquiring points from the sensor. It then moves to the point with the minimum sum of the distance from the current position, v, plus the heuristic value, $h(v')$ of the point. After the robot picks the next point to move to, v', it updates the heuristic value of the current position to $\text{EUCLIDDIST}(v, v') + h(v')$. The algorithm then repeats on the new point, v', until the goal is found. After the robot is trained, the new heuristic values help the robot to reach the goal faster.

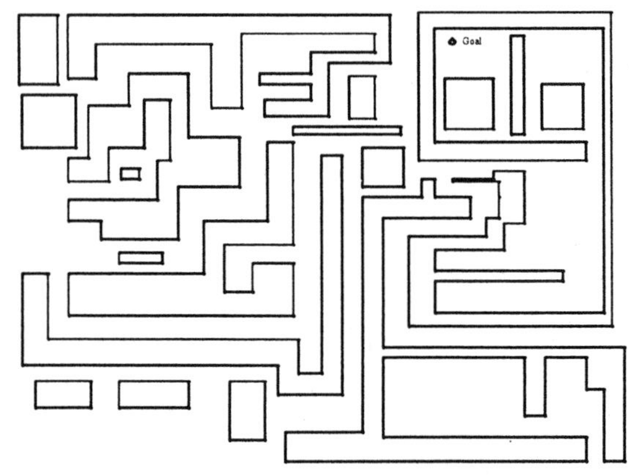

Figure 2: Test World

We have constructed a general simulator for a point robot that navigates in a polygonal world. We ran the simulator on the test world shown in Figure 2. We randomly placed the robot n times and computed the average path length to the goal with no learning. Next, we trained the robot using our method to learn heuristics. Then we placed the robot in the same random positions selected in the first experiment and computed the average path length. The average path length for no learning was 11666. In contrast, the average path length with learning was 1135. Other experiments with different initial heuristic values and different worlds produced similar results. For future work we plan to approximate the table of heuristic values with a Bayesian classifier since the table is generally to large to store.

References

[1] Benson, G. D., and Prieditis, A. "Learning Continuous-Space Navigation Heuristics in Real Time", CSE-92-22, Department of Computer Science, University of California, Davis, CA 95616.

The adaptive power of affect: Learning in the SESAME architecture

Eric Chown
AI Lab, The University of Michigan
1101 Beal Ave.
Ann Arbor, MI 48109
echown@engin.umich.edu

Summary

The SESAME cognitive architecture (Kaplan et al, 1990) provides a framework in which affect and its role in learning and behavior can be simulated and understood. The goal of the work described in this summary is to show how SESAME's learning rule, which is extremely simple and described at the level of a pair of neurons, is capable of accounting for a diverse range of learning data. This diversity is achieved through the effects of affect.

The unit of thought in SESAME is an updated version of Hebb's cell assembly (Kaplan et al., 1991). Cognition in a system constructed out of cell assemblies is based upon activation; perception of an object corresponds to the activation of a specific cell assembly. The basic cognitive structure in SESAME is a network where the nodes are cell assemblies. The network structure arises out of a simple learning rule based upon contiguity. This learning rule is a modified version of Hebb's rule which states that if one neuron repeatedly facilitates the firing of another neuron, then in the future the first neuron's efficiency in helping the second to fire will be increased. What this means in terms of cell assemblies is that when two cell assemblies are active simultaneously then there will be correlated firing between neurons between them and a link will tend to arise such that the next time one becomes active it is more likely to activate the other. Though we have modified Hebb's rule somewhat (Sonntag, 1991), it remains as a basic associative learning rule. The power of this simple rule comes in conjunction with affect, particularly the pleasure/pain system, clarity and confusion, and arousal.

There is little need to discuss what physical pleasure and pain are, but cognitive pleasure and pain is less well understood. In SESAME there are two basic types of cognitive pleasure and pain. The first comes as a result of the learning rule in a fashion analogous to temporal difference models (Sutton, 1988). Where SESAME extends the cognitive pleasure/pain concept is by providing automatic mechanisms to monitor the internal state of the system as a way of providing performance feedback. The most important of these are clarity and confusion detectors.

Clarity and confusion are indicators of how well an organism's model of the world matches the current environment. Clarity is a signal that the model is performing well and that things are under control. Confusion on the other hand is a sign of danger because the model does not correspond to the current reality. It is not surprising that such important states should be associated with pleasure and pain. Anyone who has ever been lost knows how painful it can be. Conversely, there is a real pleasure associated with making a correct prediction about an uncertain outcome. Detecting such states in the SESAME architecture is relatively straightforward. A clarity state comes when the currently active cell assemblies are receiving support from each other and from input from the environment. In such cases there will be a few intensely active cell assemblies. On the other hand confusion results when one's model supports one set of cell assemblies while the environment supports another. In such cases there will be numerous weakly active cell assemblies. It is relatively simple to construct nodes which detect each of these states.

Arousal is linked to perceived importance; the more important the current situation, the more aroused the organism becomes. In SESAME the pleasure and pain centers are considered to be positively linked to the arousal system. In addition clarity and confusion also signal importance, in one case because something is very wrong, in the other because something is very right. The effect of arousal in SESAME is that of an activity contrast enhancer. What this means is that weakly active cell assemblies will be inhibited while more active cell assemblies will become intensely active. The effect on learning is dramatic because learning is directly tied to activity. The more intense the activity of a cell assembly the more pronounced the learning effect. This means that the affect system can act as a kind of control knob for learning. Such a system automatically monitors the relative importance of events in a variety of ways and the results of that monitoring have direct effects on learning and performance.

The simulation platform for learning experiments in SESAME is called Multitrace (Sonntag, 1991). To date Multitrace has been shown to have the ability to learn basic sequences. Work is in progress to model the effects described in this summary. While the results are still in the preliminary stages, they are encouraging thus far.

References

Kaplan, S., Sonntag, M., & Chown, E. (1991). Tracing recurrent activity in cognitive elements (TRACE): A model of temporal dynamics in a cell assembly. *Connection Science.*, **3**, 179-206.

Kaplan, S., Weaver, M., & French, R. (1990). Active symbols and internal models: Towards a cognitive connectionism. *AI & Society*, **4**, 51-71.

Sonntag, M. (1991). Learning sequences in an associative network: A step towards cognitive structure. Doctoral dissertation, The University of Michigan.

Sutton, R. S. (1988). Learning to predict by the methods of temporal differences, *Machine Learning*, **3**, 9-44.

Model of a Behaviour Based Control Architecture

Luís Correia **A. Steiger-Garção**
lc@fct.unl.pt asg@fct.unl.pt
Universidade Nova de Lisboa - FCT/DI
Quinta da Torre, 2825 Monte de Caparica, PORTUGAL

Summary

The behaviour based approach to build autonomous vehicles has already proved (in research but not yet in industry) to be an alternative to traditional hierarchical models, and has been almost the only approach used in what have been called artificial creatures. Carrying on with this parallel between ethology and autonomous vehicles we are especially interested in the physiology of behaviour, meaning the implementation of the control components and architecture of animats.

We stress two issues in this behaviour control architecture: a behaviour hierarchy, and a priority resolution among behaviours. The modular structure here defined performs control of the vehicle in a completely distributed way, meaning that there is no central control entity whatsoever.

In the simplest hierarchical approach we consider animats control organized as a two layer hierarchy. The lowest level - *elementary* - includes simple behaviours (reflexes). The next level - *compound* - includes behaviours that are either sequencers of elementary behaviours thus forming a kind of motor program (in particular a fixed action pattern), or behaviour units in themselves but more complex than reflexes. Sequencers disinhibit behaviours at lower level(s), one at a time, to allow the performance of a sequence or chain of behaviour displays (actions). One behaviour can only be (dis)inhibited by behaviours of layers above. Competition among active behaviours for running (achieving effective control of) the vehicle is solved by priority assignment and resolution.

Regarding decision making on which behaviour to run the vehicle there are two functions to consider: the output function of the stimulus synthesized by each behaviour (control output); and the function that leads to the choice of one among the active behaviours (activity output). It is important to emphasize their difference, since the activity output is a measure of the need the behaviour has in expressing itself (running the vehicle) while the control outputs are the values (position or speed or other) to pass to the actuators. If we consider the activity output as a continuous function, the behaviours' priorities are produced for each behaviour as the product of a stipulated fixed priority and its activity output function. The major problem with the latter is the difficulty in tuning the whole system, adjusting the relative priorities, so that it reacts properly in "all" situations, something that genetic evolution has taken care of in biological beings.

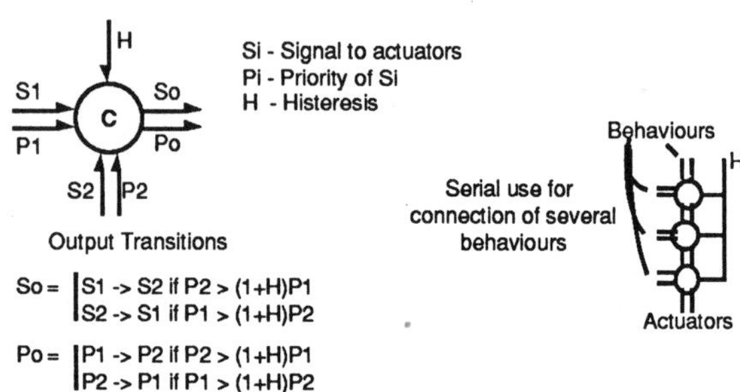

Fig.1 - Variable priority behaviour switching

To accomplish the resolution of variable behaviour priorities we propose also a sequencing solution based on the binary switch presented in fig.1. It resolves two behaviours whose priorities compare themselves by pairs. It incorporates an hysteresis in the commutation (H - global for all switches) so that oscillations are prevented when the two inputs have similar priority levels. To connect more than two behaviours we just chain as many switches as needed. A sequence of *n* of these switches, serially mounted in the supports *n+1* behaviours. Its form recalls a kind of a spinal structure as found in vertebrates. Thus it is not necessary to specify a great amount of mutual inhibiting connections among behaviours but just to define the fixed priorities and the output activity function (priority) referred to above. In fact the only inhibiting connections existent in this architecture will be those between different layers of the hierarchy.

The combination of these two structure aspects (hierarchy and variable priority resolution) plus a behaviour model incorporating a continuous activity function, provide a flexible base for the control of animats, and have a good potential to support simple forms of learning.

Comparing Robot and Animal Behavior

Bridget Hallam and Gillian Hayes
bridget@aifh.ed.ac.uk gmh@aifh.ed.ac.uk

Department of Artificial Intelligence, 5 Forrest Hill,
University of Edinburgh, Edinburgh EH1 2QL Scotland

Summary

The simulation of animal behavior on a robot is a useful undertaking for roboticists wishing to develop robots for non-predictable domains or with more generality of application than is currently possible. It can also be valuable to ethologists, as a means of testing theories of animal behavior in a modular manner, repeatably, and with identically 'naive' subjects.

Not all tasks we would like robots to undertake require high standards of accuracy, repeatability or even reliability. Some require more in the way of adaptability, flexibility of approach and robustness. Given the disparate nature of these requirements and the variety of ways in which some of these words are used, it is not always obvious what is the answer to questions such as: how can these requirements be met? how can the results be measured? how can the performance of different robots be compared? The first question requires answers which are specific to the individual robot and the preferred style of its designer and user. The second and third questions are better answered in a more general way which does not depend so much on the particular robot, environment or task. We address the second and third questions here.

Animal behavior *is* adaptable, flexible and robust. This generalization applies to many different types of animal across most taxonomic boundaries. Assuming evolution to be conservative, this implies that there is a common basic set of behavioral capabilities which are necessary and complete in terms of their ability to produce adaptable, flexible and robust behavior. The identification and use in practice of such a set would be a great step forward for many robotics applications.

In our work we have attempted to identify behavioral capabilities common to a wide variety of animals and to note which are present on existing robots (Hallam and Hayes, 1992). We have, as yet, made no attempt to identify which of the items from our list are *essential* for adaptable behavior. We have found that most mobile robots have some of these behavioral capabilities in some form or other, but we have found none which has all the items.

This list of basic behavioral capabilities includes the following: sensing of internal state, sensing the environment, mechanisms to ensure homeostasis of certain chemicals, energy management (including cyclic behavior), mechanism(s) for translatory movements, mechanism(s) for bending movements, reactions (including reflexes, taxes and fixed (or modal) action patterns), deliberative behavior, the ability to return to places seen before, communication, and plasticity of response (including associative learning and latent learning).

This list contrasts slightly with the list given by Beer (1990, pp 21-24) in that, as roboticists, we concentrate more on the physical actions and capabilities required.

We are not claiming that a robot which has all the capabilities on our list (in its current form) will automatically be a good general-purpose robot. Our intention is that this list be refined and developed as our experience progresses. We do claim that a list of this sort could function as a general standard with reference to which the behavior of real robots of different types and abilities can be measured and compared, enabling us to answer the second and third of our three questions above. Consideration of such a standard will allow designers of robots for tasks requiring adaptability, flexibility of approach and robustness to proceed in a principled manner, and adoption of a common currency will facilitate the testing of theories of animal behavior on robots.

References

[Beer, 1990] Randall D Beer. *Intelligence as Adaptive Behavior.* Academic Press, San Diego 1990. This book forms volume 6 of the Perspectives in Artificial Intelligence series.

[Hallam and Hayes, 1992] Bridget Hallam and Gillian Hayes. Comparing robot and animal behaviour. Research paper 598, Department of Artificial Intelligence, University of Edinburgh, 1992.

An embodied neurally-based algorithm for optimal action selection

Owen Holland
Artificial Life Technologies
Clinton House, Church Place,
Rodborough, Stroud,
GL5 3NF, England
(owen@tag.co.uk)

Martin Snaith
Technology Applications Group
5, Bolams Mill, Dispensary Street,
Alnwick
NE66 1LN, England
(martin@tag.co.uk)

Summary

One simple form of adaptive behaviour which an animat can display is that of optimal action selection - producing that sequence of actions in a given environment which maximises the cumulative measure over time of some quantity (reward) which is a function of the behavior in relation to the environment. Of all the architectures that can produce this behaviour, it is likely that those which can be implemented using only neural functions will be of greatest interest to those interested in adaptive behaviour.

Much analysis to date has considered systems with a finite number of environmental states and actions, and in which the reward is a function only of the present state. Two distinct kinds of information are available: the relationship between state and reward; and the relationship between state, action, and the next state. Computer-based reinforcement learning architectures using discrete states have recently evolved from those using reward information alone to those using both reward and transitional information (e.g. Sutton [1991]). However, no attempts have yet been made to embody these architectures in a wholly neural substrate, although neural networks have featured in some simulations. There are two aspects to the problem: gathering the information (exploration), and using it. This paper deals only with the second aspect, and shows how a system which always uses the available information optimally (and which will therefore outperform architectures which only approach optimality over an infinite number of trials) can be constructed from a simple and wholly neural architecture using an unusual but credible learning rule. (The presentation assumes that a one-to-one mapping of n environmental states to n neurons can be accepted as a starting point, since many networks capable of doing this have been already been studied.)

If a neuron B is stimulated immediately after a neuron A, the strength of any connections between the neurons may change. Edelman (1987) has discussed a general representation of the underlying processes, and has noted that sets of parameters may be found such that either the connections from A to B, or the connections from B to A, are affected. Holland and Snaith (1992) have called the first type of learning 'forwards association' and the second 'backwards association'. The architecture consists of two linked networks, one consisting of neurons forming forwards associations (the forwards net) and one of neurons forming backwards associations (the backwards net). The forwards and backwards nets each contain one neuron corresponding to, and excited with unit strength by, each state of the environment; each neuron in the forwards net sends a connection to its corresponding unit in the backwards net, the strength of which is determined by and equal to the average reward obtained in the relevant state. The neurons in the forwards net are fully interconnected (but not self-connected) with synapses initially of zero strength; if a transition from state A to state B occurs, the synaptic strength of the connection from the neuron corresponding to A to that corresponding to B becomes the maximum of one. The output of each neuron in the forwards net is the sum of its inputs. The neurons in the backwards net are also fully interconnected (but not self-connected) with synapses initially of zero strength; if a transition from state A to state B occurs, the synaptic strength of the connection from the neuron corresponding to B to that corresponding to A becomes the maximum of one. The output of each neuron in the backwards net is the sum of the highest input it receives from any other neuron in the backwards net and the input it receives from its corresponding unit in the forwards net; the mechanism for selecting the highest input received is proposed to be that of mutual inhibition operating between synapses rather than between whole neurons as is more usual.

We show that, within certain limits, and provided that the sequence of reward-producing states which the system can experience in a single trial in a given environment is always acyclic, then:

(i) the selection from the actions available in a given state of that action leading to the state with the highest level of output in the backwards net is always optimal

(ii) the architecture carries out a truly parallel and asynchronous version of discrete dynamic programming

(iii) the level of output of the neurons in the backwards net is equal to the expected undiscounted cumulative value of reward over time obtained by always making the optimal choices

(iv) for an environment with n states, a network of 2n neurons with ($2n^2$-n) connections is required

(v) the maximum computation time for the optimal choice is a linear function of n.

References

Edelman G.M. (1987) ***Neural Darwinism*** Basic Books, New York

Holland O.E & Snaith M. (1992) 'How to remember the future: temporal asymmetry in mechanisms of synaptic change' in ***Artificial Neural Networks 2***, North Holland, 1992

Sutton, R.S. (1991) 'Reinforcement learning architectures for animats' in ***From animals to animats*** ed. Meyer & Wilson, Bradford - MIT 1991

Why should we Build Artificial Worms and How?

Oded Maler
LGI IMAG B.P. 53X
38041 Grenoble Cedex
France
E-mail: maler@imag.fr

Summary

In this paper the author claims that developing artificial worms is *the* right thing to do. The term *artificial worm* is used to denote a class of elastic robots composed of many components, each having relatively-simple sensory-motor capabilities. The most prominent biological realizations of such robots are worms, molluscs, elephant trunks and tongues. Understanding how such mechanisms are controlled is an important stage (not to say, a prerequisite) toward the development of "truely-intelligent" autonomous agents. The arguments in favor of the worm are based on the observation that insects are too intelligent creatures to begin with, and that worm-like structures are the simplest neuro-muscular mechanisms, and that their behavior should be simpler to analyze and immitate than that of creatures having rigid joints, vision or language.

As an evidence that the author has been partially convinced by his own arguments, the rest of the paper is devoted to the description of some simulation experiments performed with the simplest model of a worm described below. The worm is made of two identical masses interconnected by a spring and having corresponding friction parameters with the ground (see figure 1). The force F applied on the masses can be either positive (causing expansion) or negative (causing contraction).

The overall dynamics is described by the following set of equations:

$$+F - k(l - l_r) - \nu\frac{dl}{dt} - m_0\frac{d^2x_0}{dt^2} - p_0\frac{dx_0}{dt} = 0 \quad (1)$$

$$-F + k(l - l_r) + \nu\frac{dl}{dt} - m_1\frac{d^2x_1}{dt^2} - p_1\frac{dx_1}{dt} = 0 \quad (2)$$

Where m_0, m_1 are the masses, x_0, x_1 denote their corresponding locations, p_0, p_1 are their "friction" control parameters, $l = x_0 - x_1$ is the actual length of the spring, l_r is its rest length, k and ν are respectively the stiffness and the damping coefficients of the spring and F is the applied force.

The controller for such a worm is essentially a program that continuously monitors the length of the spring and decides which force and friction to apply. The behavior of such a worm equipped with a given controller is tested using a numerical simulation system for equations (1) and (2). The controller is just a simple module within the simulator which computes F, p_0 and p_1 as a function of the current and previous values of x_0 and x_1. A simple strategy that achieves crawling across a large variety of environmental parameters is described.

The full paper and a draft containing a report on further experiments with more complicated models and a discussion of some methodological problems associated with simulated robotics, can be obtained upon request from the author.

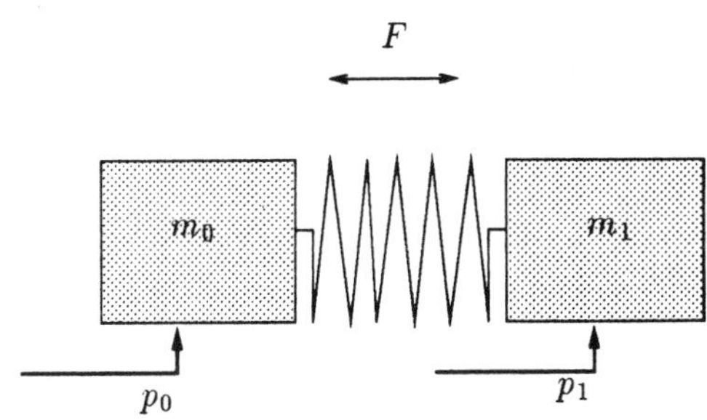

Figure 1: A mechanical model for a one-segment worm.

Acknowledgements

The work described here was done while the author was at IRISA, Rennes, France. The support of B. Arnaldi, G. Dumont, G. Hégron and C. Lecerf is gratefully acknowledged.

Creative Perception

M.A. Rodrigues **M.H. Lee**

The University of Wales at Aberystwyth
Department of Computer Science
Aberystwyth, Wales SY23 3BZ, UK
e-mail mar@uk.ac.aber, mhl@uk.ac.aber

Summary

Our current research project [Lee and McGonigle, 1991] investigates the modeling of animal behaviour in a way that may prove helpful in solving some engineering problems posed by the design and implementation of artificially intelligent systems. In particular, we are interested in emergent properties, with the long term goal of finding clues to answer the question "how does high level behaviour emerge?" This is a central issue in research on artificial life and autonomous agency. Our approach follows the philosophy introduced by Brooks [1991] by taking a synthetic approach to Artificial Intelligence (AI) as opposed to analytic. Although it has been shown that it is possible to achieve flexible robot action and to develop reliable and robust behaviour-based robot controllers [Arkin, 1989], [Brooks, 1991], [Donnett and Smithers, 1990], [McGonigle, 1990], the issues of how more complex behaviour can be generated from basic competences, and how adaptive behaviour and learning can be achieved still need extensive investigation.

We are tackling the specific problem: "for any given task, how does the control architecture select the relevant control variable(s)?" This question goes to the heart of emergent properties, since it is clear that the selection of control variables involves the structure of the entire perception-action spectrum of an organism and that selected variables not specified by design imply emergent functionality. Within this view, emergent properties are not only a function of the structure but also of perception, since only variables that can be perceived can be controlled. To emphasise our perceptual control approach [Powers 1973], as opposed to the more usual action control approach in behaviour based research, we define *creative perception* as the process that creates a new set of control variables, adding properties to the perceived environment.

We are building a case study where creative perception is generated according to the concepts of blind variation and selective retention [Campbell, 1960]. A computer simulation of a control system for a mobile robot tracking acoustic beams demonstrates our approach with an element of task discovery. Apart from position control displayed by the tracking behaviour, the simulated architecture is also able to control velocity and acceleration. The control system is able to learn a solution, or a path to the intended sound source, by trial and error through the generation of temporary meta-reference levels of control (each temporary meta-reference is a request for a perception). The generated path which is a sequence of perceptions can then be stored in memory for future reference, so that the system learns through dynamic interaction with the environment as opposed to a learning scheme imposed by the designer.

References

[Arkin, 1989] R.C. Arkin, *Motor Schema-Based Mobile Robot Navigation.* Int. J. Rob. Research, 1989, v.8, nr.4, pp. 92–112.

[Brooks, 1991] R.A. Brooks, *Intelligence Without Reason,* Proceedings of the IJCAI-91, 24-30 Aug 1991, Australia, pp 569–595.

[Campbell, 1960] D.T. Campbell, *Blind Variation and Selective Retention in Creative Thought as in other Knowledge Processes.* Psychological Review, 67(6), 1960, pp. 380–400.

[Donnett and Smithers, 1990] J. Donnett and T. Smithers, *Lego Vehicles: A Technology for Studying Intelligent Systems.* Edinburgh University, DAI Research Paper 490, 1990.

[Lee and McGonigle, 1991] M.H. Lee and B.O. McGonigle, *Cognitive Modelling and the Design of Artificially Intelligent Systems,* JCI grant MRC-G9110835 from April 1992 to March 1995.

[McGonigle, 1990] B.O. McGonigle, *Incrementing Intelligent Systems by Design.* SAB90, From Animals to Animats, MIT Press, 1990, pp 525–531.

[Powers, 1973] W.T. Powers, *Behavior: the Control of Perception.* New York Aldine de Gruyter, 1973.

Collective Behavior of Silicon Microrobots

Isao Shimoyama, Toshio Watanabe, Yoshihiko Kuwana, and Hirofumi Miura

Department of Mechano-Informatics
The University of Tokyo
7-3-1, Hongo, Bunkyo-ku, Tokyo 113, Japan
isao@leopard.t.u-tokyo.ac.jp

Summary

Several microrobot structures have been built on silicon wafers. They have an external skeleton and elastic joints just like real insects[1]. In this paper we discuss the possibility of controlling microrobots.

A simple algorithm should be used for controlling microrobots. A microrobot's behavior should simply be based upon a response to sensor input. The model for this control method is based upon the behavior of animals, especially insects.

The agents considered here are characterized as follows:

i. They can sense relative displacement and relative velocity,
ii. Each agent is controlled by the same algorithm,
iii. They do not communicate with each other.

Based upon these characteristics, we have simulated three types of models as follows:

1. Gathering together and scattering apart,
2. Following the leader, and
3. Driven by an electric field.

Models 1 and 2 are based upon using a similar algorithm, and can be quantified in the following equations:

$$\dot{q} = P(q) \tag{1}$$

$$P(q) = -\alpha q^3 - \beta q. \tag{2}$$

Varying the parameters α and β leads to quite different dynamics, as shown in Fig. 1.

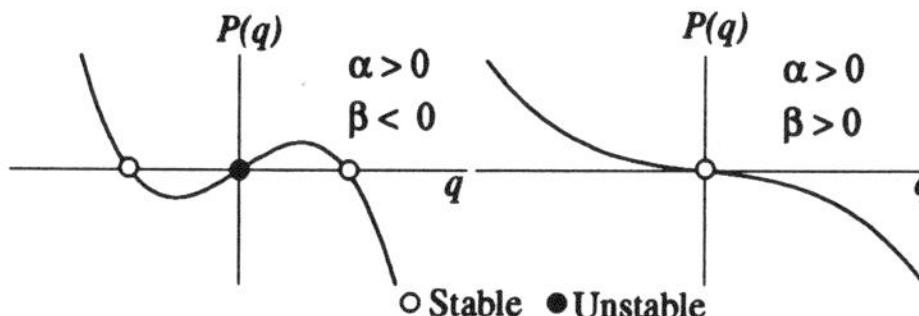

Fig. 1 Stable and unstable points of (2)

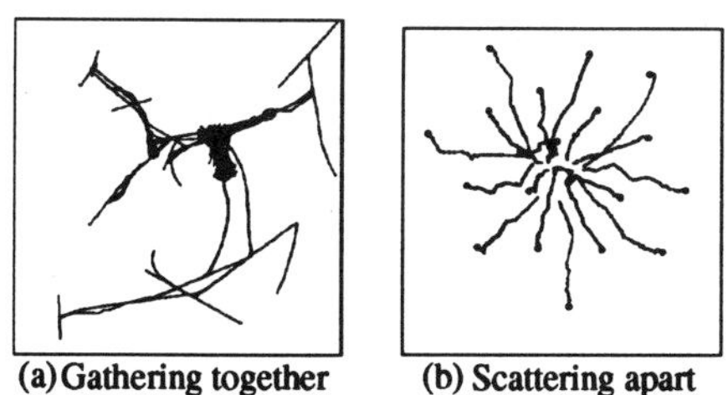

Fig. 2 Gathering together and scattering apart

Gathering Fig. 2(a) and scattering Fig. 2(b) can be simulated by applying (3) as the local interaction law among agents:

$$\left.\begin{aligned} \vec{v} &= \frac{d}{dt}\vec{r}, F_r = -\alpha_r|\vec{r}(n)|^3 - \beta_r|\vec{r}(n)| \\ \vec{v}(n+1) &= F_r\frac{\vec{r}(n)}{|\vec{r}(n)|} \end{aligned}\right\} \tag{3}$$

where $\vec{r}(n)$ and $\vec{v}(n)$ represent relative displacement and relative velocity from one microrobot to its nearest neighbor in front, in the n-th step. α_r and β_r are constant and correspond directly to α and β in (2). If $\alpha_r > 0$ and $\beta_r < 0$, $|\vec{r}| = \pm\sqrt{|\beta_r|/\alpha_r}$ is a stable equilibrium point.

By keeping the same speed as that at which a leader moves, the following motion can be realized. The leader's speed determines the shape of the group, as shown in Fig. 3. This motion is similar to that of birds flying in formation.

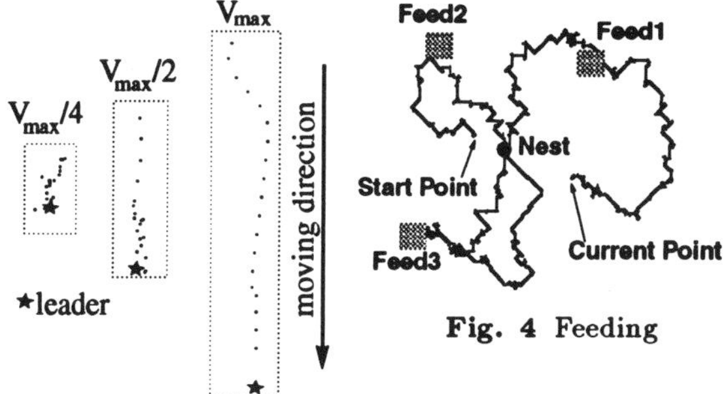

Fig. 3 Following

Fig. 4 Feeding

Model 3 is based on utilizing information contained in the field, like ants do. Ants move along a pheromone gradient. In this simulation, an agent can sense and memorize the magnitude of an electric potential, as shown in Fig. 4. If an agent can affect the field, indirect information can be exchanged through the field.

References

[1] K.Suzuki, I.Shimoyama, H.Miura and Y.Ezura, "Creation of an Insect-based Microrobot with an External Skeleton and Elastic Joints," Proceedings of IEEE MEMS '92, pp.190–195, 1992.

An Analog VLSI Model of Central Pattern Generation in the Medicinal Leech

Micah S. Siegel
Department of Electrical Engineering, Yale University, Box 4237 Yale Station, New Haven, CT 06520

Summary

This paper details the design and construction of an analog VLSI implementation of the neural system responsible for the swimming behaviors of a relatively simple organism: the Medicinal Leech (*Hirundo medicinalis*). The silicon model spans three levels of organization in the leech nervous system (neuron, ganglion, system) and, as one of the first comprehensive models of leech swimming, represents an excellent framework with which to explore adaptive response related to undulatory locomotion. The model operates on the same time- and spatial-scale as the leech central pattern generator and consumes power at nearly the same efficiency (J/cm^2).

A Central Pattern Generator (CPG) is a network of neurons that generates rhythmic output in the absence of sensory input [1]. It has been suggested that invertebrate central pattern generation may represent and excellent theatre within which to explore silicon implementations of adaptive neural systems: invertebrate CPG networks are orders of magnitude smaller than their vertebrate counterparts, much detailed information is available about them, and they guide behaviors that may be of technological interest [2]. Furthermore, CPG networks are typically embedded in larger neural circuits and are integral to the neural correlates of adaptive behavior in many natural organisms [3].

A leech swims by undulating its segmented body to form a rearward-progressing body wave. This wave is analogous to the locomotory undulations of most elongated aquatic animals (e.g. fish), and some terrestrial amphibians and reptiles (including salamanders and snakes) [3]. The moving crests and troughs in the body wave are produced by phase-delayed contractile rhythms of the dorsal and ventral body wall along successive segments.

In the leech, interneurons that coordinate the rearward-progressing swimming contractions undergo oscillations in membrane potential and fire impulses in bursts. It appears that the oscillatory activity of these interneurons arises from a network rhythm that depends on the inherently oscillatory membrane potentials in individual neurons [3]. The phases of the oscillatory interneurons form groups clustered about three phase points spaced equally around the activity cycle. To first approximation, all midbody ganglia of the leech nerve cord express an identical activity rhythm. However, activity in each ganglion is phase-delayed with respect to more anterior ganglia [3]; presumably this is responsible for the undulatory body wave characteristic of leech swimming.

The silicon analog model employs biophysical realistic neural elements (neuromimes), connected into anatomically realistic ganglion circuits. These ganglion circuits are coupled together using known interganglionic connections. The model thus spans **three levels of organization** in the nervous system of the leech (neuron, ganglion, system).

The central building block of the model CPG is the analog neuromime; like CPG interneurons in the leech swim system, the silicon neuromime integrates current across a somatic "capacitance" and uses positive feedback to generate action potentials whose frequency is determined by the magnitude of excitatory current input [5]. The silicon neuromime also employs tonic excitation, inhibitory synapses with adjustable weights and a characteristic recovery time from inhibition.

These silicon ganglia are biologically motivated, in that they have been constructed using only identified cells and synaptic connections between cells in the biological system. The model employs interganglionic connections known to exist in the biological system, generates qualitatively similar output and an appropriate time scale, and maintains this verisimilitude over a wide operating frequency range.

The analog silicon model successfully captures design principles from three levels of organization in the leech nervous system. It operates on the same time-scale as its biological counterpart and gives rise to ganglionic activity that is qualitatively similar to activity in the leech ganglion. For our purposes the current model provides an important framework for intended future implementations of adaptive undulatory locomotion.

References

1. Rowat, P.F. and Selverston, A.I. (1991). **Network**, 2, 17-41.
2. Ryckebusch, S., Bower, J.M., Mead, C.., (1989). In D. Touretzky (Ed), **Advances in Neural Information Processing Systems**, pp. 384-393. San Mateo, CA: Morgan Kaufmann..
3. Friesen, W.O. (1989). In J. Jacklet (Ed), **Neuronal and Cellular Oscillators**, pp. 269-316. New York: Marcel Dekker.
4. Mead, C.A. (1989). **Analog VLSI and Neural Systems**, Reading, MA: Addison-Wesley.
5. Friesen, W.O. and Stent, G.S. (1977). **Biological Cybernetics**, 28, 27-40.

AUTHOR INDEX